GREECE

'In isolated, god-haunted spots, flocks are
watched by shepherds who are reputedly
the last descendants of Homeric Greeks,
and werewolves, archaic even to the ancients,
still seem bone-chillingly feasible.'

Contents

Maps

About the authors

Dana Facaros, whose father is from Ikaría, started her travel-writing career with Cadogan's *Greek Islands* in 1977. She has recently celebrated getting Greek citizenship by breaking every plate in the house.

Linda Theodorou gave up teaching to live and work in Greece and follow in the footsteps of Pausanias. She has lived in the Peloponnese for more than 28 years and has never got over her love affair with the country, its people, and its kaleidoscopic history.

Authors' acknowledgements can be found at the end of the index.

Cadogan Guides
Highlands House, 165 The Broadway,
London SW19 1NE
info.cadogan@virgin.net
www.cadoganguides.com

The Globe Pequot Press
246 Goose Lane, PO Box 480, Guilford,
Connecticut 06437–0480

Copyright © Dana Facaros and
  Linda Theodorou 2003

Cover and photo essay design by Kicca Tommasi
Book design by Andrew Barker
Cover photographs: W. Bibikow / jonarnold.com,
  Tim Mitchell
Photo essay: Tim Mitchell
Maps © Cadogan Guides,
  drawn by Map Creation Ltd
Managing editor: Christine Stroyan
Editors: Dominique Shead and Linda McQueen
Art direction: Sarah Rianhard-Gardner
Proofreading: Catherine Bradley
Indexing: Isobel McLean
Production: Navigator Guides Ltd

Printed in Italy by Legoprint
A catalogue record for this book is available
  from the British Library
ISBN 1-86011-898-4

The author and publishers have made every effort to ensure the accuracy of the information in this book at the time of going to press. However, they cannot accept any responsibility for any loss, injury or inconvenience resulting from the use of information contained in this guide.

Please help us to keep this guide up to date. We have done our best to ensure that the information in this guide is correct at the time of going to press. But places and facilities are constantly changing, and standards and prices in hotels and restaurants fluctuate. We would be delighted to receive any comments concerning existing entries or omissions. Authors of the best letters will receive a copy of the Cadogan Guide of their choice.

Greece

a photo essay

by Tim Mitchell

Tholos, Delphi
(Stereá Elláda)

Ag. Triádos, the Metéora
(Thessaly)

Váthia (Peloponnese)

Odeion of Herodes
Atticus, Athens

Ioúlis, Kéa (Cyclades)

beehives, Sithonía
Peninsula, Chalkidikí
(Northern Greece)

Vouraikós Gorge railway
between Diakoftó and
Kalávrita (Peloponnese)

Fíra Cathedral, Santorini
(Cyclades)

local architecture, Kéa
(Cyclades)

mermaid carving, Galaxídi
(Stereá Elláda)

8th-century mosaic,
Ag. Dimítrios, Thessaloníki
(Northern Greece)

Chaniá, Crete

harbour, Lefkáda
(Ionian Islands)

bar, Naúplio
(Peloponnese)

Gramvoúsa, Crete

fisherman, Chíos
(North Aegean Islands)

bakery in Nidrí, Lefkáda
(Ionian Islands)

basket-weaver's
workshop, Naúplio
(Peloponnese)

Temple of Poseidon,
Cape Soúnion (Attica)

Introduction

On the face of it, Greece today is a small, mountainous and not terribly important country of ten and a half million people dangling at Europe's southeasternmost end. Tourists know it for its sandy beaches, limpid seas, myriad islands and splendid, often startling ancient and medieval ruins. Behind this travel-poster surface, however, Greece has so much more to see and do, and so many good stories to tell, that this book could easily have been twice as long. Side by side with such five-star attractions as Athens, Santoríni, Metéora, Crete, Delphi, Mýkonos, Olympia, Corfu, Mycenae, Rhodes and Thessaloníki lie layer upon layer of another, less-travelled Greece, where tiny villages are serenaded by nightingales and flocks are watched by Sarakatsáni shepherds, reputedly the last descendants of the Homeric Greeks, and where, in isolated, god-haunted spots such as Mount Lýkaio, werewolves, archaic even to the ancients, still seem bone-chillingly feasible.

Wherever you go, be warned: this is a country that threatens sensory overload. The clear light of the Aegean makes everything seem more real, more true, until it gives you goose-bumps. Sun-soaked herbs fill the air; the warm sea in a piney cove, the wildflowers in spring or the late-afternoon sky against a blue church dome are drunk with colour; the sensuous rhythms of Greek music fill the moonlit evening. And underlying all is a deeper, more terrible beauty, the creation of thousands of years of myth, poetry and turbulent history, traces of which lurk somewhere in every Greek landscape and in every Greek soul. As Katsímbalis told Henry Miller in *The Colossus of Maroussi*, 'The human proportions which the Greek extolled were superhuman. They weren't *French* proportions. They were divine, because the true Greek is a god, not a cautious, precise, calculating being with the soul of an engineer...'

Yet, for all the myth and beauty, the thousands who return year after year often cite another reason for visiting: they simply feel at home. You might say it's because Greek civilization is the heritage of all humanity; or that the ancient democratic spirit, encouraged by a climate that allows Greeks to spend so much time outside in each other's company, openly welcomes visitors to the ongoing national dialogue. Most of all, the Greeks have an infectious, almost crazy zest for life and rarely begrudge 'wasting time' enjoying it. Although epitomized by the great Alexis Zorba, this zest isn't a particularly 'Greek' trait, but an old human one that strikes a buried chord in nearly all of us, one that the Greeks have yet to forget.

Choosing Your Holiday: A Guide to Greece, and to this Guide

Most people start at **Athens**, with its sublime Acropolis and other relics of its golden age, great museums and buzzing nightlife. Its local region, **Attica**, has beaches and other ancient sites such as the imposing Temple of Poseidon at Soúnion, and the sanctuary at Eleusis (modern Elefsína), plus four islands: Aegina with its Temple of Aphaia; Hýdra, the 'Greek St-Tropez'; pretty pine-wooded Póros; and Spétses.

The nearby **Peloponnese** is the magnificent garden of Greece, and the cradle of its oldest myths: Corinth, Sparta, Mycenae, Tiryns, Argos, Pýlos, Olympia, Nemea, Epidauros, Arcadía, the river Styx and other half-legendary places are here, along with Byzantine Mystrá, neoclassical Naúplio, and an overflow of dramatic mountain scenery, beaches, olives, vines and orange groves.

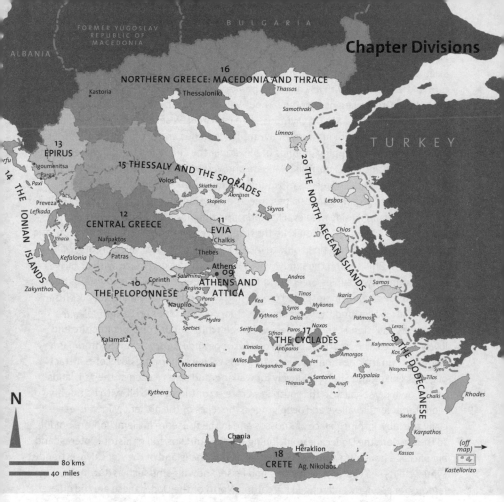

Chapter Divisions

ALBANIA

FORMER YUGOSLAV
REPUBLIC OF
MACEDONIA

BULGARIA

16
NORTHERN GREECE: MACEDONIA AND THRACE

Kastoria

Thessaloniki

Thassos

Samothraki

Limnos

TURKEY

13
EPIRUS

Corfu
Igoumenitsa
Parga
Paxi

15 THESSALY AND THE SPORADES

Volos

Skiathos
Alonissos
Skopelos

Skyros

Lesbos

20 THE NORTH AEGEAN ISLANDS

Chios

Preveza
Lefkada

14
THE IONIAN ISLANDS

12
CENTRAL GREECE

Nafpaktos

Ithaca

Kefalonia

Patras

11
EVIA

Chalkis

Thebes

Athens
09

Samos

Zakynthos

10
THE PELOPONNESE

Corinth
Salamina
Aegina
Poros

**ATHENS AND
ATTICA**

Nauplio

Hydra

Spetses

Andros

Tinos

Ikaria

Patmos

Kea

Syros
Kythnos Delos

Mykonos

Naxos

19 THE DODECANESE

Leros
Kalymnos
Kos

Kalamata

Serifos
Sifnos Paros **17**
Antiparos **THE CYCLADES**

Kimolos
Milos
Monemvasia Folegandros Sikinos

Amorgos

Astypalaia

Nissyros
Symi
Tilos

Ios

Santorini
Thirassia Anafi

Chalki

Rhodes

Kythera

N

Saria

Karpathos

(off
map)

Chania

18
CRETE
Heraklion

Ag. Nikolaos

Kassos

Kastellorizo

80 kms
40 miles

The big, mountainous island of **Évia**, also near Athens and mostly frequented by Greek families, is something of a best-kept secret. It abuts on **Central Greece** (Stereá Elláda), where ancient Delphi under Mount Parnassos is a major draw, followed by seaside Galaxídi and Náfpaktos, Mycenaean Thebes and Orchomenos, wetlands around Messolóngi to the west, and more elusive ancient sites such as Thermon.

Épirus, isolated to the northwest by the majestic Pindus range, has a character and history all its own. Its charming lakeside capital Ioánnina is full of memories of Alí Pasha; the coast is lined with handsome beach resorts such as Párga and Préveza; the breathtaking Vikos Gorge and the traditional mountain villages, especially the Zagorachória, are fascinating to explore. The lovely and very popular **Ionian Islands** that dot Greece's west coast are lusher than their Aegean cousins: Corfu with its charming Venetian-British capital; grandiose Kefalonía; relatively pristine Ithaca, Odysseus' island; Lefkáda, with its enchanting seascapes and windsurfing; intimate Paxi; and Zákynthos of beautiful beaches and unchained mass tourism.

The great plain of **Thessaly** divides Central Greece from Macedonia, with the unique monastery-topped pinnacles of Metéora, the gem-like mountain resort of Lake

Plastíra, and the bucolic Pélion peninsula. Just offshore lie the Sporades islands: racy Skiáthos with its 63 beaches, rugged tranquil Skópelos and Alónissos, and a bit further afield Skýros, with its charming traditional architecture.

Northern Greece begins over the famous Vale of Tempe by the country's highest peak, cloud-wreathed Mount Olympus. Here lies Greece's second city and port, Thessaloníki, with a unique array of Byzantine churches and art, great food, nightlife and festivals. The stomping grounds of Alexander the Great and the old Macedonians are nearby, at ancient Dion, Pélla, Náoussa and Vergína, where the gold-filled royal tumulus is now one of Greece's most unusual museums. Mountainous Western Macedonia has stunning landscapes, forests and gems such as Édessa, the city built over a waterfall, lakeside medieval Kastória, and the magical nature reserve of the Préspa Lakes. East of Thessaloníki lie the fleshpots of Chalkidikí and the holy monastic republic of Mount Athos, open only to men. Further east is the lively port of Kavála, near ancient Philippi and the sandy woody island of Thássos. Thrace, with its large Muslim minority, occupies Greece's northeast, between the Rodópi mountains and the sea; birdwatching in unspoiled forests and wetlands is a main attraction, plus traditional villages, and the venerable Sanctuary of Mysteries on Samothráki.

The rest is all islands: the **Cyclades**, with their white sugar-cube architecture and lovely beaches. The smart set parties on Mýkonos and Páros, volcanic Santoríni is a favourite romantic destination, peaceful Tínos with its charming dovecotes attracts pilgrims, Náxos and Sífnos are lovely for walking, and so on – each of the 24 islands has its own personality. To the south lies **Crete**, a continent in itself, with its mighty mountains, fertile valleys and deep gorges; the relics of the ancient Minoans, especially the labyrinthine palace of Knossos and in the museum in Heráklion, are unique. To the east are the **Dodecanese**, including Rhodes and Kos, full of historic interest and big package holiday favourites, as well as Pátmos, the island of the Apocalypse, trendy Sými with its sea captains' mansions, and lesser known gems such as Kálymnos, famous for sponges, and rugged Kárpathos. North of the Dodecanese are the quieter **North Aegean Islands**, including lovely Sámos, famous since ancient times for its wine, Chíos and Lésbos, large islands full of surprises, and wonderfully laid-back Ikaría.

A Note on Transliteration and Place Names

In Greece, expect to see slight variations in the spellings of Greek place names in Roman letters. We've tried to use the forms you're most likely to see: a D when transcribing the Greek *delta* (Δ), which you may see as DH or TH to account for its soft *th* sound, a CH when transcribing *chi* (X), which is pronounced like the CH in loch, but is sometimes written as an H; and G for the Greek *gamma* (Γ) which sounds like a guttural GH verging on a Y, and is often transcribed as a Y or a GH, as in 'saint' (*ágios/áyios/ághios*). Also note that placing the stress on the right syllable (marked with an acute (´) accent) is essential to the pronunciation of Greek.

In the text, you'll find the **Greek letters for place names** you may need when travelling, in lower case for signs on back roads (to match the road signs, for those driving), and capital letters when chances are you'll be taking a boat or a bus, especially on the islands.

History

People talk about the dead past. The past isn't dead. It isn't even past.

William Faulkner

History looms large in the Greek psyche, sometimes astonishing in its achievements, sometimes like a nagging live-in mother-in-law. Much of it is speculative, regionally fragmented, or twisted and glossed over to fit into a political agenda. This is not unique to Greece, but the Greeks have been doing it longer than most – since the 8th century BC.

20,000–3000 BC: The Stone Age

The oldest human remains in Greece, found in the Petrálona cave in Chalkidikí, date back 700,000 years. Skip ahead 650,000 years to the Mesolithic era, and permanent cave dwellings gradually replace a nomadic hunting life. The revolution in agriculture that involved the domestication of sheep and goats was first brought from Asia Minor into southern Macedonia and Thessaly. Here the oldest known Neolithic farming settlements in Europe have been unearthed, at **Néa Nikomedía** near Véria (7th millennium BC) and **Sésklo** near Vólos (6500 BC); both had simple houses around a palace-like structure, and the latter made elegant pottery and imported obsidian from Mílos. Other islands had precocious starts as well: **Polióchne** on Límnos (which had cultural links to Troy), and **Knossós** on Crete.

3000–1200 BC: Early Helladic, Minoans and Mycenaeans

A slow and somewhat shadowy incursion of foreigners began *c.* 3000 BC, bringing with it bronze metal-working techniques and the swing plough. These innovations stabilized agriculture, allowing settlements with lands radiating out several miles – about the distance it would take to travel in a day. Permanent settlements and prosperity led to craft specialization and the use of symbols such as seals or pot marks denoting a specific place, saying 'here we are and this is ours'.

The **Cycladic Islands** got off to the earliest start, trading in obsidian and learning to work in marble, producing their famous idols. On the mainland the early Bronze Age is known as **Early Helladic**, and it produced the palatial House of Tiles at Lerna in Argolís (*c.* 2200 BC). The building burned before it was completed; the fire may have been set by the next round of invaders, Greek-speaking, horse-taming, chariot-riding Indo-Europeans, with their sky god and a social hierarchy that valued warriors, sending the indigenous population, the so-called Pelasgians, to Cyprus and Arcadía.

The invaders, however, didn't make it to **Crete**, which was busily laying the foundations for the remarkable civilization we call the **Minoan**. By 2000 BC, the Minoan fleet controlled the Aegean. Writing, as yet untranslated, evolved *c.* 1900 from hieroglyphic symbols into the script known as **Linear A**. After 1700, Minoan colonies and trade counters were scattered around the Aegean as far as Sicily (most notably on Santoríni and Mílos); their elegant ambassadors figured in the tomb paintings of the Pharaohs. Crete's four great palace complexes, at Knossós, Mália, Phaistos and Zákros, attained a hitherto unknown splendour, with internal plumbing systems fed by aqueducts. The images in the Minoans' brilliant art suggest a religion dominated by the great goddess and a society where women enjoyed the same status as men. Then, some time between 1500 and 1450 BC, the cataclysmic explosion of Santoríni devastated Crete with volcanic ash, earthquakes and tidal waves. The Minoans limped on, but it wasn't long before the expanding Indo-European **Mycenaeans** filled the vacuum of power, taking over the Minoan colonies and trade across the eastern Mediterranean. Only Knossos was rebuilt, with an innovation: a Mycenaean throne room.

Mycenaean culture seems to have exploded full-grown on to the Greek scene about 1600 BC. Massively fortified palaces went up at Mycenae, Tiryns and Pýlos in the Peloponnese, while traces of others have been found in Athens and Boeotia, at Thebes and Gla. The citadel of Mycenae gave its name to the era, dominating fellow 'Mycenaeans' in some kind of loose federation; the amazing quantity of gold found there offers proof of an astonishing rise to power. Female goddesses were still important, but their male high priests were up-and-coming, holding the title of '*wanax*' or 'king'. Palaces surrounded by tremendous 'Cyclopean' walls (as later Greeks called them, believing they could only have been built by giants) were headquarters not only for government and religion, but also for the gathering and redistribution of agricultural and other goods. Mycenaean scribes kept track of these by adapting Linear A to their early Greek language in a syllabic script known as **Linear B**, crude by later standards, but suitable for documenting inventories. While the Minoans carried lilies, the Mycenaeans carried swords. One historian projects an image of a feudal-like system, with barons jockeying for position, which very soon produced too many younger sons looking for land or loot by stealing instead of by trade, and then inventing a warrior code that not only justified the process but idealized it. Certainly that is the image of the Mycenaean heroes in Homer; whether accurate or not, its literary reality became, for better or worse, the Greek *beau idéal*.

1200–500 BC: The Greek Dark Age and the Archaic Age

About 1200 BC, the Mycenaeans added major new defences around their palaces. This neatly coincides with the ancient tradition of a Dorian invasion, although hard archaeological evidence for this remains extremely elusive. For whatever reason, Troy fell in c. 1180 BC, followed shortly by the conquerors Homer made famous, one after the other. Athens and Évia alone were spared, again for reasons unknown; Athens seems to have taken in many refugees, probably too many for the thin Attic soil to support. In the 11th and 10th centuries many, calling themselves Ionians (from a legendary ancestor, Ion, the son of Apollo), set sail for Asia Minor, founding Miletus, Ephesus and other cities that would always remember their Athenian roots. Back in Greece, a much reduced population in tribal bands struggled on in isolated pockets. The Mycenaean word for 'chief' or 'baron', '*basileus*', survived to become the Classical Greek 'king', suggesting that at least some of the tribes were remnants of the Mycenaeans, led by Mycenaean nobles.

This period may be called a Dark Age, but a lot was happening while the lights were out – recently confirmed by the unexpected find of a prosperous settlement of c. 1000 BC at Lefkandí on Évia that traded luxury goods with Athens and Cyprus. When the curtain rises on the Archaic Age in the 8th century BC, what do we find?

Sea trade booming again, and diverse groups of Greeks speaking different dialects: Ionian in Attica, on most of the Cyclades and the Anatolian coast; Dorian in the Peloponnese and in an arch across the more southerly islands, including Crete and Rhodes; Aeolian in the west, Thessaly and Lésbos. All wrote in an **alphabetic script** learned from the Phoenicians; the addition of **vowels** was one of the great Greek innovations. Linear B had been used by bureaucrats to record palace stores, but some of the oldest inscriptions in the new letters show the stirrings of a new spirit: instead of lists there are dedications, curses, witticisms about wine and sly comments on romantic interests. Add to all that the first minting of **coins**, the establishment of the Panhellenic **Oracle** at Delphi as religious arbiter and political legitimizer, the founding of the **Olympic Games** (776 BC) marking the beginning of the Greek calendar, and a renaissance in the **arts**; heroic story cycles developed, including the Homeric epics.

Nurturing all of these developments is that quintessentially Greek institution, the *polis* or city-state. A 'citadel' in Homer (8th century BC), the word *polis* by Archaic times had evolved to denote a city-state not unlike the medieval *comuni* of Italy. Because of the country's geography, with its natural internal boundaries of mountains or sea, there were hundreds of city-states, many of them quite small (especially on the islands); Athens, which encompassed all of modern Attica, was exceptionally large. The city-state superseded old attachments to family and tribe with communal sanctuaries, where local guardian deities were worshipped. Mycenaean tombs were interpreted as the tombs of local heroes, leading to local cults and myths that lent each *polis* its legitimacy. Once defined on earth and in heaven, a *polis* could clone itself – population growth in the 8th century BC dictated that some citizens had to leave and found colonies among the 'barbarians' in Thrace, the Black Sea, Libya or the western Mediterranean. Or perhaps it was the pressure to colonize that focused attention on defining just what a *polis* should be. Significantly, the new writing was used very early to write down a city's laws, which were placed in the *agora* where all could read them. The days of arbitrary rule by the aristocrats were numbered.

Not without a fight. Most city-states in the 7th and 6th centuries went through an interim period of tyrants (dictators who usurped power), often supported by disgruntled noble factions. Polykrates of Sámos and Pisistratos of Athens were two of the most ambitious in their foreign policies, in founding festivals and in building lavish public buildings. Many tyrants attempted to found dynasties, although none in Greece proper lasted three generations.

Autarchy, or complete self-sufficiency, was one of the city-state's ideals, leading to endless wars in the fight for resources. Corinth, Argos and Chálki developed the new *hoplite* formations that replaced the Homeric military élite and cavalry (although these lingered well into Hellenistic times in Thessaly and Macedonia). In the *polis*, any citizen who could afford armour served as a *hoplite*. Massed together in a phalanx, shield overlapping shield, each man dependent on the next, the shared danger and need to remain fighting fit led to the social experimentation and group solidarity that produced citizens not subjects, creating a confident society ready to move towards democracy. Military training (limited to male citizens) would later be the prerequisite for participating in government.

City-states fought, but the need for the *hoplites* quickly to return to their own farms precluded long-term conquests. Sparta was the great exception, conquering her neighbour Messenía in two gruelling wars in the 8th and 7th centuries, and enslaving the inhabitants as *helots* to do all the farmwork. This left the Spartans free to train full-time as soldiers. Their political system, based as it was on the repression of a large majority, led to the creation of a military machine coupled with permanent political paranoia. Yet Sparta was only taking the whole city-state ideal, with its emphasis on citizen loyalty and pride, to the limit, highlighting the system's most serious flaw: with loyalty to the *polis* the be-all and end-all, the possibility of a larger political unity was never seriously entertained. Panhellenic shrines and games aside, the analogy that fits Hellenic culture is that of a maladjusted family whose members got together on holidays, but who had nothing good to say about the family the rest of the year, unless threatened by a real outsider – that is, any non-Greek.

500–338 BC: The Classical Moment

Meanwhile, the Greek city-states in Ionia (Asia Minor) had been gobbled up whole, first by Croesus of Lydia, who in turn was gobbled up by the Persians, at the time the greatest empire in the world. In 499 the Ionian Greeks revolted and, remembering old ties, Athens sent troops to help; they burned the Persian satrap's capital at Sardis and went home. The Persian lion quickly crushed the revolt, then sought to punish the mouse that had bitten its toe. In the long struggle that followed, the Greek city-states would band together (at least some of the time) to repel the common enemy. Athens and Plataea repulsed an expeditionary force at Marathon in 490, and a decade later, when Xerxes arrived with the biggest army and navy Europe had ever seen and things looked especially grim, 300 Spartans fought to the death in a delaying action at the pass of Thermopylae. Later, the Athenian fleet won a resounding victory at Salamis, and the Spartans led the Greek armies in trouncing the Persians and their Theban allies at Plataea in 479. Although Sparta had played a leading role in the war, most city-states, still fearing the Persians (who were ever ready to keep the pot boiling by aiding one Greek faction against another), turned for protection to Athens and its fleet in the **Delian League**, an alliance of 200 unequals that soon became a *de facto* Athenian empire. Under Pericles, Athens became a radical democracy and built the Parthenon while laying down the basics of Western civilization in art, poetry, drama and philosophy. Power and money made her the centre of the Greek world, but they would also be her downfall.

Fifty years of tension between Sparta and Athens, a simmering brew of jealousy, mistrust and self-interest, finally boiled over in the **Peloponnesian War** in 431 BC. As brilliantly described in Thucydides, every other Greek city-state became a political football on the big boys' playing field. After exhausted Athens finally collapsed in 405, Spartan hegemony lasted 30 short years; Thebes, her former ally, shattered her army at Leúktra in Boeotía (371 BC), thanks to Epaminondas and his new cavalry-infantry tactics. He brought the war to the Peloponnese and liberated long-suffering Messenía from Spartan tyranny before being killed in battle, ending Thebes' 15 minutes as big cheese in Greece.

As the city-states beaverishly undermined one another, a new actor on the stage looked down from the north and saw only ripe pickings. The Macedonians and their royal family were considered rather inferior Greeks by the Athenians, but their king **Philip II**, who came to the throne in 359, was a keen student of Epaminondas and, thanks to his gold mines, by far the wealthiest ruler in Greece. He was determined to prove them wrong, and do something not even the Athenians in their most reckless moment had envisaged: eliminate the Persian threat, once and for all. As a prelude Philip snatched up the Greek colonies in the north and annexed Thrace and Thessaly. Old enemies Thebes and Athens joined forces against him, only to be crushed at Chairóneia (338), the death knell of the old city-state. Two years later he was assassinated; his son **Alexander** shocked Greece into submission by destroying rebellious Thebes, left a viceroy in Macedonia and then led his father's planned expedition to Persia and never returned, too busy conquering the world to pay attention to Greece.

338 BC–AD 330: Hellenistic and Roman Greece

Although Alexander's death in 323 BC left a political mess as his generals fought endlessly over his conquests, his legacy would be the great cultural and economic revival in the Eastern Mediterranean known as the **Hellenistic Age**. Suddenly the Greek world had quintupled in size, while it enjoyed boom times in a great cross-cultural current. Athens still had her reputation, but the focus of cultural life slowly shifted eastwards to independent Rhodes, Alexandria and Pergamon. Demetrius Antigonas (Poliorketes), son of one of Alexander's generals, 'freed' Athens and restored democracy in 307. Greek cities would often be given their 'freedom' in the Hellenistic and Roman eras, even if it was only the freedom to do as they were told. Resistance in the Peloponnese coalesced in the **First Achaean League** (280), but it was too little, too late. Macedonia eventually succeeded in regaining control, but the struggle weakened Greece, and the endless factionalism that followed made it easy for **Rome** and her legions to wheedle in, defeating the Macondian phalanx decisively in 197. After several uprisings, Rome took direct control in 146 BC. One her first acts was to build the Via Egnatia across Greece from modern Igoumenítsa to Byzantium, opening the way to further conquests in the East.

Rome hauled off as much art as she could cram into her ships, and divided Greece into various provinces. The Romans professed to having been 'conquered' by Greek culture, a pretty compliment, and used Athens and Rhodes as a finishing school for their élite. But if the Romans considered themselves as part of the Hellenic family and went to great lengths to link themselves to the heroes of Homer, the Greeks could never really have seen them as anything more than 'Big Brothers'. Roman tourists flocked to Greece; Nero entered the games and miraculously won all events. Pausanius wrote the first guidebook. The theatres were converted into gladiatorial arenas for their entertainment and Sparta's Temple of Artemis Orthia, where boys were flogged, became a tourist attraction. Still, like every other era in history, people made the best of it; Roman rule did bring peace, and it offered a better life than the barbarians, who began knocking at the door in AD 252 when the **Goths** invaded Macedonia. By this time **Thessaloníki** up on the Via Egnatia had supplanted Athens as the most important city in Greece. As pressure from the invaders increased, the Roman empire divided itself like an amoeba into two parts; Thessaloníki briefly served as eastern capital until 330, when emperor Constantine moved to Byzantium and changed its name to his own, Constantinopolis. Historians call the resulting eastern half the Byzantine Empire, but the Greeks still referred to themselves as 'Romans'.

330–1204: The Byzantine Empire: Greece Moves East

Under the empire, Greece lost much of its importance, except for the north where Thessaloníki continued as the second city of Byzantium. **Christianity** spread early and pervasively. Edicts by the Emperor Theodosius and his mentor St Ambrose in Milan ordered that ancient temples be razed to make way for Christian churches, usually built from the same stone. Although many cities in Greece kept their chins up, the general picture is one of decline. Barbarian invasions continued periodically, and catastrophic earthquakes in 521 and 551, coupled with devastating outbreaks of plague in 541–3, left vast swathes of Greece underpopulated. The 7th–9th centuries were grim, marked by the violent controversy of **Iconoclasm** over the use of images in the Church and the **Arab conquest of Crete** (823), giving them a convenient base to raid the islands and coasts. New peoples, mostly **Slavs**, moved in to fill the gaps in Greece as the bureaucrats in Constantinople moved populations like chess pieces in order to keep up their tax base. Enough Greeks remained to absorb the invaders, and within a few generations the newcomers would be linguistically and culturally assimilated.

The light begins to flicker on again after future emperor **Nikephóros Phokás** liberated Crete (961) and **Basil II** defeated the Bulgars who had threatened the north. New churches and monasteries were built, especially on **Mount Athos**. Much of Greece, however, was deteriorating into a handful of large fiefs owned by absentee landowners (often the monasteries themselves); Constantinople's crushing taxes and clumsy statist economy meant a continuing impoverishment of the hinterlands. By 1204, the empire at Constantinople was such a remote and expensive entity that few were unhappy to see it taken over by the 'Franks' (the Greek word at the time for any Westerner) in the **Fourth Crusade**, an incursion masterminded by the merchants of Venice, who had a bone to pick over trading concessions in the East. As the Christian crusaders looted Christian Constantinople, the Venetians claimed the best art, along with control of strategic ports along the trade routes to the East, on the islands and in the Peloponnese.

1205–1821: Franks, Byzantines and Turks

Although the flimsy Latin Empire reverted to the Greeks, the Venetians held on tight to their own territories. In the 'Morea', as the Peloponnese was then commonly called, Geoffrey Villehardouin, chief of a few men in mail who had been stranded en route to the Fourth Crusade, managed to form his own Principality of Achaía, an improbable outpost of medieval chivalry. But they kept losing control of bits of it, and, after the Battle of Pelagonia in 1259, the victorious Greeks made **Mystrá** the seat of a despotate; it would be the last capital of Byzantium, before the Turks took over in 1460, seven years after the fall of Constantinople.

The **Turks** were welcome in some quarters simply because it was Ottoman policy to leave the Orthodox Church alone, something the interfering pope in Rome was loath to do. Interested only in supporting their army, the Turks left local communities alone except where taxes were concerned, combined with vicious reprisals whenever their authority was challenged. Under the Turkokratía, life for the peasants of in the north actually improved thanks to the end of the fighting that had so plagued the region in the past. Thessaloníki became the most important city, its population greatly augmented after 1492 by Jews expelled from Spain, as well as Slavs, Bulgars, Turks (Atatürk was born there) and other nationalities, planting a time bomb that would explode in late 19th-century irredentism (*see* p.520).

Significantly for the future, parts of Greece such as the Máni, western Arcadía, Souli in Épirus and Sfakiá in Crete never truly submitted to the Turks, and the pashas were constantly reduced to some form of power-sharing with local Greek leaders whom they could, of course, never quite trust. In spite of setbacks and disappointing efforts to oust the Turks by Morosini (Venice) in 1684 and Orlov (Russia) in 1770, Greek freedom fighters in *klephtic* bands, fought and were defeated again and again, then headed for the hills and bided their time. Their numbers increased dramatically in the 1700s, and an entire culture grew up around these free mountain spirits that would prove hard to give up when independence came.

1821–1922: Independence and the Great Idea

The revolutionary fires that swept through Europe at the end of the 18th century found plenty of kindling among Greeks. Poet **Ríga Feréou** of Thessaly, inspired by the French Revolution, provided the inspiration (*see* p.488), and after he was killed on the Sultan's orders, a group of diaspora Greeks living in Odessa formed the **Filiki Etaria** ('Friendly Society'). This secret society would do much to coordinate activities between well-wishers abroad and Greeks in Greece; the Ionian islands, which the British had inherited from Napoleon who had taken them from the Venetians, became hotbeds of revolutionary intrigue. The **War of Independence** began in the Peloponnese in 1821, and continued for more than six years through a parade of bloody atrocities and political in-fighting. In the end the Great Powers, namely Britain, Russia and France, came to assist the Greek cause, and the decisive **Battle of Navarino Bay** (20 October 1827; *see* p.348) gave the new Greek state the Peloponnese and the mainland peninsula up to a line between the cities of Árta and Vólos. While the Great Powers were searching about for a spare member of some inoffensive royal family to be the new Greece's king, Greece chose a president, **Iánnis Capodístria**, an ex-secretary to the Tsar of Russia. Capodístria offended the pro-British and pro-French factions in Greece with his pro-Russian policies – and also antagonized the powerful Mavromikális warlords, who had him assassinated in 1831. Before the anarchy spread too far, the Great Powers found a king: **Otto**, son of Ludwig I of Bavaria, who immediately offended local sensibilities by giving Bavarians all the official posts, including the building of the new capital over the bedraggled village that was Athens.

The fledgling Greek state was born with a mission: the *Megáli Idéa* or 'Great Idea' of liberating and uniting all the Greeks into a kind of Byzantium Revisited. Otto's arrogance and inadequacies led to revolts and his eventual dethronement in 1862, but the Great Powers found a replacement in **William George**, son of the King of Denmark (who, as a young naval cadet, learned of his new job in a newspaper wrapped around his sardine sandwich). In 1864, the National Assembly made Greece a **constitutional monarchy**, a system that began to work practically under prime minister **Trikoúpis** in 1875. During the long reign of George I, Greece began to develop, with shipping as its economic base.

In 1910, **Elefthérios Venizélos** became prime minister of Greece for the first of many terms. He deftly used the two **Balkan Wars** of 1912–13 to further the Great Idea, annexing his native Crete, the North Aegean islands, Macedonia and southern Épirus. When the **First World War** broke out, the new king **Constantine I** (married to Kaiser Wilhelm's sister) supported the Germans while remaining officially neutral, while Venizélos set up his own separate government with volunteers in support of the Allies in northern Greece. The 'National Schism' went Venizélos' way when the Allies recognized the prime minister; they blockaded the southern areas of Greece that supported Constantine and bluntly ordered the king to leave; Venizélos then sent Greek troops to the Macedonian front to fight against Bulgaria.

During the Paris peace conference, Venizélos hoped to reap the rewards of his loyalty by claiming **Smyrna (Izmir)**, which at the time had a huge majority Greek population. Turkey was prostrate, and Britain, France and America agreed to a Greek occupation as a preliminary to a local plebiscite on the future of the area. Tragically, the Greek landings were accompanied by atrocities against the Turks, who began to rally around national hero **Mustafa Kemal** (later **Atatürk**). Venizélos, meanwhile, was defeated in elections, partly from disgust with all the foreign meddling in Greek affairs, and Constantine got a royalist party elected on promises of a 'small but honourable Greece'. But Smyrna was too tempting a prize to give up. Encouraged by British prime minister Lloyd George, the Greek army marched on Ankara in March 1921. Kemal's armies routed them utterly, and by late August 1922 they threatened Smyrna; both sides committed atrocities, as thousands of Greek refugees fled the burning city. Constantine abdicated; Colonel Nikólas Plastíras took over, and in the bitterness that followed he executed five ministers and a general as scapegoats. Turkish-Greek relations had reached such an impasse that their leaders found a massive population exchange the only solution. Greece, then with a population of 4,800,000, was faced with the difficulties of finding housing and work for 1,100,000 refugees, while some 380,000 Muslims were sent to Turkey.

There were enough refugees to change the politics of Greece, and most of them supported Venizélos. The monarchy was abolished in 1924, and after a bad interlude of military dictatorship under General Pangalos, Venizélos was elected prime minister again in 1928. Trade unions and the Greek communist party, the **KKE**, gained strength. Venizélos made peace with Greece's neighbours (he visited Turkey in 1930 and even nominated Atatürk for the Nobel Peace Prize) and set the current borders of Greece, except for the Dodecanese, which Italy still 'temporarily occupied'. His term also saw the start of another headache: the first uprising by Greek Cypriots, four-fifths of the population of what was then a British Crown Colony, who desired union with Greece.

Another Catastrophe: The Second World War and the Greek Civil War

What Venizélos couldn't heal was the increased polarization of Greek political life, especially as the Great Depression led to violent labour unrest. Venizélos himself barely survived an assassination attempt; martial law was declared, coups were attempted, and in 1935, after a faked plebiscite, King **George II** returned to Greece, with General **Ioánnis Metaxás** as his Prime Minister. Metaxás assumed dictatorial control under the 'Regime of the Fourth of August', exiled the opposition, instituted rigorous censorship and crushed the trade unions and all leftist activities. Although he imitated the Fascists in some ways, Metaxás had sufficient foresight to prepare the Greek army in advance against occupation, and on 28 October 1940, as the story goes, he responded with a laconic '*Óchi!*' (No!) to Mussolini's ultimatum that his troops massed on the Albanian border be allowed passage through Greece. The Greeks heroically pushed the Italians back, but refused British offers of assistance at first in the futile hope of preventing Germany from joining the conflict. When Hitler's help came to the Italians in April 1941, it was crushing, and by mid-month the severely outnumbered British, New Zealanders and Australians, along with the Greek government, were fleeing south to the sea and North Africa.

By May 1941, after the **Battle of Crete**, all Greece was in the hands of the Nazis. The miseries of the Occupation – more civilians died in Greece than in any other occupied country; an estimated 500,000 people starved to death the first winter – politicized Greeks who in the past had hoped only to be left alone. The **EAM**, the National Liberation Front, and its army, **ELAS**, led the resistance and had vast popular support, but their politics were hardly palatable to Churchill, who was keen to restore the monarchy. He made a secret deal with Stalin to keep Greece within the British sphere of influence in the famous '**percentages agreement**'. Stalin, however, failed to tell Greek communists about his deal, and the **Greek Civil War** – the first campaign of the Cold War – broke out three short months after liberation. It began in Athens, with British troops fighting some members of ELAS, their former resistance allies, followed by long-drawn-out guerrilla campaigns in the mountains. As Britain's containment policy was taken over by the USA under the Truman Doctrine, American money and advisors poured into Greece. The Civil War dragged on until 1949; leftists who were not shot or imprisoned went into exile.

1950 to the Present: Interesting Times

The Greeks call the next two decades, up to the end of the Colonels' *junta* in 1974, the 'Years of Stone'. Recovery was slow, even if orchestrated by America, and the Greek diaspora that began in the early 1900s accelerated so fast that entire villages, especially on the islands, became ghost towns. In 1951, Greece and Turkey became full members of NATO, an uncomfortable arrangement from the start because of the unresolved issue of Cyprus. General Papágos of the American-backed Greek Rally Party won the elections of 1952. Papágos died in 1955, and **Konstantínos Karamanlís** replaced him as prime minister, inaugurating eight years of relative stability and prosperity as agriculture and tourism grew, although the opposition criticized his pro-Western policy and inability to resolve the worsening situation in **Cyprus**. Because one-fifth of the Cypriots were Turkish, Turkey refused to let Cyprus join Greece – the independence or partitioning of the island was as far as Ankara would go.

Meantime Greece was rocked with record unemployment. The royal family, especially the forceful German-born Queen Frederíka, was unpopular; there were strikes and powerful anti-American feelings. In 1963 came the assassination of left-wing Deputy Lambrákis (see Costas Gávras' film Z) for which police officers were tried and convicted. Karamanlís lost the next elections in 1965 to centre left warhorse **George Papandréou**, who gave a portfolio to his son Andréas, an economics professor at Harvard (and once Adlai Stevenson's campaign manager in Minnesota), whose mildly inflationary policies horrified the right. At the same time, King Paul died and was succeeded by his son, the conservative, 23-year-old Constantine II. The combination did not bode well; a quarrel with the young king over reforming the tradition-bound military led to Papandréou's resignation in 1966. Massive discontent finally forced Constantine to call for elections; before they could take place, a coup by an obscure group of army officers on 21 April 1967 caught both right and left by surprise. The '**Colonels**', most of whom were of peasant stock and resentful of Athenian politicians, established a **military dictatorship** and imprisoned George and Andréas Papandréou. Colonel **George Papadópoulos** made himself prime minister. Constantine attempted a ridiculous counter-coup and then fled to Rome.

The proclaimed goal of the Colonels was a 'moral cleansing of Orthodox Christian Greece'. Human rights were suppressed, absurd censorship undermined cultural life, and the secret police imprisoned and tortured dissidents – or their children. While condemned abroad, Greece's position in the volatile eastern Mediterranean and in NATO were reason enough for America, obsessed by the Cold War, to prop up the regime. The internal situation went from bad to worse, and on 17 November 1973 students of the Polytechnic School in Athens went on strike. Tanks were brought in and many were killed. Popular feeling rose to such a pitch that Papadópoulos was arrested, only to be replaced by his arrester, the brutal head of the military police, **Dimítrios Ioanídes**. Relations with Cypriot president Makários collapsed because of Ioanídes' bullying. In an insane bid for popularity, Ioanídes tried to launch a coup in Cyprus, to assassinate Makários and replace him with a president who would declare the long-desired union of Cyprus with Greece. It was a fiasco. Makários fled, and the Turkish army invaded Cyprus, occupying 40 per cent of the island. The Greek military rebelled, the dictatorship resigned and Karamanlís hurriedly returned from his exile in Paris to form a new government, release the political prisoners and order a cease-fire in Cyprus.

Karamanlís and his conservative **Néa Demokratía** (**ND**) easily won the November 1974 elections. The monarchy did less well in a subsequent plebiscite, and Greece became a republic. That same year Karamanlís realized his fondest dream when the country was anchored to the European Economic Community, of which Greece became a full member in 1981. Karamanlís brought stability but neglected the economic and social reforms Greece needed. These, along with a desire for national integrity, were to be the ticket to populist Andréas Papandréou's victories beginning in 1981. His party **PASOK** (the Pan-Hellenic Socialist Movement) promised much, beginning with withdrawal from NATO and the EU, and the removal of US air bases. A national reconciliation with the resistance fighters from the war (as long as they were ethnically Greek and not Slavs or Albanians) was at the top of the agenda; women were given more rights, and even excess accents were kicked out of the written language as a heady and hedonistic liberalization swept the land. PASOK easily triumphed again in the 1985 elections, in spite of Papandréou's failure to deliver Greece from the snares of NATO, the USA or the EU, or keep any of his promises on the economic front. Inflation soared, and Greece had to be bailed out by a huge EU loan accompanied by an unpopular belt-tightening programme. In the end scandals brought Papandréou down: corruption in the Bank of Crete, and the old man's affair with, and subsequent marriage to, a young airline hostess.

In 1990, Néa Demokratía leader **Konstantínos Mitsotákis**, a former resistance fighter, took a slim majority in the elections, promising to grapple with Greece's economic problems. His austerity measures soon proved even more unpopular than Papandréou's scandals. By late 1992 Mitsotákis had his share of political scandals as well, and in October 1993 Papandréou was re-elected. He kept Greece in his thrall as Yugoslavia disintegrated, pushing Balkan nationalist buttons over Macedonia and siding (verbally, mostly) with the Serbs, as Orthodox brethren oppressed by Muslim hordes. As Papandréou played the gadfly, the once-reviled 'capitalist club', the EU, poured massive funds into Greece, resulting in new roads, schools, sewers and agricultural subsidies.

In late 1995 Papandréou declined as well. Seriously ill, he refused to resign while his new wife's faction manoeuvred for power, thwarted in the end by a revolt led by former trade minister **Kósta Simítis**, a 'respected but bland' technocrat who toughed it out to get the party's nod. Non-dogmatic, steady and low-key, Simítis has been a hard worker for common sense. With the aid of Papandréou's son George as foreign minister, he has greatly improved relations with neighbouring states, allowing Greece to position itself as a regional leader and prime investor in the Balkans; he has also encouraged talks towards an agreement over Cyprus, as the island state prepares to join the EU in 2004. Greek-Turkish relations have improved dramatically, especially after each country rushed to the other's aid after the earthquakes in 1999.

Simítis' Greece is doggedly trying to better itself: improving infrastructure, providing a climate for capital investments, and building new ties with Eastern Europe and Russia. The biggest news, and the national deadline for every long-deferred project, is now the 2004 Olympics. A lucky break in the summer of 2002 led to the capture of members of the long elusive November 17 terrorist gang, which turned out to be a rather ordinary gang of criminals with fuzzy left-wing ideas. Fingers are crossed that diplomats will iron out the remaining snags with Turkey to allow Cyprus to slip pain-lessly into the EU in 2004. Greece has finally dropped its objections to Turkey's own application to join the club, and the two countries have put in a joint bid to host the 2008 European Football Championships.

Art and Architecture

04

Like many peoples, the ancient Greeks were inveterate storytellers, but with a twist: their focus was not so much on what happened but on how and why it happened, and here they founded one of the tenets of Western art. They were also our first over-achievers, fired with a 'divine discontent' and lust for fame that saw city-states rivalling to build the biggest temples and votaries trying to outshine their peers with showy dedications. Architects, sculptors, painters and potters constantly innovated as they strove for an ideal that became the 'classic' standard by which other artists have since measured themselves; they were the first to become celebrities, the first to sign their work, and the first to be (literally, in at least one case) worshipped as heroes.

5000–2000 BC: Neolithic and Early Helladic

Art in Greece begins in the Neolithic era, with simple paintings on the Diroú caves in the Máni and the lumpy little 'Venus' fertility figures common throughout Europe. By the 5th millennium BC, however, we get the first inklings of native talent in the pottery of Sésklo in Thessaly. The early Bronze Age, or Helladic period, began c. 3200 BC and left tantalising evidence of a sophisticated society, in the two-storey **House of Tiles** at Lérna in Argolís (c. 2500–2200 BC). Its pretty, interlaced seal impressions and other stylistic similarities with sites across the Aegean suggest an indigenous pre-Greek civilization, identified with the Pelasgians.

The Pelasgians on the Cyclades and Crete made beautiful things as well. On the Cycladic islands, the poor quality of clay limited ceramics to plain pots, but with remarkable exceptions (bird spout pitchers and 'frying pans', perhaps representing the womb). By 2600 BC their dead were buried with their trademark idols, prehistoric Modigliani-like figures of luminous white marble laboriously smoothed with emery, evolving from early quasi-abstract 'fiddles' to female statuettes with long necks and tilted oval heads; the rarer Cycladic figures of musicians and the 'toastmaster' are among the most charming prehistoric works anywhere. On Crete, the early Minoans were already demonstrating their precocious skills in pottery, stone vases and gold.

2000–1600 BC: Middle Helladic and Middle Minoan

The Middle Helladic, coeval with the Middle Kingdom of Egypt and Stonehenge, coincides with the arrival of the first Greek-speakers and the introduction of their modest but well-crafted **Minyan ware**, first discovered by Schliemann at Orchomenos in Boeotía, the seat of the legendary King Minyas. Wheel-made pottery appears at the same time as in Troy, in the same style, leading to the intriguing possibility that the Greeks were really Trojans. Or vice versa. But metals were the objects of desire: smooth **Grey Minyan** ware imitated silver, and in 1700 BC **Yellow Minyan**, fired in an oxidizing atmosphere to imitate gold, came on the scene.

The Minoans, left undisturbed on Crete, went from strength to strength. Great unfortified palaces at Knossos, Mália, Zákros and Phaistos fostered the arts: their frescoes, ceramics, jewellery and ivories cram the museum in Heráklion, filled with a love of nature and a *joie de vivre* that the old Mediterranean had never seen before. Their technique was nothing short of extraordinary: they engraved on precious stones with a precision that presupposes a magnifying glass – and one was duly found.

1600–1100 BC: Late Helladic (Mycenaean)

In the late Bronze Age (*c.* 1600 BC), Mycenaeans on the mainland came into contact with the Minoans, and within 50 years Minoan art and culture underwent a sea change. Most of the earliest finds were simply imported. But as time went on, Cretan artists made goods to suit Mycenaean tastes, which leant towards the monumental and preferred simplified versions of their more exuberant motifs; scenes of hunting and war, almost unknown in Crete, were now popular. Minoan goldsmiths crafted much of the treasure found in Mycenae (1600–1550 BC), although the famous 'mask of Agamemnon' is unlike any Minoan portrait.

Although inspired by Crete's labyrinthine palaces, the Mycenaeans built to a more regular design, in *megaron* units: each unit consisted of a gateway, a courtyard with an entrance porch (*propylon*), and a vestibule giving on to a large hall with a throne and circular hearth. Off the *megarons* were residential quarters and, beyond these, workshops. Unlike the Minoans, the Mycenaeans built citadels, of boulders so huge that they were called 'cyclopean' by later Greeks who imagined only a Cyclops could conceivably have built them. Dressed stone was reserved for gateways and corbelled *tholos* tombs, which reached an apogee in Mycenae's spectacular **Treasury of Atreus**.

Some time around 1450 BC, the Mycenaeans developed their own **Palace Style** of ceramics: stirrup-jars with 'dummy spouts' in the centre and squat flat *alabastrons*, originally made of alabaster, used to store essential oils. As time went on, potters fumblingly copied scenes from the palace frescoes, of chariots, warriors or symmetrical heraldic animals. The potters also made terracotta 'Mycenaean dollies', a minimalist version of the Minoan goddess; some resemble bud vases. Mycenaean jewellers adopted Minoan seal-engraving techniques, mass-produced gold relief beads, and may have invented enamelling (fusing molten coloured glass to the gold). Exquisite gold, silver, copper and black niello inlay work on the ornamental daggers show that Homer's description of Agamemnon's cuirass and Achilles' shield wasn't all fantasy.

1100–770 BC: The Dark Ages (Geometric Period)

In spite of their huge walls, the Mycenaean citadels began to fall around 1200 BC. Communications broke down, and with them the typical stylistic unity of Mycenaean art. Although traditional pottery forms and motifs were reused, their meaning seems confused. Some potters attempted no decoration at all, or were content with simple dark bands: this '**Granary Style**' would be the mainstay for a century or so.

The Classical Greeks knew this shadowy period as the less-heroic Iron Age, but in many ways this was the 'real' period of Homer; his description of the making of Achilles' bronze shield actually describes an iron-making process, and it was only after 1100 BC that cremation, Homeric-style, became common. Outside of Athens, at least one Mycenaean population survived the 'catastrophe' at Lefkandí, on Évia, where a royal couple were given a heroic burial in a shrine anticipating the Greek peripteral temple (1000–950 BC). Tripods found in a 'chieftain's house' at Nikchória in Messenía suggest that a similar situation may have existed there.

Although 'sub-Mycenaeans' still rattled about in the echoing halls of Mycenae and Tiryns, and Eteocretans (i.e. Minoans) survived in pockets of eastern Crete, the Iron Age seems to have been a time of large-scale migrations, when it was every man for himself. There were no new communal buildings, no multiple graves, no writing, almost no contact with the outside world. Even communications with the gods dropped off; the dolly goddesses are forgotten, and until the late 10th century the only offerings at Olympia, Tegea and other Dark Age shrines were small clay animals. It seems the wheel was forgotten also. But when potters in Athens remembered (in the Proto-Geometric era, 1050 BC), their new wheels were faster than ever, their kilns hotter, their decoration completely abstract. One of their most successful designs was the typical Greek **running meander**. The best Geometric vases are meticulous – the invention of a compass with multiple brush-ends enabled potters to draw precise concentric circles that accentuate the forms of the vessels, their lustrous sheen glowing like metal. Late in the period (800–700 BC) figurative designs began; horses, fish and birds appeared, with a few lone humans. In Athens and on the islands, vases were used as grave markers, with holes in the bottom for libations. On these, communal scenes appear, of stick figures wailing at funerals, warriors and hunters.

770–500 BC: Archaic

The peculiar Geometric interlude of self-effacement ended as abruptly as it had begun. The ferment of the 8th century BC, when the Greeks evolved their alphabet, founded the Olympics and colonized distant shores, also reawakened artistic interest in people and their doings. Inspiration may have come from hero-worship at Mycenaean tombs (and the discovery of the figurative art they contained), and certainly through renewed contacts with the East. Corinth, at the vanguard of the age, made polychrome Proto-Corinthian ware for export (c. 725–650), decorated with orientalizing images of animals and monsters, the voids filled with stylized motifs. Corinthian potters invented **black figure painting** in c. 700, and produced quality work until Athens relegated them, and all other potters, to provincialism.

Athens had the advantage of the finest clay in Greece. Iron ore was added to create its characteristic red colour, and its painters specialized in narrative scenes from the start – the Proto-Attic amphora at Eleusis showing Odysseus blinding Polyphemos (650 BC) is one of their first masterpieces. The invention of **red figure painting** in Athens in c. 530 (backgrounds were painted black, leaving inverted silhouettes, to which details were added with a fine brush) allowed painters to achieve a naturalism that no others could match; their vases were in demand across the ancient world.

The first Archaic essays into **sculpture** (c. 700–620) are small, austere, flat figures with triangular heads, called Daedelic after their legendary Cretan creator. When the withdrawal of the Assyrians from Egypt in 672 BC reopened the country to Greek merchants, the monumental statues the Greeks saw there inspired their own version, the well-known *kouros* (young man). Like Egyptian models, the *kouros* has a stiff, formal posture, one foot placed before the other, arms down by the sides. The female version, the *kore* (maiden), clothed in drapery, evokes feminine grace and modesty, right arm extended to hold an offering.

Yet from the start the Greek approach was different. While Egyptians represented specific individuals or gods, decently clad, the naked *kouros* exists in that special Greek penumbra between the mortal and divine, an ideal rather than an individual, wearing an easy, confident 'Archaic smile' as if in on a secret joke. Nor did Greek sculptors feel compelled to repeat the same conventions over and over, but each added variations, striving better to represent the appearance of nature. Towards the end of the Archaic period the Greeks learned hollow bronze casting; the Pireaus Museum has the earliest examples, found, like most surviving Greek bronzes, in shipwrecks.

Most of the *kore* and *kouros* statues were dedicated at **sanctuaries**. In the beginning these were simply a sacred precinct (*temenos*) around an altar, where sacrifices were made. With the revival of sculpture, the need arose for a shelter to protect the cult statue. Clay models show that the earliest temples were simple houses with columned fronts. The first peristyle temples (with columns on all sides) were of wood, beginning with the famous Temple of Hera on Sámos, built by 718 BC. Corinth developed the **Doric style**; the first 'classic' temple, with fluted stone columns, gable front and *metopes*, was built by her colony Corfu, *c.* 580 BC; the oldest Doric Temple still standing is the Temple of Apollo in Corinth (550 BC). Its stout bunched columns are in marked contrast to the more graceful, airier works of the following century. But in essence, the architecture of the Archaic age – buildings framed with columns and porches, so perfect for the climate – would remain the same throughout antiquity.

Adorning the temples were reliefs of battles or scenes from mythology. The desire to narrate was a powerful impetus to realism, and some of the greatest Archaic works are temple tympanums and metopes (frieze panels), among them, the formidable Medusa in Corfu, the three-headed Typhon in the Acropolis Museum, and the lively frieze from the Treasury of the Siphnians at Delphi. Some bear traces of paint. The Greeks adored colour, and all that white marble of their temples and sculpture that we find so appealing would look bare to their makers.

Funeral steles, first seen in Mycenae, returned to fashion at the end of the 7th century, often topped with concave finials evoking flowers on a grave. Sphinxes, as demon guardians of the dead, became the rage in the 6th century; tombs in Attica in particular became so elaborate that Solon subjected them to sumptuary laws. These had the effect of making artistic qualities (rather than size) the focus, leading to the exquisite funerary steles of the Classical era.

500–323 BC: Classical

The Greek fascination with maths, ideal proportions and pattern reached its apogee in the 5th century BC. For the first few decades the introspective **'Severe' Classical style** prevailed. Statues become much more naturalistic, breaking out of their stiff poses, although their smiles are replaced by brooding glances. After the defeat of the Persians in 480 BC, however, confidence ran high. The beauty of the Temple of Aphaia on Aegina and the sheer scale of the Temple of Zeus at Olympia proclaim the pride of the period. Iktinos perfected the Doric temple (and, many would say, all architecture) in his Parthenon, through the use of refinements such as *entasis* (see p.121). The Parthenon set the fashion for combining strong Doric elements with the more elegant Ionic order: the Temple of Apollo Epikourios at Bassae, also by Iktinos, is full of innovations, one of which was the first known Corinthian column, its capital modelled on the curving *volutes* of the acanthus. Innovations continued during and after the Peloponnesian War, with the Erechtheion on Athens and its famous caryatid porch, and the two beautiful, mysterious *tholos* buildings, at Delphi and Epídauros.

Sculptors vied to make figures more lifelike, on the verge of action. Yet for all the new naturalism, their work retained the Archaic ideal, concentrating on archetypes. One of the greatest 5th-century sculptors, **Polyclitus of Argos**, was celebrated for his statues of athletes and for his treatise, the *Canon*, that mathematically defined the proportions of the body that constituted beauty, each in elegant relationship to another. Extremes, personality and emotion had no place here; the beautiful gaze off into a better world with calm Classical detachment. Bronze allowed sculptors greater freedom in their poses, and became the favoured medium for life-sized figures. Unfortunately it was also the favourite medium for melting by Christians or Turks, although a handful of superb exceptions escaped: the *Zeus/Poseidon* in the Archaeological Museum in Athens, the *Charioteer* of Delphi (and the horses of St Mark's in Venice and the Riace Warriors, in Calabria). Free-standing marble statues, on the other hand, are only known through Roman-era copies, although we still have a fair amount of Classical architectural sculpture. Panhellenic themes were popular: the Labours of Heracles and the battles of Centaurs or Amazons (i.e. the 'barbarian' Persians) against the Lapiths or men (representing the 'civilized' Greeks). **Phidias**, the first real celebrity artist, was responsible for the masterpiece of the genre, the Parthenon frieze, where the theme, the great Panathenaic procession, is a unique celebration of Athens in its heyday.

Greek cities also followed patterns. The geography is such that nearly all grew up by a hill, the *acropolis*, often with fortifications and the city's oldest shrines. Below, the centre of the city was the *agora*, translated as 'marketplace', although it was much more: both the heart of civic life and a sacred *temenos*, marked by boundary stones, forbidden to the criminal and unclean. In the *agora* you'd find the Council House (*bouleuterion*), the presidential committee chamber (*prytaneion*), fountain house, and shrines, temples, altars and statues dedicated to civic gods or heroes. Along the sides, *stoas* housed shops and banks, their colonnades offering shelter from the sun and rain; one, the Stoa of Attalus in Athens, has been reconstructed. Here Greeks could indulge in their favourite pastime – talking. Planning became a science in the mid-5th century with the idealistic geometrician **Hippodamos of Miletus**, who laid out neat grids of streets to encourage *isonomia*, or social equality: Pireaus and Rhodes were two of his famous works, but Olynthos in Chalkidikí, destroyed by Philip II of Macedon after only a few decades of existence, is the best preserved example in Greece. In the early 4th century BC, Athens rebuilt its theatre in stone, and soon every city had one, many scooped into the convenient side of the acropolis hill; Epídauros has the most perfect one (380 BC). Most cities had outer defensive walls, with the great exception of Sparta, which relied on its military prowess. Their *helots*, when they were liberated, were not about to rely on any such thing, and built the still remarkable walls at Messene (begun in 370 BC). Within the walls would be a quarter devoted to athletics and the body beautiful, with a gymnasium ('place where one goes naked') attached to various schools for young men, near to the stadium.

Vitruvius wrote that the Greeks discovered **perspective** in the 5th century, and the story goes that one painter, Zeuxis, even deceived the birds, who tried to pluck grapes from his picture. **Attic vases**, with their imaginative compositions, pure line, foreshortening and realism, reached their peak in the early 5th century, before the large scale public works under Pericles lured artists away to bigger projects. The best paintings to survive are in a handful of late Classical Macedonian tombs, in particular the fabulous royal tombs in Vergína, works that prove the ancient Greeks adept at techniques that would only be rediscovered in the Renaissance.

323–30 BC: Hellenistic

In the 4th century BC, after Philip II of Macedon put paid to the Greek city-state experiment, a quiet revolt against Polyclitus' *Canon* took place. Poses and expressions become more relaxed, and there was an increase in individual 'types', although compared to the warts-and-all Roman busts that followed, they are still idealized. Alexander the Great was the first to use images of himself as propaganda. His favourite sculptor was **Lysippos of Sikyon**, who used less perfect but more lifelike proportions (with a notably smaller head) and statues meant to be seen in the round; with his brother Lysistratos he invented the life mask and lost-wax method of casting. This was also the time of **Praxiteles of Athens**, who added charm and a sensuous grace to figures in *contrapposto* poses (with the weight resting on one leg); his only surviving work, the *Hermes* at Olympia, shows his exquisite modelling that conjures flesh from marble. Praxiteles carved the first life-size female nude, of *Aphrodite*, which quickly became a tourist attraction in Knidos. Praxiteles may have been sculpting gods, but with him art had become pure art.

By the time Alexander died in 323 BC, the problems of pose, anatomy, proportions and drapery had been resolved. Now artists could only exaggerate; a Baroque sensationalism and complexity, all windswept drapery, violence and passion, became so prominent in works such as the bronze *Artemísseon Jockey* in Athens, the Louvre's *Winged Victory of Samothrace* and the Vatican's writhing *Laocoön* that reaction soon set in. The era saw the first wave of copies of older works, and others sculpted in Archaic or Classical styles, as in Damophon's statues at Lykosoúra (now in Athens).

Floor mosaics, first seen at Classical Olynthos, developed into masterly imitations of paintings in the Macedonian cities of Pella and Dion, which had some of the largest and most lavish private villas in Greece, a far cry from the simple abodes of Classical times. Other fine examples are in the once smart quarters of ancient Kos and Delos and in Rhodes' Palace of the Grand Masters.

30 BC–AD 330: Roman

The *pax romana* not only ended the rivalries between the Greeks but pretty much dried up their inspiration as well, although a stream of workmanlike sculptors, architects and other talents found a ready employment in the Roman empire, cranking out copies of earlier masterpieces. Romans bigwigs, notably the hellenophile emperor

Hadrian, liked to show their appreciation for Greek culture with public buildings, such as the Odeion of Herodes Atticus (AD 160) in Athens; the ruins of ancient Corinth, Gortyn (Crete), Nikopolis (Actium) and Philippi are essentially Roman as well. They also put Thessaloníki on the map, and even briefly made it capital of the eastern empire: the Emperor Galerius' Rotunda and arch, and the mighty walls built a bit later by Theodosius, are among the city's chief monuments.

AD 330–1452: Byzantine

The founding of **Constantinople** at Byzantium in 330 coincided with the official recognition of Christianity. The first churches were modelled on the three-aisle Roman basilica; Thessaloníki's 5th-century Acheiropoíetos, one of the oldest still in use, is a perfect example. Mosaics were relocated from the floors to decorate the walls with glittering tiny tesserae; Thessaloníki again has some of the earliest surviving works, perhaps none as charming as the church of Ósios David, where the pagan delight in the material world still lingers. In the 6th century, under the great Justinian, architects striving for a more Christian architecture placed a dome over a cruciform plan, although it took several tries to get it right (as with Basilica B, at Philippi). Most early churches in Greece, however, fell victim to the earthquakes and barbarian invasions that troubled the next few centuries. By the time the Greeks were ready to build again, the **Greek cross plan** with a dome over the crossing, supported on squinches or pendentives, had been mastered. The 8th-century Ag. Sofía in Thessaloníki is an early example, as well as one of the few surviving churches built during the puritanical fire storm of the Iconoclasm (726–843) when figurative art was equated with idolatry and icons tossed on to the pyre.

The **Middle Byzantine** or **Macedonian Age** (named after the Macedonian emperors, 844–1025) that followed the defeat of the Iconoclasts brought a cultural revival and a vast building programme of new monasteries, including the majestic Ósios Loukás in Boeotía. Painted or mosaic decoration was often in the 'hierarchical' formula that symbolically reproduced the universe; it was especially popular in *katholikóns* or monastery churches. Christ Pantocrator ('all-governing') or the Christ of the Ascension reigns in the dome of heaven, surrounded by angels, while just below the Virgin and John the Baptist intercede for humanity. The Virgin and Child occupy the central apse. The surrounding vaults and upper registers show the Dodekaorton, the 'Twelve Feasts' of the church, while in the lower, terrestrial zone are saints, prophets and martyrs (whose gory deaths are also a favourite subject in the narthex).

Yet even in the bloodiest Byzantine martyrdoms there is a certain trance-like detachment. Its saints reside on a purely spiritual plane; their most striking feature on church walls and icons is most often their intense, staring eyes. They never play on the heartstrings or ask the viewer to relive the pain of the Passion or coo over a baby Jesus; the Virgin (the Panagía, or 'all-holy'), cocooned in black like an Orthodox nun, has none of the charms of a Madonna. 'The artistic perfection of an icon,' as Timothy Ware wrote, 'was not only a reflection of the celestial glory – it was a concrete example of matter restored to its original harmony and beauty serving as a vehicle of the spirit.' An intention wholly different from that of the ancient Greeks, in fact, who were infatuated with human beauty and intellect and made divinity in their own image. The calm Classical gaze of their gods was a reflection of earthly mathematical perfection; the Byzantine stare belongs to the visionary, abstract and ascetic. Curiously, this stare annoyed the Turks no end – in many churches you'll find frescoes more or less intact except for the eyes, gouged out by their knives.

Byzantine art under the **Comnene emperors** (12th–14th centuries) marked a renewed interest in antique models: the stiff, hieratic figures are given more natura-listic proportions in graceful, rhythmic compositions. Occasionally the emperors sent imperial mosaicists to decorate their foundations – leaving exquisite examples in Thessaloníki, Dáphni near Athens, Ósios Loukás, and at Néa Moní on Chíos.

Fragmented after the fall of Constantinople to the Crusaders in 1204, Greece became a mosaic of regions under various Latin rulers and despots, some more enduring than others. Épirus, Vería and Kastoriá had thriving local schools of Byzantine art and architecture. Crete's 400-year occupation by Venice brought a cultural cross-fertilization that developed into a vibrant school of painting, best repre-sented by the frescoes in Kéra Panagía above Ag. Nikólaos and the works of Doménikos Theotokópolous, who left Crete for Venice and Spain where he became known as **El Greco**. The Crusaders for their part left mostly castles as souvenirs of their stay, often built to keep their Greek subjects in line: Chlemoútsi, Platamónas, the Acrocorinth and Karítena (where they also left a fine bridge) are among the most impressive. The Genoese left delightful villas and towns on Chíos and Lésbos; the Venetians, who lasted longer, built impressive citadels not only on Crete but at Naúplio, Pýlos, Náfpaktos, Methóni, Koróni and Corfu, where they left a charming legacy of Corfu town, one of the most beautiful in Greece. The Knights of St John, who occupied the Dodecanese after losing Jerusalem, built their share of castles too, as well as the evocative old town of Rhodes, still protected by its 15th-century walls.

The **Late Byzantine** period began in 1261, with the recovery of Constantinople by the Paleológos emperors. The humanist and naturalistic influences of the next century combined to produce, apparently independently, the Byzantine equivalent of the *trecento* art of Siena, with a greater attention to colour, perspective, landscape, and architecture. Thessaloníki's Ag. Apostóli and Ag. Nikólaos Orphanós are two fine examples; at Mystrá, the lyrical frescoes in the churches are the great poignant might-have-been of Byzantine art. After the Turkish conquest the best painters (labelled 'post-Byzantine' in the museums, a period that extends to the present day) took refuge in Venetian-ruled Crete or the Ionian islands, or the monastic republic of Mount Athos.

1460–1830: Turkish Greece (the Turkokratía)

The long centuries of Turkish rule left relatively few monuments in Greece. Much that the Turks themselves built was destroyed in the bitter War of Independence, or in its aftermath. Places that joined Greece at a much later date, such as Thrace, Rhodes town and Kos, still have Muslim minorities and the best surviving Turkish districts, with mosques, hammams and public buildings. Athens, Chíos, Thessaloníki, Ioánnina (Alí Pasha's palace) and Kavála have important monuments as well.

The Greeks of the Turkokratía are perhaps best represented by their defiant monasteries, often built in inaccessible places – on cliffs, ravines and most spectacularly on the pinnacles of Metéora. Although most people lived simply, the better to avoid the attention of the taxman, merchants in the 18th and 19th centuries left impressive mansions in Kastoriá and Siátista (Western Macedonia), in the Zagorochória (Épirus) and on the Pélion peninsula (Thessaly). In the Peloponnese, the fiercely independent Maniátes built stone tower houses that remain one of the most startling sights in Greece. Ports with their own fleets, such as Hýdra, Spétses, Sými and Líndos on Rhodes have impressive captains' mansions. It was a thriving period for textiles, costumes, jewellery, and ceramics. Local folklore and history museums are always worth a look; there are remarkable ones in Ioánnina, Kozáni, Athens, Skýros and Heráklion.

Independence to Modern Times: 1830–

After the War of Independence, Greek cities were rebuilt with a modest neoclassical flair that seemed especially suited. Athens, as the new capital, has the most lavish examples, while Naúplio, Galaxídi, and especially Ermoúpoli on Sýros, in the 19th century the most important port in Greece, reek with atmosphere and faded grandeur. One name to remember is **Ernst Ziller** (1837–1923), a German architect and friend of the archaeologist Schliemann (*see* 'Mycenae', pp.242–7), who built some of the finest neoclassical buildings and mansions in Greece, including Schliemann's own villa in Athens (now the Numanistic museum). Up until the 20th century, however, traditional vernacular styles prevailed in most places. These are surprisingly varied, and have been best preserved in more rural zones, especially mountain villages and on the islands; the Melissa Press in Athens has published a series of regional architectural guides that make a great introduction. Earthquakes, neglect, the need to provide for a million refugees overnight after the Asia Minor fiasco in 1922 and the brutality of the Occupation and Civil War have all taken a toll, as has the rash of ugly apartments and hotels that mushroomed up in the 1960–70s to cash in on the honeypot of tourism. Prosperity in recent years, however, has brought an increased interest in traditional architecture: programmes are now in place to preserve the most beautiful villages, and new laws in many areas insist that new building conform to local styles.

While modern Greeks have made names for themselves in literature and poetry (Cavafy, Kazantzákis, Rítsos, and the Nobel Prize winners Seféris and Elýtis) and in music and film (Maria Callas, Dimitris Mitropoulos, Mikis Theodorákis, Melína Mercouri, Elia Kazan, Costa Gravas, Michelis Cacoyannis, Theodore Angelopoulos among others), most people would have a hard time naming a modern Greek artist or sculptor. To get acquainted with them, visit the National Gallery in Athens, the municipal galleries in Athens and Thessaloníki, the Goulandrís Museum of Modern Art on Ándros and the Vorrés Museum in Paianía and Pierídis Gallery in Glyfáda (both in Attica). Two names to look out for are **Theóphilos Hadzimichaïl** (1873–1934), whose patriotic naïve murals of quirky charm are in Athens, Lésbos and the Pélion peninsula, and **Níkos Hadjikyriákos-Ghíkas** (1906–94), whose stunning, very personal art was initially based on Cubism (some 30 works in the National Gallery).

Topics

Losing their Marbles

Bonaparte has not got such a thing from all his thefts in Italy.
                              Lord Elgin, writing in 1801 from Constantinople

It is Greece's special sorrow that her War of Independence didn't begin two decades earlier, before the fad for antiquities swept Europe, a fad that became an international rivalry after Napoleon pillaged Italy and Egypt to fill the Louvre. But Thomas Bruce, the seventh Lord Elgin, ambassador to the Sublime Porte, trumped Boney to something even the Romans never thought of taking: the sculptures of the world's most famous building. Admittedly in 1687, after Morosini bombed the then-intact temple (even though he knew the Turks were using it as a powder store) he added insult to injury by removing the pediment showing the contest between Athena and Poseidon, only the ropes broke as it was lowered and the statues shattered into bits.

Elgin got his turn in 1801 when the Turkish military governor in Athens refused to allow his artist, Lusieri, to erect a scaffolding to paint the Parthenon frieze. Elgin went to the Sultan to get a firman, or authority, and the Sultan, pleased that the British had just rid Egypt of the French, readily provided one, not only allowing Elgin's agents into the 'temple of idols' but to 'take away any sculptures or inscriptions which do not interfere with the works or walls of the Citadel.' Elgin interpreted this as a *carte blanche*, and sent Lusieri a long list of 'samples' of various features he desired; after all, his stated goal was to take them home to improve British arts by offering a first-hand look at the greatest sculpture ever made. Besides, the Greeks 'have looked upon the superb works of Pheidias with ingratitude and indifference. They do not deserve them!' Considerable damage occurred to the marbles and the temple's structure through breakage in the removal; some panels were even sawn in two. In the meantime Naploeon's agents were sniffing around Athens for any leftovers they could lay hands on. Byron was in Athens when the last of the 120 crates were being loaded and wrote:

At this moment [3 Jan 1810], besides what has already been deposited in London, an Hydriot vessel is now in Piraeus to receive any portable relic. Thus as I heard a young Greek observe in common with many of his countrymen – for lost as they are, they yet feel on this occasion – thus may Lord Elgin boast of having ruined Athens. An Italian painter of the first eminence, named Lusieri, is the agent of devastation. Between this artist and the French Consul Fauvel, who wishes to rescue the remains for his own government, there is now a violent dispute concerning a car employed in their conveyance, the wheel of which – I wish they were both broken upon it – has been locked up by the Consul, and Lusieri has laid his complaint before the Waywode. Lord Elgin has been extremely happy in his choice of Lusieri. His works, as far as they go, are most beautiful. But when they carry away three or four shiploads of the most valuable and massy relics that time and barbarism have left to the most injured and most celebrated of cities; when they destroy, in vain attempt to tear down, those works which have been the admiration of ages, I know of no motive which can excuse, no name which can designate, the perpetrators of this dastardly devastation. The most unblushing impudence could hardly go further than to affix the name of its plunderer to the walls of the Acropolis; while the wanton and useless defacement of the whole range of basso-rilievos, in one compartment of the temple, will never permit that name to be pronounced by an observer without execration.

Another eye-witness, Edward Clarke, wrote in his *Travel to European Countries* (1811):

The lowering of the sculptures has frustrated Pheidias' intentions. Also, the shape of the Temple suffered a damage greater than the one suffered by Morosini's artillery. How could such an iniquity be committed by a nation that wants to boast of its discretional skill in arts? And they dare tell us, in a serious mien, that the damage was done in order to rescue the sculptures from ruin...

Just as the *Hydra* sailed off to Britain with its cargo of marbles, another vessel arrived in Athens, carrying architect Charles Robert Cockerell, who, inspired by Elgin, was on his way to Aegina to strip the frieze off the temple of Aphaia (which went to Munich). Even so Cockerell managed to bag the decoration from the temple of Apollo at Bassae in Arcadía; by then Greek outrage at the plundering permitted by bribe-greedy Turkish officialdom had reached such a pitch that an armed band planned to hijack Cockerell's caravan and take back the art, but it was thwarted by a forewarned Turkish army.

Nemesis saw to it that Elgin got no joy from his deed. One of his ships sank near Kýthera (although the marbles were expensively rescued by divers over the next two years). He faced constant ridicule from the British public, many of whom agreed with Byron; syphilis caused his nose to fall off, and he was divorced from his delightful Countess. On his way home to Britain he was taken prisoner in France for three years, on Napoleon's orders. His expenses totalled £63,000 (£10 million today), a quarter of which were bribes to Turkish officials (at the time, the entire contents of the British Museum were valued at £3,000), but he managed to get only £35,000 from Parliament, where several members condemned him as a dishonest looter, and he died in poverty. The current Lord Elgin wishes his ancestor had never set eyes on 'the bloody stones'.

Ever since then the issue of restoring the marbles to Greece has come up periodically in Britain, including in 1941 when they were proposed as a reward for the country's heroic resistance to the Nazis. Doubt has been cast on old claims that Elgin 'saved' the fragile Pentelic marbles, by taking them out of the Attic sun and into the London damp and smog (even Elgin noticed they were deteriorating, while dickering with Parliament over the price). The current Greek campaign for the return of the marbles received a moral boost in 1998, when William St Clair revealed in his *Lord Elgin and the Marbles* that the British Museum had 'skinned' away fine details and the patina of the marbles in 1937–8, when they used metal scrapers to whiten them. Polls say that a large majority of the British public want to return the marbles, although that number doesn't include the director of the British Museum or the prime minister. In the meantime a new $100 million museum is going up in Athens to house them, upping the ante in the war of wills.

A Greek Mythology Who's Who

Like all good polytheists, the Greeks filled their pantheon with a kaleidoscopic assortment of divinities. They may be more anthropomorphic than Egyptian or Indian gods but, having evolved over a thousand years, are nonetheless full of fathomless contradictions, subtleties and, above all, regional nuance. The Greeks had no 'Bible', no written book of dogma or ritual. About the only recognized higher authority was the Delphic oracle, which was famous for its ambiguities. The Olympians, the immortal dozen, became a recognized hierarchy by the Archaic period, mostly thanks to Homer and Hesiod, but even they were never cut and dried.

In reality, Greeks everywhere felt quite free to create their own peculiar perspective on their gods, and to hang on to any indigenous local ones they fancied as well. Naturally imaginative and idiosyncratic, they turned their stories of the gods into an art form as much as a religion. If one aspect of Zeus didn't appeal or fill the bill, he could be morphed by adding an epithet: Zeus of Oaths, Zeus the Saviour, Zeus of the Flies, ad infinitum. Different areas could claim the same divinity as their own home grown god. If none suited, a god could be borrowed: even in ancient times, equating a minor local god or a foreign god with an Olympian or other deity was something of a parlour game, one that Plutarch and company especially enjoyed. Of course, the gods were conscripted to do duty on the political level, just as in Christianity. Every city-state had stories of the gods and goddesses fighting on their side, appearing on the ramparts, providing an idea, etc. Politicians have always had a nice appreciation of the usefulness of gods, especially in time of war.

And, like elderly aunts, the Greeks could never bear to throw anything out. Once a taboo, god or ritual became part of their religious furniture, it stuck around in one form or another, resulting in early chthonic deities rubbing shoulders with later, more rationalized versions of themselves. Local nymphs, naiads, river gods and dryads ran about; a whole host of early giants, heroes, half-animal deities such as centaurs, satyrs and snake men were constantly on the loose in the 'dream time' of the Greek collective religion. Over an incredible *one third* of all days in the ancient Athenian calendar were important religious holidays just to accommodate the crowds. But we all have to start somewhere; the following is a short run down of the big guns.

The one time weather god turned big shot on Olympus was **Zeus** (or Dias, or Jupiter to the Romans), best known as a native of Crete. A version of the Indo-European sky god, he was lord of the thunderbolt, with a libido to match. Zeus was wed to his sister **Hera** (Juno), the goddess of marriage, who had the handy knack of renewing her virginity annually in a river by her great temple on Sámos (it didn't improve their relationship). Although she began in Mycenaean times or earlier as a goddess of fertility, her special role in myth was as the wronged, jealous wife. Zeus had two brothers: **Poseidon** (Neptune), who ruled the sea, managed the rivers and caused earthquakes, and **Hades** (Pluto), god of the shadowy underworld and realm of the dead, who kept a low profile except when he went hunting for a wife and kidnapped Persephone, Demeter's daughter. **Demeter** (Ceres), goddess of corn and growing things, did not need to throw her weight around – when she was unhappy, nothing grew. She and her daughter were worshipped everywhere, especially in the mysteries at Eleusis. **Aphrodite** (Venus), the goddess of love, is nearly as old as the earliest gods, and had a weird beginning. Born from the foam produced by the severed genitals of Uranos when his son Kronos castrated him, she was a force to be reckoned with: Corinth and Kýthera were her favourite abodes in Greece proper.

The second generation of Olympians were the offspring of Zeus. **Athena** (Minerva), the urbane virgin goddess of wisdom, handicrafts and ceramics, was born right out of the forehead of Zeus, his own ideal female; she was always associated with Athens in particular. **Ares** (Mars), a Thracian interloper, was the god of war. Oddly enough, given Greek history, he was not a popular god, and often resembles a whining bully. **Hermes** (Mercury), born in the Peloponnese, was a one-man courier service, a go-between who watched over travellers and merchants and took everybody on their final journey to Hades. **Hephaestos** (Vulcan), son of Hera and crippled husband of Aphrodite, was ridiculed for his less than perfect body, but revered for his fire and forge which produced the weapons and baubles of the gods; Límnos was his special island. **Apollo**, patron of the Ionians, the god of light, music, reason, poetry and prophecy, was the *non plus ultra* of a rationalized Greek god, but even he could lose his cool on occasion; his sacred places were his birthplace Délos and his oracle at Delphi. His twin **Artemis** (Diana), the tomboy, virgin moon goddess of the hunt, was a special favourite in the Peloponnese. The temperamental, cross-dressing **Dionysos** (Bacchus), god of wine, orgies and theatre, came from Phrygia and Thrace but was popular everywhere.

And we forgot **Hestia** (Vesta), the virgin goddess of the hearth and Zeus' sister, and **Helios**, the sun god and patron of Rhodes – which makes 15 (so much for the magic number 12). Among the supporting cast, two in particular stand out: **Pan**, the Arcadian deity who gave his name to posterity in the word *panic*, and **Heracles** (Hercules), a god-hero in a class by himself, and a big favourite with the Dorians.

The Environment: Endangered Animals and Plain Old Pests

Situated between east and west, the Balkans and the Mediterranean, with over 16,000km of coastline, 378 wetlands, a diversity of forests covering a quarter of its territory, and rugged mountains, Greece has one of the most diverse biospheres in the world. The flora is stunning, the bird life is spectacular, and creatures such as bears, nearly extinct in Western Europe, thrive in the mountains of the north.

For all that, much has been lost, most notably great forests of Classical times whittled away by shipbuilders, then replaced by scrub when goats were set to graze on the land. Attitudes, too, have lagged; while Western Europe was busy discovering the beauties of nature in the Renaissance and Romantic eras, Greece was fighting for survival; when the West was holding Earth Days in the 1960s and '70s, the Greeks were throwing up helter-skelter resort hotels, making Athens the citadel of sprawl it is today, merrily chucking garbage in the sea and killing off the monk seals because they ate too many fish. For decades a small but dedicated band of environmentalists sounded the alarm, but until recently many Greeks, trying to pull themselves out of poverty, saw their country only as something to exploit: if the law forbids building on forested land, the Greek solution was – and, sadly, still is in a few places – to burn the forest. The great influx of tourists is in part responsible for the severe depletion of fish stocks. Laws limiting industrial fishing and dynamiting are constantly flouted – demand has drained the Aegean's key resource by nearly 60 per cent in recent years, making what used to be the cheapest staple food in Greece the most expensive. There is often talk about a fishing moratorium of a year or two, but the economic consequences are simply too staggering to get past the talking stage. On the positive side, tourist concerns about clean beaches (and Greece now proudly claims the cleanest in Europe) have resulted in proper sewage systems and a noticeable decline in litter and junk, although there is still work to do.

Greece now has 10 national parks and several forest reserves, including virgin areas in the north where access is strictly limited, and has made great strides in saving its wetlands, 11 of which are considered of international importance according to the RAMSAR convention. In the early 1980s, efforts to save the loggerhead turtle centred on its nesting ground, which just happened to include the most popular beaches on Zákynthos. Although this began as a war between hoteliers and environmentalists, now the turtles themselves have become a selling point on the island. Another bright spot is the designation of the crystalline seas around Alónissos as a National Marine Park, encompassing untouched islets and a diversity of marine life, including the most endangered species in Europe, the monk seal. Swallows, storks, flamingos, pelicans, herons and egrets all pass at one time of the year or another. Eagles and vultures float over the mountains and cliffs, including the griffon vulture and lammergeier, with wingspans of nearly 10 feet. Dadia Forest, near the Evros Delta separating Greece and Turkey, is a haven for rare birds of prey. Closer to the ground, Greece's extraordinary wildflowers – including 6,000 native species – draws an equally colourful array of butterflies.

As for creatures unfortunately *not* on the endangered list, the wily mosquito tops the list for incivility. Most shops stock the usual defences: lotions, sprays and insect coil, or, best of all, pick up one of those inexpensive electric mosquito repellents that plug into a wall socket or run on a battery. Greek skeeters don't spread malaria, but bites from their sand-fly cousins can cause a nasty infection. Wasps may appear out of nowhere to nibble that *baklava* or grilled steak you've just ordered. Pests lurk in the sea as well: harmless pale brown jellyfish (*méduses*) may drift in depending on winds and currents, but the oval transparent model (*tsoúchtres*) are stinging devils that can leave scars on tender parts of your anatomy if you brush against them; pharmacies sell soothing unguents. Pincushiony sea urchins live by rocky beaches, and if you're too cool to wear rubber swimming shoes and step on one, it hurts. The spines may break and embed themselves even deeper if you try to force them out; the Greeks recommend olive oil, a big pin and a lot of patience. Less common but more dangerous, the *drákena*, dragon (or weever) fish, with a poisonous spine, hides in the sand waiting for its lunch. If you step on one (rare, but it happens), you'll feel a mix of pain and numbness and should go the doctor for an injection. Greece's shy scorpions hide out in between the rocks in rural areas; unless you're especially sensitive, their sting is no more or less painful than a bee's. The really lethal creatures are rare: there are several species of small viper that live in the nooks and crannies of stone walls, where they are well camouflaged, and which only come out occasionally to sun themselves. Vipers will flee if possible, but if they feel cornered they will make a hissing sound like radio static before attacking.

On *Kéfi*, Music and Dancing

In the increasingly homogenized European Union, the Irish, Spaniards and Greeks are among the very few peoples who still dance to their own music with any kind of spontaneity, and it's no coincidence that both have words to describe the 'spirit' or 'mood', whether it's *craic*, *duende* or the Greek *kéfi*. For a Greek to give his all, he must have *kéfi*; to dance without it could be considered dishonest. The smart young men in red sashes who perform at a 'Greek Night' taverna don't have it; two craggy old fishermen, in a smoky *kafeneíon* in Crete, who crank up an old gramophone and dance for their own pleasure, do. It has no age limit: many teenagers at clubs pounding out the hits are really only waiting for 1 or 2am, when the Greek music comes on and the real dancing and *kéfi* can start. You can feel the *kéfi* at Easter when an entire village joins hands to dance an elegant *kalamatianó*, an act as simple and natural as it is moving.

Musically, Greece has been influenced by her neighbours, all of whom were once influenced by the Byzantines, who heard it from ancient Greeks. The subject is not only historically vast, but each region, even each island and valley, has its own songs, still very popular at weddings and local celebrations (*panegýri*). These are most commonly played on bagpipes (*tsamboúna*), clarinet (*klaríno*) and various stringed instruments – the *violí* (violin), the *kítara* (guitar), the *laoúto* (a large mandolin, used for backing, traditionally picked with an eagle's quill), the double-stringed hammer dulcimer (*sandoúri*) and the *lýra*, a three-string fiddle, held upright on the knee, played often at a furious speed on Crete and the southern Dodecanese. Besides the notes available in the West, Greek music has a whole range of quarter tones, and time signatures (especially in the more Balkan north, in Épirus, Macedonia and Thrace) that would have made Beethoven jump out of the window if he could have heard them. Aegean island songs, *nisiótika*, are lilting and melodious; Venetian influences linger in the Ionian islands, especially in the *kantádes* of Zákynthos.

Modern Greek music owes much to the music brought over by the more 'sophisticated' Asia Minor Greeks in the 1923 population exchange, who in their longing and homesickness haunted the hashish dens of Athens and Piraeus. Here they played and sang urban songs known as *rembétika*, the Greek equivalent of the blues. *Rembétika* introduced the bouzoúki, the long-necked metallic string instrument that dominates Greek music today, to the extent that nightclubs are called *bouzoúkia* – rougher, cheaper ones are known as *skiládika* – 'dog' shops, where popular singers offer today's Greeks some of the catharsis that ancient tragedies gave their ancestors. Although expensive, a night out in one of these clubs (the locals can recommend one) is an experience; turn up after midnight, buy a bottle of wine and whisky for the table, and before you know it members of the audience are taking over the microphone, and covering the singer or each other with baskets of rose petals (baskets are sold on the spot, as plate-breaking is now illegal). If the *kéfi* is flowing, middle-aged bank managers start doing amazing feats, with wine glasses or bottles on their heads. When their wives begin to belly-dance on the table, you know it's time to leave. Besides these, there are serious contemporary composers, most famously Mikis Theodorákis, who often puts Greece's modern poetry to music. On the other end of the scale you have Greek rock bands and pop singers, who always score a 12 from Cyprus in the Eurovision song contest, but that's about all you can say about them.

Summer festivals and weddings are the places to see traditional dancing. Cretan dances are among the most vigorous and enthusiastically danced, fuelled by massive intakes of *raki*; the *pedektó* demands furious, machine-gunfire steps and hops, which resound under tall Cretan boots. Beginners would do better starting with a *syrtó*, with

Greek Recordings: What to Buy

Syllogés (compilations) or *epilogés* (best ofs) are popular with Greeks and cover every genre of Greek music, down to the Byzantine and ancient. For the tunes you usually hear in tavernas, ask for *Ta Paradosiaká* (traditional songs) or *Ta Demotiká* (popular songs). Every kind of Greek dance music is covered in *Greek Instrumental Music* (Alpha), a 3-CD set, while *A Taste of Greek Music* (Eros) offers both dances and recipes. Regional music is a more acquired taste, but abounds in regional record shops. Try Chrístos Panoutsos' *Tragoúdia tou Moriá* (Legend) for the Peloponnese; Antonis Kyrítsis's *Ta Epeirótika* (General Music) for Épirus; for Thracian, look for titles by Chronis Aïdonidis; for Cretan music, those with *lyrá* maestro Kósta Moundákis.

The best way to start of a *rembétika* collection is with a *syllogí* including the greats such as Tsitsánis, Gavalás, Vamvakáris or Bithikótsis. One, *Ta Rembétika* (EMI), has original hits by the singers who made them famous. *Ótan ta Tzouk Box Paízane Laiká* (EMI) is also excellent. Giórgos Daláras is fabulous no matter what he sings, but his *50 Chrónia Rembékiko Tragoúdi* (Minos-EMI) covering 50 years of *rembétika* is an excellent introduction to both *rembétika and* Daláras. For *bouzoúki, The Best of Bouzouki* (FM Records) is just that, plus anything by the *bouzoúki* master/composer Chrístos Nikópoulos is well worth a listen, especially his *E Zoé Mou Tragoúdi* (EMI).

Good bets by Greek divas include Glikería's *Vólta Stin Ell101da* (Lyra) singing island songs or *nissiótika*. Familiar favourites are beautifully performed by Cháris Alexíou on a CD titled *Cháris Alexíou/2* (Minos-EMI). Nana Mouskouri's *Spíti Mou, Spitáki Mou* (EMI) offers an all-Greek selection of well known songs. And a real classic collection of old favourites by one of the greats is *Marinella: E Phoní kai Mythos* (Polygram). Among the composers, try *H Ellála tou Míkis* (Minos-EMI), a 3-CD set of the best of Theodorákis; *O Mános Xatzidákis sti Romáiki Agorá* (Minos) featuring Greece's second most popular composer; *The Giánnis Markópoulos' Collection* (EMI) for 40 of this composer's greatest; or *Megáles Epitichíes* of Mários Tókas (Minos-EMI), with wonderful songs sung by the likes of Phrios, Alexíou and Kanellídou. Good sources for CDs, besides Greek music shops, are *www.greekmusic.com* or *www.gmcds.com*.

slow and somewhat shuffling pace throughout, or perhaps the *kalamatianó*, a 12-step *syrtó*, *the* national dance for many people; everyone joins in, holding hands at shoulder-level, while men and women take turns leading, often with panache. Nearly as common is the dignified *tsamikó*, where the leader and the next dancer in line hold the ends of a handkerchief; if the leader is acrobatic, the handkerchief seems to be the only thing that keeps him from flying away altogether. Everyone, women and men, loves to do the *tsíphte téli* (or 'shift the telly' as one friend calls it), a free-spirited, sensuous belly dance from Asia Minor for the loose-limbed and well-oiled.

Other dances are normally but not exclusively performed by men. The *zeybékiko* is a serious, deliberate, highly charged solo (or sometimes duo) dance with outstretched arms, evoking the flight of the eagle; a companion will go down on one knee to encourage the dancer, hiss and clap out the rhythm. An introspective dance from the soul, the performer will always keep his eyes lowered, almost in a hypnotic state; because it's private, you must never applaud. Another intense dance, the *hasápiko*, or butchers' dance, is perhaps better known as the Zorba dance. The *syrtáki* is more exuberant, traditionally performed by two men or three men, often to a *rembétika* tune; the leader signals the steps and it require practice but is well worth learning – as Alan Bates discovered, when he finally began to fathom *kéfi* from Anthony Quinn at the end of the film *Zorba the Greek*.

An Orthodox Life

With the exception of a few thousand Catholics in the Cyclades and Protestants in Athens, all Greeks belong to the Orthodox, or Eastern church; indeed, being Orthodox and speaking Greek are the criteria in defining a Greek, whether born in Athens, Alexandria or Australia. Orthodoxy is so fundamental that even atheists can hardly conceive of marrying outside the church, or neglecting to have their children baptized, even though the government legalized civil marriages in the early 1980s.

One reason for this deep national feeling is that, unlike everything else in Greece, their church has scarcely changed since the 4th century, when Constantine founded the state religion in Rome. As Constantinople took over as the capital of the empire, the Greeks believe their church to be the only true successor to the first church of Rome. Therefore, a true Greek is called a *Romiós* or Roman, and the Greek language is sometimes called *Roméika*. The Orthodox church is considered perfect and eternal; if it weren't, its adherents believe they could never expect to be saved on Judgement Day. This timelessness has spared Greeks the changes that have rocked the West, from the Reformation to Vatican II to current political questions of abortion, birth control and so on; anyone (male) interested in Orthodoxy in its purist form should consider a visit to Mount Athos, where even the clocks and calendar are Byzantine.

This determination never to change explains the violence of Iconoclasm, the one time someone tried to tinker. Back in the early 8th century, Emperor Leo III, shamed by what his Muslim neighbours labelled idolatry, deemed the images of divine beings to be sacrilegious. The Iconoclasm opened up a first major rift with the West, and it worsened in 800 when the patriarch of Rome, aka the Pope, crowned Charlemagne as emperor, usurping the position of the Emperor of Constantinople. Further divisions arose over the celibacy of the clergy (Orthodox priests may marry, and nearly all do) and the use of the phrase *filioque*, 'and the son', in the Holy Creed. This phrase caused the final, fatal schism in 1054 when the papal legate Cardinal Humbert excommunicated the Patriarch of Constantinople and the Patriarch excommunicated the Pope. Ever since then the Orthodox hierarchy has kept a patriarchal throne vacant, ready for the day when the Pope returns to his senses.

After the fall of the Byzantine Empire (that 'thousand-year-long mass for the dead' as one Greek writer put it), the Ottomans not only tolerated the Orthodox church, but had the political astuteness to impart considerable powers to the Patriarch in return for his guarantee of Greek good behaviour. The church helped to preserve Greek tradition, language and identity through the dark age of Ottoman rule and in the 18th century it involved itself in education; on the other hand, it left Greece a deeply conservative country, until the 1980s at any rate, and often abused its power on a local scale.

Greece is the only country in Europe where more churches are being built all the time, mostly on private initiatives, for any number of reasons. In keeping with the timeless quality of Orthodoxy, 99 per cent of these are in traditional styles – no architectural experiments here, thank you very much. All but the tiniest have an *iconóstasis*, or altar screen, decorated with icons, to separate the *heirón* or sanctuary, where only the ordained are allowed. Most churches are locked now thanks to light-fingered tourists; if you track down the caretaker, leave a euro or so for upkeep.

The vast majority of rural churches, especially on the islands, have only one service a year, on the name day of the patron saint (name days are celebrated in Greece rather than birthdays: 'Many years!' (*Chrónia pollá!*) is the proper way to greet someone on his or her name day. These saints are often celebrated, especially in summer, with a *yiortí* or *panegýri*, with feasts and dancing the night before or after the church service. Apart from Easter, the biggest holiday in Greece, the Assumption of the Virgin (15 August), is the most important. The faithful converge on Tínos, the Lourdes of Greece, and to a dozen centres connected with Mary.

Orthodox weddings are lovely if a bit long-winded. The bride and groom stand before the chanting priest, while family and friends in attendance seem to do everything but follow the proceedings. White crowns, bound together by a white ribbon, are placed on the heads of bride and groom, and the *koumbáros*, or best man, exchanges them back and forth. The newlyweds are then led around the altar three times, while the guests bombard them with rice and flower petals. After congratulating the bride and groom, guests are given a small gift, a *boboniéra* of candied almonds. This is followed by feasting and dancing, which once lasted up to five days.

Baptisms are a cause for similar celebrations. The priest completely immerses the baby in the Holy Water three times (unlike Achilles, there are no vulnerable spots on modern Greeks) and almost always gives the little one the name of a grandparent. For extra protection from the forces of evil, babies often wear a *filaktó*, or amulet, the omnipresent blue glass eye bead. If you visit a baby at a traditional home you may be sprinkled first with Holy Water. Compliments should be kept to a minimum: the gods do get jealous. In fact, many babies are given other pet names until they're christened, to fool supernatural ill-wishers.

Funerals in Greece, for reasons of climate, are carried out within a day of death, especially in rural areas. After funerals and memorial services mourners are given sweet buns and *koúliva*, a tasty mix of sugared wheat kernels, pomegranate seeds and nuts, a symbol of resurrection (as in the Book of John, 'unless a grain of wheat falls to the earth and dies, it remains alone; but if it dies, it bears much fruit.') The dead are buried for three to seven years (longer if the family can pay), after which time the bones are exhumed and placed in the family box in the ossuary. *Aforismós*, or Orthodox excommunication, is believed to prevent the body decaying after death – the main source of Greek vampire stories. Memorials for the dead take place three, nine and 40 days after death, and on the first anniversary. They are sometimes repeated annually. But for all the trappings of Christianity, the spirit of Charon, the ferryman of death and personification of inexorable nature, is never far away, as beautifully expressed in perhaps the most famous of *myrológia*, or dirges, still sung in the Máni in the southern Peloponnese:

> *Why are the mountains dark and why so woe-begone?*
> *Is the wind at war there, or does the rain storm scourge them?*
> *It is not the wind at war there, it is not the rain that scourges,*
> *It is only Charon passing across them with the dead;*
> *He drives the youths before him, the old folk drag behind,*
> *And he bears the tender little ones in a line at his saddle-bow.*
> *The old men beg a grace, the young kneel to implore him,*
> *'Good Charos, halt in the village, or halt by some cool fountain,*
> *That the old men may drink water, the young men play at the stone-throwing,*
> *And that the little children may go and gather flowers.'*
> *'In never a village will I halt, nor yet by a cool fountain,*
> *The mothers would come for water, and recognize their children,*
> *The married folk would know each other, and I should never part them.'*

The *Períptero* and the Plane Tree

You'll see it everywhere you go, the greatest of modern Greek inventions, the indispensable *períptero*. It is the best-equipped kiosk in the world, where people gather to chat, make phone calls or grab a few minutes' shade under the little projecting roof. The *períptero* is a substitute bar, selling everything from water and beer to ice-cream to croissants and frappé-making kits; a tobacconist; an emergency pharmacy stocked with aspirin, mosquito killers and condoms; a newsagent for magazines and papers from *Ta Néa* to *Die Zeit*; a tourist shop offering maps, guides, postcards and stamps; a general store for shoelaces, cigarettes, batteries, sunglasses and rolls of film. In towns they're at traffic lights. On the islands they are more common than donkeys.

The other great meeting centre of Greek life is the plane tree, or *plátanos*, for centuries the focal point of village life, where politics and philosophy have been argued since time immemorial. Since Hippocrates the Greeks have believed that plane shade is wholesome and beneficial (unlike the enervating shadow cast by the fig); some are hundreds of years old and considered national monuments, including the enormous 'Hippocrates' plane tree' on Kos. In Greek the expression *cheréte mou ton plátano*, 'send my regards to the plane tree', loosely translates as 'go tell it to the marines', presumably because the tree has heard all that nonsense before. The *plátanos* represents the village's identity; the tree is a source of life, for it only grows near abundant fresh water, its deep roots a symbol of stability, continuity and protection – a huge majestic umbrella, as even the rain cannot penetrate its sturdy leaves. Sit under its spreading branches and sip a coffee as the morning unfolds before you; the temptation to linger there for the day is irresistible.

Pausanias and the Golden Age of Guides

Anyone who tries to write about Greece today can hardly help envying Pausanias, the man who first put it on the tourist map. When he did his research some time after AD 150, Greece was an unimportant backwater, but the monuments of more glorious times were still in place. Stories were unencumbered by scholarly controversy, readers could be counted on to plough through whatever long boring bits an author indulged in, and history was 2,000 years shorter.

Pausanias was a Romanized Greek, born in Asia Minor. He travelled extensively in the ancient world, and his *Guide to Greece* was aimed at the well-heeled Roman élite who wanted to soak up a little culture. The fact that he wrote in Greek rather than Latin alone separated the sheep from the goats. He would settle in one area, such as Corinth, and radiate out in all directions. This was not only efficient, it was also about the only method possible when roads were mule paths, transportation was by pack animal, and inns were few and far between. Not that Pausanias mentioned food and accommodation; his wealthy readers could count on the hospitality of city officials. That meant that Pausanias could concentrate on what he liked best: history and religion. He loved any ritual, any oracle, no matter how obscure, and happily for us, he was a pushover for the weird and offbeat. He was perfectly capable of passing a landmark temple like the one to Apollo in Corinth with scarcely a mention, in order to describe Glauke's fountain, where the poor girl had landed trying to douse the flames of Medea's poisoned cloak.

He also had personality. Sometimes he affected a cynical, scientific approach, laconically offering a particular myth for those 'who want a more god-haunted version'. He wouldn't fall for just any old line, although what to his mind was acceptable and what wasn't may seem idiosyncratic: 'the story of giants having serpents instead of feet is ridiculous', he blustered at one point and yet he sat by a river in Arcadia hoping to hear the trout sing. He could be pedantic, and thank goodness for that. Scores of archaeological sites have been discovered solely because of his painstaking details, and much of our knowledge of Greek religious practice is a result of his book. Every guide to Greece since, to some degree or another, has followed in his footsteps.

Food and Drink

Life's fundamental principle is the satisfaction of the needs and wants of the
stomach. All important and trivial matters depend on this principle and cannot
be differentiated from it.

Epicurus, 3rd century BC

Epicurus may have lent his name to gourmets, but in reality his philosophy advocated maximizing simple pleasures: rather than continually seek novelty, Epicurus suggests making bread and olives taste sublime by fasting for a couple of days. In that way Greeks have long been epicureans: centuries of occupation and poverty taught them to relish food more than cuisine. What has changed in the 21st century is that cuisine has inescapably arrived. The influx of international tourists is partly responsible, but so is the rise of a well-travelled generation of Greeks. Where they travel fusion is the rage, with a broad Mediterranean slant; Athens and major resorts now have Italian, Chinese, Mexican, Indian, Japanese and Turkish restaurants.

Of course most restaurants and tavernas are still Greek, serving fish from the seas, free range chicken, lamb, fresh herbs and honey from the mountains, wild young greens from the hills, olives, fruits and nuts from the groves. Cooking methods tend to be simple, with strong Turkish and Italian influences that enhance natural flavours. A good cook almost never resorts to canned or frozen ingredients, or even the microwave – one criticism levelled at Greek food is that it's served cold. Once you get used to it, you realize that many dishes are actually tastier once they're left to cool in their own juices, especially in the summer. Anyway, the natives may be right – recent studies show that eating like a Greek is remarkably healthy.

Greek Dishes

Many Greek dishes need no introduction – *tarama*, moussaka, *gýros*, retsina, vine leaves, Greek salads with feta, Greek yoghurt and *baklava* have achieved the universality of lasagne and chicken tikka. Although some of the food may be familiar, if you've not been to Greece before you may find eating different from what you're used to, with a big emphasis on informality. Meals begin with bread (usually excellent) and starters (*mezédes*) to be communally shared: olives, *tzatzíki* (cucumbers and yoghurt), prawns, *tirosaláta* (feta cheese dip), *koponistá* (a pungent cheese dip), salted fish, roasted sweet peppers, cheese or spinach pies, meatballs, or *saganáki* (fried cheese sprinkled with lemon). These are followed (often before you've finished the starters, unless you specify otherwise) by a shared salad and potatoes, and your main course. This could be a gorgeously fresh omelette or an oven dish or stew (called 'ready dishes' as they're already prepared). Typically choices are moussaká, *pastítsio* (baked macaroni, layered with ground meat, cheese, cream and topped with béchamel), roast lamb or chicken, *makaroniá* (basically spaghetti bolognese, which has been sitting there and isn't bad), *yemistá* (stuffed tomatoes or peppers), *stifádo* (spiced beef stew with baby onions), *lagostifádo* (rabbit stew, similar but flavoured with orange), *kokinistó* (beef cooked with tomatoes and a hint of cinnamon), lamb or veal *youvétsi* (baked with tomatoes and with tear-drop pasta), *chirinó me sélino* (pork with wild celery, in egg lemon sauce) or *kréas stin stamna* (lamb or beef baked in a clay dish). Meats grilled to order come under the heading *tis óras* ('the On Times') – pork chops (*brizóles*), lamb cutlets (*paidákia*), kebabs (*souvláki*), minced steak (*biftéki*), meatballs (*keftéthes* or *sousoukákia*), sausage (*lukániko*) or chicken (*koutópoulo skára*).

Seafood is fresh and delicious, but relatively expensive, although you can usually find cheapies like fresh whitebait (*marídes*), fresh sardines (*sardínas*), cuttlefish stew (*soupiá*) and squid rings (*kalamári*). Baked or fried *bakaliáros* (fresh Mediterranean cod) is always a treat and shouldn't break the bank. Some places serve *soups – psaró-soupa* (with potatoes and carrots) or spicy tomato-based *kakavia*, a meal in themselves with hunks of fresh bread and a bottle of wine. Prawns (*garídes*) are lightly fried or baked with garlic, tomatoes and feta as *garídes saganáki*, a popular dish invented in the 1960s; spaghetti with lobster (*astakomakaronáda*) is another delicious recent addition to many Greek menus. Note that each type of fish has its own price, and portions are priced by weight; often you'll be asked to pick out the one you want cooked and the owner puts it on the scale in front of you.

Desserts are rare, although many places offer complimentary watermelon or sliced apples sprinkled with cinnamon or nutmeg; Greeks make lovely sweets, puddings, cakes and ice creams, but tend to eat them in the late afternoon after the siesta.

Eating Out

In resort areas and the touristy parts of Athens, there are plenty of places offering familiar breakfasts, lunches and dinners at familiar hours for visitors, but you may find getting into the Greek pace of life more enjoyable. This means a light breakfast (many bars sell yoghurt and honey), supplemented mid-morning with a hot cheese pie (*tirópita*). At 2 or 3pm, indulge in a long alfresco lunch with wine, followed by a siesta or *mesiméri* to avoid the scorching afternoon heat. Get up at 6 or 7pm for a swim and an ice cream. Around 8pm, it's time for the *vólta* , the see-and-be-seen evening stroll and a sunset drink. Greeks rarely eat before 10pm and meals can go on into the small hours. Children are welcome (they too nap in the afternoon) – toddlers crawl under the table, while the adults become increasingly boisterous, punctuating the meal with fiery discussions and bursts of song or dance. The more people round the table the merrier, and the more likely the meal will turn into a spontaneous cabaret. After dinner, have a brandy in a café or hit the tiles until dawn.

Restaurants and Tavernas

Because dining is an integral part of social life, Greeks eat out more than most Europeans – twice a week is the national average – and they usually order more than they can eat. At the older **estiatória** (restaurants), now becoming rare, all the Greek standards wait on the steam table for you to choose, and are served up faster than McDonald's. Newer ones tend to be like the ones back home, although it's worth looking out for ones that do regional dishes. Don't expect all the nuances of France, but there are distinct difference between the dishes of Crete (lots of cheeses and

Greek Vegetarian Dishes

Of all the people in the EU, the Greeks now eat the most meat per capita, but they also eat the most cheese, more than even the French, and follow only the Italians in eating pasta. Basically they eat a lot, which means there are plenty of dishes for vegetarians and vegans, especially if you go to a *mezedopoieíon*, where you can make a meal out of an array of little non-meat dishes ('vegetarian' is *chortofágos*). Because of historic poverty and the demands of Orthodox fasts (which forbid animal and dairy products), Greece has many traditional vegetarian dishes, and if you're a vegan Lent is an ideal time to come, because restaurants go out of their way to prepare them (especially artichokes, *angináres*). Any time of the year you should find pulses, in starters such as *gigántes* (giant butter beans in tomato sauce) or *revíthia* (chick peas, baked or in soups or fritters), bean soups (*fasoláda*) and occasionally lentils (*fakés*). Other vegan stand-bys are ratatouille-like *ládera* (fresh vegetables cooked in olive oil), a host of salads, sometimes enlivened with a handful of *kápari* (pickled caper plant which tastes delicious), *patzária* (beetroot drizzled with olive oil and vinegar), *yemistá* (peppers or tomatoes stuffed with rice), *bríams* (potato and aubergine/courgette, baked with olive oil), *imams* (aubergine stuffed with tomato and onion), various *keftédes* (vegetable fritters from carrot to courgette), *dolmáthes* (rice and dill-filled vine leaves), *oftés patátes* (potatoes roasted in their jackets) and, everywhere, endless supplies of chips, usually fried in olive oil. Although *skordaliá*, the classic garlic dip served with fried vegetables or beetroot, is traditionally made simply with puréed potatoes and olive oil, some places now do it with soft cheese.

vegetables), Corfu (a strong Italian touch) or Macedonia (hotter and spicier than the Greek norm). **Tavernas** are more like family-run bistros and can range from beach shacks to barn-like affairs with live music in the evening. Waiters will reel off what's available; if there's a menu, home-made translations may leave you more baffled than ever. **Mezedopoieíons** specialize in a host of little dishes, where you can build up an entire meal. If you're lucky, you may even find a **mageiria**, a simple place with old-fashioned pots simmering on the stove, usually only open for lunch.

At the seaside you'll find fish tavernas, **psarotavérnes**, specializing in all kinds of seafood from sea urchins and octopus stew to red mullet, swordfish, bream and sardines. Most carry one or two meat dishes for fish haters who may be dragged along. If you're a red-blooded meat eater then head for a **psistariá**, specializing in charcoal-grilled chicken, lamb, pork, beef or *kokorétsi* (lamb's offal, braided around a skewer). In some places you can still find **hasapotavérna**, a grill room attached to a local butcher's shop, with fresh carcasses on display to entice in the clientele (usually with the tail attached, as proof of freshness). Besides chops and steaks, they often offer kebabs, home-made sausages and sometimes delicious stews, usually served by the butcher's assistant in a bloodstained apron for added carnivorous effect.

Other eateries in Greece need no introduction: the pizzeria (often spelled **pitsaria**), American fast food (with local adaptations, such as non-meat meals on offer during Lent) and Goody's, the Greek chain (with lots more variety). Even the smallest islands have at least one *gýros* or **souvláki stand** for cheap greasy fills, many now offering chicken as well as the usual pork. Bakeries sell an array of sweet and savoury hot pies; a *bougatsaría* (μπουγατσαρια) specializes in them, and in northern Greece there seems to be one on every corner, often attached to cafés, where hot slices of spinach, cheese or custard pie are sold by weight. For something sweet, just look at the lovely displays in any **zacharoplasteío** or pastry shop. Greece's favourite ice cream maker, Dodóni (Δωδωνη), has a chain of shops.

Kafeneíons and Cafés

Every village larger than a dozen houses will have a *kafeneíon*: a coffee house but more importantly a social institution where men (and increasingly women) gather to discuss the latest news, read the papers, nap or play cards and incidentally drink coffee. Some men seem to live in them. They are so essential to Greek identity that in some places, where property prices make them unprofitable, people have opened municipal *kafeneíons*. The bill of fare features Greek coffee (*café ellinikó*), which is the same thick stuff as Turkish coffee, prepared in 40 different ways, although *glykó* (sweet), *métrio* (medium) and *skéto* (no sugar) are the basic orders. It is always served with a cold glass of water. Other coffees in Greece, unless you find a proper Italian espresso machine, won't make the earth move for you: '*nes*' (i.e. Nescafé) has become a Greek word, and comes either hot or whipped and iced as a *frappé*, which was invented in Greece but so far hasn't conquered many other taste buds, except in Malaysia and Thailand. Tea, soft drinks, brandy, beer and ouzo round out the old-style *kafeneíon* fare. Newer cafés usually open earlier and close much later than *kafeneíons*. In resort areas they offer breakfast, from simple to complete English, with rashers, baked beans and eggs. They also serve mineral water, ice cream concoctions, milk-shakes, wonderful fresh fruit juices, cocktails, and creamy Greek yoghurt and honey.

Bars (*Barákia*) and *Ouzeries*

Even the most flyspeck town or island these days tends to have at least one music bar, usually playing the latest hits (foreign or Greek). They come to life at cocktail hour and again at midnight; closing times vary but dawn isn't unusual in the summer. In general, bars are not cheap and are sometimes outrageously dear; it can be discon-certing to realize that you paid the same price for your gin fizz as you paid for your entire meal earlier in the taverna next door. However, remember that the measures are triples by British standards. If in doubt stick to beer (Amstel or Heineken most of the time, or the Greek brands: the slightly sweet *Mýthos*, and a recently revived old favourite, *Fix*), ouzo, wine and Metaxá brandy (Metaxá and Coke, if you can stomach it, is generally about half the price of a rum and coke).

Just when it seemed time to write the obituary on a grand old Greek institution, the **ouzerie**, it has returned as part of a national movement to hold on to Greek tradition in the face of an invasion of foreign spirits – Scotch is now the country's tipple of choice. Still, the national aperitif, ouzo (the *rakí* drunk by the Byzantines and Venetians, renamed *ouzo* in the 18th century from the Latin *usere*, 'usable'), is holding on among older Greeks. Clear and anise-flavoured, it is served in tall glasses or a *karafáki* holding three or four doses, which *habitués* dilute and cloud with water and sometimes ice. If you dislike aniseed, the Greeks also make an unflavoured grappa-like spirit called *tsikoúdia* or *rakí*. As Greeks look askance at drunkenness – as in ancient times, when they cut their wine with water and honey – ouzo is traditionally served with a plate of *mezédes*; for an assortment, ask for a *pikilía*.

Wine

Bronze is the mirror of the form; wine of the heart.
Aeschylus

Greece has 300 different indigenous vines, and there could well be something to the myths that wine was invented here. Despite this big head start, the average Greek wine has long been that – average, if not wretched. This is changing so fast it's hard to keep up: in the past two decades better education, the introduction of foreign expertise and modern techniques have improved many Greek wines. They also tend to be highly regionalized, each island and village offering their own varieties; even that humblest of bottles, Deméstica, has become acceptable and bears little resemblance to the rough stuff that earned it some unflattering nicknames. Big wineries like Achaia Clauss, Botari, Carras and Cambas dominate the market, but small independent vineyards are becoming very trendy: in 1999, they contributed greatly to the 164 new bottled wines put on the market – a 25 per cent increase. If you're buying wines, seek out a *káva*, or wine shop. If you want to learn more, there are some good books: the widely available annual *Greek Wine Guide*, by Nico Manessis, and the *Wine Map of Greece*, both by Olive Press (if you can't find it, try *olivepress@ath.forthnet.gr*, or contact them directly at 11 Stisihorou, Athens. Demitris Hadzinicolaou's *Tracing Dionyssus* (D&G Kaofolias, 1999), a beautifully illustrated coffee table book in both English and Greek, is packed full of information about Greek wines and their makers (try the Eleutheroudakis bookstore in Athens).

In a taverna, the choice of wine will probably be limited. Many serve the country's best-known (or most notorious) tipple, **retsína**, with its distinctive pine resiny taste so admirably suited to Greek food – in fact once you acquire a taste for it, other wines may taste bland. The ancient Greeks stored their wine in clay *amphorae* sealed with resin; the disintegration of the resin helped prevent oxidation and lent the wine a flavour that caught on (and is now supplied by pieces of resin). Like ouzo, though, young Greeks are turning their backs on it, and draught retsína (*retsína varelísio*) – the best – can only be found on larger islands. Traditionally retsína comes in chilled copper-anodized cans, by the kilo (about a litre), *misó kiló* (half) or *tetárto* (250ml) and is served in tumblers. Kourtaki is a reliable bottled variety and widely available.

These days, most **house wines** (*krasí chíma*) are unresinated and can be incredibly good, but there are still some stinkers around, so start with just a *tetárto* when you order. In summer, the reds often come as chilled as the whites. When eating with Greeks, keep topping up your companions' glasses, while drinking constant toasts – *steen yámass*, good health to us, *steen yássou* or *yássas*, good health to you or, in Crete, *Avíva* or *Áspro Páto* – bottoms up.

Wines of Greece

Náoussa: the best known red wine of Macedonia, cultivated from Xynomavro around Mt Vermio at 1,150ft, where winters are cold and summers are hot.

Amyntaion: similar to Náoussa, but from higher up (2,130ft). Yields dry reds and rosés.

Goumenissa: another Macedonian dry red, grown on the lower slopes of Mt Paiko in the same climate as Náoussa, but using Negoska as well as Xynomavro grapes.

Zitsa: Épirus's high altitude white wine, made from indigenous Debina grapes, cultivated 2,000ft up near Mt Pindos. Comes dry, medium dry, or lightly sparkling.

Rapsani: dry red wines from Xynomavro, Krasato and Stavroto varietals, grown on the lower slopes of Mt Olympus, where winters are cold and wet and summers very hot.

Anchialos: a soft fruity white wine from Rhoditis and Savatiano grown by the Pagasitic Gulf in Thessaly. Savatiano has long been used for retsína.

Neméa: the great noble dry red wine of the Peloponnese, cultivated southeast of Corinth from the local Agiorgitiko grapes.

Pátras: the hills around Pátras are one of southern Greece's top areas. Rhoditis is used to produce dry whites, while Mavrodaphne, blended with Korinthiaki, is aged to produce velvety **Mavrodaphne**, one of the Greece's great dessert wines, similar to port.

Mantinia: dry whites made from Moschophilero, cultivated 1,900ft up on the slopes of Mount Mainalo.

Kefaloniá: celebrated bone-dry white Robolo, from a very low yielding grape grown only on the Ionians. Kefaloniá also grows sweet red wine, related to Mavrodaphne.

Sámos: a dry muscat cultivated on steep, terraced vineyards from sea-level. The white dessert wine, with its apricot nuances, is one of Greece's finest.

Páros: windy, dry winters and hot summers yield a fine dry red wine from Mandelaria and a white from Malvazia, the grape from Monemvasia in the Peloponnese that once used to make sweet 'malmsey'. Modern wines have a peachy aromatic tone.

Santoríni: whipped by winds, with little rainfall, volcanic Santoríni produces very distinct dry white wines from Assyrtiko, one of Greece's best white grapes, blended with Athiri and Aedani, resulting in fruity, crispy or even slightly smoky wines.

Rhodes: fragrant lemony whites from Athiri grapes and reds exclusively from ancient black grape Mandelaria, grown on the northern slopes of the Mt Attaviros.

Crete: the big island has four AO wine regions: Archánes, where dry red wines are made of Kotsifali, a spicy native grape, blended with black Mandelaria. Peza are crisp whites made from Vilana, a grape indigenous to the area; the reds are similar to Archánes. Daphnes and Sitia are both dry reds from Liatiko, an Aegean variety whose name is thought to come from 'July', when these grapes ripen.

Plagiés Melítona: this is the name of the AO region of Carras' citadel in Chalkidiki, the largest privately owned wine estate in Europe and home of excellent Château Carras and Limnio, from a grape variety mentioned by Aristotle that even tastes ancient.

The Greek Menu (*Katálogos*)

Ορεκτικά (Μεζέδες)	*Orektiká (Mezéthes)*	**Appetisers**
τζατζίκι	*tzatziki*	yoghurt and cucumbers
εληές	*eliés*	olives
κοπανιστί (τυροσαλάτα)	*kopanistí (tirosaláta)*	cheese purée, often spicy
ντολμάδες	*dolmáthes*	stuffed vine leaves
μελιτζανοσαλατα	*melitzanosaláta*	eggplant (aubergine) dip
σαγανάκη	*saganáki*	fried cheese with lemon
ποικιλία	*pikilía*	mixed hors d'œuvres
μπουρεκι	*bouréki*	cheese and vegetable pie
τυροπιττα	*tirópitta*	cheese pie
αχινοί	*achíni*	sea urchin roe (quite salty)

Σούπες	*Soópes*	**Soups**
αυγολέμονο	*avgolémono*	egg and lemon soup
χορτόσουπα	*chortósoupa*	vegetable soup
ψαρόσουπα	*psarósoupa*	fish soup
φασολάδα	*fasolada*	bean soup
μαγειρίτσα	*magirítsa*	giblets in egg and lemon
πατσάς	*patsás*	tripe and pig's foot soup (for late nights and hangovers

Λαδερά	*Latherá*	**Cooked in Oil**
μπάμιες	*bámies*	okra, ladies' fingers
γίγαντες	*yígantes*	butter beans in tomato sauce
μπριαμ	*briám*	aubergines and mixed veg
φακηές	*fakés*	lentils

Ζυμαρικά	*Zimariká*	**Pasta and Rice**
πιλάφι / ρύζι	*piláfi/rizi*	pilaf/rice
σπαγκέτι	*spagéti*	spaghetti
μακαρόνια	*macarónia*	macaroni
πλιγγούρι	*plingoúri*	bulgar wheat

Ψάρια	*Psária*	**Fish**
αστακός	*astakós*	lobster
αθερίνα	*atherína*	smelt
γάυρος	*gávros*	mock anchovy
καλαμάρια	*kalamaria*	squid
κέφαλος	*kefalos*	grey mullet
χταπόδι	*chtapóthi*	octopus
χριστόψαρο	*christópsaro*	John Dory
μπαρμπούνι	*barboúni*	red mullet
γαρίδες	*garíthes*	prawns (shrimps)
γοπα	*gópa*	bogue (boops boops)
ξιφίας	*ksifias*	swordfish
μαρίδες	*maríthes*	whitebait
συναγρίδα	*sinagrítha*	sea bream
σουπιές	*soupiés*	cuttlefish

φαγγρι	fangri	bream
κιδόνια	kidónia	cherrystone clams
σαρδέλλα	sardélla	sardines
μπακαλιάρος (σκορδαλιά)	bakaliáros (skorthaliá)	fried hake (with garlic sauce)
σαργός	sargós	white bream
σκαθάρι	skathári	black bream
στρείδια	stríthia	oysters
λιθρίνια	lithrínia	bass
μίδια	mídia	mussels

Εντραδες / Entrádes / Main Courses

κουνέλι	kounéli	rabbit
στιφάδο	stifádo	casserole with onions
γιουβέτσι	yiouvétsi	veal in a clay bowl
συκώτι	seekóti	liver
μοσχάρι	moschári	veal
αρνί	arní	lamb
κατσίκι	katsíki	kid
κοτόπουλο	kotópoulo	(roast) chicken
χοιρινό	chirinó	pork

Κυμάδες / Kymadhes / Minced Meat

παστίτσιο	pastítsio	mince and macaroni pie
μουσακά	moussaká	meat, aubergine with white sauce
μακαρόνια με κυμά	makarónia me kymá	spaghetti Bolognese
μπιφτέκι	biftéki	hamburger, usually bunless
σουτζουκάκια	soutzoukákia	meat balls in sauce
μελιτζάνες γεμιστές	melitzánes yemistés	stuffed aubergines/eggplants
πιπεριές γεμιστές	piperíes yemistés	stuffed peppers

Της Ωρας / Tis Oras / Grills to Order

μπριζολα	brizóla	beefsteak with bone
μπριζόλες χοιρινές	brizólas chirinés	pork chops
σουβλάκι	souvláki	meat or fish kebabs on a skewer
κοκορέτσι	kokorétsi	offal kebabs
κοτολέτες	kotolétes	veal chops
πάιδακια	paidakia	lamb chops
κεφτέδες	keftéthes (th as in 'th')	meat balls

Σαλάτες / Salátes / Salads and Vegetables

ντομάτες	domátes	tomatoes
αγγούρι	angoúri	cucumber
ρώσσικη σαλάτα	róssiki saláta	Russian salad
σπανάκι	spanáki	spinach
χωριάτικη	choriátiki	salad with feta cheese and olives
κολοκυθάκια	kolokithákia	courgettes/zucchini
πιπεριεσ	piperiés	peppers
κρεμιδι	kremídi	onions

πατάτες	patátes	potatoes
παντσάρια	pantsária	beetroot
μαρούλι	maroúli	lettuce
χόρτα	chórta	wild greens
αγκινάρες	angináres	artichokes
κουκιά	koukiá	fava beans

Τυρια	**Tiriáv**	**Cheeses**
φέτα	féta	goat's cheese
κασέρι	kasséri	hard buttery cheese
γραβιέρα	graviéra	Greek 'Gruyère'
μυζήθρα	mizíthra	soft white cheese
πρόβιο	próvio	sheep's cheese

Γλυκά	**Glyká**	**Sweets**
παγωτό	pagotó	ice cream
κουραμπιέδες	kourabiéthes	sugared biscuits
λουκουμάδες	loukoumáthes	hot honey fritters
χαλβά	halvá	sesame seed sweet
μπακλαβά	baklavá	nuts and honey in filo pastry
γιαούρτι (με μελι)	yiaoúrti (me méli)	yoghurt (with honey)
καριδοπιτα	karidópita	walnut cake
μήλο	mílo	apple
μπουγάτσα	bougátsa	custard tart

Miscellaneous

ψωμί	psomí	bread
βούτυρο	voútiro	butter
μέλι	méli	honey
μαρμελάδα	marmelátha	jam
λάδι	láthi	oil
πιάτο	piáto	plate
λογαριασμό	logariazmó	the bill/check

Drinks

άσπρο κρασί	áspro krasí	wine, white
άσπρο/κόκκινο/κοκκινέλι	áspro/kókkino/kokkinéli	white/red/rosé
ρετσίνα	retsína	wine resinated
νερό (βραστο/μεταλικο)	neró (vrastó/metalikó)	water (boiled/mineral)
μπύρα	bíra	beer
χυμός πορτοκάλι	chimós portokáli	orange juice
γάλα	gála	milk
τσάί	tsái	tea
σοκολάτα	sokoláta	chocolate
καφέ	kafé	coffee
φραππέ	frappé	iced coffee
πάγος	págos	ice
ποτίρι	potíri	glass
μπουκάλι	boukáli	bottle
καράφα	karáfa	carafe
στήν γειά σας!	stín yásas (formal, pl)	to your health! Cheers!
στήν γειά σου!	stín yásou (sing)	

Travel

07

Getting There

By Air

The only international airports receiving scheduled flights are **Athens, Thessaloníki** in the north, and **Heráklion** (Crete); other mainland airports (Alexandroúpolis, Ioánnina, Kalamáta, Kastoriá, Kavála, Kozáni and Préveza) and many island airports can only be reached by charter flight or by onward flights from Athens.

From the UK and Ireland

As competition increases, don't automatically presume charter flights are your best buy. The one rule seems to be that the sooner you buy your ticket, the more money you save. Check the deals at your local travel agents, the websites of easyJet and other low-cost airlines and general travel websites.

Scheduled and No-Frills Flights

Scheduled flights direct to Athens operate daily from London on **Olympic, British Airways** and **easyJet**. In the peak season Olympic flies three times daily from Heathrow and twice from Manchester, and has direct flights from London Gatwick to Thessaloníki (and on to Athens). BA flies from Heathrow and Gatwick, and easyJet from Luton. Scheduled flights with one stop can be booked with **Lufthansa** (via Munich) and **KLM** (via Amsterdam). Return prices range from £80 off season to £250 high season.

Airline Carriers

UK and Ireland

Aer Lingus, t 0845 0844 444; Ireland, **t** 0818 365 000, *www.aerlingus.com*.

British Airways, t 0845 7733 377; Ireland, **t** 0044 845 7733 377, *www.britishairways.com*.

Czech Airlines, London, **t** (020) 7255 1898; Manchester, **t** (0161) 4890 241, *www.czechairlines.co.uk*; Dublin, **t** (01) 814 4626, *www.czechairlines.ie*.

easyJet, t 0870 6000 000, *www.easyjet.com*.

KLM, t 08705 074 074, *www.klm.com*.

Lufthansa, t 0845 7737 747, *www.lufthansa.com*.

Olympic Airways, t 0870 6060 460, *www.olympicairways.co.uk*.

USA and Canada

Air Canada, t 1 888 247 2262, *www.aircanada.ca*.

British Airways, USA, **t** 800 AIRWAYS, *www.british-airways.com*.

Czech Airlines, Chicago, **t** (312) 201 17 81; New York, **t** (212) 765 6545; Toronto, **t** (416) 363 3174/5; Montreal, **t** (514) 844 6376, *www.czechairlines.com/en/northamerica*.

Delta, t 800 241 4141, *www.delta.com*.

KLM, USA, **t** 800 225 2525; Canada, **t** 1800 447 4747, *www.klm.com*.

Olympic Airways, USA, **t** 800 223 1226; in Canada: Montreal, **t** (514) 878 9691; Toronto, **t** (416) 920 2452, *www.olympic-airways.gr*.

Discounts and Students

UK and Ireland

Avro, t 0870 036 0111, *www.avro.co.uk*. Charter flights (Monarch) to Athens, Corfu and Crete from Gatwick, Manchester and Glasgow.

Balkan Tours, t (028) 9024 6795, *www.balkan.co.uk*. Charter flights to Crete from Belfast.

Delta Travel, t 0870 2200 727; or Manchester, **t** (0161) 274 4444; Liverpool, **t** (0151) 708 7955; Birmingham **t** (0121) 471 2282, *www.deltatravel.co.uk*. Manchester-based agents for scheduled flights from Heathrow to Athens, and from Manchester and Birmingham for Athens and Thessaloníki; also island charters.

Eclipse Direct, reservations **t** 0870 501 0203; **t** (01293) 554 400; **t** (0161) 742 2277. Charter flights from London Gatwick, Birmingham and Manchester.

Europe Student Travel, 6 Campden St, London W8, **t** (020) 7727 7647.

Holiday Warehouse, t 0870 745 0677, *www.holiday-to-greece.co.uk*. Bargain late holiday deals and flight-only bookings.

Island Wandering, t (01580) 860 733, *www.islandwandering.com*. Helpful company offering reasonably priced accommodation and/or island-hopping packages.

JMC, flights, **t** 0870 0100 434, holidays, **t** 0870 7580 203, *www.jmc.com*.

STA Travel, 86 Old Brompton Road, London SW7 3LH, **t** (020) 7581 4132; or 117 Euston Road

Scheduled flights from Ireland to Athens on **Olympic** and **Aer Lingus** fly via Heathrow and tend to be considerably pricier than charters.

Remember to reconfirm your return flight three days prior to departure (*see* p.104 for airline addresses in Athens).

Charter Flights

The advantage of charter flights is that they go from many smaller UK or other European airports direct to many **islands** or smaller mainland airports such as **Kalamáta**, **Préveza** or **Kavála**. Check the travel sections in the weekend papers, *Time Out* or the *Evening Standard* for last-minute discounts.

Most UK charters run from May to mid-October, but some firms feature early specials, usually from London Gatwick and Manchester

in March and April, depending on when Greek Easter falls.

Charter tickets have fixed outward and return dates with often as not departure and arrival times in the wee hours. Flight-only deals are hard to find in peak season. Visitors to Greece using a charter flight may visit Turkey or any neighbouring country for the day, but must not stay overnight, at the very real risk of forfeiting the return ticket home. Travellers with stamps from previous holidays in Turkey will not be barred entry, but if you have Turkish Cypriot stamps, check with the Passport Office before you go. Returning from Greece, do confirm your return flight 3 days prior to departure (*see* p.104 for airline addresses in Athens).

NW1 2SX, **t** (020) 7465 0484; Bristol, **t** 0870 167 6777 ; Leeds, **t** 0870 168 6878; Manchester, **t** (0161) 839 7838; Oxford, **t** 0870 163 6373; Cambridge, **t** (01223) 366966, *www.statravel.co.uk*; and many other UK branches.

Student Plan, *www.interdynamic.net/intstude.php*. Internet-based travel agency specializing in student adventure holidays.

Trailfinders, London, **t** (020) 7937 1234; Birmingham, **t** (0121) 236 1234; Manchester, **t** (0161) 839 6969; Glasgow, **t** (0141) 353 2224; Belfast, **t** (028) 9027 1888; Dublin, **t** (01) 677 7888, *www.trailfinders.com*.

Travel Cuts, 295a Regent St, London W1, **t** (020) 7255 1944, **f** (020) 7528 7532, *www.travel-cuts.co.uk*

Websites

www.airtickets.co.uk
www.cheapflights.com
www.cheap-flight-offers.co.uk
www.expedia.co.uk
www.flightcentre.co.uk
www.lastminute.com
www.skydeals.co.uk
www.sky-tours.co.uk
www.trailfinders.co.uk
www.thomascook.co.uk
www.travelselect.com
www.travelocity.co.uk
www.onlinetravellers.co.uk

USA and Canada

Air Brokers International, USA, **t** 800 883 3273, *www.airbrokers.com*. Discount agency.

Council Travel, 205 E. 42nd St, New York, NY 10017, **t** 800 2COUNCIL, *www.counciltravel.com*. Student and charter flights.

Homeric Tours, USA, **t** 800 223 5570, **f** (212) 753 0319, *www.homerictours.com*. Charter flights and custom tours.

Last Minute Travel Club, USA, **t** 877 970 3500 **f** (416) 441 9754, *www.lastminuteclub.com*. Annual membership fee gets you cheap stand-by deals.

New Frontiers, USA, **t** 800 677 0720, *www.newfrontiers.com*. Flights to London.

STA Travel in the USA, New York, **t** (212) 627 3111; outside New York **t** 800 781 4040, *www.statravel.com*

Travel Avenue, USA, **t** 800 333 3335, *www.travelavenue.com*

Travel Cuts, 187 College St, Toronto, Ontario M5T 1P7, **t** (416) 979 2406. Canada's largest student travel specialists.

Websites

www.airhitch.org
www.expedia.com
www.flights.com
www.orbitz.com
www.priceline.com
www.travellersweb.ws
www.travelocity.com
www.smarterliving.com

Student and Youth Discounts

If you're under 26 or a full-time student under 32 with an **International Student Identity Card** to prove it, you're eligible for student/youth charters; these are often sold as one-way tickets, enabling you to stay in Greece longer than is possible with a regular charter flight. Students under 26 are sometimes eligible for discounts on scheduled flights as well, especially with Olympic Airways, who currently offer 25% discount to ISIC card holders on all connecting flights from Athens to the islands.

International Student Travel Service, 11 Níkis St, Athens, **t** 210 323 3767.

From the USA and Canada

Olympic, **TWA** and **Delta** offer daily non-stop flights from New York to Athens in the summer; Olympic also flies direct to Athens from Boston, and from Toronto and Montreal in Canada. American economy fares (Apex and SuperApex/Eurosavers, booked at least three weeks in advance) range from $800 return New York–Athens in low season to $1,200 high season; Canadian economy fares to Athens from Toronto or Montreal range from $1,000 low season to $1,400–1,900 high season. When ringing around, take into consideration the hefty discount offered by travel agents on domestic flights within Greece for travellers on Olympic.

From many cities in the USA and Canada, European airlines such as **KLM** or **Czech Airlines** offer the best prices to Greece, with stopovers in New York or Boston and one other European city: Internet travel companies often produce the best deals.

North American travellers can also find charter tickets, which must involve a stay of between three days and four weeks. Student charters (under 26) may be one-way. You must reconfirm your flight at least 3 days (72hrs) before departure (*see* p.104 for airline addresses in Athens).

By Train

The best and most efficient route by train from the UK to Greece is through Italy. Starting with Eurostar from London Waterloo to Paris (3hrs), the journey to Brindisi in the south of Italy should take about 24hrs, and will cost around £400 return. From Brindisi, take the ferry over to Corfu and Pátras in the Peloponnese. You can also travel by train to Venice and from there take a ferry to Pátras.

Europeans may want to consider an Interrail pass (either under-26 or over-26) if you intend to travel around in Greece; call Rail Europe or log on to *www.inter-rail.co.uk*. The North American equivalent is the Eurail pass. **Eurostar**, UK, **t** 0870 160 6600, *www.eurostar. co.uk*, USA, **t** 800 EUROSTAR, *www.eurostar. com*.

Rail Europe (UK), 179 Piccadilly, London W1V 0BA, **t** 08705 848 848, *www.raileurope.co.uk*. For information on trains from the UK to Greece, and the various rail passes available. **Rail Europe** (USA), 226 Westchester Ave, White Plains, NY 10064, **t** 1 800 438 7245, *www.raileurope.com*. Take your passport.

By Bus

Taking a coach from London through Europe to Greece is a possible alternative for those who decide that a train trip is too expensive or too easy a route to travel. It isn't cheaper than a standby flight, and can take 4 days instead of 4hrs, but it's a chance to see Munich, Belgrade and other fine bus terminals. However, as with the trains, the most direct route to take is via Italy, where ferries can be picked up in Venice, Ancona and Brindisi. **Busabout**, London Traveller's Centre, 258 Vauxhall Bridge Rd, London SW1V 1BS, **t** (020) 7950 1661, **f** (020) 7950 1662, *www.busabout.com*. Hop-on, hop-off service for backpackers who want to take in various European capitals, using bus passes that cover travel from 2 weeks to 2 months. **Eurolines**, 52 Grosvenor Gardens, Victoria, London SW1W 0AU, **t** 08705 143219, *www.gobycoach.com*. They no longer go direct to Athens, but again, they have a wide array of services that will transport you through various European cities to Athens or to Italy where you can catch a ferry.

By Sea

The most common sea route to Greece is from Italy, with daily ferry services from

Ancona and Brindisi, and frequently from Bari and Venice. Brindisi ferries connect with the night train from Rome and arrive in Pátras in the Peloponnese the next morning. Of late the ferries have been picking up speed: **Ventouris** has a high-speed catamaran from Brindisi that goes to Corfu and Igoumenítsa in under 4hrs. Passengers are usually allowed a free stopover in Corfu if that island is not their ultimate destination, before continuing to Igoumenítsa or Pátras, but make sure it is noted on your ticket.

Students, young people and pensioners can get a **discount** of up to 20%. Discounts of up to 30% on car prices are also offered when buying a return ticket. Book tickets via your travel agent or at *www.greekferries.gr*, which includes all the ferry companies and allows you to compare prices and schedules.

ANEK Lines, 54 Amalías, ✉ 10538 Athens, **t** 210 323 3481, **f** 210 323 4137, *www.anek.gr*. From Ancona.

Minoan Lines, 2 Vass. Konstantinoú, ✉ 15125 Athens, **t** 210 751 2356, **f** 210 752 0540, *info@minoan.gr*. From Ancona or Venice.

Superfast Ferries, 30 Amalías ✉ 10538 Athens, **t** 210 331 3252, *www.superfast.com*. From Ancona.

Ventouris Ferries, 91 Pireós/2 Kýthiron, ✉ 18541 Piraeus, **t** 210 482 8001, **f** 210 481 3701, *www.ventouris.gr*. From Brindisi or Bari.

By Car

Driving from London to Athens (and taking the ferry from Italy to Greece) at a normal pace takes around 3½ days. You can get your car across the Channel by ferry, but taking the **Eurotunnel** shuttle service is the most convenient way; it takes only 35 minutes from Folkestone to Calais. Shuttles through the Channel Tunnel in low season cost £169 for a standard return (much cheaper for a special day return), rising to around £200 at peak times. The most direct route is then Calais–Reims–Geneva–Milan–Brindisi/Bari/Ancona (*see* above for ferry information).

Eurotunnel, **t** 0870 53 53 535, *www. eurotunnel.com*.

An **International Driving Licence** is not required for EU citizens. Other nationals can obtain one at home, or at one of the Automobile Club offices in Greece (ELPA), by presenting a national driving licence, passport and photograph. The minimum age is 18 years.

You should check on insurance with your own company, but the **Motor Insurance Bureau** at 10 Xenofóntos Street, Athens, **t** 210 323 6733, can tell you which Greek insurance company represents your own, or provide you with additional cover for Greece.

The **Greek Automobile Club**, ELPA, in Athens at 395 Messógion Ave, Ag. Paraskeví ✉ 15343, **t** 210 606 8800, operates a breakdown service within 60km (40 miles) of Athens, Thessaloníki, Laríssa, Pátras and Herákleon: dial **t** 104. ELPA also has a helpline for medical assistance, **t** 166 (*Mon–Fri 8am–3pm*). If you belong to an automobile club at home (*see* below), breakdown service is free anywhere. Similar services are offered by Express Service, **t** 154.

Customs formalities for bringing in a car are very easy and usually take very little time. You are allowed six months' free use of a car in Greece before it must leave the country. If your visit is going to be an extended one, to avoid difficulties when you leave, make sure your car is stamped in your passport on arrival. If you leave Greece without your car, you must have it withdrawn from circulation by a customs authority. ELPA has a list of lawyers who can offer free legal advice on car problems. They also have a 24hr number of information useful to foreign motorists, call **t** 174.

AA, **t** 0990 500 600, **t** 0800 444 500, *www.theaa.com*. '5-star' breakdown cover. Can advise before you go on any matters relating to driving abroad.

RAC, **t** 0800 550 550, *www.rac.co.uk*. A similar service to the AA.

AAA, (USA), **t** (407) 444 4000, **t** 800 222 5000, *www.aaa.com*. The American Automobile Association.

Entry Formalities

Passports and Visas

All **European Union** members can stay in Greece indefinitely. The only reason you would need special permission to stay would be for working or if complicated banking procedures required proof of residence, in which case, contact the **Aliens Bureau**, 173 Leof. Alexándras, ✉ 11522 Athens, **t** 210 647 6000.

The formalities for **non-EU** tourists entering Greece are very simple. American, Australian and Canadian citizens can stay for up to three months in Greece on presentation of a valid passport. If you want to stay longer, take your passport, 20 days before your time in Greece expires, to the Aliens Bureau or your local police station, and be prepared to prove you can support yourself with bank statements and the like. If you overstay your three months without permission, be prepared to pay a fine that, at the moment is €150 for an overstay of three months, €300 if over six months.

Customs

Duty-free allowances have been abolished within the EU. For travellers from outside the EU, the duty-free limits are 1 litre of spirits or 2 litres of liquors (port, sherry or champagne), plus 2 litres of wine and 200 cigarettes. Much larger quantities – up to 10 litres of spirits, 90 litres of wine, 110 litres of beer and 3,200 cigarettes – bought locally, can be taken through customs, provided that you are travelling between EU countries and can prove that they are for private consumption only.

For more information, US citizens can telephone the **US Customs Service**, **t** (202) 354 1000, or see the pamphlet *Know Before You Go* available from *www.customs.gov*.

Getting Around

The bible of travel around Greece is the *Greek Travel Pages*, updated monthly. Check their websites at *www.gtp.gr* and *www. gogreece.com*. Bus and train information and schedules can be found at *www.ktel.org* (buses) and *www.ose.gr* (trains).

By Air

Flights from Athens to other Greek mainland airports and to a large number of the islands can be booked in advance through **Olympic** (*www.olympic-airways.gr*) or **Aegean-Cronus** (*www.aegeanair.com*); as many planes are small, do this as far in advance as possible. Some only have 18 seats, and are good fun; they seem just to skim over the mountain tops (but note, they can't take off or land in high winds, and you could end up back where you started). Because the planes are small, baggage allowances (15kg) tend to be strictly enforced – unless you've bought your ticket abroad, when you're allowed 23kg.

Olympic Airways also offer island-to-island flights in season, without going via Athens.

By Train

By European standards Greek rail (**OSE**) is somewhat patchy, slow and old-fashioned. However, train fares are cheaper than buses by up to 40%, and in a couple of places (Kalávrita in the Peloponnese and the Pélion peninsula) the old rolling stock is used for tourist routes. There's quite a variety of **passes** available, some combining air tickets to the islands; check *www.osenet.gr/eng/ sitemap.htm*. For **schedules**, call **t** 210 529 7777.

See p.104 for **stations in Athens** for journeys onwards to the mainland.

By Bus

The domestic bus service (**KTEL**), with a web of routes based in each provincial capital, is efficient, regular, and a bargain. Services start as early as 6 or 7am and run until early/mid evening, depending on the route. In August, reserve seats in advance on the long-distance buses, especially from Athens to other points in Greece. Different timetables apply at weekends; for more information, try *www.ktel.org*.

See p.104 for **bus terminals in Athens** serving the mainland.

By Sea to the Islands

The National Tourist Office publishes a **free weekly list** of ship departures, both abroad and to the islands; for serious island-hoppers, ask for their free booklet, *Greek Travel Routes: Domestic Sea Schedules*. Alternatively, visit the **website** that lists all the ferry schedules to the islands, *www.ferries.gr*. At the same time, be aware that any number of factors (weather, health emergencies and unforeseen repairs) can throw timetables out of the window, so, if you have to catch a flight home, allow for the eccentricities of the system and leave a day early to be safe. For the latest information on departures and arrivals, ring the relevant port authorities (*limenarchío*) whose numbers are listed throughout the text of this guide.

Before purchasing a ticket, check timetables in competing agencies – some ferries are faster than others, and others can take half a day, stopping at tiny island ports. On smaller islands, agents moonlight as bartenders or grocers and may only have a handwritten sign next to the door. Make sure that you have

purchased a ticket before you get on, as in most cases tickets are not sold on board, and keep it with you, in case of a 'ticket control'.

Prices are still reasonable for passengers but rather dear for cars. In most cases children under the age of 4 travel free, and between 4 and 10 for half-fare. In the summer, especially in August, buy tickets well in advance if you have a car or want a cabin. If you miss your ship, you forfeit your ticket; if you cancel in advance, you will receive a 50% refund of the fare, or 100% in the case of major delays or

Sea Travel Times and Prices

Below are some of the more popular mainland–island connections. Approximate 2003 fares and duration of each trip are given, but both are subject to change. To calculate roughly the car prices on the ferries, multiply passenger fares by three to five. *See* also the list of ferry schedules to the islands on *www.ferries.gr*.

Piraeus to Crete, the Cyclades, Dodecanese and Northeastern Aegean Islands

Heráklion (Crete)	€24	8–10hrs
Mýkonos/Páros	€18	6hrs
Sérifos	€15	4hrs
Sifnos	€16	5hrs
Folégandros	€19	10 hrs
Rhodes	€32	17hrs
Kos	€27	13hrs
Kálymnos	€25	10 hrs
Sými	€32	14–17hrs
Lésbos (Mytilíni)	€26	12–15hrs
Ikaría/Sámos	€20–23	8–11hrs

Piraeus to the Saronic Islands and Kýthera (ferry/hydrofoil)

Aegina	€6	1½hrs (F)
	€10	30mins (H)
Hýdra	€8	4hrs (F)
	€18	1½hrs (H)
Póros	€8	3hrs (F)
	€12	1hr (H)
Spétses	€23	2hrs (H)
Kýthera	€35	4hrs (H)

Sporades Line (ferry/hydrofoil)
Ag. Konstantínos to

Alónissos	€16	5hrs (F)
	€30	3hrs (H)
Skiáthos	€31	3¼hrs (F)
	€23	1½hrs (H)
Skópelos	€15	4hrs (F)
	€28	2hrs (H)

Kými (Évia) to
Skýros	€10	2hrs (F)

Vólos to
Alónissos	€14	4½hrs (F)
	€27	2½hrs (H)
Skiáthos	€18	2½hrs (F)
	€20	1¼hrs (H)
Skópelos	€14	3½hrs (F)
	€25	2hrs (H)

Rafína to Évia and Cyclades Line (ferry/cat)
Amorgós	€33	6hrs (C)
Ándros	€10	2hrs (F)
	€18	1hr (C)
Kárystos (Évia)	€8	1hr (F)
Mýkonos	€16	4hrs (F)
	€30	2hrs (C)
Náxos	€30	3½hrs (C)
Páros	€29	3hrs (C)
Tínos	€15	3hrs (F)
	€27	2hrs (C)
Psára	€18	6hrs (F)

Kéa–Kýthnos Line
Lávrion to
Kéa	€8	1½hrs
Kýthnos	€10	3hrs

Patrás and Killíni–Ionian Line (ferry/cat)
Patrás to
Kefaloniá	€13	2½hrs (F)
	€23	2hrs (C)
Corfu	€22	6½hrs (F)

Killíni to
Zákynthos	€7	1½hrs (F)

Gýthio–Crete and Kýthera Line
Gýthio to
Chaniá	€18	7hrs
Kýthera	€7	2½hrs

cancellations. If you are 'greatly inconvenienced' by a delay, you're entitled to compensation: contact the Ministry of the Merchant Marine (*www.yen.gr*), or the Piraeus or Rafína port police.

Piraeus Port Authority, t 210 422 6000/**t** 210 459 3000 (for ferry schedules).

Rafína Port Authority, t 22940 28888.

Pátras Port Authority (for the Ionian Islands) **t** 22610 341 024.

Ferries

Comfort on Greek ferries has improved by leaps and bounds, especially on the long-haul ferries, which now boast shops, video rooms, air-conditioning, disco bars, slot machines and even small swimming pools. Long-distance island ferries have two or three classes now: the first, or 'distinguished' class, with a plush lounge and private cabins (these often cost as much as flying); the second class, often with its own lounge as well, but smaller, porthole-less cabins, segregated by sex; and third or tourist class, which offers access to typically large rooms full of airline-type seats and the deck and snack bar; if you mean to use your sleeping bag, it's a good idea to get on the ferry early to claim a space. Drinking water is never very good, but all sell bottled water, beer, coffee and soft drinks (for about twice as much as on shore). Biscuits and cigarettes complete the fare on the smaller boats, while the larger ones offer sandwiches, self-service dining (usually adequate and fairly priced) or full meals served in a dining room.

Hydrofoils and Catamarans

There are several fleets of hydrofoils, several catamarans and the occasional 'sea jet' thumping over the Greek seas, and new lines are added every year. Most services (especially to ports in the Saronic Gulf) run throughout the year but are considerably less frequent between November and May. As a rule hydrofoils travel at least twice as fast as ferries and are twice as expensive. In the peak season they are often fully booked, so buy tickets as early as you can. Beware, too, if the weather is very bad, they won't leave port.

Boats to Turkey

The easternmost Greek islands have regular links to the Turkish mainland. Ferries run daily year-round between Rhodes and Marmaris (3½hrs); between Kos and Bodrum (1½hrs); from Chíos to Çeşme (1hr); from Sámos to Kuşadasi near Ephesus (1½hrs); and from Lésbos to Ayvalik (June 15–December only, 2hrs). In season, excursion boats also sail over from most of the smaller Dodecanese as well. Prices, once outrageous, are more reasonable, although there is a mysterious array of taxes on both sides (sometimes less if you only make a day excursion). Also, beware the charter restriction: if you spend a night in Turkey the Greek authorities might well invoke the law and refuse you passage home on your flight.

By Car

Petrol is cheaper in Greece than in almost any other country in the EU (around €1 a litre; unleaded (*amólivdi*) a wee bit less) and, while driving in and around Athens and Thessaloníki (and trying to find a place to park) may be a hair-raising experience, the rest of Greece is fairly easy and pleasant. There are few cars on most roads, and most signs, when you're lucky enough to find one, have their equivalents in Roman letters (good maps, such as the Michelin or the more detailed regional ROAD maps have place names in both Greek and Roman letters).

Traffic regulations and signalling comply with standard practice on the European Continent (i.e. driving on the right). Crossroads, tipsy tourists, Greeks speeding or gesticulating while driving, low visibility in the mountains and flocks of goats and sheep are the greatest hazards. Don't be shy about tooting your horn on blind mountain corners. If you're exploring off the beaten track, you may want to take a spare container of petrol along, as stations can be scarce on the ground and only open shop hours.

There is a **speed limit** of 50km per hour (30mph) in inhabited areas.

Hiring a Car

There are countless hire-car firms in the main seaside resorts and on the islands (but beware, many fewer in smaller mainland cities, even ones with airports like Kastoriá). Usually you can save money by booking a car with your flight; otherwise check the internet (*www.interdynamic.net*, or *www.hertz.gr* or *www.dilos.com* or *www.easyCar.com*), or *see* p.105 for car hire firms based in Athens. On the islands many car hire firms are family-run. If an island has a lot of unpaved roads and not a lot of competition, prices tend to be higher; at the time of writing, hiring a small car averages around €45–55 a day in the summer. In the off season, you can usually negotiate a lower rate. Arriving with brochures from the competition has been known to strengthen one's bargaining position. Most firms require that you be at least 21, some 25. Read the small print with care (look out for mileage limits, etc.) and don't be surprised if you have to leave your driving licence as security.

By Motorbike and Moped

Motorbikes and even more popular mopeds are ideal for short jaunts in the summer. It almost never rains, and what could be more pleasant than a gentle thyme-scented breeze freshening your journey? Scooters (the Greeks call them *papákia*, 'little ducks', supposedly for the noise they make) are both more economical and sometimes more practical than cars. Rental rates vary (count on at least €15 a day) and include third party insurance coverage in most cases. You will have to have a valid driving licence (for Americans, this means an international one). For larger motorbikes (anything over 75cc) you may be asked to show a motorcycle driver's licence. The downsides: many bikes are poorly maintained, many roads are poorly maintained, and everyone takes too many risks: hospital beds in Greece fill up each summer with casualties, both foreign and Greek (check your insurance to see if you're covered). Many islands and resorts have laws about operating motorbikes after midnight (the 'little ducks', often stripped of their mufflers, tend to howl like a flock of Daffys and Donalds on amphetamines), but they are as enforced as seldom as the compulsory helmet requirement.

By Bicycle

Cycling has not caught on in mountainous Greece, either as a sport or as a means of transport, though you can usually hire an old bike in most major resorts. Trains and planes carry bicycles for a small fee, and ferries generally take them along for nothing.

Hitch-hiking

Greek taxi drivers have recently convinced the government to pass a law forbidding other Greeks from picking up hitchhikers, so you may find hitching slow going; perhaps because of the law, motorized holidaymakers now seem to stop and offer more rides than the locals.

Yachting, Sailing and Flotilla Holidays

One of the great thrills of sailing the Greek waters is the variety of places to visit in a relatively short time, with the bonus that nowhere in Greece is far from safe shelter or harbours with good facilities for yachtsmen. The 100,000 miles of coastline provide a virtually inexhaustible supply of secluded coves and empty beaches, even at the height of the tourist season. The Greek National Tourist Organization has initiated a programme of rapid expansion and new **marinas** are being constructed throughout the country.

The only real problems you'll encounter are the strong winds and occasional sudden storms. **Weather forecasts** for yachtsmen are broadcast at intervals throughout the day on VHF Channel 16 (in Greek and English); security warnings are also broadcast on this channel, e.g. dangerous wrecks, lights not in operation, etc.

Yachts entering Greek waters must fly the code flag 'Q' until cleared by entry port authorities. Upon arrival the port authority (*limenarchíon*) issues all yachts with a transit log, which entitles the yacht and crew to unlimited travel in Greek waters. It must be kept on board and produced when required, and returned to the customs authorities on leaving Greece. Permission is normally given for a stay of 6 months, but this can be extended. Small motor, sail or rowing boats do not require a '*carnet de passage*', and are allowed into Greece duty-free for four

Specialist Tour Operators

In the UK

Amathus Holidays, 2 Leather Lane, London EC1N 7RA, t (020) 7611 0901 *www.amathus holidays.co.uk*. Villas, hotels and cruises.

Argo Holidays, 100 Wigmore St, London, W1 3RS, t 0870 066 7070, *www.argo-holidays. com*. Variety of holidays from painting and photography to watersports.

British Museum Tours, 46 Bloomsbury St, London WC1B 3QQ, t (020) 7436 7575, f (020) 7580 8677, *www.britishmuseumtraveller. co.uk*. Archaeological guided tours.

Equitour, 40–41 South Parade, Summertown, Oxford OX2 7JP, t (01865) 511642, f (01865) 512 583, *www.equitour.co.uk*. Horse-riding holidays on the mainland.

Explore Worldwide, 1 Frederick St, Aldershot, Hants GU11 1LQ, t (01252) 760101, *www. exploreworldwide.com*. Rambles in western Crete; caique cruises; Aegean Island hikes; Cyclades island tour.

Filoxenia, Sourdock Hill, Barkisland, Halifax, West Yorkshire HX4 0AG, t (01422) 375999, *www.filoxenia.co.uk*. Archaeological, walking, wine and cookery tours in Crete; cookery on Corfu and Léros; painting groups in Kýthera, and various holidays in Évia.

Greco-File, t (01422) 310330, *www.filoxenia. co.uk/greco.htm*. The dedicated Greek branch of Filoxenia. Expert advice on where to go, flights and 'couture' holidays.

Greek Islands Club, 10–12 Upper Square, Old Isleworth, Middx TW7 7BJ, t (020) 8232 9780, f (0820) 8568 8330, *www.sunvil.co.uk/sites/ gic*. Helpful and friendly with choice villas and a range of activity holidays on the Ionian islands, Crete, Skiáthos and Skópelos.

Headwater Holidays, The Old Schoolhouse, Chester Rd, Northwich, Cheshire CW8 1LE, t (01606) 7220033, f (01606) 7220034, *www.headwater-holidays.co.uk*. Walking holidays: mainland Greece, Crete, Kefaloniá.

Hidden Greece, 47 Whitcomb St, London WC2H 7DH, t (020) 7839 2553, f (020) 7839 5891, *www.hidden-greece.co.uk*. Organized language holidays in Athens, the Cyclades, Dodecanese, Crete and Rhodes.

Island Holidays, Drummond St, Comrie, PH6 2DS, t (01764) 670107, *www.24island holidays.com*. Nature tours : Crete, Lésbos.

Island Wandering, 51A London Road, Hurst Green, Sussex TN19 7QP, t (01580) 860733, f (01580) 860282, *www.islandwandering. com*. Hotels and studios in the Cyclades, Ionians, Dodecanese and NE Aegean.

Laskarina Holidays, St Mary's Gate, Wirksworth, Matlock, DE4 4DQ, t (01629) 822203, *www.laskarina.co.uk*. Painting holidays on more remote Islands: Chálki, Sými, Tílos, Sámos, Ikaria, Kálymnos, Léros, Lipsí, Pátmos, Alónissos and Skópelos.

Marengo Guided Walks, 17 Bernard Cresecent, Hunstanton, PE36 6ER, t (01485) 532710, *www.marengo.supanet. com*. Botanical guided trails around Épirus and other mainland locations as well as the islands.

Martin Randall, 10 Barley Mow Passage, Chiswick, London W4 4PH, t (020) 8742 3355, f (020) 8742 7766, *www.martinrandall.com*. Cultural tours to Crete and Athens.

Naturetrek, Cheriton Mill, Cheriton, Alresford, Hampshire SO24 0NG, t (01962) 733051, *www.naturetrek.co.uk*. Birdwatching and botanical trips to southern Greece, Crete and Lésbos.

Peligoni Club, PO Box 88, Chichester, W Sussex PO20 7DP, t (01243) 511499, *www.peligoni. com*. A one-off, friendly, English-run watersports club on the northeast coast of Zákynthos. They now also offer painting, sailing and relaxation holidays.

Ramblers Holidays, PO Box 43, Welwyn Garden City, Hertfordshire AL8 6PQ, t (01707) 331133, *www.ramblersholidays.co.uk*. Walking tours in the Peloponnese and on Crete and Sámos.

Simply Simon Holidays, 1/45 Nevern Square London Sw5 9PF, t (020) 7373 1933, f (020) 7370 1807, *www.simplysimon.co.uk*. Villas and hotels in Athens and the Cyclades, as well as naturist holidays.

Skýros Holistic Holidays, 92 Prince of Wales Rd, London NW5 3NE, t (020) 7284 3065, *www.skyros.com*. Creative writing courses, watersports, spiritual development courses, artists' workshops, holistic bodywork workshops in yoga, dance and massage.

Solo's Holidays Ltd, 54–8 High St, Edgware, Middx HA8 7EJ, t (0870) 0720 700, *www. solosholidays.co.uk*. Singles' group holidays in 4-star hotels. Also spring and autumn rambling breaks in Évia and a Peloponnese wine and culture tour.

Sovereign, Groundstar House, London Rd, Crawley, W Sussex RH10 2TB, t 0870 366 1634, *www.sovereign.com*. Villa parties for single travellers in traditional houses on Sými and Kálymnos. Also 'Caique Cruising'.

Swan Hellenic Cruises, 77 New Oxford St, London WC1A 1PP, t 0845 3555 111, *www.swanhellenic.com*. Cultural, archaeological and art history tours and cruises.

Travelux Holidays, 40 High St, Tenterden, Kent, t (01580) 765000, *www.travelux.co.uk*. Accommodation, fly-drive and special interest holidays in mainland Greece and the Ionian islands; painting and photography, walking, sailing and yoga.

Voyages of Discovery, Lymen House, 1 Victoria Way, Burgess Hill, BH15 9NF, t (01444) 462150, *www.voyagesofdiscovery.com*. Luxury cruises.

Waymark Holidays, 44 Windsor Rd, Slough, Bucks SL1 2EJ, t (01753) 516477, f (01753) 517016, *www.waymarkholidays.com*. Guided hiking groups in Chalkidiki, on Mílos, Crete and Sámos, spring and autumn breaks.

Yoga Plus, 177 Ditchling Road, Brighton, East Sussex BN1 6JB, t (01273) 276175, *www.yogaplus.co.uk*. In Southern Crete.

In the USA and Canada

Caravan Tours, 401 North Michigan Avenue, Chicago, IL 60611, t 800-Caravan, *www.caravantours.com*. Mainland/island tours.

Central Holiday Tours, 120 Sylvan Avenue, Englewood Cliffs, NJ 07632, t 800 935 5000, *www.centralh.com*. Tours in ancient history and archaeology, mythology and theatre.

Classic Adventures, PO Box 143, Hamlin, NY 14464, t (716) 964 8488, toll free t 800 777 8090, f 964 7297, *www.classicadventures.com*. Bicycling and walking holidays in Crete or across the north Peloponnese.

Cloud Tours, Newtown Plaza, 31-09 Newtown Ave, 3rd Floor, L.I.C., N.Y. 11102, t (718) 721 3808, toll free t 1 800 223 7880, f (718) 721 4019, *www.cloudtours.com*. Cruise and land tours, Athens and Northern Greece.

Crown Peters, 34–10 Broadway, Astoria, NY 11106, t 800 321 1199, *www.crownpeters.com*. Tours around mainland Greece and the islands, plus cruises.

Destination and Adventures International, 8489 Crescent Drive, Los Angeles, CA 90046,

t 800 659 4599, f (323) 650 6902, *www.daitravel.com*. Island cycling tours.

Flamingo Travel Group, PO Box 195, South and Urban Aves, Glenolden, PA 19036, t 800 325 PINK, *www.flamingo-travel.com*. Mainland Greece, Crete, Rhodes, Mýkonos, Santoríni.

Freedom Tour, New York, t (212) 202 5130 , f (212) 202 515, *www.freedom-tour.com*. Independent and escorted cultural tours of Athens, Delphi, Olympia, Corinth, Crete, Rhodes and many other islands.

Friends Travel, P.O. Box 691309, West Hollywood, CA 90069, t (310) 652 9600, f (310) 652 5454, *www.friendstravel.com*. Gay and lesbian cruises and tours.

www.greece101.com. Internet-based tour operator with a range of activities; many trekking/exploring tours, and kayaking.

IST Cultural Tours, 225 West 34th St, Suite 913, New York, NY 10122, t (212) 563 1202, toll free t 800 833 2111, f (212) 594 6953, *www.ist-tours.com*. Customized tours including yacht cruises and lectures on archaeology.

Meander Adventures, 2029 Sidewinder Drive, P.O. Box 2730, Park City, UT 84060, t 800 367 3230 (toll free in USA), f (435) 649 9141, *www.greece-travel-turkey-travel.com*. Organized tours, boating and sailing holidays and also personalized itineraries.

Metro Tours, 484 Lowell Street, Peabody, MA 01960, t (978) 535 4000, toll free t 800 221 2810, *www.metrotours.com*. Honeymoons and yachting holidays, Athens and Delphi.

Riding World, P. O. Box 807, Dubois, WY 82513, t 800 545 0019, f (307) 455 2354, *www.ridingworld.com/greece*. Fully organized riding holidays on Skiáthos.

Sun Holidays, 7208 Sand Lake Road, Suite 207, Orlando, FL 32819, t 800 422 8000, *www.sunholidaysusa.com*. Guided historical tours of Athens and the surrounding sites.

In Greece

Candili, Prokópi, 34004 Évia, Greece, t (00 30) 974 062100, *www.candili.co.uk*. Wide range of creative courses for all abilities. Ethnic accommodation, swimming pool, beach trips and good home cooking.

Hellenic Culture Centre, Ikaría, t (00 30) 275 061140 (00 30 2275061140 from October 2002), *www.hcc.gr*. Greek language courses pitched at all levels of ability.

Yacht Operators

In the UK

Cosmos Yachting, 6 Rocks Lane, London SW13 oDB, t 0800 376 9070, *www.cosmos yachting.com*. Charters around the islands.

Greek Island Cruise Centre, 4321 Lakemoor Dr, Wilmington, 28405, t 800 341 3030.

McCulloch Yacht Charter, 32 Fairfield Rd, London E3 2QB, t (020) 8452 7509.

The Moorings, Bradstowe House, Middle Wall, Whitstable, CT5 1BF, t (01227) 776677, *www.moorings.com*. Charters from Corfu, Skiáthos, Kos and Athens.

Odysseus Yachting Holidays, Temple Craft Yacht Charters, Middleham, Ringmer, Lewes, BN8 5EY t (01273) 812333, www.*odysseus. co.uk*. Flotillas around the Ionian Islands.

Neilson Active Holidays, Brighton Marina, Lock View, Brighton, BN2 5HA, t 0870 3333 356, *www.neilson.co.uk*. Flotilla holidays.

Sunsail, The Port House, Port Solent, Portsmouth, PO6 4TH, t 0870 777 0313, *www.sunsail.com/uk*. Flotillas, tuitional sailing and watersports.

Tenrag Yacht Charters, Tenrag House, Freepost CU986, Preston, Kent CT3 1NB, t (01227) 721874, *www.tenrag.com*. Charters from Athens, Corfu, Rhodes and Mýkonos.

In the USA

Interpac Yachts, 1050 Anchorage Lane, San Diego, CA, 92106, t 888 99 YACHT, *www.interpacyachts.com*.

Womanship, Learn to Sail Cruises for and by Women, USA, t 800 324 9295, *www.woman-ship.com*. Women-only flotillas.

Valef, 7254 Fir Rd, PO Box 391, Ambler, PA 19002, t 800 223 3845, *www.valefyachts.com*. Reputable firm, 300 crewed yachts.

In Greece

A1 Yachting, 1 Byronos and Kanada St, PO Box 393, 85100 Rhodes, t (00 30) 2410 22927, *www.a1yachting.com*.

Anemos Yachting, 39 Thoukididou, Alimos 17455, t 010 985 0052, *www.anemos-yachting. gr*.

Ghiolman Yachts, 7 Filellínon St, Sýntagma, 10557, Athens, t 010 323 3696, *www. ghiolman.com*.

months. They are entered in your passport and deleted on exit. For more information, apply to the **National Tourist Organization**, 4 Conduit Street, London W1R 0DJ, t (020) 7734 5997, who produce a useful booklet called *Yachting*, which lists all official ports of entry or exit and every marina in Greece, with a complete list of facilities offered. For more information, call the **National Tourist Organization**, Marine Division, 2 Amerikís, Athens, t 210 327 1672, or the **Piraeus Port Authority**, t 210 422 6000/ t 210 459 3000.

Yacht Charter

Chartering yachts is very popular and, as the promotional literature says, can be cheaper than staying in a hotel. Over 4,000 vessels are currently available in all sizes, with or without a crew (for a bareboat charter, both the charterer and another member of the party must show an official certificate or diploma as proof of seamanship or certification from a recognized yacht club). The National Tourist Organization has a list of Greek charter firms, or contact the **Yacht Charter Association**, Deacons Boatyard, Burseldon Bridge, Southampton SO31 8AZ, UK, t (02380) 400 7075, *www.yca.co.uk*, which supplies a list of its recognized yacht charter operators and advice on chartering overseas.

Flotilla and Sailing Holidays

If you want to float among the islands, but don't own a yacht, or lack the experience to charter one, a flotilla holiday may be the answer. A growing number of companies offer 1–2-week sailing holidays, some instructing inexperienced sailors (beginning with a week on land). High season prices for a 2 week holiday are £600–1,000 pp, on a 4-person yacht. The yachts have 4–8 berths (shared boats available for couples and singles) and sail in flotillas, usually 6–12 yachts, with experienced skipper, engineer and social hostess.

Practical A–Z

08

Children

Greeks love children, and children usually love Greece. Depending on their age, they go free or receive discounts on ships and buses. However, if they're babies, don't count on pharmacies stocking your brand of milk powder or baby foods – it's safest to bring your own supply. Take extra precautions against the strong sun. Finding a babysitter is rarely a problem: some of the larger hotels even offer special supervised kiddie campgrounds and activity areas for some time off.

Greek children usually have an afternoon nap (as do their parents), so it's quite normal for them to eat *en famille* until the small hours. Although Greek superstitions are dying out, one involving children still holds strong: if you compliment a child's beauty or intelligence, follow it with a ritual dry spit sound 'phtew, phtew, phtew' in the direction of the admired one. The 'spitting' admits the jealousy you may be feeling and wards off evil spirits. If you neglect this, don't be surprised if the old grannie, or even the trendy young mum, do the 'phtewing' for you, and add the sign of the cross and a small prayer to the Virgin to boot.

Climate and Measurements

Greece enjoys hot, dry, clear and bright Mediterranean **summers**, cooled by winds, of which the *meltémi* from the northeast is the most notorious and most likely to upset Aegean sailing schedules. **Winters** are mild, and in general the wet season begins at the end of October or beginning of November when it can rain 'tables and chairs' as the Greeks say. It begins to feel **springlike** in February, especially in Crete and Rhodes and the south coast, when wild flowers appear.

Any time is a good time to see some part of Greece. **Winter** offers wild, world-class clubbing in Athens, or gives hardy types a chance to play in the snow, or see their archaeological sites in lonely splendour (a loneliness punctuated only by a few Japanese tour buses, the only consistent winter travellers to Greece). Landscapes that seem barren in August are often wonderfully lush in January. **Spring** is a marvellous time for wild flowers, and for participating in Greek Easter, the biggest holiday on the calendar. **Late spring** or **September** and **October** are the best for hiking or travelling by car on the small unpaved roads in the mountains, since they tend to wash out in the winter rains and are rebulldozed in the spring, sometimes later rather than sooner. September and early October tend to be calm and warm without being stifling, the swimming is still excellent, and the Greeks are laid-back. That leaves **July** and **August**, the most popular months for sun lovers and people with children. This includes the Greeks themselves, so it's always the busiest, most crowded time and prices are at their highest. The islands are best from spring through to late September; after that the sea can be rough.

One uniquely Greek **measurement** you may come across is the *strémma*, a Greek land measurement (1 *strémma* = ¼ acre).

Disabled Travellers

Although increasingly hotels have facilities for wheelchair users, as do most major museums, getting around Greece can be hard. Access on trains, buses, small planes, ferries and hydrofoils poses challenges, and the steepness of the natural terrain means many villages have steps for streets and/or cobblestoned pavements. *See* box opposite for a list of organizations that can help.

Average Daily Temperatures in °C/°F

	Athens	Crete	Mýkonos	Rhodes	Corfu	Mýtilíni	Thess'íki	Vólos
Jan	11/48	12/54	12/54	12/54	10/50	10/50	6/43	10/51
April	16/60	17/62	17/60	17/60	15/60	16/60	13/55	15/58
July	28/82	26/78	25/76	27/78	27/78	27/80	24/75	25/77
Aug	28/82	26/78	25/76	27/79	27/78	27/80	24/75	25/77
Sept	25/76	25/76	23/74	25/78	23/74	23/74	21/70	22/71
Nov	15/58	18/64	17/62	17/66	15/58	15/58	12/54	15/58

Organizations for Disabled Travellers

Greece

The Panhellenic Association for the Blind, 31 Veranzérou St, Athens, 104 32, **t** 010 522 8333, **f** 010 522 2112.

UK

Thomsons, and several other big package holiday companies, have some suitable tours. Otherwise, consult:

Access Travel, 6 The Hillock, Astley, Lancashire M29 7GW, **t** (01942) 888 844, *info@access-travel.co.uk, www.access-travel.co.uk*. Travel agent for people with disabilities, with a base in Rhodes: special airfares, car hire and suitable accommodation.

Chalfont Line Holidays, **t** (020) 8997 3799, **f** (020) 8991 2982, *www.chalfont-line.co.uk*. Escorted or individual holidays for travellers with disabilities.

Greco-File's Opus 23, **t** (01422) 310330, **f** (01422) 310340, *www.filoxenia.co.uk/greco.htm*. Offers special needs holidays and accommodation on the islands.

Holiday Care Service, Imperial Building, Victoria Rd, Horley, Surrey RH6 7PZ, **t** (01293) 774535, **f** (01293) 784647, *www.holidaycare. org.uk*.

RADAR (Royal Association for Disability and Rehabilitation), 12 City Forum, 250 City Rd, London EC1V 8AS, **t** (020) 7250 3222, *www.radar.org.uk*. Publishes *Holidays and Travel Abroad: A Guide for Disabled People*. **Tripscope**, **t** (020) 8994 9294.

USA

Alternative Leisure Co, 165 Middlesex Turnpike, Suite 206, Bedford, MA 01730, **t** (718) 275 0023, *www.alctrips.com*. Organizes vacations abroad for travellers with disabilities.

Mobility International USA, PO Box 10767, Eugene, OR 97440, **t/TTY** (541) 343 1284, *www.miusa.org*. Information on international educational exchange programmes and volunteer service overseas for the disabled.

SATH (Society for Accessible Travel and Hospitality), 347 Fifth Avenue, Suite 610, New York, NY 10016, **t** (212) 557 0027, **f** (212) 725 8253, *www.sath.org*. Travel and access information.

Other Useful Contacts

Access Ability, *www.access-ability.co.uk*. Information on travel agencies catering specifically for travellers with disabilities.

Emerging Horizons, *www.emerginghorizons. com*. International on-line travel newsletter for people with disabilities.

Global Access, *www.geocities.com/Paris/1502/ disabilitylinks.html*. On-line network for disabled travellers, with links, archives and information on travel guides.

Eating Out

A Greek menu (*katálogos*) often has two prices for each item – with and without tax. In most restaurants there's also a small cover charge. If you eat with the Greeks, there's no Western nit-picking over who's had what. You share the food, drink, company and the bill, *to logariasmó*, although hosts will seldom let foreign guests part with a cent.

An average taverna meal – if you don't order a major fish – usually runs at around €10–15 a head with carafes of house wine. Prices at sophisticated restaurants or blatantly touristy places with views can be much higher. In the 'Eating Out' sections of this book, prices are only given for places that do not fall into the usual taverna price category, and are per person with house wine. Some places now offer set price meals with a glass of wine (often for under €10), some for two people, some better than others.

In many resorts, waiters are paid a cut of the profits (which is why some obnoxiously tout for custom in busy resorts); **tipping** is discretionary but very appreciated. By law, there's a little book by the door if you want to register a complaint. A law designed to catch tax evaders insists that you take a receipt (*apóthixi*) 150m from the door; the police make periodic checks.

For more on food and eating out in Greece, and a menu decoder, *see* pp.65–74.

Major Festivals

Carnival, February: biggest celebrations in Pátras, Réthymnon, Zákynthos, Naúplio and Xánthi.

Easter, March/April: celebrations everywhere.

Firewalkers, 21 May, in Langadás: *see* p.544.

Athens Festival, June–September: concerts, ballet, opera by international companies, in the Herodes Atticus Theatre, *see* p.111.

Olympus Festival, July: concerts in venues around the big mountain, *see* p.522.

Ancient Epidauros Festival, July: concerts in the 'Little Theatre', *see* p.263.

Epidauros Festival, July-August: festival of ancient Greek drama, *see* p.263.

Philippi-Thássos Festival, July–August: ancient drama and music in Philippi, Thássos and Kavála, *see* p.594.

Crete Wine Festival, July, in Réthymnon: *see* p.694.

International Pátras Festival, July–August: theatre and concerts.

Sými Festival, July–August: music, dance and films, *see* pp.788 and 780.

Sparta Artistic Summer, July–August: outdoor cultural events, *see* p.296.

Rhodes Wine Festival, late July–August.

Kalamáta International Festival of Dance, mid-July–August: *see* p.334.

International Folklore Festival, Lefkáda, August: *see* p.460.

Réthymnon Renaissance Festival, late August–September: *see* p.694.

Corfu Festival, September: classical music; *see* p.443.

The Dimitria, October and November: big name events in Thessaloníki, *see* p.529.

Electricity

The **electric current** in Greece is mainly 220 volts, 50Hz; plugs are continental two-pin. Buy an **adaptor** in the UK before you leave, as they are rare in Greece; North Americans will need adaptors and transformers.

Embassies and Consulates in Athens

Australia: 37 D. Soútsou, t 210 645 0404, f 210 646 6595.

Canada: 4 Ioan. Gennadíou, t 210 727 3400, f 210 725 3460.

Ireland: 7 Vass. Konstantínou, t 210 723 2771, f 210 729 3383.

New Zealand: 268 Kifissías, t 210 687 4701, f 210 687 4444.

South Africa: 60 Kifissías, t 210 610 6645, f 210 610 6636.

UK: 1 Ploutárchou, t 210 727 2600, f 210 727 2720.

USA: 91 Vass. Sofías, t 210 721 2951, f 210 645 6282.

Festivals and Events

Every village has its *panegýri*, or patron saint's festival, some celebrated merely with a special service, others with events culminating in a feast and music and dancing till dawn. Other events celebrate victories, liberation from the Turks, wine, music, ancient theatre, aubergines, sardines, sultanas – you'll find them listed in the text.

Health

For first aid, go to the nearest Local Health Centre (**ESY** or '*kentro e-yiée-as*') which are well equipped to deal with snake bite, jelly fish stings, stomach ache, etc. and treat foreigners for free. Where there are no ESYs, the rural doctors (*iatrós* – there is at least one on every island with more than a couple of hundred people) does the same work *gratis*. For more serious illnesses or accidents, you'll need a **hospital** (*nosokomío*); the larger islands have them, and helicopters act as ambulances.

EU citizens are entitled to free **emergency medical care**; British travellers are often urged to carry a **Form E111**, available from DSS offices (apply well in advance on form CM1 from post offices), which will admit them to the most basic IKA (Greek NHS) hospitals for treatment, but this doesn't cover medicines or nursing care. In any case, the E111 is often looked on with total disregard outside Athens; expect to pay up front, and get receipts so you can be reimbursed back home. As private doctors and hospital stays can be very expensive, consider a **travel insurance policy** with adequate repatriation cover. Non-Europeans should check their own health policies to see if they're covered while abroad.

Greek general practitioners' fees (office hours are from 9 to 1 and from 5 to 7) are usually reasonable. Most doctors pride themselves on their English, as do the **pharmacists** (found in the *farmakeío*), whose advice on minor ailments is good, although their medicine is not particularly cheap.

If you forgot to bring your own condoms and are caught short, they are widely available from *farmakeío*, kiosks and supermarkets, with lusty brand names such as 'Squirrel' or 'Rabbit'. If you can't see them on display, the word *kapótes* (condom) gets results. You can also get the Pill (*chápi antisiliptikó*), morning-after Pill and HRT over the pharmacy counter without a prescription. Be sure to take your old packet to show them the brand you use.

For some reason Greeks buy more **medicines** than anyone else in Europe (is it hypochondria? the old hoarding instinct?), but you shouldn't have to. The strong sun is the most likely cause of grief, so be careful, and stay hatted and sunscreened. *See* pp.58–9 for possibly unkind wildlife. If anything else goes wrong, do what Greeks have done for centuries: pee on it.

Internet

The Internet is big in Greece, and even the smaller islands all seem to have access of some kind available, either through Internet cafés, travel agencies or hotels.

Money

Greece now uses the **euro** (pronounced *evró*), circulating in notes of 5, 10, 20, 50, 100, 200 and 500, with coins of €1 and €2, then 1¢, 2¢, 5¢, 10¢, 20¢, 50¢ (cents in Greek are *leptá*).

The word for **bank** is *trápeza*, derived from the word *trapézi*, or table, used back in the days of money-changers. Most towns have several, and on all the islands with more than goats and a few shepherds there is some sort of banking establishment or, increasingly, at

least an automatic teller. If there's no bank, then travel agents, tourist offices or post offices will change cash and traveller's cheques. If you plan to spend time on a really remote island, such as Schinoússa, bring enough cash with you. Beware that small but popular islands often have only one bank, where exchanging money can take forever: beat the crowds by going at 8.20am, when the banks open (normal **banking hours** are Mon–Thurs 8.20–2, Fri 8–1.30).

The number of 24hr automatic cash-tellers (**ATMs**) on the islands and in smaller towns grows every year.

Major hotels, luxury shops and resort restaurants take **credit cards** (look for the little signs), but small hotels and tavernas rarely do.

Traveller's cheques are always useful, even though commission rates are less for cash. The major brands (Thomas Cook and American Express) are accepted in all banks and post offices; take your passport as ID and shop around for commission rates.

Running out? Athens and Piraeus, with offices of many British and American banks, are the easiest places to have money sent by cash transfer from someone at home – though it may take a few days. **American Express** may be helpful here; their office in Athens is 2 Ermoú St, right by Sýntagma Square, **t** 210 324 4975, and there are branches on Corfu, Mýkonos, Pátras, Rhodes, Santoríni, Skiáthos and Thessaloníki.

Museums, Opening Hours and Admission Fees

For opening hours for banks and shops, *see* 'Money' (above) and 'Shopping' (p.93).

Archaeological Sites and Museums

The usual **opening hours** are Tues–Sun 8 or 9am to 2 or 3pm, closed Mon; major attractions are open daily and have much longer hours, although these are shorter in the winter. All close on 1 Jan, 25 Mar, Good Friday, Easter Sunday, 1 May, 25 Dec and 26 Dec.

Admission fees are usually between €1.50 and €3; more expensive ones are listed as *adm exp* in the text. **Students** with valid ID usually get a discount, and in state museums visitors under 18 or over 65 with ID get in cheaper or even free. Admission is **free** to all on Sundays from 1 Nov to 31 March, the first Sundays of April, May, June and October and on 6 Mar, 18 April, 18 May, 5 June and the last Sat and Sun in September. Many are also open Wed until 11pm during the summer.

Churches and Monasteries

Because of an increase in thefts, churches only open when there is someone around, often in late afternoon (6–7pm); at other times you may have to hunt down the key (*kleethEE*). Monasteries tend to close for a couple of hours at midday. Note that visitors are expected to make a small contribution, or at least buy a candle and dress respectfully. The rule is long trousers for men, knees covered for women, arms covered for men and women. Many (but not all) provide long skirts or robes for the scantily clad.

National Holidays

Note that most businesses and shops close down for the afternoon before and the morning after a religious holiday. If a national holiday falls on a Sunday, the following Monday is often observed. The Orthodox

National Holidays

1 January New Year's Day, *Protochroniá*; also *Ag. Vassílis* (Greek Father Christmas)

6 January Epiphany, *Ta Fóta / Theofánia*

February–March 'Clean Monday', *Katharí Deftéra* (precedes Shrove Tuesday and follows a three-week carnival)

25 March Annunciation/Greek Independence Day, *Evangelismós*

late March–April Good Friday, *Megáli Paraskeví*, Easter Sunday, *Páscha* and Easter Monday, *Theftéra tou Páscha*

1 May Labour Day, *Protomayá*

40 days after Easter Pentecost (Whit Monday), *Pentikostí*

15 August Assumption of the Virgin, *Koímisis tis Theotókou*

28 October 'Ochi' Day (in celebration of Metaxás' 'no' to Mussolini in 1940)

25 December Christmas, *Christoúyena*

26 December Gathering of the Virgin, *Sináxi Theotókou*

Easter (and Lent) is generally a week or so after the Roman Easter.

In Greece, Easter is as important as Christmas and New Year in northern climes, the time when far-flung relatives return to see their families back home. It's a good time of year to visit for the atmosphere, feasts and fireworks. After Easter and 1 May, spring (*ánixi* – the opening) has officially arrived, and the tourist season begins. It's also worth remembering that the main partying often happens the night *before* the saint's day.

Packing

Even in the height of summer, evenings can be chilly in Greece. Always bring at least one warm sweater and a pair of long trousers, and sturdy and comfortable shoes if you mean to do any walking – trainers (sneakers) are usually good enough. Plastic swimming shoes are handy for rocky beaches, often the haunt of those little black pincushions, sea urchins; you can easily buy them near any beach if you don't want to carry them around with you. Greeks are inveterate night people: bring ear plugs if you don't want to hear the noise.

Serious sleeping-baggers should bring a Karrimat or similar insulating layer to cushion them from the gravelly Greek ground. Torches come in very handy for moonless nights, caves, and examining frescoes in churches.

On the pharmaceutical side, bring extras of any prescription drug you need, just in case – other items, such as seasickness remedies, sunscreen, insect repellent, women's sanitary towels and sometimes Tampax, tablets for stomach upsets and aspirin are widely available in pharmacies and even kiosks, but in remote places you'd best come prepared. Soap, washing powder, a clothes line, a Swiss army knife for picnics and especially a towel are essential budget traveller's gear.

Photography

Greece lends herself freely to photography, but a fee is charged at archaeological sites and museums for any professional-looking camera. For a movie camera, including camcorders, you are encouraged to buy a ticket for the camera; with a tripod you pay per photograph at sites, but cameras (especially tripod-mounted ones) are not allowed in museums, for no particular reason other than the museum's maintaining a monopoly on its own (usually very dull) picture stock. Film, both print and slide, is readily available, though it tends to be expensive and the range of speeds limited. Disposable and underwater cameras are on sale in larger holiday resorts. Many have one-hour developing services.

Post Offices

Signs for post offices (*tachidromío*) as well as postboxes (*grammatokivótio*) are bright yellow and easy to find. Post offices (which are also useful for changing money) are **open** from Monday to Friday 7.30am to 2pm, although in large towns they may be open till 7.30–8pm, and on Saturday morning as well. **Stamps** (*grammatósima*) can also be bought at kiosks and in some tourist shops, although they may charge a small commission. **Postcards** cost the same as letters and are given the same priority (they take about three days to the UK, unless posted from a remote island). If you're in a hurry, pay extra for an **express service**. To send a **package**, always go to an island's main post office. If you do not have an address, mail can be sent to you *poste restante* to any post office in Greece and picked up with proof of identity (you'll find the postal codes in the text, which will get your letters there faster). After one month all unretrieved letters are returned to sender.

Shopping

Official **shopping hours** in Greece are Mon and Wed 9–3; Tues, Thurs and Fri 9–7, Sat 8.30–3.30, and Sun closed; in practice, tourist-orientated shops can stay open as late as 1am. Leather goods, gold and jewellery, traditional handicrafts, embroideries and weavings, onyx, ceramics, alabaster, herbs and spices and tacky knick-knacks are favourite purchases.

Tax-free Shopping

Non-EU citizens tempted by gold, carpets, furs and other big ticket items can perhaps justify their indulgences by having the **sales tax (VAT)** reimbursed – this is 18% of the purchase price (or 13% on Aegean islands). Make sure the shop has a 'TAX FREE FOR TOURISTS' sticker in the window, and pick up a **tax-free shopping cheque** for your purchases. When you leave Greece, you must show your purchases and get the customs official to stamp your cheques (allow an extra hour for this, especially at the airport), and cash them in at the refund point as you leave. If you are flying out of another EU country, hold on to the cheques, get them stamped again by the other EU country's customs and use their refund point. You can also post your tax free cheques back to Greece for refund (10 Nikis, 105 63 Athens, t 210 325 4995, f 210 322 4701), but they skim off 20% in commission.

Sports

Greeks are fanatical about football and basketball, but in the past few years new facilities for a whole range of other sports have been built, mostly around Athens. The **General Secretariat for Sports**, 25–29 Panepistímiou in Athens, t 210 323 8025, *www.sport.gov.gr/main_en.html*, has listings of all federations and their branches.

Activity holidays are becoming increasingly popular as well; besides the specialist operators listed on p.84, contact **Trekking Hellas**, 7 Fillenion St, Athens ✉ 10557, t 210 331 0323, f 210 323 4548, *www.trekking.gr*, a great source of information for mountain walks, rafting and much more.

Watersports

Greece was made for watersports, and by law all the **beaches**, no matter how private they might look, are public. All but a fraction meet European guidelines for water cleanliness, although a few could stand to have less litter on the sand. Beaches often have umbrellas and sunbed concessions and snack bars, and if there's a breeze you'll probably find a windsurfer to rent. Bigger resorts have paragliding, jet skis and waterskiing.

New **thalassotherapy centres** have opened in hotels in Heraklíon, Loutrá Edipsóu (Évia), Vougliagméni (near Athens) and Kos.

Nudism is forbidden by law, but tolerated in numerous designated or out-of-the-way areas. On the other hand, topless sunbathing

Average Sea Temperatures in °C/°F

Jan	April	May	July	Aug	Sept	Oct	Nov	Dec
15/59	16/61	18/64	24/75	25/77	24/75	22/72	18/64	17/63

is now accepted on the majority of popular beaches as long as they're not smack in the middle of a village; exercise discretion. Even young Greek women are shedding their tops, but nearly always on someone else's island.

Scuba diving, once strictly banned to keep divers from snatching antiquities and to protect Greece's much-harassed marine life, is permitted between dawn and sunset in specially defined areas; local diving excursions will take you there. Most are listed in the text; for information contact the **Hellenic Federation of Underwater Activities**, t 210 981 9961, or the **Owners of Diving Centres**, 67 Zeas, Piraeus, t 210 411 8909, f 210 411 9967.

Land Sports

Greece, with its dramatic mountains, spectacular gorges and exceptionally rich flora and fauna, is made for hiking. There are trails and old mule paths even on the smallest island, and in the national parks and forests of Párnitha and Soúnion, near Athens, Parnássos and Oíti in Central Greece, Olympus in Thessaly, Víkos–Aóos and Vália Cálda in Épirus, Aínos in Kefaloniá, Préspa Lakes in Macedonia, Dadia in Thrace, and Samariá in Crete. The **Greek Alpine Club**, 5 Milioni St, Athens, t 210 364 5904, has shelters in these and other mountainous areas.

Greece may not be ready to challenge Switzerland, but 17 **ski centres** have sprung up on the heights from Crete to Macedonia; the most popular is on Mount Parnássos, a 3hr drive from Athens. They're listed in the text; for more information, contact the **Hellenic Skiing Federation** at 7 Karageórgi Servías, Athens, t 210 779 1615. Canoeing, rafting and canyoning are growing sports, especially in Épirus and Northern Greece.

Most resort areas, by the sea or in the mountains, are in striking distance of **riding stables**. For details, call the **Hellenic Equestrian Federation**, 55 Messeniás St, Athens, t 210 778 6297, f 210 778 1572.

Northern Greece has some of the best **bird-watching** wetlands in Europe: check out sightings on the Hellenic Ornithological Society site: *www.ornithologiki.gr/en/enmain.htm*.

Tennis is very popular in Athens with numerous municipal courts and others at major resort hotels (many are illuminated at night so you can beat the heat).

Golf courses are rare, but more are planned: currently you'll find them at Glyfáda (Athens), in Chalkidikí, Rhodes and Corfu.

Telephones

The new improved Organismós Tilefikinonía Elládos, or **OTE**, has replaced most of its old phone offices with new card phones, which work a treat. You can dial abroad direct (dial 00 before the country code). Cards (*télekartas*), sold in kiosks, come in denominations from €2.90 to €24.60. Another card, the Chronocarta (€5, €13 or €25, is good value for long-distance calls. Some kiosks (*períptera*) also have a telephone *me métriki* (with a meter), which are often more costly.

A number of places hire out **mobile phones**; one company, *www.greecetravel.com/phones*, will deliver them when you arrive.

Telegrams can be sent from one of the surviving OTE offices or from the post office.

All Greek phone numbers are 10-digit; when **phoning Greece from abroad**, the county code is 30, after which you'll need to dial all 10 numbers (those starting with 2 are standard phones and those with 6 are for mobiles).

Time

'God gave watches to the Europeans and time to the Greeks,' they say, but if you need more precision, Greek time is Eastern European, 2 hours ahead of Greenwich Mean Time, 7 hours ahead of Eastern Standard Time in North America.

Toilets and Plumbing

Greek plumbing has improved dramatically in the past few years. Tavernas, *kafeneíons*, museums, bus stations and sweet shops almost always have facilities (it's good manners to buy something), and occasionally you'll find public toilets (usually pretty grotty) in the towns. In older pensions and tavernas, do not tempt fate by disobeying the little notices 'the papers they please to throw in the basket', or it's bound to lead to trouble.

If you stay in a private room or pension you may have to have the electric water-heater turned on for about 20 minutes before you take a shower. In most smaller pensions, water is heated by a solar panel on the roof, so the best time to take a shower is in the late afternoon or the early evening. In larger hotels there is often hot water in the mornings and evenings, but not in the afternoons.

Greek **tap water** is perfectly safe to drink, and inexpensive plastic bottles of spring water are widely available (and responsible for untold pollution, taking up half the available room in landfill sites).

Tourist Information

You can contact the National Tourist Organization of Greece (in Greek the initials are **EOT**) before you go.

Australia and New Zealand: 51 Pitt St, Sydney, NSW 2000, t 9241 1663/4, f 9235 2174.

Canada: 1300 Bay St, Toronto, Ontario, M5R 3K8, t (416) 968 2220, f (416) 968 6533. 1233 De La Montagne, Suite 101, Montreal, Quebec, H3G 1Z2, t (514) 871 1535, f (514) 871 1498.

UK and Ireland: 4 Conduit Street, London W1R 0DJ, t (020) 7734 5997, f (020) 7287 1369, www.tourist-offices.org.uk/Greece/Greece.html.

USA: Olympic Tower, 645 Fifth Avenue, 5th Floor, New York, NY 10022, t (212) 421 5777; f (212) 826 6940, www.greektourism.com/. 168 N. Michigan Avenue, Chicago, Illinois 60601, t (312) 782 1084; f (312) 782 1091. 611 West Sixth Street, Suite 2198, Los Angeles, CA 90017, t (213) 626 6696; f (213) 489 9744.

Tourist Information Websites

www.gtp.gr – constantly updated and especially useful for general information.
www.gogreece.about.com – comprehensive information on all aspects of visiting Greece.

www.greekembassy.org/tourist – site run by the Greek embassy in Washington DC.
www.gnto.gr – official site of the Greek National Tourism Association.
www.greece.org/hellas – lots of useful information on current events in Greece.

Tourist Information in Greece

The multilingual tourist information number in Athens, t 171, is good for all Greece (outside Athens, call t 210 171). As the tourist industry decentralizes in Greece, many municipalities have set up local tourist offices, and most resort areas have tourist police . If nothing else, they have lists of rooms.

Legal Assistance for Tourists is available in Athens at 43–5 Valtétsiou St, t 210 330 0673, f 210 330 1137; in Vólos, 51 Hatziargiri St, t/f 242 103 3589; in Kavála: 3 Ydras St, t/f 2510 221 159; in Pátras, at 213B Korínthou St, t 2610 272 481.

Where to Stay

Hotels

Greek hotels get better by the year, but a lack of space has prevented us from listing all but a select few. On the Internet, www.greekhotel.com lists 8,000 hotels and villas in Greece, with forms for more information about prices, availability and booking. Most large hotels have their own websites as well.

Prices

All hotels in Greece are classed into six categories: Luxury, A, B, C, D and E. Prices are set and strictly controlled by the tourist police. Off season (i.e. mid-September–mid-July) you can generally get a discount, sometimes as much as 40%. Bear this in mind when looking at price categories given below and remember that walking in off the street will often

Hotel Price Categories

In this guide, accommodation is listed according to the following price categories for a double room in high season:
luxury €100 to astronomical
expensive €60 to €100
moderate €40 to €60
inexpensive up to €40

Self-catering Holiday Operators

In most resort areas it is possible to rent cottages, flats or villas, generally for a week or more at a time.

In the off season villas may be found on the spot with a little enquiry, which, depending on the facilities can work out quite reasonably per person. Generally, the longer you stay, the more economical it becomes. If you book from abroad, packages generally include flights, transfers by coach, ferry, hydrofoil or domestic planes, and possibly hire cars.

In the UK

Catherine Secker (Crete), 102A Burnt Ash Lane, Bromley, Kent BR1 4DD, **t** (020) 8460 8022, **f** (020) 8313 1431. Home-run business with the personal touch featuring luxury villas with swimming pools on the Akrotíri Peninsula near Chaniá, Crete.

CV Travel, 43 Cadogan St, London SW3 2PR, **t** (020) 7581 0851, **f** (020) 7584 5229, *www.cvtravel.net*. Upmarket villas at fair prices on Crete, Corfu and Páxos. The villas have a maid service; cooks on request.

Direct Greece, Granite House, 31–33 Stockwell St, Glasgow G1 4RY, **t** (0141) 559 7000, **f** (0141) 559 7272, *www.directholidays.co.uk*. Particularly good for Líndos on Rhodes with a wealth of traditional Lindian houses. Also villas and flats on Crete, Corfu, Lésbos, Chálki, Lefkáda and Zákynthos, and in Stoúpa in the Peloponnese.

Elysian Holidays, 16a High St, Tenterden, Kent TN30 6AP, **t** (01580) 766 599, **f** (01580) 765 416, *www.elysianholidays.co.uk*. Restored houses in Patmos, Chíos and the Kosta peninsula near Port Heli (Peloponnese).

Filoxenia Ltd, Sourdock Hill, Barkisland, Halifax, West Yorkshire HX4 0AG, **t** (01422) 371 796, **f** (01422) 310 340, *www.filoxenia. co.uk*. Haute couture holidays to Athens and a select range of islands from tiny Elafónissos and unknown Amoliani to arty Hýdra, Chíos and quiet parts of Corfu, and unspoilt parts of the mainland. Houses, villas, tavernas, pensions, fly-drive. Also **Opus 23** for travellers with disabilities.

Greek Islands Club, 10–12 Upper Square, Old Isleworth, Middx, TW7 7BJ, **t** (020) 8232 9780, **f** (020) 8568 8330, *info@vch.co.uk*, *www.sunvil.co.uk/sites/gic*. Well-run, established specialists, with helpful yet unobtrusive reps. Their new Private Collection features hideaway hotels and exclusive villas.

Greek Sun Holidays, 1 Bank St, Sevenoaks, Kent TN13 1UW, **t** (01732) 740317, **f** (01732) 460108, *www.greeksun.co.uk*. Helpful and family-run, offering Athens and a range of unusual islands. Tailor-made holidays and two-centre breaks.

Houses of Pelion, **t** (01963) 210667, *www. pelion.co.uk*. Self-catering on the Pélion peninsula.

Iglu Villas, 165 The Broadway, Wimbledon, SW19 1NE, **t** (020) 8544 6400, *www.iglu.com*. Huge choice, from basic 2-person accommodation to 6-bedroom seafront mansions, covering mainland Greece and the islands.

Kosmar Villa Holidays plc, 358 Bowes Road, Arnos Grove, London N11 1AN, **t** 0870 7000 747, *www.kosmar.co.uk*. Self-catering villas, studios and apartments from Crete to Corfu, Rhodes, Sými, Kos and the Argo-Saronics, the Peloponnese and northern Greece. Two-centre holidays, flights from Glasgow and Newcastle.

get you a lower rate than the official one quoted on the phone. Charges include an 8% government tax, a 4.5% community bed tax, a 12% stamp tax, an optional 10% surcharge for stays of only one or two days, an air-conditioning surcharge, as well as a 20% surcharge for an extra bed. All these prices are listed on the door of every room and checked at regular intervals. If your hotelier fails to abide by the posted prices, or if you have any other reason to believe all is not on the level, take your complaint to the tourist police.

During the summer, hotels with restaurants may require guests to take their meals there, either full pension or half pension, and there is no refund for an uneaten dinner. Twelve noon is the official check-out time, although on the islands it is usually geared to the arrival of the next boat. Many island hotels situated far from the port supply buses or cars to pick up

Laskarina Holidays, St Mary's Gate, Wirksworth, Derbyshire, **t** (01629) 822203, **f** (01629) 822 205, *www.laskarina.co.uk*. The largest independent programme in Greece, specializing in the Sporades, the lesser known islands of the Dodecanese and Spétses, sometimes featuring restored traditional accommodation. Two-centre holidays, out of season long stays available.

LateLet.com, The Old Bank, 247 Chapel Street, Manchester, M3 5EP, **t** (0161) 819 5100, **f** (0161) 835 2301, *www.latelets.com*. Company specializing in late-availability villa rentals in the Peloponnese and the islands.

Manos Holidays, Panorama House, Vale Road Portslade, East Sussex BN41 1HP, **t** 0870 238 7745, *www.manos.co.uk*. Good value holidays to the major resorts and lesser-known islands. Ideal for children, particularly good low season specials and singles deals.

Pure Crete, 79 George Street, Croydon, Surrey CR0 1LD, **t** (020) 8760 0879, **f** (020) 8688 9951, *www.pure-crete.com*. Anglo-Cretan company with traditional village accommodation in Western Crete.

Simply Greece, Kings House, Wood St, Kingston-upon-Thames, Surrey KT1 1UG, **t** (020) 8541 2277, *www.simply-travel.com*. Very large choice of villas on the mainland and the islands.

Simply Simon Holidays Ltd, 1/45 Nevern Square, London SW5 9PF, **t** (020) 7373 1933, **f** (020) 7370 1807, *www.simplysimon.co.uk*. Cyclades specialists, covering every island except Tínos and Ándros.

Skiáthos Travel, 4 Holmedale Road, Kew Gardens, Richmond, Surrey GU13 8AA, **t** (020) 8940 5157, **f** (020) 8948 7925. Packages to Skiáthos, Skópelos, Alónissos, Páros, Naxos, Mýkonos and Santoríni.

Sunvil, Sunvil House, Upper Square, Isleworth TW7 7BJ, **t** (020) 8568 4499, **f** (020) 8568 8330, *www.sunvil.co.uk*. Very friendly, well run company offering good value self-catering and hotel accommodation on Límnos, Chíos and Crete, plus many islands and resorts on the mainland.

Travel à la Carte, 1st Floor, 30 High St, Thatcham, Berkshire RG19 3JD, **t** (01635) 863030, **f** (01635) 867272, *www.travel alacarte.co.uk*. Select range of beach and rural cottages on Skiáthos, Corfu, Páxos, Chálki, Sými, Skópelos and Alónissos.

In the USA and Canada

Amphitrion Holidays, 1506 21st St, NWM Suite 100A, Washington DC, 20036, **t** 800 424 2471, **f** (202) 872 9878, *www.sepos.gr/ amphitrion/default.asp*. Houses, villas and apartments.

Apollo Tours, 1701 Lake St, Suite 260, Glenview, IL 60025, **t** 800 228 4367, **f** (847) 724 3277, *www.apollotours.com*. Upmarket villas and apartments.

European Escapes, 111 Ave. Del Mar, Suite 220D, San Clemente, CA 92672, **t** toll free 888 387 6589, *www.europeanescapes.com*. Luxury villas.

Omega Tours, 3220 West Broadway, Vancouver, British Columbia, **t** 800 817 0544, **f** (604) 738 7101, *www.oti.bc.ca*. A range of villas and apartments as well as fully escorted tours.

Unusual Villas and Island Rentals, 409 F North Hamilton Street, Richmond, VA USA23221. **t** 800 846 7280, **f** 804 342 9016, *www. unusualvillarentals.com*. Exceptional villas for 2–12 people, mainly on the islands but a few on the mainland.

Zeus Tours, 120 Sylvan Avenue, Englewood Cliffs, NJ 07632, **t** 800 272 7600, *www. zeustours.com*.

guests. Increasingly hotels have en-suite rooms, except for E class and some Ds, which will have a shower down the hall. In these hotels don't always expect to find a towel or soap, either, so come prepared.

Generally speaking, a hotel's category determines its price, although not always. Some B-class hotels are more expensive than an A-class and so on, as the lines between each category become more and more

blurred with the improvement of services and facilities.

Booking a Hotel

The importance of reserving a room in advance, especially during July and August, cannot be over-emphasized. Reservations can be made through the individual hotel, through travel agents, through the Hellenic Chamber of Hotels by writing, at least two months in advance, to **XENEPEL**, 24 Stadíou St, 105 61 Athens, **f** 010 322 5449, or *grhotels@ otenet.gr*, or in person in Athens, at the Hotels Desk in the National Bank of Greece building, 2 Karageórgi Servías, **t** 210 323 7193 (*open Mon–Thurs 8.30–2, Fri 8.30–1.30, and Sat 9–12.30*).

Rooms and Studios

These are for the most part cheaper than hotels. Although you can still find a few rooms (ΔΟΜΑΤΙΑ, *domátia*) in private houses, on the whole rooms to rent are in purpose-built buildings. One advantage rooms hold over hotels is that nearly all will provide a place to handwash your clothes and a line to hang them on. Another is the widespread avail-ability of basic kitchen facilities (sink, table and chairs, possibly a couple of gas rings, fridge, utensils and dishes) which may turn a room into a studio; these cost a bit more, but out of season the difference is often negli-gible. Depending on facilities, a double room in high season will cost between €25 and €40 with bath, a studio from €35 up to €75. Until June and after August prices are always nego-tiable. Owners will nearly always drop the price per day the longer you stay.

Camping

The climate of summertime Greece is perfect for sleeping out of doors, especially close to the sea, where breezes keep the worst of the mosquitoes at bay. Unauthorized camping is illegal (the law was enacted to displace gypsy camps, and is still used for this purpose) although each village enforces the ban as it sees fit. Some couldn't care less if you put up a tent at the edge of their beach; in others the police may pull up your tent pegs and fine you. It often depends on the prox-imity of organized campsites. These are liberally scattered along the mainland coasts, and most islands have at least one; you can also find them near major attractions such as Metéora and Olympia. If the police are in some places lackadaisical about enforcing the camping regulations, they come down hard on anyone lighting any kind of fire in a forest, and may very well put you in jail for two months.

Useful Websites

www.greecetravel.com/campsites
www.united-hellas.com/camping
www.interhike.com/camping.greece.html

Self-catering Holidays

See box, pp.96–7.

Women Travellers

Women travelling alone should be prepared for a fusillade of questions. Greeks tend to do everything in groups or pairs and can't under-stand people who want to go solo. The good news for women, however, is the dying out of that old pest, the *kamáki* (harpoon). These 'harpoons' – Romeos in tight trousers and gold jewellery – would try to 'spear' as many women as possible, notching up points for different nationalities. A few professional *kamákia* still haunt piano bars in the big resorts, gathering as many hearts, gold chains and parting gifts as they can.

Thank young Greek women for the decline in *kamáki* swagger. Watching the example set by foreign tourists as well as the torrid soaps and dross that dominate Greek TV, they have decided they've had enough of 'traditional values'. Gone are the days when families used the evening promenade or *vólta* as a bridal market for their carefully sheltered unmarried daughters; now the girls hold jobs, go out drinking with their friends, and move in with their lovers.

Campsite Prices

Camping prices are not fixed by law, but these are the approximate guidelines, per day:

Adult €5
Small/large tent €3/4
Child (4–12) €3
Car €7
Caravan €5
Sleeping bag €2

Athens
and Attica

09

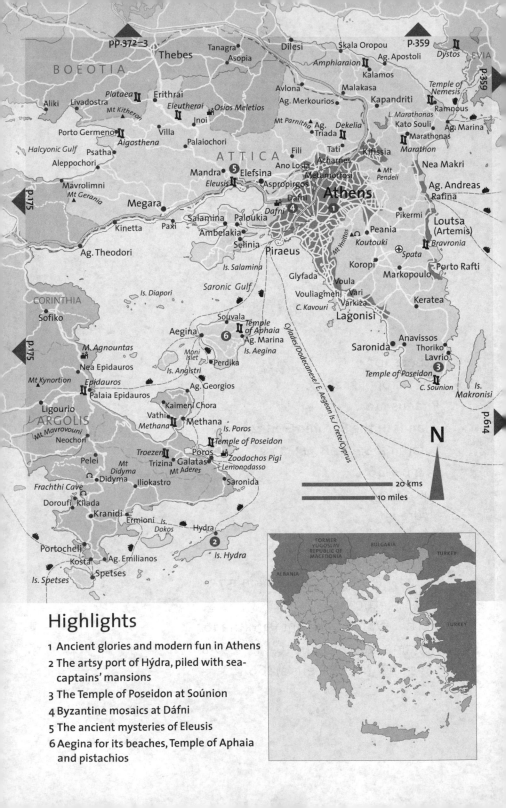

pp.372–3

p.359

p.359

p.175

p.175

p.614

BOEOTIA

Thebes Tanagra Dilesi Skala Oropou Ag. Apostoli Dystos EVIA
Asopia Amphiaraion Ag. Apostoli

Aliki Livadostra Plataea Erithrai Avlona Malakasa Kalamos Temple of Nemesis
Mt Kitheron Eleutherai Ag. Merkourios Kapandriti Ramnous
Porto Germeno Villa Osios Meletios Inoi Mt Parnitha Ag. Dekelia L. Marathonas Kato Souli Ag. Marina
Aigosthena Palaiochori Ag. Triada Marathonas Marathon
Halcyonic Gulf Psatha ATTICA Fili Tati Kifissia Nea Makri
Aleppochori Ano Losia Acharnes
Mavrolimni Mandra Elefsina Aspropirgos Metamorfosi Mt Pendeli Ag. Andreas
Mt Gerania Eleusis Dafni Rafina
Megara Dafni Pikermi Loutsa (Artemis)
Kinetta Paxi Salamina Paloukia Peania Bravronia
Ag. Theodori Ambelakia Koutouki Markopoulo
Selinia Piraeus Spata Porto Rafti
CORINTHIA Is. Salamina Koropi
Sofiko Saronic Gulf Glyfada Voula Keratea
Is. Diapori Vouliagmeni Vari
Souvala C. Kavouri Varkiza Lagonisi
Aegina Temple of Aphaia Saronida Anavissos Thoriko
M. Agnountas Ag. Marina Lavrio
Nea Epidauros Moni Islet Is. Aegina Temple of Poseidon
Mt Kynortion Perdika C. Sounion Is. Makronisi
Epidauros Is. Angistri
Ligourio Palaia Epidauros Ag. Georgios
ARGOLIS Kaimeni Chora N
Mt Mavrovouni Vathi Methana Is. Poros
Neochori Methana Temple of Poseidon
Peleï Troezen Poros Zoodochos Pigi
Mt Didyma Trizina Galatas Lemonodasso
Frachthi Cave Didyma Mt Aderes Saronida
Doroufi Kilada Iliokastro
Kranidi 20 kms
Portocheli Ermioni Is. Dokos Hydra 10 miles
Kosta Ag. Emilianos
Is. Spetses Spetses Is. Hydra

Cyclades/Dodecanese/E. Aegean Is./Crete/Cyprus

FORMER YUGOSLAV REPUBLIC OF MACEDONIA BULGARIA TURKEY
ALBANIA TURKEY

Highlights

1 Ancient glories and modern fun in Athens
2 The artsy port of Hýdra, piled with sea-captains' mansions
3 The Temple of Poseidon at Soúnion
4 Byzantine mosaics at Dáfni
5 The ancient mysteries of Eleusis
6 Aegina for its beaches, Temple of Aphaia and pistachios

Athens (AΘHNA/Aθηνα)

Who doesn't desire to see Athens is stupid; who sees it without liking it is even
more stupid, but the height of stupidity is to see it, like it, and then leave it.

Lysippus (4th century BC)

Yet modern Athens is rarely love at first sight. Under the sublime Acropolis, the
modern city pales into an urban crazy quilt of ugly architecture and congestion. At
second sight, however, you realize that it may not be uniformly pretty but it can be an
awful lot of fun. The famous sites are getting a face lift, and innumerable small oases
and tavernas wait tucked away amidst the bustle; there's the feverish pace of its
nightlife and summer festivals and, best of all, the Athenians themselves, whose
friendliness belies the reputation of most urbanites. Athens is also the least expensive capital in the European Union – although the 2004 Olympics may change that.

History

Athens was inhabited by the end of Neolithic Age (*c.* 3500 BC), but its real debut
onto history's stage began in the second millennium BC, when invaders, probably
from Asia Minor, entered Attica and established small fortified enclaves. Their descendants would claim they were 'the children of Kecrops', a half-man half-snake who
founded Kecropia on the future Acropolis. Kecrops, whose sacred bird was the owl,
gave them laws and taught them the cultivation of that all-important crop, the olive.

The next act saw the birth of King Erechtheos, 'the earth-born'. Snake from the waist
down himself, Erechtheos was the official founder of Athens, and through him and his
mother the earth, Athenians would claim an inalienable right to Attica. Erechtheos
introduced the worship of Athena; later versions of the civic myth would claim her as
his foster mother. The snake and the owl then become her symbols and, by extension,
the city's. Nor did the real thing leave the Athenian stage entirely; Classical Athenians
firmly believed that their Acropolis was guarded by a real and benevolent snake.

The city's Mycenaean rulers had a fortified palace on the Acropolis. Her hero
Theseus dates from this era. Best known for killing the Minotaur in Crete, Theseus
was also credited with unifying Attica's villages. Athenian politicians would scramble
to be associated with his exploits; at the height of Athens' glory in 475 BC, Kimon
brought his bones back from the island of Skýros and gave them a hero's burial.

The 2004 Olympics

The Athens Olympics will take place from 13–29 August, when some 11,000 athletes
are expected. Opening and closing ceremonies, track and field, gymnastics, and
swimming events will take place at the main Olympic stadium complex (*see* p.135).
Baseball, hockey, basketball, handball and fencing will happen at Ellinikó, and Fáliro
gets the discus, beach volleyball and boxing. Other venues are scattered across
Attica, although the old Olympic stadium (Kallimármaro) in the centre of Athens will
witness the end of the marathon, starting of course in Marathon. Football (soccer)
will be played in Pátras, Vólos, Thessaloníki, Heráklion and Athens.

ALEXANDRAS AV.

Athens

POULHERIAS
IRINIS ATHINEAS
ARTISSIAS
DICENI AKRITA
ASKLIPIOU

Ambelokipi

Strefi Hill

KALLIDROMIOU
ZOODOHOU PIGIS
ISAVRON
TSIMISKI
SYNESSIOU KYRINIS
SARANTAPIHOU
ASKLIPIOU
PALIGENESSIAS
ARGYROUPOLEOS

NEAPOLI

KONIARI

Lycavittos Hill

MAVROMIHALI
IPPOKRATOUS
ASKLIPIOU
LEONTOS SGOUROU

US Embassy

KOKKALI

Megaro
Mousikis

Ag. Georgios

Funicular
Railway

ARISTIPPOU
HOIDA
DORAS D'ISTRIA
ARISTODIMOU
KLEOMENOUS

Eleftherias
Park

Megaro
Mousikis

ILISSIA

SINA
ANAGNOSTOPOULOU
STATHA G.
DIMAKI P.
HERSONOS
IT IS
EVELPIDOS ROGAKOU
SINADINOU
DIMOKRITOU
MARASLI
SOUIDIAS
IOANNOU GENNADIOU
MONS PETRAKI

MANTZAROU
OMIROU
SKOUFA
LYKAVITTOS
FOKYLIDOU
PL.
DEXAMINIS
KLEOMENOUS
DINOKRATOUS
XENOKRATOUS

LYKAVITTOS
DIMOKRITOU
VOUKOURESTIOU
SKOUFA
PINDAROU
LOUKIANOU
SPEFSIPPOU
HARITOS
PATRIARHOU IOAKIM
PLOUTARHOU

Hospital
Evangelismos

SOUTSOU AL.
IRAKITOU
SKOUFA
TSAKALOF
XANTHOU
LEVENTI
KARNEADOU

KOLONAKI

KANARI
PL.
KOLONAKI

IRIDOTOU

Evangelismos

PL.
SCHOLIS

Hilton Hotel

MERLIN
SEKERI
KOUMBARI
NEOFYTOU
VAMVA
NEOFYTOU
VAMVA

UK Embassy

VASS. SOFIAS

VASS. SOFIAS

War Museum

National
Gallery

Benaki
Museum

Goulandris
Museum

Byzantine
Museum

RIZARI

Hospital

Parliament

MOUROUZI

VASS. KONSTANTINOS AV.

NIRIDON

VASS. ALEXANDROU AV.

VASS. VRASSIDA

LYKIOU

RIZARI

KRITONOS

EFRONIOU

EFRONIOU

National
Garden

RIGILLIS

VASS. GEORGIOU B' AV.

MELEAGROU

PL.
TROUMAN

ARHELAOU
HIRONOS
EILLANIKOU

ERGOTIMOU

AMASSIAS

FORMIONOS

IMITTOU

IRODOU ATT' IKOU

SPYRIDONOS
ERATOSTHENOUS

ARHELAOU
PAPSANIOU
IRONDA
PL. G. ARKTINOU
POLEMOKRATOUS
TELESSILS
POLEMONOS
ARHELAOU

SPYROU MERKOURI

STRAVONOS

THEOPOM-
POU
FEDROU
IRONOS

ZINDOTOU

ARDITTOU
MIGA M.
THEOTOKI

PL.
STADIOU

ARISTOXENOU
NIKOSTHENOUS

PANGRATI

Ardittos
Hill

Olympic
(Kallimarmaro)
Stadium

ARHIMIDOUS

PL.
PLASTIRA

PL.
EFTIHIDOU
EFTIHIDOU

SPYROU MERKOURI

DAMAREOS

N

PROKLOU

PL.
VARNAVA

PYRONNOS

IMITTOU

DAMAREOS

3 km

1 mile

Getting There

By Air

Elefthérios Venizélos Airport, 25km north-east of the centre, has shops, restaurants, banks, car hire and a tourist information kiosk on Level 0. **Airport information, t** 210 353 0000, operates 24 hours a day in English and Greek. Note that there is a charge for luggage trolleys, so bring euro coins.

Getting from the Airport

By bus: A light rail train (scheduled for some time in 2003) will link the airport to the Athens metro system. Until then there are three express 2hr buses (tickets cost €3, and are valid for 24 hours on all other forms of Athens' public transport):

E95 to central Sýntagma Square, every 10–30mins.

E94 to Ethnikí Ámyna (Line 3, the closest to the airport, on a direct line to Sýntagma), every 7mins from 5.30am until 8.10pm and then every 15–30mins.

E96 to Karaïskaki Square, by Piraeus' main harbour (3 blocks from the Line 1 terminus), every 15–30mins.

A useful **intercity bus** links the airport to the port of Rafina by way of Loútsa, every 40mins from 6am to 9.20pm (€3, €1.50 for Loútsa).

By car: Part of the road out of the airport is a toll highway (€3 – make sure you don't leave the airport without some euros). Downtown Athens can theoretically be reached in only half an hour, by taking the Pallini Junction turn-off. Taxis to the centre cost between €17–23, and double that between midnight and 5am.

Airlines in Athens

Aegean & Cronus, 572 Vouliagménis, Glyfáda, **t** 210 998 8300, **f** 210 998 2928; airport **t** 210 353 4289, *www.aegeanair.com.*

Air Canada, 8 Zirioi St, Maroussi, **t** 210 617 5321, **f** 210 610 8919.

Air France, 18 Vouliagménis, Glyfáda, **t** 210 960 1100, **f** 210 960 1457; airport **t** 210 353 0380.

Alitalia, 577 Vouliagménis, Argyroúpouli, **t** 210 998 8888, **f** 210 995 9214.

American Airlines, 15 Panepistimíou, **t** 210 331 1045, **f** 210 323 120.

British Airways, 1 Themistokléos, Glyfáda, **t** 210 890 6666, **f** 210 890 6510.

Continental Airlines, 25 Filellínon, **t** 210 324 9300, **f** 210 324 9152.

Cyprus Airways, 25 Filellínon, **t** 210 322 6413, **f** 210 323 8472.

Delta, 4 Óthonos, **t** 210 331 1668, **f** 210 325 0451.

easyJet, t 210 967 0000.

KLM, 41 Vouliagménis, Glyfáda, **t** 210 960 5010, **f** 210 964 8868.

Lufthansa, 10 Zirioi, Maroússi, **t** 210 617 5200, **f** 210 610 8919.

Olympic, 96 Syngroú, among many branches; reservations, **t** 210 966 6666, **f** 210 966 6111.

Qantas, Agent, *see* British Airways, above.

Singapore Airlines, 9 Xenofóndos, **t** 210 324 4113, **f** 210 325 4326.

TWA, 7 Syngroú, **t** 210 921 3400, **f** 210 921 3385.

United Airlines, 5 Syngroú, **t** 210 924 1389, **f** 210 924 1391.

US Airways, 65b Vouliagménis, Glyfáda, **t** 210 960 0942, **f** 210 960 0941.

Virgin Atlantic, 70 Panórmou, **t** 210 690 5300, **f** 210 699 5840.

By Train

Trains for **northern Greece** use Lárissa Station, Deliyiánni Street, **t** 210 529 7777 (Ⓜ Larissa). The station for the **Peloponnese**, **t** 210 513 1601, is behind it, over a pedestrian bridge across the tracks followed by a short hike to the south; the latter is also the terminus for **buses to other countries**.

For more information, contact OSE, 1–3 Karolou, **t** 210 522 2491.

By Bus

Athens has several long distance bus terminals. Because of the changes leading up to the Olympics, it does not hurt to call the Tourist Police at **t** 171 to get the latest update on where your bus begins its journey, or call the Attica KTEL, **t** 210 821 0872, or **t** 185.

Terminal A, 100 Kifissoú St, **t** 210 512 4910 (for buses to the Peloponnese, Épirus, Thrace and Macedonia). Take bus no. 051 from Omónia Square (Zinonós and Menándrou Sts).

Terminal B, 260 Liossíon St, **t** 210 831 7163 (for Évia, Vólos, Trikala, Metéora, Karpenísi) take bus no.024 from Leofóros Amalías in Sýntagma Square (tell the driver you want the terminal; the bus doesn't go in it).

Mavromatéon, the bus stop for eastern Attica and ports of Rafína and Lávrion. Take a tram 5 or 9 to Áreos Park on 28th Oktovríou St (just north of the National Museum). Thissío, t 210 523 5695 (hard by the metro station) is the stop for orange buses for western Attica serving Elefsína, Mégara, Vília and Pórto Gérmano.

Getting Around

By Bus and Metro

The free *Athens Public Transport Pocket Map*, distributed by EOT (*see* below) marks the main metro, bus and trolley routes. Purchase bus and trolley tickets (50¢) at the kiosks before boarding, and punch in the machine; if you're caught without a ticket the fine is €20 and up. Note that there are no transfers between surface routes, or between the metro and surface routes; you pay each time you board.

The **metro** (*see* map, p.112; tickets 75¢, sold in the stations) is an important means of getting across Athens, especially from Piraeus. **Line 1** runs from Piraeus as far as Kifissiá, stopping at Thissío, Monastiráki (near Pláka and the ancient Agora), Omónia (10mins from the National Archaeological Museum) and Plateía Viktoría (near Áreos Park). **Lines 2 and 3** run from Sýntagma Square to outlying residential districts. Line 2 goes to the Acropolis station and Lárissa train station. By 2003, a handy metro link between Sýntagma and Thissío is scheduled to open. The system should be finished by 2004.

It is possible to buy a **day ticket** for €3, good on *all* city transport, even to the airport, for 24 hours. This is a real bargain if you are moving around a lot. Note that all city transport, with the exception of the airport buses and the Piraeus–Athens bus, stops at midnight, so plan to *arrive* at your *destination* by midnight. For more info, call t 185 weekdays between 7am and 9pm; Sat–Sun 9–5.

By Taxi

Taxis are cheap. There are taxi stands in some squares, at the airport, train station and bus stations, but most cruise the streets. At the time of writing, the meter starts at 75¢ and adds 25¢ per kilometre. The minimum fare is €1.50. Rates double once you leave the city and its suburbs. There are various small surcharges and all prices double from midnight to 5am. On major holidays, such as Easter, the driver gets a mandatory 'present' of €1. From the National Archaeological Museum to the Acropolis, count on about €4.

Sharing: Because fares are so low and demand so great, Athenians often share cabs. Usually, the cabbie leaves his flag lit, even if he has passengers, to indicate that he is willing to take more. Hailing a cab this way is not for the faint-hearted; the usual procedure is to stand by the street, flag down any passing cab, and if they slow down and cock an ear, shout out your general destination. If the taxi is going that way, the driver will stop, if not, he won't. Check the meter when you board, and pay from there, adding €1.50 (the minimum fare), plus any baggage charges. If the cabbie asks for the full fare, start writing down his licence number and ask for a receipt. That usually settles the issue on the spot.

Radio taxis charge €1.50 to come from the moment you call, more if you book in advance. In many cases, especially if you're going to the airport, it is well worth it. In Athens, try: Parthenon, t 210 581 4711 & 210 581 6141; Enotita, t 210 645 9000; Ikaros, t 210 525 2800; in Piraeus, t 210 418 2333. Numbers are listed in the weekly English-language *Athens News*.

By Car

Not fun. Besides the traffic jams, the one-way system is confusing and parking is almost impossible. If you need assistance, call ELPA's (the Greek Automobile Club) tourist information service, t 174. **Car hire**: besides the major firms at the airport, there are dozens of car hire firms in Athens, concentrated around Syngroú Ave. Try:

Just Rent a Car, 43 Syngroú, t 210 924 7331, f 210 924 7248, *www.just.gr* .

Capital, 14 Syngroú, t 210 921 8830, f 210 924 6345, *www.capitalrent.gr*.

Swift Car, 21 Níkis, t 210 322 1623, f 210 325 0671, *www.greektravel.com/swift/*.

Tourist Information

The **tourist police** have a magic number: t 171. From 7am to 11pm, seven days a week, a voice in English will answer any question you may have, including lost property queries.

The **National Tourist Organization (EOT)** is at 2 Amerikís St, between Panepistimíou and Stadíou, t 210 331 0565, f 210 325 2895, *www. gnto.gr (open Mon–Fri 9–4.30)*. They also have a booth at the airport. EOT's booklet *Greece: Athens* has excellent maps of the city and Attica, with all museums and sites. The helpful weekly *Athens News* comes out on Fridays and is on sale at most kiosks.

Ticket discount: A €12 discount ticket, valid for 48 hours, will get you into the main archaeological sites of ancient Athens: the Acropolis, Agora, Theatre of Dionysos, Kerameikós, Roman Forum and the Temple of Olympian Zeus: pick one up at any of the sites.

Olympics Information: 7 Kifisias, t 210 200 4000, f 210 200 4099.

First aid (ambulance): t 166.

Police: t 100.

Fire: t 199.

Emergency hospitals (Athens/Piraeus): t 106.

Pharmacies on duty (Sun and hols): t 107.

European emergency call no. (all cases): t 112.
If you do not have a Greek speaker available, try t 171 and speak to the **tourist police**.

Useful Addresses

Main post office: Mitropóleos St, on Sýntagma Square, t 210 324 2489; *open Mon–Fri 7.30am–8pm, Sat 7.30–2, and Sun 9–1*. Use this one for *poste restante*; bring ID.

Aliens Bureau (for non-EU passport holders who need visa extensions): 173 Alexandras, t 210 770 5711.

Traffic police (for towed cars): 38 Ag. Konstantínou, t 210 523 0111.

Bureau de change: the **National Bank of Greece** in Sýntagma Square stays open longer than most: *Mon–Fri 8–2 and 3.30–5.20, Sat 9–3, and Sun 9–1*. **Eurochange**, Kar. Servías 4, t 210 322 0005, right next door is open 8am–10pm daily.

Left luggage: The airport has a facility: Pacific Baggage Storage, near Gate 1 on Arrivals Level. If you are in Athens with luggage, leave it at Bellair Travel, 40 Voulis St, t 210 323 9261 (*open Mon–Fri 9–6, Sat 9–2*). Pacific Ltd, 26 Níkis St, t 210 324 1007, offers the same facility during business hours. In Piraeus, there is a facility in the metro station.

Shopping

Athens has the same chain shops as any other European capital. Ermoú Street is the centre of **mid-range fashion** shopping; for big name **designer fashions** and their Greek counterparts, prowl the boutiques on Kolonáki, Kifissía and Maroússi. The two neighbourhoods under the Parthenon, Pláka and Monastiráki, are the place to go for your light-up Parthenons, worry beads and naughty coasters, but it's not bad for casual clothes, accessories, leather, rugs, some real antiques and genuine junk. The **Central Market** on Athinás St (*open 8am–3pm exc Sun*) is fun. Evripídou St, west of Athinás St, is the **spice** street of Athens.

The **Virgin Megastore**, 7 Stadíou St (near Sýntagma), and **Metropolis**, 64 Panepistimíou St (near Omónia), are great for Greek music (*see* p.60). The area also has some of the country's finest **jewellers**, including **Lalaounis** at 6 Panepistimíou.

For **books in English** try **Eleftheroudákis**, 17 Panepistimíou St, t 210 331 4180, or 20 Níkis St, t 210 322 9388, the latter with a good selection of guide books. **Compendium**, 28 Níkis St, t 210 322 1248, is a cosy English-only shop, with an eclectic selection of used paperbacks.

Where to Stay

Athens is a noisy city, especially so at night when you want to sleep. If you can't find a room, try the **Hotel Association**'s booking desk in the National Bank building in Sýntagma Square, t 210 323 7193 (*open Mon–Thurs 8.30–2, Fri 8.30–1 and Sat 9–1*).

Luxury

Grande Bretagne, 1 Vass Georgíou St, on Sýntagma Square, t 210 333 0000, f 210 322 8034, *gbhotel@otenet.gr (L)*. Beautiful hotel built in 1862 to house members of the Greek royal family who couldn't squeeze into the palace (the current Parliament building). It was used as a Nazi headquarters, then by Winston Churchill. Modernized in 2002, with its vast marble lobby, elegant rooms and dining room, it offers style and service that the newer hotels may never achieve.

Electra Palace, 18 Nikodímou, **t** 210 337 0000, **f** 210 324 1875, *electrahotels@ath.forthnet.gr* (*A*). Views of the Acropolis and a wonderful rooftop pool in a garden setting. Rooms are air-conditioned and there's a garage.

Royal Olympic, 28 Diákou, **t** 010 922 6411, **f** 010 923 3317, *www.royalolympic.com* (*L*). Facing the Temple of Olympian Zeus. Rooms here are American in spirit; if you get a room without a view, try the rooftop bar.

St George Lycabettus, 2 Kleoménous (Plateía Dexaménis, Kolonáki), **t** 210 729 0711, **f** 210 729 0439, *www.sglycabettus.gr* (*L*). An intimate, family-run atmosphere and wonderful views of the Parthenon or out to the sea, and a pool, too. The *Grand Balcon* dining room has views that take in most of Athens.

Titania, 52 Panepistimíou, **t** 210 330 0111, **f** 210 330 0700, *www.titania.gr* (*A*). Practically on top of lively, traffic-clogged Omónia Square. Pleasant rooms and fashionable rooftop restaurant, the Olive Garden, planted with old olive trees, and gorgeous views over the Acropolis and Lykavittós. It also has parking.

Ledra Marriott, 113–115 Syngroú, **t** 210 930 0000, **f** 010 935 8603, *www.marriott.com* (*L*). One of the many new luxury chain hotels just outside the city centre, with a Chinese-Japanese restaurant, and a hydrotherapy pool with a view of the Acropolis.

Pentelikon, 66 Diligiánni St, Kefalári, in Kifissiá, **t** 210 623 0650, **f** 210 801 0314, *www.hotel pentelikon.gr* (*A*). Out of the centre but near the metro line, with a lovely garden and pool, and the only hotel restaurant in Greece with a Michelin star.

Philippos, 3 Mitséon (Makrigiánni), **t** 210 922 3611, **f** 210 922 3615, *www.herodion.gr/ philippos* (*B*). Quiet, well-run, recently renovated. ⓦ Acropolis.

Expensive

Astor, 16 Karagiórgi Servías (just off Sýntagma Square), **t** 210 335 1000, **f** 210 325 5115, *www.astorhotel.gr* (*A*). Fully air-conditioned rooms, and a rooftop garden restaurant.

Hermes, 19 Apóllonos (near Sýntagma), **t** 210 323 5514, **f** 210 323 2073 (*C*). Comfortable and friendly, with a small bar and roof garden with Acropolis views.

Parthenon, 6 Makrí (Makrigiánni), **t** 210 923 4594, **f** 210 923 5797 *airhotel@netplan.gr* (*A*).

Great location and a pretty outdoor breakfast area. ⓦ Acropolis.

Athenian Inn, 22 Cháritos, **t** 210 723 8097, **f** 210 724 2268 (*C*). In swanky Kolonáki, this was the favourite of Lawrence Durrell.

Austria, 7 Mousson-Filopappou, **t** 210 923 5151, **f** 210 922 0777, *www.austriahotel.com* (*C*). A great location facing the Philopáppou Hill not far from the Acropolis entrance. Makes the complicated navigation required to reach it by car worth it.

Moderate

Acropolis House, 6–8 Kódrou (off Kydathinéon St in Pláka), **t** 210 322 3244, **f** 210 324 4143 (*C*). Modernized rooms but in a traditional style, with antique furnishings, frescoes and a family welcome.

Adonis, 3 Kódrou (Pláka), **t** 210 324 9737, **f** 210 323 1602 (*C*). A gem, clean and well-run by the Greek who managed the Anapolis Hilton. All rooms have balconies, and there's a lovely breakfast roof garden and bar with views (rates include breakfast).

Adam's, 6 Herefóndos (Pláka), **t** 210 322 5381, **f** 210 323 8553, *adams@otenet.gr* (*C*). Quiet but central, 3mins from Hadrian's Arch; rooms are traditional, comfortable, but go into the expensive category when busy.

Aphrodite, 21 Apóllonos, **t** 210 323 4357, **f** 210 322 6047 (*C*). In the Sýntagma-Pláka area. Basic rooms, air-conditioning and free parking in the garage.

Kouros, 11 Kódrou (off Kydathinéon St, Pláka) **t** 210 322 7431 (*E*). In an attractive old house near the Greek Folk Art Museum. Prices may be up for discussion if not full.

Art Gallery, 5 Eréchthiou and Veíkou Sts, **t** 210 923 8376, **f** 210 923 3025 (*E*). A pleasant, quiet, well-run old-style hotel. Each room with its own bathroom, and Pláka is a 15min walk away. ⓦ Syngrou-Fix.

Inexpensive

Dióskouri, 6 Pitákou (near Hadrian's Arch, Pláka), **t** 210 324 8165, **f** 210 321 0907 (*D*). Delightful old-fashioned place with high-ceilinged rooms in an old neoclassical building in a fairly quiet spot.

Phaedra, 16 Herefóndos (Pláka), **t** 210 323 8461 (*D*). An unreconstructed pre-war interior, communal facilities and a great location near the Lysikrátes Monument. Free hot showers are promised.

John's Place, 5 Patróou (behind the large Metropólis church, near Sýntagma), t 210 322 9719 (*E*). Simple and cheap, with bathrooms down the hall. No towels, though.

Tembi, 29 Eólou, t 210 321 3175, f 210 325 4179 (*D*). Nothing special, but it is cheap and has pleasant management and a good central location. Ⓜ Monastiráki.

Pella Inn, 104 Ermoú, t 210 321 2229, f 210 325 0598, *www.pella-inn.gr* (*D*). Simple but welcoming. Ⓜ Monastiráki.

Dryades, 105 Errim. Benáki and Anaxartissías (Exárchia), t 210 382 7362 or 210 382 0191, f 210 330 5193 (*C*). All rooms ensuite and the top three have lovely views. **Orion** (*D*), next door has the same management, with common facilities and a roof garden.

Marble House, 35 A. Zínni (in Koukáki, and a hike from the Syngroú-Fix Metro), t 210 923 4058, f 210 922 6461 (*E*). A comfortable Greek-French-run hotel.

Student Inn, 16 Kydathinéon (Pláka), t 210 324 4808, f 210 321 0065. Organized along youth hostel lines and ideal for the younger crowd (there is a 1.30am curfew).

Student's Hostel, 75 Damaréos St (Pangráti), t 210 751 9530, f 210 751 0616. Not far from the centre, this offers shared accommodation. The Student Card requirement doesn't seem to be taken too seriously.

Camping Athens, 198 Athinón (7km out on the main road to Corinth), t 210 581 4114, f 210 582 0353. *Open all year*.

Camping Néa Kifissiá (near the National Road in Néa Kifissiá), t 210 807 9579, f 210 807 5579. *Open all year*.

Eating Out

Athenians rarely dine out before 10 or 11pm. Glyfáda and Piraeus (Kalípoli, Mikrolímano and Zéa Marina , *see* p.142) are popular on a summer evening. Note that many top restaurants close down at Greek Easter and move to the islands (usually Mýkonos or Santoríni) until October.

Sýntagma and Around

Cellier Le Bistrot, 10 Panepistimioú (in the stoa), t 210 363 8535 (€30). Old restaurant revamped into a stylish bistro, with an Italian chandelier and the biggest mirror in Greece; Greek and international classics and a good wine list.

Aigli Bistrot, Záppeion Park, t 210 336 9363 (€40). Far from the traffic, near Záppeion palace, in the restored Aigli complex, which also includes a music bar and outdoor cinema. A lovely place to feast on taste-packed delicate Mediterranean dishes while contemplating the Acropolis.

Palea Athina, 46 Níkis Street, towards Pláka, t 210 324 5777 (€12). Pleasant, understated traditional décor. It caters to Greeks more than foreigners. *Closed Sun*.

Kentrikon, 3 Kolokotrónis, t 210 323 5623 (€11 and up). In a quiet stoa; large airy dining room, varied menu, popular with business people. *Lunch only; closed Sun*.

Loxandras, 2 Ermoú, t 210 331 2211. Sýntagma means fast food heaven and this is the best. The chicken is great; they even offer low-cal pittas. Eight tables upstairs.

Pláka

Pláka, the traditional tourist ghetto, is still fun, and it caters to the non-Greek urge to dine before 10pm. Inexpensive and moderate restaurants are clustered around Kydathinéon and Adrianoú Streets. It remains a perennial favourite with Greeks too. Touts, however, can be real pests; a blank stare tends to discourage them. Do not accept the bottled water put on your table unless you ordered it; Athens' tap water isn't bad, and its beer is better.

Daphne's, 4 Lysikrátous (by the Lysikrates monument), t 210 322 7971 (€35). In a neoclassical mansion with an elegant dining room with Pompeiian frescoes and beautiful garden courtyard – a rarity in Athens – serving generous, refined traditional dishes.

Terína, 25 Kapnikaréas, t 210 321 5015, in lovely Agorás Square (€19–22). A cut above taverna fare; decorated inside in a restrained, classic, Greek style, but it's the location that makes it a lovely place on a balmy evening.

Byzantino,18 Kydathinéon, t 010 322 7368 (€15). In the heart of Pláka, serving big portions (the fish soup and lamb fricassée are excellent) at its tables under the trees. It's also one of the few decent places open for Sunday lunch.

Bakaliarakiá, 41 Kydathinéon, **t** 210 322 5084 (€14). In a cellar supported by an ancient column; great snacks, fried cod, and barrel wine. *Open eves only; closed July and Aug.*

Eden, 12 Lissíou and Mnissikléous, **t** 210 324 8858 (€12). Athens' oldest vegetarian restaurant and very popular, even with Athenian carnivores, with vegetarian quiches and soya moussakas. *Closed Tues.*

To Xani, Adrianoú St, almost at Kydathinéon, **t** 210 322 8966 (€12–15). A taverna with a back garden which gives it the edge.

Diogénes, at 3 Shelly St, **t** 210 324 7933 (€18). Good food served at tables bordering the tiny park right by the Lysikrátes Monument. Careful choices will keep prices reasonable.

Platanos, 4 Diogénis, **t** 210 322 0666 (around €15). The oldest taverna in Pláka, near the Tower of the Four Winds, serves good wholesome food in the shade of an enormous plane tree. *Closed Sun.*

Upper Pláka

The Upper Pláka area toward the Greek Agora is the haunt of the music taverna, with bouzoukis wailing and Greek dancing.

Klimatariá, 5 Kleipsedra St, **t** 210 321 1215 (€12–15). Music Friday, Saturday and Sunday nights along with typical taverna fare.

Nefeli, 24 Panos, **t** 210 321 2475 (€12–15). Right next to the ancient Agora, and serves lunch as well as dinner. Its coffee shop has a view.

Monastiráki

Monastiráki is more for snacks than dining. If you have a hankering for good *souvláki* and *gýros* any time of day or night, get yourself to the bottom of Mitropóleos Street.

Thissío

Eat opposite the ancient Agora, concentrating at Irakleídon and Apostólou Pávlou Sts. You can have the same view for less by taking a picnic to Philopáppou hill. Many Greeks do, especially on Clean Monday before Lent.

O Kyrios Pil-Poul, 51 Apostólou Pávlou, **t** 210 342 3665. Luxurious setting with lovely Acropolis views from the terrace, to go with some of the finest French cuisine in Greece, with wine list to match (€55). *Closed Sun.*

Stavlos, 10 Irakleídon, **t** 210 346 7206 (€15–20). Housed in the old Royal Stables, an art

gallery, bar and restaurant with the old stable yard beautifully decorated to look like an old square in the Pláka.

Tourist Pavilion, opposite the Acropolis entrance just inside Philopáppou Park, **t** 210 923 1665. Café-snack bar with a magnificent head-on view of the Acropolis in a tranquil garden setting; you would swear you were out in the country were it not for the hum of traffic. The waiters have been here for years.

Dionysos, opposite the Acropolis entrance on Robérto Gálli St (an extension of Apostólou Pávlou St), **t** 210 923 3182. President Kostas Karamanlís used to head here for coffee. Lunch or dinner might be a better bet; their second floor restaurant has big windows overlooking the Parthenon, and you can get away with spending €27–30.

Psirrí

Psirrí sprouts restaurants and *ouzéries* almost as fast as the city can renovate the area, which attracts more Greeks than foreigners. It is *the* place to go, especially after 9pm, or after 1pm on Sunday, when many places have live music.

Taki 13, 13 Táki St, **t** 210 325 4707. The first, and still stands out as the most fun. It has a superb atmosphere and, though the food is simple, it's a great party bar, featuring live music (jazz/blues Tues and Wed, Greek on weekends) and sing-songs till 1.30am.

Atelier Agrotikon, 48 Sarri St, **t** 210 324 0121 (€35). Classy chef-owned, featuring simple modern cuisine, only using the finest ingredients. *Open eves only, closed Sun, Mon and June–Aug.*

Zidoron, 10 Táki and Ag. Anárgyro, **t** 210 321 5368 (€17). Always crowded for their selection of *mezédes*. Good if you arrive on the right day; try the *kolokithókéftethes* – courgette rissoles. *Closed Mon, Aug.*

Taverna tou Psirrí (Ψυρρί) 12 Aischýlou, **t** 210 321 4923 (€10–14). The last work-a-day taverna that has somehow so far resisted gentrification; it's small, plain, but homey, and good.

Gazi

Some of the best restaurants in Athens have parked themselves in this former industrial area and gas works, a short walk west of Kerameikós.

Interni, 152 Ermoú, **t** 210 346 8900 (€45). The ultimate in Athenian designer restaurants – worth a visit for the decor alone, serving exquisite Italian-Asian fusion dishes. *Open eves only, closed Sun and May–Sept.*

Kítrino Podílato, 116 Keramikoú and Iera Ódos, **t** 210 346 5830 (€35). The 'yellow bicycle' may serve the most inventive *nouvelle* Greek *cuisine* and a great Greek wine list. *Open eves only, closed Sun and June–Sept.*

Mamacas, 41 Persephonis, **t** 210 346 4984 (€25). Greek classics in an updated setting; great views of the Acropolis from the top level.

South of the Acropolis and Makrigiánni

Symposio, 46 Herodeío (very close to the Odeion of Herodes Atticus), **t** 210 922 5321 (€35–40). Upscale Mediterranean cuisine served in the garden in summer or in the conservatory of an old neoclassical house. *Open every eve exc Sun.*

Strofí, 125 Robérto Gálli, **t** 210 721 4130 (€17–20). Also close to the Odeion, this family-run restaurant has Acropolis views from its second-floor windows. It is famous for its *mezédes*. *Open every eve exc Sun.*

Koukáki (south of Makrigiánni)

Koukáki is increasingly fashionable. Pedestrian Drákou St at the Syngroú-Fix metro is at the heart, a great spot to blend in with the locals, who crowd it every evening.

Edodi, 80 Veíkou, **t** 210 921 3013 (€40). The restaurant that has put Koukáki on the gastronomic map. Superb Mediterranean *haute cuisine* – just let your waiter guide you through the day's delights. *Open eves only, closed Sun and Aug.*

Apanemiá, 2 Erecthiou (corner of Drákou and Veíkou), **t** 210 922 8766 (€15–18). Good food in a lovely traditional setting with bouzouki and guitar music thrown in on Fri and Sat evenings, and Sun midday.

Fellos, 3 Drákou, **t** 210 924 8898. A cosy wine bar restaurant.

Psitopoleío, 16 Drákou, **t** 210 922 5648. Some of the best chicken in Athens.

Omónia

Aráchova, one block east of Omónia at 8 Themistokléous, **t** 210 384 1812. Fast pittas and sandwiches in an upmarket setting. They promise home-made bread too.

Athinaikón, 2 Themistokléous, **t** 210 383 8485 (€11–14). A golden oldie and a great place to fill up on tasty mezédes (snacks) and sword-fish or lamb kebabs while watching the passing crowds. *Closed Sun.*

Andréas and Sons, 18 Themistokléous, **t** 210 382 1522(€11–14). Tasty seafood at marble-topped tables in a cosy setting at reasonable prices. It is in a quiet narrow street with some outside tables. *Open daily exc Sun 11am–11.30pm.*

Diethnés, 5 Nikitara St, just off Themistokléous, **t** 210 383 9428 (often under €8). So old-fashioned that the printed menu is unchanged since the late lamented days of the original Fix Beer (closed in the 1980s). Elderly waiters in white jackets serve a steady crowd of regulars delicious 'ready food' – great stewed dishes and tasty fish; there are a few tables out under the ivy. *Lunch only.*

Central Market

If you're near the Central Market, don't miss out on a *Les Halles à la Athènes* experience. These two places are open only in the morning and for lunch well past 4pm.

Díporto, **t** 210 321 1463, hard by Theatrou and Sofokléous (opposite the parking garage) (€8–10). An institution that needs no sign; it's down some steps and has remained exactly the same for at least 50 years, serving Hellenic soul food to hungry butchers and trendy drunkards. *Patsás* (tripe soup), the traditional hangover cure, is served on paper-covered tables set on a bare cement floor. If not the tripe, try whatever soup is on offer (the chickpea soup is delicious) and consider sharing portions; they are huge. *Closed Sun.*

Monastíri, **t** 210 324 0773 (€8–10). Inside the meat market since 1924. The food is on display to point at, but the setting is not for the faint-hearted. *Closed Sun.*

Klimatariá, 2 Plateía Theátrou, **t** 210 321 6629. Behind the vegetable market, a bit run-down but authentic, with a loyal clientele for its guitar music and taverna fare.

Exárchia

Bárba Iánnis, 94 Em. Benáki (corner of Derveníou, close to Exárchia Square), **t** 210 382 4138 (€12–15). This cheap, popular old standby has been serving wonderful Greek cooking (all on display) for years from an neoclassical house. *Closed Aug.*

Oinomayeirémata, 66 Themistokléos, **t** 210 383 1955, by Exárchia Square (€12–15). New and decorated with folk art; lots of organic ingredients, and an eager young staff.

To Stéki tou Xánthis, 5 Irínis Athinéas (on the northeast side of Stréfi Hill), **t** 210 882 0780 (around €20). For a night out, book a table in this historic house where Xánthis, disciple of Theodorákis, sometimes leads the public in old Greek songs. The food is good and plentiful. *Open eves only.*

Ama Lachi, 69 Kallidromíou, **t** 210 384 5978 (€15). Housed in an old school, the food is good and the atmosphere pleasant. *Lunch only, 7 days a week.*

Kolonáki and Around

Boschetto, signposted in Evangelismós Park off Vass. Sofías, **t** 210 721 0893 (around €46–56). One of Athens' finest, serving lovely Italian delicacies in a bosky setting, outside in the summer or in a winter garden. *Closed Sun, eves only.*

L'Abreuvoir, 51 Xenokratous, **t** 210 722 9106 (€30). Athens' oldest French restaurant, and still going strong with all the Gallic classics, down to *crèpes suzettes.*

Vlássis, 8 Pasteur St, **t** 210 646 3060 (around €20). Out towards the US embassy, a superb family-run taverna, *the* place to find true Greek cuisine and one of the rare ones with excellent wines and desserts, too; book. *Closed Sun.*

La Pasteria, 17 Tsakálof, **t** 210 363 2032 (€15–18 for the works). Great pasta dishes.

Pangráti (east of the Kallimármaro Stadium)

Spondi, 5 Pyrronos (off Plateía Varnava), **t** 210 752 0658 (€50). By common acclaim, Athens' best restaurant. True haute cuisine with imagination and flair in a lovely old mansion with a garden courtyard. Extraordinary desserts, and huge wine list, too. *Open eves only.*

Entertainment and Nightlife

The summer is filled with festivals, headlined by the **Festival of Athens**, *www.greekfestival.gr*, which runs June–Sept, attracting international stars from around the world. At other times, classical music fans should try to take in a performance at the **Mégaron Musikís**, on Vass. Sofías and Kokkáli, **t** 210 728 2333, Athens' acoustically wonderful concert hall. Maria Callas got her start at the **Greek National Opera House**, 59–61 Akademías St, **t** 210 361 2461, which is shared with the national ballet. From May to Sept there are nightly folk dance performances at the **Dora Stratou Theatre** on Philopáppou Hill, not far from the Sound and Light Show (April–Oct); for both **t** 210 921 4650 for information in English.

Rembétika, the Greek blues, is in full revival in Athens (*see* pp.59–61); the real thing may be heard live at **Stoa Athanaton**, 19 Sofokleous, **t** 210 321 4362 (*closed Sun*), or **Rota**, 118 Ermoú, **t** 210 325 2517 (*closed Mon and Tues*), and often at **Diogenis**, 259 Syngroú, **t** 210 942 5754 (also a useful street for bouzouki clubs, or if you're looking for a transvestite).

Irakleidon Street in Thissío has popular rock bars, such as **Stavlos**. For jazz, try **Jazz in Jazz**, 4 Deinokrátous St, **t** 210 725 8362, or **Half Note**, 17 Trivonianou in Mets, **t** 210 923 3460, which alternates between Greek and foreign artists.

In summer, young fashion slaves and beautiful Athenians head out to the bars and clubs in Glyfáda: here you'll find **Vareládiko**, 4 Alkondidon St, **t** 210 895 2403, the first 'hyperclub' in Greece, with the latest Greek hits; and **Romeo**, 1 Ellinikou, **t** 210 894 5345. In town, in winter, try **Club 22**, 22 Vougliamenis St, **t** 210 924 9814, for terrific, Las Vegas-style reviews.

Gay Athens gathers in Makrigiánni: **Splash**, **Lámda** and **Granázi** are popular dancing bars with cover charges, all along Lembéssi St, off Syngroú.

In the summer, outdoor cinemas are a treat and all the films are in their original language: two of the nicest are in Kolonáki: **Dexamení**, in Dexamení Square halfway up Lykavittós, **t** 210 360 2363; **Athinaía**, 50 Haritós St, **t** 210 721 5717. The outdoor **Cine Paris** on Kydathinéon in Pláka, **t** 210 322 2071, is also a good bet.

Athens Metro

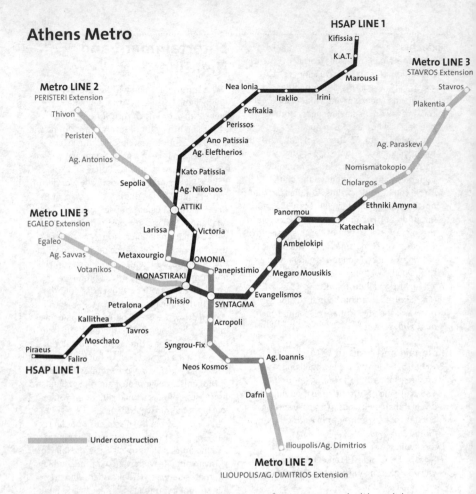

Athens managed to escape the Dorian invasions after 1200 BC and, although her culture too declined in the subsequent Dark Age, the escape was a great point of pride with Athenians, who as a result considered themselves more Greek, more legitimate and certainly more refined than their Dorian neighbours. All of this helped to create the amazing self-confidence and sense of difference that would lead to, among other things, the invention of democracy.

Some time during the 8th century BC all the towns of Attica were indeed peaceably united under the leadership of Athens. They were jointly ruled by a *basileus*, the king who doubled as the chief priest, a *polemarch* (general), and an *archon* (civil ruler), positions that by the 6th century BC were annually elected by the aristocracy in an assembly on the Areopagus. Conflict arose between the aristocrats and rising commercial classes, and reached such a point that Solon, an aristocrat elected *archon* in 594 BC, was asked to re-establish 'good order'. He complied, writing new laws in exquisite poetry. Slavery as a result of debt was abolished, existing debts forgiven, trade and crafts encouraged, and the Council of Four Hundred established to include a broader base of citizens in government. Solon's laws were carved on rotating ınoıdcıı tablets and placed in the Agora. This public display of laws and notices would become a hallmark of democracy; 7,500 inscriptions were found in the Agora alone.

But Solon's good start didn't stop his kinsman Pisistratos from making himself a 'popular' dictator or *tyrannos* in 560 BC. He began the naval build-up that first made Athens a threat to other Greek city-states. He reformed the Panathenaic Games in an attempt to rival the Olympics, instituted grandiose building projects and encouraged the arts and the planting of olives. Later, Athens would vilify his name, but there is no doubt that Pisistratos was a one-man chamber of commerce for the Archaic city. His increasingly despotic son Hippias ruled until 510 BC, when Kleisthenes, a member of the aristocratic Alcmaeonid clan, paid for a new marble temple at Delphi, and then 'suggested' that the oracle command the Spartans to liberate Athens from the tyrant. In the aftermath, as the aristocrats squabbled, Kleisthenes proposed reforms to check their power. They responded by trying to dissolve the Council of Four Hundred, and before they knew it they were cornered on the Acropolis by a spontaneous uprising; after 50 years of tyranny, the people were ripe for a new order.

Kleisthenes' reforms were revolutionary. For the first time, government would no longer merely reflect the social order, but base itself on the concept of *isonomia* or equal rights (at least for all male citizens). Ignoring previous divisions by clan or geography, he divided the population of Attica into ten political *phylae* (tribes); each of the ten would draw lots to select 50 members to serve in the new Council of Five Hundred, from which a further lot was drawn to select ten *archons*, all of whom were meant to spend a tenth of the year in central Athens. Motions for new laws were debated first by the Areopagos (the aristocrats' old assembly, surviving as a kind of House of Lords), and then by the Council, and then presented to the popular assembly for a vote. Kleisthenes also introduced ostracism – if any man was deemed too powerful, the citizens could vote him into exile for decade.

Meanwhile, as the Persian empire grew in the east, Ionian Greeks from Asia Minor (whom the Athenians regarded as cousins) urged Athens to aid them against the Persians. Recklessly, Athens agreed, and sent an army that burned the Persian city of Sardis and returned home. It was provocation enough to land the city in the soup with Darius himself, the King of Kings. In 490 BC a Persian expeditionary force landed at Marathon, only to be defeated by the Athenians under Miltiades (*see* p.161). Although Sparta and the other Greek states recognized the Persian threat, Athens was the only one to seriously prepare for it, thanks to Themistocles, a 'new man' (his father was a greengrocer), who persuaded the Athenians to invest in a much bigger navy. Perhaps even more astonishingly, in 480 BC, when Darius' son Xerxes duly returned with the greatest army and navy the ancient world had yet seen, Themistocles convinced the Athenians to abandon their city altogether and trust in their fleet. Rumours had it that even the Acropolis snake was seen beating a fast retreat, a sure sign that the rock would fall. Xerxes occupied Athens and razed it, just before he snatched defeat from the jaws of victory at Sálamis (*see* p.145).

After the allied Greeks defeated the Persians at Plataea (*see* p.376), Themistocles engaged in a diplomatic war of nerves with Athens' powerful ally Sparta, hastily building city walls in 478 BC. The Spartans strongly believed that Athens should have no such thing, ostensibly in case the Persians returned and used them to their advantage. But Themistocles kept Sparta distracted until the walls were a *fait accompli*; Athens, from then on, would be much harder to capture from land. In 477 BC Themistocles made its fleet – the only one in Greece capable of resisting the constant Persian threat – the foundation of a web of alliances that modern historians call the Delian League. Headquartered on the holy island of Delos, its membership eventually reached 200 city-states (but significantly, not Sparta), who contributed money, men or ships in return for protection. Athenian triremes challenged the Persians in Egypt and elsewhere, not always with success. Trade followed the flag, and one thing led to another; to keep the navy in fighting shape and justify its existence (and its expense), the Athenians were soon sticking their fingers in every pie around the Aegean and beyond. And what began as a league became a *de facto* empire.

Athenians were sailing in some uncharted social and political waters, and theatre played a fundamental role in helping them cope with it all psychologically; even prisoners were released so they could attend the plays. The oldest tragedy to come down to us is Aeschylus' *The Persians*, from 479 BC. Sculptors may have achieved the calm Classical ideal in art, but political change in Classical Athens continued at a breakneck pace: in 470 BC or so the brilliant but prickly Themistocles was ostracized, much to his surprise, and the popular easy-going aristocrat Kimon, son of Miltiades, became the leading politico. In 465 BC, wealthy Thássos, objecting to Athenian meddling in northern Greece, became the first major state to defect from the Delian League. Kimon took it after a two-year siege, and settled Athenians there in a *cleruchy*, or self-supporting garrison. In a far more controversial move, Kimon sent troops at Sparta's request to help it subdue the rebellious helots holed up on Mount Ithóme (*see* p.341). But Sparta suspected that the Athenians were too sympathetic to the helots and sent them home; Athens took it as a great insult.

In 463–462 BC, Kimon's absence in Thássos and the Ithóme debacle brought about the creation of radical democracy in Athens. A younger generation, led by Ephialtes, pushed through a motion that abolished nearly all the powers of the aristocratic Areopagos and established an annually-elected council in its place. Now the citizens were in control from top to bottom; even the courts, until then run by officials, adopted a jury system. More conservative Greek states viewed the experiment with the same fascinated horror as Europe would the French Revolution. It was Kimon's turn to be ostracized; Ephialtes was assassinated and Pericles emerged as the popular leader when he proposed final democratic touch: pay for jurors, for members of the Council of Five Hundred and other public servants, making it possible for even the poorest *thetes*, the lowest class who rowed the triremes, to participate.

'Born into the world to take no rest themselves and to give none to others' was Thucydides' description of his fellow Athenians. Their wealth, their feeling of unlimited potential and addiction to novelty attracted all the greatest artists and intellectuals of the time to the city: Phidias and others revolutionized sculpture; Sophocles, Euripides and Aristophanes saw the first night performances of their plays in the Great Dionysia; Herodotus wrote his history; Anaximander and Socrates philosophized. And the Athenians agreed with their brilliant Pericles, that now that they ruled the Aegean, they could only keep going forward; to where, no one was quite sure. They would use the dues of the Delian League to do it, with enough left over to rebuild the temples destroyed by the Persians, beginning with the greatest of them all, the Parthenon, completed in 438 BC.

While it was busy creating the basis of Western culture, Athens never passed a year without a war somewhere, often several, and as often as not it was Athens stirring the pot herself. The day of the independent *polis* was over: Athens signed a 30-year peace treaty with Sparta in 446 BC, each recognizing the other's sphere of influence in Greece. But Pericles always thought a showdown between the two big powers was inevitable. He linked Athens to Piraeus with long walls, ensuring the city's lifeline in a siege, and he followed policies that seemed designed to provoke the Spartans. War-weary Athenians would later come to blame him for everything.

In 431 BC, the uneasy *détente* in Greece unravelled into the Peloponnesian War. Although fighting Sparta, her allies and rebellious members of the Delian League, eager to slip away from Athens' rule and the 300 per cent increase in dues she demanded, it was still Athens' war to lose. The first year saw a Spartan army occupy Attica. Behind its new walls, the city suffered the Great Plague of 430 BC, which carried off thousands of Athenians, Pericles among them. Her new leader, the dema-gogue Kleon, refused every chance for peace, leaving the Spartans, especially their young and just general Brasidas, to pose as the liberators of Greece; when both Kleon and Brasidas were killed in the battle for Amphipolis, the exhausted sides signed the Peace of Nicias (421 BC). It wasn't worth the stone it was carved on. Egged on by flat-tering, irresponsible politicians, especially the mercurial Alcibiades, nephew of Pericles and student of Socrates, the Athenians overreached themselves by attempting to conquer Syracuse, where they suffered their gravest defeat (413 BC). An oligarchic *coup d'état* in 411 exposed Athens' divisions, though full democracy was eventually restored. Athens battled on for another seven years. Revolts of allies and a Spartan alliance with Persia sealed its doom; Lysander and the Spartans brought the city to its knees with a crushing naval defeat at Aegospotami in 405 BC.

The Spartans refused calls from Corinth, Thebes and other cities to destroy Athens; instead they merely razed the long walls and the fortifications of Piraeus. The brutal regime they installed, the Thirty Tyrants, killed over 1,500 citizens and *metics* (resident foreign merchants) with the help of the Spartan occupation force, before they them-selves were executed in a revolt. Democracy made a quick recovery. By 378 BC the city had set up a second Delian League, but the Peloponnesian War had struck a blow from which ancient Athens would never recover; though still the most important city in Greece, it would never again be a political force. Although Socrates was put to death (399 BC), partly as a scapegoat for his wayward pupils (besides Alcibiades, another one, Critias, had been a ringleader of the Tyrants), Athens' intellectual tradi-tions held true in the 4th century, the age of Praxiteles, Menander and Plato.

When Philip II made a great power of Macedonia, Athenian patriotism was briefly kept alive by the orator Demosthenes before Philip subdued all of Greece (338 BC). Losing control of its own destiny, the city was a prize fought over by Alexander's generals, beginning with Demetrios Poliorketes, who captured the city in 294 and made it the backdrop to his playboy escapades. In the new Hellenistic world, Alexandria, Rhodes and Pergamon would gradually displace Athens as cultural centres. In 168 Rome captured Athens, but left her with many privileges; 80 years later, though, Sulla punished the city for supporting Mithridates of Pontus by destroying Piraeus, the Agora and the city walls. Later Romans would remember their cultural debt; while the city dwindled, they came to attend the academies and endow the city with monuments. St Paul started the Athenians on the road to Christianity in AD 44. In the 3rd century Goths sacked Athens; in 529, Justinian closed the philosophy schools and converted the Parthenon into a cathedral.

Now a mere backwater, Athens re-enters history as the plaything of the Franks after they seized Constantinople in 1204. Guy de la Roche was made the Duke of Athens, a dukedom held at various times by the Catalans, Neapolitans and Venetians. In 1456 it was the turn of the Ottomans, who converted the Parthenon into a mosque and the Erechtheion into a harem. The Venetians made several attempts to wrench it away; in Morosini's siege of 1687, a shell struck the Parthenon, where the Turks had stored their gunpowder. In 1800, Lord Elgin looted much its surviving frieze (*see* pp.54–5).

In 1834, after the War of Independence, Athens – population 200, in a clutch of houses under the Acropolis – was declared the capital of the state for the grandeur of its ancient name. Otto of Bavaria, the first King of the Greeks, brought his own architects with him to lay out a new city, based on a grid running northeast of Stadíou and Panepistimíou (El. Venizélou) Streets. Neoclassical public buildings, evoking ancestral glory, went up everywhere, many of the more elaborate ones financed by wealthy Greeks of the diaspora, keen to show off their Hellenic credentials. By 1860 the population had risen to 30,000. Yet even the best laid plans could not cope with the flood of people from the countryside who came looking for jobs and the thousands of Greek refugees who arrived after the population exchange in 1922, and much of the rest of the city was built quickly on the cheap.

Today Athens resembles a dense domino game stacked over the dry hills of Attica. The metropolis squeezes in four million lively, opinionated inhabitants – a third of the population of Greece – who thanks to native ingenuity and EU membership are now more prosperous than they have been since the age of Pericles. Unfortunately, this translates into a million cars, though Athens' infamous smog (*néfos*) has noticeably lightened since the metro was finally inaugurated in 2000, after 35 years of delay by legal challenges from archaeologists – even then, one planned station had to be abandoned when the diggers came across a thousand tombs of plague victims from 430 BC. In the great push to put on her best face for the Olympics, buildings are being restored, trees planted, pedestrian oases created, museums overhauled; in other words, until the summer of 2004, expect a lot of scaffolding.

Sýntagma Square and Pláka

Sýntagma or 'Constitution' **Square** is the centre and crossroads of the modern city, where bus and trolley and shiny new metro lines converge, *periptera* sell newspapers from around the world, and Greeks who don't give a hang about cultural pollution pack the great big McDonald's, drinking McFrappés. The square was designed to set off the large if unremarkable royal palace, now the **Parliament Building** (Voulí), fronted by the **Monument to the Unknown Soldier**, whose guards in *evzone* uniform astonish passers-by every hour with some of the strangest steps ever invented by the military mind. Stretching beyond the Parliament are the **National Gardens**, a cool haven of shade to escape the summer heat. Finds discovered during the construction of the metro are displayed in the **Sýntagma metro's concourse**; a glass wall offers a view of the historic strata of subterranean Athens.

A short walk up Filellínon Street on the south side of Sýntagma Square will take you to Kydathinéon Street, the main artery into **Pláka**, the old neighbourhood gathered under the skirts of the Acropolis. On Filellínon have a look at the 11th-century Byzantine church of **Ag. Sotíra**, restored in the 1850s by Tsar Alexander II and now serving the city's growing Russian community, and the small, rather dour neo-Gothic **St Paul's**, serving the Anglicans. The atmosphere, however, changes when you turn down Kydathinéon: the streets of Pláka are narrow and seem to go where they please, and the cars that rule so much of Athens are almost non existent. Pláka is the Athens that became Greece's capital in 1834; since then its houses have been converted into hotels, tavernas or souvenir shops, making it the vortex of tourist Athens.

Amid the hubbub wait a smattering of museums. A handsome neoclassical building houses the new **Jewish Museum**, at 39 Níkis St (*t 210 322 5582; open Mon–Fri 9–2.30 and Sun 10–2, closed Sat*) with one of the most important collections in Europe, arranged by themes. Although Jews lived in Greece since Hellenistic times (and became assimilated as Romiótes) the majority arrived from Spain after 1492 (*see* p.533). Only a fraction survived the Holocaust. The **Greek Folk Art Museum**, opposite the little Byzantine church of the Metamorphósis at 17 Kydathinéon (*t 210 322 9031; open Tues–Sun 10–2; adm*), offers several floors of exquisite needlework, carvings, silver, weapons, jewellery, shadow puppets (*karaghiózis*), extraordinary bridal costumes and a delightful room from a house on Lésbos, painted by Theóphilos Hatzimichaíl (*see* p.825) complete with Alexander the Great, and two volcanoes. For something completely different, the **Frissíras Museum**, around the corner at 3–7 Monís Asteríou St (*t 210 323 4678, www.frissirasmuseum.gr; open Wed–Fri 11–7, Sat and Sun 10–3; adm exp*), offers an important collection of 20th-century art by Greek and foreign artists gathered together by Vlássis Frissíras; one building is used for rotating displays of the permanent collection, the other for temporary exhibitions.

Further east, Kydathinéon runs into Adrianoú, the oldest street in Athens still in use, now chock-a-block with tourist shops. Kydathinéon next meets Tripodón and Séllei Streets, once an important intersection for theatre-lovers. On the fifth day of the Great Dionysia festival (*see* below), in Academy Award fashion, a panel would choose best actor, best playwright, and best producer/sponsor (*choregós*). Every winner was allowed to put up a monument – usually a tripod – to his victory in this area and, being typical Greeks, each one did; Tripodón Street, as its name suggests, was lined with them. One of the more elaborate is just to your left along Séllei Street: the **Monument of Lysikrátes**, put up by a winning *choregós* of 334 BC. Its Corinthian columns stood under a frieze depicting Dionysos and the Tyrrhenian pirates. Much later, the monument was incorporated into a Capuchin friary to serve as a library. When Byron stayed, he was wont to do his reading there by lamplight; the ghost of Lysikrátes, recognizing a great histrionic type, would probably not have minded. In 1818 the friars were the first in Greece to grow what would become an essential ingredient of the national salad – tomatoes – in their garden.

South of the Acropolis

Continuing south of the Pláka, Séllei Street turns into Výronos and runs into Dionysíou Areopagítou Street, now pedestrianized as part of a scheme to link the chief monuments of ancient Athens. At the corner, you can pay your respect to a **bust of Makrigiánni**, the most likeable of the generals in the Greek War of Independence, who wrote a colourful autobiography in spite of being illiterate (he devised his own code). The neighbourhood south of the Acropolis is named for him. The new **Acropolis metro station** (decorated with copies of the Parthenon marbles along the platforms) is just here, as Makrigiánni Street begins; the construction site behind it extending into Mitséon is for a new $12 million **New Acropolis Museum**, designed by Bernard Tschumi, slated to open in time for the Olympics. It will be bigger than the Parthenon, will stand on pillars to protect the Neolithic to early Christian remains below, and feature a vast upper glass hall with a view of the Parthenon to display the real marbles, if and when Britain sends them back (*see* pp.55–6). West, up the hill towards the Acropolis entrance, the **Ilías Lalaoúnis Jewellery Museum** at 4a Karyátidon Street and Kalispéri (*t 210 922 1044; open Mon, Thurs, Fri and Sat 9–4, Wed 9–2, Sun 11–4, closed Tues; adm free on Wed am*) is where Lalaoúnis (b. 1920), the only jeweller ever admitted in the French Académie des Beaux Arts, displays his collection of jewellery based on designs going back to the dawn of European civilization.

The Theatre of Dionysos

t 210 322 4625; open daily 8–7, Oct–April 8–5; adm.

From the Acropolis metro station, the first monument you come to, built into the side of the big rock, is probably the oldest playhouse in the world. But its stone seats never saw a first-night performance of the great tragedies of the Classical period. In fact, no stone theatre in Greece existed before the 4th century BC; Aeschylus, Sophocles and Euripides made do with seats dug into the hill or wooden bleachers. The existing and much modified theatre was begun from 342 to 326 BC and reached its present form by the time of Nero when it seated 17,000.

Each spring in this precinct Athens, since the time of Pisistratos, attended the Great Dionysia, an *agon* or contest in which playwrights presented plays to honour the god and to be judged by their peers, a five-day theatrical extravaganza accompanied by plenty of schmoozing over the wine *krater*. On the first day, all citizens, plus aliens and colonials, took part in a huge parade displaying the hundreds of cows and bulls about to be sacrificed to the god. The custom was for each participant to hold up and wave an enormous phallus, a reminder that Greek drama sprang from much earlier fertility rites. There were political overtones as well. Dionysos' cult statue was brought 'home' to Athens every year from Eleutherai, the area of Attica closest to Thebes and Mount Kitherónas, his stomping ground, to watch the performances in his honour, and to remind the Thebans and everyone else that Athens was *numero uno*. Day two also started with a parade in front of the audience, beginning with bearers each holding aloft the equivalent of a talent in silver, until all of that year's tribute to Athens from her subject allies was lined up on display. This was meant to assure the subject states that their money was being well looked after. Then came the orphans, the state-supported children of citizens killed in battle, and so forth. Then treaties were announced and special honours given to citizens. Only then were that day's plays performed. No event shows the total unity of Athenian civic and religious ritual better than the Great Dionysia.

There were four days of plays. Each of the first three consisted of three tragedies and a satyr play. On the fourth day, five comedies were performed, one after the other. Each year's plays were under the jurisdiction of the *archon*, the annually elected leader. He chose the *choregoi*, or producers, one for each play. These ancient angels had to pay for the production for the good of the state and were also expected to fork out for a big banquet for their troupe after the performance. The *archon* chose the plays, and the lead actors presumably chose the rest of the cast. All were amateurs, but it can be assumed that the same group participated regularly. All in all, well over a thousand men and boys would be rehearsing each year. From this festival emerged comedy that even the Marx brothers could only approach, and dramas whose lyric power and brilliance has seldom been equalled. No one is really sure whether women attended these performances. Audiences were rowdy at times, and on occasion threw bits of their lunch on stage. After all, most of the masked actors were neighbours, and the plays often raised thorny contemporary issues, although ever since one play-wright, Phrynichus, got in hot water in the 490s for openly referring to the fall of Athens' ally Miletus, the dramatists took care to veil their comments in myth.

The Stoa of Eumenes and the Odeion of Herodes Atticus

Such was the reputation of Athens after its heyday that it had a slew of wealthy benefactors, all keen to enjoy a bit of reflected glory. One was Eumenes II of Pergamon (d. 159 BC) who built the long **Stoa of Eumenes** next to the theatre, where the audience could relax and buy drinks and snacks; its roof supported a road, the *peripatos*, that encircled the Acropolis. Off this was an **Asklepeion**, dedicated to the healing god Asklepios, founded after Athens was decimated by plague in 429 BC. Next to the Stoa of Eumenes is the **Odeion** (AD 161) another gift, this time from the Rockefeller of his day, Herodes Atticus, whose life reads like something out of the Arabian Nights; he inherited his extraordinary wealth from his father, who found a treasure outside Rome. Famous in its time for having no interior columns to support its long-gone cedar wood roof, the 6,000-seat Odeion hosts the excellent Festival of Athens, where modern European and ancient Greek cultures meet in theatre, ballet and classical concerts performed by companies from all over the world.

The Acropolis

In summer the site (t 210 321 0219) and museum (t 210 323 6665) are open 8–7, Oct–April 8–5. On Mon the museum opens at 10; adm for both €12.

Acropolis means 'top of the town', and although many Greek cities grew up around similar natural citadels, Athens has *the* Acropolis, a sheer limestone rock standing a proud 300ft over the city, visible for miles around. Athens would not be Athens without it; it is the key to the city's origins. Inhabited by the end of the Neolithic era, it later supported a Mycenaean palace with a Temple of Athena inside it, and was fortified by Cyclopean walls. Before democracy, the tyrants lived here as well, sharing the rock with a temple of Poseidon and Athena, built after their famous contest to become patron of the city. Poseidon struck the Acropolis with his trident to create the salt spring Klepsydra; Athena invented the olive tree, and won. In 480 BC her wooden cult statue was hurriedly bundled off to Sálamis, just before the Persians burnt everything. This allowed for renovations and the creation of the Acropolis as we see it today, a showcase dedicated to the wealth and glory of Athens.

Themistocles rebuilt the processional ramp leading to the **Propylaia**, the majestic entrance gate built in Pentelic marble by Pericles' architect Mnesikles in the 430s BC to complement the Parthenon. Take a close look at it; ancient (and many modern) architects considered the Propylaia the equal of the Parthenon itself, ingeniously built over an uneven slope, its five gates with enormous wood and bronze doors big enough to admit horsemen and chariots for the annual Panathenaic procession. On either side of its entrance are wings; the one to the north held a picture gallery (*pinakothéke*) which also served as a VIP lounge, where notables could rest after their climb up, while the smaller one to the south is a *trompe l'œil* work that appears to have the same dimensions as the *pinakothéke*, although in fact it is little more than a façade because the priests of Athena Nike refused to have a wing in their precinct.

To the right of the Propylaia, on a stone-filled bastion of the Mycenaean wall, stands the pretty little Ionic **Temple of Athena Nike** built of Pentelic marble by Kallikrates in 478 BC. In 1687 the Turks dismantled it to build a nearby wall, making it easy to rebuild it with its original material in 1835 and again in 1936, when the bastion threatened to crumble away. At the time of writing, it has been dismantled again, to be rebuilt over a titanium skeleton. A cast replaces the frieze. From the temple platform, once the site of a statue of Wingless Victory, King Aegeus watched for the return of his son Theseus from his adventure with the Minotaur. Theseus was to have signalled his victory with a white sail but forgot; at the sight of the black sail, Aegeus swooned and fell off the precipice, giving his name to the Aegean sea.

The Parthenon

The Parthenon, the glory of the Acropolis and probably the most famous building in the world, is a Doric temple constructed between 447 and 432 BC by Iktinos and Kallikrates, supervised overall by Phidias, the Michelangelo of the Periclean age. Originally called the Great Temple, brightly painted and shimmering with gold, it took the name Parthenon (Chamber of the Virgin) a hundred years after its completion. An estimated 13,400 blocks of Pentelic marble went into its construction, cut to precise mathematical calculations; the largest weighed 10 tons and no two blocks were alike. Its architects wrote the book on *entasis* or 'tension' to imitate nature, shaping the columns so they very slightly swelled in the centre as if they were live things supporting the weight. As there are no straight lines in nature, there are none in the whole building: the foundation is curved slightly to prevent the visual illusion of drooping caused by straight horizontals. The columns bend a few centimetres inward, and those on the corners are wider. These minute details, many invisible to the naked eye, give the Parthenon its incomparable life, harmony and bounce.

The Doric order, symbolic of strength, was used in the outer colonnade, of 46 columns decorated with 92 metopes, carved with scenes of conquests over 'barbarians' that echo the recent triumph over the Persians. The east side portrayed the Battle of Giants and Gods, the south that of the Lapiths and Centaurs, on the west were the Athenians and the Amazons, and on the north the Battle of Troy. Only fragments (mostly in the British Museum) survive of the pediment sculptures of the birth of Athena and her contest with Poseidon – after bombing the Parthenon, Morosini tried to take them off as a souvenir for Venice but the ropes broke and the whole thing shattered to bits. The inner colonnade was Ionic, symbolic of Athens' culture, and had a more peaceful and spiritual decoration: a sublime 524ft continuous frieze of 400 human figures and 200 animals in low relief designed by Phidias. It depicts the quadrennial Panathenaic Procession in which the wooden cult statue of Athena in the Erechtheion was brought a golden crown and a new sacred garment, or *peplos*. Here too, subtle calculations (the lower parts are sculpted to a depth of 3cm, the upper to 5.5cm) and a slight downward tilt gave them added life in their original setting. An early British traveller, Edward Daniel Clark, remarked on how 'all the strength and impression of the composition depend on the viewing of the work in relation to that exact distance and optical angle which Phidias himself had calculated.' After the passing of Elgin's agent Lusieri, only an inscription remained on the wall: *Quod non fecerunt Gothi, hoc fecerunt Scoti* (What the Goths did not do, the Scots did here).

The Parthenon was designed to hold Phidias' chryselephantine (ivory and gold covered) statue of Athena, which stood over 36ft high; small surviving copies give an inkling of its majestic appearance. Altogether, the Parthenon, with its masterful perfection and unusually elaborate decoration, was not so much a temple to the gods (it lacked even the most basic cult necessity, an altar) but to the glory, genius and wealth of Athens, leader of the Delian League. The statue of Athena was clad with 44 talents of gold, a big part of the state treasury – the goddess' robes as Fort Knox. The Romans later did the same with their statue of Juno on the Capitoline Hill.

The Parthenon later found a religious role as a church and mosque, remaining intact until 1687, when Morosini's bomb hit the Turks' powder stores and blew off the roof; an earthquake in 1894 was another serious blow. Entrance within the Parthenon has been forbidden to save on wear and tear; preserving it from smog has been part of an intense rehabilitation programme since 1983, with plans to remove the scaffolding in time for the Olympics. While discovering how to clean off a century of pollution with lasers and microwaves and using hot, pressurized carbon dioxide to re-harden stone

surfaces, Greek engineers have learned a good deal about ancient building techniques and will reconstruct as much as possible, using rust-free titanium rods.

The Acropolis Museum

In ancient times the rock of the Acropolis was thronged with exquisite Attic sculptures, including one of the city's great landmarks, Phidias' 40ft statue of Athena
Promachos, whose golden speartip could be seen miles out at sea. Some smaller
works were buried and are now in this little museum tucked behind the Parthenon,
but are destined to relocate in 2004. The Archaic works in particular stand out:
painted pediments from the 6th-century BC from the Hecatompedon (or 'Old'
Parthenon) and from the temple of Athena Polias, showing Hercules wrestling Triton
and three snake men; the smiling *Calf-Bearer* (Moschoforos) from 570 BC carrying his
offering to the goddess; lovely painted Archaic Kore statues, each with her own
personality; and the famous *Rampin Horseman*. The damaged frieze of the Assembly
of the Gods from the temple of Athena Nike is here, and several panels of the
Parthenon frieze, and the pollution-scarred Caryatids from the Erechtheion, in a
special case filled with nitrogen.

The Greek flag flying on the belvedere beyond the museum has a special signifi-
cance to Athens. The first thing the Nazis did in their occupation was replace it with
the swastika. One night in May 1941, two teenagers crept up the secret Mycenaean
stair and stole it right from under the guards' noses, in what became the opening
salvo of the Greek Resistance.

The Erechtheion

The last great temple of the Acropolis, the Erechtheion, was completed only in
395 BC after the Peloponnesian War. This complex Ionic temple with three porches
and none of the usual Classical colonnades owes its idiosyncrasies to the much older
holies of holies it encompassed – the sanctuaries of Athena Polias, Poseidon
Erechtheus, Kekrops and the olive tree planted by the goddess – yet such is the genius
of its structure that it appears harmonious.

The southern porch facing the Parthenon is supported by six Caryatids (now casts),
designed to complement the Parthenon opposite. Lord Elgin nicked one; the other
girls were said to weep every night for their missing sister. Behind the east portico,
with its six Ionic columns, the *cella* was divided up to serve both Athena Polias and
Poseidon Erechtheos, and held the primitive cult statue of Athena Polias, the wearer
of the sacred pelops and the biggest juju of them all. Down the steps is the
Erechtheion's best side: its north porch, defined by six tall and elegant Ionic columns.
Part of the floor and roof were cut away to reveal to the gods the marks left by
Poseidon's trident; when the Turks made the temple a harem, they used the sacred
place as a toilet. This porch was the tomb of Erechtheos, some say Kekrops, and the
traditional home of the Acropolis guardian snake. A small olive tree replaces the
Athena-created original in the western court of the temple.

West and North of the Acropolis

The Areópagos, Pnyx and Philopáppou Hill

Below the Acropolis entrance and slightly to the north is the bald **Areópagos**, or hill of the war god Ares, where the High Council heard murder trials, in the open, so that the councillors could avoid the pollution of being under the same roof as a murderer. It figured prominently in Aeschylus' *Eumenides* where the rule of law (albeit a shockingly patriarchal law by today's standards) defeated vengeance for the first time in history during the trial of the matricide Orestes. Although Ephialtes removed much of the power of the Council, it continued to advise on the Athenian constitution for hundreds of years. One of its tasks was to judge foreign religions, including Christianity and its Unknown God as expounded by St Paul in AD 52 (verdict: not impressed, although a certain Dionysos converted and became Athens' first bishop and saint, Dionysos the Areopagite).

Below the Areópagos and across Apostólou Pávlou Street, archaeologists are busy uncovering an ancient Athenian neighbourhood under the olive trees. An attractive stone and marble lane leads up by way of the lovely Byzantine church of **Ag. Dimítrios Lombardiaris** to the lofty **Philopáppos Monument** (AD 114) built in honour of Caius Julius Antiochos Philopáppos, a Syrian Prince and friend of Athens. Philopáppou Hill is one of the beauty spots of Athens, where you can hear the cicadas over the traffic; as the Acropolis is almost level to the monument you can even pretend that modern Athens doesn't exist. The sunsets are famous, but after dark it's very isolated, so take care. Nearby is the **Dora Stratou Theatre**, where Athens' professional folk dance troupe performs nightly in summer.

To the right of Ag. Dimítrios is the shallow bowl of the **Pnyx**, where the assembly, the *Ekklesia*, met 30 to 40 times a year and heard the speeches of Pericles and Demosthenes, or of any citizen (i.e. any free Athenian male over the age of 20 who had performed his military service) who donned a wreath and mounted the steps of the rostrum. To make sure even the poorest could attend, Pericles paid a wage of two obols. Even so it was sometimes necessary to summon the police (Scythian slaves, who were crack archers and excused from the taboo of laying hands on a citizen) to rope in citizens – literally, with a rope dipped in red paint as a mark of shame – to fill the minimum attendance quota of 5,000; for important debates 18,000 sat here. What you see dates from the 4th century BC; in Roman times the assembly moved to the Theatre of Dionysos. Today the only Pnyx assemblies are tourists watching the Sound and Light Show. Beyond this is the **Hill of the Nymphs**, where the magical maidens have been replaced by the **Observatory** (1842) designed by Theófilos Hansen.

Anafiótika and the Roman Forum

North of the Acropolis, you can descend into Pláka through its upper quarter, **Anafiótika**, a residential enclave left by the builders of Otto's palaces, who came from the island of Anáfi and, homesick, tried to recreate their village here. Still mostly residential, one handsome neoclassical mansion on its edge now holds the

Kanellópoulos Museum, at the corner of Theorías and Panós Streets (*t 210 321 2313; open Tues–Sun 8.30–3; adm*). This private collection is a sampler of Greek civilization, from Neolithic times to the 19th century, with choice *objets d'art* from every period: ancient vases; Tanagra figurines from Thebes – the first Dresden shepherdesses, but less cloying – that were the rage in the ancient world in the 4th and 3rd centuries BC; 2nd-century portraits from El Fayyum in Egypt, icons by some of the best known painters, and intricately carved crosses.

From here Itanós Street will take you down to Thólou Street, which leads shortly to the Kleánthes House (1831) – one of the very few surviving buildings that predated Athens' appointment as capital – that became the first home of the University of Athens from 1837 to 1841. From here Klepsýdras Street descends to the Romaïki Agorá, or the **Roman Forum** (*t 210 324 5220; open 8–7, Oct–April 8–5; adm*). Feeling uncomfortable in the Greek Agora, especially after they had laid waste to it (*see* below), the Romans built their own marketplace that kept its role up into Ottoman times. They knew the time day and night, thanks to a *klepsydra* or hydraulic clock in the octagonal 1st century BC **Tower of the Winds**. Once a bronze Triton weathervane spun on top, over the frieze of the eight winds; Vitruvius wrote that its builder, the astronomer Andronikos Kyrrestes, wanted to prove there were eight winds, not four. At its west end, the forum contains the **Gate of Athena Archegetis**, built by Julius and Augustus Caesar; one of its posts, still in place, has the market-pricing rules imposed by Hadrian. There is also a court and ruined stoa, and the Fetchiyé Tzamí, the Victory or **Corn Market Mosque**, now used as a storeroom. Opposite the Tower of the Winds, the **Medresse** (with Arabic script running over the mouldering door) was an Islamic seminary (1721), later used as a prison.

Near the Tower of the Winds, at 8 Kyrrístou Street, is the only surviving hammam in Athens, the 17th-century **Bathhouse of the Winds**. In operation until 1965, it now belongs to the Greek Folk Art Museum (*see* p.117) and is being restored as a museum on public bathhouses in the Balkans. At the top of Diogénous, the next street down, the **Popular Musical Instruments Museum** (*t 210 325 0198; open Tues and Thurs–Sun 10–2, Wed 12–6, closed Mon; free*) offers a fascinating collection of old and new Greek folk instruments with headphones to listen to what they sound like.

Plateía Agorás, just north of the forum, is a pleasant place to sip a drink while contemplating the ancient walls of **Hadrian's Library**, an enormous building (400 by 269ft) donated by that most philhellene of emperors, equipped with an inner peristyle courtyard and garden with a long pool. A walk west down around the ruins will bring you to the bustling **Monastiráki** metro station and opposite, the large, well preserved Tsizdaraki Mosque, built by the governor of Athens in 1759. It now houses the **Kyriazópoulos Ceramic Collection** (*t 210 324 2066; open Wed–Mon 9–2.30; adm*), another annex of the Greek Folk Art Museum, with a display of traditional Greek ceramics and pieces from some of the country's best known living potters. Monastiráki is synonymous with Athens' **flea market**, which waits to the west, where bulging shops sell antiques, fake Timberland boots, Thai trinkets and second-hand books and fridges; **Plateía Avissinías**, at the centre, is chock-full of old furniture. But this part of Athens has always been a market: the ancient Agora is only a block away.

The Heart of Ancient Athens

The Agora

*Entrance on Adrianoú, **t** 210 321 0185; open 8–7, Oct–April 8–5.*
Museum open same hours exc Mon when it opens at 11am; adm.

The Agora was the living heart of ancient Athens: not just a market, but a stage for public life, for elections, meetings, festivals and court proceedings. It had many of the characteristics of a *temenos* (sacred precinct), marked with boundary stones, with water available for purification at its entrances, and was strictly off limits to draft-dodgers, convicted murderers, traitors and other political outcasts. For citizens, the news, political manoeuvrings, verbal gymnastics and social contacts available in the shade of its stoas were life itself. By citizens, of course, we mean men. Only flute girls (prostitutes) and poor women selling fish or other goods were regulars in the Agora.

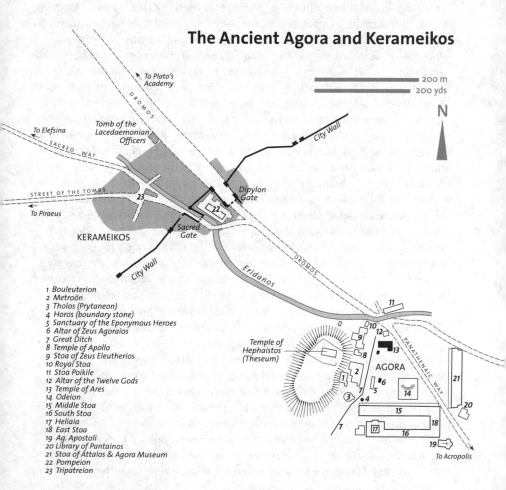

The Ancient Agora and Kerameikos

1 Bouleuterion
2 Metroön
3 Tholos (Prytaneon)
4 Horos (boundary stone)
5 Sanctuary of the Eponymous Heroes
6 Altar of Zeus Agoraios
7 Great Ditch
8 Temple of Apollo
9 Stoa of Zeus Eleutherios
10 Royal Stoa
11 Stoa Poikile
12 Altar of the Twelve Gods
13 Temple of Ares
14 Odeion
15 Middle Stoa
16 South Stoa
17 Heliaia
18 East Stoa
19 Ag. Apostoli
20 Library of Pantainos
21 Stoa of Attalos & Agora Museum
22 Pompeion
23 Tripatreion

Good girls stayed home; men even did the shopping back then. Aristophanes satirized the way they looked as they sashayed about during the Peloponnesian War, parcels dangling from their spears and knocking against their armour. Here a man could get lucky, and be buttonholed by the likes of Socrates or Demosthenes. The conversations in this highly charged public arena changed the course of Western civilization.

The Agora started out as a large open space, with stoas and buildings around its perimeter. After the Persians razed it in 480 BC, it was rebuilt on a much grander scale. Once again, after suffering desecration at the hand of Sulla's Romans, most of the structures were rebuilt, and then more added to create a clutter that a 5th-century Athenian would scarcely have recognized. Firebug barbarians didn't rebuild, however, and Athenians in need of cut stone pirated the ruins for centuries to build walls, churches and houses.

What's left covers every era of ancient history. Only foundations remain of the council house or **Bouleuterion**, built in the late 6th century BC after its establishment by Kleisthenes, and the neighbouring Temple of the Mother of the Gods, the **Metroön**, built by the Athenians as reparation for the slaying of a priest from her cult. Rooms on either side served as the public records archive and citizens' registry (to this day *mitroön* in Greek means 'register'). The annually elected *Prytanes* governed from the round **Tholos** or Prytaneon. Since some had to be on call day and night, it had kitchens and sleeping quarters. Official guests were fêted here, and honoured citizens, such as Olympic winners and their descendants, were given dining rights in perpetuity. When Socrates was on trial for his life, he was asked to choose a just sentence for himself. He answered that he should be given the right to eat free at the Prytaneon, meaning that he regarded himself as a valuable member of the state. He got to drink hemlock instead, in a building that has been tentatively identified as **Socrates' prison**.

Near the Tholos is a **horos**, one of the Agora's boundary stones still in situ. Opposite the Metroön, a stone fence and statue bases mark the remains of the **Sanctuary of the Eponymous Heroes of Athens**, which once contained the statues of the ten heroes instituted by Kleisthenes to give their names to the ten tribes of Athens. Since each tribal ward was spread shotgun fashion all over Attica to avoid one large geographical area taking precedence, members came here to read announcements (on stone stele or painted boards) concerning their tribe. The nearby **Altar of Zeus Agoraios** received the oaths of the new *archons*, a practice initiated by Solon. Running between the enclosure to the ten heroes and the Metroön is the **Great Ditch** engineered in Kleisthenes' time; it still dutifully drains rain water from the Acropolis through the Agora to the Eridanos river that flows through the Kerameikós cemetery.

The small 4th-century BC **Temple of Apollo** by the Metroön was dedicated to the forebear of the Ionians, who believed themselves descended from Apollo's son Ion. Almost nothing remains of the **Stoa of Zeus Eleutherios**, one of the recorded haunts of Socrates. It was partly built into the rock in 430 BC in honour of Zeus the Saviour for his role in saving the city from the Persians. Some of it disappears into the metro tracks. Walk over (or have a look over, if the guards haven't opened the gate) the bridge to the pathetic little strip of ruins between the tracks and Monastiráki shops to the small **Royal Stoa** (*stoa basileios*) where Athenian laws were written in stone for all to see; Socrates faced them when the indictment was read out against him. A massive slab built into the stoa's step, believed to be a lintel from a tholos tomb, was the traditional **oath stone** where the Athenians swore their most sacred vows.

In front of the royal stoa is a small, square enclosure of waist-high stone slabs, an early crossroads shrine apparently dedicated to the daughters of Leos who were sacrificed to save the city from famine way back when. It was *ávaton* (forbidden territory), but Athenians threw small tokens into it and in an adjacent circular well to honour the deified daughters – votives that offer clues into the city's religious life. If walking through the embankment north at this point were possible, you would come to the once-famed **Stoa Poikile**, decorated with paintings of the battle of Marathon, where Zeno of Kition taught in the late 4th century; hence 'Stoic' philosophy. Now it and a temple share a dismal hole on the other side of Adrianoú Street, where the Agora made a turn towards the gate that divided it from the Kerameikós cemetery.

Back over the bridge, in front and beyond the Stoa of Zeus, stands the **Altar of the Twelve Gods**, from which all distances in Attica were measured, although this too was partially obliterated with the laying of the Piraeus–Thíssio train tracks in 1868, when no one knew exactly where the Agora was; ruins lay everywhere. Beside the Altar of the Twelve Gods, right at the main entrance, is part of the **Panathenaic Way**, the ceremonial path from the Dipylon gate to the Acropolis, laid out by Pisistratos at the consecration of the Panathenaic Festival in 566 BC. In Athens' heyday, it was a gravel path; the fancy stonework that appears further up is 2nd century AD Roman.

South of the Altar of the Twelve Gods stood a 5th-century BC Doric **Temple of Ares**. But it wasn't always here: it was dismantled stone by stone, just like London Bridge, and brought to town from the suburbs by the Romans and placed here, making the Agora just that much less open. The Roman also filled in other blanks to the south. The **three giants** standing sentinel nearby were originally part of the **Odeion of Agrippa** built in 15 BC; parts of the orchestra remain intact. The massive roof collapsed in AD 190. Both the site and giants were reused in the façade of a 5th-century gymnasium. Near the 2nd-century BC **Middle Stoa** are ruins of a Roman temple and ancient shops. On the other side of the Middle Stoa was the **South Stoa**, where the rooms used for symposia can still be made out. The doors of each are slightly off-centre, allowing a long couch to fit on one side of the 'door'. Small but intimate, these were for bachelors' bashes, complete with wine, women and song. Beside it, to the west, is the large square people's court, or **Heliaia**, organized by Solon in the 6th century BC to hear political questions. It has been identified as one of the possible sites of the jury trials; since the jurors could number in the hundreds in the radical democracy, a big space was required. It was used well into Roman times.

Between the South and **East Stoa** (2nd-century BC) is the 11th-century church **Ag. Apóstoli**, built on the site where St Paul addressed the Athenians; it was restored, along with its fine paintings, in 1952. Across the Panathenaic Way run the remains of **Valerian's Wall**, thrown up in AD 257 against the barbarians, made of stone from buildings wrecked by the Romans. Between Valerian's Wall and the Stoa of Attalos are higgledy-piggledy ruins of the **Library of Pantainos**, built by Flavius Pantainos in AD 100 and destroyed 167 years later. Beside it, the **Stoa of Attalos** was built in the

2nd century BC by one of Athens' benefactors, King Attalos II of Pergamon, and carefully reconstructed in 1953–5 with funds from the Rockefellers; all the materials used replicate the original except for the rafters, which here are concrete painted to resemble wood. It now houses the Agora Museum in one large hall; the original building was divided into 42 luxury shops on two floors, leading off the shady stoa – exactly like a shopping mall. And, in case you are wondering, the **public latrines** were at the south end of this stoa, en route to the newer Roman forum.

The Agora Museum

Well laid out and varied, this museum is a far better introduction to everyday Athenian life than the blockbuster Archaeological Museum. Among its delights are a complex balloting mechanism for choosing jurors that resembles a Japanese pachinko machine, a Spartan shield that some Athenian soldier hauled home as a trophy from Sphakteria (which ended the 'come back with it or on it' legend for all time), and a 4th-century BC child's training potty. Also on display are the *óstraka* (potsherds) used to ostracize anyone whom the Athenians thought was getting too uppity. It worked this way: once a year, a referendum took place when voters were asked if they thought any citizen a danger to the state. If a majority said yes, another vote was held. On this occasion, a citizen could write the name of anyone he chose on an *óstrako*, the scrap paper of the day. If 6,000 people voted, then whoever got the most votes, no matter what the actual count, was exiled for ten years. Although not often used, Themistocles was a victim, and Pericles used it to get rid of a rival. The system was also abused: of the 190 *óstraka* found in a well, only 14 different handwritings can be discerned: someone was producing his enemy's name wholesale on pottery pieces and handing them out to anyone he could persuade to vote.

The Theseum (Temple of Hephaistos)

On the east edge of the Agora, the mid 5th-century BC Theseum is nothing less than the best-preserved Greek temple in existence. It was given this name by archaeologists who thought it was the tomb built by Kimon for the bones of Theseus (*see* p.502), but they were wrong. This Doric temple was dedicated to Hephaistos, the god of metals and smiths. It is constructed almost entirely of Pentelic marble and decorated with metopes depicting the lives of Heracles and Theseus. Converted into a church in the 5th century, it was the burial place for Protestants until 1834. The neighbourhood west of the temple, **Thissío**, has trendy cafés with lovely Acropolis views.

Kerameikós: the Graveyard Shift

148 Ermoú St, t 210 346 3552; open daily 8–7, Oct–April 8–5; adm.
Guide on sale at the site.

Extending from the Agora was the ancient Athenian West End, a large quarter known as Kerameikós, or 'pottery district'. Its great landmark was the recessed 'two towered' or **Dipylon Gate**, the city's front door and the largest gate in ancient Greece, complete with a vast courtyard for public gatherings. The marble floor of the *de rigueur* **fountain house**, where travellers abluted before entering the city, survives just inside its double doors. South of the gate stretches a marvellous section of **city walls**, then the smaller **Sacred Gate**, where the Eridanos stream made its exit.

When German archaeologists started work after 1913, the Eridanos had covered Kerameikós with 26ft of silt. They dug to the bedrock, as archaeologists do, and then did an incredible thing: they replaced just enough to recreate the area as it was in the the late 5th century BC. Even the **boundary stones** are still in place, as are the contemporary tombs and the (now filled in) moat around the walls, with the remains of the small wall or **proteichisma** in front to deter siege engines. The result is a peaceful bit of the Athens of Socrates' day, with a view back to the Acropolis just as an ancient traveller would have seen it. The value of the finds here is incalculable – not in gold but pottery, the articles of everyday life, as befits a city that made her wealth from the exceptional clay found here and the brilliance of her potters.

Kerameikós was originally much larger, extending 1.5km west to Plato's Academy. Its residents were used to living cheek by jowl with the dead. Potters potted and prostitutes hung about the gates trolling for custom (rates were regulated by law, and depended on the service on offer). Meanwhile, in the **Pompeion**, located just inside the walls, officials either organized the parade (*pompe*) for the Panathenaic festival, or lolled about on one of the 60 dining couches in rooms off the main courtyard. The Panathenaic ship carrying the *peplos* for Athena was stored here. And annually, thousands streamed through the Sacred Gate onto the **Sacred Way** (Iera Odos) leading to Eleusis (*see* p.166). Plato must have strolled and philosophized on the **Dromos**, the wide street leading through the Dipylon gate to his Academy. Merchants and sailors would have gone down the Sacred Way to the **Tripatreion**, an easy-to-spot triangular enclosure honouring all of the dead, and then left on the **Street of Tombs**, to Piraeus and beyond. And punctuating all this: funerals and burials, over 2,000 years' worth.

The Cemetery

Mycenaean Athens used the present Agora as a cemetery, but by the sub-Mycenaean period the dead were laid here in stone-lined trenches, heads oriented towards the Eleusis road, accompanied by pitchers, amphorae and mugs filled with things for the afterlife, and then covered with a mound. The Geometric period saw an increase in burials, both cremated and not (it seemed to be a matter of choice), but now the mounds were topped by vases; some of these were monumental, culminating in the enormous Dipylon Amphora in the National Museum. Offerings became ever richer to showcase a family's wealth.

By the Archaic period, clay-offering trenches were the norm. Some extended as long as 36ft from the grave, allowing ever more pots with food and other offerings to be burned and buried with the body (the link between food offerings, regeneration and the afterlife continues today; seed offerings, *spernâ*, are still part of Orthodox rites of the dead). Grave steles very like our tombstones, carved with human figures, appear. Feeling things were getting out of hand, Solon wrote a law curbing ostentatious funerals, but aristocratic tombs remained showy nonetheless. By the time of

Pisistratos, the distinctive amphorae prizes of the Panathenaic games were placed over the tombs of the victors. This was the cemetery's grandest period and many monuments survive, mostly because they were used to build Themistocles' city walls, thrown up on the double in 478 BC. Henceforth, all burials were outside the walls.

By the Classical period, inhumation prevailed and white ground *lekythoi*, jugs and clay figurines were popular grave goods. Babies, and there were many, were buried in amphorae. There were both family enclosures and collective state burials. The long narrow **Tomb of the Lacedaemonian Officers**, whose death in 403 BC was described by Xenophon, is still on the Dromos. Large marble steles, some in situ, depicting departing ladies or soldiers, became the vogue until yet another law in 317 BC prohibited ostentatious monuments. This one stuck. Little *kioniskoi*, the stubby columns you see around the museum, became the norm in the Hellenistic period. The Romans revived the splendour for a time, but slowly Kerameikós was abandoned, even by the potters who had squatted in the ruined Pompeion.

The **museum** is a treasure house of pottery finds from every era. Room B has lovely Proto-geometric bits and pieces with Mycenaean designs visibly melting into Geometric patterns, a little caryatid with an Archaic smile in case 45, and an elaborate offering vase with three roosters in case 46. The nested offering plates with the elaborate filigreed handles in case 12 would tempt any hostess today, as would the dainty 'tea cups'. Sadly there are lots of children's toys. Room C is mostly Classical. Room D is late Classical and on, with white *lekythoi* and painted Tanagra figurines. Case 33 contains a *katára*, a sinister oval lead box containing a manacled lead doll, scratched with the names of people to be cursed – a message sent express to Hades with the corpse. There are painted clay rosettes placed on the deceased's breast in case 36, and in case 37 coins placed on the corpse's mouth to pay the boatman Charon.

Around Kerameikós: Gázi and Psirrí

West of Kerameikós, down Ermoú Street, skeletons of old gasworks mark **Gázi**, an industrial slum fitfully finding a new life with galleries, clubs and some of the city's top designer restaurants. Heading east from Kerameikós on Ermoú towards the centre, the first street you come to is Melidóni, site of the Beth Shalon Synagogue (*t 210 325 2823*) and the small **Museum of Traditional Pottery** (*t 210 331 8491; open Mon–Fri 9–3, but Wed 12–8, Sun 10–2, closed Sat; adm*), dedicated to the art of Greek pottery. Although the emphasis is on the last century, techniques have hardly evolved for the big pots since the heyday of Kerameikós.

Just east begins **Psirrí** (Ψυρρή), a neighbourhood of winding little streets, where Byron rented a room. Its name comes from the slang for 'shaved' or 'fleeced', a reminder of its days as a tough quarter of warehouses and workers' tenements, where entering was something of a risk. Now one of the trendiest spots to eat and play in Athens, the city is fixing up the streets radiating out from Psirrí's centre, **Plateía Iróon**. They are almost perfect, like stage sets, an effect heightened by the squalor of the ungentrified edges. If you continue north on Aristofánous Street and turn right on Evripídou Street, you'll find **Ag. Ioánnis**, a tiny church with a Corinthian column sticking out of its roof that probably came from a temple to Asklepios. People visited it to cure their fevers; the idea was to tie the fevers to the column with string or bits of wool. Some bits still dangle away behind the iconostasis.

Evripídou Street leads west to large Koumoundoúrou Square, where the former foundlings' hospital of 1874 is now the **Municipal Art Gallery** (*t 210 324 3022; open daily 9–1 and 5–8.30, Sat and Sun 9–1; free*) devoted to Greek art since 1821, offering a fine introduction to modern Greek painting, engraving and sculpture.

Ermoú Street and Athens Cathedral

Hermes is the patron of commerce, and you may have already noticed that his street, Ermoú, is dedicated to shopping. East of Monastiráki, where the shops get fancier, it has been pedestrianized; here old men serenade shoppers with old songs on barrel organs, or *latérnes*. The Byzantine church sunken in the middle of the street – King Otto's father, Ludwig of Bavaria, just managed to spare it from the destruction decreed by his son's planners – is the late 11th-century **Kapnikaréa**; it has a charming central cupola supported by four Roman columns, and old bas reliefs and inscriptions embedded on the outer walls. Its name, from the word for smoke, '*kapnos*', refers to its founder, an official who collected the hearth tax.

The next parallel street south of Ermoú, Mitropóleos, passes large Mitropóleos Square, with its two churches. The little one is the 12th-century Ag. Elefthérios, better known as **Panagía Gorgoepíkoos**, 'Our Lady who Grants Requests Quickly'. Nicknamed 'the little cathedral', this is the loveliest church in Athens, built almost entirely of ancient marbles, one carved with a calendar of state festivals and another with the zodiac. The adjacent 'big' **Cathedral** or Metropolis was built in 1840–55 with the same collage technique, using bits and pieces from 72 destroyed churches around Athens. The kings of Greece were crowned here between 1863 and 1964, and it contains the tomb of the unofficial saint of Greek independence, the Patriarch of Constantinople Gregory V, hanged by the Sultan in 1821 for failing to prevent the uprising.

North of Sýntagma to Omónia Square

From Sýntagma Square, Ottos' planners laid out two parallel streets, Stadíou and Panepistimíou, to link up to Omónia Square in the north. If you take the latter from the top of Sýntagma, you'll soon find the wonderful new **Numismatic Museum** at No.12 (*t 210 364 3774; open Tues–Sun 8–2.30; adm*), in Heinrich Schliemann's neoclassical mansion, the Ilion Megaron (1881). Decorated with motifs recalling his discoveries, the mansion was designed by his architect friend Ernst Ziller, who had accompanied Schliemann to Troy, and later became a Greek citizen; there are displays on both men, and on the history of money (bronze weights were used from the 16th century BC on, before the first silver and gold coins were minted, in Lydia and Ionia in Asia Minor, in the 7th century BC). The 600,000 coins, in state-of-the-art displays, are one of the most important collections in the world.

If you cross from here to Stadíou via Amerikís Street, you'll meet the imposing Old Parliament building (1875–1935), guarded by a flamboyant equestrian statue of Théodoros Kolokotrónis (*see* p.285). This now houses the **National Historical Museum** (*t 210 323 7617; open Tues–Sun 9–2; adm, free on Sun*); all around the old deputies' chamber are exhibits on Greek history, concentrating on the War of Independence: famous ships' figureheads, named for ancient heroes (many have thick coats of paint – when sailing through the Bosphorus, they had to be painted black to avoid offending the Turks); the Zográfos paintings – 25 colourful scenes narrating Greek history from the fall of Constantinople to the War of Independence, commissioned by Makrigiánnis, who described the events to the painter Dimítri Zográfos; memorabilia of war heroes and of Byron, along with items and engravings used to rouse the world to the Greek cause; and a collection of folk costumes from every corner of Greece.

Two streets up Stadíou, flanking large Plateía Klafthmónos, a former residence of King Otto now houses the **Athens City Museum**, 7 Paparigópoulou (*t 210 324 6164; open Sun, Mon, Wed, Fri and Sat, 9–1.30; adm*), with photos, memorabilia and water-colours of Athens as it was. Other rooms contain memorabilia from Otto's not very successful reign. Diagonally opposite on Plateía Klafthmónos, the 11th-century church of **Ag. Theódori** is notable for its beautiful door.

Opposite Plateía Klafthmónos is the Panepistimíou metro station and, beyond that, on Panepistimíou Street, the 'Trilogy' – three huge neoclassical buildings, designed by two Danish brothers, Theophilos and Christian Hansen. The **Academy of Athens** (1886) on the right, with its huge statues of Athena and Apollo, was built with funds donated by Simon Sinas, a Vlach from Albania, who founded the National Bank of Austria in Vienna; others are the **University** (1846) and the **National Library** (1901).

Behind these at 50 Akadimías, another neoclassical pile, once the municipal hospital, now holds the **City of Athens Cultural Centre** (*t 210 32 1601; open 9–1 and 5–9, closed Mon and Sun pm; free*), which provides information on events and hosts tempo-rary exhibitions. The adjacent pink building contains the **Theatre Museum** (*t 210 362 9430; open Mon–Fri 9–3; free*), with costumes, posters and memorabilia, the recon-structed dressing rooms of Maria Callas and Melina Mercouri, displays on shadow theatre, and items relating to poet Angelos Sikelianós' revival of the Delphi festival.

At the north end of Panepistimíou, traffic spins around **Omónia** (Concord) **Square**, or 'ammonia' as Henry Miller called it in *The Colossus of Maroussi*. Once Athens' Times Square, with 24-hour dives and porn-peddling *periptera*, only a few whiffs of the old Omónia linger after a revamp: hotels and tavernas vintage 1970 and geegaw shops in piquant, dimly lit *stoas* (in modern Greek, a passage in a building; 'arcade' is too grand a word). One busy street, Athinás, leads south to the palatial **Dimarchíon** or City Hall, next to a handsome mansion by Ziller, before it divides the fruit and vegetables from the meat and fish stalls of the city's **Central Market**, open daily except Sun until 3pm.

National Archaeological Museum

Patission (28 Oktovríou) and Tossítsa Sts, t 010 821 7717. A 10min walk from Omónia or trolley 2, 4, 5, 9 or 11 from Panepistimíou St. Open April–mid-Oct Mon 12.30–7, Tues–Fri 8–7, Sat and Sun 8.30–3; winter Mon 11–5, Tues–Fri 8–5, Sat and Sun 8.30–3; adm.

This is the big one, containing some of the most sublime works of the ancient Greek world, housed in a vast neoclassical edifice begun in 1866. But note: the museum will be closed for renovations until December 2003, when some exhibits may be moved.

The museum's oldest artefacts are **Neolithic**: small schematic figures dating back to the 5th millennium BC from Sésklo and finds from Troy and its close cultural cousin, Polióchni on Límnos, the oldest site in the Aegean. The **Cycladic** civilization that blossomed in the 3rd millennium BC was famous for its startlingly contemporary-looking marble figurines; the museum has the largest complete figure ever found, the famous 4,500-year old harpist, and the 'frying pans' found in Early Cycladic graves (were they mirrors filled with water, or drums, with skins stretched over them, or did they hold offerings for the dead?) and a unique silver diadem decorated with rosettes and animals from Sýros. The longest lasting Cycladic settlement was Phylakope on Mílos; under the influence of the nature-loving Minoans, it produced the delightful frescoes of flying fish and lyrical vases shaped like birds in full song.

Among the museum's chief glories is the most important **Mycenaean** collection in the world – the treasures that convinced Schliemann that he had truly found the fief of his Homeric heroes 'rich in gold': gold masks, including the one Schliemann dubbed the 'mask of Agamemnon', bronze niello-work and cloisonnée daggers, a magnificent bull's head rhyton, boar's tusk helmet, lovely ivories (note especially the two goddesses with the child), charming frescoes from Tiryns and Pýlos, Linear B tablets, the deathly white Sphinx mask from Mycenae, delightful gold seals and signet rings, the 12th-century BC warrior *krater*, showing soldiers marching to war, a mini fresco of ass-headed demons, and the two exquisite gold cups found in a tomb at Vapheío, probably of Minoan manufacture, with vivid repoussée scenes of capturing a bull.

After the collapse of the Mycenaeans (*c*. 1150 BC), Greek art began its revival with ceramics: don't miss striking monumental **Late Geometric** grave amphorae from Dipylon (760 BC) and one of the earliest inscriptions in Greek (740 BC) on a vase found at Kerameikós. The museum also has rare examples of the sculpture of the day, flat linear 'Daedalic' figures with their triangular head, a prelude to the mid 7th-century introduction of the **Archaic** figures of the *kouros* and *kore* with their haunting smiles, as if they had 'known Divinity', as John Fowles put it. The collection spans the oldest extant *kouros*, a colossus from Soúnion (from 610 BC), to the perfect Phrasikleia Kore by Aristion of Páros, holding a mushroom, her dress painted with rosettas and solar-symbol swastikas, then to the Aristodikos Kouros (510 BC) whose vigour, muscles and relaxed pose points directly to the Classical Age. Other key Archaic works include the earliest known Nike or Victory (550 BC), from Délos, a magnificent *krater* of 640 BC showing Apollo's return to Délos after his annual confab with the Hyperboreans, a beautiful Parian marble relief of a dancer or athlete in motion, the grave stele of the Hoplite Aristion (510 BC) signed by Aristokles, and the bases of *kouros* statues found in Athens, with fascinating reliefs of athletes – wrestlers, long jumpers, hockey players and two punters egging on a cat and dog.

After the Persian Wars, the Archaic smiles are replaced by the early **Classical** 'severe style', epitomized in the relief from Soúnion of a boy crowning himself. The museum has an unsurpassed collection of Classical funerary art, including the *Stele of Hegeso*, an Athenian beauty, enveloped by the delicate folds of her bridal gown; its discovery at Kerameikós inspired a poem by Palamas. Another highlight are two exquisite votive reliefs: of *Hermes and Nymphs* and *Dionysos and the Actors*, both *c.* 410 BC. Roman copies of works by the great sculptors of the age offer hints of what's been lost: a lifeless copy of Phidias' *Athena* from the Parthenon, and the marble *Diadoumenos*, a copy of a famous bronze by Polyclitus, author of the *Canon* on the proportions of Classical beauty. Surviving Greek originals have mostly been found on shipwrecks: one is the splendidly virile bronze *Poseidon* (*c.* 460 BC), found off Cape Artemísion.

The same wreck yielded the bronze *Jockey* (*c.* 140 BC), one of the most dramatic works of the **Hellenistic** era, the horse straining and the boy's face distorted by the speed; other rescued bronze originals are the *Marathon Boy*, attributed to Praxiteles, and *Antikythera Youth*, attributed to Euphranor of Corinth. Other Hellenistic masterpieces are the beautiful and melancholy *Ilissos stele* by the school of Scopas and a striking relief of a young Ethiopian groom, trying to calm a horse, found in 1948 by Laríssa station. Also look for the bust of Plato (a Roman copy) and a bizarre double herm head of an elderly Aristotle; the *Wounded Gaul*, the base of a statue by Praxiteles, showing the music contest between Apollo and Marsyas; busts of Demosthenes and his enemy Alexander the Great in a lion helmet, with graffiti on his face; the giant heads from the Temple of Despoina at Lykosoúra in Arcadia by Damophon; and a charming group of Aphrodite, raising her slipper to whack pesky Pan. Small votive reliefs and illustrated decrees offer fascinating insights into religious life, involving plenty of bearded snakes.

From the 500 years of **Roman** rule in Greece, there's a bronze Augustus from an equestrian statue, found in the Aegean and looking very much like Roddy McDowell, and a group of 2nd- and 3rd-century AD portrait herms from the Diogeneion, an Athenian gymnasium, offering a unique look at the upper class Athenians of the day. Roman busts include ones of Hadrian and Antinous, the favourite he deified, and Marcus Aurelius, whose portrait shows a last attempt at psychological analysis before inspiration dried up altogether. A peculiar one is the bust of Julia Mamaea, mother of emperor Alexander Severus (AD 232–235); she was sentenced to death, which required that all her portraits be hammered.

And that's not all. The museum has one of the finest collections anywhere of Greek vases, and another of small bronzes going back to 1000 BC: votives from Dodona, Olympia and the Acropolis, as well as the Antikýthera device, believed to be the world's oldest computer (*see* p.315). There's an excellent Egyptian collection, and the Stathátos Collection with exquisite *objets d'art* and jewellery from all periods, including an egg-shaped red-figure vase showing a woman dowsing. Another special section is devoted to Minoan Akrotíri, on Santoríni: lovely vases and frescoes of *Boxing Children*, the *Antelopes*, and *Spring* with dancing swallows (18th–17th century BC), enough to make the Atlantis stories seem true (*see* p.664).

Around the Museum

In the same big building, but with a separate entrance at 1 Tosíta Street, the **Epigraphic Museum** (*t 210 821 7637; open Tues–Sun 8.30–2.30; free*) has an enormous collection of ancient inscriptions, mostly from Attica. Until the 6th century, all were written in *boustrophedon*, 'as the ox ploughs', back and forth (binders in the rooms have easier-to-read transcriptions, although they aren't translated into English). Stone carvers must have worked fast; one stele has the decree of Themistocles in 480 BC, ordering the evacuation of Athens.

South of the museum is the **Polytechníon** school (1880) where students began the uprising against the military junta in 1974, and met tanks in response. The neighbourhood behind this is **Exárchia**, Athens' Latin quarter, home of trendies, students and literati. *Terra incognita* for tourists, its leafy heart, **Plateía Exárchia**, is lively after dark, with traditional *ouzeries*, hip-hop music bars and smoke-filled *rembétika* clubs. Exárchia was once nicknamed 'Anarchia', but now its square shelters a huge FloCafé, which in Greece is as middle class as you can get. Above the square, there are lovely views of the Acropolis from **Strefi Hill**.

East of the Acropolis: the Záppeion and Zeus

East of the Acropolis and south of Sýntagma Square, off busy Leofóros Amalías, **Záppeion Park** is an extension of the National Gardens, surrounding the handsome horseshoe-shaped **Záppeion Palace** (1888) designed by Theophilos Hansen, and now used for summit meetings. On the corner of Amalías and Vass. Ólgas, don't miss the **statue of Hellas to Lord Byron**, in which Greece hugs the poet while sticking her hand in his pocket – a fairly accurate allegory of what occurred in the War of Independence, which Byron was the first Western celebrity to support. Since then he has been the National Favourite Brit; the first philhellene to have loved live Greeks as much as if not more than the ancient ones, and one who blasted Elgin for vandalism.

Across from here, in Leofóros Vass. Ólgas, is the entrance to the **Temple of Olympian Zeus** (*t 210 922 6330; open 8–7, Sept–April 8–5; adm*). Fifteen enormous columns and one prone and broken like spilled breath mints recall what Livy called 'the only temple on earth of a size adequate to the greatness of the god'. The spot was long sacred: not far away stood a very ancient temple to the Earth, with a cleft in the floor said to be the drain for the deluge sent by Zeus to punish humanity, killing all but Deucalion and his wife. The ambitious foundations were laid by Pisistratos, but work ground to a halt with his son, only to be continued in 175 BC by a Roman architect, Cossutius. It was half finished when Cossutius' patron, Antiochos IV of Syria, died, leaving Hadrian to complete it in AD 131. Nearby are the ruins of a well-appointed Roman bath and bits of other temples. The view to the east is tranquil, closed by the violet-tinted slopes of Mount Hymettos, while to the east, where traffic hums down Amalías, stands **Hadrian's Arch**, in Pentelic marble, erected by the Athenians to thank him for his benevolence. The complimentary inscription reads on the Acropolis side: 'This is Athens, the ancient city of Theseus', while the other side reads: 'This is the city of Hadrian, not of Theseus'.

Further east, Vass. Ólgas turns into Leofóros Vass. Konstantínos, where the land-mark is the big white horseshoe of the **Olympic** (or **Kallimármaro**) **stadium**. Another benefactor, good old Herodes Atticus, built a marble stadium for the Panathenaea festival in AD 140; it was restored for the first modern Olympics in 1896 and will be used again in 2004 for the last lap of the marathon. West of the stadium lies **Mets**, a neighbourhood popular with artists and media folk, with some fine old houses and tavernas.

East of Sýntagma Square

The Benáki Museum

t 210 367 1000; open Mon, Wed, Fri and Sat 9–5, Thurs 9–midnight, Sun 9–3; adm; book ahead for lunch or the Thurs night buffet at the popular café.

Another main artery, Leofóros Vass. Sofías, begins next to the Parliament and heads east, passing ministries, embassies and the excellent **Benáki Museum**, at the corner of Koumbári St. Antónios Benáki, born in 1873 into a prominent family in Alexandria, spent 35 years amassing Byzantine and Islamic treasures, and in 1930 was the first individual in Greece to open a museum, here in his beautiful neoclassical mansion. Hundreds of donors since have made this the best place in Athens for an overview of Greek civilization, beginning with Cycladic figurines, Minoan, Mycenaean, and Cypriot Bronze Age ceramics, Early Helladic gold cups, Mycenaean jewellery from Thebes and a lovely gold kylix decorated with running dogs from Dendrá. Next come fine Archaic and Classical sculpture and vases and some exceptional Hellenistic and Roman artefacts, including the intricate gold jewellery of the 'Thessaly Treasure'. The Christians follow, with 3rd-century El Fayyum portraits, 6th-century Coptic textiles, Byzantine earrings (that match those worn by the Empress Theodora in the mosaics at Ravenna), frescoes, illuminated manuscripts, and a superb collection of icons, including two painted by El Greco before he left Crete. A Florentine Madonna attributed to Nicoló di Pietro Gerini keeps them company; some icons show how close the Greeks themselves came to adopting the Renaissance before the Turkish conquest.

The first floor offers an overview of what the Greeks were up to under the Ottomans. There's a superb collection of costumes, jewellery, painted wooden chests, religious items, ceramics and embroideries, including a spectacular silk embroidered *spervéri* (a tent hung over the matrimonial bed) made on Rhodes. Among the marble reliefs, don't miss the one showing Constantine the Great amid trophies of Greek victories. There's a reconstructed traditional room from the plate-collecting mad island of Skýros, and two exquisite 18th-century rooms from a wealthy merchant's mansion in Kozáni, full of intricate carvings and painted decoration. Rooms 22 and 23 contain items made by visitors to Greece, including two pretty watercolours by Edward Lear. The second floor has a large room for special exhibits (which are usually excellent), folk pieces and items from the pre-War of Independence period.

The third floor covers modern Greece, from 1821 to the present: here you'll find Alí Pasha's silver and gold rifle (a gift from Britain's George IV); Byron's portable desk (the size of a laptop computer); the original score to Dionýssios Solomós' *Hymn to Freedom*, the Greek national anthem; the swords, flags and portraits of the Greek heroes; and 32 lithographs by Peter von Hess on the *Liberation of Greece*, all that survives of the murals commissioned by Ludwig I in the (now destroyed) Royal Palace in Munich. Other exhibits include the court dress of his son King Otto, memorabilia and photos of Venizélos, Cavafy's notebook, manuscripts and first editions, and the Nobel Prizes won by George Seféris (1963) and Odysséas Elýtis (1979), and the Lenin Prize won by Iánnis Rítsos in 1977.

Kolonáki and Lykavitós

Koumbári Street, next to the Benáki Museum, leads up a block to **Kolonáki Square**, Athens' Knightsbridge in miniature, complete with fancypants shops, upmarket restaurants, big cafés, the British Council and plenty of 'Kolonáki Greeks' – Athenian Sloane Rangers – to patronize them. Above **Plateía Dexamení**, the Roman aqueduct ended in a reservoir; in 1840 it was rebuilt, and still serves the city. From here, two flights of stairs lead up to the funicular at the corner of Aristippoú and Ploutarchoúis, which every 10 minutes ascends the city's highest hill, **Lykavitós** (Lycabettos), 980ft and illuminated like a fairytale tower at night. The summit offers a 360 degree view over greater Athens; here too is the white 19th-century chapel of **Ag. Geórgios**, a restaurant/bar, a lovely outdoor theatre and a cannon fired on national holidays.

Besides boutiques, Kolonáki has more museums, beginning with the sleek **Goulandrís Museum of Cycladic and Ancient Greek Art**, two blocks east of the Benáki Museum at 4 Neofýtou Doúka Street (*t 210 722 8321; open Mon and Wed–Fri 10–4, Sat 10–3, closed Sun and Tues; adm*). The collection of Cycladic art (3200–2000 BC) rivals that of the National Museum: a beautiful display of some 300 white marble statuettes as they evolved from the earliest abstract violin-shapes. Although most are female, the delightful Toastmaster who has been raising his glass now for *c.* 4,500 years steals the show. The second and fourth floors have a choice collection of art from Mycenaean to early Christian times: well preserved Corinthian helmets offered to Zeus at Olympia and exquisite vases. A glass corridor leads to the lovely **Stathátos Mansion**, designed by Ernst Ziller, now used for temporary exhibits.

Near here, a French philhellene, Sophie de Marbois the Duchesse de Plaisance, had her beautiful Villa Ilissia (1848, by Stamátis Kléanthes) on the once idyllic banks of the Ilissos. Even the river is now underground, but the villa now houses the **Byzantine Museum**, at 22 Vass. Sofías (*t 210 721 1027; open Tues–Sun 8.30–3; adm*), the most important collection in the country – not only icons but marble sculptures, mosaics, woodcarvings, frescoes, manuscripts, ecclesiastical robes, the 7th-century Mytilíni treasure, and some exquisite pieces from Constantinople brought over by refugees in 1922. Two rooms on the ground floor are arranged as chapels: one Early Christian (note the 4th-century statue of Orpheus as Christ, from Aegina) and another Middle Byzantine. The icons include the superb 14th-century *Crucifixion* from the church of Elkómenos in Monemvasiá. A new extension under the museum will be linked to the recently excavated **Lyceum**, where Aristotle, angry after failing to become Plato's successor at the Academy, set up his own school.

Just down Vass. Sofías, at the corner of Rizári Street, fighter planes mark the modern **War Museum of Greece** (*t 210 723 9560; open Tues–Fri 9–2; free*), containing weapons and battle relics from earliest times to Greece's expeditionary force in the Korean War; there's a display on the ancient beacons that just may have informed Mycenae that Troy had fallen. Opposite is the British Embassy, and next to that **Evangelismós Park**, with a useful metro; the British and American archaeological schools are above this and, at the top, the impressive neoclassical **Gennadeion Library**, one of the city's best; cases along the walls have assorted treasures, including a lock of Byron's hair.

National Gallery

t 210 723 5857; open Mon–Sat 9–3 exc Tues; Sun 10–2; Mon and Wed also 6–9pm; adm exp.

From the war museum, Vass. Sofías continues to Rizári Park, unmissable for its huge statue of *The Runner* by Kóstas Varotsos; turn right here for the National Gallery at 50 Vass. Konstantínou, across from the Hilton Hotel. The ground floor has the oldest works, among them three by El Greco from his Toledo days (the *Concert of Angels*, *St Peter* and the recently acquired *Burial of Christ*), and works painted by Greeks on the Ionian islands during Turkish rule. After independence, many Greek painters went to Munich for training and, in the polished academic style, the 'Munich school' supplied the portraits, charming genre scenes, landscapes and romantic views of the east demanded by the bourgeoisie: see Nikólaos Gýzis (*The Engagement*), Geórgios Lakovídis (*Children's Concert*) and Nikifóros Lýstras (*The Kiss*). Western artists are represented, too, among them Delacroix's *Greek Rider* and Lorenzo Veneziano's *Crucifixion*. The upper floor is dedicated to the 20th century, when attempts were made to found a national school, led by Konstantínos Parthénis (*Athanássios Diákos*). But most artists went their own way: Níkos Hadzikyriákos-Ghíkas, internationally the best known Greek painter, was influenced by Cubism, while others drew their inspiration from traditional folk themes and fairytales (Iánnis Tsaroúchis and Theóphilos Hadzimichaíl), Giórgos Gounarópolous (the Greek Odilon Redon), or from the surrealists (Níkos Egonópoulos). The last permanent section of the gallery contains postwar works by Iánnis Móralis and Spýros Vasilío, as well as changing exhibitions.

To Moní Kessarianí and Mount Ymittós

South of the National Gallery lies the essential Athenian neighbourhood of **Pangráti**, a good place to get a feel for everyday life in Athens. To escape the city altogether, take bus 224 from Akademías St (or from Vas. Sofías, by the National Gardens) up the long hump-back slopes of **Mount Ymittós** (Hymettos), where fragrant shrubs produce a honey famous since antiquity for increasing longevity. The bus leaves you a 1.5km walk from the 11th-century **Moní Kaisarianí** (*t 210 723 6619; open Tues–Sun 8.30–3; adm*), built over an ancient sanctuary at the source of the Ilissos. The oldest Byzantine baths in Greece remain visible through a grille (they were later used as an olive press) and the pretty stone church contains early 18th-century frescoes inspired by the Cretan school. The monastery was abandoned in the late 18th century; during the War of Independence the Turks took its once famous library to the Acropolis to use the paper for cartridges. In the last war, the Germans used this remote corner to execute hostages; now there are picnic tables and the lovely groves planted by the Athens Tree Society. A Roman ram's mouth fountain in the outer wall still gushes out water, and two minutes above the monastery a cistern by a cave holds the **Kallopoúla spring**, whose waters in ancient times were considered sovereign against sterility, while a bit further up, by the ruins of a Paleochristian basilica and Frankish church, is a superb viewpoint over Athens, stretching as far as the Peloponnese on a clear day.

Into the Northern Suburbs

Beyond the museums, Leofóros Vass. Sofías continues past the **Mégaro Mousikís** concert hall (1992) with its nearly perfect acoustics, and then the US Embassy and the big crossroads at **Ambelókipi**. To the left, Leofóros Kifissiás heads north towards **Maroússi**, a pleasant suburb famous for its clay and pottery, where the 78,000-seat **Olympic Stadium** (Ⓜ Iríni) was built in 1982, in anticipation of the 1996 games which ended up in Atlanta. It will have a new look for 2004, with ponds to keep temperatures cool and a roof designed by the great Spanish engineer Santiago Calatrava, made of strands of translucent glass to admit light but not the heat. Don't look for any giants – Henry Miller's 'Colossus' was a real man, the unforgettable Katsímbalis – but you may want to seek out the **Spathario Shadow Theatre Museum**, in Kastalías Square (*t 210 612 7245; open Mon–Fri 10–1.30; free*), a puppeteer's collection dedicated to the art that the Greeks know by its lead character, Karaghiózis, the 'black eyed', who came to them by way of the Turks, who came to *them* by way of 14th-century Arab merchants, who saw the shadow puppet plays in Java.

Further north, at the terminus of the metro, is **Kifissiá**, a wooded suburb under the slopes of Mt Pendéli favoured by the elite ever since the fabulously wealthy Herodes Atticus built his villa here. The **Goulandrís Natural History Museum**, 13 Levídou (*t 210 801 5870; open Sat–Thurs 9–2.30; adm*), has won awards for its displays related to Greece and the rest of the world (with explanations in English). From Kifissiá, bus 536 continues to the piney mountain resort of **Diónysos** on a spur of Mt Pendéli. This was the ancient Ikaria, where a local farmer, Ikarios, gave hospitality to Dionysos, who in return taught him how to make wine. But when Ikarios gave some to his neighbours, they killed him, thinking he was trying to poison them.

Back at Ambelókipi, a right on Leofóros Mesogion leads to **Chalandrí** and the other suburbs towards the aiport. Near here is **Moní Pendéli**, one of the biggest and wealthiest monasteries in Greece (*bus 450 from the 'Pinakothíkis' stop in front of the National Gallery to Plateia Chalandrí, and from there bus 426, 423, or the 451*). Founded in 1578, in a lovely wooded setting on Mount Pendéli, this is a popular weekend retreat, where families eat in the tavernas under a gargantuan plane tree. The monastery is near the Gothic **Rododafnis Palace**, built for the Duchesse de Plaisance; it was later converted into a royal palace, and is now used for summer concerts. Above the monastery (ask for directions) are the **ancient quarries** that yielded the famous gold tinted marble for the Parthenon; the cut blocks were sent on wooden sledges down paved paths, a few of which can still be seen. Pausanias described a large statue of Athena who once looked down on her city; she has since been replaced by a forest of masts and radar towers.

Other Sites around Athens

Plato's Academy (Akadimías Plátonos) was in a sacred wood, west of Laríssa station on a spot identified in 1966 by a boundary marker. The philosophizing here may have changed the world, but the archaeologists have yet to find anything worth seeing. There are plans to build a museum here to hold the best of the 30,000 finds discovered while digging the metro lines.

Railway Museum, 301 Liossíon Sl, Serpólia (*t 210 524 6580; open Wed 5–8pm, Fri–Sun 10–1; free*). A depot houses Greece's retired iron-horses, including the original Diakoftó-Kalávryta train and the fancy wagons made for George I and the Empress Eugénie.

Foundation of the Hellenic World, 254 Pireós St in Távros, midway to Piraeus (*take bus 149 or 914, or a cab; t 210 483 5300, www.fhw.gr; open Mon, Tues, Thurs and Fri 9–2, Wed 9am–9pm, Sun 10–3, closed Sat; adm*). An industrial complex, now used for a slick virtual reality tour of Greek civilization; their website offers a tour of Greek history.

Pierídis Museum of Ancient Cypriot Art, 34–36 Kastoriás, in the western suburb of Votanikós (*t 210 348 0000; open daily 10.30am–10.30pm; adm*). A factory converted to hold the Pierídis Foundation's important collection from prehistoric to Classical times.

Piraeus (ΠΕΙΡΑΙΑΣ / Πειραιασ)

Themistocles made Piraeus – pronounced 'pi-ray-A' – Athens' chief port in 479 BC when Fáliron could no longer meet the needs of the city. He defended its three harbours with bastions even higher than those around the Acropolis and left plans for the Long Walls (completed under Pericles) that formed a 7km corridor to Athens – lines followed today by the metro tracks and Leofóro Pireós. Pericles also hired the geometer Hippodamos of Miletus, a proto-hippie with long hair and outlandish dress, to lay out the city, which still follows his grid plan. But unlike modern grids, Hippodamos' was not designed to make land easy to parcel out and sell, but to promote equality among citizens and, for a while at least, he succeeded. All religions were tolerated in Piraeus, and women were allowed for the first time to work outside the home. Hippodamos also designed a huge *agora* in the middle, where the world's first commercial fairs and international trade exhibitions were held. Hundreds of shipsheds lined the harbours, each capable of sheltering two triremes in winter, and near Zéa Marína stood the huge *Skeuotheke*, an arsenal capable of holding the riggings and weapons for a thousand triremes (its specifications, engraved in stone, are in the Epigraphic Museum).

In 404 BC, at the end of the Peloponnesian War, the Spartans destroyed all Piraeus' fortifications. The port made a come-back under Admiral Konon, who rebuilt the walls you see today. They weren't good enough to keep out Sulla, who decimated the city in 88 BC, nor Alaric, who sacked it in AD 396. For 1,900 years Piraeus dwindled away, with a population as low as 20, even losing its name to become Porto Leone (after an ancient lion statue, carved in 1040 with runes by Harald Hadraada and his Vikings, that was later carted off by Morosini to embellish Venice's Arsenal). As port to the capital, Piraeus has regained its former glory, although much of it dates from after 1941, when German bombers hit a ship in the port loaded with TNT.

While its tall grey buildings and hurly-burly may not win you over at first glance, in a country that derives most of its livelihood from the sea, Piraeus is the true capital (and the third city in Greece, with 480,000 people) while Athens is a sprawling suburb where the bureaucrats live. It has a buzz, and excellent seafood, good museums and some interesting corners in between. Another thing to do in Piraeus: try *not* to think of the song from *Never on Sunday*, which was filmed here in 1960.

Three Harbours, Two Museums, and the Acropolis

The **main harbour** of Piraeus was known in ancient times as the Kantharos or 'goblet' for its shape, and this busy sheet of water, the metro and the ticket agencies

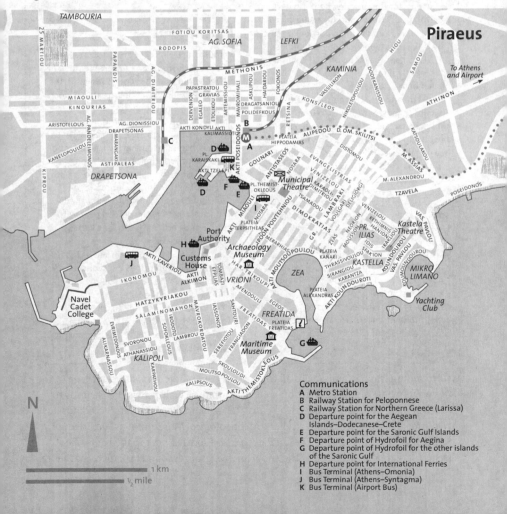

Communications
A Metro Station
B Railway Station for Peloponnese
C Railway Station for Northern Greece (Larissa)
D Departure point for the Aegean Islands–Dodecanese–Crete
E Departure point for the Saronic Gulf Islands
F Departure point of Hydrofoil for Aegina
G Departure point of Hydrofoil for the other islands of the Saronic Gulf
H Departure point for International Ferries
I Bus Terminal (Athens–Omonia)
J Bus Terminal (Athens–Syntagma)
K Bus Terminal (Airport Bus)

Getting Around

By sea: Piraeus is the main launchpad for Crete, the Cyclades, the Dodecanese, the nearby Saronic islands (see p.143), the eastern Peloponnese and most of the North Aegean islands; see the map for points of departure. The cluster of ticket agents around the port is very competitive, but prices are fixed, so the only reason to shop around is to see if there is an earlier or faster ship to your destination. For non-biased schedules call the **Piraeus port authority**, t 210 422 6000/210 459 3000 or **tourist information**, t 171. There are two **hydrofoil** companies with departures from Zéa Marína: **Minoan**, for the Saronic Islands, the Peloponnese and Crete, t 210 408 0006 and 210 324 4600; and **Ellas Flying Dolphins**, with departures for the Cyclades, t 210 419 9200 or t 210 419 9000. Note that only hydrofoils for Aegina leave from the main port of Piraeus.

By train: the station for the Peloponnese (ΣΠΑΠ) is near the metro on Aktí Kalimassióti. The station for northern Greece (ΟΣΕ) lies further on Aktí Kondíli.

By metro and bus: the metro is the quickest way into Athens, or take bus 40 from Plateía Karaiskáki, by the main harbour, which runs 24 hours to Filellínon St. The E96 to the airport (see p.104) leaves from the same square. For Zéa Marína, catch bus 904 outside the metro station. It continues around the peninsula (or Akte) including Aktí Themistokléous.

Where to Stay

Cavo d'Oro, 19 Vass. Pávlou (above Mikrolímano), t 210 411 3744, f 210 412 2210 (luxury). The swishest choice in Piraeus, with a restaurant and disco.

Kastella, 75 Vass. Pávlou, t 210 411 4735, f 210 417 5716 (luxury). A nice place above the waterfront, with a roof garden.

Mistral, Vass. Pávlou 105, t 210 411 7150, f 210 412 2096 (expensive). Comes with a pool, restaurant and air-conditioning.

Triton, 8 Tsamadou, t 210 417 3457, f 210 417 7888 (expensive). One of the best of the many in the area, if you want to be within walking distance of the docks.

Lilia, 131 Zéas, Passalimáni, t 210 417 9108, f 210 411 4311 (moderate). The pleasant owners offer free transport to the port.

Ideal, 142 Notára (50m from the customs house), t 210 429 4050, f 210 429 3890 (moderate). Offers air-conditioned rooms, but should be renamed the So-So.

Achillion, 63 Notára, t 210 412 4029 (inexpensive). Some rooms are en suite.

Glaros, 4 Hariláou Trikoúpi (near the customs house), t 210 452 5421 (inexpensive).

Eating Out

Varoúlko, 14 Deligorgi, t 210 411 2043 (€35–44). Some of the most imaginative seafood in Greece, but ring ahead, as it moves in the summer and renovations are in the works. Open eves only; closed Sun.

Jimmy the Fish, 46 Aktí Koumoundoúrou in Mikrolímano, t 210 412 4417 (€24–29). Great salads, octopus, spaghetti with lobster, or the fish of your choice, perfectly prepared.

Archaion Gefsis, 10 Epidavrou, t 210 413 8617, right off Aktí Koumoundoúrou (€20–24). Ancient Greek recipes in a unabashedly kitsch setting: try the puréed peas with garlic and cuttlefish with pine kernels. No forks allowed.

Margaró, 126 Hatzikyriákou, t 210 451 4226 (€14–17). Unpretentious but wonderful fish taverna near the naval academy; it attracts both locals and the élite.

Nine Brothers (Ennea Adélfi), 48 Sotiros (behind Plateía Kanári at Zéa Marina), t 210 411 5273 (about €9). Popular taverna with lots of locals, and a big choice.

surrounding Plateía Karaiskaki is all that 99 per cent of foreign visitors ever see of the town. From here it's only a short bus ride or 20-minute walk across the isthmus to much smaller **Zéa Marina** where you can catch a hydrofoil to the Saronic islands. Just two streets in from Zéa is the excellent **Archaeological Museum**, at 31 Har. Trikoúpi Street (t 210 452 1598; open Tues–Sun 8–2.30; adm), located next to the ruins of a Hellenistic theatre. The stars of the show are five bronzes found by Piraeus' cathedral in 1959, including a majestic *Artemis* and *Athena*, and an exquisite *kouros*, the *Apollo of Piraeus*, the oldest known Greek hollow-cast bronze statue (*c.* 500 BC). The grave stele of Pancharis is exceptional, standing over 11ft high, although it's dwarfed by the 24ft **Monument of Nikeratos** (325 BC), the largest funerary monument ever found in Greece. Nikeratos and his son were *metics* (foreign residents), many of whom were merchants and formed the bulk of Piraeus' population. It was nouveau-riche piles like this, however, that led to a law banning monster monuments a few years later.

The **Naval Museum of Greece** is a few blocks down Aktí Themistokléous, by Plateía Freatída – look for the ships' guns and torpedos in the garden (*t 210 451 6264; open Tues–Sun 9–2; adm*). Built around a section of ancient walls, the museum has plans of Greece's greatest naval battles, a model of the triremes used at Sálamis and a host of maritime mementoes. Don't miss the exquisite tiny ships made of bone by French prisoners in England during the Napoleonic Wars, which Aristotle Onassis used to keep on his yacht *Christina*.

Heading in the other direction (east), Thrasyvoulou Street leads directly to lofty **Kastélla**, the ancient acropolis, where the terrace of the Bowling Club café has gorgeous views over the city and coast. Snug in a pretty amphitheatre below, **Mikrolímano** is a nearly perfectly round harbour filled with yachts and fish restaurants. The landmark on the reclaimed land east of Piraeus at **Paléo Falíro** (Athens' original port) is hard to miss because of the dramatic ship-shaped **Peace and Friendship Stadium** (1985), used for basketball games and concerts.

Islands in the Saronic Gulf

Set in the fast lane between Athens and the Peloponnese, the five islands in the Saronic Gulf have played a disproportionate role in Greek history. Ancient Aegina was one of the most powerful maritime states in Greece, a rival to Athens itself; Póros was the holy island of Poseidon; Sálamis witnessed a famous sea battle; and Hýdra and Spétses led the Greek fleets in the War of Independence. A hundred years ago the Saronics also became the first holiday islands, when fashionable Athenians hired summer villas while father commuted over at weekends. Although modern Sálamis is mainly for connoisseurs of the Greece of 50 years ago, Aegina has all the necessary island ingredients, from a beautiful ancient temple to long sandy beaches; Póros on its 'Grand Canal' has a lovely town and easy access to the famous sights of Argolis; spectacular Hýdra has become the 'St-Tropez of Greece', and charming wooded Spétses is trendy too, but in a much quieter way.

Salamína/Sálamis (ΣΑΛΑΜΙΝΑ)

Soaking in the same bathwater as Piraeus, Sálamis (usually Salamína) is at once the most suburban and Greek of all the islands, in a gritty, authentic way that only those who know and love Greece can savour, almost as a reaction to the overpowering beauty that reigns on the other islands. The southeast coast is the prettiest part of

Getting There and Around

Car **ferry** every 15mins from Pérama (bus 843 from the metro in Piraeus) to Paloúkia and at least five a day from Piraeus; also from Megálo Péfko (by Mégara) to Pérama (the port on Salamína). The villages are connected by an efficient **bus** system, t 210 465 0803. **Port authority**: t 210 465 3252.

Where to Stay

Salamína ✉ 18900

The few hotels here are simple and 'ethnic'.

Gabriel Hotel, in Eántion, t 210 466 2223, f 210 466 2275 (*C; moderate*). The best on the island. *Open April–Sept.*

Votsalakia, 64 Themistokléous, in Selínia, t 210 467 1432 or 210 467 1334 (*D; inexpensive*). *Open all year.*

Akroyali, 92 Themistokléous, in Selínia, t 210 467 3263 (*D; inexpensive*). For the same price, and also *open all year.*

Eating Out

Because Salamína gets few foreign tourists, its tavernas are pure Greek and the food inexpensive. Seafood such as crayfish, octopus and squid are especially good – some people say it is the best place in Greece for an ouzo with octopus.

Ali, just out of Salamína town at 301 Leof. Aianteíou, t 210 465 3586. Plain and simple interior, but serving excellent Arabic specialities, besides the usual Greek fare. Wonderful kebabs.

O Christos, out of town at Resti, t 210 468 2536. Above the tiny but clean beach, with lovely view, excellent food and low prices.

Skerlou, next to the park in Paloúkia, t 210 467 7144. Hidden behind the oleanders, covering all options as a fish taverna, café, *mezé* spot and pub, run by eccentric ladies.

Vassiliou, in Selínia, t 210 467 1625. An island institution; good family-run taverna right by the water's edge, dishing up superb squid and other seafood.

the island, with its pine forests and beaches, although they are only accessible by car. Moúlki, also called Eántion, and Selínia are seaside villages, popular weekend retreats for working families from Athens and Piraeus. Salamína's weird geography and dearth of signposting means visitors with a car usually get to see every square inch of the island, whether they want to or not.

History

When the sons of King Aeacus of Aegina, Telemon and Peleus, slew their brother Phocos, Telemon fled to Salamína, where Kychreus, a shadowy character who started out as the snake in Eleusis, was king. Telemon married Kychreus' daughter to become king and fathered the great Ajax of the Trojan War. When Mégara and Athens quarrelled over Salamína, Solon visited the tomb of Kychreus to invoke his aid in the dispute, which Athens won; further evidence of his pro-Athens position was provided during the Battle of Sálamis, when the Athenians saw Kychreus appear in the form of a sea serpent to spur them on.

Salamína wasn't entirely unprepared in September of 480 BC, when Xerxes himself led the Persian fleet to conquer Greece. Athens had fortified the island's weak places, and manned them with the elderly and exiles – hurriedly recalled. After inconclusively challenging the Persian fleet at Artemission north of Évia, Athens and her allies fell back to Sálamis to join the reserves at the three ports facing Pérama. They could see the smoke rising from the Acropolis, put to the sack by the Persians. News came that the Persians would soon be advancing to the Isthmus of Corinth, and the Corinthians and Spartans were keen to abandon Athens to defend their homes. Themistocles had to resort to bribes and threats to keep them. But he was tricky, too, and sent a secret letter to Xerxes saying that the Greeks were in disarray, and about to sail home, and that the Persians could capture the whole Greek fleet if they blocked the narrow straits to the east and west of Sálamis. Xerxes fell for it hook, line and sinker. He ordered his fleet to divide and block the straits at night. But Themistocles had been warned, and careful plans were laid. At dawn half of the Greek fleet in the east pretended to flee north. The Persian commander at once gave the order to advance, and as they did the Greeks spun their triremes around and reversed in a great crescent, luring the Persians ahead, before suddenly attacking. The Persian commander was killed almost at once. After that no one was in charge, and no one could stop the momentum of the Persian ships advancing into the narrow strait where they couldn't manoeuvre, creating a log jam at the mercy of the crack fleet from Aegina, which had lain in wait. Xerxes watched in agony; the Persians managed to create a diversion to escape with their last 300 ships. As for Salamína, it gave birth to Euripides (*see* below) the very same year of the great victory, then fell back into obscurity.

Around Salamína

Salamína, the metropolis of the island, is also known as Kouloúri ('crescent') for its leisurely curl around its harbour, with numerous cafés and tavernas. A new **Museum of Folk Art**, in the town hall, at 1 Konstantínou Karamanlís (*t 210 465 4180; open Mon–Fri 8–2.30; free*), has traditional costumes and dolls, ships' models and sea paintings by naïf artist Aristídis Glýkas. From Kouloúri a bus leaves every hour for the convent of **Faneroméni**, built in 1661 on the foundation of an ancient temple. The church (*open 7–12 and 3–7.30; dress appropriately – no shorts*) is decorated with fine frescoes (all much in need of a clean), including an extraordinary *Last Judgement* containing over 3,000 figures painted in 1735 by Argítis Márkos. Above, on **Mount Pátsi**, the island's highest point, are the remains of ancient fire towers – perhaps the same that relayed the news across the Aegean that the Persians were on their way.

Six kilometres south of Kouloúri is the pleasant village of Moulki (or Eántion), set in the pines, with a nice pebble beach and plenty of weekend cottages. Ruins found at Kolonés, or 'the columns', are believed to belong to the city of Ajax Telamonios. From Moulki a bus goes to **Kakí Vígla**, a pleasant cove with a handful of tavernas, and a rough road leads south to **Ag. Nikólaos**, an abandoned monastery with a 15th-century chapel, decorated with 12th-century marble reliefs and plates from Rhodes; it also holds the island's **archaeology collection** (*t 210 465 3572; open 9–1*). Between Ag. Nikólaos and Kakí Vígla you'll find sandy beaches, especially at **Peristéria**, site of the **Cave of Euripides** (keep your eyes peeled for an obscure signpost: the path begins at the top of the dirt road). Euripides came here to write, far from the Athenian élites and rabble he detested, and they in turn detested him even while they hung on his words, hounding him and even beating him up, until he took refuge in Macedonia, where he died in 406 BC. They missed him and his plays soon enough – the playwright Philemon wrote: 'If I were certain that the dead had consciousness, I would hang myself to see Euripides' – and his cave became a tourist attraction into Roman times. Neolithic finds and votive offerings suggest that it was the lair of Kychreus the man-snake. But the most amazing find was a wine cup with Euripides' name on it, left behind 2,385 years ago.

On the east coast of Salamína, **Paloúkia** is a ferry-boat landing stage from Pérama. South of Paloúkia woebegone **Ambelákia** was the harbour of ancient Salamína that featured so prominently in the big battle. The mole and other harbour installations are visible in the shallows, but little else – it's now a smelly ships' rubbish dump. **Selínia**, a few kilometres south of Ambelákia, is a collection of summerhouses, although the beach is nothing special.

Aegina (ΑΙΓΙΝΑ)

Connections between Aegina (pronounced 'EGG-ee-na') and Piraeus are so frequent that some residents commute to work. But Aegina is no bedroom suburb, and in spite of the demands of tourism the islanders have maintained their traditional fishing fleet and pistachio groves. Aegina has a few beaches that are often packed, pretty countryside, a clutch of fine Byzantine churches and the best-preserved ancient temple on any Greek island. Just try to steer clear of summer weekends, when half of Athens descends on it.

History

Aegina was a prosperous place early on, with a major Early Helladic settlement and a precocious trading network even in the Dark Ages; in 650 BC it was the first in Europe to mint coins, which led to the creation of Europe's first banking system. Trade, thanks to a powerful fleet and exports of perfumes and pottery, made Aegina's oligarchs fat. But the island was far too close to Athens to last. In 490 BC it had sided with Persia, one of its main trading partners, until the Athenians kidnapped several prominent citizens and held them hostage. In 480, Aegina had a change of heart and sent 30 ships to help Athens, and at the Battle of Sálamis the heroism of its sailors won it the first choice of the spoils. The rivalry with Athens soon heated up again; in 458 BC Kimon captured the island. When the Peloponnesian War broke out, Athens deported the entire population; the islanders were welcomed by Sparta and later returned to their homes by Lysander.

In the 1820s, Aegina was one of the first places to be liberated from the Turks, and from 1826–28 it served as capital of Greece under president Capodístria. Fittingly the first modern drachma, bearing a phoenix rising from the ashes, was minted on the island; Aegina also had the state's first newspaper and first prison.

Aegina Town

Aegina Town, the capital and chief port, retains a whiff of grandeur from its days as capital, even if many of the 19th-century buildings are half-hidden behind shops touting Aegina's pottery and pistachios. Horse-drawn carriages wait for customers along a grand crescent harbour and mole, built in 1826 thanks to American Samuel Greenly Howe, a 27-year-old surgeon and husband of Julia, author of *The Battle Hymn*

Getting There and Around

Hourly **hydrofoil** (35mins) until late afternoon, or by boat (1–1½hrs) from Piraeus; frequent connections with Méthana and other Saronic islands, and two to three times a week with Epídavros. **Ferries** go to Aegina Town or to Ag. Marína; some call at Souvala. **Port authority**: t 229 702 2328.

Buses from Aegina Town (t 229 702 2787) depart from Plateía Ethneyersías near the quay and run to most villages, including to Ag. Marína via the Temple of Aphaia and the Nektários Monastery.

Tourist Information

Tourist police: Aegina Town, t 229 702 7777; *open all year.*

Where to Stay and Eat

Aegina Town ✉ 18010

In Aegina Town most of the accommodation is on the old side, and there are many relatively inexpensive places to stay (at least for such a popular island).
Egintiko Archontiko, t/f 229 702 4968 (*A; expensive*). Offers style in a renovated, converted 19th-century mansion, with air-conditioned rooms. *Open all year.*
Danae, t 229 702 2424, f 229 702 6509 (*B; expensive–moderate*). 20m from the sea, with many rooms and restaurant terrace overlooking a small kidney-shaped pool.
Pavlou, 21 P. Aeginitou, t 229 702 2795 (*C; moderate*). Comfortable places, a block from the waterfront. *Open all year.*
Plaza, at Kolóna, near the temple of Apollo, t 229 702 5600 (*E; inexpensive*). Pleasant and friendly, overlooking the line of fish tavernas next to the sea.

Finikas tou Lira, three blocks in, behind the Ionian Bank, t 229 702 4439. Taverna in a lovely garden setting, specializing in *mezédes.*
Bakaliarakia, south of town at Fáros. A little more expensive but serving top quality fish and lamb from the spit, with live Greek music after 10pm on Fri and Sat.
Vatzoulia's. Many locals like to hop in a taxi and eat out of town, and this place, en route to the Temple of Aphaia, is especially popular and lively. Excellent Greek food often accompanied by music. *Open only Wed and weekend eves.*

Ag. Marína ✉ 18010

Apollo, by the sea, t 229 703 2271, f 229 703 2688 (*B; expensive–moderate*). One of the quieter hotels, offering a seawater pool, tennis, and a big American-style buffet breakfast.
Galini, set in a garden 3mins from the centre of the action, t 229 703 2203, f 229 703 2216 (*C; moderate*). Panoramic pool and a decent restaurant.
Piccadilly, t 229 703 2696 (*C; moderate*). Comfortable and right on the beach; most rooms have sea views.
Tholos, t 229 703 2129. Family-run taverna with good home-cooked vegetable and meat dishes, and a view of Ag. Marina thrown in.

Pérdika/Marathónas ✉ 18010

Moondy Bay Bungalows, at Profítis Ilías, a few kilometres north of Pérdika, t 229 706 1622, f 229 706 1147 (*B; expensive*). The cushiest place to stay on Aegina, in a well-tended garden by the sea, with pool, tennis, cycling and more; book. *Open June–Oct.*
Sissy, at Marathónas, t 229 702 6222, f 229 702 6252 (*D; inexpensive*). Pleasant and includes breakfast in its room rates.
S. Stratigos, on Aiginitissa beach. Delicious grilled meat and fish in the €15 range.

of the Republic. Inspired by Byron, Howe fought in the War of Independence and later led a massive American-funded relief campaign for Aegina that employed 700 locals and refugees in public works. The first Greek government building was the medieval **Tower of Márkellos**, near Ag. Nikólaos church. It is austere, as was the hastily erected **Residence** (now the public library) on Kyvernéou Street. Capodístria, the dapper count from Corfu, slept in his office upstairs, above the national mint.

Ancient writers often referred to Aegina's 'secret port' just north of of the city – only the islanders knew the entrance. It has a pleasant little sandy beach, and overlooking it, on the hillock of **Kolóna** (*open Tues–Sun 8.30–3; adm*), is the site of a major Early Helladic settlement (2400 BC). A road and jumbly walls and a lonely Doric column from a 5th-century **Temple of Apollo** remain; the rest of the stone, with Capodístria's consent, went into building Aegina's quay. Graves here yielded the British Museum's fabulous 'Aegina Treasure' of Minoan gold, plundered by ancient robbers from Mália (*see* pp.724–5). Nearby, the **Archaeological Museum** (*t 229 702 2248; open Tues–Sun 8.30–3; adm*) replaces the first archaeology museum in Greece (1829). Items attest to Aegina's early importance: prehistoric pottery, some decorated with Early Helladic naval scenes, and vivid Archaic ceramics, including the 7th-century 'ram jug' showing Odysseus hiding to escape Polyphemus. There are 6th-century pediments from two temples; a Classical marble sphinx attributed to Calamis; fragments from the temple of Aphaia and a mosaic from an ancient synagogue.

From Kolóna, a 15-minute walk takes you to the suburbs of **Livádi** and **Plakákia**, where a plaque marks the house where Kazantzákis wrote *Zorba the Greek*. Plakákia was something of an artists' and writers' colony: the **Museum Chrístos Kaprálos** (*t 229 702 2001; open July–Oct 10–1 and 6–8, other times Fri, Sat and Sun 10–2; adm*) occupies the workshop used by the sculptor from 1963–93 and contains his most important work: the *Battle of Pindus*, a monumental limestone relief on 20th-century Greek history. If you've hired a bike, the road skirting the north coast is an easy pedal, with swimming possibilities at the rocky beaches of Leónti, and at **Souvála**, a modest resort, which lured the island's first visitors decades ago with radioactive baths.

Paleochóra and Ag. Nektários

The bus to Ag. Marína passes by the Temple of Aphaia, but most Greek visitors pile out earlier, at the **monastery of Ag. Nektários**, built by and named for the former archbishop of Libya, who died here in 1920 and was canonized in 1967 – one of the last saints to join Orthodoxy's inner circle. You can see his crowned skull in his unfinished garish blood orange church, which is claimed to be the largest in Greece. Even so, it's not big enough on 9 November, when pilgrims come for the last great outdoor festival of the Greek calendar.

If you're not in need of Nektários' services, consider climbing up to the crumbling ghost town of **Paleochóra**, just behind the monastery (*visit in the morning, when the caretaker is usually around with the keys – wear good walking shoes*). Founded in what seemed to be a safe inland location in the 9th century, Paleochóra twice proved vulnerable: Barbarossa slaughtered the men and carried off the women and children in 1538 and Morosini pummelled it in his siege of 1654. Some 28 churches still stand, many sheltering 13th-century frescoes; among the best are the **Basilica of Ag. Anárgyroi**, the **Chapel of Taxiárchis**, and the **Cathedral of the Episkopí**. Looming over all is Morosini's dilapidated **Venetian castle**.

An hour's walk south of Ag. Nektários leads to the **convent of Chrysoleóntissa** (1600) with an lovely iconostasis and a rain-making icon of the Virgin (a job once held on Aegina by Zeus). The hospitable nuns are known for the produce from their farm.

The Temple of Aphaia and Ag. Marína

East of Ag. Nektários, the road passes near the pretty village of **Mesagrós**, which is surrounded by the vineyards and pines that combine to make an excellent retsina. On a hill above stands Aegina's pride and joy, the beautiful Doric **Temple of Aphaia** (*t 229 703 2398; open Mon–Fri 8–5, Sat–Sun 8.30–3; adm*), built in the early 5th century BC. Aphaia was the name of the Great Goddess on Aegina, and she was worshipped here since 2000 BC. Several sanctuaries predated the Doric structure, with inscriptions to Artemis Aphaia (the 'not dark'), to differentiate her from Hecate, the goddess in her aspect of witch or hag. Later myths made Aphaia a child of Zeus and Leto, who often hunted with her sister Artemis. When King Minos of Crete fell in love with her, she fled him for nine months until she reached Aegina, where she threw herself into the sea and vanished, hence the Classical translation of her name, 'the disappeared one'. She suffered one last transformation, becoming Aphaia-Athena with the rise of Athens. The temple is of local golden limestone and was originally covered with painted stucco. Of the 32 columns, 25 still stand; an unusual internal colonnade surrounded the *cella*, where the cult statue once stood. The superb pediment sculptures of Parian marble, depicting scenes of the Trojan War, are Archaic masterpieces but you have to go to Munich to see them (*see* p.236). A **museum** on the site has casts and reconstructions of the temple.

The café opposite offers a splendid view of the east coast of Aegina and **Ag. Marína**, the island's busiest resort, with a long sandy beach – Aegina's best, but don't expect much in the way of elbow room. If you want to foot it from Aphaia, it's a half-hour walk. And once you get there, be prepared; all the menus are in Swedish and Russian, and cocktail hour for the big blondes starts right after lunch.

Southern Aegina

One of the most popular excursions is to cycle (or take a bus) from Aegina Town south along the coast to **Pérdika** past the attractive beach of **Aiginitíssa**. Pérdika is a pretty fishing village-cum-resort with a small beach and good fish tavernas, surrounded by Aegina's not immensely stunning but very profitable pistachio groves. Once a day a bus from Aegina Town lumbers up to **Pacheiá Ráchi**, near the **Temple of Hellanion Zeus**, dedicated to Zeus 'the rainmaker', and it's true that clouds gathering here are a sure sign of showers. Two massive terraces, cisterns and a monumental staircase remain; from here an hour's walk will take you to the summit of beautiful conical **Oros** (1,706ft), the highest in the Saronic Gulf; its name simply means 'mountain' and it enjoys magnificent views when Zeus is having a day off.

Endangered *kri kri* goats from Crete are protected on the steep little **islet of Moní**, just off Pérdika (linked by boat taxis from Pérdika or Aegina Town). Once the property of the monastery of Chrysoleóntissa, it has a small beach, ruled by nosy peacocks, a taverna and a German look-out post with a wonderful view of the Saronic Gulf. Other boats from Aegina Town sail to **Angístri**, an island of pine trees and quiet beaches, so quiet that in 2002 a wanted member of the November 17 gang, whose photo was in all the papers, camped here in a tent for weeks, unnoticed, before turning himself in.

Póros (ΠΟΡΟΣ)

If there is one dream which I like above all others it is that of sailing on land.
Coming into Poros gives the illusion of that deep dream.

Henry Miller, *The Colossus of Maroussi*

A mere 400 yards separate Póros ('the passage') from the mountains of the Peloponnese, forming a Greek Grand Canal as busy as the one in Venice; if you sail through it on a large ferry you can see what's on television through the windows of

Getting There and Around

Car ferry and hydrofoil from Piraeus, Aegina and Méthana several times a day; car ferries every 30mins from early morning to late evening to Galatás on the mainland while water taxis (*benzínas*) cross the strait 24hrs a day from June to September for a mere 30¢. Frequent passenger ships and hydrofoils run to other places in the Saronic Gulf; in high season there are weekly connections to the Corinth Canal and Naúplio. Port authority: t 229 802 2274. The one bus on Póros goes up to the monastery and back.

Tourist Information

Tourist police: on waterfront, t 229 802 2256.

Where to Stay

Póros ✉ 18020
Sirene, near the monastery, t 229 802 2741, f 229 802 2744 (*B; expensive*). The best on the island, with a salt-water pool and its own beach. *Open April–mid-Oct.*
Neon Aegli, Askéli Beach, t 229 802 2372, f 229 802 4345 (*B; expensive*). Nearer to town and with more of a Greek flavour, with a private stretch of beach and watersports; all rooms have balcony and sea view.
Pavlou, t 229 802 2734 (*B; expensive*). The best choice at Neórion, and at the lower end of the price scale; it has a lovely pool and tennis courts.
Christina Studios, 50m from the beach at Askéli, t 229 802 4900, f 229 802 4766, *askelitr@athena.compulink.gr* (*expensive*). New, sleeping 2–3, with lovely sea views.

Manessi, in the heart of the main harbour, t 229 802 2273, f 229 802 4345 (*C; expensive*). Pleasant, newly renovated rooms in a neoclassical building.
Seven Brothers, one block back from the waterfront, t 229 802 3412, f 229 802 3413, *7brothers@hol.gr* (*moderate–inexpensive*). Convenient and comfortable with air-conditioning and TV.
Douros, 9 Dimosthenous (first road right after the high school), t 229 802 2633 (*moderate–inexpensive*). Pleasant, modern rooms and apartments with air-conditioning and TV.

Eating Out

Eating out along the *paralía* is a real treat – a line of tavernas with lovely views of the Peloponnese while ridiculously expensive yachts glide silently through the strait.
Caravella, on the waterfront 100m from the hydrofoil. Excellent selection of Greek and international dishes.
Sailor Taverna, t 229 802 3096. Good for lobster and anything else from the grill.
Karavolos, t 229 802 6158. Small backstreet restaurant one block behind the cinema, popular with everybody for its good Greek fare. Get there early to find a table.
The Flying Dutchman, by the post office. The Indonesian *rijkstaffel* offers a nice change of pace, and they also do succulent steaks cooked to order in front of you.
Mourthoukos, Neorion Beach. Very good food; try the stuffed pork or the soufflé.
Taverna Paradiso, 2km from Poseidon's temple (approaching from Askéli; take a taxi or rent a motorbike), t 229 802 3419 (€12). A taste of old Greece under its pergolas of vines, with views over the forest to the sea.

houses along the quay. Of all the Saronics, Póros receives the most package tours; besides the beauty of its location, it's only an hour from Piraeus by hydrofoil, and close to the major sights in the Peloponnese.

Póros in antiquity was named Kalavria, and served as the headquarters of the Kalavrian League, a 7th-century BC amphictyony that included Athens, Aegina, Epidauros, Troezen, Naúplio, Ermióni, Orchomenos and Pasiai. One of the few things known about the league is that it operated under the protection of Poseidon. His sanctuary on Kalavria became famous in later years thanks to the great orator Demosthenes who roused Athens against Philip II.

Póros is really two islands linked by a sandy belt of land and a bridge: larger Kalávria, pine-forested and blessed with sandy coves, and little Sferiá, a volcanic bubble that popped out of the sea during the eruptions at Méthana (*see* p.267). Póros Town clambers all over Sferiá, crowned by the blue-domed campanile of the Metropolis church. These days it is given over almost completely to the needs of tourists, except for the **Naval Training School**, housed in the first arsenal of the Greek State. Póros' small **Archaeological Museum** in Plateía Koryzí has finds from ancient Troezen (*t 229 802 3276; open daily exc Mon 8.30–3; free*).

A new crop of hotels has sprung up on Kalávria, some on the beach of **Neórion** to the west, others on **Askéli** and **Kanáli**, which are rather cleaner to the east. Although they are hot stuff for Póros, true beach-lovers will turn up their noses at them; alternatives include crossing over to Aliki beach, next to Galatás, or hiring a small boat to visit the pretty coves on the north side of the island. From Kanáli the bus continues to the peaceful 18th-century **Monastery of Zoodóchos Pigí**, immersed in woods with yet another pebbly beach below. From the monastery the road (but not the bus) climbs through the pines to the plateau of Palatia and the scant remains – known locally as 'the five stones' – of the **Temple of Poseidon**. A Mycenaean sanctuary, it was rebuilt in marble in *c.* 500 BC; when Pausanias visited it, he saw the tomb of Demosthenes in the precinct. All this is dust in the wind, but the view is as spectacular as ever.

Hýdra (ΥΔΡΑ)

Hýdra had the country's largest fleet in the early 1800s, and its daring captains built the tall, grey stone mansions piled on top of each other in a magnificent amphitheatre over the harbour. Artists moved in as the last sailors moved out; the first tourist trickle was sparked off by the scenes of Hýdra in the film *Boy on a Dolphin*, starring Sophia Loren. The artsy posy tone that sets Hýdra apart, like St Tropez, Portofino and similar nooks, survives in spite of the hordes of day-trippers who haunt the sleek jewellers and galleries; at night, to the tinkling of glasses and the rhythms floating from the trendy bars, discos and clubs, Hýdra comes into its own.

History

Hýdra is a nearly barren island, and had no permanent settlers until the 15th century, when Greeks and Albanians from Épirus took refuge here from the Turks. Out of necessity the new arrivals turned to the sea for their livelihood: through ship-building, smuggling and piracy. By the end of the 18th century, Hýdra was very much an autonomous state, to which the Turks turned a blind eye as long as it paid its taxes. It boasted a wealthy population of 25,000, and the few sailors Hýdra sent as a token tribute to the sultan were prized for their prowess. Hýdra did so well under the Ottomans that the war for independence in 1821 left its captains lukewarm, until their seafaring rivals on Spétses, led by the bold admiral Bouboulína, had chalked up a few victories and the people of Hýdra threatened to revolt unless they joined the fight. But once decided, the captains threw themselves boldly into the fray. Merchants converted their fleet into warships and the Hydriot navy terrorized the Turks, especially with their fire ships: under cover of night, some 20 daredevils would sail a decrepit vessel full of explosives alongside the Turkish ships, light it, and row for their lives in an escape boat. Ironically, the independence brought an end to the island's prosperity. By the 1950s Hýdra was a ghost island, until fortune's wheel was oiled once again by the arrival of Greek painter Níkos Hadzikyriákos Ghíkas, pioneer of the artists' colony that paved the way for today's glitterati.

Hýdra Town

Just arriving is extraordinary. The island looks like a rock pile until your vessel makes a sharp turn, and suddenly – *voilà*, the pearl in the oyster shell, the scene that launched a thousand cruise ships. The grey and white mansions, built in the late 18th century, attest to the loot amassed by Hydriot privateers and blockade runners. Lanes radiate from the amphitheatre. The only motor vehicles are two rubbish trucks.

Although most of the artists have fled, a branch of the **School of Fine Arts** survives in the fine old residence of the Tombázi family. Another school, recalling an older tradition, is the **Skolí Eborikís Naftilías** for merchant marine captains, housed in the old Tsamados house. The loveliest mansions – and the largest – belonged to the Koundouriótis family, Albanians who could barely speak a word of Greek but who contributed two leaders to the cause of independence: Lázaros, who converted his merchantmen into warships at his own expense, and the fat, jovial and rather useless Geórgios, who was elected president of Greece in 1824. On the left side of the harbour, the **Museum of Hýdra** (*t 229 805 2355; open daily 9–4.30; adm*) is in a new building, built in the traditional style; it contains a rich collection of portraits of Hydriot captains and heroes, folk paintings, ships' models and weapons.

The churches in Hýdra also reflect its wealth. The most beautiful is the 18th-century **Panagía tis Theotókou**, next to the port, with a lovely marble iconostasis and silver chandelier; the cells of its former convent, now used as town offices, encompass a serene marble courtyard – the stone from Póros' temple of Poseidon. Here, too, are statues of Lázaros Koundouriótis and Andréas Vókos, better known as Admiral Miaoúlis, who is fondly remembered in celebrations called the Miaoúlia (20 June). From the church, climb up Miaoúlis Street to the lovely square of **Kaló Pigádi**, site of two 18th-century mansions and two deep wells. The one real beach on Hýdra is a 20min walk away at **Mandráki**, the old shipbuilding docks of the Hydriots, with hotel and restaurant. You can also dive off the lovely rocks at **Kamíni**.

Getting There and Around

Ferries connect Hýdra with the other Saronic islands and ports several times a day. There are up to 20 **hydrofoils** and/or **catamarans** a day from Zéa Marína or the main harbour of Piraeus, and frequent connections to Póros, Spétses, Naúplio, Pórto Chéli and Ermióni; less frequently to other Peloponnese ports such as Monemvasiá and Kýthera. **Water taxis** wait by the quay to ferry visitors to the swimming places (beach is too grand a word) at Kamíni, Mandráki and Vlíchos, and the islet of Dokós; they're cheap if you join the crowd rather than go off on your own. **Boat trips** to the far ends of Hýdra run at around €60 return. **Port authority**: t 229 805 2279.

Tourist Information

Tourist police: Votsi Street, t 229 805 2205 (summer only).
Saitis Tours, on the quay, t 229 805 2184, f 229 805 3469. Information and accommodation.

Where to Stay

Hýdra ✉ 18040
Be warned: it is madness to arrive in Hýdra in the summer and expect to find a place to stay without a reservation.

Expensive
Orloff, t 229 805 2564, f 229 805 3532, *orloff@internet.gr* (B). A beautiful restored 19th-century mansion near the port, each room on the courtyard individually designed; an added pleasure is one of the best breakfasts in Greece. *Open Mar–Nov.*
Bratsera, t 229 805 3970, f 229 805 3626, *www.hotelsofgreece.com/saronic/bratsera/* (A). Opened in 1994 in a beautifully converted sponge factory. Highly prized, combining traditional design with glamour. Most rooms overlook the colonnaded pool and lantern-lit restaurant; the Belgian chef is a creative perfectionist. *Open Mar–Oct.*
Miramare, at Mandráki, t 229 805 2300, f 229 805 2301, winter t 210 413 6406 (A). Linked to the harbour by boat, a bungalow complex built of stone, overlooking the island's sole

bit of sand, it offers an array of water sports. *Open April–Oct.*
Miranda, t 229 805 2230, f 229 805 3510, winter t 210 684 9268, f 210 804 7776 (A). Another elegant 19th-century sea captain's town house, with Venetian painted ceilings. *Open Mar–Oct.*
Leto, t 229 805 3385, *www.sofianos.gr/leto* (B). Elegant, central and a bit larger than the others with classy white and wood rooms. *Open mid-Mar–Oct.*

Moderate
Hydra, 2 steep minutes from the clock tower, t 229 805 2102, f 229 805 3330 (C). It is worth practising your mountain goat skills to stay here, but you will receive a warm welcome and have fine views over the harbour in this historic mansion. *Open all year.*
Amaryllis, t 229 805 2249, f 229 805 3611 (B). Comfortable little hotel in an old mansion, with smallish doubles with bath. *Open all year.*
Sophia, t 229 805 2313 (D). The cheapest, a friendly old-fashioned pension slap in the middle of the waterfront; no rooms with en suite but some with great views.

Eating Out

Kondylenia, on Kamíni Beach, t 229 805 3520. Particularly outstanding with views over the quaint harbour; try the squid in tomato sauce or the sea urchin dip. *Open Lent–Oct.*
Iliovassilema (Sunset), Palio Kanóni, t 229 805 267. Good food and a great place to watch the sun sink, but expect to pay a little more for the pleasure. *Open April–Nov.*
Geitoniko (also known as **Christina**), t 229 805 3615. Courtyard setting in an old stone building; excellent traditional cuisine at fair prices. *Closed Dec–Feb.*
To Steki, t 229 805 3517. Just before the clock tower; serves reliable Greek food on its veranda for even less. *Closed Nov–Dec.*
Paradossiako, t 229 805 4155. The year-round locals' favourite, serving a good variety of little dishes and delicious seafood platters.
Xeri Elia, a short walk up from the port, t 229 805 2886. Pleasant setting under the trees, serving standard Greek fare at normal prices. *Open Mar–Oct.*

Walking is a guaranteed way to escape the idle throng. **Kastéllo**, behind Hýdra town, has the ruins of a castle down near the shore. Further on, **Vlíchos** is a pretty hamlet with a rocky beach, a picturesque little bridge, and a couple of tavernas; boats and water taxis from the port also make the trip. Pine trees and swimming coves make **Mólos** a popular place for outings and for spotting Joan Collins, who often spends the summer here; in less glamorous times the steep cliffs nearby were used to throw off the aged and sick. Above town, **Profítis Ilías monastery** and the nearby convent of **Ag. Efpráxia** are about an hour on foot (or less on one of the donkeys for hire). The view is lovely and you can buy textiles woven by ancient nuns on their ancient looms.

Spétses (ΣΠΕΤΣΕΣ)

Spétses is a charming, pine-scented island, the furthest in the Saronic Gulf from Athens, a factor that long kept it more relaxed than its more accessible sisters. For all that, Spétses is an old hand at tourism – its first hotel was built in 1914. In the 1980s it was besieged by British tourists with the descriptions of John Fowles' *The Magus* dancing in their heads, but the long transfer from Athens airport has whittled away all but the most tenacious operators.

History

Spétses (ancient Pityoussa) has been inhabited since 2500 BC, but then managed to avoid history for 4,000 years. No one is even sure how it got its name; the best guess is that the Venetians called it 'Spice,' or *spezie*. The first shipyards date from the early 17th century (and survive to this day; they built Tim Severin's *Argo*, the trireme that traced the route of the Argonauts). By the 19th century Spétses was renowned for its seamanship and, like Hýdra, prospered from the derring-do of its blockade-runners.

Spétses did its bit to ignite the War of Independence. When the revolt broke out on the Peloponnese in March 1821, Old Spice sprang into action: on 2 April it raised the flag ('Freedom or Death'), and two days later won the first naval victory of the war. Then the lady admiral of Spétses, Laskarína Bouboulína, sailed her *Agamemnon*, one of the finest Greek ships, over to Naúplio and blockaded the port. A genuine military leader as well as the mother of six grown children, her chief flaw as an admiral was her predilection for abandoning ship for a horse and sabre if it looked as if the hottest fighting was on shore. The Greeks (at least the men) say she was so ugly that she could only keep lovers by holding them at gunpoint.

Spétses Town

Unlike your typical Greek island town, Spétses spreads out leisurely in the greenery, dotted with proud neoclassical captains' mansions, safely invisible from the water-front. The locals have a passion for pebble mosaics (*choklákia*); the biggest one greets you as you disembark at the **Dápia**, the elegant square that sweeps down to the quay. Bristling with cannon, the Dápia now plays a more peaceful role as the vortex of Spétses' café society. On the esplanade there's a she-means-business **statue of**

Getting There and Around

By sea: several **hydrofoils** daily from Piraeus and other Saronics, less frequently from Kýthera and Peloponnesian ports (Kósta is closest and also has *benzínas*). **Ferry** connections daily with Piraeus, other Saronics and Peloponnesian ports, although note that cars are not allowed on the island without authorization. *Benzínas* or **boat taxis** can take up to eight people to other places along the coast. Port authority: t 229 807 2245.

By road: horse-drawn **carriages** for hire along the waterfront add a touch of elegance but don't go any further than Ligonéri or Ag. Marína. Bicycles and scooters may be hired. Two **buses** run from the town beach to Ag. Marína and Ag. Anárgyri, and from Hotel Possidonion to Ligonéri.

Tourist Information

Tourist information booth on the quay.
Tourist police (also the regular police): t 229 807 3100.

Festivals

The **Armata** takes place on the nearest weekend to 8 September, when the Spetsiots commemorate their victory over the Turks in 1822. The Ottomans were held at bay throughout the day by the island's fleet, and in the end withdrew when confronted with a drifting fireboat. The battle is re-enacted in the harbour, with fireworks and dancing.

Where to Stay

Spétses ✉ 18050

For studios and apartments, try **Alasia**, t 229 807 4098, f 229 807 4053, and Tassoula at **Takis**, t 229 807 2215, f 229 807 4315, for cheaper rooms.

Possidonion, t 229 807 2308, f 229 807 2208 (*A; luxury–expensive*). Renovated under new management a few years ago, this grand old dowager on the waterfront has been the classy place to stay since 1914. *Open April–Oct.*

Zoe's Club, in town, t 229 807 4447, f 229 807 4094, *www.zoesclub.com* (*A; luxury–expensive*). Luxurious and welcoming complex, with great views, pool and the whole works (*studios for two: €105–165*).

Nissia, on the seafront (but without many sea views), t 229 807 5000, f 229 807 5012, *nissia@otenet.gr* (*luxury–expensive*). Newer, bigger, glitzier, with a magnificent, brimming pool, excellent restaurant and fully equipped studios and maisonettes (*studios from €112*).

Atlantis, t 229 807 4122/2215 (*C; moderate–inexpensive*). Modest air-conditioned rooms with balconies and pool, two minutes from the beach at Ag. Marina.

Akrogiali, at Ag. Anárgyri, t 229 807 3695 (*moderate–inexpensive*). A-class guesthouse with the feel of a small hotel, near Spétses' most popular beach; lovely breakfast terrace. *Open all year.*

Villa Christina, in town, t 229 807 2218 (*B; moderate–inexpensive*). Fairly central, charming and popular little place.

Eating Out

Patralis, a 10min walk to the right of the harbour, t 229 807 2134 (*€15–22*). Very popular, with *spetsiota* (fish baked with tomato, olive oil, garlic and pepper) on the menu. *Open Jan–Oct.*

Exedra, in the old harbour, t 229 807 3497 (*€15–22*). Also known for its excellent fish, including pasta with lobster. *Open Mar–Oct.*

Tarsanas, in the old harbour, t 229 807 4490 (*€18–25*). Owned by fishermen and serving the freshest of seafood and *mezédes*. *Open eves only, Easter–Oct.*

Liotrivi, in the old harbour, t 229 807 2269 (*€18–25*). Italian and seafood dishes in a converted olive press. *Open Easter–Oct.*

Stelios, t 229 807 3748 (*€12–18*). In addition to fish fresh from the nearby market, come here for excellent vegetarian dishes. *Open Easter–Oct.*

Lazaros, above the Dápia, t 229 807 2600 (*€10–15*). An excellent choice for the past 50 years; try their famous chicken with cinnamon. *Open Easter–Oct.*

Bouboulína, who was assassinated in her house nearby. A descendant now runs it as the delightful **Bouboulína Museum** (*t 229 807 2416; open mid-Mar–Oct, tours several times daily 9.45–8; adm*); here are her weapons, a model of the *Agamemnon*, furnishings befitting an admiral (including a wooden ceiling imported from Florence) and a dainty portrait of Bouboulína with a basket of flowers.

Behind the statue stretches the Edwardian façade of one of the first hotels on any Greek island, the Hotel **Possidonion**, built by philanthropist Sotíris Anárgyro, who, after making his fortune, decided to make that of Spétses. A dedicated Anglophile, in 1927 he founded the Anárgyros and Korgialénios College on the English public school model. John Fowles taught here and used it (not very flatteringly) as a setting for *The Magus*. The school building is only used occasionally now, but Anárgyro's third contribution to the island, the pine forests, grow luxuriantly on. Spétses' **museum** (*t 229 807 2994; open Tues–Sun 8–2; guided tours in English every eve at 6pm; adm*) is in the handsome mansion (1795) of Hadziyiánnis Méxis, shipowner and revolutionary; it has original furnishings, a box holding Bouboulína's bones, the 'Freedom or Death' flag , ships' models, paintings and figureheads.

The **Paléo Limáni**, or old harbour, is shared by caique builders, fishermen, yachts and the church, **Ag. Nikólaos**. On its bell tower the Spetsiots raised their defiant flag in 1821 – a bronze cast is displayed opposite. When the Turks came to quench the uprising, the inhabitants created mannequins out of barrels and flower pots, dressing them in red fezes, and set them up along the quay. Seeing them from a distance, the Turkish commander thought that the island had already been taken and sailed on by. Further east, near the **Fáros** (lighthouse), the church **Panagía Armata** was built after the naval victory on 8 September 1822 and has a large commemorative painting by Koutzis. Just beyond is **Ag. Marína**, site of an Early Helladic settlement, a beach and much of Spetsiote nightlife. Off the coast hovers the idyllic islet of **Spetsopoúla**, the private retreat of the Niárchos family, whose late *paterfamilias* Stávros was one of the 'Super Greeks' of the '60s and arch-rival of Aristotle Onassis. Sometimes you can see the 325ft Niárchos yacht, nearly as big as Spetsopoúla itself, topped with a helicopter pad and what looks like a surface-to-air missile launcher.

Around Spétses

The entire coast of Spétses is fringed with shingle or pebbly beaches and rocky coves; the main ones offer full watersports facilities. Heading clockwise, the first likely place for a swim is **Xokeríza**, with a pleasant shingle beach that rarely gets crowded. The opposite holds true of lovely **Ag. Anárgyri**, an irresistible bay rimmed with trees, bars and two tavernas. Continuing clockwise, some caiques continue on to **Ag. Paraskeví**, a more peaceful pebbly cove with a church and cantina, watched over by the Villa Jasemia, the house Fowles used as the residence of his tricky Magus. **Zogeriá**, to the west, is a pretty, rocky, double-coved bay, a hardish slog from the road with good swimming and a taverna. **Vrelloú** in the north is in a corner called **Paradise** for its beauty, although the beach is a litter magnet. **Blueberry Beach** and shady **Ligonéri**, a good walk or horse buggy ride from the Dápia, tend to be cleaner.

Attica (Attikí)

The dangling triangle of Attica once had 12 independent *demes*, or municipalities, which were more or less peacefully united under Athens – by Theseus himself, or so the Athenians liked to say (around 900 BC, say the historians). It was a move that contributed greatly to Athens' success, and 'Athens' in ancient times meant this entire area, its city-state. Although there are fertile patches – the Pedía, where Athens sprawls, the Mesógeia and the industrialized Thriássion plain around Elefsína – much of Attica is mountainous, 'a fleshless skeleton' as Plato called it. The mountains do what they can to keep Greater Athens from becoming greater, although developers inch a bit further up the slopes every year. Under the Ottomans Attica was so sparsely populated that Albanians were transplanted here wholesale to till the land and fish the seas; in many villages you can still hear old men chatting in Albanian.

Big changes are under way in Attica today, many driven by a revolution in regional transport. The fertile Mesógeian plain now sprouts the runways of Elefthérios Venizélou Airport, which will soon be linked by a trans-Attica highway. Even after its completion, travelling around traffic-tangled Attica is doomed to remain more wearisome than anywhere else in Greece. But if you do make it beyond the sprawl, there are bits where the famous ethereal delicacy of Attica's light and landscape can still stop the clock and make the heart sigh.

From Piraeus to Cape Soúnion

Billed as the 'Apollo Coast' by the National Tourist Office, much of the coast southeast of Piraeus is the playground of the Athenians, lined with smart suburbs, now more desirable than ever since the closing of the old airport. The first likely place for a swim is **Glyfáda**, now a rival of fashionable Kolonáki with its boutiques, golf course, gin palaces in the marina, nightclubs that dot the shore and a top notch collection of contemporary Greek art at the **Pierídis Gallery**, in a villa at 29 Poseidónos (*t 210 898 0166; open daily 9–3, closed Sat and Sun; free*). Further down the coast at **Voúla** are two sandy pay-beaches with tennis courts and windsurfers, jammed in summer with well-heeled Athenians. **Kavoúri** has posh villas in the trees, near the smart resort of **Vouliagméni** (Βουλιαγμένη) with another pay beach and excellent if pricey fish restaurants, ideal for a romantic dinner overlooking the sea. Its marina is a haven for Greek yachties and it has a year-round swimming hole, a beautiful **thermal lake** at the base of a cliff in the centre of town. The isthmus between the two bays, ancient Cape Zostor ('girdle') has the foundations of a 6th-century **Temple of Apollo** in the garden of the Astir Palace Hotel. Beyond Vouliagméni, the road continues along the coast to **Várkiza**, another beach playground with fine white sand; **Vári** just inland from here is famous for its meat tavernas. From here a stunning corniche road continues along the coast, by way of smaller resorts, to **Saronída** and **Anávissos**, with a new race track.

By the Classical age, the Greeks were as arty as they were religious, and they knew exactly where to plant a temple to its best advantage, perhaps nowhere more stunningly than the Doric **Temple of Poseidon** (*t 229 203 9363; open daily 10–sunset; adm*), 200ft over the sea at Cape Soúnion, Attica's southernmost tip. Attributed to the architect of the Theseum, it was built in 440 BC (replacing an earlier temple destroyed by the Persians) and is the same size as the Theseum but taller, made from a local marble bleached as white as bone in the clear Attic light. Fifteen of its 34 columns still

Getting Around

From Akadimías St in Athens **buses** run frequently to Glyfáda: the A2 by way of Leof. Syngroú and the A3 and B3 by way of Leof. Vouliagménis. A fast tramway to Glyfáda is in the works along Syngroú. From Piraeus, buses A1 and B1 leave for Glyfáda from Vas. Georgíou St and Plateía Ag Triáda near the port. At Glyfáda, board buses 114, 115 or 116 for Voúla, Vouliagméni and Várkiza. Buses for Cape Soúnion, **t** 210 821 3203, leave Mavromatéon terminus by Áreos Park at least once an hour until 5.30pm, either going inland via Lávrio or via the coast road (the latter can also be picked up on Filellínon St). Lávrio **Port authority** (for Kéa): **t** 229 202 5249.

Where to Stay and Eat

Glyfáda ✉ 16675

Built up and glittering, Glyfáda is convenient for the beach, nightlife and golf course, and it has excellent Greek and foreign restaurants.

Oasis, 27 Poseidónos, **t** 210 894 1724, **f** 210 894 1724, *www.oasishotel.gr* (*A; luxury*). A complex of two-room apartments, either overlooking the beach or atrium. Adult and children's pools and jacuzzi, 24hr room service and buffet breakfast.

Emmantina, 33 Poseidónos, **t** 210 898 0683, **f** 210 894 8110, *www.emmantina.gr* (*A; expensive*). Soundproofed, well-equipped rooms, 150m from the beach, with a roof garden, pool and Internet service.

Avra, 5 G. Lambráki, **t** 210 894 7185, **f** 210 898 1161, *avrahtl@hol.gr* (*C; expensive*). Older but attractive: air-conditioned rooms, all with balconies, satellite TV and fridges, and a pool (covered in winter) and sauna.

O Serkos kai ta 4 Asteria, 28 Xenofondos, **t** 210 964 9553 (€13–16). Come here for the delicious tastes of old Constantinople, from the *mezédes* to dessert, with succulent kebabs in between. *Open eves and Sun lunch.*

Far East, Lazaráki and Pandoras St, **t** 210 894 0500 (€38). Probably the best Chinese restaurant in Athens, famous for its Peking duck. *Open eves and Sun lunch.*

Vouliagméni ✉ 16671

Only 25km from the centre of Athens and 20km from the new airport, this is the area's most upscale resort with a sandy beach in a protected bay.

Apollon Divani, 10 Ag. Nikolaou, **t** 210 891 1100, **f** 210 965 8010 *www.divaniapollon.gr/divaniapollon/* (*L; luxury*). Large hotel in nearby Kavoúri, built to give each room a view over the Saronic Gulf. Spacious rooms in warm colours, beautiful suites with fireplaces, indoor/outdoor pools, new thalassotherapy centre, and more.

Astir Palace, 40 Apollónos, **t** 210 890 2000, **f** 210 896 3194, *www.astirpalace.gr* (*L; luxury*). A complex of three plush hotels on the garden peninsula, with three private beaches, watersports, indoor and outdoor pools, tennis, health club and seven bars.

Margi, 11 Litous, **t** 210 896 2061, **f** 210 896 0229, *www.themargi.gr* (*A; expensive*). Less of a resort hotel but with delightful public spaces and a pool; smallish rooms with marble baths, and an excellent restaurant.

Amarilia, 13 Ag. Nikolaou, **t** 210 899 0391, **f** 210 895 5790, *www.amarilia.gr* (*A; expensive*). Classic-styled white rooms all with sea or mountain views, outdoor pool and all mod cons, including Internet service.

Lagonísi (between Várkiza and Soúnion) ✉ 19013

Apaggio, Soúnion road at the 41km mark, **t** 229 102 6261. Specializing in traditional recipes from across Greece, this enormous restaurant is a great place to stop for lunch or dinner. Lots of seafood, but also rarely seen items like Naxian potatoes. Good wines and desserts. *Open May–Sept, afterwards Fri and weekends only.*

stand, set high on a mighty base, and there's always at least one tourist searching for the column where Byron set a example for hundreds by carving his name. The views extend to a garland of islands; here the ancients held sail races in honour of the sea god. In season, coach parties gather to drink in the sunset. The much scantier remains of a second sanctuary, the **Temple of Athena Sounias**, are 400 yards away, built in the 5th century BC over a smaller temple.

Ancient Mines: Lávrio and Thorikó

Athens 'took off' in the Classical age thanks to **Lávrio**, a name once synonymous with silver. A fabulous new vein was discovered in the early 5th century BC and, thanks to far-sighted Themistocles, the windfall went into 'wooden walls': 200 ships, more than the rest of Greece put together, which proved their worth at Sálamis. The very worst fate for a slave or captive was to be sent to the mines, where the average shaft was 3ft high and the average shift 12 hours. Life expectancy was blessedly short. By the 2nd century AD the silver had given out, but the mines were re-opened in the 19th century to extract magnesium until the 1970s. The little **Mineralogical Museum**, on A. Kordélla St (*t 229 202 6270; open Wed, Sat and Sun 10–12; adm*), displays the 280 different minerals from the area, many from ancient slag heaps in the sea (thorikosite, georgiadesite, nilite, etc.) that exist nowhere else in the world. The **Archaeological Museum** nearby (*t 229 202 2817; open Wed–Mon 10–3; free*) has the weather-worn frieze from the Temple of Soúnion with the usual battle scenes, mining tools going back to *c.* 2200 BC, the mosaic floor from an early Christian basilica, and finds from Thorikó. Woebegone now that it's been mined dry, Lávrio is still the chief port for Kéa (*see* p.616), although the bare, brooding rock just in front is **Makrónisi**, the one Greek island no one ever visited willingly: poet Iánnis Rítsos was perhaps the most famous political prisoner there during the Civil War and Junta periods.

There are more mines just north, around utterly drab **Thorikó**. Its two harbours were first used by the Minoans, who dug the first mines. The 6th-century BC **theatre** on the slopes of the acropolis (signposted) is known as the 'Arma of Thespis', the oldest surviving theatre in Attica; it has a unique irregular elliptical cavea, which was the best that the setting and probably all that local finances allowed. Archaic-era houses and workshops are nearby, along with an ore washery (restored), while further up are remains of a Mycenaean tholos tomb.

Eastern Attica

The Mesógeia: Peanía and Pórto Ráfti

Below the east slopes of long Mt Ymittós stretches the Mesógeia ('inland') plain, with some of the prettiest landscapes in Attica and red soil planted with vineyards that supply much of Athens' retsina – but the rate of encroaching concrete, however, is only bound to accelerate thanks to the new airport. **Peanía** (Παιανία), a handsome village on Ymittós' skirts, was the birthplace of Demosthenes and is now a favourite weekend destination for the lovely **Vorrés Museum**, 1 Diadóchou Konstantínou St

Getting Around

A **car**, using a good map, is by far the best, though you can use **buses** out of Athens. For Peanía and Loútsa/Artemis, take the A5 from Akadimías St, or the metro to the Ethnikí Ámina station and then bus 125 or 308 for Peanía or bus 306 for Artemis-Loútsa, to 1km from the Vravróna archaeological site. Buses leave Mavromatéon terminus by Áreos Park for Pórto Ráfti, **t** 210 823 0179, every hour; Rafína, **t** 210 821 3203, every 30mins till 6pm, every 45mins to 10.30pm; Marathon, **t** 210 821 0872, every 30mins in the morning, every hour after 1pm; Rámnous (Soúli), **t** 210 821 0872, six a day; Ag. Marína, six a day, **t** 210 821 3203; Kálamos (Amphiáraion) eight a day, **t** 210 823 0179 and *c.* every hour for Oropós/Skála Oropoú, **t** 210 821 3203. **Port authorities**: Rafína and Ag. Marína, both **t** 229 402 8888.

(*t 210 664 2520; open Sat and Sun; adm*), set in a magnificent garden. Ionas Vorrés, a Greek Canadian, spent 35 years creating the proper setting for his collections: a sleek new building containing his top collection of modern Greek art and three village houses, beautiful restored, sheltering a fascinating array of traditional art. The village is also proud of the remarkable church of **Zoodóchos Pigí**, its interior beautifully frescoed in the style of the early 15th-century Paleologos emperors – by Phótis Kóntoglou, in the 20th century. Four kilometres above the Peanía, you can also visit Attica's spectacular **Koutoúki Cave** (*t 210 664 2910; open daily 9–3.55; adm*).

Busy **Koropí** south of the airport is the Mesógeia's chief wine village; it even smells like retsina on a good day. Beyond Markópoulo lies the lovely circular bay of **Pórto Ráfti**, with sandy beaches and islets floating in the bay; one of these has a huge **Roman statue** of a seated woman that once served as a lighthouse, but the locals know her as the 'tailor' (*ráftis*). The south end of the bay, where Mycenaean tombs were found, was ancient Prasiai, from where the annual *Theoria* or sacred delegation to Délos set sail, in a ship the Athenians said was the one used by Theseus when he returned from killing the Minotaur.

Vravróna and the Sanctuary of the Little Bears

North of here, **Vravróna** (ancient Brauron), one of the twelve *demes* of Attica, gave Athens some of her leaders – Pisistratos, Miltiades and Kimon. It was famous for its **Sanctuary of Artemis Brauronia** (*off the Markópoulo–Loútsa road; t 229 902 7020, open Tues–Sun 8.30–2.45; adm*), where girls from the best families, aged between five and ten and dressed in saffron, came to serve the goddess of wild animals as Little Bears (*arktoi*), to atone for the killing of Artemis' favourite bear by two brothers. Implicit was the hope that the goddess would later protect or at least not harm them; among the dedications here were the garments of women who died in childbirth, victims of her wrath. Artemis showed her cruel side in Euripides' *Iphigenia in Tauris* and in the tradition that her wooden cult figure, brought to Brauron by Iphigenia and Orestes, demanded human sacrifices. The Persians stole the statue and took it to Susa; the site later flooded and was abandoned by the 3rd century BC. Only the steps and foundations remain of the 5th-century BC Doric **temple**, while some of the columns have been re-erected of the adjoining U-shaped **stoa** lined with dining rooms (which must have had the ambience of a school cafeteria). Next to this stands a well-preserved Classical **bridge**. On the other side of the temple is the 15th-century church of Ag. Geórgios and a shrine once worshipped as the tomb of Iphigenia. Don't miss the **museum** (*separate adm*), with a model of the site, offerings of jewellery and mirrors, statues of the little *arktoi* (many holding pets) and exquisite 5th-century BC dedicatory reliefs showing the gods and sacrifices to Artemis. If you need a swim, there are sandy strands and tavernas at **Loútsa** (aka Ártemis or Artemída).

Rafína

The long blue silhouette of Évia looks enticing from here, and if you can't resist, there are ferries to Kárystos or Marmári as well as to the nearer Cyclades from **Rafína** (Ραφήνα), the next port to the north and a good spot to stop for lunch. Not far inland, off the road to Pikérmi in the piney foothills of Mt Pendéli, is one of the more striking bits of ecclesiastical architecture in Attica, the colossal, six-domed **Moní Dáou-Pendéli**, built in the 11th century, perhaps by an Armenian, given a narthex by the Franks in the 13th century, restored in the 17th, and then abandoned until 1963. There are good sandy beaches north of Rafína at **Máti**, woodsy **Ag. Andréas**, and **Néa Mákri**, with views across the Bay of Marathon.

Marathon

In 490 BC, an expeditionary force of 25,000 Persians under Datis decimated Erétria and landed on the Plain of Marathon, following the advice of Pisistratos' exiled son Hippias, by then a bitter old man. 'The mountains look on Marathon – And Marathon looks on the sea,' as Byron wrote, but also to the north was the Great Marsh and the Kynosura ('dog's tail') peninsula; the mountain track to Athens lay to the south.

Athens was expecting the worst. Like Erétria, it had aided the revolt in Ionia; Darius, the king of kings, ruler over much of the world, wanted revenge, and his army was considered invincible. A runner Pheidippides was at once sent to Sparta to ask for aid, and so desperate was Athens' need that the city freed any slave who was willing to fight. The head *archon* Kallimachos then led ten generals (including Miltiades, who had fought as a mercenary for Darius and knew his army's ways) and 9,000 Athenians to Marathon; of all Athens' neighbours, only Plataea was willing and able to send aid – 1,000 men, all of its available force. So the Persians found their way barred by 10,000 Greeks, camped around a sanctuary of Heracles.

A four-day stand-off followed, the Persians unwilling to attack the strong Greek position, and the Greeks unwilling to leave it until reinforced by Sparta (who delayed their departure because the moon wasn't full). Finally Datis decided to send his cavalry by sea to Athens, moving them out at dawn, and covering their manoeuvres by the infantry. When they came within a mile and a half of the Greeks, Miltiades gave the order to attack, and the hoplites moved so swiftly down hill in their tight formation that they caught the Persians like a steam roller and crushed them between their two strong wings. Many who tried to flee floundered and drowned in the Great Marsh. The battle only lasted an hour; 6,400 Persians were killed to 192 Greeks, among them Kallimachos. (A much later tradition – the victory so surprised the Athenians that it at once rocketed into myth, and stayed there – claims the same Pheidippides was immediately dispatched to relay news to Athens, 26 miles away; '*Nenikíamen*' (We won!) he panted, and died.) The Spartans arrived a day late, looked at the dead, offered congratulations in a rather patronizing way and ·went home.

Although the victory at Sálamis 10 years later was more crucial, Marathon remained the proudest moment for the Athenians, and a turning point; afterwards they began to think of themselves as unique, with a chauvinistic pride that led to many of their greatest achievements. In honour of their valour, the Athenian dead were cremated and buried on the field in a 35ft-high mound, the **Marathon Tomb** or Sorós, signposted after the Golden Coast hotel (*t 229 450 5462; open Tues–Sun 8.30–3; adm*). Bits of bone, charcoal, arrowheads and ceramics from the funeral feast were found in it; today you'll see wreaths left by school outings. There are fine views over the battlefield from the top, where a statue of Nike (Victory) once stood. Another mile up the road, you'll see a sign on the left for Vrána and the museum. On the way is the sheltered Cycladic-Early Helladic cemetery of Tsépi, and the **Tomb of the Plataeans**, where eight skeletons were found (the dead Persians were tossed in a ditch).

The **museum** (*t 229 405 5155; same hours as the tomb*) has Neolithic finds from the Cave of Pan, from Tsépi and the Marathon Tomb (the ceramic offerings were important in the dating of Greek vases); there are beautiful 4th-century BC funerary steles, and Roman artefacts from the farm of Herodes Atticus, who was born here in AD 103 (including a huge statue of Hadrian's favourite Antinous, got up as an Egyptian).

Marathon is old even in myth; it was the ferocious bull of Marathon, left here by Heracles, who killed the son of Minos of Crete, leading him to demand the fateful tribute of Athenian youths and maidens. A straggling farming village bearing the august name **Marathónas** is north of Vrána; here a platform marks the starting point for the annual marathon race to Athens (other runners have replicated the real Pheidippides' run, the 140 miles between Athens and Sparta, in less than 24 hours). The winner of the first marathon in the modern Olympics in 1896 was Spíros Loúis, a postman from Maroússi, who became a national hero when he won Greece's only gold medal, running the 24.8 miles from Marathon to the stadium in two hours, 58 minutes, 50 seconds (the current 26.2-mile marathon began in the 1908 Olympics in London; it was the distance from Windsor Castle to the royal box in the stadium in White City). The bumpy preparations for the 2004 Olympics have been bumpiest here, when the fragile wetlands of the Great Marsh between Marathónas and sandy **Schiniás Beach** were flooded for the rowing centre; because of the controversy, Athens rushed it through so fast that in 2001 it became the first venue to be completed. After the games, the government promises to dismantle all and create a natural park. Eight km west of Marathónas lies **Marathon Lake**, created in 1931 by a dam – the only one in the world faced with Pentelic marble. On the way, in one of the many Attic villages named **Inoí** (Oenoë, or wine), the **Cave of Pan** described by Pausanias was discovered. Worship went back to Neolithic times, and was renewed after Pan allegedly waylaid Pheidippides as he ran to Sparta and told him how much he liked Athens.

Rámnous and the Temple of Nemesis

If you have a car, it's easy to combine Marathon with this remote corner of Attica. Beyond Káto Soúli, the road branches right for the little port of **Ag. Marína**, almost in spitting distance of Néa Stýra in Évia. In antiquity, when Évia shipped its grain to Athens, these narrows were considered too dangerous, and the cove under **Rámnous** just north was used instead, and defended by a large fortress. Now picturesque in its loneliness, Rámnous is synonymous with its mid 5th-century BC Doric **Temple of Nemesis** (*t 229 406 3477; open daily 8–6; adm; but ring a day ahead to check*). Nemesis' 'due enactment, divine vengeance' was the personification of doing the right thing, but also of retribution, ready to intervene whenever a mortal was guilty of hubris – the vain belief that one is in control of one's destiny. The temple, on a large white isodomic marble retaining wall, replaced the Archaic temple destroyed by the Persians. It was probably never finished, as the metopes and pediment were left undecorated. Adjacent stood a smaller 6th-century **Temple of Themis**, the goddess of justice and order; it too was destroyed by the Persians but never rebuilt. There are the remains of an altar, stoa and fountain house.

In the mid 1990s, thefts in the area had led to thoughts of abandoning Rámnous altogether, but since then archaeologists from the University of Thessaloníki have taken it firmly in hand. The **museum**, 400 yards north, contains the reconstructed pediment of the Temple of Nemesis, using only original bits and leaving spaces in case any new pieces are found. It also shelters part of the base of the celebrated cult statue of Nemesis in Parian marble by Agoracritus, a pupil of Phidias; according to Pausanias it was made from a block deposited here by the Persians, who, in a classic example of hubris, planned to construct a victory monument before the Battle of Sálamis. This was the only Classical-era cult statue to survive, even in fragments – the head is in the British Museum, while the base here shows Leda presenting Helen to her true mother: swan-like Nemesis, who like the cuckoo laid her egg in Leda's nest and was really behind the Trojan War. There are well-preserved tombs, steles and temple-shaped enclosures (*periboloi*). North of the museum is the 5th-century BC **fortress** with its nine towers, where some 600 soldiers lodged with such refinements as a theatre and gymnasium; one of the ancient ports has an attractive beach.

The Amphiáraion

Country roads wind to **Kálamos** and then down to the little beach resort of **Ag. Apóstoli**; another road loops down to the lush secluded valley of the **Amphiáraion** (*buses stop 3km away, at the Markópoulo cemetery; t 229 506 2144; open Tues–Sun 8–2.30*). Perhaps not a household name these days, Amphiaraos was not born of woman, but popped out of a sacred spring. Known as the Argive Seer, he joined in the Caledonian boar hunt, served as an Argonaut and was one of the famous Seven against Thebes. When that battle of champions turned into a rout and he was about to be speared, Zeus opened up the earth and swallowed him down into the under-world, where he continued his prophetic vocation, moving between worlds by way of his watery birthplace, the **sacred spring**. Next to this are the remains of a 4th-century BC Doric **temple** with the base of its cult statue, and the **altar** where those who consulted Amphiaraos first sacrificed a ram. They would then wrap themselves up in the skin and sleep on a marble bench in the long **enkoimeterion** (an impressive building with 41 Doric columns across the façade) where the god, like Asklepios, came to them in their dreams, which would be interpreted by the priests. A clutter of votive statue bases around the altar confirm a reasonable success rate. Most winsome of all is a bijou **theatre**, with five ornate marble armchairs for the priests and a restored proscenium with eight half columns in Ymittós marble. On the opposite bank of the stream are ruins of lodgings and perhaps a clinic, and a **waterclock** (*klepsydra*).

Skála Oropoú, just to the west, has tavernas and frequent ferries to Erétria, Évia. In ancient times it was sometimes under Thebes, sometimes under Athens, which increased the importance of strictly Attic Rámnous as a port. If you have a car, consider the scenic route to Athens by way of Malakása and Tatóï (*see* below).

North of Athens: Mount Párnitha

Wild and rugged Mount Parnés (Párnitha) is Attica's highest at 4,635ft, a little outpost of Switzerland covered with a surprising variety of flora – a full sixth of all the endemic plants of Greece, with plenty of Aleppo pine on the lower reaches and Greek fir high up. Although not exceptionally high, it is long; there are ski facilities near the summit, a good network of paths and a casino for those who'd rather gamble than ramble. Pick up the green ROAD map of Párnitha, which has all the paths and useful phone numbers if you want to do some serious exploring.

From **Achárnes**, an ancient *deme* now swallowed by the greater Athens octopus (or **Metamórfosi**, with an exit on the National Road), you can join the road up Párnitha to **Ag. Triáda**, a little resort at 3,600ft, by a sparkling spring. From here there is a turn-off left for the Mont Parnés casino and the Greek Alpine Club refuge (**t** *210 323 8775*); the road continues to the gates of the radar tower at the summit. A path near Ag. Triáda leads to a famous **Cave of Pan** (signposted, but you need a map and sturdy shoes).

Metamórfosi is also the point of departure for the ancient road to Párnitha's easternmost pass by way of Varimbóbi and **Tatóï** (ancient Dekelia), where the shade and rural tavernas are a favourite retreat. The Greek royal family had their summer palace here, in a lovely fenced park – a rare oasis protected from the omnipresent goats, who have made much of the rest of Attica into a museum of things goats don't like. In ancient times, when Évia was the breadbasket of Athens, the Dekelia pass was

Getting Around

There are two **buses** a day (No.713 from Acharnón St, north of Omónia Square) up to Ag. Triáda, at 6.30am and 2.30pm (check by phoning **t** 185). Bus 914 from Plateía Váthis goes twice a day to the base of the funicular. If you're **driving**, there's a Párnitha exit off the National Road; the road up to Ag. Triáda is scenic but windy – the **funicular** is faster (**t** 210 246 9111, daily exc Wed, from 3pm to 6pm every half hour and from 6pm to 3am every 15mins). For Filí, take bus A12 or B12 from Márnis St in Athens, **t** 210 520 0311.

Where to Stay

Párnitha ✉ **13610**
Grand Hotel Mont Parnés, 35km from Athens above Ag. Triáda, accessible by road or funicular, **t** 210 246 9111, **f** 210 246 0768 (*L; luxury*). At 3,444 ft, each room enjoys one of the finest views in Greece; laze by the pool with all of Attica at your feet. Evening dress and passports required for the hotel **casino** (*open daily exc Wed, 7.30pm–1.45am, till 2.45am on Sun*).

essential for transporting the grain into the city. When Alcibiades went over to the Spartans, he suggested they capture it (413 BC) and build a fortress as a base for raids into Attica (you can still see its ruins on the mountain to the left, by the royal grave-yard). Above Tatói the road climbs to the top of the pass at **Ag. Merkoúrios**, with a stunning view across to Évia, before descending to Skála Oropoú (*see* opposite).

The western route over Párnitha begins at **Áno Lósia** just west of Achárnes and leads up to **Filí**, another favourite weekend spot with tavernas. The road passes into the spectacular ravine of Goúra, where the Byzantine convent of **Moní Kleistón** (rebuilt in the 17th century) hangs dramatically over the wall of the gorge. The road rises through the crags to the 4th-century BC **fortress of Phyle** that guarded the shortest road (often closed by snow) between Athens and Thebes. Its 10ft-thick walls are well preserved, but suffered damage in the 1999 earthquake. A dirt road follows the ancient track to the Skoúrta Plateau into Boeotia.

Heading West: Athens towards Corinth

Dafní Monastery

The main highway west of Athens passes an endless array of forklift retailers before reaching Dafní park and the most important Byzantine church in Attica, part of the once grand **Dafní Monastery**, enclosed in lofty walls (*closed following the 1999 earth-quake, but due to reopen in 2004*). At this very point, the Sacred Way (Ierós Ódos) from Athens to Eleusis began its descent to the sea, and the temple of Apollo Daphneios ('of the laurel') was an important stop on the road, before it supplied both the building stone and its name to the monastery that replaced it in the 6th century. The existing church of 1080 was decorated with superb mosaics by masters from Constantinople, an unusually extravagant gesture on the part of the emperor who knew full well how vulnerable this area was to attack. After 1204, the Dukes of Athens gave the monastery to the Cistercians and made it their ducal mausoleum (hence the fleurs-de-lys and Latin crosses on the two sarcophagi). It functioned as an Orthodox monastery under the Turks, but declined after the War of Independence into a barracks, a lunatic asylum and a sheep pen before restoration began in 1887; today it's a World Heritage Site. Each of the mosaics is a masterpiece, made during the golden age of the Comneni and touched with Classical grace. Your eye, however, is drawn up at once to an implacable vision of *Christ* that makes even Michelangelo's Christ of the Sistine Chapel seem amenable in comparison. Below him are the 16 prophets, and in the squinches and along the walls scenes from the lives of Christ and the Virgin, including a *Crucifixion* (with a heartrending Virgin), a majestic *Transfiguration* and a wonderful *Descent into Hell*, with Christ shattering the door.

If one were to pin down a setting for Shakespeare's *A Midsummer Night's Dream*, Dafní's park is the most logical candidate, although these days the moonstruck are now confined to the large psychiatric hospital opposite. Further west on the Sacred Way/busy highway, the sharp-eyed may spot a few remains of a **Temple of Aphrodite**. Beyond that at **Skaramangás** are Greece's largest shipyards, founded in 1956 by

Getting Around

The A16 **bus** from Plateía Koumoundoúrou (Eleftherías) stops at Dafní and Elefsína. Local **trains** to Corinth, which haven't changed much since the 1950s, call at Elefsína and Mégara and the little towns by the sea, but take their sweet time. Orange buses from Thissío Station (*see* p.105) depart every 30mins for Mégara, and roughly every 2hrs for Vília; both stop in Elefsína.

Stávros Niárchos. Broad views of Elefsína bay are now possible, past rusting ships, to Sálamis; the famous naval battle of 480 BC (*see* p.145) was fought in this narrow strait. The **lake of Reiti** to your right was once the fish tank of the Hierophant of Eleusis (*see* below); the ancient Sacred Way crossed it on a causeway. The road then crosses into the Thirasian plain (or Rarian plain of myth), where there's a turn-off for Elefsína.

Elefsína (Ancient Eleusis)

Many are the sights to be seen in Greece, and many are the wonders to be heard; but on nothing does heaven bestow more care than on the Eleusinian rites and the Olympic games.

Pausanias

Now known as Elefsína, this Greek holy of holies and birthplace of Aeschylus (525–456 BC) is a busy industrial city, on the verge of becoming even busier as the crossroads of the new Attica highway with the E94 to the Peloponnese. In the centre of town, residential streets surround the ruins of its famous sanctuary and low acropolis. This had a Mycenaean settlement, and it is during that era that Demeter became associated with the city. Tradition has it that King Eumolpos, who had Thracian origins, was the very first celebrant of her Mysteries. Afterwards her priests were chosen from two aristocratic families, the Kerykes and the Eumolpidai, the latter providing the chief priest, the Hierophant (the 'displayer of sacred things').

The cult became truly Panhellenic after 600 BC, when Athens assimilated the Mysteries into her increasingly grandiose civic religion. Pisistratos built impressive fortification walls and towers around the site to emphasize its importance, and a 20km Sacred Way was laid out from the Dipylon gate to the sanctuary. Now Athenians could boast that *they* had introduced cultivation and the Mysteries to the world. The hereditary priests continued in office, but the Athenian *archon* took charge of the annual event. Initiation was open to all Greek-speaking men and women, slave or master, and the penalty for telling what occurred on the last night was death; Aeschylus was nearly lynched for supposedly revealing too much in one of his plays. Subsequent leaders added grand buildings and expanded the sanctuary's boundaries. Under Pericles, the hall of initiation was doubled in size, and the Mysteries remained so popular into Roman times that one writer called it 'the common precinct of the world'. Emperors, especially Hadrian and Marcus Aurelius, funded building sprees. But Theodosius's anti-pagan edit in 379 and the sanctuary's destruction by Alaric and the Visigoths in 395 marked its end. The town itself survived into the Middle Ages, and then was abandoned until the 18th century.

The Mysteria

'Thrice blessed are those mortals who see these mysteries before departing to Hades; for they alone have true life there. All that is evil besets the rest,' wrote Sophocles, and although the secret was kept too well to know what the initiates saw (one assumes, with Demeter as the focus, that it involved the regenerative cycle of nature), the build-up to the great moment is known in detail. In March, initiates would participate in the Lesser Mysteria on the banks of the Ilissos river in Athens, a necessary preliminary to the Great Mysteria that lasted for nine days in September. First the sacred objects in their baskets (*kistai*) were taken from Eleusis to the City Eleusinion in Athens. On the next day, the opening of the festival would be proclaimed by the Herald, with the proviso that murderers, desecrators and non-Greek speakers abstain. The next day the initiates went to the sea to be purified at Fáliro, where each sacrificed a piglet, bathed, and donned new clothes. The next day was in honour of Asklepios, for late comers (usually VIPs). On the fourth day, the sacred objects were returned to Eleusis, followed by the initiates who set off bearing a statue of Iacchos (Dionysos, as the lord of the dance), punctuated by cries of 'Iacchos! Iacchos!'. To stress the civic aspect of the rite, they were followed by members of the Areopagos, the council of 500, and Athenian citizens ordered by tribe and *deme*. There were frequent stops along the Sacred Way, to sing and sacrifice at shrines, and at the Kephisos bridge, where insults and jokes (*gephyrismoi*, or 'bridgery') were hurled at leading members. On their arrival in Eleusis at dusk, the initiates would be regaled in the forecourt and dance around the Kallichoron, the fountain of good dances.

The Myth of Demeter and Kore

Kore (or Persephone) was out gathering flowers when the earth suddenly opened up, a dark chariot emerged, and its driver Hades made off with her. Her mother, the goddess Demeter, disguised herself as an old woman and searched the world for her, and when she came to Eleusis she sat disconsolate on the 'mirthless rock'. Keleus, the king of Eleusis, took her in, and Iambe, his daughter tried to cheer her up by telling jokes. Touched by their hospitality, Demeter decided to make Keleus' youngest son immortal by immersing him in fire; his frightened mother intervened, thus dooming him to immediate mortality. Demeter then angrily revealed her true self and ordered Keleus to build her a house (Eleusis, according to some, means the 'temple of her in dark rage lurking'). Eventually Keleus' other son Tripolemos told Demeter that he had witnessed Hades stealing her daughter. Furiously Demeter ordered the world to stop bearing fruit until Kore was returned. Humanity was on the point of starvation when Zeus intervened with a compromise. As Kore had eaten several pomegranate seeds (symbol of the marriage bond) in the gardens of the dead, she would have to spend some time down below as Persephone, queen of Hades, but could spend the other nine months on earth with her mother. Demeter then rewarded Tripolemos with agricultural know-how: seed corn, a plough and a winged chariot pulled by snakes to travel and spread the word. With the seasons and farming taken care of, she then introduced her Mysteries of Eleusis.

The secret rites took place during the next two nights, when each initiate would be guided by a *mystagogue* or sponsor. The little that we know (mostly derived from art, literary hints and hostile Christian writers) suggests that the entire experience with its dramatic tension was as important as the 'secrets' themselves (and effects may have been heightened with drugs; the poppy, after all, is one of Demeter's symbols). At some point the initiates were blinded with a hood; a winnowing fan was passed over them, and they wandered about in the dark, disorientated, while the Hierophant beat a gong, summoning Kore from the earth. The Mysteries culminated in the Telesterion, illuminated by thousands of torches held by the Epoptai ('the beholders' or second-year initiates), with 'things shown' by the Hierophant in a transcendental moment that united the initiate with the divine, a mystic communion that offered some hope for the afterlife. Then the Epoptai witnessed 'the ear of corn, silently cut' and perhaps the epiphany of Demeter's child Ploutos 'wealth', bearing a cornucopia. The eighth day was for sacrifices and celebrations, and on the next the initiates returned to Athens.

The Site

t 210 554 3470; open Tues–Sun 8.30–3; adm.

Trying to evoke all this in modern Elefsína in broad daylight requires some imagination; the ruins wrapped around the acropolis are a somewhat confused palimpsest from Mycenaean to Roman times, surrounded by views of cranes, smokestacks and rusting tankers. At the site entrance is a portion of the **Sacred Way**, which ended in the large **forecourt** outside the walls. This was redone by the Romans, who also rebuilt the **Temple of Artemis Propylaea** and its two altars (note the gameboards carved in the steps, perhaps by idle initiates). Identical **Triumphal arches** (copies of Hadrian's in Athens) stood to the right and left of the forecourt, the latter leading into the town; the inscription 'All the Hellenes to the Goddesses and the Emperor' is still in place. Beyond are remains of hotels and baths. The ornate **fountain** near here was the Kallichoron 'of the beautiful dances', although the original was elsewhere.

Marble steps lead up to the sanctuary's monumental entrance, the **Great Propylaea**, built by Marcus Aurelius. It was modelled after the Propylaea on the Acropolis and built of the same Pentelic marble, but during the barbarian invasions in the 3rd century AD its colonnade was walled in; you can see the track in the stone where doors opened. The large medallion bust, probably of Marcus Aurelius, came from the pediment. To the right of this were the houses and meeting rooms of the priests. Further up, the **Lesser Propylaea** was a walled 40ft passage built with funds given by Cicero's friend Appius Claudius Pulcher after 50 BC. Again, grooves remain where the doors opened on their rollers. Beyond lay the sacred precinct of the Mysteries, where only initiates could enter. To the right, the small cave called the **Plutonion** is now thought to have been the location of the Mirthless Rock; a natural rock here fits the bill, and as initiates entered they would have a glimpse of 'Demeter' grieving by the flickering torchlight. The rock-cut **exedra** beyond may have been a stage for a scene in the re-enactment drama; to its left stood a **treasury** (another candidate for the Mirthless Rock) and a **temple**, perhaps dedicated to Hadrian's wife Sabina.

Beyond is the great square platform of the Hall of Initiation, the **Telesterion**. Solon built the first proper Telesterion in 590 BC, but as the cult grew it had to be enlarged, first by Pisistratos and then by Pericles. The latter ordered the design from Iktinos, the architect of the Parthenon, although it was only completed after both had died. Iktinos' Telesterion was a hypostyle hall supported by 42 columns and solid exterior walls (except for six doorways) with eight tiers of seats on each side, capable of holding 3,000 initiates. In the centre was the **Anaktoron**, which held the sacred

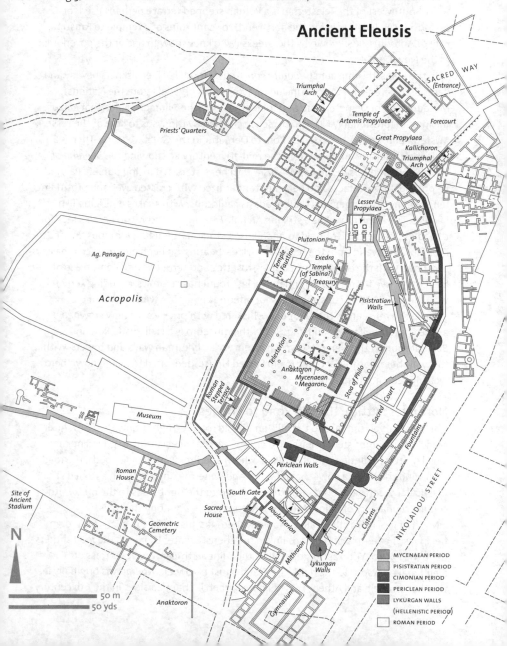

Ancient Eleusis

SACRED WAY
(Entrance)

Triumphal Arch

Temple of
Artemis Propylaea

Forecourt

Priests' Quarters

Great Propylaea
Kallichoron
Triumphal
Arch

Lesser
Propylaea

Plutonion

Ag. Panagia

Temple to Faustina

Exedra
Temple
(of Sabina?)
Treasury

Pisistratian
Walls

Acropolis

Telesterion

Anaktoron
Mycenaean
Megaron

Stoa of Philo

Sacred Court

Fountain

Roman
Stepped
Terrace

Museum

Roman
House

South Gate

Periclean Walls

NIKOLAIDOU STREET

Site of
Ancient
Stadium

Sacred
House

Bouleuterion

Cisterns

Geometric
Cemetery

Mithraion

Lykurgan
Walls

N

50 m
50 yds

Anaktoron

Gymnasium

MYCENAEAN PERIOD
PISISTRATIAN PERIOD
CIMONIAN PERIOD
PERICLEAN PERIOD
LYKURGAN WALLS
(HELLENISTIC PERIOD)
ROMAN PERIOD

objects displayed by the Hierophant at the climax of the ceremony. In all reconstructions of the Telesterion, the Anaktoron was always exactly here, right on top of the Mycenaean megaron which according to the *Hymn to Demeter* (*c.* 600 BC) was the house built by King Keleus for Demeter. Only one layman was ever allowed inside the Anaktoron: Marcus Aurelius, to thank him for all his contributions. The massive **Stoa of Philo** on the outer (southeast) side was added in *c.* 310 BC. Around this was a court, gradually filled in over the centuries but now excavated to reveal the older defensive walls. Southwest of the Telesterion is a Roman **stepped terrace** perhaps used for performances, leading up (on the north end) to scant ruins of a **temple to Faustina**, wife of Antonius Pius, known by the Greeks (who knew how to flatter their overlords) as the New Demeter.

Up the steps, the **museum** (*separate adm*) has a model of Eleusis in its heyday and items associated with the cult, including two copies of reliefs from the National Museum: one of Demeter, Kore and Tripolemos, and the 'Ninnion tablet' that shows the initiate (presumably Ninnion herself) being led by Dionysos to Kore at the Lesser Mysteria and, on top, being led by Kore to Demeter in the Great Mysteria. There's an endearingly bizarre amphora from the mid-7th century BC showing the *Blinding of Polyphemus* and *Perseus slaying Medusa*, with her sisters in dancing pursuit. Painted before the gorgons' faces had become standardized with crossed eyes and protruding tongues, the artist imagined their heads as cauldrons, with snakes emerging like handles. The same room has a striking Archaic *Fleeing Kore* from 490 BC; also look for a headless *Demeter*, attributed to Agorakritos, student of Phidias; Antinous dressed as Dionysos; a caryatid from the Lesser Propylaea, bearing on her head the sacred basket decorated with the ears of corn, poppies, rosettes and *kernoi*; and the only piece of linen to survive from Classical times. The last room has ceramics, including *kernoi*, with their many little cups and holes for offerings of grains, wine, honey or oil.

Above the museum is the **Acropolis**, whiskered with prickly pear, now crowned by a little church, bell tower and flag. Below the museum is a Hellenistic-Roman **Bouleuterion** by the well-preserved 4th-century BC **Lykurgan walls and towers**. Within the walls here was the Geometric-era **Sacred House**, dedicated to an unknown hero worshipped into Archaic times.

Northwest Attica: the Old Road to Thebes

At Elefsína, you can take to the hills on the old road to Thebes, now the E692. After Mándra this climbs steeply, passing a dozen tavernas specializing in grilled meats, a pretty little Byzantine church (at Palaiochóri) and fire-scarred pinewoods. The road then winds down to a bowl-shaped valley and wine-making **Inoí**, with a ruined Classical **tower** (to the right of the road). A road to the right leads to the pretty 11th-century **Monastery of Ósios Melétios** with frescoes, set among the trees.

North of Inoí looms the wall of Mount Kitherónas; just before it, in an overgrown field, was the Temple of Dionysos linked to Athens' Greater Dionysia. The road slithers up to the Pass of Yiftókastro, guarded by the ruined 4th-century BC fortress of **Eleutherai** on a spur to the right. Like Plataea just below, Eleutherai was originally in the Theban orbit, and Athens was delighted when it changed sides in the 6th century

BC. Once the fort had eight towers, and even today the north wall is almost perfectly intact. In 1941 British Commonwealth forces attempted to halt the Germans here; on the left side of the road is a memorial to a later Resistance action. Below lies the broad plain of Boeotia, Plataea and Thebes (*see* p.374).

The Halcyonic Gulf

Just after Inoí (*see* above) a church in a lush walled garden marks the left turn for **Vília** (Βίλια) a pleasant village famous for its clean air and handsome stone church by Ernst Ziller. In summer, frequent buses make the dramatic descent past a bizarre stone folly to **Pórto Gérmano** (ancient Aigosthena) on the Halcyonic Gulf, the eastern-most pocket of the Gulf of Corinth (the original Halcyone grieved so much at her husband's death that the gods turned them both into kingfishers, and granted seven to fourteen days of calm so they could build their nest on the sea). On summer week-ends Athenians pack Pórto Gérmano's pebbly beaches and fish tavernas, guarded by the **Fortress of Aigosthena**, the best preserved Classica-era castle in Greece. It was built by Mégara but was never of much use; today you can clamber over the walls of sun-soaked polygonal stone and its ruined towers, once fitted with catapults to smash invaders; inside are two Byzantine chapels and remains of monastic cells.

Grim **Mount Kitherónes** (4,622ft) closes off the view to the north – there's a dirt road zigzagging to the top that begins just after Vília's folly. Kitherónas was a magnet for weirdness in ancient times. It was famous for its wild animals; the baby Oedipus was exposed here, in the vain hope that one would eat him, and Dionysos' maenads, during their revels here, tore the Theban king Pentheus to pieces. Its summit saw the mother of all bonfires, the pan-Boeotian festival of the great Daidala, where every 59 years in honour of Hera each community felled a mighty oak, fashioned it into a figure of the goddess, and carted it up to the summit where huge blocks of wood had been interlocked to form a log cabin altar. Bulls and cows and other lesser animals were sacrificed, and then the altar, the sacrificed animals and the wooden dolls were ignited 'amid wine and fragrance' in a fire that could be seen all over Boeotia.

A branch off the Vília–Pórto Gérmano road descends precipitously to the long, shadeless beach at **Psátha**; here a road has been cut under the cliffs to **Aleppochóri** (ancient Pegae), a classic seaside village, with an often rubbish-strewn beach. From here you can cut across to Mégara, or continue along to the quieter cleaner coves before Perachóra (*see* p.188) and Loutráki.

Mégara to Corinth

West of Elefsína the main (toll) highway next passes into the Megarid, the ancient state north of the Isthmus and powerhouse in the first millennium BC. The chief city **Mégara** was one of the few in the Bronze Age to have a Greek rather than pre-Greek name ('the big houses'), and its Dorian population made their city a mercantile centre, specializing in woollen cloaks. But as Mégara's territory was small, it was one of the first to colonize, beginning with Megara Hyblaea in Sicily in 728 BC, followed in 660 BC by Byzantium. It produced the aristocratic poet Theognis (*c.* 570–485 BC), who wrote elegant verse for dinner parties (including the first great body of homosexual poetry); in Classical times it held annual games that featured a kissing contest between boys. Clashes over the control of Sálamis led Mégara to be squeezed like a pimple by Corinth and Athens (which eventually dominated), but it had a last hurrah under one of Socrates' pupils, Euclides, founder of the Megaran school of philosophy (440–380 BC). The modern city is still famous – for chickens. Almost nothing of its past has survived above ground besides its street plan, although there are a few ruins at Páxi, its ancient port, along with fish tavernas. A new **Archaeological Museum**, in Mégara's former town hall at 22 G. Menidiáti (*t 229 602 2426; open Tues–Sun 8.30–3; free*), has items from rescue digs – a Classical lion spout, grave steles, vases and finds from an Archaic cemetery in Aleppochóri.

West of Mégara, the old and new roads and the railway pass on narrow corniches, known as the **Kakia Skala** ('evil stair') where cliffs plunge into sea – the mythic landscape where Theseus performed his labours en route from Troezen (*see* p.267) to Athens. The old road by the sea is more fun to take if you have the time; at the 50km mark from Athens are the **Skironian Rocks**, where the nasty brigand Skiron used to kick travellers into the sea and into the jaws of a man-eating turtle, until Theseus gave him a dose of his own medicine. Here sculptor Kóstas Polychronópoulos opened the **Skiróneio Museum** (*t 229 606 1270; open Wed, Sat and Sun 10am–8pm; free*), with his own and other contemporary works. **Kinetta**, with its gardens descending to a white shingle beach, marks the end of Attica. The next village, **Ag. Theodori**, was ancient Krommyon, the lair of the man-eating sow, which Theseus also dispatched.

The Corinth Canal: The Ditch and the *Diolkos*

On the new highway bridge, you can pass the Corinth Canal, a dramatic ribbon of blue under sheer walls, before you know it. Periander, the early 6th-century BC tyrant of Corinth, was the first to start digging across the 6km isthmus, but found it too difficult and opted for the *diolkos*, a grooved stone carriageway over which ships could be towed by winch or wheeled cart from gulf to gulf on rollers. Cargoes were off-loaded and hauled overland, creating a bonanza for Corinth's teamsters. Octavian used the *diolkos* for his warships to chase Antony and Cleopatra, and records show it was in use as late as the 9th century. Intact sections (signposted) remain on the southwest bank of the canal close to the Corinth-Loutráki bridge, and on the other bank as well; it meandered a bit according to the topography.

Julius Caesar, Caligula and Hadrian all toyed with the idea of a canal. Anything cutting the trip from Piraeus to the Ionian Sea by about 200 nautical miles was worth a study or two. In AD 40 Egyptian experts claimed that the water level of the Corinthian Gulf was higher than that of the Saronic, and that a canal would inundate the Saronic islands. But Nero, not the type to worry about an island or two, went ahead in AD 67, importing thousands of Jewish slaves and personally loosening the first clod with a little golden axe. When Nero killed himself three months later, the project got the axe, too. Nobody tried again until 1881. A Hungarian went bankrupt with the effort, but Andréas Syngros took over and the first ship passed through the 'ditch', as the locals call it, on 25 July 1893. A boat from Loutráki (*see* p.187) takes tourists through twice a week.

The Peloponnese

...the place like a great plane-leaf that the sun's torrent carries away...
George Seferis

This improbable plane leaf, the Peloponnese, dangling from the mainland by a fragile, broken stem, is the real cradle of ancient Greece. Not the Greece of democracy, mathematics, science or philosophy, but something even more compelling in the cultural baggage of the West – the myths and legends. This is where Pegasus flew and Heracles laboured, where the curse of the House of Atreus devoured its victims, where the beautiful Helen hatched out of an egg, and where the Greeks themselves hatched a veritable rogue's gallery of monsters and gods: the Hydra, the Nemean lion, the Stymphalian birds, werewolves, Pan, horse-headed Demeter and Wolf Zeus and more. Names like Mycenae, Tiryns, Pýlos, Argos, Olympia, Sparta, Troezen and the River Styx hover on the fine line of dream, and startle when you first see them on the road map, cheek by jowl with the little symbols for campsites and petrol stations.

The natural beauty of the Peloponnese comes in mythic proportions as well. The decorative and quaint have no place here; the land is as dramatic and magical as the myths that flowed from its pores, sensuous in the measure of human imagination. Cool alpine pastures are disturbed only by the bells of cattle, sheep and goats, while all around mountains claw at the sky, their bowels ripped up in chasms, their cliffs shattered by the sea; the sublime and awful Taíyetos tail off into the Máni and ends in the entrance to Hades. When not impossibly vertical, the Peloponnese is astonishingly lush, a garden of olives and grapes and citrus groves, bathed in the spotlit clarity of the sun and transparent seas, wafted in the scent of pines, lemon blossoms and jasmine. It is a landscape with too many dimensions, too much history, too many monsters and heroes and gods. The latter may shy away from the busy holiday strips, but they are never very far when the noises of the modern world fall silent, either in the rosy-fingered dawn or the stillness of the noonday demon or the blazing bright starry nights where they were born.

History

Peloponnesian history is pure theatre; with dazzling actors, a great, improbable script, and a stage littered with stunning, evocative, time-worn props. **Act I** opens with the long age of the pre-Greeks, a mysterious and deep Peloponnesian *Das Rheingold*. Traces of these earliest protagonists (35,000–20,000 BC), have been found in several sites in the Máni, Argolís, Elís and Laconía. The large Fráchthi Cave in Argolís takes the prize for the greatest continuity, and produced Greece's earliest complete skeleton, c. 8000 BC. The era's most interesting artefacts are small, squat, big-breasted, full-bottomed female figures, a type common in the Mediterranean, hinting at a widespread Mother Goddess cult.

Act II begins with shadowy incursions of foreigners (2500 to 1800 BC). The current theory has two waves of migration, one in the **Early Helladic** period of non Greek-speakers culminating in the building of the House of Tiles at Lerna (*c.* 2200 BC), and another after its destruction, this time by **Greek-speaking Indo-Europeans**, the people of the Minyan ware. The Indo-European sky god cult, a social hierarchy, a tendency to

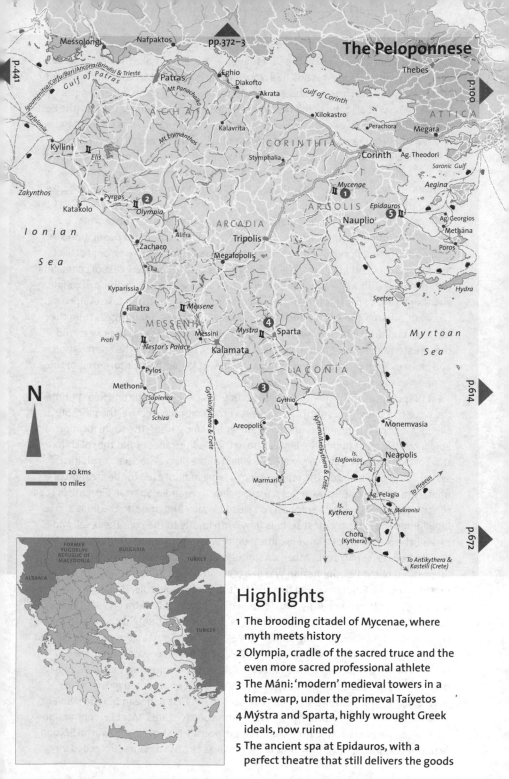

Highlights

1 The brooding citadel of Mycenae, where myth meets history
2 Olympia, cradle of the sacred truce and the even more sacred professional athlete
3 The Máni: 'modern' medieval towers in a time-warp, under the primeval Taíyetos
4 Mýstra and Sparta, highly wrought Greek ideals, now ruined
5 The ancient spa at Epidauros, with a perfect theatre that still delivers the goods

concentrate cult activity on hilltop sanctuaries, all began to make their presence felt (although mother goddesses still had clout), as the glittering **Mycenaeans** took centre stage after 1600 BC. They were backed by spectacular sets: palaces with a king, or 'wanax', who was also the high priest in residence; examples survive in Pýlos (the best preserved), Tiryns and of course Mycenae, 'rich in gold', which gave its name to the era and somehow held sway over the others. They took over Minoan palaces in Crete, assimilated both their architecture to some extent and almost all of their wonderful art, and adapted their palace script Linear A to create **Linear B** (the first written script in Greek). They built Cyclopean walls and 'beehive' tholos tombs on a scale that take the breath away.

After 1200 BC, the curtain crashes down on the Mycenaeans for reasons that are hard to determine. Their palaces burned down and a much reduced population struggled on in isolated pockets. A dark '*entre-acte*' occurs during which regional dialects appear, and conventional historical wisdom brings on a whole new cast of characters to explain the shift in the plot. These new actors are the '**Dorians**', a group of rough and tough Greek-speakers arriving apparently from points north to take over in Laconía, Corinthía, the Argolís and Messenía, leaving the rest for refugees from the last era. Hard-drinking, club-wielding, death-defying Hercules was their hero, and they created a myth that made him their forefather, so great was their admiration, and perhaps their practical need, for a past that would justify their take-over of the Peloponnese as the 'sons of Hercules'.

Act III spotlights the disjointed greatness of Classical, Hellenistic and Roman times: the wealth of naughty Corinth, Greece's first economic powerhouse; the glory of Olympia, site of the most prestigious of all panhellenic games; the sophistication of Epidauros, the most famed healing centre in the Mediterranean; and the machinations of Dorian Sparta, in many ways the villain of the piece. The Spartan political system, based as it was on the repression of a large majority, led to the creation of a military machine coupled with permanent political paranoia. Spartan extremism took the city-state ideal, with its emphasis on citizen loyalty and pride, to the limit and highlighted the system's most serious flaw: with loyalty to the *polis* the be-all and end-all, the possibility of a larger political unity was never seriously entertained. The tension between Sparta and Athens, a simmering blend of jealousy, mistrust, and self-interest, led to the **Peloponnesian War** in 431 BC. Athens lost, Sparta won, but, like most bullies, the Spartans could fight better than they could rule. Thebes, Sparta's former ally, shattered her army and destroyed her power at Leúktra (371 BC), thanks to **Epaminóndas** and his new cavalry-infantry tactics. He then brought the war to the Peloponnese and liberated long suffering Messinía from Sparta's tyranny, and created today's colossal ruins at Megalopolis and Messene. Theban power was crushed in turn by **Philip II** of Macedonia. **Alexander** was too busy conquering the world to pay much attention to the Peloponnese, and they were not enamoured of the Macedonians in any case. Resistance coalesced in the **First Achaean League** (280 BC), a significant but ill-fated attempt at a federation of city-states. Most Peloponnesian cities were members at one time or another, especially in the more powerful **Second Achaean League**, founded by Aratus of Sikyon in 245 BC. Macedonia succeeded in regaining control, but the struggle weakened Greece, making it especially easy for Rome to deliver the knockout punch in 146 BC.

Rome hauled off as much art as she could cram into her ships, and created the **province of Achaía** (the entire Peloponnese and some of the mainland), making Corinth its capital. The Odeion in Corinth became a gladiatorial arena, and Sparta's Temple of Artemis Orthia where boys were flogged was an especially popular tourist attraction; when Pausanius wrote the first guide book, the Peloponnese had the starring role. St Paul and St Andrew came and converted many to Christianity, but then it was curtains for the Peloponnese again as barbarian hordes began knocking at the Isthmus in AD 267.

Act IV begins with the Byzantines, who saw the Peloponnese as a backwater. Cities such as Corinth, Pátras, Lacedaemónia (ancient Sparta) and Monemvasiá kept their chins up, but the general picture is one of decline. Barbarian invasions continued periodically, coupled with devastating outbreaks of plague; large populations from other parts of the Byzantine empire entered the picture. **Slavs** in particular changed the face of the Peloponnese, as the bureaucrats in Constantinople moved populations inside their large empire in order to provide a lucrative tax base. One Byzantine map actually labelled the Peloponnese as 'the Land of the Avars'.

By 1204, Constantinople was such a remote entity that many Peloponnesians were not all that unhappy to be taken over by the '**Franks**' (the Greek word at the time for any European) in the Fourth Crusade. The Venetians nabbed the best art and gained control of strategic ports along their trade routes, on the islands, and at Methóni, Koróni and Monemvasiá. But most of the Morea, as the Peloponnese was then commonly called, became the **Principality of Achaía** or *La Princée de l'Amorée*, a *Midsummer's Night Dream* interlude of French knights and chivalry whose first prince was Geoffrey Villehardouin. His seat of government was in Andreville (Andravída) and his principal castle was at Glarenza (Kyllíni). Achaía was divided into 12 baronies, and its lords hung on long enough to write the most complete set of feudal law codes to come down to modern times, to institute jousts, indulge courtly manners, marry Byzantine princesses and even produce their own *Chronicle of the Morea* to immortalize their conquest. But they kept losing bits of it, especially after the Battle of Pelagonia in 1259, when they had to give back Monemvasiá and the castles of the Máni and Mystrá to the Greeks. The Byzantines then made **Mystrá** the seat of their **despotate**, from where they fitfully regained control over the rest of the Morea. More enduringly, they filled Mystrá with lovely churches; it would be the last capital of Byzantium before the **Turks** took over in 1460, seven years after the fall of Constantinople.

The Turkish turban was not an improvement over the Frankish mitre. Interested only in taxes, the Turks developed a *laissez-faire* policy except where taxes were concerned, combined with vicious reprisals if their authority was challenged. Through plague and indifference the population of the Peloponnese dropped to a mere 100,000. Many areas such as the Máni and western Arcadía never submitted to the Turks, and the pashas were constantly reduced to some form of power-sharing with local Greek leaders, whom they could, of course, never quite trust. In spite of setbacks and disappointing efforts to oust the Turks by Morosini (Venice) in 1684 and Orlov (the Russians) in 1770, Greek fighters in *klephtic* bands fought and were defeated again and again, then headed for the hills, and bided their time. An entire culture surrounding these free mountain spirits arose, and it would prove a lifestyle hard to give up when independence came. Very little cultural benefit was derived from this part of the production, but it created some terrific props. Castles sprouted like toad-stools; over 300 moulder romantically in gorgeous settings, many overgrown and haunted by foxes, birds, and gypsies.

Act V starts with the indomitable clans and captains coming down from their mountain lairs in March of 1821 to lead the **War of Independence**. Theodore Kolokotrónis (*see* p.285) took Kalamáta; the flag of revolt was raised at Ag. Lávra in Achaía by the Archbishop of Pátras on 25 March, the day later chosen as Independence Day. Kolokotrónis' successes pushed the Turks to the wall and in 1825 the Sultan called in Ibrahim Pasha of Egypt, promising him the Peloponnese if only he could win it. He almost did, in the most vicious stage of the war. Luckily, in October 1827, the allied fleets of England, France and Russia sank the Turkish and Egyptian ships in the **Battle of Navaríno** at Pýlos on the west coast. The war ended and in a comic opera dénouement, conceived by the self-serving **Powers** (England, France and Russia), the Greeks found themselves under a monarchy presided over by a teenage Bavarian king with Naúplio as the capital, before tradition insisted on Athens.

Towns razed in the war, such as Trípolis and Argos, were rebuilt, and a new Sparta was laid out with grandiose hopes. Agriculture and animal husbandry remained the focus, and transport improved with the **Corinth Canal** (1882) and the **Peloponnesian Railroad** (1890s). On the whole, however, domestic improvements ran a poor second to Greece's interest in liberating and uniting all former Greek territories around the Aegean. Wars, and the Greek Civil War stopped progress here as everywhere else, and it is only in the last thirty years or so that the Peloponnese has really picked itself up and begun to prosper again. The biggest news today, and the national deadline for every long-deferred project, is now the **2004 Olympics**, when Greece wants to look its best in the international spotlight. Even the littlest, long-shuttered archaeological museums in the deepest, darkest Peloponnese plan to reopen in 2004, restorations of major sites are also under way, and most of the huge **Río bridge** over the Gulf of Corinth is already in place. Roads, even to very remote places, improve every year; traffic jams in the cities get worse, but the international cosmopolitanism that now reigns on many Greek islands is still far from the Peloponnese; you can drive for miles and miles in the mountains and not pass a single car.

Corinthia

The modern prefecture of Corinthia continues south beyond Corinth and its isthmus to the Dervenáki pass, and encompasses the Kyllíni range to the west, giving Corinthia a beautiful mountain hinterland that it never possessed in ancient times. Agriculture is the mainstay, especially the growing of Greece's finest wine grapes and

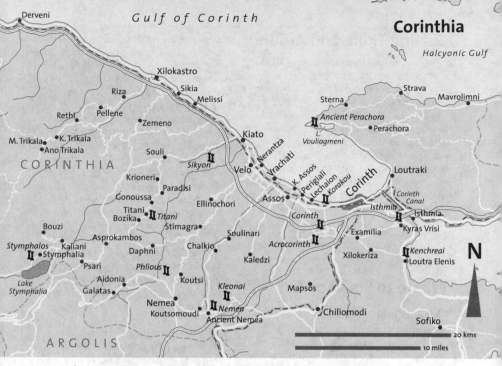

currants (the English word is derived from 16th-century raisins of Corauntz, or Corinth). And with modern systems of irrigation in place, the prefecture once again fits its Homeric description.

Corinth (Κορίνθοσ)

'Wealthy' was Homer's description, but 'decadent' is the epithet that has stuck. Corinth's natural citadel, the 1,800ft limestone Acrocorinth, is one of the great landmarks of Greece, where once a thousand sacred prostitutes plied their trade. The city-state of Corinth, which included the Isthmus – *the* Isthmus that gave its name to all isthmuses – was as wealthy and artistic as it was naughty. Two thousand years, St Paul's followers and countless earthquakes may have scoured the city clean of its fleshpots, but the fascination still lingers in the remarkable ruins near the poignantly ephemeral modern city that still bears its name.

Corinth: A Historical Outline

Corinth emerged out of the dim cocoon of the Dark Ages in the 9th century BC as a wealthy and precocious Dorian city. Perfectly placed at the narrow isthmus to control the north–south land route between the Peloponnese and the rest of mainland Greece, as well as to expand its influence both east and west, Corinth under an aristocratic family, the Bacchiads, had the talent to exploit its unique position. Her fast ships – the city probably invented the trireme – exported the distinctive Corinthian ware which dominated the Greek market all through the 8th–6th centuries BC.

Getting There and Around

There are regular **trains** to and from Athens, Pátras and Kalamáta. The station, t 274 102 2523, is three blocks east of the seaside square and has left-luggage facilities.

Buses are all clustered south of the seaside square, at Ermoú and Koliátsou Sts, t 274 107 5415. Buses to Athens and Loutráki leave every half hour from 6am to 10pm. City buses leave across the park for ancient Corinth (5km west) every hour from 8am to 9pm and go regularly to the Canal Zone. **Taxis**, t 274 107 3000, congregate near the bus station. For car hire, try Vassilópoulos, 39 Adimántou, t 274 102 5573; for mopeds: Liberópoulos, 27 Ethnikís Andistássiou, t 274 107 2937.

Where to Stay and Eat

Modern Corinth ✉ 20100

Konstantatos, t 274 102 2120, f 274 108 5634 (*C; expensive–moderate*). Just east of the Touristikí Plateía; standard but well kept. Some cheaper rooms without baths.

Neon, in the Touristikí Plateía. Reliable self-service chain with good Greek dishes.

Ancient Corinth ✉ 20100

Marinos Rooms and Taverna, t 274 103 1209, f 274 103 1994 (*moderate–inexpensive*). Set in a pine garden on the south edge of town. Best food in Ancient Corinth. *Open May–Oct.*

Shadow, t 274 103 1232, f 274 103 1481 (*moderate–inexpensive*). At the northeast edge of town. Its 12 plain rooms are modern and clean. *Open all year.*

Tassos, t 274 103 1225 (*inexpensive*). Right in town with 10 very modest rooms over a good, old-style taverna. *Open April–Oct.*

Ísthmia ✉ 20100

Kalamaki Beach, t 274 103 7653, f 274 103 7652, *kalamaki@tourhotel.gr* (*A; luxury–expensive*). Impersonal, but has a large pool, grassy grounds, tennis and a pretty beach. *Open April–Oct.*

Ísthmia Beach Camping, t 274 103 7447 (*inexpensive*). Attractive and shares its beach with the Kalamaki Beach next door. *Open April–Oct.*

Things began to go wrong for the Bacchiads when they were drawn into the first ever sea battle with their own colony Corcyra in 664 BC. That, and a refusal to share power, led to their overthrow and exile by the popular leader Kypselos around 650 BC. Kypselos and his son Periander (625–585 BC) founded more colonies and cultivated Miletus to assure trade links with Asia Minor. If Periander's private life was unsavoury (incest and necrophilia were only two of the rumours), no one doubted that he was a one-man Chamber of Commerce for Corinth. Periander instituted the Isthmian Games, built the *diolkos* (ships' tow path) across the Isthmus and translated the Temple of Apollo into stone, a lasting monument to civic prestige as well as piety.

Corinth became vulnerable when its economic dominance was challenged by Athens, particularly after 480 BC. It opted for the Spartan sphere as the lesser of two evils, and after Athens' defeat in the Peloponnesian War in 404, it, like every other *polis*, switched allegiances again and again. Yet it remained a magnet, providing all of the raunchy pleasures you might expect in a city with *two* ports of call. Even the young Alexander came to see the sights. One of these was Diogenes, the sour-tongued cynic who lived in a storage pot berating the foibles of rich and poor alike. When Alexander asked him if he desired some favour, he is reputed to have replied, 'Yes, stand a little out of my sun.'. Alexander was amused and impressed. 'If I weren't Alexander, I would like to be Diogenes,' he declared.

Corinth joined the Achaean League after 243 BC and led it in 200 BC. Its citizens thumbed their noses at Rome, at one point dumping excrement on the heads of the

Roman envoys to show the upstarts just what they thought of them. The Romans failed to see the joke and sent Mummius to destroy the city in 146 BC, appropriating its treasures and monuments for Rome and selling the saucy Corinthians into slavery. It lay deserted until Julius Caesar rebuilt it in 46 BC and Corinth boomed again, 'famous for being famous'. This attracted St Paul in AD 51 who remained in sin city for 18 months preaching and plying his trade as tent-maker, a sojourn that would inspire the two great Epistles to the Corinthians. As Rome's hold weakened, Corinth attracted the barbarians and what they did not destroy, earthquakes, especially in 375 and 521, did. Under the Byzantines, the city sank into obscurity.

The Franks wrested it from Greek defenders in 1210 after a five-year siege. Holding the Isthmus was vital for their principality of Achaía, but in 1458 the Turks took the Acrocorinth and built a city inside the walls. In the 1680s the Venetians took over for 28 years, then the Turks returned until 1822 when they were turned out during the War of Independence.

Corinthian Civic Mythology

Using bits of local myths and 'historic' (mostly Mycenaean) lore, every Greek city-state created a grand, self-serving, official history tracing its origins to gods and heroes. Corinth didn't have longstanding traditions, but it still managed to come up with two patrons, a witch, a founding father, a murderer and a horse. Helios and Poseidon (Sun and Sea), the patrons, vied for the whole city and compromised: Poseidon got the Isthmus and Helios the Acrocorinth where his worship would merge with his Olympian counterpart, Apollo. Medea, Helios' granddaughter, came next, bringing with her a whiff of oriental sorcery along with Jason, her husband of Golden Fleece fame, thus tying Corinth in nicely with the heroic past and placing the *Argo* firmly in Corinth's mythic harbour. Ten years later, Jason threw her over for the younger princess Glauke and a furious Medea sent her rival a flesh-eating cloak as a marriage gift before exiting Corinth in a huff. Corinth's citizens promptly stoned Medea's children to avenge the murder. Euripides was the first to claim that Medea killed her own children to spite Jason, a version everybody, including Freud, prefers.

Sisyphos, at Medea's behest, then took his place in the city saga. He was fraudulent, cunning, avaricious, and the Corinthians loved him. When he tried to cheat death itself, the gods punished him in Tartarus by having him roll a boulder up a hill, almost reaching the top, only to have it roll down again *ad infinitum*. Sisyphos' grandson Bellerophon became the city's hero – no matter that he got his name 'killer of Bellerus' because of murder. A Greek hero's homicidal moments were a handy way to get him off on adventures. An oracle would declare that to expiate the crime he must go off and kill a monster or two. Bellerophon's target was the lion-headed, goat-bodied, snake-tailed Chimaera. He rode Pegasus, the flying horse who hung about on the Acrocorinth, and executed a deadly aerial attack by dropping lead arrows into the monster's flaming mouth. Bellerophon then tempted fate by trying to fly to Olympus; Zeus hurled him to earth to finish his days lame and miserable. Pegasus fared better; Zeus made him into a constellation and the Corinthians immortalized him on their coins throughout their long history.

Modern Corinth: A Hub but Not a Centre

Modern Corinth stood on the ruins of the ancient city until 1858, when a devastating earthquake caused it to relocate to its present site, down by the canal. It didn't help much. Earthquakes have destroyed the new town several times (1928 and 1981 were the big ones), and now most of the buildings and houses are businesslike concrete boxes, hunkered down, waiting for the next blast of Poseidon's trident.

Corinth's pleasant seaside Elefthériou Venizélou Square is also known as Plateía Touristikoú Kéntrou: it has an interesting **Folk Art Museum** (*t 274 102 5352; open Tues–Sun 8.30–1.30; adm*) with 3,500 costumes from all over Greece.

The Archaeological Site and Museum

t 274 103 1207; open daily exc hols winter 8–5, summer 8 –7; adm exp.

With a few exceptions, the ruins you see today are of the Roman city. The 40ft-wide **Léchaion Road** is just to the east of the Temple of Apollo. Grandly paved with limestone slabs and lined with raised sidewalks, it was the main street linking the agora to the port of Léchaion. The once sumptuous **baths of Eurykles** (2nd century AD) are handy for the public **latrines**, where some of the stone seats (Corinthians must have had small behinds) are still in place. Being Corinth, the road is chock-a-block with shops. The northernmost semi-circular stoa dates from the 4th century AD, while the long southern one replaces an earlier stoa from the 1st century AD. Directly behind a row of shops to the east was the large, square 1st-century AD **Perivolos of Apollo**, with a courtyard surrounded by Ionic columns.

Large public fountains graced the entrance to all agoras, but the one here, the elaborate lower **Fountain of Peirene**, is famous. Rebuilt and renovated from the 6th century BC into Byzantine times, it still does the business, even if drinking deep is not advisable. Behind the arches are tunnels dug back into the rock, with reservoirs to gather the waters, a technique still used today in Greece. Myth has it that these were the tears of Peirene, shed over her son Kenchreus, who was accidentally killed by a hunting Artemis. In the 2nd century AD, Herodus Atticus had the entire front clad with marble and added the large vaulted apses that are so prominent. Corinth's famous mirrors and weapons were tempered in its waters.

Just west of the fountain are three steps, followed by a landing and more steps marking the spot of the once grand entrance to the Roman **forum/agora**. Measuring 690 by 300 feet, it is bounded on the west by stores fronted by six small temples and on the east by the large Julian basilica. Its east-west dimensions were determined by the huge 4th-century BC **South Stoa**, which forms its boundary on the higher of its two levels. The only Greek civic building still standing in Roman times, it had 71 Doric columns on its façade and 38 Ionic columns inside those. Of the shops on the ground floor, all but two are equipped with wells, suggesting that they served refreshments. The second floor was probably a hotel. The back of the stoa was altered again and again, one part eventually housing the Roman bouleuterion. The **Kenchreaí Gate** was punched through it at one point for the Roman road to Corinth's eastern port.

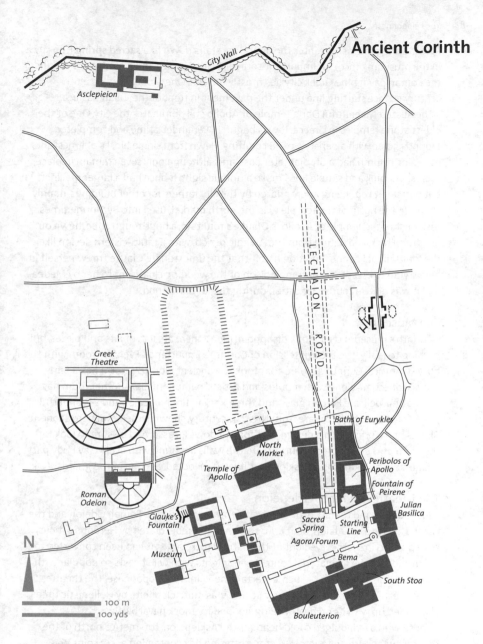

Ancient Corinth

City Wall

Asclepieion

LECHAION ROAD

Greek Theatre

Baths of Eurykles

North Market

Temple of Apollo

Peribolos of Apollo

Fountain of Peirene

Roman Odeion

Julian Basilica

Glauke's Fountain

Sacred Spring

Starting Line

Museum

Agora/Forum

Bema

South Stoa

N

100 m
100 yds

Bouleuterion

The east-west retaining wall of the forum/agora contains a **bema**, a platform from which dignitaries would address the people. On either side of it were rows of shops. It was probably in front of this bema that Paul was brought before the Roman governor Gallio, accused by the Jews of corrupting their faith. Gallio thought the charge and the new religion were small potatoes and declined to prosecute.

Just to the right, as you enter the agora, are stairs down to a **sacred spring** (the key is in the museum office), an important source in Greek times and a reminder that under the Roman paving the Greek city lies mostly unseen. One probe revealed a 6th-century BC race **starting line** under the pavement in front of the Julian Basilica.

The austerely beautiful Doric **Temple of Apollo** still dominates the city. One of the oldest stone temples in Greece, it was begun in Periander's time and completed around 550 BC with a peristyle of 38 columns. Hewn from single blocks of limestone, each 24ft column had a 6ft diameter base and, although only seven remain in place, their sheer bulk and simple lines make a unique sight. It once had a larger precinct, but parts of it kept being appropriated by the city fathers for other buildings, mainly shops. To the north of the temple was the **north market**, used into Byzantine times. Just west of the Temple of Apollo is **Glauke's fountain**, a huge rough cube, hewn out of natural rock, and dating from the Archaic period, with a multi-cistern design like the fountain of Peirene. Tradition had it that the unfortunate Glauke threw herself in here trying to escape the burning poison of the wedding cloak sent to her by Medea, and it was quite a tourist attraction during the Roman period.

The Museum

Corinth's museum is a bit of a disappointment; there are lots of bits and pieces, but nothing to really give the impression of Corinth's importance. Even the room with the busy, whimsical Corinthian ware that took the ancient world by storm has a fairly sparse collection, along with moulds and artists' paraphernalia. Another room has fascinating, delicate Roman glass and three Roman floor mosaics, and a wonderful plate of incised *sgraffito* ware from the 12th century, showing medieval hero Diogénes Akritas and a princess in a design that foreshadows Picasso. And be sure to look for the room at the back of the court where the walls are hung with every clay body part imaginable, all found in the Asklepeion. It is often locked; ask one of the guards.

The Theatres and the Asklepeion

Just outside and to the north of the site entrance stood the Roman Odeion and the Greek Theatre. The **Odeion**, built c. AD 100 and later redecorated by Herodus Atticus, seated 3,000 in seats carved out of the natural rock. By 225 it had been converted to accommodate the gladiatorial contests and fights with wild beasts so popular with Romans – the only venue of such 'entertainment' in the Peloponnese. The **theatre**, which started out in the 5th century BC and was quite elaborate by Hellenistic times, also ended up with its orchestra being flooded for mock naval battles.

Those who overindulged could head for the **Asklepeion** 400 metres north of the theatre by the Lernian fountain. A stone offering box containing a few coins was found at its entrance; the clay feet, hands, breasts, genitalia etc. found here were displayed in the temple pretty much the same way as in the museum.

The Acrocorinth: Flying Horses and Memorable Knights

A road from the lower site winds up to the Acrocorinth's massive western gates. From the Byzantine period on, this acropolis was the city centre. In 1208, after besieging the Acrocorinth for three years, the Franks built the tiny and picturesque Pendeskoufi castle on an adjacent spur to keep an eye on the fort (you can visit its ruins on foot). The big fort held out until 1210 before succumbing to Geoffrey de Villehardouin, but Leon Sgouros, its Greek defender, unwilling to be remembered as a loser, decided on the spectacular exit strategy of galloping his horse off the castle walls, where both plunged to their deaths on the rocks below.

In 1305, when the Acrocorinth was an important stronghold with a bishopric and nine dependent castles presided over by Isabelle and Philip of Savoy, seven champions from France arrived, 'challenging' the chivalry of their Achaían cousins. A tournament was held, where a thousand members of the local Frankish gentry gathered for twenty days of feasting and jousting, the likes of which the huge primordial rock had never seen before and never would again. Today the Acrocorinth is home to large green lizards, hawks and shy partridges that stare in amazement at intruders and then disappear into the weeds and broken stones.

The outer wall, almost two miles long, encircles the entire summit and is mainly of Frankish construction. The crenellated ramparts, watchtowers and dry moat were added by the Venetians. The first gate is Turkish, and the second, arched and buttressed, is Frankish, with a now empty niche, created by the Venetians for their Lion of St Mark. The most impressive gate is the third, massive and square, a good deal of it dating from the 4th century BC. Once through the gates, some ruined Venetian buildings and the extensive ruins of the Turkish city are all that remain. The upper Peirenean spring where Bellerophon caught Pegasus is to the south, not far from the square Frankish keep, and if you climb up to it the value of a flying horse does not need to be laboured.

A steep path ascends to the Acrocorinth's highest point, the eastern summit where the archaic Temple to Armed Aphrodite stood. Anyone with enough cash for the offering plate could visit the sacred prostitutes. Just how this all functioned is not known. That it was a five-star attraction goes without saying. One Lais apparently *was* one in a thousand. Diogénes enjoyed her favours on the house and poets struggled to capture her charm: 'she was more glittering than the clear water spring of Peirene'. Today this temple is a mere rectangle of stones, but the view over all of Corinthía is climactic.

Léchaion, Ancient Corinth's Northern Port

The ancient port of Léchaion is directly north of the archaeological site, and about 3km west of modern Corinth in an unkempt industrial area. Virtually unexcavated, bits and pieces of ancient cargoes and remnants of Greek and Roman buildings litter the ground along with the usual plastic rubbish. Léchaion made Corinth the power house it was in the Archaic and Classical periods, before it was superseded by Kenchreaí. It was largely artificial, a connected cluster of small boat bays dredged, excavated and protected from the sea by what is now a large sand dune. This was a tremendous advantage because the winds in the Gulf can come up quickly and make beaching a boat extremely difficult. Its eastern entrance can still be clearly seen. The busy port was connected to the city in the 5th century BC by long walls. The port's

Basilica of Ag. Leonidas was built in 450 and toppled by an earthquake in 551. At 610ft by 150ft, it rivalled the present-day St Peter's, and its huge floor is intact, with coloured marble galore, proof that Léchaion was still important at this late date.

The Isthmus: Ancient Isthmia and its Games

In myth, a certain Sinus got his jollies by asking travellers to help bend back a pine tree, and then, at the right moment, catapulting them into the sea. Theseus put a stop to that, and now only coffee and sweet shops ambush travellers crossing the famous canal (*see* p.172). Near Isthmia, on the Saronic Gulf side, the ruins of ancient Isthmia lie, massive and brooding (*t 274 103 7244; open daily 8–2.30; adm*). Buses pass the site from Corinth's centre and the Canal Zone; if you're driving follow the signs from the Canal Zone south, where almost immediately you turn right for ancient Isthmia at the village of Kryás Vrísi (Κυράς Βρύση) (badly signposted from the north, so ask). From Ancient Corinth, follow the road east via Examília.

The Isthmian Games, second in prestige only to Olympia, were instituted by Periander in 582 BC. They occurred every two years and were one of the four *stephaniteis* or crown athletic events, so called because the victors at each were crowned with wreaths – wild olive at Olympia, bay at Delphi, celery at Nemea and pine at Isthmia. Athletes called them the *períodos* or 'circuit', and there was no faster road to glory than winning at all four.

In Isthmia, the games were held to honour Poseidon, but also the youth Melicertes-Palaimon, who had drowned when his mother leapt with him into the sea after a series of adventures that would cause even a daytime soap to take pause. A helpful dolphin carried his body to Isthmia at a time when Corinth was undergoing a famine, and an oracle declared that if Palaimon were properly buried and games held regularly in his honour it would cease. So he was buried with honours under a sacred pine, and everything was fine. 'Melicertes' from the Phoenician Melkarth means 'guardian of the city', so a little political myth-making is at work too, but all crown games were funeral games (*see* p.223) and Palaimon filled the bill. The Romans loved depicting the boy on a dolphin on their coins and built the circular Temple and enclosure of Palaimon right beside the Temple of Poseidon. Only its square base can be seen today, but Plutarch tells us there were mystery rites for him at this temple. They seemed to involve many lamps; many are on display in the museum.

Isthmia suffered almost total destruction, once by the Romans in 146 BC and after that by the barbarians. As you enter the site from the back door of the museum, the **Sanctuary of Poseidon**, or what's left of it, is just on your right. Constructed with wooden columns in the 7th century BC, it was replaced by a stone temple in the 5th century, which in turn was replaced in the 4th century by a Doric temple. It was hard against the classical **stadium** whose **starting line** began at its southeast corner (all the better for the god to see the races). This stadium had quite a complicated system for ensuring that no runner 'jumped the gun'. Look for the triangular-shaped pavement of stone slabs scored with radiating grooves. The starter stood in the circular pit at the apex, holding ropes which, held by cleats, went along the grooves and held up a horizontal bar in front of each runner; when he released the ropes, the 16 starting gates opened simultaneously. Northeast of the temple are the paltry ruins of a **theatre** of the 4th century BC with enough of it left in Roman times for Nero to use. East of the theatre are the remains of a **Byzantine fortress** built by Justinian. To the southeast it abutted the Spartan trans-Isthmian wall, built in 480 BC in case the Greeks failed to hold the Persians at Sálamis and Plataea. This wall followed a natural line of low bluffs and was prominent enough in Roman times for the little town of Examília (six Roman miles, or 7.3km) to be named after it. It can still be traced almost in its entirety thanks to Justinian's massive refortification with 153 towers (using stone from the theatre and sanctuary). As a bulwark against barbarians, it failed miserably in the 6th century, and again in 1423 when the Turks came. East of the Byzantine fort, eight or nine courses of the **Spartan wall** can still be seen.

Further east, down the road from the museum and to your right, is the **'new'** **stadium**, which functioned from about 390 until 146 BC, and resumed again when Corinth was rebuilt after 46 BC. Both its starting and finish line have been discovered so we know that the one stadium race here was 181.5m. No two Peloponnesian stadiums were exactly the same length, something that must have frustrated sprinters. The variation was as great as ten metres.

The dim, rather barn-like **museum** has finds from Isthmia and Kenchreaí, including an impressive Archaic lustral basin (*perirrhanterion*) found in the precinct of the Temple of Poseidon, well-preserved helmets from 700 to 480 BC, and a strikingly contemporary Hellenistic bath tub. Beautiful glass panels in *opus sectile* with architectural and floral motifs from the 4th century AD were found still in their packing cases under water at Kenchreaí, their delivery interrupted by an earthquake. Another unusual find are the wooden doors, preserved in the formaldehyde of the sea, from the Temple of Isis – the very temple visited by the hero in Apuleius' *The Golden Ass*.

Kenchreaí: Corinth's Eastern Port and Helen's Baths

Seven kilometres south on the straight road to Epídauros, Kenchreaí's horseshoe of a harbour (signposted) had moles at its northern and southern ends, lined with stoas and temples. The exotic Temple to Isis , no doubt with pools and frescos of Nile vegetation, stood on the south mole. Many of the ruined buildings are under water because of rising sea levels. Just south along the highway are **Helen's baths** (Λουτρά Ελένης), still a little bathing area. Helen probably didn't bathe here, but the legend-loving Romans did. Then, the warm spring was on land with a reservoir and baths; it bubbles up under water now.

North of Corinth: Loutráki and Perachóra

Loutráki (Λουτράκι)

With its long arc of shingle beach, casino and spa, Loutráki has a Riviera glow. Crowded with hotels (and in summer just plain crowded), it is still compact enough to walk from end to end. The fountain-filled esplanade and lovely seaside park offer wonderful views of the Gulf, and over by the spa an elaborate artificial waterfall

Getting There and Around

The **bus** station, **t** 274 402 2262, at central El. Venizélou and Korínthou Sts, has connections with Athens (nine a day), Corinth and the Canal Zone 6km to the east, but only one a day in summer to Vouliagméni. **Taxis**, **t** 2744 06 1000, congregate near the bus station. For **mopeds** try 2B, Danaskinou St, **t** 274 402 6711.

Tourist Information

Tourist police: at Venizélou and Lekka St, **t** 274 404 2258, *www.city-of-loutraki.gr*.
Maranol Travel, 10 G. Lekka, **t** 274 406 2950, **f** 274 406 2951. Can rent you a car or bike, arrange excursions and help find you a room. They speak English too.

Where to Stay and Eat

Loutráki ✉ 20300

Poseidon Club, 3km west of town, **t** 274 406 7938, **f** 274 406 7950, *poseidonresort@ath. forthnet.gr* (*A; luxury*). Upscale holiday village. *Open April–Oct*.
Agelides Palace, 19 G. Lekka St, **t** 274 402 6695, **f** 274 406 3164 (*A; expensive*). Built in 1923, this seaside neoclassical wedding cake has been renovated with chandeliers, brass beds and gilded dining room. *Open all year*.
Mandas, I Economou St, **t** 274 402 2575 (*B, moderate*). Near the bus station; friendly and sports a small rooftop pool. *Open all year*.
La Petite France, 3 Markou Botsari St, **t/f** 274 402 2410 (*moderate–inexpensive*). By the bus station, with a small garden, run by a delightful French-Greek family. *Open April–Oct*.
Remezzo, near the bus station, **t** 274 402 1500. Home cooking and small garden.
Plaza, on the sea, **t** 274 402 2798. Has a good name for seafood.
Edem, on the Perachóra road, **t** 274 407 9111. Good view and food, even kangaroo!

Sports and Activities

Loutráki's **waters** cure stress, or will make you look and feel more beautiful; for info contact the Thermae Loutráki, 4 Venizélou, **t** 274 402 6325, **f** 274 402 1124, *www.royal-spas.com*. Daily **excursions** are offered by Albona Cruises at the quay to Vouliagméni Lake, Perachóra and through the canal. Water sports include **windsurfing** and **canoes**. And there's the **Club Hotel Casino**, 48 Possidónos, **t** 274 406 5501, if you have euros you don't know what to do with.

cascades dramatically through a trendy café. This spa existed in Roman times when Loutráki was called *Therma* in honour of its warm waters. Saline, and flowing at a constant 30°C, they help urinary disorders, arthritis, gallstones and dyspepsia. Enter the spa's temple-like confines and sip a cupful (small fee) even if you are feeling fit, just to see the décor, no doubt a pretty accurate reflection of the Roman original. Continue 17km west to **Lake Vouliagméni**, joined to the sea by a canal in 1880. It is crowded, yes, but offers good swimming, tavernas and is near Perachóra.

Perachóra: 'Over There'

Set on the westernmost tip of a narrow peninsula, tiny Perachóra, with its lighthouse, precipitous limestone shore and exquisite aquamarine bay, is a topographical poem. On a calm day, the cove is perfect for snorkelling – a good thing because some of the ruins are now under water. From the Corinthian perspective, this area was '*perachóra*' (the place over there), a strategic necessity for the big city but, because of the famous Heraion, much more than that.

Inspired by the even older Argive Heraion (*see* p.251), this sophisticated sanctuary was established by the Corinthians as early as the 8th century BC and reached its peak in the 7th and 6th when it outstripped even Isthmia. Many of its votives were rich and exotic – Phoenician scarabs, metalwork from Italy, figures of finely beaten gold. Domestic items (homely clay models of bread rings or *kouloúria* that Greeks eat to this day) reflecting Hera's role as wife, mother and fertility figure were also found amid the more extravagant offerings. Perachóra had a setback in 390 BC when Sparta destroyed it; it was rebuilt, only to be sacked again by the Romans in 146 BC. It never recovered; the Romans preferred the thermal waters at Loutráki.

Stand in the centre of the bay with the mole on your right, and the remains of the **Temple of Hera Akraias** of 525 BC are right behind you. To the left is an L-shaped outline in stone, once a two-storey **stoa** built around 400 BC. Between it and the temple are a few square stones, the foundations of the temple's **altar**. Over behind the mole was the **Greek agora** and, superimposed on it, some later Roman houses. Overlooking the port behind the small present-day church of Ag. Ioánnis stood a Hellenistic **Aspidal Temple** built over an earlier water source and reservoir; what remains is a narrow cistern, with rounded ends, about 7 feet deep with a stone stair-case leading down to the bottom. The substructure of a two-roomed **banqueting hall** is immediately to the south. East of the cistern, the ground level rises to the hard-to-decipher ruins of the **Temple of Hera Limenia**, 'of the Port', built in the 7th century BC. Over 200 curious bronze flasks with rounded, belly-buttoned shapes were found here. Just up a bit and to the east are the ruins of a settlement, including polygonal walls.

Southwest of Corinth: Nemea and its Lion

Mighty as it was, Corinth was not the only city-state in these parts: the fertile plains and valleys sheltered smaller neighbours such as Nemea, Sikyon, Phlious and Kleonai. *Neméa* means meadow or pasture, an apt description of this charming landscape of rolling hills swathed in vines. You can tell the fields bearing raisin grapes by the presence of flat cement rectangles, with bits of scaffolding where the grapes are laid out to dry in the sun – the word *currant*, after all, is derived from the *raisons of Corauntz* or Corinth. They are wonderful, but it is for wine, specifically red wine made from *agiorgítiko* grapes, that the area is famous, and Neméa has come a long way since lurid labels like Lion's Blood were flogged at rickety roadside stands. Thanks to hard work by Thanássis Pappaioánnou, the biggest producer, and others, it is now the largest, and arguably the finest, AO wine-growing area in Greece.

This fertile area has attracted people from Neolithic times, when they settled on the hill at Tsougiza near ancient Nemea. Mycenaeans were here too, at Aidónia just west of Nemea, and Hercules put paid to a Nemean lion by strangling it and using its pelt as a handy anorak. Locals swear the cave on Tsougiza's south slope was the actual lion's lair, a claim that goes down better after a few glasses of Nemean wine.

Modern Neméa is 4km west of ancient Nemea. There are exits for both from the Corinth–Tripolís toll road and from the old Corinth–Argos highway. Buses connect Corinth and the two Neméas 7 times a day.

Ancient Nemea

t 274 602 2739; open daily 8–7 in summer, 8–2.30 in winter; adm.
Museum only is closed on Mon till noon. The stadium has a separate adm.

Like Olympia, ancient Nemea was a sanctuary, not a city. The games were originally local affairs, attached to Kleonai and their Heracles cult centre, but under the aegis of powerful Argos, Kleonai instituted the games as Panhellenic in 573 BC and Zeus became the important deity. Held every two years, the Nemean Games were funeral games like those at Olympia, Isthmia and Delphi, in this case honouring Opheltes, the king's baby son, who died when his nurse forgot an oracle stating that he must never touch the ground and set him down on a patch of wild celery. A passing snake killed him, creating the required situation for the games.

Interrupted in 415 BC when the temple burned down, the games moved to Argos, resuming in Nemea again after the temple was rebuilt in 330 BC. Contests included horse races, running events, wrestling, musical contests and drama. The prizes were wreaths of wild celery in memory of Opheltes, and the judge and officials always wore black as a sign of mourning. The opening ceremonies, with mourning city officials, naked athletes and 40,000 spectators, must have been quite a sight. When they re-enacted the games in the stadium in 1996, with Greek and American politicians, thousands of spectators and a lot of TV cameras, the modest athletes opted for white robes, a deviation from historical accuracy regretted by the entire audience.

Since 1974 the University of California at Berkeley has been conducting excavations at Nemea under Stephen G. Miller. The attractive **museum**, with windows overlooking the site, displays local finds from every era. Photographs show how artefacts were found and used, and there are models of important structures. Of special interest are those exhibits relating to the games. One room displays the rich finds from the Mycenaean cemetery at Aidónia, treasures that were stolen and recovered after one of modern archaeology's great robberies, and one of the few with a happy ending.

As you leave the museum and walk towards the temple, the first ruins are of a **Christian basilica and cemetery** from AD 400, superimposed on what is assumed to be a much earlier Greek Hotel housing athletes or visitors. Beyond that, a **row of small buildings**, side by side, probably belonged to the various participating city-states; traces of a bronze-working establishment were found in one. Victors were entitled to erect statues of themselves at home and at the sites of their victories, so statues were often commissioned on the spot. Other rooms may have been treasuries, as at Delphi, but a kitchen area found out front suggests that they could have been used as entertainment centres, too – early versions of the hospitality suite. The games were a wonderful opportunity for officials to get together, party and discuss current affairs.

Three columns used to be all that remained of the original 36 of the Doric **Temple of Zeus**, designed by Scopas around 330 BC on top of the smaller 6th-century version that burned. Restorers have upped the number to five and plan to place even more on the existing 140ft by 72½ft substructure. You can descend into the temple's 6ft-deep *ádyton* under the *cella*, once a holy of holies where only priests were allowed. It suggests an oracular chamber like Delphi's, but just what went on, no one knows.

The **altar**, like all altars, received the spurting blood of the sacrificed animals. But this one was an incredible 132ft long. Sacrifices during the games must have been huge affairs, reminding us that, more often than not, the carcass was immediately butchered and roasted on spits (or boiled) – sometimes even char-broiled on the altar itself – and everyone dug in, under the approving god's statue. The official who killed and butchered the carcass was a *mageíros*, a word related to *magic* because sacrifice was a religious ritual; in modern Greek, a cook is still a *mageíros*, a magician (and may you never run into an evil one!). The 4th-century BC **baths** are so beautifully designed and complete that they seem to beg for water. Since the games were held in summer (one event was a sprint in armour), they must have been popular.

The well preserved **stadium**, built in the 4th century BC, is 500 yards east of the temple. Both starting lines have been found. Two were needed because each race, no matter what its length, had to finish at the horseshoe end of the stadium in front of the judge who sat on a special low bench. A longer race involved running around turning points placed in front of both starting lines. As at Isthmia, there were sophisticated 'starting gates' for the runners (photographs in the museum). Water for the spectators flowed around the stands in a stone ditch. If that's not enough, then surely the underground tunnel leading from the 'undressing' room into the stadium will convince you that this place was state of the art. Graffiti on the tunnel walls, mostly the names of favourites, were etched by their admirers for posterity.

A Brief Look at Other Ancient Cities in the Area

Ancient Kleónai boasts no ruins to speak of except for the intact substructure of the small Hellenistic **Temple of Heracles** in the middle of a vineyard. Hard-drinking Heracles would have loved that. To find it, follow the signs for modern 'Ancient Kleonai' from the Corinth–Argos road, cross the railway tracks, then the highway underpass and look for its sign. **Ancient Titani**, southwest of Corinth, had a famous Asklepeion, but all you will see today if you pass by modern Titáni are its picturesque acropolis walls on three sides of a hill topped by the church of Ag. Tryphon, made of ancient stones. **Ancient Phlious**, whose wine was famous in its day, doesn't even rate a sign, though the entire valley was named after it in ancient times. Its acropolis hill is about 3.5km west of modern Neméa, just south of the Petri–Aidónia road just before the turn off to Daphní. The church of the Panagía marks the site of its Asklepeion.

The Corinthian Gulf Coast to Ancient Sikyon

On the coastal strip, one market town flows into the next, and all of them slid into tourism by the accident of their proximity to Athens and the excellent swimming off their narrow shingle beaches. Used to urban density, the Athenians have no problem living the same way here in big condos, or in the villas packed between them, where at least the sea is clean and there is no smog. Many have noisy coastal roads, and all have tavernas, cafés and weirdly decorated discos. The 'strip' is a great place to see the natives in action and the views over the Gulf of Corinth are spectacular. **Kiáto** is a fair-sized port and centre for processing currants, citrus fruits and tomatoes that gets more attractive every year. Its shopping centre is great fun on a Saturday morning and the road to ancient Sikyon leaves from its centre.

Xilókastro, the westernmost town, is in a class by itself. Its lovely shingle beach stretching east from the centre is backed by a peaceful strip of pine woods which the citizens actually *voted* to preserve early in this century. A kilometre west, along a beach road lined with restaurants and cafes, is the new Marina Sports Complex, opened in 1997, with four clay tennis courts, a marina and a tiny amphitheatre.

Ancient Sikyon

The site is free. The museum, t 274 202 8900, has been closed for 17 years.

South of the village of Vassilikó, Sikyon, 'Cucumberville', is at its best in spring when the red poppies compete with wild flowers of every hue to decorate the ruins. Homer called this area *Evrichóro*, 'wide open', and it enjoys stupendous views of the Corinthian Gulf to the Acrocorinth and Pendeskoufi etched on the eastern horizon.

Sikyon, a small olive- and almond-growing city-state, was prosperous under the rule of Orthagoras. Orthagoras' brother Myron, by building the famous Treasury at Delphi to commemorate his Olympic victory in 648 BC, put Sikyon on the artistic map for the first but not the last time. Pliny wrote that outline drawing was invented here. Aristocles, Kanachos, Lysippos and, some say, Polykleitos made its school of bronze working famous. It had renowned schools of painting and pottery, and was even celebrated for its clothing and shoes. The Archaic and Classical city that produced all of this art lay somewhere between modern Sikyón and Vassilikó. Our ruins date pretty much from 303 BC, when the Macedonian leader Demetrios Poliorketes moved the city to its present site for reasons of defence. It's hard to imagine why. True, the triangular table land is raised by small bluffs and has rivers east and west, but the small acropolis backing the theatre doesn't look like it could have held out during any sort of serious siege. Aratos, Sikyon's most famous son, became the great leader of the Achaean League in 245 BC, navigating the dangerous waters of Macedonian politics until his luck ran out and he was poisoned by order of the Macedonian king. After that, Sikyon fell under the sway of Rome, even hosting the Isthmian Games from 146 to 46 BC when Isthmia lay in ruins. When it lost the games again to Isthmia, it faded gracefully into ruins.

The **Roman baths**, built in the 2nd and 3rd century AD, house the very attractive but very closed museum. Pass through a gate opposite the museum and immediately on your left is the long, narrow, 125ft by 36ft foundation of an **Archaic temple**, maybe to Apollo, which was here long before the city moved to join it. Beyond it to the right is a Hellenistic **gymnasium**, built on two levels, which has a remarkably well-preserved **fountain** with two columns still in place on the landing. Beyond the temple foundations, in a straight line and a bit to the left, is the square Hellenistic **bouleuterion** which once had 16 inner columns supporting the roof. Beside it was a 350ft **stoa** with 20 shops behind its double-columned porch. The side entrances of the charming **theatre**, just beyond the museum, are well-defined, as is the skene in front. Nine tiers

Getting Around

Buses serve the coast regularly: 14 a day, some from Corinth only, some originating in Athens. Very sporadic local buses go to mountain villages such as Tríkala, Symphalía and the Pheneós area, while 4 a day go to ancient Sikyon from Kiáto. Bus information in Xilókastro: **t** 274 302 2218; in Kiáto: **t** 274 202 2243. Kiáto has a **railway** station, **t** 274 202 2267; so does Xilókastro, **t** 274 302 2297, with several trains a day. There are exits from the toll **road** at Kiáto and Xilókastro. **Taxis** In Kiáto: **t** 274 202 8200 or 274 202 2600. In Xilókastro, **t** 274 302 2663.

Tourist Information

Xilókastro Tours, I. Ioannou 2, **t** 274 3024137, **f** 074 302 5102. Offers tours to neighbouring areas several times a week and motor bike and car hire.

Where to Stay and Eat

Kiáto ✉ 20200
Triton, Metamorphosis 2, **t** 274 202 3421, **f** 274 202 7351 (*B; moderate–inexpensive*). Central, by the port. Rooms have fridges, TV and air-conditioning. *Open all year.*
Karamaliki, **t** 274 202 4000. On the seaside and known for fish.

Xilókastro ✉ 20200
Fadira, 2 Ag. Makariou, **t** 274 302 2648, **f** 274 302 8869 (*C; moderate–inexpensive*). Functional, friendly pile. The bar and restaurant are by the waves across the road. *Open May–Oct.*
Apollon, 105 Ioannou, **t** 274 302 2239, **f** 274 302 5240 (*B, moderate*). A bargain for its class – an attractive neoclassical house and modern annexe surrounded by high hedges close to the sea, with a pool. *Open all year.*
Periandros, 3 Ag. Makariou, **t** 274 302 2272 (*C; inexpensive*). Two steps from the sea, small and friendly, with clean rooms next to the forest. *Open May–Oct.*
Touristiko Periptero, **t** 274 302 8554. A café-restaurant on the sea with its back to the forest. Well run, attractive and reasonably priced, plus showers on the beach.
Thraka, **t** 274 302 4977. Near the Hotel Fadira, with a big menu, and the usual terrace across the street on the sea side.
Psarotaverna Limanaki, **t** 274 302 5362. Fish and ouzo snacks west of the marina.

of seats remain, including many of the throne-like seats in the first row. There was an even shorter route to the theatre from the acropolis, via two vaulted tunnels built into the upper tiers. The eastern one is virtually intact. Take the dirt road in front of the theatre, and to your right as you walk up you will see a retaining wall of the **stadium**. Go right on the first dirt road and you come to the depression of the stadium, on your left.

Achaía

Achaía stretches along the north coast from Aigeíra to Kalógria, with Pátras more or less in the middle. 'It possesses a strange suggestive power,' wrote Níkos Kazantzákis, 'something feminine, fecund, and dangerously fascinating.' Most of this fascination is concentrated in eastern Achaía, where the coast, hemmed in by folded hills and hedgehogged with pinnacles of stone and pine, is only a prelude to the enchantment of the mountains behind. Here the Gulf of Corinth resembles a majestic if slightly dishevelled Italian lake, with the seigneurial villas replaced by Greek towns swathed in bougainvillaea, surrounded by vines, olive trees and emerald citrus groves growing lemons the size of a giant's fist. Yet Achaía tends to get short shrift in books because

FOKIDA

20 kms
10 miles

N

Efpalio
Nafpaktos
Glyfada
Eratini
Galaxidi
Is. Trizonia
Ag. Nikolaos
Andirio
Rio
Longos
Sellianitika
Patras
Eghio
Mavriki
Eleonas
Diakofto
Mt Panachaiko
Tuxurchion
Platanos
Akrata
Aigeira
Mamousia
Kalamias
Aigeira
Mavra Litharia
Platanovrissi
Pteri
Voutsimos
Derveni
Pyrgos
Katarraktis
Plataniotissa
Zachlorou
Aiges
Panagia ton
Katafigon
ACHAIA
Mega Spileo
Ambelokipi
Monasteri
Evrostina
Tsivlos
Exochi
Selliana
Léonidio
Kalavrita
Agridi
Sarantapicho
Rethi
Peristera
Ag. Varvara
Vlassia
Kato Lousi
Solo
M. Trikala
K. Trikala
Lousi
Zarouchla
Ano Trikala
Cave Lakes
Mt Chelmos
CORINTHIA
Mt Erymanthos
Goura
Mt Kyllini
Planitero
Ag. Georgios
Pheneos
Kleitor
Archea Pheneos
Psophis
Mosia
Bouzi
Mt Lambia
Tripotama
Kleitoria
Kastania
Kaliani
Lambia
Aroania
Stymphalia
Mt Aphrodisio
Stymphalos
Psari
ELIS
Karteri
Lake
Daphni
Lafka
Stymphalia
Kandila
Tropaia
Lake Ladon
ARCADIA
ARGOLIS
Viziki
Castle of Akova
Orchomenos
Ladon
Vlacherna
Orchomenos

it defies neat definitions and lacks a major brand-name attraction. Some of its 12 ancient cities have never been found, let alone excavated.

Called Achaía because so many Mycenaeans – Homer's Achaeans – came to the area as refugees after the lights went out in 1100 BC, Achaía managed to stay pretty much out of the history books until Hellenistic times, when its 12 cities renewed the Achaean League, a rare effort at federalization attempted by the fractious Greek city-states, which made both Sparta and Macedon sit up and take notice. In 245 BC Aratus of Sikyon was its illustrious leader, and a parliament of member states was regularly convened in Éghio. The league could not unite sufficiently against the Roman threat, and in 146 BC the Romans devoured the entire Peloponnese as *their* Roman province of Achaía in the same half-baked way that they re-named all of Hellas 'Graecia' after the first tribe they met. The Franks borrowed the illustrious name again for their principality of Achaía which at one point encompassed the entire Peloponnese. Today, Achaía has shrunk again to something resembling its ancient size.

The North Peloponnesian Mountains

Speeding along the coastal highway between Pátras and Xilókastro, tourists note the hills that make the coast so attractive and not much else. And yet, a 5-minute drive south on any road takes you into magnificent terrain; from east to west, the three great mountain ranges of **Kyllíni**, **Chelmós** and **Erýmanthos** line up, just waiting to be discovered. Back in the mists of geological time, Erýmanthos rolled over the Chelmós range and settled in its present location behind Pátras. The results of this geographical arabesque are everywhere. Mountain villages sit precariously on heights, popping unexpectedly into view around the bends of twisting roads. And while small churches dot every Greek landscape, the ones here are particularly profuse and picturesque. Out-of-the-way archaeological sites can be visited in lonely splendour; rivers rush through valleys even in the heat of summer, while all along the Corinthian Gulf busy towns are set on the small coastal plains formed by the streams on their way to the sea.

Mount Kyllíni, Áno Tríkala and the Ring Road

Born at the dawning of day, at midday he played the lyre,
and in the evening he stole the cattle of far-shooting Apollo.
Homeric hymn to Hermes

Spectacular twin-peaked Mount Kyllíni crowns the west of Corinthía, its foothills dipping into Achaía as far as Aigeíra. In ancient times, this mountain was sacred to Hermes, whose **birth cave** is about a half hour's walk from the Alpine Club refuge. No one has bothered to signpost it, but the locals know where it is (ask for the '*speeliá tou Ermí*'). Known as Zíria before independence, the mountain was given back its ancient name by the Greek government in its effort to make the modern map reflect the Classical period. Kyllíni/Zíria settled for both and the names are used interchangeably.

There are several Tríkala villages on Kyllíni's northern slope. Head for **Áno Tríkala**, sitting pretty on a lofty 3,600ft balcony overlooking the Gulf of Corinth, immersed in the fruit and nut trees that flourish at this altitude. Beneath them are terraced vineyards, even lower come olive trees, and then the citrus groves of the bottom valley – the entire spectrum of Greek agriculture spread beneath your feet. To the south, the scenery switches as abruptly as a stage set to dense spruce and pine forest, even more dramatic in winter when it's covered in snow. Little Áno Tríkala's first hotel, now a stone shell, was built in 1934. It has seen the likes of King Farouk of Egypt and is now being renovated to cash in on Greece's current 'mountain village' boom. Weekend villas have sprouted up to replace the abandoned ruins, many reusing the old stone.

Besides a crispness and clarity in the air, every mountain village has at least one huge plane tree, a fountain of running water and a little stone church. Look for these immediately east of the old hotel. The tiny church of **Ag. Nikólaos** was built in 1750 and is unusual because a residence was added onto the back of it. Its arched doorway has a small hole in the lintel. This was to accommodate a rifle barrel poked through from upstairs to blow an unwelcome visitor to smithereens. Greek hospitality is legendary, but it had its limits and was rarely extended to the Turks. Note the small windows. In times of trouble, each man's house was his fortress.

A road winds up through the forest to the wealthy convent of **Ag. Vlasíou**, 1km above Áno Tríkala; it boasts a pretty garden, picnic tables, a view, and an icon of the saint dating from 1400, to which many healing miracles have been attributed. The road continues on to the two **refuges** run by the Greek Alpine Club. From there, the walk to Kyllíni's western and **highest peak** (7,130ft) takes about 2 hours. A 28km unpaved **ring road** around the isolated western peak starts from the first mountain refuge, perfect for mountain bikes, motor bikes, walkers and 4x4s. Mountain bikers say the easiest way is clockwise. Unpaved tracks diverge from it to points south and west, but are not always passable by car. Two small mountain lakes, which fill up in the early spring from the melting snow and then dry up in the summer, can be reached on foot from the first mountain refuge or by car from Ag. Vlasíou.

Stymphalía and Pheneós: Where Still Waters Run Deep

Tucked around Mount Kyllíni, the two unusual valleys of Stymphalía and Pheneós are so close together that if you stand on the road to the Xénia hotel at Kastaniá, you can look down into both from the same vantage point. Water run-off from the mountains gathers in these valleys forming lakes, their size depending on how much of the water finds its way out through porous limestone passages called *katavóthres* (sink holes or dolines). If these work well, the result is flat, usable and very fertile land around a lake that is substantial in spring and sometimes non-existent by autumn. Catastrophe can and does occur if these sink holes become blocked.

In ancient times both valleys harboured cities by their respective lakes and flooding was attributed to the gods. One legend has it that an angry Artemis blocked the sink hole at Stymphalía with wood because her worship was not being observed. Only when a hunter, following a fleeing deer into the rising water, was swept down into the earth was her thirst for revenge satisfied and the passage cleared. Today blockages are attributed to earthquakes or human carelessness and the sink holes are covered with no nonsense grills. Both these attractive and out-of-the-way valleys can be visited in a day – enough to see but not to explore, and they are worth exploring.

The Stymphalía Valley

Rimmed by Mount Trachí to the south, Mount Pharmakás to the east and Kyllíni to the west, Stymphalía is more open to the north where a series of cultivated valleys shelve down towards the reed-ringed lake. In spring it measures about 2km by 6km, culminating in the west under **Láfka** and **Kartéri**. Its sink holes are on the eastern side. Never a very dependable water source in recent years, the Stymphalian lake dried up

Getting There and Around

Several **trains** a day stop at the towns between Pátras to Corinth along the coast. Buses on the toll road will drop you hourly at coastal towns, but in some cases it's a hike to the centre. Apart from the rail line to Kalávrita, all public transit into the mountains is by local bus or taxi. Local **buses** from Xilókastro, t 274 302 222, go three times a week to Tríkala at 5.30am and again at 2pm. Three daily buses from Kiáto, t 274 202 2240, pass through Stymphalía's villages, up to Kastaniá and over to Mosiá until Goúra. From Kaliáni, on the bus route, it's 4.5km up to the village of Boúzi, where you can hike to Kyllíni's eastern peak.

The **road** network is pretty good. Almost any seaside town can be used as a base for day trips, particularly those between Éghio and Akráta. A road links Stymphalian Kartéri and Phenean Mosiá. You can also get to Stymphalía from Neméa to the east, or reach Pheneós from the Kalávrita–Trípoli road via the Pheneós Pass.

Where to Stay and Eat

The Tríkalas ✉ 20400

Xelydorea, Méso Tríkala, t 274 309 1444, f 274 302 8691 (*expensive, moderate in summer*). Perfect down to the duvets on the brass beds. *Open weekends only in winter.*
Mysaion, Méso Tríkala, t/f 274 309 1141, *mysaion.trikalgr@hotmail.gr* (*expensive*).

New, in traditional style; it has a restaurant, and a fireplace in each room. *Open all year.*
Ta Tríkala, Áno Tríkala, t 274 309 1260 (*C; inexpensive*). Mr Korkari's hotel in the centre has good-sized rooms, balconies; fireplaces in the big dining room. *Open all year.*
Alpine refuges: the Xilócastro Alpine Club, Adamopoulou 11, 20400 Xilócastro, t 274 302 2918, holds the keys to two mountain refuges; book in advance.
Psistariá Apostólio Deláris, Áno Tríkala, t 274 309 1358. Popular with the locals.

Kastaniá ✉ 20016

Xenía Kastaniá, t 274 706 1283, f 274 706 1235 (*B; expensive*). An attractive stone hotel in the forest above the village. A good place to stop for coffee, too. Open all year.

Láfka

Xenon Láfka, t 274 703 1220 (*inexpensive*). Basic, in the middle of somewhat forbidding Láfka, a village built in the cleft of the mountain on either side of a mountain stream, and held together by bridges. *Open all year.*

Kartéti

To Kartéri, t 274 703 1203 (*inexpensive*). Simple, clean rooms. The new rooms at the back have kitchens and fireplaces.
Leonídas, t 274 703 1203. Has good country food and huge barrels of wine.
To Patrikó, Kaliáni, t 274 702 2224. Old-fashioned service and good food in a newly renovated taverna.

completely in the summers of 1997 and 1998. When it filled up again in 1999, it was immediately full of good-sized fish and other marine life, suggesting that as yet undiscovered underground reservoirs must exist. A road now circles the lake.

Stymphalía saw one of the Labours of Heracles. Foul-smelling man-eating birds with claws and feathers of bronze terrorized the inhabitants, until Heracles outsmarted them by shaking rattles and then shooting them as they rose up in confusion. Today the lake is home to herons and other bird life and the only 'monsters' to look out for are the many snakes that snooze on the rocks surrounding the lake. If you have no rattles, just make a lot of noise; they are shy.

Ancient **Stymphalos** is on the lake's west side, on a low hill immediately south of the sign-posted ruins of the 13th-century **Cistercian abbey church**. Classical stones abound in this Frankish ruin. There is no sign, but you can reach the low **acropolis** by turning east on the first dirt road south after the church. The ruins are partly submerged in the lake at times.

The Pheneós Valley

The Pheneós Valley, measuring 2km by 8km, is hemmed in by Kyllíni on the east and the highest peaks of Chelmós on the west. Its 'lake' is smaller than Stymphalía's although the flat valley floor is a sure indication that it has been bigger at times. On the mountain to the south, it is still possible to see a line marking one previous level of the lake. Pheneós' sink holes are in the south and southwest corners. The villages, all well above the old water line (just in case), work for a living, with beautiful stone houses and churches built against a truck garage or chicken shed, typical of prosperous farming communities that expanded in the 1960s and '70s. The major crop is potatoes. There are lots of shepherds, too.

Ancient Pheneos is a knob-like hill set into the flat land at the north end of the former lake, close to the village which has now renamed itself Ancient Pheneos. Ancient stones and excavated pits dot the area, all pretty obscure except to archaeologists. Hermes was worshipped here and games were held in his honour. The Pheneans claimed that Heracles passed through, fathered a mini hero with a local princess, and still had time to pierce the valley's sink holes and dredge a channel to drain the valley. It could be true. Traces of ancient drainage efforts have been detected in aerial photographs. They claimed Odysseus had a stud farm here, too. But Pheneos was Arcadian in the old days, and Arcadians loved to claim just about any god or hero as their own. In Demeter's sanctuary in Pheneos, a rock was said to have a cunningly fashioned top, opened once a year only. It contained a sacred mask which the priest wore while he beat the ground with rods – a primitive fertility rite that goes way back. Anyone swearing an oath in Pheneos, swore 'by the rock'.

Just behind modern 'Ancient Pheneos' is a delightful corner of recent origin. Follow the signs for Μονή Αγ. Γεωργίου, a short distance north, and on a pine-clad mountainside the large rugged 18th-century **Monastery of Ag. Geórgios** appears. It used to be wealthy, owning all of the land over to Neméa, which still names its famous Agiorítiko grapes after it. The large beams holding up its overhanging third floor are gnarled boughs. Although the tiny cells with their low doorways are many, at last count there were only three monks, a dog, and two cats. The door of the church is one third elaborately carved wood and two-thirds bronze, embossed with St George slaying the dragon. The frescoes of 1768 are worth a look, but today it is the setting that sets this monastery apart. A good-sized artificial lake (potatoes need water) has been created just below, leaving the monastery's tiny chapel of **Ag. Nikólaos** on a tranquil islet, reached by a short causeway from the shore. It is a beautiful sight.

Evrostína: South of Dervéni

Panagía ton Katafigíon and Ag. Geórgios: Churches with a Difference

This area was the 'Switzerland of the Peloponnese' until the devastating fire of 2000. The village of **Evrostína** was spared, an emerald on ash, with an attractive millpond, a cool shady path beside its stream, restaurants, and in June the best cherries anywhere. It also offers two unique churches with fascinating stories.

Getting There

Just west of coastal Dervéni, a road branches south via Rozená (Ροζενά) and climbs up 12km to Evrostína (Ευροστίνα), or Zácholi as the locals call it. It is also possible to arrive here from the Pheneós valley or from Méso Trikala above Xilókastro.

Eating Out

At Evrostína, eat at **H Zácholi**, t 274 303 2847, or at **Mr Golfinópoulos'** *psistariá*.

Two and a half kilometres north of Evrostína a large arched stone gateway marks the entrance of **Panagía ton Katafigíon**, Our Lady of Refuge. Walk through and down (the path and stairs are not for vertigo sufferers) until you catch sight of the tiny red-roofed church. Built into a cleft in a sheer limestone rockface, it looks like the hideaway of a misanthropic hermit. In fact, it was built in the 1780s, some time after the Russians under Orlov had entered the Peloponnese to 'liberate' the Greeks from the Turkish yoke. Only Catherine the Great made up with the Sultan, leaving the locals to suffer Turkish reprisals so vicious that the villagers fled into this valley and took up residence for years in the many caves dotting the cliff face.

Our Lady of Refuge was built to answer the need of every Greek community, no matter where, to have a church. Deserted for years, it is now being lovingly restored by a local resident and visitors are welcome. From the ante-room, before the church itself, you can ascend a rickety metal stair (if you dare) into one of the large cave refuges. They were once reached by wooden ladders. The church is modest in the extreme, but still contains many little *támata* votives with arms, legs and other appendages that attest to miracles or hoped-for ones.

Beautiful **Ag. Geórgios** in Evrostína is a 'gift' of the Turkish occupation, too, but in a very different way. In the 18th and 19th centuries, Evrostína was a thriving community of over 6,000 people but had no large church. This suited the Turks fine. Their strange relationship with Orthodoxy was a matter of policy. As long as the Church kept the Greeks in line, they tolerated it, but any church-building permissions were hedged with restrictions. The idea was to keep potential meeting places small as well as to humiliate. If a permit could be wrested from the Turkish governor in Corinth, it was a 40-day permit only, and if the walls and roof were not completed by then, the church was razed to the ground or, worse, turned into a mosque. No construction was allowed after sunset. The Evrostinians got their permit and built only a third of the church, ensuring that the Turks would order its destruction. Whereupon they carefully numbered the dismantled stones and hid them in their houses. They then applied for another permit starting from 1 June 1811, the month with the longest daylight hours, and in 39 days the church that you see now was built. A chain of 1,000 men passed each stone hand to hand from the quarry to the site. The church is 98ft by 50ft, with 17 cupolas or *troulí*, 12 for the Apostles, 4 for the Evangelists and one for God. The massive iconostasis was carved from a single tree and is ornate even by Greek stan-dards. If it's locked (try the back door), keys can be obtained from Mr Golfinópoulos' *psistariá* at the base of the steps up to the church (a road also winds up).

Akráta, Aigeíra, Plátanos and into the Mountains

Seaside Akráta with its sidekicks Aigeíra and Plátanos have developed more recently than their Corinthian neighbour, Xilókastro, but not as wisely or as well, and filled in their attractive waterfronts without a thought to nitty-gritty details like parking. The Greeks love them. Aigeíra has closed off its waterfront to cars; Akráta is thinking about it. Plátanos is the most laid back and its upper village has retained much of its former charm. The mountains just behind offer some of the Peloponnese's most alluring trips: to ancient Aigeira, to a cluster of attractive mountain villages called the Kloukinochória, to Lake Tsivlós and, above all, to the source of the hell-bent Styx.

Ancient Aigeira

The road to ancient Aigeira and Selliána (signposted) turns off to the north 1km east of Aigeíra. It then doubles back under the main road and up. The theatre is 5.2km from the turn-off. The gardening guard, Lítsa Demopoúlou, t 269 603 1717 or t 269 603 2555, is normally in every day from 8.30 till 3, but suggests you call before visiting. Adm free.

One of the 12 cities of the Achaean League, ancient Aigeira sprawls over an entire hillside overlooking the Gulf. The hill's first significant occupants were Mycenaeans, fleeing the destruction of their cities in the Argolid. As late as 688 BC, it was called Hyperesia and only became Aigeira after a famous war of nerves. It seems that the Sikyonians, informed that the bulk of the Hyperesian army was off on a foray, amassed by the sea preparing for a dawn attack. The fast-thinking Hyperesians herded all of their nanny goats onto the city walls and paraded them about with torches attached to their horns. Assuming reinforcements had arrived, the Sikyonians simply packed it in and went home. In inter-city raids, discretion was often considered the better part of valour. The relieved Hyperesians decided to rename their town Aigeira, a word meaning 'goat', and to dedicate a new temple to Artemis to whom they attributed the success of their plan. To determine *where* to place this new temple, they let the herd's chief nanny goat wander about and where she rested, built the temple. It has not been found, perhaps because no one has borrowed a nanny goat and had another go.

The **theatre**, seating 10,000, was built in 280 BC. The orchestra and most of the seats were chiselled into the slope's pebbly, aggregate rock. Like most theatres in Greece it reflects Roman alterations, easily distinguished by the brickwork. The acoustics are wonderful, and the view from the cheap seats is magnificent with the mountains of Parnassós and Helicon in the north providing a grey and purple backdrop to the blue Gulf. If you can figure out what that tunnel leading into the orchestra from backstage was for, let the archaeologists in on it.

In front of the theatre are several **basins** protected by a tile roof. A single pipe brought water to the first basin, filled it until the water overflowed into the second basin, and so on until all basins were filled; only then was the water drained away. There was no technological reason, even in Hellenistic times, why these basins could

Getting There

Several **trains** a day stop at Akráta, Plátanos and Aigeíra. The Akráta station, t 269 603 1291, is 500m from the taxi stand but has a card phone. **Taxis: t** 269 603 1892.

Every hour **buses** from Pátras or Athens stop on the toll road at Akráta. It's a 2-minute descent to the taxi stand. Local buses from Éghio go five times a day to Aigeíra, via Akráta and Plátanos on the old road. Sporadically, a bus passes ancient Aigeira to Selliána. Information: at the newspaper shop in Akráta near the traffic lights, t 269 603 1731, or in Aigeíra at the newspaper shop, t 269 603 1022. If you're **driving** on the Corinth–Pátras toll road, exit at Akráta.

Where to Stay and Eat

Akráta ✉ 25006

Ams, 200m from the sea, t 269 603 3662, f 269 603 3666 (*B; expensive–moderate*). Upscale, new, and with a small pool. *Open all year.*
Akráta Beach, t 269 603 1180, f 269 603 1813 (*C; moderate*). On the seaside strip but with quiet rooms at the back. *Open all year.*
Antónios Stavrópoulos, t 269 603 2339 (*moderate–inexpensive, expensive in Aug*). Ten apartments on the strip, with kitchens, TV, and air-conditioning.
Akráta Beach Camping, t 269 603 1988. Near the town. *Open April–Oct.*
Krioneri-Akratas Club, 3km west of town, t 269 603 1405, f 269 603 1596, *krionthe@otenet. gr.* Sometimes offers Cadogan readers ouzo.
O Thomás, t 269 603 2450. At the western end of the beach, with home-cooked meals and friendly service, all under a canopy of mulberry trees.
Veggéra, t 269 603 3000. A new Italian restaurant by the sea that has made quite a splash. It serves only Italian food, has a pizza take out, and a terrific house salad.

Aigeíra ✉ 25010

Mouriá, t 269 603 1772. Right on the sea, good for traditional fare and its *psistariá.*
Katsoúris (Κατσούρης), t 269 603 1327. On the main road in Aigeíra, complete with fountain and excellent food to distract you from the traffic.

Kloukinochória ✉ 25006

Aroánia, Zaroúchla, t 269 603 5090, f 269 603 3977 (*luxury*). A large new three-storey stone hotel with a fireplace in every room. *Open all year.*
To Pétrino, Tsivlós, t 269 603 4100 (*moderate–inexpensive*). Has 4 small rooms, with a common sitting room. Cosy and well run. Its excellent restaurant with fireplace and terrace is presided over by Mrs Vlákou, a lovely lady and a great cook. *Open all year.*
Anagnostopoúlou Rooms, Peristéra, t 269 603 3988 (*moderate–inexpensive*). This hospitable family literally welcome guests into their own living room. *Open all year.*
Taverna tou Ioánnis, t 269 603 3939 and **O Maxáiras**, in Zaroúchla: t 269 603 3928. The local specialities are bean soup, pittas made with cheese or greens, roasted meat, all served with home-made bread.
Xelmós, Peristéra, t 269 603 4076. Good for various dishes including their speciality, charcoal grilled trout from the fishery right below the village.

not each have had their own water supply and drain. And yet the same system has existed in surrounding villages, as in nearby Plátanos. Older villagers will tell you that anyone jumping the queue and using the wrong sink for the dirtiest clothes was grist for the town gossip mill and immediately labelled a *kakí neekokeirá* (bad housekeeper), still about the worst label a woman can acquire in a small village. Indoor plumbing ended the 2,500-year run of this type of washing area, an astonishing period anywhere but Greece, where time sometimes really does seem to stand still.

Beside the theatre are two fair-sized **temples**, covered by a canopy. Although a huge marble head of Zeus was found in one (now in the Archaeological Museum of Athens), it is not clear if either was dedicated to Zeus; the head seems too large for the buildings. A little in front and east of the theatre is the waist-high ruin of a

Temple to Fortune, with hollows for the bases of nine statues and a pebbled floor. Tyche or Fortune was one of the most appealing goddesses, and the enthusiasm with which she was worshipped reflects a mixture of fatalism and hope. There is some-thing very human about its scale as well, rather like the tiny Orthodox churches scattered today across the northern Peloponnese. The retaining walls of the descending fields are quite often ancient walls and some small 'fields' are actually enclosed by the foundation walls of a large building, their 'gates' an ancient doorway.

A walk up to the Mycenaean **acropolis** is best accomplished by following the first sign on the road approaching the site. This path follows the city walls; some of its stones are scattered under a large pine. The sub-Mycenaean ruins are hard to deci-pher, especially since ancient pottery kilns are superimposed. There is a large clay **cistern** covered with a tile roof. Water was brought from farther up the mountain by aqueduct, traces of which can be seen on a farmhouse wall just to the south of the acropolis. Water is still ferried from the mountains, but now in the ubiquitous black hoses you see slithering down so many mountain roads.

Vlovoká and Selliána

The Aigeíra road continues south to **Vlovoká** (Βλοβοκά), spectacularly situated at the base of a massive reddish cliff-face, a remnant of the huge Nile-like fan delta that graced this area aeons ago and deposited the fantastical, dune-like hills between Xilókastro and Akráta. If you look carefully, you will spot a Classical wall supporting a flat threshing floor and three tall cypress trees just north of the first houses.

Maps do not always mark the name in actual use. Vlovoká, for instance, has recently been renamed after a nearby ancient settlement and is now officially **Aigés**. Vlovoká, the name the villagers prefer, is related to the word 'damaged', a reminder that in past ages people with contagious diseases were left here to fend for themselves in the perpetual winter shade of the cliff. The custom of isolation, in the case of tuberculosis, persisted into the 19th century. Past Vlovoká comes **Monastéri** with a small taverna and a cypress-lined path up to a monastery with fine views. The road continues to **Selliána**, at the north end of an unusual bowl-shaped valley, a surprisingly lush and well-watered oasis surrounded by sterner, barren peaks, and great for cyclists or walkers. Traces of unexcavated ancient Phellóe can be seen by the church of **Ag. Vassílios** in the lower village.

South of Akráta: The Kloukinochória and the Styx

An excursion into this area of forested high-peaked Chelmós is beautiful in all seasons, and truly gorgeous in winter. Each small village has its own personality, at least one picturesque stone church (Sólo's is especially nice) and one cosy, family-run *xenóna* (inn). The mystery is the name; none of the locals are sure why theses villages are collectively called the Kloukinochória. They tend to fill up only on winter weekends and holidays. There are many good walks in the area, but the blockbuster is the 'walk of all walks' to the massive sheer rock face scoured by the falls of the Styx.

Unfortunately, the road to Hell is paved with bad directions, so note the following: begin in upper Akráta. Follow signs to Valimí (Βαλιμί) and Zaroúchla (Ζαρούχλα). Turn right at the river bottom, well after Valimí (look for the Pétrino inn sign) for tiny lake Tsivlós (Τσιβλός), a little mountain gem that should not be missed. For the Styx, continue towards Zaroúchla and turn right to either Sólo (Σόλο) or Peristéra (Περιστέρα). The paved straight road ends at Zaroúchla.

The **Styx** ('Abhorrent') was one of the five rivers of Hades. The gods would swear their most sacred oaths by its waters. Here Achilles was dipped by his mother Thetis to ensure his immortality, only she forgot to let go of his ankle, thus adding 'Achilles' Heel' to the lexicon. Ancient gossip held that only the hoof of a horse could hold its water (a clue that it was sacred to horse-headed Demeter), and that any other container, whether glass, agate, stone or gold, would just disintegrate. Rumours flew that Alexander the Great was poisoned by Styx water. The apparent paradox, that immortal water (*athánato neró*) could kill, is a reminder of the double meaning of 'sacred': something to be worshipped but also something to be feared and approached only when the proper preparations were made.

The same attitude comes in good stead if you decide to hike to the river's source, a good two hours each way from the start of the trail (don't try it in winter). Get there by driving from the square in the tiny village of **Peristéra** up to **Áno Mesoróugi** (Ανο Μεσορπούγι) and then along the narrow road until it ends (2km or so). Parking can be tricky as this road peters out into a path. Then follow the red trail marked with circles and arrows. Towards the end, when the path becomes steep, you can opt to go down along the river and then climb up to the trail again to the bottom of the waterfall with its little cave. The waterfall is at its most spectacular in spring and early summer, but don't stand directly under the cliff. Pieces of the rock wall often tumble down, proving once again that Styx and stones can break your bones.

If, like Achilles, you want a dip in the Styx, a road just beyond the village of **Sólo**, with its pretty church, leads down to the river. For a look at the spectacular rock face, follow the signs (by car or on foot) from Sólo's centre towards the fountain of Gólfo. It takes you round bends and suddenly the massif appears, stained black by the constant flow of water that gives the Styx yet another name, '*Mávro Néri*' or black water.

Diakoftó and the Vouraikós Gorge Railway

Diakoftó has a pleasant shingle beach by its tiny fishing port, but what has made it famous is the awesome cleft in the mountains behind it known as the **Vouraikós Gorge**. It is so narrow in places the ancients surmised that Heracles must have cut a swath through the mountains with his sword. Sir James Fraser thought it resembled 'the mouth of hell' when he passed by in 1900. But, unlike hell, you can enter its spectacular confines on the **train** to Kalávrita.

This small gauge line, built in 1889–95 by an Italian company, offers a 'fast track' into the hitherto inaccessible area around Kalávrita. In the one hour and ten minutes that it takes to get to its terminus, the train wends its way through six tunnels, crosses 40 bridges, and climbs a staggering 2,300ft in 14 miles, through tremendously grand and wild scenery. The train is aided by a rack-and-pinion system on its steepest grades.

Getting There and Into the Gorge

The Diakoftó–Kalávrita train and the Pátras–Corinth rail line share a **station, t** 269 104 3206. The Éghio–Akráta **bus** stops in front of it several times a day. The train to Kalávrita leaves four times daily, sometimes more often. It is cheap, €6.70 return at the time of writing, and in summer very crowded. Go early, or get your **tickets** the night before. The ticket sellers can be somewhat surly, but persevere.

Many people take the train to **Zachloroú**, the last station in the gorge (and the stop for Méga Spíleo), and then walk back down in about 3hrs. You can also get to Zachloroú by car. The signposted turn-off is 3.3km south of the gates of Méga Spíleo on the main highway to Kalávrita. If the train is full, an unpaved road near Diakoftó will take you into the gorge. Take the main road west from Diakoftó, cross the river and go on about 300m to a large sign on the left saying ΥΠΕΡΓΕΙΩ ΓΕΩΡΓΙΑΣ. Take this road and after 6km you can park by the river and the train tracks at the narrowest part of the gorge.

Where to Stay and Eat

Diakoftó ✉ 25003

Chris-Paul, t 269 104 1715, **f** 269 104 2128 (C; *moderate*).Small rooms with balconies, a garden, parking area, and a pool; all close to the train station. *Open all year.*

Panorama, t 269 104 1614, **f** 269 104 2608, *kargeo@greecepanorama.gr* (B; *inexpensive*). Plain, with views, and a good restaurant with terrace on the sea. *Open all year.*

Kochili, t 269 104 1844. Right by the port and known for its seafood.

Kostas, t 269 104 3228. Near the train station, a favourite winter taverna.

Zachloroú ✉ 25003

Both of these hotels have excellent restaurants deep in the gorge by the train station.

Romantzo, t 269 102 4097, **f** 269 102 2758 (D; *inexpensive in summer, moderate in winter*).

Messenia, t 269 102 2789 (*inexpensive in summer, low moderate in winter*). Slightly larger rooms, and throws in a small fridge to beat the competition.

The pretty town of **Zachloroú** deep in the leafy gorge, under the shadow of the Méga Spíleo Monastery (*see* below), was settled by refugees from Épirus, escaping the Turks. It is a perfect spot for a lazy lunch, or for a stay in one of its two modest hotels.

South of Diakoftó: Kalávrita and Around

Kalávrita, 2,460ft above sea level, is a pretty, well-watered town of 2,000, famous for its railway as well as cheeses, pasta *xilópittas* (tiny squares) and *trachaná*, a dry mixture of goat's milk and flour. It is now the closest town to the popular Chelmós Ski Centre, and that has brought trendy cafés and hotels.

Life in Kalávrita changed forever on 13 December 1943 when the occupying Germans, in retaliation for the death of four German soldiers, gathered the entire male population – over 1,200 men and boys – on the hillside below the Frankish castle and gunned them down. The women and children had been gathered together in the school to be burned alive, but a single Austrian soldier balked at this atrocity and allowed them to escape. Kalávrita subsequently became a town of widows and children. The schoolhouse has recently been made a museum; the hillside is dominated by a huge cross, and since that day the clock in the square has been stopped at 2.34 to mark the hour of the massacre.

At the monastery of **Ag. Lávra**, 6km west of Kalávrita (**t** *269 202 2363; open 8–6, but closed for 2hrs at midday*), the flag of independence was first raised against the Turks.

It now resides in the church and has become a national pilgrimage site. Ag. Lávra was founded in 961. Its present buildings were built in 1827 (although frankly, by Peloponnesian standards it's a bit dull). The bus from Kalávrita to Kleitoriá can drop you off near it. Greece's second largest **ski area** (*t 269 202 2174*), is wonderfully situated on Chelmós' north slope 14km southeast of town. Skis and snowboards can be rented, either on the slopes or in town.

Another famous monastery here is the 'Big Cave' **Méga Spíleo** (*t 269 202 3130; closed briefly in the afternoon hours, proper attire required*), 7.5km north of Kalávrita, wedged

Getting There and Around

Besides the train from Diakoftó (**t** 269 202 2245), a **bus** from Athens goes daily via Akráta to Kalavríta, **t** 269 603 1731, once a day from Éghio, **t** 269 102 2424, and several times from Trípoli. For bus information, **t** 269 202 2224.

There are many **taxis**, **t** 269 202 2127, in the main *plateía*, but no bus service to the ski area. A taxi one way costs about €15 in good weather. Icy conditions demand danger pay! The cost of a trip to either the Méga Spíleo or Ag. Lávra Monastery, with a half-hour stop and a return, is between €14 and 15.

Méga Spíleo is accessible via the Kalavríta coast road, or by leaving the train at Zachloroú (*see* p.204). From there, however, it is a steep 45-minute walk. If you do hike up, turn left at the highway to get to the monastery. **Plataniótissa** can be reached from the Méga Spíleo–Kalávrita road, via Kerpiní (Κερπινή) on a so-so road, or from the Éghio–Ftéri–Kalávrita road on a good road.

Where to Stay and Eat

Kalávrita ✉ 25001

Aphrodite, **t** 269 202 3600 (*expensive in winter, moderate in summer*). Ten well decorated rooms dramatically perched above the town, with the beds tucked up in a loft.
Filoxenía, **t** 269 202 2496, **f** 269 202 3009 (*B; moderate, inexpensive in winter*). Standard rooms in a pleasant setting right in town.
Chríssa, **t** 269 202 2443 (*C; inexpensive in summer, moderate in winter*). Six air-conditioned rooms in a new building down the street opposite the train station.
Gri-Gri Café, opposite the schoolhouse. Terrific yoghurt, *crémas* and *baklavá*.

Stani, by the National Bank, **t** 269 202 3000. Good taverna fare (shown in a glass case) in a stone and wood fireplace setting; very après ski.
Elatos, **t** 269 202 2541. The more 'traditional' stand-by, and with a nicer terrace.

Planitéro ✉ 25007

Georgia Karamánou, **t** 269 203 1689 (*moderate–inexpensive*). Modest rooms with the use of a kitchen. The owner knows the area well. *Open all year.*
Varvára Militopoúlou, **t** 269 203 1628 (*moderate–inexpensive*). Five brand new rooms with kitchens, and a common fireplace. *Open all year.*
Laléousa, on the edge of the village, **t** 269 203 2385. There are many restaurants, all featuring trout; this is certainly the most upscale.
Límni ton Kýknon or 'Swan Lake', **t** 269 203 2393. A ramshackle affair over a trout pond, and in 2001 they even added swans.

Kleitoriá ✉ 25007

Mount Helmos, **t** 269 203 1249 (*B; expensive on winter weekends; otherwise moderate*). Pleasant small hotel catering to mountain and ski lovers. *Open all year.*
Georgia Rápanou rooms, **t** 269 203 1628 (*inexpensive*). Nine new rooms 100m from the hotel, each with a small kitchen and bath, and a common room with fireplace.
Psistariá of María Kambérou. Ungentrified, in the centre of town, with oil cloth on the tables and tasty home-made food.

Plataniótissa

There are summer restaurants near the tree church, open from Easter to October. The speciality is kid boiled or roasted, so tender that no knives are needed.

into the spectacular cliffs of the Vouraikós Gorge, 3,300ft above sea level, just off the road. The monastery is not as beautiful as its setting; the original burned in 1934. Behind the ugly façade is the cave where the shepherdess Euphrosýne discovered the miraculous wax and wood icon of the Mother of God (Theotókos) in 362. It is reputed to have been made by St Luke and quickly proved its worth by zapping a dragon with a proto-laser beam. Other relics and treasures, some very old, are in the museum.

The Tree Church at Plataniótissa

That churches in Greece are varied in terms of size, magnificence and choice of building materials is readily apparent to the most casual visitor, but the church at Plataniótissa (Πλατανιότισσα) adds a new wrinkle. It is contained entirely in the bole of a huge plane tree, can accommodate 20 people and is surely the only tree anywhere with a floor tiled in blue and white. The nave, complete with chandelier, measures 10ft by 13ft. This is also, understandably, the only church where lighting candles is strictly forbidden. Notice that the tree, while having one root, appears to be three separate trees from the outside, a perfect symbol of the Trinity. That, of course, was just the icing on the theological cake. One stormy night in 840, the icon of the Theotókos from Méga Spíleo was hung inside the tree during a tour of the area. To the amazement of all, an exact replica of the icon appeared in the wood opposite where it had been hung. Sceptics may claim it was carved, but the relief has kept its shape throughout 1,160 years of tree growth (even if the face of Mary is hard to make out), and that is only one of its score of miracles. Plataniótissa's valley is especially lovely in the spring.

South of Kalávrita: Lousí, the Cave Lakes, Planitéro and Kleitoriá

A good road leads out of Kalávrita, past the turn-off for the ski area, to Lousí, situated in an Alpine valley with the peaks of the Chelmós range forming a wall to the east. Many hikers use the tiny village of **Káto Lousí** as a starting point to climb Mount Chelmós; the coffee shop owner (*t 269 208 3331*) has rooms, and there's a taverna.

This valley belonged to **ancient Lousí**, a city with enough wealth to have hosted its own games in the Hellenistic period. In 1964, the **cave lakes**, an underground water course 6,500ft long, containing 13 small lakes and connecting tunnels, were rediscovered. The ancients knew all about them, and believed, among other things, that drinking the water would make you swear off alcohol altogether. Archaeologists found a sign written in Latin inviting visitors to take a drink but forbidding them to bathe in the same water. Tourists! The **tour** (*t 269 203 1001; open all year, 9.30–4.30, sometimes until 8pm in high season; adm*) is not as exciting as it would be if they opened up one or two of the larger lakes to visitors, something they keep promising.

Lousí's other memorable sight is the entire floor plan of the large **Temple of Artemis the Tamer**, the protectress of herds, signposted from Káto Lousí. The temple, under towering trees and with views over the valley, is the perfect picnic spot. They say that water was piped directly to this temple from the cave. It isn't now, so bring your own.

After Lousí you come to the end of the road and are faced with a choice: **Planitéro**, 3.5km to the east, or Kleitoriá, 5km west. The narrow canyon leading to Planitéro was formed by the Aroánios river, gushing out from nowhere at the foot of a limestone cliff. Many rivers in the Peloponnese start like this, the outflow of the waters that disappeared into sink holes in valleys like Pheneós and Stymphalía. Thanks to the water, the plane trees here have assumed fantastic proportions and shapes straight out of a Gustav Doré fairytale illustration. This impression is marred slightly by stands flogging local produce – nuts, oregano, mountain teas, honey and dried plants in colours that nature never produced. Planitéro is a pleasant village situated on the trans-European E4 path. Trout farms take advantage of the fast waters, and restaurants take advantage of the trout. Pausanias travelled here because he had heard that the rivers contained spotted fish that sang like thrushes. He sat listening for one entire evening but heard nothing. The stone mill at the entrance to the village is still used today and has a side room as you enter to wash heavy *flokati* rugs, a process still best done with a torrent of water.

If you take the west fork, **Kleitoriá** or Mazéika is a sleepy town, reminiscent of Kalávrita in the 1960s, but its valley is much more attractive. The scant ruins of **ancient Kleitor** (signposted) moulder on the north side of town not far from a small **rug factory**, a great spot for a souvenir. It can be the stepping stone for even more obscure destinations such as **Dáphni**, 30km southwest, with an old-fashioned grocery store/butcher/restaurant squeezed into one room. The cluster of threshing-floors on the barren hill opposite is typical of many Peloponnesian villages, conserving arable land. Dáphni leads on to the isolated **Ladon dam and lake** into Arcadia after **Trópaia**. You can even visit the wild ruins of the Frankish **Castle of Akova**, a few kilometres west of **Vizíki** (Βιζίκι), on a poor but passable road (ask for the '*kástro*' in Vizíki).

On Mount Erýmanthos: Ancient Psophís and the Erymanthian Boar

Clusters of wild peaks culminate in Mount Erýmanthos to the west. For a good introduction to the area, with a spectacular view over the Kleitoriá valley, take the cliff-hugging road to the isolated little hamlet of **Aroanía**, which has more churches than inhabitants. From here, the road follows the river in 16km to **Tripótama**, a village (with restaurants) at the junction of three rivers. Tripótama is built on the site of **ancient Psophís**, which must have been truly wild and beautiful in ancient times when the surrounding area contained vast oak forests full of wild boar, bears and huge land tortoises. Psophís was named after a princess whom Heracles obligingly impregnated when passing through to kill the **Erymanthian boar** which had been ravaging the country. The city existed into the Roman period but was never very famous, except for one of its citizens, Aglaos, who was said in ancient times to be a totally happy man.

Take the dirt drive up to the gate of the high-walled monastery of **Koímesis tis Theotókou**, and you are in the middle of a city that up until now has scarcely been excavated. The extensive ruins go up the hill to the west and down the other side to the river there. Parts of Psophís' walls can be seen on the Kalávrita road in town. The monastery is built on a temple, whose truncated columns can be seen in the courtyard. Workmen renovating the building in 1999 decided that the tallest column needed a clean and sanded down its outer layers, proving not only how white all of that grey lichen coloured stone is, but also how vulnerable these unsung sites really are. The little house beside the monastery is full of ancient stones and columns. After 2,000 years or so of local attention, the archaeologists who have planned extensive excavations here had better hurry up if they want to find anything at all.

West of Diakoftó: the Coast and a Controversy

On the coast west of Diakoftó and the Vouraikós Gorge, the next chance to turn into the mountains is from **Eleónas**. Its beach, one of the best in the area, is lively in the summer, with tavernas and good swimming. From here you can make a short but scenic ascent up the mountain to **Mamousiá** (the turn-off south is east of Eleónas on the Old National Road). At 7km, just as you approach the village, you will see a sign 'Ancient Kyreneia' by a tiny church. By the road are the roofed-over remains of a **Hellenistic funerary monument**, dug up when a water pipe was being laid. Its façade (now waist-high) was made to resemble a temple entrance, only here the doors were carved in the stone. On the other side of the church, to your right, is the footpath to the **acropolis**. This was the ancient mule path to the city, partly carved into the rock. It offers a grand if precarious perch to view the countryside and to marvel at how beautifully placed these ancient cities were. The question is – is it ancient Voúra or Kyreneia? In Achaía, where there are far more ruins than known ancient place names, no one can be sure. Continue along the dirt road up past the cemetery to the top, where a wonderfully flat mesa covered with vineyards offers great walks and views. The grapes here are the prized *Rodítis*; at this height they are sun-drenched, yet the altitude allows them to mature at the slow rate necessary for top-notch wines.

If you descend to the coast by the paved road (with great views of the coastal plain), you can ponder the fate of the lost city of **Helíke** that once graced the shore. In 373 BC, an earthquake sent it into the sea; its famous sanctuary of Poseidon was visited for a time in boats. Just prior to the earthquake the people of Helíke had killed some Ionian envoys in the sanctuary, and its demise was attributed to Poseidon's wrath. If so, he still has moments of irritation, because this slippage into the sea is a phenomenon that still occurs around Éghio when the earth shakes. As for Helíke, it may no longer be lost: in 2000, scientists using magnetometry and ground-penetrating radar located what seems to be the city (now buried in the silt) near modern Helíke.

Éghio, its Ferry and Beaches

Éghio

Agamemnon gathered the Achaean leaders in **Éghio** (Aigion) to debate the expedition to Troy. It seems like a long way from the Argolid, but Mycenaean culture was far more widespread in the Peloponnese than first thought. In 276 BC, Éghio became an important member of the Achaean League. Its substantial ancient monuments were destroyed in a succession of earthquakes, and the Slavs demolished the rest in 800. Now the second city of Achaía, Éghio is a commercial and administrative centre, and really hums on Saturdays, market day.

Café-studded **Psilá Alónia**, at the top of Metropóleos Street, provides a wonderful view of the Gulf; lower down, the port is becoming more attractive as some of the 19th-century currant warehouses are being renovated. In the *plateía* east of the docks, don't miss **Pausanias' Plane Tree**, venerable even if the AD 150 date may be a exaggeration. Climb the 150 steps up to the church of **Panagía Trypití** by the ferry dock and discover the cave where yet another icon of the Virgin was found. Its feast day, the Friday after Easter, draws huge crowds. Éghio's small archaeological museum in the centre (*t 269 102 1517; open Tues–Sun 8.30–3*) is housed in a beautifully renovated market built by Ernst Ziller. The **Oinofóros Winery** (*t 269 102 9415*), in the eastern suburb of Selinoús, welcomes visitors to taste the excellent local product.

Éghio's beaches, Sellianítika and Lóngos, are side by side but **Lóngos** is by far the prettier. Set away from the highway, its lush atmosphere is almost Ionian, especially its *plateía*, shaded by a huge plane tree. **Sellianítika** is not to everyone's taste; a road runs between all the hotels and restaurants and the sea, although there are relatively quiet places at either end.

Around Éghio

The **Cliff Monastery Taxiarchón** is one of the most striking in the Peloponnese, and well worth the special effort it takes to get there. The twice-daily local bus from Éghio to Melíssia can drop you a good 4.5km walk away. If you're driving, look on the east side of central Éghio for the sign for Moní Taxiarchón (Μονή Ταξιαρχών). Drive

Getting There and Around

Éghio is served by **train**, t 269 102 2385, from Pátras and Athens several times a day and by **bus**, t 269 102 2424, hourly; local buses, t 269 102 8787, stop at the beaches of Lóngos and Sellianítika several times a day. The **ferry**, t 269 102 8888, for Ag. Nikólaos leaves nine times a day all year round, from 5.15am to 8.30pm. Cars cost €9.68; passengers €1.60. It takes about 1hr and is useful for Delphi.

Where to Stay and Eat

Éghio ✉ 25100

Galini, t 269 102 6150, f 269 102 6152 (*B; moderate*). Has the monopoly and the view. Best for winter stays really, with a cosy bar area overlooking the Gulf.

Tasos/Stathis, Plateía Polyxroniádou, t 269 102 8998. Some of best *souvlaki* in Greece.

Oinomageirión of Demétris Pléssas, t 269 102 8691. By the port near Pausanias' plane tree and run by the same family since 1960. Terrific home-cooked meals.

Lóngos

Long Beach, t 269 107 2196, f 269 107 2373 (*B; expensive–moderate*). Holiday-village style hotel with tennis, pool, and watersports. All rooms face the sea. *Open April–15 Oct.*

Spey, t 269 107 2770 (*C; inexpensive*). This plain, barn-like, 1960s-style hotel is no frills and right on the beach with large balconies, a good location, and parking. *Open all year.*

Paradis, t 269 107 2313. Coffee shop in the main *plateía* – a local hang-out and a good source of information about rooms, at a pinch.

To Baltáki. Lóngos' reasonably priced seafood emporium and taverna, also right on the sea. Follow the signs from the square.

Sellianítika

Kanelli, t 269 107 2213, f 269 107 2442 (*C; inexpensive*). At the west end of the beach, a seaside hotel with everything in miniature, including the pool. *Open all year.*

Syn Ena, t 269 107 2881. Central on the beach strip, this busy restaurant has a lovely veranda. *Open eves all year, also midday Sun and hols.*

through the village of Mavríki and continue on across the river, bearing right until you come to the monastery (*t 269 105 6208*). First built in the early 1600s, the present monastery dates from 1782; the monks here make a famous rose petal jam.

The real attraction is the upper and older monastery of the **Blessed Leóndios** (*c.* 1377), glued high on the side of a cliff and partially dug into the living rock. Two small churches grace the monastery, and a dizzying flight of 55 stairs ascends to the tiny shrine of Leónidas, which has an eagle's eye view. Mountains upon mountains surround the valley, fading endlessly into the distance as far as the eye can see. These monks may have wanted to be alone, but were never without a panoramic view of God's creation to contemplate.

Mount Panachaikó and the Ring Road between Éghio and Pátras

Mount Panachaikó is a high (6,319ft) knob-like protrusion at the northern tip of the Erýmanthos range that stretches from behind Éghio to Pátras and beyond. The scenic and easily navigable ring road from Éghio to Pátras, separating Panachaikó from Erýmanthos' highest peaks, is worth a look. From Éghio, you'll pass through **Ptéri** (not far from the tree church at Plataniótissa, *see* p.206), past the turn-off to Kalávrita which is about 12km away at this point, via **Vlassía** (Βλασία). The peaks of Mount Erýmanthos loom to the south and a footpath from Vlassía leads to one of its summits. Next comes **ancient Leondio** with its tiny theatre and then the villages of **Katarráktis** and **Platanóvrissi**, and then on to Pátras. The distance from Éghio to Pátras through the hills is about 100km.

Río and the Ferry

Like Brazil, Greece has its Río, now a wealthy suburb of Pátras, but most tourists stop only long enough to grab a *souvlaki* where the highway ends and the ferry boat begins – although this will soon bow to the bridge, due for completion in 2004. The seaside **Río Casino**, oozing ersatz splendour, is another attraction. Greeks are big gamblers every day, but the queue of cars on New Year's Eve for the traditional evening gamble for *goúri* or good luck all year is always kilometres long. The shore

Getting There and Around

Río, 6km east of Pátras, has a **train** station, **t** 261 099 1244. The no.6 **bus** from the dock will take you to Pátras in 20mins. **Ferries** (day and night) make the 20min run across the Gulf to Andírio in Stereá Ellada. Cars cost around €6.

Where to Stay and Eat

Río ✉ 26500
Rion Beach, **t** 261 099 1422, **f** 261 099 1390 (*C; moderate*). The last word in 1960s design,
and just a 5-minute walk from the train station. *Open all year.*
George, 9 Ionias St, **t** 261 099 2627 (*C; moderate*). Several blocks in from the sea, modest, but very quiet. *Open all year.*
Camping Rio, **t** 261 099 1585, **f** 261 099 3388 (*inexpensive*). Small, well-run, with an attractive fish restaurant overlooking the sea, but noisy because of the local clubs.
Rementzo, by the sea, **t** 261 099 3829. With a pine-filled terrace and fireplace inside, this restaurant is especially popular with the Pátras set for an evening out.

west of the ferry dock is chock-a-block with restaurants and bars. The **Kastelli**, or little castle down by the docks, while fairly complete, can hardly compete with the new carioca look. Used as a prison for a while, the castle sits forlornly, its moat still full of water, waiting for action. It was built in 1499 by the Turks to match the one at Andírio across the strait and saw the last stand of Ibrahim Pasha's troops in 1828 before their defeat by a combined English and French force.

Pátras

Beautifully situated between sea and mountain, Pátras is the marine gateway to the Peloponnese and its largest city. Byron first set foot in Greece at Pátras but left almost immediately, pretty much setting the pattern for the future. Today's problems include traffic snarls, near impossible parking and the prevailing box-like architecture that only an anti-seismic expert could love.

Pátras was substantial enough in Classical times to have long walls from its acropolis to the sea *à la* Athens. But the city has somehow never achieved real star status during its long history. It was a going concern in Roman times when its bizarre festival to Artemis was in full swing and Andrew, Christ's first disciple, arrived. Rich enough to attract Saracen raids in the 9th century, it became the seat of a Frankish barony and a Latin archbishopric in 1205. Sold to the Venetians in 1408, retrieved by the Greeks in 1429, it then went the way of all of Greece and was seized by the Turks in 1460 who misruled it and burned it down in 1821 during the initial stages of the War of Independence. The present plan, designed on a grid with arcaded avenues (some of which survive in the centre), was initiated by Greece's first president Capodístria, who recognized Pátras' potential economic importance to the new state.

Today Pátras is making Herculean efforts to modernize and attract business and tourism. It contains trendy corners, a huge university and quite a large industrial base, but somehow it still retains the atmosphere of a small provincial town except by the sea, where the mammoth ferries and a palm-studded square give it an indeterminate international flavour.

All of this changes radically before Lent, when the **Pátras Carnival** turns the entire city into a playground for the locals and revellers from all over Greece. In this city of 200,000, it would be hard to find someone *not* involved in the 10-day orgy of mad costumes, drinking and street parties that culminates in a parade that takes hours to pass through the city. The Carnival originated as a pre-Lenten ball held in the houses of rich merchants in the 19th century, after Independence. It assumed a wilder and more popular form when it took to the streets in 1870 and ladies began arriving unescorted, masked, dressed from head to foot in black. They chose their own unmasked and uncostumed male partners for the evening or for the night, with an abandon that only a rigid and puritanical social structure can produce. A masked ball is still held in the Municipal Theatre, and whether the old tradition is observed or not remains the secret of those who are lucky enough to be invited. It ends with the burning of King Carnival at midnight.

Pátras

500 metres
500 yds

N

To Youth Hostel

ATHINON

Ferry Terminal,
Tourist Information Office

AG DIONISIOU

To Rio and
Athens

KAROLOU

PLATEÍA
PIROVETIOU

SATOVRIANDHOU

OTHONAS AMALIAS

KAPSALI

KORINTHOU

ZAIMI

Bus Station

Train Station

Museum

ARATOU

PLATEÍA
OLGAS

KOLOKOTRONI

AG NIKOLAOS

OTHONAS AMALIAS

AG ANDREOU

REGA FEREOU

ERMOU

PLATEÍA
AG.
GEÓRGIOS

KANAKARI

PATREOS

KARAISAKI

VOTSI

Castle

PAPADIAMANDOPOULOU

D H M GOUNARI

MESONOS

Odeion

PLATEÍA
25
MARTIOU

NEOFTOU

KORINTHOU

PANOKRATORAS

SACHTOURI

TRION NAVAHIRON

Church of
Ag Andréas

PLATEÍA
PSÍLA ALÓNIA

PLATEÍA
OMÓNIAS

To Akhaia
Clauss Factory
and Kalávrita

KARATZA

To Pírgos

Waiting in Pátras?

There is lots to do in Pátras during that blank period between buying a ticket and
leaving. The port area is good for shopping, but natives prefer the streets off **Plateía
Ag. Geórgeos** and further up towards the castle. While in the Plateía, look out for the

Municipal Theatre, built in 1872 by Ziller, its interior a miniature La Scala. The **Archaeological Museum** is at the corner of Maízonos and Arátou Streets, facing Plateía Olga (*t 261 022 0829; open Tues–Sun 8.30–3; adm free*). It's far too small for archaeologically-rich Achaía. All eras are covered, and the 2nd-century BC Roman mosaic pavement displayed on the first floor is worth a look. Give **swimming** a miss in Pátras: if you have time, go instead to the beaches towards Vrachnéika, 10km west.

The Castle, the Odeion and Psilá Alónia

The **castle** (*main entrance open Tues–Sun 8–7; in winter Tues–Fri 8–5, Sat–Sun 8–2.30; adm free. The small north entrance at the top of the stairs from the city closes 30mins earlier: a pleasant path joins the two entrances*), on the site of the ancient acropolis, is best reached by Ag. Nikoláos St. The ascent involves 100 steps and is tough going on a hot day, but the view is great and the area very peaceful and pleasant. (It is possible to drive up by taking Dim. Goúrnari St to Voukaouri St and then left). The castle has an attractive keep and is a melange of Byzantine, Frankish, Venetian and Turkish architecture. The north wall, which dates from the 9th century, contains column drums and other paraphernalia from ancient temples, including the famous Temple to Artemis. These relics bring to mind Pausanias' description of the annual Festival of the Laphria, held on this very spot. Every year, a grand procession wended its way to the temple from the lower town. The last member of the procession was the priestess of Artemis, resplendent in a chariot pulled by yoked deer. Huge logs were placed in a circle around the goddess' altar the day before and, when the priestess arrived, vast

Getting There and Around

Pátras has frequent **ferries** to Italy and the Ionian Islands, and the quay is lined with ticket agencies. For more information, call the **Port authority**: t 261 034 1002.

The **train** station, t 261 063 9108, by the port, has a left-luggage facility. There are several trains daily to Corinth, Athens, Pýrgos (for Olympia) and points south.

The **bus** station, t 261 062 3886, is on Óthonos Amaliás St between Arátou and Zaími Sts, immediately east of the train station. For information on city buses, t 261 027 3936. Buses to Kyllíni–Zákynthos (4 a day) leave from 48 Óthonos Amalias St, four blocks from the main station, t 261 022 0129.

Many **car and bike rental** agencies have offices around the port area:
National, 1 Ag.Andreas St, t 261 027 3367, f 261 027 7864.
Budget, 1 Navmachias St, t 261 045 5190, f 261 023 0200.
Rent a Bike, 166 Ag. Andréou St, t 261 033 3111.

Tourist Information

EOT tourist kiosk: at the port, at the entrance to Gate 6, t 261 043 0915; *open Mon–Fri 8.30am–8.30pm, more or less*. Their useful map of Pátras notes some of the one-way streets. On weekends, you are on your own unless they answer at the **tourist police**, t 261 045 1833, located at the same gate.
Central post office: at Mézonas and Zaími Sts, t 261 027 7759; *open Mon–Fri 7.30am–8pm*.

Where to Stay and Eat

Pátras ✉ 26500
Only stay in Pátras if you're stuck; you'll do better going to points east or west.
Astir, 16 Ag. Andréou St, t 261 027 7502, f 261 027 1644, *astir@pat.forthnet.gr* (*A; luxury*). A luxurious marble pile with a rooftop pool.
Adonis, Zaími and Kapsáli St, t 261 022 4213, f 261 022 6971 (*C; moderate–inexpensive*).

numbers of wild and tame beasts – birds, bears, deer, wolf-cubs and boar, and more – were herded or thrown into the circle, and the logs set aflame. The resulting holocaust, the pride of the city fathers, must have originated as a fertility rite since the altar was also heaped high with fruits from the orchards. Pausanias notes with satisfaction that there was no record of anyone being injured by the animals. A pity.

The **Roman Odeion** (*t 261 022 0829; open Tues–Sun 8.30–3; adm free*) on Sotiriádou Street is near the castle to the west. Extensively renovated, it was built around AD 150 and seated 2,300 spectators, and is now a venue for the summer International Pátras Festival, offering music, theatre and dance (call the number above for information). When the festival is in progress, there is also a ticket kiosk in Plateía Ág. Geórgios. A stroll west along Sotiriádou Street and then right on Karatzá Street will bring you to **Plateía Psilá Alónia**, Pátras' smartest watering hole, offering cafés and a panoramic view of sea and city.

The Church of St Andrew

On the western end of Ag. Andréas St, within walking distance of the port, the church of Ag. Andréas was begun in 1908 and finished in 1974. It can accommodate 8,000 under a 141ft-wide dome complete with a huge wooden chandelier..Beside the church is the earlier basilica built by Kolokotrónis in 1835, which itself replaced an earlier church where Andrew's grave is said to be. Tradition has it that Andrew, the Apostle of Greece and Asia Minor, was martyred on this spot for refusing to deny Christ. He asked to be crucified on an 'x' shaped cross because he was too humble to

Directly opposite the bus station; a stone's throw from the train station and port.
Pension Nicos, 3 Patréos 3, at the corner of Ag. Andréou, t 261 062 3757 (*C; inexpensive*). Walking up its marble stairs is like walking back in time 30 years in a Greek village – until the traffic noise intrudes. The reception is on the third floor. By the time you navigate the stairs, any urge to clamber back down and try elsewhere vanishes.
Ichthyóskala, t 261 033 3778, on the sea in front of Ag. Andréas. Excellent restaurant, where the fish are displayed in wooden boxes and you choose as if at a market.

On the Coast West of Pátras

Although dotted with beauty spots, notably the pine forest of Strofiliás near Kalógria, as well as wetlands, dunes and beaches, the coast west of Pátras holds surprisingly little charm. The seaside road until Vrachneíka is a continuous line of villas, cafés, *ouzeries*. From Kaminía to Cape Áraxos, the water is cleaner.

Grecotel Lakopetra Beach, 35km from Pátras at Lakópetra, ✉ 25200, t 269 305 1713, f 269 305 1045, *lakbeach@otenet.gr* (*luxury*). Indoor and outdoor pools, tennis, the works. *Open April–Oct.*
Kalogria Beach, 47km from Pátras in Kalógria, ✉ 27052, t 269 303 1380, f 269 303 1381 (*B; low expensive*). All facilities and the best beach in the area, bar none. The dunes and reeds are lovely at sunrise and sunset. *Open April–Oct.*
Poseidon, 14km from Pátras in Kaminía, ✉ 25002, t 261 067 1602, f 261 067 1646, *poseidon@pat.forthnet.gr* (*C; expensive*). New, by the sea. Well appointed, with TV, small pool and a buffet breakfast. *Open all year.*
Castella Beach, 18km from Pátras at Alissós, ✉ 25002, t/f 269 307 1477 (*C; inexpensive*). Pleasant and family-run. *Open all year.*
Camping Golden Sunset, Káto Alissós, t 269 307 1276 (*inexpensive*). Offers a pool, water slides and a narrow beach. *Open Mar–15 Oct.*

be crucified on the same type of cross as Jesus. Pieces of it are displayed in the cathedral (front right) behind the glass case containing his cranium. Andrew became the patron of Pátras after 805 when his shining apparition appeared miraculously on the castle's battlements and saved the city from the Slavs.

Like so many churches in Greece, this church is built over a temple, this one to Demeter. It contained a famous oracular **well** that could tell the sick whether or not they would survive. Petitioners would tie a mirror on a string and lower it to just above water level where it would mist up, then looked in the mirror and saw themselves either alive or dead. It was believed to be infallible, so consider before you dangle any mirrors over it. It is now a Christian shrine (just to the west of the basilica), complete with icons because Andrew was said to have both slept here and baptized the first Christians using its water.

Pátras in a Bottle

About 9km from the port, the Bavarian-style **Achaía Clauss Winery** (*t 261 032 5051*) offers free hour-long tours and tastings daily from 11am to 7pm. To get there, head out of town on Dim. Goúnaris Street, following the signs for **Saraváli** (Σαράβαλι) and eventually the signs for the winery; the no.7 bus from Óthonos Amaliás St, leaves every 30mins for the 25min trip but leaves you at the gate, facing an 800m walk. The winery was the brainchild of Gustav Clauss, who in 1873 produced his first commercial batch of Mavro Daphne, a sweet, red port-like wine, named after a Greek woman Clauss admired. The winery also produced Greece's first bottled table wine when it inaugurated its legendary, and now much improved, Demestica in 1901. The newer Achaía Clauss Pátras wine is even better.

Elís

If the seven prefectures of the Peloponnese were Snow White's dwarves, soft green Elís would be Sleepy. In ancient times, it dozed on the periphery of the great events of the Peloponnese, even avoiding the Dorian invasion. The story goes that when the Dorians first landed on the coast of Elís to invade the Peloponnese, the Delphic oracle had told them to seek the guidance of 'the three-eyed' one. They came across a fellow named Oxylus riding a one-eyed horse and decided he would do. Oxylus craftily diverted them around his favourite bit of real estate, Elís, and led them on their victorious march through the rest of the Peloponnese. As a reward, they made him king of the bit they never saw. Elís' low profile made it ideally suited to host the Olympic Games, the greatest of all ancient Panhellenic events; and over time, they made it neutral holy ground. Centuries later, fertile Elís was beloved by the Franks, who called it the 'milk-cow of the Morea' and made their capital here: it was one of the few places in Greece suited to growing flax and grazing cattle, and its lush vegetation reminded them of home.

If you're looking for the arcadian scenes painted by Poussin, where shepherds watch their flocks graze in oaken groves, then come to Elís. Even the coast is gentle; sand

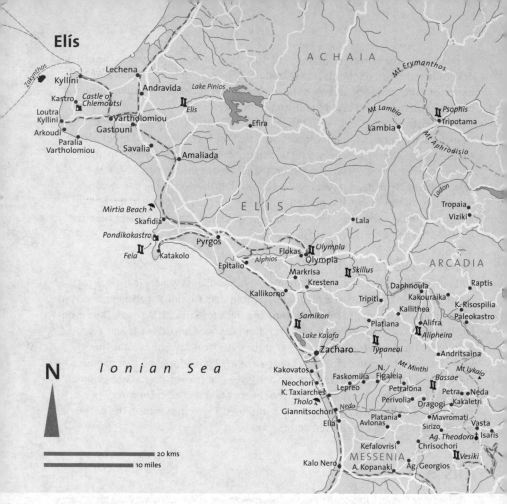

ACHAIA

Mt Erymanthos

Zakynthos

Kyllíni
Lechena
Andravida   Lake Pinios
Kastro
Loutra   Castle of
Kyllíni   Chlemoútsi
Vartholomiou   Elis
Arkoudi
Gastouni
Paralia
Vartholomiou
Savalia
Amaliada
Efira

Mt Lambia

Lambia

Psophis
Tripotama

Mt Aphrodisio

E L Í S

Ladon

Tropaia
Viziki

Mirtia Beach
Skafidia
Pondikokastro
Feia   Katakolo
Pyrgos
Epitalio
Flokas   Olympia
Alphios   Olympia
Markrisa
Krestena
Kallikorno
Samikon
Lake Kaiafa
Zacharo   Typaneai
Kakovatos
Neochori
K. Taxiarches
Tholo
Giannitsochori   Neda
Ella
Skillus
Tripiti
Daphnoula
Kakouraika
Kallithea
Platiana
Alifra
Alipheira

Lala

ARCADIA

Raptis
K. Risospilia
Paleokastro

Andritsaina

Mt Minthi
Figaleia
Lepreo
Petralona
Perivolia
Platania
Avlonas
Bassae
Petra Neda
Dragogi Kakaletri
Mavromati
Sirizo
Vasta
Ag. Theodora Isaris
Chrisochori
Vesiki

N

I o n i a n   S e a

N.

Faskomilia
Mt Lykaio

Kefalovrisi
Kalo Nero   Ag. Georgios
A. Kopanaki

MESSENIA

20 kms
10 miles

dunes and beaches line its low-lying coasts. Only at its southern frontier with Arcadía and Messenía does all turn to alpine drama. Besides Olympia, the Temple of Apollo at Bassae and the fabulous Néda Gorge are the highlights: the first an awesome work of man, the second one of the best kept secrets of Greece.

Northern Elís

Andravída and Chlemoútsi

The green, low hills in the northwest corner of the Peloponnese are grand if you're a cow, a grape or a watermelon. The coastline resembles the profile of a pig, and is a bit dull until you reach the snout. Following the highway southwest from Pátras, you may well be buzzed by training jets from the air base at Áraxos, less trouble than the persistent little vampires buzzing closer to the ground; the area is not called *Akti Kounoupéli*, or Mosquito Cape, for nothing. The first likely stop is **Andravída** or 'Andreville', once the Frankish capital of the Principality of Achaía, complete with royal

Pelops, the Eponymous Hero

Pelops got off to an awkward start when Tantalos, his father, chopped him into bits, cooked him and served him in a stew in one of the first empirical scientific experiments ever. He wanted to see if the gods would notice. It turns out they did, all except for Demeter who, mourning the loss of her daughter Persephone at the time, absentmindedly bit into his shoulder blade. So when he was reconstituted by the gods and sent off to found the Peloponnese, Pelops was sporting an ivory chip on his shoulder. He settled in Elís and married Hippodameia, daughter of King Oenomaos, but only after using his *poniría* – the cunning that to this day Peloponnesians are famous for. In order to get the girl and win the kingdom, a suitor had to beat her father in a chariot race or die. Many had already tried and failed, but that's only because they hadn't thought of paying off the king's charioteer, Myrtos, to replace the lynchpins of Oenomaos's chariot with wax so that he would be mangled to death. Pelops did, got the girl, threw Myrtos into the sea to avoid paying him the promised bribe, and lived happily ever after, basking in universal admiration, honoured above all others at Olympia. Peloponnesian leaders in ancient times bent over backwards to link themselves to his family tree; and according to myth the true descendants of Pelops, the Pelopids, were born with the same chip on their shoulder.

palace and funerary chapel, now all dust in the wind; only the transept of the 13th-century Gothic cathedral of **St Sophía** remains by the square.

Head west towards the rolling hills of the coast, and you come to one supporting the area's landmark, the **Castle of Chlemoútsi** (*open Mon–Sat 8–8, Sun 8–2.30, closed Mon in winter; adm free*). In the 1220s Geoffrey I de Villehardouin, Prince of Achaía, demanded that his clergy part with some of its gold to pay for his grand château-fort, which he called Clermont. The Pope excommunicated him for his presumption but Geoffrey didn't bat an eye, and built the finest and largest Latin building in Greece. It still dwarfs the village of **Kástro** that clings to its skirts. Geoffrey's brother William later minted the coin of the realm here, the *tournois* ('tails' showed the cathedral of St Martin de Tours), confusing the Venetians who then called Chlemoútsi Castel Torense. Inside the massive outer curtain wall is a hexagonal keep bearing a plaque to Constantine Dragatses, the last Byzantine emperor, who took Chlemoútsi in 1427 as part of his campaign to capture Pátras and put an end to the Franks' pirating ways. The keep's six lofty vaulted halls of fine ashlar masonry are impressive, even though their floors have caved in, leaving their fireplaces suspended in the air. Panels in English explain what's what. The castle is under restoration, but it was more fun, if not as safe, when you could go up the keep for the huge view enjoyed by the gentry.

Kyllíni, Loutrá Kyllíni and Arkoúdi

Just north of the castle was Clarence, or Glarentza, the chief port of Frankish Greece. Now restored to its ancient name **Kyllíni**, it's the chief port for the island of Zákynthos (*see p.475*). The medieval banks, merchants' palaces, monasteries and other institutions that made Clarence one of the richest towns in Greece are long gone; when Constantine Dragatses captured it in 1427, he razed it to the ground to prevent the

Franks from returning. Just behind the banana-lined beach is a weedy lot with some meagre remains of the castle, the equivalent of a person leaving only a toe joint behind to remember them by. Of the ancient city, zilch, not even an atom of its famous gigantic penis on a pedestal, noted by Pausanias.

The wooded setting and long, duney beach 12km south at **Loutrá Kyllíni** are attractive, but the National Tourist Organization's hotel and spa complex look as if they've been whacked by a neutron bomb. Just south of Loutrá, the delightful little oasis of **Arkoúdi** piles down a hill to a horseshoe of sand and turquoise sea. The coastal road

Getting There and Around

Three **buses** a day leave for Kyllíni from Pátras (*see* p.213). **Taxis** from Kyllíni to Chlemoútsi: about €11.

Pýrgos is Elís' transport hub, with several **trains** a day, t 262 102 2576. The bus station, just below the main *plateía*, t 262 102 2592, has 10 buses daily to Athens, hourly to Olympia, and several to Kyllíni, Katákolo and Kalamáta. Buses to the beaches or ancient Elís depart infrequently from Amaliáda, on the Pátras–Pýrgos train route.

Where to Stay and Eat

Kástro Chlemoútsi/Kyllíni ✉ 27050

Castello, Chlemoútsi, t 262 309 5224 or 262 309 5380 (*moderate*). Mrs Lepida's rooms are surrounded by greenery, and offer a common kitchen. *Open May–Oct.*
Kastro, Chlemoútsi, t 262 309 5434 (*inexpensive*). Cheaper, simple rooms. *Open June–Oct.*
Maria's Taverna, t 262 309 5439. A reliable old standby below the castle.
Seafood Garden, Kyllíni, t 262 309 2208. *The* spot for fish.
Sou Mou, Kyllíni, t 262 309 2396. Near the beach, with traditional fare.

Arkoúdi/Varthlomío ✉ 27050

Akti Rooms, Arkoúdi, t 262 309 6100 (*moderate*). Above the beach; new with fresh, airy rooms, marble baths, kitchenettes and mosquito screens. *Open all year.*
Soulis Apartments, Arkoúdi, t 262 309 6379, f 262 309 6000 (*expensive, breakfast and one meal inc.*). Lovely views and a slate central courtyard. *Open all year.*
Dougas, Arkoúdi, t 962 309 6432 (*C; moderate*). Way back from the sea but with a pool,

restaurant and grassy lawn; a good family choice. *Open all year.*
Anginara Beach, t 262 309 6211 (*inexpensive*) and **Ionian Beach**, t 262 309 6395 (*inexpensive*). Just east of Arkoúdi, two campsites with huts. *Open all year.*
Akrogiáli, Arkoúdi, t 262 309 6379. Has a big shady terrace, good food, and views of Zakýnthos through the banana fronds. *Open May–Oct.*
Arquoudi, t 262 309 6167. Right on the beach, serving snacks, drinks and meals.

Katákolo/Ag. Andréas ✉ 27067

Iónio, Katákolo, t 262 104 1494 (*C; moderate–inexpensive*). In the centre, the neoclassical Iónio is a quiet little place to stay. *Open all year.*
Zéphyros, Katákolo, t 262 104 1170 (*B; moderate–inexpensive*). Traditionally styled, and a bit fancier. *Open all year.*
Vriniótis, Ag. Andréas, t 262 104 1294, f 262 104 1402, *vrinioti@otenet.gr* (*C; expensive*). A great location by the castle, with air-conditioning. *Open Mar–Oct and in winter if you book.*

Pýrgos ✉ 27100

Olympos, Patrón and Karkavítsa 2, t 262 103 3650, f 26 2103 2557 (*C; moderate*). Near the train station. Has friendly owners, but skip the breakfast.
Letrina, inner edge of town on the Pátras road, t 262 102 5150, f 262 103 3664 (*B; moderate*). Done up for the business crowd with parking, TV and a restaurant.
Pizzeria Milano, Themistokles St (just below the big square). Serves enormous pies at rock-bottom prices, as well as other dishes, with some outdoor seating for enjoying the weather.

east of here passes other beaches and the piney **Thinon Forest** by **Paralía Vartholomioú**, with a big car park and a beach club to provide snacks and drinks.

Ancient Elis

To the east, **Gastoúni**, a prosperous livestock-rearing village, derives its name from the Frankish barony of Gastogne. It has a pretty cross-in-square Byzantine church, **Koímisis tis Theotókou**, built in the 12th century, and renovated and frescoed in 1702. In ancient times, towns were scattered all over the region. After a period of upheaval, they united in 472 BC to form a democratic polis and build a new capital at **Elis**, 15km east of Gastoúni, at the same time as Elean control over the Olympics was confirmed with the building of the great Temple of Zeus. There isn't anything half as grand here, although athletes came here to train in the city gymnasium and palaestra for the required nine months before the games, along with their relatives and friends, lending Elis a very cosmopolitan air once every four years. Because of the Sacred Truce, the city had no walls until 312 BC. By the 3rd century AD the town was gone.

The **museum** (*t 262 204 1415; open Tues–Sun 8.30–2; adm*) has finds from the site, including some rare theatre tickets (made of stone) which would admit you into the early Hellenistic-Roman **theatre**, the most intact of ancient Elis' remains. Unusually, it never had seats. The modern road cuts through the agora; there are overgrown foundations of a single and a double stoa, two Sanctuaries of Aphrodite (right next to each other – perhaps the Eleans needed double help in that area), baths and other buildings, some identified, none particularly compelling. The most popular shrine was a *temenos* to Achilles, while the most unusual one was dedicated to Hades, the god of the Underworld, and only open once a year.

Katákolo, Pýrgos, and Alph the Sacred River

The coast south of the 'pig snout' of Elís is one sweeping sandy beach dotted with campsites reached by little access roads off the Pátras–Pýrgos highway. The beaches stop at the hilly nub of **Katákolo**, dangling like the proverbial hair from the chinny chin chin. It shelters a convenient port for cruise ships, behemoths that dwarf the little town's pleasant cafés and tavernas as they disgorge passengers for Olympia.

Ancient Elis' port, where Olympic-goers from Italy landed, was located on the other side of the peninsula, at **Feia**, but a 6th-century earthquake caused most of it to subside into the sea. Its acropolis, the **Pondikókastro**, survived and was transformed by the Villehardouins into the **castle of Beauvoir** (to see it, loop around the back of the peninsula following the sign to Ag. Andréas, 1km before Katákolo). The castle has a romantically overgrown keep and pretty sunset views. Of the sandy beaches to the north of Katákolo, **Mirtiá**, north of Skafidiá, is especially nice. **Skafidiá** offers a 12th-century monastery that resembles a little castle, complete with a Venetian tower.

East of Katákolo, Elís' capital **Pýrgos** was founded around 1687 during the brief Venetian interlude. It isn't a bad place really, but there isn't much to say about it, either. Trains and buses to Olympia stop here (*see below*). At the top of the town, the stately *plateía* with a big white church of Ag. Nikólaos, neoclassical buildings, coffee shops and bars draws most of the 28,700 inhabitants in the evening.

South of Pýrgos lies the mouth of the **Alphiós**, the longest river in the Peloponnese. Its prestige was such that the Greeks put the letter *alpha* first in the Greek alphabet. Shelley unkindly labelled it a 'brackish Dorian stream' and it must have been murky, too, during Heracles' Fifth Labour, the cleaning of the stables of King Augeias of Elís, when Heracles diverted the river through centuries of manure, sweeping it away in a single day. In the 7th century BC, as the Olympics began to draw competitors from Magna Graecia, the story was told that Alphiós fell in love with the nymph Arethousa, and pursued her 'down miles measureless to man' under the Ionian Sea to Syracuse, where she turned into a spring and their waters mingled. The coastal area south of the Alphiós, once a shallow lagoon, is now usually dry; **Epitálio** on its banks has some remains of its Hellenistic–Roman namesake, and scant traces of Homeric Thryon up on the hill of Ag. Geórgios. To continue south along the coast, *see* p.233.

Olympia

The Olympic Games were the most prestigious in the ancient world, and lasted for over a thousand years. The low wooded hills in a triangle formed by the Hill of Cronus and the Alphiós and Kladeos rivers provided a wonderfully congenial setting for these great Panhellenic meetings, and to this day, no matter how many tour buses descend on the site, it retains a peaceful, almost detached quality. The presence of people from around the world and their cicerones even adds a note of realism: in ancient times, it was much the same, as visitors from around the Mediterranean were shown around the marvels by official local guides and masters of ceremonies called the *Exegetés*.

Olympia epitomizes the spirit of *agon*, the competitive drive recognized by Nietzsche as a prime force in Hellenic culture. Lovers, politicians, warriors, philosophers, beautiful girls, weavers, musicians, dramatists and artists all 'competed for the prize' *agonizesthai*; in Mégara there was even a contest for the sweetest kisser. But no contest counted for as much as Olympia. The Sacred Truce that commanded the Greeks put aside war in favour of sport is an attractive concept our nation-states still can't replicate, although the modern Olympic Games, especially now that they have been completely commercialized and professionalized, are a pretty fair version of the ancient games. The Greeks never did believe in anything as warm and fuzzy as amateur good sportsmanship. Ancient athletes were as professional and well rewarded as our modern heroes, and winning was everything, no two ways about it; the last man to finish was hooted at in derision, not clapped home.

History

Olympia is ancient – the oldest finds go back to 4000 BC, and the first apsidal houses were built in the Altis by 2000 BC. Although a Mycenaean presence is noticeably absent in the sanctuary, Mycenaean graves near the museum show they were in the neighbourhood. There is even a name for their as-yet-undiscovered city: **Pisa**, the home of King Oenomaos, who disgusted the gods by planning to build a temple with the skulls of the young men who lost the chariot race for the hand of his daughter

Getting There

For **trains** change at Pýrgos; four a day continue to Olympia. There are 16 **buses** from Pýrgos, three direct from Athens (Kifissoú terminal, **t** 210 513 4110), three from Trípolis, one per day from Lálas, and there are links to Dimitsána on Mondays and Fridays only. For a **taxi**, call **t** 262 402 2555 or **t** 262 402 2788.

Tourist Information

Kiosk on Kondilis St by the town bus stop, **t** 262 402 3100, **f** 262 402 3125; *open 9am–8pm in July and Aug, and 11–5 the rest of the year.* It lists local bus schedules.

Shopping

Besides the usual souvenirs, Olympia has a great bookshop: **Galerie Orphée**, on Kondíli Street near the youth hostel, **t** 262 402 3555. The owner sells a wonderful selection of books on Greece in English and a large selection of music. Its rival, **Atanasia**, on the same street, is no slouch either.

Where to Stay

Olympia ✉ **27065**
Hotels stay open all year, and all mentioned are close to the town centre. Do reserve.
Europa, 1 Drouva St, **t** 262 402 2650, **f** 262 402 3166 (*A; expensive*). New, modern, the best of the best, situated on the hill above town, with a nice pool garden, parking and a rooftop restaurant with a marvellous view. Cheaper than its A class rivals too.
Ilis, Prax. Kondíli St, **t** 262 402 2547, **f** 262 402 2112 (*C; expensive–moderate*). Airy, white and salmon pink. Guests can use the pool at the nearby, more pricey sister hotel.

Néda, 1 Kon. Karamanlis St, **t** 262 402 2563, **f** 262 402 2206 (*B; moderate*). This hotel's dark-panelled public rooms make it a cosy winter choice.
Pelops, 2 Vareia St (up from Kondíli), **t** 262 402 2543, **f** 262 402 2213 hotel–pelops@hotmail.gr (*C; moderate*). A small, modern hotel with balconies.
Pheidias, 2 P. Spiliopoulou St, **t** 262 402 2667, **f** 262 402 2667 (*C; inexpensive*). Plain, and a pretty good deal.
Hercules, **t** 262 402 2696 (*C; inexpensive*). On a quiet street just back from Kondíli; offers good value for its class.
Posidon, 8 Stefanopoulou St, **t** 262 402 2567 (*E; inexpensive*). A clean, family pension with a vine-covered bar and restaurant on a quiet street. It's popular, so do book ahead.
Youth Hostel, 18 Kondíli, **t** 262 402 2580 (*inexpensive*).
Camping Diana, **t** 262 402 2314 (*inexpensive*). In town, with a pool; gets the most kudos.
Camping Olympia, **t** 262 402 2745, 1km west on the Pýrgos road; has a bigger pool.

Eating Out

No lack of places in Olympia, but the locals suggest a trip to the *psistariás* at Linária.
Praxitéles, **t** 262 402 3570. One street back from Kondíli and a bit barnlike, but with a fireplace and good food.
Aegean, in the centre, **t** 262 402 2904. Considerably more upscale and a great place to people-watch as you eat.
Cafeteria Diónysos, **t** 262 402 2932. A modest beanery on Kondíli where you can go in and have a look at what you are buying.
Taverna Drosia, in Miráka, 3km east of Olympia, **t** 262 402 2311. For traditional Greek cuisine.
Bacchus, also in Miráka, **t** 262 402 2498. For grilled food, especially chicken.

Hippodameia. Pelops' victory (*see* p.217) put an end to such carryings-on, but it certainly wasn't a very sporting start for Olympia.

After the collapse of the Mycenaeans, settlement in the valleys of Elís was dispersed. Olympia itself was never a town, and its first role may have been as a central meeting place for Elean leaders. The date for the **first cult activity** has been pushed back to around 1000 BC; by the 9th century, in addition to the terracotta votives, there are pricey bronzes and jewellery from Messenía and Arcadía as well as Elís, suggesting that meetings at Olympia had expanded to include western Peloponnesian chieftains; the wealth of their offerings would enhance their status with one another and with the folks back home. As the decades passed, these dedications grew in scale; in the Early Iron Age, a great increase in large tripods, horse figures, wagons and charioteers is indicative of a new aristocratic interest in Olympia.

The 776 bc date for the first Olympic Games was first recorded by the 5th-century BC sophist Hippias of Elís in his list of Olympic victors. The archaeological evidence would push the date forward to about 720 BC, based on items found in the wells of the Altis. These wells were dug every four years and filled in at the end of the festival with junk and discarded votive offerings (votives were inalienable possessions of the god and when they were thrown out, they had to be thrown out within the sanctuary). Around 720 BC the wells show a massive increase in jewellery dedications, imports from Italy and the first plates and cups. Hippias' list of victors, even if his date is uncertain, does confirm that the festival gradually caught on throughout the Greek world. Although all the early winners come from the west and central Peloponnese, Corinth and Megara posted their first victories in the late 8th century BC, Sparta in 720 BC. The first Athenian win was 696 BC, and the first from Italy was 672 BC.

Until 724 BC there was only one event, a foot race to the altar of Zeus. The games always started with the sacrifice of a black ram to Pelops, by his tomb, followed by massive sacrifices of oxen to Zeus. Philistratos describes what happened next:

> The consecrated portions then lay on the altar, but had not yet been set alight; the runners were one stadion away from the altar; in front of the altar stood a priest who gave the starting signal with a torch. The victor put fire to the sacred portions and so went away Olympic victor.

The first to win the race to light the barbecue was, fittingly, a cook named Koroibos.

Sparta's enslavement of Messenía in 710 BC seems to have added urgency to Olympia's evolving Panhellenic status. The other city-states saw it was in their interest to meet on a regular basis, and the games offered the perfect excuse, so it became the custom to send official diplomats with the athletes to the Olympics. The development of the *polis* also encouraged the institutionalization of the games, in providing an important showcase for the status-conscious aristocrats, offering individuals glory without power and states victories in 'wars minus the shooting'. But thoughts of real war were never far off, and there were times when competitors faced real enemies in the stadiums. Weapons, once buried in the tombs of aristocrats, became conspicuous dedications at Olympia after 700 BC, while gifts of expensive tripods fall off completely by 600. Dedicating arms rather than pots was also a nice way for each city-state to advertise its prowess to the greater Greek world.

Weapons for non-votive purposes were strictly prohibited. According to legend, the **Sacred Truce** or *Ekecheiriá* was devised in the 8th century, when the kings of Elis, Pisa and Sparta agreed to its terms. Inscribed on the bronze **discus of Iphitos** in the Temple of Hera, it declared that Elis and Olympia were sacred; that no armies could set foot in their territory; that every four years a truce would be announced to the entire Greek world, during which all hostilities had to cease for three months. Then, as now, the privilege of running the games (and the economic benefits) did not go uncontested. At first run by the Elean élite, the games were taken over in 668 BC by the Pisatans, with the help of Pheidon the tyrant of Argos. Herodotus described Pheidon in shocked terms as 'the man who carried out the most arrogant action ever of all the Greeks when he expelled the Elean presidents from the Olympic Games and presided over them himself.' In 572 BC, Sparta defeated the Pisatans, and the Eleans took over again (with Sparta looking over their shoulders). Curiously, this did not help Sparta's once-

Mythic Founders and Funeral Games

The rise of a state religion with shared values, expressed in Panhellenic shrines such as Olympia, was essential in taming not only aggressive aristocrats but also aggressive states. Myth gave the Olympics their prestige, which meant the games had to have origins that went back to the dawn of time: the story goes that **Zeus** and **Cronus** wrestled for Elís, and Cronus was killed and buried under the conical hill that still bears his name. According to Plutarch, to celebrate his victory Zeus founded the first games – a foot race and a fight to the death – and the winners were crowned with apple leaves, symbol of immortality. Mirroring this is the Elean story of **Heracles**, who stopped here after cleaning the Augeian stables. He sacrificed to Pelops and Zeus, and marked the sacred precinct or *altis* around the barrow of the hero Pelops (*see* p.217). Heracles also introduced the **wild olive** to Olympia as a gift from those northern magicians, the Hyperboreans, and (re)founded games in honour of Pelops and Zeus. His younger brothers ran the first race and he crowned the victor with olive.

All Panhellenic games, at Olympia as well as at Isthmia, Nemea and Delphi, were claimed to be **funeral games** (*epitáphios agón*) in one way or another, harkening back to the games that Achilles held for Patroclos in the *Iliad*. These were seen as prestigious not only for the memory of the dead, but also for whomever held the games, determined the rules and awarded the prizes. Yet funerals and sports seem an odd combination. One explanation has it that in the development of the Olympian cult, the afterlife turned dismal. After all, for Homer's heroes, life was everything; death, especially that of a young person, caused not only grief but rage. It was a tear in the fabric of the cosmos, Order was upset; the games allowed for a physical release of the rage while confirming the struggle and victory of life.

Last but not least, Pausanias mentions that the first races at Olympia were run by girls, competing to become the priestess of Hera. Hera's temple is the oldest at Olympia, reputedly founded by Hippodameia in celebration of her marriage to Pelops. This very ancient race or *agon* suggests that the origins of all games were not funereal at all, but seasonal fertility rites. With the later dominance of Zeus, the quadrennial foot-race among youths to see who would be the consort of Hera's priestess and King of Elís became the main event, and the meaning of the games shifted to fit into the Homeric mould. But the girls' foot race was not forgotten, and it continued as part of the **Heraia**, an event open only to young women of Elis. The winner was crowned with an olive wreath, and had the right to a prime portion of the cow sacrificed in Hera's honour, and to dedicate a statue of herself to Hera.

dominant athletes; after 578 BC their victories declined, even though everyone knew they only participated in the events they felt they could win.

A Day at the Races: the Games in their Final Form

As the years passed, the games became highly regulated, with an Olympic committee setting the rules. There were divisions for boys (as of 632 BC) and grown men. To participate one had to be a free Greek and have a clean record (no murderers or temple robbers allowed). The Macedonians, for instance, were snubbed until their kings brought proof of their Argive ancestry; similar genealogical gymnastics were later performed to admit the Romans. Women were banned from the games, although unmarried women were very much on the periphery of Olympia, attracted by the aphrodisiacs of wealth, glory and toned pectorals.

Competing naked dates from 720 BC, a custom introduced by the Spartans or after a runner's pants fell down during the foot race. Coaches too had to be naked after one athlete's mother penetrated the all-male bastion disguised as his coach and as a consequence was tossed off the Typaean rock. While officially open to all free Greeks, the rules in effect limited participation to the elite. All athletes had to spend ten months **training** and were required to spend a month prior to the games at the sanctuary itself, observing a strict vegetarian diet and sexual abstinence. Coaches were highly respected, and they kept a close eye on their charges, even forbidding conversation at mealtimes to prevent the jocks from straining their brains. Their monkish regime was assuaged by admirers and agents who swarmed around the athletes, who were already the most conceited creatures in antiquity. Fashionable young men came to see and be seen, beggars to beg, actors to recite, and no doubt punters to bet. Herodotus read from his *Histories* – young Thucydides was a captive listener.

The athletes and coaches at least had roofs over their heads; everyone else below VIP status slept in conditions that make Woodstock sound cosy. Sacrifices were offered to Zeus, Averter of Flies. One anecdote tells of an unruly slave, whose master threatened to free him and take him to the Olympics unless he behaved.

Originally there was only one **umpire**, a hereditary office held by an Elean, but after 584 BC others were added until there were ten, all from Eliís, and all selected by lot. They had rods to whack athletes who jumped the gun or played dirty, and levied fines on states and athletes who cheated. The Spartans (it *would* be them) were banned from the games in 420 BC for attacking Lepreon during the Sacred Truce and were forced to pay 2,000 *minas*. The fines were spent on bronze statues of Zeus, known as **Zanes**. In some 292 Olympiads there were only 16 of these, which isn't a bad record.

The games took place over five days in July, at the first full moon after the summer solstice. The **first day** saw the opening ceremonies, the sacrifices to Pelops and Zeus, the registration of athletes and their vows to obey the rules at the statue of Zeus Horkios, the god of oaths. The **second day** was dedicated to the boys' events: running, boxing (matches were only decided when someone conceded), wrestling and the *pankration* in which the only rules were no biting or gouging out of eyes; wrestling, boxing, hitting, strangling, kicking and stomping on one's opponent were all acceptable. It too ended when one party surrendered. Or died.

On the **third day**, there was the extremely popular chariot racing in the hippodrome, which began with charioteers sacrificing to the Taraxippus, or horse-scaring
ghost of Myrtos, the charioteer of King Oenomaos whom Pelops kicked into the sea.
On the same day the men's Pentathlon (discus, javelin, long jump – with weights in
each hand – wrestling and a sprint) was held in the stadium. The **fourth day** was
devoted to the other men's sports: racing, wrestling, boxing, *pankration*, and a race
derived from military training, in full hoplite armour, huge shield in hand, held at
dawn to keep the competitors from dying of heat exhaustion. On the **fifth day** the
winners were handed a palm frond, crowned with their olive wreaths and fêted.
Sacrifices were made to the gods in thanksgiving for their victories. There were
moonlight processions and, apparently, an orgy after all that abstinence.

The victors, the *Olympioníkai*, were permitted to erect votive statues in the sanctuary. If they won three times, the statue could bear their own features. Itinerant
craftsmen set up workshops to make these on the spot; they also produced thousands of little figurines as votives and souvenirs. The prize of an olive wreath may
have been nominal, but the prestige was overwhelming. The *Olympioníkai* returned
home like triumphant Caesars dressed in purple robes, at the head of a procession of
chariots. A winner might even be invited to knock down part of the wall of his home
town, as having such men obviously precluded the need for walls. He would dedicate
his wreath to the city's patron god, receive countless gifts and an Ode in his honour,
perhaps by Pindar. More concretely, he and his descendants could expect free meals
in perpetuity at the local Prytaneion. The glory of victory, in fact, was so exaggerated
that the whole purpose of the games, at least from the point of view of the city-
states, sometimes backfired; rather than tame aristocrats, an olive wreath granted
political clout to those who knew how to use it: Alcibiades' outrageous career began
with winning the chariot race. The *Olympioníkai* were antiquity's darlings, and only a
few voices in the wilderness, among them Plato's, ever questioned the sense of it.

The End

As time went on, the lists of victors were dominated by colonists: the Olympics
assumed a special importance for them, not only in confirming their Greekness, but
also as a showcase for nouveau riche dedications. By the time of Philip of Macedon
the games had taken on a more secular character; Philip even erected a monument to
himself and his family in the Altis. The stadium, originally in view of the Altis to
emphasize the religious aspect, was now hidden with the new echo stoa (*see* p.229).
Bribing officials was not unknown, and the athletes were highly paid prima donnas.

Standards declined even further when they let the Romans in. Their senses dulled
by the brutality of gladiatorial fights, most weren't very interested, and left the
Olympics to the philhellene élite. The games reached their nadir in AD 67, when they
were delayed two years to enable Nero to participate. He inaugurated a musical
competition for himself to win, and raced a ten-horse team in the chariot race, fell
out twice and failed to finish, but won anyway, and gave the judges an ample award
for their good judgement. The thousands of statues that once crowded the Altis were
slowly filtered off to Rome and Constantinople. In 392 Theodosius banned the games,

along with every other whiff of paganism in the empire. Christians briefly occupied the complex and used some of the stone to build a wall against the Vandals. Earthquakes downed the temples, and the Alphiós and Kladeos rivers altered their course and buried the sanctuary in mud, supplemented by landslides off the Hill of Cronus. Soon only memories remained while Olympia lay under 12 feet of mud – deep enough to protect its sculptures from the Elgins of the world, at least until 1829 when the French found the Temple of Zeus and whipped some metopes off to the Louvre.

In 1875, the Germans took over, with the proviso that all the finds should remain in Greece; one big enthusiast was Kaiser Wilhelm, who fancied himself a new Achilles. In 1961, the International Olympic Academy was founded here to promote the Olympic spirit – it's just east of the site, by a memorial to Pierre de Coubertin (1862–1937), the prime mover behind the revival of the games, and whose heart is contained in a stele.

The Site

t 262 402 2517; open Mon–Sun 8–7. If you want to see both the site and museum, save money with the combined ticket.

In the Altis

The *Altis*, a super-*temenos* or sacred precinct enclosing several temples instead of the usual one, is an irregular quadrangle measuring about 200 yards on each side, surrounded by a low wall and bounded on one side by the hill of Cronus. *Altis* means 'grove', a word which goes straight back to Olympia's origins: the oldest sanctuaries were often just that, set in groves, in caves or on hilltops. Dedicated to the gods, they were also safe neutral zones for humans. The modern entrance in the northwest corner corresponds to an ancient one, where the first building you see is the **prytaneion**. This was the headquarters of the priests in charge of administering Altis and offering sacrifices on its many altars. The altar of Zeus in particular required one blood offering a day. To cook all that meat, the prytaneion had a useful feature – an eternal flame dedicated to Hestia, the goddess of the hearth. It also had kitchens and a banquet room, where the victors feasted at the end of the festival.

The circular building nearby was the **Philippeion**, erected by Philip II after his victory at Chaeroneia in 338 BC. This wasn't the first monument in the Altis celebrating a victory over Greeks, but it must have been the most galling, even though it was a pretty gazebo with 18 Ionic columns around the porch, eight Corinthian columns around the wall and a bronze roof crowned with a poppy-shaped boss. Five gold and ivory statues of the Macedonian royal family by Leochares stood inside, including one of Alexander, whose immortality was proclaimed here during the games in 324 BC.

Nearby, the **Temple of Hera** is the oldest at Olympia, as well as a key work in the evolution of the peristyle temple. The original was built of wood in the 8th century BC, but in 590 BC it was rebuilt as a long, narrow Doric temple with a peristyle (6 by 16 columns) made of limestone and bricks that could support an entablature of wood and a tile roof. The first columns were of wood, but these were replaced with stone as they rotted; their different styles show that even a Doric column can alter with fashion. When Pausanias visited in AD 160, there was still one wooden column in

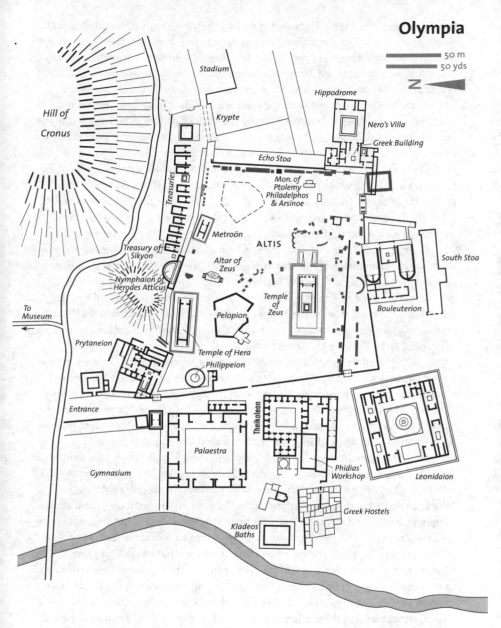

Olympia

50 m
50 yds

Hill of Cronus

Stadium

Hippodrome

Krypte

Nero's Villa

Greek Building

Echo Stoa

Treasuries

Mon. of Ptolemy Philadelphos & Arsinoe

Metroön

ALTIS

Treasury of Sikyon

South Stoa

Altar of Zeus

Nymphaion of Herodes Atticus

Temple of Zeus

Pelopion

Bouleuterion

To Museum

Prytaneion

Temple of Hera

Philippeion

Entrance

Theikoleon

Palaestra

Phidias' Workshop

Leonidaion

Gymnasium

Greek Hostels

Kladeos Baths

place. Four have been re-erected. Crowning all was a terracotta *akroterion* shaped like a disc, measuring 8ft in diameter and decorated with concentric bands of coloured decoration, resembling a giant dart-board rising out of the middle of the roof.

The temple had an Archaic statue of Hera enthroned with Zeus standing by her side. The temple also sheltered Olympia's holies of holy: the discus of Iphitos, the gold and ivory table of Kolotes where the victors came to receive their olive wreaths and the cedar chest of Kypselos. This was donated by the 7th-century BC tyrant of Corinth, who had been locked in it as a child by his mother to hide him from the Bacchiads whom he later overthrew (*see* pp.179–80). The chest, decorated with every conceivable mythological scene, merited a long description by Pausanias. He also noted a certain statue of Hermes and Dionysos by Praxiteles that was found in the *cella* in 1877.

In front of the Temple of Hera was the **Pelopion**, the low burial mound of Pelops, which was worshipped from 1100 BC. During the Archaic period, its precinct was made into an irregular pentagon, surrounded by a stone wall. It was open to the sky, with trees and a few statues, and was given a monumental entrance in the southwest corner in the 5th century BC. Here the Eleans opened the games with a sacrifice of a black ram on a fire of white poplar. Looking back towards the Temple of Hera, the great **altar of Zeus** probably stood to the right. This was elliptical, the curve filled with a 22ft-high pile of ashes of tens of thousands of victims. The new ashes would be moistened with water from the Alphiós and given a fresh coat of plaster every year.

To the right of the Temple of Hera, the semi-circular building under the Hill of Cronus is the **Nymphaion of Herodes Atticus**, which the wealthy benefactor built in AD 150 in honour of his wife Regilla. This was an elaborate fountain on three levels, with two little round fountains on either end and a two-storey exedra in the back, with niches to hold statues of the Antonine emperors. Herodes also installed the pipes and aqueducts that brought in the water, and the grateful Eleans added statues of Herodes and his missus to the ensemble.

Next to the fountain, overlooking the Altis from the wooded Hill of Cronus, are the twelve **treasuries**, all in a line. These were built between 600 and 480 BC by Dorian states: Byzantium, Cyrene (Libya), Metapontum, Elipamnos (whereabouts unknown), Sybaris, Selinunte, Gela and Syracuse (all Italy), Sámos, Mégara and Sikyon (the only three in Greece proper). Pausanias listed only ten, which has made their identification problematic. The **Treasury of Sikyon** with the column and capital is the best preserved, and made from stone specially brought from Sikyon. They served as little temple-showrooms, containing both gifts to Zeus and votive offerings for victories.

The ruined building in front of this row was a **metroön**, a late (4th-century BC) temple dedicated to the Mother of the Gods. The Romans divided it up to hold statues of their emperors. The row of pedestals between the metroön and the treasuries once held the **Zanes** (the plural of Zeus), the statues erected to stigmatize foul play, paid for by the cheaters' fines. Like the sacrifices, this is a custom that has fallen by the wayside, but an interesting one that could be revived if the Eleans ever got their wish to hold the Olympics permanently in their territory again. Beyond is the **krypte**, what remains of the vaulted passage into the stadium built by the Romans.

The Germans located the **stadium** during their first digs in 1875–81, and completed the excavations in 1960. The original stadium was 90 yards to the west and had only one embankment; this new one, laid out in the 5th century BC, had two embankments capable of seating 45,000. It must be the most famous, and the most simple, stadium in the world. There were never any seats: everyone sat on the ground except for the umpire who sat on the dias at mid field. Opposite is the stone altar of Demeter Chamyne, whose priestess was the only woman allowed to attend the games.

The track is 35 yards wide, sufficient for 20 racers, and 210 yards (192m) or one *stade* long. The starting and finishing lines are marked by low slabs; on the west end you can see the indentations made for the runners' toes. The classic race was the one *stade* sprint, but there were also the *diaulos* (two *stades*) and the *dolichos* (as many as 24 *stades*, or about 3 miles). A low stone parapet separated the athletes from the spectators; an open stone water channel, with basins at intervals, provided refreshment. To the south, in an open valley of the Alphiós, the **hippodrome** has been washed away or buried under a deep layer of mud.

In the 4th century BC the stadium was almost completely cut off from the Altis by the building of the 308ft double-colonnaded **echo stoa**, attributed to Philip II or Alexander. Little remains of it, but in its day it was one of the wonders of Olympia: any word pronounced here would echo seven times. The walls were lined with paintings which gave the spectators something to look at as they queued up to enter the stadium. The **Archaic-era starting line** was found under this stoa. In front are the ruins of the **Monument of Ptolemy Philadelphos and Arsinoe**, his wife (and sister), each of whom had a gilt statue on top of a 33ft column. The Ptolemys, who ruled Egypt after Alexander, were keen to confirm their Greekness in spite of their Egyptian-style marriage, and were great ones for showy dedications in Panhellenic sanctuaries.

A bit tacked on the echo stoa after 373 BC became known as the **Stoa of Hestia**, made of stone that had fallen from the Temple of Zeus in an earthquake. A building of unknown import was added behind (outside the Altis) known as the **Greek building**, and behind this are the remains of **Nero's villa**. Eager to curry favour, the emperor decreed that all Northern Peloponnesians were free. The locals, forced to foot the huge bill to build the villa and entertain Nero, weren't impressed.

Dominating the southern half of the Altis is the massive platform and shattered columns of the **Temple of Zeus**, one of the largest Doric temples ever built. Designed in 460 BC by Libon of Elis, the grey nubbly stone was originally covered with fine white stucco to resemble marble. Because of the low lying area, Libon made the platform unusually high and supplied a ramp on the east side. Although on a massive scale, it was otherwise a textbook peristyle temple, 6 by 13 columns, each 34ft high, with a base diameter of 7ft. The capitals supported an entablature over 13ft high, punctuated with lionhead spouts, while the pediments framed the superb sculpture in the museum – the Battle of Lapiths and Centaurs, and the Chariot Race of Pelops and Oenomaos. You can see the foundations of the *cella*, with its two vestibules. Six metopes on the Labours of Heracles decorated each end.

Inside the *cella* were a pair of colonnades, supporting an upper gallery, and one of the Seven Wonders of the Ancient World: the chryselephantine **statue of Zeus** by Phidias. Its black marble base occupied a whole third of the *cella*. Previous statues of Zeus showed him thunderbolt in hand; Phidias, taking his cue, he said, from the *Iliad*'s description of Zeus who nods to grant the request of Thetis 'and shook great Olympos', showed him enthroned in majesty, serene and aloof, his sceptre in his left hand and a figure of Nike, or Victory, in his right. At 38ft high, had Zeus risen from the throne he would have gone through the roof. But excess was the keynote: the statue was made of wood, covered with pieces of carved ivory to form the flesh, while all the rest, including his hair and beard, was covered with sheets of gold. The throne was covered with gold, ivory and ebony, inlaid with jewels and glass, and decorated all over with mythical scenes, some carved, some painted by Paionios on screens. To keep it from warping, olive oil was kept in a shallow trough in the surrounding tiles. A bigger threat came in the form of Caligula, who ordered the head of Zeus replaced with one bearing his own features. As the imperial agents were about to accomplish the dirty deed, the statue 'burst into such a roar of laughter that the scaffolding collapsed and the workmen took to their heels,' wrote Suetonius. Three hundred years later, it wasn't laughing when Theodosius II took it to Constantinople, where it burned down in 475.

According to Pliny, some 3,000 votive statues surrounded the Temple of Zeus. A few pedestals for the dedications remain. One of the largest was from Mikythos, a former slave who vowed an enormous pedestal lined with statues if his son recovered from an illness. The best was the *Nike* of Paionios (now in the museum).

Outside the Altis

The chief processional gate of the Altis was southeast of the Temple of Zeus. Outside and to the west of this are the rather confusing remains of the **bouleuterion**: two apsidial buildings linked by a colonnade, begun in the 6th century BC. This was the seat of the *Boulé* or Olympic Committee, elected from the Elean aristocracy. Between the buildings stood the statue and altar of Zeus Horkios, where competitors had to swear on gobbets of raw boar meat to abide by the rules. To emphasize the consequences, the statue held menacing thunderbolts in each hand. South of the bouleuterion stretched the **south stoa** (mid-4th century BC), which may have been the *Proedria* from where officials watched the procession of athletes. It probably contained shops as well. Directly west are the ruins of the 3rd-century BC **baths**.

Next to these begins the vast jumble that was once the **Leonidaion**, a large hotel built by Leonidas of Naxos in around 330 BC. It measured 246ft by 265ft and was enclosed by four stoas, with a peristyle courtyard within. It burned and was restored by Hadrian, who made it into an ancient Ritz, enlarging the rooms and surrounding them with canals and islands and flowerbeds; guests could watch the processions and ceremonies from the comfort of their balconies. Further west, along the banks of the Kladeos, are remains of more modest **hostels** built by the Romans and a Greek bath-house topped by the more up-to-date Roman **Kladeos baths** (2nd century AD).

In 1958, the archaeologists uncovered a **paleo-Christian basilica**, a bit ho-hum in this setting, until they realized that it was built over the **workshop of Phidias**, where the greatest artist of the ancient world made his statue of Zeus. If there was any doubt of the workshop's identity after the discovery of a mass of artists' materials – tools, clay moulds for the folds of the robe and the slivers of gold and ivory – it was laid to rest with the discovery of his cup, now in the museum. Phidias had come to Olympia under shadowy circumstances after making the chryselephantine statue of Athena in Athens. When his friend and patron Pericles fell from favour, he was accused of stealing gold intended for the statue; he was cleared, but then accused of the impiety of depicting Pericles' and his own features on Athena's shield. But making Phidias *persona non grata* in Athens was Olympia's gain.

The ruins north of here, back towards the entrance of the site, are all Hellenistic. The square **theikoleon**, which survives only in outline on the northeast corner of Phidias' workshop, was the parish house for the priests. Next to this is the charming square ruin of the **palaestra** where wrestlers, boxers and jumpers trained. The stoas around the courtyard held their dressing rooms, a room where the athletes oiled and scraped themselves, and small seating areas for spectators; 32 of the original 72 Doric columns have been re-erected. Directly abutting this is a double row of stumpy columns and the remains of a monumental entrance, all that survives of the massive **gymnasium** (2nd century BC). The walls were inscribed with the names of victors.

The Archaeological Museum

t 262 402 2742; open Mon 12–7, Tues–Sun 8–7; adm exp.

This great museum, discreetly tucked in the trees on the northwestern flank of the Hill of Cronus, houses the most spectacular of the thousands of finds the Germans have unearthed since the 1860s. Displays start in the vestibule with scale models of the Altis and a reproduction of a Geometric-era tripod dedication. **Room I** houses Neolithic tools and pottery, Mycenaean grave goods and the splendid votives from the 12th–9th century BC: the oldest bronze animal figurines and then the bronze tripods. Tripods were the Ferraris of the Geometric age, and are the first evidence of the sumptuous level of dedications that set Olympia apart. Unlike later votives, many of which were manufactured by itinerant craftsmen at Olympia, these three-legged cauldrons were made in different parts of Greece, each more elaborate than the next: note especially the leg of a Corinthian one from around 820 BC showing *Heracles and Apollo fighting for the Delphic tripod*. Some scholars believe scenes such as this didn't illustrate myths but inspired them once the original meaning was forgotten.

Later bronzes (700–625 BC) fill **Room II**: tripods and fragments decorated with Orientalizing motifs. The repoussé sheets of bronze that once covered wooden boxes and tripod legs offer fascinating 7th-century BC vignettes, including a warrior in his chariot bidding farewell to his family, and another of the *Murder of Clytemnestra*. An especially well worked one shows the *Myth of Kanieus*, the story of a Lapith woman named Kanis. When her lover Poseidon offered her a wish, she asked to be turned into an invulnerable man. Now named Kanieus, he became king, but offended Zeus by telling the Lapiths that they had to worship his spear as their god. He attended the famous Lapith wedding of Peirithoös, when the Centaurs got drunk and tried to rape the guests, and in the ensuing battle was one human casualty. The Centaurs, armed with tree trunks, pummelled him into the ground like a tent peg.

The same room contains a limestone head of Hera (*c.* 600 BC) that probably graced the statue in her temple and the greatest collection anywhere of Greek arms and armour, much of it discovered in the stadium, where it was buried when the embankments were enlarged. A 6th-century BC Gorgon gesturing to her stomach, with what look like horse legs kicking up to the left, may be Medusa giving birth to Pegasus.

Room III holds intricately decorated terracotta fragments from Archaic buildings, particularly from the Treasury of Gela. The pediment of the Treasury of Mégara has the worn remains of a clash of the Titans. In **Room IV**, the early or Severe Classical period yielded excellent painted terracottas from the 5th century: a head of Athena and a merrily pederastic Zeus striding off with Ganymede tucked under his arm. The story was immensely popular in Greece and Rome, and justified not only homosexuality but the exclusion of women from society. Other exhibits are of the kind that make history come alive: a helmet dedicated by Miltiades, the victor at Marathon; a Persian helmet with an inscription 'The Athenians to Zeus, having taken it from the Persians', and the contents of Phidias' workshop: bits of ivory, tools, moulds and his cup, engraved ΦΕΙΔΙΟ ΕΙΜΙ (I belong to Phidias).

Large **Room V** houses the sculptures from the Temple of Zeus, pieced together like a jigsaw. Key works, they were sculpted around 460 BC, when the Archaic stylization still apparent in Zeus and Ganymede had begun to relax into the naturalism of the Parthenon marbles. The figures, larger than life, were fixed to the pediments with metal clamps. The East Pediment, attributed to Paionios, shows Pelops and Oenomaos preparing for the famous chariot race (*see* p.217) that began on the banks of the Aphiós and ended at the Isthmus of Corinth. Zeus stands in the centre, Oenomaos, his wife and their charioteer Myrtos to the left, and to the right stands Pelops and Oenomaos' daughter Hippodameia. In the far corners are the personifications of Olympia's rivers Alphiós and Kladeos. The composition is static and tense, but the figure of the fearful old man behind the horses of Pelops hints of the dramatic consequences of the race: two men would be dead by the end of the day, and the curse of the charioteer Myrtos on Pelops would fall on the house of Atreus.

The West Pediment, however, steals the show. The subject is the aforementioned Battle of Lapiths and Centaurs: Apollo stands aloof in the midst of a remarkable scene of violence; a centaur grabs the bride by the breast; another has seized a woman but is about to be axed by Theseus; another centaur bites the arm of a man. The idea of civilization triumphing over barbarism was dear to the Greeks; the close call at Sálamis had only happened 20 years before. The sculptor, said to be an Athenian named Alkamenes, is also the first to show a real interest in women as women.

A third sculptor carved the metopes on the Labours of Heracles. These, with their fine moulding, innovative composition and air of calm detachment, are a genuine preview of the Parthenon marbles. The scene of Heracles cleaning the Augeian stables was the first time his Elean Labour was depicted in art, and the one in which he supports the world on his shoulders, while Atlas presents him with the apples of the Hesperides and Athena lends a hand, is sublime.

A small unnumbered room off Room IV holds the **Nike of Paionios**, sculpted by the nephew of Phidias. It was commissioned, with no little glee, by the Messenians and Naupactians (expatriate Messenians, settled there by Athens) after the defeat of Sparta at Sphakteria in 424 BC. The femininity first expressed in the Lapith women on the West Pediment has progressed to produce a real, sensuous woman in windblown drapery. Originally the Victory had wings, and stood high on her pedestal on the back of an eagle, as if she were descending from heaven. **Room VI**, also off Room IV, contains Hellenistic finds, including a bust of Alexander the Great and decorations from the Leonidaion, including its lion-head spout *sima*.

Room VIII is given over to the famous *Hermes* by Praxiteles (*c.* 330 BC), carved from the finest Parian marble and beautifully finished, standing with easy grace in Praxiteles' trademark *contrapposto* or S-shaped pose. The god holds his baby half-brother Dionysos, recently born from Zeus' thigh (a necessity after Zeus blasted his pregnant mother Semele with a thunderbolt). Zeus commanded Hermes to hide him from Hera, giving him to be raised by the nymphs of Mount Nysa. Hermes originally dangled a bunch of grapes to tease Dionysos, who reached out to grasp them. This is the only original work by Praxiteles to survive. With his work Greek art entered a virtuoso stage, to be looked at and admired as art: the once deep wells of religious aspirations and Panhellenic symbolism have dried up in elegant curly-haired Hermes.

Enter the Romans in **Room IX**, with statues from the Nymphaion of Herodes Atticus: Claudius as Zeus, his wife Agrippina, mother of Nero, Titus and Hadrian as warriors, Faustina, the wife of Marcus Aurelius, and Antinous, Hadrian's favourite. The marble bull bears the dedication to Zeus. Lastly, **Room X** contains finds from all periods concerning the games themselves; bases of statues of winners, bronze and terracotta figurines of competitors, and the 316lb (143.5kg) stone of Bybon inscribed 'Bybon, son of Phorys, threw me above his head with one hand'. He must have been a helluva guy.

Modern Olympia and Around

Modern Olympia is a 20min walk from the site over a bridge built by Kaiser Wilhelm. Nearly everything is on Kondíli street except for the **Museum of the Modern Olympic Games**, on Aginárou Street (*t 262 402 2544; open Tues–Sun 8–3.30; adm*).

Olympia has been a junction since ancient times. The road north into Achaía is by way of **Lála**, the one Greek village that sounds like a Tellytubby. Although fires have scarred the scenery, it improves above Lála, where oaks and meadows and contented cows do look like Poussin's vision of Arcadia.This road meets an east–west road along the south wall of Mt Eurýmanthos: west is the big road to Pátras. To the east is **Lámbia**, a small village with mountain views and a frescoed 14th-century Byzantine church, Ag. Triáda. You can even find a bed at the little creeper-covered **Pension Divri** (*t 263 408 1205; open all year; inexpensive*). East of here is ancient Psophís (*see* p.207).

South of Olympia: Along the Coast to Messenía

Heading south of Olympia means crossing the Alphiós (there's a bridge west of Flókas) then turning west for the alluvial plain at **Kallíkomo**. The coast here is sandy but marshy, and inaccessible except by an unpaved road that you can pick up south of **Káto Samikó**. Ancient **Samikon** was located on a spur of the mountain that hems in the coast; a scramble up will be rewarded by impressive 5th-century polygonal walls.

Under the mountain, and separated from the sea by a narrow neck of land, the picturesque lagoon of **Lake Kaïafa** is the catchment basin of sulphurous waters emitted by two cave springs. Heracles, they say, stopped here to clean his knife after slaying the Hydra, hence the aroma. Its modern name comes from another story: that Christ's judge, the High Priest Caiaphas, stopped here to bathe, and the waters in

Where to Stay and Eat

Kaïafa ✉ 27054

Kaiafas Lake, t 262 503 2954, **f** 262 503 3800 (*B; moderate*). Rooms overlooking the lake, sea, or pool, complete with mini bars, air-conditioning, and TVs. *Open all year.*

Kaiafas, by the little Kaïafa train station on the main road, **t** 262 503 1703. Kostas Gournas runs a very friendly taverna and coffee shop.

Zacháro ✉ 27054

Rex, t 262 503 1221, **f** 262 503 2035 (*C; moderate*). In town, plain, run by a dynamic lady; rooms have TV, and in off season you can negotiate. *Open all year.*

Evelyn Rooms, t 262 503 2537 (*inexpensive*). Along the road to the beach; built around a little oasis of palms and pool. *Open all year.*

Theódoro Konstanópolous, t 262 503 1724, **f** 262 503 3888 (*inexpensive*). A 5min walk from the beach, studios among the palms (follow the 'Rooms' signs).

Banana Place Rooms, 160m from the sea, **t** 262 503 4400 (*inexpensive*). Rooms and studios immersed in a huge banana plantation; tennis, volley ball, and a snack bar, among other amenities. *Open 15 April–15 Oct.*

Camping Tholó Beach, Tholó, **t** 262 506 1345, **f** 262 506 1100 (*inexpensive*). They promise 'you are not just an unpersonal camper'. *Open April–Oct.*

repugnance began to reek to repel him. None of the stories have kept the Greeks from coming here to relieve their skin ailments. There's a ramshackle **spa** run by EOT on the wooded island, reached by a causeway off the main road.

Just south is **Zacháro**, 'Sugar', the name of a woman who once ran an inn here. It's a lively town with modest resort pretensions. Down by its sandy beach, summer cottages and semi-tropical gardens form a rather sweet old-fashioned enclave and a quiet place to stay, less than a half-hour's drive from Olympia. For a radical change of scenery or just to cool off, the locals head up the mountain to **Mínthi** (20km) a pretty place with lots of fresh water and two *kafeneíons*. Further south, the beach goes on and on, with access roads at **Kakóvatos**, **Neochóri**, **Tholó** and **Giannitsochóri** before reaching Messenía and the long straight road to Kyparissía (*see* p.356); at Tholó you can pick up the road to the Néda Gorge (*see* p.237).

Kréstena to Andrítsaina, the Temple at Bassae, and the Néda Gorge

In ancient times, this southern third of Elís was called Triphyllía, a name you will still see occasionally. Although the Temple of Bassae is on the relatively beaten track, the rest of southern Elís is anything but: Andrítsaina and the Néda Gorge are lovely.

Kréstena to Andrítsaina

The road running southeast of **Kréstena** follows the route the Spartans, with their long hair, red cloaks and soft bootkins, would swish along to the Olympics. An important road, it was dotted with ancient towns, although there is confusion over which was which. Kréstena itself is near ancient **Skillus** where Xenophon lived in retirement, on an estate given to him by the Spartans. From Kréstena, signs for the Ναος Αθήνας, or **Temple of Athena Skillountia**, will take you 6km to the northeast. Only the stylobate remains, but archaeologists can somehow glean from it that it was not *the* Temple of Athena that Xenophon built. Other ruins, including a 5th-century BC

Temple of Zeus, have been found in **Markrísa**, 4.5km north of Kréstena, which some say was Skillus, or part of Skillus, or somewhere else. On a ridge just south of **Platiána**, 19km east, are beautifully preserved 3rd-century BC walls, a theatre, cisterns and two churches of ancient **Typaneai**. A few kilometres north of Platiána, lonely in a field outside **Tripití**, stands a last Gothic arch from the Frankish **monastery of Ísovas**.

East of Kréstena, the road climbs up the Alphiós valley through parasol pines, cypresses and oleanders. If you have a determined nature and a bottle of water, take the left turn 12km east of Platiána for tiny **Alífra**, another 4km; then turn right for 2km to the hill known as Kástro tis Drosítsas. This has the ruins of ancient **Alipheira**. Where the track up the hill peters out and splits in two, take the right fork and go up and up. Unfortunately there's no sign when you need one, but persevere and you'll eventually arrive at a 4th-century **Asklepeion**, while on top is the well preserved foundation of a 6th-century BC **Temple of Athena**, long (6 by 15 columns) like most Archaic temples.

Andrítsaina

Another 11km down the main road will bring you to the metropolis of south Elís, Andrítsaina, a mountain village preserved in aspic, especially around the old *plateía* that has hardly changed since the 1960s. This is roughly when Andrítsaina's fortunes began to decline. For over 150 years, the village made a good living with its fleet of mules, 65 strong, taking people up to Bassae. Now the road has improved, and tour buses lurch by but rarely stop. The square further east has a modest **Folklore Museum** and library from 1840 in a lovely old building with a satellite dish on top.

It may have been the contact with mule-needy philhellenes from abroad that led to the founding in Andrítsaina of an underground Greek school in 1764, which played an important role in sparking the independence movement in the Peloponnese. The monument in the *plateía* honours **Panagiótis Anagnostópoulos**, who was educated here. The chief advisor to Dimítris Ypsilántis, he became a leader of the secret Greek revolutionary committee, the *Philikí Etairía* ('Friendly Society'), founded in Moscow by expatriates after Napoleon's retreat.

Getting There and Around

Currently, there are **buses** down the Pýrgos–Kréstena–Andrítsaina road at 8am and 12pm, as well as from Athens twice a day. For bus information in Pýrgos: t 262 102 3703.

Taxis from Andrítsaina (t 262 602 2380 or 262 602 2160) to Bassae are €12–14 if you want the driver to wait. They will also take you to the Néda Gorge if you want to do the river trek, and arrange to pick you up downstream.

Where to Stay and Eat

Andrítsaina ✉ 27061

Theoxénia, t 262 602 2235, f 262 602 2219 (*C; moderate, breakfast inc.*). Renovated relic from the 1950s, with large rooms of the usual *Xenia* sort: stone walls, picture windows and great views. *Open all year.*

Xenónas Epikoúrios Apóllon, t 262 602 2840, f 262 602 2408 (*moderate, breakfast inc.*). A new inn with five rooms. *Open all year.*

Kafeneíon Thomópoulos, old *plateía*, t 262 602 2239. A taste of old Greece: uncompromising leather benches stuffed with horsehair.

Geórgos Sieloúli. Great food, including tasty boiled goat. A local favourite.

The Temple of Apollo Epikourios at Bassae

t 262 602 2275; open daily in summer from 8.30–8, winter 8.30–3; adm.

The bad, dangerous road and 11km in a mule saddle from Andrítsaina did add a dimension to one's appreciation of Bassae, in part for the extraordinary difficulty the 5th-century BC builders overcame to build at 3,710ft. The modern road soon leaves civilization behind, passing threshing floors under dry stone terraces wedged into cliffs, where eking out a living cannot have been easy. Soon the road leaves behind even these abandoned vestiges of life to enter some of the most grandiose, desolate and god-haunted country in Greece; in the old days, it was bandit-haunted as well. If nothing untoward happened, the mule riders would finally get their first breath-taking glimpse of the grey limestone temple, a small defiant work of art in a tremendous setting, yet one that harmonized with the surroundings in an unforget-table way – the hallmark of Iktinos, the mastermind of the Parthenon.

The harmony may strike visitors again in about 2020 when rescue operations have been completed and the massive tent draped over the temple in 1982 has finally been removed. Even though the temple owes its preservation to its isolation, weather has worn it and earthquakes have jolted it. The Greek Archaeological Service means to restore what can be restored, and make it as anti-seismic as possible. The marbles lying neatly in the yard were once part of the roof; the tiles were all of Parian marble, which must have cost a fortune to bring here. When you enter the tent, you will notice that it is an engineering marvel, dramatic on a windy day when it angrily flaps about, or when the rain pelts down. But it does make everything a bit gloomy inside.

There is some confusion about the date of the temple. It was commissioned by the small city of Figáleia (*see* below) to thank Apollo Epikourios 'the Helper' for sparing it the plague of 429 BC – the same plague that killed Pericles. This poses problems to those who believe Iktinos must have built Bassae before the Parthenon, because of its less sophisticated nature. Against that, one might argue that Iktinos had the wit to realize that the location hardly required the subtleties of *entasis*, nor were they even desirable in the local limestone. Anyway, having accomplished perfection in Athens, the architect felt free to innovate. For Bassae is a very unusual temple: in its north-south orientation (facing Delphi, Apollo's chief dwelling), in its Archaic-style length (125ft by 48ft, with a peristyle of 6 by 15 Doric columns, instead of the usual 6 by 13), and in the arrangement of the *pronaos, cella* and *opisthodomos*.

The *cella* was stripped of its frieze in 1811–12 by a pair of cat and fox antiquarians, a German named Haller and an Englishman named Cockernell, who, inspired by Elgin's 'poor plunder from a bleeding land', had already stripped the Temple of Aphaia on Aegina and auctioned its metopes off to Munich. After bribing the local Turkish authorities, they carried the 23 sections of Bassae's frieze with its vigorous scenes of battling Lapiths and Centaurs, men and Amazons, and got the highest bid (£19,000) from the British government. It's just lucky for Greece that it became independent before Haller and Cockernell came back for the kitchen sinks.

Otherwise, the *cella* is nearly complete, and although the ropes and scaffolding won't let you enter, you can see the engaged columns (a new feature) on their bell-shaped bases (another novelty). The first four columns were Ionic, while the fifth pair are the earliest known Corinthian columns, although their acanthus-decorated capitals have been lost. Another unique feature: the frieze ran along the inside of the *cella* rather than on the outside. The holy of holies, the *adyton*, was also idiosyncratic, and had an east door (possibly to admit light?) while lacking the usual wall separating it from the *cella*. The holy image was in bronze, but Pausanias wrote that it was hauled off to Megalopolis in 369 BC and replaced with stone.

Bassae means ravines. From here, or if you scramble up the side of Mount Kotilion above the temple, you can see the peaks of Arcadía, especially the bald pate of were-wolf-haunted Mount Lýkaio rising ominous in the northeast (*see* p.283).

The Néda Gorge

In myth, Néda was one of the nymphs who cared for Zeus after his mother Rhea tricked his father Cronus into swallowing a stone instead of their newborn child. Since then, Néda and her many tributaries have carved quite a gorge, surprisingly lush and green after the stark grandeur of Bassae. Often you have to make a special effort just to get down and see the river, but it's worth it: the Néda is one of the loveliest waterways in Greece, with its waterfalls, dragonflies and rock formations.

Bassae is on the road along the top of the gorge, which is dotted with small villages, fragments of old Greece, some almost abandoned in winter. You can make a complete circuit around the Néda, beginning at Kaló Neró or Elía on the west coast, taking mostly unpaved roads along the south rim, wiggling your way up to Bassae and back to the coast along the north rim. If you don't have much time, you can see many of the highlights by car, with a picnic. Visit Bassae early in the morning, then do the top

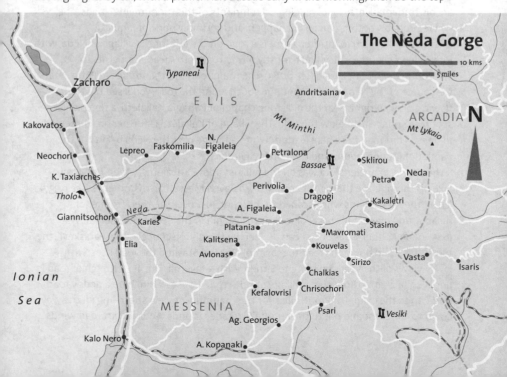

of the Néda route clockwise, crossing the river below Dragógi. From there, follow the north rim of the gorge down via Lépreo to Káto Taxiárches.

Alternatively, you can walk down the Néda – literally. The whole trek takes about three days, but you can cheat and do only certain stretches. There are five points of access to the elusive river: **Pétra** (near the source); **Kakalétri's bridge** (a quiet section); the **Koúvelas-Dragógi bridge** (where the river begins to become truly beautiful); the bridge on the new road between **Platanía** and **Figáleia** (the most dramatic, with a waterfall and the narrow gorge, passing through pink and green rock pools downstream, and a dark cave you have to swim through); and along the riverside road between **Avlónas** and **Kariés**. After Kariés, most of the water is pumped away for irrigation. Note that the trek is only possible in the high summer when the water is low. You'll need proper sturdy but lightweight footwear that doesn't mind the wet. Nor should you go alone; some parts require swimming and can be dangerous.

The Top of the Néda Gorge: Bassae to Ancient Eira to Koúvelas

The easiest way to see the Néda is to circle its upper reaches. The route begins on the Andrítsaina–Bassae road at the turn-off for **Skliroú**, 6.5km south of Andrítsaina and 4.5km north of Bassae. Skliroú is an attractive hamlet once used as a hideout for Greek guerrilla bands, or *klephts*. When news got out that the Turks were letting Haller and Cockernell strip the Temple of Apollo Epikourios, the *klephts* gathered here to stop them. The Turks, however, got wind of their plans and attacked first.

Returning to the main road, bear right at crossroads rather than turning left for Andrítsaina. After 8km you'll come to a right turn for **Ambelióna** with its chestnut groves, birthplace of film-maker Théo Angelópoulos. The slow pace and *tableaux* that are his trademark may be psychological remnants of this monumental landscape, where probably nothing much did happen, and certainly none of it quickly.

Return to the main road. After 2.5km is a road on the left for the village of **Néda**, with lovely views over the valley, and a mostly paved road into Arcadía, for visits to Lykósoura and Mount Lýkaio (*see* p.283). The main road then continues to **Pétra**, near the source of the Néda. As you continue south along the road, you'll see the Néda flowing on your right, near the old stone **chapel of Panagía Kakalétri**, a fine picnic spot by a spring, just below the road. The village of **Kakalétri** is further on, immersed in trees. A dirt road from here leads down to a bridge over the Néda by way of the hamlet of **Marína**, pop. 6, and then up to Skliroú.

The citadel of ancient **Eira** was on the hill just above Kakalétri, a steep, hot 45min hike up through the thorns. When Sparta enslaved Messenía, Aristoménes (*see* p.337) led all the Messenians who escaped to this spot, just over the then-frontier of Arcadía, and made it his base for raids into Laconía in the Second Messenian War (685–68 BC). Other walls of Eira can be seen by the hilltop chapel of **Ag. Paraskévi** (the turn-off is 1.2km down the road to Stásimo). Beyond **Stásimo** the road rises, with lovely views of the valley en route to **Sírrizo**, with a taverna. The next stretch of road is unpaved (4.2km) to **Koúvelas**, a village of tidy stone houses. From here a dodgy road leads up to the chapel of **Profítis Ilías** for the magnificent view stretching all the way down to the coast and out to the remote Strofades islands. Another dirt road winds down from Koúvelas to the ghost village of **Mavromáti**, where the chapel of Ag. Dimítrios has frescoes. The river below is lovely, with a **bridge** crossing to **Dragógi**, which has something rare in the Néda villages: new houses.

The North Rim of the Gorge: Bassae to Figáleia, Lépreo and the Coast

The other approach to **Dragógi** is to drive directly west of Bassae. At the next village west, **Perivólia**, you'll come to a giant plane tree, where you should turn left and continue 2.9km to a rural crossroads. The unpaved road to the left doesn't look promising, but if you don't give up it will eventually take you to the very traditional but nearly empty village of Áno Figáleia that has superseded **ancient Figaleia** (and whose new bridge can now take you to the south side of the gorge). You can see the ancient **fountain house** by the church with the graveyard.

Backtrack to the crossroads and take the right fork. To the left, just before the houses start, are remains of a **temple** with a well-preserved altar. Walls and towers, once extending 4.5km, can be discerned on the steep cliffs. Ancient Figaleia must have been quite a place. It made its living as a transit point between Arcadía and the sea, sending goods up and down the Néda. It was briefly captured by Sparta in 659 BC, and somehow it came up with the readies to build Bassae. Yet by all accounts Figaleia was a hard-drinking, wild town not averse to a little sorcery. One temple (perhaps this one?) was dedicated to Dionysos Kratophoros 'of the wine-mixing vessel', whose statue was placed in the middle of the vineyards, painted with cinnabar to glow red in the sun. East of town flowed the Lymakos, a tributary of the Néda, considered sacred for washing away Rhea's afterbirth (*lymata*) after she produced Zeus. There Figaleia built a sanctuary of Eurynome, the daughter of Oceanus, which they visited once a year. Inside, the cult statue resembled a mermaid, half woman and half fish, and was bound to the place by golden chains (a reminder that ancient Figaleia was in Arcadía, where gods never quite evolved into human form). The Figaleians were proudest of their two-time Olympic *pankration*-winner Arrhakion, who was choked to death but won posthumously. His statue stood in the middle of the agora. What happened to his murderous opponent remains a mystery, but he probably got a statue, too.

After the temple the road arrives in steep Káto Figáleia. Signs point the way (or ask) to the Áspro Neró, the enchanting **white water waterfall**. Plane trees provide the shade, and there are pools downstream where you can pretend to be the star of a shampoo ad. The bit downriver is the steepest and most dramatic part of the gorge.

As you return to Perivólia and the main road, you'll see a driveable track leading off 3km to the left to **Stómio**, another lost hamlet of stone houses. This was part of ancient Figáleia, where a cave in the wall of the gorge (near the picturesque **chapel of the Panagítsa**) was dedicated to Demeter Melaina, 'Black Demeter'. Here, Pausanias found a seated statue of the goddess with a mare's head, holding a dove in one hand and a dolphin in the other, recalling that she was the ancient goddess of the horse cult, the oak (dove) cult, and the dolphin cult. She is known as Black Demeter because she dressed in black and took refuge here after losing her daughter to Hades and being raped by her brother Poseidon in the form of a horse. It would depress anyone. But as Demeter was also the corn goddess, her sadness drove humanity to the brink of starvation until Pan cheered her up and coaxed her out. The image in the cave was made of wood and caught fire, and on cue Figaleia's crops at once failed. They urgently sent to Aegina to commission the very expensive sculptor Onatas to make a bronze copy, which sorted things out.

The scenery along the gorge road becomes distinctly greener as you approach **Petrálona**, with a pair of cafés and a sprinkling of stone houses. **Néa Figáleia**, next to the west, seems like a metropolis with its many *kafeneíons* strung out along the road.

The last village, **Lépreo**, is high over the Gulf of Kiparissía. According to the myth, ancient Lepreon was founded by Minyans, whom the Argonauts had fathered on the women of Límnos (*see* p.832) and who sailed to Triphyllia. The town was named after King Lepreo, who had foolishly advised King Augeias to chain Heracles up after he cleaned out his stables; years later when Heracles came to sort him out, Lepreo's mother persuaded him to ask Heracles' pardon. Heracles agreed, but on the condition that Lepreo compete with him in three contests: throwing the discus, drinking the most water, and eating an ox the quickest. Heracles won the first two, but Lepreo was the first to wolf down the ox. In the excitement, Lepreo at once challenged him to a duel, and Heracles squashed him like a fly with his club. But in the odd logic of myth, it was Heracles who henceforth was known as *Bouphagos*, the ox-eater.

Entering Lépreo from the west, a hill resembling a giant tooth greets you; this was the site of the **prehistoric acropolis** – of the Minyans, one imagines. On the east side of town, past the leafy cafés, a road lined with prickly pear leads up on the right 1.7km to the **Hellenistic acropolis**. The first thing you'll see is a stable in a little **Hellenistic building**, still using the ancient door and window. The foundations of a limestone peristyle **Doric temple** are just beyond. Bits of column look as if they've been stubbed out like cigarettes around the peristyle, and there's a large, long **altar** (especially designed for ox barbecues, one supposes). The altar looks odd tucked around the back on the east side of the temple, when the view to the west over the Gulf of Kiparissía is so splendid, but rules are rules. From Lépreo the road down to the sea passes charming churches, chickens, a lovely pine forest and a jet-setter's helipad.

South of the Néda Gorge

The deep ravines of the Néda's tributaries make a direct route around the south edge of the gorge difficult, but you could do worse than to spend a few hours in northern Messenía (the Néda forms its border with Elís). If you're in a hurry, take the mostly dirt road west of **Koúvelas** (*see* p.238) to **Avlónas**, **Panórama** and the coast.

If you have a couple of hours to spare, however, head south of Koúvelas to the old villages of **Chalkiás**, **Chrisochóri** and **Psári**. From Psári, follow the road east towards Mélpia for 3km to the turn-off for **Vesíki**, where you can drive up part of the way, but have to continue on foot to reach a well-preserved Mycenaean **tholos tomb**, 17ft in diameter. It seems rather lonely here; perhaps it was built by a family that didn't get along with the others in Peristería (*see* p.356).

Return to Psári and continue 4km southwest to **Ag. Geórgios**, where a giant mulberry tree shades a perfect old-fashioned *kafeneíon*. Continue southwest to Áno Koranáki, then loop up north towards **Kefalóvrisi**, with an enchanting *plateía* by an ice-cold spring. A road heads north 8km to **Platánia**, which enjoys fine views down to the Gulf of Kiparissía. Over the Figáleia bridge, you can follow the river down to the chapel of the Panagítsa (*see* p.239).

On the main road west of Platánia, the next village is hilltop **Avlónas**, a village founded in the early 19th century by a Turkish aga who couldn't bear the mosquitoes on the coast. The village bore his name, Kara-Mustafa, until 1922, when it was changed to Avlónas after an ancient city that no one has yet rediscovered. From Avlónas, a decent unpaved road runs west through the nearly abandoned village of **Ptéri**, then up to **Panórama** – the latter lives up to its name, with lovely views down the Néda valley to the sea, which has made it a favourite for holiday homes. The road descends to **Kariés** on the river bank, where the Néda begins to peter out due to agricultural demand. But from Kariés you can backtrack along an unpaved road to its old river mills, including the Marmaras Mill (1500) used for grinding wheat.

The mouth of the Néda, below the village of **Eliá**, is, after Zákynthos, the biggest nesting ground for *Caretta caretta* turtles in Greece. In the summer volunteers mark the nests to protect them until the baby turtles hatch. Their biggest enemies here, however, aren't humans but foxes. To continue down the coast, *see* p.356.

Argolís

Cut off by mountains and the sea, Argolís may be a place apart from the rest of the Peloponnese, but in Greek history and myth it has often held centre stage – Mycenae, Tiryns, Troezen, Epidauros, Argos and Lerna are here, and for anyone who has dined, or

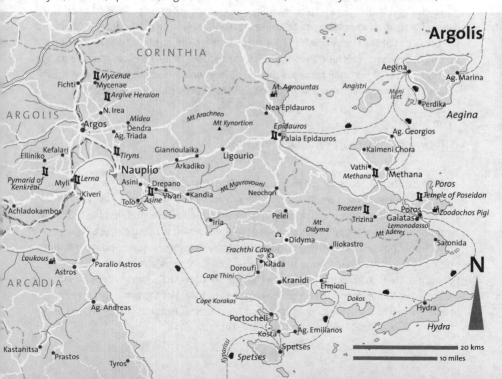

even snacked, on the classics, the province is a five-course banquet. For dessert there's the capital of the Argolís, Naúplio, the Peloponnese's most beautiful city. And as a garnish, you'll find good beaches along Argolís' lovely island-ringed coast, flashy resort hotels (or old-timer inns) and more than a dollop of wild Peloponnesian grandeur, topped off with a volcano. Nowadays, ferries and hydrofoils from Athens make access to Argolís easy, too easy, perhaps: it's really at its best on either side of the summer, and it stays open all year.

Mycenae

Approaching Mycenae (ancient ΜΥΚΗΝΑΙ, modern Μυκήνες) from Corinth on the old national road means crossing the **Pass of Dervenáki**. By the Neméa-Dervenáki train station, a road goes left to a heroic statue of Kolokotrónis. In the adjacent gorge, on 6 August 1822, a band of insurgents led by Kolokotrónis ambushed Dramali Pasha's Turkish force of 6,000, causing 4,000 casualties. Greek losses were minimal. Edward Trelawney, riding through a year later, found the gorge thick with the skeletons of men, horses, mules and camels, all positioned just as they had fallen. The road pierces the twin peaks of Mount Tretós and descends to the Argive Plain. On a clear day you can spot not only the lofty castle of Argos, but also Naúplio's Palamídi fortress. Next comes the busy crossroads at Fíchti, with the turn-off for Mycenae, the ancient citadel set on its 1,000ft-high spur under Mounts Zara and Elias, watchful and terrible.

The City that Imagination Built

Surcharged with myth and history, Mycenae captures the imagination at once: the sheer barbaric power of the citadel makes it the ideal setting for the fatal playing out of the Curse of the House of Atreus. Heinrich Schliemann, the true believer, certainly thought he was unearthing those bloodstained stones when he excavated the palace in 1874. But, as at his other fabulous discovery, Troy, what he actually found was much older and perhaps even more intriguing than the Homeric heroes he sought.

The Myth

These things never happened, but are, always.
                         A Greek philosopher

Acrisios, King of Argos, locked his daughter Danaë in a vault, because an oracle had proclaimed that her son would kill him. Zeus visited her in a shower of gold and Perseus was born, grew up, killed the snake-haired Medusa and fulfilled the oracle by accidentally killing his grandfather. One day, when he was walking in the hills, a mushroom popped out of the ground, followed by a spring, reason enough to found a new city called Mycenae (*mykos* means mushroom). Perseus' son married Pelops' daughter. Their child Alcmene became the mother of Heracles, whom Zeus had fathered with the intention of making him the High King of Mycenae. But jealous Hera delayed his birth long enough so that his cousin Eurystheus was born first and became king, and set Heracles on his Twelve Labours.

When he died, the Mycenaeans chose Atreus, a son of Pelops, to be king. Not a nice type, Atreus feared his brother Thyestes' dynastic ambitions, so ended them by cooking up his nephews and serving them to their father. He kept his throne, but Thyestes laid a curse upon his family which fell on Atreus' son, Agamemnon. Agamemnon led the Greeks to Troy but first sacrificed his daughter Iphigenia to gain fair winds for the fleet. His wife, Clytemnestra, did a little cursing of her own, and killed Agamemnon in his bath when he returned from Troy. Their son Orestes, goaded by his sister Electra, then killed his mother and was hunted by the Furies until Apollo and Athena decided enough was enough and justified the matricide on the grounds that females only provided space for a foetus, so killing them didn't count as a family crime. That bit of genetic flummery absolved Orestes, who went on to become King of Sparta. The barest outline of the story, first mentioned in the *Odyssey*, is complicated enough. Add 2,500 years of poets and playwrights, and these stories have gathered enough critical mass to keep psychiatrists, sociologists and historians busy forever.

With so much written *about* them, we have to keep in mind that the Mycenaeans themselves left no written historical or mythical records. In Homer, Aeschylus and co, what we have is the ancient Greeks' *perception* of Mycenaean culture, its traditions hugely subverted by Greece's post-Mycenaean overlords in order to flatter their own warlike ways and patriarchal religion. The Trojan War occurred, but what really happened and why it happened will forever remain a mystery. That is part of Mycenae's boundless appeal to the imagination: facts gleaned by the archaeologist's spade collide and merge with the myth. Schliemann came to Mycenae seeking Agamemnon, and it's hard to resist doing a 'Schliemann' when coming here, looking for the bath where Agamemnon was killed, the ravine where Clytemnestra's body

Getting There

There are several **buses** a day direct to Mycenae from Naúplio and Argos, and another 15 from Athens.

Several **trains** go as far as Fíchti on the main road, a mile from Mycenae. You can wait for the Naúplio bus or take a taxi which the Fíchti KTEL office, t 275 107 6206, will call for you.

Anna's Stathmos Café opposite the bus station has left luggage facilities and showers.

Where to Stay and Eat

Mycenae ✉ 21200

Modern Mycenae (Μυκήνες) is a small town where the people not involved in tourism grow oranges. The reason to stay is to get to the site before the tour buses.

La Petite Planete, t 275 107 6240, f 275 107 6610 (*B; expensive*). Quiet, air-conditioned hotel with a pool and a view similar to the citadel's. Book ahead. *Open April–Nov.*

Marion Dassis, t 275 107 6123, f 275 107 6124 (*inexpensive*). Airy rooms in the centre (two for families); great bathrooms, parking and a small travel agency. *Open all year.*

Belle Helene, t 275 107 6225, f 275 107 6179 (*E; inexpensive*). Built around room 3 where Schliemann stayed in the 1870s, with memorabilia of the great archaeologist. Virginia Woolf stayed here too. *Open April–Oct.*

Atreus Camping, t 275 102 1200 (*inexpensive*). On the edge of town with a lot of shade and a small pool. *Open all year.*

Camping Mycenae, t 275 107 6121, f 275 107 6247, dars@hol.gr (*inexpensive*). Right in town and somewhat eclipsed by Atreus; it tries hard to please. *Open all year.*

Point Bar and Restaurant, t 275 107 6096. Has a small menu of its own specialities.

Spíros' Restaurant and Tavern, t 275 107 6115. Traditional fare just opposite.

was hurled, and trying to figure out if those signal fires mentioned in Aeschylus could really have been seen from the citadel. Even the Archaeological Service gets into the act and labels tombs after Clytemnestra and Aegisthus, when the dates could not possibly jibe...and about those signal fires – they could have been seen from the citadel. So it must have happened, right?

The Citadel and its History

Surrounded by half a mile of massive Cyclopean walls, Mycenae's citadel is solid, impressive, and barren. Walk over the ridge towards the Lion Gate, with the deep east–west Kokorétsa ravine running behind the site, and you realize how defensible it was. The palace commanded a view of the entire Argive Plain, and for centuries it commanded its political life as well, giving its name to an entire culture.

The hill was occupied from 3000 BC on, and by 2000 BC the inhabitants may well have been Greek speakers. They used the valley just west of the citadel to bury their dead and by 1600 BC they were rich enough to have buried those bodies in what we call Grave Circle A, along with weapons, more homely articles and over 14 kilos of gold – the richest grave-find in Greece. Homer knew; he called Mycenae 'rich in gold'. And since there are no gold mines associated with the Mycenaeans, the big question remains: where did it come from? Informed gossip suggests that the warlike Mycenaeans either hired themselves out as mercenaries in Egypt, who paid in gold, or that they were one of the large bands of marauders in the Mediterranean at this date, and that they got their gold by plunder. If the Mycenaeans used Minoan ships to come and go on their expeditions, it would be possible to explain the well-off warrior society with Minoan religious and artistic habits that these graves reveal. It also nicely encompasses the Mycenaean take-over of Minoan palaces on Crete. There are other hints: the Mycenaean habit of burying their dead with rich goods and gold face masks has an Egyptian ring to it, and many legends suggest Egyptian connections.

The descendants of the people found in these graves went from strength to strength, their artistic and technical achievements culminating in the numerous tholos tombs and in the two-storey palace whose floor plan crowns the ruins. In this palace-centred culture, accounts were kept in Linear B (*see* pp.352–3). Finds show that trade relations extended from Egypt (ostrich eggs) to the Baltic (amber). At its height, from 1400 to 1100 BC, Mycenae controlled all of the cities in the Peloponnese in some kind of federation. Roads criss-crossed the landscape.

The physical development of the citadel is a 'record' of sorts. Before 1350 BC, a palace existed, but no walls. Cyclopean walls were built at the same time as the palace whose ruins we see today. In 1250 BC, more walls were added, extending the citadel to the southwest and refortifying it. Changes included the construction of the Lion Gate. Civil expansion partly explains the changes, but they were increasingly defensive in nature. Whether the threat was external or internal is moot. The further extension of the walls on the northeast to enclose a water source in about 1200 BC indicates a real fear of siege, a fear that was well-founded; *something* terrible and final did happen. The palace-based Mycenaean culture collapsed in flames about 1100 BC, leaving remnants, and no Peloponnesian-based victors.

The Site

t 275 107 6803; open April–Sept 8am–7pm, winter 8am–5pm; adm exp.
Tickets cover the site and the Treasury of Atreus. Bring a torch for the cistern.

Mycenae's **Cyclopean walls** are simply astounding. The average weight of the boulders is six tons, and they were held in place by smaller stones at their interstices. It may sound clumsy, but the results are not. Standing 15ft thick and about 50ft high in

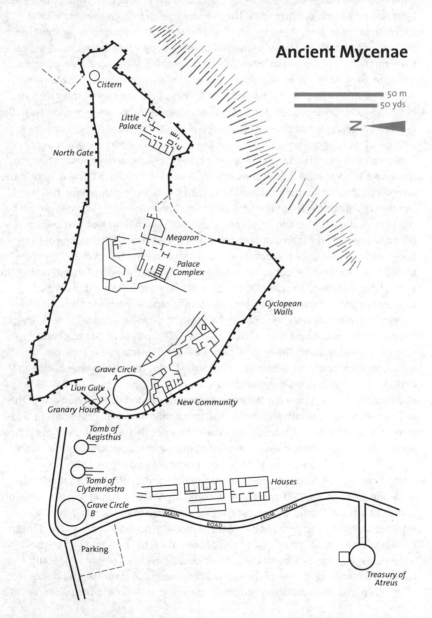

Ancient Mycenae

50 m
50 yds

Cistern

Little Palace

North Gate

Megaron

Palace Complex

Cyclopean Walls

Grave Circle A

Lion Gate

Granary House

New Community

Tomb of Aegisthus

Tomb of Clytemnestra

Grave Circle B

Houses

MAIN ROAD FROM TOWN

Parking

Treasury of Atreus

places when new, they were attributed to the Cyclops by awed later generations who had lost the ability to move such massive rocks. Not all of the walls are Cyclopean. In the impressive 48ft **corridor** leading up to the Lion Gate, equally huge stones were used, but dressed into rectangular blocks and arranged quasi-isodomically. As you approach the gate, the citadel wall is to your left, while the wall on your right belongs to a bastion and tower built to enhance the defences.

The **Lion Gate** makes the perfect introduction to the citadel, conveying power, prestige and just a touch of brute force. The gate consists of four massive monolithic stones creating an almost square opening, the gateposts narrowing slightly at the top. A sculptured relief of (now headless) lionesses, supporting a pillar, is set in the relieving triangle of the 12-ton lintel. This fairly common Minoan heraldic motif was no doubt adopted as the royal coat of arms, and enlarged on a scale the Minoans never attempted. The threshold was scored for better chariot access. The gate had huge, hinged double wooden doors sheathed in bronze. Look for the pivot holes in the lintel and doorway. In the gateway to the left is a cleft, for guard dogs, guards, or a shrine – a lot of conclusions drawn about Mycenaean ruins are pure guesswork.

Inside and immediately to the right is the two-storeyed **granary house**, which may really have been a guard house. Immediately beyond this is **Grave Circle A**. Here in the summer of 1876 Schliemann believed he beheld the face of Agamemnon before it crumbled to dust as he lifted the golden mask. What a moment! His date was out by 300 years, but no matter. This royal compound, with six shaft graves, was used over a period of time and contained 12 men, five women, and two children; some of the bodies were judged to be six-footers – unusually tall for the time. When they were buried, there were no Cyclopean walls. When the southwest extension was added, the sloping ground behind the new Cyclopean wall was filled in with rubble until it reached the present level, burying the original grave circle. However, the stelae covering the mounds were removed and a new 85ft diameter double circle of upright stones capped by horizontal ones (that you see today) was built on the new level, copying, in grander form, the original circle; and the old stelae were replaced. This deep reverence for ancestral tombs, when larger tholos tombs for royals had been the custom for over 200 years, is remarkable.

Just south of Grave Circle A is the **new community** created by the extension of the walls after 1250 BC. The labyrinth of foundations would have supported one- or two-storey houses that probably belonged to officials since this was a citadel, not a city. Some buildings may have been used for cult purposes because so many idols were found. If so, Mycenaean indoor shrines were pretty poky affairs.

A 79ft **ramp** ascends to the upper **palace complex** and its propylon on the north-west side. This entrance led into a narrow corridor going south, and had two corridors off it leading east. The northernmost corridor ascended to the family quarters, which were totally obliterated by buildings in the Hellenistic period. The second and south-ernmost corridor led to the public rooms of the palace, the area that can be most imaginatively grasped today. Its outer court would have been open to the south, taking in a magnificent view of the Argive Plain. The grand **staircase**, still visible, led up to this public area and was no doubt used by official visitors to the palace. To enter the megaron, the most important room in any Mycenaean palace, you passed through the two-columned porch which faced the court (the little stairway on its north side leads to the rest of the palace) into the **prodomos**, or vestibule, and then into the **megaron** itself. This was a fair-sized room (42ft by 39ft) with a circular central hearth that can still be seen; it was decorated in spirals and flame motifs. Four wooden columns sheathed with bronze held up the roof, and the area above the hearth would have been open to the sky. The floors were paved with painted gypsum tiles with linear patterns and the walls were alive with brightly coloured frescoes. One portrayed a battle scene with Mycenaean ladies cheering on the menfolk from the ramparts. The throne must have been on the south wall, a part of the megaron that had fallen into the ravine by the time Mycenae was excavated, although it has since been reconstructed. The rooms to the west of the open court were probably guestrooms. The **bathroom** where Clytemnestra killed Agamemnon or, at any rate, a bathroom, is immediately adjacent to the megaron to the northeast.

East of the palace were **workshops**, and beyond that a colonnaded building called the 'little palace' because it, too, contained a megaron. The exact use of some buildings in the upper citadel is conjectural, but we can assume they were the store rooms, treasuries and administrative areas required by a palace-based economy. From here, you can visit the **North Gate**. It was erected at the same time as the Lion Gate but like most back doors is not quite as grand. The area further east was the last part of the citadel to be walled in, in order to defend a cistern that received water via an underground terracotta conduit from a spring, now called the **Spring of Perseus**, 500 yards outside the walls. This cistern with its corbelled roof in the form of an inverted 'V' is one of the most impressive technical works of the Mycenaean period; 16 steps descend to a sharp turn and then there are 83 more down to the water level. It is open, but you need a torch – it has the spooky quality of all old underground places.

Outside the Citadel

North of the Lion Gate, the ravine has a large tholos tomb and a new **museum**, designed to be invisible from the citadel. It was built to house 17,000 Mycenaean artefacts that have hitherto been locked away. In view of its isolated setting, the fabulous Mycenaean gold will stay in Athens and only copies will be displayed here. The target opening date is 2004.

Southeast of the Lion Gate is **Grave Circle B**, earlier or contemporary with Grave Circle A, which produced finds almost as rich and equally fascinating. South of this are several **houses** of the 1200s BC, perhaps belonging to merchants since they lay outside the walls. That's the logic behind the name of the Oil Merchant's House; it appears he traded in aromatic oils, and rows of oil jars lined the wall when it was excavated. Other houses are named after the finds they yielded: the House of Sphinxes and the House of Shields. Linear B tablets found here suggest that the script may have been used in ordinary business transactions, not just for palace inventories. Also of note are the tholos tombs, the most important being the so-called **Tomb of Clytemnestra** (c. 1300 BC), quite refined, possibly the last tholos tomb built at Mycenae. Notice the single row of seats of a **Hellenistic Theatre** above its narrow *dromos*; when it was built, no one remembered the existence of the tomb. The nearby **Tomb of Aegisthus** is much earlier, as early as 1470 BC.

The Treasury of Atreus

On the road to the site, 400 yards before the Lion Gate, the magnificent Treasury of Atreus is the largest of Mycenae's nine tombs. This is the acme of tholos or beehive design, not to mention the largest single-span building in antiquity before Hadrian built the Pantheon in Rome. Built *c.* 1300 BC, two centuries after the first tholos, it was a family tomb like the others, and used many times over. A majestic 120ft entrance passage, or *dromos*, leads to a 34ft door, supporting a 120-ton lintel, curved to match the once elaborate decorative scheme inside and out. The triangle above the lintel, similar to the Lion Gate, shifts the weight above the door to the jambs on either side. Originally it was masked by a red marble plaque carved with spirals, fragments of which are in the British Museum, thanks to Lord Elgin, who visited a few decades before Schliemann. The Green marble half-columns (in the Athens museum) that stood either side may have been the inspiration for the Doric column and capital.

The tholos stands 48ft and measures 47½ft in diameter. Notice how the stones overlap each other to create the dome and then are capped by a single stone, a corbelled technique that required some pretty astute engineering. The small room off the tholos is not typical, and may have been used as an ossuary. Originally the dome would have stuck out over the top of the hill, and been covered by a mound of earth. The tholos tombs were all robbed in antiquity, so perhaps bigger isn't always better. Pausanias, who toured the Lion Gate and tholoi of Mycenae in the 2nd century AD much as we do now, gets the blame for the 'treasury' misnomer. Since no burials were found, he assumed they must have been storehouses.

Argos and the Argive Plain

The fertile Argive Plain south of Mycenae was always inhabited, according to the Argives who described themselves as 'born of the soil'. Hera won this plain from Poseidon and her sanctuary, the Argive Heraion, was one of the oldest and most important in Greece.

Argos

If you come at night, Argos puts on a good show with its illuminated Castle of Larissa suspended in the darkness like an ethereal beacon. In the harsh light of day, however, there is nothing ethereal about the city's box-like buildings, its tile and brick factories, and its river bed gouged out and festooned with garbage. Industry has to be somewhere, but surely the Inachos river, the city's mythical founder, deserves a better wreath than plastic bags and bald tyres.

Argos is backed by two hills which intrude into the flat plain. The lower, rounded one was named Aspida or 'shield' because of its shape, and the 900ft conical one, now topped by the castle, was named Larissa in honour of perceived Thessalian roots. With

Getting There

The Argos bus station, **t** 275 106 7324, has buses to N. Iréa; from there a well-marked road leads to the Argive Heraion in a kilometre or so. From Mycenae, the old road goes to N. Iréa from the centre of the village, or you can do what the Mycenaeans did and walk to the temple (*see* below).

Where to Stay and Eat

Argos ✉ 21200

Telesilla, 2 Danáou St, **t** 275 106 8317 (*C; moderate*). Refurbished with TV and air-conditioning. *Open all year*.

Mycenae, 10 Plateía Ag. Pétrou, **t** 275 106 8754, **f** 275 106 8317 (*C; moderate, expensive in Aug*). Rooms with balconies overlooking the busy square. *Open all year*.

Apollon, by the indoor market, **t** 275 106 8065 (*E; inexpensive*). Very basic; run by a nice lady who never stops ironing. *Open all year*.

Aegli, Plateía Ag. Pétro, **t** 275 106 7266. For a good plate of *kokonistó me patátes* or *mouskári lemonató* (veal in lemon sauce), an Argive speciality.

O Opsimos Psistaria, Korinthos St, **t** 275 102 0149. Grilled chicken in an uncompromisingly Greek provincial atmosphere.

---

these two *acropoli*, Argos was so perfectly sited that its centre has been in exactly the same place for 5,000 years. Poseidon's curse on the Inachos was not a problem, as water is present in aquifers and wells have existed since time immemorial. The fifty daughters of Danaos may have originally been nymphs, each presiding over a well, toiling endlessly to draw water for the herds and gardens.

Although powerful enough for Homer to call the Greek force at Troy the 'Argives' and the 'Danaans' (after Danaos), Argos was subordinate to Mycenae for most of that era's history. It reached the height of its power between the 10th and 7th centuries BC, and was famous for its pottery, especially during the Geometric period. It had an acclaimed school of bronze sculpture, the most famous exponents being Ageladas and Polykleitos. Its most famous figurehead king, Pheidon, made the leap to 'tyrant' thanks to his commercial acumen. He introduced the first coinage on mainland Greece, improved the standard weights and measures and was the only military leader with the muscle to stand up to Sparta (he may have invented the hoplite shield known as an 'argive'). In 669 BC he led the Argives to victory over the Spartans at Hysiai; he even took over the Olympian Games in 668 BC (*see* p.223).

Argive-Spartan rivalry continued into the mid-6th century, when the two cities held a strange, Wild West-style 'Battle of the Champions': 300 Argives versus 300 Spartans on the disputed plain of Thyreatis (modern Ástros). One Spartan and two Argives survived, but the Spartans claimed victory because the two survivors ran off first to proclaim their victory. This resulted in an all-out battle that the Spartans won, which so infuriated the Argives that they swore to shave their heads until they regained Thyreatis. Hearing that, the Spartans vowed never to cut their hair. Coiffure aside, it permanently embittered Argos against Sparta; whatever Sparta did, Argos did the opposite. Once, when the Spartans moved to capture Argos, the Argive women under the poetess Telesilla rallied to defend the city. The Spartans, thinking it would look unsporting to slaughter women, or even worse to be defeated by them, gave up and went home. Sir James Frazier in *The Golden Bough* thinks the Telesilla story has something to do with the fact that Argive brides wore fake beards on their wedding nights.

Mythic Argos

When Hera and Poseidon quarrelled over Argos, Inachos, the local river god, chose Hera. In revenge, Poseidon dried up its water for most of the year: 'thirsty Argos' was its Homeric epithet. Phoroneos, son of Inachos, instituted the worship of Hera and taught his subjects the uses of fire, while his sister Io invented the first five vowels of the alphabet. A few generations later Danaos, a great-great-great grandson of Inachos, arrived back in Argos from Egypt and took over. The story goes that Danaos, who had fifty daughters, the Danaids, was compelled by his brother Aegyptos to marry them to Aegyptos' fifty sons. Not trusting his brother, he ordered his daughters to kill their bridegrooms. Forty-nine of them did, presenting their heads to their father the next morning. Hypermnestra disobeyed. Her husband then killed Danaos, took over the kingdom, and everyone lived happily ever after, except the 49 daughters who were offered to Argos' athletes as prizes. When they died, they were further punished in Tartarus by having eternally to collect water in leaky jars.

Thwarted of wider influence by Sparta, Argos contented itself with trying to control Nemea and the Akte peninsula, not always with success. After sitting out the Peloponnesian War (to avoid siding with Sparta) they embraced the Macedonians, joined the Achaean League in 229 BC, but were annexed by Rome anyway. Earthquakes, barbarians and plague diminished the city. Leon Sgouros was the last Greek to have control before the Franks took over in 1212. Turks, Venetians, Turks, Kolokotrónis, wholesale destruction by Ibrahim Pasha's troops, and eventual independence followed. In its fallen state Argos even lost its status as provincial capital to Naúplio, its port. With a sigh, it rebuilt itself and, like Candide, returned to its garden.

The City

Argos' past can only be examined in the time it takes between an old building being torn down and a new one being put up. Only the most significant finds are preserved, leaving a few pockets of limestone ruins that only archaeologists could love. Exceptions are the much remodelled 5th-century **odeion**, and the **theatre**, built around 300 BC. This was one of the largest in Greece, seating 20,000, with its 81 rows still more or less intact. Legend has it that Perseus buried the Medusa's head – the one that turns viewers to stone – in Argos' ancient agora. That should make excavating more interesting.

Modern Argive life revolves between two central squares. One has a church in the centre of a score of cafés; the other gives onto the arcaded **old market**, and fills up completely on Friday nights, Saturday and Wednesday with a vegetable and clothes market, where the spirit of old Argos is probably reflected more truly than in its ruins. Between the two squares, on Olga Street, the **museum** (*t* 275 106 8819; open Tues–Sun 8–2.30; adm) has a choice selection of artefacts from Argos and around – pretty Mycenaean things, excellent Geometric pottery decorated with horses and warriors, a sherd from a krater depicting the blinding of Polyphemos from the 7th century BC, a well preserved suit of late Geometric armour, a Classical vase showing Theseus, Ariadne and the Minotaur, and Roman mosaics depicting the seasons. The lower level is devoted to finds from Lerna (*see* below) – a fine Neolithic female figure from 3000 BC, dainty Early Helladic sauce boats, three-spouted ceremonial drinking vessels, a hearth and the clay **seals** from the House of Tiles, as well as Minyan ceramics.

High above Argos, conical **Larissa Hill** has a panoramic view and a double row of walls, First built in the 6th century BC, they ring a Byzantine-Frankish-Venetian-Turkish castle made of ancient masonry from Argos' acropolis. There is a road up to it, or a steep, overgrown footpath above the theatre if you're spoiling for a sweat (40mins to an hour). The **monastery of Panagía Katakriméni**, halfway up, is on the site of the temple to Hera Akraia; then have a look at the Aspida Hill (now Profítis Ilías), site of a Mycenaean necropolis and the Argives' first acropolis.

The Argive Heraion

For 2,000 years Argive Hera was worshipped at the Heraion, the local holy of holies where Agamemnon was sworn in as leader of the expedition to Troy. You can get there from Argos by bus, following the route of the heroes Kleobis and Biton, who harnessed themselves to their mother's chariot to take her to the sanctuary. She was a priestess there and the usual oxen were unavailable. She was so proud of her boys that she prayed to Hera to grant them the greatest happiness humans could wish for. They slept in the temple that night and in the morning both were dead – an insight into the ancient Greek concept of happiness. Or you can take the well-worn path from Mycenae, crossing the Mycenaean bridge in the Chávos ravine, about 500m south of the citadel, and heading along the side of the mountain; the Heraion was within easy distance of all of the local Mycenaean settlements. Her classical cult statue, made in 420 BC, was described by Pausanias: 'The statue of Hera is enthroned and very big, made of gold and ivory by Polykleitos. She wears a diadem worked with Graces and Seasons; in one hand she holds a sceptre, in the other a pomegranate... they say the cuckoo sits on her sceptre.'

Contemplating the Ruins

The fenced-in part of the dig (*open 8–2.30; adm free*) lies on three levels; take the path to the top to survey the entire site. As you ascend, notice the enormous, rough, stone blocks of the uppermost retaining **wall**, built in the early Geometric period (*c.* 900 BC) to shore up the top platform. They lack the polish of Mycenaean walls, another reminder of how much was lost after the palace cultures disintegrated. On

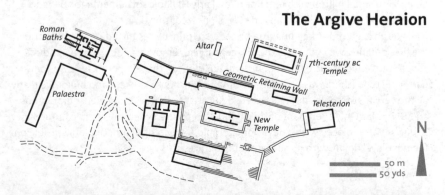

The Argive Heraion

Roman Baths

Altar

7th-century BC Temple

Palaestra

Geometric Retaining Wall

Telesterion

New Temple

N

50 m
50 yds

Hera's Dual Nature

This majestic figure is so different from the jealous wife of so many stories that one can't help but wonder, who was Hera really? Etymologically, her name suggests 'master', 'earth' and 'sky'. Her peacock represented the constellations and her white veil the Milky Way. She embodied the annual cycle of life so important to prehistoric people. That is why she bathed every year in the spring of Kanathos, to renew herself (as a virgin girl), the crops, and all life; that is why the Graces and Seasons sat on her diadem. The pomegranate in her hand signified female fertility. The cuckoo, sacred herald of rain, sat on her sceptre. Her power was venerated on hilltops, and she ruled alone, at least until Mycenaean civilization collapsed.

Four hundred years later, she emerged as a poor second to Zeus on Mount Olympus. Her sacred bird, the cuckoo, was made his attribute. The story told in Classical times was that Zeus had turned himself into this bird to 'woo' her, that she found him in a storm, took pity and held him to her breast at which moment he turned himself back into a god and raped her. Aside from what this incident tells us about sexual attitudes, it is also a telling description of a significant religious moment. In this rape and forced marriage we can actually see the shift from an earlier female-centred religion to the male-dominated Homeric and Classical one. Zeus and Hera struggle constantly; Hera was a threat. Her symbols were trivialized; the peacock became an emblem of her vanity, her veil a symbol of her subjection to Zeus in marriage. Since myth reflects cultural attitudes, there is no getting around it; ancient Greek men considered their wives something of a necessary evil. If Hera's honeymoon lasted 300 years, she spent the rest of eternity facing Zeus' infidelities, and being depicted as a shrill, vain scold. Freud developed his theories of sexuality by studying Greek mythology; he seemed to find this conflict depressingly contemporary.

Although diminished and hemmed in, Hera never lost her primacy at the Heraion. In the Classical period, Argive chronology was still based on the years of service of the priestesses at this shrine. Her worship went underground, becoming a mystery religion, and initiates swore to keep its secrets – hence the Heraion's telesterion (*see* opposite). And annually, her priestess still led a procession in an ox-drawn cart, carrying the mature Hera (or her statue) to bathe again in the Kanathos spring, where she become once more the Girl. And the rains returned, too.

top, the flat stone **paved court** commands a breathtaking view of the Argive Plain. Behind is a small hilltop with remains of an **Early Helladic settlement** (3000–2200 BC), a natural little fortress inhabited even since Neolithic times.

Although it's tempting to imagine Mycenaean priestesses presiding in a hill shrine, the first building we know of is the **7th-century BC temple** standing just behind the paved court. One of the earliest peripteral buildings in the Peloponnese, it was only partly of stone (there was some unfathomable link between Hera and building; nearly all the very first temples in Greece were dedicated to her: here, at Paleochóra, Sámos and Olympia). Only a remnant of the stylobate remains. When the temple burned in 423 BC, it was replaced with a **new Doric temple**. Its rectangular floor plan is visible on the next level down, with its altar in front to the east.

All other structures played a supporting role to these two temples. A 6th-century BC **stoa** directly under the Geometric retaining wall has a low square basin and tunnel for waterworks. Whatever decoration it had is gone, except for a lovely carving of two doves. The other stoa, from the 5th century BC, is at the lowest level towards the entrance and is the best preserved structure in the complex. In front of the new temple to the east (to your left if you have stayed put on the upper terrace) are the ruins of a 5th-century building with a triple row of interior columns. The fact that it is reminiscent of a similar structure in Eleusis suggests that this was the **telesterion**, or Hall of Initiation, built for the Mysteries involving Hera during the Classical period. A coeval square building down one level from the new temple to the west may have been a **banquet hall** (note the three small rooms on its north side). To the west, well outside of the fence, are a **Roman bath** and a **palaestra**.

East of Argos to Midéa

East of Argos and south of the Heraion, the village of **Ag. Triáda** is named for its lovely 12th-century Byzantine **church**. Follow the signs northeast of here for **Dendra**, where Swedish archaeologists in the 1930s discovered a tholos tomb – the first one intact, with all of its grave furnishings (now in Athens). The relics of a royal cremation were found in another tomb; some have interpreted the remains as a case of suttee, a practice vaguely hinted at in a myth or two (but then again, there is little in human experience that Greek myths *don't* contain. There's even a story about Siamese twins). The tombs belong to Mycenaean **Midéa**, of which only the Cyclopean walls remain, a 15-minute walk up, south of the modern village of Midéa.

South of Argos: a Holy Cave, a Pyramid, a Hydra

Five kilometres south of Argos, off the Trípolis road, **Kefalári** is named for the spring that wells out at the base of a limestone cliff into pools. The two caves here were sacred to Pan and Dionysos. The larger, shaped like a Gothic arch and framed by a truly enormous bougainvillaea, is 195ft deep, spacious enough to have hosted Kolokotrónis and his entire army before the battle of Dervenáki. It sheltered a lot of sheep too, until an icon of the Virgin was discovered inside and the tiny church of **Panagía Kefalariótissa** was built in the smaller cave; the grapes on the white iconostasis are especially *à propos*, given who was worshipped here first. At the same time, Kefalári often flummoxes foreign visitors. This beauty spot has an electric cross on the hill with a tangle of wires, a bare concrete weed-filled basin for the spring and, inside, a plywood Christ wreathed in plastic flowers. Patrick White once called Greek churches 'a combination of magnificence and squalor', a feature not unknown in ancient temples: consider the boar's tusk at Tegea (*see* p.279). While not an endangered species, sites like Kefalári are being tidied up and made 'respectable' for the 2004 Olympics, but as it is, its splendour and kitsch reflects a way of thinking that accepts both with equal aplomb, a kind of magnificence all by itself.

A mile west of Kefalári, in **Ellinikó**, the 4th-century BC **Pyramid of Kenkreaí** is impressive, even if it now surveys a football pitch. Six tiers of massive blocks, polygonal and squared, and part of the corbelled arch leading into its hollow centre survive. Who built it and why? Someone reviving the saga of the Argos' Egyptian connections? Perhaps it was an ancient folly; there's another one near Ligourió. Mountains close the Argive Plain just to the south, leaving only a narrow gap along the coast. This enabled Dimítrios Ypsilántis and his 227 troops to hold back Ibrahim Pasha in 1825 and spare Naúplio the razing received by Trípolis (*see* pp.275–6). The gap is guarded by a Frankish castle, and during the last war the Germans added three forts.

Lerna and the House of Tiles

Four km or so south of Kefalári, the Trípolis road passes through the centre of **Mýli** ('the Mills'), the heir of ancient **Lerna**. Lerna's bottomless lake is one of several entrances into the Underworld, reputedly the place where Hades dragged down Persephone. The potential for a mythic frisson is hijacked by the lake's meta-morphosis into a sump pond feeding a waterworks. In the old days, a sanctuary to Persephone's mother Demeter stood on the banks, and there was a later one to Dionysos, who went down to Hades via the lake to bring back his mother Semele.

Lerna was the home of the original swamp monster, the **Hydra**, that Heracles faced in his Second Labour. The Hydra's breath was bad enough to kill, and it had anywhere between seven and 10,000 heads; one was immortal, and the others grew back, two or three at a time, as soon as Heracles, holding his own breath, lopped one off, until his charioteer Iolus came to the rescue with a firebrand to sear the stumps. It is now assumed that the Hydra's heads represented the many outlets of the rivers that flow into the area, and that Heracles' feat in fact represented early attempts at hydraulic engineering.

The main attraction today is Lerna's **House of Tiles**, signposted in a citrus grove just outside of Mýli (*t 275 104 7597; open daily 8.30–3; adm*). Excavations here by John Caskey in the 1950s revealed a *millefeuille* of successive habitation from the Neolithic period (*c.* 6000 BC) to the Bronze Age. In the layer known as Early Helladic II (*c.* 2200 BC), a period coeval with Troy II and Schliemann's 'treasure of Priam', Caskey unearthed a circuit wall with a row of rooms built into it, along with the foundations of dwellings, including one of unguessed at sophistication for the time: a large (82ft by 40ft) house, the first storey of stone, the second of mud brick, topped by a roof of neat square tiles. Fragments of these oldest Greek tiles are on view, as well as the sub-structure of the house, with its curious long entrance corridor.

By 2200 BC, farmers had perfected the triad of vines, olive and wheat. Crafts had also become specialized. This new sophistication required a centre to tabulate, record and redistribute wealth; one small outer room (XI) contained some 60 clay seals of deli-cate beauty (now in the Argos Museum) that were fixed to jars and chests. The House of Tiles was getting its finishing touches – plaster was laid on the walls, in some places divided into panels as if in preparation for frescoes – when it was destroyed by a devastating fire. Perhaps the invaders had studied it before setting it alight because it seems to foreshadow Mycenaean buildings. Its entrance corridor, found in other Early Helladic sites, looks ahead to the labyrinthine ramps at Mycenae and Tiryns.

The next (Early Helladic III) inhabitants did something peculiar to the ruined House of Tiles: they built a round tumulus on top of it, surrounded by a ring of stones, as if ceremoniously *burying* it. They built their own houses around this sacred mound in an apsidal form hitherto unknown in Greece, although common hundreds of years earlier on the lowest level of Troy. Like the early Trojans, these newcomers were familiar with the potter's wheel; one red-brown jar found on this level was even imported from Troy. All this adds fuel to the speculative theory that the invaders, perhaps the first Greek speakers, may have actually come from Troy.

Naúplio and Around

Blessed by nature, decorated by history and preserved with good taste, Naúplio (pronounced Náfplio) is a rarity in the Peloponnese: a beautiful city. Sheltered in the upper pocket of the Argolic Gulf and guarded by the tiny island castle of Boúrtzi, its tall neoclassical houses rise up in tiers to the Turkish fortress of Its Kalé. The commanding hill of Palamídi and its Venetian citadel provide a stupendous backdrop, especially when floodlit at night. Naúplio isn't only lovely; it's also one of the few cities that demonstrates that Greece didn't really spend the period between the Middle Ages and mid-19th century in suspended animation.

History: A Capital City More Than Once

The port of ancient Mycenae and Argos, Naúplio was never large. By the Classical period, it had acquired the usual political myth to explain its names. In this one, Naúplios was a son of Poseidon. His son, Palamedes, fought and died in the Trojan War, but not before he managed to invent the lighthouse, measures, scales, dice, 11 consonants of the alphabet (to go with the five vowels invented by Io of Argos), and donate his name to the hill behind the city. Naúplio also possessed the spring of Kanathos, sacred to Hera (*see* pp.251–2). This has been identified as the fountain in the courtyard of the 12th-century convent of Zoódochos Pigí (Fountain of Life), 3km out on the Epídauros road, although the virgin-wives tending it now are of an entirely different faith. If you care to test the waters, visitors are welcome.

Geoffrey de Villehardouin wrested Naúplio from the Greeks in 1210 and gave it to Otho De La Roche, the Duke of Athens. The Venetians bought it in 1388 from Marie d'Enghien and, with their usual efficiency, assumed residence, changed its name to Napoli di Romania and repelled several Turkish attempts to take it over until 1540, when the Turks won and made it their capital of the Morea. This was followed by a tug of war over the Acronauplía: the Venetians regained it in 1686, and to consolidate their position built the fortress of Palamidi on the heights in 1711. The Turks waited until the Venetians had done all the work and took it back in 1715. The Russians occupied it briefly in 1770, when the Turks concluded that this seaside capital was attracting too much attention. They moved their capital inland to Trípolis; but remained in control of Naúplio until 1822 when Kolokotrónis captured the prize.

Kolokotrónis declined to give up the fort to any of his fellow freedom-fighters until 1824, a stand-off that led to bloodshed. All sides were convinced of the double dealing of the others, and they only buried the hatchet temporarily in order to repel fresh

Getting There and Around

Naúplio's **bus** station, **t** 275 202 7323, is located on Sigróu St, on the edge of the old town. A schedule in English covers the frequent buses to every major town, beach and archaeological site in the province, as well as to Trípolis, Sparta, Corinth, and Athens; special buses commute to Epídauros during the festival. The **train** station, **t** 275 106 7212, at the foot of Sigróu St by the port, is a renovated railway coach; there are three slow trains a day to Corinth, Trípolis and Kalamáta. There's **free parking** on the mole facing Plateía Iatróu. **Car hire**: Auto Europe, 51 Bouboulínas, **t** 275 202 4160, **f** 275 202 4164, *carrental@naf.forthnet.gr*.

Tourist Information

City office, 25 Martíou St, **t** 275 202 4444; *open daily 9–1 and 4.30–8*.

Tourist police: 25 Martíou St and Anapavseos, by the Kýknos factory, **t** 275 202 1051; *open 7am–10pm*.

Where to Stay

Naúplio ✉ 21100

Naúplio stays open all year.

Xenia Palace Bungalows, **t** 2752 02 8981, **f** 275 202 8987 (*L; luxury; half board obligatory*). Situated within the walls of Its Kalé; luxurious, with a pool.

Byron, 2 Plátanos, **t** 275 202 2351, **f** 275 202 6338, *byronhotel@otenet.gr* (*C; expensive–moderate*). A beautiful renovation in the old town; air-conditioning on request.

Dioscouri, 6 Vironos, **t** 275 202 8550, **f** 275 202 1202 (*C; moderate*). Modern and functional; the same view as the Byron, with balconies and air-conditioning.

Marianna Pension, 9 Potamiánou, **t** 275 202 4256, **f** 275 209 9365, *petros@otenet.gr* (*C; just expensive, breakfast inc.*). Traditional decor with mod cons; great views from the terrace, and parking at the old Xenia hotel.

Park, 1 Dervenakión, **t** 275 202 7428, **f** 275 202 7045 (*C; expensive–moderate*). By the municipal park; plain, sympathetic, air-conditioning on request, and the parking is not bad.

Acropole, 9 Vas. Ólga, **t** 275 202 7796 (*D; inexpensive*). Old, attractive, two streets up from the port car parks.

Acronaúplia, 6 Ag. Spyrídon, **t** 275 202 4481, mobile **t** 694 459 3680 (*moderate–inexpensive*). Five houses offering charming period rooms (air-conditioning on request).

Dimétris Békas, 26 Efthiopoúlou behind the Catholic Church, **t** 275 202 4594, mobile **t** 693 758 8903 (*D; inexpensive*). The old town bargain; the hall has a fridge.

Económou, 22 Argonauftón, **t** 275 202 3955 (*D; inexpensive*). Clean if a bit shabby; some rooms ensuite. Parking is easy. With a map, it is a 10-minute walk into the old town.

Eating Out

Along the port, Bouboulínas Street has a long line of restaurants. In the evening, narrow Staikopoúlou St is charming.

Savoúras, Bouboulínas St, **t** 275 209 4374. Fish.

Taverna Tou Stelára, Bouboulínas St, **t** 275 202 8818. Pretty blue and white decor; stresses *laderá* (vegetarian fare).

O Basílis, Staikopoúlou St, **t** 275 202 5344. A touch of class with candles and flowers.

Taverna To Fanária, Staikopoúlou St, **t** 275 202 7141. On a small side alley that is a very pleasant place to sit, though the dining room leaves a lot to be desired. Excellent food.

Carrera's, facing Plateía Kapodístria, **t** 275 202 4985. Great for pizza and beer.

Nightlife

Café Benetsjanjko, Akti Miaoúli. As picturesque as its view.

Nápoli Di Romaniá, Akti Miaoúli, **t** 275 202 7840. A favourite of locals and foreigners alike since the 1960s.

Naúplio's clubs, 2–3km west on the Neas Kios road, lend surreal glamour to the waste land along the beach. If you don't have a car, arrange for a taxi for the return trip.

Shiva of Liquid Club, **t** 275 202 6542. An expensive cross between the Alamo and a Moroccan fort complete with palms.

Rusty, nearby. Has gone for a post-industrial Mad Max look.

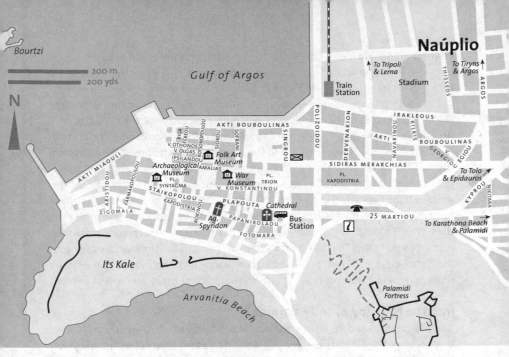

Turkish attacks. After a lot of wrangling, Naúplio was named the capital of Greece in 1828 by Capodístria, the first president of the Greek state. The six short years of its mandate witnessed his assassination and the arrival of King Ludwig I's son, the 17-year-old Otto as King of the Hellenes. His arrival in Naúplio with his Bavarian battalions in 1833 marked the shaky start of the modern era.

The Old Town

Café-studded **Aktí Miaoúli** is a beautiful place to sit and contemplate the sea, with the **Boúrtzi**, the exceedingly picturesque little castle built by the Venetians in 1471, just off shore. A seaside walk will take you around the peninsula of **Its Kalé**, the Turkish name for the Acronaúplio. In the case of both castles, a distant view is more romantic than a close up. Behind Its Kalés' lovely walls the brash Xenia Palace hotel dominates the lower town, a fitting symbol of Naúplio's new master, tourism. The Boúrtzi, once a retirement home for Turkish executioners, is a deserted hulk awaiting a new role.

Up from the seaside, every narrow street has neoclassical houses with balconies festooned with flowers, Turkish wall fountains, ruined mosques and even a Turkish hammam; Venetian, Turkish and Greek buildings stand cheek by jowl more harmoniously than their builders ever did. There is even a Catholic church, the **Metamórphosis**, at the corner of Potamiánou and Kapodístria Streets, built by Otto I, its entrance inscribed with the names of Philhellenes who died during the War of Independence. At 13 Sofráni St, a **Folk Art Museum** (*t 275 202 8379; open Wed–Mon 9–2*) contains over 20,000 items that cover the range of Greek traditional arts, and has an excellent shop selling the same. Just above it, the **War Museum** on Amaliás Ave (*t 275 202 2591; open Tues–Sun 9–2*) occupies Greece's first Military Academy; displays focus on the burning of Smyrna in 1922 and the Second World War.

Sýntagma Square is especially attractive with the **Archaeological Museum** (*see* below) in the Venetian barracks, and a **Turkish Mosque**, now a theatre, opposite. The area is great for shopping, whether you're looking for museum replicas, silver and gold, or seashell tack. Behind the square, Staikopoúlou St has, amid the restaurants, the first **Hellenic Parliament** building. On parallel Kapodístria St, the church of **Ag. Spyrídon** witnessed the death of Capodístria one Sunday morning. The aristocratic president was unsympathetic to the anarchistic aspirations of the clans from the Máni, who had fought so hard for independence and were proving resistant to political unity as a constitution was being hammered out. Capodístria arrested the great Petróbey (*see* p.323) in an effort to tame the Maniátes, and when his kinsmen came to sue for his release, he arrested them, too, but made the mistake of allowing them the freedom of the city. When they approached him, he seemed to think they wanted to greet him. They did, with a yataghan and a bullet, the Maniáte calling card throughout its bloody history. Behind a glass plaque is the hole made by the fatal bullet, a reminder that, politically speaking, Greeks can be their own worst enemies.

Into the New Town, and Palamídi

From Sýntagma Square, V. Konstantínou St will take you into the parks and squares that separate the old and new towns. A walk in this area is very pleasant and, if you follow Sigróu or Polizoidou Streets to the right, you can ascend the hill, with Palamídi looming on the left and the Grimani Bastion on the right, to **Arvanitiá**, a saddle of land between the two castles which contains the Xenia Hotel. This offers a panoramic sea view and access to Naúplio's only in-town **beach**. Arvanitiá is also the traditional way up to the **Palamídi fortress** (*t* 275 202 8036; open summer Mon–Fri 8am–7pm, Sat, Sun 7.30–3; winter daily 7.30–3; adm) if you have the puff to face the legendary 999 stairs (there's really only 857, but that's still more than enough). By car, you can follow 25 Martíou St out of town and up to the castle the back way; in summer the bus to Karathóna Beach will drop you off close to the entrance. This was the last fortress built by the Venetians in Greece, and it was state-of-the-art, with layer upon layer of walls, eight little forts and one big daddy fort in the centre, all made of fine cut stone. Nonetheless, Jan Morris was right to describe it as a 'Piranesi prison, whose staircases lead nowhere after all, and whose vaulted arches support nothing but themselves'. When the Turks returned, the Venetians gave it all up with scarcely a struggle.

Just up 25 Martíou St, carved in high relief in natural rock, is the **Bavarian Lion**, created in 1834 to commemorate King Otto's Bavarian troops, who had died of the plague so far from home, in a country where they were reviled and whose complexities they could never have understood. The lion is very sympathetic; it seems as if he, too, wonders what in the world he is doing so far from home, lording it over a postage-stamp park full of children playing.

Karathóna Beach is 2km out of town, on the same road as Palamídi fortress. This long stretch of lovely seaside has so far escaped development, other than a couple of tavernas and places to rent windsurfers and canoes. This could change at any moment, but so far so good.

The Archaeological Museum

Sýntagma Square, t 275 202 7502; open Tues–Sun 8.30–3; adm.

This museum is well stocked, although the exhibits are inadequately displayed and labelled. It starts with finds from the prehistoric to the Mycenaean eras, including gravestones from Grave Circle B at Mycenae and part of the entablature from the Treasury of Atreus. The star of the collection is a unique set of **Mycenaean armour** found at Dendra, made of bronze strips to form a flounced full metal jacket, complete with a **boar's tusk helmet** (15th-century BC) just as Homer described it. A brightly coloured **Mycenaean fresco** shows female figures, perhaps goddesses, priestesses or just plain citizens. A unique series of mysterious **terracotta figures**, about a foot high and wheel-made in the early 1300s BC, were found in what are assumed to be small shrines; probably goddesses, they have stylized floral dresses, prominent eyes and pointed breasts. Sharing their case is a solid-looking coiled **snake**, also unique and belonging to the same cult centre. Perhaps the sacred household snake, the *oikouros ophis* of the Classical Age is a direct descendant of this fellow. Today in mountain villages, house snakes are considered good luck and food is often left out for them.

The Mycenaean **pottery** is often exquisite, full of a love of nature and a freedom that would disappear with the palace culture. The **Bird Pitcher** in the third free-standing case from the door on the right seems to be singing its heart out in sheer ecstasy. Octopi are another favourite motif; none is exactly the same. Some look harassed, others benign and playful. The case on the left hand wall contains some small clay **tablets** etched with Linear B (*see* pp.352–3).

The upper floor covers the rest up to the Hellenistic period, stressing Geometric finds from Mycenae, Tiryns, Asini, and the area around Naúplio. Beautiful as they are, it is hard not to see them as sterile compared to their counterparts downstairs. On the back wall is an interesting collection of terracotta Archaic figurines, somewhat crudely done but powerful. Just at the door as you leave, notice that modern-looking Hellenistic clay bath tub with the seat and the depression for the feet.

Tiryns

t 275 202 2657; open summer daily 8–7, winter daily 8–3; adm. 5km north of Naúplio, just off the highway; the Argos–Naúplio bus passes every 30mins.

In 1884, Schliemann turned his spade to Homer's 'wall-girt' Tiryns. Rising only 87ft above the Argive Plain, incongruously tucked in beside an orange-processing factory, it may not look wildly impressive from the highway, but get closer: its massive Cyclopean walls are absolutely extraordinary. The historical vicissitudes of Tiryns pretty much echo Mycenae's, although its first walls predate Mycenae's by 50 years or so. Tradition has it that Heracles was born here, and lived here until King Eurystheus of Mycenae sent him on his Labours. Tiryns likewise was somehow subordinate to Mycenae, although it must have been a very favoured dependent; the entire citadel bespeaks wealth, prestige and power. Earthquakes have rendered sections of the walls dangerous, so expect to find areas cordoned off.

The main entrance is formidable, but hardly straightforward. The wide **ramp** built against the east wall leads into the citadel, and then requires a sharp right turn in order to reach an inner ramp hemmed in by massive walls. A sharp turn left, and the path up to the palace passes through two gates and into a courtyard. Here another sharp right turn is required to enter the **Great Propylon** leading to the **outer courtyard** of the palace. Turn right again past the two small guard rooms, through the **second propylon** to the **palace courtyard**, and on via a porch and a vestibule into the **Great Megaron**. Of course, some of these twists and turns were defensive, but it may be that Mycenaeans, like the Minoans, just enjoyed building labyrinths.

The Great Megaron, laid out as neatly as an architect's plan, measures 38ft by 32ft, and was set up like its counterpart at Mycenae, with a circular hearth, four columns and a throne, on the east wall this time. The walls were gaily frescoed with a boar hunt and ladies in procession, and floors stuccoed and painted with very Minoan dolphin and octopus motifs. The three doorways leading into the vestibule resemble the ones at Knossos, too. A very early **Temple to Hera** (8th century BC) was fitted into this area, making it hard to decipher. It's also a nice physical reminder that Hera most likely began her career as a Mycenaean goddess.

The same maze-like plan can be seen in the once luxurious and frescoed **west apartments**. Here the 20-ton monolithic slab of the **bath** has a drain and holes around it for *orthostats* (upright stone panels with pegs chiselled into the base to join the walls to the floor). The palace complex had decent plumbing, with four drains – another idea borrowed from the Minoans, whose craftsmen often worked on Mycenaean projects. Note the little 'T'-shaped **light well** beside the bathroom and the stairwell beside it for an upper floor. A narrow corridor goes right around behind the Great Megaron to the **east apartments**, where the courtyard and megaron arrangement reappear on a smaller scale. Exit from the back door of the west apartments into the **middle acropolis** to check out (if it's reopened) the remarkably preserved **long stairway** down through the bastion to the west gate. A gap left between the top of the staircase and the landing was covered by planks in peacetime and removed to create a pitfall in war.

The famous **underground casement gallery** in the east wall of the citadel is underneath the first palace courtyard and linked the storerooms built in the walls themselves. The sheer massiveness of the corbelled vaults is stunning. Shepherds discovered these ruins open to the east hillside and used them for generations as sheep folds, hence the lanolin-polished stones along the walls. The **lower acropolis** was the last part to be surrounded by Cyclopean walls. Square storage chambers were cut into the walls, and two 66ft galleries tunnelled beyond it, forming **cisterns** that assured Tiryns' water supply. At present, it is only for archaeologists. About 2km into the orange groves beyond the site is Tiryns' only known **tholos tomb**, and a fine big one it is, too. It is signposted and only a short walk from the narrow road.

Beaches and Resorts South of Naúplio

Southeast of Naúplio a string of seaside towns offer convenient beach hotels. The coast is flat except for rocky headlands, a terrain very typical of the Argolís, and perfect for cycling.

Getting There and Around

Buses between Toló and Naúplio run from 7am to 10pm, and many continue to Drépano; other connections are less frequent. **Boats** in Toló offer day trips. Try Pegasos, t 275 205 9430, for cruises to Hýdra, Spétses and Monemvasiá.

Where to Stay and Eat

Toló ✉ 21056

In winter, it rolls up its streets.

Christina, 7 Bouboulínas, t 275 205 9001 (*C; moderate*). Air-conditioned, on the strip; popular for years, with a sea view restaurant. *Open Mar–Oct.*

Epídauros, 52 Sekeri, t 25 705 9219, f 275 205 9219 (*C; moderate, breakfast inc.*). On the main street; air-conditioned; new and nicely decorated. *Open Feb–Dec.*

Ingrid Bungalows, t 275 205 9747, f 275 205 9871 (*moderate*). Just east of Asine's beach. Perfect if you want Toló, but not the noise. Large island-style apartments with balconies and a garden; free bikes for the 5min cycle into town. *Open all year.*

Drépano and Vivári ✉ 21060

Dante's Beach, Drépano, t 275 209 2294, f 275 209 2193, *dantis@otenet.gr* (*B; expensive*). A pretty choice with its pool and tennis court, in a green setting. *Open April–Oct.*

Eleni-Chrisoula Apartments, Drépano, t 275 202 2623, f 275 209 2489 (*moderate–inexpensive*) Plain, clean, set back from the sea in a garden. *Open April–Oct.*

Plaka Beach Camping, Drépano, t 275 209 2294 (*inexpensive*). The best camping in a string of campsites, with the least number of permanently parked caravans.

Aretí, Vivári, t 275 209 2391 (*C; inexpensive*). An old-fashioned hotel with a view makes up for the road between it and the sea. No heating. *Open all year.*

Camping Leukas Beach, Vivári, t 275 209 2334. On a sloping hill among poplar trees, less than a mile from town.

O Dimítris, Vivári, t 275 209 2125. A good view and good fish; on the beach.

Toló, 10km from Naúplio, is Coney Island, Greek style, with strings of hotels, campsites and clubs. It is on a beautiful, wide, south-facing bay, with a charming island centrepiece and a narrow sandy beach (the best in the area). Just east lies the small rocky headland that was ancient **Asine**, a fortified town inhabited from the Early Helladic period on down. In the 1920s the Swedes, led by archaeology boffin King Gustav Albert, found the striking clay portrait of the 'Lord of Asine', now in Naúplio's museum. You can swim off the tiny beach while having a look at its crumbling walls; doing just that inspired one of George Seferis' most haunting poems, seeking the King of Asine 'unknown, forgotten by all, even by Homer'. One of these kings of Asine made the mistake of joining Sparta to ravage the Argolís in *c.* 720 BC. The Argives destroyed Asine in turn, and the inhabitants moved to Koróni (*see* p.342).

Drépano, 3km east, has a long narrow beach, less inviting than Toló's, but the town itself is set back so its seaside is quieter. So close to Drépano as to seem a suburb, lovely, tiny **Vivári** is a fishing port on an exquisite sea lake. Just over the next headland is **Kándia**, artichoke capital of Greece – in spring, try them with fresh peas.

East to Epidauros

A good 25km road links Naúplio to Epídauros by way of **Arkadikó**, where you may want to keep your eyes peeled for a perfect little **Mycenaean bridge** with its single arch, a ruined **tholos tomb**, and the impressive 5th-century BC polygonal walls of the **acropolis of Kazarma** on the hill, all visible from the road. Handcarved briarwood pipes are a local industry, and you can examine them in the shop in **Giannoulaíka**. Bustling **Ligourió** has some too, as well as a privately run **Natural History Museum** (*open daily 9–8; adm*), with a well-displayed collection of fossils and rocks and sea shells. In Ligourió you'll also see a sign for its **Pyramid**, similar to the one at Kenkreaí (*see* p.253), but not as well preserved; it stands 1.5km west of the centre. You'll also see signs for an old and new Epídauros on the coast, but the Epidauros with the famous theatre is, properly, Asklepeion Epidaurou, signposted 2.5km east of Ligourió.

Epidauros

A site full of pines and oleanders, Epidauros attracts thousands to its magnificent ancient theatre. When *it* was new, visitors came for quite a different reason – to consult Asklepios, the god of healing and one of Greece's most beloved deities. A sanctuary functioned here for 2,000 years on two areas of Mount Kynórtion. Similar gods were worshipped under different names. Even more curiously, it was a city cult centre without a city. A little history is in order.

History: Chthonic Gods, Snakes, and Politics

It all began as a Mycenaean open air sanctuary high on Mount Kynórtion, dedicated to a chthonic deity. Chthonic 'earth' gods presided over the annual cycle of planting

---

The Dream Cure and the Epiphany of the God

So how did it work? After being purified with holy water and offering a holocaust (*see* opposite), the pilgrim was left to sleep in the *enkoimeterion* (sleeping place) or *ávaton* (literally 'no go' to the unpurified). Here Asklepios, or his snake or faithful hound, appeared in a dream, which his priests would interpret, then proceed with the therapy. The surgical instruments found at the Asklepeion indicate that they were adept medical practitioners, not just dream catchers – the famous Hippocrates of Kos was a priest of Asklepios. Case studies were recorded and a medical library was open to patients and priests. Not exactly a hospital, but not Lourdes either (although Epidauros records some 40 miracle cures); healing hinged on practical experience, but faith was the key. 'Purity is to think pious things' was engraved over the entrance.

Testimonials recorded on stone plaques by satisfied customers were left in the sanctuary. Rich gifts or buildings were donated, enhancing the sanctuary's status. Clay votives in the shape of body parts would be placed in the sanctuary, either in supplication or in thanks, a practice that has continued in an unbroken line in the little stamped metal *támata* that hang from icons in Greek churches today.

If aspects of this process seem primitive, much has stayed the same: the god-like aura of the specialist, the shrine-like lobbies of medical buildings, dedications and donations, and the close connection between the healing arts and faith, whether in God or science. The psychology is the same. One practice in Epidauros might also be envied today. Visitors were charged according to their ability to pay, so even a person of humble means could hope for a cure.

Getting There

Ligourió/Epídauros is served by six **buses** from Naúplio, Portochéli and even Galatás (three a day in summer). Do make sure you're on the bus to the right Epídauros (the ones for the ancient site usually say Theatre or Asklepeion). On **festival nights** there are special buses from Naúplio and Athens. From June to mid-Sept, Minoan **hydrofoils** link Palaiá Epídauros to Piraeus via Aegina. In Epídauros the agent is M. Syrogiannouli, t/f 275 304 2010. **Port authority**: t 275 304 1216.

Where to Stay and Eat

Ligourió/Epídauros ✉ 21052

Alkion, t 275 302 2002, f 275 302 2552 (*D; inexpensive*). 20 adequate rooms.

Taverna Leonides, t 275 302 2115. The place to dine in Ligourió; in the garden, with good food and atmosphere.

Palaiá Epídauros ✉ 21059

Mike, on the port, t 275 304 1213, f 275 304 1502 (*C; moderate*). Most rooms have views, and a good restaurant by the sea. *Open all year.*

Poseidon, next door, t 275 304 1211, f 275 304 1770 (*C; moderate*). Newer, whiter, balcony-rimmed, with another good restaurant by the water. *Open April–Oct.*

Elena and **Astéria**, on a quiet side street, t 275 304 1207 (*moderate–inexpensive*). Air-conditioned studios. *Open all year.*

Bekas Camping, on Gialási Beach, t 275 304 1394. Big; well equipped for sports. *Open April–Oct.*

Nikolas II Camping, nearby, t 275 304 1445. Friendly and shady. *Open Mar–Oct.*

Amyelóesa, t 275 304 1287. For a fish feast by the port that won't break the bank, get a table on the Gini family's long veranda.

Néa Epídauros ✉ 21054

Avra, t 275 303 1294 (*expensive–moderate*). Colourful, relaxed little place with a restaurant. *Open April–Oct.*

Mariléna, t 275 303 1279 (*moderate–inexpensive*). A better sea view. *Open April–Oct.*

Camping Diamantis, t 275 303 1181. With a pool, windsurfers, disco, the works.

The Epidauros Festivals

The **Epidauros Festival** takes place on weekends in July and August, concentrating on the classics (in modern Greek), performed by the Greek National Theatre. The enormous size of the theatre means it is rarely filled up, so even if you get a seat in the gods you can move down closer once the show starts. For information, contact the **box office**, t 275 302 2006, or the **Athens Festival Box Office**, t 210 322 1459, *www.greekfestival.gr*; tickets can be purchased at the gate (from €15–62 for front row thrones).

Musical events take place on July weekends at Palaiá Epídauros' **Mikro Theatro** and the calibre of the performances is not small; Maria Farandoúri and Paco Pena have performed here. For information, t 275 304 1250 or contact the Mégaron Musikís in Athens, t 210 728 2333.

and reaping, and were propitiated by early agricultural societies with rituals involving water and ash, two elements that made things grow. Even when the worship of the Olympians became the norm, chthonic worship continued alongside it, and in many cases, as in Epidauros, became incorporated with it. The hallmark of chthonic sacrifices was the *holocaust* (the burning of the entire animal), as opposed to the fat and thigh bones burned for the ethereal Olympians (it was the vast amount of ash from holocausts near a water source that identified Epidauros' Mycenaean god as a chthonic one). Chthonic gods also had therapeutic powers because of their ability to bring the dead earth to life. Snakes, who appeared rejuvenated by sloughing off their skins and who were equally at home under the earth or on it, were associated with them, and were favourite symbols of resurrection and rebirth on ancient grave stelae.

After the Mycenaean period, the hilltop sanctuary was given over to Apollo. Only here he was worshipped here as Apollo Maleatas, an epithet probably referring to the earlier chthonic deity. The ritual still involved holocaust sacrifice, so it is hard to say exactly who appropriated whom.

The site might have remained just another country shrine, except that in 640 BC the seaside city-state of Epidauros was nervous about the expansionist propensities of Argos. To discourage Argos, Epidauros' tyrant, Prokles, entered into an alliance with Corinth. As a compliment to Apollo, Corinth's patron, he declared the shrine of Apollo Maleatas the Official City Cult Centre of Epidauros, in spite of the fact that it was a 2½hr walk away. This proved to be an astute political move. The sanctuary just happened to be on the disputed border, so any attack on Epidauros' shrine now meant offending Corinth. Prokles further stacked the cards against Argos by instituting Panhellenic Games on the site, timed to follow the Isthmian Games.

In the 6th century BC, the sanctuary expanded to the present site and its focus shifted to Asklepios, a chthonic healing god from Thessaly, who with his companion snake made himself perfectly at home here. He was neatly incorporated into the existing cult by making him the 'son' of Apollo and the princess Koróni. Polytheism is nothing if not elastic. Apollo, the story goes, sent him to learn the healing arts from the centaur Cheiron, and he learned so well that he started to raise departed friends from the dead. Zeus, at Hades' request, zapped him underground with a thunderbolt. From there Asklepios helped humans recover from the 'little death' of illness by appearing to them in dreams. Symbolic of his status as the ancient Greek's best friend is his dog; no other god had a pet. Apollo never lost precedence, but it was the cult of the compassionate Asklepios that made Epidauros famous until Theodosios II closed its doors in AD 426. The cult then gave way to the Christian son of God and snakes developed a bad name, but not before they had became the symbol of the medical arts on the caduceus.

The Museum, the Asklepeion and Theatre

t 275 302 2009; open summer 7.30–7pm, winter 8–5. The museum hours are the same except on Mon when it opens at noon; adm exp.

The **museum** by the entrance is a warehouse of marble parts – pieces of temples, croterions, votive offerings, dedicatory plaques and what have you. What with the medical instruments, one can imagine an architectural Dr Frankenstein doing his stuff in here one night and producing an entire temple by morning. These, and the extensive ruins reflect 800 years of building and rebuilding. As you go north from the museum, to the right was a large 4th-century BC **hotel**, which had two floors and four atriums. What remains are some low polygonal walls and the thresholds to the lower rooms. They weren't en suite, but next door were **baths** offering both tubs and basins. Built in the 3rd century, one wonders what visitors did before that. Over time, Epidauros grew into a major entertainment centre. The **stadium**, first used in the 5th century BC, occupies a partly artificial depression. There was an underground vaulted passage leading through the seats on the north side to a **palaestra**. The large

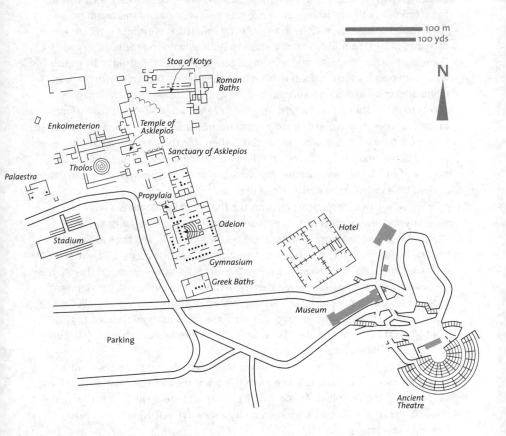

Epidauros

100 m
100 yds

N

gymnasium, 230ft by 249ft, had a grand **propylaia** (entrance) on the north side. The lower parts of the walls are well finished limestone, showing its layout, but the rest was brick work and perishable, and a lot of its superstructure went into the construction of the Roman **odeion**, now in ruins itself in its centre. In Roman times the propylaia was a Temple to Hygieia, or Health. The **Stoa of Kotys** may just have been shops; lots of visitors were well off.

Unfortunately, the remains of the **Sanctuary of Asklepios** itself are sparse. Surrounded by the ruined walls built in AD 395 to protect the holy of holies from the Goths are the remains of the old 6th-century BC complex and new 4th-century BC one. Both had an all-important temple and altar, a water source for purification and an enkoimeterion. You can make out the plan of the 4th-century Doric peristyle **Temple of Asklepios**, which had six columns on the front and 11 on the sides and measured a modest 43 by 40ft, with a ramp leading up. In contrast, the 4th century **enkoimeterion** (*see* p.262) was 232ft long, allowing plenty of people to dream at the same time. The 6th-century water source was incorporated into this building.

The **tholos** or rotunda, built in 360–320 BC by Polykleitos, is intriguing. There are drawings of it in the museum: it once had 26 Doric columns on the outside and 14 Corinthian on the inside. All that remains is the basement, consisting of six concentric walls with openings to form a maze. The floor over this was covered with black and white diamond-shaped tiles, surrounding a circular stone which opened to give access to the subterranean maze. It may have been a sacred snake pit. All Asklepeions in the Graeco-Roman world ordered a snake from Epidauros as a seal of legitimacy, so they must have kept quite a collection somewhere. The tholos is being partially reconstructed. The **library** was north behind the enkoimeterion; the other buildings to the north and east were **Roman baths**, gateways, and so on. The **propylaia**, the entrance in ancient times, was on the north side of the site.

Designed with mathematical precision, the **theatre of Epidauros** is a work of harmony and beauty, both within itself and in its relation to the landscape. Built in the 3rd century BC to accommodate 6,000 people in 34 rows, and then expanded in the 2nd to accommodate 6,000 more in another 20 tiers, the acoustics are perfect; even the sound of a match being struck in the orchestra carries loud and clear to the top seats. This is the best-preserved theatre in Greece; the entrances, the *skene* and *proskene* are still pretty much as they were. Note how the seats were all hollowed underneath so that the audience could tuck in their legs to allow people to pass in front. VIPs sat in the moulded seats in the first row. The circular orchestra is the only one to survive intact from antiquity.

The ruins of the older sanctuary to **Apollo Maleatas** near the eastern summit of Kynórtion can be reached by car or on foot but ask at the museum first, as they must send a guard. The **Temple to Apollo** is under a shed and the **prehistoric settlement** is above it. The Romans were here too, creating perceptual confusion to those deciphering the ruins.

Down on the Coast: Palaiá Epídauros and Néa Epídauros

Ten kilometres up the road, **Palaiá Epídauros** (Αρχαια Επιδαυρος) concentrates on the pleasures of sea and beach. Its yacht-filled port is closed in by a wooded headland to the south on which is a well-preserved, rather sweet 4th-century BC **theatre** set in an olive grove. This *Mikro Theatro* has a mere 18 tiers of seats, including ten moulded throne-like ones in the front for the big shots, some still bearing the names of their donors. Remains of the **ancient city** are scattered about: some Roman bits, Cyclopean walls and foundations of a paleo-Christian basilica. South beyond that, a long sandy **beach** is protected by a big red boom from debris blown over from Aegina.

Néa Epídauros, 7.5km north, holds tight to the slopes of Mount Árkos with the remains of a Frankish castle of Nicholas de Guise guarding the gorge. Its 15 minutes of fame occurred on 20 December 1821, when Greek revolutionary leaders gathered here in their first assembly to declare the country's independence. A road leads down 2km past the orchards to the narrow **beach** on a pretty bay, with a blue and white church and views over mountains and cliffs. The **Agnoúntos Monastery**, 5km north on the Corinth road, is known for its remarkable 18th-century frescoes.

Akte: The Dewclaw of the Morea

If the Peloponnese is a paw, Akte, the jaggedy rugged peninsula that dangles east, is its dewclaw, dividing the Saronic and Argolic Gulfs. Where arid Mount Adéres relents you'll find lush valleys and sandy beaches – plus a volcano, a Devil's bridge, a lemon forest and a nearly perfect fishing village.

Méthana and the Volcano

South of Palaiá Epídauros, the corniche road eventually descends to the peninsula of Méthana. Attached to the mainland by only a tenuous 100yd-wide umbilical cord at Stenó, it looks like a hot air balloon on the map. In a way it is: the peninsula is made up of a volcano that popped out of the sea. Méthana's nickname is 'stinky lake', and it has three sulphurous **springs** to soothe your rheumatism and tickle your nose. The whole of Méthana is an old-fashioned kind of place, with a yacht-crammed port and a wooded islet, topped with the inevitable church. You can swim nearby, but you'll do better by following the coastal road north to the golden sands of **Limniónas**.

Steep volcanic slopes prevent the two roads trying to encircle the peninsula from succeeding, but they give on to paths that are lovely in early summer with orchids. One road continues up to the fishing village of **Ag. Geórgios**, then ends at the '**Baths of Pausanias**' (Ag. Nikólaos on some maps), another hot spring. To reach the ancient city of Méthana visited by Pausanias, take the west coast road to **Vathí**, a potential hideaway with tiny beaches and a handful of rent rooms. Vathí means 'deep' – the sea here plunges 1,300ft. Classical walls and gates to the acropolis remain on the hill above Vathí at **Paleókastro**; the rest of it fell into the sea after an eruption.

The coastal road north of Vathí ascends to the peninsula's star attraction: the volcano. Leave the car or bus in **Kaiméni Chóra** ('Burnt Village'), a white hamlet wedged into the black volcanic rock. Wear sturdy shoes, take water and a hat, and follow the path from the church (marked προς Ηφαίστειο) which in 20 to 30 minutes, with some scrambling, leads to the lip of the volcano. In this alien world of savage black, red and green crags and sharp abysses, the perfect silence is relieved only by a breeze rustling in a few brave pines and the sighing of the indigo blue sea far below. The Peloponnese may be the 'Cradle of Hellenism', but here, by this pitiless crater, it seems more like the cradle of the world itself. Or a preview of its end.

Trizína: Ancient Troezen and the Devil

South of the Méthana peninsula, **Trizína** sits on a wooded shelf of Mount Adéres, surveying the sea, citrus groves and cultivated fields of flowers. This coast was once a marsh; the ancients planted it with clover for the famous horses bred here.

Getting There and Around

Ferries and summer **hydrofoils** ply the Piraeus, Aegina, Méthana, Póros, Hýdra, Spétses route five times a day in summer; less in winter. In Méthana the agent is at 52 Akti Saronikou, **t** 229 809 2071. A local **car ferry** (every 30mins) or **water taxis** flit across the strait from Gálatas to Póros. Three **buses** a day, **t** 229 802 2480, link Epídauros (the theatre), Naúplio, Méthana and Trizína, and Gálatas. **Hire a car** in Galatás from Top, **t** 229 802 2909, mobile **t** 693 279 8876 or Pop, **t** 229 802 4910, **f** 229 802 5716. There are also **taxis**.

Buses from Naúplio run to Ermióni and Portochéli four times a day. The ports, including Hýdra's, are linked to one another and Piraeus daily, all year, by Minoan Flying Dolphins (in Ermióni, **t** 275 403 1170; Portochéli, **t** 275 405 1543). Spétses is linked by **waterbuses** from Kósta (around €10). **Hire a car** in Ermióni at Pop's, **t** 275 403 1880, **f** 275 403 1881; and at Portochéli at Alias, opposite the bus station, **t** 275 405 1313. For a **taxi** in Ermióni, **t** 275 403 1060.

Where to Stay and Eat

Méthana ✉ 18030

Avra, **t** 229 809 2382 (*B; moderate–inexpensive*). On the sea; the nicest and most comfortable of several waterfront hotels. *Open April–Oct.*

Saronis, **t** 229 809 2312, **f** 229 809 2001 (*B; inexpensive*). Eager to please. *Open April–Oct.*

Small tavernas dot the waterfront to keep you from starving, and in the evening, bop by the beach at La Playa disco.

Galatás ✉ 18020

Galatia, **t** 229 802 2227 (*C; inexpensive*). Right on the sea, with the best views of Póros; pure Greek 1970s, from its lobby to its awnings. *Open all year.*

Papassotiríou, **t** 229 802 2841, **f** 229 802 5558 (*C; expensive–moderate*). By the sea in town; offers meals as well. *Open all year.*

Koulis Rooms, **t** 229 802 2322 (*inexpensive*). Down at the far east end of town; quiet.

O Vláchos. The best taverna is near *Koulis*; the real McCoy, with tables by the sea.

Ermióni and Around ✉ 21051

Porto Hydra Village, 14km east of Ermióni, **t** 275 404 1270, **f** 275 404 1295 (out of season, **t** 210 360 6447, **f** 210 360 4305), *www.portohydrahotel.gr* (*A; luxury*). On the beach at Plépi, massive hotel and villa-style accommodation, with a taverna, nightclub, gym, pool, sea sports and activities for 2–14-year-olds. *Open April–Oct.*

Paladien Lena-Mary, 7.5km south, **t** 275 403 2166, **f** 275 403 1451 (*A; expensive*). At Petrothálassa Beach, a luxury compound that could be anywhere. *Open April–Oct.*

Philoxenia, **t** 275 403 1218 (*inexpensive*). Near ancient Hermione; handsome, quiet and well furnished rooms and studios. If no one's there, ask at **Taverna Ganossis** right on the port, **t** 275 403 1706 (the food is pretty good, too).

Akti, **t**/**f** 275 403 1241 (*E; inexpensive*). A modest waterfront choice. *Open all year.*

Psitariá To Vitsi, near the pines. A good bet for succulent grilled meats.

Portochéli ✉ 21300

Porto, **t** 275 405 1410, **f** 275 405 1869 (*C; moderate–inexpensive*). Portside, if you are stuck. *Open all year.*

Porto Heli, **t** 275 405 3400, **f** 275 405 1549 (*A; luxury–expensive*). All the beach amenities; rooms have kitchenettes, satellite TV and so on. *Open all year.*

Ververoda, **t** 275 405 1342, **f** 275 405 1345 (*B; expensive–moderate*). More modest, back from the sea, but still well equipped. *Open May–Oct.*

O Kostas. At the end of the main drag for good homestyle cooking.

Kósta ✉ 21300

Cap d'Or, **t** 275 405 7360, **f** 275 405 7067 (*B; luxury–expensive*). A French Riviera experience with a Greek touch. French food in the dining room looking out over the channel to Spétses. They will take in anglophones if they have room. *Open April–Oct.*

Lido, **t** 275 405 7393, **f** 275 405 7364 (*B; moderate*). Plain, motel-like, right on the beach between the water taxis and the swimming beach; a perfectly fine lodging for a night or two.

One of the oldest cities in Greece, Troezen's myths are beyond the pale of Peloponnesian story cycles. Instead they are linked with Athens (even today, Trizína is administered from Piraeus) and much earlier, with Egypt: the first man in these parts was Oros (Horus) and the name for the area was Oraia. Later came Troezen, a son of Pelops and his half brother Pittheos, 'the wisest man of his time' and the first to teach oratory. Pittheos founded the Sanctuary of Oracular Apollo (the equivalent of Horus), said to be the oldest shrine in Greece. The son of his daughter Aethra was Athens' hero Theseus. Just who the father was is more complicated: Pittheos gave his visitor, king Aegeus of Athens, too much to drink, so he mistook the door of Aethra's room for his. Later, that same evening, 'Deceitful Athena' willed that Aethra go down to the shore to make a sacrifice to Poseidon, who ravished her as well; when it came to Theseus' paternity, the Athenians wanted it both ways. In the morning, Aegeus commanded Aethra to raise any child they might have in secret, and to send him to Athens *only* when he proved himself by lifting a boulder and taking the tokens – a sword and sandals – he had hidden. Which Theseus, of course, did.

Theseus' son Hippolytos became heir to Pittheos and another story cycle. Devoted to physical fitness and chastity, he ignored women and instead built Artemis a temple and stadium in Troezen where he trained. Miffed by his neglect, Aphrodite caused Theseus' wife Phaedra to fall in love with him. Phaedra erected a nearby temple to Peeping Aphrodite in order to spy on Hippolytos as he trained, naked. Then the familiar story, retold in Euripides' *Hippolytos* and Racine's *Phèdre* plays itself out. Back in Athens, Phaedra confessed her love to her stepson, was rebuked, and hanged herself, leaving a letter accusing Hippolytos of attempted rape. Theseus cursed his son, and called on his divine father Poseidon to kill him. As Hippolytos rode his chariot by the sea near Troezen, a monster (or wave) spooked the horses, and he was dragged to his death. This Athenian version probably never washed in Troezen, where Hippolytos, a horse god, was far more important than Theseus. Some say Artemis had Asklepios bring Hippolytos back to life, the last straw for Hades, who asked Zeus to strike Asklepios with a thunderbolt. And there was even a tablet in Epidauros recording a gift of 20 horses from Hippolytos to thank Asklepios for his resurrection!

The 'real' history of Troezen confirms the city's special relationship with Athens. When the Persians menaced in 480 BC, the Athenians sent their women and children to Troezen for safety – as many as 70,000 in all. By all accounts, they were treated well. In 1827, the town was briefly in the limelight again when it hosted the third Greek Assembly, which produced a third constitution and elected Count Ioánnis Capodístrias, then the foreign minister of Russia, as first president of Greece.

Follow the signs up from Trizína into the olive groves, where at 500m a fork in the road is marked by the **Theseus Rock**, under which the hero found the sword and sandals. The right-hand road passes first the turn-off (on the right) for a **palaeo-Christian church**, made of ancient blocks, and continues over the river to the bare foundations of the **Temple of Hippolytos** and a 3rd-century BC **Asklepeion**. It preserves some of its plumbing (water being an important part of the cure) and a curious room that may have been a morgue when the cure didn't work. Phaedra's Temple of Aphrodite Kataskopeia, 'Peeping Aphrodite', is believed to be on the site of the ruined Byzantine church of the **Episkopí**. Unfortunately, there's no sign of the sanctuary of the Nine Muses, built by Ardalos, the inventor of the flute. The ancient Greeks had a sense of humour; it had an altar dedicated to Sleep.

Return to the Theseus Rock and take the left fork, passing a prominent **tower**, 2nd-century AD on the bottom, medieval on top. Shortly beyond, a grove of enormous plane trees marks the **Devil's Gorge**. It is an idyllic place, where nymphs seem to lurk just behind the ferny drippy boulders and crystal pools fed by Troezen's 'golden stream that never dies'. The small **bridge** was built by the devil, they say; someone has painted his picture on the wall. A third road from Trizína heads up the slopes of Adéres for the **Monastery of Ag. Dimítrios** (1.5km) with fine frescoes restored in the 17th century and excellent views across to Póros.

Galatás, the Lemonodássos, and Eastwards

Sailing through the 400 yards that separates Galatás on the mainland from the island of Póros (*see* p 150) is unique; if you've drunk as much as Henry Miller, you may even find that it recaptures 'the joy of passing through the neck of the womb'. But wherever you end up, on the island or mainland, you'll find yourself irresistibly drawn to this Greek Grand Canal. Although Póros is far more fashionable, Galatás has the better view – of Póros and its delightful pile of houses, churches and bell towers.

Galatás is an easy-going workaday place, stretched thinly along the waterfront. Dairy products (*gála* means milk) gave the town its name, but today's residents are more concerned with their orchards and flowers. There are two beaches to the east: **Pláka** (2km) and **Alykí** (4km; on an unpaved road, with a good taverna). Near the Alykí turn-off, at the sign for the Cardassi restaurant, is the entrance to Galatás' citrus groves, the **Lemonódassos**, lemon forest. The blossoms from *one* lemon tree can scent a garden; on a warm spring day, a stroll here among 30,000 is a full dose of undiluted aromatherapy. Follow the trails up to the delightful taverna for a glass of lemonade.

The road east of the Lemonódassos to the **tip of the Akte peninsula** is lovely, especially at dawn or at twilight, when Póros and its baby islands and rocks are stained violet in the mirror of the sea. Past **Saronída**, 8.5km from Galatás, the coast is dull; an alternative is the unpaved road west along the spine of Andéres to Ermióni, with the ruins of ancient **Eileoi** (polygonal walls and a temple) at **Iliókastro** along the way.

Ermióni, Portochéli and Kósta

Akte's southerly nub is a favourite among yachties. Ermióni and its coast bask in the reflected glow of glittering Hýdra (which unlike Ermióni has no beaches at all), while Portochéli's satellite Kósta is the nearest landfall to stylish Spétses.

Ermióni occupies a long narrow headland; one side has a handsome waterfront and port, while the other side, **Mandráki**, has pretty rocks you can swim off under white, island-style houses. The sparse ruins of **ancient Hermione** with some stones from a temple to Poseidon, lie scattered in a pine grove at the tip of the headland, but fluorescent blue birds (European rollers) steal the show as they flit over the sea. Hermione's claim to fame is that it was the only ancient city in Greece to hold nautical games – boat races and diving and swimming, all in honour of Dionysos of the Black Goat.

Portochéli, ancient Halieis, services yachts and package tour groups, and has as much personality as a doorknob; it is one of the very few ports in Greece that feels suburban. Even its beautiful, sheltered little bay is wasted as roads and car parks separate the sea from the shoulder-to-shoulder hotels and restaurants. Its tentacles have spread north towards **Ververóda** and south to **Ag. Emilianós**, where huge hotels await their charter flight passengers, and flats their time-sharers.

Kósta, to the south overlooking Spétses, is much nicer. There is a lovely beach with a terraced restaurant, a small hotel, and not much else. The wealthy Athenian villas on the western headland may explain why Kósta has not gone ballistic; they have *méson* (influence) where it counts. With any luck it will stay that way.

Back towards Naúplio: Big Holes

The main road north of Portchéli passes through the market town of **Kranídi**, where secondary roads go west, one to pretty little beaches and one to **Kiláda**. Kiláda is that *ava rara*, an unspoiled fishing village, full of no-nonsense boats and fine fish restaurants along the port. So tuck in (and keep it under your hat). From Kiláda's esplanade you may have already spotted the awesome gaping maw of the **Frachthi Cave** (Σπηλιά Φραγχθι), where the oldest skeleton found in Greece (8000 BC) was unearthed. Arrange a ride over with a fisherman, or follow the dirt road around the bay and walk the last bit. Inhabited from the Mesolithic to recent Neolithic eras, the cave has proved of fundamental importance in dating other sites around Europe. Bring a torch: it has a water source and lots of bats, but that's about it.

After Foúrni, the roads ascends towards **Dídyma**, a village to the right of the road. Your eye, however, will be drawn to the left, where the flank of the mountain is scarred by yet another startlingly enormous **hole**. Actually there are two craters, formed by meteors in the 19th century; the sign calls them *spilia* (caves). Access to the first is by way of a subterranean passage (signposted Ag. Geórgios), leading to a ledge that supports two chapels, apparently to encourage God to keep the stars in the sky where they belong. The second, even larger one, if you scramble up to the brim, is just a great big hole, but dramatic nonetheless. Once past the holes, the road climbs into a saddle of **Mount Dídyma**, affording views over the Argolic Gulf; bigger views await if you take the road to the right that zigzags 10km up to the 3,678ft summit.

Arcadía

In spite of possessing a familiar name, Arcadía is a well-kept secret. A place that seemed ancient even in ancient times, it lacks big league attractions, but is full of sublime minor ones, both natural and man-made, where the getting there is half the fun. Most tourists making the circuit around the Peloponnese scarcely set foot in it, although in the past few years Greeks in the know have made it a favourite weekend bolt-hole. Now it can be hard to find room at the inn on a Friday night.

Arcadía can look forbidding, even dreary, from the main highway. With the exception of the east coast strip of Kynoúria, the province is a combination of wild forested

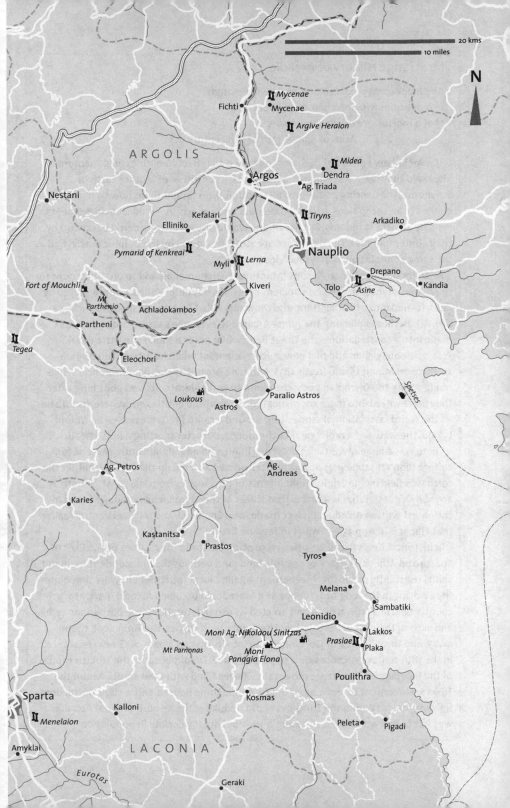

The Strange History of Arcadía

And black earth produced god-equalling Pelasgos
in mountains with long hair of tall trees
that a mortal race might come to be.

Asios of Samos (7th or 6th century BC)

The Arcadians' version of their origins may well reflect Neolithic tribal memories. They said they were descendants of Pelasgos, a son either of Mother Earth or Eurynome, the dancing goddess of all creation, who taught them how to make clothes from sheep skins, to build rude huts and eat acorns – modest achievements, even by ancient standards. But Arcadians would always be considered backward by their contemporaries. The name 'acorn eaters', bestowed by the Delphic oracle, had the same connotation as 'hayseed' does today.

Pelasgos produced enough sons (Mantineos, Orchomenos, and so on) to account for the names of most of Arcadía's ancient cities. His daughter Kallisto, impregnated by Zeus, turned into a bear by Hera, and promptly killed by Artemis, died producing a son, Arkos, thus explaining the name Arcadía to everyone's satisfaction (she was made into a constellation – the Great Bear, while Arkos became the Little Bear). Pelasgos' son Lykaion added a new cultural element when he introduced human sacrifice on Mount Lýkaio (*see* p.283). And here Arcadía shows her difference. While not ignoring the Olympian gods, she clung to earlier local cults and gods long after they had evolved into more sophisticated, rationalized entities elsewhere. Its lore has all the weird fascination of stories told around a camp fire: werewolves on Mount Lýkaio, the statue of a rapist near Orchomenos, Demeter sporting a horse head.

There was a large Mycenaean presence in Arcadía and, significantly, Mycenaean culture didn't disappear as abruptly after 1100 BC as it did on the coast. Whether the torch was held by the original inhabitants or by refugees from the coast, or both, is anybody's guess. What is a fact is that traces of the Mycenaean language found in the oldest written Arcadian dialect made John Chadwick and Michael Ventris realize that Linear B (*see* pp.352–3) must indeed be Greek.

In historical times Arcadian cities were often pawns in the rivalries of the likes of Sparta and Athens. The lack of useable land (and perhaps the independent highland spirit) constantly pitted local settlement against local settlement in wars that benefited no one in the long run. Thebes and Macedonia occupied Arcadía, partly to counter Sparta. Rome arrived and erected its usual decorations; the barbarians came and caused their usual destruction. The Franks built castles, the Turks took them away, and the wild area of Gortynía came into its own as a base of Greek resistance. In the 18th century, Arcadía was a populous place. Trípolis became the Turkish capital of the Peloponnese, the large mountain villages filled with freer spirits whom the Turks were content to leave more or less alone; some housed entire clans of freedom-fighting *klephts* whom the Turks never did find. After the revolution, rural Arcadía was left to its own devices, suffering a slow but steady decline in population.

mountains scored by rivers and deep gorges, and flat alpine valleys drained by sink holes. Arable land is scarce, drought and floods a constant threat. Such terrain could never support large numbers, and Megalopolis, the one artificial attempt at creating a great pan-Arcadian city-state, was a mega-flop.

The province was once rich in game – deer, bears and boars in particular – that were suitable company for Arcadía's uncouth, not quite anthropomorphized gods, such as Hermes and Pan. Rough shepherds compelled their children to learn music to soften the harshness of their existence. These few facts were enough for Virgil to spin his lyrical web; Arcadía became synonymous with the idealized pastoral life in his *Eclogues*. The idyllic representation was continued in the Renaissance and later by painters and poets. But the real Arcadía is far more stunning and as Alice would say, curiouser, than Poussin and Claude's painted imitations.

Upland Arcadía divides itself naturally into three main areas: **Trípolis and its plain**, **Megalopolis and surroundings** and **Gortynía**.

Trípolis

Home to 22,000, Trípolis is Arcadía's capital and its farming and industrial heavy-weight, producing textiles, building materials and leather products. A dense town without suburbs, it can feel like New York after you've spent a week in the wilds of Arcadía. They say its climate is one of the worst in Greece – too hot in summer, too cold and rainy in winter – and those are the residents talking, The three central *plateías* are giant roundabouts, with roads radiating out in every direction. This makes passing through an adventure as well as something of a necessity. One gets the feeling that the Tripolistiótes on their lonely plain rather enjoy compelling everyone travelling across the Peloponnese to run the gauntlet. Come on 23 September, when Trípolis celebrates its independence from the Turks, or for Easter in Plateía Areós .

History

Trípolis' history is short and bleak. It was the small village of Droboglitsa when the Turks took over in the 1700s and made it the seat of the Pasha of the Morea. They renamed it Tripolitsá, *Three Cities*, for the three ancient cities of Mantinea, Tegea and Pallantio – whose stones went into its building. By the late 18th century, Trípolis had 10,000 people, three quarters of whom were Greek, most of them involved in business, some of them very prosperous. When Veli Pasha arrived in 1807 with 12,000 Albanian and Turkish soldiers it became the biggest Turkish stronghold on the Peloponnese. That made it a prime target for Kolokotrónis (*see* p.285). In 1821 he took the town, and over 10,000 people were slaughtered in the subsequent three-day orgy of looting and slave-taking that in those days passed as army pay. Kolokotrónis wrote that when he entered Trípolis, his horse's hooves never touched the ground, so thick were the bodies. The plunder financed the war – one reason for Kolokotrónis' success and independence is that he invested his share wisely, in the banks of the then-British Ionian islands. The Turkish reprisal, a few months later, was the massacre of

Getting There and Around

The **highway** and the Artemision tunnel have cut the Athens–Trípolis journey to 2½hrs (the train is more dramatic but takes twice as long). Distances in the mountains are not great, but they can seem long because of the twisting roads and frequent stops for sheep or goats.

The **Arcadías bus station**, Plateía Kolokotrónis, t 271 022 2560, has the following connections: Athens, 12 daily (to the Kifissos station, t 210 513 2834); Megalópolis, nine daily; Pýrgos, two daily; Andrítsaina, 2 daily; Stemnítsa and Dimitsána twice a day and once on weekends; Vitína several times a day; Alonístaina twice; and Karítaina (bottom of the castle hill only) twice. For Messenía and and Laconía, the **KTEL bus station**, t 271 0 24 2086, is 400m east of the Arcadías station, opposite the train station. Buses ares: Sparta, 8 daily; Kalamáta, 12 daily; Pýlos, 5 daily; and Pátras, 2 daily. Local buses in Plateía Areós leave every hour to Mantinea and Tegea.

The **train station**, t 271 024 1213, is 400m east of Plateía Kolokotrónis. Trains go four times a day either to Naúplio–Corinth or to Kiparissía–Kalamáta.

All **roads** but one lead to and out of the centre of Trípolis and, once you get there, expect confusion and impossible parking.

Tourist Information

Tourist office: in the city hall on Ethnikís Antistaseos St, just north of Plateía Petrinou, t 271 023 1844; *open Mon–Fri 8.30–12.30.*

Where to Stay and Eat

Trípolis ✉ 22100

Trípolis' so-so hotels are central, open all year, and on busy streets. Tripolisiótes eat and drink in style, though. Deligiánni St, a pedestrian lane one block south of Plateía Areós, is the favourite watering hole for the under thirty set.

While in Trípolis, stock up on **Arcadian wines**. This area is one of the Peloponnese's finest growing areas, home of the well-known Cambas label, but also of some terrific smaller ones such as the Tsélepos estate near Tegea. Try their excellent white Mantinéia.

Arcadía, Plateía Kolokotrónis, t 271 022 5551, f 271 022 2464 (*B; moderate*). The smartest, with five parking spots in front on the square.

Menalon, Plateía Areós, t 271 022 2450 (*C; moderate–inexpensive*). Older, quieter, with high ceilings, balconies over the *plateía* and a charm that even the brown wallpaper cannot erase. Cars are banned in this square, but there is a car park in the rear.

Klimataria Piterou, 11a Kalavriton St, t 271 022 2058. Serves wonderful pork with celery and other delicious dishes.

Menalon, Plateía Areós, t 271 022 3442. Old fashioned, good food and a great location.

Mélathron (Μέλαθρον), 2km north of town on the Trípolis–Levídi highway, t 271 024 2148. Its drab location belies upscale amenities. Dine on succulent wild boar or rooster with pasta, around a kidney-shaped pool. Around €15 a head with wine.

25,000 Greeks on Chíos, and the enslavement of 47,000 more. Ibrahim Pasha got Trípolis back in 1825 and started his own reign of terror. When he was driven out, he destroyed what was left of the town. Not one inch of its old walls remain.

The Town and its Museum

The Trípolis that rose out of the blood and ashes is a lively place full of young people, thanks to Greece's largest military training base. It has some lovely squares, excellent restaurants and two parks, including an extensive pine forest on the west side of town. Its bland block architecture won't win any prizes, but the museum designed by Ziller, the courthouse and the Malliaropoúlio theatre are three lovely neoclassical exceptions to the rule. A magnificent equestrian **statue of Kolokotrónis** in his famous Frankish helmet lords it over Plateía Areós.

Trípolis' underrated **Archaeological Museum**, 6 Evangestrías Street, between Kolokotrónis and Ag. Basileiou Squares (*t 271 024 2148; open Tues–Sun 8.30–2.30; adm*), displays finds from all over Arcadía. It lists the contents of each numbered room in the foyer in English; when they get around to numbering the rooms, the system will work perfectly. There are wonderful finds from prehistoric Arcadía. The two four-handled, 3ft-high **clay storage jars** are unique to this museum. Sophisticated, with ripple patterns in the clay, they prove our 'acorn eaters' had enough leisure to enjoy artistic, not just utilitarian, creations. Along with early tools, there is a choice array of those tasty little **Neolithic fertility figurines**, or 'Venuses', so typical of the era.

The **Mycenaean pottery** found in the tombs at Paleókastro on the Alphíos River is exceptional. On the main floor, notice the fair-sized pot from tomb 7 with braided handles, fish and birds, and every kind of wonderful Mycenaean 'filler' design. Some finds raise questions about the Greek 'Dark Age'. The small, round-lidded pot from tomb 22, adorned with a pattern of lines and weaving-type motifs, looks Geometric, but is Mycenaean. And how about those big **fibulas** that scholars claim were introduced by the Dorians? Well, Mycenaeans wore them in Arcadía. This museum suggests a seamless continuity of habitation and gently reminds us that the more we learn about Greek history, the less we know. In the room to the far right of the entrance called 'Arcadian Sanctuaries' are **votive offerings**; small and sympathetic, they give some idea of the hope and devotion evoked by these shrines. There are interesting **Roman artefacts** too, especially from Hadrian's villa at Loutrá.

Around Trípolis: The Flood Plain and Water Wars

Ancient Tegea, Mantinea and Orchomenos occupy the same smallish flood plain, partially separated from each other by low barren hills. Dry and brown in summer, one writer likened the plain to a lunar landscape, an effect heightened by the scarcity of buildings. The citizens of these cities had the same obsession, displayed by so many city-states: to destroy each other whenever possible. Their very proximity, with no more than 35km between them in the relative isolation of Arcadía, makes the absurdity of Greek city-state rivalry especially poignant. Low-lying Mantinea and Tegea would stop up the others' river exits in order to flood their cities and grazing lands. Since most buildings were mud brick, it was an unedifying spectacle. No wonder the ruins of these three cities are not extensive.

As a footnote, there was a fourth city on the plain, **Pallántion**, just south of Trípolis. Only its name has survived, in our word 'palace' (its stones went into the building of Trípolis). Legend has it as the birthplace of the mysterious King Evander, son of Hermes, who founded a colony called Palatine on a hill over the Tiber. The Roman emperors believed in the connection, and accorded Pallántion privileges because of it.

Mantinéa: the Case of the Disappearing City

Mantinéa lies 12km due north of Trípolis off the Levídi road, and has a folly for a landmark: the church of **Ag. Foteiní**, a hodgepodge of bits of ancient Mantinea. Built between 1970 and 1978 in a quirky mix of Minoan, Classical and Byzantine styles, and dedicated to 'the Virgin, the Muses and Beethoven', it is opposite the ancient agora.

Excavations on Gourtsoúli, the rounded hill just north of the theatre, indicate an acropolis inhabited from the Geometric to Classical times. During the Persian Wars Mantineans fought beside Sparta, but, like all of Sparta's subjects, they tried to get out from under the big thumb whenever the coast looked clear. They took their chances with Athens in the Peloponnesian War, and in 418 BC were soundly trounced by Sparta in the First Battle of Mantinea. By this time, downtown Mantinea had moved from Gourtsoúli onto the flat plain by the then meandering Ophis (Snake) river and surrounded itself with high mud brick walls – another bad decision, but that wasn't obvious until 385 BC, when they rebelled against Sparta again. The Spartans trooped up, surveyed the situation and for once used their imagination instead of their phalanx. They dammed up the natural outflow of the Ophis, waited for the water to rise, and literally dissolved the city's defences.

The Mantineans regrouped and raised their mud-brick walls again after the Battle of Leuktra in 371 BC with the blessing of their new patron Epaminóndas of Thebes, but this time they prudently built the lower courses of stone. These walls were 4km in circumference, and had 122 towers. Mantinea, whose rulers were doggedly thick, turned against Thebes just in time to be soundly trounced by Epaminóndas in 362 BC in the Second Battle of Mantinea. In 223 BC the Macedonians took over and dissolved the city – politically this time. Built up again by the Romans in AD 125, it became a centre for the worship of Hadrian's deified boyfriend Antinous. The Mantineans equated his worship with Dionysos. Those were the days...

The Ruins

Mantinea (*always open; adm free*) is one of the oldest excavated sites in Greece, dug up in 1887–88 by Fougeres, who found it using Pausanias and the stunted growth of wild hashish as his guides. The low hump of the **theatre** is the most prominent ruin, with many of the large polygonal stones used to build up the cavea still in place as well as two stairways on its outer circumference. The two identical **temples** directly in front are Roman, and immediately to their south are the ruins of a **Temple to Hera**. Just north of the Roman temples is the **Hero's Shrine to Podares**, a monument that shows a certain greatness of soul since he *lost* the battle against Thebes in 362 BC. The entire area in front of the theatre is the **agora**, which still has traces of the paved roads and of the **bouleuterion** on its south side and **colonnades** on its north. Although the ruins are sparse, it gives an idea of the mix of shrines and buildings that could rub shoulders in a small area. Mentally add a score of plaques, statues, memorials, shops and huddles of Mantineans plotting their next blunder, and you get the idea. Stones from the lower courses of the city's walls are in the surrounding fields.

Orchomenos

Orchomenos' small valley lies in moody Wild West scenery between Levídi and Vlachérna, off the Trípolis–Pátras highway. Homer called it 'rich in sheep', and there are still quite a few mooching around. In the Classical period, Orchomenos often made alliances with Sparta or Athens, merely to spite Mantinea. It never moved entirely onto the flood plain and so has bequeathed some ruins to posterity. The small **acropolis** and **theatre** on a high hill enjoy grand views. Two **temples**, one to Apollo and one to Artemis higher up, plus a **bouleuterion** with a stoa and a cistern complete the picture. The small defile to the east has **Venetian towers** guarding what was once the ancient and medieval road to Pheneós, now passable only by jeeps or mules. It was on this road that Pausanias saw the monument to Aristokrates, who had raped the virgin priestess of Singing Artemis. Not only were monuments awarded for this, but the act itself was considered so natural that the Orchomeniótes decided to reduce the odds on its repetition by switching the job prerequisites: virgins were replaced by old married women well past their prime. Even Delphi had to do the same.

Tegea

Tegea, 7km south of Trípolis on the Sparta road, was a conglomerate of villages rather than a city. Famous for its dauntless warriors, Tegea considered itself especially favoured by Athena and built a splendid temple in her honour. One story goes that during the 600s BC when the Tegeans were proving less than enthusiastic allies, the Spartans came marching north to put things right. In a crude but typically Spartan gesture, they came bearing the chains they intended to use to truss up rebellious Tegeans to drag them home as slaves. With Athena's help, of course, the Tegeans routed the Spartans in the 'Battle of the Fetters'. The chains were triumphantly hung up in her temple alongside a tooth from the Caledonian boar. But even Athena's patronage couldn't prevent Tegea from becoming a vassal state to Sparta by 560 BC. The Tegeans tried to throw off the yoke on various occasions, didn't succeed, then astutely decided to side with them in the Peloponnesian War, unlike Mantinea. After Leuktra in 371 BC, Tegea joined the Arcadian League and stayed loyal to Thebes in 362 BC. It flourished under the Romans, was destroyed by Alaric in the 5th century, and sank into oblivion until 1209 when it was made the Frankish barony of Nikli.

Ancient Tegea covered a large area, and only a small part has been excavated. What civic buildings have been brought to light are in the middle of a work-a-day farming community which probably in many ways resembles the ancient city. The substructure of the famous **Temple of Athena Alea** is not far from the museum. Built in 370 BC and decorated by the great Skopas, it was second in size only to the Temple of Zeus at Olympia, with a Doric peristyle (6 by 14 columns) and an internal colonnade of Corinthian half columns with Ionic above, all made of local marble. The East Pediment depicted the Caledonian boar hunt and the huntress Atalanta, a native of Tegea who made good in spite of being exposed at birth because she was not male. The West Pediment depicted the fight between Telephos and Achilles. There is no sign of the chains, or boar's tooth: Augustus took the mighty cuspid to Rome to punish Tegea for siding with Antony and Cleopatra. The **theatre**, built in the 2nd century AD, is a 20min walk from the temple and somewhat difficult to see because the church of Palaiá Episkopí (built in 1888) was erected inside its cavea. This church replaced the earlier Byzantine chapel of Nikli and has preserved its venerated mosaic icons.

The Museum of Tegea and a Hmmm on Herms

Tegea's small **museum** (*t 271 055 6540; open Tues–Sun 8.30–3; adm free*) has marble **thrones** from the theatre, **acroteria** from the Temple of Athena Alea and part of its altar, all pretty standard fare. But two sets of stone **herms**, each about two feet high, are unique. Both consist of stone columns stuck together, one set having human heads on each column, the other mere triangular appendages. In the Classical period, herms were placed at crossroads all over the Greek world (apparently the number of herm columns indicated the number of roads leaving from the crossroads), but their usual form at that period was a column with a human head and *membrum virile* that you could hang your hat on. Their function was prophylactic, so they were also set outside houses to guard the entrance. Hermes became the patron saint of merchants because he guarded them on their travels, hence the name Ermoú Street (Hermes' Street) for the main commercial street in virtually every Greek town today. Hermes, unlike the other Olympians, never entirely shed his non-human form. He existed simultaneously as a stone column and as an anthropomorphic deity. In primitive Arcadía, where he originated, he kept his original form even longer than elsewhere.

The Megalópolis Valley and Around

At intervals in its history, areas of the Megalópolis valley would spontaneously catch fire because lignite deposits lie so close to the surface. This bonanza was exploited in the 20th century by power-starved Greece with the construction of two huge coal-burning power plants. From the surrounding hills, you'll catch sight of these

Getting Around

The Megalópolis **bus** station, **t** 279 102 2238, one block from the main *plateía*, has nine buses a day to Trípolis, several to Kalamáta, and two to Andrítsaina. A local bus goes into the villages of Karítaina and Lykosoura every day, but Vásta just gets one on Fridays. Happily, there is a **taxi** stand, **t** 279 102 2551, in the town square.

Where to Stay and Eat

Megalópolis ✉ 22200
The hotels in Megalópolis are open all year and close to the main *plateía*. They cater to businessmen, and for that reason alone they will probably be enchanted if you stay.
Apollon, 49 Tourlende and Kolokotrónis, t/f 279 102 4828 (*C; moderate*). The smartest in town, and comfortable.

Paris, 9 Ag. Nikolaou, **t** 279 102 2410 (*D; moderate–inexpensive*). Old-fashioned, family-run, just renovated and with TV and air-conditioning; offers more than its class suggests.
O Antónis. Fine food in the main *plateía*.
Isareiko Spiti, Ísaris, **t** 279 108 1200 (*inexpensive*). Simple rooms in a traditional *xenóna*, towering over the main square. The restaurant is famous for rooster with pasta and *kayianá*, a tomato omelette. *Open all year.*
Psistariá Nerómylos, Ag. Theodóra, **t** 279 108 1208. Not far from the church, with an old-fashioned wood-burning oven. They are open all year, but phone first.

Karítaina ✉ 22025
Kondopoúlos, **t** 279 103 1262 (*inexpensive*). Two plain rooms near the castle.
To Konaki, **t** 279 103 1600. Good food in a traditional setting.
Cafe Brenthe, **t** 279 103 1650. A surprisingly trendy bar and café.

fire-breathing behemoths at every turn. They rule the valley, digging huge pits to fuel themselves and creating Athens-level smog on the days when the wind doesn't blow.

Along with its own lacklustre ruins, Megalópolis offers a convenient base (it isn't *that* bad) for the much more interesting remains of ancient Lykósoura as well as two of Greece's strangest shrines: Ag. Theodóra and the summit of Mount Lýkaio. These, along with Karítaina to the northwest, are not visited as much as they deserve to be.

Megalopolis (Μεγαλοπολη)

After the Theban general Epaminóndas amazed the ancient world by defeating Sparta at Leuktra in 371 BC, he founded two new cities in the Peloponnese: Messene by Mount Ithóme and Megalopolis, both to act as bulwarks against future Spartan aggression. Megalopolis was to be a capital for a new Panarcadian League and, to populate his ancient Brasilia, Epaminóndas emptied 38 small cities. Anyone reluctant to move was either dragged there or killed, an inauspicious start for the 'Great City' and perhaps the reason why the league lasted only a few years, and why many of its citizens secretly preferred Sparta, which had at least left them slaves in their own towns. Many of these reluctant Megalopolítes would later support the Macedonian army when it invaded. Briefly repopulated in Roman times, Megalopolis then sank into oblivion, never really famous for much except its size.

The **ruins** lie on both banks of the Hellisón river, 1km north of town. The main attraction is the **theatre**, the largest in Greece, seating 21,000. Built in the 4th century, it had 59 rows of seats divided by 10 aisles. Its orchestra measures 99ft in diameter, but the only spectacle you're likely to see from the cavea is the belching saga of the power plants. Immediately in front of the theatre are the ruins of the square **council house** of the Panarcadian League, a nice symbolic reminder of the shambles of the league itself. Across the river are scanty remains of the city, still mostly unexcavated.

Under the smoke stacks, **modern Megalópolis** is an unassuming tiny country town with a lazy, nothing-much-ever-happens-here atmosphere. Sit in its central *plateía* and you can imagine you are back in 1965. About the most exciting event is the placement of three huge red plastic eggs, complete with yellow chicks, every Easter.

Around Megalópolis: Ag. Theodóra, Lykósoura and Lýkaio

The journey to these shrines offers lovely and quite different scenery. While it is just possible to rush down to Ag. Theodóra and then reverse to take in the other two in a single day, it would not be advisable unless you just want to say you did it. But Lykósoura and Mount Lýkaio are feasible in a one-day duet. Lunch possibilities are limited, so pack a picnic.

The starting point for all three is Apíditsa, on the Kalamáta road, 8km south of Megalópolis. There is a sign for **Ag. Theodóra**. Go 8km or so up to Ísaris; from here a twisty little road winds down from **Vásta** through a forest to a car park and kiosks touting religious bric-a-brac. Beyond that by the river is the tiny 10th-century **church of Ag. Theodóra**, with 17 large oak trees growing up from its slate roof. Walk around, take a peek inside (it only holds about eight people), and you will still see only a single root, about as thick as your wrist, to the left of the entrance. The rest are all thin as hairs and have somehow threaded their way *inside* the church walls between the roof and ground to form the miraculous canopy. Some claim that the origin of this miracle is the spring under the church, but the 'real' story began in the 9th century when each local family had to provide one son for a year to guard a nearby (now defunct) convent. Having no son or money to pay a substitute, Theodóra's parents dressed her as a man and sent her on guard duty. A nun became pregnant, and was locked up until she would reveal her lover's name. Only Theodóra showed her sisterly compassion. For this kindness she was accused of the crime and condemned. The nun, trying to protect her real lover, said nothing. Too ashamed to reveal her identity, Theodóra uttered only one prayer before she died: that her body become a church, that her flowing hair become trees and that her blood become a rushing river. When the horrified executioners realized their error, they built this church and the rest is history.

Lykosoura

*Site and museum, **t** 279 108 1344; open Tues–Sun 8.30–2; adm free.*

Lykosoura (head about 2km northwest of Apíditsa and then turn left) claimed to be the oldest city in the entire world. When the Thebans gathered the other Arcadian citizens to inhabit Megalopolis, they left the Lykosouriotes at home out of respect. Goat-legged Pan had an early oracle here before Apollo took over the prophecy business, and as late as Roman times a flame was kept eternally lit at his shrine for old time's sake. In the Classical period, visitors thronged here to the Mysteries celebrated at the Temple to the Mistress, or *Déspoina*, Arcadía's version of Persephone who, in their tale, was the daughter of Demeter and Poseidon. They claimed Demeter had turned herself into a mare to escape Poseidon's advances, but he turned himself into a stallion, and the result was 'Déspoina', the Maid, whose real name only initiates knew. The mysteries were similar to those at Eleusis, with vegetative symbols, baskets of fruit and so on, but with a theriomorphic, primitive undertone so typical of Arcadía. The ladies' dress code was found, inscribed in the stoa north of the temple: no provocative dress, no rings, no rich materials, no make up and no fancy hairdos.

The ruins and museum are at the top of a short, steep road on the south edge of town. From the vantage point of your arrival on the road, with the museum to the right, the **acropolis** covers the hill in front of you. The Temple of the Mistress is to the right, underneath the small museum. To your left, on the other side of the road, a path leads to a **bath** and **fountain** that probably belonged to a hotel. Some of the city **walls** are intact but buried in undergrowth and are most easily seen from the modern village on the road to Lýkaio. The substructure of the **Temple of the Mistress**, built in 180 BC to replace an earlier, smaller 4th-century one, measures 70ft by 28ft. It had six Doric columns on a paved mosaic porch and **three altars** in front. What intrigued punters in the old days was a mirror hung on the wall by the entrance, which blurred the reflections of those gazing into it, but revealed the cult statues a treat. On the south side an intriguing **'wall' of stepped stones** goes up the hill. They are believed to have been seats for spectators, whose eyes would have been glued to the unusual small doorway built into the side of the temple – surely something significant must have manifested itself during the Mysteries to account for this departure in design. The cult statue of Demeter and the Maid seated on a throne, with Artemis-cum-hound to the left and Anytos, the Titan who raised the Maid to the right, was carved by Damophón of Messene out of a single block of stone. If true, it must have been carved first and the temple built around it. Its total height was 19ft and it fits into the temple with only 19 inches to spare at the back and very little on the sides. Parts of this are in Athens, and other bits are in the small **museum**, along with curious clay votive offerings with human bodies and animal heads. The remains of the **long stoa** are visible beside the temple, and on the hillside in front, going up to the museum level, stood the multi-levelled **megaron** of Déspoina, where the votives were left.

Mount Lýkaio

Et in Arcadia Ego. As the expression goes, death exists, even in Arcadía, but even without werewolves and human sacrifice the isolated top of Lýkaio, or 'Wolf' Mountain, would be worth visiting (from Lykosoura, head on up past Áno Kariés; much of the road is unpaved, but it's a good road). The stupendous view reveals at least a third of the Peloponnese on a clear day. The dome-like summit, the deserted terraced fields, stone walls and slate grey huts create an austere backdrop for a shrine that goes back to the earliest Greek rain-making rites. Somewhere up here was a spring called Hagnos and, during droughts, the priest of Lykaion Zeus dipped an oak branch in it; hopefully, a mist would arise, and cover the mountain top and it would rain – sympathetic magic, pure and simple. Arcadians claimed that Zeus was born here, not in Crete, and during droughts the people of the plains would arrive here in such desperation that it was rumoured all through antiquity that human sacrifices were offered on Wolf Zeus' altar, a rite initiated by Lykaion, son of Pelasgos. And when a child was sacrificed, it changed into a wolf as its blood splashed on the altar.

Zeus, according to the more civilized Greeks, took umbrage at this, and turned Lykaion himself into a wolf and struck his house with lightning. When Lykaion's sons still brazenly offered Zeus a bowl of humble soup made from one of their brother's guts, he was so disgusted that he released too much rain – a flood, in fact, to kill off all humanity. But even these extreme measures failed to do the trick. Besides Deucalion and Pyrrha (the Greek Noah and his wife) a band of Parnassians survived the flood, migrated to Arcadía and, as soon as there was another drought, revived the wicked rites of Wolf Zeus. (No one seemed to mind the fact that Zeus comes out in this attempt to reconcile different traditions as a deranged schizophrenic.) A system of sorts developed on Mount Lýkaio: a shepherd, chosen by lot, would eat the soup prepared from the human sacrifice and turn into a werewolf. If he didn't kill anyone, he would regain his human shape after eight years. One famous ex-werewolf, Damarchus, went on after his eight-year stint to win the boxing at the Olympics.

The ruins are not up to much. Ascending after Áno Kariés, you come to a flat area containing the paltry bits of a 4th-century **stoa** and small **hotel**, a **Temple to Pan**, a **stadium**, and the very obvious **hippodrome**. If you walk up, you'll be inclined to think prizes should have been awarded just for getting here. The road ascends above the hippodrome and divides almost immediately. The left fork goes to the summit with the **altar** and **temenos**, near the little **church of the Profítis Ilías** (aka Elijah, the Christian version of the weather god, and quite fitting under the circumstances). The altar in Classical times was flanked by two columns surmounted by golden eagles that faced east and the rising sun. The image evoked seems more Hollywood than holy, but the two column bases and part of a column are still there to back up the story. Strange taboos surrounded this shrine. Part of it, no doubt the part struck by Zeus' lightning bolt, was fenced in by stones and no one was allowed to enter; it was *ávaton*. Those who did would lose their shadow and die within a year. Even animals wandering in would be seen to have no shadow, no matter what the time of year. The other fork continues quite a way further up to the very scarce remains of the Archaic **Temple of Parnassian Apollo**, just to the north of the church of Ag. Ioánnis which itself incorporates ancient stones. Also a weather shrine, a boar was sacrificed annually in Megalopolis and brought here to encourage the god to bring rain. Its bones and thighs were burned on the altar and the rest was cooked and eaten on the spot.

The Castle of Karítaina: 'the Toledo of Greece'

Northwest of the Megalópolis plain, the picture-perfect castle of **Karítaina** crowns a cone-shaped hill, dramatically overhanging the river 650ft below. The site of ancient Brenthe, it came into its own in 1254 when Hughes de Bruyères built the castle as a bulwark against the Slavic bands then living wild in Skorta (the medieval misnomer of ancient Gortys) just to the north. Hughes' son, Geoffrey, the Sire de Caritaine, was the flower of chivalry whose romantic exploits get full treatment in the *Chronicle of the Morea*; captured by the Greeks and held in Constantinople along with his lord, William de Villehardouin, Geoffrey charmed the emperor and was able to arrange for William's ransom. Although the castle looks impregnable, the Franks never gained control of the area and sold it in 1320 to Byzantine despot Andronikos II Paleológos. The Turks took over from 1460 until the War of Independence, when Kolokotrónis made it his headquarters. The last war-like use of the castle occurred during the Second World War when the Germans constructed gun emplacements to control the Andrítsaina road. The **castle**, a fine example of feudal fortifications, can be reached from the village by a short, steep path. In the east curtain wall, the main gate has a square niche over it, no doubt for the long-gone de Bruyères coat of arms. It is flanked on the north by a square tower topped by three stone brackets which would have held a platform for showering missiles on attackers. Once inside, an ascending vaulted passage leads to the triangular enceinte. On the south side, the ruins of a large, vaulted hall have four north-facing windows and a vaulted cistern in front.

The small **village** of Karítaina is made up of old houses with wooden balconies on narrow, winding streets. Towards the end of Turkish rule it was a prosperous town of over 35,000 with a soap and silk industry and water mills. It has two other souvenirs of the Franks. The separate bell tower of the 11th-century Byzantine **church of the Panagía** at the beginning of the town is the only Frankish-Italian architectural innovation that ever caught on in the Peloponnese. The second is the pretty **bridge** over the Alphiós. Originally of six arches, with a tiny chapel built on a

Theodore Kolokotrónis: Klepht and Warrior

Born in Messenía in 1770, to a clan that had never submitted to the Turks, Kolokotrónis became a *kapi* or leader, as his father had been before him, at the age of 15. Intelligent, shrewd and with exceptional natural ability, he inspired great love among his followers. When the uprising in the Mani started, Kolokotrónis went to Karítaina and gathered his men, many of whom called him king. He was largely responsible for the victories in the Peloponnese during the War of Independence. He took Trípolis from the Turks in 1821, defeated Dramali at Dervenáki in 1822 and was sent to lead the fight against Ibrahim Pasha, even though the other Greek leaders were as sceptical of his motives as he was of theirs. Kolokotrónis fortified Karítaina at his own expense in 1825 and made it his headquarters. He took to wearing a Frankish helmet he found buried there; it would become his trademark. Ibrahim Pasha's reign of terror was the low point of the war. Ibrahim insisted on papers of submission from the terrified towns and, fearing death or worse, they gave them. Then Kolokotrónis came promising the same for any town who did not take them back. He realized that these 'submissions' would be used politically by Turkey to claim that ordinary Greeks were against independence. It seems as if every town in Arcadía has a story of Kolokotrónis arriving either to encourage – or to punish.

It was a brutal and horrible phase in a brutal and horrible war, fought out under medieval, not Marquess of Queensberry, rules. At this time Kolokotrónis was offering a dollar apiece for Turkish heads, an echo of the Turks' own method of verifying and rewarding their soldiers' kills. Many a headless body, including Kolokótronis' own father, was buried by a family while the head was piled in the enemy's gruesome trophy display. From Karítaina he conducted a resourceful guerrilla war without enough men, supplies or ammunition until the decisive Battle of Navaríno Bay ended the nightmare. After the war, Kolokotrónis found favour with Capodístria, but after the latter's assassination he was arrested, kept in solitary confinement for months, charged with treason and condemned to death – a not uncommon fate for Greek military leaders. He was pardoned five months later by King Otto because of his service and because his popularity would have made it imprudent to do otherwise.

Soldier, warlord, rogue, 'Kolokotrónis, with all his faults and virtues, is one of the leaders of our race,' wrote Kazantzákis, and his frank autobiography makes gripping reading to anyone who wants to understand the complexities of modern Greek history and the Greek character. One thing is certain; he had style. When Otto arrived in Naúplio, Kolokotrónis grandly offered him Karítaina as a personal gift. What more royal gesture could there be than that from one 'king' of a castle to another? And what better example of submission to the new Greek political reality? When he died in 1843, he was affectionately known to all as the Old Man of the Morea.

middle pier, it was later reduced to four. Now it sits forlorn under the modern bridge. Locals claim that the castle is haunted by de Bruyères; if so, the wrong ghost is in residence. The dominating spirit here was the more powerful and charismatic Theodore Kolokotrónis.

Gortynía

Named after ancient Gortys, this corner of Arcadía has rugged alpine scenery and stupendous monasteries. Here the Ládon, the Erýmanthos and the Loúsios leave precipitous north–south ravines and rush into the fertile Alphiós valley. The forested and craggy mountains were a refuge in times of trouble and a bandit enclave all of the time. This is Kolokotrónis country; no Turk ever entered willingly. But today you can, and at any time of year. Vitína, Dimitsána and Stemnítsa make wonderful bases; the more adventurous may prefer the *xenónas* in the hamlets. Ideally, spend a few days and loop back around on the spectacular Vitína–Stemnítsa road.

Stemnítsa

Bustling and lively Stemnítsa (Slavic for 'forested area') has the most beautiful collection of stone houses in the Peloponnese. They sit in tiers on a steep precipice, while one long main street overlooks the Loúsios Gorge to the west and the Megalópolis valley to the south. Keep your eyes open for some of its 18 churches, especially the 12th-century **Panagía ee Baféro**, **Ag. Nikólaos** and the 15th-century **Zoodóchos Pygí**. The substantial grey houses have blank walls on the lower floors (storerooms and stables) and living quarters on top. It was 'Queen for a Day' in 1821 when it was declared the capital of Greece. Many Peloponnesian towns had this honour, showing just how unclear the geography of the new Greek state was as independence was established, but Stemnítsa was *numero uno*. Always famous for its metalwork, it now has a school for gold and silversmiths attended by students from all over Greece. Housed in a renovated five-sided building in the centre, it looks quite grand with black and gold double doors. Several shops sell its products. Stemnítsa is famous for sweets, especially *skaltsoúnia* (little socks), a clam-shaped pastry filled with walnuts and honey and then covered in sugar.

Dimitsána, the Loúsios Gorge and Ancient Gortys

The 'balcony of the Loúsios', lovely Dimitsána has the most dramatic setting of Gortynía's villages, piled on a 3,150ft amphitheatre high over the gorge. It stands on the site of ancient Teuthys, the walls of which can be seen here and there among the handsome stone buildings of the upper town. Substantial, even in the 11th century, it became a centre of learning during the Turkish occupation. Today, Dimitsána is the main town in the Gortynía, with banks and a post office. There is a **museum** (*t* 279 503 1219; open Mon–Fri 9–1.30; adm free) displaying rare old books, a collection much diminished in the War of Independence when their pages were pirated by guerrillas to make cartridge cases. Dimitsána's water mills, which once numbered over 90, functioned as tanneries, grain mills, *nerotrivés* to wash blankets and rugs, distilleries making *tsípoura*, and, from 1700 on, as factories for making gunpowder. This area is now a **Water Mill Museum** (*t* 279 503 1630; open Wed–Mon, summer 10–2 and 5–7, winter 10–4; adm); it has videos in English and sells a cultural map of the area.

The narrow, wild and beautiful **Loúsios Gorge** extending from Dimitsána to Karítaina is criss-crossed in places by unpaved roads, now slowly being asphalted,

Getting There and Around

Buses sporadically connect the villages from Trípolis (**t** 271 022 2560), Megalópolis and Kalávrita. Vitína gets several a day; Dimitsána and Stemnítsa, two; Alonístaina and Chrisovítsi, one. **Taxis** can be got in Dimitsána, **t** 279 503 1237, and Vitína, **t** 279 508 3359, **t** 279 503 1100, or **t** 279 502 2619. **Hikers** love the Loúsios Gorge, and **cyclists** will enjoy the 24km road linking Vitína to Stemnítsa via Eláti.

Where to Stay and Eat

Hotels are more expensive in winter, especially on weekends and holidays.

Stemnítsa ✉ 22024

Trikolonion, t 279 508 1297, **f** 279 508 1483 (*C; inexpensive*). Built of stone in the traditional style by the town. Breakfast is included in its low price. *Open all year.*

Stemnitsa Restaurant, t 279 508 1371. In the main square beside the bell tower. Traditional hearty mountain fare.

Maria Baroutsa. A small coffee shop at the back of Ag. Geórgios church in the main square. Try her wonderful sweets, especially the *skaltsoúnia*.

Dimitsána ✉ 22007

Dimitsána, t 279 503 1518, **f** 271 023 9061 (*C; moderate*). On the south edge of town; roomy, convenient, and nicely situated, but missing something nonetheless.

Georgos Belisaropoulos, t 279 503 1617 (*moderate–inexpensive*). Offers several rooms with a view high up in the main part of town.

Vasilis Tsiapa, t 279 503 1583 (*inexpensive in summer, moderate in winter*). Rooms with kitchenette, bath, and TV, in a wonderful old stone house with a living room and fireplace, overlooking the Loúsios Gorge; parking nearby.

O Tholos, t 279 503 1514. The Polýxronos family offers good food in a barrel-vaulted room in the centre of town. *Open Thurs–Sun in winter and daily in summer.*

Psistaria Demitsana, t 279 503 1680. Small, family-run, at the bottom of the town hill, with great charcoal-grilled lamb.

Vitína ✉ 22010

Mainalon Art Hotel, t 279 502 2217, **f** 279 502 2200 (*C; expensive, breakfast inc.*). Right in the centre of town, new and well appointed.

Aigli, t 279 502 2216 (*C; moderate–inexpensive*). Attractively renovated, with a restaurant and bar. *Open only in winter, Thurs–Sun.*

Sinoi, t 279 502 2354 (*inexpensive, on holidays moderate*). Central, small, plain rooms in the upstairs of a private house; also a small living room with fireplace and TV for guests.

Taverna Klimatariá, t 279 502 2226. An old favourite; has two dining rooms, each with a fireplace and lots of dishes to choose from.

Vitina Club, 1km west of town, **t** 279 502 2960. Posh café-restaurant with a big pool.

The Small Villages of Gortynía

Kentrikon, Langádia ✉ 22003, **t** 279 504 3221, **f** 279 504 3221 (*C; inexpensive*). North of Dimitsána. Cheap for its class, with TV and a lift (there are enough stairs in the village). It has a taverna complete with fireplace and its own barrelled wine.

Xenónas Kosmopoulos, Valtesiníko ✉ 22026, **t** 279 508 2350 (*moderate*). In a lovely old stone house with wooden floors, facing a forested mountainside west of Vitína.

Kyriákos Katsigiánnis Xenónas, Nimfasía, mobile **t** 694 024 8488 (*inexpensive*). 2km north of Vitína; comfortable, new; en suite, but the nightingales may keep you awake.

Xenónas Theoxénia, Alonístaina ✉ 22100, **t** 271 073 1363 or **t** 210 360 0829 (*expensive*). South of Vitína, a renovated, neoclassical house tucked in a narrow mountain pass. *Open all year; in winter weekends and holidays only.*

meaning the dreaded tour buses will eventually be able to enter. The best place to see the river is from ancient Gortys, the best place to see the entire gorge is from Dimitsána or Zátouna, and the best way to explore it is to take the roads to the monasteries. It is possible to get to the Prodrómou monastery from Stemnítsa, and to the Philosóphou from Zátouna and Márkos, but both, along with the Emialón, can be reached from the road between Dimitsána and the Dimitsána hotel. If you choose only one monastery, choose Philosóphou, just for its location.

The **Emialón** (*t 279 503 1273*), the most accessible of the big three, is built into a rock face, 3km south of Dimitsána. A road goes to it from the water mill museum. Built in 1625 on the ruins of an older monastery, it is worth a look, and would be considered spectacular were it not for its two neighbours. Robes for visitors hang at the entrance.

Large **Prodrómou** (*t 279 503 1279*) was founded in 1167, again at the base of a huge rock, on the east side of the gorge. Its frescoes date from the 16th century. Kolokotrónis used it as a refuge and it was also a hospital for the wounded during the War of Independence (note the bullet holes in the door). Some of the monks fought in the war and the monastery, once wealthy, gave much of its gold to the cause.

The **Philosóphou** (*t 279 508 1447*) is so close to the edge of the west side of the gorge that it looks ready to spill into it. Approaching it from the gorge, you cross the Loúsios on a lovely old stone bridge. What you see on arrival is the church of the 'new' monastery, dating from 1691, with excellent frescoes. The cells have disappeared. A guest house is being built for pilgrims, but it's no place for sleep walkers. The original monastery, built in 927, is 400m away, clinging to a niche at the base of a huge rock.

Ancient Gortys is best reached by a 4km unpaved road from **Ellinikó**. Park beside the river near the old stone bridge. The site is extensive; Gortys' **acropolis**, in ruined walls from the Macedonian period, is a half-hour walk above Atsícholos. Other ruins on the west bank of the river include the **Asklepeion** where Alexander was said to have dedicated his breast plate and spear. According to myth, the Loúsios, 'the wash', was the place where Zeus' swaddling clothes were cleaned. It was also said to be the coldest river in the world, so put your picnic wine in to cool before you do the archaeology bit.

West of Dimitsána: an Excursion into the Alphiós River Valley

This itinerary into the heart of rural Arcadía could allow a visit to Bassae (*see* p.236) if you get an early start. A lookout at the 4km mark just before the attractive village of **Zátouna** offers the best panoramic view of the **Loúsios Gorge**. Go on via **Ráptis** and **Kakouraíka**, cross the river to **Daphnoúla** and go on to **Andrítsaina** and **Karítaina** from there. These roads pass through small working mountain villages; donkeys abound, and so do villagers in straw hats and women dressed in black. The lower Alphiós valley is Mycenaean country, and at **Paleókastro** many Mycenaean tombs were found.

Northwest of Dimitsána: Langádia and Ancient Thelpousa

On the main road to Olympia, **Langádia** is reminiscent of one of Italo Calvino's fantastical *Invisible Cities*. Its old stone houses are built in an almost perpendicular, vertiginous setting (*langádia* means ravine) in a bleak, forbidding landscape. Even in death, the inhabitants cannot escape the vertical; the town cemetery is built on four levels, counting the church. Langádia offers two interesting side trips. The first takes you 13km west of town, then 2km north, to **Vizíki**, and then even further north to the pretty lake formed by the **Ládon Dam**. A 3km detour due east of Vizíki on a dirt road (ask for *to kástro* in town) leads to the picturesque ruined castle at **Akova**. For the second possibility, head 22.5km west of Langádia and turn north for a scenic drive up the Ládon river to ancient **Thelpousa**. Once you find the sign follow these directions carefully: go 500m on the signposted road, past a small farm house, then turn left for 200m and left again (don't go farther up the hill) for 50m. You will be rewarded with a ruined **Roman bath** and a marvellous view over the Ládon river. The river is wide here and has plenty of sand bars, reminiscent of Milton's 'by sandy Ladon's lilied banks'.

Vitína and Mount Maínelon

Little Vitína, with its dark grey stone houses, had a sanatorium in the 19th century and has been something of a resort ever since because of its dry and cool climate. It occupies a flat, open meadow under Mount Maínelon, whose looming dark fir forests form a stunning backdrop in winter when coated with snow. Small shops flog Vitína's wood carvings, ranging from the mesmerizingly tacky to beautiful pieces in olive wood. Nearby **Mount Maínelon** (6,500ft) was sacred to Pan; its wooded slopes once crawled with tortoises but no one touched them because they belonged to the god. Maínelon's current charmed species are snow bunnies who crowd the slopes at **Ostrakína** wherever there is enough snow. Maínelon is not ready to challenge the Alps, but there are plans to expand, and the 10km road to it south of Levídi is always ploughed. There is a 50-bed **refuge** at Ostrakína and lots of gorgeous scenery. For information, contact the Trípolis Alpine Club at 6 Ag. Konstantinou St, **t** 271 023 2243.

The 'balcony of the Morea', **Magoúliana** is 10.5km northwest of Vitína and the highest village in the Peloponnese; the coffee shop under huge plane trees has the view. The church of the **Panagía** in the lower village has an elaborate wooden iconostasis, a reminder that this local craft was honed over centuries into an art. After Magoúliana, the road ascends, affording the kind of views you usually get from a small plane, and then descends to **Valtesiníko**, a going concern in the Frankish period, and on to meet the Vitína road 4km east of Langádia.

South of Vitína through the Forest to Stemnítsa

The magnificent paved road linking Vitína (west of town) and Stemnítsa should not be missed. It winds majestically through a full-grown forest, where that old saw about sentinel pines is absolutely true for miles and miles. At about the 12km mark an unpaved road detours to **Libovísi**, the village that the Kolokotrónis clan called home. The Turks never did locate it. A small, sometimes open, one-room **museum** (*free*) has been set up in a typical home of the period, complete with a Kolokotrónis *fustanella* (gun) in a glass case and family pictures. The whitewashed family church still stands. And that's it. This village, once populated by 60 families, has returned to nature. The scenery is grand, especially the view to the east. The main forest road then leads past some seriously monied private mountain retreats and on to Stemnítsa.

The Arcadian Coast: Kynouría and the Tsakonians

Cut off from the rest of Arcadía by the wild sierra of Mount Párnonas, the eparchy of Kynouría was terra incognita until recent years, accessible only by mule path or by sea. And, like the Maniátes, who claim Spartan descent, the Kynouríans are believed to be a race apart, hardly a single malt but one blended by Greece's many invaders. Their soft, rich language, Tsakoniká, still widespread a century ago, has been intensely studied by linguists. A German professor named Thiersch devoted his life to it, and found that while many words were similar to ancient Dorian, its basic structure predates even the Dorians, with elements going back to the early-Bronze Age Pelasgians. By 1573, the Tsakonians are recorded in Constantinople as 'a people not understood by the rest of the Greeks'. A number of older people still speak Tsakoniká fluently and there is a proposal to teach it in schools. It may be too late. Kynouría's isolation has ended: a coastal road is being dynamited into the crinkle-crankle coast south of Poúlithra, and the master-blasters are back every summer, extending it another few yards towards Kápsala in Laconia. Except for the occasional yacht flotilla from Spétses, Kynouría is as yet relatively unknown but, with its dramatic mountains and sandy beaches on the Myrtóan Sea, it will not stay unknown for long.

From Trípolis to the Coast

The main road from Trípolis to Kivéri heads straight east, then past **Mount Pathenío** (on your right), the second Arcadian mountain sacred to Pan, and one where the goat-footed one made a famous cameo appearance: in 490 BC, as the Athenian runner Pheidippedes was carrying news of the Persian invasion to Sparta, he encountered Pan. Unlike the Spartans, Pan offered to help, and was duly seen by the outnumbered Athenians at Marathon, panicking (his contribution to the English language) the Persians. About 3km east of Agiorgítika are the ruins of **Mouchli**, a Byzantine fort inherited by the Franks and destroyed in 1460. Ancient **Hysiai**, a mile or so from **Achladókambos**, has disappeared apart from some handsome polygonal walls around the acropolis. Stop for a coffee 3km further down for the grand view over the Argolic Gulf and to steel yourself for the loop-the-loops curling down to Kivéri. Little roadside shrines mark each bend in the road. These mark accident sites and close calls as well as the proximity of a church, and in this case the former seems to be the rule.

Parálio Ástros

South of Kivéri, a corniche road skirts the sea cliffs before descending to the orchards of the Thyreatic Plain and the easygoing village of **Parálio Ástros**, out on a spit of land shared by a minor Frankish castle and scant ruins of ancient Nisi. Newer villas mingle with old houses, overlooking a horseshoe port with plenty of ducks, while on either end of the village are beaches, one sandy and one pebbly. **Ástros**, 3km inland, is best known for its juicy peaches; 4km inland on the Trípolis road, the **Moní Loukoús** stands next to a ruined Roman aqueduct; visit the nuns to see their garden and Byzantine church from the 1100s, a collage of pagan temples, with ancient reliefs embedded in the walls next to ceramic plates. A road twists up to **Prastós**, in Turkish times the centre of Tsakonia, once the subject of numerous ballads. It is deserted now except for one elderly couple. In still lively **Kastánitsa** across the ravine are some of the best decorated churches in the area, and some wonderful stone houses.

Getting Around

Buses from Trípolis and Athens go down the coast: for information in Athens, t 210 513 2834; Tyrós, t 275 704 1467; Leonídio, t 279 102 2255. Hydrofoils link Tyrós and Leonídio to Piraeus (t 210 428 0001), Portochéli, and other eastern Peloponnesian ports; local agents are P. Politis, Paralía Tyrós, t 275 704 1692, and S. Kounia, Pláka Leonidíou, t 279 102 2206.

Tourist Information

Atrapós, on Tyrós Beach, t/f 275 704 1713. Devoted to environmental tourism.

Where to Stay and Eat

Parálio Ástros ✉ 22001

Crystal, t 275 505 1313 (C; moderate). A block in from the beach, with a restaurant, bar, air-conditioning and balconies; rather spartan rooms sleep 2–6. Open all year.
Golden Beach, t 2755051294 (D; inexpensive). Typical seaside hotel, with air-conditioning. Open all year.
Remezzo, t 275 505 1494. By the marina, with the best food in town – onion soup, a wide variety of salads, seafood, pizzas and more. Open 20 May–20 Oct.

Kastánitsa

Xenonas Andoníon, t 275 505 2296, info@sun-mountain-snow.gr (expensive). A fine, renovated old house. Breakfast is included; nice view across the ravine. Open all year.

Paralía Tyroú and Around ✉ 22300

Kamvissis, t 275 704 1242, f 275 704 1685 (C; moderate). Most rooms have sea views and so-so wallpaper. Open all year.
Four Stars Rooms, t 275 704 1437 (inexpensive). All the Kótsyfa family rooms have balconies with sea views. Open April–Oct.
Zaritsi Camping, t 275 704 1429 (inexpensive). In a sandy cove; very agreeable with a restaurant, bar, kitchen and watersports.
Taverna Manoleas, Livádi, t 275 706 1092 (inexpensive). Simple rooms to rent all year and delicious aubergine dishes, prepared to traditional recipes.

Leonídio and Around ✉ 22300

Ta Kamaria, t 275 702 2395 (C; expensive, sometimes moderate). Isolated by the sea in Lakkós; good for families, with flats, tennis, volleyball and a garden. Open April–Oct.
Diónysos, t 275 702 3455 (D; moderate). In Pláka Beach in an old ice factory; nearly all rooms overlook the beach. Open all year.
N. Troúbas Rent Rooms, t 275 702 3660 (inexpensive). In Pláka; a bargain.

Restaurants in season will regale you with dishes featuring the King of Eggplants.
Taverna Mouria, Leonídio, t 275 702 3292. Has delicious mezédes, kid baked in paper, mountain greens and sautéed potatoes, all washed down with barrelled wine.
Michael-Margaret, Pláka, t 275 702 2379. Right on the water, and in the same spot since 1830, serving seafood on its wide veranda; specialities include mussel pilaf, stewed octopus and baked aubergine 'special imam with cheese'.
Café Pizza Panorama, Pláka, t 275 702 3366. Offers lovely views over the bay, pies made in a real Italian pizza oven and those delicious honey-drippers, loukoumádes.

Poúlithra ✉ 22300

Akrogiali, t 275 705 1262, f 275 705 1501 (expensive–moderate). Traditional, with quiet studios and a lovely view of the sea.
Andréas Stágias, t 275 705 1466 (moderate). Air-conditioned studios and apartments in season, sleeping up to four people.
Zavalis, t 275 705 1341. In a pretty setting by the beach; good homecooking.
Heraklis, t 275 705 1480. By the port; specializes in mezédes, fish and aubergines.

Kosmás ✉ 22300

Maleatis Apollon, t 275 703 1484 (moderate–inexpensive). Handsome restored mansion of 1876, with traditional-styled rooms sleeping up to four. Good restaurant.
Kosmas Studios, t 275 703 1483 (moderate–inexpensive). Well-equipped rooms with kitchenettes and TVs; warm in the winter and cool in the summer.
Taverna Elatos, t 275 703 1427. Next to the plateía's lion fountain. Try the charcoal-grilled lamb, local pasta and tasty dishes from the traditional oven.

South of Ástros, and **Ag. Andréas**, the mountains close into the sea; little shingle coves offer a chance for a swim or a quiet place to sleep in rooms or campsites. The cliffs give way briefly at **Tyrós**, the modern centre of the Tsakoniká language, to allow for terraces of olives, a beach, a port and some low-key development under its ruined windmills. Further south, a by-road leads up to **Mélana**, which claims to be a 'typical Dorian village'. The coastal road then passes the sandy coves at **Livádi** and **Sambatikí**, and winds down to a dramatic change of scenery at Leonídio.

Leonídio and Poúlithra: Aubergine Country

A vertical wall of red cliffs rings whitewashed **Leonídio** and its emerald coastal oasis, the 'garden of Dionysos' according to Pausanias, although vines are not the main crop now: this is the home of long, pale, purple-striped *tsakónikis melanzánas*, the *ne plus ultra* of aubergines. Tiny ones are used to make a sweet called *melitzanáki leonidíou*. A late August aubergine festival attracts chefs from across Greece, who compete to use them in the tastiest and most original dishes. Leonídio is a fine old town (note the Greek welcome sign, Καλας ηλθατε, written in Tsakoniká, Καουρ εκανετε), but not one designed for all the traffic funnelling through around the tightest corners; a series of mirrors somehow manages to prevent collisions, and the bottlenecks caused by any bus or truck offers much amusement to *kafeneíon* habitués. Most visitors stay by the sandy beaches, **Lákkos** and **Pláka**, on either end of town; Pláka, the site of ancient Prasiae, with its little port, friendly geese and protected sandy beach, wins the charm prize – a great place to hole up for a few days and do nothing.

At one point, however, make the loop south of Leonídio: a so-so unpaved road leads up the cliffs to the **Moní Ag. Nikoláou Sínitzas**, a monastery built by a cave. On a clear day you can see Spétses, Spetsopoúla and Hýdra. All around the monastery are the ruins of hermitages in the cliffs. Circle down from here to **Poúlithra**, with another long white sandy beach. The mountain villages above Poúlithra – **Peletá** and **Pigádi** – have lovely views, and from **Choúni** there's a panoramic unpaved road to Kosmás.

From Leonídio to Kosmás

Until the road engineers conquer the coastal mountains, the only way to head south of Leonídio is by way of the mountain road to Kosmás. After about 20 minutes, you'll see, hanging high overhead, the vertiginous **Moní Panagía Élona**, founded around 1500 to house a miraculous icon – one of the 70 supposedly painted by St Luke. Frequently burned, the church was last rebuilt in 1809, and in 1821 the monks joined the War of Independence. Besides the superb natural setting, Élona, a convent since 1972 (*open dawn to dusk – ring the bell if necessary*), has a chapel containing a fine carved iconostasis as well as the famous icon, all clad in silver, and a holy spring.

From Élona the road winds up to **Kosmás**, 'the balcony of Kynouría'. Surrounded by orchards, Kosmás has a perfect *plateía* encircling its stone church, ringed by *kafeneíons* under enormous plane and horse chestnut trees, next to a splashing lion's head fountain. The ancient name of the region was Maleas, and in recent years an Archaic bronze statue of Apollo Maleatis was found in the village, and carted off to the National Museum in Athens. The road continues to Geráki (*see* p.306).

Laconía

Níkos Kazantzákis was so overcome by Laconía's beauty that he proposed a theory about the relationship between the landscape and the human soul. Some cultural gene must have been at work, he mused, that allowed the Mycenaeans to see only the green and fertile valley, and the Spartans only the implacable chasm of Kaiádas. How else could the same Eurótas valley produce both perfumed Helen and Sparta, a single-minded culture of war and death?

Since Laconía's men have always been Greece's proudest, toughest *hombres*, we can only assume that the hard and flinty gene has dominated, just as the region's two mountain ranges dominate its horizons. Spine-chilling Taíyetos and its rough and tumble sidekick Párnonas stretch their mighty vertebrae south to give the Peloponnese its middle and eastern peninsulas. Monemvasiá's position as the Gibraltar of the east ensured its unique history; the Máni, the last refuge of the unwanted and hunted, is in a dazzling class by itself, as is Mystrá, the last outpost of the Byzantine empire. But it was the Spartans, the most famous Peloponnesians of them all, who made their name synonymous with Laconía.

Sparta

Sparta. The very name still has the power to make you stop slouching and sit up straight. Get to know her, however, and words like paranoia, weird and '1984' come to mind. Tracing its development is not easy. The 'laconic' Spartans, after a brief cultural fling in the Archaic period, seldom bothered to immortalize their attitudes in print or stone. It was their enemies, the Athenians looking at Sparta through the lens of their own experiment in radical democracy, who made Sparta famous and every succeeding age has given Sparta the meaning it chooses.

History

Homer called it Hollow Lacedaimon. Tucked down in the Eurótas river valley, between Taíyetos and Párnonas, it was inhabited in Neolithic times and went on to become an important Mycenaean centre. From here Paris stole Helen from Menelaos, igniting the Trojan War. The Spartans were part of the Dorian push into the Peloponnese some time after 1200 BC. But while most of their fellow Dorians settled down, built splendid cities, fostered the arts and founded colonies, Sparta, never big on foreign travel or architecture, focused instead on Messenía, her neighbour to the west, and conquered her in two bitter wars (743–24 BC and 685–68 BC). They also put in place the world's very first constitution, the great Rhetra, supposedly handed to them by Lykourgos, a legendary king (or god – they weren't sure). The lynchpin of this 8th-century document was the total equality between free citizens, the Spartiátes, who lived in a loose conglomeration of five townships around their low acropolis. One feature was the dual kingship, one king being chosen from the Agiad family and and one from the Eurypontids, two clans who traced their ancestry back to Heracles and were forbidden by law to intermarry. Once elected, the kings functioned as judges,

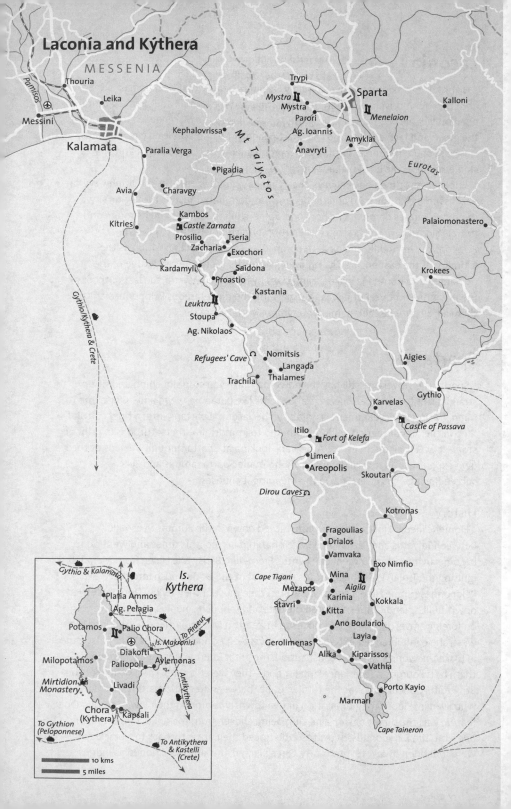

Laconia and Kýthera

MESSENIA

Pamisos

Thouria

Leika

Messini

Kalamata

Kephalovrissa

Paralia Verga

Mt Taïyetos

Trypi

Mystra Ⅱ
Mystra

Parori

Ag. Ioannis

Anavryti

Amyklai

Sparta

Kalloni

Menelaion Ⅱ

Eurotas

Pigadia

Avia

Charavgy

Kambos

Kitries

Castle Zarnata

Prosilio   Tseria

Zacharia

Exochori

Kardamyli

Saidona

Proastio

Kastania

Palaiomonastero

Krokees

Leuktra Ⅱ

Stoupa

Ag. Nikolaos

Gythio/Kythera & Crete

Refugees' Cave Ω   Nomitsis

Langada

Thalames

Trachila

Aigies

Karvelas

Gythio

Itilo

Fort of Kelefa 🏰

Castle of Passava 🏰

Limeni

Areopolis

Skoutari

Dirou Caves Ω

Kotronas

Fragoulias

Drialos

Vamvaka

Exo Nimfio

Mina Ⅱ

Aigila

Karinia

Kokkala

Kitta

Ano Boularioi

Layia

Gerolimenas

Alika   Kiparissos

Vathia

Porto Kayio

Marmari

Cape Taineron

Cape Tigani

Mezapos

Stavri

Gythio & Kalamata

Is. Kythera

Platia Ammos

Ag. Pelagia

Potamos

Palio Chora Ⅱ

To Piraeus

Is. Makronisi

Milopotamos

Diakofti

Paliopoli

Aylemonas

Mirtidion Monastery 🏰

Livadi

Antikythera

Chora
(Kythera)   Kapsali

To Gythion
(Peloponnese)

To Antikythera
& Kastelli
(Crete)

10 kms

5 miles

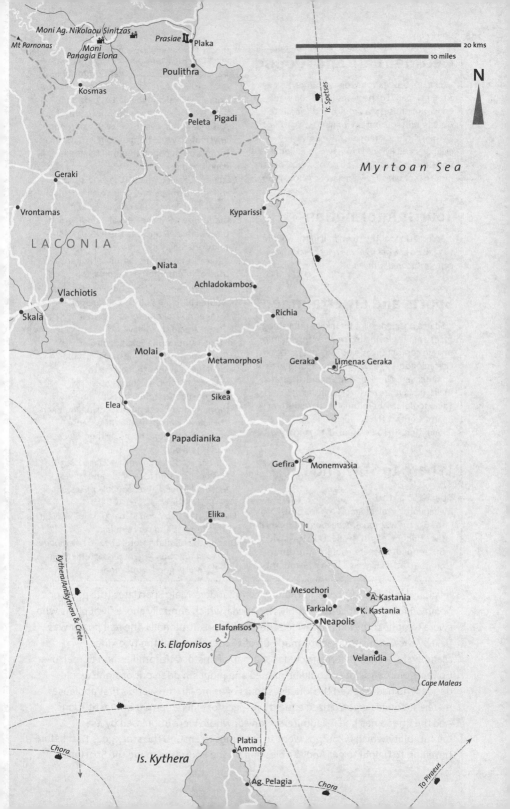

Getting There and Around

Sparta's **bus** station is on Lykoúrgou St, **t** 273 102 6441. Daily connections (fewer on weekends): nine buses via Corinth and Trípolis to Athens' Kifissoú Station (**t** 210 512 4913); five to Gýthio; three to Areópolis, Monemvasiá, Neápolis and Pýrgos Diroú; two to Kalamáta and Geroliménas. **Taxis**, **t** 273 102 4100. For **car hire**, try Kotsáras, 50 Menélao, **t** 273 102 9966.

Tourist Information

Second floor of the town hall in the square, **t** 273 102 6772; *open Mon–Fri 8–2*. Pick up a copy of *Laconía's Traveller*.

Sports and Entertainment

Sparta has done a lot for **hikers**, publishing maps and improving old mule paths; for information contact the Alpine Club of Sparta, 97 Gortsológou, **t** 273 102 2574. The **Sparta Artistic Summer** sees Greek drama and music, and modern plays are performed at the **Sainopoúleion Amphitheatre**, 5km south of Sparta. Contact the Sainopoúleion Foundation, 86 Paleológou St, **t** 273 102 8878.

Where to Stay and Eat

Sparta ✉ 23100

Menelaion, 91 Paleológou, **t** 273 102 2161, **f** 273 102 6332, *www.hotel-menelaion.gr* (*B; expensive*). Built in 1935 in the neoclassical style, this refined, renovated hotel in the centre offers an attractive pool with a restaurant.

Sparta Inn, 105 Thermopylón, **t** 273 102 1021, **f** 273 102 4855 (*C; moderate*). Comfortable enough, if less grand, with two small pools.

Laconía, 61 K. Paleológou St, **t** 273 102 8951, **f** 273 108 2257 (*C; moderate–inexpensive*). A standard business hotel which may not be anything to write home about, but its price is right, often negotiable, and it has air-conditioning.

Cecil, 125 K. Paleológou St, **t** 273 102 4980, **f** 273 108 1318 (*D; moderate*). This small, popular hotel has been totally renovated and modernized. But the new air-conditioning hasn't affected one iota the warm hospitality offered by its very welcoming owners, Katerína and Ioánnis Katránis. They are a fund of information on Laconía, too.

The Spartans of old favoured black broth flavoured with pig's blood and vinegar; the new ones don't. Remember, too, that Mystrá or Paróri are not far away.

Taverna Lámbrou, 82 Paleológou St. Good Greek country food. One of the last old-fashioned eateries that caters to villagers in town for the day, serving *patsas* (sheep's stomach soup) from early morning and Greek home cooking for lunch. They never did open at night because everyone had gone home by then. *Open noon–3pm only*.

Diethnés, 105 Paleológou St, **t** 273 102 8636. Has been around for a while and serves reasonable food at reasonable prices; small garden at the back.

Elyssée, 113 Paleológou St, **t** 2731 02 9896. Near the Diethnés and very similar.

Dias, in the Mániatis Hotel at 72–6 Paleológou St, **t** 273 102 2665. A genteel pastel setting and a pretty good reputation.

religious leaders and, above all, military commanders. Male Spartiates (the peers or *homoioi*) formed a citizen assembly, the Apella, which annually chose five Ephors who swore to uphold the kings, provided they acted constitutionally. The real power was held by the Gerousia or senate, made up of 28 members and the two kings. Membership was for life, restricted to a group of aristocratic families and to men over 60 years old. Candidates would be named and judges, hidden out of sight, would decide who had received the loudest shouts of approval (the world's first applause meter). It sounds great; citizen equality, respect for elders, permanent institutions. And the Rhetra has had its admirers, many of whom were impressed by its immutability, which Lykourgos went to extremes to ensure. The story goes that before travelling to Delphi to get Apollo's blessing on the Rhetra, he made the Spartans swear by terrible oaths that they would not change a word of it until he returned in person. When the Rhetra was duly blessed, Lykourgos starved himself to death and asked that his ashes be scattered at sea to prevent anyone repatriating his remains and using them as an excuse to change the Rhetra.

The guarantee of equality for each free citizen has a hollow ring when you consider that the Spartiates were always a small minority in Sparta (even at their height they only numbered nine or ten thousand), and that their so-called freedom was based on the ruthless subjection of the majority; both the indigenous population and semi-Dorian Messenians were *untermenschen* under the Spartan jackboot. The luckier ones, the *perioikoi*, 'those who lived around' were tradesmen, artists and craftsmen in surrounding towns, with very limited self-rule, no citizen rights, and an obligation to provide troops for Sparta's army. The vast majority were despised helots, slaves with no rights at all, but whose presence was essential to perpetuate Spartan society.

The Life of the Spartan Élite

Every Spartiate was a soldier, liable for military service until age 60 and prepared for his role from the cradle. A *Leske* or group of citizens appointed by the state decided if a newborn child was fit to live or be thrown from Kaiádas, a rocky ravine of the Taíyetos. Each new male citizen was allotted an equal share of state land to be worked by state-owned helots, allowing him the freedom and wealth to become a part of the state military machine.

Boys were taken from their mothers at age seven and raised in barracks until age 20. Brutal games including beatings where the victors were the ones who did not flinch, theft exercises where being caught was severely punished and even a spell in the infamous Spartan secret police (where helots were hunted and killed) were all part of the educational programme, the *agogé* instituted by Lykourgos, aimed at creating the perfect warrior. Retreat was not an option: 'Either return with your shield or on it,' was the Spartan motto and shame or death awaited anyone who disobeyed. It led to the morale-boosting heroics at Thermopylae in 480 BC (*see* p.380). The down side was the fear this same military ethos inspired in their fellow Hellenes. The Spartan phalanx, the only army to march lock step into battle to the sound of heredi-tary pipers, struck terror into Greeks whose armies were made of everyday citizens and whose major preparation for battle was a pep talk from their current leader.

And Spartan women? If dying in battle was the only way for a man to have his name on a grave stele, the only way for a woman was to die in childbirth. In death they were equal: heroes of the state. Women were as fanatical as men and full of contempt for 'tremblers'. Marriage customs show just how far off the norm Spartan society became. The bride, her hair shorn, was dressed in male attire and left lying in a dark room where her new husband would visit, exercise his conjugal rites, and then return to his barracks. They would continue to meet in this fashion until the man was thirty and he was allowed to live with his wife. Why? Since homosexuality was common, even encouraged, in the Spartan army, it may have been a way to make sex with a woman more palatable. It certainly ensured that Spartan males kept their minds on soldiering, rather than on hearth and home.

To say that the Spartiates were unloved by their subject people would be an under-statement. When on campaign, the Spartan army posted two rows of sentries every evening, one looking outward to the visible enemy and one looking inward to the piled arms cache, to make sure the *perioikoi* and, later, helots (who were brought into service as the Spartiates declined) did not grab them and revolt. A militaristic society with paranoid tendencies was inevitable. Sparta boasted that she needed no walls; her soldiers were her walls, which was true. By the Classical period, the system had created Spartiates with the fortress mentality par excellence.

By 500 BC, Sparta controlled most of Arcadía, Argolís and Elís. She was the force to be reckoned with, coercing other states to form alliances with her, or to fight and be beaten into submission. She was Athens' great rival, a situation that exploded into the Peloponnesian War in 431 BC. Even then many great Athenians admired Sparta, including Socrates and Xenophon. Democracy was messy; the Spartan system brutal but neat. Since then utopian idealists and socialists of all stripes have idealized the ethos, taking a leaf out of the Spartan notebook, from eugenics to brutal military training to suppression of minorities on the basis of their 'natural' inferiority.

Sparta won the Peloponnesian War, but did not know what to do with her victory. Like other states that exist by suppressing their majorities, she lived in terror of revolt, and it was only a matter of time before her greatness dimmed. Constantly at war, Spartiate numbers dwindled, and there was no provision in the constitution allowing the formation of new citizens. The surrender on Sphaktería in 425 BC (*see* p.348) put paid to the myth of fighting to the last man. Epaminóndas of Thebes proved that Sparta could be defeated in 371 BC; the Macedonians conquered them; they were defeated by the Achaeans in 222 BC. By the Roman period, the Spartans were reduced to living on their fame. Tourists crowded into a brand new amphitheatre built around the Temple to Artemis Orthia to see the young boys beaten, a spectacle designed to show just how tough the Spartans were, way back when.

Modern Sparta (Spárti)

Sparta, occupying the same spot as the ancient and medieval city, is a thriving agri-cultural centre, producing olive oil, figs, honey, tomatoes and oranges, oranges, oranges. Refounded in 1834 by King Otto and designed to hold 100,000 in an efficient grid system, its open, pleasant atmosphere might be attributed to the fact that only 15,500 people actually live on its wide streets, some of which are lined with lovely neoclassical buildings. The two principal avenues are north–south **Paleológou** and east–west **Lykoúrgou Streets**, the names pretty compliments to Sparta's medieval and ancient heroes. Paleológou is the showplace, with a palm-studded median. Plainer Lykoúrgou has the museum to the east; the main *laikó* or villagers' shopping district lies west of the square that knots the two streets together. Sparta's lively atmosphere reflects the pride her own citizens feel for their home. The setting helps. It may be far from the sea, but to the west the Taíyetos range rises so abruptly it looks like a painted backdrop of Himalayan proportions – magical in the winter and spring when the upper 'wall' is covered in snow, above the valley full of olive and orange groves.

Remnants of Ancient Sparta

'The day will come when you will seek the traces of Sparta, and not find them,' predicted Thucydides, and he was right; the Spartans left the big civic building projects to the Athenians. The low Spartan **acropolis**, on the north edge of town past the modern stadium, is now a pleasant park. A large **Roman theatre** was built on the south side of the acropolis in the Imperial period. Its orchestra is 82ft in diameter and its cavea 459ft, making it the third largest in Greece, seating 16,000. Large holes were found for wooden posts to hold up shades during the performances. On the acropolis are traces of the **walls** built to keep out the barbarians after AD 267 as well as the 10th-century ruins of the **basilica of Ag. Níkon**, a reminder that this was the site of medieval Lacedaimonia until it moved to Mystrá. Near the Roman theatre is a ruin turned into a little street park, said to be the **memorial to Leonídas**, the hero of the famous last stand at Thermopylae. His modern statue, looking suitably heroic and sporting a great pair of legs, stands at the north end of Paleológou Street.

The **Temple of Artemis Orthia** (*entrance free*), an easy walk north from the centre, is signposted just south of the Eurótas bridge. It is uncharacteristically shabby for tidy Sparta. A temenos existed here from the 10th century BC, a temple from the 8th. The existing remnants date from the 6th century BC: the remains of a *cella*, a *pronaos* and two Doric columns remain; an oblong altar can be seen to the east of the temple.

In the historical period it was said that Artemis' statue was found standing (*órthia*) in a thicket, and its discovery coincided with an outbreak of madness, murders and epidemics. These could be stopped only by offering human sacrifice to the goddess. By Spartan times, the 'sacrifice' was somewhat mitigated. Young boys were whipped and prizes given to the ones who did not flinch, or posthumously to the ones who died. A macabre detail has the statue of Artemis being held by a priestess; if the flagellation slackened, she would bend under the weight of the displeased goddess until the beatings became more severe. Many clay masks were found at the site. Masks and flagellation suggest early fertility rituals as do the sickles embedded in stone on the winners' trophies. The hillside above the temple accommodated spectators. After AD 100, the Romans built the horseshoe-shaped amphitheatre whose remains can just be deciphered. In this construction, the temple was in the place of the raised stage in a normal theatre, and the altar, where the whipping took place, was right in the middle of the orchestra.

Archaeological Museum

On Lykoúrgou St, just west of Paleológou, t 273 102 8575; open daily exc Mon, 8.30–3, Sun 10–2; adm.

The museum, a neoclassical pile built in 1875, is not large, but covers the ground in Laconía from the prehistoric to Roman art. Distinctive 4th-century BC **stone plaques** inset with sickles are inscribed with the names of 'victors' of the contests held at the festival of Artemis Orthia, along with the statue base of a *vomonikes*, a young lad who endured the flogging and won. There are two cases of uncanny 7th- and 6th-century BC **clay masks** from the Sanctuary of Artemis Orthia. The museum has over a hundred; they have bizarre expressions and seem to represent real people. In the second room to the right are some powerful Achaic **votive offerings** either to chthonic deities or heroized ancestors. Note the double-handed cup, the snake motifs, and the horses and dogs. Were they clan signs? On the right wall are plaques of snakes, which always seem to be more in evidence when Mycenaeans were in the area. The so-called **statue of Leonidas**, found in the Temple to Athene Chalkioikós on the acropolis, dates from the 5th century BC.

Ancient Sites Close to Sparta: the Menélaion, Amýklai and Vapheío

The **Menélaion** is 5km southeast of Sparta. Take the side road immediately north of the Eurótas bridge that goes to Geráki and go south until you see the sign. A large Mycenaean settlement existed here. What remains is the **Sanctuary of Menelaos and Helen** on three raised ramps, with the remains of an Archaic temple and a great view.

There is a lot more to Helen than the *Iliad* tells, where she is just a prize to be stolen or recovered. The most likely theory has her as the focus of a local vegetative cult where her fetish, or statue, was annually 'stolen' (causing the land to be barren) and then 'returned' (causing the land to blossom). Even the tough Spartans considered the Helen saga of utmost importance; one of their most treasured relics was a piece of shell of the egg from which Helen, daughter of the swan-raped Leda, was hatched.

The Sanctuary of Apollo and Vapheío are both in **Amýklai**, 7km south of Sparta, on the west bank of the Eurótas. To reach the famous **Sanctuary of Apollo**, turn off from the main road just north of the Shell station and head 1km east. The discovery of sub-Mycenaean (12th century BC) and Geometric votives on this pleasant low hill point to a continuous cult site. Only a few large stones erected at a later date survive. The sanctuary surrounded the tomb of Hyakinthos, a pre-Greek deity, as the ending *–inthos* indicates. The Greeks incorporated him into their pantheon by making him a young friend whom Apollo killed by mistake and whose blood created the flower. Apollo buried him here with honours, instituted the ancient festival Hyakinthia, and then took over his name, thus becoming Apollo Hyakinthos. The Hyakinthia was famous for its cult hymns to Apollo called *paeans*, which Plutarch wrote were brought to Sparta from Crete in the 7th century. A small church now marks the spot.

The **Vapheío** turn-off is just a little further south and 3km in from the road. The huge tholos tomb, in a pit and destroyed except for its lower courses, yielded two magnificent golden cups now in the Athens National Archaeological Museum.

Mystrá

From Sparta, it's a lovely 6km drive to Mystrá. The modern village has a tiny *plateía* with a majestic plane tree, water flowing from its bole and, around the bend, a bronze statue of **Constantine Dragatses Paleológos**, the last emperor of Byzantium. Mystrá is his town. The yellow Byzantine flag with its black double-headed eagle (one head for Rome, the other for Constantinople) flies everywhere; signs are written in Byzantine lettering and bakeries bake Byzantine biscuits called *kaloudia*. Legend states that

Getting There

Buses from Sparta to Mystrá leave hourly between 8am and 8pm from the bus station or on Lykoúrgos St, two blocks west of the main square. All go to the lower gate by the Xenía Tourist Peripteron. This same bus can also drop you at the two local campsites and at modern Mystrá. Some go to the site's top gate. Since the two gates are over 2km apart, and the site is steep, it may make sense to take the bus to the top, enter there and then walk down through the ruins, returning to Sparta from the stop near the bottom gate; t 273 102 6441 to find out the times for buses to the upper gate.

For **taxis** in Mystrá, call t 273 108 3450.

Where to Stay and Eat

Mystrá ⊠ 23100

Byzantion, t 273 108 3309, **f** 273 102 0019 (*B; expensive–moderate*). In spite of its pretty balconies, it seems a little forlorn for such a lovely setting. *Open April–Oct.*

Christina Vachaviólou (Βαχαβιόλου), **t** 273 102 0047 (*inexpensive*). This hospitable lady offers three plain rooms in an old-fashioned house behind the hotel; communal baths and fridge, plus an apartment that can sleep four in a modern wing.

Camping Mystrá, t 273 102 2724, **f** 273 102 5256 (*inexpensive*). A tiny site on the road to Mystrá with a small pool and playground. *Open all year.*

Castle View, t 273 108 3303 (*inexpensive*). Larger, with a slightly bigger pool; it offers bungalows at a very reasonable price. *Open April–Oct.*

Taverna O Éllenas, t 273 108 2666. In Mystrá's main *plateía*, complete with little black cannons and a pretty side garden. This is the nicest one in town.

Marmara, t 273 108 3319. Farther up the road towards the site, this well established taverna has a terrace overlooking Sparta and piano music on weekends.

Xenía, t 273 102 0500. Bar/coffee shop and a pizzeria-restaurant above. Its large terraces with a huge mulberry tree overlook the entire valley, showing 'hollow Lacedaimon' at its best. No better place to be at dusk.

Paróri/Anavrytí

Anavrytí Hotel, t 273 102 1788 (*inexpensive*). Plain, nice and cheap, in a great location, if you can just brave either the road or footpath to it. *Open all year.*

Psistariá Drosopigí, t 273 108 3744. Offers trout, among other delights.

O Kéramos, t 273 108 2833. Serves traditional Greek oven dishes in a pleasant spot.

Constantine has been preserved in marble in a secret cave, awaiting the moment when the Greeks return to Constantinople (they rarely say Istanbul), an ambition most Greeks have relinquished in practice, but almost none have in their dreams.

The ghost town is above the modern village, high on an outcrop of Taíyetos. This was the last sigh of Byzantium, where the last Despot held on for three years after the fall of Constantinople. Now cypresses, olives and flowers grow where 40,000 people lived, their memory kept alive by the grace of their churches and the bittersweet splendour of their frescoes, painted with the intense spirituality that informs all Byzantine art, yet with a vitality, colouring and delicate charm as if they were harbingers of spring instead of doom.

History

In 1249, after subduing the fierce Melingi Slavs, William II de Villehardouin, the most Philhellene of the Franks, found a perfect pedestal for his castle, located at the mouth of the Gorge of the Melingi, with impossible cliffs falling to the south. He called it after the Greek name for the mountain, Myzithra ('goat cheese'), and it became his favourite residence. In 1259, the Byzantines captured him in the battle of Pelagonia, and he spent three years in the clink, before his barons agreed to the ransom: Mystrá, Monemvasiá and the Máni – but only because in their absence, their wives got to vote, and they tipped the 'yeas'. When the Franks tried to recapture Mystrá, two years later, the citizens of Sparta, who until then had camped out in the ruins of the classical city, relocated here, literally, stone by stone.

In 1348, Emperor John VI Cantacuzenós made Mystrá the seat of the Despot ('Prince') of the Morea; John himself, one of the great scholars of his age, came to Mystrá when he abdicated, and died here in 1383. Ruling the Morea was tricky; harassed by Franks and Turks, the Despots brought in Albanian mercenaries in such numbers that occasionally they too became a threat. It made for interesting times – Slavs in the mountains, Albanians on farms, Greeks and a fair number of Jews in the towns, and Franks. As policy, the Despots married Frankish princesses just as the Franks took noble Greek wives. As Constantinople frayed, isolated Mystrá became a centre of scholarship, attracting the likes of Gemistos Plethon – the scholar who introduced Plato to the Florence of the Medici, and hence to the rest of the West. Constantine Dragatses served as Despot before becoming emperor; his brother, Demetrios, allowed the Turks to take Mystrá in 1460.

Mystrá prospered again when the Venetians regained it in 1687, and made it an important silk manufacturing town. It fell again to the Turks in 1715 and was burned badly twice, in 1770 by the Albanians in the employ of the Sultan and in 1825 by the Egyptian troops of Ibraham Pasha. In 1831, when King Otto founded modern Sparta, many of the ancient stones were carried down to the plain again to build the new city. Salvage work by the French at the turn of the century and restorations in the 1930s saved the churches and their lovely frescoes.

The Site

t 273 108 3377. High season open daily, 8am–7pm, Sat, Sun and hols 8.30–3; off season daily 8.30–3; adm exp. Keep your ticket, wear sturdy shoes and come in the morning, when the sun illuminates the best frescoes, in the Perívleptos.

Mystrá is divided into three levels; the oldest and uppermost, built around Villehardouin's castle, has an entrance that can be reached by bus or car (*see* 'Getting There'). The main entrance at the bottom leads through a vaulted passage in the walls into the **lower town**. Here, for the sake of the best light, take the path to the left, past the **Lascaris House**, once one of the grandest mansion in Mystrá, to the **Perívleptos**. This 14th-century cross-in-square church is set against a vertical rock face, which gave rise to its irregular plan; the door is located behind the apses, and the entrance is through a rock passage. The relief of a lily and lion rampant in the apse suggests that the Despot Manuel Cantacuzenós and his wife, Isabella de Lusignan, were the founders. Its frescoes are among the most beautiful in Greece and are lavish with detail: note the playing children in the foreground of the *Entry to Jerusalem* and the beautifully coiffed angels, the fish and tiny people swarming in the river in the *Baptism of Christ*. The *Descent from the Cross* recalls Duccio di Buoninsegna.

Hodegétria
(Aphendikó)

Brontóchion

Evangelistra

Museum

Mitrópolis
(Cathedral)

Palace of
the Despots

lower entrance
gate

Ag. Sophia

top
entrance
gate

Ag.
Nikólaos

Lascaris
House

Monemvasiá
Gate

Pantanassa

Ag. Geórgios

Castle

Peribletos

A steep path ascends to the **Pantánassa**, the loveliest church, set in a commanding position above a convent whose nuns are the only residents in Mystrá. The Pantánassa was dedicated in 1428, making it one of the last churches and the culmination of the Mystrá style. The builders followed the same plan as the Aphendikó (*see* below), but the apses are even higher and narrower, windows more numerous, the architectural features emphasized in masonry, especially in the sanctuary. The Frankish-style bell tower with its little melon dome fits in with rare harmony. The narthex is frescoed with nasty martyrdoms, while the inner doorway has what looks like Kufic script, apparently made by a Greek who simply liked the design. The poorly preserved frescoes on the lower level of the nave are 17th and 18th centuries; the upper ones, as in the Perívleptos, show a love of detail, softer modelling of the figures and bright clear colours. The *Entry into Jerusalem* is especially fine.

From here the path leads up to the **Monemvasiá Gate**, under an impressive battlemented house from the 15th century. Above, in what was once the main square, stands the massive **Palace of the Despots** (currently undergoing restoration). Many

19th-century travellers mistook it for the Palace of Menelaos. Begun by Villehardouin, the Paleológoi later added the vast throne room. Originally stuccoed and painted, this was heated by no fewer than eight fireplaces. The church to the left, **Ag. Nikólaos**, was built during the Turkish period, while to the west, up from the Palace of the Despots, is the church of **Ag. Sophia**, built as the *katholikón* of a small monastery by the first Despot Manuel Cantacuzenós (1348–40). It represents the simpler style of Mystrá church, the cross-in-square, but with unusually tall and narrow proportions and two exterior colonnades, a feature common in Constantinople but rare in Greece.

High above is Villehardouin's **castle** where he and his wife Anne-Ange Comnene ('as beautiful as a second Helen', according to the *Chronicle of the Morea*) held a chivalrous Franco-Greek court. It's easy to understand why the Franks were loathe to give it up. The walk is steep; if you have a car, drive up. The views are spectacular.

From the Despots' palace, the path descends back through the Monemvasiá Gate, past the 14th- or 15th-century **Evangelístria**, used as a mortuary chapel and ossuary. At the bottom, turn left for the **Brontóchion**, once a vast monastic complex with two large and impressive churches. One, the octagonal domed **Ag. Theódori** (1290s), was probably copied from the Ag. Sophía in Monemvasiá. A unique feature, however, is the east façade, with its triple broken roof and bands of grey stone and red ashlar; the west is similar but hidden by a later narthex. The second church, the **Hodegétria**, now better known as the **Aphendikó**, was built 20 years later and designed as if to remind the citizens of Mystrá of their imperial lineage – it's a tall, complex fusion of a basilica with a cross church and five domes, and a lovely campanile; the view from above on to the Aphendikó's garden of tiled roofs is perhaps the best way to appreciate the architectural sleight of hand. The interior, with its marble facings, is elegantly proportioned. The frescoes are excellent: saints and Hierarchs, and lively scenes of the *Miracles of Jesus*. In the north chapel of the narthex is the tomb of Theodore II Paleológos, showing him dressed as a Despot and as a monk (it wasn't uncommon for Byzantine rulers to abdicate and enter a monastery). Copies of chrysobulls (imperial decrees) to the Brontóchion are on the walls.

The last church before the entrance is the **Mitrópolis**, or cathedral, built in 1291 when the Bishop of Lacedaemonia transferred his seat to Mystrá. It has a confusing plan: originally built as a basilica and divided into three barrel-vaulted aisles, it suffered from an insensitive 15th-century bishop who whipped off the roof and beheaded the upper rank of frescoes to give it a women's gallery and five domes, and built a heavy bell tower over a chapel. In the courtyard, a Roman sarcophagus decorated with maenads and griffons was once used as a fountain; it is the only classical artefact ever found in Mystrá. Inside, the Mitrópolis has a wonderful marble iconostasis carved with dragons. The inscriptions on the columns were left by bishops, describing their good deeds. The frescoes were painted at various periods: the *Miracles of Jesus* and the *Saints*, the *Cycle of Feasts*, and the *Passion* and *Resurrection*; the *Last Judgement* in the narthex is the most recent, showing the *Preparation of the Throne* (the *Etoimasiá*) and scenes of hell, where lustful women are wrapped in coiling snakes. The marble plaque on the floor marks the spot where the gentle, reluctant Constantine Dragatses was crowned emperor in 1449. Four years later, he died defending Constantinople from the Turks, shedding his imperial regalia to fight like a common soldier by the gate. His body was never identified, leaving him to became the marble fairytale prince in his countrymen's dreams.

There is a small **museum** off the Mitrópolis' courtyard, with architectural fragments, icons, part of a silk dress and a plait of hair recovered from a noblewoman's tomb, jewellery, a relief of the arms of Isabella de Lusignan, a fine 12th-century plate showing an eagle attacking a hare and a peculiar metal cross sprouting baby crosses.

Paróri: a Short Detour into the Taíyetos

Paróri, 2km due south of Mystrá, offers lovely restaurants by a small waterfall and a 20-minute walk into a typical, albeit miniature, Taíyetos gorge housing the tiny cave church of **Panagía Langadiótissa**. The atmosphere is suitably eerie, especially towards dusk when bats flit about. The church has a flat platform in front to sit on and contemplate the scenery. This gorge may have been the infamous *Kaiádas* where the Spartans tossed their unwanted babies. There is another candidate on the Kalamáta road, but this one has practicality on its side: it is closer to town. Getting rid of imperfections would not have seemed an important enough task to Spartans to warrant a long journey. Three hundred metres past Paróri towards Ag. Ioánnis, a 5km footpath twists up the mountain to lofty **Anavrytí**. It can also be reached by car via Ag. Ioánnis up a steep secondary road with spine-chilling hairpin bends. The straight road from Paróri back to Mystrá offers a marvellous view of the castle.

Roads and Hikes over the Taíyetos

The great spine of the southern Peloponnese is a force to be reckoned with. 'Look at the Taíyetos and your chest expands, petty calculations vanish, you are ashamed of the tiny, meaningless life that you have led,' wrote Kazantzákis. You can get a spellbinding taste of the Taíyetos on the 60km route over the celebrated 4,265ft-high **Langáda Pass**, on the road built in 1940 between Sparta and Kalamáta. Just past **Trýpi** the road enters a sinister gorge, steep enough to be a candidate for *kaiadás*. A more circuitous paved road further south snakes over from **Aigiés**, 5km north of Gýthio, via Kastaniá, Saidóna and on to Stoúpa in the Outer Máni. This one is for the bold.

The highest reaches of Taíyetos are better left to hikers with proper equipment and maps such as the ROAD *Taíyetos*. There is a footpath right over the mountain range and down to Kardamýli, but there is plenty of scope for duffers on the lower slopes near Sparta on old mule paths and cobblestoned *kalderími*. A brochure available at Sparta's tourist office shows each trail, giving its height, difficulty and the time required. Although labelled in Greek, it is still possible to decipher the main points. Roads occasionally intersect these paths – a paved one at Anavrytí, and unpaved ones to Tauyéti, Sochá, and to the Alpine Club refuge near the highest peak of the Taíyetos, **Profitís Ilías**, (7,897ft) – so it's possible to combine driving and hiking.

Mount Párnonas, east of Sparta, is not as majestic as the Taíyetos, but Laconía's number two range is easier to reach by way of **Vamvakoú** (the turn-off is 12km up the main Trípolis road.) From Vamvakoú a path leads due west and in 2 hours (or the unpaved road twists around for 26km) to the **mountain refuge Arnomousga** (4,593ft) run by Sparta's Alpine Club (*35 beds, kitchen facilities: call* **t** *273 102 6518*). From here you can drive or walk (3 hours) to the 6,348ft summit **Megáli Toúrla or Krónion**. The lonely villages of Párnonas are famous for their mountain teas; stop and try some.

Geráki: a Mini-Mystrá

Southeast of Sparta, the Eurótas river wends through empty, undulating country dignified by views over the Taíyetos backbone. In the Middle Ages, the strategic hotspot between Mystrá and Monemvasiá was Geráki ('falcon' in Greek). Captured by the Franks in 1245, William II de Villehardouin gave it to Guy de Nivelet, but the Franks had to hand it over to the Byzantines in 1262 after the Battle of Pelagonia; Geráki was thereafter ruled by Mystrá.

Modern Geráki is piled over ancient Geronthrai, famous in Spartan times for its festival in honour of war-like Ares. **Old Geráki** is 4km above the modern town, a kind of third-division Mystrá in a rugged setting, all abandoned in the 1800s. The mobile phone-toting caretaker is around in the mornings and late afternoons; once your car is spotted by his lookouts heading up to the site, he'll be on his way. He doesn't speak English, but do give him a tip. And wear sturdy shoes – the paths are rocky. The three small frescoed churches here are far more typical of the period than the ones in that imperial hothouse orchid, Mystrá. The first is **Ag. Paraskeví**, a cross-vaulted church built by the French, with traces of their 13th-century sculptural decoration and Greek frescoes from the 15th century. The back wall has portraits of the donors who paid for the paintings. The simple, aisle-less **Zoodóchos Pigí** has paintings from the same period: note the priests dedicating the church, John the Baptist, sadly contemplating the head in his hands, and a lovely enthroned Virgin. The most remarkable Franco-Greek fusion is at the top, in Guy de Nivelet's **castle**, emblazoned with his moon and star coat of arms, with superb views towards the Taíyetos and the Máni. Inside, the little basilica of **Ag. Geórgios** boasts the only Gothic tabernacle in Greece, a curious, rugged work in stone, its knotted columns decorated with the Villehardouin fleur-de-lys and Nivelet stars. The frescoes are currently being restored; note the ancient column and relief.

Eastern Laconía: Epídauros Limerá

With the exception of Monemvasiá, the *eparchy* of Epídauros Limerá or far east end of Laconía is the back of beyond, stretching from the formidable slopes of Mount Párnonas down to storm-tossed Cape Maléas. Plenty of beaches rim the Laconían Gulf, but they are wind smacked and more suited to the sea turtles who nest there; the Eurótas Delta is an important wetland. Some creatures are rare, like the black pelican and a unique fish, the *tropidophoxineius Spartiaticus*. The islands are the main lures: Elafónisos with its fine beaches and Kýthera, the island of the goddess of love.

Down the Myrtoan Coast

'Down the coast' is a bit of a misnomer since your chances of touching the sea are limited by the austere eastern flanks of Mount Párnonas. But if you like long, lonesome drives over the wild mountains, scooting along at eagle level, this is *the* place for you. By car, the easiest way to reach the little port of **Kyparíssi** is to take the turn-off to Metamórphosi from either Molái or Sikéa on the Sparta–Monemvasiá road, and continue 40km over the mountains through the villages of Achladókambos, Lambókambos and Chárakas, and then wind down, down, down with a sigh of relief to the first white houses and gardens, next to a silvery plain of olives.

The extra effort makes Kyparíssi (pop. 400) a spot to linger. It has a perfectly clear sea and pebbly beach, a few *kafeneíons*, a couple of shops and tavernas, and that's it. You can, with your map, backtrack towards Metamórphosi, only turning left after Achladókambos at the crossroads for Richiá. After this the asphalt gives out for a few kilometres, until you come to the left turn for the coast and the **Convent Evanglístrias**, perched high above the sea with lovely views. The main road continues to **Géraka** and its charming fjord-like port, **Liménas Géraka**, with its three little tavernas and swimming coves just south of the village.

Monemvasiá

Monemvasiá is one of the natural wonders of the Peloponnese – an unassailable rock-berg tied to the coast by a bridge, dyed a soft purple in October by a massive carpet of cyclamens. The town, once home to 40–50,000 people, is invisible from land and had only one entrance (*moni emvasis*), and getting through it, if one wasn't welcome, was next to impossible. This sense of security, similar to that of Venice in her lagoon, allowed the Monemvasiótes to create the Greek equivalent of an Italian mercantile republic, ruled by an oligarchy who were also pirates as the need arose; the Rock overlooked the main sea lane between the Bosphorus and the west.

Monemvasiá's individual history began in AD 375 when a mighty earthquake rent the rock from the mainland. Founded by Byzantine Emperor Maurice in 585, the town on the rock, or Kástro, quickly became a refuge for those fleeing the Slavs and Avars, while the mainland was given over to growing food and what would become the most prized wine of the Middle Ages, malmsey, shipped to England in butts big enough to drown in, as demonstrated by the Duke of Clarence. The impregnability of Monemvasiá's defences was severely tried in the 800s by the Saracens from Crete; they stood up to an onslaught of the Norman army from Sicily in 1147. By this time the emperors, especially the Comnenes, had seen the wisdom of granting the Monemvasiótes every possible privilege to keep their loyalty.

As the Rock was the key to the southeastern Peloponnese, it was a thorn in the side of the Franks. To blockade Monemvasiá, William de Villehardouin borrowed four ships from Venice, and only after three years, when the Monemvasiótes were reduced to eating cats and dogs, they surrendered – on the condition that they maintained all their privileges. William agreed, and went on to capture Sparta and the Máni and control the entire Morea – with the exception of the ports of Methóni and Koroní, the price Venice charged for her aid. William kept his prize for all of 14 years (*see* Mystrá).

Getting There

Monemvasiá

Hydrofoils, from Marina Zea, Piraeus, **t** 210 419 9200, head out via Portochéli daily in late June–mid Sept (weekends only in winter) to Kyparíssi (**t** 273 205 5275), Liménas Géraka (**t** 273 205 9214) and Monemvasiá (**t** 273 206 1219). Some go direct to Monemvasiá from Piraeus in 2½hrs.

Buses from Athens, **t** 210 512 4913, go direct to Monemvasiá (by way of Geráki) twice daily, and there are three daily from Sparta. In Monemvasía, **t** 273 206 1752. Local buses to Kyparíssi go once or twice a day from Molái.

Parking in Monemvasiá along the road outside the gate can be exasperating. In the summer (weekends in winter), a minibus from the bridge links the medieval town with the mainland every few minutes, or it's a 20min walk. **Hire a car** or **motorbike** at Christos, **t** 273 206 1581, **f** 273 207 1661, or contact **Malvásia Travel** to book a car or a room, **t** 273 206 1752, **f** 273 20 6 1432, *malvtrvl@otenet.gr*.

Neápolis and Elafónisos

Buses, t 273 402 3222, link Neápolis to Athens and Sparta at least three times a day, and to Poúnda (for Elafónisos) four times on most days. For a **taxi** in Neápolis, **t** 273 402 2590. **Hydrofoils** (**t** 273 402 2940, **f** 273 402 3590) call

here daily in summer en route to and from Kýthera, less often in winter. A **car ferry** goes every half hour from Poúnda to Elafónisos in season, and one caique daily connects it to Neápolis. **Port authority: t** 273 402 2228.

Where to Stay and Eat

Kyparíssi ✉ 23052

Katína's Studios, t 273 202 3775, **f** 273 205 5238 (*inexpensive; moderate in high season*). Katína offers air-conditioned rooms for two, three or four. *Open all year.*

Myrtoo Rooms, t 273 205 5327 (*inexpensive; moderate in high season*). New; rooms with balconies, in a little garden. *Open all year.*

Monemvasiá Kástro ✉ 23070

A number of Venetian mansions have been restored as hotels and are open all year.

Malvasia, t 273 206 1323, **f** 273 206 1722 (*A; expensive–moderate*). Three buildings, all air-conditioned, with beautiful traditional furnishings. One, the Stelláki mansion, is the most imposing in town.

Byzantino, t 273 206 1254, **f** 273 206 1331 (*A; expensive*). A choice of rooms, some large and furnished with antiques, some smaller under vaulted roofs, all reeking with local tradition.

When Monemvasiá returned to the Greeks, it became the port of Mystrá, a golden period when libraries and over 40 churches were founded.

Although it managed (with a ruse) to escape capture by the Turks, Monemvasiá was completely isolated in the mid-15th century, and put itself under the protection of former enemy Venice. The Venetians confirmed the privileges of Napoli di Malvasia, as they called it, and strengthened its fortifications. But in 1537, when Suleiman the Magnificent defeated the combined fleet of Venice, Charles V and the Pope at Préveza, a treaty was signed handing Monemvasiá over to the Turks. The citizens were allowed to leave if they wished, and many did, taking their malmsey vine-roots to Crete and Santoríni. The Turks, who arrived when the cyclamens were out, named their new acquisition Meneksche, the 'Violet City'.

The Venetians made several attempts to regain Monemvasiá. Their technique, bombing and starving out the defenders, finally succeeded in 1690, after Francesco Morosini captured the rest of the Morea. The Venetians repopulated the town with many of the families who left in 1540. There was a building boom of churches and fancy palaces. But in 1715, the Turkish army that had re-conquered the rest of the Morea turned up at the gate, and the Venetian governor surrendered without a fight.

Lazareto, t 273 206 1991, **f** 273 206 1992 (*A; luxury*). Large rooms and suites, all with sea views, in the old Venetian quarantine station 700m before the gate.

There are a few **rooms**, although these cost over the odds. Try **Zambelli, t** 273 206 1212, mobile **t** 694 620 7515, or **Dina, t** 273 206 1311. **Matoula, t** 273 206 1660. The oldest and prettiest garden restaurant – delicious *dolmades* in lemon sauce overlooking the wine dark sea. Go early; it's popular.

Kanoni, t 273 206 1732. Greek and international dishes served with a sea view.

Pizza Athanasakou, t 273 206 1361. Pies near the entrance for more than 20 years.

Géfira ✉ 23070

Géfira has easier parking, lower prices, and mosquitoes.

Filoxenia, t 273 206 1716, **f** 273 206 1143 (*B; moderate*). Overlooks the rocky town beach; its balconies offer fine views of the Rock. *Open Mar–Oct.*

Petrino Rooms, t 273 206 1136 (*moderate*). By the sea; a stone building with traditionally styled rooms with balconies. One of the prettiest places to stay. *Open all year.*

Paradise Camping, t 273 206 1123 (*inexpensive*). South of Géfira on the beach.

T'Agnantio, t 273 206 1754. One of the last tavernas to the south. Tables overlook the sea and views of Monemvasiá; excellent shrimp *saganáki*, in a hot tomato and feta sauce to mop up with your crusty bread.

Neápolis ✉ 23053

Limira Mare, t 273 402 2236, **f** 273 402 2956 (*B; moderate*). A bargain by the sea with air-con, and water sports. *Open April–Oct.*

Vergina, t 273 402 3445 (*B; inexpensive*). More modest. *Open all year.*

Aïvali, t 273 402 2287, **f** 273 402 2777 (*inexpensive*). 22 rooms north of the centre on the sea, with air-conditioning. *Open all year.*

Elafónisos ✉ 23053

Linardo's Rooms, studios and suites, **t** 273 406 1137, winter **t** 210 807 1698 (*moderate; expensive in Aug*). Set back in the trees, with balconies, air-con, café. *Open May–Sept.*

Lafotel, t 273 406 1138, **f** 273 406 1183 (*expensive–moderate*). Similar, but right on the beach. *Open May–Oct.*

Asteri tis Elafonissou, t 273 406 1271 (*C; moderate*). In town, back from the sea; offers rooms with fridges. *Open all year.*

Simos Camping, t 273 402 2672. Four km south of town. *Open June–Sept.*

Elafonissos , t 273 406 1268 (*C; inexpensive*). Smack on the beach, offering breakfast, a lunch barbecue and bar in the evenings. *Open Easter, and June–Oct.*

Monemvasiá knew its last minute of importance in 1821 when, after a four-month siege, it became the first fortress captured by the Greeks in their War of Independence. Although once again many of the old Monemvasióte families moved back, the Rock went into decline as people abandoned their old houses for the mainland, leaving the Byzantine and Venetian mansions in Kástro, strictly protected by a preservation order. Over the past 30 years, about half of the crumbling mansions have been restored as holiday homes, hotels, trendy bars and restaurants.

The Kástro

Géfira or 'bridge', Monemvasiá's mainland extension, is a typical Greek seaside town, with a beautiful view of the Rock and and the causeway to the **Kástro**. The road to the gate passes the **cemetery**, last resting place of poet Yannis Ritsos (1909–89), who was born in Monemvasiá. Elaborate fortifications were destroyed in order to build the road, although the entrance, as ever, is through a single **gate**. The massive wooden doors, once closed every evening at sundown, are scarred by bullets holes.

Within, the cobbled main street is little more than an alley, lined with arty tourist shops and bars. It leads straight back to the main landmark of the lower town: the bell tower and church of **Christós Elkómenos** (the 'dragged Christ') named for an icon it once had, which was so marvellous that the Emperor Isaac II had it stolen for a church near Constantinople in the 12th century. The curious relief over the door, of two peacocks grabbing a snake with a cow's head in between, is a relic of the original 11th-century church; other marble bits were incorporated into the portal in the Venetian restoration of 1697. The interior is a fine example of Italo-Byzantine architecture, with a neoclassical veneer. Many of the icons show an Italian touch as well, as in the 14th-century icon of the *Crucifixion*. According to legend, the church's two painted thrones were placed there for the first King and Queen of Greece. The church square has a cannon dated 1763, a cistern (Monemvasiá has no springs, so every house had a cistern) and a **mosque**, or *tzamí*, where architectural fragments are stored awaiting its metamorphosis into an archaeological museum. Below the square you can wind your way down to the **Portello**, or little sea gate; the locals swim off the rocks below.

The lower town's Byzantine, Venetian and Turkish houses were built and rebuilt so often that it's hard to distinguish which is which. The Kástro's most popular church, the white 17th-century **Panagía Chrysaphítissa**, is down by the sea along the eastern walls; the tiny chapel next to it is dedicated to a holy spring, although the water turns out to be salty. Another important church, **Panagía Myrtidiótissa** ('Our Lady of the Myrtle'), is near the Elkómenos bell tower and is the finest example of the Italo-Byzantine style in town. It has an elaborately carved iconostasis (the church is usually locked, but you can see it through the window).

From Panagía Myridiótissa, the upper path zigzags up to the **Upper Town**, 1,000 feet over the sea. The thousands of people living at the top were totally dependent on this path and it was designed to make access difficult for an attacker. It also defeated the residents; the last person turned out the lights in 1911. The door of the gate on top is marked with bullet holes, while a little plaque above informs all comers that 'Christ reigns here'. Anyone who didn't care and got past that faced the **vaulted passage**, lined with nasty boobytraps, while defenders poured hot oil from the roof.

Although the walls up here are fairly intact, what stood inside them is mostly a desolate ruin. The exception is **Ag. Sophía**, a beautiful cross-in-square church with an octagonal drum and round dome, balanced on the lip of the precipice. Although attributed to Emperor Andronicos II in the late 1200s, it may be older – no one can make out the inscription of its foundation. Unusually for a Byzantine church, it has a two-storey loggia in front, built during the first Venetian period. Pretty carved capitals decorate the windows. The frescoes, mostly damaged, are from the 13th century: you can make out the Pantocrator, bishops and an angel.

South of Monemvasiá: Neápolis, Elafónisos, Cape Maléas

The road from Monemvasiá over the mountains has an austere charm, which is more than could be said of **Neápolis**, the 'new city' born after Greek independence when the farmers came down from the hills. In ancient times this was Boeae, a Spartan port during the Peloponnesian War. Today the action is still concentrated along the port, where leaving is the main reason for coming.

The best swimming in the area is out on Elafónisos, but if you want to pootle about, take the road up to **Mesochóri**, a medieval village now all but abandoned, where the Byzantine chapel of Agii Theodóri has the remains of some fine frescoes. The next village, **Farkaló**, 'the Balcony of Vatíka', was the local capital. From here you can circle around the hamlets of **Áno Kastaniá**, at the top of a gorge, with a road winding down to a quiet sandy beach, and **Káto Kastaniá**, with a clutch of little Byzantine chapels.

Another option is to take the vertiginous road above **Láchio** and zigzag up the mountain then down again through Gothic pinnacles of rock to the remote village of **Velanídia** (17km). Or head south to **Ag. Nikólaos**, with a tiny fisherman's cove below called **Ag. Lias**, continuing down on a mostly unpaved road to **Cape Maléa**. This is liable to be gusty., and was dreaded by ancient sailors; the storms here blew Odysseus to the land of Lotus-Eaters, which everyone has been looking for since. The cape is marked by the chapel of **Ag. Iríni**; a hermit lived here in the early 1800s, living off alms from sailors. Another landmark is **Ag. Geórgios**, built in the cliff near the lighthouse.

Elafónisos

The Venetians called this rocky island Cervi for the sake of its deer-shaped head; Ελαφόνησος means the same thing. It was linked to the mainland until a few centuries ago, but became island enough (it's only 300m from Poúnda) for the Venetians to hold on to it after the Turks occupied the Peloponnese, and for it to pass like Kýthera to the British in 1815, before being ceded to Greece in 1864. It has gorgeous beaches, white crescents of sand and dunes on a transparent sea at **Símos** and **Leúki** in the south (unpaved road) and at **Nisiá tis Panagías**, 5km south of the port (paved road), with its cluster of offshore baby islets.

The dunes, lakes and lagoons on the mainland opposite Elafónisos are important wetlands, where the occasional loggerhead turtle comes to nest. Similar areas exist up the peninsula's west coast, with dirt roads leading to long empty stretches of sand; **Archángelos**, a fishing village with a long beach and hotel, is one of the nicest spots. **Eléa**, on a little cape, has views across to the Máni, places to eat, and rooms.

Kýthera (ΚΥΘΗΡΑ)

Tucked under the Peloponnese, Aphrodite's island is on the way to nowhere, and owes a good part of its attraction to that fact. Today some 100,000 people of Kýtheran origin now live in Australia or 'Big Kýthera' as the 3,000 who still live on Kýthera call it. All who possibly can return to little Kýthera each summer, but few are interested in developing the island's tourist potential; they like it fine the way it is.

At first glance, the island may seem a forbidding place of scrub and rock, but don't be fooled. If it can't equal the luxuriance of Watteau's *Pèlerinage à l'Ile de Cythère*, Kýthera is in many places a green island with a very human landscape. In summer the land is lent a golden sheen by fields of *sempreviva*, which when dried keeps 'forever' or at least a few years, rather like love itself.

Getting There and Around

By air: three flights a day from Athens in season; airport information: t 273 603 3292. Tickets from the Olympic Airways office at 49 El. Venizélou, Pótamos, t 273 603 3362, or try Porfyra Travel in Livádi (*see* below).

By sea: Kýthera has two ports, small Ag. Pelagía and the newer Diakófti. In season the ferry goes daily from Neápolis, three times a week from Gýthio; in June–Sept there are hydrofoils from Piraeus, some making the trip in only 3½ hours. **Port authority**: Diakófti, t 273 603 4222; Ag. Pelagía, t 273 603 3280.

By road: The roads are good, but in the absence of buses, expect to rely on **taxis**, which charge set fees (e.g. Diakófti–Kapsáli €18). If there are no taxis, ask the port authority to call one. For **cars and moped hire** try Panayiotis in Kapsáli, t 273 603 1600, f 273 603 1789; in Ag. Pelagía, t 273 603 3194; or in Chóra, t 273 603 1551, *panayioti@otenet.gr*.

Tourist Information

Porfyra Travel, Livádi, t 273 603 1888, *porfyra@kythira.com*. For help with accommodation in the south. They also organize walking tours of the island. The tourist guide *Kýthera* is freely available and full of interesting titbits.

Where to Stay and Eat

Chóra (Kýthera) ✉ 80100

Margarita, off the main street, t 273 603 1711, f 273 603 1325, *fatseas@otenet.gr* (*C; expensive*). Attractive blue and white hotel in a former bank, with an impressive wooden spiral staircase. *Open May–Oct.*

Castello, t 273 603 1069, f 273 603 1869. Three studios (*moderate*) and 6 rooms (*moderate-inexpensive*) leading off a lovely walled garden near the fortress; immaculate and well-designed, rooms all have telephone, fridge and overhead fans. *Open all year.*

Zorba's, in Chóra's main street. Nicely old-fashioned taverna.

Belvedere, on the road to the port, t 273 603 1705. Pizzeria-cum-grill house with a magnificent view.

Kapsáli ✉ 80100

Raikos, between Chóra and Kapsáli, t 273 603 1629, f 273 603 1801 (*B; expensive*). One of the island's posher places, with a pool. *Open May–Sept.*

History

When Zeus took his golden sickle and castrated his father, Cronos, he cast the bloody bits into the sea. This gave birth to Aphrodite, who rose out of the foam at Kýthera. She found it too puny for her taste and moved to Cyprus, but her sanctuary on Kýthera was the most sacred of all her temples in Greece. The Minoans were here early on, and the Phoenicians, who came for its murex shells, the source of purple dye. Most of the time its location, at the crossroads between Crete and the mainland, the Aegean and Ionian Seas, brought trouble: Kýthera was invaded 80 times in recorded history. The rulers of Kýthera in the Middle Ages were the Eudhaemonoyánnis family from Monemvasiá, and it served as a refuge for Byzantine nobles until 1537, when Barbarossa stopped on his way home from his unsuccessful siege of Corfu and destroyed the island. The Venetians took over and called the island 'Cerigo', the name you'll see in old history books. In 1864 it was ceded to Greece by the British with the rest of the Ionian islands.

Chóra (Kýthera Town)

Chóra, the capital, is a pretty-as-a-postcard blue and white Greek village, 900ft above the port of Kapsáli, and guarded by a ruined fortress furnished by the

Poulmendis Rooms, t 273 603 1451 (*moderate–inexpensive*). Perfectly clean and comfortable, at the other end of the price range.

Daponte Stella, t 273 603 1841. Peaceful and private, with access to the gorgeous secluded beach of Sparagário.

Iannis Avgerinos, on the beach. Rooms (*moderate*) and apartments (*expensive*) converted from fishermen's huts, in an olive grove.

Camping Kapsáli, t 273 603 1580. Good facilities, set amongst cypress trees.

Magos, t 273 603 1407. Taverna with lovely views, serving all the usual.

Venetsianiko. Blue and white, for that island feel. Try the *ladopaximado*.

Filio, in Kálamos, t 273 603 1054. Impressive taverna on several levels where locals go to sample traditional Kythniot cuisine. There are also rooms for rent (*inexpensive*).

Livádi ⊠ 80100

Aposperides, t 273 603 1656, f 273 603 1688 (*C; expensive*). Pristine. *Open all year*.

Pierros. Probably the oldest and most traditional taverna on Kýthera, with authentic home cooking and kind prices.

Eleni, near the 'British bridge'. A favourite for *mezédes*.

Avlémonas ⊠ 80100

Poppy's, t 273 603 3735 (*expensive*). Self-catering, good for families.

Sotiris, t 273 603 3722. Taverna prettily set in a small square overlooking the sea, preparing excellent seafood as fresh as can be, caught by the owners themselves.

Skandia, just outside nearby Paliópoli, t 273 603 3700. Greek specialities served under an enormous elm tree – a great place for lunch.

Diakófti ⊠ 80100

Sirena Apartments, t 273 603 3900; winter, t 210 481 1185 (*A; expensive*). For peace and quiet right on the sea, with big verandas and kitchens.

Petroheílos, t 273 603 4069 (*moderate*). Rooms in an old mansion overlooking the sea.

Maistali, t 273 603 3760 (*inexpensive*). Simple, decent rooms.

Mitáta ⊠ 80100

Michális, an informal taverna, with panoramic views. People come from right across the whole island to eat here; Michális' wife cooks island specialities, including cockerel and rabbit, prepared with vegetables from their own garden.

Venetians. Ten **Venetian mansions** still retain their coats-of-arms, and a two-room **museum** (*open 8.30–2.30, closed Mon*) contains artefacts dating back to Minoan times. Shops sell handmade rugs, ceramics, ethnic-style jewellery and local wine, honey, chutneys and oils. Below, **Kapsáli** has two pebble and sand beaches, one very sheltered and boaty, the other only a bit more exposed. Little 'Egg islet' offshore is said to be the spot where Aphrodite was born. **Kálamos**, just east, is within walking distance. Its church of Ag. Nikitas has a pretty bell tower, and there is a restaurant and rooms for rent. Dirt roads continue to various beaches; nearest is pebbly **Chalkos**, set in a beautiful, almost enclosed bay, with a snack bar.

Northwest of Chóra

From Chóra, a paved road heads north to **Livádi**, with a stone bridge of 13 arches, built by the British in 1822; the story goes that its considerable length is a result of the British engineer's affair with a local girl and his desire to prolong his stay. Heading east, **Káto Livádi** has a **museum** (*t 273 603 1731; open Tues–Sun 8.30–2.30*) with Byzantine and later items. A 4km dirt road leads on to the dramatic beach of **Fíri Ámmos** ('red sands'); in an ordinary car, the final descent is manageable, if a little hair-raising. West of Livádi via Drimónas is the important monastery of **Panagía**

Mirtidíon, magnificently set on the wild west coast among cypresses, flowers and peacocks. The monastery is named after a much venerated gold-plated icon of the Virgin and Child, whose faces have blackened with age. Two islets offshore are said to be pirate ships that the Virgin turned to stone for daring to attack the monastery. Unfortunately she was unable to protect the surrounding landscape from fire.

North of Drimónas, **Milopótamos** is the closest thing to Watteau's vision, a pretty village criss-crossed by tiny canals, on either side of the Neraída (Nymph) valley; an old watermill lies along the somewhat overgrown path to the waterfall at Foníssa, surrounded by plane trees, flowers and banana plants, where nightingales sing. The ghost town **Káto Chóra** lies just below Milopótamos, in a Venetian fortress of 1560, although some of its houses and churches are being restored. A road here descends steeply to the secluded sandy beach of **Limiónas**. Signs from Milopótamos point the way to the cave of **Ag. Sofía**, at the end of a rugged track (*usually open Mon–Fri 3–8 in summer, weekends 11–5, but check in the village or call t 273 603 4062/3397*). In the past, the cave was used as a church, and inside there are frescoes and mosaics, as well as stalactites and stalagmites and small lakes.

The East Coast

From both Fratsiá and Frilingianiká in the centre, roads branch east to **Paliópoli**, a tiny village on the site of **Skandeia**. A Minoan trading settlement found here has bestowed archaeological status on the long and lovely beach, which remains untouched except for a good taverna. Locals can direct you to 'Helen's throne'; nearby is an Minoan cave dwelling resembling a five-roomed house. In ancient times, devotees would climb to the Temple of Urania Aphrodite, 'Queen of the Heavens'. Pausanius wrote that her temple was one of the most splendid in all Greece, but the Christians destroyed it and used the stone to build the church of **Ag. Georgíos**; now only the acropolis walls remain at the site, called **Paliokástro**.

From Paliópoli the coastal road descends to **Avlémonas**, a fishing village with good restaurants. The Venetians left a small octagonal fortress by the sea, with a few rusting cannon inside. To reach one of the island's finest beaches, **Kaladí**, follow signs marked ΠΡΟΣ ΚΑΛΑΔΙ along 2km of dirt road which leads past a blissful little chapel and stops; from here there's an abrupt, but mercifully short, climb down to the pebbly coves. Another dirt road north of Avlémonas leads in 7km to **Diakófti**, a scrap of a resort popular with Greek families, now Kýthera's main port; it has a strip of white sand, protected by a pair of islets.

Palio Chóra and the North

Palio Chóra is Kýthera's Byzantine ghost town, this time with real ghosts. It was founded by the Eudhaemonoyánnis clan, who carefully hid it from the sea, high on the rocks – the dreaded Turkish admiral Barbarossa only found it by torturing some locals until they gave away the secret. Beside the ruined fort is a terrible 330ft abyss, the Kakiá Langáda ('bad gorge') into which mothers threw their children before leaping themselves, to avoid being sold into slavery. The gorge is magnificent – you can walk down it in five hours and end with a refreshing dip at **Kakiá Langáda Beach**.

Palio Chóra is near **Potamós**, the largest village in the north, all blue and white. On Sundays it hosts the island's biggest market. West of Potamós, **Ag. Elefthérios** is a lovely secluded beach, and a good place to watch the sunset. From the pretty village of **Karavás**, the road continues to the fine beach and good taverna at **Platiá Ámmos**. **Ag. Pelagía**, Kýthera's northern port, also has a long pebble beach and a few more facilities, if not a lot of soul. There are some excellent beaches to the south including another by the name of **Fíri Ámmos**.

Antikýthera (ΑΝΤΙΚΥΘΗΡΑ) and its Ancient Computer

Utterly remote Antikýthera lies midway between Kýthera and Crete. If the *meltémi* wind isn't up, as it often is, ships call twice a week en route between Kýthera and Crete. Fewer than 100 people live in its two villages, **Potamós** and **Sochória**, and the rest is very rocky with few trees. Water is a luxury and the few rooms available are primitive. Potamós has a taverna, but food can also be scarce.

In 59 BC, a Roman ship sailing from Rhodes, laden with booty that included the 4th-century BC bronze *Antikýthera Youth* (one of the celebrities of the Archaeological Museum in Athens), went down off its coast. The wreck was discovered by chance in 1900. by sponge divers from Sými, and became the world's first underwater archaeo-logical dig. One item (also in Athens) was a wooden cabinet about a foot high which quickly deteriorated, leaving a calcified hunk of metal that broke into four bits. Archaeologists were astonished to see that they belonged to a mechanical device – in fact an astronomical computer, operated by a complex mass of clockwork. The captain may have been bringing it to Rome for Cicero, who knew of a 'future-telling astronom-ical device' on Rhodes. 'It is a bit frightening to know,' wrote Derek Price, who studied it, 'that just before the fall of their great civilization, the Ancient Greeks had come so close to our age, not only in their thought but also in their scientific knowledge.'

The Máni

South of Sparta lies the Máni, one of the most distinct regions in Greece. Actually there are two Mánis. The **Outer Máni**, the part that belongs to Messenía, stretches from Kalamáta to Ítilo, a marvellous blend of hills, bays and seaside villages (Kardamýli is the most important) backed by the rugged Taíyetos. And while not lush, the Outer Máni's olive groves and plane-shaded *plateía* assume paradisiacal propor-tions in comparison with the **Inner (or Deep) Máni**, the part that belongs to Laconía. Gýthio is the Máni's gateway, but its core is the tower-studded middle finger of the Peloponnese where the Taíyetos hunkers down in a no-frills cascade of barren lime-stone south to Cape Taíneron. There is virtually no water, and little arable land. In spring, the rocks have an ephemeral covering of green, and the Inner Máni becomes a yellow and pink rock garden. But the rest of the year, it displays grey rocks, prickly pear, seared grass, and olive trees knuckled down in rocky terraces – so stunted that they never impede the view. The landscape is austere, almost inhuman. But so beau-tiful is this mountain desert surrounded by pounding surf on both sides that even the driest and dustiest historical account waxes poetic. Together, these isolated regions produced a unique and warlike culture which reached its heights in the 17th and 18th centuries, and was still going strong until well after 1850.

History

Inhabited since Neolithic times, the Máni in the Bronze Age saw both Phoenician traders and Mycenaeans, and was important enough for Homer to mention eight of its cities. After 1200 BC it became Dorian and was subject to Sparta. Early in this period, Cape Taíneron was an important shrine to chthonic Poseidon, and its *temenos* a place of asylum. In the Roman period, the Máni boasted several cities of the Free Laconian League, a league, like so many in Peloponnesian history, founded to impede Spartan ambitions. But even then, Taíneron was garnering a dark reputation as the gathering point for mercenary adventurers, taking advantage of the shrine's asylum and ready to hire themselves out to anyone offering enough gold. During the Byzantine period it was not showered with attention, partly because of its isolation and partly because of its increasingly anarchic reputation. At this point remnants of the wild Slavic tribes then in the Taíyetos began assimilating with the already independent-minded natives.

Who were the Maniátes? Theories based on linguistic analysis suggest that the core Maniátes were Spartans fleeing Slavic invasions; the eight-syllable *myrologia* (dirges) of the Inner Máni do display Dorian origins. Others may have arrived from the Frankish principality of Nikli and other centres in Arcadía when the Turks came. Certainly their hierarchical and warlike social system has Spartan and feudal overtones. Cretan refugees from the Turks in the late 1600s definitely added to the mix, and probably to that one could add just plain loose ends from anywhere and everywhere else. The Máni's isolation and Greece's turbulent history combined to make this a cultural melting pot, or rather a constantly bubbling cauldron.

The earliest churches date from about the 6th century, although the Máni was not totally converted until the 800s. At that point the Máni was under Byzantine control to the extent that they could at least map it, put it into organized units, and give it the name 'Castle Maina', which it has retained until today. The most arresting etymological theory has it coming from the word *manes* (or *mánii*), the name given to the Furies, those frightening harridans with home bases in Taíneron and Hades, and who were worshipped in Arcadía and elsewhere. 'Maniac' and 'manic' come from the same root. It would be a fitting etymology for the warlike culture that was already coalescing in the background.

With no authority in place, except in a castle or two, the law of the sword prevailed. Barbarian invasions, unrest and plagues sent a growing number of refugees to the area. Farming could not possibly have sustained the population and, by the late Byzantine period, it wouldn't have suited their temperament either. More lucrative activities such as piracy and the slave trade blossomed. The Franks came and fortified the castle of Maina near Mézapos, but did not attempt inroads into the hinterland. And thus, over time, the free-wheeling, weapon-toting Maniátes developed their own social system. An aristocratic few, the Nikliáni, had political clout and their houses sprouted high narrow towers with tiny openings for guns, and often a platform on top for a cannon. The lower echelons of society were called Achamnómeri; they had few rights, and were not only obliged to help the Nikliáni in their wars, but were forced to live in low houses with flimsy roofs within shooting range of the towers, so retribution would be swift if they rebelled. This explains the compact quality of Maniáte villages. Enemy towers, bristling with weapons, implacably at war, were often so close they could shout insults at each other with ease. In other cases, families held larger areas like the Mavromichális clan at Tsimova (Areópolis) and Liméni. Many grandly claimed to descend from Byzantine royal houses.

In the Máni, the lawless, warlike ethos joined seamlessly with the Christian church in a symbiotic relationship that can only be marvelled at for its sheer chutzpah. There are tiny churches everywhere, and when fighting made going to church difficult, churches were added to the tower compounds. Ritual was observed; a Maniáte was perfectly capable of making the sign of the cross before a church he was going to blow to smithereens if it sheltered a rival clan member. It speaks volumes for life in the Máni that there are no large churches at all.

Turf wars over scarce land resources may explain how the fighting became institutionalized into vendettas with elaborate rites regarding truces, treatment of women and so on. By the time outsiders visited the Máni and recorded its strange ways, etiquette and murder went hand in hand, and the vendetta was an accepted, even glorified way of life. The birth of a male was announced as the birth of a new 'gun' in the family, and the Maniátes raised the presence of death to the heights of poetry in their wonderful *myrologia*. These long-drawn-out extempore funeral songs chanted by black-garbed women (*mirologístres*) could go on for hours, in praise of the dead, in lamentation against 'fate' (*myrologia* means 'fate words'), and, in the many cases of violent death, actively encouraging revenge. They were as practised and passionate in their recitals as any Homeric bard.

> God made so many good things, but one thing failed to make,
> A bridge athwart the sea, and a stair to the underworld,
> That one might cross, one might descend and go to the world beneath,
> And see the young folk where they sit, the old folk where they lie,
> And see the little children, how they fare without their mothers.

The Turks tried various strategies to control the area. In 1669, they allowed the Maniátes 'privileges' denied to other Greeks, namely permission to ring their church bells, put crosses on their belfries and pay lower taxes. They also rescinded the child tax law, so Maniáte first sons did not have to be sent to the Porte to become Janissaries as they did in the rest of Greece. Of course, they were just making a virtue of necessity, because no one was about to enter the Máni to enforce the law. The Turks built forts at Kelefá and Pórto Káyio, just to keep their foot in the door, and to try to counter growing Venetian influence. The Máni was a virtual recruitment centre for Venetian and Russian efforts to harass the Sultan.

Like other freedom fighters in Greece, the Maniátes were left in the lurch again and again as the Great Powers, influenced by larger political interests, briefly helped, then pulled out and left them to Turkish reprisals. But the Maniátes never gave up. By 1776, the Turks, somewhat at their wits' end, formally invested all local powers in Beys, chosen from the Máni's important clans. In return for collecting taxes and keeping order, these Beys were offered protection from other clans by the Turkish Captain Pasha of the area. Not surprisingly, the Maniáte Beys simply managed to wrest more privileges from the Turks while doing very little in return. It was a dangerous job: out of the seven Beys from 1776 to 1821, three were executed by the Turks, and three summarily dismissed. The last was the famous Petróbey of the Mavromichális clan, a clan that provided many 'guns' for the War of Independence when it finally came.

Ironically, the victory they fought so hard and well for would turn out to be the death knell for their own way of life. Constitutional rule and a foreign king did not sit well with Maniátes, who would have preferred to carry on as before, or even to enlarge their territory. In 1831, after members of the Mavromichális clan had assassinated Capodístrias, Greece's first president, the young King Otto's advisors decided that the Maniátes needed to be 'civilized'. One of the king's first edicts was that the towers in the Máni and Arcadía had to go. Arcadía complied, but the Máni didn't.

A Note on Maniáte Churches and Towers

Maniáte churches are fascinating. All are small, but their exteriors and interiors are lovingly decorated, often with childlike charm. The Máni is simply so rich in them that the most dilapidated ones have been left to moulder away, doubling as animal shelters, bird houses and bat caves. Some churches resemble piles of enormous stones, but are decorated with care inside. Ag. Pandaleímonos in Boulárioi is a good example of the type. There has been quite an effort recently to signpost churches and monuments. Those in isolated spots are invariably locked; ask at your hotel or in the nearest village coffeehouse about keys.

Towers exist everywhere: all alone as watch towers, in company with one-storey houses or most commonly with two-storey houses. Villages resemble medieval Italian hill villages – Kítta or Váthia look like miniature San Gimignanos. Since the Franks were mostly Italian in the last part of their Peloponnesian interlude, and the Venetians from Koróni and Methóni were a constant influence, there may have been some borrowing. Certainly in the beginning the towers were home-made versions of the Venetian watch towers that dot the Peloponnese – no-nonsense affairs, meant to give height, not to display wealth. They become more elaborate as building techniques improved and their owners grew richer; some have the trappings of little castles. This effect is heightened by the tendency, as time went by, to put walls around the house and tower, creating an inner courtyard, and adding a church as well. These tower complexes exist in the Inner Máni, but they positively proliferate in the richer Outer Máni. The stone work could be rough, almost megalithic, as if the Cyclops had come to town. But this, too, changed over time, and became more sophisticated, especially among the Maniáte clans with pretensions, and there were a lot of those. You would be on precarious ground dating buildings by their architectural style, however; what makes the Máni so remarkable is that their 'medieval cities' were built from 1600 on, and were being added to as late as 1850.

How to Visit the Máni

The **Outer Máni** can be traversed easily in a day in the 80km from Kalamáta to Areópolis, although to do so would be to miss a lot of its charm. The **Inner Máni** is also small enough to drive around in a day, and many visitors do just that, using Gýthio as a base. A day or two in three or more places would be ideal. In the high season, book ahead. Many of the hotels are in traditional buildings, and run by locals who have a story to tell, making the choice of accommodation part of the experience.

When King Otto sent his Bavarian troops down to the Máni on a tower-destruction mission, the entire army were captured, stripped naked and held for ransom. A typical example of the Maniáte sense of humour is the price they asked the king to pay: 20 cents a soldier, 10 cents an officer, and 2 dollars for a donkey.

Eventually even the Máni was brought to heel, but not until the tower order, luckily for posterity, was rescinded. But it was a slow process. The common expression in Greek, to hold something *Maniátiko*, still means holding an implacable grudge that demands revenge. *Mirologístres* exist, although diminished in ranks. And reading the death notices in the local paper proves that poetic eulogies have not yet gone out of style in the Máni. One family in Areópolis buried a loved one recently and commissioned a *myrologístra*. Her lament 'broke the heart of the rocks,' the satisfied funeral-goers proclaimed.

Water is now piped into the Inner Máni, making it difficult to comprehend just how barren it was. For years, the young defected to the cities en masse. How many years longer will old women in black be seen sitting in front of low tower doors, with huge Kelvinator refrigerators sent by the kids gleaming in the depths behind? A few young people are coming back to help with the new tourist boom; there is building going on everywhere, almost all in the native style. Right now, the Máni, at the start of a new millennium, still looks back to the old. Visit now, before it changes utterly.

Gýthio: the Gateway to the Inner Máni

Gýthio was founded by two gods after a dispute over a pot. Heracles was miffed because the priestess at Delphi refused to purify him after one of his forays into mayhem and murder, so he stole the famous tripod she sat on while receiving oracular messages. Apollo went after him and fisticuffs broke out at Phenéos in Arcadía. Zeus stepped in, reclaimed the tripod for Delphi and made the boys shake hands. As a sign of their new bond, they built Gýthio. Gýthio was a Mycenaean settlement and port; tholos tombs at nearby Mavrovoúni were used by the Germans as bunkers during the Second World War. During the Classical period it was Sparta's port and a town of *perioikoi* (*see* p.297), famous for its murex molluscs that produced a purple dye so prized it became the colour of royalty. The town thrived when the Romans created the Free Laconian League, as a buffer against Sparta. Today Gýthio claims 4,000 inhabitants, and tourism is big business.

Overlooking the curve of the bay, Gýthio's pastel houses tumble down from the ancient acropolis, Laryssion, to its long seaside street. The renovated hotels and restaurants, with newer rivals, have transformed the once down-at-heel port. Always

Getting There and Around

The **bus** station, **t** 273 302 2228, is close to the sea on the Sparta road. Six buses per day go to and from Athens (in Athens: **t** 210 512 4913) via Corinth-Trípolis-Sparta; Kalamáta via Ítilo has two per day; Areópolis and Geroliménas, four per day. These last pass the campsites at Mavrovoúni and Passava; you can even get to Váthia on some days. For Monemvasiá, you'll have to take a bus 17km up the Sparta road to Xánia, and wait for a connecting bus.

Ferries to Crete and Kýthera are sporadic, and depend on the season. Contact the Rozakis Travel Agency, **t** 273 302 2207, **f** 273 302 2229, on the waterfront near the docks; they also do **car rentals**.

Mopeds can be hired at Super Cycle, **t** 273 302 4407 on the main *plateía*. **Taxis**, **t** 273 302 2601, are at the taxi stand opposite the KTEL station.

Tourist Information

EOT tourist booth (summer only): in the centre at Vas. Georgiou 20, not far from Aktaeon Hotel, **t** 273 302 4484. Two **bookshops** by the bus station, the Ladopoúlou and Andreíkos, have books on the Máni.

Where to Stay

Gýthio ✉ 23200

All hotels overlook the sea, are open all year, and most offer off-season discounts. Gýthio's campsites are lined up along the sandy beach at Mavrovoúni.

Aktaion, **t** 273 302 3500, **f** 273 302 2294, *www.hotelakteon.gr* (*B; expensive–moderate*). A gem of a period renovation from its reception to its air-conditioned bedrooms.

Gythion, **t** 273 302 3452, **f** 273 302 3523 (*B; moderate, breakfast inc.*). A small hotel with spacious rooms and a large piece of the natural cliff face jutting into its lobby.

Kranai, **t/f** 273 302 4394 (*D; moderate*). A wonderful façade with traditional rooms in a variety of sizes and shapes following the original plan.

Pension Saga, **t** 273 302 3220, **f** 273 302 4370 (*inexpensive*). Modern, family-run, nice.

Kalliope Andreakou, **t** 273 302 2829 (*inexpensive*). Beyond the ferry port by the causeway to Marathonísi; rooms with large balconies and shared kitchens.

Xenia Karláfi's Rooms, **t** 273 302 2719, **f** 273 302 2991 (*inexpensive*). By the causeway to Marathonísi. Mrs Karláfi's 'hotel' started many years ago when two people knocked on her door looking for a place to stay. With true Maniáte hospitality, she and her husband gave them their own bedroom, refusing payment, naturally. The visitors left some much-needed cash on her pillow and her guest house was born.

Gythion Beach Camping, **t** 273 302 2522. *Open all year.*

Eating Out

Saga, **t** 273 302 3220. Run by Mr Kolokotróni and his French wife; has a good reputation and a pleasant décor with fireplace.

To Akroyiáli, **t** 273 302 2943. Claims to have an astounding 80 different dishes on any day.

Psarotavérna Constantínos Drakoulákos, **t** 273 302 4086. Near the Hotel Kranai; a picturesque choice for fish with its old blue wooden chairs.

Touristikó Períptero, **t** 273 302 2282. Start your evening with an ouzo in this trendy spot by a lovely park on the sea right in front of the bus station.

---

a popular stop-over (Paris and Helen spent their first amorous night on Kranai island, now **Marathonísi**, before departing for Troy), many use it as a base to explore the Máni, or as a jumping-off point for Crete and Kýthera. The fishing port is huddled to the south by the causeway that ended Marathonísi's days as an island in 1896. Good **beaches** are to the north towards Monemvasiá past the headland, or 2km to the south at Mavrovoúni. Shod in plastic beach shoes to avoid the sea urchins, you can have a pleasant swim off piney Marathonísi and visit the **Museum of the Máni** (*t 273 302 2676; open daily 9.30–5; adm*) at the same time. This is housed in the late 18th-century fortress tower of Zanetbey Grigoráki and offers a good introduction to the Máni, with excellent exhibits of typical houses and portraits of the locals, as well as foreign visitors, during the Turkish period. There is a wonderful one of the great Petróbey, mustachioed, and smoking a *chibouk*, a pipe so long its bowl goes right down to the floor. Big pantaloons, tightly fitting calf-leggings and slippers complete the picture of the great man 'at home'.

The **Roman theatre** is signposted, if you look carefully, on the coastal road on the northern edge of town. Even before its marble pieces were hauled off by all and sundry, it was tiny, with the entire *cavea* a mere 246ft across. Several tiers of marble seats can be seen, including some of the front row VIP seats. The foundations of *skene* remain. For a climb and a view, go behind the causeway and head up to **Laryssion**. There is nothing to see in the way of ruins, but you get the view the Romans got when the acropolis was a going concern.

The Highway from Gýthio to Areópolis

The road stretches west past the campsites and into small scrub and pine clad hills; one at the 9.5km mark is crowned by the **castle of Passava**. Built by Geoffrey de Villehardouin in 1254, the Franks had to abandon it to the Byzantines by 1263. The Turks took over, then the Venetians for a time and then the Turks again. It was not a lucky castle. As in Corinth, the Turkish population lived here along with the soldiers, and in 1780, in retaliation for the execution of a family member, Zanet Grigorákis of Gýthio and his clan overran the castle and killed all 700 men, women and children who lived there. *Myrologia* praised the deed, of course. Astonishingly, this same Zanet was later made an offer by the Turks that he couldn't refuse – to become the Máni's third Bey in 1784, or die. For the best view of the castle, follow the road a short way north towards the nearby village of **Karvelás** and look back. From there its nearly complete 40ft walls can be seen to best advantage. The ruins inside are Turkish, although stones from Homer's city of Las are built into the cisterns. The panoramic views will reward the 15-minute scramble up the hill. After Passava, a road goes south to the very good beach at **Skoutári**, with a couple of towers and tavernas but not much else, then continues, unpaved, to Kótronas and the east coast of the Inner Máni.

Towards Areópolis, the hills become more scoured and barren, except for prickly pear (a trademark of the Inner Máni), its flat dinner plate leaves often the only touch of green. Ten km or so after Passava there is a marked turn-off for the large, ugly, no-nonsense Turkish **fort of Kelefá**, built in 1670 to keep an eye on the roads leading to Areópolis. The best view is from the coast road up to Ítilo.

Areópolis, Ítilo and the Diroú Caves

Areópolis

Once called Tsímova and renamed **Areópolis**, 'the city of Ares', as a compliment to Petróbey Mavromichális and his contribution to the War of Independence, small and compact Areópolis is a perfect introduction to the Inner Máni. Its narrow streets evoke the old days, especially at Easter when they echo with exploding firecrackers at

Getting There and Around

You cannot rent a car or bike either in Areópolis or points south, so plan ahead. The bus station, t 273 305 1229, is the Europa Grill in the main *plateía*. There are two daily buses to Geroliménas and Váthia in summer (three times a week in winter) and one daily to Kótronas. Service to Gýthio, four a day; to Kalamáta three daily with a change at Ítilo; and three to Sparta. Weekends have fewer.

A **bus** to the caves at Diroú leaves at 11am and returns at 12.40pm, just enough time to see the caves if there is no queue. **Taxis** come in handy here, t 273 305 1382, or t 273 305 1588, and prices are roughly €6 to Diroú, €14 to Váthia, and €4 to the beach at Liméni.

Tourist Information

The town publishes a brochure in English with a map, and lists the towers. Ask at the city hall (*dimarchío*) past Plateía 17 Martíou. Areópolis has a bank and a post office.

Shopping

Areópolis is the place to buy *síglino*, a smoked pork that was a Máni staple and is extremely popular to this day, either by itself, baked in oven dishes or in omelettes.

Where to Stay and Eat

Areópolis ✉ 23062

Londas Traditional Hotel, t 273 305 1360, f 273 305 1012 (*expensive*). A beautiful renovation of a Maniáte tower. Try it and live like a modern Petróbey. *Open all year*.

Bozagregos Traditional Guest House, t 273 305 1354/51403 (*low moderate–inexpensive*). A tower house behind the Taxiarchón church. Great hospitality from a barrel-vaulted bar area. There is an outside terrace on the second floor. *Open all year*.

Xenónas Tsímova, t 273 305 1301 (*inexpensive*). By the Taxiarchón church. Mr. Versákos has quite a little war museum below his rooms, and is proud of the fact that Kolokotrónis not only slept here but sent the family a thank you note. He also has two studios, generally inexpensive depending on when. *Open all year*.

Máni, t 273 305 1190, f 273 305 1269 (*C; moderate–inexpensive*). Has a very attractive new stone wing. Each room has a balcony, and two have fireplaces. *Open all year*.

all hours of the day and night, pretty much as they must have during a clan war. Another good time to come is Independence Day, which Areópolis celebrates a week earlier than the rest of Greece, on March 17, the day the Máni rose up. This is a good time to get a look at the Maniáte flag with its two mottos: 'Freedom or Death', from the Greek War of Independence, and 'Return with your Shield or on it', from ancient Sparta. Both sentiments are well within the Maniáte tradition.

The work-a-day main square, **Plateía Athanáton**, is dominated by a huge bronze statue of Petróbey Mavromichális, looking splendidly ferocious and entirely at home among the small business emporia and pick-up trucks. The beautiful old town stretches to the west, down a narrow street which leads to the church of the **Taxiarchón** and Plateía 17 Martíou. This church, with its wonderful stone reliefs of angels, suns, eagles, lions and signs of the Zodiac inside and out and its high bell tower, added on in 1836, is the town landmark. Stroll past this square and head west and in ten minutes you come to the cliffs overlooking the sea. The marvellous view extends as far south as the forbidding bulge of Cávo Grósso. Note the low stone walls everywhere, the tiny fields, and remember that this was the *fertile* area of the Inner Máni. Some of the more famous **towers** are signposted.

Nicola's Place, in the square, t 273 305 1366,. Don't be put off by the awful pictures of what's on offer; the dynamic Démitra takes a real interest in her cooking.

Tsímova, t 273 305 1219. A nice raised terrace in the main square, the better to see Petróbey while dining.

O Barba Petros, t 273 305 1205. In an old stone building en route to Plateía 17 Martíou; this eatery is well established and popular.

March 17 restaurant, Plateía 17 Martíou. A renovated stone house, complete with marble table tops and a huge gilt mirror, the height of Maniáte chic.

Ítilo ✉ 23062

Ítilo, t 273 305 9253, f 273 305 9234 (*A; expensive, luxury in high season*). Quite isolated on a good beach with a nice terrace, but not a lot of Maniáte atmosphere. They also rent rooms in a stone building on the other side of the road. *Open all year.*

Aleuvras Tower Guest House, t 273 305 9388, winter t 210 664 5023 (*A; expensive*). Set up on a hill; large rooms for three people, complete with kitchen, a pool in the garden and a view of the bay. *Open May–Oct.*

O Faros, in Karavostasi, on the road to N. Ítilo. Welcoming taverna on the water's edge, serving fresh fish as well as usual Greek fare.

Also four rooms upstairs (*inexpensive*). *Open all year.*

Liméni ✉ 23062

Liméni Village, t 273 305 1111, f 273 305 1182 (*expensive*). High above Liméni, a new stone complex, with pool, classy lobby – the Máni *à la* Palm Beach. Getting down to the pool is a hike; getting to the beach even more so. *Open all year.*

O Koyrmas Pension, t 273 305 1458 (*inexpensive*). *Very* basic, over a pleasant restaurant, overlooking the rocky shore, by the tower of Petróbey. *Open April–Oct.*

Diroú ✉ 23063

Diros, at the turning to Diroú from the main road, t 273 305 2306 (*C; moderate*). A plain hotel offers air-conditioning and screens, but far from the sea. *Open all year.*

Panorama, t 273 305 2280 (*low moderate*). Close enough to the caves to be in walking distance; air-conditioned, too. The owner promises fresh fish from his taverna downstairs and the use of his fridge. *Open April–Oct.*

Villa Koulis, 7km south of Diroú, t 273 305 2350 (*inexpensive, moderate in Aug*). New, built of traditional stone, in a big garden; large, with balconies and kitchens. *Open all year.*

Ítilo and Liméni

Ítilo, the capital of the Inner Máni, is an unremarkable town 10km north of Areópolis. At the southern end of Ítilo's bay, **Liméni** was the stronghold of the Mavromichális clan, and here **Petróbey's tower** stands perfectly preserved. Petros Mavromichális became Bey in 1815. He impressed the English traveller Colonel Leake as a 'gentleman', praise indeed from Leake, who had a very jaundiced view of the Máni. While he was Bey, he and his clan plotted with the expatriate Greek revolutionaries of the *Philiki Eteria*, and it was Petróbey who stood outside the church of the Taxiarchón in Tsímova and declared the Máni's independence. Forty-nine members of his family would die in the subsequent fighting, not an unusual statistic in the Máni during this war. It was his arrest that led his clan to assassinate Capodístria in Naúplio. Petróbey himself survived incarceration and returned to the Máni to fight another day, this time for the Greek government – when it suited his own plans for the area, of course.

The Caves at Diroú and the Museum

Caves, t 273 305 2222, open June–Sept 9–5, Oct–May 8.30–3.30; adm exp.

Museum, t 273 305 2233, open all year Tues–Sun 8.30–3.30; adm.

Eleven kilometres south of Areópolis, the spectacular caves at Diroú lie hidden on the south side of a large bay. The cave of **Vlychada** is part of a large subterranean lake system in which, so far, over 5km of passages and great halls have been explored and mapped. Parts are open to the public, who float through in small boats, a journey that, in spite of the sardonic guides and hype, is awe-inspiring. The water temperature inside averages 18°C, and at its deepest point is 100ft. There are stalactites in fantastic shapes and colours, and even stalagmites under the water, formed before sea levels rose. Fossils over two million years old have been found. Two other caves, **Alepótripa** (the foxhole) and **Kataphygí** (the refuge) are not yet open to the public. In the former, the 'great hall' measures 330ft by 100ft. The Alepótripa yielded extensive Neolithic remains and rock paintings, which are very rare in Greece. These finds feed the museum and continually push the date back for man's first step on the Máni.

South of Diroú: Into the Bad Mountains

South of Diroú, the tail end of Taíyetos becomes the **Kakovoúnia**, the Bad Mountains. They don't look more evil than others in the Máni, and Patrick Leigh Fermor, in his excellent book *Mani*, puts forth a convincing argument that the alternative name for the region, *Kakovoúlia*, the Land of Evil Council, is actually a misinterpretation of *kakkavoula*, the Cauldroneers. The name recalls the Maniáte habit of converting their three-legged cauldrons into helmets when they attacked a passing ship; there are records of them doing just that into the 18th century.

There is no road over the Bad Mountains until Álika and Pórto Káyio, although one or two hikers' paths exist. The best of these is from **Karínia**, south of Mína, over to **Éxo Nímfio**. This leaves the west coast, the 'Shadowy Coast', and the east coast, the 'Sunny Coast', quite separate. Small towns are hemmed in by the sea on one side and the mountains on the other, so it isn't easy to get lost. The main road goes south 9km to the turn-off for Mézapos. In order to get a close look at several small villages, try the parallel unpaved road through **Fragoúlias**, **Dríalos**, **Vámvaka** to **Mína**. Vámvaka's lovely cruciform church, with elaborate cloisonné brickwork, dates from 1075. The stone walls snaking down the bald mountain behind these villages is a reminder of the

Where to Stay and Eat

Stavrí and Geroliménas ✉ 23071

Michális Georgoulákos, t 273 305 6244. Mézapo's only eatery: plain, no-frills; fish taverna that has been there for years.

Pirgos Tsitsiri, Stavrí, t 273 3056297, f 210 685 8962 (*B; expensive–moderate, breakfast included*). A renovated tower house with some thoughtful extras. Larger windows, and a terrace in the courtyard. Its dining room is a barrel-vaulted basement; its position on the Cávo Grósso makes it ideal for rambling, especially towards Tigáni. *Open all year.*

Faros Apartments, Geroliménas, t/f 273 305 4271 (*just moderate*). Air-conditioned, quiet; two rooms have large balconies overlooking the stunning cliffs of Cávo Grósso. Its seafront is rocky; there's a wooden dock for swimmers or a walk to the shingle beach.

Akropoyiáli, t/f 273 305 4204 (*E; moderate–inexpensive*). On the beach, run by Mr. Theodorakáki and his Canadian wife, a sculptor. Their terraced restaurant under the hotel has a good reputation. *Open all year.*

Porto, Porto Kayio, t 273 305 2033. A fish taverna on the beach run by a member of the Grigorákis clans. For dessert, it offers an art gallery with 'subjects from the Máni'.

once intensive efforts at farming. Just past the turn-off to Mézapos, on the right, is **Ag. Nikólaos**, a nice combination of tower house and church.

Mézapos, Tigáni and Cávo Grósso

Sleepy, out-of-the-way **Mézapos** was a pirate centre once, and an important stop for the ferries that plied the Inner Máni before the road was built. Now it is almost deserted. Down by the mole to the right is a small, almost perfectly circular bay completely surrounded by high cliffs, tempting a swim. Mézapos offers fine views of **Tigáni**, a long bone-white causeway of jagged rock that curves a kilometre out into the bay and widens at the end to support the imposing ruins of a castle. *Tigáni*, 'frying pan', describes it perfectly. Behind it, the 1,000ft cliffs of **Cávo Grósso** rise to the south in one of the grandest spectacles the Máni has to offer. These limestone precipitous cliffs are riddled with caves, called *thyrides* or 'windows' by locals. The same word, *thyrides*, is used today for safe deposit boxes in Greek banks, no doubt partly because these particular windows were used by Maniáte pirates over the years expressly to stash their loot. The top of the cape is a fairly smallish flat area by anyone else's standards, but it's the great plain of the Inner Máni.

Tigáni can best be reached on foot from **Stavrí**, on the heights of Cávo Grósso. The going is tough. Tigáni's arm is pock marked with salt pans, 365 of them, an old song claims. Gathering salt was an industry in the Máni at one time, and the villagers still produce their own. Tigáni's castle, the famous Byzantine **Castle Maina**, probably stands on Homer's 'dove haunted Messe'. Its 2,460ft perimeter encloses cisterns, incomprehensible ruins, Cyclopean walls from about 1300 BC, and the foundations of a large (by Máni standards) Byzantine church, 72ft long. This was probably the cathedral for the bishopric formed in the 9th century. Tigáni has garnered innumerable stories, including one about a princess who was loved by Death. He came and swept her away, leaving his horse's hoof print on the stairs to the castle. In the Máni, Death was admired for the invincible warlord he was. If the walk to Tigáni's castle is too daunting, take the road from Stavrí towards Tigáni right to the end for the view.

Kítta and Geroliménas

Kítta sits half way between Mézapos and Geroliménas, and offers a view over the entire Cávo Grósso and a marvellous collection of tower houses and churches. Its name could come from *cittá*, city in Italian, reinforcing some theorists who find an Italian influence on the Máni's towers. They say Kítta was settled by Niklians from Arcadía when the Frankish empire collapsed. In 1805 it had 22 towers and was the biggest settlement in the Inner Máni. Today, it has even more towers, a reminder that many were built after 1800.

Geroliménas, with its good-sized shingle beach, is what passes for civilization in these parts. It was important in the 1800s, when it rivalled Mézapos. Now it contains a cluster of restaurants and hotels along with more traditional houses. The massive cliffs of Cávo Grósso loom over the bay, creating quite a shadow in the late afternoon. It's a good base for exploring nearby **Upper and Lower Boulárioi**. The two Boulárís have between them an astonishing 21 churches dating from the 10th to the 18th centuries; the most important is the domed, cruciform church of **Ag. Strátigos**, which dates from the 11th century and contains marvellous frescos. This area was the baili-wick of the Mantoúvali clan. Upper Boulároi has the earliest tower built in the Máni (*c.* 1600) and, nearby, the restored Mantoúvalos family tower.

Kipárissos, Váthia and Pórto Káyio

South at **Kipárissos**, a road by the river bed takes you to a beach with a headland on its left. This was Roman **Kenípolis**. Water under this area made wells and the estab-lishment of a busy town possible. It is still a little oasis today with small gardens and robust olive trees, and ruins, including temples to Aphrodite and Demeter. On the inner slope of the headland are the remains of the 5th-century **Basilica of Ag. Pétrou** mouldering in a private garden. (Try asking for the '*Archaíos Naós tou Agioú Pétrou*'.) At 70ft by 62ft, it was a fair size, and one of the Máni's earliest churches. These ruins still create a certain *frisson*, as if ghosts linger here.

The road then climbs to **Váthia**, an especially photogenic nest of tower houses, this time crowning a hill. The inhabitants were apparently involved in a feud that lasted 40 years. It is so compact that it is hard to imagine how even complicated rules of etiquette could have handled the usual truces, breaks for holidays, harvesting and so on. The road continues south to a point so narrow that a single glance encompasses the wonderful small bays of **Marmári** to the west and **Pórto Káyio** to the east. Pórto Káyio, the port of quails (from the Italian *Porto Quaglio*) was a popular hunting ground for these birds as they migrated. The Turks placed a **fort** here in 1669 which, with a few lovely stone houses and a little monastery, offers a great view across the bay. On 29 March 1942, Allied forces were evacuated from here to Crete. While a single German Stukka divebombed the battleship, a returning hail of bullets from the battleship missed the plane, but hit the castle, the last time it was ever involved in a battle. Pórto Káyio with its little tavernas is a popular spot for lunch and a swim.

Up the Sunny Coast

At this point, most visitors head back up the 'Sunny' east coast and back to Gýthio. The intrepid may wish to carry on to Cape Taíneron, an isolated piece of real estate with a unique history (*see* below).

Five km north of Pórto Káyio, **Láyia** has a large collection of tower houses, some of them very old – you can recognize them by their tapered tops. At 1,300ft, it offers a vista and a coffee shop. Northwest of Láyia are quarries of *antico rosso*, a red-hued marble that was much sought after even in Mycenaean times; some of it graced the treasury of Atreus. The road north is hemmed into an extremely narrow space between mountain and sea. Three km past **Kokkála**, turn left at Éxo Nímfio and drive up to Mésa Chóra, then make the hike up to the **Moni Panagías Kournoú**, by a never-failing spring. The rare water source made this isolated spot the site of a small city; the ruins of two Doric **temples**, all that remains of ancient Aígila, sit on a plateau about 500m beyond the monastery. Pleasant **Kótronas** at the top of the east coast has a sandy beach and tavernas, but seems just a tad too civilized after the journey south. From here, roads go inland to Areópolis or around the cape north to Skoutári.

Cape Taíneron and the Underworld

From Pórto Káyio an unpaved road continues south to the ruined chapel of **Ag. Asomáton** and a coffee shop, set on a little oval bay. Ag. Asomáton occupies a rectangular building dating from Hellenistic times; its name ('the bodiless') refers to Archangel Michael, who, in the Greek church, is the 'gatherer of dead souls'. His presence here is no accident: 60 yards away is the cave occupied by the famous **Sanctuary of Poseidon** at Taíneron, which was both *asyla* and *ávaton* (not to be violated and not to be trodden). Besides the usual priests, it had a resident *psychopompeion*, escorter of souls of the dead and representative of the border-crossing god Hermes, who bore his chthonic staff, the *kerykeion*, with its stylized copulating snakes. The sanctuary was one of the few where a killer, with the aid of the *psychopompeion*, could summon up the soul of his victim and placate him with a sacrifice.

This sanctuary also had connections with other marginal types – outlaws, mercenaries (in Hellenistic times it was the greatest 'man market' in Greece) and escaping helots. The destruction of Sparta in an earthquake in 464 BC was attributed to the wrath of Poseidon after the Spartan ephors had dragged helots out of this sanctuary and murdered them, an act that shocked the entire Greek world, and was the subject of a lost play by Eupolis called *The Helots*. Traces of the sanctuary can be seen: cuttings on the north side of the entrance, where stelae recorded the emancipation of slaves, and numerous rock-cut foundations. These are believed to have been used for the construction of huts for supplicants; apparently there were many. Silician pirates were not impressed and destroyed the sanctuary in the 1st century BC.

A path from the end of the road leads in a half hour to the lighthouse of **Cape Taíneron** (or **Matapan**), the southernmost point of continental Greece, and the southernmost point in Europe with the exception of Tarifa in Spain. On the other side of the cape (accessible only by boat; ask around in Marmari) is the **entrance to hell**, locally known as η σπηλια του αδη. Taíneron was one of most famous of Hades' ventilation shafts, favoured by mortals on quests, although the results were mixed. Theseus and his friend Peirithous descended here to kidnap Persephone; Heracles used it to kidnap the three-headed dog Cerberos in his Twelfth Labour; Orpheus descended in search of his Eurydice; and Psyche went down to find Aphrodite's beauty kit.

The Outer Máni: Kámbos, Kardamýli and Stoúpa

The Outer Máni is remarkable for its small Byzantine churches, its stunning scenery and beautiful seaside towns, Kardamýli and Stoúpa in particular. With its blend of olive trees, cypresses, limestone mountains and blue sea, it is a place the term 'Mediterranean landscape' was invented to describe, particularly the area between Kardamýli to Ítilo. Cut off in the old days from Kalamáta by the rocky prominence of Mount Kaláthi and Capes Kitriés and Koúrtissa, today's road heads for the hills, marked with guard towers here and there until Kámbos and points south.

Kámbos and the Castle Zarnata

The substantial village of **Kámbos** is set in a fertile upland plain of olives and meadows that attracted the Mycenaeans. To the south, it is overlooked by the

Getting Around

Kardamýli's **bus** station, **t** 272 107 3642, is in Evangelos Troupákis' ouzerie in the centre of town, making waiting for a bus part of the holiday. There are three to four buses a day to and from Kalamáta, and three from Ítilo that pass through Stoúpa as well.

Taxis are plentiful: call Níkos, **t** 293 297 7929; Vassílis, **t** 272 107 7477; or Geórgos, **t** 272 107 3382. The taxi drivers hang about at Mr Troupákis', hopefully drinking coffee, not ouzo. A taxi ride to Stoúpa is €5–6. **Best Car Rent a Car, t** 272 107 3940, is in Kardamýli on the main street. For information in Stoúpa, ask at **Travel Agency Zorbas, t** 272 107 7735, **f** 273 107 7754, at the north end of the beach.

Where to Stay and Eat

Kardamýli ✉ 24022

Anniska Apartments, t 272 107 3600, **f** 272 107 3000(*C; moderate, expensive in high season*). Modern seaside apartments in three buildings, run by a hospitable Greek-Australian family. There is a large common terrace, and a binder in every room describes local attractions, including hiking trails with maps. *Open May–Oct.*

The Castle, t 272 107 3226, **f** 272 107 3685 (*inexpensive*). Traditional; small rooms with balconies in a garden, each complete with fridge and tiny kitchen. *Open May–Oct.*

Léla's Pension, t 272 107 3541, **f** 272 107 3730 (*moderate*). Five rooms above the seaside taverna. Book early; it has a loyal and regular clientele. *Open Mar–Oct.*

Olympía Koumanákou Rooms, t 272 107 3623 (*inexpensive*). Behind Léla's, a bargain with a large common kitchen, a garden and very friendly hosts. *Open all year.*

Joan Stephanéa Rooms, t 272 107 3242 (*inexpensive*). On the main road, by the bus station. Three rooms, with baths and a shared kitchen. Mrs Stephanéa will help the 'roomless' using her family network – good to know in August. *Open all year.*

Melítsina Beach Camping, t 272 107 3461 (*inexpensive*). On the stretch of beach north of town among olive trees. *Open April–Sept.*

Kalamítsi, t 272 107 3131, **f** 272 107 3135 (*B; expensive*). In the bay south of town. Rooms with mini-bars and separate bungalows. Well built in an idyllic setting overlooking its own cypresses and olives. As a bonus, you are sharing the bay with Patrick Leigh Fermor, who made the Máni famous, and who may be regretting it now. His house is almost a national shrine. *Open April–Oct.*

Léla's Taverna, t 272 107 3541. Fabulous views and good food served at old-fashioned tables on different levels overlooking the sea, and a room with fireplace for the winter.

Taverna Kikí, t 272 107 3466. Family-run; offers a large variety of Greek fare on its attractive seaside terrace.

O Kýpos tis Kardamýlis, t 272 107 3516. Just behind Kikí's; tables set out in a large garden under grape vines.

Stoúpa ✉ 24024

Stoúpa, t 273 107 7308, **f** 272 107 7568 (*C; moderate*). Modern, nice, set back from the beach; much cheaper out of season; mini-bars in each room. *Open all year.*

Leuktron, t 272 107 7322, **f** 272 107 7720, *leftrone@otenet.gr* (*C; moderate*). Beside the Stoúpa and very like it. *Open April–Oct.*

Apartments To Pefko, t 272 107 7177 (*moderate*). Complete with kitchens and prices which drop dramatically in the off season. *Open all year.*

Apartments Kalógria, t 272 107 7479, **f** 272 107 7679 (*moderate*). Right on the beach at Kalógria, with wonderful views. The Balaktári family offer rooms with fridges, and very good off season prices as well. *Open April–Oct.*

Camping Kalógria, t 272 107 7319. Close to Kalógria Beach, on the other side of the road; lots of shade. *Open June–Sept.*

Akrogiáli, t 272 107 7335. The blue and white terrace is the perfect place to view the bay over a plate of fresh fish.

To Pefko, t 272 107 7452. A terrace, a fireplace. Coffee or food day and night.

Psistariá Stoúpa, t 272 107 7516. At the north end of the bay; grilled meat on a terraced site full of picturesque pine trees overlooking the bay.

perfectly conical hill of the **Castle Zarnata**, a stronghold straight from the pages of C. S. Lewis. Walls, as high as 33ft, encircle the lower part of the hill like the fringe of a monk's tonsure, and much higher up on the 'crown' is a circular keep, topped today by a square Maniáte tower. Bits and pieces of prehistoric and ancient debris stud the hill, suggesting it was Homeric Enópe and Classical Gerínia – the Máni's ruins can only hint at their past as there is very little written or verifiable historical data. The present castle started out as a Byzantine fort, and the Franks are likely responsible for today's outer wall. In the early 1400s Thomas Paleológos, the last Emperor's brother, had control. Then, the castle contained many small houses, each with its underground cistern, a fact it is best not to forget when exploring medieval ruins in Greece.

When the Turks came, they razed the castle and houses and, in 1670, rebuilt the castle as a frontier post to contain the Maniátes. Its circular outer wall enclosed 22,000 square metres, and had a walkway all around, with six towers. To ensure their supremacy (and safety), they added 51 cannons. They built a mosque, too, with an imposing minaret, a type of 'tower' not often seen in the Máni. The Venetians got it for a while after 1690, not by outfacing all those cannons but by treaty, and, in their organized way, mapped the area, giving the settlements around the castle Latin names like today's 'Malta', just west of the castle. The ruined square tower and house were built during the period of the Beys. The little church of **Zoodóchos Pigí**, inside the castle walls, is practically derelict, although it has a wonderful wooden iconostasis and frescoes depicting the signs of the Zodiac, flying horses, and sea creatures.

Around Kámbos

At Charavgý, 6km north of Kámbosa, a paved road will take you up and up to **Vérga**, for a great view of the Messiniakós Gulf and Kalamáta. Continue up the road and you arrive, inevitably in Greece, at a church of **Profítis Ilías**, at about 4,265 ft. Instead of turning left to Vérga on this same road, it is possible to turn right after 4.5km, past the monastery of Ag. Georgíou and up on unpaved roads into the fastness of Taíyetos. The scenic road through **Pigádia** (spring) and **Kephalóvrissa** (spring head), their names reminders of the all-important water source that settlements in these mountains depended on, can even take you to the Sparta road just west of the Kaiádas. Ask in Kámbos about this road before trying it.

Kardamýli

Six kilometres south of Zarnata, and you'll suddenly find yourself circling down like an eagle, with a tremendous view of the Viros Gorge cutting deep into Taíyetos and the small coastal plain of Kardamýli. Lush and small, Kardamýli is also extremely pretty. In spring, its flowering shrubs and aromatic bushes will make you wish you were all nose. Happily, it lacks a coastal road. The town shore is rocky, and although swimming is possible, especially off the dock, there is also a sand and pebble beach stretching for quite a way, within walking distance north of town.

Even in the Mycenaean period, Kardamýli was popular. In the *Iliad*, Agamemnon offered it to Achilles, to mitigate his famous 'wrath'. The fact that he refused shows just how mad he was. And the Dioschouri, the twins Castor and Polydeuces, were born in Kardamýli, hatched from the same nest as Helen and Clytemnestra by a brooding Leda after Zeus' notorious visit to her in the guise of a swan. The twins remained popular gods of the Spartans as well as gods of sailors and of hospitality. Zeus turned them into the constellation Gemini when they died and they are generally depicted in flowing white gowns with stars in attendance around their heads. The fact that stars and celestial bodies are a popular Outer Máni motif carved on lintels and doorways may be just coincidence, but it is nice to think it's a tribute to two home boys who made good. The **graves of the Dioscouri** (Mycenaean tombs, carved in the rock) can be visited on the path up from 'Old Kardamýli to Ag. Sophía church.

Not much is known about Classical Kardamýli. Pausanias described an acropolis and temples. Under Augustus, the Romans were in a sufficiently expansive mood to offer Kardamýli as a gift to Sparta, so it could have a port (Roman benevolence didn't run to giving them Gýthio back). Sparta accepted with alacrity. If you consider the hike from Sparta over the Taíyetos, it was a gift only a Spartan could have construed as a favour.

This past, however, was a prelude for Kardamýli's great historical moment that produced the wonderful conglomeration of ruins of 'Old Kardamýli' at the north end of the town. Most of it was built in the late 1700s. These medieval-looking settlements, represented most fully by the Troupákis, Moúrtzinos and Petréas enclaves, are wonderful examples of the acme of Maniáte tower-complex-building, and the feudal way of life they represented.

Old Kardamýli

Following the signs to 'Old Kardamýli' will take you up the river bed a short way and to the main gate of the **Moúrtzinos compound**, now minus its massive wooden door. Inside the courtyard is the church of **Ag. Spyrídon**, built, they say, at the beginning of the 18th century. Dates are tricky in the Máni. Its 56ft Frankish bell tower sports ornamental designs showing the sun, moon, stars and the double-headed eagle, a lovely mixed bag of symbols, here in marble rather than the usual sandstone. The church's eight-sided dome is Byzantine; its slightly pointed arched window, Frankish.

The **houses**, too, displayed not only superior workmanship and wealth (the use of ceramic tiles for the roof, rather than slate, meant money), but a mixture of Byzantine, Latin and even Turkish architectural styles that is dazzling in its own right. Inside the courtyard is a two-storey house, which like all Maniáte houses has narrow windows topped by an arch and, in the corner, the important defensive tower, with its many wooden floors packed with all the paraphernalia needed in times of siege. This one has a ground floor storeroom and a stairway up to its entrance. Unlike the houses, the towers were all business, and not comfortable. Various other storerooms, sleeping quarters and a spring or cistern for gathering rainwater make up the rest. In short, a miniature medieval castle. These families controlled trade, functioning as self-proclaimed customs houses and overseeing all aspects of local life. All in all, it was a more genteel existence for the wealthy than in the parched Inner Máni. Kolokotrónis slept here. He slept in more places than Napoleon or George Washington. And, like everyone else, he slept on the floor. As in many village houses in Greece until the 1950s, bedding was folded up in the corner by day, and spread over the floor at night.

The Moúrtzinos family not only had a resident priest – handy in times of vendettas – but a full time paid storyteller. Those other towers overlooking the complex probably belonged to allies. In any case, the Moúrtzinos would have owned other towers at strategic points in the area. Maniátes rarely put all of their 'guns' in one basket.

Twice a day the church bell would ring and the wooden doors were thrown open to welcome a queue of citizens and retainers who came for meals that may have been cooked in the small ruin just to the left, inside the main gate. This Maniáte custom was widespread. The Grigoráki in Gýthio were also famous for this kind of hospitality. In a second courtyard, also with its own tower, lie ruins of the olive press and mill stones. The **enclave of the Petréas Family**, just to the southeast, is composed of three fortified towers, various living quarters and storerooms, a small family cemetery and a spring with an arched entrance from 1734. Many old compounds are still inhabited by family members, who have renovated them with varying degrees of aesthetic success, and some offer a good idea of what Maniáte life must have been like.

Around Kardamýli: Walking and Hiking

With a copy of the town's map called *Hiking Routes and Walking Times*, you can walk through the entire Víros Gorge: paths go from **Prosílio**, 8km north of Kardamýli, east to **Tséria** or **Zachariá**, and hence into the gorge. Alternatively, the two-hour walk to and from Kardamýli to the church of **Ag. Sophía** is not too strenuous, and it takes you past the 'graves' of the Dioscuri. Stick to the river bed only and you can go to the **Monastery of the Sotíros** and back in two hours. A 4- to 5-hour walk starting at **Exochóri**, way above town, will take you into the gorge and back to Kardamýli, via great natural scenery, some ruined mills, a cave or two, and some water springs.

Go south of Kardamýli a bit and then up to **Proástio**, which has the greatest ratio of religious to secular buildings of any village in the Máni – one church or monastery for every eight houses. The really keen can hike up to the church of Profítis Ilías on top of the Taíyetos (*see* p.305). In some cases, taking a taxi and walking back is a good idea.

Stoúpa

Stoúpa has a beautiful sandy beach in a picture-perfect semicircular bay that is its honeypot and its curse. Tourists swarm to Stoúpa, and they have brought intensive development in their wake, creating a dense hive of attractive seaside dwellings that overpower the beach. Foreign-owned condominiums dot the area as well. With its blue waters and shallow sea it is still a wonderful choice in the off season; a less attractive one in August when the beach might be hard to find under the bodies. In winter, Stoúpa is pretty much deserted except on weekends. If peace and quiet is your goal, leave Stoúpa in the high season and head for Kardamýli.

Past the north end of Stoúpa's beach, but on the road into town, is the beautiful little bay of **Kalógria**, also with a beach, where Níkos Kazantzákis lived between 1917–18 trying to run a lignite mine with a certain Macedonian miner and skirt-chaser named Geórgios Zorbas, in the saga that would become *Zorba the Greek*. The residents insist that many of the other characters in the novel were portraits of locals.

Around Stoúpa

Ancient Leuktra sits on a table top rock just north of Kalógria. Experts claim it was also the site of the Castle of Beaufort built by William de Villehardouin. The ruins of both are sparse, but the setting is great. Straight up from Stoúpa, a scenic route leads into the mountain to **Kastaniá**, **Saidóna**, and after that the sky's the limit. This road can take you to the other side of Taíyetos in good weather. On no account miss the small secondary road leading several kilometres south from the seaside town of Ag. Nikólaos to **Trachíla**, where the white rocky prominence in front has summer fish tavernas. The view is lovely and the stones form a kind of miniature Tigáni (*see* p.325).

Between Stoúpa and Ítilo

The main road between Stoúpa and Ítilo is lined with hedgerows of prickly pear and great views of the sea, and passes through a series of charming villages, each one with at least one show-stopper medieval church. In **Nomitsís** it's the frescoed chapel of the Anárgiri, while the practically twin villages of **Thalámes** and **Langáda** are both worth exploring. The church in Thalámes is little 13th-century **Ag. Sophía**; Thalámes also has a coffee shop named **Oasis**, which is no exaggeration. Its car park sports what looks like an ancient statue base, an ancient something or other in any case, just to set the tone. (Don't expect the locals to enlighten you about ancient stones. They have been looking at them all their lives and are not impressed.) The entire village is built on top of ancient Thalámes. But even if it wasn't, the plane-shaded terrace of Mr Pávlos Michaléakos' *kafeneíon*, surrounded by old stone houses, is worth a stop for its sheer beauty alone. For the ultimate experience, see if you can persuade him to make you a delicious omelette with *síglino*, the smoked pork the Máni made famous.

Langáda has gorgeous stone houses and **Ag. Sotíros**, a marvellous little church containing icons from the 10th century. Towers rise in tiers up the hill; the signposted **Pýrgos Kapetsino** is one of them. The tiled roofs here have quite an unusual turned-up edge. Farther south at **Ag. Níkon**, the church of the same name deserves a look and the coffee shop in the square, by the heroic monument crowned by an eagle, just begs you to stop for a coffee. The road continues south to Ítilo, *see* p.323.

Messenía

Down in the southwest Peloponnese, Messenía is the luxuriant land of King Olive. Here, groves in thick canopies produce not only fine oil but also fat, tapering, purply brown Kalamáta olives that make a much appreciated addition to any Greek salad and are grown according to a secret farming technique. Everyone in Messenía owns a few trees, and although you may find smaller hotels that stay open after October, they come with the caveat that it may be hard to find the owners during the harvest. The province is also famous for its figs – it produces over half the national total.

In the *Iliad*, Messenía was the home of King Nestor, 'the flower of Achaean chivalry', whose calm reasonableness provided a foil for the hotheads at Troy. Unlike the other bossy Dorian states of Argos and Sparta, Messenía didn't have a central kingship, but

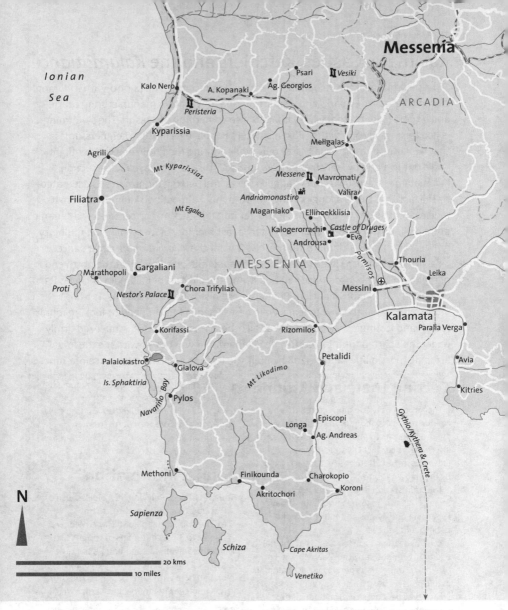

Messenía

Ionian Sea

ARCADIA

Kalo Nero
Psari
Vesiki
A. Kopanaki
Ag. Georgios
Peristeria
Kyparissia
Meligalas
Agrili
Mt Kyparissias
Messene
Mavromati
Andriomonastiro
Valira
Filiatra
Mt Egaleo
Maganiako
Ellinoekklisia
Kalogerorrachi
Castle of Druges
Androusa
Eva
MESSENIA
Pamisos
Thouria
Marathopoli
Gargaliani
Leika
Proti
Chora Trifylias
Nestor's Palace
Messini
Korifassi
Rizomilos
Kalamata
Paralia Verga
Palaiokastro
Petalidi
Avia
Is. Sphaktiria
Gialova
Mt Likodimo
Kitries
Navarino Bay
Pylos
Episcopi
Longa
Ag. Andreas
Gythio/Kythera & Crete
Methoni
Finikounda
Charokopio
Akritochori
Koroni
Sapienza
Schiza
Cape Akritas
Venetiko

N

20 kms
10 miles

was divided into small self-governing units. By the 8th century BC, this state of affairs
was far too mellow for the jealous military egos next door, and after a long war
Messenía was captured and enslaved by the Spartans. Their subjugation finally ended
in the 4th century BC, when they became free to share fully in the vicissitudes of the
Peloponnese during the Hellenistic and Roman periods. In the Middle Ages, contact
and trade with Venice brought prosperity, then bitter battles with the Turks; during
the War of Independence, Messenía witnessed the sea battle at Navaríno that led
directly to Greek independence. For the visitor today, it offers beautiful sandy
beaches, a decent dose of culture and a convenient airport in Kalamáta.

Kalamáta: Castles, Kerchiefs and the *Kalamatianó*

The second city of the Peloponnese is actually a nice town of 44,000, with a vibrant cultural life, galleries, parks and a smart marina for yachts. A manufacturing centre and oil port (olive oil, that is), Kalamáta is also something of a resort. The swimming is good, especially out by the Filoxenía hotel's pebble beach. Still, foreigners, unless they're plane-spotting, usually stay only while waiting for a train or a charter flight.

Laid out in a grid by French engineers in 1829 after Ibrahim Pasha's destruction, Kalamáta has the usual traffic-clogged streets and parking nightmares, exacerbated by the fact that this is a long narrow city, stretching almost two kilometres from its medieval castle down to the port. If you get into (or stuck in) the centre, buy a ceramic pot, a big industry here, or a silk headscarf, a last memory of Messenía's old mulberry groves. Kalamáta is as famous for these as it is for the *kalamatianó*, a circle dance.

Kalamáta's **Frankish castle** (*open during the day*) sits on a low hill at the north end of the town. It looks good once you find it, and the old part of Kalamáta encircles its enceinte. It sits on top of ancient **Pharai**, whose history is as obscure as its ruins. Suffice to say that the Mycenaeans were here (Telemachus dropped by looking for his father) and it suffered the same fate as all other Messenían cities – squeezed firmly under the Spartan thumb. Geoffrey de Villehardouin was not slow to see the low acropolis' possibilities and in 1208 he built the fortress with the outer enceinte, inner

Getting There and Around

The **airport**, t 272 106 9442, complete with car hire offices, is about 6km west of town. There are flights to and from Athens daily. For information, contact Olympic Airways, 17 Siderodromikóu Stathmou St, t 272 102 2376, by the train station.

The **train** station in the centre on Frantzi Street, t 272 109 5056, has two trains a day to Kyparissía and Pýrgos and four to Trípolis, Corinth and Athens.

The **bus** station, t 272 102 2851, is at the north end of Artémidos St by the New Market. For Athens, 11 connections per day via Megalópolis and Trípolis; Pátras two per day via Pýrgos; Sparta two per day; Mavromáti (ancient Messene) two per day; Koróni eight per day; Pýlos nine per day; Finikoúnda two per day (where you can change for Methóni); Areópolis four per day.

The **city bus** depot is near Plateía 23 Martíou. Bus no.1 goes down Aristoménous and east along the waterfront as far as the Filoxenía Hotel every 12 to 15 minutes.

For a **taxi** in the centre: t 272 102 1112; on the seaside, t 272 102 8181. For a 24-hour radio taxi: t 272 102 1112. For **car rental**, *see* Maniates Travel

(*below*), or Avis, t 272 10 2 0352, f 272 102 2428, which has offices both at the airport and at 2 Késseri St. For **motorbikes** try Alpha, t/f 272 109 3423, at 156 Vironos St up from 45 Navarínou St.

Tourist Information

Tourist Office, 6 Polyvíou St, a block south of Plateía 23 Martíou, by the City Hall (*dimarchío*), t 272 108 6868; *open Mon–Fri 7.30–2.30.* Gives out maps of the city.
Maniates Travel, 1 Iatropoúlou St, t 272 102 5300, f 272 102 8136, *maniatis@kal.forthnet. gr.* Can help with hotels, car hire and tours. It has branches in Stoúpa and Kardamýli.

Festivals

On 23 March, Kalamáta celebrates **Independence Day** two days before the rest of Greece. No two areas joined the fray at the exact same moment, and any city that feels it 'jumped the gun', so to speak, is very proud of it. In the open air theatre near the castle, Kalamáta hosts an **International Festival of Dance** from mid-July to mid-August.

redoubt and keep that you see today. William de Villehardouin was born here. The castle then passed to the Slavs (1293) back to the Franks, to the Byzantines in 1423, then to the Venetians, the Turks, the Venetians, and so on. No wonder it is the worse for wear. Walking in it is restricted in areas. The last big earthquake in 1986 put some ominous cracks in the walls and devastated the nearby metropolitan church. Near the castle on Benáki Street, the **Archaeological Museum** (*t 272 102 6209; open Tues–Sun 8–2.30*) covers the Classical period up to the War of Independence. The museum is located in the handsome Benáki mansion, and its small collection is excellent.

In the Middle Ages, the city was called Kalámai. It got its name *kalamáta* (good eyes) when an icon of the Virgin, remarkable for her sympathetic eyes, was found. You can check out the truth of this in the **Church of the Apostles** in Plateía 23 Martíou, where the icon holds pride of place. Kalamáta's last dramatic appearance in war occurred nowhere near the castle, but on its **beaches**. In 1941, 7,000 Allied troops fell into German hands here before they could be evacuated by the Royal Navy.

While still inside Kalamáta proper, on the main Sparta road, look for the turn-off to the village of **Leíka**, then immediately look for the sign to the now deserted **Velanidiás monastery**. Its hill offers the best panoramic view of Kalamáta and the castle. The monastery got its name in 1884, when an icon fell out of the centre of a lightning-blasted oak (*velanídi*): a rather Nordic hiding place for an icon in Greece.

Where to Stay

Kalamáta ✉ 24100

Many hotels in Kalamáta are on Navarínou Street, the long coastal road leading to the Máni, served by the no.1 bus.

Filoxenía, Navarínou-Paralía, in a little park on the beach on the east edge of town, t 272 102 3166, f 272 102 3343, *sales@ath.grecotel.gr* (*B; expensive–moderate*). This well run hotel has a great pool and a tennis court.

Flisvos, 135 Navarínou, t 272 108 2282, f 272 109 0080 (*C; moderate*). On the coastal strip, between the Filoxenía and the centre.

Nedon, 153 Navarínou, t 272 102 6811, f 272 102 5044 (*C; moderate*). Close enough to the 'Flisvos' to tempt comparison shopping and a tactful bargaining foray.

Haicos, 115 Navarínou, t 272 108 2886, f 272 102 3900 (*C; moderate*). Slightly closer to the centre, with air-conditioning.

Avra, 10 Santa Rosa, t 272 108 2759 (*E; inexpensive*). Quiet, simple (shared bath), cheap, and has the advantage of being a street back from Navarínou and close to Fillellínon.

George, Frantzi St and Dagre St, t 272 102 7225 (*E; inexpensive*). A seven-room bargain hotel by the train station.

Camping Marias, t 272 104 1314 (*inexpensive*). This is the best one; on the shingle beach beside the Filoxenía hotel. *Open all year.*

Eating Out

Most restaurants are also on Navarínou St, where the busy road separates kitchens from their seaside terraces, makes work a death-defying dodge for the waiters and a rather noisy meal for the customers.

Psaroúla (Ψαρούλα), on the beach at 14 Navarínou St, t 272 102 0985. For fresh fish and friendly service.

Zesti Goniá, on Santarosa St and Kanári St, just back from Navarínou St, t 272 108 9558. This taverna is quieter, moderately priced, and close to the budget hotels.

The marina west of Kanári St just beyond the port offers easy parking and quieter restaurants on a pedestrian-only mall overlooking the yacht basin. Although swish looking, places are so untouristy that they have not yet Romanized their signs.

Liméni (Λιμένι), t 272 109 5670.

Pyrofáni (Πυροφάνι), t 272 109 5386.

Kanná (Καννά), t 272 109 1596.

New Messíni to Ancient Messene, through the Blessed Land

Just west of Kalamáta and the airport, the modern but excruciatingly dull town of **Messíni** is located in one of Greece's prime rice-producing areas. Originally named Nísi, it has shanghaied the proud name of ancient Messene, and the turn-off for the same is about the only reason to cross the city limits. The direct route to ancient Messene passes through **Éva**, 8km north of Messíni, a town once sacred to Dionysos and named after the cry *'evoi! evan!'* of his maenads. It then continues north of Lámbena and then left to Mavromáti.

There is, however, a tempting back way starting at **Androúsa**, 2.5km west of Éva. Here a down-at-heel, gypsy-haunted Frankish pile known as the **Castle of Druges** commands a splendid view over the Messenian plain, known since ancient times as Makária, the 'blessed land', still a wide glimmering plain of olive groves, dotted by cypresses, the whole watered by the Pásimos, the mightiest river in the south Peloponnese. Today it's one of the most densely populated rural corners of Greece. Byzantine churches dot the area, starting with the single-nave **Ag. Geórgios** in Androúsa itself. Go northwest through **Kalogerórrachi** and on towards **Ellinoekklesía** and you come to the ruined 14th-century **Samarína Monastery**, founded by the Empress Theodora; its beautiful church, **Zoodóchos Pigí**, was built over an ancient temple and incorporates some of its columns under the dome. From here, continue west towards Maganiakó, where you'll come to the dirt road that leads to Petrálona. Along it stands the **Andriomonástiro**, another imperial monastery, this one built by Andronicus II Paleológos above the spring that still provides Androúsa with its water. Head northeast to Mavromáti and back even further in time to ancient Messene.

Mavromáti and Ancient Messene

Ithóme means 'step', and at 2,630ft it was a giant one, a natural citadel over the plain of Makária to the south and the plain of Stenyklaros to the north. Underneath it, in a fold closed off by the austere slopes of Mount Eva, lies ancient Messene, enclosed in its magnificent late Classical walls. On the plan of the ancient city, the modern village of **Mavromáti**, 30km from Kalamáta (and linked to the same by bus) resembles a few grains of rice lost in a large frying pan, barely keeping alive the promise of the oracle: 'The bright bloom of Sparta shall perish and Messene shall be inhabited for all time.' Since 1986, Pétros Themelís of the University of Crete has unearthed all but one of the buildings mentioned by Pausanias.

History

Legend tells that Queen Messene, daughter of King Triopas of Argos, built the altar of Zeus Ithomátas on Mount Ithóme and founded the earliest city here. When the Spartans coveted Messenía, they came up with one of the kinkiest provocations of all time. A group of armed young Spartans in drag went into a room full of Messenian worthies, at first pretending to entertain them, then pulling out the daggers hidden

Where to Stay and Eat

Mavromáti ✉ 24002
Pension Zeus, t 272 405 1426 (*moderate–inexpensive*). A handful of rooms with kitchenettes owned by the friendly Kouvelakis family.

A Mr Grumpy also offers rooms near the Klypsedra, the Messenian exception that proves the rule.

There's also a single restaurant, its terrace patrolled by the very chickens who may appear on your plate.

under their skirts. The Messeníans were quicker and killed the phoney girls, which was enough for Sparta self-righteously to declare the First Messenian War.

The Messeníans, under their king, Aristódemos, fought long and hard, but eventually the Spartans cornered them on Ithóme. It was a long, bitter siege. Aristódemos, remembering Agamemnon's sacrifice of his daughter Iphigenia, announced he would sacrifice his pure virgin daughter on the altar of Zeus Ithomátas for the sake of victory. The night before, her lover eliminated her from the ranks of the virgins in the hope of sparing her life, but Aristódemos killed her anyway in a spate of paternal fury.

The Delphi Oracle then told them they could defeat the Spartans if they first dedicated a hundred tripods to Zeus on Ithóme. The Messenians set to work making tripods, but word leaked out to the Spartans, who defied their reputation for stupidity by quickly whipping up a hundred *toy* tripods and sending them up to the sanctuary with one of their spies. The Messenians saw them and simply gave up.

Sparta's defeat by Argos at Hysiae in 669 BC encouraged the Messenians to revolt unsuccessfully under their gallant hero Aristoménes in the Second Messenian War. The Third Messenian War (465–459 BC) occurred in 465 BC, when Sparta was devastated by an earthquake. The helots saw their chance and attacked, were defeated but then retreated to Ithóme and made a stand. Sparta, desperate, asked Athens for help, invoking a treaty the two had signed after the Persian Wars. The Athenians, not entirely convinced it was a good cause, sent 4,000 hoplites. The Spartans soon regretted their request and, nervous at the 'adventurous and revolutionary' behaviour of the Athenians, insulted their pride by telling them to go home because 'they weren't needed after all'. Although Sparta prevailed at Ithóme, Athens resettled the helots who escaped in Náfpaktos and allied herself with Sparta's enemy Argos, beginning the Cold War that would lead up to the hot Peloponnesian War in 431 BC.

In 369 BC, after defeating the Spartans at Leúktra (*see* p.176) Epaminóndas was determined to bottle them up in Laconía and founded Messene for the former helots. Diodorus Siculus wrote that it was built in an incredible 85 days, which seems impossible when you look at its 9 kilometres of walls. All Greece guaranteed the new city's autonomy – except for bad fairy Sparta, which looked on with impotent fury. The Messeníans, keen to make up for four lost centuries, built like crazy, held games in honour of Zeus and participated fully in the alliances and betrayals of the Hellenistic age. Loathing and distrust of Sparta dictated most of their policy, but not always.

The walls proved their worth in 295 BC against the famous Demetrios Poliorketes, 'the Besieger'; then in 214 BC, against an even stronger Macedonian army led by Demetrios, son of Philip V, who was killed with nearly all of his phalanx when citizens of both sexes bombarded them with boulders; and then again in 202 BC, when the

Spartans made their last play to take over the Peloponnese. On this occasion, they were repulsed by the general of the Achaean League, Philopoemen of Megalopolis. But gratitude was as sadly lacking in Messene as in Athens: in 183 BC, a demagogue led a faction to revolt against the Achaean League; Philopoemen attacked them, was captured and forced to take poison. The Romans had the city soon after, and in AD 395 the Goths overran it before it faded from history.

The Site

Mavromáti is a bucolic little place, offering a fine overview of the ruins and a peaceful spot for an overnight stay. Its fountain is ancient and still fed by Messene's famous spring, **Klepsydra**, brought down by an aqueduct from Ithóme. The **museum** (*t 272 405 1201; open Tues–Sun 8.30–3; adm*) has mostly statues and architectural fragments from the site. Next to this, a road descends to the ruins (same hours) and the car park near the **theatre**. This theatre was built to a revolutionary design, the *cavea* cupped in an artificial slope supported by a semi-circular wall, made from the same fine limestone blocks as the city walls, with pointed entrances every 65ft. This was the

Ancient Messene

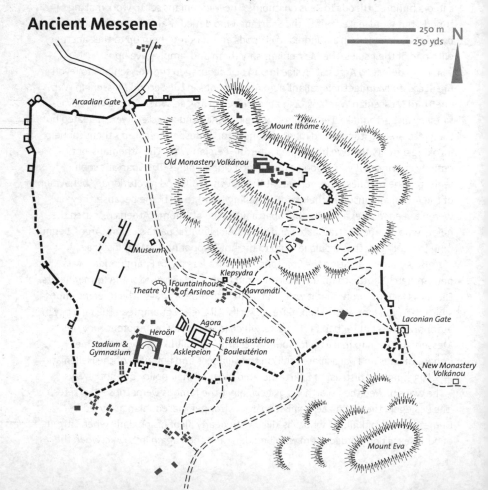

first known example of what a modern designer would call the 'fortified-look', a style that become popular in large-scale, freestanding Roman theatres and amphitheatres.

No one felt like going to the theatre any more by the time of Diocletian (early 4th century AD) and some of its blocks were used to restore the nearby **fountain house of Arsinoe**, which received water from the Klepsydra. A coin of Leo VI (d. 912) and a quantity of Byzantine pottery from as late as the 13th century found here confirm that Messene carried on quietly for centuries. Little remains of the **agora**, its northern extent marked by a semicircular **exedra** and a great 330ft **stoa**, shaped like the Greek letter P. Fragments from the Temples of Poseidon and Aphrodite described by Pausanias are in the museum.

The centre of action in the ancient city was the nearby **Asklepeion**. The Messenians regarded Asklepios not as the god of healing, but as an important member of their royal family, in the time before the Dorian invasion. In 214 BC, they erected this Asklepeion over a 7th-century Asklepeion in a flurry of patriotic pride after defeating the Macedonians. As Pausanias describes it, it was used as a sculpture gallery and civic centre; statue bases (originally there were over 140) clutter the space around the temple and altar. No one is quite sure of the dedication of the **Doric temple** with its large altar in the middle of the Asklepeion, but it held a giant chrysolith (gold and marble) statue of the heroine goddess Messene, so it was probably hers.

A quadrangle of stoas (200ft by 215ft) surrounded the temple. Attached to the east end was the **ekklesiastérion**, a roofed and elegant little theatre, used for meetings of the Assembly as well as for concerts. It was surrounded by a strong retaining wall and the floor of its orchestra was paved in Roman times with red, white and blue stone. Next is an imposing gateway or **propylaia** with three doorways. Beside this is the **bouleuterion** (or synedrion), where the councillors or *synedroi* of the independent cities of Messenía met; a continuous bench running along three sides of the room could seat 76 in comfort. Next to this were their **archives**.

The **west wing** of the peristyle court held what we would call today terrace temples: a row of four connecting **cult rooms** that once held statues by Damophón, a 2nd-century BC native of Messene. A roof shelters the best preserved room, dedicated to **Artemis Orthia**, where the body of Damophón's statue of Artemis was found, along with bases for statues of priestesses and girls initiated in the rites of Artemis. According to Pausanias, the room dedicated to Epaminóndas held a statue of the city's founder made in iron, as a sign of the tremendous respect the Messenians felt for him. The stout northern wing contained public dining halls that were later converted into the **sevasteion** or caesareion, dedicated to the worship of the goddess Roma and the emperors, with two compartments divided by a monumental staircase.

Northwest of the Asklepeion are the ruins of the first **Sanctuary of Orthia**, with a square shaped cella, and west of that are the poorly preserved **Sanctuary of Demeter and the Dioschouri**. Its east end was demolished for a drainage channel in 1960; problems with flooding on the site were resolved when this and the ancient drains were restored. The foundations of **Hellenistic baths** are just east of the Asklepeion; cuttings for clay tubs and some of the terracotta pipes have survived, as well as a hoard of bronze coins, many in identical pairs: the charge for a bath was two pennies. Near the baths stood a rectangular funerary monument, or **heroön**, erected in the mid-2nd century BC. A column was found here, inscribed with honours from seven cities to Damophón for his talent, generosity and skill at restoring cult monuments.

Some 80 yards east of the Asklepeion, a very late but lavish Roman building known as the **room with opus sectile** was uncovered, the interior faced with marble, the floor paved with slabs and a marble opus sectile geometric pattern. Excavations are continuing to the east of the Asklepeion, where a street over another drain was found, along with a stone *hecataión*, or column. Its side was sculpted with three aspects of Artemis, a nice reminder that even in Roman times her original role as a seasonal fertility symbol was not wholly forgotten. South of the Asklepeion is the **heirothysion** (*heiróthyta* were the parts of an animal eaten after a sacrifice), used by the magistrates responsible for running Messene's festivals and games. According to Pausanias, this held the tripods that appear on Messene's coins and were given as prizes in the Ithomaian Games (a generous gesture, considering the story of Spartan trickery).

South of the heirothysíon are the well-preserved **stadium** and **gymnasium**, built as a single unit. Entrance was by way of a Doric **propylaia**; note the ruins of a stairway on the south side, made in late antiquity out of statue bases, and carved with a board for playing dice. The stadium, host to the Ithomaia Games, had stone seats (including fancy ones for members of the festival committee), and its horseshoe curve is surrounded on three sides by **stoas**; the one of the east, built on the cheap without iron clamps and dowels, has completely collapsed. The gymnasium, abutting the west stoa, had a sanctuary of Heracles and Hermes, and between the columns you can see statue bases for various gymnasiarchs, or coaches. Many prominent Messeníans chose to face eternity from the vicinity of the stadium; the biggest tomb, the late Hellenistic **heroön of the stadium**, belonged to a high priest named Saethidas. The lofty podium is intact, and there are plans to restore the shattered monument.

The Walls of Messene

Messene's 9.5km circuit of walls are the most spectacular in Greece, their ashlar limestone blocks so finely and precisely cut (from quarries on the slopes of Ithóme) that all subsequent fortifications look a bit shoddy. Standing only 20ft high in most places, they take advantage of the escarpments in the terrain, rendering most ancient siege machinery and scaling ladders impractical. Thirty powerful square or horseshoe-shaped towers stand at the most vulnerable points. The walls were designed to enclose enough farmland to keep the city from starving during a long siege (with Sparta nearby, no precautions were too great). Enough survives of the entire circuit to trace it entirely, but the northwest section up by the circular **Arcadian gate**, with its mighty limestone lintel half-fallen, is the best preserved and easy to reach up the main road from the museum.

The second best preserved gate, the **Laconian gate**, can also be reached by car, winding up through the centre of Mavrománti (signposted). From the gate you have a fine view of the chain of walls rising precipitously up the slopes of Ithóme. If you follow the road through the gate you'll soon come to the impressive 'new' **Monastery Volkánou**, which in the 15th century briefly belonged to the Knights of St John.

Mount Ithóme

Off the road to the Laconian gate is a zigzagging path and unpaved road to the flat top of Mount Ithóme. Strabo considered it the strategic equal of the Acrocorinth, yet it twice (in the First and Third Messenian Wars) proved to be an Alamo for its defenders. Their ancient citadel is long gone; the view sublime. Blood was often spilled here, and it wasn't all in battle. On the way up are the foundations of an Ionic **Temple of Limnatis**, dedicated to Artemis Laphria, who, as in Pátras (*see* p.213), demanded cruel animal holocausts. On the summit, the original, abandoned 13th-century Byzantine Monastery of Voulkánou was built over Queen Messene's **Sanctuary of Zeus Ithomátas**. On the east side, some ancient foundations may be seen; the discovery of a leg from a Geometric-era tripod confirms its antiquity. As a primordial weather god, Zeus Ithomátas is associated with memories of human sacrifice; here Aristódemos either sacrificed his daughter or, according to another account, killed 300 Spartan captives, including their king Theopompos. Messenían coins showed the cult statue, holding a thunderbolt in one hand and an eagle in the other.

Meligalás

If you go through the Arcadian gate, it's 9km to the land of 'milk and honey', **Meligalás**, the largest village of the northern plain of Stenyklaros, famous for the triple **Mavrozoúmenos bridge**, built over the Pámisos where it is formed by the conjunction of the Mavrozoúmenos and Amphitos rivers. The piers are from the 3rd or 4th century BC; the arches are Turkish.

South from Kalamáta to Koróni

Unlike much of Messenía's Ionian coast, this easterly shore facing the Gulf of Messenía is lined with good beaches with the added plus of views across the water to the jagged profile of the Taíyetos. The first town on the coast is stretched-out **Petalídi**, 15km southwest of Messíni. In August 1828, General Maison landed on Petalídi's sandy beach with 14,000 French troops, which encouraged Ibrahim Pasha and his Egyptians to leave the Peloponnese once and for all, ten months after Navaríno.

Episcopí, 10km south of Petalídi, is almost entirely made of holiday flats and studios, while **Ag. Andréas**, a few miles beyond, is less cosmopolitan but more of a real place, its little port and small beaches shaded by eucalyptus trees. This was the ancient port of **Longá**, where the **Shrine of Apollo Korythos** was rebuilt four times, from the Geometric period on; in the Christian era the temple was replaced with a basilica, which was later replaced by the current church of Ag. Andréas. As you head south, vines and cypresses line the road as you approach the crossroads at **Charokopió**, a fine old-fashioned Messenían village. Koróni is just to the east.

Koróni

Koróni is a wonderful quirky old place full of character, with a long sandy beach, a Venetian castle, and its piquant old town piled on narrow, steep, zigzagging streets with splendid views across the Messiniakós Gulf to the Máni.

Getting There and Around

Koróni is linked by **buses** from Kalamáta. In Koróni the bus stop is in the square behind the seafront: get your tickets at the astonishing news-stand of Takis Stampatópoulis, t 272 502 2231. Moto Koróni hires **bikes** and **motorbikes**, t 272 502 2980. In August, **boat excursions** cross the Gulf to Stoúpa and the Diroú Caves.

Where to Stay and Eat

Petalídi ✉ 24005

Sunrise Village, t 272 203 2120, f 272 203 1799, *sunrisev@hellasnet.gr* (*expensive*). An all-in family resort, with a lagoon-style pool, gym and health club and a diving centre. The restaurant serves Greek and Cypriot cuisine. *Open Mar–Oct.*

Erato Studios and Apartments, t 272 203 1719, f 272 203 1965 (*inexpensive, moderate in Aug*). Up in a residential neighbourhood, 100m from the main *plateía*. Spotless, and all with kitchenettes and verandas, run by welcoming Mrs Níkki.

Petalidi Beach Camping, t 272 203 1154 (*inexpensive*). With bungalows.

Ag. Andréas ✉ 24100

Longas Beach, t/f 272 503 1583 (*C; moderate*). Isolated; the most upscale. *Open April–Oct.*

Angelos, t 272 503 1268, f 272 503 1368 (*C; moderate–inexpensive*). Pleasant and right on the sea. *Open April–Sept.*

Francisco, t 2725 03 1396, f 272 503 1096 (*C; inexpensive*). Modern, with a restaurant.

Camping Ag. Andreas, t 272 503 1880, f 272 509 5393. Well-shaded sites by the sea and a few camping bungalows. *Open April–Sept.*

Koróni ✉ 24004

Auberge de la Plage, t 272 502 2401, f 272 502 2508 (*C; expensive–moderate*). Over Zága Beach; a great location, pretty garden, air-conditioning, mini-bus, and steps to the sea.

Marinos Bungalows, t 272 502 2522 (*C; inexpensive*). On the north entrance to town; a lovely view over the sea and town. There's a small beach below, 200m away, and easy parking. *Open April–Oct.*

Diana, t/f 272 502 2312 (*E; inexpensive*). Down near the port; tasteful, air-conditioned and immaculate, even if the rooms are small.

Christos Mállios Rooms, t 272 502 2229 (*inexpensive*). Past the neoclassical port-side *plateía*, under the castle. Rooms in a neo-classical building, with high ceilings and a shared kitchen; the same owners have flats (*moderate*), sleeping four. *Open April–Oct.*

Koroni Camping and Bungalows, t 272 502 2884, f 272 502 2119 (*moderate*). North of town, with a pool under a big palm tree, a playground, restaurant, and bungalows with TVs and kitchens. *Open April–10 Oct.*

As usual, most of the restaurants and bars are on the waterfront. Try **Flísvos** for seafood, or **Ifigénia** next door for *mezédes*, moussaka or a big 'farmer steak'. Bakeries are particularly good here, especially **To Koroneika** on the main street.

Koróni's history closely parallels that of Methóni on the opposite end of the penin-sula, only it went through even more name changes. It was originally Asine, a colony founded by refugees from Asine, who were sent packing when they sided with Sparta (*see* p.261). In the 9th century AD, more refugees, this time from ancient Korone (modern Petalídi) fled here, when pirates and other marauders trickled into their terri-tory. They took the town name with them, and rebuilt Asine's acropolis as their citadel, which in turn was taken over by the Franks in 1204 and Venetians in 1207. The Venetians rebuilt the castle and, like their fort in Methóni, considered it an 'eye of the Republic'; it was also an important port for olive oil and the red dye cochineal. In 1500, when Bayezit II appeared fresh from crushing Methóni, the disheartened inhabitants gave up without a fight and moved to Kefaloniá, which belonged to Venice.

In 1532, the Genoese admiral Andrea Doria captured Koróni in the name of the Holy Roman Emperor, but the dread pirate admiral Barbarossa came fast on his heels, forcing Doria to evacuate the town; those left behind were slaughtered. In 1685, Francesco Morosini (who superstitiously always dressed in red and never travelled without his cat on the poop deck) recaptured Koróni for Venice and in turned massacred its 1,500 Turks. Again the Greeks and Venetians came back, and again they had to leave in 1718 when the Turks regained Koróni.

The picturesque, irregular **castle** (*always open*) sits on the bluff, its round bastions surrounded by water on three sides. The curtain walls are made from stones of ancient Asine, while the Venetians added the romantic Gothic gate, reached by a cobbled ramp from the north. Inside the walls are tiny houses and churches (one, Byzantine Ag. Sophía, is built over a Temple of Apollo). A stair leads down to a little plateau occupied by the church of the **Panagía** and a palm grove as well as a **historical and archaeological collection** that you can skip without feeling too guilty. Long, sandy **Zága Beach** begins below the walls to the south.

On the north side of the castle, the **medieval town** spills down narrow cobbled streets. A fondness for primary colours, folk art and flowery gardens add to its charm along with the fact that cars can't squeeze into many of its lanes. The port is lined with fish tavernas and *ouzeries*. Beyond is a wonderfully romantic view of the castle on its rock, rising over the waves, guarded by cypresses, golden in the setting sun.

The Southwest Coast

Finikoúnda

Although this squared-off westernmost prong of the Peloponnese isn't as mountainous as the others, the southern coast is craggy enough and dotted with islets. There's one point, however, where a river has muscled its way through to make a series of sandy beaches. In the early 1970s, the village by the beaches, Finikoúnda, was a fishing port with a Phoenician-sounding name, a vaguely Spanish air and the same climate as Ierápetra on the south coast of Crete. A few beachbums found their way to this isolated, sheltered haven, followed by campers and watersports lovers, a holiday company or two, some palm trees and whoosh!

Finikoúnda has a sandy in-town **beach**, prettily framed by headlands and Schiza Island, and a broader one, **Anemómilos**, just over the hill to the west, with a taverna, campsite and watersports. Schiza Island, closing off the sea view, offers a goal for sailors, with its low white cliffs, wild goats and sheltered cove on its southwest side. It's also a target for Greek air force bombers, so don't venture over unless you're sure the coast is clear. To the east, off the southern point of **Cape Akrítas**, the islet of **Venetikó** has a little lighthouse, a dramatic rocky coast and a rudimentary beach.

Methóni

In the extreme southwesternmost corner of the Peloponnese, Methóni is a pleasant sun-soaked town with white streets charmingly lined with red and green hibiscus trees. Venetian walls enclose its thumb-shaped promontory, now inhabited by lizards; its once bustling harbour, partly sheltered by the Inoússai islands, is now a long sandy

Getting Around

Regular buses go between Pýlos, Methóni and Finikoúnda. There are **caiques** from Pýlos to Sapienza in the high season. Pýlos **port authority**: **t** 272 302 2225. In Methoni, Apostolídi, **t** 272 30 7 1452, has a cheaper boat called 'Bebé' going out from the beach.

Where to Stay and Eat

Finikoúnda ✉ 24006

Avoid driving down Finikoúnda's seaside road if at all possible; parking is a headache, and even moving can be difficult in summer.

Finikoúnda, **t** 272 307 1208, **f** 272 307 1400 (**t** 272 307 1408 or **t** 272 307 1308 during olive season) (*C; moderate–inexpensive*). In town with parking nearby; quiet if smallish rooms around a central courtyard, with a shady upstairs terrace. *Open all year.*

Aktí Rooms and Studios, **t** 272 307 1316 (*inexpensive, moderate in Aug*). Just off the beach; a friendly place immersed in bougainvillaea, with a few parking places. *Open April–Oct.*

Dímitra Tomará, **t** 272 307 1323 (*inexpensive*). On the upper edge of town, above the fishing port; nice rooms sleeping up to three, with overhead fans and balconies. *Open all year.*

Korakákis Beach, **t** 272 307 1221, **f** 272 307 1132, *koracaci@otenet.gr* (*E; moderate– inexpensive*). Offers parking, air-conditioning, and simple rooms. *Open all year.*

Camping Loútsa, **t** 272 307 1169, **f** 272 307 1445 (*inexpensive*). Niko Tsónis' at Loútsa Cove is a favourite, with a restaurant and family atmosphere. *Open April–Oct.*

Camping Tsápi, Chryssokellariá, **t** 272 305 1521 (*inexpensive*). Shares its fine sandy beach with a couple of tavernas and a chapel. *Open April–Oct.*

All the restaurants along the strip have seaside terraces overlooking the fishing port. **Oméga**, **t** 272 307 1227. One of the better and more popular ones.

Ta 5 F, **t** 272 307 1242. For seafood.

Kýma, **t** 272 307 1224. There are good 'ready' dishes made by mama; it's also one of the few restaurants that remains open all year.

Hellena House. On the point, with big views; perfect for an evening drink.

Methóni ✉ 24006

Achilléus, 100m from the beach, **t** 272 303 1819 (*B; moderate*). New in 1998, with air-conditioning, TV and fridge; large, airy rooms, some with balconies. *Open all year.*

Odysseus, **t** 272 303 1600, **f** 2723 03 1646 (*B; expensive–moderate*). Comfortable and has a decent restaurant. *Open all year.*

Ánna, on the main street, not far from the sea, **t** 272 303 1585 (*C; inexpensive*). A homey place with a deep shady tunnel to its door and a terrace.

O Fáros, **t** 272 303 1449 (*moderate–inexpensive*). Close to the beach; four well-furnished studio flats with kitchenettes, air-conditioning and TV that sleep up to four.

Castéllo, **t** 2723 03 1280, **f** 272 303 1300 (*D; inexpensive, moderate in high season*). Modern, near the sea, with views over the castle; plain rooms and breakfast in the garden.

Taverna Klimataria, opposite the Castello hotel. Wonderful stuffed courgette flowers and cheese and onion tart.

beach. As much as a town can, Methóni has retired from history, with a sigh of relief, for this is one of those places where every stone has been stained with blood.

History

In Homer, Methóni was Pedasos, 'rich in vines'. In the 7th century BC, the Spartans allowed a group from Naúplio (exiled by Argos for their support of Sparta) to settle Méthoni as *periokoi*, to perform the commercial and artisan tasks forbidden to the Spartan overlords and the Messenian helots. The Messenians didn't mind the Argives, and allowed them to remain after they became independent. In the 4th century, Methóni was recorded as a bishopric, but in the troubled times that followed it became a nest of pirates, and was razed by the Venetians in 1125. The Venetians coveted Methóni, or Modon as they called it, and in 1204 claimed it as part of their 'quarter and a half' share of the Byzantine empire.

Venice used Greece's ports as stations for her Eastern fleet, but none was as important to her as Methóni, 'the receptacle and special nest of all our galleys, ships and vessels'; it and Koróni were the *Oculi capitales communis*, the 'Eyes of the Republic'. Venice's trade routes to the Black Sea and Middle East converged here, and every year two convoys of galleys would set sail together out of Venice as far as Methóni. On board were not only goods to trade, but also pilgrims bound for the Holy Land. At Methóni they would pick up water and provisions, and silk and wine to barter; on the return trip they picked up bacon. Methóni supplied nearly all of Venice. Relations with the locals were good, and the Greek light horse, or *stradioti*, were responsible for land defences. The most famous commander of the *stradioti* was Graitzas Paleológos, who fought so bravely against the Turks in the 1450s that he became the commander of all the Serenissima's cavalry. When the Turks prevailed over the Peloponnese, the Venetians were confined within their walls, here and at Koróni and Pýlos.

In 1500, the Turkish fleet of Bayazit II, manned with 100,000 Janissaries, cut off all Methóni's supply routes. Nevertheless, the 7,000 defenders held out for a month and fought back so fiercely that Bayazit was on the verge of sailing away, especially when five Venetian supply ships slipped past the Turks' blockade. The besieged were so thrilled by the arrival of food and munitions that they forgot to man the walls. The Turks noticed and stormed Methóni, and beheaded every male over the age of ten. In 1531 Fra Bernardo Salviati, a nephew of the Pope, led the Knights of St John to Methóni, on the chance that if they liked it, they could seize it and stay there instead of Malta. The Knights mistook the Greeks for the Turks, pillaged their houses and carried off all their women to Malta (there *are* reasons why the Greeks are mistrustful of the West). The Venetians were more earnest, and recaptured Methóni on their sixth attempt in 1685 under Morosini, who so impressed the Turks with his flamboyant red clothes and courage that they surrendered. But in 1715 Venice lost Methóni, again through a muddle; the Turks were again besieging the walls and the Commander of the Fleet came to succour the defenders. A Turkish fleet appeared, the Commander made an undignified dash for it, and once again the defenders were massacred.

In 1825, during the War of Independence, the Greek admiral Miaoulis sailed into Methóni and directed his trademark fireships at the fat Turkish frigates. All caught fire, but so did Methóni when the powder in the cargo ships exploded. Not long after, Ibrahim Pasha landed his troops here, beginning their rampage of the Peloponnese, and the town remained Turkish until 1828, when it was liberated by the French under General Maison. During the Second World War, the castle played its most recent military role, housing an Italian garrison.

The Venetian Castle

Even in its damaged state, the castle (*open 9–7; adm free*) is still a bold sight, surrounded by the sea on three sides and a wide dry moat on its landward side, now used by the locals to gather wild *hórta* for their salads. Two **reliefs of the Lion of St Mark** embedded in the walls smile down upon them; note that the books they hold are open, a sign of favour (places in the Republic's bad books would get scowling lions with closed books). The moat is spanned by a handsome 14-arched stone **bridge** built by the French to replace the original wooden structure, and leads to a fancy **monumental gate** built by the Venetians in 1700, adorned with a pair of Corinthian columns and warlike trophies. Inside are two more **gates**, one with a neatly made round hole on the side that looks as if it were a measure for cannonballs. In the masonry you can see the Classical stone of the ancient city, completely cannibalized by the Venetians. The medieval town that once stood inside the walls was completely cannibalized in turn by the French in 1828 when they built the new town, leaving only a ruined Latin church and Turkish bath. Through the old sea gate, a causeway leads to the picturesque **Bourtzi**, the little octagonal Turkish fort built on the spot where the last hapless Venetians and Greeks were cornered and beheaded in 1500. In the late afternoon sun it takes on a rich pink hue. Methóni's big sandy **beach** is a few steps away.

The Island of Sapiénza: Strawberry Trees and Neutrinos

Sapiénza, the large uninhabited island south of Methóni, means 'wisdom' in Italian. Although its small ports have often provided shelter (and bases for attacking Methóni), many ships didn't quite make it, coming to grief on its rocks. One, a Venetian galley filled with granite columns from Herod's Great Peristyle in Kessaria, was wrecked on Sapiénza's north cape, **Karsi**. This, and other wrecks, provide fascinating diving, and there are plans to make Karsi an underwater park. Near Karsi there's a pier by the sandy beach **Ammos** where a path, overgrown in places, departs towards the south of the island, passing through a valley containing a unique arbutus forest. Arbutus is a typical *maquis* shrub; in autumn, red strawberry-like fruit and white blossoms appear at the same time in its dark green foliage. Here the bushes, isolated for thousands of years, have grown into trees, standing up to 40ft high. So much pollen has accumulated that it has formed a unique orange 'rock' in the middle of the island called *spartólaka*. Sapiénza is also home to 200 *kri kri* goats from Crete.

At the end of the path, on a height overlooking the south of the island, stands a handsome **lighthouse**, built by the English in 1890. Just below are two sea rocks, and just beyond them is one of the deepest places in the Mediterranean, the **Well of Inoússes**, plunging 16,801ft. On a plateau, 12,467ft under the sea, physicists have constructed a massive submarine telescope to study star dust – neutrinos – from extragalactic sources, deep down where they are unaffected by cosmic rays.

Navaríno Bay

Navaríno Bay is one of the most beautiful, fragile and evocative areas of Greece, besides being one of the best natural harbours in the Mediterranean. For the best view of its complicated topography, stand at its centre, at the end of the mole at Giálova Beach, at sunset when the hills turn purple and the water melts from blue to rose to gun-metal grey. Modern Pýlos tumbles down the hill around the Turkish castle to the south. In front, low and barren Sphaktiría Island, the Waterloo of the Spartan army, broods lengthwise across the large bay, leaving a wide channel at Pýlos town

Getting There and Around

The **bus** station on Pýlos' main square, t 272 302 2230, has a services to Giálova, Chóra and Kyparissía (five per day), Methóni and Finikoúnda (four per day), Kalamáta (nine per day) and Athens (two per day). For Koróni you have to go via Kalamáta.

There are **caiques** from Pýlos to Sapiénza in the high season. **Port authority**: t 272 302 2225. To **rent a bike**, call t 272 302 2707. For a **taxi**, call t 272 302 2555.

In Pýlos, the **water taxis** have a stand on the pier. If no one is there, try the Aetos Café on the waterfront. Prices to visit the bay, Golden Beach, and the war memorials vary according to the number of passengers. Unless you get a deal, you can give Sphaktiría a miss. Other than the 'monuments' to the dead, it has only a few Cyclopean walls.

Where to Stay and Eat

Pýlos ✉ 24001

Karalís Beach, t 272 302 3021, f 272 302 2970 (*B; expensive – just*). Quiet, and nice; tucked under the new castle. Rooms have balconies that overhang the sea and offer fantastic views of the bay. No real beach, though. The glorious location draws plenty of non-guests to the rooftop café. *Open April–Oct*.

Karalís, on the main road, t 272 302 2960, f 272 302 2970 (*B; expensive*). New, tastefully built in the neoclassical style; two minutes up from the square. *Open all year*.

Miramare, t 272 302 2751, f 272 302 2226 (*B; moderate, more in July and Aug*). Just south of the *plateía*; pleasant, and right by the bathing ladders. Some rooms have terrific

views. Perhaps one day they will rethink the colour scheme. *Open April–Oct*.

Galaxy, t 272 302 2780, f 272 302 2208 (*C; moderate–inexpensive*). The economic choice, right in the *plateía* and handy for buses. *Open all year*.

12 Gods Rent Rooms, t 272 302 2179, *12gods@otenet.gr* (*inexpensive*). One of the nicest of the rent room places that congregate just up from the *plateía*. A lovely terrace overlooks the sea. *Open April–Oct*.

Diethnés, t 272 302 2772. Has been by the quay for years and is a good bet.

1930, t 272 302 2032. An outstanding restaurant run by Michael Kyriazákos, near the Karalis hotel. Even if you eat outside on the small terrace, don't miss the interior, decorated to imitate the Plateía Navárkon as it was in 1930. The food, Greek and international (with a leaning towards French cuisine), is excellent. *Open eves only*.

Giálova (6km North of Pýlos)

Giálova has an attractive pier and sandy beach (where the swimming is pretty good).

Zoe, t 272 302 2025, f 272 302 2026 (*C; low moderate–inexpensive*). Has enchanting views over a garden to the bay. The rooms are small, the balconies large and the hospitality offered by the Giannóutsos family superb. Their restaurant **Oasis**, t 272 302 4001, where Mr Giannóutsos is the chef, is one of the best, supplied by their organic garden and local fishermen. They also rent apartments on the shore. *All open April–Oct*.

To Spitiko. Excellent food, with friendly attentive service, served on wooden platforms on stilts over the sea.

Navaríno Beach Camping, t 272 302 2973. Plain, but has a great view of the bay.

but a much narrower one to the north. Above this the ancient and medieval fortress dominates the sloping hill. Just beyond that, a headland marks the Voïdokiliá, 'the cow's belly', a perfectly round bay as stunning as it was when the Mycenaeans used it as their harbour so long ago.

A Short History of Navaríno Bay

The entire bay was Mycenaean country, overlooked by Nestor's Palace on the low hill of Epáno Englianó. Tholos tombs are everywhere, suggesting a conglomeration of settlements that owed allegiance to the palace. When it was destroyed after 1200 BC, the centre of habitation gravitated to the northern part of the bay, to the more

Two 'Untoward Incidents' in Navaríno Bay

Navaríno Bay saw two blunder-filled defeats that changed history. The first occurred during the Peloponnesian War, in the summer of 425 BC, and involved incredible misjudgements on the part of the Spartans. Never great sailors, and even worse swimmers, at sea the Spartans were always nervous of the Athenians, who were skilled in both. So when the Athenians came to Navaríno Bay and threatened the Spartans' soft Messenian underbelly by fortifying Koryphasia and leaving behind five triremes to guard it, Spartan antennae were quivering. They sailed in and landed 420 men on the island of Sphaktiría to keep an eye on the big fort and to deny the Athenians its use, while they deployed the rest of their army on the mainland to obliterate Koryphasia. The Athenians called for more ships which somehow escaped the Spartans' notice until they sashayed into the bay from both entrances and trounced the Spartan navy.

That left the 420 Spartans stranded on Sphaktiría with shields as sun shades, and not much else. Sphaktiría's narrow 2¾-mile length was never well wooded, and has only one brackish well. The Athenians were not much better off in their fort, surrounded by Spartans. Talks were held and food sent to the stranded Spartans, until the talks broke down. Things remained at an impasse for 72 days, until fresh Athenian troops arrived under Kleon and attacked the island from all sides. The fact that the Athenians were less than eager to engage the enemy although they outnumbered them by 25 to one speaks volumes for the Spartan reputation.

Fighting valiantly, but unable to ward off this concentrated horde, the Spartans sent a lone swimmer to the mainland for advice. The laconic reply was: 'The Lacedaimonians order you yourselves to consider your own situation, provided that you do nothing dishonourable'. After a fierce battle, the 292 surviving Spartans came up with their own interpretation of 'dishonour' and surrendered. The propaganda value of this defeat was all out of proportion to the number of soldiers captured. Suddenly the Spartans were no longer invincible. Athenian soldiers rushed to grab Spartan gear as souvenirs (one shield is in the Agora museum in Athens), the captives were hauled off to Athens to be put on display (shades of Rome) and the magnificent Victory of Paionios was erected at Olympia for all the Greek world to see.

defensible hill, known as Koryphasia in Classical times. On its north side is Nestor's Cave , inhabited from time immemorial; and under it, ancient settlements spilled down to the Voïdokiliá Bay. The Slavs and Avars had their innings here between the 6th and 9th century, leaving the name Avarino-Navaríno but not much else. The Franks came in 1278 when Nicholas II of St Omer built the wonderful castle that now crowns the hill. This castle bore the brunt of Genoese, Venetian, even Austrian attentions and then fell to the Turks in 1501. But the Turks felt too exposed to unfriendly fire here and in 1572 moved lock, stock and mosque to the so-called 'new castle', Neókastro, which guards the southern gap of Navaríno Bay.

In 1825, the Neókastro became the headquarters of Ibrahim Pasha, when he made his devastating sweep through the Peloponnese; the Sultan had promised him that if he conquered it, he could keep it. A large part of his strategy was eliminating as many

The next 'incident' occurred on 20 October 1827, when the British, French and Russian fleets massed together in the vicinity of Navarino Bay under the command of Admiral Codrington. He had been given the unenviable if not impossible task of 'guaranteeing the autonomy of Greece', while not offending the Sultan. This contradictory policy foreshadowed subsequent relationships between the Great Powers and Greece, right up to the Cyprus crisis in 1974.

The mere presence of the fleet sent Ibrahim Pasha packing from the fort, but not from the area. That left 82 Turkish warships bristling with 2,438 guns and 16,000 of Ibrahim's men riding anchor in the bay, while the Allied fleet of 26 ships and 1,270 guns cooled its heels outside in the open sea. Negotiations on land had hit a stalemate; the allies called for an armistice which was promptly accepted by the Greeks and ignored by the Turks, who figured they had nothing to gain by accepting and were only too aware that the dithering by the Great Powers helped their own side. What they hadn't taken into account was the Philhellenic bias and the enterprising spirit of the allied admirals. Using the Turkish refusal to sign the armistice as a pretext, they sailed into the bay through the southern gap (they would later claim that the Turks shot first) and by nightfall the Turks were left contemplating their ruined fortunes and the watery grave of 6,000 of their men and 53 of their ships. The allies lost only 145 men, and every timber of their fleet was intact. The French and Russian governments didn't even bother to conceal their delight at what the British, weeping crocodile tears, would refer to as an 'untoward event' in parliament, thus washing their hands of any responsibility (while accepting the kudos for their help).

It was the battle that ended the war and guaranteed Greek independence, and if you're in Pýlos on 20 October you can take part in the annual celebration. Navies from the three allies send ships full of sailors in full dress uniforms to decorate the square, politicians bask in reflected glory, and citizens line up to take the water taxis to the three burial grounds of the allies, or to see the rotting timbers of the Turkish ships hard by Sphaktiría if the sea is calm. Interestingly, the British monument to their dead is on the tiny island of Chelonáki ('little turtle') smack in the middle of the Bay, well away from the other monuments, as if even in perpetuity they are not sure to what extent they want to claim participation in the 'incident'.

Greeks as possible; the ones he didn't kill were sold in a slave market he set up in Navarino. He remained until the gathering naval forces from France, Great Britain and Russia began to focus on the bay. Discretion forced him to abandon the fort, just before the decisive Battle of Navarino (*see* above) ended his hopes for good.

Modern Pýlos

Modern Pýlos is a pleasant, sleepy little town (except on 20 October), built amphitheatrically around the enormous **Plateía ton Trion Navárkon**, framed in arcaded neoclassical and *faux* neoclassical buildings and open on its west side to the sea. This is the place to come for a drink under the huge plane trees. The centrepiece is a **monument to the Battle of Navarino**, with Admirals Codrington (British), de Rigny (French) and von Heydon (Russian) looking majestically at the sea, the *kafeneíons* and the fruit stand respectively. If it all seems slightly Gallic, thank the French, who held down the fort after the big battle and laid out the town. The quay is only a minute away and offers a great view of the bay and dramatic cliffs and islands by the southern channel. This is where the battleships moor for the 20 October festivities. There is no good swimming in town, although ladders are built into a platform just south of the mole. For beaches, try Giálova, 6km to the north, or Methóni, 11km south.

The small **museum** (*t 272 302 2448; open Tues–Sun 8.30–3; adm*) on the road to Methóni has minor finds from some of the many Mycenaean and Hellenistic tombs in the area. They are proud of their Hellenistic glass; some of the pots are lovely, too.

The large **Neókastro** (*t 272 302 2010; open Tues–Sun, 8.30–3; adm*) crowns Pýlos but, in spite of its size, it is not especially obvious unless you take the shore road to the Karalís Beach hotel. From the sea, however, it dominates the town. The Turks began it in 1572, and the entire Turkish population lived inside its walls. The Venetians gave it their own particular signature when they held sway from 1686 to 1718. The Russians under Orlov occupied it in 1770 very briefly. A bloodcurdling massacre of the Turks took place in 1821, before it played its most famous role as the headquarters of Ibrahim Pasha. The walls now have the same, almost too perfect atmosphere of Palamídi in Naúplio. Inside, the Turkish barracks hold a museum of engravings from the War of Independence; unfortunately the engravings are labelled only in Greek. The church of the **Metamorphosis tou Sotiros** (the Transfiguration) in the middle of the castle was a mosque, speedily metamorphosed into a church after independence.

The Old Castle, the Voïdokoiliá, and Nestor's Cave

The Old Castle has too few visitors, whereas the Voïdokoiliá has far too many. It's not hard to understand why: under a steep headland this perfectly round shallow bay (hence the name 'cow's belly') that was the ancient harbour of sandy Pýlos is enchanting. You'll see it on the postcards, deserted and pristine, the way it was a few years ago. Now a parade of cars and camper vans, undeterred by the very poor pot-holed road from Petrochóri, clutters up the entrance, even in October, threatening the fragile ecosystem. A few herons are still in evidence, but they look sadly out of place. Now that Voidokoiliá is no longer a secret, perhaps the only way to keep tourists from destroying it is to cordon the area off to cars, and patrol at night to rout out the campers who see a golden opportunity for a free night's stay and then leave all of their debris behind. Go early to enjoy it alone, for a while anyway.

On the main road just north of Giálova, there is a signposted road to Golden Beach and St-Omer's Castle, now better known as the Old Castle or **Palaiókastro**. The path to the castle is on the sea side, near the narrows, and its entrance is obvious from this vantage point. It is an easy if steep 25-minute climb, rewarded with wonderful views along the way. The castle has crenellated walls (partly built on Cyclopean or Classical bases), square towers and an inner and outer court. Quite an array of wild creatures call it home and seem, understandably, to resent intrusions. But don't worry; their reaction is a startled stare and a hasty retreat.

It is possible to clamour down to the Voïdokiliá from the north side of the castle and have a look at **Nestor's Cave** en route. (If that seems too precarious, retrace your steps and walk to Voïdokiliá from sea level along the footpath at the base of the castle hill, on the landward side.) Nestor's cave is 60ft deep and 40ft high. Because the stalactites were thought to resemble animal hides, this was supposed to be either a stable for Nestor's cows, or the place where Hermes hid Apollo's herd after he stole it. People have lived here from Neolithic times on, and there were settlements around it both in the Mycenaean and the Classical period. The wonder is that some shepherd or shepherdess has yet to find an icon buried in its depths and claim it for Christendom. There is a path to the headland north of Voïdokiliá which leads to a Mycenaean **tholos tomb**, said to belong to Thrasymedes, the son of Nestor. The Messeníans made it a hero shrine; excavators found an entire sacrificed bull inside, as well as 4th and 3rd century BC votives. If you continue along this path beyond the tholos, you can also scramble down to a lovely small beach facing the open sea.

The Wetlands: the Giálova Lagoon

The wetlands at the north end of Navaríno Bay are fed by two rivers and encompass Voïdokiliá and the area up to the old castle. It's now a Natura 2000 site, and none too soon; loggerhead turtles (*Caretta caretta*) nest here, and the lagoon is the only habitat of the African Chameleon in Europe. These insect-eaters change colour rapidly and lay their eggs in the sand, making them very vulnerable. Ospreys and flamingoes are among the 245 species of birds that visit.

Nestor's Palace

Pýlos is practically synonymous with Nestor, the respected, hospitable, garrulous old trout who ruled for three generations. At Troy his 90 ships were second only to Agamemnon's, but in the *Iliad* he is more than a warrior; he is also a sage and peacemaker – a thankless task with that unruly lot. But as a reward he got to be one of the very few Achaean chieftains who arrived home safe and sound.

Homer contradicted himself on the location of Nestor's Palace: in the *Iliad* he places it on the banks of the Alphiós, and in the *Odyssey* he writes that Telemachus found it near the shore, but later he places it on a crag overlooking a plain. As far back as the 3rd century BC, scholars were arguing over the location. In 1939 Carl Blegen, fresh from excavating Troy with the University of Cincinnati, decided to look for himself. His first hunch, the hill of Epáno Englianó, 14km north of the modern Pýlos, was right on the money. The war broke out right after he started digging, and Blegen had to wait until 1952 to finish the task.

A Mostly Mythic History

Pýlos was the home of Melampos the Magician, the first mortal to practise as a physician, to build temples to Dionysos and to mix water with his wine. Because he understood the language of the birds, he was also the first 'seer' or *mantis*. Many seers in Classical times traced their genealogies back to Melampos; the Spartans employed his descendant, Teisamenos, whose reading of a sacrifice's entrails before battle accurately led them to five great victories, including Plataea.

Melampos was brought to Pýlos by Neleus, son of Poseidon, when he arrived with a mixed band of Achaeans and Aeolians and chased out the natives. Neleus had 12 children. The youngest was Nestor; he was the only one of his family to receive Heracles when the big guy showed up in Pýlos, asking to be purified after murdering a house guest. Heracles later attacked Pýlos for aiding King Augeias of Elís and killed the entire royal family except for Neleus and Nestor. Pýlos was rebuilt by the Eleans, but they insulted Neleus and stole the horses he sent up to compete in an Olympic chariot race. To retaliate, he sent Nestor up to raid their cattle, provoking a general war. In the subsequent truce Nestor won nearly all the events in the funeral games, as he informs everyone in the *Iliad*. After he returned to Pýlos from Troy, he entertained Telemachus who came to ask about his father Odysseus, but otherwise bows out of history, living peacefully among his sons.

The Palace

t 276 303 1437; open 8.30–3, winter 8.30–2.30; adm.

Fitting in nicely with the peaceful reputation of Nestor's reign, 'his' palace has none of the awesome Cyclopean walls of Mycenae or Tiryns, although its hilltop situation did allow the residents to survey all who approached. It was built around 1300 BC, and went up in flames like Mycenae and Tiryns after 1200 BC. Although the highest walls are only waist level, this is the best preserved example that we have of a Mycenaean royal residence, surrounded by its storerooms and magazines. The large roof sheltering the remains seems to disappoint many, but does add a note of realism: the palace was originally roofed, after all, all in wood. It stood two storeys high, stone on the bottom and half-timbered in the Tudor manner on top, the walls made of rubble braced in timber. The exterior walls were faced with squared limestone blocks and interior walls were plastered. Important ones were frescoed.

The original entrance is the one still used today, with an **outer and inner propylon**. To the right of the outer entrance was a **guard room**, while directly to the left, with an outward facing door, are the two **archive rooms**, with remains of a staircase leading to an upper floor, which may have been a watchtower. Here Blegen unearthed a cache of hundreds of **Linear B tablets** in the very first hour of digging – on the same day that Italy invaded Albania. Preserved by the conflagration that destroyed the palace, these tablets were the first found on mainland Greece, and were quickly spirited away to spend the war in an Athenian bank vault.

Linear B tablets (along with the older, rarer Linear A) had already been found by Arthur Evans at Knossos. Blegen shared Evans' opinion that both scripts belonged to a long-lost language, and their presence at Pýlos was evidence of Minoan imperialism. That is, until Michael Ventris, an architect with a bent for languages, put his mind to the task of deciphering Linear B. At first he thought the language might be Etruscan but, when he reached an impasse, he turned to Greek. He taught himself the language and the results were encouraging, only the script still didn't fit because of the endings. In 1952, John Chadwick, an expert on ancient Greek, heard Ventris explain his difficulties with the word endings on a radio programme, and at once realized

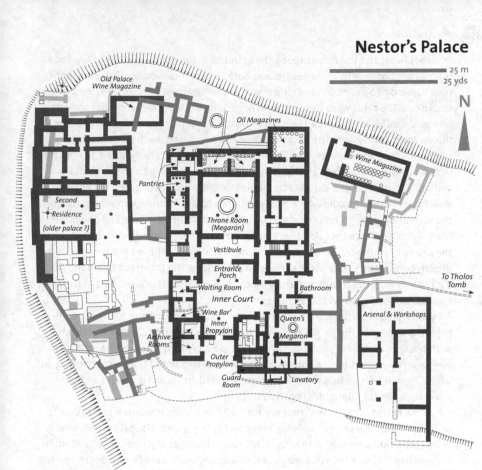

Nestor's Palace

25 m
25 yds

N

Old Palace
Wine Magazine

Oil Magazines

Wine Magazine

Pantries

Second
Residence
(older palace ?)

Throne Room
(Megaron)

Vestibule

Entrance
Porch

Waiting Room

Bathroom

Inner Court

'Wine Bar'

Inner
Propylon

Queen's
Megaron

Arsenal & Workshops

Archive
Rooms

Outer
Propylon

Guard
Room

Lavatory

To Tholos
Tomb

that they fitted the ancient dialect that had survived in the hills of Arcadía. When
Ventris and Chadwick deciphered the tablets conclusively in 1952–3, it forced a
rewriting of history; what were Linear B and Greek doing in Crete? Mycenaean incursions had never been considered until then. Other examples of Linear B were found
by Alan Wace at Mycenae in 1952; there are a few fragments at Tiryns, and on pots in
Thebes, where clay tests proved much to everyone's surprise that they were Cretan
imports. The language was syllabic – fine for the number crunchers, but basic enough
to ensure no poetry would ensue. The tablets concern taxes, debts, distribution of
goods and other administrative business – not compelling reading, but a big insight
into the operation of a palace economy. The most startling discovery was a reference
to Dionysos, which undercut the long-held belief that he was a relatively recent
arrival from Thrace. It also jibes nicely with stories about Melampos the Magician.

Once past the gates is the large **inner court**, which was open to the sky. To the left is
a **waiting room** with a bench; wine jars and cups found in the adjacent room suggest
guests were served wine while they waited. When the king was ready to receive
them, they would continue straight into the state rooms or megaron, where all the
walls were colourfully frescoed: the **entrance porch**, the **vestibule** (where a stair led to

an upper floor) and the **throne room**, the grandest in the palace. Similar to Mycenae, this has a round hearth in the centre, and bases where four wooden fluted columns once supported a gallery. An opening over the hearth would have allowed light in and smoke out. The walls were frescoed with lions and griffons (a creature that appears on a gold seal found in one of the royal tombs, and was painted on the walls of the throne room of Knossos). The floor was divided into squares, each colourfully decorated with geometric or wavy designs. The throne, inlaid with ivory, stood against the right wall, by a shallow trough that may have allowed the king to offer a libation without getting up. Pýlos exhibits the same maze-like quality of other Mycenaean royal houses. The vestibule was the only entrance to the throne room, and to reach the surrounding rooms required backtracking through the vestibule and down the narrow corridors on either side. Five small rooms off the left corridor were **pantries**, the source of all the crockery in the Chóra museum. Those off the right corridor, and directly behind the palace, were used as **oil magazines**. The tablets found in the two back rooms were descriptions of the various olive oils, their flavours and qualities. Even back then Greeks were connoisseurs.

If you walk back through the vestibule to the inner courtyard and turn left, you'll enter the section of the palace known as the **Queen's megaron**. The small hall has a round hearth, and there's a room with a drain (possibly a **lavatory**), and a little room everyone remembers best: a **bathroom**, complete with painted terracotta bathtub on a base. Homer tells us that when Telemachus visited, he received a scrub and rub-down from Nestor's daughter Polykastra.

A gateway from around the corner of the bathroom leads towards a pair of courts and a multipurpose second building, identified as the palace **arsenal** and **workshop**, with a little **shrine** similar to the small cult rooms found at Mycenae. A large room to the north of this was the **wine magazine**, where clay seals were found identifying the sources of the large jars. On the west side of the palace, separated by open **courts**, is a second **residence**, tentatively identified as an older palace. It had its own **wine store** as well, to the north. Royal **tholos tombs** have been found around the palace; one, about 100m northeast of the gate, has been restored.

Chóra Trifylías and the Archaeology Museum

Four kilometres north of the Palace of Nestor, the market village of **Chóra Trifylías** is distinguished by a big square full of cafés and a small but important **Archaeology Museum** (*t 276 303 1358; open Tues–Sun 8.30–3; adm*), housing finds from the area. In Room I, your eye is at once drawn to the **gold cups** found in the tholoi of Peristeriá, glittering in their central case with gold **jewellery**, a diadem and bee beads, nautilus shells and tiny owl rivets, all done in loving detail. Cases on the left hold the more utilitarian Mycenaean finds: double axes, arrow heads, seal impressions, tweezers, a rhyton with three deer heads, and good – if surly-looking – octopi to the right of the door. Room II is dedicated to artefacts from Nestor's Palace. Compared to Mycenae, the tombs yielded few works in gold, jewellery, bronze and ivory, but what was found is of a high quality, and all in the National Archaeological Museum in Athens. Here at Chóra you'll find cupboards of **crockery**, 20 different kinds of cups and plates, handy for royal banquets. The star attractions are remnants of the **frescoes**, offering little windows into a lost world: there's a war scene showing the boar tusk helmet and a rather gruesome spearing of a warrior, doves, a bull-leaper and a lyre-player. The room also has casts of Linear B tablets. Room III has more finds from the palace of Nestor: stone horns of consecration, reminiscent of those found in Knossos, giant storage pithoi, loom weights, chimney pipes, a rhyton decorated with palm trees, stacks of what look like tea cups, a *souvlaki* grill and a fine vase decorated with stylized ivy. The pots show signs of the intensity of the fire that destroyed the palace.

Up the Ionian Coast: Chóra to Kyparissía

Northwest of Chóra, the main road goes through busy hilltop **Gargaliáni,** which pulls in crowds on Wednesday for its market. It has lovely views over the fishing village of **Marathópoli** and the island of **Próti**, which floats off shore like a giant beaver. If it's time for lunch or a swim, you could do a lot worse. Regular boats go out to Próti, which in ancient times had a little market town. One of its small bays is known as Gramméno or 'written' bay for the inscriptions sailors carved in the rock, wishing for a safe voyage. A handful of monks live at the **monastery Theótokou**, named for an icon found on the shore in 1984. The anniversary of its discovery, 23 September, is an excuse for a big *panegýri* with a fish feast. Próti was long an island for hermits, so perhaps it's not surprising that it still has a few icons on the loose.

North of Marathópoli and Gargaliáni is more of the low hilly country that the Mycenaeans liked best. To the east rises nubby Mount Egáleo (3,937ft). Down below, orchards and olive groves surround **Filiatrá**, a market town that tries harder than the rest: bell towers sport bright island-style domes and a miniature version of the **Unisphere** from the 1964 New York World's Fair and a 40ft model of the **Eiffel Tower** stand on either end of town. If you're intrigued, there's more: Mr Fouraráki, the artist behind it all, left a fairytale castle called the **Pýrgos ton Thaumaton** in the seaside hamlet of **Ágrili**, 6km north of Filiatrá.

Getting There and Around

There are four daily **trains, t** 276 102 2283, from Pátras or Kalamáta to Kyparissía. The **bus** station, **t** 276 102 2260, near the train station, has four buses a day to Athens (via Trípoli), four to Kalamáta, three to Pýlos, two to Pátras. For a **taxi: t** 276 102 2666.

Where to Stay and Eat

Kyparissía ⊠ 22500

Kyparissía Beach, t 276 102 4492, **f** 276 102 4495 (*B; expensive*). In a garden by the sea; large rooms and balconies. *Open all year.*

Kanellakis, t 276 102 4464, **f** 276 102 4466 (*B; expensive*). Stylish, with an attractive pool area and a beautifully landscaped setting; 100m from the sea. *Open all year.*

Tsolaridis, t 276 102 2145, *tsolaridis@conxion.gr* (*B; expensive–moderate, breakfast inc.*). A startling purple and white confection, with a truly lovely terrace. *Open all year.*

Camping Kyparissia, t 276 102 3491, **f** 276 102 4519. The only one; right down by the sea. *Open April–10 Oct.*

For dinner try the beach tavernas or the three little restaurants up by the castle, with lovely views (the latter open eves only in the off season).

Kyparissía and Peristería

Kyparissía has the landmark on this stretch of coast, the 500ft crag of Mount Psychro by the sea, which made it just the spot Epaminóndas wanted as a port for ancient Messene. Today a modest resort, Kyparissía is famous for sunsets and sandy beaches, some of which are also favoured by loggerhead turtles for their nests. Needle-sharp cypresses rise on the hill under the **castle**; get there by way of a sign-posted road from the main square. Ruined along with the rest of the Kyparissía by Ibrahim Pasha, it has a big keep built with masonry from the time of Epiminóndas to the Franks and views as far as Kefaloniá. Around the castle are little medieval streets, stairways and houses with tiled roofs, a favourite place to spend the evening.

Before Epaminóndas, the Mycenaeans were here, and buried their important dead inland at the three tholos tombs in **Peristería**. The signpost just north of Kyparissía says 4km, but the gate is actually 5.5km away; the guardian, Mr Kanelópoulos, is there from 8.30–3, but doesn't always take the same day off – to make sure he's around, ring Olympia, **t** 262 402 2529. It's worth the trouble: Peristería has the perfect setting, among rolling hills over a quiet river valley, a beautiful and unspoiled landscape. As you follow the winding road, you'll see the knob of a corbelled dome protruding from the ground like an omphalos or stone breast. The three tholoi here, the source of the gold cups and jewellery in the Chóra museum, were discovered by accident in 1960, when a dog fell through one of the domes. The archaeologist Spiros Marinatos reconstructed the best preserved one: it stands 33ft high, with a 25-ton lintel and a faint relief of a dove (*peristéri*) and olive branch, preserved under glass on the door jamb.

Évia
(ΕΥΒΟΙΑ / Ευβοια)

11

Évia – Classical Euboea – is often lumped together with Central Greece in the next chapter, yet at the same time it has kept something of its island remoteness, even if it's the only one accessible by train and only 88km from Athens. The second largest island after Crete, its landscapes of olive groves, orchards and vines alternate with forests, wild cliffs and snow-capped mountains, while nearly every hill is crowned with a Frankish or Byzantine castle. Its name means 'rich in cattle' and animal husbandry remains important. But Évia also has plenty of beaches, and gets throngs of Greek tourists, especially in July and August. This essential Greekness also means reasonable prices for an island and excellent tavernas but, on the other hand, it also means that car hire, travel agencies and English speakers are thin on the ground.

History

Two of the most precocious city-states in the 8th–7th centuries BC were Evian rivals Chalkís and Erétria, both located on the Evripós Strait, a busy shipping lane in antiquity, when mariners shunned the stormy east coast of the island. Both traded far and wide and had colonies in Italy, but between them lay the Lelantine plain 'rich in vineyards'; both cities claimed it and extended their disagreement into international affairs. In 506 BC Chalkís joined Boeotia against Athens, only to be conquered and divided; Erétria joined Athens in supporting the Ionian revolt in Asia Minor, and in retribution was sacked and enslaved by the Persians en route to Marathon. In the

Getting There and Around

By Sea

Ferries link Évia with the mainland from Rafína to Kárystos (just over 1½hrs; twice a day), Rafína to Marmári (six to seven times a day), Ag. Marína to Néa Stýra (at least five times a day), Arkítsa to Loutrá Edipsoú (12–14 times a day), Skala Oropóu to Erétria (every half-hour) and Glífa to Agiókambos (every 2hrs). Ferries also link Skýros daily from Kými. In the summer, there are connections from Ag. Konstantínos to Oreí and Péfki.

Summer **hydrofoils** to Loutrá Edipsoú, Oreí, Péfki and the other Sporades; others sail from Vólos to Kými and Oreí; from Trikéri to Oreí; from Ag. Konstantínos to Chalkís, Loutrá Edipsoú and Porto Limini; and from Kárystos to several Cyclades islands.

Port Authorities

Kárystos, t 222 402 2227; Marmári, t 222 403 1222; Néa Stýra, t 222 404 1266; Kými, t 222 202 2606; Alivéri, t 222 302 2955; Erétria, t 222 106 2201; Chalkís, t 222 102 2236; Péfki t 222 604 1710; Oreí, t 222 607 1228; Agiókambos, t 222 603 1107; Loutrá Edipsoú, t 222 602 2464.

By Road

Évia is linked to the mainland by a bridge over the Evripós Strait; there are **buses** every half-hour, and **trains** every hour from Athens to Chalkis (1½hrs); train information in Chalkís, t 222 102 2386. The bus terminal in Athens is Liossion, from where you can also travel direct to Kými , Erétria, Amárinthos, Edipsós or Alivéri; for Rafína, Ag. Marína and Oropós, *see* p.160.

A good bus service connects Chalkis (the station is in the centre, t 222 102 2640) with all the major villages of Évia as well as Thebes (twice a day) on the mainland.

Note that Chalkís and Erétria are the only places on Évia where you can rent **cars and motorbikes**. You'll also need a compass and the newest map you can find: signposting ranges from the minimal to the non-existent.

Tourist Information

Tourism Promotion Committee of Évia: 10 Charalambous St, Chalkís, t 222 108 2677. **Tourist police**: 2 El. Venizélou, Chálkis, t 222 107 7777; Edipsós: t 222 602 2456.

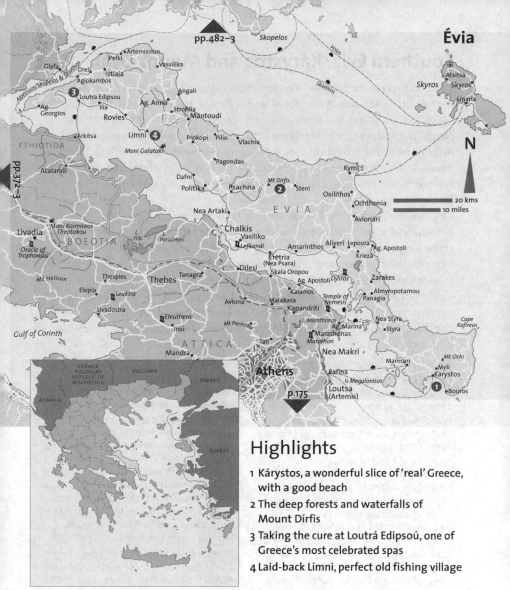

pp.482–3

pp.372–3

N

20 kms
10 miles

Highlights

1 **Kárystos**, a wonderful slice of 'real' Greece, with a good beach
2 The deep forests and waterfalls of **Mount Dírfis**
3 Taking the cure at **Loutrá Edipsoú**, one of Greece's most celebrated spas
4 Laid-back **Límni**, perfect old fishing village

5th century BC, the two cities and the rest of Évia came under the rule of Athens, which regarded it as its personal granary.

Under the Franks, the island was divided it into three baronies, initiating an intense castle-building spree. Over the next hundred years Évia came under the direct rule of the Venetians, whose mushy accents mangled Evripós (the channel) into 'Negroponte', a name they used for the entire island. When the Turks took Negroponte in 1470, they did not even allow the usual puppet Venetian governor to hang around as a tax farmer, but settled the fertile prize themselves. In the 19th century 40,000 refugees from Albania and Épirus settled in the south, and a small Turkish minority remained on the island by special agreement in 1923.

Southern Évia: Kárystos and Mount Óchi

The best way to see Évia, with a minimum of backtracking, is to take the 1½hr ferry from Rafína to **Kárystos**, at the foot of Mount Óchi, at the extreme southern tip of the island on the Myrtoan Sea. Renowned for its green cipollino marble, Kárystos so caught the fancy of Greece's first king Otto that he renamed it Othonoúpolis and declared he would make it the capital of Greece. He summoned an architect from Bavaria to lay out the town plan, who left the wide, straight streets that set Kárystos apart. Whiffs of neoclassical grandeur linger in 19th-century buildings like the Dimarchíon (town hall).

Othonoúpolis fell by the wayside like Otto himself, leaving Kárystos to carry on peacefully as a typical Greek town with a long sandy beach that is perfect for snorkelling and windsurfing. The evening stroll, or *vólta*, endures with enthusiasm, along a *paralía* crowded with excellent *ouzerie* and tavernas; these are heaving on the third or fourth weekends of August, when Kárystos puts on its wine festival. The waterfront is defended by a four-square 14th-century coastal fort, or **Boúrdzi**, its walls incorporating sculpted marble from a 2nd-century AD mausoleum. Opposite, the Cultural Centre houses the **Archaeological Museum** (*t 922 492 2471; open Tues–Sun 9–5*), with pottery and reliefs from Classical to Roman times.

Where to Stay and Eat

Kárystos ✉ 34001

Apollon Suites, on sandy, if sometimes windy, Psilí Ámmos beach, t 222 402 2045, f 222 402 2049 (*A; expensive*). Air-conditioned apartments and a heated pool.

Karystion, t 222 402 2191, f 222 402 2727 (*C; expensive–moderate*). Surrounded by the park near the *bourdzi*; all rooms with sea view, air-conditioning and TV.

Als, t 222 402 2202, f 222 402 5002 (*C; moderate*). Comfortable, on the waterfront; you can watch all the action from your balcony.

Hironia, in town by the sea, t 222 402 2238 (*C; inexpensive*). Battered but budget-friendly.

Mount Ochi Shelter, ring Mr Sákis Biniáris, t 222 402 2378. Fully equipped with a capacity for 30 people.

Cavo D'Oro (€10–12). Besides the waterfront tavernas; it's worth hunting up this one on a side street off the main square.

For local colour, eat on Kotsíka St, next to the Als hotel. This area was the old Jewish quarter, and now buzzes with grill houses. Try:

To Obpaïïka, at the top of Kotsíka St. Tables are shared with other diners as well as cats and dogs, and the food is good and cheap.

Néa Stýra ✉ 34015

Sunday, t 222 404 1300, f 222 404 1205 (*C;moderate; rates include breakfast*). Family-run hotel with big green awnings on the balconies overlooking the sea.

Venus Beach, 2km from town, t 222 404 1226, f 222 404 1209 (*C; moderate*). Twin bungalows in a lovely garden setting with a pool, restaurant and its own beach.

Castello Rosso, near the Venus Beach, t 222 404 1547/780, (*C; moderate*). Nice small hotel with a pool, 50m from the beach; rates include a buffet breakfast.

A small group of tavernas on the north end of town (turn left at the Lemonías sign) serve most of the usual Greek dishes, but specialize in fish.

Akroyiali, past the ferry docks. *Ouzerie*/taverna serving good dishes in attractive setting by the water.

Kými ✉ 34003

Korali, t 222 202 2212, f 222 202 3353 (*C; moderate*). A decent choice. *Open all year.*

Beis, at Paralía Kými by the quay, t 222 202 2604, f 222 202 2870 (*C; moderate*). Large, if rather anonymous hotel often used by people sailing out to Skýros. *Open all year.*

For most of the Middle Ages, the safest spot for miles around was the huge citadel above Kárystos, the **Castel Rosso** (or **Kókkino Kástro**, or Red Castle), built in 1030 by the Byzantines, rebuilt by the Franks in the 13th century, and purchased by the Venetians in 1366. Although the citadel, with its deceptive multi-level layout and labyrinth of entrances, was believed to be impregnable, to the extent that only 30 men were needed for its defence, the Turks captured it. Four hundred Turkish families were settled within its walls and the rulers, unusually, gave local Christians the chop if they refused to convert to Islam.

The road to Castel Rosso passes by **Mýli**, a good lunch stop in a ravine, then continues over a handsome stone bridge crossing another ravine at Graviá. The ancient cipollino quarries are nearby. A 3hr path from Mýli continues to the mountain refuge and then, through ever more dramatic and barren scenery, to the summit of **Mount Óchi** (4,586ft), crowned by a 'dragon's house' – the large blocks of a Pelasgian building, perhaps a beacon or peak sanctuary. In **Aetós**, close to Mýli, the church of **Panagía tis Theoskepástis** was abandoned by the villagers when they could not afford to cover it; then one night Mount Óchi dropped a massive boulder on top of it, without harming the walls, hence the name 'roofed by God'.

If Kárystos is too crowded, there's another long sandy beach 13km away at **Boúros**, where free camping is usually tolerated, although you'll have to bring your own

There are also a few rooms and waterfront tavernas, including the **Valedi** and **Aegio**, which serve good, standard fare while waiting for your ship to come in.

Amárinthos ✉ 34006

Stefania, on the north end of town, t 222 903 8382, f 222 903 8384 (*B; expensive*). Large, comfortable hotel with a pool. *Open all year.*

Flisvos, t 222 903 6071 (*C; moderate*). Smaller choice, without pool. *Open all year.*

Limanaki, t 222 903 6609 (€12–18). Decent fish taverna on the water, with extensive selection of starters.

If you need meat, little Gymnó, 8km north, is famous for its dozen tavernas drawing dedicated carnivores from as far away as Athens.

Erétria ✉ 34008

Erétria has many hotels, as does Malakónda (just east), a beach-side resort that has mushroomed up for the package holiday crowd.

Palmariva Eretria Beach, 2km from Erétria, t 222 906 2411, f 222 906 2418 (*A; expensive*). Recently renovated, with everything a seaside resort hotel should have – sea sports, pools, tennis, gym, disco and a wide choice of bars.

Holidays in Evia, on the beach in Erétria, t 222 906 2611, f 222 906 1300 (*B; expensive*). Another sports- and fun-orientated resort complex and conference centre, with a good restaurant by the water. *Open all year.*

Malaconda Beach Vogue Club, at Malakónda, t 222 906 2510, f 222 906 2518 (*B; expensive*). Prettily set among the olives and cypresses, with a pool. *Open Mar–Oct.*

Delfis, t 222 906 2380 (*C; moderate*). An old favourite. *Open June–Sept.*

Dreams Island, on the peninsula with sandy beaches, t 222 906 1224, f 222 906 1268 (*moderate–inexpensive*). Fancy name for town-run complex of two hotels, bungalows, restaurant, bar, barbecue and disco with a not-so-glorified campground atmosphere.

Eva Camping, at Malakónda, t 222 106 1081. The nicest campsite, with good shade.

Ligouris, opposite the ferry, t 222 906 2352. Specializes in seafood, especially lobster; set menus range from €25 up to €38 for lobster, with ouzo and barrelled wine.

Psiteria, a few yards further along. Try the stuffed *biftéki* washed down with their excellent chilled white wine, and pay pennies for it.

water. Near Boúros, at **Nikási**, experienced speleologists can visit an enormous cave, once a Palaeolithic shelter, with the little church of **Ag. Triáda** at the entrance. Below, an underground river flows from the bowels of Mount Óchi; outside there is cold spring water to drink and a grove of plane trees, perfect for a picnic on a hot day. A road with occasional rough patches continues along to the southeasternmost tip of Évia, the notorious, tempest-tossed **Cape Kafiréus** (the Venetian Cabo d'Oro), where to avenge the death of his son Palamedes King Nauplios (*see* p.255) lit fiery beacons to mislead the Greeks returning from Troy. Cabo d'Oro still has a few woebegone ruins of a fortress, repaired in the 1260s by Admiral Likarios, the right-hand man of Michael Paleológos, who after the depredations of the Fourth Crusade restored the Byzantine Empire – beginning in Greece at this weatherbeaten fort.

Up the West Coast

The road north of Kárystos follows the spectacular west coast of Évia, along a corniche at times half a mile over the sea; the cliffs below are a favourite nesting place for hawks and eagles. There are two small resorts here: **Marmári**, named for its quarries of green marble, with a long beach and little port, sheltered by islets, and **Néa Stýra**, a lazy holiday base with a long sandy beach and excellent swimming. Near Néa Stýra are more 'dragons' houses', a terrace with three buildings believed to have been Homeric watch-towers (finds in the Kárystos museum). Old **Stýra** lies under the mammoth Venetian fortress of Larména on Mount Kilósi; you can seek out the ruins of ancient Stýra near the meagre remains of Mycenaean **Dryopes**, a once important town that did its bit against the Persians at Artemission and Salamis.

After Néa Stýra, the road rises to **Almyropótamos**; side roads lead down to barely developed beaches around **Panagía**, on the west shore. Further north, just before the crossroads at Lépoura, a dirt road from Kriezá leads in 5km to the well-preserved polygonal walls, gate and 11 square towers of 5th-century BC **Dystos**. Spread over a hill by Évia's largest lake (which in summer dries up to form Évia's biggest vegetable garden), you can also trace the foundations of ancient houses set on terraces and streets; the tower was renovated by the Venetians. Fossils of prehistoric beasts have been discovered by the sea below Kriezá, at **Ag. Apóstoli**, a sheltered little fishing harbour with a beach tucked in the rocky cliffs of Évia's east coast.

Lépoura to Kými

At **Lépoura** the road forks, one branch heading towards Chalkís (*see* p.364) and the other north to Kými. On the Kými road, a turn-off to the right leads down to **Avlonarí**, a fine old village topped by a small fortress and home to the lovely 12th-century Venetian church of Ag. Dimítrios. Further on, **Ochthoniá** is a busy village crammed beneath a Frankish castle, overlooking a set of quiet sandy beaches. After the Ochthoniá turn off, the Lépoura–Kými road plunges and writhes through a lovely and pastoral valley, dotted with Frankish towers to **Oxílithos**, named for its landmark, a volcanic precipice crowned with a church.

Kými, the main port for Skýros, is a low-key resort, lush, surrounded by vineyards and fig orchards, perched on a shelf high above the sea, with a front-row view of the dawn. Many Greeks have summer villas in the hills, including some ambitious nouveau riche designs. The **Museum of Popular Art**, in a neoclassical mansion (*t 222 202 2011; open 9–1 and 5–7*), houses costumes, tools, furnishings and a display on Kými's famous son, Dr George Papanikoláou, who invented and gave the first syllable of his name to the smear test every woman knows so well. Pretty footpaths and the road wind down to the port, **Paralía Kými**, near a beach sheltered by pampas grass. It's not particularly inspiring, but there are lovely beaches a short drive away at Platanás and Chiliádou. A fine walk along the road north of Kými leads to the sheer rocky ledge that was the acropolis of Homeric Kyme Phyrkontis. The stone of its temples went into the precipitous Byzantine/Frankish castle of **Apokledí** and the handsome convent **Sótiros** (1634) with a beautiful tile roof (*women only admitted*).

Lépoura to Erétria

Back on the main road from Lépoura to Chalkís, the first major village is **Alivéri**, its old red-roofed houses inhabited by men working in the nearby power station. Pylons and a cement factory protect it from any tourist pretensions, but the seaside tavernas and beach can make for a pleasantly lazy afternoon. Three ancient towns stood nearby: Tamynae above Alivéri, Porthmos by the beach, and **Amarinthos** by Alivéri, now marked by a Venetian tower called Pyrgáki with its door suspended 24ft above ground level. Amárinthos is a lively little resort popular for its fresh seafood (some plucked direct from the offshore fish farms) and has two Byzantine churches in the environs, **Metamórphosis** and **Kímissi tis Theotókou**, and a Macedonian tomb – rare this far south – at **Vlichó**. In the hills above Amárinthos, the pretty village of **Áno Vátheia** has another Byzantine church, **Zoodóchos Pigí**.

Ferries from Oropós sail to **Erétria**; its alternative name, Néa Psará, recalls the refugees from Psará (*see* p.821), who built their new town and fine captains' mansions on top of the old. Even so, Erétria is the most complete ancient site on Évia, as well as its biggest holiday resort after Loutrá Edipsoú. Ancient Erétria, under its own Mount Olympus, reached its prime during its rivalry with Chalkís over the lush Lelantine Plain that lay between them. In the end the two cities decided to leave their weapons at home and meet at a midway point, where a general free-for-all punch-up decided all. Erétria lost, then suffered an even worse disaster in 490 BC when the Persians razed the city, thinking to have Athens for dessert (*see* p.161). But the Erétrians rebuilt, and earned a reputation for ceramics and a school of philosophy, founded in 320 BC by Plato's student, Menedemes. Then in 87 BC Mithridates of Pontus sacked the city, and that was it; Erétria was never rebuilt. Nowadays Erétria is something of a French colony, with a line of smart cafés, and takes itself a little too seriously.

The **museum** at the top of Arkaíou Theátrou St (*t 222 906 2206; open Tues–Sun 8.30–3*) has a striking Proto-Geometric centaur and figurative ceramics, derived from old Mycenaean designs, from Lefkándi (*see* below). Erétria's finds are displayed by theme, and include fragments of Archaic sculptures from the pediment of the Temple of Apollo Daphnephoros. The adjacent excavations (*same hours; pick up the key for the Macedonian tomb at the museum*) have revealed **walls** of excellent trapezoidal masonry, an elaborate **west gate** with a corbelled arch that once extended over the moat, a 4th-century BC peristyle **palace** (complete with a clay bathtub), a **House of Mosaics** from the same period, and a **gymnasium** which has some plumbing in situ on its east end. Although the upper stone tiers of seats of the **theatre** were cannibalized to build the modern town, the stage has the world's only survival of a *deus ex machina*: an underground passage from the orchestra that leads to the built-up *skene* behind the stage, where gods could suddenly appear to resolve a tangled plot. A path west of the theatre leads to the tumulus of a **Macedonian tomb**, its square chamber holding well-preserved painted marble couches, two thrones and a table. Another path from the theatre leads in 15 minutes up to Erétria's walled **acropolis**, affording an excellent view of the Lelantine plain, and, on a clear day, Mount Parnassós on the mainland. Down in the centre of the modern town, you can see the foundations of the **Temple of Apollo Daphnephoros**, 'the laurel bearer', who enjoyed a fervent following in Évia: the 6th-century Doric temple was built over a 7th-century BC Ionic temple, with wooden columns.

Recent discoveries suggest that **Lefkándi**, 2km below Vassilikó off the Chalkís road, may have been the Erétria listed in the Homeric *Catalogue of Ships*. Inhabited from the Early Helladic period, it is one of the very few places in Greece to have carried on in style in the Dark Ages, maintaining trade links with Athens throughout the Proto-Geometric era. On the cemetery *toumba* (mound), just north of Lefkándi port, a giant roof covers the most astonishing find: a huge building (177 by 33ft) from *c*. 1000 BC, built in mud brick over stone foundations (*no adm, but you can walk around the outside*), surrounded by a wooden colonnade – predating the 'first' peristyle Temple of Hera on Sámos by two centuries, as well as revealing a complete break with Mycenaean styles. A tomb in the centre was divided into two compartments: one held a man, his bones wrapped in fine cloth in a bronze vase, with his iron sword and spear, and a woman with lavish gold, iron and bronze ornaments. The other had the skeletons of four horses with iron bits. The implications are still being debated: who were these conspicuously wealthy people? The building was filled in with earth shortly after their burial (perhaps to make a hero mound?). The rest of the community prospered, trading gold and ceramics with Athens and Cyprus, until it was mysteriously abandoned in the 8th century BC.

The Centre of Évia: Chalkís and Mount Dírfis

Chalkís or Chalkída (ΧΑΛΚΙΣ / Χαλκις or ΧΑΛΚΙΔΑ / Χαλκιδα), the bustling industrial rhinoceros-shaped capital of Évia, occupies the narrowest point of the Evripós, only 130ft from the mainland. Its location has been the source of its prosperity, not least through its potential of seriously blocking ancient sea trade between Athens and the north. Its name comes either from copper (*chalkós*), another early source of wealth, or perhaps from *chalki*, the murex mollusc prized in antiquity for making royal purple dye. Mentioned in the *Iliad* as the home of the great-hearted Abantes, the city by Archaic times had so many colonies in northern Greece that it gave its name to the peninsula, Chalkidikí; in Italy it founded Messina, Reggio Calabria and Cumae near

Where to Stay and Eat

Chalkís ⊠ 34100

Lucy, 10 Voudouris, t 222 102 3831, f 222 102 2051, *www.lucy_hotel.gr* (*A; expensive*). An old waterfront hotel, now refurbished; one of the Best Western chain.

Paliria, Leof. Venizélou 2, t 222 102 8001, f 222 102 1959 (*B; expensive–moderate*). A modern building in the centre, overlooking the Evripós, with a snack bar and roof garden.

John's, nearby at 9 Angéli Govioú, t 222 102 4996 (*B; expensive–moderate*). Comfortable rooms, all with air-conditioning and TV, and parking.

Kentrikon, 5 Angéli Govioú, t 222 102 2375 or t 222 102 7260 (*C; inexpensive*). Old and old-fashioned, with helpful English-speaking owners.

Stavedo, 1 Karaóli St, t 222 107 7977 (€20–30). Upscale restaurant-cum-bar on the waterfront, specializing in Mediterranean cuisine, especially seafood with pasta.

Ta 5 F, 61 Evias, t 222 108 5731 (€15). Old classic in a new location, famous for its succulent prawns.

Kotsomoura. In a quiet spot by the hippodrome, traditional taverna. *Open eves only*.

On Ermoú St, just in from the sea, a handful of little tavernas (signs in Greek only) serve up the real thing. Try **Koutsocheras**, serving fish, **O Thanassis**, with big simmering pots of meat and vegetable dishes, or **Kavithas**, with grilled meats. There are also three excellent tavernas on Ag. Minás beach, 3km over the bridge, and a nest of authentic *ouzerie* and fish tavernas 3km south in Néa Lampsakós.

Steni ⊠ 34014

Dirphys, in the village t 222 805 1217 (*C; moderate*). Small and open all year.

Steni, t 222 805 1221 (*C; moderate*). Similar but slightly pricier.

Hellenic Alpine Club Refuge at Lirí (3,773ft). To book, call t 222 102 5230, or t 228 805 1285 for information.

Naples. Modern Chalkís has a glamorous side on the promenade, where you can sit in chic cafés looking at the mainland, and back streets where charming little houses with wooden balconies still exist, but for how much longer is anybody's guess as the bulldozers are hard at work demolishing anything that looks vaguely quaint or old.

The city's first **bridge** was built in 411 BC (the modern sliding drawbridge dates from 1962), but before crossing it have a look at Chalkís and Évia from the walls of the Turkish castle of the **Karababa** ('black father') built in 1686 over Chalkís' ancient acropolis. Once over the bridge, note the modern metal **sculpture** donated to the city by its ancient colony Giardini-Naxos in Sicily, and turn left to find a row of smart cafés and *ouzerie* where you can sit and ponder the mystery of the 140ft-wide **Evripós channel**; the dangerous currents inexplicably change direction every few hours – sometimes only once a day, on rare occasions 14 times day – a phenomenon that so baffled and bothered Aristotle that he threw himself into the waters in frustration. Current thought (excuse the pun) has it that there are two separate streams in the Evripós, and a host of factors determines which dominates at a given moment.

The main attraction in the new part of Chalkís is the **Archaeological Museum** on Leof. Venizélou (*t 222 107 6131; open Tues–Sun 8.30–3*), housing some of the finest artefacts from Erétria, including a headless statue of Athena, the Archaic marble pediment from the Temple of Apollo Daphnephoros showing the rape of Antiope by Theseus, and a bas-relief of Dionysos. Nearby, there's a pretty 16th-century **mosque** with a marble fountain, marking the entrance to the **Kástro**, the old Turkish quarter. Nearby **Ag. Paraskeví** is a Byzantine basilica converted in the 13th century by Crusaders into a Gothic cathedral, resulting in the curious architectural collage inside, with 14th-century inscriptions and coats of arms. Every year, in late July, a market for the feast of Ag. Paraskeví enlivens Chalkís for 10 days, attracting bargain hunters from all over Évia and the mainland, while the lovelorn beseech the icon of the saint for their hearts' desire; in the old days they would press a coin against the picture, and if it stuck there it meant their love would not go unrequited. Also in the Kástro, note the arcaded **Turkish aqueduct** that brought water from Mount Dírfis. There's a delightful little **Museum of Folk Art** on Skalkóta Street (*t 222 102 1817; open Wed–Sun 10–1*), containing traditional costumes, icons, the interior of a home and a printing press from the 1920s. Chalkís' Romaniot Jewish population goes back an estimated 2,500 years; the **synagogue** at 27 Kótsou (*open after 6pm*) was built in the mid-19th century, but re-uses a number of marble fragments from the original, which burned down. In the Jewish quarter, off Avantón Street, is a marble bust of Mórdechai Frízis of Chalkís, the first Greek officer killed in the Second World War.

Beaches North of Chalkís, Mount Dírfis and Stení

Buses run to the shingly beaches to the north, all enjoying views of the mainland: **Néa Artáki**, **Paralía Politiká** and best of all **Dáfni**, a green oasis like all the other places in Greece that share the name. Just inland are two of Évia's most distinctive white-washed villages, **Politiká** with a late Byzantine church and a castle and cosy little square, and **Psachná**, a little market town with another castle. Boats leave Chalkís daily for the islet of **Tonnoíro**, with a hotel and beach; the *Eviokos* makes 'mini-cruises' to Límni, Edipsós and other places to swim and eat.

The real beauty spot within easy striking distance (25km) of Chalkís is **Mount Dírfis**, Évia's highest peak at 5,725ft. Wrapped in firs, it supports a surprising quantity of alpine flora, and there's a shelter, at Liri (3,674ft), if you want to do some serious walking (*see* 'Where to Stay'). Buses go as far as **Stení**, a delightful village of wooden houses, chalets and waterfalls in the midst of an 'aesthetic' chestnut forest that's particularly refreshing in summer. From Stení a well-marked if rather strenuous path climbs to the summit of Dírfis, and a magnificently scenic road goes over the pass, towards Strópones; it continues in a bumpy way down to the east coast and the splendid, pebble beach of **Chiliadoú**, with summer tavernas and places to camp.

Northern Évia

Parts of the northern half of Évia are so lush and green that you could be forgiven for thinking you were in Austria, although here the coast has long stretches of beaches lined with whitewashed houses and rose-filled gardens. Unfortunately, it has suffered more than its share of forest fires in recent years.

Prokópi and Around

North of Psachná, the road to Pagóndas rises high into the mountains, permeated with the scent of pine forests; beehives everywhere attest to the potency of local herbs and wildflowers, and the honey offered in roadside stands comes close to nectar. Tavernas with outdoor terraces take advantage of the views. **Pagóndas** (35km from Chalkís) is a typical mountain settlement; further north, a striking castle piled on a nearly inaccessible precipice signals **Prokópi**, a village set near the end of the magnificent narrow, wooded ravines of the Kleisoúra valley, where the road offers fine views over the Sporades. This is prime picnicking territory, and, if extra thrills are called for, wobble over the ravines on the rickety wooden suspension bridges.

Sometimes called by its Turkish name, Ahmet Aga, Prokópi is populated by Greeks from the fantastical Cappadocian town of Ürgüp, who came over in the 1923 population exchange. They brought their holy relics, the bones of St John the Russian, a soldier in the Tsar's army who was captured by the Turks and sold as a slave in Ürgüp (1730), then canonized by the Russian Orthodox Church (in 1962); he attracts his share of pilgrims at his church, **Ag. Ioánnes tou Rossou**. In the centre of Prokópi, the Turkish Pasha's estate and his tulip and rose gardens were bought in 1832 by Edward Noel, a relative of Byron, who set up the North Euboean Foundation to provide health care and education for the Greek refugees who poured into Évia after the War of Independence. The estate is now home to the **Candili Centre** (*see* 'Where to Stay').

From Prokópi, a road to the east leads steeply down through forests of planes, pines and firs to **Pílio**, set in rocky mountain scenery. There are tavernas and rooms to rent, and lovely old houses with goats in the garden alternating with the usual concrete monstrosities. The sandy bay below looks across to Skópelos and still has only one taverna; if you want somewhere even less civilized, brave the rough road east along the coast to the pebbly beach beyond **Vlachiá**.

From Prokópi, the main road continues north through **Mantóudi**, with its pretty square and great *ouzerie*. At **Strofiliá** you can turn west for Límni (*see* below) or continue to **Ag. Ánna**, a traditional village located above two very long beaches, **Paralía Ag. Ánna** (with a campsite, t 222 706 1550) and **Angáli**, just north. **Vassiliká**, further up, looks directly across to emerald Skiáthos; the sign for **Psarodóuli** points the way to a long, sandy beach.

Around the Top of Évia

The north coast of Évia, dotted with fine beaches, looks across to the Pélion peninsula and the mainland; Greek families settle in here for the entire summer, making accommodation for only one or two days problematic. **Artemísseon** witnessed the first but indecisive naval battle between the Greeks and the Persians in 480 BC. Near the shore are the ruins of the vast **Temple of Artemis Proseoa**, although the greatest treasure was a shipwreck of ancient bronzes, discovered in 1928, the source of the National Archaeological Museum's splendid Poseidon (or Zeus) and the Cape Artemisseon Jockey. Continuing east of Artemísseon, **Péfki** has an extensive sand and pebble beach popular with Hungarians and Slovaks, and splendid views across to the Pélion and Skiáthos, which you can reach by hydrofoil.

Cattle belonging to Hera grazed at **Istiaía**, described by Homer as 'rich in vines'. It was founded by Thessalians who thumbed their noses at Athens so often that Pericles captured the town and booted out the inhabitants, repopulating it with

Tourist Information

Hydro/Physiotherapy Centre: 3 Okeanídon, Edipsós, t 222 602 3500 (*summer only*).
Tourist police, Edipsós: t 222 602 2456.
Bus station, Edipsós: t 222 602 2250.

Where to Stay and Eat

Prokópi ✉ 34004

The Candili Centre, *www.candili.co.uk* (*expensive*). Luxury at the idyllic estate of the Noel-Baker family, with inclusive painting, ceramics or music courses, and lots of delicious food served in the evening. Large family suites are available, with a pool, and more.

Péfki ✉ 34200

Galini, towards the east end of the waterfront, t 222 604 1208, f 222 604 1650 (*C; moderate*). Cheery furniture and lovely sea views. English-speaking owners.
Amaryllis, on the waterfront, t 222 604 1222 (*C; moderate*). Pleasant, comfortable hotel with friendly owners. *Open July–Sept.*

Camping Pefki, t 222 604 1161. A good site with some bungalows.
Kati Allo. Get here early if you want a table to enjoy their delights from the grill.

Oreí ✉ 34012

Porto Kairis, t 222 607 1055, f 222 605 2888 (*C; moderate*). Right on the pebble beach, with a little dipping pool.
Leda, t 222 607 1180 (*C; moderate*). Studios on the pebble beach, within easy walking distance of a stretch of sand.
Byzantium, t 222 607 1600 (*C; moderate*), and **Akroyalis,** t 222 607 1375 (*D; moderate–inexpensive*). Just west at Néos Pírgos; comfortable and convenient for the beach.

Loutrá Edipsoú ✉ 34300

There's no shortage of accommodation, although it's impossible to find a room in August without booking; **Lokris Tours,** 2 Ermóu St, t 222 606 9044, f 222 606 0300, *root@nikolaos.hlk.forthnet.gr*, can help. Live Greek music attracts the crowds to various venues – just follow the noise.
Thermae Sylla Spa-Wellness Hotel, on the waterfront, t 222 606 0100, f 222 602 2055,

Athenians. Although attractively situated in an amphitheatre of hills, the Athenian colonists didn't find Istiaía to their liking, preferring to found nearby Oréi instead; when they in turn were driven out by the Spartans in the Peloponnesian War, the Istianians returned. The whole population of Évia contributed to the construction of Istiaía's Venetian **Kástro**, built right in the centre of town; a second medieval fortress, to defend the narrow strait, was built over the ancient acropolis.

The Athenians may have been right: **Oréi** is still a lovely place to while away a few hours. It is renowned for its *ouzerie* which line the pleasant waterfront under the feathery tamarisks. The grid-based backstreets don't yield much, however, but the central square is guarded by a Hellenistic marble bull found offshore in 1962, which in turn is protected by an unappealingly salt-sprayed display case. These days the treat offshore is the islet of **Argirónisos**, abandoned at the turn of the century and now the only private island in Greece taking paying guests. West of Oreí, **Néos Pírgos** is an attractive little resort with a couple of hotels and beach tavernas and, further on, the beach at **Agíokambos** has a row of good seafood tavernas.

Loutrá Edipsoú to Límni

Magnificently set in a giant wooded bay, **Loutrá Edipsoú**, a once glamorous neo-classical spa, is still invaded every August and September, especially by Greek matrons seeking rejuvenation in the fountains of youth. There are 80 hot sulphurous springs

www.thermaesylla.gr (*L; luxury*). Fabulous, palatial spa hotel with every type of hydrotherapy and thalassotherapy, and extremely well-appointed rooms. The two restaurants serve delicious (and healthy) meals for €20–30. *Open all year.*

Aegli, on the waterfront, **t** 222 602 2216, **f** 222 602 2991 (*A; expensive*). Run by the delightful Alkis, and great for wallowing in the faded spa atmosphere. Equipped with mini spas in the basement. Good restaurant, too. *Open May–Oct.*

Giórgos, opposite the bus station, **t** 222 602 3285 (*D; inexpensive*). Small, convenient and lighter on the pocket.

Folia. Away from the waterfront in the market up some inauspicious-looking steps, and set under a canopy of vines; probably the best taverna in town.

O Glaros, in the suburb of Ag. Nikólaos, **t** 222 606 0240 (around €16). The local favourite for fish.

Ag. Geórgios ✉ 34300

Alexandros, **t** 222 603 3208 (*B; moderate*). In the middle of the waterfront, with sea and mountain views. *Open June–Sept.*

Kineon, **t** 222 603 5066, **f** 222 603 3066 (*C; moderate*). The second place to try. *Open April–Oct.*

Límni and Around ✉ 34005

Vateri, 2km from Límni, **t** 222 703 2493, **f** 222 703 1228 (*expensive*). Stay among the vines, orchards and olives of a Greek farm, with beautiful views over the gulf. Six rooms with fireplaces and balconies, good breakfast.

Límni, at the quiet south end of the bay, **t/f** 222 703 1316 (*C; moderate–inexpensive*). Basic rooms, some with balconies on the water.

O Platanos, on Límni's waterfront, **t** 222 703 1686. Excellent grilled fish and meats under the huge reassuring limbs of a plane tree.

Astron, at Katounia, 3km south on the road past the Limni Hotel, **t** 222 703 1487 (€12). The best taverna for grilled fish and meat.

Roviés ✉ 34005

Alexandridis, **t** 222 707 1272, **f** 222 707 1226, www.anzwers.org/trade/alexandridis (*C; expensive–moderate*). Atmospheric studios wih balconies in a handsome old hotel.

Camping Rovies, **t/f** 222 701 1120. Immaculate site by the sea. *Open all year.*

squirting out of the ground at up to 160°F, some cascading from cliffs into the sea where you can stand as in a hot shower, others tumbling over a spread of rocks filling little pools where you can laze as in a bath.

Since antiquity these waters have treated rheumatism, arthritis, gallstones and even depression. The ancients believed that Loutrá's source was connected under the sea with the hot springs at Thermopylae; Aristotle praised the waters; the gouty Sulla, Augustus and Hadrian called in for lengthy soaks in the now ruined Roman baths. Tasteful and low-key Loutrá Edipsoú certainly isn't, but it has its own quirky charm mixed in with the night-time clamour of live Greek music and noisy Athenians promenading the wide avenues until early morning. It also has a long, lovely beach, and excursion boats to Skiáthos, Alónissos and Skópelos.

Follow the road along the bay to Évia's westernmost promontory and a second, more modest spa, **Loutrá Giáltron**, with its frescoed church and boaty beach made picturesque by an old windmill. There are more worthy beaches further west. Club Med had to import lorryloads of sand to make its hideaway at **Gregolímano**, but the immense stretch of sand and pebbles at **Kávos** is open to everyone. Watch out for noticeboards announcing the ferociously fast-changing tides, which, though fascinating to watch, can make for dangerous swimming. Nearby, **Ag. Geórgios** is a laid-back fishing village, with an eponymous church that makes an attractive focus for its cheery waterfront. There's a stalactite cave at Profítis Ilías, and places to picnic and snooze under the plane trees, especially at a spot called Paleóchori.

The road south of Loutrá passes the seaside villages and beaches of **Ília** and **Roviés**, immersed in olive groves; there are fine 17th-century frescoes in the church of **David tou Géronta**, 8km away (check around for the key before setting out). **Límni**, 15km south of Roviés, is many an old hand's favourite place on Évia: a friendly old white-washed fishing village around a sleepy bay with mediocre beaches. The sailing is good, and the waterfront is just right for lazing with the village cats and watching the world go by. According to myth, Zeus brought Hera to Límni (then called Elymnion) during their honeymoon. The temple that marked the spot keeled over in an earth-quake, but in its place Límni offers a pretty paleo-Christian mosaic floor in the chapel of **Zoodóchos Pigí**.

An 8km track from Límni leads south past a lovely strip of sand and pebble beaches to **Moní Galatáki**, a Byzantine monastery (now a convent) in a beautiful, peaceful setting, built over a temple dedicated to Poseidon. The church has fasci-nating 16th-century frescoes, including portraits of the two sea captains who became the monastery's great patrons after they were shipwrecked nearby and saved by divine intervention.

Central Greece:
Stereá Elláda

12

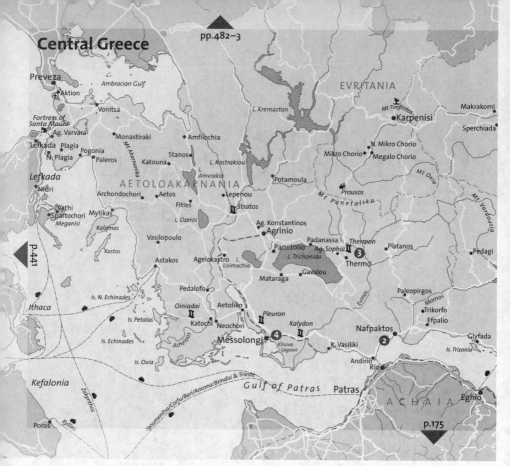

North of the Gulf of Corinth and south of a line between Lamía and the Ambracian Gulf lies what is known poetically as Roúmeli, but administratively as Stereá Elláda (Στερεά Ελλάδα), 'Continental Greece', a term coined around 1830 to describe the part of the mainland and Évia wrested from the Turks in the War of Independence. In ancient times the region consisted of Boeotía, Phocia, Locria, Aetolía and Akarnanía – never quite household words, but encompassing places that resound in myth and history such as Thebes, Delphi, Parnassós, Helicon, Hippocrene, Thermopylae, Orchómenos, Lepanto (Náfpaktos) and Messolóngi. Boeotia, Plutarch's 'dancing-floor of war', saw the Battles of Plataea, Leúktra, and Chairóneia. And one small tribe near Tanágra, the Graioi, who migrated in the 8th century BC to Cumae in Italy, gave their name through a Latin misunderstanding to the Greeks (Graecus) as a whole.

Yet while the names resound, the actual places in Stereá Elláda often thud. Thebes has only a museum to recall its fabled past, and Orchómenos with its Mycenaean fortress at Gla only does a little better. The battlefields that changed history lie in featureless terrain, and Mount Helicon's valley of the Muses didn't even inspire Hesiod who lived in nearby Askra: 'accursed...bad in winter, unbearable in summer,' he called it – an exaggeration, but it is true that Helicon's eastern foothills and the Copáis basin look more like a corner of Arkansas than an Aegean postcard.

pp.482-3

20 kms
10 miles

N

Artemission
Pefki
Glyfa
Orei   Istiaia   Vassilika
Lamia   Stilida   Agiokambos
Loutra   Ypatis   Alonissos/Skopelos & Skiathos
Ypati   Oíte   Thermopylae   Loutra Edipsou   Ag. Anna
National   Molos   Ilia   Strofilia
Park   Thermopiles   Kammena   Ag.   Rovies   Mantoudi
Mt Oíte   Vourla   Georgios
Brallos   Mendenitsa   Ag.   Arkitsa   Limni
Konstantinos   Livanates   Moni Galataki
FTHIOTIDA

Polidrosos   Amfiklia   Elatia   Atalandi
Eptalofos   Malesina   Dafni
FOKIDA   Parnassos   Martino   Politika
Lidoriki   National Park   Parnassos
Amphissa   Davlia   Orchomenos   Gla
L. Mornou   Arachova   Chaironeia   Orchomenos   Kastro   Loukisia
Chrisso   Delphi   Moni Koimiseos   L. Copais
Itea   Distomo   Theotokou   (drained)   L. Yliki   L. Paralimni
Eratini   Osios   Livadia
Galaxidi   Andikira   Loukas   Oracle of   BOEOTIA
Ag. Nikolaos   Aspra Spitia   Trophonios   Aliartos
Askra   Vagia   Tanagra
Mt Helicon   Thespies   Thebes   Asopia
Valley of   Thespai
the Muses   Elopia   Leuktra
Plataea   Erithrai
Aliki   Livadostra   Eleutherai   p.100
Mt Kithéron

p.482-3
P.359
p.100

Highlights

1 Delphi, Apollo's Oracle under Mount Parnassós
2 The medieval dream port of Náfpaktos
3 A sumptuous 'city' shrine in a grand setting, at Thermon
4 Messolóngi's fish-filled lagoon and hinterland of archaeological surprises
5 Orchómenos and Livadiá, where Mycenaeans shared a lake with an offbeat Oracle

West of Livadiá, Stereá Elláda is another story. There are lovely things to see, although apart from Mount Parnassós and Delphi, the 'navel' of the ancient world, their names may not ring any bells. North lies Lamía, gateway to Ypáti on fabled Mount Oíte, and Karpenísi, one of Greece's nicest mountain resorts, with a back road to ancient Thermon. The watery oasis at Livadiá, once famous for its subterranean dream oracle of Trophonios, is well worth a stop, as are the superb Byzantine mosaics at Ósios Loukás, the sea captains' village of Galaxídi, historic Messolóngi, the Venetian castle at Náfpaktos, and lovely Mýtikas, a slice of vanishing Greece.

Thebes (Thíva / Θνβα) and Around

Thebes

Even in ancient times Thebes was *the* city of legend, and names like Cadmus, Semele, Dionysos, Tiresias, Pentheus, Oedipus, Jocasta and Antigone have permeated our Western literary consciousness via college syllabi ever since the Renaissance. Its kaleidoscopic mythological heritage stemmed from its rich Mycenaean past.

The Thebans remained plentiful and powerful enough during the subsequent Dark Ages to keep these Bronze Age story cycles alive until two locals, Hesiod, who mapped Mount Olympus in his *Theogony* and Boeotía in *Works and Days*, and the 'divine' Pindar, composer of myth-studded odes to Olympic victors, immortalized them in print. It also helped that the great Athenian playwrights, fascinated by Theban story cycles, appropriated them wholesale, holding them up as mirrors to their own *polis*.

Getting There and Around

By Bus

From Athens' Liossíon station (**t** 210 831 7179) hourly from 6am to 9pm (fewer on weekends) to the Theban terminal, south of the Kadmeía on Estias St, **t** 226 202 7512; among the local buses based here is one to Chalkída twice a day. The Athens-Livadiá bus is also pretty much hourly and leaves Liossíon (**t** 210 831 71730) to 'Terma Charoneías' in Livadiá (**t** 226 102 8336). From here, well over 10 buses a day go to Orchómenos and Dístomo; three to Kástro (in walking distance of Gla), four to Chairóneia, and three to Aráchova, which has good connections to Delphi. A useful intercity bus connects Thebes and Livadiá six times a day. In Thebes, this bus leaves from in front of the Astoria sweet shop, not far from the Niobe hotel.

By Train

Ten trains a day connect Thebes, Livadiá, Athens and points north. The Thebes station (**t** 226 202 7531) is on the very north edge of town. The Livadiá station, **t** 226 102 8046, is miles from town in the old lake bed, but there is a connecting bus.

By Taxi

Thebes, **t** 226 202 7077; Livadiá, **t** 226 102 2322; Dístomo, **t** 226 702 2799.

Where to Stay

Thebes ✉ 32200

Accommodation in Thebes is humble and its huge army base sometimes block-books.

Niobe, 63 Epanimonda, **t** 226 202 9888 or **t** 226 208 9094, **f** 226 202 7949 (*C; moderate, breakfast included*). A second-floor reception and tiny breakfast area, and neat rooms with TV. To avoid leaving the Niobe 'all tears', call or book ahead.

Meletiou, **t** 226 202 7333. Just in case; across the street.

Livadiá ✉ 32100

The three hotels here are unaccountably grand; curiously, the best is the cheapest.

Philippos, Leofóros Papaspirou (on the Thebes road), **t** 126 102 4189, **f** 226 102 0121 (*A; expensive*). In a field, far from town; a new, well designed convention-orientated hotel with a spacious marble lobby and a posh restaurant. Crossing this lobby in a bathing suit to the pool would require nerve. Elsewhere, it would be in the luxury class; here, it's just over moderate.

Dístomo ✉ 32005

Koutriaris, 6 Plateía Ethnikis Antistassis, **t** 226 702 2268 (*C; moderate*). Neat and modern.

America, 1 Kastriti, **t** 226 703 3079 (*C; moderate*). Opposite, and a tinge cheaper.

History

In myth, Cadmus (a Phoenician in some versions, or an Egyptian), was told by the Delphic oracle to follow a cow into Boeotía and build a city where she rested. When she sank down on a long, low plateau overlooking Lake Copáis, Cadmus killed the resident dragon, and, on the advice of Athena, sowed its teeth. They promptly became armed men (Sparti, 'the sown ones') who killed each other except for five who stuck around to father the Theban race on the acropolis-hill named the Kadmeía after Cadmus, where they have lived ever since. The poor cow was sacrificed to Athena for her pains; Cadmus married Harmonia, daughter of Ares and Aphrodite, fathered Semele, Agave and Polydoros, and produced the alphabet before he was turned into a snake. Not an auspicious start, but myths have their own strange logic.

The Kadmeía, inhabited in Neolithic times, became a large fortified Mycenaean city, with an Old Palace that burned down in *c.* 1350 BC; a New Palace, built from scratch and completely reorientated, suffered the same fate in *c.* 1250. In the earliest historical times, 'Seven-gated Thebes' was always the local powerhouse, rivalled only by smaller Orchómenos across the lake; by the 6th century BC (most probably earlier), it formed and headed a federation of Boeotian cities.

Thebes sided with the Persians at **Plataea** in 479 BC. That annoyed Athens, who attacked Thebes in 457. This in turn annoyed Thebes, who wholeheartedly backed Sparta in the Peloponnesian War. Taking advantage of Athens' and Sparta's battle-fatigue, Thebes made a bid to control Greece under her brilliant leader **Epaminóndas**. He had two secret weapons. The first was his innovative military tactics, using a deep phalanx to draw in the enemy for his cavalry to clobber from the side. The second was the **Sacred Band**, an army of paired lovers who presumably would fight harder to impress their beloveds and were universally admired by the Greeks for their prowess. After demolishing forever the myth of Spartan invincibility at **Leúktra** in 371 BC, Thebes controlled much of Greece for nine years, freeing enslaved Messenía from Sparta before Epaminóndas was killed in battle near Mantinea in 362 BC. That was the beginning of the end. Thebes resisted the blandishments of Philip of Macedon, was defeated by his army at **Chairóneia** in 338 BC, then besieged by Alexander the Great in 335, who completely razed the city (except for the temples and Pindar's house) *pour encourager les autres* – an act that so shocked the Greeks that for the first time ever the mysteries at Eleusis were cancelled after they started. Thebes suffered the same fate at the hands of the Romans in 86 BC. Local tenacity and the fertility of the Copáis region allowed it to recover. By the 9th century, it was probably the biggest city on the Greek mainland, with a silk industry that was the envy of the world – until the invading Normans carried off the silk workers, many of whom were Jews, to Sicily. After 1205, Thebes was the capital of the Frankish Duchy of Athens. Its castle was destroyed by the Catalans in 1311, and the Turks let it decline into an obscure village because they preferred well-watered Livadiá.

Thebes Today

Thebes may be the dullest market town in Greece. Like the riddling Sphinx that plagued the ancient city, modern Thebes hunches over the Kadmeía Hill, where each successive generation buried its past under its present, throwing its rubbish in the gullies below. Now that it's all anti-seismic reinforced concrete, archaeologists have to excavate in basements for clues to the past. On Pindárou Street, two nondescript excavations mark the once grand (300,000 sq. metre) 14th-century BC 'New' **Mycenaean palace**, identified by the many Linear B tablets (*see* p.352) unearthed here; the tablets, known in antiquity, may be behind the legend that Cadmus invented the alphabet, albeit an undecipherable one to later Greeks. Important Mycenaeans were buried in frescoed **chamber tombs** on Megáli Kastélli hill east of the Kadmeía; one has escaped being buried in turn by sprawl and can be visited. That's about it, except for the 4th-century BC **Electra Gate** (one of the famous seven) at the southeast end of the Kadmeía by the cathedral. The brow of the Kadmeía has been pedestrianized; head there for refreshment.

The Archaeology Museum

Pindárou St, at the north end of Kadmeía, t 226 202 7913; open Tues–Sun 9–3.

Set in a marble-filled courtyard, under a square Frankish tower (last relic of the medieval castle), this museum is alone worth the visit to Thebes. The present jail of a building is about to be replaced by a much nicer and larger one, commensurate with the city's growing collection of unique and marvellous artefacts. The intricate lapis lazuli Mycenaean **seals** made in the palace workshop speak of taste and wealth. The palace also yielded a vast number of **Linear B tablets**, and stirrup jars that have used Linear B labels – a unique find – and intriguingly new-looking terracotta **larnakes** from the extensive Mycenaean cemetery of ancient Tanágra, the only ones found so far in mainland Greece although common enough in Minoan Crete. The mourning women depicted on them, hands raised to their heads and scratched faces, offer insights into burial rituals; many of these small coffins were for children. The Archaic, Classical and Hellenistic eras of the Copáis basin are not ignored, with Archaic idols and charming **Tanágra figurines**, some with their paint; these were named after the town east of Thebes, where they were first discovered.

South of Thebes

Plataea, the 'Finest Victory in all History'

Modern **Erithraí** (or Kriokoúki), 13km south, in effect replaces ancient Plataea, which stood 5km to the west. Thanks to the long memories of the Greeks, this area is still an enclave of Attica: Plataea hated Thebes so much that in 519 BC she allied herself with Athens, and in 490 sent her entire army to help at Marathon. Yet her loyalty to Athens would cost her dearly.

In 479 BC, after Sálamis and Xerxes' retreat, the Persian army still occupied much of Greece except for the Peloponnese. The Persian general Mardonius wintered in Athens, then he heard that a Greek army under the Spartan Pausanias was on its way north. Mardonius retreated to Boeotía, land of his Theban allies, and chose Plataean territory, pro Athenian and therefore dispensable, as a battle ground suitable for his cavalry. Here he waited for the Greek League who (after the usual bickering) massed their forces, and sent the largest Greek army in history – some 60,000 hoplites and 40,000 light infantry – through the pass at Yiftókastro (*see* p.170) and camped in the foothills of Kitherónas. Although Herodotus as usual exaggerates the size of the Persian army (at 1.7 million, no less), modern historians believe the two sides were probably more or less equal, although the Greeks were handicapped by their lack of cavalry. As the days wore on, neither side was keen to engage; when the generals did move it was because they were short on provisions. Pausanius moved his thirsty Greeks into the lower hills by the Asopos river where there was a spring; Mardonius poisoned the spring, but still delayed an attack in the hopes that the Greeks would get into a more vulnerable position for his cavalry. Pausanius then made a strategical retreat by night into the foothills of Kitherónas, but confusion and quarrelling between the Spartan leaders left the army split into three at dawn. Mardonius saw his chance and attacked, but the Greeks' furious resistance caught the Persians by surprise, and in the bloody battle that ensued it became a matter of raw guts and soldiering, and here the Greeks proved superior. The Spartans took on the Persian cavalry and killed Mardonius; the Persian camp was taken by storm and the Persians annihilated. It was 'the finest victory in all history' according to Herodotus. On the same day the Greeks defeated the last of the Persian fleet at Mykale; a 'paradigm coincidence,' wrote Aristotle.

Plateia for its part was rebuilt, and remained loyal to Athens. During the Peloponnesian War, it was besieged for two years by the Spartans (429–27 BC), who then destroyed it and killed everyone. It was rebuilt only to be destroyed by Thebes, then rebuilt again by Philip of Macedon after the Battle of Chairóneia to show Thebes who was boss, then it simply dwindled away. Just a hodgepodge of worn walls litter the now peaceful plain, crossed only by lizards and the shadows of summer hang-gliders drifting off Kitherónas' foothills.

Leúktra, Thespies, Askra and the Valley of the Muses

Leúktra, where the Spartans were spectacularly defeated in 371 BC, is signposted a few kilometres west of Plataea. The battlefield is marked by an ancient plinth with triglyphs topped by nine stone shields; only the bronze warrior placed on top to remind the world that Thebes won is missing. A small road goes south to **Livadóstra**, a small swimming beach and site of Kreusis, the ancient port of Thespies. **Thespies** itself, just northwest of Leúktra by way of Elopía, honoured Eros above all gods, proof that love can flourish just about anywhere. The modern town is modest in the extreme. It must have been much more interesting to visit when the courtesan Phryne lived here; her statue by her lover Praxiteles was still in the **temple of Love** into Roman times. A short drive west gets you to **Askra**, the not-so-beloved home town of Hesiod, ancient Greece's answer to Eeyore the donkey; 'It's only me,' you can almost hear him mutter. A lot of farmers here are now doing quite well, using modern agricultural techniques rather than his dour and sour directions in the *Works and Days*. The very keen can ascend Mount Helicon at this point looking for the once well wooded, now sad and denuded **Valley of the Muses** (ask in modern Áskri), where the *Mouseion Games* were held (poetry and drama) every four years with the addition of the *Erotica* games dedicated to Love, which rather disappointingly turn out to have been musical contests. You can also seek out the **Hippocrene fountain** on an eastern summit of Mount Helicon, the most famous of the many springs made by the flying horse Pegasus by striking the ground with his hoof, but it's more fun to take the road south of Elopía to **Alikí**, and have a swim in its pretty bay.

North of Thebes

Lake Copáis, Gla and Orchomenos

Pancake-flat, the Copáis basin, 67km in circumference and now planted with cotton and cereals, was the biggest lake in Greece when the Mycenaeans built **Orchomenos** on its northwestern shore opposite Thebes. Gla, a stronghold belonging to Orchomenos, was built 16km east on raised ground in the shallow lake bed itself. Sometimes Lake Copáis drained entirely by late summer, but when the sink holes in its eastern section were blocked, the lake just got bigger. From Mycenaean times on, there is evidence of frequent efforts to drain it altogether. It was a bog in 1311 when the Catalans and Franks squared off for battle in front of Orchomenos. The Catalans, then the local bullies, lured the unwary Frankish cavalry onto the lake which looked like a meadow, and then mowed them down when their horses floundered in the mud. Drained once and for all in 1931, everyone still pretty much respects the old shore line except the Athens–Thessaloníki National Road, which cuts right through the old lake bed leaving **Gla** and its impressive 3km circle of Cyclopean walls just east of the highway. Take the Kástro turn-off (a bridge crosses the highway here if you come from the direction of Orchomenos) for a closer look. A road encircles it. Note the impressive south gate with bastions on either side, forming a narrow outer court to flummox enemies, just as in Mycenae. Clamber up to enjoy the extensive view that the Orchomenos garrison would have had in 1300 BC, and see if you can figure out what it was used for. Since no Mycenaean megaron has been found, it probably wasn't a city, and what good would a citizen's fort be in the middle of the lake, so far from Orchomenos? Traces of grain were found in its buildings, and one theory is that it was a silo, or maybe just the best fortified corral ever built. The cattle raised hereabouts were famous (Boeotía itself means 'cow land') and made Orchómenos rich. Perhaps they got their own Cyclopean walled citadel when winter rains made it impossible for them to be grazed on the lake bed.

Ancient Orchomenos

Orchomenos was very wealthy, according to Homer, and inhabited by the legendary Minyans, who had perceived Egyptian roots. A distinctive Middle Helladic pottery (wheel-made, grey and smooth) was first excavated by Schliemann here, and has been called Minyan ware ever since. Thebes' traditional rival throughout its turbulent history, Orchomenos nevertheless followed Thebes and sided with the Persians, an alliance hardly calculated to win them many friends. In antiquity it was famous as the first town to worship the Three Graces.

The ruins on the long, low acropolis, continuously inhabited from Neolithic into Roman times, are complicated, and include buildings from every era. The biggest draw, at the narrow east end, is a large **Mycenaean tholos tomb** (*t 226 103 2474; open Tues–Sat 9–2.30, Sun 10–2; adm free*), dubbed the treasury of Minyas, with a grey marble lintel and no roof at present. Tholos tombs were not in style in Mycenaean Boeotía, so this very rich one is an oddity. Remarkable bronze rosettes decorated the walls, and it had a side room like the Treasury of Atreus, carved out of the rock. Beside it, dug into the flank of the **acropolis**, are the remains of a smallish 4th-century BC **theatre**; 12 rows are preserved. Opposite the theatre, surrounded by lush greenery, is the the the wonderful **Moní Koimíseos Theotókou Skripoús**, a Byzantine gem built in 874 when the Thebes-Copáis region was the wealthiest in Greece. It stands over the Mycenaean palace. The *katholikón* made use of the handy stone quarry opposite; the only glimpse you will get of the famous Temple of the Graces are its column drums, beautifully incorporated into the *katholikón*'s façade in two neat rows above the door.

Northern Stereá Elláda

Gla to Thermopylae

After Gla, the National Road continues across the ancient lake bed to meet the attractive Lokrian coast, with views across to Évia. The big town here is **Atalándi**, 6km inland, with a new **Archaeology Museum** at 21 Var. Velliou St (*t 223 302 3355; open Tues–Sun 8.30–3; adm*), with local finds from all over Locria. The small ports of **Arkítsa** and **Ag. Konstantínos**, between the highway and the sea, have become small resorts because of their links to Évia and the Sporades respectively, ensuring a steady stream of passing tourists; many still head to the once fashionable thermal spa **Kamména Voúrla**, squeezed in between sharp green slopes and sea, where the waters are good for arthritis. Another 17km further on, a road on the left winds up to a modern war memorial at **Mendenítsa**, just below the romantic, ruined **Castle of Bondonitsa**, partly built out of marble from a Temple of Hera. The Italian Marquisate of the Pallavicini (1205–1414) had the seat of his elegant court here; his allegiance to Venice protected him from the rampaging Catalans, but not the invading Turks. The grotesquely outnumbered Greek and Italian defenders made a heroic stand and were enslaved for their trouble; the capture of Bondonitsa gave the Ottomans Central Greece.

Getting There

By bus: buses to Ag. Konstantínos leave hourly from the Liossion St terminal in Athens, t 210 831 7147; you can get off at Arkítsa for the Évia ferry boat, but it is a kilometre hike to the quay from the bus stop.

By sea: Arkítsa has ferries to and from Loutrá Edipsoú on Évia every hour from 7am to 9.30pm (every 2hrs in winter); Port authority: t 223 309 1290. Ag. Konstantínos has ferries and hydrofoils to Vólos and the Sporades; Port authority: t 223 503 1759. Ticket offices portside: t 223 503 1614 or t 223 503 2445.

Thermopylae

In 480 BC, as the great Persian invasion force approached by land and sea, a small Greek army under Leonidas, one of the two kings of Sparta, was sent to occupy Thermopylae as a first defence; with him were 300 handpicked Spartans, all of whom had living sons. Other troops from the Peloponnese, along with several thousand Locrians and Phocians and 400 Thebans, made up the Greek contingent. The other allied states intended to send contingents as soon as the Olympic Games were over, but Xerxes and his army – modern estimates suggest that the Persians numbered some 300,000 rather than the three million in ancient histories – reached Thermopylae first.

Herodotus writes that in the face of such an overwhelming foe the Peloponnesians were all for retreating to their newly built wall on the Isthmus of Corinth to defend their own lands, but Leonidas voted to stay with the Phocians and Locrians, advising only that they call for reinforcements. Xerxes sent a scout ahead to count the Greeks, who returned with the surprising news that there were only a handful of Spartans and they were combing their long hair, which a Spartan in the Persian army explained as a sign that they meant to fight to the death. Xerxes gave them four days to do the sensible thing and retreat, then sent in his best troops. For two days his army was pummelled in the narrow pass, where it could take no advantage of its huge numbers, and Xerxes was on the point of retreating when the traitor Ephialtes came forward and offered to take the Persians over the mountains by night to turn the Greek position, surprising and routing the Phocians who were guarding that little known mountain path.

Having been warned by his soothsayer that they were doomed, Leonidas had already sent most of his army home, keeping with him his 300 Spartans (and the 900 helots who tended them, but who always get left out of the account) as well as the 700 Thespians who refused to abandon him, and the Thebans whom Leonidas kept as hostages. He suspected them, quite rightly, of secretly sympathizing with the Persians. The Greeks then prepared to fight to the death; when told that the Persian arrows were so many they blackened the sky, one Spartan made the famous laconic remark that it was pleasant news: 'if the Persians hide the sun, we shall have our battle in the shade.' The Thebans changed sides after Leonidas was killed, and in the end the Greeks fought with their hands and teeth. Only two Spartans survived; one hanged himself in shame, and the other, vilified as 'the Trembler', redeemed his Spartan honour at Plataea. An epitaph composed by the poet Simonides marked Thermopylae's grave mound:

Go tell the Spartans, you who read:
We took their orders, and lie here dead.

But of course they were only repeating what happened just up the road at **Thermopylae,** 'the hot gates' (*see* box, above). The pass was named for its thermal springs, and hot water is certainly what its defenders inevitably found themselves in throughout history. It is also one of the most disappointing places in Greece: the once narrow 6.5km defile between the cliffs of Kallídromo and the sea is now a 5km plain formed by silt from the Sperchios river. Modern **Thermopíles** is a spa with a hot waterfall, the **grave mound** where the Three Hundred (plus the 3,700 killed before the last stand) were buried, and an impressive **Monument to Leonidas** (replacing the original ancient lion) erected in 1955 with funds from America, decorated with reliefs of the battle and the famous epigram: *Four thousand here from Pelops' land/Against three million once did stand.* Of the many other fierce contests fought here, the Greeks best remember the battle in 1821 at the Alamanas Bridge to the north, which the heroic young Athanasios Diakos, the Bishop of Salona and 700 Greeks tried to hold against a Turkish army led by Mehmet Pasha; Diakos was captured, and roasted alive in the main square of Lamía. Just north of Thermopylae, there is a turn off south for Ámphissa (*see* p.399) through the Brállos Pass.

Lamía

South-facing Lamía sprawls down a steep hill with two summits, four major *plateías* and a rabbit-warren of streets and stairs. Only the attractive castle, on the northeastern summit, provides a focal point, lit up at night in case you lose your bearings. Once you manage to negotiate your way into Lamía, you'll find it the area's most sophisticated town, with great restaurants for visitors and wealthy farmers alike.

Lamía's position made it a bone of contention between Athens and Macedonia in the Hellenistic period, between the Latins and the Byzantines after 1205, and between

Getting There and Around

By bus: for **Athens** (every hour) and **Thessaloníki**, go to 27 Papakiriazí St, t 223 105 1346. For **Karpenísi** (five daily) go to 3 Bótsari St, t 223 102 8955. Local buses for **Thermopylae** (five daily) and **Ypáti** (10 daily) leave from 2 Konstantinopóleos St, t 223 105 1347. These three are clustered around the town train station. For **Vólos** (two daily) go to 69 Rozáki Angelí and Kopodistríou Sts, t 223 102 2627. For **Delphi** (three daily) go to 58 Thermopylón, t 223 103 5494. For **Lárissa** (three daily), **Tríkala** (eight daily) and **Pátras** (two daily), go to the **Praktorío Karditsa**, 62 Thermopylón St, t 223 102 2802. The last two are 1.5km south of town and need a taxi.

By train: There are two stations: in town at 1 Konstantinopóleos, t 223 102 3201, and the Lionokladíou Station, t 223 106 1061, 6km west at Stavrós, with better connections. A railway company bus connects them.

By car: Parking in the centre is no fun; try the car park on Botsári St, behind the train station. **Taxis** abound, t 223 103 4555.

Tourist Information

EOT: 3 Plateía Laoú, t 223 103 0065; *open Mon–Fri 8–2.20.* Help with accommodation.

Where to Stay and Eat

Lamía ✉ **35100**
Fthia, 5 Andréas Papandréou St, t 223 105 3111, f 223 103 1443 (*B; expensive*). East of the castle on the Stilída Rd. Modern, comfy, views, parking and a lavish breakfast.
Neon Astron, 5 Plateía Laoú, t 223 102 6245 (*D; inexpensive*). In the heart of town; a simple budget hotel with en suite baths and TV. It beats the nearby so-so C-class hotels.
Boston Art, 15 Satovriándou St, t 223 104 7237 (€20). A great innovative Swedish chef, in a renovated mansion in the centre.
Gogos Taverna, 3 Aristotélous St, t 223 102 3501. Right by Plateía Laoú. Three floors of an old house and terrific *dolmades* (cabbage rolls) and rolled pork with egg-lemon sauce. *Closed Sun, July and Aug.*

the Catalans and everybody else until the Turks took over. The Catalans came as mercenaries employed by the Latins and Byzantines, but they stayed, and their habits of piracy and banditry made them a curse on everybody. They called Lamia *El Cito*, the city. The **castle** is their effort, built on the foundations of a Classical fort with views east to Thermopylae and west towards the spa of Ypáti. After independence, it functioned as a frontier fort until the Ottoman Empire ceded Thessaly to Greece in 1884. Its barracks do nicely for the **Archaeological Museum** (*t 223 102 9992; open Tues–Sun 8.30–3; adm*), with exhibits of local finds from Palaeolithic to Roman times.

Up towards the northwestern summit of Profítis Elías, attractive **Plateía Ag. Louká** is backed by pleasant gardens. Two other squares offer a graphic illustration of 21st-century Greece. **Plateía Laoú** (the 'People's Square') has plane trees, old shops with local produce, and worry-bead-flicking codgers sitting about in old-fashioned *kafeneíons* discussing the events of the day. Two minutes up, big, slick and shiny **Plateía Eleutherías** cannons you into the future. Expensive restaurants and bars cater to perfectly dressed trendies who don't need to go to Athens for exciting nightlife. Knitting the two squares together are a couple of pedestrian streets lined with *chasapotavérnas* specializing in roast meat.

Ypáti

The road west to Karpenísi runs through the wealthy and lush Spercheiós river valley. At the 13km mark, you can turn south for **Loutrá Ypátis**, a spa since the 4th century BC, and **Ypáti**, an eagle's nest sitting pretty 1,312ft above the valley floor. An earthquake in 60 BC destroyed ancient Ypáti and when Byzantine emperor Justinian rebuilt it he renamed it Neopatras. Its position assured it a turbulent history as a stronghold of the Byzantines, the Franks and then the Catalans, who made it their capital. The Turks took their turn in 1393. It is a pleasant town, with a water mill, restaurants and hotels, and is a base for walks into nearby **Mount Oite National Park**, 42,000 square meters of wilderness where it is easy to get lost. The castle can be visited on foot via the path to the mountain refuge (ask in town). Ypáti has a small couscous factory, not something you find every day in Greece.

Karpenísi and Around

The main road from Lamía carries on to **Karpenísi**, capital of Evritanía, Greece's smallest mainland prefecture. A once plain Jane town of 10,000, built on the slopes of Mt Timfristós (or Veloúchi), its nearby ski area has transformed it into a resort, but one that has not quite shaken off its village aura. Many prefer it to Parnassós' Aráchova for just that reason. Trekkers come for the mountains, white-water enthusiasts for the rivers, passers-by for **Agrinio**, 117 rough-and-tumble kilometres west, and everyone for the gorgeous views. The area is justly called the 'Switzerland of Greece', and the gorge south of town harbours villages much nicer than Karpenísi itself.

Karpenísi stands at the pleasant open northern end of a spectacular 30km gorge that grows increasingly sinister as you penetrate into its depths. Midway, at pretty

Getting Around

The **bus station**, t 223 708 0013, has daily runs to Karpenísi and Agrínio, and a much poorer service (twice a day usually) to Mikró and Megálo Chorió. **Taxi stand**: t 223 902 2100.

Tourist Information

Tourist office: near the bus station on Tsamboúla St, Karpenísi t/f 223 702 1016; *open Mon–Fri 9–2 and 5–9, Sat 9–2 and 5–8, Sun 10–2*. Maps of the area are available.

Sports and Activities

Trekking Hellas, Zinopoulou St, t/f 223 702 5940, offers organized kayaking, rafting, trekking and mountain-biking. The **Ski Centre** is 13km from Karpenísi, t 243 409 1385 or t 243 409 1558. **Horses** are for hire at 'The Saloon', 4km from Karpenísi on the Prousós road. A **pool club** sits on the Prousós road at the Korischádes turn-off.

Where to Stay and Eat

Winter is the main season here, but everywhere is open all year, and you can bargain in the villages except on weekends. Almost all hotels are new, with kitchens and TV.

Karpenísi ✉ 36100

Montana Club, t 223 708 0400, f 223 708 0409, *montana@otenet.gr* (*L; luxury*). Great style 1.5km from town at Soulia, pools, individual fireplaces, restaurant, the works.

Villa Verginia, t 223 702 5133, f 223 702 2264, mobile t 6974 046 6857 (*luxury–moderate*). South of Karpenísi off the Prousós road in Voúteros, a small village surrounded by pines. The charming Mrs Verginia has added a luxurious wing to her comfortable inn. Lounge and pool.

Anessis, 50 Zinopoúlou St, t 223 708 0700, f 223 702 3021, *ANECIC@otenet.gr* (*B; expensive*). In the centre, recently renovated, cosy; the back rooms have the view.

Helvetía, 33 Zinopoúlou St, t 223 702 2465, f 223 708 0112 (*C; moderate*). Right in the centre.

Panórama, 18 Riga Fereou St, t 223 702 5976. Large courtyard for dining on traditional casserole dishes and roast meat. Trout, too.

Megálo Chorió ✉ 36075

Antigóne Hotel, t 223 7041395, f 223 704 1486 (*D; moderate*). In the *plateía* with a great view and a good restaurant to boot.

Fróso Giannakopoúlou Rooms, t 223 704 1191 (*moderate; expensive at weekends*). Big, clean, a shared kitchen, a great view, balcony and very nice owners.

To Pétrino Rooms, t 223 704 1187, mobile t 697 297 1734 (*inexpensive summer, moderate-expensive winter*). A beautiful new stone *xenóna*. Pleasant owners; a nice setting on the 'main' street.

To Spiti Tou Psará, on the main road under Megálo Chorió in an area called Gávros, t 223 704 1202. The homiest of a series of tavernas strung along the road, and the one the locals like. Terrific pittas, and trout in season, all with home-made bread and sweets.

To Hagiati, by the Spiti tou Psará, t 223 704 1200. This one is more upscale and has quite a name. The food is good and, like its neighbour, it overlooks the river at the back.

Néo Mikró Chorió ✉ 36075

Basiliki Nasopoúlou Rooms, t 223 704 1257 (*inexpensive summer, moderate midweek and expensive weekends in winter*). By the village bus stop; friendly; great restaurant.

Foteiní Zára Rooms, t 223 7041 236 (*inexpensive in summer, expensive–moderate in winter*). Good rooms with a cosy common room and kitchen. Mr Zara knows everyone in the village and can help you if he is full.

Mikró Chorió ✉36075

Messandra at the Hellas Country Club, t 223 704 1570 (€20–25). The hotel, a favourite of fashionable skiers, is overpriced, but the restaurant serves excellent Greek and international cuisine.

Prousós ✉ 36074

Agathides, on the road to Thérmo, t 223 708 0813, mobile t 6974027680 (*inexpensive to just moderate in winter*). 'Monastic' is the word for this little *xenóna* in this ungentrified town, offering a taste of village life.

Mikró and **Megálo Chorió**, placed well up from the river bed, there are still trees along the river and wooded peaks crisscrossed by trails. If you sit in the *plateía* of sympathetic little Megálo Chorió, however, you can see the huge scar where a landslide obliterated most of Mikró Chorió opposite, necessitating the building of *Néo* Mikró Chorió 3km north. Someone is now building a large inn in the old scarred village, presumably for people who need an adrenaline rush greater than white-water rafting, skiing or hiking can provide. The many small villages hereabout offer both fancy and simple accommodation, absolutely terrific food, and great scenery. To the south, the gorge becomes an inhuman bare bones canyon of dark brooding rocks under the alpine village of **Prousós**, an incongruous spot for the sophisticated monastery of **Panagía tis Prousiótissa**. An icon of the Virgin was found in a cave by the river, so here the massive monastery stands. Russian Orthodox in atmosphere, it has a square clock tower stuck onto a skeletal pinnacle of rock, an ecclesiastical exclamation mark in an alien world. Virtually unknown to foreigners, the monastery is an important pilgrimage site. A hair-raising, but good paved road goes south of here through wildly scenic country in one and one half hours to Thérmo (*see* p.405).

Livadiá to Delphi

Livadiá and the Oracle of the Snake God

Livadiá, Boeotía's sprawling modern capital, contains a luscious beauty spot at the source of the Erkyna river, where a narrow gorge in Mount Helicon opens and the stream gathers force to rush pell mell through town. The water mills and tanneries here made Livadiá one of the largest towns in Greece by 1830. Overlooked by an 18th-century clock tower and a large **castle**, the Erkyna's source, *Kría* (cold), has been converted into a stunning oasis, its flagstoned paths lined with attractive cafés and restaurants. If lost in town (it easily happens), ask either for *Kría* or the *Xenía Café* which sits opposite one of the castle's imposing square towers. You can climb up to this 14th-century fortress, a plaything of Franks, Catalans, Venetians and Turks, by following the flagstoned path up the gorge, noting the church high up in the rock face – legend has it that there was an underground route to Delphi from this cleft.

In ancient times, this area was the site of the famous **Oracle of Trophonios**, a chthonic rain-making snake god, whose story got rationalized and mixed up with that of Asclepius the healing god. Trophonios' ritual involved several days of sacrifices, with lots of feasting and entrail reading, and bathing in the cold river. The suppliant then bathed in the Pool of Forgetfulness (Lethe) to empty his mind, then in the Pool of Memory to remember what he saw, and then got dressed in a linen tunic, boots, with honey cakes in hand (for the snakes presumably) before walking down a ladder into a small domed underground chamber, a bit like a Greek outdoor bread oven. Here he placed his feet first in a niche in the rock, from which he apparently disappeared immediately. Some unspecified time later he returned feet first (no mention of wear and tear on the boots, but suppliants had to wear them). The priests set him on the 'throne of memory', a handy rock, and interpreted his story. It was said initiates could not laugh for days afterwards. That didn't stop the likes of Croesus and Mardonius from consulting the oracle, or Pausanias in the 2nd century AD, who left us our most detailed account. Unfortunately stories from the Underworld were recorded on wooden tablets, rather than stone or lead, so we don't know what initiates found out. Right at the foot of the castle's tower, an underground archaeological museum (empty at the moment), in the style of Trophonios' crypt, is due to open in 2004.

Today, park along the river to visit the small underground **Ethno-Historical Museum** (*t 226 102 6366; open Tues–Fri 11–2 and 7.30–9.30pm, Sat–Sun 7.30pm–10.30pm*), or the Nerómilos Restaurant, where a wide waterfall cascades from the upper terrace, next to a huge water wheel. The trendy Xenía Café overlooks the actual source, identified as the Pool of Memory, where you can soothe your tired feet under the plane trees. Note the niches in the nearby cliff face, made for ancient votives; the big one, a tiny room really, was the Turkish governor's favourite spot to meditate. The Pool of Forgetfulness is buried some 30ft in the rock and its narrow passage is off limits.

The Triodos, Chairóneia and Dístomo

En route from Livadiá to Dístomo, you come to the bleak *tríodos*, 'three roads' (you will see a sign to Dávlia), the crossroads where legend has it that Oedipus killed his father. Turn right for 19km and then right again for six for ancient **Chairóneia**, where in the battle of 338 BC Philip II's Macedonians defeated Athens and Boeotía and put an end to southern Greek independence. You can't miss it; a large bluish marble stone lion (28ft high with its plinth) sits on its haunches guarding the common tomb or **Polyandron** containing 254 members of the Theban Sacred Band, who fought to the death against the 18-year old Alexander's cavalry. The skeletons were found stacked inside; presumably the famous lovers locked in an eternal embrace, along with their armour. Chairóneia's ancient **theatre** is built into the acropolis hill nearby. It doesn't look like much now, but Chairóneia was cosmopolitan enough when the gentle Plutarch (*c.* AD 42–120), a priest at Delphi, and his friends sat around discussing the events of the day, religion and history.

South of the Thebes–Delphi highway, little **Dístomo**, the jumping-off point for Ósios Loukás monastery, is not a bad place to stop for a taste of a small-town life. Once drab, it is now rather nice thanks to a dynamic mayor, with a cobblestoned centre, nice restaurants, cafés, two hotels, and even a small **Archaeological Museum** (*t 226 702 2000; ask at the town hall*). A depressing monument on the hill commemorates the 218 villagers massacred by the Germans on 10 June 1944; their relatives' legal struggle for reparations, begun in 1997, has embroiled the foreign ministries of Greece and Germany. From Dístomo it is 9km to the sea at **Áspra Spítia** (big aluminium factory and a shingle beach off to the right), and 13km to Ósios Loukás.

The Byzantine Monastery of Ósios Loukás

t 226 702 2797; open May–Sept 8–2 and 4–7; winter 8–5; small adm.

'Blessed' Luke, a Greek (not the apostle), was born near Delphi and died in 951 in Steíri, a village halfway between Dístomo and the monastery. He was noted for his holiness, his cures and his prophecies (the most notable was that Crete would be liberated from the Arabs by a Byzantine emperor named Romanós), and such was his reputation that his splendid monastery was begun as soon as he died.

The setting, on Mount Helicon's wooded west flank, is superb, with marvellous views over an olive-studded valley. From the visitors' courtyard (with a coffee kiosk, WC, cats and a shop selling icons and guides to the mosaics), enter the gates – note the bullet holes from the War of Independence, when the monastery was a fort. Just inside the gates the **Refectory** contains the ticket booth and a museum in progress. The grand and harmonious **Katholikón** (*c.* 1020), built by imperial builders by order of the emperor himself, is an octagon made of ancient blocks on its lower courses and porous stone and cloisonné brickwork on the upper, all held together by attractive buttresses. A magnificent dome, 29ft in diameter, spans the luminous interior, clad with marble and covered with some of the finest 11th-century gold ground **mosaics** anywhere. These are characterized by the use of outline to indicate the figures and the large ecstatic eyes set in the elongated faces of the saints. They are static and formal, suggesting the eternal quality of the Orthodox world. Set pieces, such as the *Crucifixion* and the *Descent of Christ to Hades* in the narthex, are especially severe in composition. Women were allowed to attend services in the upper gallery. The crypt, predating the church, has 11th-century frescoes and the Blessed Luke's marble tomb. To the left of the Katholikón is the oldest building in the complex, the **Theotókos chapel** (begun before 1020), a tetrastyle church dedicated to Mary, copying a Constantinople style. The interior looks strangely modern because of renovations after earthquake and fire damage. Note the elaborate exterior cloisonné masonry, decorated with deep dog-tooth brickwork and a kufic frieze. Inside, it has a remarkable inlaid marble floor and black granite columns, probably from the Temple of Demeter in Steíri. Each one is solid granite; an Egyptian influence is suggested.

The cells on two sides of the courtyard once housed 200 monks, leaving a lot of extra room for the six who now hold the fort (the oldest is 80, and the youngest, brother Chýsanthos, is 30), and no one really needs the curious little multi-domed structure behind the big church. This is a *fotánama*: its central dome, held up by columns, is pierced with holes for the smoke from the fire (*fotiá*) that was laid on the floor, while monks and visitors huddled on the stone benches around the walls, trying to get warm. All the big monasteries had them, and if you visit in winter you'll see why. While there, note the low door to the right of the gate, a stable, and part of the fortified tower, all that remains of the monastery's stout walls and four towers.

Aráchova and Mount Parnassós

Steep **Aráchova**, at 3,300ft above sea level, and famous for rugs, goat's cheese (ask for *formaélla*), pasta, spoon sweets and *tsípouro* (Greek *grappa*), has recently added another feather to its cap to become the biggest ski resort in the Parnassós area. As a result, this already attractive town, sporting an old clock tower on a dramatic pinnacle and the imposing double-towered church of **Ag. Geórgios** (lit up at night), has undergone a facelift that puts Delphi to shame. All new structures must be built in the

Getting There and Around

Aráchova, 12km east of Delphi, is linked by five to six **buses** a day. For more bus information, *see* Livadiá (p.384) and Delphi (p.390). **Taxis: t** 226 703 1566.

Tourist Information

Tourist office: on the short road to the Xenia Hotel, **t** 226 702 9170, **f** 226 702 9170, *detpa@internet.gr*; *open Mon–Fri 8am–10pm, weekends 8–12.* They have accommodation lists for the whole Parnassós area and local bus schedules.

Aráchova's dragon-slaying patron **St George** is honoured with gusto on 23 April – although check with the tourist office, as the date has to fall after Orthodox Easter. There are folk dances, a procession and athletic contests – a memory, perhaps, of the games held in honour of another dragon-slayer, Apollo, at Delphi.

Sports and Activities

The **Parnassós ski area** (with restaurants, bars, a rental outlet), **t** 223 402 2689 or **t** 223 402 2695, is 25km from Aráchova on the north slope of Parnassós' second peak, Gerondóvracho. There are two lift areas: Fterólakka at 5,900ft and Kelária at 5,741ft, with a total of 20 runs covering every level of difficulty and a special area for snowboarders. It offers hot skiing on sunny days and stupendous views to Mount Olympus.

Because of the snow, July and August are the only practical months for **climbing**; the alpine club refuge, Katafígion Sarantári at 6,200ft, is the traditional base for the classic pre-dawn ascent, but the ski service roads can get you much closer. Check at the information office for details; the green ROAD map of Parnassós is also helpful.

Where to Stay and Eat

Aráchova ✉ 32004

With its handsome traditional-style inns, which are not at all expensive except on winter weekends, Aráchova is a terrific alternative to staying in Delphi. In summer prices plummet without any effort on your part (average €32–35; winter weekends €73–76). Besides the following, there are 200 rooms available through the Women's Rural Tourism Cooperative, **t** 226 703 1519 – it's a good

traditional stone style, and the long narrow main street is lined with them, punctuated now and then by tiny indentations – *plateías*, though barely big enough to be given the name. Navigating by day is hazardous – it is the main highway – but by night it is magical, especially in winter. It even has a 'make to order' worry-bead store on the main street, the Gobologádiko (Γομπολογαδικο), **t** 226 703 2868.

Mighty **Parnassós** rears up dramatically behind Aráchova and Delphi. It was the Greek Mount Ararat, where after the flood Deukalion's boat beached between the highest peak Lykeri (8,061ft) and Gerondóvracho (7,988ft). Much of the mountain is now part of Parnassós National Park, with a network of scenic roads and paths linking the mountain resorts, such as **Amfíklia** (17km from the ski centre; two buses daily from Livadiá) on the north side. A road now goes up to the **Corycian Cave** (4,462ft), a surprisingly small (now, at any rate) north-facing cave with stalagmites and stalactites. Sacred to Pan and the Nymphs, the first Delphians sheltered here in the Neolithic era; it was used in Mycenaean and Classical periods, and always served as a handy hide-out for the locals in times of trouble. Some consider it the lair of Python, and the place where the oracle of Gaia gave the first pre-Delphi divinations; in winter, the Dionysiac orgies of the Herois (*see* below) were held here. Don't be surprised if you meet a wild boar along the road.

opportunity to meet the locals and try some of the local produce for breakfast.

Anemolia, t 226 703 1640, **f** 226 703 1642, *anemolia@cybex.gr (B; luxury)*. Impersonal luxury at the west end of town with a great view. The draw here is the glassed-in indoor pool and grand buffet breakfast. If not packed with tours, you may get a good deal.

Villa Filoxenia Apartments, t 226 703 1406, **f** 226 703 1215, *bkatsis@filoxenia-arachova.gr (expensive–moderate)*. Opposite the Sfalákia on a quiet street; new with traditional decor, and fully equipped with sitting room, bedroom, kitchens; great for more than two or for longer stays.

Xenía, t 226 703 1230, **f** 226 703 2175 (*B; moderate in summer, low expensive in winter, breakfast inc*). A cosy Xenía Hotel sounds like a contradiction in terms, but this one has achieved it. The public rooms are lovely; the views excellent.

Xenónas Sfaláki, just after the turn for the ski area (look for the signs), **t** 226 703 1970, **f** 226 703 1097 (*moderate, but expensive winter weekends*). Cosy, quiet, well run; with charming rooms for four; a cute breakfast area with tiny fireplace.

Pension Nóstos, by Plateía Xenía, **t** 226 703 1385, **f** 226 703 1765, *nostos@otenet.gr*

(*moderate–inexpensive*). This traditional inn oozes charm, from its owner to its tiny enclosed stone courtyard and glassed-in upper porch. The Beatles stayed here and liked it well enough to have their picture taken with the owner. Mini bus service to the ski area.

Apollon Inn, at the bottom of the road to the ski centre, **t** 226 703 1057, *apolloninn-arachova@united-hellas.com (moderate, often less)*. New, neat, not fancy, and friendly staff.

Apollo, on main street at east end of town, **t** 226 703 1427 (*inexpensive*). A bargain oldie with shared baths, run by the Apollon Inn in the summer months.

Taverna Agnantio, towards the east end of town on the main road, **t** 226 703 2114. Specializes in grilled meats.

Taverna Karathanási, on the main street in the centre, **t** 226 703 1360. Plain but cosy, specializing in casserole dishes since 1930; in summer dine on the upstairs terrace.

Prin & Metá (Before and After), at beginning of road to the ski centre, opposite the Avalanche ski shop. Off the beaten track, a pretty restaurant that tries hard with an Italian and French flavour to its reasonably priced cuisine.

On Parnassós' west slope, 22km from Aráchova, **Eptálofos** (or Agoriánis) was once a bustling market town, where the 400 year-round residents have built many attractive inns and tavernas to cater to the snow crowd (for hotels there, see Aráchova's information office). Streams rush through its forests, the former dancing grounds of the Muses. You too can dance your way from Eptálofos to Delphi on a trail.

Delphi

Modern Delphi

Before the French could excavate Delphi in 1891, they had to move the village on top of the ruins to its present site. The new Delphi is a small, rather ordinary town split by the highway into two frumpy one-way streets, Vas. Pávlou & Frideríkis and Apóllonos. Parking is not easy except at either end of town, so take what you can get.

Ancient Delphi

The greatest oracle of the ancient world occupies one of the most spectacular, lyrical settings in Greece: a shelving ledge below the sheer Phaedriades (the Shining Cliffs), with a wild glen and dense olive groves at its feet, and the Gulf of Corinth

2,000ft below. Like Olympia, Delphi was a holy place that all Greeks shared; it was the centre of the world – when Zeus released an eagle in the east and an eagle in the west, Delphi is where they met; it was *the* great authority appearing somewhere in nearly every Hellenic myth and saga. And the whole – the stories, the temples, the art in the treasuries – was a masterpiece, albeit with a pinch of humbug.

The Myth

Gaia, or Earth, had the first oracle here, with her consort Poseidon. Her daughter Themis, goddess of justice and order, inherited it, then Phoebe the Moon goddess, who 'as a birthday gift' gave it to Phoebos Apollo – a succession that mirrors the interests of religion itself, from early fertility cults to the great cosmic patterns of the sun and stars. The oracle's first name was Pytho, and it was watched over by Earth's guardian, Python, who like the Athenian Kerkops was a hero-snake, a sacred king, who had to be killed to make way for the new. To get there from his natal Délos, Apollo turned himself into a dolphin (*delphinos*, hence Delphi) and hijacked a Cretan ship; he shot Pytho, and the Omphalos, the navel, the holy of holies, was his tomb.

Apollo evolved into what must have been the ideal of every Greek man – handsome, lusty, arty, an ace at the bow or lyre, the ultimate Olympian, the god of truth and light. Although the rationalizers made Python into an evil monster, Apollo had to be cleansed of the murder, and he spent eight years in self-imposed exile as a slave of the King of Thessaly in the Vale of Tempe, tending his flocks. When he returned to Delphi, he instituted the Pythian Games to celebrate. His first priests were Cretan captains from Knossós' fleet, recalling the Minoan roots of his cult.

Apollo, however, didn't spend the whole year at Delphi, but in November went north for his annual confab with the Hyperborians. For the three months when no oracles were given, Apollo's youngest brother Dionysos took over the sanctuary. Women from Athens and Delphi, known as the Thyiads, would join in orgiastic rites on Mount Parnossós, culminating every nine years in a festival called the Herois, in which the Thyiads 'brought up Semele' (the mother of Dionysos, who was really Gaia) from Hades to bless the earth. The priests would later downplay this side of Delphi a bit, better to promote the Apolloine message of truth and light; the Romans, who lacked the psychological fine-tuning of the Greeks, would deny it altogether, and propagated the story that Parnassós was the home of Apollo and the Muses.

History

The long continuity of the sanctuary in myth has physical evidence in Delphi's Minoan finds, traces of Mycenaean building under Apollo's Temple and a cache of 200 Mycenaean terracotta statues found under the Temple of Athena Pronaia. This Athena superseded a Bronze Age goddess, who was remembered perhaps by the fact that it was always a woman, the Pythia, who spoke for Apollo. The oracle, originally in the middle of a village, was in business by the time of the *Iliad*. It gained more than local importance in response to a very precise need in the late 8th–7th centuries BC: to offer guidance to the newly emergent land-hungry city-states, especially in directing and sanctioning the founding of colonies abroad. Delphi was the first shared oracle and as such specialized in community issues, legitimizing crucial decisions made by oligarchs, kings and tyrants alike. Although remote (which helped maintain its neutrality), the frequent comings and goings made Delphi the central

Getting There and Around

The **bus** station, t 226 508 2317, is at the west end of modern Delphi at Apóllonos and Vas. Pávlou & Frideríkis St. There are six buses a day to Delphi from Athens' Liossion terminal, t 210 8317096, via Thebes, Livadiá, and Aráchova; twice a day from Pátras; once from Thessaloníki (via Lamía and Lárissa) except Fri and Sun; four from Ag. Nikólaos (ferry boat) via Itéa. For Ósios Loukás, there are four buses a day to Dístomo and then by taxi (t 226 702 2797 in Dístomo). **Taxis**: t 226 508 2000.

Tourist Information

Town Hall information office: 12 Vas. Pávlou & Frideríkis, t 226 508 2900; open Mon–Fri 7.30–2.30. Pick up the free 'Green map' with simple plans of Aráchova and Delphi.

Where to Stay and Eat

Delphi ✉ 33054

Hotels here are nondescript but comfortable, and every one above D class has room for a tour bus or two. All are open all year.

Amalía, Apollónos St, t 226 508 2101, f 226 508 2290, hotamal@hellasnet.gr (A; luxury). At the west end of town, with views. Garden setting, buffet breakfast in the large restaurant area and spacious lounges. There is an outdoor pool, too.

Xenía, t 226 508 2151, f 226 508 2764, delphtis@otenet.gr (A; luxury). The most expensive, right under the Amalía. It has a large indoor year-round pool, and gardens.

Vouzás, 1 Vas. Pávlou & Frideríkis, t 226 508 2232, f 226 508 2203 (A; luxury). At the east end; a marble pile spilling down the hill with views from the rooms. No pool.

Acropole, 13 Filellinon (down from the Vouzas), t 226 508 2675, f 226 508 3171, delphi@otenet.gr (C; expensive). All the mod cons of the luxury hotels (but no pool), at half the price; many rooms have perfect views of the valley. They claim to offer parking.

Hermes, 27 Vas. Pávlou & Frideríkis, t 226 508 2318, f 226 508 2639. (C; expensive). Neat, new, white with brown trim; some rooms with view. Bargain gently in the off season.

Varónos, 25 Vas. Pávlou & Frederíkis, t/f 226 508 2345 (C; moderate). The jungle of potted plants helps to obscure the boring furniture in the spacious lobby. Clean and modern, and some rooms with a view.

Pan, 53 Vas. Pávlou & Frideríkis, t 226 508 2294, f 226 508 2320. (C; moderate). Not new, but clean, and many rooms have a view. Some sleep five, so it is a great family choice.

Sun View Rooms, 84 Apollónos, t 226 508 2349, f 226 508 2815 (inexpensive in summer, moderate in winter, buffet breakfast included). Friendly Mr Kalénzis' seven new rooms may be Delphi's best bargain with TVs and balconies with unimpeded views. They claim they spend €20 a week on cleaning products, and it shows.

Pension Sibylla, 9 Vas. Pávlou & Frideríkis, t 226 508 2335, f 226 508 3221 (inexpensive). A bargain with a friendly English-speaking owner. High-ceilinged ensuite rooms.

Camping Apollon, t 226 508 2750 (inexpensive). The closest (1.5km west) of three good campsites with pools by Delphi. This one has a couple of inexpensive chalets to let.

Taverna Váchos, 31 Apollónos, t 226 508 3186. Dusky pink tablecloths, an expanse of marble floor, and a great terrace form the backdrop for this upmarket, reasonably priced family taverna.

Epíkouros, 33 Vas. Pávlou & Frideríkis, t 226 508 3250. This elegant restaurant with a terrific view belongs to the Acropole Hotel and is well cared for and caters to groups.

Lechariá, 33 Apollónos, t 226 508 2864. A few steps west of Váchos. Nicely decorated with blond wood and red-checked curtains; this cosier spot has good food and the killer view.

Ómphalos, at the east end of Apollónos St, t 226 508 2484. This corner restaurant is more intimate than the others, and no wonder with a name like 'Belly Button'. Try the grilled meats: the owner's wife runs the butcher shop.

switchboard of the Greek world. Its festival, held every eighth year, featured a competition of songs performed on the lyre.

The first Temple of Apollo was built between 650 and 600 BC, when the Delphians were forced to move outside the holy precinct. It marked a crisis in relations between the locals and outside interests in the sanctuary – the so-called First Sacred War of 600–590 BC – which may not even have really happened, but nicely explained the rise of the Amphictyony ('those who dwell around') of 12 tribes (the Ionians, Dorians, Achaeans, Thessalians, etc.) that took control of the sanctuary, declared Delphi an independent city, put the fertile Crisaean Plain below off limits to the plough, and reduced the locals to temple servants. The Amphictyonic League, a kind of proto-United Nations, met twice a year, once at Delphi and once at Thermopylae. The *Homeric Hymn to Apollo* also appeared at this time, and emphasized the panhellenic aspect of the cult; the old Delphic festival was reorganized as the quadrennial Pythian Games, one of the four crown events of Greece (*see* pp.186 and 223). But the music competitions remained as important as the usual athletic contests and chariot racing on the Crisaean Plain. Winners were crowned with bay from the Vale of Tempe.

Although participation in the Pythian Games was limited to Greeks, the Delphic oracle acquired international prestige: Egyptians, Etruscans and Persians all made the arduous journey to consult it. In 548 BC, the sanctuary was destroyed by fire, but the temple and the treasuries were soon rebuilt on a grander scale with money sent from all over the known world. No one, however, contributed as much as the Alkmaeonids of Athens, who took over the temple project and paid for it to be faced in Parian marble. The grateful oracle then ordered the Spartans to oust the Alkmaeonids' enemies, the Pisistratids, from Athens. This serious breech of ethics was followed by a second scandal in 490, when the Spartan king Cleomenes I paid the oracle to declare his fellow king Demaratus illegitimate, but was caught and committed suicide.

Trying to preserve its reputation, the oracle became cautious, and took the Persian side in the wars. Xerxes showed his gratitude by sending an expedition to pillage Delphi, but Apollo knew how to 'protect his own' with a miraculous rock slide. The whole saga of the oracle's advice to Athens, to rely on its 'wooden walls' and 'divine Sálamis' may even have been invented by Themistocles to increase support for his naval plans; many famous oracles were actually made up after the fact, back when a *polis* had time to 'improve' history. By the time of the Peloponnesian War, when Thucydides interviewed eye-witnesses, it couldn't 'use' the oracle as freely; also, Athens began to keep records on stone, making the past harder to tweak. But perhaps most importantly, the Greek states, especially the democracies, felt sufficiently legitimate to not want any second guessing from Apollo.

In spite of the fall-off in big state oracles, Delphi continued to be honoured as the ultimate authority on religion. Victors in war felt obliged to send Apollo a tithe of the spoils, which were used to create works of art in a fever of one-upmanship. In 448 BC a Second Sacred War broke out for local control of the sanctuary, with Athens taking the Phocian side and Spartans the Delphian side. In 373 rocks from the Phaedriades cliff fell on the Temple of Apollo, and in 356, while contributions came in for its rebuilding, the Phocians started the Third Sacred War by rifling the treasuries to pay

The Pythia and the Oracle

The Pythia was a local woman chosen by the Delphians; at first they selected beautiful virgins, but, after a sex scandal in the temple, stuck to women over 50. She was assisted by two *Prophets* (priests appointed for life) and five *Hosioi*, who came from Delphian families that claimed descent from Deukalion and who attended to religious duties, mainly the winter rites of Dionysos. At first the oracle was open only on Apollo's birthday, the 7th Bysios (February), but such was the demand that eventually consultations were held every month on the 7th day from February to October; at Delphi's peak, three Pythias worked shifts.

Most pilgrims (*theopropoi*) arrived by sea at Crisa's port, where extortionate landing fees were said to be the cause behind the First Sacred War. At Delphi, they would purify themselves in the Castalian spring and pay a fee, which varied whether the pilgrim was an individual or a state envoy. The pilgrim then offered a goat for sacrifice, but first a pitcher of cold water was poured over it; if it shuddered it was a sign that the god would respond. Then lots were drawn to determine the order of consultation; states that sent Delphi major donations like Náxos and Chíos were given the privilege of jumping the queue (*protomanteia*). When it was a pilgrim's turn, he (no women were allowed) would be admitted to a room next to the *adyton*, the holy chamber in the Temple of Apollo, to ask his question of the Pythia. She too would have ritually prepared for the moment, by fasting and bathing in the Castalian spring, and burning bay and barley on the altar. She wore a bay leaf crown, sipped water from the Kasiotis spring, held a sprig of bay in her hand and sat on a tripod.

Where this tripod was and how she actually delivered her answer is a subject of lively debate. Legend has it that a shepherd first noticed that vapours emerging from a cleft in the earth allowed humans to see the future, and that this power had been harnessed and limited to the Pythia, who descended into a cave to sit by the cleft, mildly poisoned herself by chewing laurel leaves, and then replied to the question in an excited frenzy, blurting out gobbledegook which the two prophets interpreted and put into hexameter verse. But the archaeologists found no sign of a cleft, and the whole idea of a mad frenzy was apparently derived from Latin authors who confused *mantic* (prophetic) and *mania* ('the feeling of participating in the divine'), which they mistranslated as 'madness'. All historical records of Delphic consultations have the Pythia making articulate responses directly to the pilgrim. Sometimes, however, when a individual or state sent an envoy and the question was personal or secret, it would be written on a lead tablet and sealed in an envelope. The priest would then copy down the Pythia's reply and send it back, similarly sealed.

Because the oracle was a private affair, few genuine responses have come down to us (Joseph Fontenrose has catalogued them all in his book, the *Delphic Oracle*). Most of these are straightforward; ambiguous ones, not surprisingly, were issued when the outcome was doubtful. But even if the 'big oracles' such as the one that misled Croesus into attacking Persia ('If you cross the Halys you will destroy a great empire'), are really the result of the Greek urge to improve a story, the Greeks themselves *believed* it happened, and that belief kept Delphi in business for a thousand years.

their army; after their 15 minutes of fame as a Greek powerhouse, Philip II of Macedon smashed them, kicked them out of the Amphictiony and made them repair the damage (346 BC). In 279 BC the Galatians tried to seize Delphi, but a combination of local heroics and another timely landslide from the Phaedriades saved the day. The Romans did some repair work when they weren't pillaging (Sulla took all the gold and silver in 83 BC; Nero, who competed in the games and naturally won a music prize, pinched 500 statues). In the 2nd century AD, Hadrian and Herodes Atticus restored it all and the Pythia spoke again, mostly for Roman tourists. The last oracle was given to Julian the Apostate in the 360s, whose envoy received the apocryphal reply: 'Tell the king, the fair-wrought hall has fallen to the ground. No longer has Phoebus a hut, nor a prophetic laurel, nor a spring that speaks.'

The Huns and Goths finished it off, and in the 7th century a new hamlet, Kástri, grew up over the remains. In 1861, the French, who received the much-sought permission to excavate, began to dig, only to be delayed 30 years because of a wrangle over French taxes on Greek currants. Their exciting discoveries inspired the poet Angelos Sikelianós and his American wife Eva to found an International Delphic centre and host a festival of drama, dance, music and sports, in an attempt to 'restore the basic principles of Classical civilization', which Sikelianós thought had been misinterpreted and corrupted over history (one festival did take place in 1927 before the Depression dried up the funds). In 1960, Sikelianós' idea was given a new lease of life with the creation of the European Cultural Centre of Delphi, near the Amalía Hotel, to revive the place as an intellectual and cultural centre. It hosts congresses (2003 offers a series of symposia on ancient Greek drama), and has purchased the Sikelianós' house and made it into a museum of Delphic Festivals (contact them at 9 Frynihou St, 10558 Athens, t 210 331 2781, f 210 331 2786, and ask for their booklet in English).

The Sanctuary of Athena Pronaia

Pausanias, as usual, was the first to leave a traveller's account of Delphi, and today the traditional tour follows in his footsteps. There are two sacred zones, roughly a mile apart, and, if you approach from the east, the area called Marmária with the Sanctuary of Athena Pronaia is the first place you'll come to; steps lead down to it from the road. The Mycenaean finds here indicate that this was the original pre-oracle sanctuary of the village. On the terrace are two ruined temple-like buildings, one of which was dedicated to Philakos, a local hero who helped rout the Persians from Delphi in 480 BC. Below are remains of altars and the **Old Temple of Athena Pronaia**, 'the Temple Guardian', which was built of porous stone in the mid-7th century (the surviving capitals are among the oldest in Greece). It was a particularly unlucky Doric structure, rebuilt in c. 500 BC, damaged by the landslide in 480 and then the earthquake in 373; even when it was excavated, another landslide ruined all except for three columns. Next to it was a **Doric Treasury** (c. 480 BC), the Parian marble **Treasury of Massalia** (Marseille) from 530 BC, and the loveliest and certainly most mysterious building in Delphi, the partly reconstructed **Tholos** (c. 390 BC). A rotunda in Pentelic marble, topped with a conical roof and surrounded by a ring of 20 Doric columns, with an inner circle of 10 Corinthian columns, it resembles the equally mysterious Tholos in

Epidauros and could be by the same architect. Old Pausanias didn't mention it, however, leaving us clueless as to its purpose; one guess is that a chthonic deity presided here. Next to it stood the **New Temple of Athena Pronaia**, from c. 360 BC, built in the local limestone. A path west of here leads to the 4th-century BC **Gymnasium**, which was rebuilt by the Romans. The steepness of the site forced it to have two levels: on top was the **xystos**, a covered running track, while below was the **palaestra**, built around a court with a circular pool. The nearby café has lovely views.

Back on the road, where it bends around the ravine that separates the cliffs of the Phaedriades, rises the clear, cold **Castalian spring**, hopefully accessible again after a recent rock slide. Here pilgrims, priests and the Pythia bathed and in particular purified themselves by wetting their hair (murderers, however, required full immersion) before participating in any religious activity. The **Archaic fountain house** (c. 590 BC) was found by accident by the modern road; some 50 yards further up the slope is the Hellenistic **fountain house**, cut out of the rock.

The Sanctuary of Apollo

t 226 508 2312; open daily 7.30am–7pm; adm exp. Bring a bottle of water.

From the fountain house, a pilgrim would continue east to the Sanctuary of Apollo. The trapezoidal perimeters of its precinct, established in c. 600 BC, were enclosed by a wall or **peribolos** that had several gates into the surrounding town. Within these walls was a permanent Greek World's Fair, chock-a-block with magnificent showcases – each city state rivalling the others in the splendour of its treasuries and monuments, which because of the steep setting stood on large bases or platforms.

Between the ticket booth and main gate are extensive remains of a 4th-century AD **Roman Agora**, where the last pilgrims (or more likely, the first tourists) could shop. The **Sacred Way** begins up a few steps, and still has some haphazard paving from Roman times. Past the gate and just to the right is the base of the bronze **Bull of Corcyra** (480 BC), dedicated by Corfu after it landed an enormous catch of tuna. This has a certain innocent charm compared to what follows. Opposite stood the overweening **Monument of the Navarchs**, dedicated by Lysander in 403 BC to celebrate Sparta's victory over Athens at Aegospotami with 37 bronze statues of Spartan admirals and gods. Facing them (and in their face) were the **Offerings of the Arcadians**, nine bronze statues erected to celebrate a successful invasion of Sparta in 369 BC. Back on the left side, the Athenian **Offering of Marathon** (460 BC) was erected as a tardy tribute to Miltiades. It set a lofty standard for victory monuments with 13 bronzes by the great Phidias (the 10 eponymous heroes of Athens plus Miltiades, Apollo and Athena); three more were added later. Next to this are remains of two **Argive Monuments**, showing the Seven against Thebes and the revenge of their sons, the Epigonoi (the large semicircular niche) erected after a victory over Sparta in c. 460 BC. For Argos, any thumping of Sparta was worth celebrating: to mark her defeat by Epaminondas of Thebes they erected the **semi-circular niche** on the left, with statues of the 10 mythical kings. The colonies got into the act too – next to the 10 kings is a large rectangular base that supported the **Offering of the Tarentines**, donated by Sparta's colony in southern Italy.

Delphi

The Sanctuary of Athena Pronaia

1 Temple-shaped Buildings
2 Altars
3 Old Temple of Athena Pronaia
5 Treasury of Massalia
6 Tholos
7 New Temple of Athena Pronaia
8 House of the Priests

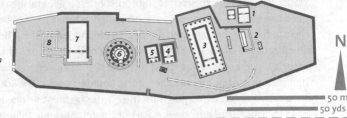

N

50 m
50 yds

The Sanctuary of Apollo

↑ To Stadium

1 Roman Agora
2 Bull of Corcyra
3 Offering of the Arcadians
4 Monument of the Navarchs
5 Argive Monuments
6 Semi-circular Niches
7 Niches
8 Offering of the Tarantines
9 Treasury of the Sikyonians
10 Treasury of the Sifnians
11 Treasury of the Megarians
12 Treasury of the Syracusans
13 Treasury of the Cnidians
14 Treasury of the Aeolians
15 Treasury of the Thebans
16 Treasury of the Athenians

17 Bouleuterion
18 Rock of Sybil
19 Rock of Leto
20 Naxian Sphinx
21 Stoa of the Athenians
22 Treasury of Corinth
23 Tripod of Plataea
24 Altar of the Chians
25 Statue of Eumenes II
26 Statue of Attalos I
27 Stoa of Attalos I
28 Offering of Daochos
29 Lesche of the Cnidians
30 Temple of Apollo
31 Offering of Krateros
32 Theatre
33 Stoa of the Aetolians

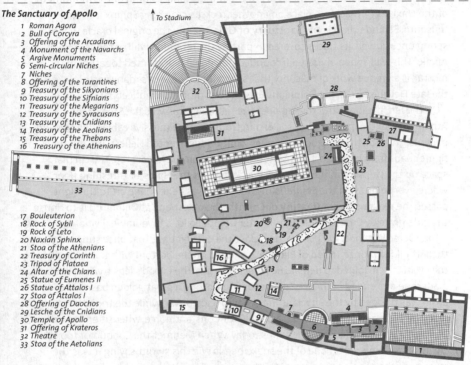

Next come the first of 27 once dazzling treasuries, most now reduced to rubble. On
the left beneath the Sacred Way lie the square foundations of the **Treasury of the
Sikyonians**, built c. 580, and rebuilt after the big fire; it had an open pavilion that may
have displayed the chariot of the Sikyón tyrant Kleisthenes, victor of the first Pythian
Games. Next to it are the huge foundations of the **Treasury of the Sifnians** (c. 530 BC),
the most splendid of all, an elegant Ionian building in Parian marble funded with
tithes from the island's gold mines (see p.621); its magnificent frieze is in the
museum. At a bend in the Sacred Way stands the platform (on the right) of the
Treasury of the Megarians; there are scanty remains of the Treasuries of the
Syracusans (erected after their great upset victory over Athens), Cnidians and
Aeolians; on the right, half of the foundations survive of the **Treasury of the Thebans**,
built after they defeated Sparta at Leúktra (371 BC). Just up from here on a triangular

platform stands the Doric **Treasury of the Athenians** in Parian marble, where Athens proudly displayed the spoils of Marathon. It offers a general idea of what the others looked like; in 1906, Athens paid 35,000 gold drachmae for it to be reconstructed.

Next to this are the damaged rectangular foundations of the **Bouleuterion**, or council house of the Delphians, and the **Rock of the Sibyl**, a chunk fallen from the Phaedriades where tradition has it that the first Pythia, Herophile, stood and sang when she came from Troy. Another of the boulders here is the **Rock of Leto**, where Apollo's mother stood and gave him the encouragement he needed to slay Python, whose lair was the nearby crevice. Part of the mighty Ionic column of the **Monument of the Naxians** (570 BC) is in place on another rock; its crowning Sphinx is in the museum. Behind this was the **Sanctuary of Gaia-Themis**, the original oracle where a spring once flowed, its traces covered in part by the **retaining wall** of the Temple of Apollo. This wall, made of irregular rounded polygonal blocks fitted together without mortar, is a unique work of masonry that stood up to the area's many earthquakes. In the late Hellenistic era, the Delphians used it for a municipal noticeboard.

On the left, the long structure against the retaining wall was the **Stoa of the Athenians**, built in 478 BC to house Persian trophies – the massive cables of linen and papyrus, 3ft thick, that had bound Xerxes' boat bridge over the Hellespont and the figureheads from his ships; the inscription is intact on the lower step. The circular space up the steps in front of the stoa was known as the **Halos**, or threshing floor, where every ninth year the *Stepteria* mystery play was held. A lane off to the right passes the remains of the **Treasury of Corinth**, the oldest one at Delphi, built to house the gifts given by Croesus, hoping to butter up Apollo for a favourable divination.

The Sacred Way, now well paved, rises past the circular base that once supported the 18ft gilded bronze **Tripod of Plataea**. Inscribed on the bottom with the names of the 31 cities who joined to defeat the Persians in 479, the tripod's legs twisted like a giant rope and ended in three snake heads, supporting a great golden basin. The basin was pillaged by the Phocians in the Third Sacred War, while the tripod was taken by Constantine the Great as a bauble for Constantinople, where it ended up in the Hippodrome, and where it remains today. When Mehmet the Conqueror took the city in 1452, he lopped off one of the snake heads with his sword, saying it was the revenge of the peoples of Asia against the Greeks. The plinth near here held the **Chariot of Helios**, a dedication from Rhodes (c. 304 BC); there is some evidence that the magnificent Horses of St Mark's in Venice may have started their long and varied career pulling the chariot here. North of this are two **pedestals** for gold statues of Eumenes and Attalos of Pergamon, and the ruined Stoa of Attalos.

At the top of the Sacred Way are the bases of the **Tripods of Gelon and Hiero**, all that remain of four huge golden tripods on a vast monument commemorating Syracuse's victory over the Carthaginians at Himera in 480 BC – but they too fell victim to the Phocians in 353 BC. To the left is the 28ft **Altar of the Chians** in black and white marble, offered in the 5th century BC in thanksgiving for their liberation from the Persians. In 1920, after being liberated from the Turks, the islanders paid for its reconstruction.

In spite of all the competition, the Doric **Temple of Apollo** dominated Delphi and still does today, with its six re-erected columns. Tradition says the first temple was built of bay wood and leaves, the second in feathers and beeswax, and the third in bronze, before the legendary architects Agamedes and Trophonios built it of stone in the 7th century. After the fire in 548 BC this was replaced by the splendid Alkmeonid temple, on the same scale as the Parthenon; after rocks fell on it in 373 BC, it was rebuilt in local limestone, with pediment sculptures of Parian marble that have curiously vanished without the slightest trace. The French excavators dismantled the temple, searching for signs of the famous cleft and the *adyton* – where the omphalos was kept, where the sacred spring Kassiotis was piped, and where the Pythia sat on her tripod – and for all their pains found only hints of a small underground structure.

Delphi's moralizing bent was concisely expressed by the two famous maxims that were inscribed in the pronaos: 'Know Thyself' and 'Nothing in Excess'. The first one didn't quite have the meaning we give it today, but advised knowing one's limitations before the gods, while the second expressed the moderation, the *sophrosýne* that the Greeks idealized, perhaps because they so rarely if ever achieved it outside of art. Pausanias on his visit saw an altar of Poseidon, a gold statue of Apollo (where Nero dedicated his harp), statues of Homer, the Fates and the iron throne of Pindar (who, to the chagrin of Hellas, had supported Delphi's defeat in the Persian Wars) where his ghost was invited to an annual feast with Apollo. Here too was the hearth of the eternal flame, made of fir branches and tended by women past menopause. If any Greek city's sacred fire was somehow religiously 'polluted', all the fires in the city would have to be extinguished and a messenger sent on the double to bring back a new clean flame from Delphi.

The Sacred Way follows the length of the temple; to the west, a gate in the peribolos led to the large **Stoa of the Aetolians**, dedicated after their victory over the Galatians in 278 BC. Before that, to your right, is the rectangular exedra that held the **Offering of Krateros** (320 BC) dedicated by the companion who saved Alexander the Great's life during a lion hunt in Susa – here bronzes by Lysippos and Leochares represented the scene depicted in the mosaic in Pélla (*see* p.548). A Roman stair next to it ascends to the 4th-century BC **Theatre**, which hosted the musical and poetry contests of the Pythian Games. It is beautifully preserved (the Romans were the last to restore it, in grey limestone) and it enjoys a magical view that becomes especially lovely in the late afternoon light. The orchestra still has its irregular pavement and water channel; the 35 tiers of seats are divided two thirds of the way up by a *diazoma* (landing). A path to the east leads to a rectangular exedra that was the **Offering of Daochos of Thessaly** (330 BC) – some of its statues are in the museum – and the site of the **Temenos of Neoptolemos**, honouring the son of Achilles who was killed here by a priest of Apollo. The ruins further on belonged to the **Lesche of the Knidians** (*c.* 450 BC), a ritual dining-hall/clubhouse that once had an extraordinary painting by Polygnotos, of which Pausanias' lengthy description is all that survives; it was so complex that it included 'viewing instructions'.

Two fountains that once held the water of the now dry Kossotis spring lie between the Theatre and **Stadium**. The latter is at the top of Delphi, proof that even spectators in ancient times had to be fit. It too is one of the best preserved in Greece, and was last renovated by the ever-generous Herodes Atticus, who added the **triumphal arch** on the end. Stands seating 7,000 on the north and west sides cut into the rock, while the south side (with no seats) was made level by a support wall in the 5th century BC. The track here was 177m, or 600 Roman feet.

The Museum

Open Mon–Fri 7.30am–7pm, Sat and Sun 8.30–3; adm exp.

Located just west of the site, this museum, full of beautiful things, is Delphi's modern treasury. A large floor mosaic of animals at the entrance came from a 5th-century church on the site. At the top of the stairs an iron tripod and bronze cauldron from the 7th century BC offer an example of the favourite trophy of ancient times. Next to it is a Hellenistic copy of the omphalos, the navel of the world, found just outside the Temple of Apollo (it was definitely an 'outie', a shape that recalls that it was also Python's tomb); marble fillets and knots represent the wool and precious jewels that covered the original. Even Delphi's earliest votives had an aristocratic quality: Room II has three bronze shields from the late 8th century BC and a small Daedelic *kouros* perhaps representing Apollo (*c.* 650 BC). The next room has two bold early 6th-century BC *kouroi* from Argos, *Cleobis and Biton* (*see* p.251), signed by Polymedes, a small bronze Apollo and five damaged but intriguing Archaic metopes on the story of the Argonauts from the first Sikyonian Treasury (560 BC).

Once an item had been dedicated to a god, it had to stay in the holy precinct, and if damaged it was buried in a dump. One of these dumps, from the mid-5th century BC, yielded the beautiful works in Room IV: a life-sized bull made of silver sheets, originally attached to a copper frame, and beautiful ivories, including the heads of Artemis and Apollo (with long golden tresses) from chryselephantine statues, along with some of the golden sheets, decorated with animals, that adorned their garments (6th century BC, Ionian work). Room V has the enigmatically smiling Naxian Sphinx, young and lithe on her very fluted Ionic column; sphinxes were frequently placed on Archaic tombs as guardians, and this one may have served the same role, replacing Python as the oracle's protector. Here, too, is some of the finest and liveliest Archaic sculpture to come down to us, from the Treasury of the Sifnians (*c.* 535 BC), which justifies the building's reputation – a delightful caryatid, the great pediment sculpture of the impetuous Heracles stealing Apollo's tripod while Athena tries to referee, and the two surviving friezes by an unknown master, in places still retaining their original paint. On the east frieze, the gods are assembled (pro-Trojan deities on the left, the pro-Greek faction on the right) while the Greeks and Trojans fight over a body. The north frieze shows the Gigantomachy, where the gods do battle with the giants.

The next room has the original metopes (*c.* 490 BC) from the Treasury of the Athenians, showing the labours of Theseus and Heracles, notable for their daring composition. Rooms VII and VIII contain the remains of the Archaic Alkmeonid Temple of Apollo, and two hymns to Apollo from the 2nd century BC, found engraved in the wall of the Athenian Treasury; they are among the few to survive complete with their musical notation in Greek letters. Rooms IX and X have grave steles and fragments from the Tholos – its Hellenistic metopes are remarkable, sadly damaged. Room XI contains statues from the Offering of King Daochos of Thessaly (330s BC) celebrating his boss Philip II's victory at Chairóneia. The five, representing Daochos' ancestors, are copies of bronzes; at least one, Agias (14-time victor in the Olympic, Pythian, Nemean and Isthmian Games), was by Lysippos. Here, too, is the giant 4th-century BC acanthus column topped with three dancing girls, who once held a tripod.

The museum's star, the bronze Charioteer of *c*. 475 BC, stands in Room XII, along with bronze fragments from the rest of the monument, which was smashed in the earthquake of 373 BC. It was dedicated by Polyzalos of Gela in Sicily, who won the chariot race – a sport that became an obsession among Gela's tyrants. A great work of the Severe Classical style, the charioteer is calm, having already won his victory; even the eyes of magnesium and onyx, with their eyelashes, are well preserved and slightly uneven, which combined with other slightly less-than-perfect features give the cool figure his individuality. His body, which resembles a fluted column, was disproportionately elongated, perhaps because it was meant to be seen from below. The last room is dedicated to the handsome Parian marble figure of Antinous (2nd century AD), a laughing little girl (3rd century BC) and a fine Hellenistic portrait bust, believed to represent Titus Q. Flamininus, who defeated the Macedonians in 197 BC. Small bronzes and ceramics are here too, some going back to Mycenaean times and some from the Corycian Cave. A new modernistic mausoleum-style **museum** has just been built, tucked under the road, which will display some of Delphi's many other finds.

From Delphi to Náfpaktos

Ámphissa, Itéa and Galaxídi

West of Delphi, the road winds down 13km past **Chrissó** (campsite and a nice *xenóna*) to a crossroads. The road north goes to the **Brállos Pass** and Lamía (*see* p.381) by way of modern **Ámphissa**, presiding over a vast sea of olives just as it did in ancient times. Known as Salona in the Middle Ages, it boasts an attractive **Frankish castle** (*c*. 1205) on Classical foundations; although seldom visited now, it got far too much attention in the past, changing hands from French to Catalans (1311) to Turks in 1394. The Brállos road eventually passes a signposted turn-off to **Heracles' Funeral Pyre** on Mount Oíte, where the big guy laid himself to escape the pain of the centaur Nessus' flesh-eating shirt and Zeus blasted his mortal parts away with a thunderbolt and made him god. But don't expect to see anything much except mountain scenery.

The road south from the crossroads goes through olive groves to workaday **Itéa**, ancient Delphi's port, where most pilgrims landed. It has a pretty seaside promenade, a wide shingle beach, and a view of the entire bay with its small islands. Other than that, you could give Itéa a miss, and hightail it past the dark red mounds of bauxite and the fish farms in the deep bay west of town, and on to much nicer Galaxídi.

Galaxídi's densely stacked houses and tiny gardens cover two lovely, low headlands punctured by little fjords. A road circles around the edges, but it is sometimes one-way, forcing you into charming twisty back lanes. One house, built right on top of an ancient city wall, reminds us that maritime Galaxídi has been a going concern for a long time. In the 14th century BC it was called Oianthe and had an acropolis on the

Getting There and Around

Easy **access** from the Peloponnese make this area not quite as remote as it looks on the map. In 2004 the Rio bridge is destined (they say) to replace the Rio–Andírio ferry (see p.210), but the Éghio–Ag. Nikólaos ferry (see p.209) will still be going strong. The towns en route can be reached on the twice daily Pátras–Delphi **bus**. In Pátras: **t** 261 027 4938. Five buses a day link Ag. Nikólaos with Delphi.

Where to Stay and Eat

Itéa ✉ 32200

Kalafáti, 1 Giónas St, **t** 226 502 2945, **f** 226 503 2986 (B; expensive). This is the nicest place, set back from the beach.

Panórama, 153 Aktí Poseidónas, **t** 226 503 4715 (B; moderate). A new, stark, white and blue trimmed pile, but right on the sea.

Ayánnis Camping, t 226 503 2555. The best one on a beach of sorts, but the campsites in Chrissó and Delphi with their pools look more inviting. Open May–Oct.

Seafood Taverna Zephyros, t 226 503 2666. A great terrace right on the best part of the beach by the Panórama Hotel.

Galaxídi ✉ 33052

Soaring prices in summer are higher than average, but Galaxídi is open all year and its tavernas serve all day long. Ask at the hotels for the brochure put out by the town.

Argo, t 226 504 1996, **f** 226 504 1878 (B; expensive). A small hotel in a neoclassical house in a garden – you would never guess that it was new. White marble stairs lead into a cosy modern and traditional interior.

Ianthia, t/f 226 504 2434 (expensive). Maybe the classiest of the classy; a renovated mansion behind the town hall in the southern bay, with stained glass.

Ganymede, 20 N Gourgouri, **t** 226 504 1328, **f** 226 504 2160 (expensive–moderate). A neat white confection with a round window and cosy courtyard, run by an Italian who loves

---

headland where the church is today. Shipbuilding was its mainstay, with a little piracy thrown in; all kinds of ancient gold and silver coins have been found in the harbour. After a bad patch of barbarian incursions and earthquakes in the 6th century, it was favoured by the Byzantines and had a monastery built by Michael Comnenus himself. It continued to thrive except for a glitch in 1660 when pirates destroyed the town. Even the Turks granted it privileges, but it reached its zenith after independence. By 1890 it had a fleet of 550 ships, seaside mansions and forest (still there, on the south side of the fishing port) especially planted for its boat builders. The **Archaeological-Nautical Museum** (*t 226 504 1558; open Tues–Sun 9–2.30*) tells the tale.

Galaxídi ran out of steam when it ran into steam. No one needed its lyrical sailing boats any more, and the locals contented themselves with captaining the ships of others, something they still do. Meanwhile the town looks better than ever: in the last 30 years, foreigners and Greeks have renovated its imposing neoclassical houses, and the tasteful and laid-back result is part gay resort, part family resort, and a popular destination for yachties. The town 'beach' and others around the southern headland are less than stellar, but the swimming is good and its narrow fishing port is just lovely, for both people and ducks.

Ag. Nikólaos and Trizónia

The indented coast to Náfpaktos can be navigated in under an hour; several small settlements grace the coastal flats or tumble down hills to narrow shingle beaches. Halfway along, **Ag. Nikólaos**, terminal for the Éghio ferry (see p.209), has a small, pleasant beach at its west end and inexpensive rooms to rent, a campsite and

his work; famous for serving the best breakfasts in town. Some rooms have kitchens.

Galaxídi, 11 Syngroú, behind the narrow end of the fishing port, t 226 504 1850, f 226 504 1206 (*C; moderate, expensive in summer*). Quiet, with a pretty garden and parking.

Koukoúnas, 31 Pappa, t 226 504 1179 (*C; moderate*). Beside the Galaxídi; a tinge less charming, but pretty good and cheaper.

Porto, t 226 504 1182. The old standby at the port, with great octopus and pasta.

To Barko tis Maritsa, t 226 504 1059. The current favourite, with seafood and tasty dishes made with courgettes.

Trizónia ⊠ 33058

Drymna, on the island, t 226 607 1304 (*C; moderate*). Pleasant little summer hotel.

Náfpaktos ⊠ 30300

Plaza House, Psáni Beach, t 263 402 2226, f 263 402 3174, info@plaza-house.com (*moderate*). New, with TV, air-conditioning, fridges and a beach view. The owner speaks English.

Golden Beach (Ξρυση Ακτη), Psáni Beach, t 263 4021444, f 263 402 4625 (*moderate*). New, built over a lobby that is the Internet café; good-value apartments with view.

Regina Apartments, Psáni Beach, t 263 402 1556, f 263 402 1556, mobile t 694 255 5203 (*moderate to inexpensive in winter*). Attractive white and blue trimmed studios with air-conditioning and TV. On the beach, cosy and friendly.

Spitikó, Grýmvovo Beach, t 263 402 6524. Looks upscale, but the prices are fair and the food good; try the soufflés or cabbage rolls.

Tsaras, in the port, t 223 402 7809. An attractive and cosy café.

Ároma Café, on the port, t 263 402 9664. Best for contemplating the fishing boats, the circular moles, and walls.

Stredo Café, t 263 402 6426. On the left side of the port by one of Náfpaktos' five mosques, a friendly place with music and a fireplace. Tony, who presides in this former smugglers' den, is a great source of local information.

tavernas, handy if you arrive too late for the ferry. **Glyfáda**, next to the west, looks across at **Trizónia**, an island almost close enough to swim to (or take the cheap hourly water taxi), with villas, tavernas and a small hotel. As you meet the Mórnos river, you can detour north to **Tríkorfo**, home to a monastic rock band, popularly known as the '*paparokádes*' (monk-rockers), who have swept the Greek charts and rocked the ecclesiastical boat in recent years. The road leads almost immediately to Náfpaktos, a little bit of Aetoloakarnanía (*see* below) that in any case is a place apart.

Náfpaktos (Lepanto)

Modern, busy, straggling Náfpaktos is the last place you would expect to suddenly come across a tiny **medieval port**, so complete it only lacks a chain placed across its mouth every evening. The delightful port is a prelude to the imposing castle set high above the town in a beautiful forest of pines. Inhabited by Locrians, the site was taken over by Athens in 455 BC and given to displaced Messenians (*see* p.337). Even then it was an important supply depot for ships bound for Italy. Fortified again in Byzantine times, the Franks changed its name to Lepanto and used it as a stopover to the Holy Land; the Despot of Épirus used it when things were too hot in Épirus; and Albanian tribesmen just used it. Finally it came to the Venetians in 1407. They did the decorating, building one of the finest fortifications in Greece, and that in spite of the Turkish occupation after 1490. The core was the castle or **Fortezza** (*open daylight hours*), surrounded by walls and square and round towers; from here two walls descend to enclose the port, joined by four transverse walls to create five defensive zones. The walk up through impressive gates (and past two cafés built into the walls) is delightful and the view superb; a church of Profítis Elías, a Byzantine bath, cisterns and mosque still stand in the castle.

Fortezza notwithstanding, the most famous battle hereabouts was fought on sea, not on land. In 1571, a Turkish admiral took on supplies here before what became the **Battle of Lepanto**, fought to the west, where a Western allied fleet under Emperor Charles V's son, Don Juan of Austria, dealt such a crippling blow to Turkish sea power that it turned the tide of Ottoman expansion in Europe, and incidentally spared the castle and the port for posterity. Cervantes lost an arm in the fray and left us the best description of the battle; other survivors told how confusion reigned at Lepanto from one end to the next; on some ships, heads rolled without mercy, while on others, Turks and Christians hurled lemons and oranges at one another, laughing.

The port area is about to be pedestrianized. It is framed by long, wide, shingle beaches; the western one, **Psáni**, is the most sympathetic, and the eastern, **Grýmvovo**, is fancier. Businesses are run by young people with New York and Sydney accents, the first generation of expatriates to return to Greece looking for streets paved with gold. They may find them when the Río-Andírio suspension bridge (10km west of town) makes Náfpaktos and the unexplored mountains beyond easy to reach.

Western Stereá Elláda: Aetoloakarnanía

Many travellers pass through Aetoloakarnanía on their way between the Peloponnese and Épirus, but few tell. How can they? Its name is the biggest tongue-twister in Greece. Bounded by the Ambracian Gulf on the north, the Gulfs of Pátras and Corinth on the south, the Ionian Sea on the west, and a rabbit-warren of isolated mountains and river gorges on the east, it was easier to pronounce in ancient times when it was two separate regions. Mostly mountainous Aetolía was east of the mighty Achelóos river, and mostly flat, muddy Akarnanía, west of it. The Aetolíans and Akarnaníans shared a tendency to piracy and banditry, a habit of eating raw meat, and a language different enough from mainstream Greek to get called barbarians by fellow Hellenes. They were also vociferous enemies, forming rival federated states. This meant that when they did build settlements, they were very well fortified indeed.

Getting There and Around

By air: Aktion is the nearest airport.

By car: there are two major routes: Andírio to Messolóngi and Vónitsa via Astakós, or Andírio to Messolóngi and then to Amfilochía on the inland route, the latter a mere 108km.

By bus: Agrinio's bus station, t 264 102 2538, has several buses a day to Thérmo, Amfilochía, Vónitsa, Messolóngi and Pátras, and can drop you at points in between. Buses leave Athens' Kifissós station (t 210 512 4910) hourly for Agrínio, and stop on request after Andírio. Pátras' Aetoloakarnanían bus station, 5 Norman St, t 261 042 1205, connects with Messolóngi (eight daily), Agrínio (three daily) and Vónitsa (three daily). A few daily buses from Messolóngi (t 263 10 2 2371) go on the coast to Mýtikas; local buses serve villages between Mýtikas and Vónitsa.

By taxi: taxis exist in all towns. In Messolóngi: t 263 102 2655.

'Civilization' came late – in the 5th century BC for the Akarnaníans and the 3rd century BC for Aetolía. The Akarnanían capital was Strátos, a huge stronghold by the Achelóos 11km north of present-day Agrínio; the Aetolían capital and cult centre was Thérmon, a large mountain hideaway just west of Lake Trichonída. In the 3rd century BC, the Aetolíans were a force to be reckoned with, taking over a lot of territory, even Delphi briefly. Alliances with the Romans went sour, reducing both federations to ashes, their populations decimated or forced to populate Octavian's Nikopolis (*see* p.415).

Modern Aetoloakarnaníans live in workaday villages, with only an occasional church to catch the eye. Flat fields grow tobacco, corn and cotton. Cows, pigs, sheep and goats abound. Aetoloakarnaníans tend to leave them loose, even the pigs, by the roadsides. Not on many people's 'must see' list, Aetoloakarnanía nonetheless has a lot to offer: Messolóngi, which saw the last of Byron, the surprisingly large archaeological sites of Strátos, Thérmon, Kalydon, Pleúron and Oiniádai, lakes, and an absolutely superb coastline on the Ionian Sea.

Andírio to Messolóngi: Kalydon Country

After the turn-off to Náfpaktos (*see* p.401), at around the 14km mark, the highway passes near little Káto Vasilikí (last chance for a good swim) and descends into the wide **Évinos river valley** and Mycenaean country. Up the first hill past the Évinos bridge, a blue sign points east to ancient **Kalydon** (*adm free; a guard's kiosk marks the entrance*). The extensive ruins, now someone's olive grove, run beside and parallel to the highway. They date from historical times, when Kalydon was an Aetolían League member, but the name recalls Meleager's famous boar hunt that attracted an all-star cast of ancient heroes – although Atalanta, the lone woman, made the kill, causing some serious testosterone problems. Mycenaean Kalydon remains the only legendary Mycenaean centre still to elude the archaeologists' spade, but those who 'know' are sure it is here somewhere. The depression just past the guard's hut contains a **Bouleuterion**, of which two walls with tiered stone benches set at right angles survive. Ascend the gravel path and turn left a bit; a sign points right for the large 1st-century BC **Heróon**, dedicated to Leon, a local worthy (his tomb was the barrel-vaulted room in the basement). Another sign points left, past a ruined Hellenistic stoa, to the infamous **Temple of Artemis Laphria**. Once the city's pride and joy, all that remains is its massive platform, built for show in 370 BC. It once had a peristyle of six by thirteen Doric columns and a cult statue of Artemis in the guise of an Amazonian huntress (the Atalanta story was still remembered). Annually, a huge bonfire immolated live animals for the goddess, a gruesome fertility rite with deep cultural roots; this temple sits on the ruins of a 7th-century temple to the great goddess (bits are in the Athens museum). The Romans, never ones to miss out on a bit of fun, adopted the cult in Pátras (*see* p.213). Apollo, Artemis' twin, gets a nod, but rough and tumble hunts seem to have appealed more to ancient Aetolians than Apollo's cool rationality; his temple is the small one, out the back. A long **Sacred Way** went in a line from Artemis' Temple up to the **Acropolis**, whose 3rd-century BC walls are meagre, but the view is good.

Messolóngi

Aetoloakarnanía's capital Messolóngi is situated on the huge, shallow Klísova lagoon, the second largest in the Mediterranean and a Natura 2000 site. Birds love it, and it teems with fish. Not a big city (pop. 18,000), nor long-standing (pirates settled it in the 1600s), flat Messolóngi is set out in a grid, the pleasant old centre with narrow streets, surrounded by new broad avenues. Its name means 'middle of the lake' and the lagoon vistas from the attractive port show why. A 5km causeway leads out to the Tourlídas swimming beach. Messolóngi has excellent seafood: eels, smoked, spitted or baked in the oven are a favourite, and there is a great variety of fish from the open sea or local fisheries, some still using the shacks built on stilts.

Byron left his heart in Messolóngi, and not metaphorically either. On 19 April 1824 he died here, with a momentous sense of anticlimax, of fever, while trying to raise money and troops for the Greek War of Independence. His body went to England but his heart lies beneath his statue, in the **Heróon** or **Heroes Park**, buried among other luminaries of the war. The park (*adm free*) is on the edge of town closest to the highway, and bounded on one side by a long stretch of old city walls.

Messolóngi was unlucky during the War of Independence. Hemmed in by Ibrahim Pasha's troops for 12 months, the desperate, starving population attempted to break out en masse under cover of night on 22 April 1826. Of the 9,000 who tried, only 1,800 survived the enemies' guns and knives. The *Exodus* is commemorated annually on the day by a solemn procession.

Inland Aetoloakarnanía

Messolóngi to Amfilochía

Between Messolóngi and Aetolikó (due east of the salt works), the highway passes **ancient Pleúron**. There are signs on the highway, but you have to be ready; the turn-off is abrupt in both directions. This huge seven-gated, 3rd-century BC Aetolían fortress is 2km straight on and remarkably hard to see until you are almost there. A map in English inside the gate explains the highlights. The tiny theatre backed by the city wall suggests that the citizens were not exactly culture vultures (was it used for out-of-town try-outs perhaps?). Near the agora, a huge (now roofless) water cistern holding 55,000 gallons still sports four massive brick division walls. Note the triangular openings in the walls that kept the water level uniform. Wonderfully preserved walls, pseudo-isodomic and trapezoidal, reinforced with 36 towers, still enclose the town and fortified acropolis; all for nothing. Augustus demanded its citizens move to Nikópolis and it was abandoned. The view over Messolóngi's lagoon is worth the trip.

The highway passes through the Kleisoúra, a narrow cleft in the limestone mountains, and past **Lake Lisimáchia** and the much bigger **Lake Trichonída** (*see* below), past **Agrínio** (give it a miss) and on 11km up to low-lying, but massive **ancient Stratos**. Akarnanía's ancient capital was and is on the Achelóos, all the better to guard its rich farmland and discover the Aetolíans' next nasty move. Now neglected and down-at-heel, it straddles four hills, big enough for two signs off the highway and two

Tourist Information

Messolóngi: the Municipality, 20 Máyer, t 263 105 5120, f 263 102 4372.

Where to Stay and Eat

Messolóngi ✉ 30200
Theoxenía, 2 Tourlídas, t 263 103 3683, f 263 102 2493 (*B; expensive–moderate*). Big, by the lagoon and port, amid trees; renewed and well equipped. *Open all year.*
Avra, 5 Har. Trikoúpi St, t 263 102 2284. (*D; moderate–inexpensive*). Central, with TV and air-conditioning. *Open all year.*
Mezedopoleío of Ioánnis Demitroúkas, 11 Pazikóstika St, t 263 102 3237. In the old town; this local favourite is a stand-out. Try the heavenly baked eel ('*chéli* / χέλι), with greens (*chórta*).

Mourágio, the port, t 263 102 5138. Piles of fish on ice; choose, and take in the port from its terrace. The parking is easy here, too.
To Iliovasílema, t 263 102 2577. A fish taverna in Tourlídas. Go for the sunset.

Thérmo ✉ 30008
Modern Thérmo's pleasant flagstoned *plateía* offers meat tavernas with home-town produce, amid shade and running water.
Aetolía, 35 Har. Trikoúpi, t 264 402 2394. Ungentrified and cheap; in the *plateía*. *Open April–Oct.*
Thermios Apollon, t 264 402 4024, f 264 402 4025 (*moderate*). This brand new hotel, isolated way up the mountain, has large rooms with kitchenettes, TV, balconies and a fantastic view of the ruins in the distance. Book in Aug. *Open all year.*

entrances. The northernmost takes you past the Texaco station, up a hill where you turn right and then turn left at a cement retaining wall sporting huge water pipes. This unassuming road leads shortly to a footpath that goes up to the large 4th-century peripteral Temple of Zeus built on Stratos' west wall (just the substructure and part of the *cella* remain), and incidentally goes on to follow the impressive city walls for a long way. The southern sign takes you up the hill and through a gate (unlocked) pretty much in front of the old agora with a city cross wall on your right, a theatre east beyond it and the small acropolis straight ahead. No one seems to care if you visit, but it is worth the effort just to grasp its sheer size (consider its picnic possibilities). Stratos was Akarnanía's largest city, and in the good old days, ships could navigate from here right to the Gulf of Corinth. Today, the drab modern town drapes itself uninterestedly around the crumbling walls.

The highway continues north 30km or so to Amfilochía, the beginning of a nice Gulf-side drive to Vónitsa (*see* p.407). It makes a good café stop, too, before tackling the 41km north to Árta in Épirus (*see* p.412).

Lake Trichonída to Ancient Thermon

Trichonída's north shore offers views and pleasant villages (lakeside Padánassa with cafés and a taverna is lovely) and a bevy of Byzantine churches; the most spectacular, 13th-century **Ag. Sophía** (in the town of the same name), is built from bits and pieces of a Temple of Aphrodite. There are lots of unsung ruins, too, and, at the end of the road, wonderful **ancient Thermon** (*a map in English at the entrance labels the important buildings*). Aetolía's premier archaeological site sits on a large plateau 1.5km from the modern town, a pleasant spot that was home to Mycenaeans and then morphed fairly seamlessly into a cult centre in historical times. By the 3rd century BC it was the fortified stronghold, capital and treasury of the Aetolían League, and home of a pan-Aetolian fair (with games). That lasted until the Macedonians and then the Romans snuffed out the league for good.

The elevated visitors' entrance is near the sanctuary's north gate. The main gate is still visible in the southeast wall, beyond two massive parallel **Hellenistic stoas** (540 and 567ft), which by the 3rd century BC boasted 2,000 or so statues and lots of treasure. This ancient Fort Knox was far too tempting to Philip V of Macedon, who impiously attacked in 218 BC and stole all of the portable treasure, callously burning the rest. The entrance is the best spot for a long view of the entire rectangular site, within the fortifications that failed so miserably, as well as a close-up of the 7th-century BC Archaic **Temple of Apollo Thermios** (40 by 124ft), one of the first Doric temples in Greece. It is covered by a tile roof now, held up by stubby round wooden cylinders, faint reminders of its tall wooden columns. Only column bases and the perimeter wall foundations were of stone; the rest, of mud bricks and wood, had to be protected from the elements by huge roof tiles and highly decorated clay revêtments, many of which are in the museum. Behind the temple are the stone foundations of sub-Mycenaean houses, distinguished by their aspidal back walls. A so-called Megaron B (matching the visible Megaron A), built in the 10th century BC, must have been a cult centre: when the Temple of Apollo Thermios was built on top of it, it followed the same north-south orientation, a deviation from the west-east norm that

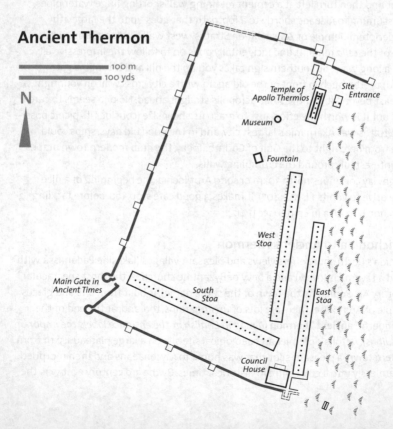

Ancient Thermon

100 m
100 yds

N

Temple of
Apollo Thermios

Site
Entrance

Museum

Fountain

West
Stoa

East
Stoa

Main Gate in
Ancient Times

South
Stoa

Council
House

cannot be easily explained otherwise. The **museum** (*t 264 402 2131; open Tues–Sun 9–2.30*) is a treasure trove of Archaic art, with brightly painted artefacts stacked on shelves, warehouse-style. The antifixes, small clay squares with painted Archaic smiling faces, are superb, as are vases from every era and clay metopes from the temple. There are bits of a Mycenaean boar's tusk helmet, too. The large square stone **fountain** in front of the museum still does the business with a substantial pool of cool spring water. For motoring thrills, take the back road to Prousós (*see* p.384) for Karpenísi.

Coastal Aetoloakarnanía

Messolóngi's shore road north passes the **Kálas Salt Works**, with lagoony pans and glittering white mountains of the stuff. Across a bridge, dense **Aetolikó** seems to be pressing its island foundation into the sea. Watch for the characteristic shallow-bottomed boats and square-rigged fishing nets. Attractive cafés and tavernas (even a modest old hotel) line up under the palms by the island's second bridge and the road to Astakós, where you soon cross the wide and elusive green Achelóos river, hard to spot in such flat country. Consider here a detour straight through workaday Katochí, and on to ancient Oiniádai.

Ancient Oiniádai

On the far side of Katochí, turn left into the road with a BP station on it. Down this road a short way, look on your right for a small sign recessed ridiculously far back and turn for 5km or so to the ruins (signposted properly, just when it doesn't matter).

Stone for Oiniádai's amazing 5km of polygonal **walls and towers** (5th–3rd century BC) was shipped down-river on the Achelóos. It was once a sea port and withstood Pericles in 454 BC, allied itself with Athens in 424, and was captured by rival Aetolía twice, once in 330 and once and for all in 260 – until Philip V of Macedon took over in 219, that is. The real master of Oiniádai, however, is the river. The Achelóos has embraced Oiniádai with so much silt over the centuries that it is now a low hill amid flat fields, fully 7km from the sea. The road past the guard's shelter leads to the fenced remains of a small 4th-century BC **theatre**. The flat road to the right leads around outside the walls and through a gate (just open it), to the massive, more evocative stone ramps hard against the citadel's ramparts. Substructures intact, these six **ship ramps**, once colonnaded and tile-roofed, stand at the ready – to launch vessels into surrounding fields. If the gate is locked, walk around the fence a bit.

Up the Ionian Coast: Astakós to Vónitsa

Pretty, clean-cut **Astakós**, set in a fjord-like bay, was once a mule train destination and is now a port for an intermittent ferry to Itháki and Kefaloniá. It has good water-front restaurants, an expensive hotel behind a postage stamp bathing beach and a nicer hotel hidden up by the old castle, with bird's eye views of the **Echinádes islands**

Tourist Information

Nikopoli Ellas Tour Agency, Páleros, 300 12, t/f 264 304 2114, *csoldato@otenet.gr*. From April to October, Christos Soldatos can find you rooms, cars, bikes and boats, or arrange day trips as far afield as Párga and Léfkada. In winter write to 17 Speliadou St, ✉ 49100 in Préveza, or try *www.nicopoli.com*. Ask him for a copy of the municipality's guide to the area in English.

Mýtikas: get info 'old style' at the Super Market of Mr Nikólaos Sideroménos (his kids speak English). He knows about rooms.

Where to Stay and Eat

Astakós ✉ 30006

Bungalows Lemon, t 264 604 2346, mobile t 693 283 2639 *(moderate)*. Up by the *kastro*. Large, modern studios in a garden with an unparalleled view. *Open April–Oct.*

Psarotavérna Spíros, t 264 604 6642. Serves a great and inexpensive fish soup, port-side with no cars allowed.

Mýtikas ✉ 30019

Mitika Hotel Apartments, t 268 204 1618, mobile t 694 646 2561, *MitikaHotelAp@ yahoo.com (expensive–moderate)*. New, friendly, roomy studios with garden 50m from sea. *Open April–Nov.*

Hotel Simos, t 264 608 1380, f 264 608 1245 *(C; inexpensive)*. Central, very sixties and plain as a fence post. *Open April–Oct.*

Akroyiáli, t 264 608 1206 *(E; inexpensive)*. Teensy, old-fashioned rooms in the town core, over the owner's seaside café. *Open April–Oct.*

Camping Alizia, t 264 608 1454. On a shingle beach 2km south of Mýtikas. Big, not fancy, with a summer taverna. *Open April–Oct.*

Vónitsa ✉ 30002

Bel Mare, seaside *plateia*, t 264 302 2563, f 264 302 2564 *(C; moderate)*. The nicest of the three hotels in town; its restaurant is popular year round.

O Faros, t 264 302 2410. A simple, local favourite; a seaside, shaded terrace near the *plateía*. Excellent *kalamáres*; good prices.

---

and the sea. The road from Astakós to Mýtikas is lovely. Simply gazing out to sea from **Mýtikas** itself is one of Greece's great experiences, looking towards sparsely populated **Kálamos Island**, its cone summit and forested slopes mirrored in the bay; no wonder Onassis wanted to buy it before settling for Skorpiós. A water taxi goes over several times a day; there are a few rooms to rent, and a pair of tavernas on the beach. In Mýtikas fishermen and tourists rub shoulders in cafés. It's the kind of spot old Greek hands love, like Mýkonos' little Venice, in pre-tourism days. Local fishing boats supply the tavernas and sport triangular flags that are placed in the water along with the nets. If the flags are low or submerged, it's time to haul up the catch.

Pretty **Páleros** is next, a tourist mecca on a hill with 300 beds on offer and a narrow sandy beach, a Párga (*see* p.417) in embryo thanks to Actium's airport, 28km away. Just north of town, the stubby **Plagiá Peninsula** stretches over to the ship canal and Lefkáda (*see* p.458). This route offers a great sandy beach at **Pogónia** (fronting the Paleros Club, UK package tours only), the obscure ancient site of **Kekropia** (for fanatics only) and wonderful views of Lefkáda from the eerie ghost village of **Plagiá**. Néa Plagiá and Ag. Varvára both have small Turkish castles spying on Léfkas. Sleepy little **Vónitsa**, on the Ambracian Gulf, is a cosy spot to while away a day or two, wandering through its attractive bijou Venetian castle, or swimming in town or at Panagía Beach 5km away. Vónitsa is 20mins by road from Lefkáda (*see* p.458) and the airport at Actium. From there, a 3km tunnel (toll) leads to Préveza, in Épirus (*see* p.415).

Épirus

13

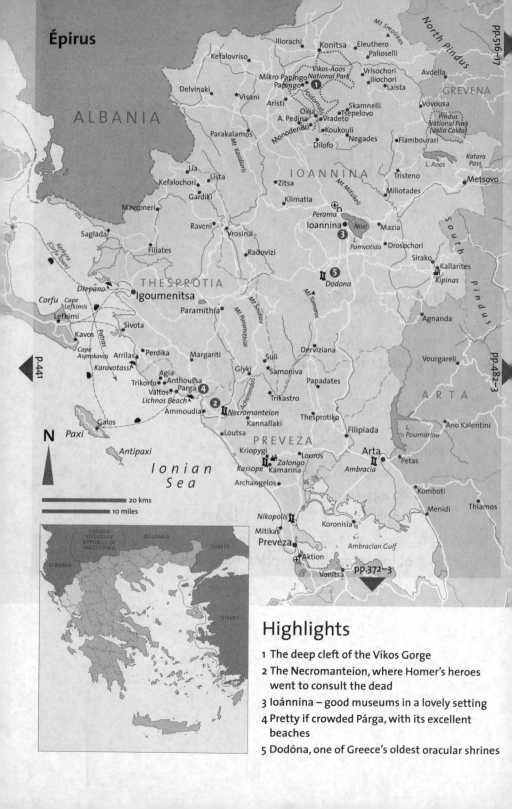

Épirus

Mt Smolikas
North Pindus
pp.516-17

Iliorachi   Konitsa   Eleuthero
Kefalovriso   Palioselli

Vikos-Aoos   Vrisochori
Mikro Papingo   National Park   Iliochori   Avdella
Papingo ①

Delvinaki   Visani   Laista   GREVENA

ALBANIA   Aristi   Skamnelli   Vovousa
          Oxia   Isepelovo   Pindus
        A. Pedina   Vradeto   National Park
Parakalamos   Monodendri   Koukouli   (Valia Calda)
          Negades   Flambourari
       Dilofo

      Katara
      Pass
Lia   IOANNINA   L. Aoos
Kefalochori   Lista   Tristeno
    Zitsa   Metsovo
Gardiki   Miliotades

Mavroneri   Raveni   Klimatia
        Perama
Saglada   Vrosina   Ioannina ③   Mazia   South
           Nissi
Filiates   Radovizi   L.   Drosochori
         Pamvotida   Sirako
              Kallarites
Drepano   ⑤   Kipinas
Corfu   Cape   Igoumenitsa   Dodona   Pindus
(Corfu Town)   Lefkimis
Lefkimi   Paramithia

Kavos   Sivota   Agnanda

Cape   Arrilas   Perdika   Margariti   Suli   Derviziana   Vourgareli
Asprokavos   Karavotassi
      Agia   Glyki   Samoniva   ARTA
p.441   Trikorfo   Anthoussa   Papadates
   Valtos   Parga ④
Lichnos Beach   ②   Trikastro
Ammoudia   Necromanteion   Thesprotiko   Ano Kalentini
Galos   Kannallaki   L.
N   Paxi   Loutsa   Filipiada   Pournariou
        PREVEZA
Antipaxi   Kriopygi   Louros   Arta   Petas
      Kassope   Zalongo   Ambracia
Ionian   Kamarina   Komboti
Sea   Archangelos   Menidi   Thiamos

20 kms
10 miles

Nikopolis   Koronisia
Mitikas
Preveza   Ambracian Gulf
Aktion   pp.372-3
Vonitsa

p.441
pp.516-17
pp.482-3
pp.372-3

Highlights

1 The deep cleft of the Víkos Gorge
2 The Necromanteíon, where Homer's heroes went to consult the dead
3 Ioánnina – good museums in a lovely setting
4 Pretty if crowded Párga, with its excellent beaches
5 Dodóna, one of Greece's oldest oracular shrines

Bounded by Albania on the north and the Ambracian Gulf on the south, beautiful Épirus has historically played as hard-to-get as a fairytale princess; the starched, vertical pleats of the Pindus range skirt her eastern side, an implacable barrier to admirers and assailants alike, while the breath from her malarial swamps along the Ionian Sea promised danger and death to those foolhardy enough to attempt her western defences. *Noli me tangere* could have been her motto, right up until the 20th century. Now modern roads have breached her mountain fastnesses, and determined agriculturalists have painstakingly tamed her swamps. Rapists or lovers? It's a matter of opinion, but the result has been to make her intricate, varied and extravagant beauty accessible to all. Although most come for the beaches around Préveza and Párga, the sheer glory of the lush green Pindus mountains and the stunning Víkos Gorge ensure a steady stream of hikers, kayakers, rock climbers and paragliders, along with birdwatchers and botanists. The archaeological sites – Roman Nikopolis, beautiful Kassope, the very ancient oak tree oracle at Dodóna and the oracle of the dead at the Necromanteíon – are choice. Yet even as Épirus yields to her suitors, she hasn't surrendered her soul: each corner has kept its personality, costumes, music and dialect, especially in the unique mountain villages of the Zagorochória, one of the most enchanting regions of Greece.

History

Impassable mountains and swampy coasts always discouraged civilization. The Mycenaeans were here, but not in force; in historical times, the Molossian tribe had royal dynasties and grandly claimed descent from Achilles, but Épirus' early history is pretty much a blank until the 7th century BC when wealthy Corinth took an interest, founding **Ambracia** (at present-day Árta) and other small cities. Except to visit Dodóna and the Necromanteíon, Classical Greeks didn't pay much attention to Épirus, nor did they write much about it. In 400 BC Tharypas, the Molossian king, tried to form a federation of states and raise the cultural level of his pastoral countrymen. **Olympias**, wife of Philip of Macedon and mother of Alexander the Great, came from this dynasty, a connection that would henceforth give the Macedonians a tie to and claim upon Épirus. In 307 BC **Pyrrhus** became king and instituted all the trappings of a respectable Hellenistic city-state. He took on the up-and-coming Romans in Italy won a few costly battles, but had to retreat, and died, never dreaming that *Pyrrhic victories* would become a byword for battles won at too high a price. Squeezed by Rome on one side and Macedonia on the other, the Epirótes threw in their lot with the latter. When they were trounced in 168 BC, they suffered Roman reprisals; 70 towns were levelled, thousands killed and 150,000 sold into slavery. Épirus never recovered and its villages were decimated again in 38 BC when Octavian needed citizens for **Nikopolis**, the grandiose city he founded after defeating Antony and Cleopatra at Actium.

The enforced pax romana didn't last long. After 90 BC, one horde after another decimated Épirus – Thracians, then Germanic tribes, the Bulgars in 502, then the Slavs, even Saracens (in 877), then Bulgars again, then the Normans. The only infiltrators to stay, aside from **Slavs**, were the **Vlachs**, nomadic shepherds who speak a Latin language (although every other fact about them is disputed) and who still live in

Épirus. After the capture of Constantinople in 1204, many Greeks fled to Épirus, and in 1205 Michael Angelos founded a breakaway Greek state, the **Despotate of Épirus**, with Árta as its capital. This gave the region a little breathing space, and a lot of new churches. In 1349 the Serbian kral **Stephan Dushan** had his Epiróte interlude. Then the local Albanians and Serbs entered the field, vying for the tattered football that was Épirus; both factions bolstered their sides with **Turks** who took the ball themselves in 1431 and played it better than most. Ottoman Épirus was actually prosperous, although there were uprisings by the Greek **Súliots**; the Venetians kept the pot boiling, as did the Great Powers. Ioánnina's **Alí Pasha** brought a kind of peace and prosperity until his death in 1822, then factionalism and rebellion reigned as the Épirótes tried to join the new Greek state they had helped create. Although the Árta area joined in 1881, the rest had to wait until 1913. That should have been the happy ending, but there was one last drama to be played.

On 28 October 1940 **Mussolini**, without provocation, invaded Greece through Épirus. The bulk of the Italian army moved to Kalpáki north of Ioánnina, while the rest infiltrated the mountains. The Epirótes joined the Greek army in defending their homes, the women carrying ammunition when the pack horses died of cold. It was a heroic effort and the Italians were driven back, a victory celebrated in Greece every 28 October as **Óchi Day**, the day Greece said 'no'. The Germans came in 1941 and burned towns and villages in reprisal for fierce resistance which just would not stop, leaving Épirus decimated in 1944, and the **Civil War** that followed completed the process. Nowadays the invaders are tourists, and Épirus has managed to take them in its stride, even if Párga does look under siege in August. At least these hordes have brought prosperity, and in their own way have made it possible for the Epirótes to continue living in their villages, just as they always have.

The Ambracian Gulf

The Ambracian Gulf, almost closed on its western end by the Préveza peninsula (where a new underwater tunnel makes getting around much easier), harbours fish, sea horses and jellyfish, including one bruiser that looks like a giant fried egg and can navigate, too. Octavian chose its sheltered waters to build his winner's city, Nikopolis, now an extensive ruin brooding just north of Préveza. Historic Árta, at the northeast end, is separated from open water by silt, marshes and shallow lagoons, favoured by thousands of migrating birds. And, speaking of that, a perfect bird's eye view of the gulf awaits the visitor from the heights of ancient Kassope.

Árta

Árta, capital of the long-gone Despotate of Épirus, displays glittering gems of Byzantine architecture in a very plain setting. It occupies a height in a loop of the Árachthos river with a large 13th-century castle firmly planted on classical blocks to the northeast; it would be impressive if the main highway to Ioánnina and Préveza

River Arachthos

200 m
200 yds

N

Kastro

P

P

PERIPHEREIAKH ODOS (RING ROAD)

AMVRAKIAS

KRYSTALLI

To
Bus Station

TZAVELLA

SKOUFA

Ag. Vasilios

PRIOVOLOU

Ag. Theodora

VASSILEOS PYRROU

PLATEIA
E. ANOISTASSIS

Church of
Constantinou
and Eleni

VASSILEOS KONSTANTINOU

SKOUFA

Theatre

Temple
of Apollo

PERIPHEREIAKH ODOS (RING ROAD)

PLATEIA
KILKIS

SKOUFA

Ag.
Parigoritissa

PLATEIA
SKOUFA

TZOUMERKON

Archaeological
Museum

To Bridge of Arta (600m),
Ioannina & Preveza

didn't occupy the same space. Motorists should park off the highway near the **castle** (the adventurous can follow signs to the 'κεντρο' and Plateía Kilkís for the few parking places there). Downtown Árta is compact; the walk down Pýrrou Street from the castle clock to Plateía Kilkís takes all of 20 minutes. En route you'll pass **Ag. Vasílios**, a small 13th-century church famous for its brick and tile decoration. Just past that to the right (near No. 27) look for **Ag. Theodóra**, built in the same era by Theodóra, wife of

Getting There and Around

Árta is easy to get to by **bus**. Eight daily connect it to Athens' Kifissós station (**t** 210 513 3139) and there is a regular service from Ioánnina, Préveza and Pátras. Árta's bus station, **t** 286 102 7348, is on the highway in Plateía Krystálli.

Taxis abound for the short trip to the centre. Radio taxis: **t** 268 107 8332.

Tourist Information

Árta tourist office: Plateia Krystálli, **t** 268 107 8551; *open Mon–Fri, 8–2.30.*

Where to Stay and Eat

Árta ✉ 47100

Staying in Árta has a certain charm, a bit of small-town life.

Hotel Cronos, Plateía Kilkís, **t** 268 102 2211, **f** 268 107 3795 (*C: moderate*). Large, plain, with TV, air-conditioning and balconies.

Taverna-Spíros Thomás, Plateía Kilkís, **t** 268 102 7708. Homey, red and white checks within, tables in the square without, where you can study an equestrian statue of King Pyrrus. Popular and friendly; great grilled food.

The En Arti...1887 Café. Upscale and in a great outdoor setting in Plateía Skoufá.

the Despot, with elaborate brick and tile work in its narthex. Recessed in its own little square (once it was surrounded by a monastery), it has no sign, perhaps because it is occasionally used for services. Inside, Theodóra's tomb has capitals snitched from Nikopolis. Just before Pýrrou Street flows into small **Plateía Kilkís**, the plain Byzantine **church of Constantínou and Eléni** is signposted on the left (beyond 'Pizza Venezi'). It shares a tiny square with a 4th–3rd-century BC **theatre**, now well below ground level. Árta is built over ancient Ambracia, bits of which appear whenever holes are dug; just beyond the theatre, practically in the square on Pýrrou Street, are the ruins of a 6th-century BC Temple of Apollo.

All this is prelude to Árta's jewel, the fabulous 13th-century **Panagía Parigorítissa** (*t 268 102 8692; open Tues–Sun 8.30–3; adm*), sitting pretty and alone by marble-tiled Plateía Skoufá, cornerwise to Plateía Kilkís. This unusual square church with imposing brickwork is topped by six cupolas (*trouli*), the central one on three tiers of ancient columns, each tier resting on the butt ends of two columns. The refectory houses a small **archaeological museum** with finds mostly from local cemeteries. The clay votives are lovely, including a terrific little cockerel. One case has the moulds from which many were made – votives were quite an industry in Árta. Even then, funerals were big business. There is a big bronze pail with a handle too, just to remind us that these people were farmers.

The famous **bridge of Árta**, a multi-arched bridge for packhorses built in the 17th century, is easily visible from the modern bridge at the west end of town. Legend and a popular song say that during its construction its tower piles collapsed each night until the master mason buried his wife in the foundations. Folklore, maybe, but even now in many villages chickens are slaughtered and their blood drained into the foundations of new structures. Maybe it's a good thing Árta has only one stone bridge.

The 27km road south to Koronisía (with fish tavernas) is a good way to visit the shallow lagoons of the **Ambracian Gulf Wetland Reserve**, one of the most important in Greece for rare birds and plantlife, hosting one of the last colonies of silver pelicans in Europe; the Amvrakikós Office of Environmental Awareness in Préveza, **t** 228 202 2224, has details.

Préveza, Nikopolis, Kassope and Zálongo

Préveza

Préveza's 20,000 citizens live in a new city by Greek standards, just 700 years old, decorated with a Venetian castle and a newer one built by Alí Pasha. Once a dull provincial town with so-so beaches, linked by a rust bucket car ferry with Actium, it appealed only to duck-hunters. But Préveza has improved. It now has a pretty waterfront along Venizélou Street closed off to traffic, popular tavernas lining its pedestrian streets, a good market area, and a brand new tunnel whisking visitors three kilometres from Actium (Aktion) to the south side of town. The swimming is not bad near Ag. Geórgios castle, south of town.

Nikopolis

t 268 204 1336; open daily 8.30–3; site free, museum adm.

Octavian trounced Antony and Cleopatra on 2 September 31 BC at Actium and promptly built his trophy, 'Victory city', on the site of his army camp, emptying most of Épirus and Aetoloakarnanía to populate it. He made it part of the Amphictyonic League, inaugurated the quadrennial Actian Games, and along the way gave Rome a base ideally located for her interests in the east. Nikopolis was a success. **St Paul** visited in AD 64 and wrote his epistle to Titus; in the 3rd century it had 300,000 inhabitants and the games were still going strong. It didn't begin to lose its lustre

Getting There and Around

Préveza's **airport**, t 268 202 2089, just south of the 'channel tunnel' at Actium (Aktion), gets plenty of regular charter flights from the UK and elsewhere, as well as daily local flights from Athens. The **bus station**, on Leofóros Irínis, t 268 202 2213, is 500m north of the port, with regular buses to Ioánnina, Igoumenítsa (95km), and Árta (47km). **Taxis**: t 268 202 2887. Parking's tough: try south of the pedestrian area.

Tourist Information

On the waterfront by the post office, t 268 202 8120; *open Mon–Fri 7–2.30 and 6–8, Sat 9–1.*

Where to Stay and Eat

Préveza ✉ 48100

Hotels here are open all year.

Magarona, t 268 202 4361, f 268 202 4369, *www.amalia.gr (B; expensive).* Préveza's best, 1km north on the waterfront road, with no beach but a nice large pool.

Avra, 19 El Venizelou St, t 268 202 1230, f 268 202 6484 *(C; moderate).* At the south edge of the waterfront walk. Modest and convenient; TV and air-conditioning.

Dione, Plateía Th. Papageorgiou, t 268 202 7381, f 268 202 7394 *(C; moderate).* Off Leof. Irinis, 10 minutes south of the bus station; quiet, and in walking distance of the port.

Alexandros Rooms, t 268 202 9454 *(inexpensive).* A real bargain; the nicest of a row of rent rooms out by the castle south of town. All have lawns leading to the sea.

Camping Kalamitsi, 4km north of town on the Igoumenítsa road, t 268 202 2192. With a pool.

Psátha, 2 Dardhanéllou, in the pedestrian centre. Every local swears by it, especially for its casserole dishes.

Taverna Ambrósios, nearby. Fish restaurant.

Nikopolis Club Restaurant, Monolithi Mýtikas, t 268 204 1985. Upscale bar-café-restaurant with a pool and views of the Ionian Sea that Octavian himself would have enjoyed.

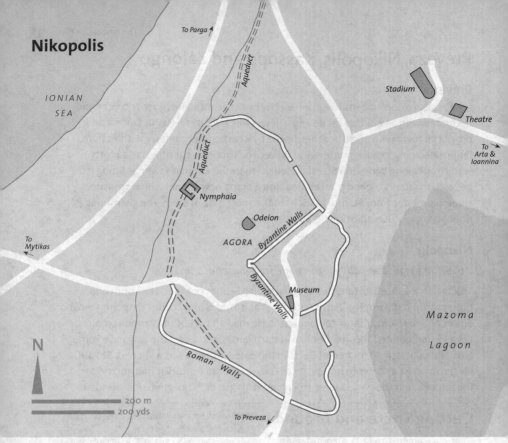

Nikopolis

IONIAN
SEA

To Parga ↑

Aqueduct

Aqueduct

Stadium

Theatre

To
Arta &
Ioannina

Nymphaia

Odeion

Byzantine Walls

AGORA

Byzantine Walls

Museum

Mazoma

Lagoon

To
Mytikas

Roman Walls

N

200 m
200 yds

To Preveza ↓

until the Goths invaded and Justinian had to refortify its core as a stronghold of last resort in the early 6th century. Even then, five good-sized basilican churches were built, proving that it had weathered that particular storm. Subsequent Slav invasions convinced the Byzantines, Nikopolis was too big and open a target, and more defensible Náfpaktos on the Corinthian Gulf became the new government seat.

The ruins of Nikopolis are melancholy although the countryside is grand; crumbling Roman brick is just not as attractive as Greek marble, and long, weed-choked grass adds to the sense of faded glory. The huge **theatre** is at the north end by the main road; its proscenium walls still stand as does some of its upper portico, where you can see holes for the canvas awnings to protect the audience, *à la* Sparta. The depression that was the stadium is just to the east. Further south, to the west of the Préveza road, the city stretches out; the best view of its massive and arched **walls** is from the side road to Mýtikas. The two-room **museum**, with Roman bits and pieces, is built inside the two right-angled walls added by Justinian. Near here, the 6th-century mosaics of the **Basilica of Doumetios** are unfortunately covered up, as are other fine mosaics of that era. Pass through the impressive gate in the Justinian wall east of the museum and you come to the once-covered **Roman Odeion**, still in a good state of preservation. Beyond it to the west are the ruins of two elaborate fountain houses, the **Nymphaia**, built opposite each other just inside the Roman walls. Even now they stand 27ft tall, and would have impressed newcomers arriving via Komares (today's Mýtikas), the city's port. The Nymphaia were the terminal of the **Nikopolis Aqueduct**. This aqueduct was an engineering marvel, and it's worth seeking out its pictur-esque, multi-tiered ruins arching over the Loúros river at **Ag. Geórgios**, 30km north on the Ioánnina road. Just south of that, signposted on the main highway, is the begin-ning of the **Nikopolis Tunnel** that took the water the rest of the way to the city. Clamber up to the top of it and you will be rewarded with another marvel: the remnants of the **red desert**, a dune-like formation, now partially covered in vegeta-tion, left over after Africa and Greece went their separate ways.

Kassope and Zálongo

8.5km north of Nikopolis on the coast road, a road diverges east 2.5km to Archángelos, and then up 10km via Kamarína to Kassope (signs) and Zálongo. It can also be reached from the Árta road, and from Glyki and Kannalláki via Kriopygí.

Kassope (*open 8.30–3 daily; adm free*) wasn't very important but is just plain pretty. A lovely walk through a pine forest leads to the entrance, where a sign in English explains the site's history. It became a city in the 4th century BC and was built on a Hippodamian grid that once boasted 500 houses. Their layout is still discernible past the agora, where you'll also find the perfectly preserved substructure (neat as an architect's plan) and lower polygonal walls of a building identified as a **Katagogeion** (hotel), or possibly a market. A small **Theatre** graced the slope just above. The remaining stoas, temples and so on pale in comparison with the view. The remnants of the small 2,000-seat **Odeion**, used for assemblies, provide a great spot to look over the entire Préveza–Árta plain 600 metres below. How did they ever concentrate on business? Perhaps that's why they stayed a minor Thesprotian city. Being forced to move to low-lying Nikopolis in 31 BC must have been traumatic.

While at Kassope look up to the east towards the monastery of **Zálongo** to see a row of women apparently ready to dance off the mountain top. That is exactly what they did in 1806. Sixty Súliot women and children, trapped by the Turks, chose this dance of death rather than be captured (*see* p.422). Go no closer.

Párga and the Coast

The highway from Préveza north to Loútsa passes resort after resort on an indented, lush and beautiful coast, and many are filling up with flats bought by foreigners, thanks to the proximity of Áctium's airport. But the beaches from Ammoudiá to Sívota are simply stunning, with Karavotássi, north of Párga, just maybe taking the prize. The attractive villages, Párga in particular, attract thousands of tourists, many of whom never leave their sunbeds. But there are treats in store for those who do. From the mysterious Necromanteíon to the fabled Súliot villages and the attractive castles studding greater Párga, coastal Épirus pulls out all the visual stops and still manages to accommodate nature in the marshes and the narrow Achérondas Gorge.

Getting There and Around

By bus: buses from Párga, **t** 268 403 1218, go several times daily to Igoumenítsa (47km), Préveza (60km), Athens and once to Thessaloníki. In summer 2 daily to Sívota via Pérdika, but not to Pérdika's beaches. There is no bus to Ammoudiá, but several a day to Kannalláki, from where buses go to Glykí.

By boat: ferries link Corfu and Párga two days a week. Water taxis connect Párga to Líchnos and Váltos beaches (about €3) all day. Caiques (about €9) to the Necromanteíon leave regularly from the town pier. Tour boats to Páxi leave every day except Saturday, fewer out of high season.

Port authority: **t** 268 403 1227.

By car: Párga's waterfront Anexartisías St is a pedestrian walk, splitting the driver's Párga in two. As the main highway descends almost to the sea, a road up and to the right goes to the town centre, and on to Váltos Beach. Continue down to the sea and you must turn left on Ag. Athanasíou in front of Krionéri Beach, a busy road that will eventually allow you to loop back to where you started. Parking is difficult; take what you can get and walk.

By taxi: rank on Al. Bága St, outside the OTE offices. Radio taxis: **t** 268 403 2332.

Tourist Information

Municipal tourist office, on the quay at 9 Anexartisías St, **t** 268 403 2107, **f** 268 403 2511, *parga@otenet.gr*. They offer a list of every room in the area, handy in high season. and a good map including the Achérondas Gorge. Also try *www.parga.gr*.

Synthesis Travel, 6 Al. Bága St, **t** 268 403 1700, **f** 268 203 1203, *synthesitr@otenet.gr*. Offers a rainbow of services, from booking ferries to car rentals, to tours (the Necromanteíon, the Achérondas river, Páxi, etc); plus itineraries for hikers, divers and mini-cruises with wine, or walks with snacks. *Open all year.*

Kanaris Travel, 51 Anexartisías St, **t** 268 403 1490, **f** 268 403 1977. On the quay; with a handy service point listing local bus schedules and prices. They also rent bicycles.

Internet café: Try the Terra Bar on the waterfront; *open 7.30am–3am.*

Sports and Activities

Párga has a diving club, waterskiing and parasailing on its larger beaches, along with canoe rentals and the like. In Glykí the Pony Club, **t** 266 604 1223, mobile 697 299 3744, offers rafting, tours through the gorge and riding (ponies for children).

Párga

A Venetian castle attractively set on a headland marks the west end of Párga, which then spills down to a quay packed with restaurants and bars as far as the narrow beach of Krionéri, which is separated by another mini headland from boulder-strewn Píso-Krionéri Beach. Its eastern boundary is still being defined by new development. Párga is not so much a town as a dense holiday village, its pleasant pastel, red-roofed houses hijacked by tour companies. The medieval stepped lane to the *kástro* is a shop-lined pedestrian highway to even more restaurants and bars and the pleasures of Váltos Beach. Two or three streets above Plateía Andístassis still harbour Greek homes, but most of the locals running the Párga machine live in outlying villages such as Ag. Kyriakí or Anthoússa. It sounds awful (and it is in August), but Párga is still as pretty as its setting. The 100 metres of water separating the beach from small Panagía Island may not be pristine, but there are other beaches nearby and the island and castle (lit up at night), combined with the dense vegetation and rocky headlands, are hard to beat. If restaurants use foreign names like Villa Rossa and Rudi's, rest assured that their Greek owners are just doing what Párga has always done: dealing with foreigners as best they can.

Where to Stay and Eat

Párga and Around ✉ 48060

Párga's hoteliers block-book some rooms but wisely keep others (usually with the best views) for independent travellers. Ignore the plaques of tour companies and go in and ask. All have balconies, the largest space you will have to yourself in high season. Expect big reductions in April and October. Book ahead in high season.

Pension Adam's Edém, t 268 403 2160, **f** 268 403 2690 (*expensive*). All mod cons in a rather grand building above a good-sized pool. Lots of olive trees and parking. Almost 1km from the beach on the road into town, though. *Open April–Oct.*

Villa Koralli, 7 Ag. Athanasiou St, **t** 268 403 1069, **f** 268 403 2469 (*low expensive*). Friendly, new, with a few parking spaces, on the road backing Krionéri Beach. The view of Panagía Island and the castle from the terrace is perfect. *Open all year.*

Rezi, 12 R. Fereou, **t** 268 403 1689, **f** 268 403 1627, *hotelrezi@otenet.gr* (*C; moderate–expensive*). Left on the road to the sea as you enter town. Just back from the beach, with a pool, and quieter than some. *Open May–Oct.*

Torini, t 268 403 1219 (*C; moderate, inexpensive off season*). One of many on Spíros Livadá St, up from the main *plateía*. Friendly and adequate. *Open all year.*

Angela, 12 Ag. Athanasiou St, **t** 268 403 1614, **f** 268 403 1927 (*moderate, inexpensive in off season*). Marvellous views; just its own garden and café terrace stand between it and Píso-Krionéri Beach. *Open April–Nov.*

Dolphin Apartments, Líchnos Beach, **t** 268 403 2439, **f** 268 403 2574 (*expensive*). Big rooms with kitchens, balconies with a fabulous view, and far enough up from the beach that you may enjoy their pool (kiddies' pool attached). *Open April–Nov.*

Gialós Rooms, Líchnos Beach, **t** 268 403 1979 (*inexpensive–moderate in Aug*). Simple rooms by the beach; well kept with nice owners. *Open April–Oct.*

Líchnos Camping, t 268 403 1171. Spills down the hill to what is effectively its own beach. Has a modern restaurant, big shop and rent rooms. *Open April–Oct.*

Párga has a lot of restaurants, but *adequate* comes to mind rather than *outstanding* – lots of fast food places, Italian restaurants and even a highly decorated Chinese one near the main square. Most are open from May to October. In winter, take what you can get.

Párga began as a precarious Norman settlement-cum-castle in the 12th century. A treaty with Venice was signed in 1401 to keep it from falling into Turkish clutches. The castle, with its Lion of St Mark above the gate, stayed Venetian with two brief interruptions (Barbarossa in 1537 and the Turks in 1571) until 1797 when the Turks took it again, only to lose it in 1801–7 when Párga had a brief fling at independence under Russian protection. Then the French had it, just long enough to build the fort on the island that crumbles so romantically today, followed by the British, who sold it to Alí Pasha. The Pargiótes were paid compensation, but being forced to move to Corfu did not sit well. When Párga joined Greece in 1913 its citizens returned, bringing their flag and icons. The annual *Barcarole* on 15 August re-enacts the return of these *Holy Articles* in a nautical torchlight parade followed by fireworks.

Beaches and Castles in and around Párga

Long, wide, and sandy, **Váltos Beach** is immediately west of Párga and linked by a footpath from the **Venetian castle** (*open all day; free*), itself worth a visit for its tranquillity and views. **Líchnos Beach,** 4km east, is a spectacular, south-facing sandy bay with a fabulous view of Ammoudiá's dune-like headlands over the water. Water taxis

Rudi's, t 268 403 1693. Yellow neoclassical decor on the quay. Good food and good service at higher than average prices.

Villa Rossa, t 268 403 1952. On Krionéri Beach, with two potted shrubs trimmed as dolphins flying through hoops. The same ingenuity is not lavished on the food but it is good, as are the prices. Try the ostrich steaks, fresh from a farm in the hills.

Romantic, by the castle, **t** 268 403 1944. Run by the Rizos family, with a stupendous view of Váltos Beach and a large menu of traditional Greek fare.

Argo, Platéia Andístassis, **t** 268 403 1238. In a central square that still has character near Vizinoú St. Nice at night.

Gialós, Líchnos Beach, **t** 268 403 1979. A terrific traditional taverna with home cooking by mom, right on the beach presided over by the charming Kyriákis family. It is big, but the family take that in its stride, and the view from the terrace is great.

Tango Club, Váltos Beach, **t** 268 403 1252. A restaurant–pool–café complex that has good food and an upscale atmosphere.

Ammoudiá and Glykí ✉ 48062

Ammoudiá's vast apartment complexes are not very appealing, but the pension at nearby inland Glykí is.

Pension Bournás, t 266 604 1416 (*moderate*). Eleven new, large studios over a very good restaurant right by the river. A summer disco is the rub. *Open all year.*

Pérdika ✉ 46030

Regina Mare, t 266 509 1560, **f** 266 509 1118, *regina@otenet.gr* (*A; luxury*). 120 rooms spread in gardens on a hill facing the sea; a cable car to Karovotássi Beach! *Open full tilt April–Oct, diminished amenities in winter.*

Sívota ✉ 46100

Sívota Travel, t 266 5093264, **f** 266 509 3355, *info@sívotatravel.gr*, can help with rooms.

Méga Ámmos, t 266 509 3447, **f** 266 509 3305, *sesi@compulink.gr* (*B; expensive*). A hotel–bungalow complex 2km south of Sívota's centre within a 2-minute walk of small Méga Ámmos Beach. You would need a car. *Open April–Oct.*

Hellas, t 266 509 3227, **f** 266 509 3294 (*E; inexpensive–moderate*). Very simple, in the centre; for bargain hunters. *Open May–Oct.*

Trehantiri, t 266 509 3232. Fish restaurant on the quay. *Open all year.*

George's Family Restaurant, t 266 509 3266. Dishes out great green beans and stuffed tomatoes with the same great view on the quay. *Open all year.*

are the best way to go; parking is almost impossible, and pricey. There are other, less crowded beaches, all marked on the maps handed out by the municipality. **Alí Pasha's castle**, picture-perfect, was built to make sure the town knew who was boss by an Italian engineer in 1814. It looms high over Párga and can be reached from Váltos by a footpath. **Anthoússa**, north, sports another castle, accessible from the Tríkorfo road.

South of Párga

The approach to the **Achérondas Delta** offers a vista of flat agricultural land, punctuated by the raw new tourist town of Ammoudiá, which almost but not quite spoils the lovely sandy beach where the river flows into the sea. Part of the delta, still willow- and cane-bordered marsh, is a Natura 2000 site, where 150 species of birds, along with otters, turtles, foxes and badgers and 450 species of flora, draw naturalists in spring and autumn. A swampy lake in ancient times, the draining of the delta's malarial waters in the 1950s has turned the Shrine to Hades and Persephone from an island near ancient Ephyra into a knobby hill beside the Igoumenísta–Préveza highway. Better known as the **Necromanteíon**, visitors once came here in trepidation to communicate with departed loved ones.

The Necromanteíon

Open daily 8–3; adm. The site is well signposted from the highway, but the nicest way is to go by boat up the Achérondas, now a pleasant narrow river.

The Oracle of the Dead developed early. In Homer, Odysseus came to its 'wild shore' to consult the seer Teiresias about how to get home. Suppliants underwent complicated rituals, including a special diet, animal sacrifices, all-night vigils and maybe hallucinogenic drugs before being led through a dark labyrinthine corridor and lowered by winch into a vaulted underground chamber. Flanged bronze rings and ratchet wheels belonging to this mechanism are in the Ioánnina museum. Exactly what transpired is not known. Corinth's tyrant Periander sent envoys to contact his wife Melissa. He had misplaced something given him in trust when she was alive and couldn't find it anywhere. So she was raised from the dead to answer the archetypal male question: 'Honey, what did you do with the...?' She told him, but only after he had guaranteed her a new wardrobe.

The **ruins**, topped by the small 18th-century church of Ag. Ioánnis, were discovered in the 1950s by Sotiris Dakaris and date from the late 4th to early 3rd century BC. There are three rooms on the left of a corridor, which may have been where suppliants stayed; bones and ash found in the long corridor at right angles to this suggest ritual animal sacrifices. Another right-angled turn leads to the small labyrinth, and right again to the central chamber, 72ft square with very thick (11ft) polygonal walls and adjacent storerooms. Disappointingly, the winch has been replaced by a metal stair. Some have suggested that this is not the Necromanteíon at all but the foundations of a Hellenistic tower fort, with a catapult (the bronze bits), an underground cistern and clay storage pots in case of siege. Well, archaeology is not able to answer all questions, but the matter could be settled easily if we could just contact Melissa. While on the hill, squint and you can see the shores of the old lake.

The Achérondas Gorge and the Súliot Villages

The Achérondas river runs through attractive country for all of its 64 kilometres, but when it turns north near **Tríkastro**, up to the small stone **Dala bridge** (opposite Samoníva), and then west as far as Glykí, a narrow gorge makes it one of the most beautiful rivers in Greece. The gorge is accessible, too; a 10km (4 to 4½ hours) trail follows its rim from Tríkastro. At **Glykí**, the little town at the gorge's mouth (most easily reached from the Necromanteíon via Kastrí and the market town of Kannalláki), the green river widens and meanders placidly to the sea; summer restaurants place tables on its shady gravel bed. A second trail from Glykí (a bit over an hour) goes past the Dala bridge and up to **Samoníva** and **Kiáfa castle**, brooding against the hillside. In summer many people wade down the river narrows (6–8 hours; swimming is required in places; go on a tour or with plenty of company), and rafting is popular in spring. A less strenuous wading experience can be had from Glykí up to the **Dragon's Cave** (Spiliá tou Drákou). The water is cold.

A road just north of Glykí will also get you up to the **Súliot villages**, including Samoníva. In the 16th century, these 11 remote villages formed the Súliot Federation,

12,000 members strong, and all dedicated to freedom from the Turks. They were an ornery lot, and their consistent resistance has made them popular heroes today. A blood and thunder film called 'The Súliots' is shown like clockwork every 25 March (Independence Day) on Greek television. Their independence lasted until 1803 when Alí Pasha dislodged them, only to ally himself with them 17 years later against the Sultan. The Sultan prevailed in 1822, and the vanquished Súliots abandoned their villages, strongholds and curiously shaped wells forever. Even today, only a few old-timers and romantics inhabit this once powerful stronghold.

North of Párga to Sívota

The coastal road past Párga's Váltos Beach is lined with rent rooms and olive trees right up to **Anthoússa**, a pleasant village full of the same that takes the overflow from Párga. After **Tríkorfo** the road ascends through barren windswept **Agía**, which incredibly has one pension (for Heathcliff and Cathy?) and down again through olive groves to clean-cut **Pérdika** (Partridge town). A tourist stopover perched high above the sea, Pérdika is at the junction of the road to sandy **Arrílas** and **Karavotássi** Beaches (taxis will take you there). The main road past Pérdika offers bird's-eye views of the indented coast north to **Sívota**. Tucked in a small bay on the northern pod of an amoeba-shaped headland, Sívota hides its charms until you arrive at its wide flagstoned quay lined with palms, old-fashioned street lamps, restaurants and coffee shops. It is more upmarket than Párga and a lot smaller. But it is growing, with travel agencies, a water taxi for the sand beaches nearby, a boat service to Páxi, and lots of fairly pricey rooms. There is no beach in Sívota proper, but there is a busy one within walking distance.

Igoumenítsa

Igoumenítsa calls itself the gateway to Europe, but most tourists think of it as the back door to Greece. Its busy port is the third largest in the country, and its 10,000 inhabitants quite like their home, but there is no compelling reason to stay unless your ferry leaves or arrives at an awkward time (most do). If you have hours to wait, try **Drépano Beach** (snack bars) 5km west of Igoumenítsa and serviced by city buses, or head south by car to **Kalámi Beach** (9km).

Igoumenítsa to Ioánnina

The road to Ioánnina is a yawner by Greek standards, but a pleasant stopover can be made at **Vrosína**, an old-fashioned village in a dip in the road that has a stone bridge over its river and several reasonably priced restaurants (try *The Vrosina* (Η Βροσηνα), **t** 265 803 1234). There is a tempting detour north of Vrosína to **Lía** (Λια), 24km away, (the town made famous by Nicholas Gage in *Eléni*); it is a picturesque drive on an unpaved road via Ravení (Ραβένη), Gardíki (Γαρδικι) and Kefalochóri (Κεφαλοχωρι). Return (or go) via Lísta (Λιστα) on a paved road; both roads terminate in Vrosína. Lía takes you a few kilometres from the Albanian border, and back in time. It takes three hours, with a coffee break in Lía.

Getting Around

The waterfront has a long north–south axis. **Ethnikís Andístassis St** backs the **Old Port** and has banks and travel agencies galore where tickets for Italy can be bought. Tickets to Corfu are sold on the quay in the Old Port. As Ethnikís Andístassis heads south, it turns into **Ag. Apolstólou St**, backing the **Corfu Ferry Docks**, and then the **New Port** which is still under construction. Signs in English attempt to route ferry passengers; ask where yours leaves from when you buy your ticket.

By bus: 47 Kípou, t 266 502 2309, with nine daily buses to Ioánnina; five to Athens and Párga; two to Préveza and Thessaloníki.

By sea: ferries to Italy are: Ancona: 2 per day (24hrs), Bari: 1–2 per day (12hrs), Brindisi 4–6 per day (8hrs), Venice 1–2 per day (25hrs). For **Corfu**, there are 21 ferries a day from 7.30am to 10pm. **Port authority**: by the Customs offices, t 266 502 2235.

Car rental: Budget, 14 Ag. Apostolou St, t 266 502 6226, f 266 502 7949.

Tourist Information

EOT in the Old Port by the customs offices, t 266 502 2227; *open 7–2.30.*

Where to Stay and Eat

Igoumenítsa ✉ 46100

Angelica Palace, 145 Ag. Apostólou, t 266 502 6100, f 266 502 2105 (*B; expensive*). On the Sívota road. As good as it gets, with a pleasant atrium. *Open all year.*

Actaeon, 17 Ag. Apostólou, t/f 266 502 2330 (*C; moderate*). Business hotel, recently built, with TV. *Open all year.*

Stavrodromi, 14 Soulio, t 266 502 2343 (*E; inexpensive*). The best budget hotel; inside the town over its own restaurant. *Open all year.*

Camping Kalami Beach, t 266 507 1211 (*inexpensive*). By a nice beach. *Open April–Oct.*

As far as eating out is concerned, words fail. Try *souvlakis* and pizzas, or a good bakery. The locals go to outlying villages like Sívota.

Ioánnina

Ioánnina, a sophisticated university town of 100,000 and the commercial and cultural centre of northwest Greece, is beautifully situated on a plateau 600m above sea level, with a picturesque citadel jutting into the shallow waters of Lake Pamvótis. Full of garden-like *plateías*, it has an island anchored off its leafy shore exactly where any landscape architect would have placed it. With excellent museums and remnants of its fascinating past, Ioánnina also makes a great base for the Pérama Caves, Dodóna and its beautiful surrounding villages.

History

Named after a monastery to John the Baptist, Ioánnina was founded *c.* AD 527. It didn't get its first official mention in Constantinople till 879, then stayed out of the limelight until the disastrous Crusade of 1204, when refugees crowded in from Constantinople and the Peloponnese. Fortifications began in earnest in 1205, after Michael I Comnenus Ducas founded his breakaway Byzantine state, the Despotate of Épirus, and made Ioánnina the second city after Árta. Churches and monasteries were founded in and around Ioánnina, a trend that would continue after 1335 when the Despotate reunited with the ragtag remnants of the Byzantine empire. In 1430 it surrendered to the army of Sultan Murad II, a defeat which marked the beginning of Ioánnina's golden age. Under the Sinan-Pasha's Declaration of 1430, Murad granted Ioánnina tax privileges, left its churches entirely alone and even placed the *kástro* off limits to Turks, a privilege that a Christian rebellion in 1618 put paid to. But in spite of

Ioánnina

Lake Pamvotida

Aslan-Pasha Mosque
(Municipal Museum &
Fotis Rapakousi Museum)

Boats to Nissí Island

To Airport,
Perama Caves,
Zagori &
Igoumenitsa

PAPAGOU

PAMVOTIDOS

PAPANDREOU

EVANGELIDOU

KOUDOURIOTOU

KARAMANLIS

KASTRO

A. PALEOLOGOU

Silver
Collection

Victory
Mosque

Byzantine
Museum

ZOSIMADON

ANEXARTISSIAS

Bus
Station

Old
Bazaar

PLATEIA
GEORGIOU

TSIRIGOTI

KORAI

VYRONOS

AVEROF

28 OKTOVRIOU

M. BOTSARI

KOLETTI

AVEROF

Archaeological
Museum

Litharitsia
Park

GARIVALDI

Popular Art
Museum

M. ANGELOU

POL

Tourist
Police

PLATEIA
DEMOKRATIAS

METSOVOU

KATSARI

PLATEIA
PYRROU

NAPOLEON ZERVAS

Olympic
Airways

VIZANIOU

Bus
Station

DODONIS

PLATEIA
TZAVELA

To Dodona,
Arta & Athens

N

200 m
200 yds

that glitch, Ioánnina and its district remained wealthy and relatively free compared to
southern Greece. Silver guilds thrived; churches were frescoed by painters adept
enough for critics to refer to a school of Epiróte painting. Educational institutions
sprang up using easily available Greek books, and wealthy families sent their children
abroad for schooling or on business. Greek women had quite a lot of freedom, too,
given the times, although they did not always use it in edifying ways. One contemporary wrote that fashionable ladies waddled in the streets, just like geese.

By the time Alí Pasha took over in 1788 Ioánnina was booming, with a population
of 35,000, of which only 5,000 were Turks. He managed to get the fortress into

A Little Orientation

Plateía Pýrrou, high above the lake, is the core of this expanding city. It spills into **Áverof Street**, with innumerable shops selling Ioánnina's famous silverware, icons, bowls and every imaginable type of jewellery. Towards the bottom, a rabbit warren of streets on the left is all that remains of Ioánnina's **bazaar**. As Áverof turns into **Karamanlís Street**, the gate leading into Ioánnina's *kástro* comes into view on the right. This fortress, with impressive walls which once dropped directly into the limpid waters of the lake, is still a vital precinct of the city, and easier to reach now that the moat has been filled in. Its quiet cobbled lanes are filled with houses, mostly built after 1900, but with architectural hints of their medieval predecessors. Karamanlís Street ends at student cafés by the lake and landing where boats leave for the island. These cafés, all offering table games, are great places to soak up the local atmosphere. The tree-lined lakefront street to the right leads all around the *kástro*.

splendiferous shape by 1809, in time to impress Byron. The burning of Ioánnina in 1820, some say by Alí, others by the Sultan's forces, marked the decline of the city's fortunes. In 1878, the Congress of Berlin assigned Ioánnina and the rest of Épirus to Greece, but nobody took them up on it until 21 February 1913. This late start has left Ioánnina's lakeside *kástro* with its minarets intact, a rare exotic eastern touch.

Nissí: Ioánnina's Island

Boats leave from the quay by the kástro every half-hour from 7am to 11.30pm in summer (10pm in winter) and cost around €1 each way. In summer, the 'En Plu', looking as if should be on the Seine in Paris, offers dinner cruises.

Ioánnina's reed-fringed wooded island is a popular destination. The small white-washed houses that greet you on the quay, all with typical Epiróte white lace curtains, are the remains of a settlement of Maniátes who sought refuge here in the 16th century. These 'protected' houses can only be handed down to family members now, so there is a certain clannish solidarity among the residents. Trout, frog's legs and other goodies are on offer at a cluster of restaurants. Although they say the lake struggles with pollutants these days, the frog population seems to be coping, and it's hard not to feel a little guilty listening to them croaking while a steaming plate of their comrades is delivered to the table. A wide footpath circles the island. Just east of the village is the small 16th-century **Pandeleímonos Monastery** (*open 8am–8pm; adm*) where visitors come to see the holes in the floor made by the bullets which ended the life of Alí Pasha. Some Alí paraphernalia make up a small 'museum'. Close to it, the attractive façade of the monastery of **Ioánnou Prodrómou** has parts going back to the 13th century and 19th-century frescoes. A longer and more interesting walk, west of the village, takes in the churches of **Ag. Nikoláou Philanthrópinon**, **Ag. Stratigopoúlou Dilíou** and **Ag. Eleoússas** (*closed during the siesta*). Parts of Ag. Nikoláou date back to the 13th century. Its fine frescoes are from the Turkish occupation, more tactfully referred to as the 'Post-Byzantine Era', when the local school of painting was at its height; in the additions of 1560, Solon, Aristotle and Plutarch were

Getting There and Around

By air: Ioánnina airport, **t** 265 102 6218, is 4km north on the Kónitsa road. Olympic has connections to Athens twice most days and to Thessaloníki five days a week. In town, contact Olympic, 1 Napoléon Zérvas, **t** 265 102 6218.

By bus: the station for Athens (450km), Thessaloníki and Igoumenítsa, is at 4 Zosimádon St, **t** 265 102 6211, five short blocks north and one west of Plateía Pýrrou. The bus station for Préveza, Pátras and Dodóna is at 19 Vizaníou St, just south of Plateía Pýrrou, **t** 265 102 2014. Local buses, **t** 265 102 2239, depart from Plateía Pýrrou; nos. 1, 2 and 7 ply the airport route every 15mins from 6.30am to 10.30pm; 8 and 16 do the same to Pérama.

By car: For parking, try the waterfront or inside the *kástro*. All car rental agencies are represented. Budget is at 109 Dodónis St, **t** 265 104 3901, **f** 265104 5382.

By taxi: cruising taxis abound, or hang about the castle entrance on Karamanlís St. For radio taxis: **t** 265 104 6777.

Tourist Information

EOT: 39 Dodónis St, near the Xenia hotel, **t** 265 104 8442; *open Mon–Fri 7.30–2.30 all year, in July & Aug Mon–Fri 5.30–8.30 and Sat 9–1.* A summer information kiosk is open all day lakeside by the island water taxis.

Tourist police: 28 Oktovríou St, just off Plateía Demokratías, **t** 265 102 5673; *open 8am–9pm every day.*

Central post office: 28 Oktovríou St, by Plateía Pýrrou; *open Mon–Fri, 7.30–8.*

Bookstore: Papasotiríou, 6 M. Angélou St, **t** 265 106 4000. An excellent selection of books on Épirus in English.

Where to Stay

Ioáninna ✉ 45221

Hotels here are open all year. For inexpensive rooms, try Pérama's main street.

Du Lac, t 265 105 9100, **f** 265 105 9200, *www. dulac.gr (A; luxury).* By the lake, a long walk south of the *kástro*; done up in a pleasant, pared-down Epiróte style with pool and a neutral air that convention-orientated hotels acquire.

Xenia, 33 Dodónis, **t** 265 104 7301/5, **f** 265 104 7189 (*B; expensive*). Privatized and renovated; package tour comforts without pool. Its great virtue is the garden setting right in the middle of town and the parking facilities.

Kástro, 57 Andréas Paleológou, **t** 265 102 2866, **f** 265 102 2780, *www.epirus.com/hotels. kastro (B; expensive).* A lovely renovated old house with seven rooms inside the *kástro*; perfectly located, quiet, well run and with easy parking. The rooms for three on the second floor are terrific. (Enter by the *kástro*'s sea gate, past the island boats, and follow signs to the Byzantine museum).

Astoria, Áverof & 2a Paraskevópolis, **t** 265 102 0755, **f** 265 107 8410 (*C; moderate–expensive*). Standard businessman's hotel with a good

added to the usual Orthodox worthies – not the first time ancient Greeks have been lovingly placed in the company of saints. They look quite at home.

The *Kástro* and Its Museums

The *kástro* took its present shape when taken in hand by Alí Pasha early in the 19th century. It boasts two heights. The largest, on the southeast, is **Its-Kale** (Turkish for 'inner fortification'). Entered through an impressive gate (*open 8am–10pm; adm free*), it is like a park, with views that must have been appreciated by all of Alí's visitors. His palace and seraglio were here. To fit them in, he flattened part of the hill and incorporated a Norman round tower, the calling card of Bohemond who passed through in the 11th century but didn't have Alí's staying power. The **cook house** with its four distinctive round and multi-sided chimneys, has been nicely transformed into a café

central location, offering parking next door for €3 a day.

Tourist, 18 Kolétti, t 265 102 6443, f 265 102 0002 (*C; moderate*). Off Áverof St right behind the Metropolis Hotel; adequate, clean, with cheaper rooms without bath.

Metropolis, Áverof & 2 C. Kristáli, t 265 102 6207 (*C; inexpensive*). Ioánnina's nicest budget hotel in a neoclassical building. Shared baths, marble halls, and lots of street noise unless you ask for a room at the back.

Sotiris Dellas Pension, Nissí, t 265 108 1494, f 265 107 9380 (*inexpensive*). Near the boat landing; the only rooms on the island, two of which are en suite. Even with the fare to the island, these simple rooms are a bargain.

Camping Limnopoúla, Kanári 10, 455 00, t 265 102 5265, f 265 103 8060. Ioánnina's only campsite, on the road to Pérama.

Eating Out

In Ioánnina, where life doesn't revolve around tourism, the best restaurants are often closed in July and August. Aside from Plateía Pýrrou and its views, it's a good idea to head for the lakeside at the bottom of Áverof and Karamanlís Sts. The many coffee shops and ouzeries under the plane trees in Plateía Mavíli are local favourites. Go past them (away from the *kástro*) until you come to the row of popular restaurants on Pamvótidos St whose look-alike terraces fringe the lake. Don't forget to sample Dodóni ice cream.

Agnánti (Αγναντι), 2 Pamvótidos, t 265 102 4200. Try this one for fish, and snacks.

Límni (Λιμνη), 26 Pamvótidos, t 265 107 8988. Has very reasonable prices, perhaps because you have to pass so many others in between.

Nyssi, t 265 108 1253. Near the landing; Panagiótis Xaratsáris' taverna is one of the most popular on Ioánnina's island. Like others, it specializes in trout and frog's legs, along with more traditional Greek fare.

Evi, 4 Plateía Neomártyros Georgíou, t 265 107 3155. A hole in the wall catering to students and tourists, at the bottom of Áverof St. There are seats outside.

Presveía, 17 Karamanlís, t 265 102 6309. Typical of the many trendy beer bar-restaurants in this area catering to young people. It has lots of pricy imported beer, inexpensive food, and live entertainment late in the evening.

ES-AEI, 50 Koundouriótou, t 265 103 4571. The best room is the glassed-topped, stone-walled back garden with fireplace, and bric-a-brac-from Ioánnina's past. They offer snack plates with different meats, cheeses or other specialities so you can try a lot at one sitting. *Open eves only; closed June–Aug.*

Gástra, Leof. Kostáki-16a Eleoúsa, t 265 106 1530. Six km from the *kástro* gate, past the airport, on the Kónitsa road opposite the Dodóni ice cream factory. All Ioánnina comes to this large restaurant for *gástra*, tender lamb or kid titbits that fall off the bone after being cooked in large round casseroles (made originally of clay) in a special oven on the terrace. The food is placed in the oven, and a lid full of burning coals is lowered over it to do the cooking. *Open all year, lunch and dinner, but don't arrive before 9pm.*

and there's a **Byzantine Museum** (*t 265 102 5989; open daily 8am–7pm, Mon 12.30–7; adm*), built in 1958 to resemble an Epiróte mansion of Alí's era. It displays art (with English explanations) into the 19th century, but no matter. An adjacent building (*same ticket, but open 8.30–3, closed Mon*) houses a large **silver collection** with explanations of guilds and the silver market. Buyers came from as far afield as the Roumanian Principalities and Russia, and master craftsmen, like the Kouyoumtzídes family of Kalarrýtes, grew wealthy supplying them. Its-Kale contains the nicely proportioned Fetihie Cami, or **Victory Mosque**, built in 1611 (remodelled in 1795) and the modest **tomb of Alí Pasha**, topped by a black metalwork cage. It is hard to decide if it's intended to commemorate Alí or to keep his restless spirit firmly underground.

A five-minute walk through the *kástro*'s streets takes you to the so called **northeast height**, once site of the Byzantine palaces. Past a ruined cook house, stacked cannon

Everybody's Favourite Despot: Alí Pasha (1744–1822)

I talk not of mercy, I talk not of fear
He neither must know who would serve the Vizier:
Since the days of our prophet the Crescent ne'er saw
A chief ever glorious like Ali Pashaw
                    Byron, *Childe Harold's Pilgrimage*, 1812

Many historians present Alí Pasha as simply another in the series of ruthless, cruel double dealers created and fostered by the chaotic, despotic Ottoman empire. But Alí, who defies neat definition, was much more. Born in Tepelini (in present day Albania), he began as a well-connected bandit with a terrifying Greek mother, Khamco, who could have shown the Hell's Angels a thing or two and was the source, Alí said, of his early dreams of 'power, treasure, and palaces'. He helped the Sultan in the war of 1787 against Austria and got appointed pasha of Tríkala for his pains. But Alí wanted Ioánnina. He curried favour with the local Greeks and then forged a decree from the Sultan who, short-handed at the time, honoured it. He ably administered Ioánnina, at the same time swallowing Préveza (1798) and having the poor Súliots for dessert (1803). Aided by his sons, Veli and Mukhtar, he instituted a rough and ready order in his expanding territories which at one point included much of present-day Albania, Épirus, Macedonia, Thessaly and even the Peloponnese. By 1807, this charming, wily sociopath was more a king than Sultan's representative, allying himself with the French when it suited him or the British, who gave him Párga in 1817.

Illiterate, but clever enough to employ the wealthy, literate Greeks he admired, Alí created a court that, when it suited him to thumb his nose at the Sultan, hosted Greek freedom fighters Karaiskákis, Botsáris and Androútsos, and intellectuals such as Kollétis. He was called the 'Lion of Ioánnina' and he *was* lionized by the many

balls and the narrow, colonnaded **Medresse** (Ottoman seminary), the **Municipal Museum** (*t 265 102 6356; open daily, summer 9–4, winter 8–3; adm; an A4 sheet in English is handed out to visitors*) occupies the **Aslan-Pasha mosque**. Built in 1618, with a well-proportioned dome, it functioned until 1928 and still has recesses in the vestibule for the shoes of absent worshippers. It holds a somewhat tired and eclectic collection of Epiróte costumes and everyday objects of the Christian, Jewish and Muslim communities. The collection is overshadowed by the wonderful **Fótis Rapakoúsi Museum** (*same hours; adm free*), opened in 2001 in the small Medresse. Mr Rapakoúsi, a dynamic Danny De Vito lookalike, speaks no English, but the collection speaks for itself. Fabulous *spathiá* (swords) and *enxeirídia* (daggers) share space with an amazing array of firearms, including muskets with balls the size of hen's eggs, an efficient looking 19th-century switchblade with a deer-foot handle and two *cheirovomvídes* (hand grenades) that look like festive candles. Especially interesting are the silver *baláskes* (shot holders), shaped like and worn somewhat like Scottish sporrans from the belt, and the small intricately decorated *medoulária* (tiny square containers holding grease, for cleaning the guns). These beautifully mounted,

foreign Philhellenes who came his way. These included Byron (1809), who was especially susceptible to Ali's blend of magnetic charm and amoral cruelty. Visiting Ali's sumptuous court, with its blend of oriental barbarism veneered with Hellenic sophistication, became something of a literary industry, and his hospitality was as effusive as his pockets were deep. Even today, when Greeks want to say that they have it made, they will invariably say that they are like the 'Pasha in Ioánnina'.

His horrendous crimes were legendary even in his own time. He roasted an enemy of his mother's on a spit, to honour her dying wish. In 1801 he drowned Kyra Frosyni, a Greek woman who rejected his advances, by throwing her along with seventeen companions into the handy lake, and he had Katsandónis, a prominent Greek independence fighter, publicly executed by breaking every bone in his body with a sledgehammer. Considering the atrocities Ali admitted to, along with some apocryphal ones, he has had amazingly good press. And when all is said and done, Ali Pasha was good for Ioánnina, and not as hated in his lifetime as some historians have made out. He did not consider himself, nor was he then considered, as much an outsider as the British, or French, or even some of the more sophisticated expatriate Greeks who visited.

The Sultan, not the Greeks, ended his amazing career. He began by placing Ioánnina under siege and burning it in 1820. Ali, who never believed there was a corner he couldn't get out of, waited on Ioánnina's island for a pardon that never came. He was executed in 1822 and the Sultan insisted on his head being sent to the Porte, just to be sure. Ali's resistance to the Sultan gave Greeks the opportunity to start background planning for their own uprising and, in some cases, the venue to plot it. Perhaps that is why many Greeks look on him with a certain affection today. Most portraits displayed in Ioánnina depict him as a benevolent old codger, quietly smoking his famous pipe.

exquisitely worked and polished items, along with more homely silver belt buckles and pen holders, graphically show how war and everyday life were inextricably mixed in Épirus. Weapons, made for death, were meant to be treasured for life. When fully kitted up, it can truly be said that Epiróte warriors were 'dressed to kill'.

Mr Rapakoúsi plans to add three more rooms for his collection. In the meantime, ask to see Ali Pasha's *chiboúki*, the 63-inch decorated pipe with a rosewood bowl.

Archaeological Museum

Plateía 25 Martíou (Litharitsia Park), t 265 103 3357; open Tues–Sun 8.30–3; adm.

This excellent museum houses artefacts from the Palaeolithic up to the Roman period from all over Épirus, with good explanations in English. In Room A, one case displays some of the 150 lead sheets found at Dodóna, on which questions were written for the oracle. Another contains intricate nails and the round 'handle' of the bouleuterion's door at Dodóna. This bronze disc has holes for string coming from the latch inside. Pulling it down released the latch; pulling it taut from the inside locked the door. Many mountain houses still use the same system. The Necromanteíon is well represented with terracotta figurines of Persephone, votive hydrias and, in case 10, fragments of the so-called windlass mechanism for lowering supplicants into its inner sanctum (*see* p.421). The finds from Vítsa are especially graceful; some from the 8th century BC in case 8 are reminiscent of Mycenaean pottery. Don't miss the clay baby's bottle in case 7. Opposite Room C are grave goods from a Molossian cemetery (13th–4th century BC) from Liatovoúni near Kónitsa. The museum's most impressive prehistoric object is a triangular stone axe the size of a fist from 200,000 BC; its edges still look like they could do the trick. Found in Préveza in 1991, it is the oldest palae-olithic tool ever found in Greece. Room E, opened in 2001, offers gold jewellery from Ambracía (Árta), coins, pretty clay jugs, some small blue and yellow glass phials and a turtle's carapace used to make a lyre.

Popular Art Museum

42 M. Angelou St, t 265 102 0515; open Tues, Thurs, Fri 9–2; Wed, Sat 3–5; adm.

The wonderful **costumes of Épirus** are the stars here, ranging from elaborate waist-coats embroidered with silver and gold thread to the black and white geometrical costumes of the Sarakatsáni shepherds from the austere skirts and headscarves of the ladies from Pogóni to the famous black flower-embroidered aprons still seen in Métsovo. Fine silver is displayed and traditional working methods explained in English; *symateri* (or filigrana), Ioánnina's trademark, involves intricately lacing silver wire, with a blend of Byzantine, Baroque and Arab influences guaranteeing complex and unique designs. *Savati* (niello), where black enamel is used on a recessed back-ground to highlight embossed metal designs is especially dramatic, and goes back to the Mycenaeans.

Outside of Ioánnina there are two other attractions: the **P. Vrelli Museum of Waxworks**, 12 km south of town on the Árta road (*t 265 109 2128 ; open daily 9.30–5; adm*), an extensive adaptation of Madame Tussaud's to Greek history, not lacking in gruesome displays or visitors. The **Pérama Caves** (*t 265 108 1521; open daily in summer 8–8, winter 8.30–6; adm*) are 5km away on the lake's north shore, in a down-at-heel suburb by the airport with lots of cheap restaurants and rooms on offer. Underground, Pérama is more interesting. Tours go every 15 minutes into this 1,100m complex, distinguished by the remarkable size of its chambers. To exit, you must climb 163 stairs, but the temperature stays at a nice, constant 17° C.

Around Ioánnina

The scenery around Ioánnina is lovely, and its many villages shared the city's pros-perity. To the west is **Zítsa**, famous for its monasteries (the icon screen of Profítis Elías is elaborate even by Epiróte standards) and for its terrific high altitude white wine. To the north and west in the Pogóni region near Kónitsa are **Molyvdoskepastós** and **Doló**, the latter's churches built in a squat, muscular basilica style with tall cupolas that Pogónians still prefer. Southeast in the Tzourmérka region are **Siráko** and **Kallarítes**, both studded with mansions, and the nearby Kipínas Monastery, mouldering in its sheer rock face. Any and all are worth a visit, but the **Zagorochória** (Zagóri villages. *see* p.432) directly north of Ioánnina are in a class by themselves.

Dodóna: From Tree Shrine to Wind Chime

t 265 108 2287; open summer 8–7, winter 8–5. Dodóna is in an isolated valley 22km southwest of Ioánnina, off the Árta road. Buses from Ioánnina Mon, Wed and Fri only.

They say Dodóna's oracle was founded in 1900 BC by a clan of prophets, the *Selloi* or *Helloi*, who never washed their feet and slept on the bare ground to be in contact with a sacred oak whose roots harboured the god, and whose leaves whispered prophecies, intelligible to their ears alone. Not for the faint-hearted: Epiróte winters are bone-chillingly cold. Jason incorporated some of Dodóna's oak as a powerful charm in the *Argo* and Achilles himself invoked 'Zeus of wintry Dodóna' in the *Iliad*. But by historical times a steady stream of ordinary people came, seeking solutions to everyday problems. Questions, scratched on lead tablets, remained much the same: *Am I her children's father? To which god should I pray for my fortune, my children and wife? Should I sail to Syracuse at a later date?* and *To which god should sacrifice be offered as to govern the land the best way and have an abundance of good things?* The response to the last one would be worth having, but answers were not recorded.

In the Archaic period, the tree was surrounded by a ring of bronze cauldrons, the offerings of wealthy petitioners. By the 5th century, it 'got civilized' when a small stone temple was built beside it. In the 4th a circuit wall surrounded both and a small fortified city formed around that. During the reign of King Pyrrhus (297–272 BC), a gigantic 17,000-seat theatre was built, along with a stadium to accommodate the *Naia*, a festival featuring horse races, drama and athletic contests, all to enhance the king's prestige as well as to compliment Zeus. By Plato's day, barefoot prophets were out; frenzied priestesses received the oak's message. By Hellenistic times, the tree was a wind chime, its message amplified by cauldrons suspended in its branches. Even later, a bronze statue of a boy held a baton; when the wind moved it, it struck a row of contiguous copper pots and *that* sound was interpreted. At some point, the oak was cut down by marauders, which may account for the last refinement. Or perhaps it was just a case of 'different strokes for different folks'. Cult practices may have been written in stone, but they altered over time to meet the needs of new generations.

The Site

Visitors enter through the remnants of a **stadium**. Some of its seating remains up against the retaining wall of the **theatre**, built into the acropolis hill. Destroyed by Aitolíans in 219, it was rebuilt by Philip V of Macedon soon after from the spoils of Thermon. The Romans damaged it, then patched it up as an arena during Augustus' reign, replacing the front rows with a protective wall to shield audiences from wild beasts. Note the rusticated isodomic ashlar masonry of the *cavea*'s retaining walls, once buttressed by towers – an unusual touch for a Greek theatre. Double gateways with Ionic half columns lead to the *parados* and orchestra where the horseshoe drainage channel is still in good shape. A ceremonial entrance led to the topmost gallery from the once grand **acropolis**: this is roughly quadrilateral with thick walls and towers on three sides and not much else. Beside the theatre, the large 3rd-century BC **bouleuterion** or council house had a porch with Doric columns and an inner roof supported by Ionic columns. Like many buildings in this era, only its base was of stone, the upper walls being mud brick; wooden bleachers provided seating. The complicated ruins of the **prytaneion** south show that a hospitality suite was required as early as the 4th century BC. Further east, are a cluster of small temples to Aphrodite, Themis, Dione and Heracles, built from the mid-4th century on, and amid them, a **Temple of Zeus**. Only the unusual relationship of its temple wall to later colonnades indicate that the oak must have been on the east side of the court. The archaeologists have planted a new one, so you can pose questions of your own.

The Zagóri and the Zagorochória

The Zagóri (Slavic for 'land behind the mountain') is surrounded by spectacular peaks and scored by ravines, including the fabulous Víkos Gorge. At its core is the Víkos-Aóos National Park, created in 1973, and *its* core, the jagged 8,133ft Týmphi range, aptly nicknamed the 'Greek Alps', forms a backdrop to 46 settlements, so small and isolated that they evaded the devastation caused elsewhere in Épirus by the Germans during the Second World War. Now designated a national treasure, it is the totality of the Zagorochória that takes your breath away. Grey stone houses, many of them mansions, and grey stone churches are knitted together by lanes and *plateías* paved with the same ubiquitous stone. The stone was always there; the prosperity came when these resourceful highlanders took over the lucrative Pindus trade routes during Turkish times. Many became stone masons who exported their talent throughout the Balkans until well into the 20th century. At home, they built paved

The Zagorochória

10 kms
5 miles

N

Mt Smolikas

Iliorachi
Konitsa
Eleuthero
Palioselli
Kefalovriso
Stomiou Aoos
Vrisochori
Vikos-Aoos National Park
Mikro Papingo
Papingo
Mt Tymphi
Iliochori
Laista
Delvinaki
Vikos
Voidomatis
Visani
Aristi
Skamnelli
Elafotopos
Óxia
Tsepelovo
Kalpaki
A. Pedina
Vradeto
K. Pedina
Kapesovo
Monodendri
Koukouli
Negades
Parakalamos
Vitsa
Kipi
Dilofo
Flambourari

Zagóri Architecture

Zagóri houses are surrounded by stone walls, just high enough for looking over to be impossible. Doorways with triangular stone lintels lead into flower-decked flag-stoned courtyards, which often have low stone benches outside the house entrance. Arched doorways and windows exist, but rectangles dominate. Symmetrical windows, sheathed in thin black bars, have drab wooden shutters that often turn in rather than out, giving houses a blank expression. But Zagóri houses, like *geodes*, are grey on the outside only. Raised wooden floors flank the fireplace to accommodate mattresses covered in fluffy *flokáti* rugs or brightly embroidered blankets and pillows – seating by day, beds at night. The typical fireplace is a plastered apron projecting into the room over an open stone hearth. In summer, an embroidered cloth or '*tzakó-pano*' is placed over the mantel, as important a piece in any dowry chest as embroidered linen or the white lacy half-curtains that grace every window. Houses with separate living rooms have closed wooden benches lining the fireplace wall and sides of the room, all topped with embroidered cushions. Ceilings are board and batten, but wealthier houses go over the moon with elaborate criss-crosses over tiny squares, and special mouldings for the chandelier. Cupboards are built in, with matching wainscotting so that some walls are all wood, painted bold dark blues, greens, even red, providing the background for folk art motifs that sometimes spill over to the white plastered walls. Deep windows are lined with wood; doorways can be low. Where space was at a premium, the animals lived downstairs and their owners up, and outside stone staircases often added an ornamental flair. Other mountain houses have similar features. But here, utility became an art and many of Greece's best designers have taken leaves out of the Zagóri's book.

Even looking down is interesting. Village lanes are stone-paved with precision, and without the benefit of cement. Many were constructed in a shallow 'v' so rainwater drained away from the walls. Steep paths have a stepped strip in the middle, so animals could navigate while the wheels of their carts ran smoothly on either side. On gentle inclines the entire road might be lined with steps shallow enough for cart wheels to roll over. Some are decorated with a median strip, some are rounded, others flat.

Zagóri churches are basilican and quite grand, frescoed by a local school of painters. Arches are more popular here, especially in the colonnaded porch that inevitably runs down the one side and sometimes two, with benches perfect for inclement Sundays. The isolated bell towers were made to impress, but cupolas or *troúlis* are rare and restricted to one per church, if at all. The style is so uniform that it is only the crumbling stonework that distinguishes a very old church from a new.

mule paths and connected rocky chasms with poetic stone bridges that have become the region's trademark. Today, these are being repaired at a great rate, not as difficult a task as you might think; they were the only roads in the Zagóri until the 1950s.

The Zagóri encompasses three mountain zones. Arbutus, holly oak, pine and cypress are found with cyclamens, anemones and camomile in the 'maquis' (1,600–2,600ft).

Getting There and Around

The Zagóri is bounded by the Ioánnina–Kónitsa highway to the west, the Aóos river to the north and east and the Ioánnina–Métsovo highway to the south. The densest cluster of villages are the **central Zagorochória** around Monodéndri: Elafótopos, Áno and Kato Pediná, Vítsa, Vradéto, Kapésovo, Koukoúli, Kípi; Negádes, Tsepélovo, Skamnélli, Iliochóri and Vrisichóri; with little Láista farthest east. The **western Zagorochória** consist of Arísti, Víkos, Pápingo and Mikro Pápingo. The less visited and less spectacular **eastern Zagóri**, best represented by Flambourári and Vovoúsa, are most easily reached en route to Métsovo.

By bus: Buses are in short supply. There are two a day from Ioánnina to Monodéndri, Vítsa, Pápingo, Tsepélovo and Skamnélli on Mondays and Fridays. In summer, they sometimes add a bus. There are regular buses from Ioánnina to Kónitsa (60km) and Métsovo (58km) however. Forget about **taxis** unless you arrange one from Ioánnina.

By car: The network of narrow roads is good and mostly asphalt, except in the eastern Zagóri. The central Zagorochória are an hour from Ioánnina (53km to Monodéndri) and most easily approached by turning east from the Ioánnina–Kónitsa road just north of Kalpáki. Three kilometres north of that is the road to the western Zagorachória.

On foot: The Zagóri is criss-crossed with trails and has a well-placed mountain refuge. Inns offer advice; some even pack a lunch.

Tourist Information

Mikró Pápingo information centre: t 265 304 1931; *open daily 10.30–2.30 and 4.30–8, closed Wed, Sun 11–5 only.*

ANAVASI's *Zagóri* **map** (easily found in the Zagóri's main towns and Ioánnina) is excellent, with names and text in English and Greek. Roads, footpaths, old bridges, inns and restaurants are marked, along with kayaking runs and paragliding areas. Long and short treks are suggested, with approximate times and levels of difficulty. They leave out the less visited eastern Zagóri. For a wider perspective, get the *Road* map.

A fax to **EOT** in Ioánnina (*see* p.426) will get you useful information, including phone numbers for all village inns.

Excursions

Robinson Club, 8 Marakias St, Ioánnina, t 265 102 9402, *www.Robinson.gr* (on the airport road). English-speaking Constantine Vasilíou offers tours for hikers, rock climbers, kayakers, rafters and mountain bikers.

Trekking Hellas, 7 Napoleon Zervas St, ✉ 45332 Ioánnina, t 265 107 1703, f 265 107 4190, also offer tours.

Ioánnina Mountaineering Club, 2 Despotátou Epírou, t/f 265 102 2138; *open 7–9pm except in July and Aug.* This friendly club runs the Týmphi Alpine Refuge.

Where to Stay and Eat

The Zagóri is open all year and the inns and hotels are good. You will eat simply but well: even tiny settlements have restaurants serving local meat and *pittas*, large flaky pastry pies loaded with cheese and spinach.

Kónitsa ✉ 44100

Hotel Gefyri, t 265 502 3780, f 265 502 2783, *gefyri@yahoo.com* (*expensive–moderate*). On

In the mountain zone (2,600–6,500ft) the oak, black fir, beech, maple and chestnut share space with lilies, peonies and crocuses. The alpine zone, above 6,500ft, is carpeted with rare blooms in spring. Many species are unique to the Zagóri and many have been used for centuries for their medicinal properties. The **K. Lazaridi Museum,** t 265 305 1398, in Koukoúli houses over 2,500 dried species of local plants and herbs, all from the Zagóri. Monodéndri is the most visited village, the Pápingos perhaps the most dramatic, but each and every Zagóri village has its own style and atmosphere.

the river by the old bridge; attractive, with a small pool.

Bourazani, 12km west of Kónitsa, on the road to Molyvdoskepastós, t 265 106 1286. This unusual restaurant serves deer and wild boar grown on their private game park.

Monodéndri ✉ 44007

Pension Víkos, t 065 307 1332 (*moderate*). New, but built in traditional style, with a terrace.

Kikítsa Restaurant, t 265 307 1340. In the *plateía* near Ag. Athanásios, Kikítsa's cheese pie (one feeds three!) is so good, the recipe hasn't changed in 42 years.

Pápingo ✉ 44004

Saxonis, t 265 304 1890, f 265 304 1891 (*B; expensive*). Three houses with a charming connecting courtyard and a hearty breakfast included in the price.

Xenonas Astraka, t/f 265 304 1693 (*moderate, expensive in winter*). A perfectly traditional Zagóri house with mattresses framing the fireplace and a common living room. All rooms sleep four; the price is by the room.

Pension Koulis, t 265 304 1138, f 265 304 1138, mobile 693 284 7752 (*moderate*). Still the family home with a small shop in the courtyard and a terrace where drinks are served along with home-made spoon desserts.

Kaiti's Pension, t 265 304 1118, f 265 304 1422 (*moderate*). Six big new rooms, each with kitchen, run by the lovely Kaiti; for a third person add 20%.

Lakkis, t 265 304 1087, f 265 104 1120 (*inexpensive, moderate in Aug*). Five good, plain rooms over a café; the courtyard parking is a blessing. A kettle, with cups, waits in the hall for those who have brought tea bags.

Dias, Mikró Pápingo, t 265 304 1257, f 265 304 1892 (*moderate*). A well run, traditional inn;

12 airy rooms. The courtyard is cosy, the food is terrific and the Tsoumánis family make visitors feel at home.

Nikos Tsoumánis, t 265 304 189. Has good food, but so does the more upmarket Ioannides, t 265 304 1124, by Ag. Vlássios.

Arísti ✉ 44004

Taxiarches, t 265 304 1888, f 265 304 2200, *taxiarches@hol.gr* (*B; expensive*). Large, new, with extensive grounds by Zagóri standards (a pool is planned). Has its own restaurant and a great view.

Xenona Zissis, t 265 304 1147, f 265 304 1088 (*B; moderate*). 36 beds in a traditional house with an attractive courtyard and a terrace restaurant.

Aphrodite Rent Rooms, t 265 304 1181 (*inexpensive*). Friendly Mr Bellos has two rooms with fridge, TV and '*mati*' for heating water; plus an apartment for four–six with separate bedrooms, kitchen and living room.

Tsepélovo ✉ 44010

Drakolimni, t 265 308 1318, f 265 308 1311 (*C; expensive*). New, big, impersonal, on the main road at the entrance up to the main *plateía*; it even has a parking lot.

Pension Fanis, t/f 265 308 1271 (*B; inexpensive in summer, moderate in winter*). Old, simple, but nice. Fanis' new flats in front will spoil the view, if not the welcome.

Pension Gouri, t 265 308 1214, mobile 694 478 9909 (*inexpensive*). Eight simple but nice rooms, some with balconies (a luxury in this area) and a common room.

Taverna Gerasimou, t 265 308 1088. Blue painted arched windows and seating area in the *plateía*. Stavros and Maria cook up a storm. Sweets and coffee as well.

Monodéndri

Once wealthy, Monodéndri has the best collection of mansions. The attractive main *plateía* by the imposing 19th-century church of Ag. Athanásios is especially attractive, and the 15th- century **Ag. Paraskeví Monastery** is worth a look if only to see the sheer drop to the bottom of the Víkos Gorge that it provides. The monks took advantage of it; their loo is perched right over the drop. Just taking one of its round seats would have been an act of faith. A scary path leads from the monastery to Megáli Spiliá, a cave used as a hideout in tough times.

An 8km road ascends from Monodéndri through fantastical heaps of flysch, the naturally fissured flagstone that made the Zagorochória possible, and on to **Oxía** and the **Víkos Balcony** with a heart-stopping view of the Víkos Gorge from the rim at its highest point. Its great depth is emphasized by the closeness of the canyon walls. *Víkos* means echo; you can easily test it out.

The Pápingos

The road to the two Pápingos passes through lovely Arísti village and then descends to the **Voidomátis river**, here serene and bubbling in a wide bed festooned with plane trees. The 16th-century **Moní Spiliótissa**, perched on the rock face above the river, is beautiful, as are the views from its bell tower. The road then corkscrews up to Pápingo's first house, where prosaic asphalt ends and perfectly set stone paving begins. Visitors are invited to leave their cars in a field (you can drive in Pápingo, but reconnoitre first). The church of Ag. Vlássios (1851) guards the entrance to the village. Compact, neat and homogenous, Pápingo is so like a stage set you almost expect Dorothy and the Scarecrow to round a corner and break into song.

Wide **Astráka**, Týmphi's most imposing peak, aptly nicknamed 'the tower', looms above, impossible to escape, softening only at sunset when it is dyed a glowing pink. The famous 'view' lives up to its reputation. Two short kilometres of asphalt gets you to lusher **Mikró Pápingo** (no cars), closer to Astráka and a village from another time. Trails leave from here to the small lake of Drakolímni, to Týmphi's peaks, and to the Víkos Gorge.

Between the Pápingos, and handy to both, are the sign-posted *kolymbýthres* (swimming holes) where a picturesque stream has been dammed up. Paddling here amid the fractured flagstone, so typical of the Zagóri, is one of life's great experiences.

A Circle round Mount Týmphi

This is an excellent day trip by car, but could easily stretch to two or three. From **Kónitsa** head for **Eleúthero**, then **Paliosélli**. At the 10km mark, the peaks of Týmphi are lined up, an amazingly long and jagged panorama that makes the bone-rattling dirt road down to the Aóos river from just past Paliosélli worth it. A new bridge over the Aóos gives hope that this 12km stretch is due to be paved. At pretty **Vrisochóri** (an inn, a restaurant, lots of water, and its own private gorge) the asphalt continues and whizzes you past **Iliochóri**, through the forest, past the turn-off to tiny **Láista** and on to the **Gyftókambo** (Gypsies' meadow). In this area of pine and fir trees a good number of nomadic Greek Sarakatsáni shepherds gather for an annual fair in the first week of August. The Sarakatsáni have lived in the high mountains of the Balkans since the cows came home; there is even speculation that they are the last 'pure' ancient Greeks, a branch of the family who took to the hills some time after the first Slavic speakers arrived, became shepherds and never built permanent homes. The closing of the northern borders in 1923, however, undermined their traditional way of life, and since 1950 they have increasingly become more settled. Several of their traditional thatched shelters are fenced in by the road, but are pretty tame stuff;

many Sarakatsáni now book at the inns for their jamboree, although presumably the sheep still camp out. **Skamnélli** is next, sitting pretty on an open hillside with vistas to the south as well as to Týmphi's peaks (for a closer look, try the marked trail from here to Kónitsa). Skamnélli is famous for the murals in its houses and the churches of Ag. Athanásios and Ag. Paraskeví. Then comes **Tsepélovo**, a metropolis by Zagóri standards, with 180 people, inns, a post office, high school and a lovely main *plateía*. Home owners have kicked over the traces and painted their exterior woodwork bright greens, reds and blues. The nearby **Rongovoú monastery** (1050) has interesting frescoes. Wind down the tour by descending past **Koukoúli** to charming, low-lying **Kípi** and the beautiful triple-span **Bridge of Plakída**. The road to Dílofo will get you back to the Ioánnina-Kónitsa highway.

A Trek in the Víkos Gorge

Over aeons and aeons, the **Voidomátis** ('bulls eye') river ground its way through Týmphi's limestone tablelands to produce the **Víkos Gorge**, a narrow 10km phenomenon with walls 3,400ft high in places, the steepest in the world and second only to the Grand Canyon in depth. It begins in earnest just north of Kípi and ends near the village of Víkos. Navigable in summer and autumn, the most popular trek is from Monodéndri's *plateía* to either Víkos or the Pápingos: it takes seven hours, and you will need a big water bottle, proper walking boots and a stick. The 45min walk down the stepped mule path is enough to discourage duffers. Once down, a path runs parallel to the river following part of the marvellous **o3 trail** which begins in Ioánnina and ends on Mount Grámmos. After 4½ to 5 hours, the steep walls recede, the **Voidomátis springs** come into view and an ascent can be made either to Víkos (½ hour) or to the Pápingos (1½ hours). Happily, Heraclitus was not thinking of mule paths when he said 'the path up and down is one and the same'; going up is a lot easier on the legs. The trail from Monodéndri south to Vítsa also goes to the bottom of the gorge, but is shorter (2 hours or so). Of similar duration but less strenuous is the route from Kípi up to the beginning of the gorge and on to the Misíou bridge, and then up to Vítsa.

Kónitsa

Kónitsa is a convenient gateway to the Zagóri for those without cars; bus services are regular, and there are lots of rooms and small hotels (the *dimarchío* in the main *plateía* has a list). The town spills down Mount Trapezítsa as far as the majestic Aóos river and a delicate single-spanned **bridge**, the longest in the Zagóri at 131ft, and built in 1870 by master stonemason Kostas Frontzos. Many walks begin here, including one to the abandoned **Stomíou Monastery**, sitting on a small plateau of Týmphi over the narrowest part of the **Aóos Gorge**. This 1½ hour trek is an excellent introduction to the Aóos, a gorge some prefer to Víkos. The intrepid can hike the Aóos from its source near Métsovo or kayak down its rushing waters. Kónitsa means 'horses' and it still has plenty of grazing on its doorstep in the huge flat and green valley created by the confluence of the Aóos and Voidomátis rivers, where trout fishing is popular.

East of Ioánnina:
Métsovo, Vovoúsa and Válía Cálda

The 52km from Ioánnina to Métsovo offers great views of Lake Pamvótis and then heads east to Mázia. After 8.5km you can pick up a paved road snaking 50km north via Miliotádes, Trístano, Flambourári and on to scenic **Vovoúsa**, in the heart of the eastern Zagóri, where a beautiful stone bridge crosses the Aóos river. It has an excellent restaurant and two small inns catering mostly to hikers.

With no detours, the main highway takes less than an hour to reach **Métsovo**, where everyone traversing the Katára Pass into Thessaly congregates for an hour or two, taking the steep road down to its pretty cobblestoned *plateía* to check out the most astonishing tourist tack this side of Athens (you could also try the local honey or *metsovóne*, Métsovo's famous smoked cheese). Ladies hang about in traditional aprons, interesting monasteries are nearby, and the town boasts a good folk art museum.

Aside from skiing in winter, the compelling reason to stay is the nearby **source of the Aóos river** (a small lake really) and the enchanting **Pindus National Park**, better known as **Válía Cálda** (Vlach for 'Warm Valley'), due north of town. This is your best chance to spot some of Épirus' shy wild animals including bears, wolves and tiny wild cats. The closest asphalt approaches to the park are from the Aóos lake or Vovoúsa. But hiking is a much less intrusive way to see one of Épirus' last wilderness areas, or there is a riding stable, **t** 265 604 1696, at Profítis Ilías near the turn-off for the springs. A 33km paved road goes from the source of the Aóos down to Trístano and on to Vovoúsa, handier for those approaching from the east. All the dirt roads in the area are pretty good, except in winter.

Where to Stay and Eat

Métsovo ✉ 44200

Victoria, 500m from the town centre, **t** 265 604 1771, **f** 265 604 1451 (*B; expensive*). Quiet, pretty, with a sauna and an outdoor pool and jacuzzi. It's large reception-bar is in the Epiróte style, with a fireplace, and lots of wood trim.

Galaxy, **t** 265 604 1202, **f** 265 604 1124 (*C; expensive*). A traditional-style wooden balcony overhangs the main *plateía* and it has a good garden restaurant.

Asteri, 58 Th. Tossítsa, **t** 265 604 2222, **f** 265 604 1267 (*C; moderate*). On the road to the main *plateía*; traditional style, some rooms with views.

Athinae, 1 Kentriki Plateía, **t** 265 604 1332, **f** 265 604 2009 (*E; inexpensive*). Metsovo's only budget hotel; Mom does the cooking in its restaurant.

Psistariá To Katoi, **t** 265 604 2024. A small *psistariá* in the main square, with a fireplace and small terrace. A great location for people-watching.

Vovoúsa ✉ 44200

Niki Akrivi Rooms, by the bridge, **t** 265 602 2863 (*inexpensive*). Four plain rooms, two en suite.

Sophia Stavroyánnis Rooms, **t** 265 602 2846 (*inexpensive*). Two with shared bath, one ensuite, by the bridge.

Angelos, **t** 265 602 2841. A grocery-cum-taverna with a great view of the river, excellent grilled meat, fresh vegetables and watermelon preserves to end the feast. Mr Angelos himself presides over this dying breed of wonderful eateries.

The Ionian Islands

Sprinkled randomly across the Ionian Sea, from Corfu in the north to Kýthera at the southern end of the Peloponnese, the Ionians are known in Greek as the Eptánissa, the Seven Islands. Lumped together politically since Byzantine times, they share a unique history and character; they are more Italianate, more luxuriant than the Greek island stereotype, swathed in olive groves and cypresses and bathed in a soft golden light very different from the clear solar spotlight that shines on the Aegean. They also get more rain, especially from October to March, and are rewarded with a breathtaking bouquet of wild flowers in spring and autumn, especially on Corfu. Summers, however, tend to be hot, lacking the natural air-conditioning provided by the *meltémi* in the Aegean. Weather and history aside, each of the Ionian islands has a strong personality. Connections between them are not the best, but with a little forward planning you can hop from one to the next, depending on whether you want to boogie in a loud Zákynthos nightclub, windsurf below the cliffs at Lefkáda, hike among the olive groves of bijou Paxí, swim under the white cliffs of Kefaloniá, or seek Odysseus' beloved home on Ithaca. Corfu is a major international destination, with its gorgeous beaches and historic town, once labelled in the British press as a 'Venice without canals, Naples without the degradation'. Only beautiful and distant Kýthera remains aloof and today belongs to the district of Piraeus; you'll find it on p.311.

History

Settled in the Stone Age by people from Illyria (present-day Albania), the Ionian islands were first mentioned by Homer and, were he the last, they would still be immortal as the homeland of Odysseus. Corinth colonized the islands in the 8th century BC and, as trade grew between Greek cities and their colonies in southern Italy and Sicily, the Ionians became important ports of call; Corfu, the richest, with a fleet second only to that of Athens in Classical times, grew so high and mighty that she broke away from mother Corinth and proclaimed herself the ally of Athens (433 BC). This forced Sparta, Corinth's ally, either to submit to this untoward expansion of Athenian influence or to attack. Two years later they attacked. The result was the disastrous Peloponnesian War.

The Romans incorporated the Ionian islands into their province of Achaia. After the fall of their empire, Ostrogoths from Italy overran the islands, only to be succeeded in

When the Cow Jumped Over the Sea

If the Ionian islands spent centuries out of the mainstream of Greek politics, their inhabitants have been Hellene to the core from the beginning. Not to be confused with Ionia in Asia Minor (named after the Ionian people's legendary father Ion, son of Apollo), the Ionian Sea and its islands are named after lovely Io the priestess, who caught the roving eye of Zeus. When the jealous Hera was about to catch the couple *in flagrante delicto* Zeus changed the girl into a white cow, but Hera was not to be fooled. She asked Zeus to give her the cow as a present, and ordered the sleepless hundred-eyed Argus to watch over her. When Hermes charmed Argus to sleep and killed him, Io the cow escaped, only to be pursued by a terrible stinging gad-fly sent by Hera. The first place she fled to was named after her, the Ionian Sea.

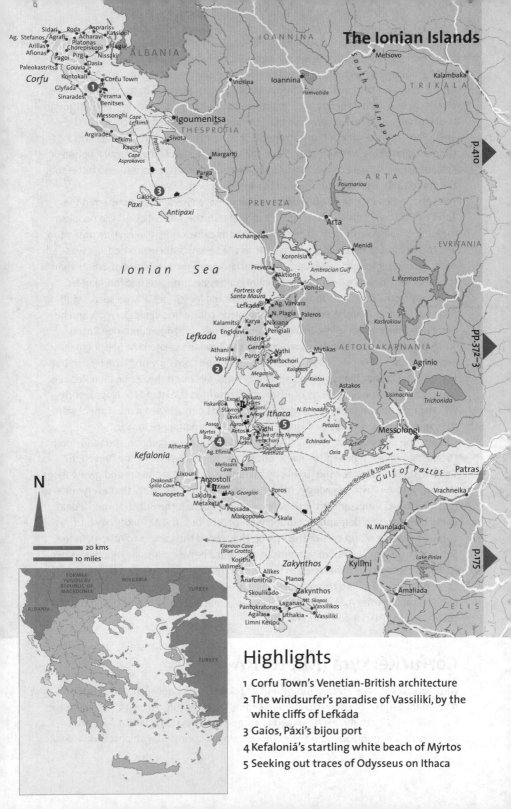

The Ionian Islands

Highlights

1 Corfu Town's Venetian-British architecture

2 The windsurfer's paradise of Vassilikí, by the white cliffs of Lefkáda

3 Gaíos, Páxi's bijou port

4 Kefaloniá's startling white beach of Mýrtos

5 Seeking out traces of Odysseus on Ithaca

the Greek–Gothic wars by the Byzantines, who valued them as a bridge to Rome. In 1084, during the Second Crusade, the Normans under Robert Guiscard, Duke of Apulia, captured the Ionians by surprise attack and established bases to plunder the rest of Greece. With difficulty the Byzantines succeeded in dislodging them, although the Normans were no sooner gone than the Venetians claimed the islands in the land-grab after the sack of Constantinople in 1204. After crucifying the Sicilian Norman pirate king, Vetrano, they made the southern islands the County Palatine of Kefaloniá. Fate, however, gave Corfu to the Angevins for 150 years, a rule so bitter that the inhabitants willingly surrendered to the 'protection' of Venice.

Venetian rule was hardly a bed of roses. The average Greek, in fact, preferred the Turks to the bossy Catholic 'heretics': if nothing else, the Turks allowed the people a measure of self-government. Some of the Ionians came under Turkish rule until 1499, and the Ottomans renewed their assaults as the Serenissima weakened; life was never secure. Yet for all their faults, the Venetians were more tolerant of artists than the Turks, and in the 17th century the Ionian islands became a refuge for painters, especially from Crete. Their Ionian school was noted for its (not always successful) fusion of Byzantine and Western styles. Napoleon conquered Venice in 1796, and he demanded the Ionians in the Treaty of Campo Formio. In 1799 a combined Russo-Turkish fleet took the islands from him, and the Russians created the Septinsular Republic under their protection – shielding the islands not only from the French but from the designs of the tyrant of Épirus, Alí Pasha. Although the Septinsular Republic was nullified by the 1807 Treaty of Tilsit which returned the islands to Napoleon, it was the first time in centuries that any Greeks had been allowed a measure of self-rule, an experience that helped kindle the War of Independence in 1821.

In 1815 the British took the Ionian islands under military protection and re-formed the quasi-independent Septinsular Republic. Sir Thomas Maitland, the first High Commissioner, infuriated the Greeks by assuming dictatorial powers and giving Párga (*see* p.419) to Alí Pasha, obeying an obscure clause in the 1815 treaty that everyone else had forgotten. During and after the War of Independence, the British turned a deaf ear to the islanders' demands for union with Greece, but in 1864, once they had Cyprus as well as Malta to take their place, they ceded the Ionians to Athens. In the Second World War, Mussolini's dreams of creating a new Septinsular Republic under Italian protection were shattered in 1943 when the Germans occupied the islands. Large numbers of Italian troops joined the Greeks to fight them, only to be slaughtered by their former Axis allies. When the news reached Italy, it contributed to the collapse of the Fascist government.

Corfu/Kérkyra (ΚΕΡΚΥΡΑ)

In contrast with the austere mountains of Épirus and Albania just opposite, Corfu is a luxuriant Garden of Eden. Its Venetian capital is one of the loveliest cities in Greece; the (few) beaches that have managed to escape the infectious claw of package tourism are still gorgeous; and the mountain slopes, sprinkled with pastel villas and

Getting There and Around

By air: frequent charter flights from the UK and many European cities; daily from Athens. **Airport information**: t 266 103 0180 or t 266 103 7398. No airport bus, but there is a regular bus stop on the main road, several hundred metres away, or a taxi for €5.

By sea: year-round ferries from Brindisi, Bari, Ancona and Venice stop en route to Pátras (*see* p.213). Ferries sail daily between Corfu Town or Lefkími to Igoumenítsa; Paxí gets year-round ferry service, but travel to Eríkousa, Othoní and Mathráki is less frequent (t 266 103 6355). **Port authority**: t 266 103 2655.

By bus: several daily buses connect Athens and Thessaloníki with Igoumenítsa ferries. For travel on Corfu, there are two bus stations in Corfu Town: Plateía Theotóki (San Rócco Square), t 266 103 1595, has blue buses to Kanóni, Pótamos, Konokáli, Goúvia, Dassiá, Pérama, Ag. Ioánnis, Benítses, Pélekas, Kastelláni, Kouramádes, Áfra, Achilleíon and Gastoúri. From Avramíou Street, t 266 103 9985 or t 266 103 0627, green buses run to the more distant Ipsos, Pírgi, Glyfáda, Barbáti, Kassiópi, Paliokastrítsa, Sidári, Ag. Stéfanos, Róda, Kávos, Messóghi, Ag. Górdis and both resorts named Ag. Geórgios.

By car: International Rent a Car, t 266 103 3411 or t 266 103 7710, f 266 104 6350, *slemis@ otenet.gr*, is at 20a Kapodistríou St, Corfu Town. The best **map** at the time of writing is *The Precise All New Road Atlas of Corfu*.

By bicycle: rent in Corfu Town at the Dutch Bicycle Company, Ag. Ioánnis Tríklino, t/f 266 105 2407, or at Dassiá's Mountain-bike Shop, t 266 109 3344, f 266 104 6100.

Tourist Information

All in Corfu Town.

EOT: 7 Rizospastón Vouleftón, t 266 103 7520, f 266 103 0298; *open weekdays 8–2*.

Tourist police: Samartzi Street, near San Rocco Square, t 266 103 0265; *open Mon–Fri, 8–2*.

Post office: 26 Alexándras, t 266 103 9265; *open Mon–Fri, 8–8; Sat 7.30–2.30; Sun 9–1.30*.

Consulates: UK, 1 Penekratous, t 266 103 0055/7995; Ireland, 20a Kapodistríou Street, t 266 103 2469/9910.

Hospital: 1 Andreádi St, t 266 108 8200; some staff speak English.

Scuba diving: Contact Waterhoppers, Ípsos, t 266 109 3867, Paleokastrítsa t 266 103 7118; Corfiot Diving Centre Diving Centre, t 266 103 9727.

Festivals

Procession of **Ag. Spyrídon** in Corfu Town on Palm Sunday, Easter Saturday, 11 August and first Sunday in November. **Easter Saturday** is celebrated in Corfu town with a bang – the sound of everyone to sling out their chipped crockery. 21 May, big celebrations for **Union with Greece**. July sees a prestigious **guitar festival**; the **Corfu Festival** in September brings concerts, ballet, opera and theatre, followed in early October by a delightful **Chamber Music Festival**.

---

farms, could be in Tuscany. Homer called it *Scheria*, the happy isle, where the shipwrecked Odysseus was found washed up on a golden beach by the lovely Nausicäa. Shakespeare had it in mind when he created the magical isle of *The Tempest*, and Edward Lear and Gerald and Lawrence Durrell evoked its charms so delightfully that it found a special niche in the British heart – with staggering consequences. During Corfu's first British occupation, it learned to play cricket and drink ginger beer; during the second, the Corfiots have been stunned by the Calibanish behaviour of British lager louts, then stung by negative reports of their island in the British press.

The rotten publicity spurred an intense 'culture versus crud' debate. Although way too late for the coastline on either side of Corfu Town, a new sewage system, stricter building regulations and a spit and polish has set the tone for a more genteel Corfu. Classical music festivals (*see* box, above) entice a new breed of tourists, and Count

Spíros Flambouriári, member of an old Corfiot family, has set up an island 'National Trust' to restore the once mouldering country estates scattered in the gorgeous hinterland. Seek out these and the old cobbled mule paths between the villages – you'll be rewarded with a poignant vision of the old Corfu, strewn with wild flowers (including 43 kinds of orchids), scented with blossoms and silvery with billowing forests of ancient olives. They still outnumber tourists by three and a half million.

History

In ancient times Corfu was *Corcyra*, named after a mistress of the sea god Poseidon. In 734 BC the Corinthians founded a colony at Paleopolis (the modern suburbs of Anemómylos and Análypsis), and built a temple to house the sickle that Zeus used to castrate his father Cronos (whose testicles, by the way, are the two hills around the Old Fortress). Perhaps it was this inauspicious start that cursed the island with violent internal rivalries and bloody wars. Corcyrans fought the first sea battle in Greek history, against mother Corinth in 664 BC, and in 435 BC their quarrel with Corinth over a colony in Albania set the stage for the Peloponnesian War. It was captured by Syracuse, then by King Pyrrhus of Épirus, and in 229 BC by the Illyrians, and its loyalty to Mark Antony brought down Octavian's army in a reprisal that destroyed every civic monument on the island. Yet ancient Corcyra never lost its reputation for fertility and beauty; Nero paid it a special visit in AD 67 to dance and sing at the Temple of Zeus in modern Kassiópi. The remnants of the population that survived the Goths in AD 550 decided to rebuild on the more defensible site of the present Old Fortress.

In 1204, Venice claimed Corfu, but the inhabitants put up a stiff resistance, aligning themselves with the Despotate of Épirus. Fifty years later, when Charles I of Anjou snatched Corfu along with the Peloponnese, Angevin misrule made the Corfiots swallow their pride and petition Venice to take over. In 1537, Suleiman the Magnificent landed at Igoumenítsa, intending to make Corfu his base to attack Italy. The frantic Corfiots tore the stones from their houses to bolster the fortress, and thousands who had been abandoned outside the walls were caught in the lethal crossfire before Suleiman, discouraged by the resistance, lifted the siege. The Turks tried again 21 years later, this time decimating the island's villages, trees and vineyards, and slaughtering everyone they found. Two years later, the pirate admiral, Sinan Pasha, did it again; by 1573, the population was one tenth what it had been fifty years before.

In 1576, the Venetians undertook to protect the surviving Corfiots. Their crack fortifications expert Michele Sammicheli built the state-of-the-art 'New Fortress', and they jumpstarted the economy by paying for every olive tree planted (today there are some 4.5 million, producing 3 per cent of the world's olive oil). They allowed wealthy Corfiots and other Ionian islanders to purchase titles, creating the only aristocracy in Greece, and offering them limited self-rule.

Sammicheli's walls were tested in 1716, when the Turks went all out to seize Corfu. The stratagems of a German mercenary, Field Marshal Schulenberg, and a timely tempest sent by Corfu's patron saint, St Spyrídon, saved the day. After Napoleon captured Venice, the French occupied Corfu, but lost it two years later in a fierce battle against the Russo-Turkish fleet. When Napoleon got it back, he personally designed new fortifications for the town, with walls so formidable that the British, when allotted the Ionians in 1815, did not care to argue the point when the French commander Donzelot at first refused to give them up. Count Ioánnis Capodístria, the first president of Greece, was a product of this unique era.

British and Greek Corfu

The British took it upon themselves to run all the affairs of the Ionian State, which they 'legalized' by a constitution imposed by the first High Commissioner, Sir Thomas Maitland ('King Tom'), who kept the peasants in near-feudal conditions while denying Corfu's educated and middle classes any political role. He built new, stronger walls around Corfu Town and then called upon the Greeks to cough up more than a million gold sovereigns to pay for them. He imposed neutrality on the islands when the Greek War of Independence broke out, disarming the population and imprisoning and even executing members of the revolutionary Friendly Society. Still, new roads, reservoirs, schools and even a university (the 'Ionian Academy', founded by Hellenophile Lord Guilford) were established, and Edward Lear spent happy months there, painting pretty watercolours and writing in his journal.

In 1858, the political situation was so tense that Gladstone was sent down to sort things out, but, constrained by British distrust of King Otto and Greek support of Russia (Britain's enemy in the Crimean War), he had little to propose. The overthrow of Otto (1862) gave Britain a chance to cede the islands gracefully to Greece in 1864, as the 'dowry' of the new Danish-born king, George I. There was one ungracious hitch: to ensure 'neutrality' the British blew up Corfu's fortresses. An even worse bombardment occurred in 1943, when the Germans blasted the city and its Italian garrison; a year later, the British and Americans bombed the Germans. By 1945, a quarter of the old city was destroyed, including 14 of the loveliest churches.

Corfu Town

Corfu Town, or Kérkyra (pop. 40,000), the capital of the Ionian islands, was laid out by the Venetians in the 14th century when the medieval town, crowded onto the peninsula of Cape Sidáro (where the Old Fortress now stands), had no room to expand. They began with the Campiello (from *campo*, Venetian for 'square'), where three-or four-storey houses still loom over the narrow streets. By the time the new walls were added in the 16th century, the Venetians built in a more open style, laying out an exquisite series of central streets and small squares; some of the finest houses, decorated with masks and half-moon windows over the door, can be seen along the upper Esplanade. The British knocked down the Venetian walls to allow the town to grow, and added a set of elegant Georgian public buildings.

The old city is divided into smaller quarters such as Garítsa, the 19th-century residential district to the south. The Old Port, on the east side of the New Fortress, is used only by the excursion boat to Paxi; all the other ferries and boats come in and out of town through its back door at Mandoúki, or New Port, west of the New Fortress.

The New Fortress Area

The Venetian **New Fortress** (*t 261 103 3324; open daily 9–8.30; adm; entrance from Solomós Street*), built after 1576, bore the brunt of the great Turkish siege of 1716. Over the gates, Lions of St Mark and inscriptions erode genteelly away; there are excellent views of Corfu Town from its bastions, two tunnels to explore, and the town **market** (G. Markorá St) in its moat. To the west, beyond the hospital on Polichroni Konstantá St, the **Monastery of Platýteras** contains two icons given by Catherine the Great in honour of Count Capodístria, the first president of Greece, who is buried there. You can reach the town centre from the Old Port through the 16th-century **Spiliá Gate** incorporated into a later structure, or take the steps up into the medieval Campiello Quarter (*see* below); the **Jewish Quarter**, equally old, lies south of Plateía Solomoú. A synagogue and a school remain in Velissáriou Street; only 170 out of the 1,800 Jews sent to Auschwitz returned to Corfu after the war.

The Esplanade (Spianáda), the Listón and the Old Fortress

A series of long parallel streets all lead to the town's centre, the Spianáda or Esplanade, one of the largest public squares in Europe. It took its present form as a garden and promenade when Napoleon had the arcaded **Listón** built on the west side, in imitation of Paris' Rue de Rivoli. Reserved for the aristocracy (those on the Liste d'Or, hence its name), then, as now, the Listón was a solid row of elegant cafés.

The north end of the Esplanade is filled by the Georgian **Palace of St Michael and St George**, with its two grand gates and symbols of the seven islands on its Maltese marble façade. Designed by Sir George Whitmore for Sir Thomas Maitland, it became the summer residence of the King of Greece in 1864. It now houses the magnificent **Museum of Asiatic Art** (*t 266 103 0433; open Tues–Sun 8.30–3; adm*), a gift from Greek diplomat Gregórios Mános and others, containing 10,000 masks, ceramics, armour and much more, some dating back to 1000 BC; the palace also has an **Art Café** that puts on local art exhibitions. Adjacent to the palace is the *loggia* of the **Reading Society** (*t 266 102 7277; open daily 9–1*), founded in 1836 by a group of young Corfiot idealists who studied in France. Just in front of the palace is the **cricket ground**, where six local teams take on all comers.

In the centre of the Esplanade's Upper Plateía where local bands serenade the crowds are the **memorial to Sir Thomas Maitland**, and a marble **statue of Marshal Schulenberg**, the crafty soldier of fortune from Saxony who outwitted the Turkish High Admiral in the Great Siege of 1716. The **Guilford Memorial** is to Corfu's favourite Englishman, the Hellenophile Frederick North, Earl of Guilford (1769–1828), here dressed like the ancient Athenians he so admired. Another statue, of Count Capodístria, stands on the southern end of the Esplanade.

The **Old Fortress** (*t 266 104 6919; open daily 8.30–2.30; adm*) on Cape Sidáro is separated from the Esplanade by the moat, or *contra fosse*, dug over a 100-year period by the Venetians. The medieval town of Corfu was located on the two little hills of the cape, and scholars have identified the site with the Heraion acropolis mentioned by Thucydides. The fortress walls were badly damaged by the British, but you can explore

Corfu Town

Vido Island
OLD PORT

ARSENIOU
Byzantine Museum
Solomos Museum

SPILIA
DONZELOT
PROSFOROU
CAMPIELLO
RARTOUROU
APOLODOROU

POL
ZAVITSIANOU
PROSSALENDIOU
MITROPOLEOS
AG. THEODORAS
AC. NIKOLAOU
THEMISTOKLI
DOUSMANI
AG. ELENIS MANESSI
EKATERINIS LEONDOS

PLATEIA SOLOMOU
SOLOMOULGOU
PALEOLOGOGU
N. THEOTOKI
Cathedral
PHILARMONIKIS
AG. NIKOLAOU
AG. SPIRIDONOS
THEODOSSIOU

Palace of St Michael and St George

NEW VENETIAN FORTRESS
HISTORICAL CENTRE
TENEDNIOU
VELISSARIOU
PALEOLOGOU
AG. PATERON
Ag. Spyridon PARGAS
N. THEOTOKI
SEVASTIANOU
AG. PANTON

MANDRAKI
Offshore Sailing Club

National Bank
PLATEIA M. THEOTOKI
VOULGAREOS
Town Hall
Cricket Ground
Buses for Kanoni
LISTON

Sound and Light
OLD VENETIAN FORTRESS
Cape Sidaro

Market
G. MARKORA
VOULGAREOS
G. THEOTOKI
DIKASTIRION
MANOU
EPARHOU
DOUSMANI
Statue of Schulenburg
ESPLANADE
ESPLANADA

Ag. Georgios

To Avrami Hill and KTEL Long Distance (Green) Bus Station
I. THEOTOKI
PANDOVA
ARISTOTELOUS
KAPODISTRIOU

Municipal Theatre
DESSILA
MANTZAROU
N. POLITI
N. ZAMBELI
MOUSTOXIDI
MAVILI
SOULIOU
DIMODOKOU
Maitland Rotonda

PLATEIA SAN ROCCO
City (Blue) Bus Terminal
MITROPOLITI METHODIOU
SAMARA
GUILFORD
G. ASPIOTI
AKADIMIAS
Corfu Nautical Club

ALEXANDRAS
RIZOSPASTON VOULEFTON
ZAFIROPOULOU
I. ROMANOU
VAAILA
POLILA
Tennis Courts
MARASLI

Archaeology Museum

G. KALOSGOUROU
British Cemetery

Garitsa Bay

Prison
Tomb of Menecrates
MENEKRATOUS
DIMOKRATIAS

KIPROU
MARASLI
ALKINOU
M. ATHANASIOU
GARITSA

N

To Kanoni

300 m
300 yds

Venetian tunnels, battlements, a drawbridge, and **St George's**, the British garrison church, now an Orthodox chapel. The café here has an alluring sea vista; best of all, however, is the view of the city from the two hills.

Where to Stay

Corfu Town ✉ 49100

Hotels are open all year. EOT (*see* above) or the Association of Room Owners, 24 Adr. Iakovou Polyllá, **t** 266 102 6153, **f** 266 102 3403, can help if you are stuck.

Cavalieri Corfu, on the end of the Esplanade at 4 Kapodistríou, **t** 266 103 9336, **f** 266 103 9283 (*L; luxury*). An elegant 17th-century palazzo; air-conditioned with a magnificent roof garden bar (open to non-guests).

Corfu Palace, 2 Dimokratías, over Garitsa Bay, **t** 266 103 9485, **f** 266 103 1749, *www. corfupalace.com* (*L; luxury*). The prestige hotel on Corfu since 1953, with a recent major face lift. The spacious rooms have marble bathrooms and sea views, but can cost as much as €205 in summer. Pool, beautiful garden, excellent breakfast.

Corfu Holiday Palace (*née* Hilton), 2 Nafsiká St in Kanóni, **t** 266 103 6540, **f** 266 103 6551 (*L; luxury*). Hotel and bungalow complex with casino, bowling alley, pools, water sports, etc., etc.; rooms have sea or lake views.

Bella Venezia, just back from the Esplanade at 4 N. Zambeli, **t** 266 104 4290, **f** 266 102 0708, *belvnht@hol.gr* (*B; expensive*). Renovated old mansion in a quieter, yet central, part of town, with a pretty garden terrace for sumptuous buffet breakfasts.

Arcadion, 44 Kapadistríou, **t** 266 103 7671, **f** 266 104 5087, *info@arcadionhotel.com* (*C; expensive*). Comfortable, central, on the Liston.

Konstantinoupolis, 11 Zavitsianou St, on the waterfront in the Old Port, **t** 266 104 8716/7, **f** 266 104 8718 (*C; expensive*). A good choice since 1878.

Ionian, 46 Xen. Stratigoú, **t** 266 103 9915, **f** 266 104 4690 (*C; moderate*). Conveniently located in town between the old and new ports; plain but decent, with en suite baths.

Royal, 110 Paleopolis St, in Kanóni, **t** 266 103 5345, **f** 266 103 8786 (*C; moderate*). Enjoys a commanding position and could be a class higher with its three swimming pools on descending levels and roof garden with views over Mouse Island and the airport.

Hermes, 4 Ger. Markóra, **t** 266 103 9268, **f** 266 103 1747 (*C; inexpensive*). On the inland side of the New Fortress, next to the morning food market.

Europa, 10 Gitsiáli, at the New Port, **t** 266 103 9304 (*D; inexpensive*). A modern choice.

Eating Out

Corfu shows its Venetian heritage in the kitchen, too. Look for *sofríto*, a veal stew

Ag. Spyrídon and Around

The church of Corfu's patron Ag. Spyrídon – the original Spíros, the most common given name on Corfu – is in the old town; its campanile soars above the town like a mast, bedecked with flags and Christmas lights. Spyrídon was a 4th-century bishop of Cyprus, buried in Constantinople; when the city fell to the Turks, his bones were smuggled in a sack of straw to Corfu. The church was built in 1596 to house them in a silver reliquary. Spyrídon 'the Miracle-Worker' has brought Corfu safely through many trials, frightening both cholera and the Turks away. At one point the Catholics considered placing an altar in his church, but the night before its dedication, he blew up a powder magazine in the Old Fortress with a bolt of lightning to show his displeasure. Four times a year (Orthodox Palm Sunday, Easter Saturday, 11 August and the first Sunday in November) his reliquary gets a processional outing, and the faithful gather from all over Corfu and the mainland to kiss the lid for good luck.

The Ionian Bank, two blocks south in Plateía Iroon Kypriakou Agona, houses a **Museum of Paper Money** (*t 266 104 1552; open Mon–Sat 9–1*); opposite, the church of the **Panagía Faneroméni** (1689) contains fine icons of the Ionian school. The square gives on to the main street, Nikifórou Theotóki, one of the prettiest in town. From

flavoured with garlic, vinegar and parsley; *bourdétto*, a fish stew, liberally peppered; and *pastitsátha*, a pasta and veal dish.

The island's own sweet is *sikomaeda*, or fig pie.

Rex, 66 Kapodistríou, one street back from the Listón, t 266 103 9649 (€12–15). Inexpensive, reliable and good – try the *pastitsátha*, *sofríto* and other Corfiot dishes.

Venetian Well, in Kremastí Square, t 266 104 4761 (€22–28). Stylish and romantic, with a varied menu and a wide choice of costly Greek wines. *Open Mar–Oct.*

La Cucina, 17 A. Giallini, t 266 104 5029 (€17–20). At the corner with Guilford St. Arty Italian with good fresh pasta dishes.

Nausicaa, out in Kanóni, 11 Nafsiká, t 266 104 4354 (fairly dear, but they take credit cards). Delicious Greek, French and Eastern dishes under the garden trellis.

Traditional, 20 Solomoú (€10–12). As authentic an old Greek taverna as you could hope for, with old pots bubbling away in the kitchen and ready oven dishes; try their pickled octopus (*ochtapóthi xytháto*).

Becchios, in Mandoúki (€12), opposite the ferries to Igoumenítsa. For carnivores; splendid charcoal-grilled meats.

Yannis, in Garítsa, near Ag. Iássonos and Sosipater. One of the few remaining tavernas where you are still invited to go into the kitchen and choose your own food in the traditional fashion.

Taverna Tripa ('Hole in the Wall'), in Kinopiástes, 3km from Gastoúri, t 266 105 6333 (€25). Cluttered with knick-knacks and photos of celebrity diners; on the ceiling strings of salamis, sausages, peppers and garlic are linked by cobwebs. Greek nights with up to 10 courses are renowned; the food and service are excellent.

Entertainment and Nightlife

Apart from the disco ghettoes north of town and clubs in Kanóni, most of Corfu's nightlife revolves around the **Listón**, with a smattering of music bars.

The best live Greek music, with dancers and the works, is at the **Loutrovio** restaurant in Kefalomandoukó, on the hill overlooking 'disco strip'. **The Gallery**, on Ag. Spyrídon Street, is a favourite watering hole of Greeks and ex-pats. The **café/bar** in the Old Fort is also a scenic spot, with music and an alluring view (*open 9am–2am*).

there, head up E. Voulgáreos Street to Corfu's **Town Hall**, a Venetian confection begun as a noblemen's club in 1691; grotesque faces grimace from the building and a bas-relief shows a triumphant Doge. In 1720, it was converted into the Opera dell'Oriente, the first opera house in Greece. The nearby Catholic **Cathedral of San Giacomo** (1693) was hit by German bombs in 1943. Only the bell tower survived; the rest was rebuilt.

Campiello

The Campiello quarter between the Old Port and the Esplanade offers the **Orthodox Cathedral** (1577), dedicated to Ag. Theodóra Augústa, Empress of Byzantium (829–42), who was canonized for her role in restoring icons following the Iconoclasm. She lies in a silver casket in the chapel to the right of the altar; if the priest likes the look of you, you can kiss her and take home fragments of her slipper. The **Byzantine Museum** (*t 266 103 8313; open 8.45–3, Sun and holidays 9.30–2, closed Mon; adm*) isn't far, by the sea and up the steps from Arseníou Street in the beautifully restored 15th-century Antivouniótissa. This typical single-aisle Ionian church has a timber roof and exonarthex, or indoor porch, that runs around three sides of the building, and an elaborately decorated ceiling or *ourania* ('heaven') that the Ionians were so fond of, as well as a stone iconostasis, Italianate 17th-century murals on Old Testament themes, and wonderful icons. On a narrow stair off Philharmoniki Street is **Ag. Nikólaos**, once the parish church of the king of Serbia. After the defeat of the Serbian army by the Austro-Hungarians in 1916, the king and 150,000 Serbs took refuge on Corfu. A third of them died shortly thereafter from the flu and are buried on **Vído island**. Caiques regularly make the trip; the islet still has its Venetian fortifications, footpaths and a little beach.

South: Garítsa and the Archaeological Museum

Garítsa, just south of Corfu Town, was fashionable in the 19th century and has plenty of neoclassical mansions to prove it. It also has Corfu's excellent **Archaeological Museum** (*A. Vraila St, t 266 103 0680; open Tues–Sun 8.30–3; adm*), housing statuettes from Archaic to Roman times, a horde of 6th-century BC silver coins and even Cycladic sculptures, discovered in 1992 by an alert customs officer. Upstairs are Archaic *kore* and *kouros* statues, the snarling 'Lion of Menecrates' from the 7th-century BC **Menecrates tomb** (the rest is in a garden, at the junction of Marásli and Kíprou Streets, three blocks southwest of the museum) and the powerful **Gorgon Pediment** (585 BC) discovered by the Temple of Artemis in Kanóni, the oldest of its kind, and one of the largest (56ft wide). A relief of a Dionysiac Symposium (*c. 500 BC*), shows the god with a youth, their eyes focused intently on something lost forever.

Also in Garítsa, on Kolokotróni Street, the beautiful **British cemetery** is something of a botanical garden, with rare species of wild flowers; the headstones date from the beginning of the British protectorate.

Southern Suburbs along the Kanóni Peninsula

City bus no.2 from Corfu Town takes you to the garden suburbs draped over the little **Kanóni peninsula** dangling south of Garítsa Bay. Ancient Corcyra occupied much of this peninsula and had two harbours: the Chalikiopóulos lagoon to the west and the ring-shaped 'harbour of King Alcinous' (now filled in) in the northeastern corner at Anemómylos. Here, a few lanes back, the 10th-century Byzantine church of **Ag. Iássonos and Sosipater** is Corfu's oldest; it has an octagonal dome, handsome masonry and incorporates ancient columns.

The coastal road continues to the villa of **Mon Repos**, built by Sir Frederick Adam, the second High Commissioner of the Ionian State, for his Corfiot wife. The Greek royal family later adopted it; Philip, Duke of Edinburgh, was born here on a kitchen table in 1921. A Roman villa and **Roman baths** lie opposite the 5th-century basilica of **Ag. Kérkyra** of Paleópolis, itself made of the ruins of a Doric temple (by the crossroads, opposite the gate of Mon Repos). A minor road leads to the Doric **Temple of Artemis** (585 BC), source of the Gorgon Pediment in the Archaeological Museum. Little **Mon Repos Beach** is just below if you need a dip, or you can follow the seaward wall of the villa to the path to the spring of **Kardáki**, which flows icy cold year-round from the mouth of a stone lion fountain, used by the Venetians and British to supply their ships. From here it's an easy walk to the lush residential area of Análypsos. **Kanóni**, further south, is named for the cannons once situated where cafés now overlook the

the harbour of ancient Corcyra. Two islets protected it: one with the convent **Panagía Vlacharína**, linked by a causeway, and **Pondikonísi**, 'Mouse Island', with its 13th-century chapel, Ag. Pnévmatos. Legend has it that the ship that was taking Odysseus home to Ithaca was turned into a rock, 'fast rooted in the bed of the deep sea', by Poseidon. An unlovely airport runway crosses the west end of the lagoon, and big hotels have toadstooled nearby.

Pérama, Gastoúri and the Achilleíon

Past the Kanóni peninsula and linked to it by a pedestrian causeway over the lagoon, **Pérama** claims to be the site of King Alcinous' fabled garden. **Gastoúri** provides the lovely setting for the one and only **Achilleíon** (*t 266 105 6210; open for tours daily in summer, 8–3.30; adm*), built in 1890 by the beautiful, melancholy Empress Elisabeth ('Sissi') of Austria and dedicated to her hero Achilles. Eight years later, she was assassinated by an Italian anarchist and it was bought by Kaiser Wilhelm II. It contains the swivelling saddle chair from which he dictated plans for the First World War. Amid this mix of bad art and power, note, over the gate of Troy in Franz Matsch's painting of the *Triumph of Achilles*, a prophetic little swastika. The villa itself was sufficiently kitsch to have been used in the James Bond film *For Your Eyes Only*.

North of Corfu Town

Immediately north of Corfu Town sprawls a 10km stretch of beach, hotels, campsites and restaurants, most intense at Kontókali, Goúvia, Dássia, Ipsos and Pírgi; there's visual redemption only in the dishevelled beauty of the surrounding hills and olive groves. At **Gouviá** the lagoon was once the Venetian harbour; remains of the **arsenal** brood over the marina. Further north, emerald **Cape Komméno** extends out, looking far better from a distance. Then comes busy **Dassiá**, a long, narrow sand and shingle beach fringed by olives, a favourite for sports from waterskiing to paragliding. Excursion boats from here run as far as Kassiópi (north) and Benítses (south). **Ípsos** and **Pírgi**, at either end of Corfu's 'Golden Mile' north of Dassiá, offer carousels of inflatable crocodiles and 'I ♥ Corfu' postcards on their long scimitar shingle beach. From Ípsos, you can escape inland to **Áno Korakiána**, with an olive wood workshop and delightful folk sculpture at the **Museum of Aristides Metalinós** (*t 266 302 2317; open Tues–Sun 8.30–2.30*). The road into the Troumpétta range via Sokráki is an awesome series of hairpins through green and gorgeous country. From Pírgi, noodle up though Spartílas to Strinílas for lunch and excellent wine in the beautiful square.

The Northeast Corner: Barbáti to Ag. Spirídon

After **Barbáti**'s stretch of crowded pebble beach, the coastal road wiggles its way to cosier resorts, where hints of traditional village charm peek through: the quiet cove below **Nissáki** is one, with two good tavernas, and another is **Kamináki**, a pebble bay bordered by villas and tavernas, perfect for snorkelling and watersports. Still heading north is the picturesque bay of **Agní**, with crystal-clear waters and three outstanding

Where to Stay and Eat

Dassiá ✉ 49100

Corfu Chandris and **Dassia Chandris, t** 266 109 7100, **f** 266 109 3458, *www.chandris.gr* (*A; luxury*). Huge, on the beach; with bungalows, villas; pools, tennis, playground, restaurants and a free shuttle service into Corfu Town. *Open April–Oct.*

Scheria Beach, t 266 109 3233, **f** 266 109 3289 (*C; moderate*). Rather more modest but perfectly pleasant and family-run; try to get a sea-facing balcony. *Open June–Sept.*

Camping Kormari, t 266 109 3587; **Camping Karda Beach, t** 266 109 3595. Both offer ample facilities, including pools.

Etrusco, in Kato Korakiana, between Dassiá and Ípsos, **t** 266 109 3342 (€22–35). Corfu's best: the Botrini family serve exquisite delicacies such as pappardelle with duck and truffles, plus mouthwatering desserts and great wines. *Open April–Oct, eves only.*

Nissáki/Kalámi/Ag. Stéfanos/Agní ✉ 49100

You can rent villas here, including the upstairs of Lawrence Durrell's White House in Kalámi; book through **CV Travel** (*see* p.96).

Sol Elite Nissaki Beach Hotel, t 266 309 1232, **f** 266 302 2079, *nissaki@otenet.gr* (*A; luxury*). The only big hotel on this stretch of coast; a mammoth eyesore with great views, a pool, gym, shops, restaurants and good facilities for kids. *Open April–Oct.*

Vitamins, up on the coast road through Nissáki. Smart and friendly taverna with excellent food and a lovely terrace.

Mitsos, on Nissáki Beach. Always busy for lunch, with good reason.

Kassiópi ✉ 49100

Kassiópi bulges with Italians in August and unless you are pre-booked forget it. **Kassiopi Travel Service, t** 266 308 1388, or **The Travel Corner, t** 266 308 1220, **f** 266 308 1108, may be of help.

Kassiopi Star and **The Three Brothers** (€12–15) on the waterfront serve Greek and Corfiot specialities.

Imerolia Beach Taverna. Good food, and dancing every other night.

Ag. Spyrídon ✉ 49100

St Spiridon Bay, 100m from the sea, **t** 266 309 8294, **f** 266 309 8295, *norcorfu@otenet.gr* (*B; moderate*). Tucked away in the olive groves; quiet, unpretentious bungalow complex with pool, only open in season.

Olive Bar, opposite. Mellow place to eat, with good fresh fish and the beach nearby; ask here if you're looking for a room.

Róda/Agnos/Astrakéri ✉ 49081

In season nearly every room in Róda is blockbooked.

Village Roda Inn, t 266 306 3358 (*C; moderate*). Friendly Greek-Canadian-run hostelry; they'll organize a boat trip for you, too.

Roda Beach Camping, t 266 306 3120. An alternative if all else is full.

Kind Hearted Place, at the eastern end of the waterfront. Once the only taverna in town, offering a Greek menu since the early '60s.

Angela Beach, in Agnos, 1km from Róda, **t** 266 303 1291, **f** 266 303 1279 (*C; moderate*). Uninspiring, but does offer a pool, and is minutes from a couple of good-value fish tavernas.

Perouládes ✉ 49083

Villa de Loulia, t/f 266 309 5394, *www.otenet. fr/villadeloulia* (*luxury*). An oasis of class: big, elegant rooms in a 19th-century garden villa with a pool. *Open May–Oct.*

Othoní/Eríkousa/Mathráki ✉ 49081

Locanda dei Sogni, on Othoní, **t** 266 307 1640. Pretty rooms (but book early) and good Italian food.

Rainbow. A good taverna on Othoní.

Erikousa, t 266 307 1555 (*C; inexpensive*). The only hotel on Eríkousa; on the beach.

tavernas, all with sunbeds on the beach, and the popular pebble beach of **Kalámi**. Nearby **Kouloúra** is a lovely seaside hamlet on a narrow horseshoe bay where the brothers Durrell lived; here the 16th-century Venetian Koúartanou Gennatá is part villa and part fortified tower, and there are two 17th-century mansions, Vassilá and

Prosalenti. The next beach north is **Kerásia**, a white pebble strip with shade and a taverna, reached by doubling back 2km from Ag. Stéfanos, playground of the Rothschild set.

Kassiópi, founded by Pyrrhus of Épirus in 281 BC, is the largest resort on the northeast coast. The Romans surrounded it with great walls; its famous shrine of Zeus Cassius was visited by Cicero and Nero, and Tiberius had a villa here. Its ruined Byzantine fort now guards wild flowers, its main street groans with tourist trinkets. Four small, well-equipped beaches can be reached by footpath from the headland and two of Corfu's most tastefully developed beaches, **Avláki** and **Koyévinas**, are a quick drive, or 20–30-minute walk, south of Kassiópi.

Continuing west beyond the grey sand beach of **Kalamáki**, a sign for Loútses and Perithía announces the way up the brooding slopes of 2,953ft **Mount Pantokrátor**, Corfu's highest point. You can drive as far as **Perithía**, a charming cobblestoned village abandoned by all but three families, one of whom runs a nice taverna. The path from here to the summit of Pantokrátor takes about an hour, offering a wondrous display of wildflowers, even in summer, and a bird's-eye view of the emerald island and the white-capped Albanian peaks. The rutted road from Perithía by way of Láfki takes in some of Corfu's most enchanting countryside.

Back down on the coast, **Ag. Spyrídonos** may be the small sandy beach with simple tavernas and rooms that you've been looking for, most days anyway. It fills up on Sundays with locals.

The North Coast

Almirós, at the quiet east end of Corfu's longest beach, is a shallow lagoon with trees and migratory birds. From **Acharávi**'s pretty beach to **Róda**, egg and chips are on every menu; it's packed by package tourism, but there's enough sand to spread out.

Inland from Acharávi, **Ag. Panteléimonos** has a ruined tower mansion, used as a prison by the Venetians; another Venetian manor lies further up in **Episkepsís**. Inland from Róda, **Plátonas** is kumquat country. These sour little fruits look like baby oranges and were introduced from the Far East over half a century ago; the 35-ton annual harvest is distilled into kumquat liqueur (using both blossoms and fruit) or preserved as jam. Inland from Astrakerí, pretty **Karoussádes** has the 16th-century Theotóki mansion as its landmark.

Sidári has surrendered wholesale to package tourism and mosquitoes. If you're passing through, you may want to take a dip in the **Canal d'Amour**, a peculiar rock formation said to be two lovers – swim between them and you are guaranteed eternal love. Less crowded beaches await west of Sidári below **Perouládes**, where the wind-sculpted cliffs cast the beach into shade by early afternoon.

Offshore Islands: Othoní, Eríkousa and Mathráki

Caiques from Sidári (and ferries from Corfu Town, or summer caiques from Ag. Stéfanos) sail to three sleepy islets: Othoní, Eríkousa and Mathráki, the western-most territory of Greece. Criss-crossed with paths and planted with olives and aromatic table grapes, each has a handful of rooms to rent. **Othoní** is the largest, pop. 150, and has two exceptional beaches, one directly under a precipice and the other the sublime Aspri Ammos, of white sand, accessible only by boat. It has trails up to the pretty, nearly abandoned villages and a medieval fort on a pine-covered hill. **Eríkousa** has the most in the way of facilities and good beaches. Bijou **Mathráki**, the smallest, also has a lovely beach – a nesting place for loggerhead turtles.

Western Beaches: North to South

Forested northwest Corfu is off the beaten track; the 'roads' can bottom out your shock-absorbers. The main road from Sidári cuts off the corner en route to **Ag. Stéfanos** (not to be confused with the Ag. Stéfanos on the east coast), a large, uninspiring bay with brown sand; **Aríllas** just south has a wide, sandy, sleep bay with an attractive backdrop of green hills. The village of **Afiónas** is on a headland with magnificent views in either direction, its sandy beach steadily developing. Best of all is **Ag. Geórgios** (Pagoí), a long, magnificent stretch of beach under the cliffs. It offers watersports (especially windsurfing), tavernas, discos and rooms.

One of Corfu's celebrated beauty spots, **Paleokastrítsa** spreads out from a small horseshoe bay, flanked by sandy and pebbly coves, olive and almond groves, mountains and forests. Although chock-a-block in the summer, in the early spring it's easier

Where to Stay and Eat

Paleokastrítsa ✉ 49083

Akrotiri Beach, t 266 304 1237, f 266 304 1277, *belvnht@hol.gr* (*A; luxury*). Five minutes uphill from the beach, great views and a seawater pool.

Casa Lucia, 12km from Paleokastrítsa, t 266 109 1419, f 266 109 1732 (*expensive–moderate*). A cluster of small houses nicely done out with kitchens in a converted olive press; lovely garden, a pool. Ideal for young families.

Fundana Villas, 4km from the sea, t 266 102 2532, f 266 102 2453 (*expensive–moderate*). Rooms with kitchens in a Venetian villa, with lovely surroundings. *Open Mar–Oct.*

Apollón, t 266 304 1124, f 266 304 1211 (*C; moderate*). A more modest affair, with balconies facing the sea.

Astacos ('Lobster'), t 266 304 1068. Restaurant popular with residents and long-term visitors; also has quiet, good-value rooms (inexpensive rooms, not so for the lobster).

Paleokastritsa Camping, t 266 304 1204. Probably the nicest campsite on Corfu.

Chez George. Seafood restaurant, in a prime location and prices to match.

Fisherman, just north by Ag. Giorgi ton Pagon Beach. Corfu's best and cheapest seafood restaurant is hidden off a dirt road in an olive grove by the sea and has neither electricity or phone (so stop by earlier to find it and book a table). *Open May–Oct.*

Glyfáda/Pélekas ✉ 49100

Pelekas Country Club, a few minutes from Pélekas, t 266 105 2239, f 266 105 2919, *www.country-club.gr* (*A; luxury*). A touch of genteel old Corfu in the wonderful wooded grounds of an 18th-century villa with pool, tennis courts and stables, if you want to bring your horse. The antique-furnished rooms, all with kitchenettes, are in the outbuildings. *Open April–Oct.*

Louis Grand, t 266 109 4140, f 266 109 4146, *www.louishotels.com* (*A; luxury–expensive*). Elegant and smack on Glyfáda Beach, with a pool and lots of watersports.

Glyfada Beach, t/f 266 109 4257 (*B; moderate*). A cool, pleasant alternative.

Levant Hotel, Pélekas, t 266 109 4230, f 266 109 4115, *levant@otenet.gr* (*A; expensive*). Perched on top of Pélekas; superb views and a pool, away from it all. *Open April–Nov.*

to see what all the fuss is about. On a low promontory above town, **Zoodóchos Pigí** (or Paleokastrítsa) monastery was built in 1228 on the site of a Byzantine fortress and tarted up by an abbot with rococo tastes in the 1700s. For an even more spectacular view of the magnificent coastline, make the steep climb (or drive) out of Paleokastrítsa through cypresses and pines up to the village of **Lákones** and its Bella Vista Café. Lákones offers some of the loveliest walks on Corfu, especially to Kríni and the formidable ruins of the 13th-century **Angelókastro**, built by the Despot of Épirus, Michael Angelos. This castle sheltered villagers and the Venetian governor during raids and is still impressive, clinging to the wild red rocks over a 1,000ft precipice. The mountain roads from Lákones north to Róda through the little villages of **Chorepískopi**, **Valanión** (3km on a by-road) and **Nímfes** offer a bucolic journey through the Corfu of yesteryear. In spring and early summer the air is laden with herbs and flowers; little old ladies line the road selling oregano, honey, almonds and olive oil.

South of Paleokastrítsa is the **Rópa valley**, where Homer's description rings true: 'Pear follows pear, apple after apple grows, fig after fig, and grape yields grape again.' Rópa boasts the **Corfu Golf Club**, once rated as one of the best in the world, but now a bit woebegone (*green fees €38–44*, **t** *266 109 4220*). Ropa's **Riding Club** (**t** *266 109 4220*) offers rambles across the countryside. Westwards on the coast, **Ermónes**, with its pebble beaches and hotels, is another candidate for Odysseus' landing point. **Pélekas**, a 17th-century village up on a mountain ridge, was Kaiser Wilhelm II's favourite spot to watch the sunset; coachloads arrive every evening at his observatory to do the same. Pélekas was a naturist beach until a road built from Gialiskári brought in crowds; now the unadorned walk down the steep track to lovely **Mirtiótissa** Beach (the half by the monastery is not nudist). **Glyfáda**, with steep cliffs dropping straight down into the bay, is one of the island's best beaches, a long, gentle swathe of golden sand that fills up during the day, but in early evening is perfect for a swim.

Southern Corfu

The southern half of the island has majestic olive groves and the worst excesses of budget tourism. **Benítses** was the worst offender, a British package resort bubbling with hormones and baked beans. It is a gentler place today, although its beach is too close to the coastal highway for comfort. The arches and mosaics just behind the harbour belonged to a Roman bathhouse. A walk through the old residential quarter takes you through delightful rural scenery towards **Stavrós**, site of the Benítses Waterworks, built by Sir Frederick Adam in 1824–32. Benítses hosts the **Corfu Shell Museum** (**t** *266 107 2227; open daily 10–8; adm*), with thousands of beautiful sea treasures. Further south, nearly continuous resort sprawls past the beaches of **Moraítika** and **Messónghi**, a cut above Benítses. If you're down here for the scenery, skip the coast and take the inland route, beginning at Kinopiástes (near Gastoúri), passing by way of **Ag. Déka** (one of Corfu's prettiest villages), Makráta, Kornáta and Strongilí.

The west coast is more worthwhile: **Ag. Górdis**, one of Corfu's more attractive village-resorts. has a sheltered 2-mile-long beach of soft golden sand and minimal

Where to Stay and Eat

Benítses ✉ 49084

All Tourist Services, t 266 107 2223, on the main road, can find you a room.

Marbella, a few kilometres past Benítses at Ag. Ioannis, **t** 266 107 1183, **f** 266 107 1180, *marbella@otenet.gr* (*A; luxury*). Luxurious and recently refurbished in grand style, it exudes tranquil opulence. The à la carte restaurant is reasonably priced.

Avra, t 233 107 2367. Excellent little Italian place on the beach. *Open April–Oct.*

Paxinos, in the old village, **t** 266 107 2339. Serves some more traditional fare.

Ag. Górdis ✉ 49084

Karoukas Travel, t 266 105 3909, **f** 266 105 3887, *karoukas@otenet.gr,* on the main street, may be able to fix you up with a room or apartment.

Ag. Gordis, t 266 105 3320, **f** 266 105 2237 (*A; expensive–moderate*). Large, ultra modern, and endowed with pool, tennis courts, etc.; right on the sand.

Dandidis Pension-Restaurant, t 266 105 3232 (*moderate*). Plain doubles with fridge and balcony on the beach.

Pink Palace, t 266 105 3103 (*E; inexpensive*). Resort complex run by Americans for backpackers who want to party the night away.

Moraïtika ✉ 49084

It's fairly easy to find a rent-room here. Ask at **Vlachos Tours, t** 266 107 5723.

Miramare Beach, t 266 107 5224, **f** 266 107 5305, *cfumiram1@otenet.gr* (*L; luxury*). Complex set in 200-year-old olive and citrus groves, with pool, tennis and disco.

Margarita Beach Hotel, t/f 266 107 5267 (*C; moderate*). Offers more modest seaside doubles with balcony.

Bella Vista, up in the old village. Promises a calm dinner in a garden with views.

Messónghi ✉ 49080

Messonghi Beach Hotel and Bungalows, t 266 107 6684, **f** 266 107 5334, *aktimess@otenet.gr* (*B; expensive*). Giant, self-contained family fun complex.

---

waves. Inland, pretty **Sinarádes**, surrounded by vines, is home to a fine folk museum (*t 266 105 4962; open Tues–Sun 9.30–2.30; adm*). The road south to **Ag. Mattheos** is a delightful meander through olive groves and cypresses; the village has old houses with wooden verandas overflowing with flowers, and a 4th-century monastery, Christos Pantokrator, on top and peaceful beaches below. The octagonal Byzantine castle at **Gardíki**, south of Ag. Mattheos, was built by the Despot of Épirus, Michael Angelos II. A minor road leads in 4km to the lagoony **Límni Korissíon**, where the mosquitoes grow as big as pterodactyls and 14 kinds of orchids bloom.

The scenery from here down to Corfu's tadpole tail is flat and agricultural, but the beaches are sandy and clean. South of Lake Korissíon a family resort has grown up around (another) **Ag. Geórgios. Linía**, the northern extension of Ag. Geórgios beach, is tranquil and backed by dunes; the beach of **Marathiás** has a few tavernas. **Lefkími**, the largest town, is dusty and uninviting; the nearest beaches, **Mólos** and **Alykés**, 2km away, are flat and grey.

At **Kávos**, once a fishing village, the 24-hour rave party has got so out of hand that locals refuse to work there. At the southernmost tip of Corfu, the quieter beaches of **Asprókavos** and **Arkoudílas** (near a ruined monastery, reached by a path from Sparterá) have white sand; the pretty beach below **Dragotiná** is a long walk from the village but never crowded.

Paxí (ΠΑΞΟΙ)

The island of 20 fabled secrets, tiny Paxí (or Paxos) is traversed by an 8km road that twists through immaculate olive groves, source of the liquid gold that has won international medals and is so good that you can drink it straight. Besides the beauty of its 300,000 silvery trees and tidy stone walls, Paxí has some of the friendliest people in Greece. Together with little sister Antípaxi and its wonderful beach, it is a perfect small-is-beautiful escape, although the Italians and yachties who descend on it in July and August strain the facilities.

Plutarch recounts a strange incident that took place at sea near Paxí at the beginning of the 1st century AD. The passengers of a ship passing en route to Italy all heard a loud voice call out from the island commanding the ship's pilot: 'When the ship comes opposite Palodes, tell them the Great God Pan is dead.' He did so, and great cries of lamentation arose, as if from a multitude of people. The story went around the world, and when it came to the attention of Emperor Tiberius, he appointed a commission of scholars to decide what it might mean. What they determined was never entirely disclosed, but any astronomer or priest (as Plutarch was) in that period would have been aware that times, as measured on the great dial of the firmament, were changing – a new World Age was at hand, the Age of Pisces, whose cold chaste fish the Christians adopted as a symbol of Christ.

Gáios, Lákka and Longós

The streets are too narrow for cars in **Gáios**, the island's toy capital, named after a disciple of St Paul who is buried here. There's a small sandy beach and most of Paxí's facilities, a fleet of yachts and a tiny **aquarium** of critters who are released and replaced pot-luck every year. On a rocky islet facing the harbour is the **Kástro**

Getting There

There are daily **ferry** connections with Corfu; twice a week (daily in season) with Párga on the mainland; also infrequent connections with Pátras, Kefaloniá and Ithaca. In summer you may have to have a room reservation before boarding a ferry. **Port authority:** t 266 203 2259.

Where to Stay and Eat

Paxí ✉ 49082

Official accommodation is limited and block-booked in the summer. Everyone else stays in rent rooms, which are invariably pleasant, tidy and double, and average €20–25. **Bouas Travel**, t 266 203 2401, *info@bouastours.gr*, can help.

Paxos Beach, t 266 203 1211, f 266 203 2695, *www.paxosbeachhotel.gr* (*B; expensive*). Pleasant chalet bungalows near the beach in Gaiós; try in the off season.
Paxos Club, 1km from Gáios, t 266 203 2450, f 266 203 2097, *paxosgr@otenet.gr* (*luxury*). With a large pool and very comfortable rooms. *Open May–Sept*.
Taka Taka, t 266 203 2329. One of the handful of tavernas in Gáios serving solid Greek fare and fish, for about €12 for a meal. Mongoníssi has an excellent restaurant (€12) and a pleasant beach.
Ilios, t 266 203 1808 (*E; inexpensive*) and **Lefkothea**, t 266 203 1408 (*E; inexpensive*). In Lákka; both small and open all year, but fill up in season.
Rosa, t 266 203 1471, in Lákka. A pretty little Italian restaurant featuring a wide variety of pasta dishes. *Open May–Sept*.

Ag. Nikólaos, built by the Venetians in 1423, and an old windmill, and beyond it, the islet of **Panagía**, which on 15 August is crowded with pilgrims. **Mongoníssi**, another islet, is connected by boat taxi belonging to a pretty, family-run restaurant that brings customers over for dinner, music and dancing. A minibus winds through the olive groves north to **Lákka**, a tiny port, within easy reach of small pebble beaches; the Venetian **Grammatikoú mansion** nearby is fortified with a tower. Laid-back **Longós**, Paxí's third minute port, is about midway between Gáios and Lákka, and gets fewer visitors; there's a pleasant rocky beach (and others within easy walking distance to the south) and a few bars.

Excursion boats circle the island, offering a look at the dramatic scenery. Paxí's **sea caves** among the sheer limestone cliffs on the wind-beaten west coast were famous even in antiquity; one, **Kastanítha**, is 600ft high. Another distinctive cave, **Orthólithos**, has a monolith standing sentinel at its entrance; **Grammatikó** is the largest of all.

Antípaxi

South of Paxí, tiny Antípaxi has only a few permanent residents. In summer caiques leave Gáios daily for the 40-minute trip to its port Agrapídias. Although the coast facing Paxí looks as if it had been bitten off by a Leviathan, Antípaxi's gentle side is graced with fine sandy beaches, 'softer than silk'. There are two tavernas in the itty-bitty village and port at **Ormós Agrapídias** (do try the local wine) but no accommodation; if you want to stay, bring a sleeping bag; Voutoúmi Beach has a small campsite.

Lefkáda (ΛΕΦΚΑΔΑ)

Lefkás, or Lefkáda, named for the whiteness (*leukos*) of its southern cliffs, became an island some time after 640 BC when Corinthian colonists dug the 66ft-wide Lefkáda ship canal to separate the peninsula from the mainland (today, a swing bridge joins it up again). Although a rather dreary lagoon and town zapped by earthquakes stand at the entrance, the rest of the island beyond, with its long sandy strands, lush beauty and traditional mountain villages, is a delight. Lefkáda is famous for lace and embroideries, and many women still keep a loom in the back room. It is just as celebrated for its windsurfing at Vassilikí and idyllic sailing. Dolphins like it, too: there are more varieties seen off the coasts of Lefkáda than anywhere else.

Colonized by Corinth in Archaic times, Lefkáda had a rocky history: it was devastated by the Corcyraeans and the Athenians during the Peloponnesian War, then by the Macedonians and the Romans who siphoned survivors to populate Nikopolis (*see* p.415). In the Middle Ages the Orsini, Venice, the Despotate of Épirus and then the Turks took turns. The Venetians built the formidable fortress of Santa Maura, the island's 'front door', and its name came to refer to the entire island. When the Turks ruled, they linked Santa Mavra to Lefkáda Town with a mighty causeway–aqueduct of 260 arches across the lagoon (its ruins can still be seen north of the present-day causeway). In 1807 the French and then the Russians grabbed it; even Alí Pasha of

Ioáninna tried to buy it. It was a hotbed of rebellion during the Greek War of Independence, providing refuge for the likes of Theodore Kolokotrónis, but like the other Ionians it had to wait until 1864 to join Greece.

Lefkáda Town and Around

The Venetian and Turkish **Fortress of Santa Maura** has its feet in the sea as you approach the island. Blown up in an accidental powder explosion in 1888, it continued as a military camp and, after the 1922 Asia Minor Disaster, as a refugee camp. It survived the local earthquakes better than the island's capital, **Lefkáda Town**, which collapsed like a house of cards in 1948, and was hit hard again in 1971. In spite of all its knocks, it has a genuine Greek atmosphere, narrow lanes of colourful houses, made of stone below and light anti-seismic wood or corrugated metal above. **Bosketo Park**, a shady square by the causeway, displays busts of Lefkáda's *literati*: the poet Valaorítis, Angelos Sikelianós (*see* p.393) and Lafcadio Hearn (1850–1904). The latter went to Japan in 1890, took the name Yakomo Kuizumi and became an expert on Japanese language and culture.

Lefkáda's stone, domeless churches have largely survived, under anti-seismic iron bell towers that resemble oil derricks. **Ag. Minás** (1707) contains fine examples of the Ionian school of painting; the **Pantokrátor** has a pretty façade, last reworked in 1890, with an atypical curved roofline; **Ag. Spyrídon** (17th century) has a fine carved wooden screen. Near Ag. Spyrídon, the **Orpheus Folklore Museum** displays beautiful embroideries and weavings, and old maps, including one of Lefkáda made by the Venetian cartographer Coronelli in 1687. The **Archaeological Museum** (*t 264 502 3678; open weekdays 10–1; adm*) on the north seafront houses finds from cave sanctuaries and the 12th-century BC tombs discovered by Dörpfeld in Nidrí; the **Post-Byzantine Museum** (*t 264 502 2502; open 10.30–12.30; adm*), with works of the Ionian school, is housed in the library; and the **Lefkáda Phonograph Museum** at 12–14 Kalkáni Street (*open 10–1.30 and 6.30–11*) contains old gramophones and recordings of the 1920s.

The closest place for a swim is the **Gýra**, the sandy if often windy lido by Santa Maura. Above town in the pinewoods, the **Faneroméni Monastery**, rebuilt in the 19th century, offers bird's-eye views over the town and lagoon. Two kilometres south, the stone church of the **Panagía Odigýtria** (1450) is the island's oldest.

East Coast Beaches and Islets

Lefkáda's east coast is lush green and bedecked with beaches. A few kilometres south of town at Kaligóni are bits of **ancient Nerikus**: scramble through the olives to find its Cyclopean walls, a theatre and early Byzantine ruins. Further along past the overbuilt fishing village of **Lygiá** is attractive **Nikiána**, with striking views of the mainland. Further south is **Perigiáli**, with a fine beach, and then **Nidrí**, Lefkáda's busiest most cosmopolitan resort.

Nidrí lines the busy main road, but its taverns look out over lovely Vlýcho Bay, closed in by the Géni peninsula, its still waters dotted with the private wooded islets of **Mandourí**, **Sparti**, **Skorpídi** and **Skórpios** (the last belonging to the Onassis family; excursion boats sometimes land on Skorpiós if no one is in residence). A small army

Getting There and Around

By air: Several flights weekly from Athens and regular charters from England to nearby Aktion (*see* p.415); a bus plies the 26km between Lefkáda and the mainland airport from May to Oct. **Information**: Olympic Airways, **t** 264 502 2881.

By sea: Summer excursion boats connect Nidrí and Vassilikí to Sámi, Fiskárdo and Póros (Kefaloniá) and Kióni (Ithaca). Daily boat from Nidrí to Meganísi. Ferries leave Vassiliki once or twice a day for Kefaloniá and Ithaca. **Port authority**: Lefkáda, **t** 264 502 2322; Nidrí harbour: **t** 264 509 2509.

By road: **Buses** from the station, **t** 264 502 2364, on Golemi St by the marina go to Athens (five a day). Connections to Nidrí, Ag. Nikítas, Vassilikí and beaches are frequent, but consider hiring a **moped** at Vassilikí and Nidrí.

Tourist Information

Tourist police: 30 Iroon Politechníou in Lefkáda Town, **t** 264 502 6450.

In Lefkáda Town, try friendly **Iris Travel**, Akarmanias & Golemi St, **t** 264 502 1441, and in Vassilíki, **Samba Tours**, **t** 264 503 1520, *samba tours@otenet.gr*.

Festivals

In August there is a large **International Folklore Festival**, in Lefkáda Town. Karyá offers festivities including the re-creation of a traditional wedding, with fine old costumes.

Where to Stay and Eat

Lefkáda Town ✉ 31100

Ionian Star, by the beach, **t** 264 502 4762, **f** 264 502 5129, *ionstarh@otenet.gr* (*A; expensive*). The smartest and most comfortable hotel in town, with pool and roof garden.

Nirikos, **t** 264 502 4132, **f** 264 502 3756, *nirikos@lefkada.gr* (*C; expensive*). Most rooms face the water, and there's a nice café-bar downstairs. *Open all year.*

Pension Pirofani, **t** 264 502 5844 (*moderate*). Renovated; spacious, air-conditioned rooms with balconies looking on to the pedestrianized main street. *Open all year.*

Byzantio, **t** 264 502 1315, **f** 264 502 2629 (*E; inexpensive*). Basic but well-kept and friendly at the waterfront end of the same pedestrianized street. *Open all year.*

Sto Molo, 12 Golemi, **t** 264 502 4879. Delightful new place serving tasty *mezédes*, with tables set out by the boats.

O Regantos, on D. Vergoti, near the Folklore Museum, **t** 264 502 2855. Blue and white and cute, with solid fare for around €12.

Nikiána/Lygiá ✉ 31100

Red Towers, **t** 264 509 2951, **f** 264 509 2852, *www.red.towers.gr* (*C; expensive*). Part new, part old, a charming place with a lovely pool, and apartments for families. *Open May–Oct.*

Aliki, **t** 264 507 1602, **f** 264 507 2071 (*C; expensive*). Small apartment hotel in a superb location; pool and air-conditioned rooms overlook its own small beach. *Open all year.*

of locals maintain the island in accordance with Onassis' will. His power and obsession with privacy kept Nidrí's tourist facilities sparse during his lifetime, but locals have since made up for lost time and much of the old beach was sacrificed for a quay. Still, sit at any seaside café in Nidrí at twilight just to watch **Mandourí**, 'the poet's island', float above the horizon on a magic carpet of mist. Its mansion belongs to the family of Aristotélis Valaorítis (1824–79), one of the first poets to write in demotic, everyday Greek rather than in stilted, formal *katharévousa*.

One of the nicest excursions from Nidrí is the 45-minute walk by way of the hamlet of Rachí to the **waterfall**, at the end of the Dimosári Gorge. In summer, it's wonderfully cool and there's a pool for a swim. Charming **Vlyhó**, the next village south, is famous for its boat-builders. Sandy **Dessími** Beach lies within walking distance, as does the olive-clad **Géni peninsula**, offering stupendous views of Skorpiós and

Konaki, 300m from the sea at Lygiá, **t** 264 507 1397, **f** 264 507 1125 (*C; expensive–moderate*). In a garden setting, overlooking a large pool. *Open May–Oct.*

Kariotes Beach Camping, just north of Lygiá, **t** 264 507 1103. A pool but no beach!

Minas, **t** 264 507 1480. Excellent fish soup and seafood on the road to Nidrí.

Nidrí ✉ 31100

George Kourtis' agency can fix you up with a room, **t** 264 509 2494.

Armeno Beach, **t** 264 509 2018, **f** 264 509 2341, *www.armeno.gr* (*C; expensive*). Modern and right on the beach, with watersports available.

Nidrí Akti, **t** 264 509 2400 (*B; moderate*). Good views and open all year.

Bella Vista, **t** 264 509 2650 (*moderate*). Set in a garden 500m from Nidrí and two minutes from the beach; studios have pretty views of Vlýho Bay.

Gorgona, **t** 264 509 2268, **f** 264 509 5634 (*E; moderate*). Set in its own quiet garden.

Desimi Camping, Simi Bay, near Vlýho at the end of the peninsula, **t** 264 509 5374.

Póros/Sívota ✉ 31100

Sívota has rent rooms and fish tavernas, where you can pick your own live lobster.

Okeanis at Mikrós Gialós, **t** 264 509 5399 (*moderate*). Relatively quiet place on the beach with comfortable rooms. *Open May–Sept.*

Poros Beach Camping, **t** 264 502 3203. Luxurious, with bungalows (*moderate*).

Ag. Nikítas ✉ 31080

Odyssey, **t** 264 509 7351, **f** 264 509 7421, *filippas@otenet.gr* (*C; expensive*). One of the island's nicest hotels, with a roof garden and pool.

Ag. Nikítas, **t** 264 509 7460, **f** 264 509 7462 (*C; expensive–moderate*). Tastefully decorated, tranquil hotel at the top of the village. *Open May–Oct.*

Ostria, **t** 264 50 7483, **f** 264 509 7300 (*A; moderate*). Pretty blue and white house in a great spot, overlooking the bay. *Open May–Sept.*

Sappho, on the beach, **t** 264 509 7497 (€14–18). Tasty fish and pittas (an island speciality) and local wines. *Open May–Oct.*

Vassilikí ✉ 31082

Ponti Beach, **t** 264 503 1572, **f** 264 503 1576 (*B; expensive*). Smart option here above the bay, air-conditioned, with a pool and fabulous views.

Wildwind apartments, **t** 264 503 1501, **f** 264 503 1610 (*moderate*). A few yards from the beach, with sailing and windsurfing, volleyball and croquet.

Katina's Place, **t** 264 503 1262 (*moderate–inexpensive*). Simple, clean and tremendously hospitable place with great views over the village and port.

Surf Hotel, in Pondi, **t** 264 503 1740, **f** 264 503 1706 (*C; inexpensive*). New, with balconied rooms by the beach.

Vassilikí Beach Campsite, **t** 264 503 1308, **f** 264 503 1458. Halfway along the bay.

Meganísi from its heights. The archaeologist Wilhelm Dörpfeld, Schliemann's assistant, who excavated 30 Bronze Age tombs near Nidrí (and theorized that it was Odysseus' Ithaca), is buried by the Géni's white church of Ag. Kyriakí. Further south, **Póros** is near the white pebble beach of **Mikrós Gialós**. **Sívota**, the next town south, has an exceptionally safe anchorage that draws so many yacht flotillas you can cross the bay on boats in winter; the nearest swimming is at **Kastrí**, to the west.

Inland Villages: Lace and Lentils

Old villages occupy the fertile uplands, and it's not unusual to encounter an older woman dressed in traditional brown and black, with a headscarf tied at the back. **Odigytría** (near Apólpaina) has a good 15th-century church, Ag. Geórgios, its design showing Byzantine and Western influences. The large village of **Karyá** is the centre of the island's lace and embroidery industry; its **Museum Maria Koutsochéro** (*t 264 504 1590; open 9am–8pm in high season; adm*) is dedicated to the most famous needle-worker of them all, whose pieces were in international demand: if you want to buy, follow the KENTHMATA signs. Another traditional lace town, **Englouví**, is tucked in a green valley; it's the island's highest village (2,395ft), and famous for its lentils. **Drymónas** to the west is a pretty village of stone houses and old tile roofs.

Down the West Coast to Vassilikí

Under the cliffs of Lefkáda's rocky, rugged west coast lie some of the most stunning stretches of sand in the Ionian. From **Tsoukaládes**, southwest of Lefkáda Town, a 2km road leads down to narrow pebbly **Kalímini** Beach and the most turquoise water imaginable. Next, the long sandy **Pefkóulia** Beach stretches south to **Ag. Nikítas**, a village with tile roofs, old tavernas and narrow streets overhung with flowers and vines. The sea is crystal-clear, pale blue and cold. Don't let your windsurfer run away with you, though – the odd shark fin has been spotted off the coast. Just south, **Káthisma** has a taverna on the wide beach of golden sand. The beach below **Kalamítsi** is set among giant rocks, with rooms that make it a good, quiet base.

The road south passes the leafy villages of **Chortáta** and **Komíli**, where the road forks. Buses go down the southwest peninsula as far as **Atháni** (*tavernas with rooms*). **Gialós** Beach can be easily reached by a path from Atháni; the golden sands of **Egrémni** further south are at the end of a long unpaved road and 200 steep steps. After that, the sands of sublime **Pórto Katsíki** ('goat port') lie under pinkish white cliffs below another long walkway-stair (*parking fee*); it's a popular excursion boat destination and has a taverna. At the southern tip are the 190ft sheer white cliffs of **Cape Doukáto** or **Kávo tis Kyrás** (Lady's Cape), the 'lady' being Sappho, who, rejected by Phaon, supposedly leapt to her death. It was always a popular jumping-off place. The ancients forced lunatics or criminals over as sacrifices to Poseidon. Later, priests of Apollo Lefkáda, like the divers at Acapulco, would make the jump – *katapontismós*, with live birds tied to them to slow their fall. Hang-gliders make the leap today.

The left-hand fork at Komíli passes through inspiring scenery to shady **Vassilikí**, a windsurfer's mecca and Lefkáda's second biggest resort, where brightly coloured sails flit like butterflies across the bay. The mid-morning breeze is perfect for beginners; by mid-afternoon it's blowing strongly for experts; by evening it takes a break, allowing a pleasant dinner by the sea. For a swim, walk along the sand to Pondi or catch a caique to Pórto Katsíki (see above) or the white beach of **Agiofýlli**, accessible only by sea.

A road from Vassilikí passes fields of flowers (seeds are a leading export) to **Sývros**, with Lefkáda's largest cave, **Karoúcha**. The road then tackles the increasingly bare slopes of Eláti, Lefkáda's highest peak (3,799ft), to **Ag. Ilías**, with magnificent views.

Meganísi (ΜΕΓΑΝΗΣΙ)

Spectacular Meganísi, an hour and a half by daily ferry from Nidrí, lies off the south-east coast of Lefkáda. Its 1,800 inhabitants are employed in traditional occupations –

seafaring for the men, embroidery and lacemaking for the women. Ferries call at **Váthi**, a pretty port with good fish tavernas, rooms to rent and a campsite. From the cheerful hamlet of **Katoméri**, a track heads down to the beach in narrow Athéni Bay, site of the **Hotel Meganísi** (*t 264 505 1049, f 264 505 1639 B; expensive*). The road continues to **Spartochóri**, a charming island village of 50 years ago, with good tavernas and rooms, and back to Váthi. Excursion boats from Nidrí usually call at the yawning 295ft deep **Papanikólaos' Grotto**, the second largest in Greece and named for the daring Greek resistance submariner who used to hide here and dart out to attack Italian ships, and at the sandy beach of **Ag. Ioánnis**, with a summer cantina.

Kefaloniá (ΚΕΦΑΛΟΝΙΑ)

'The half-forgotten island of Kephaloniá rises improvidently and inadvisedly from the Ionian Sea,' writes Louis de Bernières in *Captain Corelli's Mandolin*. Its Jabberwocky silhouette contains 781 square kilometres, making it the largest Ionian island by far. It has fine beaches, lofty fir forests, two lovely caves and Robóla wine. Kefalonians have the reputation of being cunning, ironic, tight-fisted and the worst blasphemers in Greece, swearing at their patron Ag. Gerásimos one minute and swearing by him the next (although they treat visitors with friendly courtesy). Thanks to Captain Corelli, the island is now anything but 'half-forgotten'. It's essential to book (British holiday firms have most of the properties); in summer the big island bursts at the seams, but there are still quiet corners, if you have wheels.

Getting There and Around

By air: daily from Athens and frequent charters from Britain. The Olympic Airways office is in Argostóli, at 1 R. Vergotí, **t** 267 102 8808; the **airport** is 9km south of Argostóli, **t** 267 104 1511, and reachable by taxi (€10–12).

By sea: Kefaloniá has five ports. Starting at the north, Fiskárdo has ferry links to Ithaca and Lefkáda; Sámi with Ithaca and Pátras; Póros with Kyllíni (Peloponnese); Pessáda, in the south, with Zákynthos; finally, Argostóli with Kyllíni. Schedules change frequently. **Port authorities**: Fiskárdo, **t** 267 404 1400; Sámi, **t** 267 402 2031; Póros, **t** 267 407 2460; Argostóli, **t** 267 102 2224. A ferry between Argostóli and Lixoúri goes every half-hour in season and otherwise hourly.

By road: The Argostóli station is at 4 Tritsi St (left of the causeway as you enter town), **t** 267 102 2281; in Lixoúri, **t** 267 109 3200. Argostóli to Lassi: six buses daily in high season, two or more to Fiskárdo, Ag. Evfimia, Sámi and Skála. No lack of **taxis**, or **car and moped rentals**.

Tourist Information

EOT: Argostóli, on the waterfront across from the Star hotel, **t** 267 102 2248, **f** 267 102 4466; *open weekdays 8–2.30.*
Tourist police: Argostóli, **t** 267 102 2815.
Filoxenos Travel, 2 Vergoti, **t** 267 102 3055, **f** 267 102 8114, *filoxenos-travel@galaxy.gr*, are very helpful.
Proper Cefalonian Travel, 13 Rizopaston, **t** 267 102 6924, **f** 267 102 6925, *ecco@ath.forthnet. gr*, can arrange rooms, tours, dives and yacht rentals.

Festivals

21 May, **Festival of the Radicals** (celebrating union with Greece) in Argostóli; 15 August, **Markópoulo** (with little snakes); 16 August and 20 October, **Ag. Gerásimos**; first Saturday after 15 August, **Robóla festival of wine** in Fragáta.

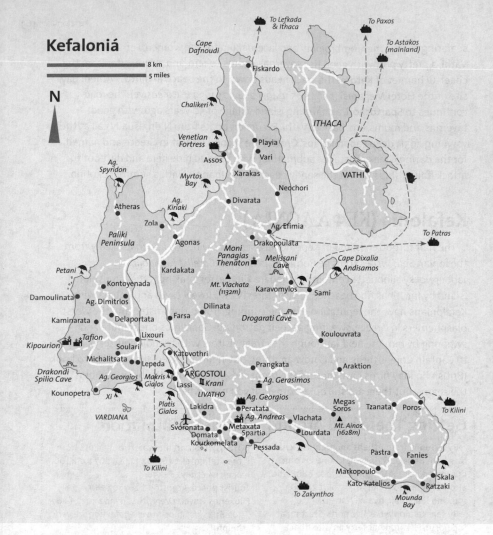

Kefaloniá

8 km
5 miles

N

Cape Dafnoudi

To Lefkada & Ithaca

To Paxos

To Astakos (mainland)

Fiskardo

Chalikeri

ITHACA

Venetian Fortress

Playia

Vari

Assos

Ag. Spyridon

Myrtos Bay

Xarakas

VATHI

Neochori

Ag. Kiriaki

Divarata

Atheras

Zola

Ag. Efimia

Paliki Peninsula

Agonas

Drakopoulata

To Patras

Petani

Kontoyenada

Moni Panagias Thenaton

Melissani Cave

Cape Dixalia

Andisamos

Kardakata

Damoulinata

Ag. Dimitrios

Mt. Vlachata (1132m)

Karavomylos

Sami

Kaminarata

Delaportata

Farsa

Dilinata

Kipourion

Tafion

Lixouri

Drogarati Cave

Koulouvrata

Soulari

Katovothri

Michalitsata

Lepeda

Prangkata

Araktion

Drakondi Spilio Cave

Ag. Georgios

Makris Gialos

ARGOSTOLI

Krani

Ag. Gerasimos

Kounopetra

Xi

Lassi

LIVATHO

Ag. Georgios

Platis Gialos

Lakidra

Peratata

Megas Soros

Tzanata

Poros

To Kilini

VARDIANA

Ag. Andreas

Vlachata

Mt. Ainos (1628m)

Svoronata

Metaxata

Spartia

Lourdata

Pastra

Fanies

Domata

Kourkomelata

Pessada

Markopoulo

Skala

To Kilini

Kato Katelios

Ratzaki

To Zakynthos

Mounda Bay

History

Four independent city states, Sami, Pali, Krani and Pronnoi, divided Kefaloniá between them in historic times, and even earlier may well have formed part of Odysseus' kingdom of Ithaca (*see* p.472). The discovery of a kingly Mycenaean tomb by Póros, containing what looks like Odysseus' seal, has started a race to find the jackpot – his palace. In Byzantine times the island's prosperity attracted pirates and it became the plaything of the Normans, the popes, and most of all of the Venetians. It also attracted a motley assortment of dukes and counts, including Count Matteo Orsini, who founded a murderous, dowry-snatching dynasty at the end of the 13th century. In 1483 the Turks captured the island, but lost it again in 1504 when Venice and Spain under the Gran Capitan, Gonzalo Fernández de Córdoba, took the fort of Ag. Geórgios.

In 1823, Byron spent four months on Kefaloniá before going to die from fever in Messolóngi. During the British occupation the Kefalonians revolted, demanding union with Greece, and 21 nationalists were hanged in 1849 for their pains. This was not the last atrocity in Kefaloniá. In 1943, after Italy's surrender, the occupying Italian Acqui Division joined the Greeks and fought the Germans. More than five thousand Italians died in the subsequent mass executions ordered, it is said, by Hitler himself; their bodies were burned to hide the evidence. Greeks call them the Kefaloniá martyrs – all now familiar to the world through *Captain Corelli*.

A decade later, in August 1953, Nature herself struck, repeatedly: 113 tremors over a five-day period reduced nearly all the island's 350 towns and villages to dust; the first earthquake had the force of 60 atomic bombs. Money for reconstruction poured in from all over Europe and the tens of thousands of Kefalonians who live abroad.

Argostóli (ΑΡΓΟΣΤΟΛΙ)

Big, busy Argostóli (pop. 10,000), set magnificently on a thumb in the island's west bay, has an especially deep and safe port, used as a winter anchorage. As Ag. Geórgios, the Venetian capital, declined, the residents petitioned Venice to make Argostóli the island capital and in 1759 their wish was granted, to the everlasting disgust of arch-rival Lixoúri across the bay. After the earthquake of 1953, Kefalonians abroad lavished money to rebuild the town around central, palmy **Plateía Vallianóu**, the city's surprisingly sophisticated centre. There are two museums to see: the **Koryalenios Historical and Folklore Museum** (*t 267 102 8835; open Mon–Sat 9–2; adm*), on Ilía Zervoú Street, is one of the best of its kind, its contents ranging from the Venetian *Libro d'Oro* listing the local nobility to photos of of pre-1953 Argostóli. The **Archaeological Museum**

Where to Stay and Eat

Argostóli ✉ 28100

White Rocks, at Platís Gialós Beach, 3km from Argostóli, t 267 102 8332, f 267 102 8755 (*A; luxury–expensive*). A swanky choice, with an older clientèle. *Open April–Oct.*

Irilena, on the Lassí peninsula, t 267 102 3118 (*C; moderate*). Family-run, cosy, pleasant choice near a little beach. *Open May–Oct.*

Ionian Plaza, in central Plateía Valliánou, t 267 102 5581, f 267 102 5585 (*C; moderate*). Stylish hotel, rooms with balcony. *Open all year.*

Tourist, on the waterfront, t 267 102 3034, f 267 102 2510 (*moderate–inexpensive*). Comfy old-fashioned rooms, with TV.

Hara, 87 Leof. Vergotí, t 267 102 2427 (*D; inexpensive*). Basic, but cheap. *Open all year.*

Argostoli Beach Camping, 2km north, by the lighthouse, t 267 102 3487.

Casa Grec, 10 Metaxas, t 267 102 4091. Widely considered the best place for dinner. Light classics served in an elegant dining room and courtyard. (€18–22).

Indian Queen, 2 Lavranga St, t 267 102 2631 (€20). Your big chance for something hot and spicy. Excellent balti and other delights; English owned. *Open in season.*

Patsoúras, 26 I. Metaxas, opposite the Sailing Club, t 267 102 2779 (€12). Popular for its local meat dishes, spicy sausage, *panzeta* (smoked pork) and pasta with squid.

Mythos, 13 Rizopaston, t 267 102 2663 (€18–22). For something different, such as *panzeta* in vinegar, honey and thyme (sweet and sour pork), an ancient delicacy.

Kyani Akti, I. Metaxa, t 267 102 6680 (€12–16). Wonderful taverna, excellent fish.

Lixoúri ✉ 28200

Cefalonia Palace, by Xi Beach, t 267 109 3112, winter t 267 109 2555, f 267 109 2638, cphotel @hol.gr (*A; luxury*). New hotel offering half-board accommodation with pools; all rooms have a sea view and balcony. *Open April–Oct.*

La Cité, 28 Octovríou, t 267 109 3501 (*moderate*). Quiet, friendly, with a pool and garden.

Akrogiali has good fish in season and **Zorbas** has a nice terrace garden.

(*t 267 102 8300; open Tues–Sun 8.30–3; adm*), on R. Vergóti, contains ex-votos to the god Pan from the Cave of Melissáni, a room of Mycenaean finds and coins from the four ancient cities of Kefaloniá.

The 800m **Drapanós bridge**, built by the British in 1813 over the shallowest part of the bay, somehow survived the earthquake. Across it, it's a short drive to Razáta, where a dirt road leads up to ancient **Krani**, the best preserved of the island's four ancient cities, where Cyclopean walls of huge stone blocks snake through the trees.

The Lassí Peninsula

The little Lassí peninsula, just north of Argostóli, has some sandy beaches and a clutch of bars, tavernas and discos leading to the somewhat forlorn **Katovothri**, or swallow holes, where the sea is sucked deep underground. In 1963 Austrian geologists poured 140 kilos of green dye into the water. Fifteen days later it appeared in the Melissáni cave lake and at Karavómylos, near Sámi, on the east coast. Sea mills, once used to harness the rushing water for electricity, were destroyed by the earthquake (which also diminished the suction). One has been half-heartedly reconstructed. At the peninsula's tip, the **lighthouse of Ag. Theódori** in a Doric rotunda was built by one of Kefaloniá's great benefactors, British High Commissioner Charles Napier.

The coastal strip just south of Argostóli with its huge beaches, **Platís Gialós** and **Makris Gialós**, was once a place of great natural beauty. Now the locals steer clear and leave it for package tourists; don't feel too deprived if you give it a miss.

Lixoúri and the Palikí Peninsula

Regular ferries ply from Argostóli to Lixoúri, Kefaloniá's second city (all new houses on wide streets) on the bulging Palikí peninsula. Lixoúri values humour and in its central square has a dapper statue of Andréas Laskarátos (1811–1901), a poet and satirist who typifies the Kefalonian wit. He criticized the Orthodox church so much, it excommunicated him – in Greek, *aforismós*, meaning that the body will not decompose after death. Laskarátos, who was poor, promptly gathered his many children's worn shoes and returned to the priest, asking him to excommunicate them too. The **Iakovátos Mansion** (*t 267 109 1325; open Mon–Fri 8–1.30, Sat 9.30–12.30*), an earthquake survivor, is now an icon museum. North of Lixoúri, on Paliókastro Hill, are some of the walls of ancient Pali (or Pale).

The under-populated Palikí peninsula is well endowed with beaches, churches and caves. Four km south of town are sandy **Michalitsáta** and **Lépeda**. **Soulári's** church of Ag. Marína has fine icons and a handsome Venetian doorway; the next village, **Mantzavináta**, has good frescoes in its church of Ag. Sofía. From here a road leads south to the lovely beach of **Ag. Geórgios** (or **Miá Lákko**), a long stretch of golden-red sand. It merges to the west with **Xi**, a crescent of pinkish sand, with sun beds and a taverna (bus service in summer). The huge seaside monolith, the **Kounópetra** just south, once rocked to and fro, pulsating at a rate of 20 beats a minute until the earthquake of 1953 fouled up its magic by stabilizing the seabed. A paved road west of Lixoúri takes you to the rebuilt **Kipouríon** monastery, perched on the west cliffs, with spectacular sunset views. **Drákondi Spílio,** a cave 130ft deep, can be reached from this monastery with a guide. The northern part of the Palikí has a scattering of pretty villages such as **Damoulináta**, **Delaportáta** and **Kaminaráta** and more beaches: the large, white sands of **Petáni** are rarely overcrowded. Even more remote is sandy **Ag. Spyrídon**, tucked into the tip of the Palikí peninsula, via the village of Athéras.

Southern Kefaloniá

Southeast of Argostóli: The Livathó, Wine, and Mount Aínos

Most of Kefaloniá's rural population is concentrated southeast of Argostóli in the attractive fertile rolling hills called the Livathó. **Miniés** is home to a ruined 6th-century BC Doric temple and some of Greece's finest wine made from Robóla, a grape variety introduced by the Venetians in the 13th century that ferments into a distinctive lemony dry white wine (Gentilini and Calligas are two of the best). The coastal road south of Miniés continues to **Svoronáta**, where the red sands of **Avithos Beach** look out to the tiny islet of Días which had an altar to Zeus. Sacrifices were coordinated by smoke signals with those on Mount Aínos. **Domáta**, the next village east, boasts Kefaloniá's oldest olive tree (able to squeeze 20 people in the hollow of its trunk) and the church of the **Panagía**, with a pretty reconstructed Baroque façade and a giant 19th-century carved iconostasis gilded with 12,000 melted gold sovereigns.

Nearby **Kourkomeláta** was rebuilt by the wealthy Kefalonian shipowner Vergotís; everything is as bright and new as a Californian suburb. At **Metaxáta**, where printing was introduced to Greece, Byron lived for four months in 1823, and finished *Don Juan*. Just northwest, **Lakídra** is a suspected site of Odysseus' palace; in the suburb of Kallithéa, near the little church of **Ag. Nikólaos ton Aliprantídon**, four Mycenaean tombs (1250 to 1150 BC) were found. Byron used to come here and, inspired by the view, wrote: ΑΝ ΕΙΜΑΙ ΠΟΙΗΤΗΣ ΤΟ ΟΦΕΙΛΩ ΕΙΣ ΤΟΝ ΑΕΡΑ ΤΗΣ ΕΛΛΑΔΟΣ ('If I am a poet, I owe it to the air of Greece').

Inland: Ag. Andréas, Ag. Geórgios and Ag. Gerásimos

North of Metaxáta, more Mycenaean rock-cut tombs are signposted at Mazarakata, on the way to the Byzantine convent of Ag. Andréas. The 1953 earthquake shook loose its whitewash, revealing frescoes that date back to the 13th century (in the chancel) and the 17th and 18th centuries (along the nave). Now the **Ag. Andréas Monastery Museum** (*t 267 106 9700; open Mon–Fri 9–1.30 and 5–8, Sat 9–1.30; adm*), it houses ecclesiastical exhibits, among them the Veneto-Byzantine icon of *Panagía Akáthistos*, painted in 1700 by Stéfanos Tsankárolos from Crete. The new basilica was built to house the sole of St Andrew's right foot.

Above the church and village of Peratata looms the massive bastioned **Castle of Ag. Geórgios** (*open June–Oct Tues–Sat 8.30–3, Sun 9–3*), spread over a 1,050ft hill, offering truly grand views over the island. The Byzantine citadel was completely rebuilt by the Venetians, who made Ag. Geórgios the island capital until 1757. Store rooms, prisons, Venetian coats-of-arms, churches and a bridge built by the French during their brief occupation have recently been shored up. To the east of the castle lies the green **plain of Omalós** and the **monastery of Ag. Gerásimos**, founded by

Kefaloniá's patron saint in 1560, and now named after him; his bones rest in a silver reliquary in a church built over his grotto hermitage. He is immensely popular; every second male on the island is named after him. Gerásimos' forte was helping farmers dig wells, but posthumously he is renowned for curing mental illness, especially if the patient keeps an all-night vigil at his church on his feast day (20 October) and lays on the ground during the procession so the reliquary passes over his or her body.

From the Argostóli–Sámi road, a branch winds up the slopes of **Mégas Sóros** (5,341ft), the highest of the majestic Aínos range, as far the tourist pavilion (4,265ft); from there you can easily hike the rest of the way, among the tall, scented trees, seemingly on top of the world. Once the Aínos was blanketed with *Abies cefalonica*, indigenous bushy black firs with upward-pointing branches, so dense that Strabo called the island Melaina ('the Dark'). Venetian shipbuilders over-harvested them and fires in 1590 and 1797 destroyed most of what remained. In 1962 the remnants were made into **Mount Aínos National Park**, where little wild horses, descendants of ancient stock, gallop free. The foundations of the 8th-century BC Sanctuary of **Aenesian Zeus**, lord of the mountain, are just below Mégas Sóros; until recently you could see the piles of ash from the animal sacrifices that took place there.

The South Coast and the Virgin's Little Snakes

Kefaloniá's south coast is trimmed with calm sandy beaches: **Spartiá** under sheer white cliffs and **Trapezáki**, 1.5km from **Pessáda**'s tiny harbour, where ferries chug across to Zákynthos. East, below **Karavádos**, is another pretty sandy beach with plane trees and reeds spread behind. But the longest and most crowded is **Lourdáta**, named after the English milords who came here in the 19th century to enjoy its warm micro-climate. Its village square is the beginning of a 2½-hour walk on a nature trail through orange and olive groves, *maquis* and scrubby phyrgana, pines and kermes

Where to Stay and Eat

Pessáda ✉ 28083

Sunrise Inn, 1.5km from the port, t 267 106 9586, f 267 106 9621 (*B; luxury*). Comfortable and air-conditioned, set in the trees, with a pool and children's activities.
Karavados Beach Hotel, near Ag. Thomas Beach, t 267 106 9400, f 267 106 9689 (*B; expensive*). Offers two pools, tennis and a mini-bus service to Argostóli.

Lourdáta ✉ 28083

Lara, t 267 103 1157, f 267 103 1150, *lara@hol.gr* (*C; expensive–moderate*). Pleasant hotel with a pool, near the sea. *Open May–Oct.*

Skála ✉ 28082

Nine Muses, by the beach, t 267 108 3563, f 267 108 3560, *www.9museshotel.com*

(*expensive*). Tasteful bungalow complex, set in lush gardens with a pool. *Open May–Oct.*
San Giorgio, t 267 108 3267, f 267 108 3557, *www.sangiogiohotel.com* (*luxury–expensive*). A charming place, with lots of old elements in the design. Plus a pool. *Open May–Oct.*
Aliki, t 267 108 3427, f 267 108 3426 (*B; moderate*). Good value, overlooking the sea.

Póros ✉ 28082

Seagull Holidays, t 267 407 2001, f 267 407 2002, *seagull@otenet.gr*. Ten simple rooms with balconies (*inexpensive*); they rent cars or bikes, too. *Open April–Oct.*
Pantelis Rooms, on the busy waterfront, t 267 407 2484, *pantelis-rest@usa.net* (*moderate–inexpensive*). Basic rooms with fridge and air-conditioning, over a good taverna.
Romanza. Perched one flight up on a rock; Greek cuisine and the best view.

oaks, passing the ruined **Monastery of Síssia**, founded in 1218 by St Francis of Assisi on his return from the Crusades. **Káto Kateliós** is a small resort, pretty, with springs, greenery and a beach that curves along Moúnda Bay. Just east, **Potomákia Beach**, below Ratzaklí, is a favourite nesting place of loggerhead turtles.

Markópoulo, set over the sea on a natural balcony, is famous for a unique rite: during the first 15 days of August, small harmless snakes with little crosses on their heads suddenly appear in the streets. Formerly they slithered into the church and mysteriously disappeared near the silver icon of the Panagía Fidón ('Virgin of the Snakes'). Nowadays, because of the traffic, the villagers collect them in glass jars and bring them to the church, where they are released after the service and immediately disappear just as before. Sceptics argue that the church is simply along the route of the little snakes' natural migratory trail; the faithful point out that the snakes failed to appear when the island was in distress – during the German occupation and in 1953, the year of the earthquake.

Low-key **Skála**, with its long beach and low dunes, is a good-sized resort with plenty of watersports, sunbeds and bars. It has always been popular: a 2nd-century AD **Roman villa** here has pretty mosaic floors, one showing Envy being devoured by wild beasts. Two km north of Skála, a 7th-century BC Temple of Apollo has been cannibalized to build the nearby chapel of Ag. Geórgios. Some Cyclopean walls of Pronnoi, one of the island's four ancient cities, are located above the village of **Pástra**. In the nearby hamlet of **Tzanáta**, signs point to the 12th-century BC **Mycenaean tholos tomb**, 23ft in diameter, discovered in 1992 and the most important discovered in western Greece (there's usually a guardian there to show you around). Although the vault has collapsed, the tomb was unpillaged – its bones, jewellery and seals (including the one that may have belonged to Odysseus) are at the University of Pátras.

From Tzanáta the road descends through the narrow 'Póros Gap', carved, they say, by Heracles who was in a hurry to cross the mountains. **Póros**, on three turquoise bays, with ferry links to Kyllíni, was ancient Pronnoi's port. It is the most 'Greek' of the resort towns, with a pleasant waterfront, shingle beach, and food that isn't all tourist fare.

Northern Kefaloniá

Plain Jane **Sámi** is the port for Pátras and Ithaca. For the shooting of the film of *Captain Corelli*, it got a wonderful mock-Venetian waterfront that left many older residents dewy-eyed as they remembered how their town used to look. All gone now except for some unsightly dumps where the sets were tossed. The two hills behind Sámi sport **ancient walls**, where the citizens put up a heroic four-month resistance to the Romans in 187 BC before their defeat and sale into slavery. Five kilometres east, there's an exquisite pebble beach, **Andisámos**, set in a bay of exceptional beauty with forested hills spilling down to a crystal sea.

Magnificent grottoes are nearby. Magical sheer-sided **Melissáni** (*t 267 102 2997; open 9–6, July–Aug 9–9, closed after Oct; adm exp*) is a half-hour walk from Sámi; local gondoliers paddle you across its salt water lake (supplied by the swallow holes near Argostóli), immersing you in a shimmering play of blues and violets as the sun filters through a hole in the roof, 100ft above. The **Drogaráti Cave** (*t 267 102 2950; open 9–6,* *closed after Oct; adm*), near Chaliotáta, is a lugubrious den of orange and yellow stalactites and stalagmites; it has such fine acoustics that Maria Callas came here to sing.

Pretty **Ag. Efimía**, at the base of the island's northern peninsula, is more upmarket than Sámi, although it still has a handful of simple rooms to rent. The pretty village of **Drakopouláta**, a few kilometres above the port, was a rare one spared by the earthquake. Goats grazing on the slopes of Mount Ag. Dinatí sport silver-plated teeth because of the soil's high mica content.

Up the Northwest Coast: To Mýrtos, Ássos and Fiskárdo

The journey from Argostóli north to Fiskárdo is magnificent. Two kilometres below **Divaráta** curves the stunning, oft-photographed U-shaped bay of **Mýrtos**, where sheer white cliffs carpeted with green *maquis* frame a crescent of tiny white pebbles and sand against a sea so blue it hurts. Bring provisions (and a hat – there's no afternoon shade) or settle for a pricey sandwich at the café. The road continues along a corniche

Where to Stay and Eat

Sámi ✉ 28080

Sámi Travel, by the dock, t 267 402 3050, f 267 402 3052, *samitrvl@otenet.gr*, can help find rooms and issue tickets. **Aris Rent A Car**, t/f 267 402 2239, has bikes, too.

Pericles, t 267 402 2780, f 267 402 2787 (*B; expensive*). Large-ish unexceptional complex on the edge of town, with two round pools, tennis and a nightclub. *Open May–Oct.*

Athina, at Karavomilos, 2.5km from Sámi, t 267 402 3066, f 267 402 3040 (*expensive*). New, nice, with rooms and apartments sleeping four with sea views.

Melissani, t/f 267 402 2464, in Athens t 210 417 5830 (*D; moderate*). Small and friendly hotel set back from the waterfront in greenery. *Open April–Oct.*

Kastro, t 267 402 2656, f 267 402 3004 (*C; moderate*). Sea views and handy for ferries. *Open April–Oct.*

Karavomilos Beach Camping, 1km from town, t 267 402 2480. Well equipped.

The **Delfini**, **Adonis**, **Port Sámi** and **Dionysos** are reliable. Look out for octopus pie and meat cooked in a ceramic *stámna*, and expect to pay around €12.

Ag. Efimía ✉ 28081

Gonatas, Paradise Beach, a 5-minute amble from the port, t 267 406 1500, f 267 406 1464 (*B; expensive*). Family-run and smart, with a pool and sea views. *Open April–Oct.*

Paradise (also known as Dendrinos, after its owner), at Paradise Beach, t 267 406 1392. Taverna which has earned itself a big reputation for Greek dishes.

Ássos ✉ 28084

Beds fill up fast in the summer; book ahead through a package company or try:

Linardos Apartments, t 267 405 1563 or winter in Athens, t 210 652 2594.

Platanos. Good food and Kefalonian humour offered by the English-speaking owner.

Fiskárdo ✉ 28084

Pama Travel, t 267 404 1033, f 267 404 1032, *pamatravel@compulink.gr*, can help.

Agnantia Apartments, t/f 267 405 1801, *www. agnantia.com* (*luxury–expensive*). Charming studios with gorgeous views. *Open May–Oct.*

Kiki Apartments, t 267 404 1208 (*expensive*). Attractive; on the waterfront in the back bay.

Stella, t 267 404 1211, f 267 404 1262, *stella@ kef.forthnet.gr* (*B; expensive–moderate*). Furnished apartments right on the water.

Dendrinos, t 267 404 1326 (*moderate–inexpensive*). Just out of town, in traditional style.

Nikolas, t 267 404 1307, on the harbour opposite the town. Rooms (*expensive–moderate*) and a good restaurant with Greek dancing.

Sotiria Tselenti, t 267 404 1204 (*inexpensive*). Rooms over the Fiskárdo bakery.

Tassia, t 267 404 1205 (*€25–30*). Rub shoulders with visiting celebrities in the heart of the harbour. Seafood is the order of the day.

> ### Robert Guiscard: A Stormin' Norman
>
> Fiskárdo's name comes from Robert Guiscard, the *terror mundi* of his day. Born in Normandy in 1017, Robert began his career as a mercenary adventurer with an eye for the main chance (*Guiscard* means 'crafty'). He made himself Duke of Apulia, the master of southern Italy, while his brother Roger founded a dynasty of Norman kings in Sicily. In 1085 Robert was here on his way to conquer Constantinople when typhoid struck, and he died in the arms of his warrior wife Sichelgaita. John Julius Norwich described him as 'a gigantic blond buccaneer who not only carved out for himself the most extraordinary career of the Middle Ages, but who also, quite shamelessly, enjoyed it.' Such was the power of his name that the old pirate was granted a posthumous reputation as a virtuous Crusader, and two centuries after his death Dante installed him in *Paradiso*, probably the only way he would ever have landed there.

to the unforgettable view over **Ássos**, where the gorgeous Venetian castle and colourful little fishing hamlet look like toys. Package tour companies have replaced the Venetians and the once pristine causeway to the fortress, lined with maisonettes, resembles a modern Ponte Vecchio. A path leads up to the **Venetian fortress** (1585), with gorgeous views that are especially lovely at sunset. It was used as a rural prison until 1815; deserted now, it awaits a better idea.

A secondary road rises up through the inland villages of the peninsula; here **Varí** has the late Byzantine church of **Panagía Kougianá** (*ask in the village for the key*), frescoed by a folk artist with delightful scenes of hell and paradise. Heading up Kefaloniá's northernmost cape, the road passes the white rocky beach of **Chalikéri**, where people soak in the exceptionally briny water and leave pleasantly pickled. In **Ántipata Erissóu**, the unusual Russian church (1934) was built by a local who made it rich in the USSR.

Fiskárdo is the most picture-postcard-perfect, trendiest and most expensive village on the island, its 18th-century houses gathered in a brightly coloured apron around a yacht-filled port. A fluke in its geological depths spared it from the 1953 earthquake and it's a poignant reminder of Kefaloniá's former glory. Some of the houses have been fixed up for guests; others are decorated with folk paintings of mermaids and ships. Four carved stone sarcophagi and the ruins of a Roman bath are fenced off by the Panormos hotel. The tiny **Nautical and Environmental Museum** (*open 10–2 and 5–9*) displays objects trawled up from the depths (including the Bristol Beaufighter, shot down in 1943). Fiskárdo's beaches are so-so, but there are caiques to others.

Ithaca/Itháki (IΘAKH)

Ithaca, in brief, is one of the most likeable islands in Greece. As Homer sang, it is 'narrow', 'rocky' and 'unfit for riding horses', with a jagged, indented coast that make it a favourite with sailors. Best of all, Ithaca has changed little over the years; the atmosphere is relaxed and low-key, and most islanders like it that way. Itháki, as they call their home, is the eternal symbol of all homes 'even if you find it poor,' as Caváfy wrote, 'Ithaca does not deceive. Without Ithaca your journey would have no beauty.'

The Myth: There and Back Again

Arkikious of Kefaloniá annexed Ithaca and made it the centre of his realm; his son, Laertes sailed with the Argonauts, then married Anticleia, who gave birth to Odysseus. Homer says his name (it means either 'angry,' or ' hated by all'), arose because gossips suspected his dad was really Corinth's cunning Sisyphus (see p.181), and Arkikious, who named him, knew it.

Odysseus sought Helen's hand in marriage, then wed Penelope instead and had a son, Telemachus. An oracle warned that if Odysseus went to Troy (as he was bound by oath to do, as a former suitor of Helen), he would be absent for 20 years and return alone without booty, so Odysseus pretended madness by ploughing sand and sowing it with salt when Menelaus' representatives came to fetch him. To test him, the representatives placed his baby son Telemachus in front of his oxen, and Odysseus diverted his course; the game was up, and off he went to fulfil the oracle. After his delayed homecoming and murder of Penelope's suitors, Homer's story ends, but myth tells how Odysseus wasn't permitted to die until he appeased the anger of his old enemy Poseidon. The only way to do so was to take an oar and walk until he came to a land where people asked him what he carried. Then, after a sacrifice to the sea god, he sailed home, and was drowned on the way.

History

Communal life on Ithaca goes back to 3000 BC, and by Mycenaean times its settlements had coalesced into an organized kingdom (c. 1200 BC) that scholars believe included Kefaloniá, Zákynthos, Lefkáda and part of the Peloponnesian coast. Inscriptions found on Ithaca show that Odysseus was worshipped as a divine hero; coins bore his picture, and pottery was decorated with his cockerel symbol. Homer says his palace was above 'three seas' and, on the hill near Stavrós, overlooking three bays, Schliemann duly unearthed a large structure here he labelled 'Odysseus' Palace', although it dates from only 700 BC. Other Homeric sites have been tentatively identified, such as the Fountain of Arethusa and the cave where Odysseus hid the treasure given to him by the Phaeacians (see p.474).

Ithaca later became so unimportant that at times it was simply known as 'Little Kefaloniá', and was all but abandoned because of pirates. The Venetians offered generous incentives to anyone who would settle there but, unlike the other Ionian islands, it was always too poor to have an aristocracy. Many have emigrated to Australia, South Africa and perhaps even a few to Ithaca, New York. Most who stayed are sailors, and spend much of the year away at sea.

Váthi (ΒΑΘΥ)

Váthi (pop. 1800), at the bottom of a narrow horseshoe bay, has been the capital of the island since the 16th century. Its beautiful harbour, surrounded by mountains, embraces a wooded islet called **Lazaretto** after a quarantine station established in 1668 by the Venetians. Two ruined forts, **Loútsa** and **Kástro**, built in 1805 by the French, guard the harbour entrance.

Although shattered in the same 1953 earthquake that razed Kefaloniá, Váthi was reconstructed as before with red tile roofs. One building that survived, a neoclassical mansion, is now the **Archaeological Museum** (*t 267 403 2200; open Tues–Sun 8.30–2.30*) housing vases, coins and Mycenaean and Classical artefacts. The little **Folklore Museum** near Polyctor Tours (*t 267 403 3398; open 8.30–2*) has reconstructed rooms of old Ithacan homes. The church of the **Taxiárchos** has an icon of Christ attributed to a young El Greco. Every four years, Váthi's Centre for Odyssean Studies has hosted an International Congress on the *Odyssey*. If it's a swim you need, make use of the caique services in Váthi port for **Gidáki** Beach. Otherwise, some small pebble beaches are accessible by car to the east.

Getting There and Around

By sea: Ithaca has three ports: Váthi, connected at least twice a day with Sámi (Kefaloniá), Pátras and occasionally with Astakós; Píso Aetós, 7km west of Váthi, has a faster, cheaper ferry to Sámi (Kefaloniá) and occasionally to Fiskárdo (Kefaloniá) and Vassilikí (Lefkáda). Fríkes, in the north of Ithaca, connects with Lefkáda and Sámi (also daily caiques between Váthi and Fríkes). Schedules do change. **Port authority**: Váthi, t 267 403 2209; Píso Aetós, t 267 403 2104.

By road: One **bus** (two in July and August) a day plies up and down the island from Kióni to Váthi and back. **Taxis** abound. **Car hire**: Mr Koutavás, by Váthi's town hall, t 267 403 2702; for **motorbikes** Mákis Grívas, by the port, t 267 403 2840.

On foot: There are some wonderful walks (see the excellent free pamphlet, 'Trails of Ithaca'). Ian Peters, PO Box 2 Váthi, t 267 403 3592, offers walking tours.

Where to Stay and Eat

Váthi ✉ 28300

For help with rooms, try **Polyctor Tours**, t 267 403 3120, *polyctor@otenet.gr*, or **Delas Tours**, t 267 403 2104, f 267 403 3031, *delas@otenet.gr*, both in the main square in Váthi.

Perantzada, 821 Odyssea Androutsou, t 267 403 3496, f 267 403 3493, *arthotel@otenet.gr* (*A; luxury*). Overlooking the port, a plush designer 'art' hotel in the former naval school, each room a delight. *Open all year*.

Captain Yiannis, t 267 403 3173, f 267 403 2849 (*C*). Appealing bungalow complex with kitchenettes etc., pool and tennis, east across the bay from the hub of the town.

Odyssey Apartments, t 267 403 2268, f 267 403 2668, *www.one-world.net/hotels/odyssey* (*expensive*). Well equipped, with lovely views. *Open April–Oct*.

Maroudas Rooms, t/f 267 403 2451. Studios (*moderate*) and rooms (*inexpensive*).

There's a smattering of tavernas around the harbour and back lanes, with good food.

Kandouni, on the waterfront, t 267 403 2918 (€12–15). Plain taverna, but the kitchen has a few treats, *soutzoukákia* and pasta with lobster among them.

Trexandiri, set back from the port (€10–12). Small and inexpensive with good food.

Sirines ('Sirens'), nearby, t 267 403 3001 (€15–18). A romantic courtyard setting; tasty *mezédes* and hearty main dishes, including pasta. *Open eves only*.

Tsibiris, 800m east of the ferry dock. Fresh fish by the water, with a view of town.

Fríkes/Kióni ✉ 28301

Try **Kiki Travel** in Fríkes, t 267 403 1387, f 267 403 1762, *kikitrav@otenet.gr*.

Nostos Hotel, Fríkes, t 267 403 1644, f 267 403 1716 (*C; moderate*). Set near the beach.

Kionia, in Kióni, t/f 267 403 1362 (*luxury*). Elegant, but mostly block-booked.

Maroudas Apartments, t 267 403 1691, f 267 403 1753 (*moderate*). Pleasant self-catering option that may have vacancies in season. *Open all year*.

Calypso, t 267 403 1066. Sweet little taverna in Kióni, with a dab hand at the hob.

Southern Ithaca: On the Odysseus Trail

Some sites identified with places in the *Odyssey* make pretty walks. West of Váthi, it's a 4km walk (or drive) to the **Cave of the Nymphs** or Marmaróspilia (*signposted, but often closed*), where Odysseus is said to have hidden the gifts of King Alcinous. The cave has a hole in the roof – 'the entrance of the gods' – which permitted the smoke of the sacrifices to rise to heaven. Below, the narrow **Dexiá** inlet may be the 'Harbour of Phorcys' where the Phaeacians gently put the sleeping Odysseus on shore.

South of Váthi, an unpaved road runs 7km to the pretty Maráthias plateau. About 4km along, a path to the left is signposted Κριν Αρεθουσα, the **Fountain of Arethusa**, an hour and a half walk. According to the myth, Arethusa wept so much when her son Corax 'the raven' was killed that she turned into this spring. Just to the south, at **Ellinikó**, Odysseus, disguised as a beggar, met his faithful swineherd Eumaeus; excavations have uncovered Mycenaean odds and ends. From the Arethusa fountain a rocky descent leads to a pretty beach, facing a tiny islet where the murderous suitors hid, awaiting to ambush Telemachus on his return from Pýlos.

The only other village in the south is **Perachóri**, on a 984ft-high balcony covered with vineyards, where a pair of seasonal tavernas serve local wine and *tserépato*, meat slowly roasted in a clay pot. Nearby is crumbling **Paleochóra** (signposted), where a church has fading Byzantine frescoes and the view is superb. Another road – four-by fours only – climbs 3km to the earthquake-blasted **Monastery of the Taxiárchis** (1645) near the top of Mount Stéfano.

North of Váthi

Ithaca has an hourglass figure, its waist the narrow mountain stretch of **Aetós** (Eagle). Overlooking the bays below is what Schliemann called the **Castle of Odysseus** with Cyclopean walls. Recent excavations around Aetós' church of Ag. Geórgios unveiled a site occupied since the 13th century BC, but no palace. There's a pebble beach in the bay below to the east and an excellent one at **Píso Aetós** in the west, where the local ferry boats come in.

Just north of Aetós, near Agrós, is the **Field of Laertes**, with its 2,000-year-old 'Laertes' olive' where Odysseus encountered his father after killing the suitors. From here a road ascends **Mount Níritos** (2,572ft) to the **Monastery of the Katharón** (t 267 403 3460), built on the site of a Temple of Athena, its church containing an icon attributed to St Luke. When Byron visited in 1823 a special mass was held in his honour; today pilgrims walk up from Váthi and spend the night of 14 August. From its bell tower you can see the Gulf of Pátras. A paved road continues 3km up to **Anógí**, 'at the top of the world', passing odd-shaped boulders, including a phallic 25ft monolith named Araklís, or Heracles. The village has Venetian ruins and a 12th-century church dedicated to the **Panagía** with frescoes; clay amphorae embedded in the walls improve the acoustics. Ask at the *kafeneíon* for the key.

A second and easier road from Agrós follows the west coast. At Ag. Ioánnis is a lovely, seldom-used white beach, Aspros Gialós. **Lévki**, a small village to the north, was a base for the resistance during the war; Britain officially adopted it after the 1953 quake and helped rebuild it. There are small beaches below and a few rooms to rent.

The two roads meet at **Stavrós**, overlooking lovely **Pólis Bay** ('city bay'), its name referring to the Byzantine city of Ierosalem, which sank into it during an earthquake; Robert Guiscard (*see* p.471) had been told by a soothsayer that he would die after seeing Jerusalem, but he never thought it would be on Ithaca. Stavrós' **Cave of Loízos** was an ancient sanctuary, where prehistoric pots, Mycenaean amphorae, bronze tripods from 800–700 BC, and an inscription to Odysseus were found before the cave and the path to it collapsed.

Another plausible Odysseus' palace is **Pilikáta**, just north of Stavrós. It fits the Homeric description perfectly, in sight of 'three seas' (the bays of Frikés, Pólis and Aphales) and 'three mountains' (Níritos, Marmakás and Exógi or Neion). Although the ruins are of a Venetian fort, under it excavators found evidence of buildings and roads dating back to Neolithic times, and a pit containing sacrifices and two ceramic shards engraved in Linear A, from c. 2700 BC. Finds from Pilikáta and the Cave of Louizos are in the small but interesting **Stavrós Archaeological Museum** on the Platrithiás road (**t** 267 403 1305; open Tues–Sun 9–2).

From Stavrós a road leads north to lofty, deserted **Exógi** ('beyond the earth'); above the village is Ithaca's oddball attraction, three narrow pyramids built in 1933 by a fellow named Papadópoulos. He is buried under one; his mother under another; the third guards his coin collection. Further up, the disused monastery of Panagía Eleoússa offers extraordinary views over the sea. Between Exógi and Platrithiás are hewn blocks called '**Homer's School**'. This fertile area is one of the most pleasant on the island. **Platrithiás** is the biggest hamlet; another, **Kóllieri**, has an outdoor 'folklore museum', with obelisks made out of millstones.

North of Stavrós, **Fríkes**, a favourite pirates' lair into the 19th century, is now a fishing village and port-of-call for flotilla yachts, with two tiny beaches nearby. Pretty **Kióni**, around a bijou harbour, is also popular with the yachting set; landlubbers can hire motorboats to the beaches. Kióni means 'column', and an ancient one still stands on the altar in the church of Ag. Nikólaos. There are Cyclopean walls nearby, at Roúga.

Zákynthos/Zante (ΖΑΚΥΝΘΟΣ)

Of all their Greek possessions the Venetians loved soft luxuriant Zákynthos most. *Zante, fiore di Levante* – 'the flower of the East' – they called it, and built a city even more splendid than Corfu Town, which the earthquake of 1953 turned to rubble. Many islanders have Venetian blood, and Cretan, too, after Heráklion fell to the Turks in 1669. This shows up in their names and their love of singing. Their painters led a school of painting; poets Andréas Kálvos and Diónysios Solomós were born here, and the island's politics were the most progressive in Greece. Sad, then, that this once charmed island has bellied up whole hog to the trough of brash tourism.

History

The story goes that when Odysseus killed Penelope's suitors (20 were nobles from Zákynthos) the island rebelled and became independent. Levinus took for it Rome in 214 BC, and when the people revolted he burnt every building on Zákynthos. The

Getting There and Around

By air: various UK charters and flights from Athens; the Olympic office is at Alex. Róma 16, Zákynthos Town, t 269 502 8611. **Airport information**: t 269 502 8322. The airport is 6km from town; a taxi costs around €6.

By sea: Many connections with Kyllíni, southwest of Pátras, plus a couple daily from Pessáda (Kefaloniá) to Skinári–Ag. Nikólaos. Local excursion boats visit the west-coast beaches; caiques sail several times a week from Laganás to the Strofádes islands. **Port authority**: 1 El. Venizélou, t 269 502 8117.

By road: the central **bus** station is on Filíta Klavdianoú in Zákynthos Town, t 269 502 2255 for long-distance buses; t 269 504 3850 for local buses. Buses hourly to Laganás, 10 times daily to Tsiliví, four to Alikés, twice to Volímes, three to Vassilikiós and Porto Roma, eight to Kalamáki, twice to Kerí Lake and Skinári-Ag. Nikólaos. **Car hire**: National, 18 Lombárdou, t 269 504 3471; Budget, at the airport, t 269 504 3680. Sáki, 3 Leof. Dimokratías, t 269 502 3928, rents **mopeds** for around €15.

Tourist Information

Tourist police: 62 Lombárdou, Zákynthos Town, t 269 502 7367. Get the free *Zante Moments*. **Pilot U**, 78 Lombárdou, t 269 502 8207, f 269 502 8208, for scuba diving and horse-riding.

Festivals

A lively **carnival** initiated by the Venetians remains strong in Zákynthos and lasts for two weeks prior to Lent. In July the **Zakýnthia** takes place, with cultural activities. For the major **feast days of Ag. Diónysios** on 24 August and 17 December, Zákynthos town is strewn with myrtle and there are fireworks at the church.

Saracens captured it in AD 844; the Byzantines expelled them until 1182, when the Norman-Sicilian pirate Margaritone took over. The Venetians acquired it in 1209 and held on to it for almost 350 years, with a Turkish interlude (1479–84). The privileges of the wealthy Venetians and the local nobility provoked a rebellion among the *populari* or commoners, who seized control of the island for four years. When the Septinsular Republic established an aristocracy of its own in 1801, Zákynthos rebelled again. During the War of Independence mainland rebels often found asylum and help on the island which, like its Ionian sisters, had to wait until 1864 to join Greece.

Zákynthos Town

Zákynthos Town (pop. 10,000), rebuilt after 1953, is saved from anonymity by its superb setting – the ancient acropolis hovering above crowned by a castle, and the graceful sweep of the harbour, punctuated to the right by the striking silhouette of Mount Skopós. Wrapped along the waterfront, the streets of the long, narrow town are sheltered by arcades, just as they were before the earthquake. Houses are smothered with bougainvillaea and hibiscus. Shops sell *mandoláto* (nougat with almonds).

Zákynthos' churches had to be reconstructed after 1953; one, **Kyrá tou Angeloú** (1687) in Louká Karrer Street, contains icons by Panagiótis Doxarás of Zákynthos and a pretty carved iconostasis. Only the concrete reinforced **Basilica of Ag. Diónysios** at the south end of town, built in 1925 to house the relics of the island's patron saint, survived the earthquake. Gold and silver ex-votos bear witness to his influence in heaven; pilgrims pile in every 24 August. Formal **Plateía Solomoú** at the north end of town is too large and open, its small cafés uncomfortable by the solemn Town Hall, the Cultural Centre and the sailors' church, **Ag. Nikólaos tou Mólou** (1561), pieced

Where to Stay and Eat

Zákynthos Town ✉ 29100

Friendly Tours, 5 Foscolos, t 269 504 8030, f 269 502 3769, can help with rooms.

Bitzaro, on the waterfront, t 269 502 3644, f 269 504 5506 (*C; expensive*). Glam reception, smart rooms with balcony.

Strada Marina at 14 K. Lombárdou Street, t 269 504 2761, f 269 502 8733, *stradamarina@hotmail.com* (*B; expensive–moderate*). Larger, older hotel well located for ferries, good views of town and a pool. *Open all year.*

Phoenix, Plateía Solomoú, t 269 504 2419, f 269 504 5083 (*C; moderate*). Comfortable, air-conditioned rooms with TV. *Open all year.*

Apollon, 30 Tertséti, t 269 504 2838, f 269 504 5400 (*C; moderate*). Small; good central choice. *Open April–Oct.*

Aresti, by the Krionéri lighthouse, t 269 502 7379 (*€16–22*). Zákynthos' finest dining in a lovely setting. *Open eves only.*

Karavomilos, on the road to Argássi, by the basilica of Ag. Diónysos (*€15–20*). Has the name for fish; the friendly owner will recommend the best of the day's catch.

Malanou, 38 Ag. Athanásou, t 269 504 5936 (*€10–12*). In a similar direction, for lunch.

Aresti, on the coast road near Stávros, t 269 502 6346 (*€12–15*). Onassis and Maria Callas came here often for live traditional *kantádes*.

Pórto Zóro/Vassilikós

Aquarius, t 269 503 5300, f 269 503 5303 (*B; expensive*). Prettily set in greenery, advertising itself as 'a place to forget the world'.

Locanda, t 269 504 5563, f 269 502 3769 (*C; moderate*). Well-run family hotel.

Louis Royal Palace II, t 269 503 5492, f 269 503 5488, *www.louishotels.com* (*A; luxury*). One of several Louis resort hotels in Vassilikós.

O Adelfos tou Kosta, Vassilikós, t 269 503 5347 (*€12–15*). Traditional taverna with some of the best *kantádes* and delicious *mezes*.

---

together like a jigsaw after the quake. Here too is the **Neo-Byzantine Museum** (*t 269 504 2714; open Tues–Sun 8–2.30; adm; free Sun*) housing art salvaged from Zákynthos' shattered churches, including paintings by Michael Damaskinós, El Greco's teacher, excellent 16th-century frescoes from Ag. Andréa at Volímes, and superb 16th- and 17th-century icons of the Cretan-Venetian school. There is a model of the town before the earthquake. In from Plateía Solomoú is the social centre of town since the 15th century, marble-paved **Plateía Ag. Márkou**, site of the **Solomós Museum** (*t 269 504 8982; open daily 9–2; adm*), with mementoes of the poet, other famous Zantiotes, and old photographs. Adjacent are the tombs of Diónysos Solomós and Andréas Kálvos.

Filikóu Street, behind Ag. Márkou, leads up to **Bocháli**, the upper quarter of town. En route, in Tsilívi, a small **Maritime Museum** (*t 269 502 8249 or t 269 504 2436; open 9–1.30 and 6–8.30*) may lure you with its imposing torpedo display. Bocháli's **Ag. Giórgios Filíkou** was a hotbed of resistance during the War of Independence and, on the hill of Lófos Stráni, a bust of Solomós marks the spot where he composed the *Ode to Liberty* (now the Greek national anthem) after hearing of the death of Lord Byron. Another road leads to the Venetian **Kástro** (*t 269 504 8099; open Tues–Sun 8–2.30; adm*); ruins of churches and walls of the ancient acropolis stand amid the pines, and nearby cafés take in the grand view. **Akrotíri** (take the north road at the Bocháli crossroads) was the centre of Zantiote society during British rule. At one house, the Villa Crob, the British laid out Greece's first tennis court.

Beaches and Mount Skopós

The town beach isn't too good – try the south beaches along the rugged peninsula under Mount Skopós beyond **Argássi**, itself a soulless assembly line of hotels and tavernas. Further along, however, there's wide, sandy **Pórto Zóro** (**Banana Beach**), strewn with sea daffodils, followed by **Ag. Nikólaos**, **Mavrándzi** and the thin crescent at **Pórto Róma**, all with tavernas. Its 16th-century Domenegini tower was a rebel depot during the War of Independence. To frighten off busy-bodies, the fighters installed someone as a a 'ghost' at night to holler and throw stones at passers-by. Tiny **Vassilikós** with its resort hotels is at the end of the bus line. **Gérakas** has the finest stretch of sandy beach, popular with nesting loggerhead turtles, and has been designated as a conservation area, easier to do here than in crowded Laganás.

From the edge of Argássi, a road leads up to **Mount Skopós** ('Lookout'). On the way note the picturesque ruins and mosaic floor of the 11th-century **Ag. Nikólaos Megalomátis**, built on the site of a Temple to Artemis. Views from the top take in all of Zákynthos. By the rocky summit stands the venerable white church of **Panagía Skopiótissa**, atop another Temple to Artemis. The frescoed interior has a carved stone iconostasis; the icon of the Virgin was painted in Constantinople, and there's a double-headed Byzantine eagle mosaic on the floor.

Laganás Bay and the South

Zákynthos looks like a big fish whose gaping jaws are about to devour a pair of small fry islets in Laganás Bay. Tourist strips follow the sandy beaches every inch of the way. **Laganás**, set on flat, hard sand beach, is Zákynthos' Blatant Beast, a 'Golden Mile' of open bars, throbbing music and flashing lights. A bridge leads out to the attractive islet of **Ag. Sostís**, topped with pines and, this being Laganás, a disco.

The lush, gently inclined plain behind Laganás is dotted with country estates, vineyards and current vines. Aim for **Pantokrátoras**, near three fine churches: the beautiful **Pantokrátor**, founded by Byzantine Empress Pulcheria; **Kiliómeno**, restored after the quake, with beautiful icons; and the medieval **Panagía**, with a pretty bell tower and stone carvings. The picturesque ruins of the Villa Loundzis, one of Zákynthos' wealthiest estates, are in **Sarakína** nearby. **Lithakiá**, south of Pantokrátoras, has a restored 14th-century church, **Panagía Faroméni**, with art gathered from the area's ruined churches. Lithakiá's long stretch of sand has stayed Greek, with half a dozen tavernas (hardly a baked bean sign in sight) and has the pleasant Michailitis rooms for rent, t 269 505 1090, f 269 505 2710.

At Loggerheads over Loggerheads

Laganás Bay is the world's single most important nursery of loggerhead turtles (*Caretta caretta*), who dig some 1,000 nests a year on 4km of beach. They are among the oldest species on the planet, and every June until September they crawl up onto the beaches at night and lay between 100 and 120 eggs the size of golf balls. For 60 days the eggs incubate in the warmth of the sands, and then the baby turtles make a break for the sea. It is essential that the nesting zones remain undisturbed – that people stay away from the beaches between dusk and dawn, and do not poke parasols into the sand or run vehicles over it. Even the lights in the bay are liable to distract the baby turtles from their all-important race to the sea. In 1983 the Sea Turtle Protection Society was formed to monitor and mark nests, and in 1999 a Marine Park was established. Yet opposition among developers remains.

From Lithakiá the main road continues south over the Avyssos Gorge – a rift made by the 1633 earthquake – to the coastal swamp of **Límni Kerioú**. Look carefully at the roots of the aquatic plants for the black natural pitch that once welled up in sufficient quantity to caulk thousands of boats; both Herodotus and Pliny described the phenomenon. From the sea (*caique excursions from Kerí Beach*) this coast is magnificent, marked by sheer white cliffs, deep dark-blue waters and two towering natural arches at Marathía. The mountain village of **Kerí** offers fine views, especially from the nearby white lighthouse. A road winds westward to remote **Agalás**, passing the two-storey grotto called **Spiliá Damianoú**, where one formation resembles a horse.

Heading Northwest

North of Zákynthos Town, the **Krionéri Fountain** was built by the Venetians to water their ships. Beyond that, pretty sandy beaches are backed by orchards, vineyards and holiday developments: narrow **Tsiliví**, **Plános** (overlooking Tragáki Beach), little **Ámpoula** with golden sand, and **Alikanás**, where a long stretch of sand goes to **Alikés**, named for the nearby saltpans. In the rich agricultural interior look for **Skoulikádo**, a village with several handsome churches including **Panagía Anafonítria**, with stone reliefs and a lovely interior, and **Ag. Nikólaos Megalomáti**, whose 16th-century stone icon has unusually large eyes. **Ag. Marína**, a rare survivor of the earthquake, has a cell behind the altar where the insane would be chained in hope of a cure.

A newish coastal road follows the sea north to Korithí. It starts with a sequence of beautiful pebbled beaches, such as **Makri Aloú** and **Makrí Giálos**, becoming more dramatic, volcanic and inaccessible as it wends north. **Ag. Nikoláos** (ferry from Kefaloniá) nestles in a beautiful bay. The white coast is pocked with caves, cliffs and natural arches and, most spectacularly, one hour by boat from Skinári, **Kianoún Cave**, glowing with every shade of blue. Excursions from Ag. Nikólaos run around the north tip of the island and south to **Xinthia**'s sulphur springs, where the sand is so hot that you need swimming shoes – and to the cave of **Sklávou**.

Up the Southwest Coast

Much of western Zákynthos plunges abruptly into the sea, 1,000ft in places. Head to **Macherádo** where the ornate church of **Ag. Mávra** has Venetian bells famous for their clear musical tones. Macherádo's **Domaine Agria**, run by the Comoutós family since 1638, is the oldest winery in Greece. From Macherádo a road rises to **Koiloménos**, with a curious belltower from 1893, carved with Masonic symbols. A secondary road leads to the wild coast and **Karakonísi**, an islet resembling a whale, with great plumes of spray when windy. At Ag. Léon (with another striking bell tower, converted from a windmill) there's a turn-off to the dramatic narrow creek and minute sandy beach at **Limnióna**. Just before Exo Chóra, a road descends to **Kámbi**, where tavernas on the 650ft cliffs offer spectacular sunset viewing.

The main road continues to **Anafonítria** and the frescoed 15th-century **Monastery of Panagía Anafonítria**. Below is **Porto Vrómi**, 'Dirty Port', because of the natural tar that blankets the shore. Around the corner is a perfect white sandy beach, wedged under sheer limestone crags, with Zákynthos' **'shipwreck'**, a scene that graces a thousand

Where to Stay and Eat

Tsiliví to Ag. Nikólaos ✉ 29100

Book through a holiday firm in season. Lots of throbbing bars/clubs everywhere.

Louis Plagos Beach, at Ámpoula Beach, Tsiliví, t 269 506 2800, f 269 506 2900, www. louishotels.com (A; luxury). Complex, near the sea, with gardens, pool, tennis.

Contessina, Tsiliví, t 269 502 2508, f 269 502 3741 (C; moderate). Might be able to squeeze you in if everything else is full.

Olive Tree. The first taverna in town and one of the few playing Greek music.

Caravel at Plános, t 269 504 5261, f 269 504 5548 (A; expensive). Sister to the one in Athens; will lighten your wallet, but has all the trimmings. Open April–Oct.

Nobelos, Ag. Nikólaos, t 269 503 1400, f 269 503 1131, www.nobelos.gr (luxury). Five sumptuous suites in a beautiful stone villa, with flowers and sun platform by the sea.

Pension Panorama, Ag. Nikólaos, t 269 503 1013, f 269 503 1017 (moderate–inexpensive). Pristine. Open May–Oct.

Taverna Xikia, t 269 503 1165. On the coast road, not far from Koroní and worth a detour, serving tasty Greek food in an idyllic clifftop setting.

postcards and a prime destination for excursion boats. The ship was run aground by cigarette smugglers in the late 1980s when they were about to be nabbed by the coastguard; word spread quickly to the villages and by the time the police arrived there wasn't a pack of Marlboros in sight. You can see it from the path near the abandoned monastery of **Ag. Geórgios sta Kremná**.

The road passes through an increasingly dry landscape on route to **Volímes**, the largest village on the west coast, billowing with bright handwoven goods for sale. Seek out the church of Ag. Paraskeví and the 15th-century Ag. Theodósios, with its carved stone iconostasis.

The Strofádes Islands

A couple of times a week caiques from Laganás sail south to the Strofádes (there are two, **Charpína** and **Stamvránio**), passing over the deepest point in the entire Mediterranean, where you would have to dive 1,449ft down to reach Davy Jones' locker. Strofádes means 'turning': according to myth, the Harpies, those female monsters with human heads, hands and feet, winged griffon bodies and bear ears, were playing their usual role as the hired guns of the gods, chasing the prophet Phineas over the little islets, when Zeus changed his mind and ordered them to turn around and come back.

Although little more than flat green pancakes in the sea, the Strofádes offered just the right kind of rigorous isolation Orthodox monks crave, and accordingly in the 13th century Irene, wife of the Byzantine emperor John Láskaris, founded the **Pantochará** ('All Joy') monastery on Charpína. Pirates were a problem, and in 1440 Emperor John Palaeológos sent funds to build high walls. No women or female animals were allowed in, and the 40 monks who resided there (among them the future saint Diónysos) spent their days studying rare books. In 1530, however, the Saracens breached the walls, slew all the monks and plundered it; in 1717 the body of Ag. Diónysos was removed to Zákynthos. The evocative, desolate citadel is now owned by the monastery of Ag. Diónysos, and remains in a fine state of preservation.

Thessaly and the Sporades

15

Thessaly

pp.516–17

KOZANI

Grevena

GREVENA

Trikomo

Venetikos

Aliakmonas

Mt Kamvounia

Krania
Elassonas

Deskati

Elassona

Vovousa

Pindus
National Park
(Valia Calda)

Flambourari

Katara
Pass

L. Aoos

Mt Chasia

Fotino

Verdikoussa

Mesochori

Tristeno

Miliotades

Metsovo

Orthovouni

M E T E O R A

Great Meteora

Ag. Nikolaou

Kastraki

Roussanou

Kalambaka

Mt Zarkou

IOANNINA

Mazia

Drosochori

Sirako

Kallarites

Kipinas

Polithea

T R I K A L A

Mt Koziakis

Megarchi

Zarko

Farkadona

Trikala

p.410

S
o
u
t
h

P
i
n
d
u
s

Pertouli
Pertouli Ski Resort

Agnanda

Mesochora

Ag. Vissarion

Stournareika

Megala Kalivia

Pyli

Agnandero

Mouzaki

Proastio

Palamas

Itea

Vourgareli

A R T A

Oxia

Mesenikolas

Karditsa

K A R D I T S A

Artesiano

Mataranga

Sofades

Kalivia

Pezoulas

Neochori

Karitsa

Mitropoli

L. Plastira

Ano Kalentini

L.
Pournariou

Megalochari

Kedros

Anavra

Leondari

Ekara

Arta

Petas

Ambracia

Mt Valtou

Raftopoulo

Agrapha

Komboti

Thiamos

FORMER
YUGOSLAV
REPUBLIC OF
MACEDONIA

BULGARIA

TURKEY

ALBANIA

TURKEY

E V R I T A N I A

pp.372–3

Makrakomi

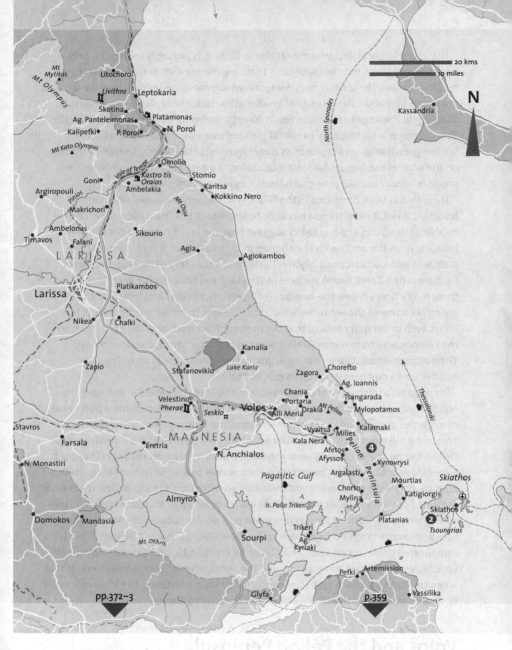

Highlights

1 The Metéora – other-worldly monasteries, hanging in an extraordinary mountain setting

2 Gorgeous Koukounariés Beach, on Skiáthos, island of beaches

3 Lake Plastíra, a lost piece of Switzerland right beside the 'unwritten' mountains

4 The Pélion Peninsula, for sandy coves and old-fashioned mansions

Thessaly's fertile plain, by far the largest in Greece, is probably something only a farmer could love, but the mountains that ring the big dish preserve some truly magical corners. The otherworldly Metéora, where monasteries defy the laws of gravity on perpendicular rocks, is a five-star attraction; the idyllic Pélion peninsula dangling in the Aegean is famous for its forests, charming villages and beaches; the Vale of Tempe, a dramatically beautiful glen between Óssa and Olympus, has a lingering enchantment in spite of its busy highway; Lake Plastíra, a sapphire mirror on the edge of the rugged Ágrapha mountains, is a best-kept secret, whereas the province's four delicious pine-clad islands, beginning with Skiáthos, are not.

Thessaly has been compared to the Nile Delta. Densely inhabited since early Neolithic times, it nevertheless has little to show for itself thanks to a reliance on mud brick. Tradition and linguistics suggest that the very first proto-Greek speakers, invading from the north with their horses in c. 2500 BC, got this far, saw that the plain was good, and stopped. Myth reflects this in the story of Hellene, the son of Deukalion (the Greek Noah). He lived in Thessaly and fathered the ancestors of the three major Greek tribes, the Aeolians (of Thessaly), Dorians and Ionians, before giving his name to the entire 'Hellenic' race. The epic tradition was born here, too: critics even in antiquity believe that the heroes of the Iliad were 'dragged down to the Peloponnese from homes in Northern Greece'. Agamemnon started off as a Thessalian chieftain; 'horse-rearing Argos' was originally the plain of Thessaly. Achilles was a rare hero who stayed put, in Phthia.

In c. 1140 BC, a fresh wave of Greek speakers, the Thessali, moved in and gave the region their name. With the best cavalry in Greece, they developed into a horsey set of oligarchic squires under a chieftain or *tagos*, and reduced everyone else to serfs. They were big news in the 6th century BC, when they controlled the Amphictyony at Delphi, but on the whole they were considered backward by other Greeks (the poet Simonides wrote that the Thessalians were the only people he had never cheated, because they were too stupid), and their alliance with Persia in 492 BC lost them what remained of their Panhellenic clout. Gobbled up by Philip of Macedon after foolishly asking for his assistance, Thessaly remained part of Macedonia until becoming a Roman province in 168 BC. Later overrun by Huns, Goths, Slavs and Bulgars, it hosted a complicated game of Risk after 1204 played by Frankish barons, Catalan mercenaries, Epiróte despots, Byzantine emperors and the Serbs, who so wore themselves out that when the Turks arrived in 1396 they encountered little resistance. The Turks remained until 1881, when the Ottoman empire ceded Thessaly to Greece.

Vólos and the Pélion Peninsula

Vólos

Magnesía, the region of eastern Thessaly around Mount Pélion and the Pagasitic Gulf, has long been famed for its beauty and climate. Vólos is the current capital, but

Getting There and Around

Six or so **trains** a day link Vólos by way of Lárissa to Athens or Thessaloníki. There are also direct trains from Vólos to Kalambáka by way of Stávros, Kardítsa and Trikkala. Tickets at the station or by the quay at the corner of Iásonos and Rozou, **t** 242 102 8555 (*open 8am–8pm*).

Buses from Athens to Vólos leave Liossíon station, **t** 210 831 7186, and end up at the terminal by the port at A. Zachou and G. Lambráki Sts, **t** 242 103 3253; there are frequent connections to Lárissa, Thessaloníki, Kalambáka, Néa Anchíalos, Almyrós, Velestíno, one daily to Pátras and Arkítsa for Loutrá Edipsoú, plus three weekly for Ioánnina and Igoumenítsa, **t** 242 102 5537. For the Pélion, frequent buses run to Portariá, Makrynítsa and Káto Lechónia, and five or so a day to the other villages, but to really see the peninsula you need a **car**. Hire one from European, 79 Iásonos St, **t** 242 103 6238, or Hellas, 79 Iásonos, **t** 242 103 6238. **Taxis: t** 242 102 4911

Ferries and **hydrofoils** from Vólos sail to Skiáthos, Skópelos and Alonissós, and weekly to Skýros; others sail to Ag. Konstantínos.

In summer hydrofoils from Thessaloníki, Skiáthos and Néa Moudania (Chalkidikí) call at Choreftó, Ag. Ioánnis, Plataniás and Vólos. **Port authority: t** 242 102 8888.

Tourist Information

EOT: Plateía Ríga Feréou (off Iásonos St), **t** 242 102 3500, **f** 242 102 4750; *open summer Mon–Fri 7–2.30 and 6–8.30, Sat, Sun 9–12 and 6–8.30*.
Tourist police: t 242 107 2421.

Sport and Activities

Pélion, criss-crossed with old cobblestone paths (*kalderimia*), is splendid **walking** country; ROAD publish a 1/50 000 map with hiking suggestions in English, or contact the **Greek Alpine Club**, 94 Dimitriades St, Vólos, **t** 242 102 5696.

Pélion **train**, **t** 242 102 8555 or **t** 242 102 4056. On summer weekends, this narrow-gauge train travels the beautiful 28km from Káto Lechónia to Miliés in 90 minutes. It leaves at 11am and returns at 4pm; €12 return.

over the centuries Magnesía's centre has bounced all over the map. Its Mycenaean-era inhabitants, said to be Pelasgians descended from a certain Magnes, had their capital at Iolkos, up in the northernmost recess of the gulf, and saw off Jason and the Argonauts, whose search for the Golden Fleece mirrored early Greek explorations of the Black Sea. With the arrival of the Dorian Thessalians (the 'palace' at Iolkos burned down in c. 1200 BC), Magnesía became a tribute-paying fief and Pagasae replaced Iolkos as the big town on the gulf. In early Christian times the action moved further south to Fthiótides Thebes (Néa Anchíalos), and in the 12th century it moved south again to Almyrós. Under the Turks, the coast was abandoned for the safer mountain villages of Pélion, but in the 19th century Iolkos was reborn as Vólos. A new harbour was built in 1912 and, with the population boost of Asia Minor refugees a decade later, the city grew quickly, processing and shipping local cotton, fruit, cereals and tobacco.

Shattered by earthquakes in 1954 and 1955, modern Vólos (pop. 120,000) is just that – modern, rebuilt on a waffle plan, yet busy and likeable, a good place to watch the world go by over a glass of *tsípouro*. Central **Plateía Ríga Feréou** overlooks the hyperactive fishing port. Just west, on Mitropoliti Grigoriou St (by the train station), a hill with signs of habitation going back to 2500 BC was 'spacious' **Iolkos**, where Pelias usurped the throne from his half-brother Aeson, father of Jason. Traces of a 130ft palace from 1600 BC lie in the weeds along Souílou Street, much of it destroyed in the building of a Byzantine castle. The quay for the Sporades is east of the fishing port,

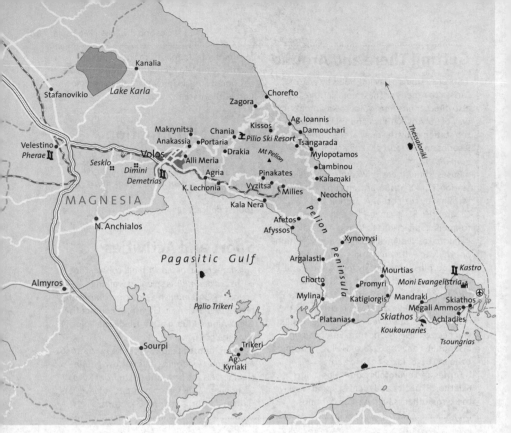

where the waterfront, lined with *tsipourádika*, has a bronze model of the *Argo*. At nearby Metamorphósis and Dimitriádos Streets, visit the **Giorgio de Chirico Art Centre** (*open Tues–Fri 6–9pm, as well as Thurs–Sat 10–1*). The designer of the Pélion railway was an Italian, Evaristo de Chirico, whose painter son Giorgio was born in Vólos.

The **Archaeological Museum**, on Athanasáki Street is on the east end of town, behind the hospital (*city bus no.1 or 3, t 242 102 5285; open Tues–Sun 8.30–3*). Famous for a collection of unique painted marble funerary steles from Demetrias (3rd century BC), the museum's contents reflect Magnesía's true age: artefacts from Sésklo from 6500 BC, Mycenaean-era finds from Iolkos, and a large room devoted to the Neolithic that makes the era come alive, with a delightful portrait gallery of little faces, seals, clay models of houses, the wild wheat (*triticu Boeoticum*) they planted, and reproductions of tools, looms and more. In the same neighbourhood, at 38 Afentoúli (K. Makris St) north of Alexandras Avenue, the **Kitsos Makris Ethnographic Museum** (*t 242 103 7119; open Mon–Fri 8.30–2, Sun 10–2; adm free*) has folk art, including paintings by Theóphilos Hadzimichaíl (*see p.491*).

Ancient Places around Vólos

Other ancient cities near Vólos have more to show for themselves. **Demetrias**, 3km south of Vólos (take bus 6 from the Dimarchíon), was the Hellenistic capital founded by warlord-playboy Demetrios Poliorketes, who made it his base when he wasn't out

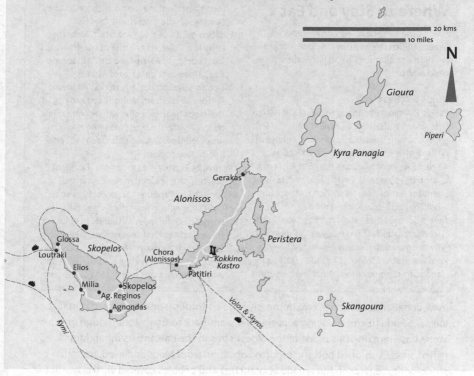

besieging Alexander's successors (most famously at Rhodes, *see* p.771) or holding
orgies in the Parthenon. A large theatre is the most prominent souvenir, and walls
and towers reconstructed in the 1st century BC, using as stone and preserving for
posterity the painted steles in the museum. The road (signposted Pefkákia, itself an
important Neolithic site) circles the promontory where Demetrios' city and
Macedonian palace stood, atop the ruins of Bronze-Age Pagasae, where Jason built
the *Argo*. Further south was Phthia, the homeland of Achilles, where the star attraction is **Néa Anchíalos**, a small resort built over **Phthiotic Thebes**, one of the most
important Early Christian sites in Greece (*open daylight hours, at least in principle*). So
far nine basilicas and a sumptuous baptistry, all from the 4th to the 6th centuries,
have been found strung out along the main road, some with pretty mosaic floors and
lovely carved columns; the portable finds are to the south in the **Almyrós
Archaeological Museum** (*t 242 202 1326; open Tues–Sun 8.30–3*). Achilles was born
inland at **Fársala**, which was shattered in the 1954 earthquake; there's nothing to see,
but the name may ring a bell: the Romans called it Pharsalus and it was here, on
9 August 48 BC, that Caesar defeated Pompey and decided the fate of Rome.

West of Vólos, you can visit two of the oldest Neolithic farming settlements in
Europe, both south of the Lárissa road (*both t 241 102 8 563; open Tues–Sun 8.30–3*).
Dimíni (6.5km) was inhabited in the 4th millennium BC – it had a central megaron
and smaller houses enclosed by rings of walls that hint of a troubled time; resettled

Where to Stay and Eat

Don't miss the best seafood *mezédes* in Greece, which the locals wash down potent *tsípouro* – similar to raki – in bars called *tsipourádika*.

Vólos ✉ 38221

Park, 2 Deligiórgi, t 242 103 6511, f 242 102 8646, *amhotels@otenet.gr* (*B; expensive*). Overlooking the sea and gardens, between the centre and archaeological museum.

Aégli, 24 Argonaftón, t 242 102 5691, f 242 103 3006 (*B; expensive*). On the seafront, convenient for ferries. Two renovated 19th-century buildings, air-conditioned rooms.

Ávra, 5 Sólonos, t 242 102 5370, f 242 102 8980 (*C; moderate*). Not too noisy, on a side street by the port and recently renovated.

Roussas, 1 Iatrou Tzánou, t 242 102 1732, f 242 102 2987 (*E; inexpensive*). Near the museums (bus no. 1). En suite rooms with air-conditioning, on the waterfront garden.

Pacifico, 7 P. Melá, t 242 102 0002. Near the central market, a favourite of the smart set for its delicate Asian-Med cuisine (around €28). *Open eves only, closed Mon.*

Inopolío-Spyrópoulos, 7 Ferrón St (in an old factory by the train station), t 242 103 0588. Delicious hearty cuisine with an Anatolian touch. Try the flavoursome lamb *ampelourgoú*; around €20. *Open eves only, but be sure to book.*

Remvi, 25 Plastíra, t 242 102 7952. Excellent starters and seafood in the €15 range.

Tsipourádiko Papádis, 3 Sólonos, t 242 102 9360. Poky place near the fishing port, considered the most authentic in Vólos for its perfect seafood snacks. *Closed eves.*

Tsipourádiko Pyrofani, 1 Tsopotou, t 242 103 1370. Sip *tsípouro* with grilled shellfish, and watch the comings and goings of the port.

in Mycenaean times, it has two impressive tholos tombs (some think it may in fact be Iolkos). **Sésklo** (18km), enjoying a lovely view, goes back to 6500 BC; although only a stone base remains, this is one of the oldest sites in the Balkans. Its inhabitants fished, made sun-dried pottery, imported obsidian from Mílos and lived around a stone-built megaron in huts made of branches and pebbles covered with clay – but without an outer defensive wall. Further west, apple-growing Velestíno was ancient **Pherae**, famous in myth as the kingdom of Admetus; his noble wife Alcestis volunteered to die in his stead. Of its real rulers, Jason (d. AD 370) put all of Thessaly under his rule; his autocratic successor Alexander was murdered in 358, leading the ruling Aleuadae family in Lárissa to beg for help, first from Thebes, and then from Philip of Macedon who came and annexed the country while he was at it. Pherae is completely covered by modern Velestíno, although the fountain in the town garden may just be the fountain of Hypereia, where Hera was said to bathe. The town is proudest of poet Ríga Feréou ('of Pherae', 1757–98), who, fired by the American and French Revolutions, proposed that Greeks and Turks alike should fight for liberty and rule by law in a pan-Balkan revolution against the arbitrary power of the Sultan –'better an hour of freedom than forty years as a slave'– before he was captured in Trieste and murdered in Belgrade on orders from Istanbul.

The Pélion Peninsula

Just behind Vólos rises Mount Pélion, the 'healing mountain', covered with medicinal herbs, wild strawberries, vineyards and orchards, standing at the head of a peninsula that resembles a sock with a ball stuck in the toe. The Greeks know it as one of their country's most idyllic corners, but foreigners, who tend to fly into the honeypot of Skiáthos and get stuck there, are relatively few. Yet gorgeous beaches dot the dramatic Aegean coast, and in the winter Pélion, which gets more rain than any place on the Greek mainland, goes all misty and romantic, with a mantle of snow on top. And, unlike Skiáthos, hotels tend to stay open year round.

Although Pélion was inhabited in antiquity, piracy forced its abandonment in the Middle Ages, except for a string of monasteries high on the mountain. Villages sprouted up near them in the 15th century and they grew rich on silk and woollens, thanks to the benign neglect of the Turks. The traditional houses are a delight; thick walls of grey stone support an overhanging wooden floor, painted white and lined with windows and wooden shutters. A frustrated desire for stained glass led to the custom of painting colourful geometric motifs over the real windows; lintels around the front doors are often of carved stone or marble; older houses have magnificent slate roofs. Flower pots crowd every inch of space outside. Fountains plash, brooks gurgle, cobbled paths (*kalderímia*) link the villages and enormous plane trees shade

Where to Stay and Eat

Archontikó means mansion, and many in the Pélion have been converted into small luxurious inns, serving sumptuous breakfasts. Nearly all stay open all year, but beware; few take credit cards. Pélion hotel association web site: *www.travel-pelion.gr*.

Portariá/Makrynítsa ✉ 37011

Portariá, t 242 809 0014, f 242 809 9066 (*B; luxury–expensive*). New hotel in the Pélion style, with indoor and outdoor pools, sauna, jacuzzi and gym, open to non-guests.

Diakoumís, Portariá, t 242 809 9898. Reasonably priced and tasty local dishes.

Archontiko Karamarli, in Makrynítsa, t 224 809 9570, f 242 809 9779 (*B; luxury*). Nine rooms, each one decorated in a different period in a 250-year-old mansion, with a garden bar and lovely neoclassical tea room.

Archontikó Xiradakis, Makrynítsa, t 242 809 9250, f 242 809 0151 (*A; expensive*). Traditional mansion with five rooms furnished with antiques and canopied beds.

Theodóra, Makrynítsa, t 242 809 9179, f 242 809 9189 (*B; expensive–moderate*). Rooms with a view, complete with satellite TV.

Pantheon, in Makrynítsa Plateía, t 242 809 9143. Tasty Pélion specialities.

Theóphilos. *Kafeneíon* in Makrynítsa with murals (1910) by Theóphilos Hadzimicháïl (*see* p.491).

Zagorá/Choreftó ✉ 37001

Villa Horizonte, Zagorá, t 242 602 3342, f 242 602 3176, *www.villa-horizonte.com* (*expensive–moderate*). Six delightful rooms with gardens run by an English-speaking Swedish-German couple, who put on a lavish buffet breakfast and run workshops in music, Greek dancing, cuisine and language; on request they serve Greek, exotic or vegetarian meals with ingredients from their organic garden, orchard and vineyard.

Rousis Rooms, Zagorá, t 242 602 3407 (*inexpensive*). Pleasant en suite rooms.

Pétros, Zagorá, t 242 602 2666. A favourite for grilled meat dishes.

Aoilós, 20m from Choreftó Beach, t 242 602 2910, f 242 602 3390, *www.greecetravel.com/hotels/aiolos/* (*expensive*). Lovely studios around a small pool, in a quiet walled garden of olives and lemons. *Open Mar–Dec*.

Akrogiáli, t 242 602 2892. Fresh fish, right by the water for around €15.

Tsangaráda/Damoúchari ✉ 37012

Kastanies, Ag. Stéfanos, t 242 604 9135, f 242 604 9169 (*A; luxury*). Beautifully restored mansion surrounded by flowers. Hand-crafted furniture, big American-style breakfast of local produce.

Thyméli, Ag. Geórgios, t/f 242 604 9595 (*B; expensive*). Five rooms in a charming old farm house in an enchanting setting. Once

the squares. The churches are different, too: rectangular with small apses and wide overhanging roofs, their frescoes and iconostasis often full of rustic charm.

Pélion's special symbol are Centaurs ('those who round up bulls'), who may have been ancestral memories of horsey Thessaly's first cowboys. A later myth has it that Centauros was the product of the union between Ixion, the king of the Lapiths, and a cloud shaped like Hera, created by Zeus to confound Ixion's lusty designs. For his presumption, Ixion ended up tied to a fiery wheel for eternity, while Centauros mated with the mares of Pélion to create the centaurs. Their wise and immortal king Cheiron tutored Asklepios, Jason, Aeneas and Achilles, and arranged the wedding party of Thetis and Peleus, attended by all the gods – although they forgot to invite Eris ('strife'), who in revenge set the Trojan War in motion by sending a golden apple inscribed 'to the fairest'. Accidentally shot in the foot by Heracles, Cheiron was in such pain that he asked Zeus to give his immortality to Prometheus. Zeus complied, but immortalized the centaur anyway as Sagittarius, the constellation with the arrow pointing the way to the Golden Fleece. Pélion weddings had a habit of going wrong;

owned by Greek actress Jenny Karezi, whose belongings give it a personal touch. Homemade bread and jam for breakfast.

Aléka, t 242 604 9380, **f** 242 604 9189 (*expensive*). Mrs Aleka's house has ten handsome guest rooms with lots of added touches; her taverna features good home cooking.

Diakoumís Rooms, 1km from Milopótamos Beach, **t** 242 604 9203 (*moderate*). Rooms with balconies hanging over the cliff, all traditionally furnished.

Dipnosophistis, t 242 604 3295. Atmospheric wine bar under the plane trees on the road down to Mylopotámos Beach, with great food and music. *Open eves only, daily July–Sept, other times Fri, Sat and Sun only.*

Miliés/Vyzítsa/Pinakátes ✉ 37010

Paliós Stathmós, t 242 308 6425, **f** 242 308 6736 (*A; low expensive–moderate*). A small guest house near Miliés station, its restaurant fabled for its oven dishes.

Glorious Peleus Luxury Castle, Vyzítsa, **t** 242 308 6671, **f** 242 308 6611 (*L; luxury*). Mansion full of antiques and attention to detail, plus a sauna and jacuzzi.

Xénonas Thétis, Vyzítsa, **t** 242 308 6111 (*C; moderate–inexpensive*). Excellent value; traditional inn with traditional furnishings, not all rooms en suite.

Archontiko Anastássi Xiradáki, Pinakátes, **t/f** 242 308 6375 (*A; expensive*). Six traditionally furnished rooms, some with lovely sea views, and a charming Pélion lounge.

Xenónas Allatinou, Pinakátes, **t** 242 308 6995 (*expensive–moderate*). Another hotel in an old mansion, if a bit more monastic in the decor. Good breakfast on the lovely terrace.

Inosíphylos, Pinakátes, **t** 242 308 6897. Family-run taverna serving an excellent *koukiofava* and other traditional Pélion dishes at reasonable prices.

Mylína ✉ 37013

Xenon Athina, t 242 306 5210 (*inexpensive*). Nice budget choice by the sea; the owner is usually behind the counter in the nearby souvenir shop.

Camping Olizon, by the sea in an olive grove, **t** 242 306 5236. *Open mid-April–Sept.*

O Pinguínos, on the Trikéri road, **t** 242 305 1865. Absolutely delicious fresh fish, the way penguins like it, at kind prices – usually under €11.

Palío Trikéri ✉ 37009

Galatía, t 242 305 5505 (*C; expensive*). Furnished flats a stone's throw from the port and 200m from the beach. Restaurant, bar and watersports. *Open April–Oct.*

Palió Trikéri, t 242 309 1432 (*E; moderate*). The island's one hotel. *Open all year.*

one hosted by Peirithoös the Lapith, the king of Magnesía, led to the drunken misbe-
haviour of the Centaurs that Greeks so liked to depict in art (*see* p.231).

The road up Pélion from Vólos passes through the suburb of **Anakassiá**, where a
sign on the left indicates the delightful **Theóphilos Hadzimichaíl Museum** (Οικια
Κοντου), a 5-minute walk up the lane and turn to the right (*open Tues–Sun 8–3; free*).
The little painter from Lésbos (*see* p.825) spent 30 years wandering around the Pélion,
painting for his supper. In 1912 Yánnis Kontós took him in, and he decorated the walls
of his house – this museum – with scenes of the village, Greek gods, heroes of 1821,
Kontós on horseback, crocodiles and a giraffe. In 1928, just before he returned to
Lésbos, Theóphilos was 'discovered' by painter Geórgos Gounaropoúlos, who took
photos of his work to Paris. Sadly most of his other murals have been lost, but some
survive at the Melini bakery at nearby **Álli Meriá**.

At **Portariá**, the next village, the air is already noticeably cooler, and *kalderímia* offer
beautiful walks. A 2km turn off leads to the car park at the entrance to lovely
Makrynítsa, 'the balcony of Pélion' and a favourite of Sunday coach parties.
Markynítsa's mansions, piled on the steep slope, are especially charming; some have
their front doors on the third floor. Everyone congregates in the deeply shaded
plateía, where a huge hollow plane tree dwarfs the church of **Ag. Ioánnis** (1806), with
a bijou apse covered with marble plaques, echoed in the decoration of the pretty
fountain. The **Museum of Popular Art** (*t 242 809 9505; open Tues–Sun 10–5, in summer
10–2 and 6–10pm*) is in a mansion just below the square; just above the square is the
13th-century church of **Panagía Theotokou**, a secret Greek school during the Turkish
occupation, decorated with more marble plaques and stones bearing ancient and
Byzantine inscriptions. Come on May Day, when the lively celebration is a descendant
of an ancient rainmaking rite, involving men in black and white sheepskins.

The road continues above Portariá to the 3,940ft pass at **Chánia**, with spectacular
views over the Pagasitikós Gulf, but you can go even higher. Two roads branch out
through beech forests, one to the summit of **Mount Pélion** (5,282ft), the other to the
ski centre at **Agriolefkés**. From Chánia the road to the Aegean coast hairpins through
forests of *firikia* apples, walnuts and chestnuts that seem more Corsican than Greek.
After 13km is the turn for Pélion's largest village, **Zagorá**, spread out in four hamlets.
It took advantage of its isolation in Ottoman times to prosper, producing 32 tons of
silk a year; in 1712 its merchants opened a high school (where the Revolutionary poet
Ríga Feréou studied) and later a library, now housing over 18,000 books. In the square,
the church of **Ag. Geórgios** has a huge gilt iconostasis with lacy carvings. **Choreftó**
(8km), the old silk port, is now a resort, thanks to a long sandy beach.

From Zagorá, you'll have to backtrack to continue south along the Aegean coast, a
stunning stretch of cliffs and sea. Popular **Ag. Ioánnis** has three long beaches of
coarse white sand, and a summer hydrofoil to Skiáthos; if you prefer pebbles, try
Damouchári to the south, a charming hamlet with a Venetian tower and minuscule
port. **Kissós** up above has a pretty square and the 17th-century church, **Ag. Marína**,
with a beautiful iconostasis (1802) called 'the treasure of Pélion' and made by the
local sculptor Ioánnis Pagónis. There's another wonderful iconostasis in the church at

Moúresi, the next village, where every house has a minimum of a hundred pots of gardenias, roses and camellias on its terrace.

Huge boulders, deep forests and streams cutting into ravines surround **Tsangaráda**, another village spread out in hamlets. One, Ag. Taxiárchi, has the best centrepiece: a church of 1746, a pretty fountain and a truly magnificent thousand-year-old **plane tree**, just over 49ft in circumference. There are more beaches below: sandy **Fakistra**, closed by promontories, is hard to reach, but there are few people to share it with, and **Mylopótomas**, with three sandy/pebbly beaches, separated by a mighty rock pierced by a natural tunnel. A breathtaking corniche road continues south to **Lambinoú** and **Kalamáki** (overlooking more pretty and quiet beaches). Beyond Kalamáki you can cross the Pélion's waist to Vyzítsa (*see* below) or continue south by way of Neochóri.

The Gulf Coast and Southern Pélion

Beaches along the Pagasitikós Gulf coast are more sheltered, but less spectacular and pristine because of the busy shipping lane. Cultivated flowers – especially roses and their attar – are big business here, although if coming from Vólos you first must pass a less aromatic refinery and cement factory. At Agriá, there's a 12km turn-off for **Drákia**, a village of traditional houses, among them one of Pélion's most lavish, the 18th-century **Triantáphyllou Mansion**. Back on the coast, **Káto Lechónia** has the station for the little **Pélion train** to Miliés (*see* 'Activities', p.485) which departed from Vólos until 1971 and is now restored for tourists on weekends.

Further south, **Kalá Nerá**, a little family resort, has the turn-off for **Miliés**, a mountain village where Cheiron had his cave and the library has 4,000 rare volumes. The church of the **Taxiárches** has a superb gilded iconstasis and pulpit; here the locals proclaimed Thessaly's allegiance to Greek independence in 1821. The town hall contains an excellent little **Museum of Popular Art** (*t 242 308 6602; open Tues–Sun 10–2, and 6–8pm Thurs and Sat in summer; free*). From here it's 4km to **Vyzítsa**, a beautiful village among the plane trees, with Pélion's largest collection of mansions and tower houses, many restored as luxury inns. For less restoration and lower prices continue west of here on the new road to lovely **Pinakátes**.

The southern Pélion, with its olives, pines and cypresses, is more typically Greek, and, just as typically, swathes were scarred by a fire in July 2000. **Áfyssos**, the busiest resort on the gulf, has three beaches, campsites and lots of German holiday homes. From **Argalastí**, the largest village in the south, you can descend to the Aegean by way of **Xynóvrysi** to the superb sandy beach framed by giant rocks at **Potistiká**, or continue south to the turquoise coves dotting the gulf shore from **Chórto** to **Mylína**, the latter a quiet resort with banana plants, sunset view and a whimsical 'Euro-garden' (proof that the Pélion folk art spirit lives on). East of Mylína, a road winds up through a forest of olives to **Plataniás**, looking across to Évia with two-day-old English newspapers mellowing on the racks and a long sheltered crescent of sand; other beaches are below Promýri at **Mourtiás** (with 'sculpted' rocks) and **Katigiórgis**, with an end-of-the-world air, rooms and a riding stable.

A road (built only in 1987) goes to the toe of the peninsula, passing several pretty coves to **Trikéri**, which overlooks the narrow strait where the Greek triremes first tried to squeeze the Persian navy in 480 BC. Trikéri was long accessible only by boat; here the men spend so much time at sea, women run things and even pass property down the female line. Tavernas at the port of **Ag. Kyriakí** serve the day's catch, and hydrofoils link it to Vólos in the summer, stopping at the islet of **Palio Trikéri**. The islet offers a monastery, hamlet and peaceful places to stay.

Magnesía's Islands: The Sporades

The Sporades, the 'scattered' islands off Pélion's Aegean shore, are as lovely as the peninsula itself, but because they are poor in antiquities or names that anyone remembers from school history, they were among the last Greek islands to be 'discovered'. Then an airport was built on Skiáthos, word spread, holiday photos were passed around showing beaches and villages that fit many people's image of a holiday paradise, and the rest is history. There are four Sporades: babylonian Skiáthos, closest to the Pélion, with the most beautiful beaches; dignified Skópelos, that has kept much of its Greek character; Alónissos, gateway to Greece's first national marine park; and tradition-loving Skýros, scattered so far that it has a separate history and is easier to reach via Kými, Évia (see p.362), although it too has a small airport.

Skiáthos (ΣΚΙΑΘΟΣ)

One of the most popular destinations in the country, racy, cosmopolitan Skiáthos is not for the shy teetotaller or anyone looking for a slice of 'authentic' Greece. An isolated peasant community in the early 1970s, Skiáthos catapulted faster than any other island into big money tourism, so fast that corruption and violence have long been a factor in local life. Away from the main road, it is as stunningly beautiful as ever, and its 62 beaches provide some of the best swimming in Greece. Add to this

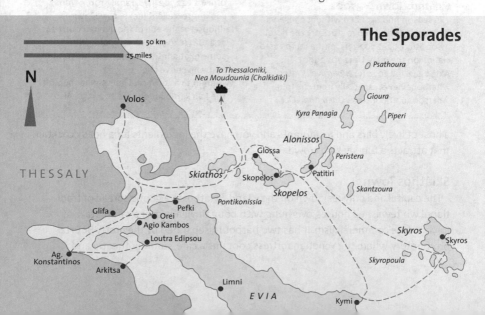

Getting There and Around

By air: daily from Athens, and countless charters from European cities. Olympic Airways, at the airport, **t** 242 702 2040. **Airport information**: **t** 242 702 2049. The 2km to the airport can be taxied for around €8.

By sea: ferries and frequent hydrofoils connect daily with Ag. Konstantínos, Vólos, Skópelos and Alónissos (combined bus/ferry tickets available in Athens from Alkyon Tours, 97 Akademías, **t** 210 384 3202, **f** 210 383 3948); also several times weekly with Thessaloníki and Péfki (Évia). **Port authority**: **t** 242 702 2017.

By road: buses (often packed) run every 15mins in season until the wee hours from the new harbour to Koukounariés. The harbour is lined with places to rent **cars** and **scooters**. Taxis, **t** 242 702 4461, are a popular option; never be shy of sharing.

Tourist Information

Tourist police: Papadiamánti St, **t** 242 702 3172; *open 8am–9pm in season.*

Geof Baldry, **t** 242 704 9607/9473, *www.skiathosinfo.com*. A great source of information; he also organizes painting, riding or sailing holidays.

Where to Stay and Eat

Skiáthos Town ✉ 37002

In season finding a bed without a reservation is the devil. If you're stuck, try the hotel association, **t** 242 702 3314, or the rooms association on the quay, **t** 242 702 2990 .

Akti, **t** 242 702 2024 (*C; expensive*). Watery harbour views, especially from the four-person top-floor suite. *Open April–Oct.*

Alkyon, on the new harbour, **t** 242 702 2981, **f** 242 702 1643 (*B; expensive–moderate*). The town's biggest hotel with an airy lobby and comfortable rooms overlooking gardens.

Meltemi, nearby, **t** 242 702 2493 (*C; expensive–moderate*). Has a loyal following and is generally booked solid; their bar is a good vantage point for the antics of the flotilla crowd. Conveniently near the bus stop. *Open all year.*

Pothos, Evangeslistrías St, **t** 242 702 2694 (*D; expensive*), and **Bourtzi**, **t** 242 702 1304 (*C; expensive*). Two central sister hotels away from the harbourfront, set in delightful little gardens. Both are charming, but Pothos just has the edge. *Both open May–Oct.*

Messinis Family, up in nearby Ag. Fanourios, **t/f** 242 702 2134 (*moderate*). Quiet rooms with panoramic views from the balconies, carefully tended by a master craftsman.

Australia Hotel, just off Papadiamántis Street, behind the post office, **t** 242 702 2488 (*E; inexpensive*). Central and cheaper, with simple en suite rooms.

San Remo, **t** 242 702 2078, **f** 242 702 1918 (*D; inexpensive*). Colourful hotel whose terraced rooms give you dress circle seats to observe the harbour traffic.

Mesogia, in the backstreets, **t** 242 702 1440. The oldest taverna on Skiáthos has an excellent repertoire including outstanding courgette balls (*kolokythiakéftedes*).

I Roda, Evangelistrías St, up from the post office, **t** 242 702 3178. Family-run, home cooking, excellent inexpensive taverna.

Jailhouse, at the end of the old harbour, **t** 242 702 1081 (€20–25). Very popular with visitors; some exotic, international delights conjured up by inventive chef.

Windmill, in a converted guess-what behind the San Remo hotel, **t** 242 702 4550. Also

a host of lively bars and restaurants and you have the ingredients for a heady cocktail that attracts a fun-seeking crowd.

Skiáthos Town

The capital and only real town on the island, Skiáthos is a gentle spread of traditional whitewashed houses, overhung with bougainvillaea over a razzmatazz of in-your-face commercialism. It has two harbours, separated by the pretty **Boúrtzi** promontory, where the Venetian fortress contains a café, summer theatre and

with an international flavour and a lovely view; popular, though a little pricey.

Agnantio, t 242 702 2016, on the road to the Evangelístria monastery, overlooking the sea. A popular delight with its chic navy and white interior, and its terrace with beautiful views over the Pounta promontory, serving tasty Greek fare.

Anatoli, in the same area as Agnantio, past the turn-off to the monastery, t 242 702 1907. Family-run with tasty home-cooking and a gorgeous view from the terrace.

Panorama, further inland on the road to Profítis Ilías. As the name promises, fabulous views over Skiáthos Town and over the sea to Skópelos. Good oven-baked pizza.

Kanapítsa/Achládies ⊠ 37002

Plaza, t 242 702 1971, f 242 702 2109, *plaza@ n-skiathos.gr* (*B; luxury*). Among pines and olives 100m from Kanapítsa Beach; pool, gym and the inevitable Greek nights.

Esperides, Achládies, t 242 702 2245, f 242 702 1580, *www.esperides.gr* (*A; luxury*). All rooms have balconies, sea views and air-conditioning; tennis, pool, sea sports, etc. among the many features. *Open April–Oct.*

Villa Diamanti, at Kanapítsa, t 242 702 2491, Athens t 210 590 3280 (*A; expensive*). 50m from the sea; stylish apartments in a garden setting with a barbecue. *Open May–Oct.*

Angeliki, t/f 242 702 2354 (*E; moderate*), or smaller **Rea**, t 242 702 3065 (*C; inexpensive*). Both at Megáli Ámmos Beach; the flora on the terraces lends an exotic atmosphere.

Koukounariés/Ag. Paraskeví/Inland ⊠ 37002

Skiathos Palace, Koukounariés Bay, t 242 704 9700, f 242 704 9666, *www.skiathos-palace.gr* (*L; luxury*). Overlooks the bay amid pines, with pool, tennis, massage and roof garden. *Open May–Oct.*

Skiáthos Princess, Ag. Paraskeví, t 242 704 9731, f 242 704 9740 (*L; luxury*). Bright and airy, on one of the best beaches, plus a diving school. *Open May–Oct.*

Atrium Hotel and Bungalows, t 242 704 9345, f 242 704 9444 (*A; expensive*). Near the Princess, a 5min stroll from the beach, with excellent views. *Open April–Oct.*

La Luna, overlooking Troúlos bay, t 242 704 9262 (*A; expensive–moderate*). Well-equipped studios and maisonettes, a lovely pool and great views, 10 minutes' walk from the sea.

Zorbathes, t/f 242 704 9473, *geof@skiathos info.com* (*expensive–moderate*). Two stone, wood and terracotta houses sleeping 4–6 in a lush peaceful valley; book in advance.

Camping Koukounaries, t 242 704 9250. The nicest campsite on the island (and the only official one), at the east end of the eponymous beach.

Entertainment and Nightlife

You'll be spoilt for choice when it comes to bars, but they're not cheap. The **Admiral Benbow Inn** (Polytechníou St) provides a corner of old England while, next door, the Aussie/Brit **Kazbar** is compact, noisy, friendly and fun, with live music. **Adagio** in Evangelístrias St is a friendly and non-exclusive gay bar, an oasis of tranquillity. **Kentavros** near Papadiamántis' house promises a funky jazz and blues atmosphere. On a summer evening, the waterfront bars come into their own; **Jimmy's** is one of the best. For a blaring bop, try **Kavos**, **Remezzo** and the ever-popular seafront **BBC**.

cultural centre. You can dive off the rock here and pretend you're in a Martini ad, or take a morning boat to **Tsoungriás** islet, floating just offshore. In the '60s the Beatles tried to buy it. It's an ideal place to escape the crowds, with its fine sand and snack bar and two beaches, accessible only by foot, where you can play Robinson Crusoe.

If hedonism palls, get a shot of culture at the **house of Alexander Papadiamántis** (*t 242 702 3843; open Tues–Sun 9.30–1 and 5–8*). Papadiamántis (1851–1911) was one of modern Greece's first and finest novelists. Twelve of his stories have been translated by Elizabeth Constandinides as *Tales from a Greek Island*, complete with a map (it's usually available at the house) – a perfect read on a now radically changed Skiáthos.

Koukounariés and Other Beaches

Beaches, beaches, beaches are the key to Skiáthos' success, and they rim the emerald isle like lace. Mobile sardine tins called buses follow the south coast, stopping within walking distance of the best strands, all equipped with tavernas and watersports. The most convenient is **Megáli Ámmos**, but it's generally packed, followed to the west by busy **Achladiés Beach**. Beyond that, the **Kalamáki** peninsula juts out with a coating of holiday villas. Beaches here include **Kanapítsa**, a popular cove, and **Vromólimnos** ('dirty lake'), hard to find but one of the finest places to swim, with powderpuff-soft sand. **Plataniás/Ag. Paraskeví** is a lovely long beach with sun beds. **Troúlos** has tavernas and more good swimming.

The last stop, 12km from town, is the legendary **Koukounariés**, the 'Best Beach in Greece': a superb crescent of soft sand that somehow escaped from the South Pacific, fringed with pine trees, although in August towel space is at a premium. Tavernas, hotels and a campsite are hidden away behind trees and a rather uninspiring lagoon. Hyper-trendy **Krássa**, or **Banana Beach**, is up the hill with the sea on your left when you get off the bus at Koukounariés. At gay/nudist **Little Banana** (or Spartacus) next door, you can peel off everything and lie cheek-to-cheek in a bunch. Next is the lovely **Ag. Eléni**, the last beach accessible by road, a quieter spot with views across to Pélion.

Beaches on the north coast are subject to the *meltémi* winds. **Mandráki** is reached by a pretty footpath from the lagoon behind Koukounariés, with two stretches of sand and a snack bar. Further east, sandy **Asélinos** is in an arcadian setting with a taverna and reed shelters, but beware the undertow in the sea. Just off the road to **Mikro Asélinos** is the exquisitely painted 17th-century chapel of **Panagía Kounistrá**, overlooking the north coast. Past Kástro, **Lalária** (accessible only by sea) is a marvel of silvery pebbles, shimmering like a crescent moon beneath the cliff, with a natural arch.

Inland to Kástro

For a break from charter-set life, take the 4km road just before the airport to **Moní Evangelístria** (*open 8–noon and 4–8pm; proper attire required*), founded in 1797. A lovely, peaceful place, it became a refuge for the *armatolés* (revolutionary militia) from the Olympus area, who, with the support of the Russians, had raised a small pirate fleet to harass the Turks. When Russia made peace with Turkey in 1807 the *armatolés* were abandoned, and many came here; under Yiánnis Stathás they formed an irregular army, and over the monastery hoisted the blue and white Greek flag that they had just invented. The Ottoman fleet soon put an end to their pretensions, but a statement had been made that would inspire the War of Independence 14 years later. A rusting cannon and a small museum recall the monastery's belligerent past.

From here you can cross the island to **Kástro**, a town founded on a windswept niche in the 14th century, when pirates were on the warpath, and inhabited until 1829, when everyone moved down to Skiáthos Town. One of the eight surviving churches, **Christós**, has good frescoes. In 1941, the locals smuggled out trapped Allied troops from the beach below. A detour on the path leads to the 15th-century monastery **Panagía Kechriá**, and lovely isolated **Kechriá Beach**, where a goatherd runs a taverna.

Skópelos (ΣΚΟΠΕΛΟΣ)

Where Skiáthos has given its all to tourism, beautiful Skópelos has remained aloof. Entirely covered with fragrant pine forests, the island has pebbly beaches almost as lovely as the sands flaunted by its rambunctious neighbour, and two pretty towns, Skópelos and Glóssa, that attract 'the more discerning traveller' (as the more discerning package companies call them). Skópelos was colonized by Prince Staphylos of Crete, a tradition given dramatic substance in 1927 when two rich Minoan tombs were discovered by the cove that has always borne his name. Staphylos means 'grape' and the local wine was famous. In the Middle Ages the Venetian renegade Filippo Gizzi was based on Skópelos, and his capture by the Byzantines meant a decline in local excitement until Barbarossa decimated the island in 1538. In later years Skópelos was a refuge from the Turks, who called the Sporades the 'demon islands' because of their pirates. The Skopelitians joined Skiáthos in the revolt of 1805, and tens of thousands of refugees poured in during the War of Independence.

Skópelos Town and its Harbour

Skópelos Town, artfully arranged in an amphitheatre around the port, is a handsome collage under old blue slate and post-earthquake red-tile roofs. The newer houses incorporate traditional features, while the national obsession for planting a seed wherever it has half a chance has resulted in a lush growth of flowers. The town claims 123 churches, many with charming iconostases; two to look out for are **Zoödóchos Pigí** and **Christó** (above the Commercial Bank) with a triangular, Armenian-style apse. At the top rise the walls of the Gizzi's **Kástro**, so formidable that Skópelos was left alone during the War of Independence. A row of chapels along the edge offers saintly defence against the storms that crash into the island, and the 9th-century church, **Ag. Athanásios**, has damaged frescoes from the 1500s. On the other side of town, the **Museum of Folk Art** has a fine collection, especially of embroideries, in a rebuilt 18th-century mansion. **Panagía Eleftherótria**, beyond **Plateía Plátanos** and its enormous plane tree and fountain, is a handsome 18th-century stone church. At the end of town, the fortified monastery **Episkopí**, built by the Venetians, shelters a 17th-century basilica. Further on, **Ag. Regínos** has the sarcophagus of Ag. Regínos, the first Bishop and patron saint of Skópelos who was martyred in 362. There's a mediocre town beach, where cafés scent the evening with honeyed *loukoumádes*.

Around Skopelos Town

The hills over Skópelos' large, windswept harbour shelter no fewer than five monasteries. A lovely path links all, beginning just beyond the strip of beach hotels, or you can go by road as far as the Metamórphosis. The closest, **Evangelístria**, with a magnificent view over town, was founded by monks from Mount Áthos, but is now occupied

Getting There and Around

By sea: ferries connect daily with Vólos, Ag. Konstantínos, Skiáthos and Alónissos, and several times a week with Thessaloníki. Most call at both Skópelos Town and Glóssa. Hydrofoils daily to Skiáthos, Alónissos, Vólos and Ag. Konstantínos. Port authority: t 242 402 2180; Glóssa, t 242 403 3033.

By road: buses run several times a day across the island from Skópelos Town to Glóssa, stopping by all the paths down to the beaches.

Tourist Information and Excursions

Website: www.skopelosweb.gr.

Regular police: Skópelos Town, t 242 402 2235; Glóssa, t 242 403 3333.

Thalpos Travel, upstairs on the waterfront, t 242 402 2947, f 242 402 3057, can help with accommodation and excursions such as night fishing trips, round-island sails in a schooner, and diving trips with marine biologist Vassílis Kouroútos (€130 for two days).

Heather Parsons, author of Skópelos Trails, offers intimate, in-depth views of the island (t 242 402 4022, hevskop@otenet.gr).

Festivals

Carnival (Apokriés) is fun, but can be dangerous to your health. A boat, the tráta or trawler, is made of cane and decorated with rubbish and has a smoke-stack spewing fumes from burning wet garbage. This foul vessel is borne through the streets, while its bearers, bodies painted, drink and sing lewd songs until they finally make it to the harbour, where the boat is hurled into the sea and the merrymakers jump in after it.

Where to Stay and Eat

Skópelos Town ⊠ 37003

Like Skiáthos, Skópelos is expensive; unlike Skiáthos, there are no huge hotels. Some of the most characterful accommodation can only be had through package firms. For rooms, you'll have no problem; offers as you step off the boat are plentiful and honest.

Skopelos, across the bay at Livádi, 600m from town, t 242 402 2517, f 242 402 2958 (L; expensive). Seafront bungalow complex and a pool. Open April–Oct.

Prince Stafilos, nearby, t 242 402 2775, f 242 402 2825 (B; expensive). A rustic feel with a small pool and gardens. Open May–Nov.

by nuns who offer their weavings for sale (open 10–1 and 4–7). Further afield, fortified but abandoned **Ag. Bárbara** has frescoes from the 15th century. The **Metamórphosis** too was abandoned in 1980, but is now being rehabilitated. Over the ridge, looking towards Alónissos, is the convent **Timíou Prodromoú**, with a beautiful iconostasis (same hours as Evangelístria). The path continues to the abandoned **Taxiárchon**, where the Resistance hid Greek and Allied soldiers before they were smuggled to Turkey.

On the other side of the harbour, **Ag. Konstantínos** has a pleasant shingle beach and the ruins of a Hellenistic water tower. If it's too crowded, try **Glystéri** to the north; there's a pleasant taverna and a campsite amid the olive groves. Caiques also sail to the sea cave of **Tripití**, or to the islet of **Ag. Geórgios**, with a 17th-century monastery and wild goats.

Across Skópelos to Glóssa

Buses from Skópelos Town to Glóssa pass the island's best beaches. **Stáphylos**, where the Minoan tombs were found, is now a popular family beach. **Agnóndas**, the next stop, is a boaty little bay with good tavernas and a pebbly beach. Greeks have long memories: Agnóndas was named after a local victor in the 569 BC Olympics, who disembarked here to wild acclaim. Nearby sandy **Limonári** is one of the finest beaches

Dionysos, nearer the centre, t 242 402 3210, f 242 402 2954, *dionysco@otenet.gr* (*B; expensive*). Upbeat hotel in the Pélion style, with a large pool and gardens; comfortable rooms, some with sea views. *Open May–Oct.*

Kyr Sotos, t 242 402 2549 (*A; moderate–inexpensive*). A popular and traditional pension. Each room has its own character and views of the harbour or flower-draped courtyard.

Aegeon, 300m above the beach, t 242 402 2619, f 242 402 2194, in winter t 210 902 4825 (*C; moderate*). Stylish small hotel, with panoramic views.

Perivoli, near Plátanos square, t 242 402 3758. Greek food with a French touch; try the pork roll filled with plums (€15–20).

Ouzeri Anatoli, set in the Kástro, serves excellent *mezédes* on a panoramic terrace. The owner, Giórgos Xintáris, if he's in the mood, plays *rembétika* songs after 11pm.

Mourayo, by the ferry port, t 242 402 4553. One of the best tavernas on the island.

Finikas, t 242 402 3247. Further up into town, a friendly, lantern-lit taverna with delicious regional specialities and a huge palm tree.

Pánormos ✉ 37003

Afrodite, by the beach, t 242 402 3150, f 242 402 3152 (*B; expensive*). Air-conditioned, with a gym and bikes to rent. *Open May–Oct.*

Adrina Beach, t 242 402 3373, f 242 402 3372, *adrina@otenet.gr* (*A; luxury–expensive*). Above the beach, a child-friendly complex in traditional style with a pool and restaurant open to non-residents. *Open May–Sept.*

Terpsi, on the main road, t 242 402 2053. A garden restaurant, where everyone goes for roast chicken stuffed with walnuts, chicken livers and pine nuts (book ahead).

Ostria, t 242 402 2220, f 242 402 3236 (*B; moderate*). A well run family hotel with a lovely pool and sea views, a few minutes walk down to Stáphylos Beach.

Agnóndas ✉ 37003

Paulina, t 242 402 3272/3634 (*A; expensive*). Lovely apartments with beautiful sea views.

Pavlos, t 242 402 2409. The choice of four fish tavernas, shaded by myrtle.

Vangélis and Geórgios, at Limonári, t 242 402 2242. Pleasant rooms and a taverna.

Glóssa ✉ 37004

Zanetta, in Néa Klíma, t 242 403 3140, f 242 403 3717 (*C; moderate*). Complex in the woods with a pool, popular with Greek families.

Agnanti, t 242 403 3606 (€14 –18). Arrive early in Glóssa to get a table at this popular taverna's roof terrace; traditional cuisine, with some unusual fish dishes.

(although the bus stops 800m short), and from Agnóndas a road cuts through the pines to pebbly **Pánormos**, set in a magnificent bay. **Miliá** has a beautiful pebbly beach. Further along, Élios is a small resort that got its name from a dragon who demanded an annual tribute of human flesh, until St Reginos took the place of one of the victims and asked God for mercy (*eleos*); the dragon then let Reginos lead it over a cliff. At **Káto Klíma**, a lovely road goes up to **Athéato**, the oldest village on the island.

At the north end of Skópelos, the traditional settlement of **Glóssa** spills prettily over a wooded hill. Three ruined 4th-century BC towers watch over it, and a track leads in an hour to the monastery of **Ag. Ioánnis**, an eagle's nest with real eagles often soaring overhead; the last leg of the walk is 100 steps carved in the rock. A steep 3km below Glóssa, there's an untidy beach and tavernas at **Loutráki**, the port of Glóssa.

Alónissos (ΑΛΟΝΝΗΣΟΣ)

Long, skinny Alónissos is the queen of an archipelago of nine islets. But while Skiáthos and Skópelos became tourist destinations, Alónissos sat on the sidelines, recovering from a nasty earthquake in 1965, and from politicians who contrived to retard its development. This suited visitors in search of peace and quiet just fine.

Nine-tenths of the island were accessible only by foot, making it great walking country. Then, in 1992, Greece's first National Marine Park was set up around its archipelago to protect the monk seal – the rarest animal in Europe. The donkey tracks have been paved and package holiday makers and flotilla yachts have arrived, but fairly discreetly; this is as close to ecotourism as you get on a Greek island.

Alónissos' history is complicated by the fact that the modern Alónissos is not ancient Halonnesos, but bore the name Ikos – a confusion resulting from an over-eager restoration of ancient place names. Ikos/Alónissos was famous for its wine and spent much of its career under Athenian rule. As for ancient Halonnesos (wherever it may be), Philip of Macedon and Athens quarrelled over it, its port subsided into the sea, and even its location faded from human memory.

Patitíri and Chóra (Alónissos Town)

In 1965, when an earthquake shattered the island's principal town, Chóra, the junta in Athens forced the homeless into prefab relief housing at the port, **Patitíri**, and prevented their return to Chóra by cutting off the water and electricity. Patitíri has since spread its wings to merge with the fishing hamlet of **Vótsi**; in between, a few families are still stuck in the relief village. Charming it ain't, but bougainvillaea covers many a sin. Right by the quay, the **Society for the Study and Protection of the Monk Seal**, and the **European Natural Heritage Fund** (*open 9–2*) will both make you aware of the odds against the little grey *Monacus monacus*; some 300 of the last 500 seals live in Greece, and the 30 or so on the islet of Pipéri form the largest community. The National Marine Park is off limits, unless you go on a tour (*see* Skópelos, p.498). There's a small beach at Patitíri, and a prettier one at Vótsi, just to the north. To the south **Marpoúnta** has the submerged remains of a Temple of Asklepios; beyond are much nicer beaches at **Víthisma** and **Megálos Moúrtias**.

Chóra, set high up above the sea, has outstanding views, especially of the frequent cinemascope sunsets. After the 1965 earthquake, Germans and Brits bought the houses for a song and restored them, agreeing to do without water and electricity (although now they've been hooked up, as the resentment of the former residents has diminished). From Chóra it's a 20-minute walk down to sandy **Vrisítsa Beach**.

Beaches around Alónissos

Boats from Patitíri go to the best beaches, such as **Chrysí Miliá**, in a small cove enveloped with pines. The 5th-century BC capital of ancient Ikos was found by the rose-tinted beach **Kokkinó Kástro**, which was also busy in the Middle Palaeolithic era (100,000–33,000 BC) – the stone tools, now in Vólos Museum, are among the oldest ever found in the Aegean. Further north, **Stení Valá** and **Kalamákia** have beaches sheltered in the embrace of Peristéra islet, and good watersports. **Ag. Dimítrios**, the next beach up, is lovely and usually deserted.

Alónissos' Archipelago

The islets around Alónissos are veritable fish magnets. The most important are olive-covered **Peristéra** to the east, with plenty of sandy beaches and barbecue

Getting There and Around

By sea: ferries connect at least once a day with Vólos, Skópelos, Skiáthos and Ag. Konstantínos; three times a week with Thessaloníki. Daily **hydrofoils** to Skópelos, Skiáthos, Vólos and Ag. Konstantínos. **Excursion boats** from Patitíri go up the coast, and to the islets of Peristéra, Kyrá Panagía and Yoúra. **Port authority: t** 242 406 5595.

By road: buses link Patitíri and Chóra 5 to 10 times a day, depending on the season.

Tourist Information

Ikos Travel, **t** 242 406 5320, **f** 242 406 5321. Pakis here is helpful and ecologically minded. For **tourist police**, see regular police, **t** 242 406 5205.

Where to Stay

Alónissos ✉ 37005

The spiffier places tend to be booked by packagers in summer, but there are generally plenty of room offers as you disembark.

Expensive

Paradise, t 242 406 5160, **f** 242 406 5161 (*C*). On the promontory, beautifully tiered terraces below the pool make a perfect spot for evening drinks. *Open May–Oct.*

Archontiko, near the beach at Patitíri, **t/f** 242 406 5004, winter **f** 210 683 2044. Comfortable apartments with fridges, some with full kitchens. *Open May–Oct.*

Milia Bay, 3km from the port, **t** 242 406 6032, **f** 242 406 6037, *www.agn.gr/hotels/miliabay*. Pretty flats with views and a pool. *Open May–Oct.*

Atrium, Vótsi, **t** 242 406 5749, **f** 242 406 5152 (*C*). Modest complex with quiet, comfortable rooms overlooking the sea and its own pool.

Moderate

Liadromia, directly over the fishing boats on the cliffs of Patitíri, **t** 242 406 5521, **f** 242 406 5096 (*B*). Full of rustic character, with clean rooms and a breakfast terrace.

Alkyon, on the sea, **t** 242 406 5220, **f** 242 406 5195 (*C*). Modern white hotel with rooms and studios overlooking the centre of the action.

Alonissos Beach, Vótsi, **t** 242 406 5281, in Athens **t** 210 223 0869 (*C*). Bungalow complex with a pool and tennis. *Open July–Sept.*

Hiliodromia Studios, t 242 406 5135, **f** 242 406 5469, and **Constantina Apartments, t** 242 406 5900. Good Class A guest houses in Chóra.

Inexpensive

Panorama, in Vótsi, **t** 242 406 5006. In the trees, with a small beach below and a restaurant and bar; the owner speaks good English. *Open May–Sept.*

Dimitris, in Vótsi, **t** 242 406 5035, **f** 242 406 5785. Also with its own bar, pizzeria and terrace, and six rooms with balconies over the little harbour.

Votsi, in Vótsi, **t** 242 406 5818, **f** 242 406 5878. A bit cheaper; a two-minute walk up from the waterfront, with good-sized rooms, a communal kitchen and sea-view terrace.

Eating Out

If you've ever wanted to splurge on Mediterranean lobster (*astakós*), Alónissos is the place for it; the Aegean, for some reason, is quite salty here and the fish especially tasty.

Ouzeri To Kamáki. The local consensus for the best fish in town.

Argos, t 242 406 5141. For an excellent meal in a pretty setting under the trees, follow the path around the rocky promontory to the left of the port. Has a wider than usual selection of fresh fish and lobster and a good wine list. *Open May–Oct.*

Babis, on the way up to Chóra, **t** 242 406 6184 (€12–15). Views over Patitíri from the terrace of this family-run taverna serving island specialities with vegetables from their own garden; try the *bouréki* (cheese pie) and the *xinótiri* (sour cheese).

Paraport Taverna, Chóra. Magnificent views, but arrive early to get a table.

Steni Vala, at Steni Vala, **t** 242 406 5590 (€15–20). Family-run fish taverna, supplied by the owner's fishing boat. Also serves local cheese and vegetable dishes.

evenings. **Psathoúra** has one of the most powerful lighthouses in Greece; beneath it lies a submerged city (possibly Halonnesos) and a sunken volcano. Lovely, wooded **Kyrá Panagía**, two hours by caique from Patitíri, has a sunken 12th-century Byzantine ship, sandy beaches and a stalactite cave (reputedly of the Cyclops). A rare breed of goat skips about the rocks on **Gioúra**, which has another wonderfully dramatic 'Cyclops' cave, although you need a torch, stout shoes and a fit constitution to see it; the island guardian will unlock the gate. **Pipéri**, on the north end of the National Marine Park, is home to rare Eleanora falcons as well as its small colony of monk seals.

Skýros (ΣΚΥΡΟΣ)

Long-isolated Skýros is exceptional in many respects. It has two distinct geological regions, squeezed in the middle by a girdle where everybody lives; the southern half is rugged, ringed with cliffs, and home to a race of tiny ponies, the Pikermies; the north is fertile and pine-forested. Guests at the Holistic Skýros Centre drink ouzo with old men in traditional baggy trousers and sandals. Traditional houses are decorated with plates brought back from around the world by Skyriot sailors, with American refrigerators gently purring in the back room. In other words, the outside world has arrived, but the Skyriots are determined to set the rules by which it operates on their island.

Achilles, Theseus, and a Bit of History

When it was prophesied that Achilles would either win glory at Troy and die young, or live peacefully at home to a ripe old age, his mother Thetis hid him from the warlords by disguising him as a girl and sending him to live at King Lykomedes' palace in Skýros. Achilles didn't mind, and took advantage of his stay by fathering a son, Neoptolemos. But another oracle declared that the Greeks would never win the Trojan War without Achilles, and Odysseus was sent to find him. He brought gifts for the women when he called on Lykomedes – perfumes, jewellery, finery – and a sword, which the young transvestite seized and betrayed his identity. When an arrow in his heel ended Achilles' life, Odysseus, obeying another oracle, returned to Skýros to fetch his son Neoptolemos to Troy: with his help, the war was eventually won.

Lykomedes plays a less benign role in another story: when Theseus returned to Athens after spending four years glued to the Chair of Forgetfulness in Hades, he found the city divided into factions against him. Theseus sought asylum in Crete, but was blown off course to Skýros, where he was received with such honour by Lykomedes that he announced that he would retire on an estate his family owned on Skýros – an estate coveted by Lykomedes himself. So after a drinking party the king took Theseus to Skýros' acropolis and gave him a push. Theseus' memory was neglected by the Athenians until his spirit was seen at Marathon. The Delphic oracle then charged Athens to bring his bones home – just the excuse the Athenians needed to nab Skýros. In 476 BC Kimon captured it and, guided by a she-eagle, found a tall skeleton buried with his weapons. Certain that it was Theseus, Kimon carried the bones back to Athens, and enshrined them (*see* p.128).

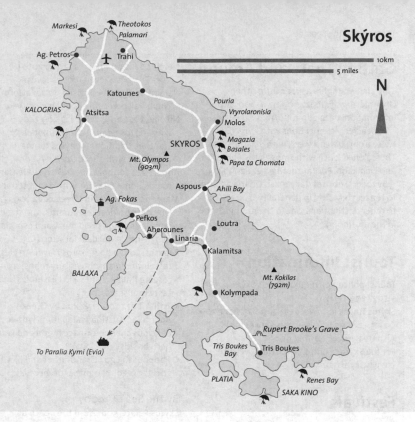

Skýros

N

Skýros Town

Skýros Town, or Chóra, wouldn't look out of place in the Cyclades, its white houses stacked along narrow lanes and steps, sweeping like a full skirt around the rocky precipice of the acropolis. The main street curls past grocers and hardware shops, cafés, tavernas and cocktail bars catering to the needs and desires of both locals and visitors. The path up to the acropolis and **Kástro** passes by way of the monastery of **Ag. Geórgios**, founded in 962 by Nikephóros Phókas, 'the Pale Death of the Saracens' and liberator of Crete, who gave it to his saintly friend Athanásios, future founder of the Great Lávra on Áthos. The church has a fine painting of St George and an icon of the same with a black face, brought from Constantinople during the Iconoclasm. A lion of St Mark (1354) marks the gate of the Byzantine-Venetian citadel, built over a Classical fort; where Lykomedes gave Theseus his fatal shove over the sheer drop.

Brooke Square, at the end of town, seems neglected, although the willy of the gormless *Statue of Immortal Poetry* (1931) is administered to weekly by spray painters. The **Archaeological Museum**, along the steps down to Magaziá (*t 222 209 1327; open Tues–Sun 8.30–3; adm*) has finds from Copper Age Palamári and proto-Geometric Thémis, plus a traditionally furnished Skyriot home, 35 sq m in size – the average living space per family. The nearby **Faltaits Museum of Folklore** (*t 222 209 1232; open 10–1 and 6–9 in summer; otherwise 5.30–8*) has a first-rate collection of domestic items, costumes, and embroideries covered with mermaids, double-headed eagles, pomegranates and hoopoes - and an excellent shop.

Getting There and Around

By air: two flights a week from Athens; Olympic Airways, **t** 222 209 1123/1600; **airport information: t** 222 209 1660/1625.

By sea: ferry connections with Kými (Évia) twice a day; twice a week with Skiáthos and Thessaloníki; once with Tínos, Páros, Santoríni and Heráklion. **Port authority: t** 222 209 1475.

By road: six **buses** daily reach Linariá and up to ten reach Mólos; in general two buses a day to other destinations, one in the morning, one in the afternoon.

Tourist Information

Tourist police: see regular police, Skýros Town, **t** 222 209 1274.

Skýros Travel, in town, **t** 222 209 1123, **f** 222 209 2123. Leftéris Trákes here is very helpful. Also try *www.skyros-net.gr*.

For the **Skýros Centre**, check their website, *www.skyros.com*.

Festivals

Skýros preserves vestiges of ancient goat and cattle cults during its **Carnival**, when three characters dance down the street: the 'Old Man' in a goatskin costume, mask and sheep bells, followed by the *Frángos* (the Frank, or foreigner), dressed in motley clothes, with a mask and bell, blowing a conch shell to scare children, and the *Koréla*, a man dressed up as a woman. These perform the *Horós tou Trágou*, or the Goat Dance, possibly a relic of the *tragoudía* or 'goat song' that gave us the word tragedy. Every day during carnival the Old Man, the *Frángos* and the *Koréla* make their way through town, joining in satires until they end up at the monastery of Ag. Geórgios.

Where to Stay and Eat

Skýros Town ✉ 34007

Buses from the port are besieged by little old ladies, offering horribly overpriced rooms in traditional houses. If you take one, mind you don't break the plates.

Nefeli, t 222 209 1964, **f** 222 209 2061 (*B; expensive*). The best; seven rooms have a traditional *sfa* (bed raised on a platform). There's also a roomy pool. *Open all year.*

Nikolas, t 222 209 1778, **f** 222 209 3400, *www.skyrosnet.gr/nicholas* (*moderate*). Tranquil, traditionally styled rooms (complete with a *sfa*). *Open all year.*

Anna, t 222 209 1941 (*inexpensive*). Pleasant rooms, some en suite, with a roof terrace.

Margetis, on the main street, **t** 222 209 1311. One of the oldest restaurants, and the most popular, serving good meat and especially fish dishes in an ideal location (€15).

Pegasos, 20m below Skyros Travel. An elegant restaurant in a 19th-century mansion, serving Italian dishes, kid casseroles and tasty moussaka.

Kristina, t 222 209 1778. Run by Greek-Australian Kristina Tsalapatani, with a delicious change-of-pace menu and warm herb breads.

O Pappous Ki Ego ('Grandfather and I'), **t** 222 209 3200. Popular place for *mezédes*.

By the Sea ✉ 34007

Skýros Palace, 50m from the beach at Grismata, **t** 222 209 1994, **f** 222 209 2070, winter **f** 210 275 2094, *www.skiros-palace.gr* (*B; expensive*).Built in the traditional Skýros-Cyclades style, it has a lovely sea-water pool and restaurant. *Open mid-May–Sept.*

Skýros Studios, Mólos, t 222 209 1376, in winter **t** 210 723 0871, **f** 210 723 0957 (*B; expensive–moderate*). Set in a large garden, built and furnished in the traditional Skyriot style.

Molos, nearby, **t** 222 209 1381, in winter **t** 210 262 7513 (*moderate–inexpensive*). Offers pleasant garden studios, with big discounts in May and June. *Open May–Sept.*

Perigali, set back from the sea in Magaziá, **t** 222 209 1889, **f** 222 209 2061 (*moderate*). A handful of well-kept studios and rooms circling a luscious garden. *Open May–Oct.*

Efrosýni Varsámon, Magaziá, **t** 222 209 1142 (*moderate*). Charming rooms above a pottery shop.

Thoma to Magazi, Mólos Beach, **t** 222 209 1942. Excellent seafood, and not too dear.

A 10-minute walk below Skýros Town stretches the long sandy beach of **Magaziá**, named after the Venetian powder magazines once stored here, and next to it is **Mólos Beach**; most of the island's accommodation and nightlife are concentrated here. Other beaches are in walking distance; avoid sewage-prone Basáles, but continue south to **Papá ta Chómata** ('Priests' Land'), where not even the priest minds if you sunbathe nude. From **Órmos Achílli** Achilles embarked for Troy; a new marina allows yachties to do the same.

Around Skýros

The only way to visit the rest of the island is by foot, taxi or hired wheels. The pine-wooded north half of Skýros has better roads and the fine sandy beach of **Ag. Pétros** past the airport. A path (taking about 3 hours and not always easy to find) crosses the island from Skýros Town to **Atsítsa**, where a taverna sits on a rocky beach, near a branch of the Skyros Centre. A second path to Atsítsa begins in the port **Linariá**, built after 1860; it passes by way of **Achérounes** and the pretty beach and tavernas at **Péfkos**. Even prettier **Ag. Fokás Beach**, with white pebbles, is further north, with a basic taverna and a few rooms. From Linariá, caiques sail to the islet **Skyropoúla**, home to two beaches and a cave, and a herd of munchkin ponies.

The beaches in the rugged south are less appealing, with the exception of sand and stone **Kalamítsa**, fronted by tavernas and a few rooms. Taxis offer excursions (for about €32) to **Tris Boukés** and the **grave of Rupert Brooke** – 6ft of official British soil – at the southernmost point of Skýros. On 23 April 1915, the 27-year-old poet, en route to Gallipoli, died of blood poisoning and was buried in this olive grove. His epitaph came from his own pen:

If I should die, think only this of me:
That there's some corner of a foreign field
That is for ever England.

Among the boat excursions on offer, the one to Sarakíno Beach and Platý island, and around the cliffs at Renés, is spectacular; Eleanora falcons nest on the heights.

Back on the Mainland: Lárissa and Around

Lárissa

Lárissa (pop. 115,000), the capital of Thessaly and a major industrial city, sits on the banks of the Piniós, in the middle of the plain that is one of the hottest places in Europe – hitting 48°C (118°F) in the summer of 2000. Its name is a Pelasgian word for 'citadel' and it has been inhabited since Palaeolithic times; in the Classical age, the ruling family, the Aleuadai, were often the big cheeses in all Thessaly, and patrons of both Pindar and Hippocrates (who died here). Nowadays it's one of those cities you may remember best for its gridlock traffic, but there are a few things to see, all in walking distance of huge central **Plateía Sápka**. The **Archaeological Museum** is in a mosque, by the covered market on Kíprou St (**t** *241 028 8515, open Tues–Sun 8-1; free*), and offers a rich display of Palaeolithic and Neolithic artefacts, a rare Greek menhir from a Bronze Age tumulus, Archaic weapons, massive Thessalian fibulae, bronzes and Roman steles. Northwest of Sápka square on Papanastasíou St, a large 3rd-century BC **theatre** has been excavated; from here Venizélou St leads to the new bridge over the Piniós, its banks dotted with mansions and luxuriant gardens. The wooded **Alcazár Park** on the opposite bank offers respite if the sun is blistering.

From Lárissa, the National Road skirts the west flank of 6,490ft **Mount Óssa** (or Kíssavos), the big cone rising over Thessaly's plains. In myth, the giant twins Otyus and Ephialtes piled Pélion on top of Óssa to reach Olympus and seize Hera, only to be seized instead by Zeus and hurled to their deaths. Yet compared to the two splendid mountains on either side of it, Óssa is something of an intermission. Still, if you want to see a bit more and aren't in a hurry, drive through the cotton fields to **Agiá**, a big farming town above **Agiókambos**, with a good campsite and what is claimed to be the longest (14km) beach in Greece. To the north, Óssa's skirts are fringed by scrappy beach resorts, of which the nicest is **Kókkino Néro** ('red water'), with big plane trees, a Byzantine bridge, a spa oozing reddish water, and lots of Russian tourists. From here the road rises up the mountain to **Káritsa**, before embarking on a narrow, windy descent down Óssa's steepest slope to the long beach at **Stómio**, a small resort famous for its bottomless springs. At **Omólio**, where the landmark is a bizarre top-heavy church, you can join the National Road thundering through the Vale of Tempe (*see* below).

On the National Road from Lárissa, just before the Tempe toll booth, a narrow road on the right winds 5km up to **Ambelákia**, on Óssa's west slope. Named for its vine-yards, what has made Ambelákia, pop. 480, a subject of international study was the

Getting There and Around

By train: Lárissa's station is south of the centre, off Iroon Politechníou St, t 241 059 0161, and has several direct trains from Athens, Thessaloníki and Vólos.

By bus: Six a day to Lárissa from Athens leave from Liossíon station, t 210 831 1434. Lárissa's main bus station, t 241 053 7737, is 150m north of Plateía Laoú on Ólympou St; there are also 13 buses to Thessoloníki, 12 to Vólos, three to Kastoriá, and two to Ioánnina. For Tríkala (21 a day) and Kardítsa (11 a day) take a taxi to the much remoter station on Iroón Polytechníou, t 241 053 7777.

Tourist Information

EOT: 18 Koumoundoúrou, on Plateía Ríga Feréou, t/f 241 025 0919.
Tourist police: 86 Papanastasíou, t 241 062 3158.

Where to Stay and Eat

Lárissa ☒ **41222**
Elena, 13 28 Oktovríou, t 241 028 7461, t 241 053 7251, f 241 028 7463 (*B; expensive*). In the centre, with more character than most; pretty furnishings and air-conditioning.
Rodi, Filellínon St (just off Plateía Sápka), t 241 053 2326. Delicious Greek starters and main courses served in a neoclassical house.

Ambelákia ☒ **40004**
Ennéa Moúses (Nine Muses), t 249 509 3405 (*moderate*). Traditional hotel by the square with its plane trees and fountain.
Women's Agrotourism Cooperative, t 249 509 3487 or t 249 509 3362, f 249 509 3349. They offer a dozen rooms in village houses and run the Rodi café with good *mezédes*.
Taverna tou Daniil, in the square, t 249 509 3356. A place to dawdle over succulent meat and potatoes while quaffing the local wine.

founding, in 1780, of the world's first co-operative, the *koiné syntrophiá* ('common company') by the producers of a glossy red cotton thread that was in demand across Europe, especially in Germany and Austria. In its heyday there were 24 dyeing mills and a population of 6,000, most of whom were bilingual (one bylaw of the company provided that merchants should be sent abroad to learn languages). Although the cooperative didn't last long – the Napoleonic Wars wreaked havoc on the trade and Alí Pasha demanded 60,000 pilasters a year in tribute from the village – the **Mansion of George Schwartz** (German for his name, Mávros), built in 1787 by the president of the cooperative, offers a glimpse into how successful it once was (*t 249 509 3302; open Tues–Sat 8.45–3, Sun 9.30–2.30; adm*). Its three floors are decorated with charming murals of real and imaginary landscapes, carved wood and stained glass from Vienna – a delightful mix of Balkan, Islamic and Central European.

The Vale of Tempe

In the Quaternary era the great plain of Thessaly was a lake. A cataclysm then rent Óssa from Olympus, creating a narrow 10km cleft under sheer mountain walls that allowed the lake to drain in the sea, a course now followed by the Piniós river. The ancient Greeks liked to imagine the mountains had been savagely torn in the war of the gods and giants, and they considered the glen in the cleft, the lush Vale of Tempe (Tembi) a hallowed beauty spot sacred to Apollo. Legend has it that he served eight years here as the shepherd to the king of Thessaly after slaying Python in Delphi. He fell in love with Daphne, the daughter of the river god, but as he pursued her she begged the gods to save her, which they did, more permanently than she may have wished, by turning her into a laurel tree (*dafni*). Apollo plucked a branch and replanted it in Delphi, and used it to crown the victors of the Pythian Games.

The Vale of Tempe provided a convenient gate between southern and northern Greece, but not one that could be closed; attempts to block invaders (the Persians in 480 BC, the Romans in 168 BC, Germans in 1941) never succeeded, because they all too soon located the mountain track inland to Gónnoi and turned the position. The ruined medieval **Kástro tis Oraiás**, or Castle of the Beautiful Maiden, near the south entrance of the glen, is built over one of many ancient fortresses. Today the busy National Road drowns out the nightingales, but you can pull over to the car park for a hint of what the poets sang about, and walk over the suspension bridge for the chapel and grotto of **Ag. Paraskeví**. The '*Love Boat*' (presumably named for Apollo and Daphne) makes half-hour river trips, or you can continue on a bit further to the cool, less overrun **Spring of Daphne**. To continue north, *see* p.521.

Inland Thessaly

Due west of Lárissa, **Tríkala**, except for a few pleasant squares, a pretty clock tower and a nice park beside the Lethéos river, is as flat and featureless as the landscape. For something more picturesque, head 20km southwest to little **Pýli**, also a river town, but at the mouth of a narrow gorge directly under a vertiginous wall of the South

Pindus range. Pýli means 'gate' and a road does continue west past the gate deep into the mountains to the ski centre at **Pertoúli**; it then wiggles its way to Kalambáka, a good choice if you have a sense of adventure. At the west end of Pýli, a pretty stone bridge arches across the river. Now just a photo opportunity, it was part of a major highway during the Byzantine period. Cross the modern bridge, where a sign points left to **Pórta Panagía** (*the crabby caretaker is usually around from 8–12 and 3–5*), a small hodgepodge of a 13th-century church built by Ioánnis Doukas, the Despot of Épirus, who liked it well enough to be buried in it; a fresco over his tomb shows him being led to Paradise. Its mosaics, especially of the Virgin and Christ, are renowned, albeit the worse for wear. Mary stands on Christ's right, an unusual honour; both mosaics are framed by attractive marble frames. The domed narrow ceiling is still impressive.

Continue beyond the bridge where a sign for Ag. Vissaríonos' monastery will send you left and 5km straight up a dirt road with terrific views of the plain. A mere hour by car from Metéora, **Ag. Vissaríon** (*open daily 8–12 and 3–7*) is worlds apart: this is the real McCoy, a fully functioning monastery. Founded in 1530 by St Vissaríon of Lárissa, it's an austere square fortress, equipped with 366 cells, one for each day of the year. Only the maroon and white cupolas of its *katholikón* add a little whimsy; inside are excellent 16th-century frescoes and an 18th-century gilded iconostasis carved by artisans in Métsovo. Admission is forbidden to women, a rule written into the founder's will. Exceptions are made for the small upper chapel to the left of the entrance if women beg earnestly enough (and many do; the saint is renowned for his cures), but never anywhere else; the monks swear that every time the rule was violated, catastrophes occurred. *Kourabiédes* (almond sugar cookies) are offered as consolation to those left on the doorstep. By the outer wall, just beyond the old windlass gallery, a tiny trout fishery has been made out of an old water tank. The monks eat no meat, so the trout and their garden make them almost self-sufficient. Go soon; the road is being graded for asphalt, the kiss of death to monastic solitude, and a spiffy new stone church is being built outside the walls for ladies. Orthodoxy's slight nod to women here will probably spell the end to those delicious *kourabiedes*, too.

Pýli is the back gate to gorgeous Lake Plastíra, and the 20km drive through mountain villages from Pýli is a much nicer prelude to this pocket Eden than the highway from Kardítsa.

Lake Plastíra

At 2,624ft the highest artificial lake in Europe, Lake Plastíra stretches 14km from Krionéri village in the north to the Plastíras dam in the south, its indented sand-coloured shore emphasizing its impossibly blue water. In places 195ft deep, it holds 400 million cubic metres of water for Thessaly's dry plains. So far this area is unknown to foreigners but it won't stay that way. The surrounding hills are all forest, perfect for walking, mountain biking, paragliding, skiing and horseback riding, and everything is so neat and pristine it could be in Switzerland, an effect heightened by the newness of the lake hotels and the generous intervals between them; so far, no crowding in Paradise. The road that circles the lake is perfect for Sunday cyclists.

Getting There and Around

By bus: the Trίkala bus station, at the corner of Όthonas and Giravάldi Sts, **t** 243 107 3130, has 20 connections daily to Kalambάka, 22 to Lάrissa, eight to Athens, six to Thessaloníki, four to Vόlos and two to Ioάnnina. There are hourly buses to Kardίtsa and 3 daily to Pýli.

The Kardίtsa bus station on Leofόros Demokratías (Terma) by the national stadium, **t** 244 102 1411, has three buses a day to Plastίra (as far as Kardίtsa), and hourly ones to Trίkala, Lamía and Lάrissa.

By train: Trίkala train station: **t** 2431 02 7214. Kardίtsa train station: **t** 244 102 1402. The train service north to Thessaloníki and south to Athens is regular and frequent.

Maps: the *Road* map of Épirus and Thessaly is fine unless trekking or driving west and south of Lake Plastίra, when you'll need the *Road* Ágrapha map.

Activities

Christos Zapéta Riding Club, **t** 244 109 2855. On the north shore, east of Krionéri.

Tavropόs Nature and Sport Adventure Centre, Kalίvia Pezoúlas, **t/f** 244 109 2552. Friendly Dimítris Charalambίdis rents mountain bikes, offers guided tours, hands out a great map of the lake, and can find you a room.

Plastίra Mountain Club, **t** 244 109 2552. There are two refuges in the area.

Pezoúla Beach, turn at sign for Kalίvia Perzoúlas, **t** 244 109 2477. This narrow spit of land south of Krionéri juts into the lake. Aside from drinks or food, you can swim, or rent a canoe or a small sail boat.

Festivals

Trίkala: end of May, the **Hadjipetria Festival**, with athletic contests and national dances. Kardίtsa: 20–30 May, the **Karaiskáki**, with traditional dancing, parades and pageantry, honouring the guerrillas of the War of Independence.

Where to Stay and Eat

Trίkala ✉ 42100

Lithaéon, 16 Όthonos St, **t** 2431020690, **f** 243 103 7390 (*B, expensive*). By the river, on top of the bus station, renovated; breakfast included in the price. *Open all year.*

Pallάdion, 4 Víronas St, **t** 243 102 8091 (*inexpensive*). Two streets back from Όthonos, fine for overnight. *Open all year.*

Pýli ✉ 420 32

Pýli, **t** 243 402 3510, **f** 243 402 3510. (*C; moderate*). Plain, modest, new, over the bridge to Pόrta Panayίa. Breakfast. *Open all year.*

Babanάra, **t** 2434022325, **f** 243 402 2242 (*D; moderate–inexpensive*). Big rooms, TV, and the village coffee shop downstairs, to get to know the locals. *Open all year.*

Limni N. Plastίra ✉ 43067

Lake Plastίra makes a wonderful base for the Ágrapha.

Naiádes, Neochόri, **t** 244 109 3333, *naiades@ hol.gr* (*A; expensive*). New, Plastίra's most luxurious hotel, with views of the lake, a pool, tennis, a piano bar and a lot of antique furniture. Fireplaces in the rooms.

Liápis Rooms, Kalίvia Pezoúlas, **t** 244 109 2424, mobile **t** 697 709 5695 (*moderate–inexpensive*). New large rooms, 50m from the lake.

Kardίtsa ✉ 43100

Kiérion, Vlatsoúka and Tzélla Sts, **t/f** 244 107 1923, *www.karditsa-net.gr/kierion* (*B; expensive*). A new central hotel with a summer pool and buffet breakfast.

Ástron, 47 Iezekiél St, **t** 244 102 3552, **f** 244 102 3551 (*C; moderate–inexpensive*). No pool but central, by the *dimarchίon* (town hall).

Neochόri, on the west shore, is the largest town, and a lot of it is new; the old village is under water. Nine km southwest is **Karítsa**, an old village immersed in trees with the 15th-century monastery of **Panagías tis Pelektís** at 4,920ft, and a trout farm and restaurant by its river. Cross the dam for the east shore, where there's swimming at Lamberό Beach just north of Tsardάki. The fortress-like 16th-century **monastery of Korόnas** ('the crown') has stupendous views of the plain of Thessaly to the east.

A 25km highway leads east to **Kardítsa**, Thessaly's 'little heart', a smaller version of Tríkala, with a university, a lovely park in its centre, and a trendy indoor market. If civilization doesn't yet appeal, those with sturdy cars (or boots) can navigate the capillaries of the **Ágrapha Mountains** west of Lake Plastíra towards Karpenísi, a fascinating wilderness so little travelled in Byzantine and Turkish times that it was called *Ágrapha*, ' the unwritten'.

The Metéora

The road from Tríkala northwest to Kalambáka is mesmerizingly boring – until suddenly out of nowhere a massive cluster of sandstone cylinders appear, rising straight up from the valley floor. Eroded, iron grey and water scarred, their sometimes stubby, sometimes pointed pinnacles are visible for miles, and from a distance they look as two-dimensional and contrived as a cartoon backdrop. Over 800 smooth and windswept rocks, some as high as 1,200 feet, cover 20 square kilometres. Geologists drily call this unique massif debris left over from a primeval river delta, but it's really the mighty Pindus' last and greatest conjuring trick, a spectacular geographical *non sequitur*, before it releases its spell on the landscape and subsides into the dull Thessalian plain. Even if monks had not built in its improbable recesses and inaccessible peaks, it would still be visited for the sheer grandeur of its scenery. Metéora means 'things hovering in the air', as apt a name for the rocks themselves as it is for the stupendous and unforgettable monasteries that crown them.

History

In the 11th century, a ragtag group of misanthropic hermits arrived seeking salvation in Metéora's clefts and caves. A small proto-monastic community developed at Doúpiani (present-day Kastráki), its small church serving their few communal liturgical needs. Then, in 1336, Athanásios, a monk from Athos, founded the Great Metéora, the first monastic settlement on the rocks themselves. This and subsequent monasteries were coenobitic, which stressed hierarchical communal living – the kind of monasticism preferred by the Orthodox church to the spiritual athletes in lonely caves who often ignored or, worse, challenged the church's authority and its more worldly approach to salvation. Each monastery had its own constitution, but the local bishop, as representative of the church, invested its abbot and gave him legitimacy. As these grander monuments to Orthodoxy sprang up, the hermits in their clefts might have been forgiven for doubting whether the absence of solitude and conspicuous wealth made Holy Contemplation any easier.

The monasteries got an improbable boost in the Middle Ages during the short-lived Serbian interlude in Thessaly, thanks to the piety of their kings. During the Ottoman period, after serious initial setbacks, Metéora recovered and by the reign of Suleiman the Magnificent (1520–66) there were 13 substantial monasteries, replete with wooden galleries, corniced rooftops, and frescoed *katholikóns*, each one more beautifully situated than the next, along with 20 smaller establishments. They were well

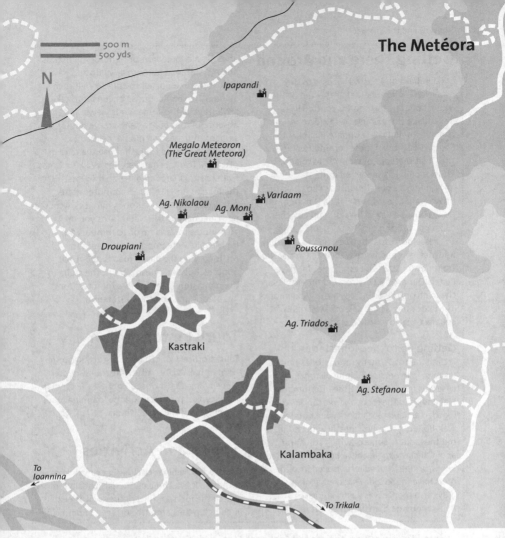

500 m
500 yds

N

Ipapandi

Megalo Meteoron
(The Great Meteora)

Ag. Nikolaou   Varlaam

Ag. Moni

Droupiani   Roussanou

Ag. Triados

Kastraki

Ag. Stefanou

Kalambaka

To
Ioannina

To Trikala

endowed, owning lands as far away as Moldavia and Wallachia. Ironically, their ultimate decline was caused by Greek independence. The new state did not include
Thessaly, and so the monasteries were left suspended in the Ottoman empire, as
monks went to monasteries in the new Greek state.

Metéora's renaissance as a mega-tourist attraction (700,000 people visit yearly) has
a downside. These are no longer working monasteries unless you count the harassed
monks and priests, their habits covered in sawdust, organizing the endless renovations that these old structures demand. If the mere fact of coenobitic monasticism
made contemplation difficult early on, then any monk at today's Metéora is surely
facing an uphill battle to sanctity, guarding the door against insensitive tourists with
uncovered knees, and flogging postcards, cushions and varnished stones larded with
inspirational messages. The six functioning monasteries, its massif and Kastráki are
now a World Heritage Site. Greeks are allowed in free, but the admission (€1.50)

Getting There and Around

Kalambáka and Kastráki (closer to the monasteries) sit together at the feet of the Metéora. Public transport is centred in Kalambáka, but 24 buses a day (6.30am–9pm) from the main Plataía Dimarchío link it to Kastráki. Several of these continue as far as the Great Metéora, passing Ag. Nikoláou, Roussánou and Varlaám en route.

Kalambáka's **bus** station, t 243 202 2432, is on Averoff St, 50m from Plateía Dimarchío. It has 24 buses a day to Tríkala, eight to Athens (Lióssion station, t 210 831 1434) and Lamía, six to Thessaloníki, four to Vólos, two to Ioánnina and Métsovo, and twice weekly to Pátras. The **train** station, t 243 202 2451, is not far from Plateía Dimarchío. Services and timetables to the main north-south lines are in flux; phone. The **taxi** stand is near Kalambáka's main square: t 243 202 2310 or 243 202 2822.

Getting up to the Monasteries

Until the 1920s, many monasteries hauled visitors up in nets; the 'flight' distance in one case was 150 feet; flight time interminable. Handholds in the rocks, and precarious rope or wooden articulated ladders were employed as well. Building supplies are still winched up, but the ladders, some of which still hang about at crazy angles, have been abandoned. Roads, bridges and stairs chiselled into the rocks have made today's ascent a lot easier.

By car: a road leaves Kastráki, passes Roussánou and then branches left for Varlaám

and Megálo Metéoron, or right for Ag. Triádos and Ag. Stefánou. You can drive up and have a look at the exteriors of the big six in less than an hour. Do this at sunrise or sunset to take advantage of the stupendous views, and the absence of tour buses. Keep an eye out for the smaller churches and monks' cells.

On foot: marked trails that use the road in places go to all six monasteries. Walking times from Kastráki: Droúpiani 15–20 minutes; up the road to Ag. Nikoláou 10 minutes more; Ag. Nikoláou to Roussánou 15 minutes. A footpath just past Ag. Nikoláou takes you up in 30 minutes to Varlaam or 20 minutes more for Megálo Metéoron. From Varlaám to Ag. Triádos on the paved road is about 30 minutes, but that doesn't count the stairs to the monastery. Twenty more minutes from Ag. Triádos gets you to Ag. Stefánou.

Tourist Information

Tourist office: 1 Vlakáda St, t 243 207 5306, in Kalambaka's city hall, by the main square; *open May–Oct*. If closed, contact the regular **police**, t 243 207 6100, on the Ioánnina road, 1km west of the main Plateia.

Sports and Activities

Metéora is a big **rock climbing** centre and, although it is technically illegal, just sit and watch the rocks a while; figures will appear inching up their smooth surfaces, or bouncing

charged to others emphasizes the fact that Metéora's once vital monasteries have become museums, glorious paeans to things that were and never will be again.

The Monasteries

We follow the road up from Kastráki, going left after Roussánou to Varlaám and the Great Metéora, then double back east to Ag. Triádos and Ag. Stefánou.

Ag. Nikoláou tou Anapavsá was built by Dionysios, the bishop of Lárissa, in the 16th century on the foundations of an older building. Restored in 1960, its *katholikón* boasts frescoes painted in 1527 by Theophánes the Cretan in his then trend-setting style. The *katholikón* in the centre of every monastic square, symbolizing the church as the centre of the human cosmos, traditionally faces east, but here it faces north; Metéora's topography required some rearrangements. Before leaving, glance up at nearby **Ag. Moni** sitting on its needle-like pinnacle, a mere ruin since an earthquake in 1858. A footpath to Varlaám leaves just after Ag. Moni. Even if you are not travelling on

down their vertical walls on flimsy ropes. Paragliding is now strictly forbidden, and this one is enforced. Metéora's unique rocks go as far north as Gávros, and there are **hiking** trails throughout the area. Most campsites and a couple of hotels have **pools**; non residents can swim for a fee.

Where to Stay and Eat

Hotels are open all year, and bargains can be had outside of July and August. Bypassing Kalambáka for Kastráki is best for a cheaper, homier experience. For food, stick to Kastráki unless you love the greasy fast stuff.

Kalambáka ✉ 42200

Motel Divani, t 243 202 3330, f 243 202 3638, *divanis@divaniacropolis.gr* (*A; luxury*). Popular with tour groups for its so-so luxury.

Amalia, way out of town on the Tríkala road, t 243 207 2216, f 243 207 2457, *www.amalia.gr* (*A; luxury*). As much personality as an airport, but lovely views of the rocks.

Edelweiss, 3 Venizélou, t 243 202 3966, f 243 202 4733 (*B; expensive*). A reasonable hotel in the centre of town, with a pool.

Kastráki ✉ 42200

Kastraki, t 243 207 5336, f 243 207 5335 (*B; moderate; expensive in season*). Comfortable, buffet breakfast; pseudo luxury with parking. A good choice if you can get the upper rooms with the view.

Doupiani House, t 243 202 4078, f 243 207 5326, *doupiani-house@kmp.forthnet.gr* (*moderate*). A winner, with a clear panoramic view to the rocks (book). If you can't get a room, go for a coffee on its terrace, and walk over to Droúpiani, a chapel built in 1861 on the site of the original.

France, t 243 202 4186, f 243 207 5186 (*moderate*). Typical of the family-run hotels along Kastráki's main road.

Papastathis Rooms, t/f 243 207 7782 (*inexpensive*). Brand new, on the edge of town, closest to the monasteries. Large rooms, some with the view.

Tsikáli, t 243 202 2438, f 243 207 7872 (*E; inexpensive*). This one is just down from the main road, with a lawn and tables for 'the view' and the welcoming K. Chrissoúla.

Pantavális Rooms, t 243 202 2801 (*inexpensive*). On the main road, with 'healthy hot water'. Views from its upper terrace.

Camping Vráchos-Kastráki, t 243 202 2293. In the centre of Kastráki with a pool and view.

Camping 'The Cave', t 243 202 4802. Has the same view and a pool, too.

In the evening all of Kastráki's tavernas roast meat on outdoor spits.

Metéora, opposite the Kastráki hotel, t 243 202 2285. Inexpensive, good food.

Filoxénia, t 243 202 3514. A pleasant garden-like terrace and a big menu.

ABC Pub, t 243 207 5627. A nicely decorated spot to chill out at night, right in the centre of town on the main road.

foot, follow it the short distance to the base of Varlaám's pinnacle for a look at the 300ft-deep Dragon's Cave.

Roussánou, compact, with its walls exactly in line with the edge of its pedestal, looks precarious; a frightening narrow bridge built in 1868 between two mini peaks replaced an earlier, even scarier approach. Founded in 1545 by Maximos and Joseph of Ioánnina, it is now a convent , whose new kitchen inside the entrance nicely highlights an ongoing dilemma for monasticism. How much of the modern world should this conservative institution embrace? Formica and spiffy new kitchen cupboards look wildly incongruous after the gruesome frescoes in the *katholikón* (the nun's habits haven't changed much, though).

Varlaám is wonderful. Founded in 1517 by Theophánis and Nektários Apsarádas from Ioánnina, it was named after the hermit who originally built on the spot. It is approached by a flight of 195 stairs added in 1932, and its overhanging tower room contains a windlass and rope still in use. Varlaám boasts quite a little museum in the

Visiting the Monasteries

Women must wear skirts covering the knees; arms may not be bare and no low-cut blouses. Men must wear long trousers and shirts.

Ag. Nikoláou, t 243 202 2375; *open daily 9–3.30, closed Fri in winter.*

Roussánou, t 243 202 2649; *open daily 9–6.*

Varlaám, t 243 202 2277; *open daily 9–2 and 3–7, closed Thurs.*

The Great Metéora, t 243 202 2298; *open daily 9–1 and 3–6, closed Tues.*

Ag. Triádos, t 243 202 2220; *open daily 9–12.30 and 3–5, closed Thurs.*

Ag. Stefánou, t,043 202 2279; *open daily 9–1 and 3–5, closed Mon.*

old refectory, with relics and ecclesiastical treasures. The *katholikón*, built in 1544, has a carved and gilded iconostasis, frescoes by Frángos Katelános and two charming cupolas, one in the main body of the church and one in the narthex. The *katholikón* has retained the original church built by Varlaám as a side chapel, although its frescoes date from the 1600s.

The **Great Metéora** (Μεγαλο Μετεωρων), on *Platys Lithos* (flat rock), is the big one, and well worth the trek up its 146 steps. Founded by Ag. Athanásos, who flew here on the back of an eagle (or so they say), it's also called the **Monastery of the Transfiguration** (*Moní Metamórphosis tou Sotíros*). Its privileges were guaranteed in 1362 by the Serbian emperor Symeon Uros whose son, taking the name of Joásaph, became monk here. That did the monastery's finances no harm. Joásaph built the first *katholikón* at his own expense in 1387–8, and subsequent alterations never needed to be done on the cheap. The result is today's cross-in-square church under a 12-sided dome 79ft high, and a series of frescoes by Theophánis depicting all the gruesome details of the Roman persecution of the Christians. Joásaph's original *katholikón* is now the *ierón* behind the iconostasis. This charming incorporation of older structures within newer ones, like so many Russian dolls, is common in Byzantine monasteries. On the north side of the *katholikón*, the vaulted refectory (*c.* 1557) is a museum now – a sea shell incense burner is one of its less serious efforts. The domed kitchen is interesting, as is the library, noted for its fine manuscripts and rare books – if they allow you in. Before leaving, consider the 30-minute path to the 14th-century church of the long-gone **Monastery of Ipapandí**, built inside a small cavern.

Farther east, 15th-century **Ag. Triádos** on an isolated pillar with ravines on either side will look familiar to James Bond fans, who will recognize the spectacular backdrop for some of the skulduggery in *For Your Eyes Only*. The 140 or so step approach is mostly through a dramatic tunnel, offering some relief for vertigo sufferers. It still boasts a few 'real' monks as well as a small folk museum, with kitchen and farm implements.

The convent of **Ag. Stefánou** is easternmost. A deep gorge separates its pinnacle from the road; the two rocks are connected by a bridge. It was bombed during the war, so has a newer look in places, and a fabulous view out over Kalambáka and the plain beyond that is alone worth the journey. Its church of Ag. Stefános (*c.* 1350) has a timbered roof, some gold leaf wood carvings and wall paintings (*c.* 1545) by a local priest, Ioánnis of Stagoi (Kalambáka's earlier name). The *katholikón* dedicated to Ag. Charálambos (*c.* 1798) contains the said saint's skull, a gift of Vladislav of Wallachia.

Northern Greece:
Macedonia and Thrace

Northern Greece

God-haunted Mount Olympus guards the entrance to northern Greece, where everything is at once more Balkan: the winters are colder, the climate more humid, the light softer. Deeply forested mountains, lakes, fertile valleys and plains watered by year-round rivers make up a land where tobacco and cotton thrive, as do cattle; in fact, a beefy diet helped to make Alexander's army the tough *hombres* they were. A complex history has slowed modern development, leaving much of the north's natural beauty intact. Rare pelicans nest in isolated wetlands, some of Europe's last bears and wolves roam the remote corners, and storks tonsure domes with their nests; the possibilities for hiking, rafting and skiing are many and varied. But it's a long sandy coastline that attracts the lion's share of tourists, especially on the rugged promontory of Chalkidikí, studded with resorts but also home to the unique monastic republic of Áthos.

Politically, northern Greece is divided into three administrative regions – Macedonia; West (or Upper) Macedonia; and East Macedonia and Thrace. The regional capital Thessaloníki, at the top of the Thermaic Gulf, is a vibrant city that many prefer to Athens, and it lies within easy striking distance of the ancient stomping grounds of Philip and Alexander at Pélla, Díon, Naoússa and Vergína, where the spectacular royal tombs are one of Greece's top attractions. All across the north,

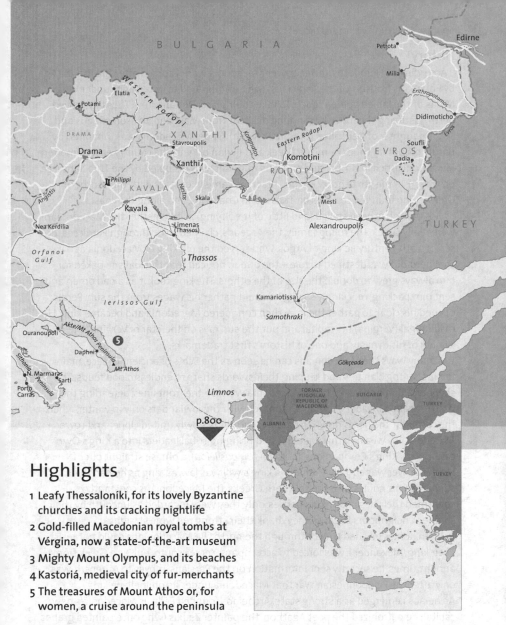

Highlights

1 Leafy Thessaloníki, for its lovely Byzantine churches and its cracking nightlife
2 Gold-filled Macedonian royal tombs at Vérgina, now a state-of-the-art museum
3 Mighty Mount Olympus, and its beaches
4 Kastoriá, medieval city of fur-merchants
5 The treasures of Mount Athos or, for women, a cruise around the peninsula

dense little cities turn into buzzing mini-Manhattans when the sun goes down; the most interesting by day as well are Édessa with its lovely waterfall, fur-making Kastoriá where grand mansions are piled high over a mountain lake, Véria with its Byzantine monuments, Kavála, near the extensive ruins of ancient Philippi, and Komotiní, where Greeks and Turks (or properly, Muslim Greeks of Turkish origin) live side by side. As an added bonus, two unique islands beckon on the horizon: sand-rimmed Thássos, with pretty villages and an ancient city, and Samothráki, where the Mountain of the Moon watched over the night Mysteries of the Great Gods.

History

According to Herodotus, fertile Lower Macedonia was occupied after the Bronze Age by Phrygians (cousins of the Thracians), who immigrated to Asia Minor under King Midas of the fabled golden touch. To take their place, Dorians from Thessaly moved north, justifying the move by claiming descent from Makedon, the son of Zeus and Thyia, daughter of Deukalion (the Greek Noah). Upper Macedonia was inhabited by unruly mountain tribes of mixed Greek and Ilyrian origins; the country east of modern Thessaloníki, rich in timber and precious minerals, was occupied by the Thracians (*see* pp.582–3). In the 7th century BC the Thracians came in contact with the southern Greeks, who founded colonies on Thássos, in Chalkidikí, and along the coast.

A lot of ink has been spilled (and little of it edifying) as to whether the Macedonians were really Greek. The ruling family, the Argeads, claimed to be through Perdiccas, the son of a 7th-century BC king of Argos, who served the old king of Macedonia as a shepherd but was destined to rule – the queen noticed that the loaf she baked for him always grew to double the size of the others. The king took it as a bad omen and sent him packing, mockingly saying he could gather his wages from the sun. Perdiccas opened his cloak to gather the rays; then conquered Macedonia and became king. He made Aigai (Vergína) his capital and put the sun rays on the 'star of Vergína', the symbol of his dynasty and one of history's first trademarks.

In many ways the Macedonians can be seen as the Scots of ancient Greece, maintaining strong clan ties and keeping their swords sharp in endless blood feuds. The shepherd highlanders of Upper Macedonia were on the front lines, defending the passes against invaders, coming in contact with the lowlanders only in winter, when they brought the herds down to pasture. The kings slowly united Upper and Lower Macedonia by weaving marriage ties and bringing tribal leaders into a King's Own cavalry, the 'King's Companions' (*hetaíroi tou basileíou*), a phrase straight out of Homer. Power was equally Homeric: a king's will was law, as long as he had the support of his nobles. Like the southern Greeks, the Macedonians constantly confirmed their ties in drinking parties, only they were regarded as uncouth by their southern neighbours because they drank their strong red wine straight.

When Xerxes invaded Greece through the north the Macedonians could not resist. Their king, Alexander I, was forced to accompany Xerxes south, but 'as a Greek from ancient times' he secretly sent information on the Persians' moves to Athens. It was only after the Peloponnesian War that Macedonia under its philhellene king Archelaos I emerged as a strong state. Archelaos founded Pélla as Macedonia's new capital; he patronized the poet Agathon, the painter Zeuxis (who once painted grapes so lifelike that birds tried to eat them) and Euripides, and founded the Olympian Games at Dion before he was assassinated in 399 BC – something of an occupational hazard for Macedonian kings.

Forty years of confusion followed, before the extraordinary Philip II took power in 359 and made Macedonia a major player on the Greek stage. Philip consolidated his hold on the north by capturing the Greek colonies on the coast and the fabulous gold mines of Mount Pangéo, before turning his attention south, using the Amphictyonic League as sheep's clothing to gain entry. The orator Demosthenes encouraged Athens to stop him: the city united with its hated rival Thebes, and both were defeated at Chaironeia in 338, leaving Philip *hegemon* or leader of Greece. When he was assassinated two years later, his plan to invade Persia as revenge for Xerxes (already 140 years past) was inherited by his 20-year-old son Alexander; acting with his trademark swiftness, Alexander clobbered the border tribes who rose against him, then burned rebellious Thebes to the ground *pour encourager les autres*. Once Greece was secure, he left a Companion, Antipater, as regent, and never returned (*see* p.36).

Alexander's sudden death in Babylon resulted in turmoil back home; Cassander, the son of Antipater, made himself king and put Alexander's wife Roxane and son to death, and restored Macedonian hegemony over Greece. After a quick succession of rulers, the son of Demetrios Poliorketes, the stoic 'Philosopher King' Antigonos II Gonatas, brought a measure of peace (277 BC). Later kings tried to regain control over Greece in three Macedonian wars, before a last moment of glory and prosperity under Philip V (188–179 BC), just in time for the Romans to mop it all up by defeating his son Perseus at Pydna (168 BC). Macedonia became the first Roman province of the east (even then there were difficulties over the exact borders) with Thessaloníki as capital. To expedite the legions eastwards, the Romans built the Via Egnatia (148–120 BC) from Dyrrachium (Durrazo, in modern Albania) to Byzantium. The cities along the road thrived; Philippi, Thessaloníki and Véria were among the first places in Europe to hear about the new religion of Christianity, from St Paul himself.

Byzantine and Ottoman Macedonia

Although the Gauls marauded through Macedonia in 252, Roman collapse was postponed by Diocletian's reforms of 293 that divided it into more manageable portions: Galerius Maximian, emperor of the east, made Thessaloníki his capital (289–311) before Constantine moved it to Byzantium. The next centuries saw incursions by Goths, Bulgars, Slavs, Huns, Serbs and Normans, but few breached the walls of Thessaloníki; the 11th and 12th centuries were a golden age of Byzantine art and scholarship here and in smaller cities such as Kastoriá, Véria and Kavála, and in the recently founded monastic republic of Mount Athos.

After the Fourth Crusade (1204) Macedonia was made into Baldwin of Monferrat's Kingdom of Thessaloníki, ushering in a period when it was the prey of all comers from Bulgarian Tsars (Ivan Asen II) to the Despots of Épirus, and Catalan mercenaries who wrecked Chalkidikí and Mount Athos (1308). Stefan Dushan, the greatest of Serbia's medieval kings, briefly incorporated all of Macedonia except Thessaloníki into his empire (1346–55). Turkish Sultan Murat I took over the Balkans in 1364, but Tamerlane restored the Christian princes after defeating the Turks at Ankara in 1402. It was only a temporary setback: by 1444, all of the Balkans were part of the Ottoman empire.

The Turks called their European conquests Roumelia (the 'land of the Romans', who in this case were the Byzantine Greeks), and they administered it by cavalry officers and locals who converted to Islam. Located at the great Balkan crossroads, Macedonia became so ethnically mixed that it gave the French their word for mixed fruit salad – *macedoine*: Greeks, Turks, Jews, Vlachs, Slavs, Serbs, Albanians, gypsies, Pomaks and Bulgarians all lived in relative harmony in a ramshackle Ottoman empire that gave

The M Word

Under the Byzantines and Ottomans, the modern Greek region of Macedonia became, because of the cosmopolitan nature of its sea ports, a microcosm of the Balkans, inhabited by Greeks, Slavs, Turks, Vlachs, Jews, Serbs and more, most of whom, thanks to the Ottoman *millet* system, maintained their ethnic identity through language and religion. Since the break-up of the Ottoman empire, forging the Balkans into smaller nation states has been a gruelling process, causing no end of bloodshed and misery, all based on selective views of history. For example, during the Second World War Stalin and Tito, in order to justify claims over northern Greece and its Aegean ports, insisted that there had been an ethnic Macedonian people since ancient times, complete with their own language and culture. Under this scenario, even Philip and Alexander were not Greek at all. Greece for its part has obscured well documented Slavic immigrations into its modern territory since the 7th century AD, preferring to think that Macedonian history stopped with Alexander, who of course, *was* Greek (and who, ironically, was an early promoter of multi-ethnic harmony).

During the Greek Civil War in the late 1940s, some 40–50 per cent of the left-wing EAM-ELAS members were ethnic Slavs, and part of their party platform was the creation of a much larger independent 'Macedonia' that would include 'Aegean (read Greek) Macedonia' along with southern Yugoslavia. This lost EAM much of its support in Greece – and explains why ethnic Slav members of the Resistance were

each *millet*, or people, autonomy in religious and judiciary matters, as long as they paid their taxes. Peace encouraged people to return to the countryside to farm, and an influx of Jews from Spain brought skills in silk-weaving, textiles, leathers and furs and metal-working to the towns, which flourished particularly in the 18th century, thanks to trade networks in Central and Western Europe.

The Greek War of Independence in 1821 unleashed a new highly combustible ingredient into the mix: nationalism. People who had been simply 'Christians' to the Turks were now encouraged by irredentists to be Greek, or Bulgarian, or Serb, and to aspire to national sovereignty. The interests of the Great Powers and Russia's wars with the Ottoman empire confused issues further; most alarming for the Greeks was Russia's support in the treaty of Santo Stefano in 1878 for a 'Great Bulgaria' that encompassed much of the territory they claimed. In the early 1900s, irregular bands of Greeks, Bulgarians and Serbs fought the Ottomans (what the Greeks call the 'Macedonian Struggle'), before uniting to win the First Balkan War (1912). Bulgaria, not satisfied with the division of spoils, began the Second Balkan War, lost, and got even less territory in the Treaty of Bucharest (1913) that ceded the modern regions of Macedonia and Thrace to Greece, and with them their Slav and Turkish populations.

Bulgaria invaded again in the First World War, but the Greeks, with their British and French allies, managed to hold the frontier and the Strymónas river . After the 1922 population exchange, the tens of thousands of Greek refugees in the region were just settling in when Mussolini attacked western Macedonia in November 1940. German ally Bulgaria, still pumped full of dreams of an Aegean port, set up a puppet regime in

not included in Andréas Papandréou's amnesty of former Communists who were offered the chance to return to Greece. When Yugoslavia imploded in 1991 and the tiny breakaway province in the south became a state calling itself the 'Republic of Macedonia', it brought forth a blast of Greek hysteria that few outsiders could understand. Papandréou blanketed the country with the badly worded slogan 'Macedonia is Only Greek', confusing many foreigners who thought that Greece was claiming part of the former Yugoslavia. Nor did politicians up in Skopje help matters with loose talk about open borders of a 'spiritual Macedonia' that stretched all the way to Chalkidikí. The only winners in this debate were makers of nationalist key-chains, bumper stickers and lapel buttons, both sides using the Star of Vergína liberally on their trinkets to prove their point.

At the height of the dispute Athens blocked the landlocked country's access to the sea, forcing a compromise that soothed Greek concerns: the new country would be called the Former Yugoslav Republic of Macedonia, or FYROM, a name which itself causes a lot of confusion. There is a movement afoot for an agreement with Athens to adopt the Macedonian-language 'Republika Makedonija', which just might make everyone happy, if such a thing is possible in the Balkans. But as trade and investment do their bit to normalize relations, and as Greece, the regional economic powerhouse, becomes increasingly multicultural (yet again) due to current immigration, the devisive M word dispute seems to be on the verge of slowly receding into the complex mosaic that is Greek history.

northern Greece and behaved so badly that the Gestapo, not known for its finer feelings, dismantled it. The subsequent Civil War (1946–49) was extremely painful here, especially along the frontier where children were kidnapped and taken behind the Iron Curtain; many never returned, or couldn't, during the 'Years of Stone' (1950–74).

The *pax sovietica* and closed borders to the north brought Macedonia and Thrace a truce of sorts and a military garrison in every town. Then, just as detente took hold and post-junta Greece began to prosper as a member of the European Union, the collapse of Communist regimes to the north in the early 1990s inexorably dragged the region back into the quagmires of Balkan nationalism. Although issues remain (*see* box), there are signs that the region is regaining its historic position as the crossroads of southeastern Europe as Greece invests billions of euros in the Balkans, opens its ports to the hinterlands and improves transport (the Via Egnatía motorway project, linking east and west, is well under way). Human contacts through business and tourism also slowly help to dispel the legacy of mistrust.

Mount Olympus to Thessaloníki

Approaching from the south, through Tempe (*see* p.507) the first province of Macedonia is Pieria, famed in antiquity as the birthplace of the Muses. Mount Olympus is its landmark, and the coast, the 'Olympus Riviera', consists of one vast sandy beach after another, rimmed with hotels and campsites popular with Central

Getting There and Around

By bus: the Athens–Thessaloníki **bus** stops at the Litóchoro crossroads, where a connecting bus will eventually take you to the town; alternatively take the bus to Kateríni from Athens' Liossin station, **t** 210 831 7059 or Thessaloníki, **t** 231 051 9101; from Kateríni (**t** 235 102 9317) there are frequent buses to the coastal resorts, Díon and Litóchoro.

By train: Kateríni also has the most convenient **train station** to Olympus, **t** 235 102 3709, on the Athens–Thessaloníki line.

Tourist Information

Litóchoro: by the bus stop, **t** 235 208 3100; *open June–Sept, 9–12.*
Greek Alpine Club near the tourist information, **t** 235 208 2444. Can advise and organize stays in a refuge; *open summer 9.30–11.30 and 6.30–8.30.*
Trekking Hellas, *www.trekkinghellas.gr.* Offers excursions with English-speaking guides, including a women-only ascent of Olympus.
National Park information booth, 4km up the road from Litóchoro.
Kateríni tourist police: **t** 235 102 3440.

Festivals

The summer **Olympus Festival** shindig features ancient drama and concerts by top Greek performers in the theatre of Díon, the Byzantine church of Panagías Kontariótissas and Platamón Castle. For information contact festival headquarters: 69 Eirínis, Kateríni, **t** 235 107 6041, **f** 235 107 6042.

Where to Stay and Eat

Litóchoro ✉ 60200

It's absolutely essential to book ahead for July and August.
Villa Pantheon, **t** 235 208 3931, **f** 235 208 3932 (*C; expensive–moderate*). On the edge of town, on the road leading to the gorge, a new hotel with big rooms and wonderful views from the rooms, eight of which have their own fireplaces. *Open all year.*
Villa Drossos, in Ag. Geórgios outside the centre, **t** 235 208 4561, **f** 235 208 4563, *grigoris@kat.forthnet.* gr (*C; expensive*). New hotel with pool and garden, and tidy if smallish rooms. Choice of continental or American breakfasts. *Open all year.*
Archontikó Aphroditi, Plateía Eleftherías, **t** 235 208 1415, **f** 235 208 3646 (*D; low moderate*). Friendly atmosphere and air-conditioned rooms (including some triples), and useful mosquito nets over the beds. *Open all year.*
Stavrós Refuge, on the National Park road, **t** 235 208 4519 (*inexpensive*). Café, restaurant and dorm rooms. *Open daily in summer and winter weekends.*
Park, 23 Ag. Nikolaou, **t** 235 208 1252 (*D; inexpensive*). Tired decor but a balcony, TV and fridge with each room. *Open April–Oct.*
Erato, on the square, **t** 235 208 3346. A municipally run restaurant with tables outside in the summer, by the fireplace in winter. Feast on hearty baked or stewed dishes such as stuffed cabbage, rabbit or pork; in the evening they do pizza, too.
Myli, **t** 235 208 3111. Lovely spot by an old water mill at the entrance to the Enipéas Gorge, with good regional dishes. *Open daily in summer, weekends only in winter.*

Platamónas ✉ 60065

Zeus, **t** 235 204 2888, **f** 235 204 2888 (*C; moderate*). New, quiet, a bit kitschy, 60m from the beach, but *not* block-booked like the rest. *Open April–Oct.*

Díon ✉ 60100

Dion Resort Hotel, by the beach, **t** 235 202 2731, **f** 235 202 2335 (*A; luxury*). New, smart, with lots of sports and activities, and a beautiful pool and garden.
Dion, **t** 235 105 3222, **f** 235 105 3222 (*C; moderate*). Pleasant little hotel, 100m from the archaeological site. *Open all year.*

and Eastern Europeans; signs and newspapers come in a bewildering array of languages and alphabets. The only minus is one this Riviera shares with the Italian one: the proximity of the railway to the shore and the night trains that use it.

Two of the nicest beaches are the southernmost, **Néa Póroi** and **Platamónas**, both with theatrical views of the **Castle of Platamónas** on its headland and Olympus soaring behind. The castle (*car park off the National road; open daily 8.30–7; free*) was built by the Lombards under Orlando Piche in 1204 to guard the entrance into the Thermaic Gulf, but was taken after a terrible siege in 1218 by Theodore Angelus, Despot of Épirus. Within the walls are bits of ancient Heraclea, a Macedonia frontier town, and the 'black plane tree' where the Turks hanged rebels during fierce fighting in 1912. Traditional villages, just inland – **Ag. Panteleímonas**, **Paléo Póroi** and **Skotína** – offer a slice of old, pre-tourist Greece. The next resort, **Leptokariá**, is the biggest on the coast. A road begins here around the south flank of Olympus into Thessaly; 5km up this is the ancient site of **Livithra** or Leibethra (path near the roadside café) inhabited from Mycenaean times to the 1st century BC. It was here that the Maenads buried the limbs of Orpheus, after tearing him to bits (*see* pp.582–3); the women of Leptokariá re-enact some of this at carnival time, so look out.

Mount Olympus

Olympus (Greeks pronounce it *Ólymvos*) originally meant 'mountain', and scattered around the Mediterranean some 20 others bear the same name. But this one, the highest peak on the Balkan peninsula (9,570ft), set on the fringes of the Classical Greek world, its summits wreathed in cloud, its precipices echoing with thunder, was always *the* Olympus, the abode of Zeus and his argumentative clan. In Homer, the palaces of the gods lay in the mountain's 'mysterious folds'. At the tallest peak, the Pantheon (now Mýtikas, 'the needle'), where the sun always shone and the air was too thin for humans to breathe, they would gather to hear Zeus arbitrate from his Throne, the sheer armchair today known as Stefáni (9,543ft).

Olympus was one of the last famous European mountains to be climbed (in 1913) – not because of Zeus' thunderbolts, but because of the *armatolí* (nationalist partisans) and kidnapping bandits who haunted it until Macedonia became part of Greece in 1912. In 1938, High Olympus and its deeply wooded eastern slopes and ravines were designated Greece's first National Park. Some 1,700 Mediterranean and Central European plants have been found (25 per cent of all the flora in Greece), and of the rare little plants above the tree line, 23 species are unique to Olympus. The lions who attacked the camels in Xerxes' army are gone, but Zeus' eagles still float overhead.

Litóchoro, the classic gateway to Olympus, is in a superb setting just 5km up from the coast. The ascent of Mýtikas is not difficult, although the very last leg is a precipitous scramble and can be dangerous. The climbing season begins in late May–June, after the snows have melted, but even then winds and storms are not uncommon; check the weather report in Litóchoro before setting out. The path (part of the European Long Distance Trail E4) follows the sheer-sided **Enipéas Gorge** – the first part is so easy that it's a favourite of local promenaders – and passes near the hermitage and **monastery of Ag. Dionysios**, founded in *c.* 1500 by St Dionysios of Mount Athos. Damaged for resisting the Turks in 1848, bombed in 1943 for resisting the Germans, it is currently being restored. From Litóchoro it takes about five hours to reach **Prióna** and its restaurant (you can also drive up from Litóchoro). From Prióna it is another two and half hours to the **Spílios Agapitós refuge** (6889ft; *t 235 280 1800; open mid May–Oct*), and another three hours to the top of Mýtikas. The second route, the more beautiful, begins 15km up the same Priónia road, starting at the Gortisa car park, from where a five-hour walk leads to the **Plateau of the Muses**, site of two refuges (*book with the Alpine Club*); from here it's an hour to the top.

Ancient Díon

t 235 105 3206; open daily 8am–7pm, winter till 6pm, adm. An excellent guide by Dimitrios Pandermalis, Díon's archaeologist, is available at the site.

Another name for Zeus was Dias, and this ancient city north of Litóchoro supposedly stood where Deukalion erected the first altar to the father of the gods after the flood. As the Macedonian kings claimed Zeus as an ancestor, Díon became important in the late 5th century BC under King Archelaos, who founded the Olympian Games in honour of Zeus and the Nine Muses. It was during these games that his descendant Philip II was given a superb but skittery stallion, which no one could mount until the eight-year old Alexander piped up and asked to try, then rode into the sun because he had noticed the horse was startled by his own shadow. 'Oh my son, look thee out for a kingdom equal to and worthy of thyself, for Macedonia is too little to hold thee,' his proud father exclaimed. Alexander named the stallion Bucephalas, and later rode him to India. Díon was also the place where the Macedonians sacrificed before leaving for battle, as Alexander did in splendid style before going to Persia, presiding in a tent that held a hundred dining couches. After suffering destruction by the Aetolians in the 3rd century BC, Díon carried on under the Romans, who made off with its most famous monument – 25 bronze statues by Lysippus of Alexander's Companions who fell at the battle of Granicus.

Díon lies by a stream, among lawns and duck ponds; pretty blue dragonflies dart over the ruins. Off to the right of the entrance stands the **Hellenistic theatre**, with modern seating for the Olympus festival. It has a rare surviving feature: a 'ladder of Charon', a corridor with two little rooms under the orchestra that allowed actors to emerge from the 'Underworld'. Under Philip II, the surrounding meadows were used to drill the Macedonian phalanx, which with its full body shields and long spears was said to resemble a charging porcupine. This acted as an 'anvil' to hold the centre, while the heavy cavalry (mostly recruited from horsey Thessaly) would swing around and 'hammer' the enemy. Philip learned the tactics as a hostage of Epaminóndas in Thebes, and Alexander would use them over and over, with a hundred variations.

Towards the woods you'll find a **Sanctuary of Asklepios** and a **Sanctuary of Demeter** (from the 6th century BC, predating the rest of Díon). A bridge crosses the Vaphyras river, which was navigable in antiquity, to the often-flooded Hellenistic **Sanctuary of Isis**, a pretty complex, decorated with copies of its statues. The rulers who followed Alexander adopted his syncretizing ways, and replaced Artemis with the gentler Egyptian Isis as their goddess of childbirth. The sanctuary had side temples dedicated to Isis the goddess of fortune and to Aphrodite Hypolimpidia ('under Olympus').

Backtrack to the entrance into the city itself, still enclosed in well-preserved **walls**; except for a protruding bit by the river – possibly a jetty – it was nearly perfect square grid. The main street is wide and was nicely paved by the Romans. Immediately on your right are Roman **workshops** and a big stone façade, decorated with shields and cuirasses from the 4th century BC, which may once have been the base of a victory monument disassembled and moved here. Further on and down to the right are villas with excellent Roman mosaics, especially the vast **Villa of Dionysos** (*c.* AD 200), which had a row of shops facing the street, baths, a shrine to Dionysos, four peristyle courts with pools and a banquet hall with a superb mosaic of the epiphany of Dionysos in a chariot borne by amphibious panthers. On the other side of the main road from here are private houses and a large **Early Christian basilica**.

Back towards the entrance (up the steps from the workshops) note the well-preserved public **lavatory**, where citizens socialized while relieving themselves. Behind this is a luxurious **bath complex**, the most important of the 10 found in the city, its mosaic floors and hypocaust system impressively intact. Statues of Asklepios and his children (now in the museum) found at the north end suggest that at least part of the complex was used for therapeutic purposes. A path leads to the **Roman Odeion**, used for concerts or lectures.

The new, well-arranged **Archaeological Museum** (*t 235 105 3206; open Tues–Sun 8am–7pm, Mon 12.30–7; adm*) in the centre of modern Díon has mostly Hellenistic and Roman finds: statues of the philosophers from the Villa of Dionysos, others from the sanctuaries and baths, and funerary steles, including an expressive one of a mother and child by a 5th-century BC northern sculptor. Upstairs, don't miss the 1st-century BC **hydraulis**, the oldest example yet found of the world's first keyboard instrument. Invented in the 3rd-century BC by Ktesibius of Alexandria, an engineer who specialized in air- and water-powered mechanisms, it was a hit in ancient Rome (Nero claimed to perfect it). It was later forgotten in the West until 757, when the Byzantine emperor sent one as a gift to Rome, where it developed into the modern church organ. Díon's hydraulis was reproduced by the European Cultural Centre at Delphi – it sounds like a melancholy train whistle heard underwater, the rhythms emphasized by the clack of the keys and creaking water pump. Another musical find in Díon was a woman's funeral stele that yielded our first image of a *nabla*, a six string instrument with a soundbox on the bottom and two tuning strings on the sides, often played at ancient banquets, and known in the Temple of Solomon.

Kateríni, Pydna and Methóni

Kateríni, Pieria's capital, has a fine view of Mount Olympus and seriously crazy traffic that makes you just want to get out as soon as possible. The road to Thessaloníki from here follows the coast and isn't too exciting, although remains of Byzantine **Kítros** were recently uncovered near the modern town, where you can also have a look at the most important salt pans in Greece. In ancient times this was **Pydna**, where Alexander's meddlesome mother Olympias was stabbed to death by Cassander's assassin employed in the fight between the Successors, and where in 168 BC the final battle of the Macedonian Wars pitted 38,000 Romans under Lucius

Amelius Paulus against 43,000 Macedonians under King Perseus. The Romans laboriously brought their secret weapon – 22 elephants – over Olympus, but in spite of the common belief that Pydna once and for all proved the superiority of the legion over the phalanx, most military historians in fact blame Perseus' failure to follow Alexander's tried and true methods of bringing in the cavalry 'hammer' for Macedonia's wretched defeat (20,000 killed and 11,000 imprisoned, compared to 1,100 Roman dead). Perseus fled to Samothráki, but he was captured and forced to take part in Amelius' triumph in Rome before he died.

Methóni, the last Blue Flag beach before Thessaloníki, was an Athenian colony, the last one to survive in northern Greece until Philip II besieged it in 354 BC; he lost an eye in the battle, and when Methóni surrendered he sent the Athenians home and gave their land to his men.

Thessaloníki (ΩΕΣΣΑΛΟΝΙΚΗ)

Thessaloníki, or Salonica, the 'Bride of the Thermaic Gulf', was the second city of the Byzantine empire, and now with a population of 1.5 million it's the second city of Greece. But you'll rarely hear Greeks indulge in the banter and rivalry that often characterizes relations of first and second cities, like Barcelona and Madrid, or Rome and Milan; in fact, many Athenians will admit that Thessaloníki is a much nicer place to live, with its seafront and trees, less hectic pace, its universities and cultural life, its great restaurants and sizzling nightlife.

They are very different cities. Thessaloníki boomed in the Middle Ages while Athens snoozed, and its most compelling monuments are Byzantine: 22 churches still stand, several of which – the Rotunda, Ósios David, Ag. Dimítrios, the Acheiropoietos, Dodéka Apostóli and Ag. Sofía – are World Heritage Sites for the sake of their dazzling mosaics. The upper city is cocooned in towering Theodosian walls, while the lower city stands on tiers like a choir singing to the sea. Once the heart of Jewish Thessaloníki, the lower city was rebuilt after a huge fire in 1917: here you'll find the remains of the ancient city, Turkish baths and mosques, most of the hotels, and the shopping mecca of the Balkans. Thessaloníki has always been a cosmopolitan city, and the dozen languages you'll hear in the streets somehow seem perfectly natural.

History

Thessaloníki is one of the few Greek cities to know its birthday – 315 BC, when King Cassander founded a new city named Thessaloníki after his wife, a half sister of Alexander. To populate his foundation, Cassander used carrots and sticks to merge the inhabitants of 26 older towns in the area, the largest of which, Therme, gave its name to the *Thermaïkós Kólpos*, the Thermaic Gulf.

Even so, the city only really blossomed when the Romans conquered Macedonia in 146 BC, blazed the Via Egnatia and roads north into the Balkans, and made Thessaloníki into a leading commercial and military port. St Paul came twice, and later addressed two epistles to the church he founded. In the late 3rd century AD, as

To Eptapyrgio

PARASCHOU

Moni
Vlatadon

ANO POLIS

Osios David

Taxiarchon

Ag. Nikolaos
Orphanos

EVANGELISTRIA

Aristotle University

Atatürk's House

Byzantine
Baths

Alaca Imaret
Mosque

Telloglio
Foudation

Profitis
Ilias

Yeni Hamam

Ag. Ekaterini

Ag. Dimitrios

Rotunda

Arch of Galerius

Ag. Pandeleimonos

Helexpo
International Fair

Sotir

Ministry of
Northern Greece

Roman
Agora

Acheiropoeitos

Archaeology Museum &
Museum of Byzantine
Civilization

Ag. Sofia

Hippodrome

Palace of
Galerius

Dodeka
Apostoli

Bey
Hamami

Panagia
Chalkeon

Ag. Ioannes
Prodomos

Town Hall

Hamza Beg Cami

Ag. Gregorios Palamas

White
Tower

Bezesten
(Indoor market)

Modiano
Market

Museum of the
Jewish Presence

Ag. Minas

Museum of the
Macedonian Struggle

N

To Railway
Station

LADADIKA

Thermaic Gulf

Vardari
Fortress

Museum of Ancient &
Byzantine Musical Instruments

28 OCTOVRIOU

500 m
500 yds

Customs House

the vortex of the Roman empire moved away from Rome, Caesar and later Emperor
Galerius made Thessaloníki his capital. Although the city was severely disappointed
when Constantine passed it by in favour of puny Byzantium for his 'new Rome',
Constantinople, the emperor did finance a new artificial port as compensation.
Theodosius the Great (379–395) often made Thessaloníki his base; in 380, when he
thought he was dying, he converted to Christianity and issued the Edict of
Thessaloníki, banning pagan practices such as the Olympics, although the more
subtle lessons of the faith were lost on him (*see* p.536).

By Justinian's time, Thessaloníki was the second city of the Byzantine empire, much
visited for its fair and the relics of its patron saint Dimítrios. It remained a Greek
outpost even when the Avars and Slavs occupied the rest of Macedonia, and in the

Getting There

By air: Macedonia airport, **t** 231 098 5177, 15km south of town, is served by direct scheduled and chartered flights to London, daily to Athens, several times a week to Límnos, Lésbos, Chíos, Rhodes, Ioánnina, Corfu, Chaniá and Heráklion. Bus 78 runs roughly every 40 minutes from the train station to the airport, by way of Mitropóleos and Tsimiskí. **Airlines**: Olympic, 3 Kountourióti, **t** 231 023 0240. Aegean/Cronos, 2 Venizélou, **t** 231 023 9225. Britannia is handled by Doucas Tours, 8 Venizélou, **t** 231 026 9984, who are generally good for finding cheaper flights.

By sea: ferries at least twice weekly to Límnos, Mytilíni, Chíos, Sýros, Íos, Tínos, Mýkonos, Páros, Santoríni, Heráklion, Skiáthos and Skýros, plus hydrofoils to Alónnisos, Skiáthos, Skópelos, Moundaniá (Chalkidiki), Ag. Ioánnis (Pélion) and Ag. Konstantínos. For all, contact **Karacharísis**, 8 N. Kountourióti, **t** 231 051 3005 or **t** 231 052 4544, **f** 231 053 2289. The quays are a 15min walk from the buses or train station. **Port authority**: **t** 231 053 1502.

By train: all, including the 6hr Intercity to Athens, use the 'new' station on the west end of the city on Monastiríou, **t** 231 051 7517, but you can buy tickets at the OSE office at 18 Aristotélous (*open Mon and Sat 8–3 and Tues–Fri 8.30am–9pm*).

By bus: the disdained new bus station in the western suburb of Sfagiá stands empty as buses still depart from a score of KTEL offices, mostly clustered near the train station, except for the Chalkidikí and Mount Athos station, at 68 Karakási on the east end of town (bus 10 from Egnatía), **t** 231 092 4444. For Athens: 12 a day until midnight from 67 Monastiríou, **t** 231 051 0834. Ioánnina: 19 Ch. Pípsou, **t** 231 051 2444. Vólos: 79 Monastiríou, **t** 231 091 2122. Lárissa: 4 Enotikón (by Anagenísseos), **t** 231 054 4133. Corinth: 69 Monastiríou, **t** 231 052 7265. Pátras: 75 Monastiríou, **t** 231 052 5253. Kavála: 59 Langadás, **t** 231 052 5530. Náoussa, Véria, Édessa: 75 Monastiríou, **t** 231 052 2160; Kastoriá: 6 Anagenísseos, **t** 231 051 0042.

Coach services to Albania, Bulgaria and Turkey, **t** 231 053 8367, leave from the train station. For other buses and their departure points, try EOT or the tourist police (*see* below).

Getting Around

By city bus: orange buses circulate in the city; blue or red ones go to the suburbs or neighbouring villages; tickets on sale in the *periptera*. While most sights are within walking distance in the centre, city buses that may come in handy are nos.10 or 11 from the train station across town on Egnatía St; no.22 from Plateía Eleftherías to the upper city; no.5 from Plateía Eleftherías to along the sea front to Néa Kríni, passing near the Archaeological Museum and the museums on Vas. Ólgas.

By taxi: as in Athens, it's common to share. If you can't find one, try **t** 231 021 4841 or 231 021 4900. To summon a radio taxi, **t** 231 055 0500 or **t** 231 055 1525.

By boat: in summer, boat buses from the White Tower cross the bay to the beaches at Aretsoú, Peraía and Ag. Triáda; ring EOT for schedules.

By car: the one-way system and local tendency to double- park everywhere can drive you buggy. The biggest central car parks are in Plateía Eleftherías, by the train station, and behind the Archaeological Museum. If you do find a spot in the street, you're supposed to buy parking discs (€1 per hour) in a *períptero* to fill in and display on the dashboard.

Car hire: Europcar, 5 Papandréou, **t** 231 082 6333, airport **t** 231 047 3508; **Avis**: 3 Níkis, **t** 231 022 7126; **Budget**: 15 Angeláki, **t** 231 022 9515, airport **t** 231 047 1491. **Hertz**: 4 Venizélou, **t** 231 022 4906, airport **t** 231 041 9852. **Sixt**: 35 Papandréou, **t** 231 042 7886.

Tourist Information

EOT: 8 Aristotélous, **t** 231 026 3112 or **t** 231 022 2935; *open Mon–Fri 7.30–3, Sat 8–2*. They also have an information desk in the airport.

Tourist police: 4 Dodekaníssou St, in the centre, **t** 231 055 4871; *open daily 7.30am–10pm* .

Post office: main branch at 26 Aristotélous; *open Mon–Fri 7.30am–8pm, Sat 7.30–2.15, Sun 9–1.30*.

Consulates

Bulgaria: 12 N. Mávou, **t** 231 082 9211. **Canada**: 17 Tsimiskí, **t** 231 025 6350. **Denmark**: 26 Komninón, **t** 231 028 4065. **Netherlands**: 26

Komninón, **t** 231 023 4065. **Romania:** Níkis 13, **t** 231 024 4793. **Turkey:** 151 Ag. Dimitríou, **t** 231 024 8452. **UK:** 8 Venizélou, **t** 231 027 8006. **USA:** 43 Tsimiskí, **t** 231 023 2905. **Yugoslavia:** 4 Komninón, **t** 231 024 4265. For visas to **FYROM** (Republic of Macedonia) or **Albania**, see their consulates in Athens.

Festivals

In July and August an **outdoor theatre festival** takes place up at Shéikh-sou Forest and at the city theatre in the park. A **Festival of Greek Song** is in September; the **International Fair**, two weeks in mid-September. This also kicks off the **Dimítria**, a cultural festival culminating in celebrations, from 26 October (Ag. Dimítrios day) to late November. There is an **International Film Festival** for 10 days in November. For details on any event, contact the Department of Culture, 25 Theofílou St, ✉ 54635, **t** 231 028 1068, **f** 231 028 6519.

Shopping

Lower Aristotélous Street neatly divides the city's commercial districts. To the east are the food markets, **Modiáno** and **Vláli**, surrounded by pedestrian streets with household goods and inexpensive clothes spilling over the pavements. To the west, designer shops and boutiques for fashion-obsessed Thessaloníkians are clustered on Mitrópolis and its side streets. A flea market, still known by its Turkish name, **Bit Bazar**, takes place on Saturday mornings along Venizélou, Olýmpou and Filíppou Streets. For **English books and papers:** try Molho, Tsimiskí 10, which publishes a useful map of Thessaloníki; another good place to buy English language papers is the News-stand, near the middle of Aristotléou St, on the west side. Byzantine art lovers should pick up an in-depth local guide; *Monuments of Thessaloniki* or *Wandering in Byzantine Thessaloniki* are both widely available.

Where to Stay

Autumn is high season, especially during the International Fair in September when it can be next to impossible to find a room if you haven't booked. At other times prices tend to be over the odds. While the city sparkles with new hotels, the cheap ones are mediocre compared to what the same money buys elsewhere, and ear plugs may be a good idea.

Luxury

Hyatt Regency, by the airport 13km south of town, **t** 231 040 1234, **f** 231 040 1100, *www.thessaloniki.hyatt.gr* (*L*). Opened in 1999 and rated one of the top hotels in the Balkans – beautiful rooms with all mod cons, voice mail, modem jacks and digital phones; excellent restaurants, tennis, sauna, fitness centre, indoor pool, outdoor pool the size of a small lake, congress centre and casino.

Mediterranean Palace, 3 Salamínos St, **t** 231 055 2554, **f** 231 055 2622, *www.mediterraneanpalace.gr* (*L*). The city's grandest hotel when it collapsed in the 1978 earthquake, but now rebuilt. Neoclassical design in a great location by the sea and Ladádika nightlife; restaurant and parking.

Capsís Bristol, Katoúni & 2 Elia Oplopiou, **t** 231 050 6500, **f** 231 051 5777, *www.capsisbristol.gr*. Stylish, luxurious and central, with only 16 rooms close to a 24hr car park and nightlife. Excellent French restaurant, **Dipnossofistis**.

City, 11 Komninón, **t** 231 026 9421, **f** 231 0274358, *www.cityhotel.gr*. Swish, central hotel, completely renovated in 2001, cosy earth tone furnishings, computer facilities and good restaurants nearby.

Egnatía, 6 Antigonidón, **t** 231 053 0675, **f** 231 053 1761, *egnatia@aegeon-com*. New hotel near the Egnatía with an Art Deco flair, where each of the 46 rooms is complete with satellite TV, in-house movies and hydromassage in the bath. Internet and disabled access. Bottom of this price range.

Expensive

ABC, 41 Angeláki, **t** 231 026 5421, **f** 231 027 6542, *www.hotelabc.gr*. Recently renovated, soundproof rooms in Syndrivaniou Square, near the Archaeological Museum.

Tourist, 21 Mitropóleos, **t** 231 027 6335, **f** 231 022 6865. An atmospheric old favourite with a recent face-lift. Breakfast included.

Le Palace, 12 Tsimiskí, **t** 231 025 7400, **f** 231 022 1270, *www.attract.gr*. Hotel of character from the 1930s, recently renovated; soundproofed windows. Price includes a big traditional Macedonian breakfast spread.

Pella, 65 Dragoúmi, **t/f** 231 052 4221. Archetypal Greek salesmen's hotel, in the heart of the city just off the Egnatía.

Oceanis, 49 N. Plastíra, in the suburb of Aretsoú, **t** 231 044 7789, **f** 231 044 7811. On the east end, overlooking the marina (take bus No. 5 from Venizélou St); popular taverna-*mezedepoleion* downstairs.

Moderate

Atlas, 40 Egnatía, **t** 231 053 7046, **f** 231 054 3507. Pleasant and friendly; rooms minus bathrooms are cheaper.

Ilios, 27 Egnatía, **t** 231 051 2620. En suite rooms with air-conditioning.

Averof, 24 Sofoú, **t** 231 053 8840, **f** 231 054 3194. Adequate and jovial; most rooms en suite.

Nea Metropolis, 22 Sygróu, **t** 231 052 5540, **f** 231 053 9910. Just off the Egnatía, a reliable choice; again, not all en suite.

Inexpensive

Oréstias Kastoriás, 14 Agnóstou Stratiótou, **t** 231 027 6517, **f** 231 027 6572. A pleasant and (relatively) quiet choice off Olympiádos St.

Emborikón, 14 Sygroú, **t** 231 052 5560. Old hotel with a certain charm, on the corner of Egnatía (even the sign is from the 1930s). Rooms have balconies, but the bathrooms are down the hall.

Kastoriá, 17 Sofoú, **t** 231 053 6280. Very basic rooms just off the Egnatía, a few eccentrically en suite. On the plus side, **Nea Ilysia** restaurant is right downstairs.

Outside the Centre

Panórama, 26 Analípseos, Panórama, **t** 231 034 1123, **f** 231 034 1266, *www.hermes.gr/ panorama* (*A; luxury*). On the hill, 11km east of Thessaloníki. Comfortable, stylish rooms with a great view and friendly service (bus 58 from Plateía Dikastiríon).

Péfka, Analípseos 92, Panórama, **t** 231 034 1153, **f** 231034 1035 (*C; expensive*). Quiet rooms in a garden, with a lovely view (bus 58).

Galaxías, 2 Lambráki, Ag. Tríada, **t** 239 202 2291, **f** 239 202 4364 (*C; expensive*). Recently renovated and probably the most popular out-of-town hotel, 23km southeast of the city (bus 72 from Plateía Dikastiríon).

Camping Akti Thermaïkou, Ag. Triáda, **t** 239 305 1360. EOT-run campsite, the closest to Thessaloníki (bus 72). *Open all year.*

Eating Out

Thessaloníki is famous for its restaurants. Good traditional tavernas are concentrated around Áthonos square in the Upper City, and between Dímitsa and Palanoú Sts, near the Modiáno meat market. Many places serve the city's classic *méze, mythia saganáki* (mussels in a spicy tomato sauce and melted feta).

Expensive

Porphýra, 2 Megálou Alexándrou, the 9th floor of the Macedonia Palace, **t** 231 086 1400 (around €70). The city's best, featuring innovative dining based on French traditions in an elegant setting, with views over the Thermaic Gulf. *Open eves only.*

Olympos Veria, 6 Chapsa St in Ladadiká, **t** 231 054 1778. Excellent Greek and international dishes prepared from top organic ingredients by the celebrated Mrs Magda, followed by one of the best cheeseboards in Greece, and accompanied by a seriously impressive wine list. Book. *Closed 15 June–Aug, and Sun.*

Living Room, 100 Th. Sofoúli St, **t** 231 041 1784. On the east end, just past the Yacht Club with a lovely garden and views over the city, a cool 'lounge restaurant' serving good Mediterranean dishes. *Open eves only.*

Shark, Argonaúton 2 and Sofoúli, **t** 231 041 6855. In spite of its name, a lovely, romantic place right on the sea, with first-class cuisine, with an Italian touch. *Open eves only 9.30pm–3.30am.*

Miami, 18 Thétidos, Néa Kríni, **t** 231 044 7996. With tables under a huge awning right next to the sea, fresh blue and white decor and wonderful fresh fish (bus 5 or a taxi).

Taste of China, 64 Analípseos, Panórama (11km east of town), **t** 231 034 3880. Considered the best Chinese restaurant in Greece, specializing in lobster dishes.

Moderate

Ta Nisiá, 13 Proxénou Koromilá 13, **t** 231 028 5991. Perhaps the most extensive Greek menu in Thessaloníki; excellent chef and a well stocked cellar. *Closed Sun.*

Krikélas, 32 Ethnikís Antístasis (eastern extension of Vas. Olgas), **t** 231 045 1289. In business since 1940: great food, great wine cellar, and live Greek music at night. *Closed Sun.*

Mare e Monte, 16 Kalapothaki St, near Plateía Eleftherías, **t** 231 027 1074. Fine Italian restaurant on a pedestrian street with a delicious range of antipasti and pasta dishes, and pizzas cooked in a traditional oven. *Closed mid-July–mid-Aug, Sun eves and Mon lunch.*

Neo Porto Marina, 2 Kountouriótou, Néa Kríni, **t** 231 043 9000. Excellent and affordable seafood; indulge in the tasty starters.

Tiffany's, 3 Iktínou, **t** 231 027 4022. South of Plateía Ag. Sofía; the gems here are the moussaká and classics with a home-made touch. Tables outside under the parasols.

Inexpensive

Ta Louloudádika, 22 Komninón St, **t** 231 022 5624. Next to the flower market, a taverna with lots of fish on the menu and outdoor tables, always crowded.

Plateía Áthonos, Dragoúmi 24, up on the edge of the Áno Pólis, **t** 231 026 4418. Popular taverna, open day and night, with game dishes in season.

To Makedonikó, **t** 231 062 7438. One of the most popular tavernas in the Áno Pólis, on the Sykiés, i.e. west side of the walls (bus 28 passes nearby), with live music in the eves.

Soutzoukákia Rogoti, 8 Venizélou St, **t** 231 022 3306. Classic market restaurant in business since 1928, famous for its spicy meatballs. *Closed Sun and some eves.*

Nea Ilýsia, 17 Sófou, Resolutely old-fashioned restaurant down to the tablecloths with classic 'ready' dishes served from 8.30am to 2am. Tables inside and out.

Bars/Cafés/Ouzerie

De facto, Paúlou Melá St. Favourite of the arty set; try coffee boiled slowly on hot sand.

Ethnic, 1 Proxénou Koromilá, **t** 231 027 2940. For a wide variety of coffees to go with the world music; moves out to Marmará in Chalkidiki in summer.

Aristotélous, 8 Aristotélous, **t** 231 023 3195. Exceedingly pleasant *ouzerie* in a leafy back courtyard, serving tasty snacks.

Balkan, 3 Proxénou Koromilá 3, **t** 231 026 5050. Atmospheric place for a cocktail.

Zýthos, 5 Katoúni, **t** 231 054 0284. The oldest bar in Ladádika, with lovely high ceilings, 50 kinds of beer and delicious *mézes*. *Open midday till 2am.*

Dore-Zýthos, 7 Tsirogiánni (by the White Tower), **t** 231 027 9010. Same owners, similar old-fashioned trendy style. *Open till 2am.*

To Kourdistó Gourouni, 31 Ag. Sofías, **t** 231 027 4672. The 'Wound-up Pig' is in a café founded in 1928 in a 'Turkish Baroque' mansion; over 80 kinds of beer. *Open till 2.30am.*

Mistral, 4 Tinou, Néa Kríni, **t** 231 044 4845. Romantic place for a drink by the sea.

Entertainment and Nightlife

Mégaro Mousikís, by the sea at 25 Martíou and Megálou Alexándrou, **t** 231 024 4480, is where big name concerts and ballet performances take place in a nine-storey hall. Many **cinemas** play English-language films with subtitles. Outdoor ones include: **Ellenis** in Plateía XANTH; **Alex**, 106 Olýmpou; **Aigli**, in the Yeni Hamam at Ag. Nikoláou and Kassándrou, just off Ag. Dimítriou, which also has a lovely bar and performance area inside the old Turkish baths.

The huge influx of Greek refugees from Anatolia in the 1922 made Thessaloníki a close rival to Athens in music and culture; it was one of the cradles of *rembétiko*, and any night of the week you can hear good live Greek music, none of it processed for tourists. Xyládika, the neighbourhood by the old railway station (buses 9 or 53 from Plateía Dikastrírion) has become the focus of the city's exciting contemporary art and music scene. **Mylos**, in a converted flour mill at 56 Andréou Georgíou, **t** 231 055 1836, *www.mylos.gr*, is a polyvalent centre that put Xyládika on the map, with spaces hosting concerts, plays, art exhibitions, films, etc., and an excellent *mezedopoleíon*. **Vilka**, in a former brewery, is at 21 Andréou Georgíou, **t** 231 051 9923.

Ladádika is another favourite spot for night owls, with music bars and clubs of every description: just head to Plateía Morichóvou and follow your ears. The barn-sized clubs are out towards the airport; there's a glitzy one by the airport at the Hyatt, along with a **casino**.

9th century it became the cultural centre for the entire Balkan region after two Thessalonian brothers, Methodius and Cyril, converted the Slavs to Christianity and created an alphabet for their language. Its prosperity attracted unwelcome visitors, too: among them the Saracens, who captured and sold off 22,000 inhabitants as slaves in 904. After the Fourth Crusade in 1204, the city briefly became the capital of the Latin kingdom of Thessaloníki before returning to the Greeks.

In the late 13th century, Thessaloníki became the fulcrum of the Orthodox Hesychasm ('Quietness') movement, which advocated the contemplation of God through 'total' prayer that concentrated body, mind and soul. Their regard of the body as a healthy, godly thing was revolutionary at the time; a suggestion by St Nicephoros the Hesychast that young monks should fix their eyes on their navels, to 'attach the prayer to their breathing,' led to the accusation that the Hesychasts were '*omphalopsychoí*', having their souls in their navels. The nobility supported the Hesychasts, while a popular party, the Zealots, found it distinctly non-Greek. Under Thessaloníki's Hesychast archbishop and later saint Gregory Palamas (1296–1359) the pot boiled over; anathema followed anathema, and in 1342 the Zealots hurled the nobles over the walls. Yet the Hesychast period coincided with a splendid age of painting and church building. Thessaloníki fell to the Ottomans in 1387; Tamerlane restored it to Constantinople in 1403 but, realizing he couldn't defend it, Emperor Andronikos Paleológos gave it to the Venetians for safekeeping. But in 1430, with its population reduced to 7,000, Sultan Murat II captured it once and for all.

An important military base and Janissary command post, Ottoman *Selanik* soon regained its stature as a major port and transit node; every week caravans set off for Skopje, Sofia and Vienna. Even by Balkan standards, the city was an ethnic mix where everyone spoke half a dozen languages; more than half the population was Jewish (*see* box), a third Greek and the rest Turks, Serbs and Bulgars, with a smattering of others. It worked well enough until the 1800s: after local attempts to join in the War of Independence were crushed, many Greeks moved south to the new state, leaving only 4,000 Greeks in the city. The Turks then gave the city a new lease of life, building a port for steamships and rail links to Skopje (1871) and Constantinople (1896). As mansions went up, the Thessalonikians were moved to modernize in other aspects: the Young Turks rallied here for equality for all religions and the decentralization of the Ottoman empire before overthrowing Sultan 'Abdul the Damned' in 1908.

In the Balkan Wars that followed soon after (1912–13), Thessaloníki was claimed by both Greece and Bulgaria, but the Greek army arrived first, by a few hours, and kept it after fierce street fighting. In August 1917, the lower city, including the Jewish quarter, went up in flames, leaving 70,000 homeless. Greek refugees from Asia Minor multiplied their forlorn numbers in 1922; Thessaloníki became known then as the *Phtochtómana*, the 'Mother of the Poor'. The influx of the Anatolian Greeks, however, did more than any post-Balkan War Hellenization scheme to make the city definitively Greek once more. An earthquake in 1978 caused severe damage, especially to the Byzantine churches, but most were restored in time for Thessaloníki's year in the limelight as the Cultural Capital of Europe (1997).

The Mother of Israel

By Hellenistic times, there were Jewish communities in all the commercial cities of the eastern Mediterranean, including the Thessaloníki visited by St Paul. By the 12th century, as the traveller Benjamin of Tudela reported, they had become so assimilated that they spoke Greek as their first language and called themselves Romiots, citizens of the 'Rome' (the Byzantine empire). The emperors tolerated them as God's chosen people and the Ottomans, when they took over, treated them like the Christians, as a *millet*, or nation, with religious and, to a large extent, legal autonomy.

Their attitude was in stark contrast to the persecutions in the West. When Spain expelled its Jews, the Sephardim, in 1492, Sultan Bayezit II welcomed them, and some 20,000 settled in Thessaloníki, their numbers soon augmented by thousands of Jews from Central Europe, Naples and Sicily. The Sephardim outnumbered the local Romiots, and their liturgy and language, Ladino (derived from medieval Spanish), dominated; their prominence in the city's business community made Ladino the local language of commerce. They called Thessaloníki 'the Mother of Israel'. Their 36 synagogues, with names such as Aragon and Toledo, did much to keep medieval Spanish culture alive; mystic cabbalist schools flourished. In the mid-17th century, the city was visited by the charismatic false messiah Shabbetai Tzevi, a native of Smyrna; many in Thessaloníki followed him in his 'sacred sin' of converting to Islam in 1666, an act explained as the ultimate sacrifice of the Messiah. The essential thing was to remain inwardly a Jew and secretly maintain Jewish ritual.

Because of their close association with the Ottomans, Jews were massacred in southern Greece during the Greek War of Independence. Survivors fled north to Thessaloníki, swelling the Jewish population to its peak at *c*. 90,000. Troubles came again after the Balkan Wars, when Athens sought to drag the idiosyncratic old city into contemporary Greek life. Greek was imposed as the official language, and many traditional religious laws had to be adapted to the laws of the new state. After the great fire of 1917, many Shabbetaians moved their businesses to Istanbul; in 1923, the influx of Greek refugees from Asia Minor made the Jews a minority in the city and, as Athens became the centre of national life, many moved to the capital or to Palestine.

By 1939 there were only 56,000 Jews in Thessaloníki. The German consulate had been taking notes on them during the 1930s, and the Occupation began with the plundering of their most precious books, manuscripts and ritual items. Families were evicted and their apartments taken over by Germans. There were systematic desecrations of the Jewish cemetery, and all Jewish men were mobilized for civilian labour under appalling conditions. The chief rabbi raised a huge sum to pay for their release, but in February 1943 Eichmann's right-hand man, Dieter Wisliceny, arrived to implement the 'Final Solution' and sent 48,974 to Auschwitz. Suspicions about their fate led the Resistance in Athens and other Greek cities to kidnap local rabbis – without them, the Nazis had a much more difficult time identifying and rounding up the Jews, so some escaped. Still, Greece as a whole lost 97 per cent of its Jews in the Holocaust. In 1945, only 10,000 remained in Greece; today the population is half that.

The White Tower and Around

Thessaloníki's famous landmark began as part of the seafront walls of Theodosius, but at the end of the 15th century it was rebuilt as a stout 105ft cylinder, probably by the Venetians. Under the Janissaries, the Sultans' praetorian guard who became a law until themselves, it earned the name Bloody Tower for the frequent executions within its walls. When Sultan Mahmoud II purged the Janissaries in 1825, the tower was whitewashed and has been the **White Tower** (*Lefkós Pýrgos*) ever since.Today, its six floors are used for special exhibitions.

A statue of **Philip II** scrutinizes the tower with his one bad eye, while in the nearby garden, the thoughtful city has installed a colourful pigeon hotel. On the edge of this green space, on Plateía Xanth (ΧΑΝΘ; Greek for YMCA), a Flash Gordon telecommunications tower marks the grounds of the **International Fair of Thessaloníki**, the biggest event of its kind in the Balkans, founded in the early Middle Ages and revived in 1926. Behind it stretches **Aristotle University** on what was a massive Jewish cemetery before the Germans bulldozed it.

The Archaeological Museum

Plateía Xanth, t 231 083 1037; open summer Tues–Sun 9–7 and Mon 12.30–7; winter Tues–Sun 8–2.30, Mon 10.30–5; adm. Bus 11 or 12 from the train station.

Although the fabulous treasures from the tomb of Philip II are now in Vergína, the museum remains a showcase of the wealth and craftsmanship of ancient Macedonia. This is dazzlingly displayed in the gold from 121 6th-century BC tombs found at Síndos, in the suburbs of Thessaloníki; to pick out the granulation and filigree on the necklaces you almost need a magnifying glass. Men were buried with their weapons, women with their jewellery, and both with miniature items useful in the afterlife – furniture and mule carts, one pulled by terracotta mules. Five tombs contained gold masks; others had gold lozenges that covered the mouths of the dead.

From the Síndos rooms, cross the foyer for Room I, with fragments of an Ionian temple. Next come sculptures from Archaic to Hellenistic times, including the torso of a *kouros* in a clinging robe; a lovely Classical funeral stele of a girl holding a dove; and an excellent if headless 5th-century BC 'Aphrodite of Thessaloníki', dressed to make modern wet T-shirt competitions on the islands seem tacky. The next large room focuses on ancient Thessaloníki, with displays on Galerius' ambitious building programme, a virtual reconstruction of the Rotunda and mosaic floors discovered under the modern city, most notably a painterly one of Ariadne and Dionysos from the 3rd century. Among the Roman statues, there's an Augustus as a hero, an early example of the 'propaganda' statues erected across the empire (later, the Romans would save money by sending out bodies with replaceable heads).

The gold of Macedonia, the same that funded Philip II's meteoric rise to power in Greece, is covered in the next section. A cemetery in Dervéni, southwest of Thessaloníki, yielded a glittering horde from the second half of the 4th century BC, along with one of the masterpieces of Hellenistic art: the bronze **Dervéni Krater** (*c.* 320 BC). The only intact relief metal vase to survive antiquity, it was made with such a high quantity of tin in the alloy that it looks gold-plated. According to an inscription on its shoulder, its owner was a nobleman of Lárissa, probably a hostage of Philip II; its creator was a Greek Cellini, who some critics have tentatively identified as Lysippus. The theme is a Dionysian revel. Hammered out in the most exquisite repoussée, ecstatic bacchants whirl in their fluttering garments across the main body of the vase, watched by a man wearing one boot, identified as the Thracian king Lykourgos, who was punished by Dionysos with madness for his impiety. Ariadne and Dionysos are shown seated, Ariadne pulling back her veil as her husband stretches a sensuous leg over her thigh. The other elements are of cast bronze – the extraordinary four figures weary from the dance around the neck: Dionysos and a maenad, and a satyr and maenad who are the very definition of erotic languor. Even the handles are unique, anticipating rococo soup tureens, decorated with bearded heads framed in screw-tailed snakes.

From here stairs descend to the prehistoric finds discovered in the mounds that dot the plains, which later inhabitants considered magical places. Back upstairs, there are local funerary reliefs and sculpture from the 3rd and 4th centuries AD, still vigorously pagan and imbued with a homely charm as proportions begin to waver from the golden mean. The last room is dedicated to Macedonian tombs (*see* p.551). The superb 4th-century BC marble door with all its bronze fittings came from Thessaloníki: wheels once allowed it to open effortlessly. A tomb at Potídaea in Chalkidikí was robbed just before its official discovery in 1984 and, although they tried, the robbers couldn't remove the beautiful marble couches painted with griffons, a bull, gods and a red-shoed Silenus that Giambattista Tiepolo would have been proud of.

The Museum of Byzantine Civilization

2 Leof. Stratoú, t 231 086 8570; open Mon 12.30–7, and Tues–Sun 8–7; adm.

Where the archaeological collection ends, this new museum, directly behind, picks up the story of Thessaloníki. Early Christian art shows the continuity of pagan styles, even in the tombs, although instead of 'Farewell' they now read 'Sleeping' or 'At Rest'. The earliest art here emphasizes hope – the young, beardless Good Shepherd amid sweet visions of a heaven filled with birds, fruit and wine: crucifixions wouldn't become popular until the 6th century. And judging by the mosaic floor and paintings from a 5th-century dining room, life on earth, at least for some, was good, too. There are bittersweet photos of the mosaics in Ag. Dimítrios, lost in the fire of 1917, and a fresco showing Susannah and the Elders, unique in Greece. After the puritanical Iconoclasm, there was an explosion of art to fill the new monasteries founded by the Macedonian emperors (867–1056). There's also a video installation on the Byzantine castles built along the Via Egnatía, and a collection of icons.

Galerius' Capital: the Arch and Rotunda

When Galerius made Thessaloníki his capital in AD 300, he built a complex to match his imperial dignity, covering some 45 acres. Of the **Palace of Galerius**, a courtyard and rooms from the southeast corner of the complex are visible in Plateía Navarínou, a short walk from the museums; the adjacent **octagon**, with lavish marbles, was prob- ably the throne room. Nearby Plateía Ippodrómou's name recalls that it was the site of the **Hippodrome**, or 'Theatre called Stadium' as the Byzantines called it. Racing was very popular in Thessaloníki, and in 390 the city's favourite charioteer tried to seduce a boy slave of Emperor Theodosius' commander, the stern Goth Botheric. Scandalized, Botheric imprisoned the charioteer; the outraged Thessalonians murdered Botheric; the furious Theodosius invited them to the Hippodrome to watch their favourite, then locked the gates and set his army on them. In a three-hour killing spree, over 7,000 were massacred. St Ambrose, the bishop of Milan, made Theodosius pay penance for it – a first for an emperor, setting an important precedent for the Church.

From the palace, a covered portico went up modern Dimitríou Goúrnari Street to what has been Thessaloníki's thoroughfare since its foundation, misleadingly called **Egnatía Street** (the famed Roman Via Egnatía passed northwest of the centre). The crossing point of street and portico was marked by the **Arch of Galerius** (or *Kamara*, as the locals call it). Only a quarter of the domed double gateway survives, with reliefs all crowded and busy in the Late Imperial style celebrating Galerius' triumphs in Persia: although the faces have been carefully hacked off, you can see the emperor fighting on horseback, addressing his troops, riding his chariot and reigning and sacrificing with his father-in-law Diocletian, who fancied that he was the incarnation of Jupiter and Galerius was his Hercules. The two were rabid persecutors of Christians – Galerius alone martyred some 3,000, to please Diocletian – but on his deathbed in Sofia Galerius felt which way the wind was blowing and signed an edict of tolerance.

Just up from the arch, the portico continued to the **Rotunda** (*t 231 021 3627; open Tues–Sun 9–7; free; bring your binoculars*). If the arch looked to Roman models, this great round building referred to the Pantheon. Yet no one is sure what it was meant to be – Galerius' mausoleum, perhaps (although his body was never brought here), or possibly a Temple to Zeus. The walls of brick and rubble masonry, 20ft thick, enclosed a space 80ft in diameter, covered with coloured marbles and relieved by barrel-vaulted niches for statues. The tremendous dome, 98ft high, was made of brick, and like the Pantheon there was a central hole to let in light and air – and rain; the floor was equipped with drains.

In the 4th century, when the Rotunda was converted into the church of the Asómatoi (Archangels), a now-destroyed ambulatory was built around it; mosaics, the oldest in Byzantium, were lavished on its walls; and the east bay was widened to make a sanctuary, which unfortunately undermined the integrity of the circular struc-ture. In an earthquake, perhaps in the 10th century, the dome collapsed and had to be repaired, and two buttresses were built to shore up the sanctuary. In 1591, it was converted into a mosque, and has the only minaret in Thessaloníki that survived a nationalist rampage following the assassination of King George I in 1913. The earth-quake of 1978 severely damaged the building and the decoration, but at the time of writing the scaffolding is slowly being taken down.

In its prime, the church glittered with mosaics made up of *c.* 34 million tesserae, which survive only in fragments. But what fragments – still fresh and glowing from the cusp of a world age, Hellenistic in style but full of the wonder and promise of the new religion. In the centre was the figure of Christ Pantocrator (now lost), in a lush heavenly garden in a rainbow supported by four angels, whose heads, wings and hands survive. The next band contained the Apostles, although they too have been lost, except for their feet. Below them are eight saints martyred under Diocletian, their arms spread in the *orans* or prayer gesture, standing before delightful stage façades studded with gems and hung with pearls, where peacocks frolic. Some of the bays have retained their mosaics as well. After the 10th-century earthquake, the mosaics in the sanctuary were replaced with paintings of the Ascension.

Down from the Rotunda's entrance is medieval **Ag. Pandeleímonos**, a nubby quilt of brick and tile, and one of several churches in the city whose original name and date are disputed: by the architecture it is late 13th century, a good example of the complex tetrastyle cross-in-square plan; but only a few of its damaged wall paintings survive. Across Michaíl Street, turn right to see the sunken little church of the **Sotir** (*c.* 1350), its jauntily tilted octagonal dome surrounded by restaurant tables. The earthquake of 1978 revealed its secrets: its rare plan, a tetraconch (four-sided shell) inscribed in a square, and forgotten wall paintings.

Panagía Acheiropoéitos and Ag. Sofía

The nearby basilica of the **Acheiropoéitos** (*west on the Egnatía and a right on Ag. Sofías; open 8–12 and 5–7*) was built shortly after the Council of Éphesus recognized Mary as the Mother of God (431), making it one of the oldest churches in the world still in use. Its name, meaning 'made without hands', was derived from a medieval icon of the Virgin reputedly painted by angels. Converted into a mosque in 1430 and restored after serving as emergency shelter for refugees in 1923, the interior is impressive in its simplicity, its three aisles divided by monolithic colonnades. The columns have superb 5th-century 'Theodosian' capitals, named after Theodosius II, decorated with Corinthian acanthus leaves perforated to resemble lace, which either stand upright or blow in a violent wind, sometimes every which way: similar ones do duty in Istanbul's Ag. Sophia. Charming golden mosaics of fruit, flowers, fountains, birds and geometric designs from the same late 5th-century school as the Rotunda decorate the soffits of the arches. Of the frescoes, all that remains are portraits of 18 martyrs along the right arcade. In the left aisle, look for the floor mosaics, once part of the Roman bath.

Across Egnatía Street waits Thessaloníki's Byzantine cathedral, **Ag. Sofía** (*open 8.30–2 and 5.30–8*). Built over a 5th-century church built over a Roman bath, it was once much grander, with a large atrium (now marked by a palm garden) and elaborate Turkish portal from its days as a mosque, both victims of an Italian air raid in 1941. The interior, however, with its huge dome on pendentives is reminiscent of the Ag. Sofía in Istanbul. It is filled with a mosaic of the *Ascension*, dated to shortly after the end of the Iconoclasm and showing the same scene in the Rotunda: the Pantocrator on a rainbow is supported by two angels, although the artist's attempt to adapt the figure of Christ to the curved surface gives him a curiously stumpy look. All around him, standing in a stylized rocky landscape, are the apostles, gazing up in astonishment and consternation while the Virgin stands serene between a pair of angels;

the quotation is from Acts I ('Men of Galilee, why do you stand gazing up into heaven?'). The golden mosaic of the Virgin and Child in the apse, also from the 9th century, replaced the original simple cross (you can still see its 'ghost'); the mosaics in the barrel vault, with monograms of Constantine VI and Empress Irene, are rare survivors from the Iconoclasm. The subterranean chapel just to the right of Ag. Sofía, labelled the 'catacombs' of **Ag. Ioánnes Pródomos**, was really the 5th-century church's baptistry, built over a Roman nymphaeum.

Further down Ag. Sofías street, at the corner of Mitropoléos, stands the city's current cathedral, **Ag. Gregórios Palamás** (dedicated to the Hesychast leader, who was re-buried here); it was rebuilt after a fire in 1890. Next to it, at 23 Proxénou Koromilá, is the **Museum of the Macedonian Struggle** (*t 231 022 9778; open Tues–Fri 9–2, Wed 6–8pm, Sat and Sun 11–2; free; in Greek, but English translation available*), housed in a handsome neoclassical mansion designed by Ernest Ziller. It was the Greek consulate during the years leading up to the Balkan Wars, where the Procouncil Koromilá was instrumental in assuring that Thessaloníki became Greek instead of Bulgarian (there was fierce hand-to-hand fighting nearby, the Greeks having the advantage with a machine gun in Ag. Sofía's old minaret).

Around Plateía Dikastiríon: the Roman Agora

Three blocks to the east of here, broad **Aristotélous Street** is a favourite promenade, lined with bookshops and cafés, where old men debate and protesters march. It links the seafront to Egnatía Street and **Plateía Dikastiríon**, a large space cleared after the 1917 fire, except for two landmarks. On the east corner, the **Bey Hamami** (*open Tues–Sun 8am–7pm; free*) was the first Ottoman bathhouse in the city, built in 1444 by Sultan Murad II. It had sections for men and women, the former more opulent, with a special apartment for the bey under a stalactite ceiling. The Greeks who used it until 1968 called it Loútra Paradeisos (note the painting of a woman, contemplating a bill-board advising baths for health and beauty). Today the baths house exhibitions.

In the west corner, the church of **Panagía Chalkeón**, 'Our Lady of the Coppersmiths' (*t 231 027 2910; open 8–11 and 7–9*), was founded in 1028 by one Christóphoros, a *kapetan* of Lombardy, who was buried there; it earned its name while serving as the mosque for Turkish coppersmiths from 1430 to 1912. Like all Byzantine churches in Thessaloníki, it is made of brick, in a cross-in-square plan, with an attractive angular style in various textures and patterns; a tall narrow dome rises out of the centre and a pair of smaller ones mark the narthex. The frescoes are dark, but are of special interest because they date from the early 11th century: the *Last Judgement* in the narthex is especially good.

In the 1960s, while digging foundations for its law courts at the top of the square, the city stumbled across the 1st-century AD **Roman Agora** and its three stoas. Now that it's been excavated, a scheme is underway to integrate the ruins into the city: the impressive **cryptoporticus** under the south stoa will host special events, the 3rd-century **Odeion** will be used for concerts again, and the rest of the square dedicated to cultural activities. The **library**, reduced to a large apse on nearby Agnóstou Stratiótou Street, will be used for exhibitions.

The Basilica of Ag. Dimítrios

Another block up, overlooking the Agora, is the city's holiest spot and the largest church in Greece (*t 231 027 0008; open Mon 1.30–7.30, Tues–Sun 8am–7.30pm*). Yet Dimítrios, Great Martyr of the Greeks and second only to George as a military saint, patron of children and horses, is a rather elusive character. In Thessaloníki they say he was a Roman soldier, born in 280, who taught Christianity to children, although what led to his martyrdom in 304 was his blessing of his friend Nestor, who defeated Galerius' favourite gladiator at wrestling. The emperor, a sore loser, imprisoned Dimítrios in the Roman baths, where he was run through with a spear. A myrrh-scented oil oozed from his wounds; hence his epithet, *Myrovlítis*. The Christians built a chapel over his grave as soon as it was permitted, in 313. In the 5th century, when the Prefect Leontius was cured of paralysis by the sacred oil, he founded a large church, which was rebuilt in the 7th century after a fire. It was converted into a mosque in 1491, and when it became a church again in 1907 and its whitewash cleared away, its 141ft nave was found to have splendid mosaics – just before most of them vanished forever in the 1917 fire.

The basilica was rebuilt as it looked in the 5th century, preserving as much of the original as possible; the result resembles its contemporaries in Ravenna. The baptismal font in the square, the size of a paddling pool, originally stood in the atrium. As you enter the long rectangular nave from the narthex, you'll see on the left an engraved 15th-century Easter calendar and the elegant Florentine Renaissance **wall tomb of Lukas Spantounis** (1481), not something you see every day in Greece; on the right, there's a curious wall painting of a man being chased by a unicorn. Arched colonnades divide the nave into five aisles, each with their own roof. Originally the walls were clad in marbles, but as time went on the faithful replaced them with votive mosaics and paintings. Two **mosaics** survive on the west wall: a beautiful fragment of *Dimítrios with an Angel* blowing a trumpet in a rainbow-coloured background, and on the right a garden scene showing the *Dedication of Two Children* to the saint. Most of the **columns** are survivors from the 5th-century basilica, and their capitals offer a rare ensemble of early Christian sculpture: animals, geometric figures or lacy Theodosian acanthus.

The other mosaics (5th–9th century) are on the piers around the sanctuary. On the right are a young, wide-eyed *Dimítrios with Two Founders of the Church* stands before the walls of Thessaloníki; *Dimítrios and a Deacon* (who was told by the saint in a dream that the church would be rebuilt after the 7th-century fire), and an excellent *St Sergius*, dressed as a Roman military officer, hands raised in prayer; on the left there's a sombre *Virgin and St Theodore*, and the charming *Dimítrios with Two Children*. All the saints wear mantles with a different coloured fabric sewn on the left, a convention showing their status. To the right, a baby basilica stuck on to the church by a donor, the **Chapel of Ag. Euthémius**, has expressive paintings of Christ's miracles (1303).

The labyrinthine **crypt**, long forgotten, was revealed by the fire in 1917. Now used to display sculptural fragments, it incorporates a stretch of Roman road and baths (other jumbly remains lie outside the basilica) where Dimítrios was martyred. Here too is the apsidal *martyrium* of 313 and the fountain into which the miraculous myrrh seeped from the wall of the saint's tomb, which pilgrims collected in lead flasks. A phial of earth soaked in blood (presumably Dimítrios') was discovered under the altar; similar phials were valued gifts for emperors.

Just north of the basilica, at Ag. Nikoláou and Kassándrou Streets, the 16th-century **Yeni Hamam** (*t 231 027 0715; open 9–1 and 5–9, closed Mon and hols*) is now a bar and concert venue; the nearby **Alaca Imaret mosque** (1484) on Kassándrou is used for municipal cultural events. West on Ag. Dimitríou St, the **Ministry of Northern Greece**, which devotes itself to Macedonia and Thrace, overlooks the extensive Hellenistic- and Byzantine-era ruins and the **Prefecture** (1891) in Plateía Dioikitíriou.

Into the Old Commercial District

Venizélou Street descends from Ag. Dimitríou Street into the old commercial heart of the city, lined with grand buildings: the **Dimarchíon** at No.45, built over the old merchants' caravanserai, and the **Hamza Beg Cami**, at the intersection with Egnatía. Founded in 1468, it is one of the finest Ottoman mosques outside Turkey, but currently suffering from neglect and earthquake damage; its peristyle courtyard, unique in Greece, is now filled with shops. Another landmark here, visible down Egnatía St, is **Greece's largest shoe**, a glittering pump, rotating over a shoe shop.

Venizélou continues down to the 15th-century Ottoman **Bezesten** – an indoor market, still in use, where the most precious textiles, perfumes and jewellery were sold (and could be guarded); in its heyday this had 100 stalls, where, according to the 17th-century traveller Evliya Çelebi, 'visitors literally lose their senses from the scent of musk, amber and the other perfumes.' The food markets are just east: meat and fish in the **Modiáno Market** (1922), named for its architect, Elí Modiáno, scion of a promi- nent Jewish family; and fruit and vegetables in the **Vláli Market**. **Plateía Eleftherías**, at the south end of Venizélou, is surrounded by elaborate banks from the 1920s.

The most important church in the area is **Ag. Mínas**, at Dragoúmi and Iraklíou Sts (*t 231 027 2700; open 8.30–1 and 6–8*). Founded in the 5th century and nicknamed the 'Ark' for the many animals sculpted on its cornice (now in the Museum of Byzantine Civilization), it was one of the few churches in Thessaloníki not converted into a mosque, but it burned and was rebuilt in 1852 with tear drop windows and a surprise: a creamy Central European rococo interior, part of the city's attempt to modernize itself in the 19th century. The **Museum of the Jewish Presence** is nearby, upstairs at 13 Ag. Mínas (*t 231 025 0406; open 11–2, Wed and Thurs also 5–8, closed Mon and Sat*), with photographs and historical documents. At the corner of Iraklíou and Kominón, the 16th-century **Ioudi Hamam** (Jewish baths) is now a flower market, the **Louloudádika**.

In 323, when Emperor Constantine built a new artificial harbour for Thessaloníki, the sea reached in as far as Frágon Street. It silted up over the centuries, and a new quarter, the **Ladádika** (olive oil market), grew up on little lava-paved lanes, now all fixed up, brightly painted and converted into bars, clubs and restaurants. Katoúni is one of the prettiest streets with its colourful façades and old street lights; here at No. 12, the Piraeus Bank set up in 1997 the **Museum of Ancient and Byzantine Musical**

Instruments (*t 231 055 5263; open 9–3 and 5–10, Mon 9–3; adm exp*), which turns out rather disappointingly to be three silent floors of wooden reconstructions of ancient Greek instruments. The view from Ladádika to the modern port is closed off by the huge customs house, another work by Elí Modiáno (1910).

Remains of the 16th-century **Vardári Fortress**, built by Suleiman the Magnificent over layers of walls that once protected Constantine's port, are set in a park at the east end of Frágon Street. Just north, busy **Plateía Dimokratías** was the location of the fabled Golden Gate, Thessaloníki's front door until the 19th century, now gone without a trace and replaced by a statue of Prince Constantine, liberator of the city in 1912. The moving **Memorial to Thessaloníki's Jews** (1962) is just up Langadá Street.

The Upper City (Áno Pólis)

Above Ag. Dimitríou Street, the mood changes as you ascend to the Upper City or Áno Pólis, the part of Thessaloníki still guarded by the mighty **ramparts** erected by Theodosius in 390. Built of rubble masonry and brick and standing up to 50ft high, Hellenistic masonry in places suggests that they follow some of the original walls of Cassander. Rectangular towers are interspersed at irregular intervals over the 4km that have survived, and in places incorporate brick arches for support in case the walls were sapped. Here and there inscriptions in red brick testify to repairs over the past 1,400 years. An inner wall protecting the acropolis runs along Eptapyrgíou Street. This is the best preserved stretch, although also the bloodiest; in 1345, in the Hesychast revolt, the Zealots tossed aristocrats off these walls onto stakes. The stout tower of the south acropolis wall, the **Chain Tower**, replaces the Byzantine Trigonion, focus of the Turkish assault in 1430. It still fires cannons – at midnight on New Year's Eve.

At the top the acropolis, the seven-towered fortress, the **Eptapýrgio**, is still often known by its Turkish name, Yedi Koulé (bus 23; *t 231 020 4734; open Tues–Sun 8–7; free*). It was rebuilt by the Turks soon after their conquest, and housed the city's governor until the 19th century, when it was converted into a prison. This closed in 1989, and a small part of the fortress is open to visits; the splendid main gate, with a Turkish inscription of 1431, is prettily studded with Byzantine reliefs of peacocks. Behind it is Thessaloníki's only active Byzantine monastery, **Moní Vlatádon** (*t 231 020 9913; open 7.30–11 and 5.30–8*), founded in the mid-14th century by the Hesychast Dorotheos Vlatis, a pupil of St Gregory Palamas, who directly attached it to the Patriarchate in Constantinople. The church was rebuilt over an 11th-century predecessor, and unusually the dome is supported directly on the walls. The frescoes, uncovered in 1981, date from *c.* 1370. The right chapel marks a spot where St Paul preached in AD 51, but his message wasn't well received by some of the local Jews, who attacked his lodgings. Outside, the monks' peacocks enjoy a superb view over the city.

Byzantine Churches in the Upper City

How letters ever get delivered in the Áno Pólis, where narrow streets turn into stairs with names invisible to the naked eye, is a credit to the city's postmen. Yet living here, in one of these old Turkish houses with gardens, far from the cars triple-parked below, must seem a lot like bliss. Signposts point in the general direction of Byzantine churches tucked in tangles of stairs and one-way lanes. The most winsome, 5th-century **Ósios David** (*t 231 022 1506; open Mon–Sat 8–12 and 5–7, Sun 8–10.30; donation*), is down the steps of Diamádou St from the Moní Vlatádon, in a side street off Timothéou St. From the outside it looks like someone's home: a tile porch faces a little courtyard where potted plants thrive, a canary sings and a table with a couple of chairs wait in the shade, all cared for by the gregarious caretaker. Its story is typically obscure: no one knows the original name, or when the nave was amputated for conversion into a mosque.

If mosaics could sing, Ósios David's 5th-century *Epiphany* would warble like a nightingale. Hidden under layers of plaster in the semi-dome, it has survived nearly perfectly intact and shows a young, beardless but serious-minded Christ, surrounded by the light of glory (*doxa*). Under his feet the rivers of Eden, Physon, Geon, Tigris and Euphrates flow into the Jordan, personified as a man with fish swimming along his body. Symbols of the Evangelists surround the *doxa*: an endearing ox and lion earnestly clutch their books. Next to the lion, Ezekiel (whose vision this is), is bent over in fear and ecstasy; on the right, the prophet Habakkuk smiles in deep thought. Although overshadowed by the mosaic, also take a close look at the 12th-century wall paintings discovered in 1976: the *Nativity*, the *Bathing of the Christ Child* and *Baptism* are among the finest surviving works from the Comneni era.

Heading east of here, just off Akropóleos Street, the 14th-century **Taxiarchon** is a handsome little stone and patterned brick church that lost most of its frescoes when it served as a mosque. Just down from here, on Theotokopoúlou, you'll find the best preserved **Byzantine baths** in Greece, built in the late 13th-century but modelled after those of ancient Rome, with tepid, hot and cold rooms, and in constant use until the last bather towelled off in 1940.

Heading east, in a walled courtyard between Apostólou Pávlou and Irodótou Streets, is the monastery church or *katholikón* of **Ag. Nikólaos Orphanós** (*t 231 021 4497; open Tues–Sun 8.30–2.45*), built in the early 14th century by the Serbian king Milutin, who married a daughter of a Paleológos emperor and frequently visited Thessaloníki. The church was originally a three-aisle basilica, but was amputated like Ósios David; the brickwork is simple by standards of the day and most of the sculpture is recycled early Christian. The vivid frescoes (1310–20), however, are the best preserved in the city, and show a fresh naturalism and concern for colour and feeling typical of the Paleologian era. In the *Marriage of Cana*, the Virgin, usually a sorrowful character in Byzantine art, whispers to her Son, just as any mother would, that their hosts have run out of wine and need a timely miracle to fill the carafes.

Down Apostólou Pávlou St, by the Turkish consulate, stands **Atatürk's House** (*151 Ag. Dimitríou; to visit, t 231 024 8452*). The founder of modern Turkey was destiny's child; when he was born here in 1881, his father hung his sword over his cradle to dedicate him to a military career; his maths teacher later gave him his name Kemal, 'the perfect one'. After attending a military academy in Istanbul, Kemal was appointed in 1907 to a unit in Thessaloníki, at the time a hotbed of the Young Turk movement. He joined the march on Istanbul to depose the reactionary sultan Abdul Hamid, but never returned; after the First Balkan War, his family was forced to leave Thessaloníki. Nearby, the **Telloglio Foundation**, 159a Ag. Dimitríou (*t 231 02 4 7111; open Tues–Fri 10.30–1.30 and 5.30–9, Sat 5.30–9, Sun 11–8.30; free*), has a noted collection of modern Greek art.

Olympiádos Street leads west to the last three jewels in Thessaloníki's Byzantine crown, beginning with another great Paleologian church, the 14th-century **Profítis Ilías** (*t 231 027 3790; open 6–12 and 6–8*), built in a wonderfully panoramic setting. Its original name, long forgotten, is the subject of much dispute. It is the only Athonite church in the city (tetrastyle cross-in-square plan with side choirs), a style invented by St Athanásios with the Great Lavra on Mount Athos; its masonry (white ashlar alternating with courses of brick) is rare in Macedonia, but common in churches in Constantinople. Unfortunately only a few of the rich wall paintings of 1360 survive – the *Massacre of the Innocents* is strikingly realistic in its cruelty. Another church from the same period, **Ag. Ekateríni**, is west along Olympiádos St, turning at Tsamadoú St (*t 231 022 5580; open 10–12 and 6–8*). A complex tetrastyle cross-in-square church with a closed ambulatory, its decorative brick work gives it a nubby texture. Only fragments of its frescoes of 1315 survived its conversion into a mosque in 1500.

From here, follow the west walls down to Ag. Dimitríou Street, where the Roman Letaia Gate once stood. Near here is a church that resembles Ag. Ekateríni, the **Dódeka Apostóli** (*t 231 053 7915; open daily 7.30–12 and 5.30–7.30*). Founded by Patriarch Niphon I in *c.* 1312, it was one of the largest and richest foundations in the city, its grounds incorporating a vast cistern that gave it a later name, the Cold Water Mosque. The domes are pierced with numerous openings, letting in beams of light to show up the elegant mosaics, inspired by the Chora monastery in Constantinople, although as they were never completed. Yet they represent the summit and one of the last examples of Paleologian mosaic art – more naturalistic and earthy in detail, yet endowed with the Hellenistic grace that marked the curtain call of Byzantium. In the dome, as usual, there is the *Pantocrator*, surrounded by prophets and Evangelists, while the *Dodekaorton* (the Twelve Holy Feasts) decorate the vaults and west wall – scenes of the *Nativity* (with a nurse testing Jesus' first bath), *Resurrection*, *Transfiguration*, and *Entry into Jerusalem*. When the patriarchal largesse dried up (Niphon was deposed in 1314) the remaining walls were painted: the *Tree of Jesse* in the ambulatory, the *Hand of God* holding the souls of the righteous, the *Birth of John the Baptist*, *Herod's Feast*, and *Salome* performing an unusual feat – dancing while balancing the Baptist's head on a tray on her own head.

Outside the Centre: Views, Villas, Beaches and Fire-walkers

A ring road heaving with traffic skirts the city to the north, running along the edge of the city's famous pine groves, although they're a bit worse for wear from fires and exhaust fumes. Within the ring, and above the university, is Thessaloníki's biggest city park, **Sheikh-sou** (or Kedrinós Lófos, or Chília Déndra; bus 24 from Plateía Eleftherías) a favourite place for walks; the bus goes as far as the zoo at the top of the park. A spot called **Kará Tepé** has excellent views over the city and gulf, although the best views of all are from the aptly named **Panórama**, 11km east on the slopes of Mount Chortiátis (bus no.58 from Plateía Dikastiríon). The village, burned by the Nazis in a horrific reprisal, has been rebuilt as a slick resort, with weekend villas, hotels and restaurants.

Thessaloníki's modern residential districts stretch miles to the southeast of the centre. Just before the Balkan Wars beautiful mansions went up, especially along Vas. Ólgas Street. One, built by Giakó Modiáno in 1911, was quickly converted into the Government House, and now serves as the excellent **Folk and Ethnological Museum** (*68 Vas. Ólgas; t 231 083 0591; ring to see if it's reopened*), with a large collection of items from northern Greece and explanations in English. The nearby **Yeni Cami**, at 30 Archaiologikoú Mouseíou (*t 231 085 7978; open 9–1 and 5–9*), was built in 1902 by the Shabbetaians – a mosque with a charming garden and ravishing interior that recalls the city's lost Spanish synagogues; it's now used for exhibitions.

There are fancy mansions on Vas. Ólgas at Nos. 108 and 131 (the latter a brick castle of 1890 called ΣΑΤΟ ΜΟΝ ΜΠΟΝΕΡ – aka Château Mon Bonheur). The **Municipal Art Gallery**, at 162 Vas. Ólgas (*t 231 042 5531; open Tues–Fri 9–1 and 5–9; free*), in an eclectic mansion of 1905 surrounded by luxuriant gardens, contains works by local artists from 1900 to 1967, as well as modern Greek etchings and sculpture. Further east, note the Art Nouveau **Villa Bianca** (1911) at 180 Vas. Ólgas and the big brick **Villa Allatini** (1898) at No. 198, now the Prefecture. Turn right here for the city's marinas and priciest seafood restaurants in **Aretsóu** and **Néa Kríni** (bus 5 from Venizélou St). There are beaches here, but the water is much cleaner further east; city buses go out to Finikas (no.2 or 3 from the train station). Here you'll have to change for **Ag. Triáda** (No. 72) or **Órmos Epanomís** (No. 69), where the beach and campsite are a bit nicer.

Langadás 16km northeast of Thessaloníki, is famous for its fire walkers, the *Anastern árides* ('groaners'), who on the evening of 21 May dance barefoot over burning coals to the drum and *lýra*, holding aloft icons of SS. Constantine and Helen. The story goes that in c. 1250, in Kósti, Thrace, when the church of Ag. Konstantínos went up in a blaze, its icons could be heard groaning, and some of the villagers rescued them without coming to any harm. Since then, both the icons and the ability to walk on fire in a trance have been passed down in their families. The families moved to Macedonia in 1914 when Kósti was joined to Bulgaria; besides Langadás, other Anasternárides live in Ag. Eléni (south of Sérres) and Melíki (by Véria) where the ceremony also takes place, and usually includes the sacrifice of a garlanded bull or calf. The Dionysian echoes of all this hardly meets the approval of the Orthodox church, which in the past has excommunicated the fire-walkers and done all it could to suppress the rite. These days, however, the Anasternárides have taken on the trappings of a folklore troupe: special buses come up from Thessaloníki (from Langadás St), admission is charged (get there by late afternoon for a good view), and the fire-walking takes place over three evenings to accommodate the crowds. If you can't make it in person, check it out on Greek TV.

West of Thessaloníki: Alexander Country

West of Thessaloníki lies the heart of the ancient kingdom of Macedonia, where Alexander was born and educated, and where he buried his father Philip in Aigai (Vergína), now the most glittering and compelling archaeological site in northern Greece. The surrounding hills produce a lovely, leggy red wine. By making a circular route in this relatively small area, you can also take in Édessa with its beautiful waterfall, Lefkádia with some of the best surviving Macedonian tombs, and the old Byzantine town of Véria. If you have more time, this loop could easily be enlarged to include the highlands of Upper Macedonia, *see* p.557.

Ancient Pella

From Thessaloníki, head northwest (following signs to Édessa) and continue on the E86 – the Roman Via Egnatia. This, as in ancient times, goes through the centre of Pélla, and in the busy traffic it's easy to drive straight past it. The car park is next to the museum, on the left. The site and museum, **t** *238 203 1160, are open Tues–Sun 8.30–3; adm.*

Pella was founded on the grand scale by King Archelaos, who moved his capital here from Aigai at the end of the 5th century BC; Euripides wrote his most uncanny play, the *Bacchae*, for his new theatre not long before he died. Pella soon became the largest city in Macedonia, and boomed when Alexander's Companions returned from Asia with gold burning holes in their pockets. But Pella gradually lost its importance to Thessaloníki, and some time in the 1st century BC it was hit by an earthquake and vanished in the mud, to be replaced by a Roman colony (modern Néa Pélla). Rediscovered by chance in 1957, excavations so far have only revealed a fraction of the city and **palace** where Philip II and Alexander were born. The latter was famous in its day, a 60,000 square metre complex with a swimming pool, set on the hill to the north, built as a giant belvedere over the Thermaic Gulf. 'Nobody would go to Macedonia to see the king, but many would come far to see his palace,' commented Socrates, who was invited to take refuge there but still preferred to drink hemlock.

Although it's hard to imagine now, Archelaos chose the site for its natural defences. Pélla was built on reclaimed marshland, surrounded by a wall and moat, with access to the sea via a shallow lagoon. A small island in the swamp, linked by a wooden draw bridge, doubled as a prison and treasury. As in Díon, Archelaos chose the fashionable Hippodameian grid for his plan, but with wider streets and blocks and an excellent water and drainage system, all built around a massive square **agora** that takes up ten city blocks. The scale allowed for palatial villas like the **House of Dionysos**, extending over a hundred yards, with courtyards and *androles* (men's entertaining rooms) decorated with superb pebble mosaics; a vivid *Stag Hunt* is still in place, the violence of the scene in marked contrast to the exceptionally lovely floral border.

The **museum** has a room dedicated to the 16 *toumba* (mounds marking Neolithic settlements) found in the area: one, Mandalon, goes back to 4600 BC. There are other

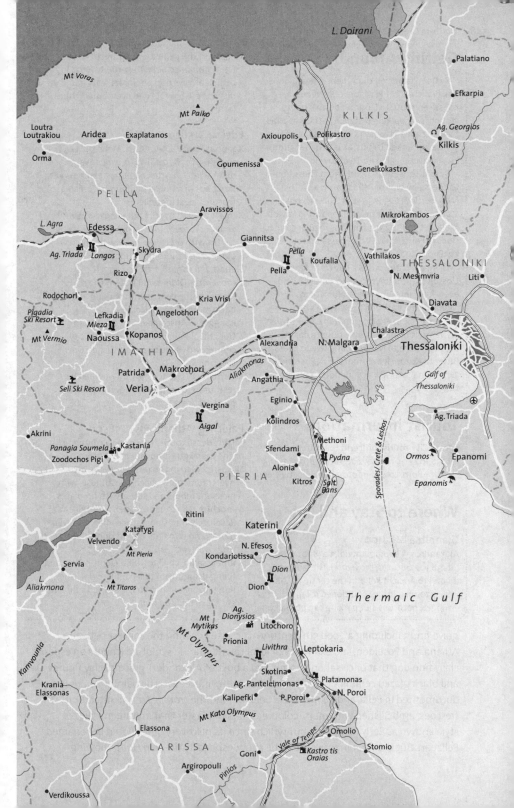

Getting Around

By train: trains on the Athens–Thessaloníki line branch off at Platí for Véria, Náoussa, Édessa en route to Flórina. Édessa's train station is in walking distance of the waterfall, t 238 102 3510. Náoussa's station is out of the centre but linked by bus; as is Véria's station, t 233 102 4444, 3km north of town.

By road: **buses** run hourly from Thessaloníki to Édessa by way of Pélla from 319 Monasteríou, t 231 059 5435. Édessa's bus station is in the centre at Filippou and Pávlou Melá St, t 238 102 3511, and has regular connections to Loutrá and Véria. Édessa **taxi** stand: t 238 102 3392.

There are three buses a day from Athens' Liosson station to Véria, t 210 525 2548, and every half hour from Thessaloníki, 319 Monastiríou, t 231 059 5404. Véria's bus station, t 233 102 2432, is on Trebesinas St, just off Venizélou, and has nine buses a day to Vergína, more to Náoussa, and five to Édessa. Buses to Kozáni leave from the KTEL station 3km from town; ask at your hotel. **Taxi** stand: t 233 106 2555.

Tourist Information

Édessa City tourist office: in the waterfall park, t 238 102 0300, www.edessacity.gr; open daily 10am–8pm. Lots of information on activities.

Where to Stay and Eat

Giannitsá ⊠ 58100

Alexandros, 5 Kougioumtzídi, t 238 101 4700, f 238 102 6800 (*C; moderate*). The closest hotel to ancient Pélla, in the centre of the busy town; big air-conditioned rooms, fridges, bathtubs, but parking can be tricky.

Vaggos. In the pedestrian centre, t 238 202 8523. *Simpatico* old family-run taverna in the centre, always popular for its tasty game dishes, roast meats and dishes made from local produce.

Édessa ⊠ 58200

Xenónas Varósi, 45–47 Arch. Meletíou, t 238 102 1865, f 238 102 8872 (*B; expensive*). In the quiet Varósi quarter, eight pastel rooms with iron beds in a house built in 1818; breakfast features local ingredients.

Xenia, t 238 102 9706, f 238 102 9708, www.xenia-edessas.gr (*B; expensive*). Near the centre with pretty views, now under new owners and thoroughly updated.

Elena, t 238 10 3218, f 238 102 3951 (*D; moderate*). Older hotel just off the main square in the centre, with parking at the back; rooms have balconies.

Passaggio, 11 Arisotelous St, t 238 102 4000. Delightful Italian restaurant in the city centre, with delicious pasta dishes. *Open eves only*.

Katarraktes, t 238 102 3101. City-owned bar-restaurant over the falls; lovely views, fair prices, fat cats.

Paléo Ag. Athanásios ⊠ 58500

The Édessa tourist office has a complete list of the many guest houses in the area.

Lithos, t 238 103 1996 (*expensive*). An attractive, traditionally styled guesthouse, with pleasant rooms and suites with fireplaces.

Metochi, t 238 103 1890 (*expensive–moderate*). Resolutely traditional stone inn with seven rooms and two flats, built around a beautiful courtyard.

Kaimaktsalan, t 238 103 1882. Good, hearty and filling dishes from this border region: suckling pig, pork and cabbage, stuffed cabbage, etc. *Open daily all year*.

---

grave finds, including a good 5th-century Attic vase showing the contest between Athena and Poseidon, and examples of local talent: marble sculpture (there's an especially fine dog that once sat on a tomb, and a bust of Alexander), graceful clay figures and black glazed ceramics prettily decorated with vine leaves. The painter Zeuxis is documented in Pella, and he may have been behind the *trompe l'œil* architectural frescoes, embellished with multi-coloured coats of plaster that imitate marble – a style known as Early Pompeian, but which since its discovery here should be renamed Pellaean. But the floor mosaics steal the show, especially the *Lion Hunt*, showing

Náoussa and Around ✉ 59200

Vermion, t 233 202 9311, **f** 233 202 9311, *deth@nao.forthnet.gr* (*expensive*). Large city-run hotel and restaurant just 2km from the centre in a lovely setting in Ag. Nikólaos park. Guests can use all the municipal sports facilities. The restaurant is good, too, and famous for its fresh trout.

Ampelonas Valtadrou, Ag. Nikólaos, **t** 233 205 2300, **f** 233 202 1540, *www.hotel-ampelonas.gr* (*expensive*). Owned by local wine-producers, bright airy rooms and suites and access to the city's indoor pool, tennis, riding, etc.

Hayati (Χαγιατι), Ethnikis Anistasi (100m from the main square), **t** 233 205 2120, **f** 233 205 2121, *hayati@mail.gr* (*expensive*). A classy *xenónas* with big rooms, beautiful bathrooms and a pleasant bar downstairs. Delicious breakfast. Try to get a room in the back, as the street can be noisy.

Vila Anthemia, 1km from Aristotle's School by Kopanós, **t** 233 204 3480, **f** 233 204 2808 (*expensive–moderate*). A newish *xenónas* bungalow style, with air-conditioned rooms, pool, bar in the kiwi orchards, with views over Mount Vérmio; quiet guaranteed.

Grameni Highland Camping, 15km above Náoussa on Mt Vérmio, **t** 233 204 9271. Small campsite with a taverna and mini market.

Inomagiremata, 1 Stefanou Dragoumi, **t** 233 202 3576 (around €15). In the centre of Náoussa, a great place to try local cuisine, lovingly prepared, to go with a bottle of Náoussa wine. *Closed Mon.*

Taverna Arapitsa, 3 Dimokratias St, by the bridge, **t** 233 202 3068. A charming location on the river bank, especially in summer. Lots of good *mezédes*. *Open eves only.*

Boutari, south of Kopanós in Stenímachos, **t** 233 204 2678. If you ring in advance, you can not only have a wine tour, but lunch with dishes built around Boutari's wines. There are three menus to choose from, ranging from €11–22. *Open Mon–Fri.*

Véria ✉ 59100

Makedonía, 50 Kontogeorgáki St, **t** 233 106 6902, **f** 233 102 7900 (*B; expensive*). Smart modern hotel on the edge of the old town, a favourite of local businessmen.

Veria, 6.5km along the Náoussa road, **t** 233 109 3112, **f** 233 109 3556 (*C; low expensive*). New comfortable air-conditioned hotel in a garden setting with a large pool.

Villa Eliá, 16 Eliás St, **t** 233 102 6800 (*low expensive*). Old Greek provincial design near the park and belvedere, with air-conditioning, smack in the centre; parking fairly easy.

Verói, Plateía Orologíou (Raktivan), **t** 233 102 2866, **f** 233 102 7923 (*moderate*). A bit basic but conveniently located, at the bottom of Mitropóleos St.

Petrino, 11 P. Ioakím, **t** 233 107 4110, in the old town. In a pretty old mansion, where you can dine on 'stuffed chicken chest with mushroom sauce' and other Francohellenic dishes; around €18. *Closed Mon.*

Erateinon, opposite on Angélon St, **t** 233 107 2571. The prettiest café-bar in the city, in a handsome old courtyard. *Open till 2am.*

Vergína ✉ 59 100

Pension Vergina, **t** 233 109 2510 (*moderate–inexpensive*). Simple but friendly in an overgrown house, with a monopoly on local beds.

Filippion, **t** 233 109 2892. The place to dine *après* tombs, and equally full of surprises, especially out of season when you can dine on pheasant and boar, and even crocodile. In summer it's more predictable. *Closed Sun and Mon eves.*

Alexander and his companion Kraterus in Susa, when Kraterus saved Alexander's life; note how use of various sized pebbles and lead strips lend the work its dynamic volume. Others show a rare *Female Centaur*, the *Abduction of Helen by Theseus*, with a powerful quadriga of rearing horses, and a rather girlish *Dionysos Riding a Panther*.

Around Pélla: Giannitsá

Industrial and commercial **Giannitsá**, the big town near Pélla, is one of those intense bits of urbanity that dot an otherwise very rural landscape; at night, when everyone is out and about, you may as well be in Manhattan. Few tourists venture here; a dilapidated mosque is all that recalls that this was a holy Turkish town in its day. The battle of Giannitsá, which won Macedonia for Greece in 1912, is celebrated with the 'Black Statue' in the centre, by Gregorios Zevgolis.

Édessa: the Castle of Waters

The Byzantines called Édessa 'the god-defended castle of Vodena' (its Slavic name, meaning 'waters'). Waters is no exaggeration: streams lined with plane trees and cafés gurgle through town, culminating in a bosquey park over a 78ft **waterfall** (*katarráktes*), unique in Greece, plummeting down through the trees and maidenhair ferns before a gargantuan pipe carries it all away. The rights to the thundering waters, which were once voluminous enough to run textile, wheat and sesame mills, were sold to the electric company in 1954, and by 1962 the mills were out of business. Mostly dating from the mid-19th century, the mills are now being converted into an 'open air water museum'; one holds a little **aquarium** (*open Wed–Mon 10–2 and 6–10; adm*). Glass lifts descend to Greece's only **hemp factory** (*kannavourgeío*), with its original machinery intact, soon to become a museum on water power. There's a **little waterfall** just off Dimokratias Street and if you follow the stream up from here you'll come to **Kiouprí**, a park with a **Roman bridge**. To the south, the pretty **Yeni Mosque** is the only one still standing, and holds a never-open archaeology museum. Another Turkish legacy is carpet-making, which is still going strong.

Varósi, Édessa's old Christian quarter, is just south of the waterfall park, around the highest edge of the bluff. Before Édessa became an industrial centre, it all looked like this; Edward Lear wrote the city was 'difficult to match in beauty.' A nest of resistance in the war, most of it was torched by the Germans, and what remains is being fixed up in an EU pilot plan. Here you'll find a little **Folklore Museum** (*24 Makedonomáchon St, t 238 102 8787; open Tues–Sun 10–6*), a girls' school of 1877, the **Parthenagogeío**, now used for art exhibits, and the **Psilos Vrachos** 'High Rock' café with magnificent views. Two churches here, **Ag. Petrou and Pavlou** and the 14th-century **Koímisis tis Theotókou**, re-use columns from the acropolis of ancient Édessa, which was enclosed in a triangle of walls that incorporated the waterfall. A path from Varósi leads down to lower ancient Édessa at **Longos** (*t 238 102 5261; open Tues–Sun 10–7; free*), which you can also reach by car off the Thessaloníki road. It reached its peak in Hellenistic and Roman times, and has walls standing 20ft high in places, and a colonnaded main street. Part of the temple of a local goddess called Mas has survived with inscriptions related to the freeing of slaves, which seems to have been her speciality. In Byzantine times Longos was abandoned for the safety of the acropolis; much of the old stone went into the adjacent 19th-century monastery of **Ag. Triáda**.

Around Édessa

Just past the train station in Édessa, a narrow road winds up 21km to a plateau of red pepper and tobacco fields, where **Aridéa** is the main town. The frontier to the

Macedonian Tombs

No one will never know for sure, but it seems that the Macedonian élite at the end of the Classical age turned to Plato when designing their last resting places. In the *Laws*, he describes the tombs for his Custodians of Law: 'Their tomb shall be constructed underground, in the form of an oblong vault of poros stone, as long lasting as possible, and fitted with couches of stone set side by side; in this when they have laid him who is gone to rest, they shall make a mound in a circle round it and plant thereon a grove of trees, save only at one extremity, so that at that point the tomb may for all time admit enlargement.' And so the Macedonians built, with simple or elaborate house or temple façades (no two are alike) on their underground tombs, closed by a marble door on metal hinges. Most had two vaulted chambers: an antechamber in the front, sometimes with a marble throne, and a tomb chamber in the back, with marble banquet couches for the deceased (although bodies were cremated on pyres just outside the tombs and placed in urns) and tables for offerings. Where they varied from Plato is in the frescoes they lavished on the walls, in vibrant reds, blues, pinks, greens, violets and blacks. Favourite subjects were garlands, hunting and battle scenes, architectural features, the myth of Persephone and portraits – the best examples of Classical and Hellenistic Greek painting.

north is marked by the Vóras Mountains, but the prettiest places are west of Aridéa. One is **Loutrá**, a funny old down-at-heel spa (with a hot outdoor pool great for winter dips) in a lovely glen shaded by plane tree groves; there's a beautiful 9km path up the canyon along a rushing stream. **Órma** just south is the base for walks in the dense **Mávros Dássos** (Black Forest) and for the scenic mountain road to the **Vóras Ski Centre** (or Kaimaktsalán), the highest in Greece (*t 238 108 2169; open Dec–early May*). It has given a new lease of life to the nearest village, **Paléo Ag. Athanásios**, classed a 'traditional settlement' where many old houses have been converted into inns. Another old village, Panagítsa (east, on the far side of 'new' Ag. Athanásios) has, thanks to its updraughts, found a new life as well as Greece's most important hanggliding and lighter-than-air centre. To continue west, *see* pp.564–7.

Lefkádia (Ancient Mieza)

South of Édessa, Lefkádia lies on the edge of Homer's 'lovely Emathia', the rich plain now densely planted with peach and apple orchards, a gorgeous frilly sight in spring before the blue backdrop of Mount Vérmio. The precise location of Mieza, the ancient city in these parts, is still a mystery, but bits of it keep cropping up in the orchards in a triangle between Lefkádia, Kopanós and Náoussa, most prominently a little Hellenistic **theatre** (signposted) and four Macedonian tombs, three of which can be visited. Signs point to the **Tomb of Judgement**, where the guardian is based (*t 233 204 1121; open Tues–Sun 8.30–3*). Now protected by a concrete hanger, this is the largest Macedonian tomb (28ft high) and it reeks of new wealth, probably acquired by the occupant's campaigning with Alexander. The façade was given the works: four Doric half columns decorate the lower zone, with figures of the dead man, Hermes Psychopompos, and the judges of the dead, Aeacus and Rhadamanthys. Above, metopes showed the Centaurs and Lapiths; the next register has a frescoed frieze in stucco relief of Macedonians fighting the Persians, above that an Ionic colonnade, with fake doors between the columns; the pediment's frescoes are too faded to see.

From here the guardian will hop in your car or walk with you to the **Tomb of the Palmettes**, some 200m away. This was discovered in 1971 by grave robbers, although it had already been broken into in antiquity, through the roof. It has four Ionic columns, painted to resemble marble, under a pretty frieze of palmettes and lotus flowers highlighted in blue and red. Three windblown palmettes in deep relief stand proud on the pediment, which is frescoed with a reclining mature couple; the key in the man's hand suggests that he held an important office. The great marble door leaves and lock mechanism were discovered *in situ*, having fallen in. The ceiling in the antechamber is painted with a charming pattern of stylized palmettes and waterlilies on a sky blue background, perhaps a reference to Lake Acheron in the Underworld.

The third tomb, the 2nd-century BC **Tomb of Lyson and Kallikles**, is a few minutes' drive away in a farmer's field. In order to preserve its colours it has been left in its mound, so entrance (not for the stout) is through a hatch in the roof and an iron ladder. The tomb was used by several generations of the descendants of Lyson and Kallikles, whose ashes were laid in 22 niches, husbands on top, wives on the bottom. The painted decoration almost seems new: a garland of pomegranates and ribbons links painted columns on the four walls, and *trompe l'œil* weapons look as if they were hanging on nails or sitting on a shelf. The tiny antechamber is painted with a snake by an altar. It's a funny old place, and can get claustrophobic after a few minutes. In more than one case, Macedonian tombs have been found with skeletons intact – of would-be robbers who couldn't escape.

Aristotle's School (the Nymphaion)

In late 343 BC Philip II invited Aristotle, the most prominent philosopher in Greece and son of a Macedonian court physician, to tutor his 13-year-old son Alexander and his contemporaries far from the court intrigues at Pélla, in Mieza's **Sanctuary of the Nymphs** (*signposted from the centre of Kopanós, on the Náoussa road, open daylight hours*). Identified by descriptions left by Plutarch, it is an idyllic place, set on a ledge above a spring. The three natural caves may have served as dormitories; the square cut walls were the back of a stoa. For nearly three years Aristotle taught natural sciences, maths, philosophy and poetry on these 'shaded walks' and made it his task to mould Alexander into a new Achilles, giving his pupil an annotated copy of the *Iliad* that he always kept by his side. The philosopher's spirit of inquiry may also have rubbed off, in the keen interest Alexander took in the geography and customs of his conquests. Many have speculated why Aristotle never mentioned Alexander in his writings; it may have been personal (he had Aristotle's nephew put to death on suspicion of treason), but it may also have been his disregard for some of Aristotle's dearest precepts, most notably that non-Greek 'barbarians' should be treated as slaves – to the extent that he compelled his officers to marry Persians, just as he married Roxane.

Náoussa

Just above Lefkádia, Náoussa enjoys a beguiling setting on the slopes of Mount Vérmio, overlooking orchards and the vineyards that yield its excellent red wines. The town has a few streets of old houses, but its setting and climate are the main attractions; it is a favourite resort for basketball and football teams in training, and is a good place to go for carnival, when two masked figures, Genítsari and Boúles, lead the Dionysian revels. **Ag. Nikólaos**, 2km away on the Arapitsa river, is a pretty oasis, where springs bubble under plane trees. Roads hairpin up deeply forested **Mount Vérmio**, where in autumn russet and gold are woven in the green. On top are two well-equipped ski centres: **3–5 Pigádia**, 16km northwest (*t 233 204 4981*), which also has cross-country trails, and the National Ski Centre at **Séli**, 20km southwest (*t 233 104 9226*); if you're not in a hurry, the latter makes a scenic route to Véria.

Véria (Βεροια)

Under Mount Vérmio, on a tributary of the Aliákmonas river, Véria was an important city in ancient Macedonia. In myth, King Midas' gardens were here 'where roses grow wild – wonderful blooms, with sixty petals each, and sweeter smelling than any others in the world'. One day his gardeners found Dionysos' tutor Silenus under the roses, sleeping off too much wine. When Midas safely delivered Silenus back to

Dionysos, the god offered him a wish; he asked that all he touched turned to gold, and nearly died of thirst and starvation before Dionysos told him to go east to the Pactolus river and wash it off. Midas stayed in the east to become the heir to the childless Phrygian King Gordius (tier of the famous Gordian knot cut by Alexander), leaving Macedonia to be occupied by the Dorian heirs of Makedon.

In historical times, Véria was the cradle of the Antigonides, Macedonia's last ruling dynasty, and was famous for games held in honour of Alexander. Véria (the Berea of the Bible) also had an important Jewish community; Acts VII tells how St Paul and Silas came here and noted that the local Jews 'were more noble than those in Thessaloníki...they searched the scriptures daily.' Under the Byzantines, it became the most important city in the region after Thessaloníki, nicknamed 'Little Jerusalem' for its 72 churches, many of which were provincial versions of churches of Constantinople; today some 48 have survived, 40 with frescoes.

It's easy to get lost in Véria, although you're never far from the main streets, Mitropóleos and Venizélou. These meet at a Y-shaped angle with Eliás Street, which leads to the garden belvedere **Eliá**, with a café and views east across the Imathian plain. Aníxeos St follows the gardens to the **Archaeological Museum** at No. 47 (*t 233 102 4972; open Tues–Sun 8.30–3*), where a giant Medusa head (formerly embedded in the walls, to scare off attackers) now greets visitors. Bronze funerary vases, a handsome 2nd-century AD bust of the river god Olganos, a table support showing the rape of Ganymede and gold jewellery are the highlights; stacks of Roman steles and sculpture litter the garden. There are plans to display artefacts from Néa Nikomédia, one of the oldest Neolithic farming settlements ever found in Europe (7th millennium BC) – it had walls and what seems to have been a palace, as at Sésklo (*see* pp.32 and 488).

Mitropóleos Street was a branch of the **Via Egnatía**; the deeply grooved paving stones, discovered in 1997, await their next chariot. **Christoú** (*open Tues–Sun 8.30–3*), at the lower end of the street, is Véria's most important church, beautifully frescoed in 1315 with the only signed work by Geórgios Kalliérges of Thessaly, an elegant painter of saints and angels, although someone else painted the curious scene under the porch, of a river and men hugging each other, wearing flying saucers halos. Many of Véria's other Byzantine churches (several originally camouflaged in houses, hidden from pesky Turkish officials) are tucked behind Mitropóleos Street in the **Kyriótissa** quarter, where old houses have been converted into restaurants, cafés and clubs. Be sure to walk down the steps to see the Roman-Byzantine **walls** along Thomaídou Street, supporting rickety old houses and balconies. Véria's brand new **Byzantine Museum** is here in a restored flour mill (*t 233 102 5847; open Tues–Sun 8.30–3; free*). The art (a pretty mosaic floor) goes back to the 5th century, and the good icon collection includes a *Virgin Hodgetria*, attributed to Kalliérges. Near the top of Kyriótissa, Loutrá Street is named for its well-preserved **Ottoman baths** (*no admission*).

On the other side of Mitropóleos Street, little shops and the market take care of business in Véria; in their midst stands the **Old Cathedral**, built in the 5th century, with a handsome inlaid apse. Busy Plateía Orologíou, at the top of Mitropóleos, was the acropolis; towards the river the Jewish **Barbouta quarter** preserves a 19th-century synagogue and 18th- and 19th-century mansions. On the other side of the square,

Bótsari St leads shortly past a mosque, near the **Bema of St Paul**, set up in 1961 to mark the spot where the Apostle preached.

Vergína and the Royal Tombs of Aigai

East of Véria, past the dam over the Aliákmonas river and a dozen fruit stands, the road rises into the gentle foothills of Mount Pieria to a village created by 1922 refugees. One hill had some old stones that the locals said was the 'little palace' of a certain queen Vergína, who gave her name to the village. In the 1860s, the French began excavations on the palace and found a Macedonian tomb, but wars and troubles prevented any further investigations until 1937, when it became one of the first projects of the new University of Thessaloníki. War stopped work again until 1959 when Manólis Andrónikos returned to the site. Convinced by NGL Hammond's theory that Vergína was ancient Aigai, the sacred capital of Macedonia, he set to work on the Great Tumulus, the largest in Greece at 360ft in diameter. Five seasons of excavations showed that the clay and gravel of the tumulus had fragments of damaged funerary steles from 300–250 BC – which slotted in with the historical fact that Galatian mercenaries of King Pyrrhus, left to guard Aigai in 274 BC, had plundered its cemetery. And in 1977–8 Andrónikos found, under all the rubble, what he had sought: the royal tombs. What he hadn't expected was to find one unplundered, with the fabulous treasure and ashes of Philip II – confirmed by the forensic reconstruction of the skull showing the horrific eye wound he suffered at Methóni.

History and Murder

A vast **Iron Age cemetery** with hundreds of tumuli shows that Aigai was inhabited in the 11th century BC by a Central European people; one curious find was a triple double-headed axe. King Perdiccas, the founder of the Argead dynasty, made it his capital, and even after Archelaos built Pélla, Aigai retained its importance, especially as a royal burial ground; a saying warned that if a king were buried elsewhere the dynasty would end (proved correct when Alexander was buried in Egypt). In 336 BC, when Philip II was at the height of his fortunes and had already sent an expeditionary force into Asia, he invited his nobles and representatives of the Greek city-states to attend the wedding of his daughter Cleopatra (Alexander's sister) to her maternal uncle. It was a magnificent ceremony, designed to impress the Greeks, and after the wedding Philip invited everyone to a ceremony at Aigai's theatre, which he planned as a send-off to his conquest of Persia. Signs for the latter were auspicious: there had been double poisonings in the Persian royal family, the Greeks in Asia Minor were ripe to revolt and the Delphic oracle had told him 'Wreathed is the bull; the end is near, the sacrificer is at hand.' Philip, of course, interpreted the 'bull' as the king of Persia.

The **theatre** has been found under the palace, just past the village (*open daily 8am–7pm; adm*). Only one row of seats survives, but try to imagine the bowl filled with dignitaries in the cool of a summer's dawn. First, splendid statues of the Olympian gods are carried in in a solemn procession, followed by what may have been a surprise, a statue of Philip himself, enthroned as a 13th god (a conceit later adopted by the Roman emperors). Then his 20-year-old son Alexander and new son-in-law, Alexander the Lyncestian, entered the theatre, just before Philip was to enter, alone. Instead – a horrible shout, as Philip's bodyguard Pausanias stabs him to death. In the confusion Pausanias almost got away to the waiting horses before he was killed. Conspiracy theories began immediately, many pointing to Alexander's mother, Philip's estranged wife Olympias, although the only contemporary account to survive, by Aristotle, says a tawdry sexual humiliation was the motive. After the murder, Alexander the Lyncestian stood beside Alexander in the theatre to nominate him as successor, and the assembled Macedonians raised their shields and beat them with their spears, to signify their accord.

The **City of Aigai** extended to the north of the theatre; so far a pair of sanctuaries near the theatre have come to light, one to Cybele and one to Euclia. A track leads up to the **Palace**, on a commanding height guarded by a big oak; 350ft long, it had a triple gateway and large peristyle courtyard that may have been a secret garden; the banquet hall still has a superb floral pebble mosaic. This palace was probably built by Antigonas Gonatas (320–240 BC); where earlier kings may have lived no one knows. Along the road back to Vergína you can have a look at the **Rhomaios Tomb** (sign-posted 'Macedonian tomb') named after its discoverer; a royal tomb, it has a pretty Ionic façade and an impressive marble throne, over 6ft high and carved with sphinxes. The nearby **Tomb of Eurydice** is the oldest Macedonian tomb found so far (*c.* 340 BC). It too contained a marble throne, painted with the *Rape of Persephone*, set before a delightful *trompe l'œil* façade in coloured plaster with four Ionic columns; its date and splendour suggest it was the tomb of Philip II's mother.

The Great Tumulus (Vergína Museum)

t 233 109 2347; open Tues–Sun 8am–7pm, Mon 12–7; adm exp. Cars are banned from the street in front, but there's a big car park 100m away.

In 1998, the Great Tumulus, now wearing a neat grass crewcut, was arranged as the most spectacular new museum in Greece. Here the bright light of day is left behind for the atmospheric penumbra of the tomb, where golden treasures glow magically, just out of reach (thanks to fibre lighting in almost invisible cases). Ideally, start your visit with the film shown to the left of the entrance, which puts all in perspective.

Manólis Andronikos discovered four tombs in the big mound. One was next to a heröon, built for the worship of Philip, but destroyed when the tumulus was built. The second, the **Tomb of Persephone**, takes its name from the finest ancient wall painting to come down to us, a frieze of the *Rape of Persephone* attributed to Nikomachos, a painter famous for his speedy work, who captured motion with quick brushstrokes, subtle colours and an unerring line – Hades, sceptre in one hand and the despairing Persephone in the other, leaps into his chariot, drapery flapping, while the maiden's companion crouches in fear and Hermes assists Hades; Demeter on her 'Mirthless Rock' and the three Fates are much fainter. This tomb may well have belonged to King Antigonas Gonatas, who may have ordered the building of the enormous tumulus to protect it after the sacrilegious depredations of the Galatians – only it didn't work, because the tomb was plundered in antiquity.

It did, however, distract robbers from the **Tomb of King Philip II**, its façade decorated with a faded but excellent frieze of Alexander hunting lions. 'In the funeral which Alexander arranged for his father, in accordance with tradition, the magnificence of the ceremony surpassed all expectation,' wrote Diodorus Siculus. The treasure he buried with Philip is certainly breathtaking. A gold chest emblazoned with the star of Vergina held the king's remains and a superb gold wreath with 313 oak leaves and 68 acorns; there's an exquisitely worked gold and ivory shield and other armour, silver and bronze vessels and a magnificent chryselephantine burial couch; among the delicate surviving ivories are portraits of Philip, Olympias and Alexander. The tomb's antechamber yielded a smaller gold chest containing burnt bones, remnants of gold and purple cloth, a gold wreath of myrtle and a splendid diadem; these belonged to one of Philip's wives, probably a Thracian, who committed suttee and so was specially honoured by Alexander. Others were cremated on top of Philip's tomb to placate his ghost: the crucified corpse of the assassin Pausanias, his sons and presumed co-conspirators, and even the getaway horses. Homer's heroes would have approved, but the average 4th-century BC Athenian would have found it all a bit *de trop*.

Next to it, the **Prince's Tomb** is believed, by virtue of the age of its occupant and wealth of its fittings, to have belonged to Alexander IV – the 13-year-old son of Alexander the Great, who was assassinated with his mother Roxane in 323 BC on the orders of Cassander. A decorative red, blue and white frieze in the antechamber shows a chariot race. The burial was in a silver hydra with a gold wreath around its shoulder; a gold-plated collar and ivory miniatures, including a remarkable Dionysos and Ariadne following Pan, were among the offerings.

Western (Upper) Macedonia

Mountainous Upper Macedonia is an often strikingly beautiful corner of Greece, but not one that ever makes it on tourist posters of Aegean daydreams. Parts of it could be in the Scottish Highlands; bears live here and one of the biggest industries is fur coats. The names of its ancient kingdoms – Orestis, Tymphaia, Lyncestis, Elimeia, Eordaia and Pelagonia – are not exactly household names. By the 5th century BC, they were allied to lowland Macedonia; by 358 BC they had one king and his name was Philip II. Although Upper Macedonia saw a bit of history during the medieval incursions of the Bulgarians and Normans, its remoteness enabled merchants in the towns of Kozáni, Siátista and Kastoriá to amass fortunes in Central Europe without much interference from the Ottomans. Their old way of life began to change under Ali Pasha of neighbouring Épirus and vanished in the turmoil of the 20th century, culminating in 1947–49 when Upper Macedonia became the last bitter battleground of the Civil War. Besides the Greeks and Slavs, there are quite a few Vlachs (presumed descendants of the ancient Romans in Dacia – modern Romania), many of whom still follow their traditional pastoral vocation in the mountains.

Getting There and Around

By air: there are several flights a week from Athens to Kozáni (Olympic Airways, **t** 246 103 6463) and Kastoriá (15 Megálou Alexándrou, **t** 246 702 4648), although note that neither town has a car hire office.

By train: four trains a day from Thessaloníki go to Kozáni (**t** 246 103 4536).

By bus: buses from Athens' Kifíssou station run three times a day to Kastoriá (**t** 210 515 2548) and twice to Flórina (**t** 210 513 0427). Services are at least once daily between the major centres, but can be sparse in the countryside; Kozáni, **t** 246 103 4455, has hourly services to Thessaloníki, and two a day to Kalamáka and Ioánnina, four to Athens and six to Lárissa. Kastoriá bus station (**t** 246 708 3455) located by the sports ground, a short walk from Daváki Square, has frequent buses to Thessaloníki, usually via Édessa, and one a day each to Kozáni and Flórina.

Tourist Information

Kastoriá: Ioustriarou St, just off Plateía Daváki, **t/f** 246 702 6777.

Sport and Activities

Lake cruises: the *Kastoriá* goes out at noon and 6pm, mobile **t** 6932 002973; *Mavormori* goes out at 6.30pm, mobile **t** 6932 634244.

Contact the Kastoriá Yacht Club, **t** 246 702 8956, for information on boating, fishing or waterskiing.

Trekking Hellas, *www.trekkinghellas.gr*, offers walking and other excursions in the area. They have an office in Grevená at 3 Pindou St, **t/f** 246 208 2858.

Skiing: Kastoriá has a small resort on Mt Vitsi, at 5,909ft, **t** 246 702 4884.

Riding: Kentro Ipassias in Nymphaío, **t** 238 603 1132.

Where to Stay and Eat

Siátitsa ✉ 50300

Archontikó, **t** 246 502 1298, **f** 246 502 2835 (*C; moderate*). Attractive traditionally styled hotel with big balconies and a good restaurant, with grills on weekends.

Kastoriá ✉ 52100

It's always best to book, especially in May when the fur fair takes place.
Archonitkó Aléxiou Vérgoula, 14 Aidítras, **t** 246 702 3415, **f** 246 702 3676, *sfinas@otenet.gr* (*A; expensive*). A traditional mansion on the south side of town, with beautiful lake views, large rooms (some sleep four) and traditional furnishings, including fireplaces in some. The restaurant on the ground floor serves home-made continental breakfast and turns into a wine bar in the evening.

Heading southwest from Véria (*see* above) the scenic but busy E90 rises rapidly to the mountain village of **Kastania**, a woodsy resort built around the **Monastery of Panagía Soumelá**, 'the palladin of Asia Minor Greeks', founded in 1930 by Pontic refugees from Soumela. They installed their icon attributed to St Luke in a church with mosaics that offers a good idea of what a Byzantine church may have been like when new. Further up, take in a dizzy view over the Aliákmonas Valley from **Zoodóchos Pigí**, where shops sell *gýros* or soup to tired truckers before descending into lignite-mining and power plant country and its capital Kozáni.

Kozáni

Kozáni was settled by families from Kosdiani, Épirus, who in 1389 were the beneficiaries of a *firman* that put them under the protection of the Sultan's mother, so they paid no income tax, enjoyed complete freedom of religion and had no Turkish officials

Aeolis, 30 Ag. Athanasíou, t 246 702 1070, f 246 702 1086 (*A; expensive*). Small, elegant hotel in a lovely cream-coloured mansion, half way up the hill.

Kastoriá, 122 Níkis, t 246 702 9453, f 246 702 9500 (*B; expensive*). Right on the lake, on the north shore, with comfy rooms a 10min walk from the Plateía Daváki.

Tsamis, 4km south in Dispilió, t 246 708 5334, f 246 708 5777, *htsamis@otenet.gr* (*B; expensive*). Hotel vintage 1978 right on the lake, with pretty public spaces but rather plain rooms, although many have splendid views.

Venetoúla's House, 6 Ag. Theológos, t 246 702 2446 (*moderate*). Charming bed and breakfast in a traditional mansion, with a bar and en suite rooms; parking close by.

Filoxenia, Profítis Ilías, t 246 702 2162 (*moderate*). Rooms on the peninsula hill, with lovely views of the lake from its balconies.

To Krontiri, 13 Orestiados St, t 246 702 8358. Lovely and very popular place to eat on the south shore of the lake with outdoor tables, where local *mezédes* hold pride of place, from beef with plums to pickled cabbage. Count on €13 for a full meal.

Omonia, Plateía Omónia, t 246 702 3964. Great old-fashioned restaurant with old-fashioned prices in upper main square; delicious 'ready' dishes.

Kratergo, 19 Orestion St (by the north shore), t 246 702 9981. The former prison, now a *mezedopolion* where you can fill up on tasty

titbits. *Open weekdays eve only, weekends and hols all day*.

Hagiati, 8km south in Ambelókipi, t 246 708 5107. A local favourite for excellent grilled meats, served in the summer in a pretty garden. *Open eves and Sun lunch*.

Nymphaío ✉ 53078

Do ring ahead; some places may close on weekdays and weekends are very busy.

La Moára, t 238 603 1377 or 231 028 7626, f 231 028 740 (*luxury, but includes breakfast and dinner*). In 1990 Yiánnis Boutaris of the big wine clan converted an old stone watermill (*moára* in Vlach) into a lovely small hotel with views over the garden and mountains. Excellent meals prepared by hosts Anna and Stelios Zezios, accompanied by bottles from the vast wine cellar. *Closed July*.

Ta Linoúria, t 238 603 1133 or t 231 030 0050 (*expensive*). Handsome stone inn and restaurant, with lovely rooms and tasty bean soup and other local dishes.

Athená, t/f 238 601 1141 (*expensive*). Five attractively furnished rooms with lots of antiques and pretty views; delicious home-made breakfast included in the price.

Névesca, t 238 603 1442, f 238 603 1442 (*expensive*). At the bottom end of this category, a pleasant, village-run guesthouse and meals prepared with a Vlach touch. The restaurant doubles as the local coffeehouse, so it's a good place to find out what's going on.

---

in their midst. Thanks to these privileges, Kozáni became a major crafts centre, trading with Vienna, Budapest and Bucharest; one merchant, a certain Karayannis, was the great grandfather of conductor Herbert von Karajan. Today it's a prosperous little city, with bars that bop until dawn (especially around Gouvedariou Street).

Besides a bop, there is one reason to stop in Kozáni: the wonderful **Museum of History, Folk Life, and Natural History**, on I. Dragoúmi Street, halfway down the big hill (*t 246 103 0997; open 9–2 and 5.30–8; adm*); it covers six floors, and is in the throes of doubling in size. The ground floor has charming mechanical dioramas made by local boffins (photos attached); there are petrified trees, elephant fossils and nature's hiccups – a five-legged lamb, a goat with one head and two bodies, and an impressive mess of rope found in the stomach of a cud-crazed cow. Upstairs are 19th-century photos, costumes, Neolithic art, memorabilia from the wars and, at the top, beautiful rooms reconstructed from old mansions – one, belonging to a doctor, with intricate floral decoration and figures from Euclid's geometry. The **Archaeological Museum** nearby on Dimokratías Street (*t 246 103 3978*) has a small but choice collection of artefacts, including a unique 7th-century BC copper amulet from Apidéa.

South of Kozáni: Aianí and Lake Polifito

Saffron was first used in Greece by the Minoans, but today most of it is grown south of Kozáni in, appropriately enough, **Krókos** ('crocus'), where you can visit the saffron co-operative. From here the main road continues 20km south for **Aianí**, capital of the ancient Macedonian kingdom of Elimeia. Recent excavations of **ancient Aianí** (signposted at Megáli Ráchi) have revealed some surprises: that it was a major producer of matt-painted pottery in the Middle Helladic period (1900–1600 BC) and had close contacts with the Mycenaeans. Nor were the Upper Macedonian kingdoms as uncouth as previously thought: the oldest buildings date back to the early 5th century BC – a century before Philip II united Macedonia – and yielded the oldest Greek inscriptions yet found in the area. The **Royal Necropolis** is 700m away, and has impressive Archaic and Classical tombs in precincts that once had painted interiors, stone roofs and temple features. Finds in the new **Archaeology Museum** under the hill (*t 246 109 8800; open Tues–Sun 9–2, but ring ahead*) are also very much in the Greek orbit: beautiful Archaic ivory plaques, *kouroi*, lions, clay figurines with traces of paint, and a striking terracotta head from the 6th century BC called the '*kore* of Aianí', wearing heavy make-up and the blank, unsmiling stare of a modern fashion model.

Below Aianí, **Lake Polifito** is swollen by the dammed waters of the Aliákmonas river, although recent droughts have made it more like the Bonneville salt flats by summer's end. The road swoops over the lake on a curve of a bridge and joins the E65 to Lárissa, 4km from **Sérvia**. Sérvia was named for the Serbs who settled here in the 7th century under Emperor Heraclius to defend one of the most important passes into the heart of Greece. Their ruined **castle** overlooks vaguely anthropomorphic rocks in the gorge that are said to be the defenders, petrified when the castle was captured by the Turks in 1393. The path up to the castle passes the impressive ruin of the 11th-century basilica of Ag. Dimítrios. **Velvendó**, a large village further down the lake, is famous for its fruit and jams; 23km up from here, the little village of **Katafýgi**, on the wooded slopes of Mount Pieria, was the native village of the most famous modern Greek – Geórgios Zórbas, the original for Kazantzákis's *Zorba the Greek*.

West of Kozáni: Siátista and Grevená

From Kozáni, the E90 passes through a strikingly empty landscape as you approach the turn for **Siátista**, a town founded after the fall of Constantinople, under the barest, greyest limestone mountains in Greece. The Turks certainly didn't care for it, and left Siátista to its own devices. Merchants from across Macedonia took refuge here, and by the 18th century it was a wealthy fief sending caravans to Épirus, Vienna, Venice and Russia; like Kastoriá (*see* below) it produced furs and leather. Because of its isolation, brigands were always a problem and the surviving 18th-century **mansions** (*archontiká*) scattered around town had heavily fortified ground floors. Four of these have interiors from their long lost world, lavishly decorated with murals, wood carvings, stained glass and more; to arrange a visit, t 246 502 1253. The **Botanical Museum** in the former high school (*t 246 502 2805; open by appointment*) has palaeontology and butterfly collections as well as plants and flowers.

South of Siátista, the road forks south for nondescript **Grevená**, capital of a province that takes in the eastern Pindus range and its enchanting mountain scenery and beech forests. The road from Grevená south to Kalambáka is perhaps the most stunning approach to Metéora (*see* p.510), and to the west the green mountains are dotted with the summer settlements of Vlach shepherds. Aim for **Spílaio** with an impressive clifftop monastery of the Assumption (1633), then follow the signs down the blue **Venétikos river** (ideal for rafting) to the 18th-century **Portitsa bridge**, next to a gorge of sheer 650ft cliffs, at places only 18ft wide. A lovely road from Spílaio leads into the **Vália Cálda**, now a National Park (*see* p.438) and important habitat of the brown bear. An isolated village just to the north of it, **Avdélla**, was the birthplace of Yiánnis and Miltiadis Manakis, 'the Fathers of Balkan cinema', who shot their first film, the *Weaver Girls*, here in 1905. In **Tríkomo**, just south of Spílaio (as the crow flies, anyway), there's the 232ft single-span **Aziz Aga bridge** built when Alí Pasha improved the roads linking the Zagorachória to Thessaloníki. It is so big that a bell was hung over the arch to tinkle when the wind was up and warn that crossing was dangerous.

Kastoriá

Ringed by mountains reflected in the moody waters of its lake, Kastoriá is the most attractive city in Upper Macedonia, and one that has managed to both prosper and maintain its character. Traditional houses spill over the neck of a mallet-shaped peninsula, where cobbled lanes are crammed with grand mansions and Byzantine churches. The lake once had a considerable beaver population, who left their name (*kástoras*), and perhaps provided the impetus for the fur trade that made Kastoriá rich. Instead of beavers, the lake now supplies tasty perch; even when it freezes in winter, the locals go out after them in ice boats (*plaves*). Summer comes late here, and, although the water is unpolluted, it often wears a stunning coat of green slime. Rowing is another obsession: Kastoriá has one of the best clubs in Greece.

Ancient Keletro, in the kingdom of Orestis, the city was taken by the Bulgarians under Tsar Samuel in 990–1018, and in 1083 by Robert Guiscard and the Normans, in spite of 300 members of the Emperor's English Varangian Guard sent to guard it; the Serbs and Albanians took turns, too, before the Turks in 1385. Not long after, the local Jewish tailors acquired a reputation for matching scrap strips of pelts and sewing them seamlessly together. The Greeks learned from them, and now 90 per cent of all the world's furs made of strips are sewn in the 3,000 shops in Kastoriá, as well as a large percentage of the whole furs and 30 per cent of the leather piece work, a market that has boomed since the fall of the Iron Curtain (note the signs in Russian). Besides the countless shops, you can buy one at the permanent **Furs Exhibition** (Έκθεση Γουναρικων) off the Flórina Road (*t 246 702 7771; open Mon–Sat 9–5*).

All roads to Kastoriá converge on **Plateía Daváki**, midway between the two lakefronts, near the covered market and remains of the walls built under Justinian. To the

Kastoriá

Florina &
Furs Exhibition

To Lakeshore Drive
Moni Panagia Mavriotissa

Kastoria Lake

KORYTSAS

PLATEIA
MAKEDONIAMACHON

To
Argos Orestiko
GRAMMOU

3 SEPTEMVRIOU

Bus Station

Sports
Ground

PLATEIA
DAVAKI

DALIPI

AG. ATHANASIOU

FANEROMENIS

LEOFOROS NIKIS

CHRISTOPOULOU

MERACHIAS

Sapoutzis
Mansion

OLYMPIADOS

VARDAKI

Tsistsiara
Mansion

Ag. Anargyroi
Varlaam

Post Office

MAKEDONOMACHON

MITROPOLEOS

M. ALEXANDROU

Byzantine
Museum

PLATEIA
DEXAMENIS

Panagia
Koumbelidiki

MALENGANOU

Ag. Nikólaos
Kasnítsi

PLATEIA
OMONIA

KAPLANI

ELOUSIS

AG. MINA

Ag.
Stefanos

PINDOU

PHILOTOU

NOSTOMIOU

Kastoria Lake

PAPARESKA

PLATEIA
PAVLOS MELAS

Taxiarches
Mitropoleos

Ag. Athanasios

MANOLAKI

Ag. Anargyroi

KOSMA

OLYMPIOU

PAPANIKOLAOU

PAPAKONSTANTINOU

EVRAIDOS

PLATEIA
EMMANOUIL

Ag.
Apostoloi

ARCHOLOGOS

LAZOU

FEREIOU

DOLTSO

Archontiko Nazim

ORESTIADOS

PAPATHOMA

Folklore
Museum

ORESTIADOS

MAVRIOTISSAS

To Lakeshore Drive

N

north, boats bob by the fish market near leafy **Plateía Makedoniamachon**, which honours General Van Fleet, who led the American forces here in the last bitter battles of the Civil War. If you're driving, a one-way system takes you up Mitropóleos Street and circles around to Ag. Athanasíou Street; keep an eye peeled for the steep turn to the left to the top of the town, Plateía Dexamenis, site of the old Xenia hotel and the **Byzantine Museum** (*t 246 702 6781; open 8.30–3; free*), dedicated to Kastoriá's other claim to fame, its school of Byzantine painting, from the 12th century. Ask here about the keys to the city's churches; there are 54 of these, most of them little basilicas with rustically ornate brick and stone work. About half have frescoes.

Just south of the museum is one of the most striking churches, the 11th-century **Panagía Koumbelídiki** with its tall drum of a dome and 13th-century frescoes, with others from 1946 on the exterior. Just below in Plateía Omonía, **Ag. Nikólaos Kasnítsi** has vigorous 12th-century frescoes, including portraits of the donors, a magistrate and his wife. Manoláki Street descends from here to the 10th-century **Taxiárches Mitrópoleos**, in Plateía Pávlos Mélas; this has three aisles and unusual 15th-century portraits of the people buried inside, and a 13th-century Virgin and child; within are fragments of even older frescoes and others of 1395, signed by the monk Daniel. On the other side of the 19th-century cathedral is **Ag. Athanásios**, built by the Albanians during their brief tenure in Kastoriá (1380–85) and decorated with scenes of saints dressed in Byzantine finery. **Ag. Anárgyroi** to the east, below Plateía Emmanouil, has an excellent painted iconostasis.

This is the Doltso quarter, where cobbled lanes have mansions crowned with storks' nests; the **Archontikó Nazim** is especially charming (ask about visits at the tourist office). Another mansion, the Archontikó Nerantzi Aivazi on Lázou Street holds the **Folklore Museum** (*t 246 702 8603; open Mon–Sat 10–12 and 3–6*), containing reconstructed interiors of local mansions, costumes and an old fur workshop. Below you can follow the lake shore around Kastoriá's peninsula (*see* below). Returning towards the centre, **Ag. Apóstoloi**, a block above the folklore museum, has more good frescoes (1545). Further up, another dense cluster of churches includes two of Kastoriá's oldest: lofty 10th-century **Ag. Stéfanos** (on Elousis St) with decorative brick work, a women's gallery and sombre 10th-century frescoes, and even taller **Ag. Anárgyroi Várlaam**, founded by Basil the Bulgar Slayer in 1018, after an earlier church was destroyed by his army. Dedicated to Cosmas and Damian, the doctor saints, it has severe 11th-century frescoes in the narthex and others from a century later in the nave.

Descending to the north shore, look for two fine mansions on Christópoulou Street: the **Sapoutzis Mansion** and the recently restored **Tsistsiara Mansion**, a rare one with two wooden upper floors. Century-old plane trees rim the lake along Leofóros Níkis, at the start of the delightful **lake shore drive** that encircles the Kastoriá's peninsula; on Sundays the locals come here to walk, cycle, fish, and eat in the tavernas. On the way don't miss the **Moní Panagía Mavriótissa** (*open sunrise to sunset*), with expressive if not expertly drawn early 13th-century frescoes in the nave of the *Dormition of the Virgin* and the *Ascension*. The monastery may have been founded by emperor Alexis Comnenus in 1085, to mark the spot where he landed to boot out the Normans – note the two headless imperial portraits by the Tree of Jesse. There's a lively *Last Judgement* in the narthex, and in the chapel a wonderful *Last Supper* painted without a clue about perspective.

Around Kastoriá

You can also make a scenic 32km drive around the entire lake, a favourite haunt of frogs and ducks – and adders, in the undergrowth, so take care. There's a great view over the lake from **Apóskepos**, 10 minutes north on the Flórina road. South at **Dispilió**, a **Neolithic lake settlement** (*t 246 707 4289; open 7–1.30; adm*) of *c.* 5000 BC has been excavated, revealing a boat, jewellery and ceramics; some of the thatched huts on stilts have been reconstructed. There are other uncommonly old things to see in these parts, including a **petrified forest** (*Apolithoméno Dásos; t 246 708 4566; open 10–2 and 5–8; adm*) with trunks going back 15–20 million years at **Nóstimo**, southwest of Árgos Orestikó. Southwest of Kastoriá, **Omorphoklisiá**, 'beautiful church', is named for the 11th-century **Ag. Geórgios**. This houses a wooden statue in high relief of St George, brought here in the 1200s by two nuns from Ioánnina pulling a sled. Pilgrims press coins to the statue; if they stick, it's a sign that their prayers will be answered. In August, **Nestório** on the upper Aliákmonas river hosts an annual River Party with concerts that attract thousands of Greek and foreign campers. Nestório is the gateway for exploring the network of roads and paths on the east slopes of 8,267ft **Mount Grámmos**, the source of the Aliákmonas, on the border of Macedonia, Épirus and Albania; you can drive on a dirt road (but make sure you have a good map) through the splendid black pines of Barougas forest, past abandoned villages where people come to free camp by the streams.

East of Kastoriá, among the beech forests of Mount Vitsi, **Kleisoúra** was a flourishing Vlach village with a huge library before it suffered two 20th-century disasters, at the hands of the Turks in 1912 and the Germans in 1944; a sole survivor of the old village is the **Monastery of the Panagía** outside town, with a gorgeous gilt iconostasis. A bit further east, with grand views across to Mount Olympus, the traditional Vlach settlement of **Nymphaío** (formerly Neveska) was a silver- and gold-working centre until the 1929 stockmarket crash. Abandoned after the Civil War, the village has been restored as a fashionable weekend resort. A new museum in the 19th-century **Neveska House of Goldsmiths** (*t 238 103 1382; open Mon–Fri 10–2 and 5–8, Sun and Sat 10–2 and 3–8; adm*) has rare goldsmith's tools, murals, local furniture and costumes. In nearby Aetós, you can visit the **Arktoúros Bear Sanctuary**, t 238 604 1500, where rescued dancing bears live in a 50-acre fenced ravine, where they are unintrusively fed and cared for.

The Préspa Lakes and Flórina

The Prespa Lakes

To cross the last mountain pass in northwesternmost Greece is to descend into 'a giant and totally secluded cradle' of magical remoteness and stillness. Austere mountains surround two limpid sheets of water: Great Préspa, the largest lake in the Balkans, the liquid frontier between Greece, Albania and the FYROM, and Lesser Préspa, mostly Greek but with a tail poking into Albania. The three governments are not exactly chums, so it came as a surprise to many when their leaders met in October 2000 to designate Préspa an international park (a Balkan first) to preserve its fragile wetlands – the result of a decade of hard work by Geórgios Kastadorákis and Myrsini Malakou, founders in 1990 of the award-winning Society for the Protection of Préspa (SSP). The lakes are home to the world's largest colony of Dalmatian pelicans, as well as 260 other birds and 1,500 different plants. Although separated only by a spit of land, the lakes have diverse fish populations, including species unique to each.

While the wildlife flourishes in blissful ignorance of borders, the humans here have led complicated lives. At the end of the 9th century, Préspa belonged to the Western Bulgarian empire. When it was dissolved in 971, the son of the last emperor, Tsar Samuel, took refuge here, reorganized and made Préspa his base to seize much of Greece, until Emperor Basil II reconquered all the lost Byzantine territory (1018) and

Getting There and Around

Buses from Athens' Kifissou station run twice daily to Flórina (**t** 210 513 0427). Flórina's **train** station, **t** 238 502 2404, and **bus** station, **t** 238 502 2430, have several daily connections with Thessaloníki, and there are frequent buses to Kastoriá. Buses to the Préspa villages run only once a day to three times a week, depending on the season. Flórina **taxis: t** 238 502 2800. There are plans to start international cruises on Great Préspa Lake; check at the information office.

Tourist Information

Préspa Lakes Information Centre:
Ag. Germanós, **t** 238 505 1452; *open year round 9.30–2.30, closed hols*. They can arrange guided tours and accommodation.
Níki: frontier tourist office, **t** 238 609 2203.
Tourist police: t 238 505 1203

Where to Stay and Eat

Préspa Lakes ✉ 533077

Accommodation is simple and the lake fish is delicious; if it's on the menu, try *stifádo me grivádi*, a delicious stew made with onions and a fish that lives only here. Bring cash; the nearest banks/automatic tellers are in Flórina and no one takes credit cards.
Liakoto, in Lémos (by Ag. Germanós), **t** 238 505 1320, **f** 238 505 1205 (*expensive*). Intimate and stylish, the smartest place to stay by the lakes, with a lovely veranda and views.
Xenónas Ag. Germanós, **t** 238 505 1397, mobile **t** 6972 076654 (*moderate*). In a recently restored old stone house in the village

centre; rooms have little fireplaces and traditional furnishings. *Open all year.*
To Petrino, Ag. Germanós, **t** 238 505 1344 (*inexpensive*). Six rooms in an old stone house, run by the hospitable Thomai Tsikos.
Xenónas Ag. Achilliou, on Ag. Achíllios island, **t** 238 504 6601, **f** 238 504 6112 (*moderate*). Traditional, with breakfast and restaurant; a great place to hear yourself think.
Psarádes Hotel, Psarádes, **t** 238 504 6015 (*C; inexpensive*). Simple place by the water.
Syntrofia, Psarádes, **t** 238 504 6107 (*inexpensive*). Charming guesthouse and one of the best fish tavernas, right on the lake.
Women's Rural Tourism Cooperatives offer inexpensive accommodation. Contact them at Ag. Germanós, **t** 238 505 1329, or Psarádes, **t** 238 504 6015.

Pisodéri ✉ 53076

Modéstios, **t** 238 506 1345, **f** 238 504 5801 (*C; moderate*). Stone school building of 1903, converted into a guesthouse in a little village in the bosom of the mountains, midway between Flórina and Préspa.

Flórina ✉ 53100

Philippeon, 38 Ag. Paraskevís, **t** 238 502 23346, **f** 238 502 4477 (*B; expensive–moderate*). Flórina is surprisingly well endowed with B-class hotels. This is one of the nicest, on a hill on the edge of town, new and well kept, with a restaurant.
Hellinis, 31 Pávlou Méla, **t** 238 502 2671, **f** 238 502 2815 (*C; moderate*). Central, if a bit basic; the best bargain in town.
Olympos, 30 Mégas Alexandros. Authentic old *mageireío*, where good Greek fills are displayed in big pots and pans. *Open lunch only, closed Sun.*

put an end to Préspa's day in the sun. During the Frankish and Turkish periods, the utter remoteness of the place attracted monks and hermits. Life was never easy for the rest of the population, and the Civil War made it intolerable; most people simply left, moving into the Balkans or to Australia, to the extent that the government offered free empty houses and land to Vlachs just to have warm bodies on the frontier. Today the SPP is aiming to strike a delicate balance between the needs of humans and nature: encouraging organic farming, sound fishing practices, modest tourism (converting traditional buildings into guesthouses) and a revival of cattle rearing; Préspa's dwarf cows are needed to eat the reeds, to prevent them from taking over the lakes while leaving sufficient cover for the pelicans to nest. So far it all seems to be working; bird numbers are on the increase, and new jobs are keeping young people in the area. In August the Préspa Festival brings in big name performers, including the likes of Míkis Theodorákis; in winter locals flock to the ski centre at **Vigla Pisoderíou** (*t 238 502 9939; open weekends*) on the Flórina road.

Préspa's dozen friendly hamlets (pop. 1,300 in all, down from 13,000 a century ago) are an echo of the Greece of decades ago. All but one are on Lesser (or Mikró) Préspa, which has the best pelican watching. Isolated **Mikrolímni**, the first hamlet, has a charming fish taverna; **Ag. Germanós**, the biggest village and designated traditional settlement, is named for its 11th-century church, covered top to bottom with 18th-century frescoes. There are more frescoes, good expressive ones from the 16th century, in the otherwise nondescript chapel of **Ag. Nikólaos** near the top of nearby **Platí** (ask for the key in the village).

On the north end of the lake, **Ag. Achíllios Island** (pop.27) was linked to the mainland in 2000 by a pedestrian causeway, which hasn't spoiled its time warp, or threatened the ratio of 25 chickens per person. Yet back in the 10th century, this was the capital of Tsar Samuel. Like any medieval ruler he needed holy relics to get on the map, so he pinched the body of St Achíllios in Lárissa and installed him in the elegant **basilica of Ag. Achíllios**. Although sacked in 1072 by the Alemanni as they passed through, the church remained in use until the mid-15th century; one of the graves here yielded a rare piece of Byzantine gold cloth now in the museum in Thessaloníki. Folksy 15th-century frescoes decorate the church of **Ag. Geórgios** (again, you'll need to seek out the key). Back on the mainland, there's a beach nearby at Koúla, by the military post.

The only Greek village on Great Préspa Lake, **Psarádes**, is another traditional settlement, where boatmen offer Byzantine lake tours that take in the rock frescoes on the vertical cliffs and three 13th-century **hermitages** tucked in the steep cliffs; one, dedicated to Panagía Eleousa, is covered with pastel frescoes from 1410.

Flórina

Flórina is a pleasant little city of modest neoclassical-Art Deco-Macedonian buildings strung out along the duck-filled Sakoulévas river . Much of it post-dates the Civil War, when it was the target of EAM's last offensive in 1949; today, bitter feelings linger among the many Macedonian Slav speakers, who call the town Lerin, and who in 1995 founded their own political party, Rainbow, which has faced local harassment.

In ancient times Flórina was near the border of Eordaia and Lyncestis, the latter the proudest of Macedonia's highland kingdoms, whose rulers were descended from the Bacchiads, the royal family of Corinth (*see* pp.179–80). Philip II's mother was a Lyncestian, and her kinsmen Leonnatus, Alexander's Companion, was so feisty that he took camel-loads of sand to Persia so he could challenge anyone, any time, any where to a wrestling match. Flórina has a well- arranged **Archaeological Museum** by the train station (*t 238 502 8206; open Tues–Sun 8.30–3; free*), with finds from Armenochóri, home of a Neolithic acorn-eating people (5800 BC). Funeral steles, with robust provincial carvings, stress the importance of the horseman in Macedonian hero cults; later steles identify the mortal dead with the gods (young women and concubines with Aphrodite, merchants with Hermes, etc.). There are frescoes and items from the Byzantine churches at Préspa, and the first floor is devoted to a well-planned Hellenistic town by Pétres (no one is sure of its name) founded in the 3rd century BC as part of Antigonos Gonatas' settlement policy. Finds include a clay drinking horn in the shape of a young man's foot, a blob of blackened resin (used for wine-making?) and a little pot with a satyr's grinning face in the early Disney style. Another building by the station contains the local **art gallery** and workshop. Towards the centre, have a coffee in the historic **Kafeneíon Diethnés**, used as a setting by Theodóros Angelopoúlos in several of his films. Flórina also has a **Modern Art Museum**, founded in 1977 in a big pink house by the river at 103 Leof. Eleftherías, with a collection of 20th-century works (*but closed at the time of writing*).

Heading back east of here towards Édessa, you can visit **ancient Pétres**, 1.5km from the modern town, by little Lake Petrón. Next to this is much larger **Lake Vegorítida**, filled with trout and a rare fish, the *korigonos*. Its southwest shores are lined with the vineyards of **Amíndeo**; the beach at **Ag. Pantelémonas**, a handsome village of old stone houses, is a growing resort where the locals offer sunset fishing excursions.

East of Thessaloníki: Chalkidikí

Hanging from Macedonia like a giant paw, Chalkidikí has a history and spirit as distinctive as its geography. The paw's 'pad' is farmland, forest and mountain, while its three claws, softened with pines and sandy beaches, beckon with a come-hither look. The westernmost Kassándra peninsula, brash and overbuilt, is the summer

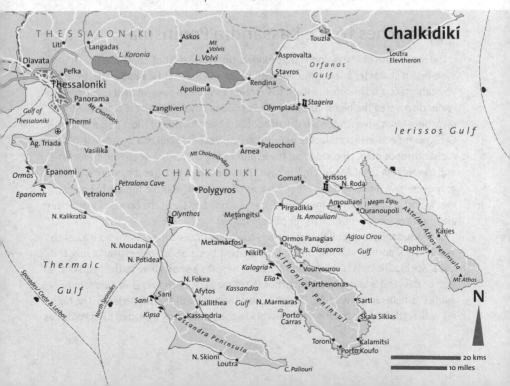

resort of half of Thessaloníki, Germany and Austria. The middle Sithonía peninsula is lovelier, less infested and classier. The eastern Akte peninsula, the most beautiful of all, is the way station to another world: Mount Athos, the last theocracy in the West.

Chalkidikí owes its name to 8th-century BC colonists from Chalkís, Évia, who, along with their land-hungry rivals from Eretria, founded the first Greek settlements along the coast. They intermarried with the local Thracian tribe, the Paeonians, and traded grain, timber, gold, slaves, and silver with southern Greece. After being conscripted into Xerxes' invading army, the Chalkidikians were compelled to join Athens and pay a crushing tax, the 'Thracian tribute' that left the door open to Spartan and Macedonian intrigue; when one colony, Potidea, rebelled in 432 BC, Athens besieged it, helping to ignite the Peloponnesian War. In the 390s, the 32 city states of Chalkidikí formed their own league under their aegis of their own capital Olynthos, a rare, progressive example of ancient Greek cooperation that excited the jealousy of neighbouring Apollonia and Acanthus, who found a pretext for Sparta to interfere and conquer. Weakened and subsequently caught in the meshes of Philip II, the cities turned to Athens for help, and Philip responded by destroying every last one. Depopulated, Chalkidikí slipped out of history until the 9th century, when the first monks came to Athos. Over the centuries, the emperors granted the rest of Chalkidikí to the monasteries as dependencies (*metóchia*) to support the holy men. Settlements grew up around their fortified towers and life carried on pretty much the same until 1923, when the *metóchia* were confiscated to provide land for the Asia Minor refugees, who built some 30 new towns on the promontory, most of them named after their old homes with a 'new' (*Néa*) in front.

Approaches to the Kassándra Peninsula

The road south of Thessaloníki that follows the west coast of Chalkidikí doesn't have much character but is trimmed with beaches. One is at **Néa Kalikrátia**; from here you can make a 14km detour inland to Petrálona, where in 1959 villagers searching for water discovered the beautiful stalactite **Petrálona Cave** (*t 237 307 1671; guided tours daily 9am–7pm, 5pm winter; adm*). Palaeontologically it's one of most important in Greece; embedded in a stalactite was a 700,000 year old skull of a 25–35-year-old Archanthropos man, who stood on the evolutionary ladder between *Homo erectus* and the Neanderthal. Models in the cave show how he lived. Like a modern Greek he may even have dined on *souvláki*: the traces of a million-year-old fire are the oldest ever found. If open, a small museum displays stone tools and the bones of giant bears and panthers who kept Archanthropos company.

Néa Moudanía, south by the crossroads to Kassándra, is a lively town with a beach and a handy port for slipping off to the islands; it hosts a Sardine Festival in July and has a waterpark for your own small fry. From here it's a short drive to the head of the Gulf of Kassándra and ancient **Olynthos** (*t 237 192 2148; open Tues–Sun 8am–7pm; adm*). Pre-hellenic for 'wild fig', Olynthos occupies a pair of flat topped hills. The higher hill was settled by Bottiaians from Imathia in the 7th century BC, when King Perdiccas

Getting There and Around

Buses from Thessaloníki (t 231 092 4444, *see* p.528) serve all of Chalkidikí, where the main bus stations are at Néa Moudaniá, t 237 302 1228 and Polýgyros, t 237 102 2309. In summer **hydrofoils** link Néa Moundaniá to Skiáthos and the other Sporades; for information, t 237 302 1172.

Tourist Information

Tourist police: Kassandría, t 237 402 3333; Polýgyros: t 237 102 3496. The website *www. halkidiki.com* has good coverage of the area.

Where to Stay and Eat

Chalkidikí has the plushest hotels in Northern Greece. For more listings, look at *www.halkidiki-hotels.gr*; for a preview of the many campsites, try *www.campsites.gr*.

Sáni (Kassándra) ✉ 63077

Sani Beach, t 237 403 1231, f 237 403 1292, *www.saniresort.gr* (*A; luxury*). Immaculately landscaped complex encompassing seven sandy beaches, a bird sanctuary and 1,600 acres of old pines: facilities include a beauty-fitness centre, Internet cafés and 15 pools, plus 10 private pools for the bungalows.

Áfytos (Kassándra) ✉ 63077

Petrino Suites, 700m from the sea, t 237 409 1635, f 237 409 2659 (*C; luxury–expensive*). Suites in 28 stone houses, with traditional furnishings, fireplaces and air-conditioning in a pretty setting with a pool. The hotel taverna serves tasty dishes (with lots of game in season) prepared in an outdoor wood oven. *Open all year.*

Blue Bay, 200m from the sea, t 237 409 1644, f 237 409 1646 (*D; expensive*). Warm and welcoming hotel in a quiet setting on the edge of town, with lovely views over the gulf. Pool and beach bar. *Open May–Sept.*

Soussourada, t 237 409 1594 (around €25). One of the best restaurants in Chalkidikí, serving refined nouvelle Greek cuisine with an emphasis on top quality ingredients. You won't find a wider choice of aged Greek cheeses and wines, brandies and cigars – the works. *Open May–mid Oct, eves only and weekend lunch.*

Nikíti and Beaches to the South (Sithonía) ✉ 63088

Danai Beach Resort, t 237 502 2310, f 237 502 2592, *www.danai-beach.gr* (*A; luxury*). A member of the Small Luxury Hotels of World club. Elegant bungalows most with sea views, jacuzzis, CD players and plenty of marble; the suites, some with private pools, are simply divine. Excellent breakfast buffet

conquered their homeland (*see* **History**). In 480 BC, Xerxes drafted them and their ships to his cause, but when the city rebelled the next year, the Persians destroyed it. In 432 BC, the Chalkidikians built a new Olynthos on the north hill, with 30,000 inhabitants, and made it the seat of the Olynthian Confederacy. Philip II courted it after it was fatally weakened by its Spartan overlords, but the relationship went sour in 349 BC, and he besieged it. In Athens, Demosthenes in his three Olynthiac speeches rallied the Athenians to its defence, but the wily Philip caused a diversion by attacking Évia and obliterated Olynthos before the Athenians arrived, leaving behind his calling card for archaeologists: arrowheads inscribed 'Philippos'.

Because it had lasted only 84 years, Olynthos is the best preserved example of a purely Classical city in Greece, laid out in a Hippodameian grid in blocks of ten houses, in two rows of five, with a channel between to take rain water from the roofs. Walls on rubble foundations were built with sound anti-seismic flexibility, their baked bricks strengthened with timber ties. Uniformity ended indoors, however, where householders arranged rooms as they pleased around stone-paved courtyards, each with their own cistern, family altar and pastas (portico), leading into the residential

and restaurant featuring organic ingredients. *Open April–Oct.*

Anthemus, Eliá Beach, t 237 507 2001, f 237 507 2201, *www.anthemus.gr* (*A; luxury, but half the price of the Danai*). On a private cove, with a pool in a garden setting, a modern complex ideal for families, with an airport shuttle and Internet café. *Open April–Oct.*

Virginia, Eliá Beach, t 237 502 2022, f 237 508 1283, *virginia@hal.forthnet.gr* (*C; luxury–expensive*). Family-run hotel and restaurant that has won prizes for its ecologically-sound management, down to the special anti-allergy cleaning systems. Car and bike hire available. *Open May–Oct.*

Elia Beach, Eliá Beach, t 237 508 1250, f 231 081 5257 (*C; expensive*). Studios with big verandas by the beach in a garden setting, good for families. *Open May–Oct.*

Néos Marmarás (Sithonía) ✉ 63081

For rooms, contact the rent rooms association, t/f 237 507 1158.

Meliton, Porto Carrás, t 237 507 1381, f 237 507 1502, *www.ellada.net/meliton/* (*A; luxury*). The height of 1970s resort design, a cross between Inca temple and cruise liner, with a huge range of facilities from open air movie theatre, 18-hole golf course, riding stable, tennis, diving school, and much more. There are two other hotels in the Porto Carras complex, the **Sithonía Beach** (with a casino)

and the more intimate **Village Inn**, on 10km of coast dotted with 34 sandy coves. *Open mid-April–Oct.*

Villa Karavitsi, t 237 507 2197, f 231 053 1545 (*C; expensive*). Modern stone buildings and characterful rooms in a garden setting by a pebble beach, serving great home-made breakfasts. *Open mid-April–mid-Oct.*

Kyrani Akti, on the beach road, t 237 507 1290 (*inexpensive*). Rooms and restaurant for a flavoursome bit of old Greece.

Ta Kymata, t 237 507 1371 (around €25). Excellent seafood restaurant with tables on the sands, overlooking the fishing boats, one of which belongs to the owner.

Parthenónas (Sithonía) ✉ 63081

Xenónas Parthenon, mobile t 6944 382384 (*A; moderate*). Lovely traditional rooms that sleep up to four; rates include a delicious home-made breakfast. *Open all year.*

Paul's, t 237 507 1349. A little oasis of a taverna at the end of the village, with beautiful views and light meals served on rustic tables. *Open May–Oct.*

Vourvouroú (Sithonía) ✉ 63078

Thalassokipos, t 237 503 1945, mobile t 697 706 4945 (*D; expensive–moderate*). Studios with balconies and lovely views.

Gorgona, t 237 509 1461. For tasty fresh fish on the beach.

area. *Androns* (men's banqueting rooms) were decorated with the oldest floor mosaics ever found, including one of Bellerophon on Pegasus attacking the Chimera. One house still has its bathtub. Of the Archaic era city on the south hill, recent excavations have revealed two avenues, the agora and the prytaneion.

The Kassándra Peninsula

Kassándra is technically an island, cut off at its narrow neck by a canal at **Néa Potídea**. Potidaea was Chalkidikí's one Corinthian colony – the settlers obviously felt at home on an isthmus – and it maintained a close relationship with its mother city, which encouraged it to revolt against Athens in 432 BC. A two-year siege ensued (Socrates was one of the hoplites, and was famous even then – for going barefoot on ice) before Athens prevailed and replaced its population with Athenians. Philip II snatched it from them and gave it to Olynthos to curry favour, then razed it. His son-in-law Cassander, king after Alexander, refounded the town as Kassandría. He dug the canal and made the city Macedonia's ship-building centre. You can see ruins of the great walls built out of ancient buildings under Justinian; they were last repaired by the Venetians in 1426 in a vain attempt to turn back the Turks.

Kassándra is the most fertile of Chalkidikí's prongs, and was the most prosperous until 1821 and the War of Independence, which Kassandrans enthusiastically joined, only to realize that they were hardly prepared to fight. They backpedalled, but the Pasha of Thessaloníki would have none of it and slaughtered them, demolishing their villages; for decades it was given over to shepherds. The road passes through flat lands to reach **Sáni** on the Thermaic Gulf, site of an ancient Eritrean colony and now one of Greece's top luxury hotels. The hinterland has thick pine forests and a billion bee hives; the 16th-century tower on the coast is typical of the ones built by the Athonite monasteries. A similar one guards **Néa Fókea** to the south, where the road crosses over to the east side of the peninsula. Next down the east coast, **Áfytos** (ancient Aphitis) is Kassándra's prettiest village, its traditional stone houses hugging the slope down to the beach. **Kallithéa**, next south, has a good white sandy beach adorned with the foundations of a 4th-century **Temple of Zeus Ammon**. This was one of the most important dedicated to the Egyptian deity in Greece, and has an unusual north-south orientation. Otherwise, Kallithéa sets the tone for the rest of the penin-sula – fast food and pop music clubs, heavily patronized by teenagers and large red people wearing money belts and little else. If you're not deterred, continue south for fine views over the Aegean from **Cape Palioúri** (or Kalogriá), or to soak in the hot springs at **Loutrá**, with an attractive beach under the cliffs. The nearby fishing village of **Néa Skióni** occupies the site of ancient Skioni, which was besieged by Athens in 423 BC for welcoming the Spartan general Brasidas; it resisted heroically, and when it fell the Athenians slaughtered every male.

Polýgyros and the Sithonía Peninsula

North of the cleft between the Kassándra and Sithonía peninsulas under Mount Cholómondas, Chalkidikí's capital **Polýgyros** replaces Apollonia, the same city that invited Sparta to Chalkidikí and caused so much grief. Its **Archaeological Museum** (*t 237 102 2148; open Tues–Sun 8.30–3*) is a good one; it has the treaty made between Philip and the Olynthos in 356 BC, and clay figurines from Acanthos that offer a glimpse into everyday life in the 4th century BC (kneading bread, washing up, bathing, but also riding giant ducks). There's a beautiful painted stone larnax from the late 6th century BC from Aphitis, and finds from Stageira.

The Sithonía peninsula offers most in the way of postcard visions of Chalkidikí – deeply wooded ravines ending in delectable coves, with pines running down to the white sand, lapped by a turquoise sea. All this begins in earnest at **Nikíti**, which had a Paleo-Christian predecessor, **Ag. Geórgios**, 2km away; here the 5th-century basilica of Bishop Sophronios has good mosaics and bits of fresco. After Nikíti, lovely beaches, one after another – **Ag. Ioánnis**, **Kalogriá**, **Spathiés** and **Eliá** – scallop the coast south to **Néos Marmarás**, a town founded by refugees from Marmaras and now a big jumbly resort village with a few fishing boats bobbing in the port. Sithonía's nightlife is concentrated on the surrounding coast road, but in the hills above, the traditional village of **Parthenónas**, immersed in quince and pomegranate groves, is a remnant of quieter days; from here you can gain the unpaved road that follows Sithonía's lofty backbone. South of Néos Marmarás, the vast **Porto Carrás** estates stretch from Mount Melíton to the shore. In 1965 shipowner John Carrás of Chíos founded this experimental farm producing organic olive oil and Plagiés Melítona AO wine. At 450 hectares it's the largest privately owned wine estate in Europe; their Limnio and Château Carrás wines are among the best in Greece (*see also* 'Where to Stay').

From here a road crosses over the saddle of Sithonía, or you can continue south to make a complete circuit around the peninsula by way of the huge, scarcely developed beach at **Toróni**. At its end lie the foundations of two 5th-century basilicas and a little promontory, Cape Lekythos, sprinkled with the walls of ancient Torone, a Bronze Age settlement and then a leading Greek colony that became, like so many, a battleground in the Peloponnesian War. South of Toróni, *maquis* covers the rugged shores around **Pórto Koufó** (Thucydides' Kofos Limenas), the most sheltered anchorage in Chalkidikí, a pretty lake of a bay with a beach and a couple of hotels. The wild south of Sithonía is fire-scarred and dotted with corrugated metal goat sheds, many of them virtual goat condominiums, but offers a peaceful haven at **Kalamítsi** with an excellent beach, fish tavernas and a handful of rooms to rent. There's a magic moment as you approach **Skála Sikiás**, when the whole Akte peninsula comes into view, the tremendous cone of Mount Athos piercing the sky through a necklace of clouds. Skála Sikiás has a set of beautiful small beaches (signposted Linaráki), and there are others to the north, by **Sárti**, that are even finer: **Platanítsi** and **Kavourótrypes**, where the white sands are decorated with pale granite, whipped by the elements into petrified froth, and, 8km further north, **Armenistís**, where the sea comes in every shade of blue and green. There's another excellent beach, **Karýdi**, with pine trees and a great bar just south of the resort with the fun-to-pronounce name, **Vourvouroú**. **Órmos Panagiás** to the north is a laid-back little fishing village with excursion boats around Mount Athos. You can cut across back roads from here to Ierissós and Athos by way of Gomáti, although don't count on any help from the signposts.

Across Chalkidikí towards Mount Athos

Two roads from Thessaloníki cross Chalkidikí to the coast, then head south for the Athos peninsula. The northerly one passes two shallow, bird-filled lakes, **Korónia** and **Vólvi**. Forests border the latter around **Apollonía**, an ancient Ottoman station on the Via Egnatía (there are remains on the edge of the village). At **Rendína** the road enters the Straits of Rendína, the so-called 'Macedonian Tempe', where the Richios river, draining Lake Vólvi, splashes through the plane trees under cliffs. In 406 BC, Euripides went hunting here with King Archelaos and was torn apart by his hounds (animals had it in for Greek playwrights; Aeschylus died when an eagle dropped a tortoise on his bald head); his tomb was a landmark for Roman travellers. Not far from Rendíni

Where to Stay and Eat

Stávros ✉ 57014

Athos, t 239 706 1353 (*C; moderate–inexpensive*). Just outside the centre; simple rooms with balconies facing the plane grove and beach. *Open May–Oct.*

Aristostelis, t 239 706 5616 (*C; moderate–inexpensive*). Adequate and open all year.

Kozi, by the beach in the plane forest. A great summer bar, magically lit at night with fountains under the plane trees, while ducks, rabbits and sheep toddle on the lawn.

Olympiáda ✉ 57014

Germany, t 237 605 1362, **f** 237 605 1255, *hotel-liotopi@hal.forthnet.gr* (*C; moderate*). Greek in spite of its name, and right on the beach, with an excellent taverna. Owner Dimitris is a fund of information on ancient Stageira; he also runs the quieter **Liotopi**, further along the waterfront.

Arnéa ✉ 63074

Oikia Alexandrou, t 237 202 3210, *www.oikia-alexandrou.gr* (*expensive*). Six charming rooms in a historic house of 1812, lovingly restored by its architect owners. Big breakfasts; lunch and dinner available on request.

Oikia Mitsiou, t 237 202 2744, **f** 237 202 2988 (*C; expensive–moderate*). Art Nouveau mansion converted into a hotel by the village, preserving its original furnishings and bygone charm. *Open all year.*

Ouranoúpoli ✉ 63075

Eagles Palace, 4km from town, **t** 237 703 1047, **f** 237 703 1383, *www.eaglespalace.gr* (*A; luxury*). Where the Aga Khan and Maria Callas stayed: beautiful gardens, luxurious rooms or bungalows, on an immaculate private white sand beach. *Open April–Oct.*

Xenia, t 237 707 1412, **f** 237 707 1362, *www.papcorp.gr* (*A; luxury*). Former state hotel vintage 1963 right on the beach. Converted into a plush inn, with sea water swimming pool and playground; good for young families. *Open April–Oct.*

Hellinikon, t 237 717 1138, **f** 237 707 1043 (*C; moderate–inexpensive*). On the edge of the village, 200m from the beach. Breakfast in the garden. *Open April–Oct.*

Xenios Zeus, t 237 707 1274, **f** 237 707 1185 (*D; inexpensive*). Simple but welcoming, a favourite hotel for pilgrims to Athos (they will store your bags). *Open all year.*

Kritikos, just in from the shore, **t** 237 707 1222 (around €25). Come here for spaghetti with lobster – or just about any other fish you fancy – and leave with a smile.

Amouliani Island ✉ 63077

Agionissi Resort, a mile from the village, linked to Ouranoúpolis by private boat, **t** 237 705 1102, **f** 237 705 1180, *www.papcorp.gr* (*A; luxury*). Lovely rooms and studios in bungalows around a delightful garden and pool. Three beaches are in easy walking distance (and there are boats you can hire); breakfast and sumptuous buffet dinners are part of the deal. *Open May–Oct.*

you'll see a sign for the **Kástro** (over the footbridge), a hill site inhabited from Classical to Byzantine times, only to be forgotten by the 14th century. It has impressive walls and towers, a striking if ruined church, remains of ancient temples and baths, and a secret passage to the cisterns.

At the end of the ravine the road forks. Sandy beaches line the Orfanós Gulf to the north (*see* p.584). But if you need a beach, try **Stavrós**, on the Chalkidikí road, an unpretentious resort, with a huge beach backed by a glen of century-old plane trees that resemble dancers frozen in the middle of a fandango. Another plane tree in Stavrós, the huge **Plátanos of Apollonía**, is an official 'monument of nature'. **Olympiáda** to the south is another low-key resort, known as Kaprus but re-named after Alexander's mother when she was exiled here by Cassander. It was the port of **ancient Stageira**, founded in 650 BC by colonists from Ándros. As a member of the

Olynthian League, it was destroyed by Philip II in 349 BC, much to the chagrin of its native son Aristotle. Alexander did his old tutor the favour of rebuilding Stageira, and in 322 BC the philosopher's bones were brought here from Chálkis, and a festival, the Aristoteleia, inaugurated. Yet when Strabo visited 300 years later, Stageira was abandoned. Aesthetics weren't the reason because the site, on a pair of hills over a little cape, couldn't be more fetching. Excavations (*open 8am–8pm daily; free; for info try Olympiáda town hall, t 237 605 1275*) since 1990 have revealed Archaic to Hellenistic fortifications, the acropolis in triangular walls, roads, two 6th-century BC temples (including a circular *thesmophoríon* of Demeter) and a Classical agora and stoa.

The shorter road from Thessaloníki through the heart of Chalkidikí rises as it nears lovely **Arnéa**, a Brigadoon of stone and wooden houses, cobbled lanes and fountains, surrounded by orchards and vineyards; it lies at the beginning of a lovely road through sunny vales of chestnut, oak and beech that twists south to Polýgyros over Mount Cholomóndas. The main road continues east through the charming smaller villages of **Paleochóri** and **Neochóri** before reaching modern **Stágeira**, so-named before the rediscovery of the ancient city. Above the village, in the remains of a Byzantine fort, a large, inane statue of Aristotle broods over the sea; below, at **Stratóni**, an end-of-the-world place where mussels are farmed and ancient gold mines have been reopened, the road turns south to Ierissós.

Ierissós and Ouranoúpoli

A large beach and boat building yards signal **Ierissós**, the port for eastern Athos and site of ancient Acanthos ('Thorn'). The story goes that in 655 BC colonizing expeditions from Chalkís and Ándros arrived here at the same time, and both sent scouts racing to claim the spot. When the scout from Ándros saw that he would never catch his Chalkís counterpart, he hurled his javelin ahead, and in arbitration Ándros was declared to have won the site 'by the point of their spear'. Acanthos grew rapidly, thanks to nearby mines, minting coins by 530 BC. Jealous of Olynthos and its confederacy, it proved true to its thorny name in 382 BC by inviting in the Spartans. Bits of the ancient city are signposted off the main road (on the right): amid the chicken coops look for a Classical temple and altar under a metal roof, and further up the walls of the citadel. Just beyond Ierissós on a steep hill is a chapel dedicated to **Ag. Pávlos**, where St Paul stopped and enjoyed a great view over Mount Athos.

In 492 BC, the Persian invasion fleet was shipwrecked in a horrible storm off this peninsula. A decade later, Xerxes was determined to avoid the same fate by having an army of slaves dig a canal wide enough for two triremes to sail abreast at **Néa Róda**. Although Herodotus wrote that the Great King wanted 'to leave something to be remembered by', its 2.9km have silted up so completely that the modern road now follows its traces; the curious little hills by the side were the excavated mounds. In the past few years, a more tangible Hellenistic temple and Archaic house were excavated at Néa Róda, associated, respectively, with Alexarchos and Sane (*see* below). **Trípiti**, at the south end of the ex-canal, has ferries to the island of **Amoulianí**, with quiet beaches, hotels and a campsite; until 1922, this entire area belonged to the monastery Vatopedíou; the monks' boathouses are still intact.

Sandy coves line the coast south to **Ouranoúpoli**, the 'City of Heaven' complete with the usual Greek seaside charms and end of the road for women, children and permit-less men, unless they take an Athos sightseeing cruise. Surprisingly, its name predates any monasteries, or even Christianity: Ouranoúpoli was founded in 315 BC near an older city, Sane, by proto hippie guru Alexarchos, the brother of King Cassander; he fancied he was the Sun and founded a commune here, imposing his own alphabet and a dialect 'incomprehensible even to the god of Delphi'. The picturesque **Tower of Prosphórios** (1344), the tallest monastic watchtower on Chalkidikí, watches over the village fishing fleet. It was the home of Joyce and Sydney Loch, workers for a Quaker refugee organization, who came here for a holiday in the 1920s and never left, helping among other things to promote the local carpet weavers. Now restored, the tower houses a chapel and a museum of Christian antiquities (*hardly ever open*).

Mount Athos (Ágion Óros)

One of the great landmarks of the Aegean, the 6,660ft pale marble cone of Mount Athos punctuates the end of a magnificent 56km peninsula mantled in virgin forests and wildflowers. The Greeks call it Ágion Óros, the Holy Mountain, and there is no place like it; a thousand years of isolation and devotion have permeated the land to create a mystical otherworldliness, offering, for many who have been there, a fore-taste of paradise. The monasteries resemble castles, and in their walls they have safeguarded the soul of Orthodoxy, shielding it from a millennium of Western influ-ences and ecumenicalism. Together, they form the world's greatest museum of Byzantine art, but a living museum – the monks sing Byzantine hymns, paint icons and prepare incense as they've done for centuries, keeping safe exquisite reliquaries, icons and some 12,000 illuminated manuscripts – nearly half of those in Greece. The days are marked by the Julian calendar (putting Athos 13 days behind the rest of the world), the hours by Byzantine time, which starts the clock for each new day at sunset. Even the flora is Byzantine, and incredibly rich and diverse – thanks to a ban on grazing animals for the past 1,000 years. Jackals still roam the wilder reaches. The recent (and controversial) building of roads on the Holy Mount has disturbed some of

Getting There

Buses from Athens (**t** 210 515 4800) and Thessaloníki (**t** 231 092 4444) go direct to Ouranoúpoli to meet the 9.45am boat (**t** 237 707 1248) to the monasteries of Zográphou, Konstamonítou, Docheiaríou, Xenofóndos and Ag. Panteleímonos, and Dáphni; visitors to Simonópetra, Grigoríou, Dionysíou, and Ag. Pávlos can change boats at Dáphni. Although subject to windy weather, caiques also sail out of Ierissós in summer (check with the port police, **t** 237 702 2576) for the east coast monasteries of Chelandaríou, Esfigménou, Vatopedíou, Pantokrátor, Stavronikíta, Ivéron and the Great Lávra. Summer cruise boats from Ouranoúpoli and Ierissós sail around Athos at 500m – which is as close as women are allowed (although you can bring binoculars).

A **bus** at Dáphni meets the boat for Athos' capital Kariés, and there are two buses from Kariés that cross the peninsula to Ivéron at 8.15am and 1.30. Where roads exist, there are four-wheel-drive **taxis** driven by monks, **t** 237 702 3266, mobile **t** 694 430 2451. Otherwise expect a one- to three-hour walk between monasteries.

Athos Practicalities

Mount Athos is the Garden of the Virgin, and she will brook no rivals: it has been *ávaton* or off limits to all females since 1063, with the exception of hens and cats. To visit, you need a permit from the Pilgrims' Office (*Grafío Proskynitón Agíou Órous*) at 14 Leofóros Karamanlís, ✉ 54638 Thessaloníki; *open Mon–Sat 8.30–1.30 and Mon, Tues, Thurs, Fri 6–8, t 231 083 3733 (English spoken)*. Each day 100 permits (*diamonitíria*) are reserved for the Orthodox and 10 for non-Orthodox, who should ring at least six months in advance to set a date and receive a code number (you will have better luck in winter; in summer facilities are strained to capacity). The *diamonitírio* gives you four days on Athos, but you can apply for a 2-day extension at the Holy Community in Kariés. Before embarking from Ierissós or Ouranoúpoli (arrive at least an hour early) you will need to show your passport, *diamonitírio*, and pay around €20 if you are non-Orthodox or €12 if you are (check the fee when you apply). Non-Greek Orthodox should bring their baptismal certificates or other proof from their church. While many monks now speak English, it's a disadvantage on Athos not to have any Greek at all. Four monasteries (*see* below) speak other languages.

All visitors are expected to stay at the monasteries and you'll need to ring ahead to reserve a bed (but not on Sundays or holidays, when no one will answer the phone). Gates close at sunset. On arrival, the gatekeeper will check your *diamonitírio* and direct you to the guest master (*archontáris*) who will offer you *tsípouro, loukoúmi*, cold water and coffee, give you the timetable of services and meals, then escort you to the dormitory (equipped with toilets and basins; some now have hot showers). Hospitality is free, although an offering 'for the church' might be accepted.

After resting, at around 4pm, monks and visitors attend Vespers in the monastery church (*katholikón*) in the courtyard, next to a small pavilion (*phial*) holding spring water that is blessed in special services. After Vespers the bells summon everybody to

its medieval peace, but the income from a discreet increase in logging and tourism has enabled the monasteries – wonderfully rambling complexes that have evolved (or devolved) over time – to make much-needed repairs and renovations.

History

Athos could have had a different fate, had the Macedonian architect Deinokrates had his way. One day he appeared in Alexander the Great's court in Asia, naked except for a lion skin and club. Intrigued by the Heracles get-up, Alexander heard his proposal: to sculpt Athos into his likeness, with a fortified city in one hand and a lake in the other, which would spill over as a waterfall into the sea. History doesn't record how long Alexander mulled over the idea (he rejected it because there wasn't enough farmland to support the city), but he was impressed enough to hire Dienokrates and later to commission him to lay out his grandest foundation, Alexandria in Egypt.

Legend has it that the Virgin Mary was heading for Cyprus to visit Lazarus when her ship was blown in a storm to the Bay of Ivéron. Enchanted by its beauty, she prayed that it might be hers, and heard a voice from heaven: 'Let this place be your

the refectory (*trápeza*) opposite the *katholikón*; the Abbot (*Igoúmenos*) enters first, followed by the monks and the visitors (note that some monasteries have special customs about church attendance and meals for the non-Orthodox). Meals are eaten in silence, while a monk reads aloud from the Bible, and consist of olives, vegetables, rice, pasta, beans, fruit, cheese and good Athos wine. Meat is never eaten, and fish is only served on feast days. On fast days (Monday, Wednesday, Friday and before major feasts) monks abstain from wine, oil, and dairy products. After supper, visitors then return to the *katholikón* for Compline (the evening liturgy), after which relics are displayed for the veneration of Orthodox pilgrims. Afterwards there is free time, when you can chat with the monks. All retire with the sun at around 9 or 10pm, then wake up at around 3 or 4am to attend Matins, Hours and the Divine Liturgy, immediately followed by breakfast (similar to dinner) at 7am. The monks then go about their work and visitors are expected to continue their pilgrimage of Athos (you can stay at a monastery for more than one night, but only by special request).

Because of the walking, take as little as possible, but do pack a good map, water bottle, stout shoes, hat, insect repellent, snacks, a torch and matches (many monasteries have no electricity). Dress is casual, but shorts are out. The monks don't swim; if you do, do it out of their sight. Photography is allowed, but you will need the Abbot's permission to take pictures of the monks or any interiors. Video cameras and tape recorders are strictly banned. Kariés, the 'capital', has basic shops, post office, doctor, restaurants, a simple hotel and police station, but no bank or money-changing facilities. For more information, try the following:

The Station by Robert Byron. By far the zestiest traveller's account, written in 1928 and reissued by Phoenix Press in 2000.

Mount Athos by Sotiris Kadas. A guide to the monasteries, available in Greece.

www.medialab.ntua.gr/athos/uk/ Practical and spiritual information, and photos.

abacus.bates.edu/~rallison/friends/friendsguide.html Site of the Friends of Athos.

inheritance and your garden, a paradise and a haven of salvation.' The first hermits arrived in the 8th century, fleeing the Iconoclasts, and as the influx of spiritual athletes grew, Emperor Basil I proclaimed the peninsula their exclusive domain (885). In 963, the first monastery, the Great Lávra ('community of hermitages') was founded by St Athanásios with funds from a guilty Nikephóros Phokás, who had promised Athanásios that he would become a hermit if he succeeded in taking Crete, but instead fought for the imperial throne. A faction of ascetic hermits, led by Pávlos Xeropotomíou, accused Athanásios of introducing luxury to Athos. But Athanásios had friends in high places, and in 971 his rules were inscribed in the *Próto Typikó*, or charter that governs Athos. Other holy men, many financed by princes, established monasteries (180, or so they say) including Moldavian, Albanian, Bulgarian, Russian, Romanian, Serbian, Georgian, Wallachian and Amalfitani houses, with a population of 40,000 monks. Their wealth attracted pirates – hence the high walls. More trouble began in 1204 with the Latin occupation, but the restoration in 1261 of Michael VIII Paleológos in Constantinople brought no respite: attempting to bully Athos into accepting the union of the Eastern and Western churches, his men tortured and burnt 26 monks alive. Although his son Andronicus II was an anti-Unionist, his Catalan mercenaries, when dismissed for bad behaviour, occupied the Kassándra peninsula and spent the next two years plundering and burning, leaving only 25 monasteries standing.

In 1453 Athos submitted at once to the Turks, and in return the Sultans let the peninsula maintain its independence, although heavy taxes took a toll. There was a revival in the 18th century, when the Mount took a leading role in the Greek enlightenment, with the founding of the Athonite Academy near Vatopedíou; in 1821, many monks joined the Greek War of Independence. In 1926, after the monasteries were compelled to give up most of their dependencies to the Asia Minor refugees, a new charter made Athos an autonomous part of the Greek state, subject only in its external relations to the Ministry of Foreign Affairs.

Mount Athos Today

The peninsula is divided into 20 territories, each controlled by a 'ruling monastery'. Each has a deputy on the Holy Council that governs Athos in conjunction with an annually elected executive board of four. The 20 monasteries follow a rigid hierarchy of precedence, from the Great Lávra, Vatopedíou and Ivéron down to the newest, Konstamonítou. Although several were idiorrhythmic (each monk 'going his own way', working and providing his own food), as of 1992 all monasteries are coenobitic, where the monks live and eat communally. Most have several dependencies. These include mini-monasteries or skete (skítis) ruled by a prior; kelliá, like farmhouses with a chapel and usually three or four monks; even smaller kalýves and kathiímata; and smallest of all hesychastéria, huts or caves in the cliffs, mostly in the 'Desert of Athos' at the south end of the peninsula, where hermits live in complete isolation, devoting their lives to prayer, living off what passers-by drop in their baskets. Today some 2,000 monks and novices live on Athos, including many young, better educated monks (so don't expect to find only doddering eccentrics, as most travellers found a few decades ago). The Bulgarian, Russian, Romanian and Serbian houses are undergoing such a renewal that there is fresh concern over maintaining the Mount's 'Greekness.'

Since permits are checked before you embark, it's no longer necessary to go to **Kariés**, the seat of the Holy Community (and only capital in the world without a women's WC) unless you want a two-day extension on your permit. The oldest building on Athos is here, the 10th-century church of the **Protáton**, with lovely 14th-century frescoes by Manuel Panselinos.

The Monasteries

In four or six days on Athos, it's impossible to see everything. While all the monasteries have relics and icons, works of art and rich libraries (to examine them, you'll need a letter of introduction, preferably from an Orthodox bishop), you may want to concentrate on the famous ones, such as the Great Lávra, Vatopedíou, Ivéron and Simonópetra. Check the aforementioned books and websites for more information; the following are thumbnail sketches of the monasteries as you'll find them sailing from Ouranoúpolis, and then from Ierissós.

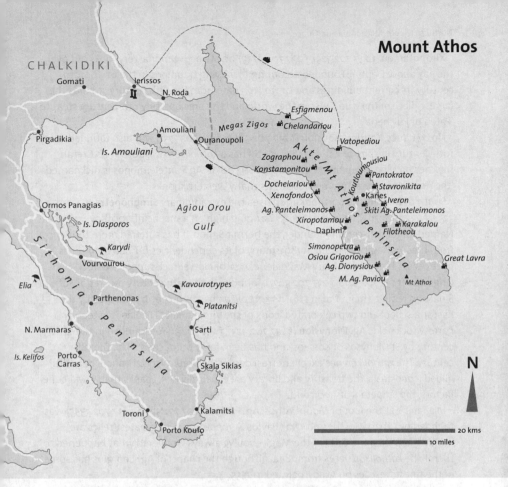

CHALKIDIKI
Gomati
Ierissos
N. Roda
Esfigmenou
Megas Zigos
Chelandaríou
Amouliani
Ouranoupoli
Is. Amouliani
Vatopediou
Pirgadikia
Zográphou
Koutloumousiou
Konstamonítou
Pantokrator
Docheiaríou
Stavronikita
Xenofondos
Kariés
Iveron
Ormos Panagias
Agiou Orou
Ag. Panteleimonos
Skiti Ag. Panteleimonos
Is. Diasporos
Gulf
Xiropotamou
Karakalou
Daphni
Filotheou
Karydi
Simonopetra
Vourvourou
Osiou Grigoríou
Ag. Dionysiou
Great Lavra
Elia
Kavourotrypes
M. Ag. Paviou
Mt Athos
Parthenonas
Platanitsi
N. Marmaras
Sarti
Is. Kelifos
Porto
Carras
Skala Sikias
N
Toroni
Kalamitsi
Porto Koufo

20 kms
10 miles

Sithonia Peninsula

Akte/Mt Athos Peninsula

   The first (hidden from the sea) is the Bulgarian monastery **Zográphou** (*t 237 702
3247*), founded in the 10th century and famous for its miraculous icons. Its name 'the
painter' comes from one of St George that mysteriously appeared here. Half hidden in
a wooded ravine, **Konstamonítou** (or Kastamonítou, *t 237 702 3228, f 237 702 3901*)
comes last in Athos' hierarchy; its *katholikón* dates from 1871. Next is **Docheiaríou**
(*t 237 702 3245*), founded by a companion of St Athanásios who was in charge of
stores (the *doleiarios*). Its buildings, mostly 16th-century, were a gift from the prince of
Wallachia; the *katholikón*, with excellent frescoes of 1568 by the Cretan master
Tzortzis, houses the famous icon of the Panagía Gorgoepikoös, 'she who grants
requests quickly'. Very near by, **Xenofóndos** (*t 237 702 3249, f 237 702 3660*) was
founded in the 900s by the Blessed Xenofóndos but was largely rebuilt after a fire in
1817; it has an enormous *katholikón* (1809–1919), containing two 13th-century mosaic
icons, and also an older *katholikón*, frescoed in 1544 by the Cretan School. Green onion
domes, symbolizing heaven, mark Russian **Ag. Panteleímonos** or the 'Roussikon' (*t 237
702 3252, f 237 702 3682*), founded in the 10th century. In 1765 the Russians built a vast
new monastery closer to the sea that resembles a walled city and once held 1,500
monks, in a failed attempt to take over Athos by sheer force of numbers.

Xiropotámou (*t 237 702 3251, f 237 702 3733*), an attractive monastery, looks out over the bay above Dáphni. Founded according to varying traditions in the 6th or 10th century, its current buildings and *katholikón* date from the 18th century; it holds the largest piece of the True Cross in the world and the precious, tiny 6th-century steatite 'Paten of Pulchería'.

Up by Kariés, **Koutloumousíou** (*t 237 702 3266, f 237 702 3731*) was also founded in the 10th century. In spite of a fire in 1870 it still has a *katholikón* of 1540, but its Cretan frescoes have been repainted. The monastery's Skíti Ag. Panteleímonos is nicknamed 'the American monastery' because of its many Western monks.

South of **Dáphni**, the port for Kariés, rises the extraordinary **Simonópetra** (*t 237 702 3254, f 237 702 3707*), its seven storeys hanging high on a sheer cliff, 700ft over the sea. Named for its 13th-century founder, the hermit Simon, it has suffered more than most from fires, having been razed in 1891; many of its dependencies burned in 1990. Its prize relic is the hand of Mary Magdelene. A rather lower rock supports **Osíou Grigoríou** (*t 237 702 3218, f 237 702 3671*), founded in the 14th century by Gregory of Sinai and rebuilt after a fire in 1761; its *katholikón* has 18th-century frescoes by the Kastoriá school and two celebrated icons of the Virgin and St Nikólaos. A steep and narrow rock holds **Ag. Dionysíou** (*t 237 702 3237, f 237 702 3686*), founded in the 14th century by St Dionysos of Korseos, and has been fairly untouched since the 18th century. The *katholikón* has excellent frescoes by the Cretan Tzortzis, and a beautiful gilded iconostasis; the treasury and library are especially rich, thanks to its royal bene-factors, the emperors of Trebizond.

In a ravine at the foot of Mount Athos, **Ag. Pávlos** (*t 237 702 3250, f 237 702 3355*) was founded by Athanásios' hermit rival, Pávlos Xeropotomíou. Its greatest relics are nothing less than the Gifts of the Magi – you've always wondered what happened to them! The *katholikón* dates from 1844, although the chapel of Ag. Geórgios has some of the finest frescoes on Athos, painted in 1555.

Sailing down the east coast from Ierissós, the first monastery is **Chelandaríou** (*t 237 702 3797*), only a short walk from the sea but hidden in wooded hills. Its founders, Prince Stefan Nemanja and his son St Sávvas, gave up thrones to become monks, and the monastery was given in perpetuity to the Serbs by Emperor Aléxis III in 1198; even Tito sent the monks a tractor. The *katholikón* has frescoes of 1320 (unfortunately repainted) and a fine mosaic floor; it possesses a piece of Christ's shroud, cameos and important icons. In rough weather waves lap the walls of **Esfigménou** (*t 237 702 3796, f 237 702 3937*), 'tied with a very tight cord', a late 10th-century monastery; among its treasures is the most bizarre relic in Greece, a large piece of the tent Napoleon used at Moscow, donated by pious pirates.

Next is **Vatopedíou** (*t 237 7023219, f 237 702 3657*), a great rambling country estate of a monastery, founded in *c.* 980 by three monks from Edirne, although the derivation of its name 'bramble field' is unknown. Its 10th-century *katholikón* has excellent fres-coes of the Macedonian school (although repainted) and its treasury houses major relics: the Virgin's girdle, the rod that held the sponge soaked in vinegar given to Christ, plus a superb diptych, portable icons, and 2,000 illuminated manuscripts. On a headland, **Pantokrátor** (*t 237 702 3253, f 237 702 3685*), was founded by two Byzantine nobles in the 14th century, but suffered fires in 1773 and 1948; it has a famous icon of the Virgin known as the 'Elder'. **Stavronikíta** (*t 237 702 3255, f 237 702 3908*), the smallest monastery on Athos, resembles a little castle and has great views over the big mountain. Its foundation in the 10th century is lost in legend; its *katholikón* has frescoes by the great Theophanes (*c. 1520*), although its most famous icon is that of St Nicholas of the Oyster, named for the creature stuck to it (the mark is still visible) when the monks pulled it from the sea. Both it and **Ivéron** (*t 237 702 3643, f 237 702 3248*) are linked to Karíes by road. Ivéron was founded in the 900s by John Tornikios, a courtier of the king of Iberia in Georgia; when its famous jewelled icon of Panagía Portaitissa cured the daughter of Tsar Alexis in the 17th century, the monks were given the monastery of St Nicholas in the middle of Moscow. Its *katholikón* (11th–16th century) has a fine mosaic floor; the rich treasury includes the robe of Emperor John Tzimiskés (the successor to Nikephóros Phokás) and the library has three 10th-century chrysobulls and 2,000 codices.

Filothéou (*t 237 702 3256, f 237 702 3674*), another late 10th-century foundation, sits on a plateau that once had an Asklepeion, and shelters one of Orthodoxy's most famous icons, the Glykophiloúsa or Sweet-Kissing One. High above the sea, a picturesque 16th-century fort, **Karakálou** (*t 237 702 3225, f 237 702 3746*), has a mighty defence tower and *katholikón* with frescoes from the 1700s.

Lastly, on the wild slopes where its founder battled with demons, is the most venerable and imposing **Great Lávra** (*Megistís Lávras*) (*t 237 702 3758, f 237 702 3766*), home to 420 monks. The refectory and *katholikón*, built by St Athanásios and the model for every subsequent monastery church, have superb frescoes by Theophanes (1535); its treasury and library are the richest on Athos and house the magnificent imperial robe and crown of Nikephóros Phokás. It has the most important dependencies as well, including the **Pródromos**, inhabited by Romanian monks, and the hermitages in the sheer cliffs of Karoulia. From the Great Lávra you can make the ascent of **Mount Athos**; Robert Byron claimed he could see the plains of Troy from the summit.

Eastern Macedonia and Thrace

You could subtitle this 'Almost, but not quite Unknown Greece'. Its beach-fringed island of Thássos has put it on the package holiday map, and anyone who has dabbled in the classics will recognize its other island, Samothráki, and the two ancient cities of Amphipolis and Philippi. Naturalists will know it for its wetlands; they say as many different species of flora and fauna have been spotted between the Rodópi mountains and the Évros Delta as between Sweden and Italy. Inveterate starers at maps may know its provincial capitals: Kilkis, Sérres, Dráma, Kavála, Xánthi, Komotiní and Alexandroúpoli – all buzzing little cities, and not bad as starting points for heading off the beaten track.

Eastern Macedonia and Thrace are dotted with *toumbas*, the mounds of Neolithic and early Bronze Age settlements, whose pottery resembled that of Troy. In the 13th century BC, these early inhabitants were overrun by the Thracians, probably from

Central Europe, whose territory at its greatest extent stretched from Bulgaria to Évia and Gallipoli. They were Indo-European, but spoke a non-Hellenic language and had neither script nor literature, so most of what we know about them is through the Greeks, who usually gave them a bad press, as 'gods of war' (Thrace was the home of the violent Ares, as well as of Boreas, the North Wind) or lazy drunkards who would sell their own children as slaves. In art, you can tell Thracian women by their tattoos, the men by their long embroidered cloaks, boots and foxskin caps, tails dangling *à la* Davy Crockett. These 'Butter-Eaters', as the Greeks called them (olive groves being rare), were tall, grey-eyed and fair or red-haired, and famous for their music, like their cousins the Phrygians. Thanks to their gold mines, they had a remarkably rich material culture – in Bulgaria, excavations have revealed superb gold work and frescoed tombs. The latter show how Hellenized the Thracian nobility was by the 4th century BC; several kings even claimed to be Greek through ancestral gods and heroes.

Thrace with its 50 tribes was the most populous land after India, wrote Herodotus. 'If the Thracians could be united under a single ruler or combine their purpose, they would be the most powerful nation on earth and no one could cope with them.' Instead Thrace became the Persians' first European conquest under Darius I in 512 BC. After the Persian defeat in Greece, the Greek colonies made a comeback along the coast until Philip II gobbled up southern Thrace in 358 BC. It took the Romans until the

Thrace's Mystic Thread

Where the Greeks anthropomorphized and distanced their gods, the ancient Thracians wanted to become them. Warriors identified with the 'Hero-rider', lord of the Sun and of the Underworld, who appears on funerary steles across northern Greece. The Thracian Great Gods, the Kabeiri, 'Earth and Sky', offered a mystic communion with divinity on Samothráki (*see* p.610) that attracted initiates from the Greek world; significantly, one of the two hereditary families of high priests at the Eleusian Mysteries was Thracian. Most Greeks, however, drew the line at the most fundamental of all Thracian beliefs, that they were immortal and after death would go to paradise with their god-prophet Zalmoxis.

Yet the idea of achieving divinity in this life, for a moment if not for eternity, came to Greece in that most revolutionary of all Thracian religious imports, Dionysos, the god of wine, and secondly by following the teachings of another Thracian, Orpheus. During his orgiastic rites, Dionysos' followers, most famously the Maenads, were intoxicated with an enthusiasm that made them one with the god, capable of inhuman tenderness or inhuman cruelty, nursing wild fawns at their breasts or sinking their teeth into their raw flesh. Their rite of *Omophagia*, the eating of raw flesh, was a primitive version of communion with the godhead. Several myths attest to the arrival of Dionysos' cult in Greece, warning, too, of the terrifying consequences of denying his power. The 'rational' Greeks did their best to tame him. The idea of impersonating the god led to the impersonations of the stage and invention of theatre, the god as 'art'. On the religious side, the poet/prophet/shaman/religious reformer Orpheus invented the 'Mysteries of Dionysos', where spiritual ecstasy was

late 1st century BC to subjugate all the tribes, and then their lives were harsh; Diodorus Siculus wrote that in some places a Thracian slave was only worth a jar of wine. Their language was extinct by the time of the Byzantine empire, their land north of the Rodópi mountains occupied by Slavs and proto-Bulgars.

In the power intrigues of late 19th century, Russia offered southern Thrace to Bulgaria, and it became a fixation that guided Bulgaria through the Balkan and World wars; now Bulgarians flock over the border again to frolic on Thrace's beaches. Borders dividing Western (Greek) and Eastern (Turkish) Thrace were drawn in 1922, although Muslims in Western Thrace were exempted in the exchange of populations in a deal to safeguard the once sizeable Greek population of Istanbul. There are now 120,000 Muslims in Thrace, half of whom are of Turkish origin, while others are Roma Gypsy, Pomaks (who live in the Rodópi mountains and speak their own southern Slav language, and are claimed as long-lost brethren by Greeks, Bulgarians and Turks, although they themselves tend to identify with the Turks) and Athingani (descendants of Greek heretics expelled from Asia Minor under the Byzantines, who later converted to Islam). The great thaw between Greece and Turkey that began with the earthquakes in 1999 has already brought benefits to the region, symbolized by the Egnatia motorway project cutting across the Thracian plain, and plans to share energy resources and reopen rail links.

achieved, not through drunkenness, but by Apolline purification, symbolized by his music; in early Greek art, he plays his lyre not to tame wild beasts, but to enchant uncouth Thracian tribesmen. But like Huck Finn, something in the nature of Dionysos refused to be 'civilized', and Orpheus was a martyr to his own reforms; the Maenads, feeling he had missed a point or two, tore him to pieces. He became the patron of the Orphics, who in their 'secret *logoi*' codified rules of living with the goal of attaining divine rapture in this life as well as the next. By Classical times, Orphism existed alongside Dionysian revels, sometimes in competition, sometimes closely intertwined, both subtly undermining the resolutely non-mystic pile that was Olympus.

References to the lost 'secret *logoi*' survive in Euripides and Plato (who were steeped in Orphism) and in the golden Orphic inscriptions discovered in southern Italy. The early Church identified Christ with Orpheus, and since then Orphism has led to some surprising destinations, not least Renaissance Florence when Orphic 'natural magic' was revived by Marsilio Ficino (who also translated Plato for the Medici), and inspired the allegorical paintings of Botticelli. But such magic is a fragile thing, as Jane Ellen Harrison wrote in her classic *Prolegomena*:

> The religion of Orpheus is religious in the sense that it is the worship of the real mysteries of life, of potencies rather than personal gods; it is the worship of life itself in its supreme mysteries of ecstasy and love. It is these real gods, this life itself, that the Greeks, like most men, were inwardly afraid to recognise and face, afraid even to worship. Now and again a philosopher or a poet, in the very spirit of Orpheus, proclaims these true gods, and asks in wonder why to their shrines is brought no sacrifice.

Eastern Macedonia and Kilkís

Amphipolis and Mount Pangaíon

After passing over the top of Chalkidikí, the E90 – our old friend the Via Egnatía – continues east past the wide sandy beaches of **Asproválta** to the mouth of the Strymónas river. Flowing down from the Bulgarian frontier, this river has seen a heavy dose of history, both in antiquity and in the 20th century, when it marked the border between the Allies and the Central Powers in the First World War and between the occupation zones of the Germans and Bulgarians in the Second.

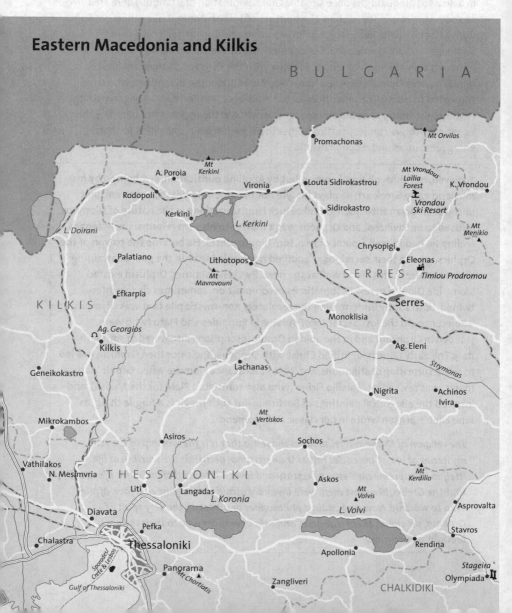

Eastern Macedonia and Kilkis

On the east bank of the river the landmark is 'golden' Mount Pangaíon, the ancient El Dorado. It lured the Mycenaeans and in the 6th century BC the Athenians, who founded the colony of Eion at the mouth of the Strymónas (and minted a curious coin, showing a goose and a geometer's right angle). The Athenian tyrant Pisistratos raised a fortune from its gold mines for his comeback from exile, and Athens, always remembering, founded a colony further inland in 465 BC that was wiped out by the Thracians; then sent Agnon to try again in 437 BC. He named the site **Amphipolis** – a name now familiar to millions, as the home of TV's *Xena the Warrior Princess*.

In real life, the paint was still wet in 422 BC when the Spartan general Brasidas seized it. Athens' general, Thucydides, rushed to the rescue with seven triremes, but

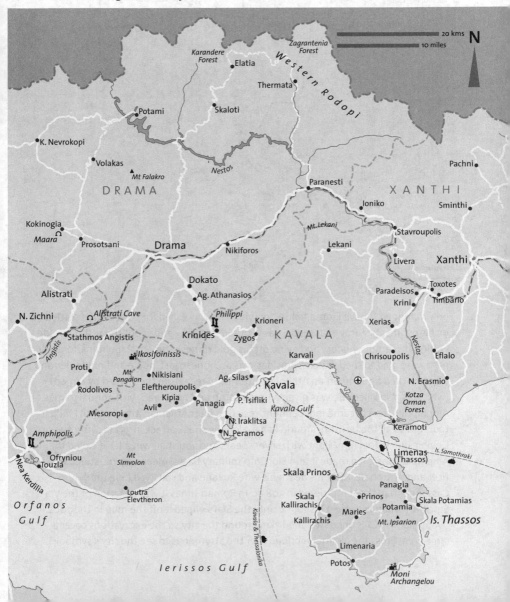

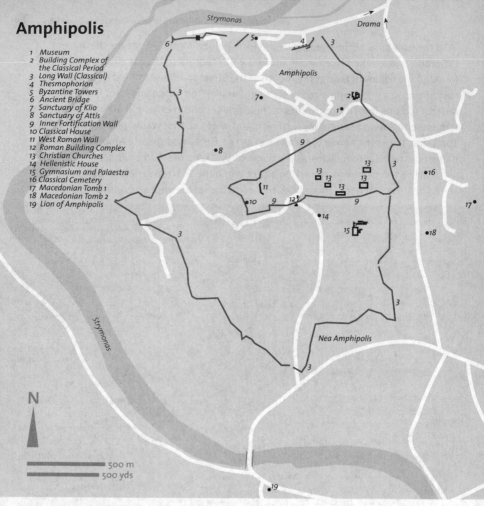

Amphipolis

1 Museum
2 Building Complex of
   the Classical Period
3 Long Wall (Classical)
4 Thesmophorion
5 Byzantine Towers
6 Ancient Bridge
7 Sanctuary of Klio
8 Sanctuary of Attis
9 Inner Fortification Wall
10 Classical House
11 West Roman Wall
12 Roman Building Complex
13 Christian Churches
14 Hellenistic House
15 Gymnasium and Palaestra
16 Classical Cemetery
17 Macedonian Tomb 1
18 Macedonian Tomb 2
19 Lion of Amphipolis

Strymonas

Drama

Amphipolis

Nea Amphipolis

Strymonas

N

500 m
500 yds

only managed to save Eion, a failure for which he was exiled for 20 years (he settled on his estate at nearby Skaptesyle – as yet unidentified – and spent the rest of his life writing his famous history and living off his gold mines). The Amphipolitans, for their part, were glad to shed Athens; Brasidas was an honest, just, noble and mild ruler, and when he died fighting off an Athenian attempt to recapture the city led by Kimon (who was also killed), he was given a hero's tomb and honoured with annual games. Amphipolis then became independent, resisting later Athenian attacks until Philip II took it (and all the territory around Panagaíon) by sneak attack in 357 BC, after the Delphic oracle told him 'Fight with silver spears and you shall win all'. He exiled the Amphipolitans, then made it and Eion into military bases; Alexander mustered his fleet and army here. After his death his wife Roxane and son lived here until Cassander had them murdered in 308 BC. In Roman times it was a station of the Via Egnatía; it then became a bishopric until the Slavs wiped it off the map in the 700s.

Amphipolis' walls once stretched 7km around the city, so the excavations cover a large area. Cross the old metal bridge over the Strymónas to see the city's symbol:

the huge 4th-century BC **Lion of Amphipolis**, broken to make a dam in the Middle Ages but now reconstructed; it probably honoured Laomedon, one of Alexander's companions who settled here. The road then passes the signs for two **Macedonian tombs** (finds from the unplundered one are in the Kavála Museum), then a track (signposted 200 yards below the modern village) to the 3rd century BC **gymnasium** and **palaestra**, both among the best preserved in Greece, with a wrestling court, tiled exercise rooms, drains, pipes and basins. Nearby were two tracks, including a covered *xystus* wide enough for six runners to race abreast. A shelter nearby covers a well-preserved **Hellenistic house** with wall paintings similar to the Pélla style.

At the top of the modern village, recent excavations have revealed a portion of Agnon's Athenian colony, next to the new **museum** (*t 232 203 2474; open Tues–Sun 9.30–3, in summer also Wed to 11pm; adm*). It houses Amphipolis' beautiful coins, jewellery, painted busts, a stele of 21 BC from the gymnasium inscribed with rules on the education of youths aged 16 to 18, and a golden oak garland and silver ossuary from a cist tomb in the city centre that may have belonged to Brasidas. An inner wall defended the acropolis, where so far the chief finds have been five 6th-century

Getting There and Around

By train: several daily from Thessaloníki to Kilkís, Siderókastro, Sérres, and Dráma.

By bus: for Sérres, there are three a day from Athens, **t** 210 512 0212, and a service every half hour from Thessaloníki, **t** 231 052 6582. From Sérres, buses to Athens and other provincial capitals depart from 5 Kerasoúntos St, **t** 232 102 2822; local buses (for Amphipolis, Alistráti and points north) leave from Plateía Emboríou, **t** 232 103 6731. Rent a **car** from Roulis, 46 Merarchías, **t** 232 102 4526. Sérres radio **taxi**: **t** 232 105 9100. Buses from Kavála (*see* below) serve Eleftheroúpolis.

Sport and Activities

Kerkíni: the Lake Kerkíni Information Centre, **t/f** 232 702 8004, *www.kerkini.gr* (*daily 10–2*) and Ecopoereigitis (*see* below) offer a range of lake activities.

Sérres: Xtreme eXperience, **t** 232 403 2020, mobile **t** 6977 685714, **f** 232 109 8587, offers rafting, kayaking, skiing, rock climbing, etc.

Where to Stay and Eat

Proti ✉ 62047

K. Karamanlis Hotel, **t** 232 406 1112, **f** 232 406 1112 (*B; moderate–inexpensive*). Pleasant seven-room inn with a coffee-shop, a good base for exploring Mount Pangaíon and Amphipolis.

Áno Poróia ✉ 62055

Viglatoras, **t** 232 705 1231, **f** 232 705 1330 (*expensive*). Rooms and studios in a traditionally styled mansion; rooms are charmingly furnished, and have mini bars, TVs and lovely views. Bar and breakfast. *Open all year*.

Panorama, **t** 232 705 1363 (*C; moderate*). Simple; a favourite of hikers. *Open all year*.

Pestrofotaverna, **t** 232 705 1375. Wonderful old atmospheric taverna on a trout (*péstrofo*) farm, serving you know what, freshly grilled or smoked.

Kerkíni ✉ 62055

Ecopoereigitis, **t/f** 232 704 1450, *rekl1@otenet.gr* (*expensive–moderate*). Ideal for bird watchers; attractive apartments and studios with local character and good breakfasts in a peaceful setting near the lake. Jeep, bike and canoe hire, and excursions on the lake with telescopes.

Dionyssos, **t** 232 704 1215. A taverna that doesn't look like much, but the food is the finest on the lake, and well priced, too.

Siderókastro ✉ 62300

Pigi, at Loutrá Siderokastrou, 7km from the centre, **t** 232 302 2422, **f** 232 302 4858 (*C;*

Christian **churches**, one hexagonal, and others (especially Basilica C) with lavish mosaic floors. Heading north, a left turn off the Dráma road leads to an abandoned train station by a **Byzantine tower** and **Classical walls** of fine isodomic masonry, 24ft high in places and equipped with an impressive drainage system. The three gates here, one defending the river crossing, confirm the accuracy of Thucydides' account of the battle between Kleon and Brasidas in 422 BC. A unique find, a hundred fossilized wooden piles of the **ancient bridge**, is now protected under a roof.

The road east of Amphipolis to Kavála passes the silted-up port of **Eion**, the hilltop site of its acropolis and the 10th-century walls of Chrysoupolis, its Byzantine replacement. The new coastal road to Kavála continues to **Touzla**, a pretty beach resort at the start of a 50km of undeveloped sandy coast and a spa, **Loutrá Elevthéron**.

The shorter old road – the same one used by Xerxes' armies – runs through the rich valley and orchards between Mounts Símvolon and **Pangaíon** (6,417ft). A whiff of the uncanny lingers about Pangaíon's knobby marble peaks; Dionysos had an oracle here, tended by the fiercest of Thracian tribes, the Satrai (who would be 'demonized' in the Greek mind as Satyrs), where white horses were sacrificed and a priestess gave

expensive–inexpensive). In a panoramic position, a large municipally-run spa hotel equipped with such features as hot baths, hydro massage and sauna and two indoor pools.
Olympic, t 232 302 3811, f 232 302 3891 (C; moderate). Typical Greek provincial hotel with a restaurant in the main square.

Sérres ✉ **62100**
Elpida, 66 Merarchías, t 232 105 9311, f 232 103 6301 (B; expensive). The smartest hotel in town, with modern air-conditioned rooms, mini bars, sauna and more.
Xenia, 1 Ag. Sofías, t 232 102 4752 (B; moderate). Popular hotel a bit to the east of town, near a pretty wooded park.
Metropolis, 49 Solomou, t 232 105 4433, f 232 102 2271 (C; expensive–moderate). Restored neoclassical building, all rooms with TV and air-conditioning.
Park, 18 Plateía Eleftherías, t 232 102 2133, f 232 102 3533 (C; moderate). Overlooking the main square, and okay for overnight.
Petrino, t 232 105 2713. A fine restaurant in the bosquey suburb of Ag. Ioánnis, 2km east of the centre, serving some unusual dishes (there's an ostrich farm nearby) and the city's classic akanedes, sweets made of roasted almonds and fresh butter.
If you have a car, try the tavernas in **Chrisopigí** or **Elaónas**, 11km north.

Alistráti ✉ **62045**
Archontikó Boziki, t 232 402 0400, f 232 402 0408, www.hotelboziki.gr (A; expensive). Follow the signs to this yellow mansion of 1924, lovingly converted into a hotel in 2000, with a pool and café terrace overlooking the town. Beautiful antiques in the rooms, linen sheets, delicious breakfast and friendly, English-speaking owners.

Dráma ✉ **66100**
Kouros, 3km south on the Kavála road, t 252 105 7200, f 252 102 5800 (A; expensive). Brand new hotel and best in the area, with smart contemporary furnishings, a fine restaurant and a pool.
Emboriko, 8 Ethn. Amýnis, t 252 103 7969, f 252 103 4969 (B; moderate). Nice central hotel by the park.
Lucullus, Próto Iouliou St, t 252 102 1200 (around €28). Dráma's most ambitious restaurant, in a neoclassical mansion with all the trimmings; food and service two cuts above the norm.
Ydrama, 14 Ag. Varvara, t 252 103 4266. Restaurant in a former tobacco warehouse, with tables flowing into the city's pretty municipal park; excellent lamb dishes.
Idonas, 32 D. Gounari, t 252 103 2192. Towards Dráma's park, known for its succulent meat dishes. Especially fun on weekend evenings, when there's live music.

ambiguous oracles, similar to Apollo's Pythia. Today monasteries dot the wooded slopes, along with grill houses and tavernas popular on summer evenings. **Mesorópi**, just north of the road, is a pretty village with a lush oasis of plain trees; another, **Avlí**, has a mountain path through beech trees and giant ferns. Yet another, **Kipía**, has remains of a 5th-century basilica (fenced in, to the left of the road); a track east from here leads to another, built inside a ruined shrine of the Thracian Hero-rider.

Eleftheroúpolis, Próti and Rodolívos

Eleftheroúpolis, the local crossroads and market town, is dotted with old tobacco warehouses. One road from here (by way of Panagía) goes down to the convivial beach resorts west of Kavála. Another road leads to the summit of Pangaíon (with a ski run and alpine refuge); at the top, look for the curious rock incisions of horsemen, suns and weapons that date from the Iron Age to Archaic times. A third road from Eleftheroúpolis goes around to the mountain villages on the north slopes such as **Nikísiani**, where the last twelve days of the year are celebrated by the 'Arápedes', locals who don capes of animal skins and huge bells to re-enact Dionysiac rites of death and rebirth. There are traces here of the ancient mines, which were still a going concern in the 1st century AD. A winding road through beech and chestnut groves leads to Pangaíon's most important monastery, **Moní tis Ikosifoiníssis**, reputedly founded in the 4th century by the Blessed Germanós. Destroyed by the Turks in 1507, and the Bulgarians in 1917 and 1943, it has since been rebuilt and is now inhabited by nuns, who safeguard an icon of the Virgin 'not made by human hands'. **Próti**, on the road along Pangaíon's north flank, is proud of the neoclassical summer villa of the late Greek prime minister and president Konstantínos Karamanlís. Nearby **Rodolívos**, a traditional settlement, is believed to be the site of the oracle of Dionysos, where Orpheus climbed to watch the glory of sun god Apollo, and was torn apart by the jealous Maenads. But they repented when they came to themselves for, as Jane Ellen Harrison says, the Maenads were the same as the Muses, and they buried his limbs by Mount Olympus and took his head, still singing away, to Lésbos.

North from Thessaloníki: Kilkís and Lake Kerkíni

There are two major roads from Thessaloníki that meet up at Sérres. The more northerly road goes by way of **Kilkís**, a garrison town but not unpleasant provincial capital, with a big monument to a victory over the Bulgarians in 1913. The **Archaeological Museum** (*t 234 102 2477; open Tues–Sun 8.30–3*) stars a late 6th-century BC *kouros* with rather willowy features that show a strong Ionian influence. Near the top of the steep hill that distinguishes Kilkís, the **Cave of Ag. Geórgios** (*t 234 102 2233; open Tues–Sun 9am–7pm; adm*) offers a 40-minute musical tour of its formations covered with what looks like petrified popcorn. The naturally moist air has special properties that help children suffering from respiratory diseases, according to Czech, Bulgarian and Ukrainian 'cave therapists', who began a programme of cures in 2002. **Geneikókastro**, 15km southwest of Kilkís, is named for its 'Castle of Women' built by Emperor Andonicus III in 1341, who made the walls so strong that women alone could hold them; it's still impressive, and undergoing restoration.

The road then continues to the frontier **Lake Doiráni** and much larger **Lake Kerkíni**, formed by the damming of the Strymónas river in 1932 to create farmland out of the marshes for Asia Minor refugees. Birds (including the rare pygmy cormorant, pelicans, herons, spoonbills and ibis) have taken to its wetlands, and wolves, jackals and otters live in the forests to the north, although the animals you're most likely to see are water buffalo. The lake's fishermen are staunch defenders of the pelicans and feed them during lean times, but the wildlife is under serious threat: a new dam has brought dramatic changes in water levels. There are places to stay in leafy **Áno Poróia** or in **Kerkíni**; if you're pressed for time, an easy way to see the lake is by way of the 17km drive along with southwest shore to the dam at **Lithótopos**. The main road continues to the spa of **Loutrá Sidirokástrou**, where it joins the E79 to Bulgaria by way of **Promachónas** and the stern Rupel Pass. Take the E79 south for the now peaceful small town of **Sidirókastro** named for its 'Iron Castle' on the hill, built by Basil the Bulgar Slayer and rebuilt by Andronicus III in the 14th century. The nearby church of Ag. Dimitrios has a curious iconostasis – the façade of an ancient Macedonian tomb.

Sérres

On the edge of the broad Strymónas valley – hot in the summer, freezing in the winter – Sérres is one of Macedonia's larger provincial capitals, a well-run city brimful of new Balkan optimism in spite of a history that has seen it devastated on more than one occasion – most thoroughly in 1913, when the retreating Bulgarians burned it out of spite. With 70 workshops, jewellery is a major concern, and there's increased use of local geothermal fields, especially for heating asparagus greenhouses.

On the north edge of town, you can walk or drive up to a ruined tower of the **castle** (1350) built under Serb ruler Stephan Dushan; next to the walls and café stands a little Byzantine jewel of a church, **Ag. Nikólaos**, from the same period. Below to the east, the pretty **Ag. Anargyri valley** has little waterfalls, restaurants and nightclubs. The city's proudest monument, the lofty Byzantine ex-**Metropolis of the Holy Theodores**, is at the bottom of the castle on Padazi Street, restored after the 1913 fire with a little striped chapel stuck on the end. Nearby, a new **Folk Museum of the Sarakatsáni** at 62 Konstantinoupóleos (*t 232 106 2528; open Tues–Sun 9–2*) is devoted to Greece's ancient pastoral people (*see* p.606). In shady Plateía Eleftherías, the **Archaeological Museum** (*t 232 102 2257; open Tues–Sun 8.30–3; free*) occupies the 15th-century six-domed Bezensteni or cloth market: it has steles and votive plaques featuring the Hero-rider, a vase from Tragilos (*c.* 400 BC) with a big fight scene, marble doors from a Macedonian tomb, and art that survived from the Holy Theodores: a figure of St Andrew from a once grand 11th-century mosaic, and a relief of Christ Pantocrator.

Around Sérres

When they feel like getting out of town, the inhabitants of Sérres are spoiled for choice. The north (by way of the summer resort of **Chrysopigí**) is ruled by the **Vrondoús** mountains, named for the thunder that resounds in its peaks, said to be louder than anywhere else in the world. Near the 6,064ft peak with an Arabian Nights name, Ali-Babas, grow the lofty beeches and pines of **Laïliá Forest**, where the local Beys once sent their harems in the summer, and the locals ski in winter (*t 232 105 8784*). Yet another road to the north, by way of **Eleónas** (with tavernas) offers splendid mountain and forest scenery en route to **Áno Vrondoú** (32km), a hamlet dominated by an enormous poplar. Closer, 10km northeast of Sérres, a wooded ravine shelters the important **Monastery Timíou Prodrómou**, founded in 1270; Gennádios Scholários, the first Patriarch of Constantinople under Ottoman rule, lived here from 1457 to 1462 and 1465–72 and was buried here. For 300 years the monastery's school offered Greeks a university-level education, but in 1941 it was wrecked by the Bulgarian army and the monks massacred. Now restored and home to nuns, it looks like the monasteries on Athos; there are remains of the frescoes in the *katholikón*.

Thracian refugees of 1922 brought their old customs to the villages near Sérres: firewalkers on 21 May (*see* p.544) in **Ag. Eléni** to the south and the *Gyneikokratia* or Rule of Women on 8 January (Midwife's Day) in **Monoklisiá** to the west, where men stay home with the children to do the housework while women take over the coffee-houses. Men who try to escape are lewdly teased or get a bucket of water over the head and a thrashing with a broomstick. It may be a last memory of a Dionysian festival, when women were likely to do much worse to men who didn't keep their heads down; these days it's an excuse for a big hen party.

Alistráti and Dráma

The road from Sérres to Dráma enjoys sweeping mountain views, south towards Mount Pangaíon and north to Mount Meníkio. Big bustling **Alistráti**, in between, has traditional houses and, to the south, the **Alistráti Cave** (*6km, well signposted, t 232 408 2045, www.alistratycave.gr; open daily 9–5, till 9pm in summer; adm exp*). Discovered only in 1975, its stalactite formations include the finest gravity-defying eccentrics in Greece. At the time of writing a trail from the cave is being laid out to the nearby Angístis Ravine, where the steep walls are decorated here and there with primitive rock etchings dated to the 5th century AD. The Angístis river is a favourite for rafting, with a 15km course; there's a good view and easy access at **Stathmós Angístis**.

The road continues to **Dráma**, a thriving tobacco town, with big *plateías*, a lovely park and the Ag. Varvára quarter with its streams, ponds and cafés; otherwise it's one of those places that should be more interesting than it is, especially given its name. Even the **Archaeology Museum**, at Patriárkou Dionysíou (*t 252 103 2365; open 8.30–3*), isn't very compelling. Nature is the main attraction: at **Kokinógia** (20km west) near the upper Angístis you can take a boat tour on a subterranean river in **Maara Cave** (*book, t 252 206 0460*), and to the north are the summits of Mount Falakró (Bald Mountain), the deep forests of Rodópi and the lakes of the Néstos (*see* p.600).

Ancient Philippi: the First Christian City of Europe

t 251 051 6470; open Tues–Sun 9–3; adm. Located on the KTEL bus route between Dráma and Kavála; car parks by the theatre or off the Via Egnatía.

In 360 BC, the Thássians (*see* below), already occupying Kavála, founded the colony of Krenídes ('fountains') to exploit new gold discoveries and the timber of Mount Pangaíon. Four years later it was wrenched from them by Philip II, who, not one for false modesty, renamed it Philippi and whose Macedonian settlers laid out a new town in the Hippodameian grid. It replaced Amphipolis as Macedonia's gold and silver centre, and was so important that the Via Egnatía was specially diverted north of Pangaíon for its sake in the 2nd century BC.

In 41 BC, the plain of Philippi witnessed a turning point of history. In the aftermath of Caesar's death, the legions of Brutus and Cassius, occupying Rome's eastern provinces, met the nearly equal force of Mark Antony and Octavian, in the biggest confrontation ever between Romans. In the first round, Brutus defeated Octavian (who was ill but managed to escape to Antony's camp), and Antony defeated Cassius, who committed suicide. Twenty days later Brutus let himself be drawn into battle in the same place and was crushed by Antony, bringing the Roman republic down with him as Brutus, too, committed suicide. Antony settled his veterans in the town, and in 30 BC Octavian (now Augustus) granted others land in his Colonia Augusta Iulia Philippensis. With his patronage it soon grew into a large Roman city. In AD 49 or 50 St Paul came here to preach Christianity for the first time in Europe, and baptized his first convert, Lydia. Otherwise, he and Silas had a rough time of it, attacked and imprisoned after Paul exorcised a demon from a fortune teller. Paul returned six years later, and seems, by his Epistle to the Philippians (c. AD 64), to have had a soft spot for the city. The 5th century brought the first barbarian raids; a massive 7th-century earthquake toppled the city. The Byzantines strengthened its walls, and it was still thriving when the Arab geographer Idrisi visited it in c. 1150. But by the time of the Turkish conquest, the fertile plain was a marsh. Excavations, begun in 1914, continue apace.

Most of Philippi's visible remains date from the Roman or Early Christian period. At the base of the pyramid-shaped acropolis hill, however, is the large **theatre** built by Philip II and remodelled to give it an extra large orchestra for Roman blood spectacles. It was partly restored in the 1950s for the summer Festival of Philippi, one of the most important ancient drama festivals in Greece; the relief figures of Victory, Nemesis and Ares that decorate it are from the 3rd century AD. Around the hill, a large terrace was built for the 5th-century **Basilica A** and baptistry (with a mosaic floor) that collapsed in the 7th-century earthquake; off to the right, carved into the rock, are niches and walls that belonged to several small 3rd-century AD **sanctuaries**, dedicated to Sylvanus, Bendix (the Thracian Artemis), Heracles, Dionysos and Hermes. The paved atrium in front of the basilica incorporates parts of an older heröon; the crypt below, supported by props, is said to be the **prison of St Paul**, where he and Silas were liberated by a timely earthquake; their guards, impressed, at once converted. Further west are the remains of 6th-century **Basilica C** and the **archaeological museum**, with exhibits from nearby Dikili Tass, an important Neolithic settlement just south, and from Philippi – mosaics, capitals, glass, coins and part of an inscription sent by Alexander for the town plan. From here a path winds up to the shattered bits of the **Sanctuary of the Egyptian Gods**, then up to the top of the **acropolis**, with three stark Byzantine towers built over the ancient originals, offering an excellent overview.

The rest of the city lies across the modern Via Egnatía, paralleling the ancient **Via Egnatía** – which doubled as Philippi's *decumanus*, or main north-south street – with its large paving slabs and sidewalks. Two side passages linked it to the vast **Forum**, which had two fountains for travellers on the north side. The **marketplace** was just to the southwest, although much of its stone was reused for the giant **Basilica B**, erected in the reign of Justinian. Like the Ag. Sophia in Constantinople, it was an experiment on the evolutionary road from Roman basilica to cruciform Byzantine church, and like the Ag. Sophia the dome collapsed, only here the discouraged architects abandoned the project, leaving only the mighty piers standing against the bluish backdrop of Mount Pangaíon. Several capitals, with their deeply incised acanthus leaves, are still in place. By the entrance arch lie scant remains of the **Palaestra**, but with beautifully preserved public **latrines**, a veritable monument where some 50 Philippians could take their ease at the same time. Further south are the **Roman baths** and a clubhouse (3rd century AD), stripped of their mosaics by the Bulgarians in 1941.

East of the forum, the **Octagon** was Philippi's cathedral, built in the mid-5th century over an earlier chapel dedicated to St Paul. Cubic on the outside, with a dome on top, the beautifully paved interior (including colourful mosaics) had an interior colonnade of 20 columns and a horseshoe apse projecting from one side; the original effect must have been similar to Ravenna's San Vitale. Beneath this is a vaulted Hellenistic funerary **heröon** belonging to a certain Euephenes Exekestou (whose name is also recorded as an initiate at Samothráki), who was somehow important enough to be buried in the city centre in the 2nd century BC. There are more **baths** just north of the Octagon (from the Christian era, and linked directly to its baptistry) and extensive remains of the **Bishop's Palace**, with storage vases in situ.

Just west of Philippi, on the little Zygaktis river, the **baptistry and church of Ag. Lydía** marks the first baptism in Europe. Other remains, including a large cemetery basilica and tombs, are scattered around modern **Krinídes**. Further south, on the last height before the road swoops down to Kavála, is the modern **Monastery of Ag. Sílas** near a pavilion with a stunning view down to the city, Thássos and Samothráki.

Kavála (Καβαλα)

Kavála, second city and port of northern Greece, has an enchanting amphitheatrical setting under Mount Símvolon, looking towards Thássos, a green mountain in the sea. Thássos made it a colony in the 7th century BC and called it Neapolis, but it knew its greatest prosperity as the Roman port of Philippi. Renamed Christoúpolis by the Byzantines, it prospered until the Normans burned it in 1185 during their failed attempt to take Constantinople. In the 19th century, elegant mansions went up, paid for by tobacco, the golden weed that made Kavála's fortune.

Just in from the waterfront, in a nest of public offices, the **Archaeological Museum** at 17 Erythroú Stavroú St (*t 251 022 2335; open Tues–Sun 8.30–3, till 11pm on Wed; adm*) shelters finds from Neapolis, including architectural elements from the 5th-century BC sanctuary of the virgin goddess Parthenos. One section has finds from Amphipolis – lovely jewellery, a silver mirror, gold wreath, a painted bust of a woman and a reconstruction of a Macedonian tomb with painted couches. Other artefacts come from other Greek colonies, including a painted sarcophagus (c. 300 BC) and a Cycladic amphora, with animal figures and patterns (630 BC). Venizélou Street, just in from

Getting There and Around

By air: Kavála airport, 29km east of town, t 259 105 3273, receives international charter flights and daily flights from Athens and Heráklion (on Aegean). Olympic is at 8 Eth. Anisasseos, t 251 083 0711; for Aegean information, t 259 105 3333.

By sea: frequent **ferries** from Kavála to Thássos, and at least once a week to Samothráki, Límnos, Lésbos and Chíos. **Port authority**: t 251 022 3716.

By road: There are **buses** to Kavála from Athens' Kifissou station three times a day, t 210 514 8572. The long distance bus station is by the quay, t 251 022 2294, and has connections to Thessaloníki (25 a day), Sérres, Xánthi and three a week to Lárissa, Tríkala and Ioánnina. Local buses, t 251 022 3593, from Plateía K. Dimítríou, on the east end of the quay, run every half hour to Dráma (with the nearest **train** station) by way of Philippi, to Eleftheroúpolis; to Chrisoúpolis and the beaches to Néa Péramos, and every hour to Keramotí. **Taxis**: t 251 022 1433 or t 251 023 2001 (radio taxi). **Car hire**: Budget, 35 El. Venizélou, t 251 022 8785, or Europcar, 24 El. Venizélou, t 251 023 1096, airport t 259 105 3222.

Tourist Information

EOT: Plateía Eleftherías, t 251 022 2425; open 9–2.
Tourist police: 119 Omonías, t 251 022 2905.

Festivals

Kavála and the State Theatre of Northern Greece sponsor the **Philippi-Thássos drama festival** in July and August; for information contact the Kavála Municipal Theatre, 10

Kyprou St, t 251 022 3504, f 251 022 0510. From 25 June –5 July, the city celebrates its **liberation** in 1913 from the Bulgarians.

Where to Stay and Eat

Kavála and its Beaches ✉ 65302
Egnatia, 139 7th Merarchías St (the road to Dráma), t 251 024 4891, f 251 024 5396, *egnatiah@otenet.gr* (*A; expensive*). Swish new hotel on top of town, with parking, and panoramic views from the roof garden.
Oceanis, 32 Erythroú Stavroú, t 251 022 1981 (*B; expensive*). Central; air-conditioned rooms, with a pool, bar, and more.
Galaxy, 27 El. Venizélou, t 251 022 4811, f 251 022 6754, *www.hotelgalaxy.gr* (*B; expensive–moderate*). Big hotel overlooking the harbour, with air-conditioned rooms.
Nefeli, 50 Erithroú Stavroú, t 251 022 7441, f 251 022 7440 (*C; moderate*). Pleasant little air-conditioned place near the archaeological museum, with a restaurant.
Ocean View, Paralía Eleochoriou (6km from Néa Péramos), t 259 402 3059, f 259 402 1848 (*B; expensive*). Small beach hotel with spacious rooms. *Open all year.*
Vournelis, Néa Iraklítsa, t 259 402 1353, f 259 402 2502 (*C; moderate–inexpensive*). Modest hotel by the beach. *Open all year.*
Miramare, Néa Péramos, t 259 402 2425, f 259 402 1035 (*C; moderate–inexpensive*). Seaside studios. *Open all year.*
Panos, Plateía Dimitriou, t 251 022 7978. Classic old-fashioned restaurant by the port.
Vangelis, 15 Thassou St, t 251 022 0997. Great place for delicious seafood on the coast, along the road to Xánthi. *Open all year.*
Athánato Neró, opposite the Imaret. Trendy restaurant with good *meze* and tables along the pavement for afternoon dawdling.

Erythroú Stavroú, marks the original waterfront; the large tobacco warehouses (which are more stylish than they sound) are now being converted into nightclubs and cafés. Nearby Kýprou and Filíppou Streets were the addresses of the tobacco princes; one, a mansion, a white folly modelled on a Hungarian castle, now serves as Kavála's city hall. The **Municipal Museum** on Filíppou has costumes, jewellery, needlework, paintings, stuffed birds and sculptures by Polýgnotos Vagis of Thássos.

Before it sprawled all over the place, Kavála was squeezed in the walls of its promontory, now a peaceful district of leafy cobbled streets, stepped alleys and neoclassical and Turkish houses. The crenellated Venetian-Turkish **citadel** on top was supplied with water by means of Kavála's landmark, the three-tiered **Kamáres** aqueduct, of Roman inspiration but built in 1550 by Suleiman the Magnificent. Just up from the port on Theodórou Poulídou Street, stop for a drink in the rambling yellow **Imaret**, bubbling with little metal-coated domes; in 1817 when Mehmét Alí (*see* below) asked Kavála what favour he could grant it, the answer was this, an almshouse for 600 boarders, a soup kitchen and a seminary, all funded by the rents Mehmét received from Thássos. It closed in 1923, but is still owned by the Egyptian government, and houses a café.

The same street continues up to a flamboyant equestrian **statue of Mehmét Alí**, sheathing his scimitar, paid for by Greeks in Egypt to honour the founder of the dynasty that endured until King Farouk. This stands next to the handsome **House of Mehmét Alí** (*open 10–2 and 5–7; donation*), built in 1720 and equally unrestored – don't jump up and down on the chestnut floors. Son of a prosperous Albanian farmer, Mehmét (1769–1849) was born here and spent much of his youth on Thássos. He left for good at age 35 to further his meteoric military career and was made viceroy of Egypt, where he massacred the Mamelouks, modernized the state, conquered the Sudan and with French assistance challenged the Sultan himself. The house, with its panelling and harem (he had six wives), kitchen and stable and rather rudimentary bath offers a glimpse of 18th-century life, but the only surviving piece of furniture is Mehmét Alí's desk, covered with pictures of his descendants (one of whom was Ibrahim, the terror of the Peloponnese). You can continue up on foot to the castle for the view; below the promontory to the east are the boat yards and marina.

Sandy beaches, hotels, villas, tavernas and campsites dot the 'Gialochória' west of Kavála, and all fly the Blue Flag thanks to the most modern biological sewage treatment plant in the Mediterranean. Closest to town are **Kalamitsa** and **Vatis**, both of which charge a fee for their facilities; next is **Tosca**, with a big hotel, then upscale **Paléo Tsiflíki** (or just 'Paléo') with its nightclubs and bars. **Néa Iraklítsa** still has a little fishing port tucked in its piney cape, and **Néa Péramos**, with a ruined Byzantine castle on the headland and a beautiful stretch of sand dunes, is lapped by a crystalline sea.

Thássos (ΘΑΣΟΣ)

Most of Kavála's visitors are en route to Thássos, Greece's northernmost island, ringed with soft beaches and mantled with pinewoods, plane trees, walnuts and chestnuts. It has a moist climate, subject to lingering mists; on hot days the intense scent of the pines by the sapphire sea casts a spell of dreamy languor. The opening of Kavála airport to charter flights brought in package tours from Britain and Germany, but these days the island, a short drive from Bulgaria and Romania, is in the throes of becoming the morning star of the Balkan Riviera. Wherever you sleep, come armed: the mosquitoes are vivacious, vicious and voracious.

In *c.* 710 BC Thássos was invaded by Greek colonists from Páros. The Parians dominated in the end, and it was worth all the fuss: they annually extracted 90 talents of gold and silver from their mines on the island and mainland colonies; its marble, timber, fine oil and wine were in demand across the Aegean. Trouble came in 490 BC,

Getting There and Around

By sea: ferry from Kavála to Skála Prínos almost every hour and to Liménas once a day; also frequent links from Keramotí to Liménas. There are **hydrofoils** from Kavála to Liménas (at least eight a day), Limenária, Liménas Potós and Kallíráchi. **Port authorities:** Keramotí, **t** 259 105 1204; Liménas, **t** 259 302 2106.

By road: the **bus** service, **t** 259 302 2162, is good; from Liménas quay there are at least 10 services daily to Skála Prínos, Skála Potamiá and Limenária, and six to Theológos and all around the island. **Car hire** is available at the agencies around the central *plateía* in Liménas; try Ladicas Travel, **t** 259 302 3590, **f** 259 302 3402.

Tourist Information

Tourist police: in Liménas, on the waterfront, **t** 259 302 3111.

Where to Stay

Package firms rule here, but fluctuate; one year a hotel will be block-booked, the next year not. Whatever the case, be sure to have a reservation before you arrive.

Liménas (Thássos Town) ✉ 64004

Makryámmos Bungalows, t 259 302 2101, **f** 259 302 2761, *makryamo@otenet.gr* (*A; expensive*). The poshest place to stay, on the soft sandy beach of the same name, with watersports, tennis, pool, fine restaurant and a nightclub. *Open May–Oct.*

Ethira, on the edge of Liménas, **t** 259 302 3310, **f** 259 302 2170 (*B; expensive–moderate*). White bungalows, green lawns and a pool.

Amfipolis, one street back from the waterfront, **t** 259 302 3101, **f** 259 302 2110 (*A; expensive*). Spacious, converted from a tobacco warehouse, with a pool.

Filoxenia Inn, t 259 302 3331, **f** 259 302 2231, *Philoxenia-Thassos@hotmail.com* (*C; moderate*). An old white villa near the port with a petite pool.

Villa Molos, t 259 302 2053 (*moderate–inexpensive*). Bed and breakfast near the sea in a quiet garden setting.

Alkyon, t 259 302 2148, **f** 259 302 3662 (*C; moderate–inexpensive*). Welcoming, airy place by the harbour.

Asteria, one street back from the main seafront. In business since 1962, with lots to offer from the spit including revolving goats' heads sporting lascivious grins.

New York, on the east end of the harbour (about €15). Covers all options with

when the invading Persians razed the city walls. When they reappeared a decade later under Xerxes, the Thassians cleverly prevented another attack by hosting a fabulous banquet in their honour. Thassos later revolted against the Delian League, and in 463 BC Athens sent Kimon to teach it a lesson, which took a two-year siege. After that Thássos was ruled by Athens, until Philip II seized it and its gold mines. In 1813, when the Sultan gave the island to Mehmét Alí, brought up in the village of Theológos, he lowered taxes and granted Thássos virtual autonomy. Benevolent Egyptian rule lasted until 1902, when the Turks returned briefly before union with Greece in 1912.

Liménas (Thássos Town)

The bustling capital and port of the island is officially Thássos, but is better known as **Liménas**. It may not be pretty, but it's lively; massive plane trees shade the squares, and shops wait to sell you walnut sweets and honey. Abandoned between the Middle Ages and the 1850s, the town's 2,300 inhabitants can hardly begin to fill the shoes of **ancient Thassos**; bits of it crop up everywhere and give the town its character.

The contents of the recently expanded **Archaeological Museum** at Megálou Alexándrou (*t 259 302 2180, to see if it's re-opened*) hint at the wealth of the ancient city-state: there's a 7th-century BC plate showing Bellerephon on Pegasus slaying the

traditional Greek food, giant pizza for five, pasta dishes and occasionally fresh mussels.
Syntaki, in the same area. For home-grown vegetables and good fish.
Marina's. Long-established, British-owned bar right on the waterfront; a friendly jam-packed place to begin and end the evening.

Panagía ✉ 64004

Thassos Inn, t 259 306 1612, f 259 306 1027 (*C; moderate*). Charming place. *Open all year.*
Helvetia, t 259 306 1231 (*E; moderate*). Small and perfectly reasonable.
Kosta. One of the most popular tavernas, packed on Sunday afternoons with locals.
Tris Pigés Taverna, next to the church. Bouzouki nights with dancing on Fri, Sat, Sun and Mon nights.

Skála Potamiás/Kínira ✉ 64001

Sylvia, at Kínira, by the sea, t 259 304 1246, f 259 304 1247 (*C; expensive*). Quiet, medium-sized and modern, with a pool and playground.
Miramare, t 259 306 1040, f 259 306 1043 (*B; expensive–moderate*). Moderate-sized, with a restaurant and pool close to the sea.
Blue Sea, t 259 306 1482, f 259 304 1278 (*C; moderate*). Better than Miramare, if you can nab one of its 12 rooms.

Camping Chrysí Ammoudiá, t 259 306 1472. A fine campsite by the sands.

Limenária/Potós ✉ 64002

Garden, Limenária, t 259 305 2650, f 259 305 2660 (*C; inexpensive*). Studios and a pool.
Alexandra Beach, Potós, t 259 305 2391, f 259 305 1185, alexandra@tha.forthnet.gr (*A; expensive*). Handsome hotel with nearly every imaginable watersport, tennis and a pool. *Open April–Oct.*
Coral Beach, right on the sea on the south end of Potós, t 259 305 2402, f 259 305 2121 (*B; expensive*). Cheaper but still has all kinds of mod cons and pool.

Skála Prínos/Skála Rachóni ✉ 64004

Xanthi, t 259 307 1303 (*C; inexpensive*). Good guesthouse on the edge of town. *Open June–Sept.*
Kyriakos Taverna, Prínos quay. Good fresh food and a wider than average selection.
Zorba's, next door. Just as popular; an added treat is the traffic policemen assailing your eardrums with their whistles.
Coral, Skála Rachóni, t 259 308 1247, f 259 308 1190 (*C; moderate*). A well-scrubbed, stylish place to stay with a pool amid the olives, and there's a row of beach tavernas.

Chimera; a 6th-century BC *Kriophoros* (a young man bearing a lamb) over 11ft high, but left unfinished when the sculptor discovered a flaw in the marble by the ear; an Archaic relief (550 BC) of a hunting scene and a beautiful ivory lion's head from the same period; a lovely, effeminate head of Dionysos from the 4th century BC; an elegant Hellenistic Aphrodite riding a dolphin; and Roman busts, including a fine one of Hadrian and another of Alexander the Great.

Mount Ipsárion, a solid block of white and greenish marble in the middle of Thássos, provided the raw material for the ancient city. In the centre of Liménas, the **agora**, much rebuilt under the Romans, is the most prominent survivor, with foundations and columns of porticoes and stoas, sanctuaries and a massive altar. A **heröon** in the centre of the market honoured the astonishing mid-5th-century BC athlete Theogenes, who won 1,400 victories in his career. The mysterious paved 'Passage of Theoria', predating the rest of the agora by 500 years, leads back to the sparse remains of the **Artemision**, where some of the most precious votives in the museum were found. On the other side of the agora are a **Roman street**, an **exedra** and a few tiers of the **Odeion**. East, towards the ancient naval port, another group of ruins includes a **Sanctuary of Poseidon**, with two altars on its terrace; next to it, another **altar** remains in good enough condition to accept sacrifices to its divinity, Hera

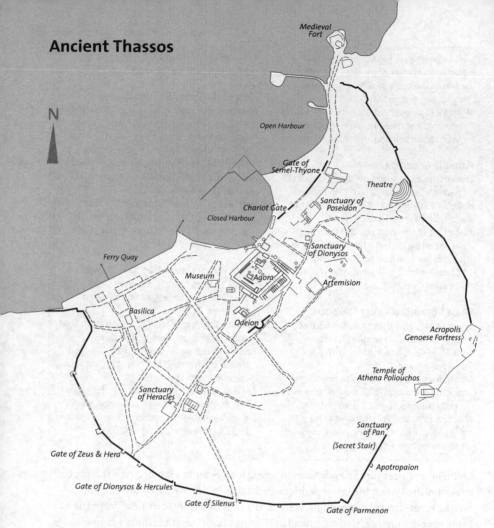

Ancient Thassos

Medieval Fort

N

Open Harbour

Gate of Semel-Thyone

Theatre

Chariot Gate

Closed Harbour

Sanctuary of Poseidon

Ferry Quay

Museum

Agora

Sanctuary of Dionysos

Artemision

Basilica

Odeion

Acropolis Genoese Fortress

Sanctuary of Heracles

Temple of Athena Poliouchos

Sanctuary of Pan

(Secret Stair)

Apotropaion

Gate of Zeus & Hera

Gate of Dionysos & Hercules

Gate of Silenus

Gate of Parmenon

Epilimenia, guardian of ports. Remains of the naval gates with bas-reliefs survive here: the **Chariot Gate** (with Artemis in a chariot) and the **Gate of Semel-Thyone** (with Hermes and the Graces). From here, a path leads to the ruined medieval fort and the beginning of the city's **walls**, last rebuilt in 411 BC but kept in repair by the Genoese.

Unless you're really keen, however, there's a shortcut to the acropolis by way of the **Sanctuary of Dionysos** (south of the Sanctuary of Poseidon), with its 3rd-century BC choreographic monument, erected by the winner of a drama prize. From here a path rises to a charming 5th-century BC **Greek theatre**, affording a fine view over the pines and sea. Above, the **acropolis** is spread across three summits of a ridge. On the first stands a **Genoese fortress** built out of the Temple of Pythian Apollo, whose Delphic oracle had encouraged the Parians to colonize the island; a relief of a funerary feast (4th century BC) can be seen near the guardroom. The second hill has the foundations of a 5th-century BC **Temple of Athena Poliouchos**, while the third and highest summit was a **Sanctuary of Pan**. An eroded relief shows Pan piping to his goats.

Around the back of the sanctuary, the vertiginous **Secret Stair**, carved in the 6th century BC, descends precipitously down to the remaining **walls and gates** (be careful if you attempt it: the stair-rail is rusted and there are big gaps between the steps). Here you'll find the watchful stone eyes of the **Apotropaion** (to protect the walls from the Evil Eye), the well-preserved **Gate of Parmenon**, still bearing its inscription 'Parmenon made me' and, best of all, the large **Gate of Silenus** (by the intersection of the road to Panagía), although a vigorous bas-relief of the phallic god (6th century BC) has lost its most prominent appendage to a 'moral cleansing' in the 20th century. Continuing back towards town are, respectively, the **Gate of Dionysos and Hercules** with an inscription, and the **Gate of Zeus and Hera** with an Archaic relief; this last one is just beyond the Venus hotel if you gave the Secret Stair a miss.

The sandy town beach is small and shaded, but tends to be crowded. **Makryámmos**, 3km to the east, is lovely, and defends its chic aura with an entrance fee; just west, buses or boats will take you to **Chrysí Ámmos**, **Glyfáda** and **Papalimáni**, all free.

Clockwise Round the Island: Beaches and More Beaches

A road encircles Thássos, and in July and August expect it to be busy. Directly south of Liménas, charming **Panagía** is the prettiest traditional village in Macedonia. Down by the sea, tavernas line the lovely town beach **Chrysí Ammoudiá**. To the south of Panagía, another large, well-watered mountain village, **Potamiá**, has two museums: a small **Folk Art Museum** (*closed Tues*) and the **Polýgnotos Vages Museum** (*t 259 306 1400; open Tues–Sat 9–1 and 6–9, Sun 10–2*), dedicated to the local sculptor (d. 1965) who made it big in New York. A path from Potamiá leads to the summit of **Mount Ipsárion** (3,697ft), taking about seven hours there and back, while below stretches the excellent beach of **Chrysí Aktí** (or **Skála Potamiás**). Quiet **Kínira** has a small shingly beach closed off by an islet; just south are the white sands of **Paradise Beach**.

The hamlet of **Alikí**, set on a headland overlooking twin beaches, thrived on marble exports in ancient times and has the ruins of an Archaic Doric double sanctuary. Further along, the slate-roofed **Monastery Archángelou** is perched high over the sea on arid cliffs. Its cloistered nuns are in charge of a sliver of the True Cross, but the pretty courtyard and church may be visited (*proper attire, even long sleeves, required*); paradoxically, the pebble beach in the cliffs below is frequented by nudists. The lovely beach of **Astrís**, above Cape Sapúni, is still defended by medieval towers. Continuing clockwise, much of Thássos' resort development (and worst forest fires) have happened above the sandy beaches around **Potós**, golden **Pefkári** and white **Psilí Ámmos**, with plenty of olive groves in between. Potós is a good place for a drink over the sunset, and for exploring inland; a handful of buses each day make the 10km trip up to the handsome slate-roofed **Theológos**, the former capital of Thássos.

The island's second town **Limenária** is surrounded by trees and endowed with a huge stretch of shady beach. In 1903 the German Spiedel Company mined the ores in the vicinity; the company's office, the 'Little Palace', is prominent on the headland. Cruise boats depart for Mount Athos. Some 15km inland, **Kástro** sits high on a sheer precipice, a refuge in the days of piracy, where the abandoned houses are now being converted into holiday homes. From here the road joins the flatter west coast of

Thássos, farm country, where the beaches are less crowded. **Tripití** has fine sands near the somewhat ramshackle little port of **Skála Marión**, while **Mariés** proper, 10km inland, is perhaps the least changed of the island's traditional villages. **Skála Prínos**, the ferry port to Kavála, enjoys views of an oil platform.

Down the Néstos River

Some of the north's finest natural features lie along the Néstos river. It rises in Bulgaria, then enters Greece for its last 140km, weaving between Mt Falakró north of Dráma and the lush Rodópi Mountains, home to Greece's largest forests. The dammed upper lakes have a sprinkle of villages on their mostly inaccessible banks, and only forest roads penetrate the **Karándere Forest** (by way of Skalotí and Elatiá) and the **Zagranténia Forest** (north of Thermatá); the latter is among the last virgin 2,650 acres in Greece, a 'Monument of Nature' where Egyptian vultures and eagles breed.

Downstream, 40km east of Dráma, **Paranésti** is a quiet village; here the Néstos meets the Dráma–Xánthi railroad, laid out in the 19th century by Ottoman engineers concerned to protect it from coastal bombardments. Defensive considerations are nothing new here: take the road 15km east at Neochóri then north to **Ionikó** and the marble hilltop **Fortress of Kalyva**, built by Philip II in 340 BC, with a deep beehive cistern and a well-preserved relief of Priapas on the gate. **Stavroúpolis**, the largest Néstos village, has a well-preserved **Macedonian tomb** of c. 200 BC, with marble couches and painted decoration; to visit, ring the guard, **t** 254 202 2040.

Below Stavroúpolis begin the beautiful **Narrows of the Néstos**, the 'Thracian Tempi' where the river coils like a clock spring through the wooded limestone hills. Rare flowers dot the banks; Levant sparrow hawks and lesser spotted eagles hover

Sports and Activities

Strovilos, t 254 109 3870, **f** 254 109 3871, *ico@otenet.gr*, offers rafting and kayaking down the Néstos and parasailing.
Maíandros, t 254 206 2690, for rafting trips.
Néstos Delta Visitor Centre, t 259 105 1831. Behind the high school in Keramotí; *open daily 8.30–2.*

Where to Stay and Eat

Paranésti ✉ 66035
Filoxenia, t 252 402 2001, **f** 252 402 2031 (C; *moderate*). New hotel set up above town, with comfortable rooms and balconies.

Stavroúpolis ✉ 67062
Iniochos, just south in Komniná, **t** 254 202 2678, **f** 254 202 2483, *perinest@otenet.gr*

(*luxury*). Three separate houses, comfortably furnished with kitchens and fireplaces around a garden, pool and bar. *Open all year.*
Xenios Zeus, t 254 202 2444 (*moderate*). Charming traditional guesthouse in the centre of the village with a little courtyard, located just above the village square.

Chrisoúpolis ✉ 64200
Irene, 13 Venizélou St, **t** 259 102 2163, **f** 259 102 2718 (C; *moderate*). Fairly quiet hotel, convenient to the airport and the Néstos Delta. *Open all year.*

Keramotí ✉ 64011
Karagianis, t 259 105 1471, **f** 259 105 1077 (B; *expensive–moderate*). Comfortable studios, 50 yards from the sea. *Open summer only.*
Xastero, t 259 105 1212, **f** 259 105 1230 (C; *moderate*). A bar and restaurant and disabled access. *Open all year.*

overhead, nightingales and Orphean warblers serenade from the trees; wild Liverian horses roam the meadows. The train (there's no road) is an easy way to see it (although there are lots of tunnels), or you can float down the Néstos in a canoe, raft or kayak. Or follow the long distance path E6; for a lovely four-hour stroll, start at the abandoned train station at **Liverá** and end at Galani, by **Toxótes**, where there's a big sandy beach and a delightful restaurant, the Touristiko Katafygio (swimming can be dangerous, though, because of sudden releases from the hydroelectric plants).

Wetlands (and Kavála's airport) surround **Chrisoúpolis**, a big market town to the south, while coastal **Keramotí** with a sandy peninsula is a low key resort with excellent beaches and tavernas, specializing in mussels and offering the most frequent ferries to Thássos. It's also the base for visiting the beautiful **Néstos Delta**. Lagoons stretch for 50km east and west of the river mouth, and encompass the **Kotza Orman** (Turkish for 'Legendary') **Forest**, the last luxuriant remnant of a once vast coastal woodland. Stop at the visitor's centre (*see* above) for directions. The delta is home or way station to over 300 kinds of birds, including rare avocets and collared pratincoles.

Thrace (Thráki): Xánthi to Turkey

Modern Thrace (for its history, *see* pp.581–3) has often served as a buffer zone, and frankly this is not the first place for anyone in search of a classic Greece experience – although it's a good place to find an authentic one, as well as experiences that cross ethnic and religious borders. Ornithologists can have a field day at Lake Vistonída, the Évros Delta and Dadiá National Forest; there's a major ancient site on Samothráki, itself a best-kept secret, and minor ones at Abdera and Marónia. Best of all is the new spirit that has emerged with the relaxing of tensions between Greece, Bulgaria and Turkey, and the feeling that Thrace may no longer be a far-flung buffer on the edge of Greece, but in the forefront of pan-Balkan co-operation.

Xánthi (ΞΑΝΘΗ)

With 50,000 souls, Xánthi owes its name either to a Thracian tribe, the Xanthons, or Xanthos, one of the carnivorous horses of Diomedes (*see* below). At the foot of the Rodópi mountains, it was a summer resort of the Ottomans before the railway turned it to business, especially in golden *xanthíyaka*, the finest Turkish tobacco. These days sugar beet is as important – hence the giant refinery. Xánthi may be the most Balkan city in Greece, especially on Saturday when Greeks, Turks and Pomaks pour into town to haggle around the market and the cluster of squares that make up Xánthi's heart. Under the scant remains of a Byzantine fort on the north side, the granite paved streets of **Old Xánthi** twist up, lined with traditional houses and colourful tavernas; the neighbourhood even holds its own September festival. But the Xanthiots are a fun-loving lot: they put on the liveliest carnival in Thrace, and at Lefkos Pyrgos just to the northwest there's a flash casino, with a five-star hotel in the works.

North of Xánthi you can slip off the beaten track to visit the **Pomak** villages of the Central Rodópi. One theory (supported by Ottoman tax records) has it that the

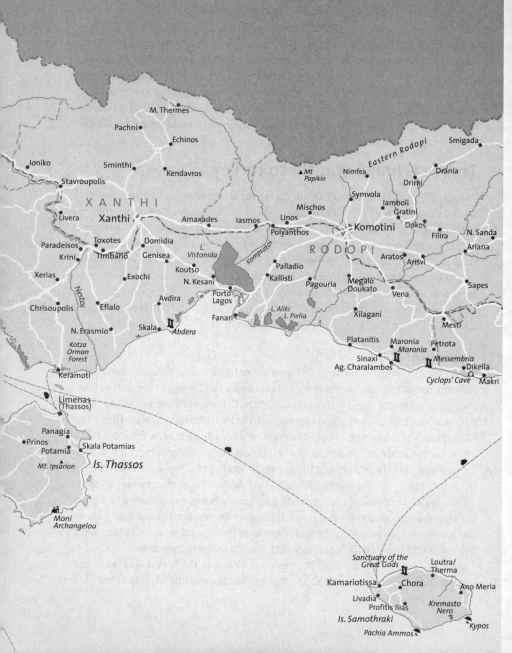

Thrace

Svilengrad
Ormeni
Petrota
Dikea
Edirne
Kastanies
Rizia
Ardas
Milta
Valtos
Kavili
Orestiada
Doxa
Evgeniko
Metaxades
Erithropotamos
Mavroklisi
Didimoticho
Pythio
Petrades
Mikrochori
Mikro Derio
Protoklisi
Mt Virsinis
Kechros
K. Kambi
Mega Derio
Soufli
EVROS
Evros
Dadia
Likofi
Dadia National Forest
Leptokaria
Lefkimi
Tichero
Esimi
TURKEY
Kirki
Kipi
Avantas
Ardani
Ipsala
Feres
Loutros
Doriskos
Traianoupoli
Alexandroupolis
L. Nimfes

BULGARIA

TURKEY

Getting There and Around

By air: Xánthi has a bus to Kavála airport from the Olympic office at 6a Michael Vogdou St, t 254 102 6497. To the east, Alexandroúpolis has three flights daily from Athens, t 255 104 5198; the Olympic office is at 6 Ellis & Kolleti Sts, t 255 102 6207.

By sea: Alexandroúpolis is the main port for Samothráki (*see* p.610) and usually has two ferries a week to Límnos, Psára, Ag. Efstratios, Lésbos, Chíos, Sámos, Kos, Rhodes and Rafína; for information, t 255 102 5455.

By train: several a day to Xánthi, Komotiní, Alexandroúpolis, and to the towns along the Évros en route to Svilengrad in Bulgaria. For schedules (and for info on buses to Turkey and Bulgaria) contact the stations in Xánthi (Kondili St, t 254 102 2581), Komotiní (2.5km west of town, but there's an OSE office at 50 S. Kyriákos, t 253 102 6804), and Alexandroúpolis (east end of the port, t 255 102 6398).

By road: from Athens' Kiffisou station **buses** go to Xánthi, t 210 513 2084, Komotiní and Alexandroúpolis, t 210 513 3280. A daily service to Istanbul begins in Xánthi (tickets from Tarpidou Travel, t 254 102 2277); for Bulgaria, t 254 102 2277. For local services, contact KTEL: Xánthi, t 254 102 2684 (long distance) or t 254 102 2740 (provincial); Komotiní, t 253 102 2912; Alexandroúpolis, t 255 102 6479. **Car hire**: try Budget in Komotiní (62 Plateía Irínis, t 253 103 6903) and Alexandroúpolis (t 255 102 9028).

Tourist Information

EOT: 14 Ap. Souzou, Komotiní, t 253 107 0996, f 253 107 0995.
Tourist police: Alexandroúpolis, Karaïskáki St, t 255 103 7411.

Where to Stay and Eat

Xánthi ✉ 67100

Zita Palace, G. Kondyli, t 254 106 4414, f 254 106 4410, *z-palace@otenet.gr* (*A; luxury*). The smartest, on the west end of town, and the only hotel with a pool; good French as well as Greek dishes are on the menu of the restaurant, L'Étoile (around €20).

Elena, 2 Stratoú, Av, t 254 106 3901, f 254 106 3906, *elenahotel@internet.gr* (*B; expensive*). Located on the northeast side of town, near Old Xánthi; modern, cosy and air-conditioned. Ask for a room with a view.

Natassa, just outside town on the Kavála road, t 254 102 1521, f 254 102 1525 *www.hotel natassa.gr* (*B; expensive*). Large and recently renovated, with a welcoming atmosphere. Good Continental breakfast.

Xanthippion, 214 28th Oktovríou, t 254 107 7061, f 254 107 7076 (*C; high moderate*). Fairly central hotel, but parking isn't easy.

Ta Fanarakia, 14 G. Stavroú, t 254 107 3606. Good food, including some unusual meat dishes from the grill.

To Ktima, 4km east on the Komotiní road, t 254 102 1010. A big favourite, using only organic ingredients on its wide-ranging menu; some seafood and a good wine list.

Xanthippi, on the Dráma road, t 254 102 3627. On top of the city by the theatre, famous for its wild boar and offers a view over every roof in Xánthi. Stop for a drink opposite at the **Alexandra**, a bar in an old mansion.

Komotiní ✉ 69100

Try Komotiní's famous *soutzouk lukum*, long ropes of Turkish delight with walnuts.
Astoria, 28 Plateía Irínis, t 253 103 5054, f 253 102 2707 (*B; expensive*). Komotiní's oldest

---

Pomaks, originally Christian, were forced to convert to Islam in 17th century, when their mountains were the favoured hunting grounds of the Sultan and his retinue. They required a large number of servants, who by law had to be Muslims. One place to aim for is north, to the little spa village of **Thérmes**, where a rock is carved with a vivid relief of the 2nd century AD, showing the Persian sun god Mithras (a favourite of the Roman legions) sacrificing a bull.

By the sea south of Xánthi, at Ag. Panteleímos, lie the rather meagre remains of ancient **Abdera** (*t 254 105 1988; open daily 8–2; free*). For his Eighth Labour, Heracles had to capture the four man-eating horses of Diomedes, the king of the war-like

and most attractive hotel, right in the heart of town, overlooking the garden.

Democritus, 8 Plateía Vizínou, **t** 253 102 2044, **f** 253 102 3396 (*C; expensive*). Central, a short walk from the park.

Giaxis, 8 Kilkis St, **t** 253 103 3786. Handsome restaurant near the market, with shady outdoor tables serving the best seafood in town, brought in from Pórto Lágos.

T'aderfia, 33 Orfeos St, **t** 253 102 0201. Good, popular taverna with a big choice of dishes and very friendly prices.

Ydrohoos, Plateía Irínis, **t** 253 103 3786. Cosy 24-hour restaurant featuring *laderá* dishes.

Marónia/Platanítis ✉ 69400

Platanitis, **t** 253 306 1065, **f** 253 306 1067 (*A; expensive*). Classy big rooms in a small hotel with a pool, across the road from the beach.

Roxani, 3km from the sea, **t** 253 304 1391, **f** 253 304 1258, *www.ecoexplorer.gr* (*expensive*). Traditionally styled hotel, with big comfortable rooms, a restaurant (vegetarian meals available on request), bar, cigar humidor and Internet access. Delicious breakfasts of home-grown products. Free transport from Alexandroúpolis airport or Komotiní train station. Works with Ecoexplorer (*see below*).

Women's Rural Tourism Cooperative, **t** 253 304 1258. Inexpensive rooms in local houses; a chance to try local cuisine and gain insights into everyday life.

Alexandroúpolis ✉ 68100

Astir, 280 Dimoktrias St (1km west of the centre), **t** 255 102 6448, **f** 255 102 4651 (*A; luxury–expensive*). Long-established hotel with the city's finest rooms in a garden by the beach. Pool, good restaurant, and friendly service. *Open all year*.

Alexander Beach, 2km west of town, **t** 255 103 9290, **f** 255 103 9070, *www.alexbh.gr* (*B; expensive*). Newish tranquil hotel with a seawater pool and tennis, most rooms with sea views. *Open all year*.

Park, 458 Dimokratias St, **t** 255 102 8607, **f** 255 103 1002 (*C; moderate*). Tidy new hotel with a small pool in the courtyard, between the centre and a park of pinewoods that tries hard to please.

Erika, 110 Karaoli Kimitriou, **t** 255 103 4115, **f** 255 103 4117 (*D; moderate*). Closest to the ferries, but can get noisy in the evening.

Camping Alexandroupolis, **t** 255 102 8735. Big, municipally run site out by the sandy town beach, just west of the city.

To Charama, 30 Kessanis St, **t** 255 103 5833. The best of several tavernas on Kessanis Street.

Dadiá/Souflí ✉ 68400

Ecotourist Hostel, Dadiá **t** 255 403 2263, **f** 255 403 2463 (*inexpensive*). A 10-room hostel ideal for vulture watchers. Women in nearby Katratzides run an agrotourism restaurant, the **Buzzard**, **t** 255 403 2209, serving traditional dishes.

Orpheus, Vas. Georgiou, Souflí, **t** 254 402 2922, **f** 255 402 29233 (*C; moderate*). Pleasant hotel in a pleasant village. *Open all year*.

Lagotrofio, 4km west on the Yiannoúli road, by the municipal pool, **t** 255 402 2001. A lovely setting for a renowned restaurant, famous for succulent meat and game dishes. *Open June–Sept daily; other times w/e only.*

Didimóticho ✉ 68300

Plotini, 1 Ag. Paraskeví, **t** 255 302 3400, **f** 255 302 2251 (*B; expensive*). Large, comfortable hotel on the south end of town, with a pool in the garden.

Bistonians. The horses were tethered with iron chains to bronze mangers in their stables by Lake Vistonída; Heracles killed their guards, and was leading the horses to his ship when Diomedes led an attack that Heracles crushed with his club. But when he returned to the shore, he found that the horses had devoured his friend Abderus; to honour his memory he founded the city and games, although out of respect horse-racing was always banned. Historically, the site was settled in 656 BC by Ionian colonists from Clazomenae and then in 545 BC by new arrivals from Teos. Abdera hosted Xerxes' army in 480 BC and nearly went broke as a result – which may be why its inhabitants had a reputation for stupidity in spite of the fact that it was the birthplace of Democritus, the father of atomic theory (c. 460–355 BC) and Protogoras, the first and wisest of the Sophists, who gave his name to one of Plato's *Dialogues*. But the Romans had little use for it, as it was too far south of their Via Egnatía. The most prominent remains are the seaside acropolis, where the Byzantines built a fortress, **Polystylon** ('many columns'), over the Classical walls. Within the fenced site are remains of a gate and walls, houses and a workshop where votives were made. The new **Archaeological Museum**, up in modern **Ávdira** (*t 254 105 1003; open daily 11–2; free; explanations in English*), has items from everyday life – a medical kit, perfume pots, coins, knucklebones (used as toys), jewellery and bronze 'key rings' from Roman times, a painted sarcophagus, and vases going back to 650 BC.

To the east, the new Via Egnatía cuts south of **Lake Vistonída**, where vast flocks of herons, swans, ducks, silver pelicans, flamingos and spoonbills feel perfectly at home; the **visitor centre** at Néa Kessáni (*t 254 109 6646; open Mon–Fri 9.30–3*) offers guided ornithological tours by arrangement. **Pórto Lagos**, the largest village on the lake, has a pretty landmark – the church of Ag. Nikólaos on an islet, reached by a causeway. A series of sandy beaches backed by lagoons begins on the east coast of Vistonía Bay at **Fanári**, which has hotels, rooms and a good campsite (*t 253 503 1217*); the huts you see belong to a reconstructed Sarakatsáni settlement. Until borders closed in the 20th century, the nomadic Sarakatsáni wandered on either side of the Rodópi mountains; now many have settled in **Palládio**, just northeast.

If you take the older (and shorter) road from Xánthi to Komotiní, a dirt road to the left just before **Amaxádes** leads to **Anastasioúpolis** (or Peritheorion) on the north shore of Lake Vistonída. Known as Stabulo Diomedis (Diomedes' Stable) until it was rechristened by Emperor Anastasius (d. 518), the city wall and towers built by Justinian survive, and on the south side the main gateway to the harbour still bears its imperial monograms. The city was destroyed by the Bulgarian Tsar Kaloyan in 1296, but it was rebuilt in 1341 and given the name of Peritheorion. Just east of **Iasmós**, near the road, an impressive triple-arched stone **bridge** carried the Via Egnatía over the Kompsátos stream; the locals claim it was built by Alexander the Great, but what now stands dates from the 18th century. At Linós you can take the prettier road to Kominití by way of **Míschos**, a typical Pomak village with an elegant minaret and watermill in a gorge.

Komotiní

Komotiní, the capital of Thrace and seat of its university, is a relative newcomer as Greek cities go, a mere fort on the Via Egnatía while nearby Maximianopolis (Byzantine Mosynopolis) was the big news until the latter's destruction by the Bulgars. First documented in 1331, it was the battleground in the civil war between the Emperor Andronicus III and Prince Omur of Smyrna; in 1363 it was taken for the Ottomans by a Greek convert to Islam, Gazi Evren Bey. When treaties following the First and Second Balkan War left this part of Thrace to Bulgaria, local Greeks and Turks united in resistance to form the short-lived Republic of Gumuljina (from Komotiní's Turkish name, Gümülcüne). It is also playing a role in the new Balkans: a natural gas pipeline from Russia is being constructed to Komotiní, and there are plans to use it to fire a power station on the Turkish border, to provide power for both countries.

Komotiní is already a shining example of Greeks and Turks living together; if you come on a Tuesday, when the **Pazari** (bazaar) takes place out by the swimming centre, you'll hear Turkish, Greek and Pomak in the scrum for bargains. Unfortunately, the town lost much of its character in the 1960s when the Boukloudzas river was diverted and its bed filled in to form a long winding avenue, taking with it old cobbled streets, a covered market, inns, baths, gardens and tanneries. Today the **Clock Tower** of 1884 and the minaret of the domed **Yeni mosque** mark the centre of what remains of the old town; nearby **Plateía Iféstou** and the surrounding lanes, the most colourful part of the city, are called the *tenekedzidika* ('tin-ville') for their traditional workshops. Pedestrian-only Plateía Irínis is a favourite meeting place, by the shady **Municipal Gardens**, with a memorable war memorial – a giant sword.

From here busy Ap. Soúzou Street passes the sign for the **Folklore Museum** (*13 Ag. Georgíou St; open Mon–Sat 10–1; adm*) in a 19th-century merchant's mansion, with beautiful costumes, music boxes, and elaborately worked guns and yataghans. The **Archaeological Museum**, further west on A. Symeonídi and Výronos Streets (*t 253 102 2411; open daily 9–6; free*), offers a good introduction to ancient Thrace; there's a relief of the Hero-rider, and another of Priapus; the iron soles of a soldier's sandals; a phallic altar dedicated 'to all the gods'; gold and silver votive plaques from a Sanctuary of Demeter ; a mask of Dionysos from Marónia, and a golden bust of Septimius Severus. Other finds come from the tomb of a landowner of the 1st century AD: a bronze ink box, lampstands, carbonized walnuts and other things you don't see every day.

Bulgaria is only 22km north, and to defend the defile 11km north of Komotiní in the Rodópi mountains the Byzantines built the **Nimféa Fortress**. In the Second World War it was returned to duty, when the 360 defenders resisted the invading Germans so tenaciously that the German commander warmly congratulated his counterpart when they were finally forced to surrender. There are pretty picnic spots in the woods and, just below the fortress, a tourist pavilion with broad views over the plain.

Marónia and the Coast to Alexandroúpolis

Marónia, 32km south of Komotiní, is a pleasant village with a scattering of old houses and roads down to the beach resorts of **Platanítis** and **Ag. Charálambos**. The latter replaces **ancient Maronia**, a once vast coastal city named after Maron, the priest of Apollo who rewarded Odysseus with strong wine, which he used to intoxicate the miserable Cyclops – and sure enough this area is the one part of Thrace with lots of vineyards. The city, founded by colonists from Chíos in the 7th century BC, was taken by the Persians in 513 BC, prospered again under Athens in the 5th century, and again under the Romans. Bits of the ancient city are scattered among the trees; 4km on the road from modern Marónia, on the left-hand side of the road, are parts of the west wall and two square 4th-century BC towers. Further along (signposted 'mosaic') is a Hellenistic **villa**, with a fireplace, mosaic floor, a room used for weaving and a bath-room. Near the car park by the sea are the ruins of a monumental marble double **gate**, built by Hadrian in AD 124, and the remains of a Byzantine church. A dirt road leading to the coast passes the 4th-century BC **Sanctuary of Dionysos**, and a sweet little Hellenistic **theatre**, with three tiers of marble seats and parapets added by the

Romans to protect the audience in gladiator shows. Beyond at Marmaritsa are **marble quarries**, where the speciality was millstones. At **Sínaxi**, the ruins of a Byzantine monastery stand over an ancient sanctuary, where pilgrims set sail for Samothráki; east of here mountains crowd the shore, although there's a beach below at **Petrotá**. Inland, a low altitude **black pine forest** is a botanical fluke, where the trees stand only 7–10ft tall. You can get to know the area through **Ecoexplorer** in Marónia (see 'Where to Stay'), which offers birdwatching, canoeing, speleology, archery and star-gazing.

East along the coast there's a good beach at **Mesembría**, by the foundations of a colony founded by Samothráki in the 7th century BC to trade with the Thracians. The ancient city (*t 255 109 6214*) has well preserved walls, blocks of houses, the Sanctuary of Demeter that yielded the votives in the Komotiní museum, and a Sanctuary of Apollo. After **Díkella**, a sign points the way to the **Cyclops Cave**, one of hundreds scattered across the Mediterranean; this area around **Mákri** has been inhabited since Neolithic times, although the excavations you see are of early Byzantine churches. From here it's 11km to Alexandroúpolis.

Inland, the new Via Egnatía motorway is finished between Komotiní and Alexandroúpolis, so you can zoom across the cotton and tobacco fields in about an hour. Or there's an older, slower route by way of the charming old **Gratíni** with a ruined Byzantine fortress. At **Arianá** you can make a detour way off the beaten track, north into the isolated villages of the east Rodópi, to the Pomak village **Kéchros**, where some of the older inhabitants still wear their traditional costume. Another scenic road begins east of Arianá at **Néa Sánda**, winding up and down to Alexandroúpolis by way of **Leptokariá** and the **Ávantas Gorge**. Or there's an older road, where you can seek out a pair of **Roman bridges** that carried the original Via Egnatía, at **Arísvi** and **Sápes**; from there the scenery is best by way of the village of **Kírki**.

Alexandroúpolis

Alexander the Great founded a score of cities that he named after himself, but this isn't one of them. Originally Dedeagaç, a holy town of dervishes, it became important in the 19th century with the railroad and artificial harbour, and in 1919 it was renamed after Greece's King Alexander (who died the following year from a bite from his pet monkey). It has the largest group of Gagauz (Christian Turkish-speaking people) in Greece, plus sizeable Armenian and Pontic communities. All gather in the evening to make a *vólta* along the waterfront, under a big lighthouse.

'Provincial' was long the word for Greece's easternmost port (for Samothráki, see p.610) but this is ripe to change: in 2002, the Novorossisk–Bourgas–Alexandroúpolis pipeline was begun alongside a European Urban Pilot Project to make the town a link between the Balkans, Black Sea and the Mediterranean. A high-tech information network is being installed in a former flour mill on the east end of town, near a new state-of-the-art **Natural History Museum**. Until it's ready, the first floor of the Cultural Centre in Plateía Polytechníou (*t 255 102 6200; open Mon–Sat 9–1*) has displays of stuffed creatures from the Évros; although the collection is only 50 years old some birds are already extinct. Alexandroúpolis also has a good **Folklore Museum**, at 319 Dimokratías St (*t 255 102 8926; open Tues–Sun 9–1*).

East of Alexandroúpolis: Up the Évros Valley

Thanks to decades of geopolitical turmoil, this easternmost corner of Greece has never been exploited the way it would have been had everyone been lovey dovey. Although it's been bad for humans, it has been great for nature, in particular for some of the rarest birds in Europe, including the slender-billed curlew. Many nest along the **Évros** (Meriçi in Turkish) **river**, the second longest in the Balkans after the Danube. It rises near Sophia and flows 530km into the sea, for 204km forming the border between Greece and Turkey. Just east of Alexandroúpolis, much of the shore is taken up by the Évros Delta, one of the richest natural habitats in Europe, where 304 of the 423 birds recorded in Greece have been sighted. Although irrigation on both sides between 1950–70 has reduced the delta to a fifth of its original size, it is now protected by the Ramsar convention. Because of the border, you can't just show up to visit, but need to arrange a bus, boat or bike tour two to three weeks in advance through English-speaking Andréas Adanasiádes at the **Évros Delta visitor centre** in **Traïanoupoli** (*t 255 106 1000, f 255 106 1020, euroswet@hol.gr; open Mon–Fri 8.30–2.30; email or fax your name, nationality, date of birth, and passport number*). September and October are the best times to visit (but drench yourself in mosquito repellent).

Named after the Emperor Trajan, Traïanoupoli was an important station on the Via Egnatía and is now a popular rural spa. Its landmark is an **Ottoman inn** from 1375 that in its current state resembles a Nissen hut (similar inns can be found in Turkey, every nine miles along the old Persian Royal Road). At nearby **Loutrós** there are picnicking spots along the torrent and a road north to Dadiá (*see* below). The main road east passes **Dorískos**, once a Persian fortress town, where proud Xerxes stopped to count his invading army, by building a corral that could hold 10,000 men at time. **Féres** up the road was an important defensive outpost of Constantinople; it has a ruined Byzantine aqueduct and, at the top of the town, the church **Panagía Kosmosotíra**, built by Isaac Comnenus in 1152, with a spacious interior and five domes; remnants of its frescoes and carved capitals hint of its once imperial decoration. **Ardáni** has the turn off for Istanbul, following the route of the ancient Via Egnatía; **Ipsala** on the Turkish side was once Kypsela, the largest city of the ancient Thracians.

Following the river north, just past Likófi, is the turn-off for **Dadiá National Forest**, famous for its birds of prey – altogether 36 of the 38 species remaining in Europe pass through in winter and spring, while 20 live here year round; with Extremadura in Spain it's the last European refuge of the black vulture. Wolves, jackals, roe deer, bats, squirrels, turtles and over 40 kinds of reptiles keep them company. The WWF-sponsored **Ecotourist Centre** (*t 255 403 2210*) has a mini bus to take visitors out to the observation post and feeding table where you can watch the big birds tuck into carrion; the centre also distributes a map showing the footpaths in the forest. On the edge of the protected area, **Souflí** has some fine old houses on the Évros, where mulberry trees fuel the local silk worm industry. An old mansion belonging to a silk manufacturer is now a **Silk Museum** (*t 255 402 3700; open Wed–Mon, 10–2 and 5–7, mid-Oct–mid-April 10–4*) with interesting displays on how it's all done.

The most important town in these parts, **Didimóticho** is piled theatrically on a steep hill where the Erithropótamos river flows into the Évros. Originally Plotinopoulis, founded by Trajan and named for his wife Plotina, it was captured by Frederick Barbarossa during the Third Crusade; in Byzantium's Civil War (1341–47), John Cantacuzenós, Andronicus III's Grand Domestic, was proclaimed emperor here by the army. In 1361 it fell to Sultan Murad I, who made it his capital and built the large square **mosque** with a pyramid roof in Plateía Dimarchíon; the original interior decoration is well preserved. A bit further up is the pride of Didimóticho, its excellent **Folklore Museum** (*t 255 302 2236; ring ahead*) with displays that cover the gamut of a vanishing way of life. Further up are the walls of the **castle**, built by the Byzantines and Turks over Plotinopoulis, with good views of the Évros. The back streets in and around the walls are especially picturesque, lined with old Turkish houses and hammams. There's an even better intact Byzantine castle, overlooking the river to the east at **Pýthio**, used as a retreat by John Cantacuzenós. In the other direction, up the Erithropótamos, **Metaxádes** has some well preserved stone mansions from the days when its merchants travelled the Ottoman empire.

To the north, sugar beets grow in the flat lands around **Orestiáda**, a town with wide streets and more than its share of bored young soldiers. At **Kastaniés**, the border was drawn west of the river to encompass greater **Edirne** (Adrianoúpoli), the Ottoman capital after Didimóticho and before Constantinople (1367–1458) and now the big market city in the area, where many Greeks go over to shop; it has a beautiful mosque designed by Sinan. To the west of Kastaniés, the Árdas river is an important tributary of the Évros and the scene of a summer youth festival. **Orméni** is the last stop in Greece before Bulgaria and the frontier town Svilengrad.

Samothrace/Samothráki (ΣΑΜΟΘΡΑΚΗ)

Samothráki is an island of lingering magic, of cliffs, nightingales, plane forests and waterfalls around the 5,459ft Mountain of the Moon (Mount Fengári), where Poseidon sat to observe the tides of the Trojan War. Although lacking a natural harbour, Samothráki was one of the most visited islands of antiquity, thanks to its Sanctuary of the Great Gods; people from all over the Mediterranean came here to be baptized in bull's blood and initiated into its Mysteries.

Kamariótissa and Chóra

Samothráki's workaday port, **Kamariótissa**, has an exposed rocky beach and most of the island's modest tourist facilities. High above, safely hidden from raiding pirates, the whitewashed houses of **Chóra** occupy an amphitheatre below a broken tooth of a ruined Byzantine castle. Designated a 'traditional settlement', it has a charming old bakery and a little **Folklore Museum** (*open summer 11–2 and 7–10pm*).

Pretty agricultural hamlets dot the slopes of southern Samothráki: **Alónia**, the largest, has ruins of a Roman bath, while **Profítis Ilías** is famous for tavernas serving kid. From delightful **Lákoma**, a windy 8km road leads to the turn-off for the church of **Panagía Kremniótissa**, tottering high on rocks and taking in huge views as far as the Turkish island of Imbros. Below is the island's main sandy beach, **Pachiá Ámmos**, with

Getting There and Around

A new airport is being built. Daily **ferries** cross from Alexandroúpolis, and at least twice a week from Kavála. From Feb–Nov, daily **hydrofoils** go from Alexandroúpolis (t 255 102 6721) to Samothráki; also frequently from Kavála. **Port authority:** t 255 104 1305.

Buses run from Kamariótissa to Chóra, Alónia, Palaeópolis, Loutrá/Therma and Pachía Ámmos; for schedules, t 255 104 1505.

Car hire: Budget, t 255 104 1100, f 255 103 8233.

Taxis: t 255 104 1341.

Tourist Information

Tourist police: in Chóra, t 255 104 1218 or t 255 104 1790.

Where to Stay and Eat

Kamariótissa ✉ 68002

Aeolos, t 255 104 1795, f 255 104 1810 (B; expensive). Family-run hotel with a modest pool, 300m east of town; all rooms have balconies, some with views. Open April–Oct.

Klimatariá, t 255 104 1535. For traditional Greek fare, the best value in town.

Limanaki, t 255 104 1987 (moderate). Smart new place on the far end of town, with delicious seafood (around €20) and spanking new and quiet rooms.

Chóra ✉ 68002

Sotiros, t 255 104 1500. Open summer only, but a real must – lovely old farmhouse by a stream, where the wine and beer are chilled, to accompany Samothráki's famous succulent kid and crispy potatoes, all for around €12.

Thérma ✉ 68002

Kastro Bungalows, t 255 108 9400, f 255 104 1000 (B; luxury). Smartest hotel on the island with a pool and sea sports, and a restaurant overlooking the sea. Open all year.

Mariba, t 255 109 8230, f 255 109 8374 (moderate). Bungalows covered with ivy in the midst of the plane tree forest; friendly and quiet. Open 15 May–15 Oct.

Stoa, in the centre of the village. The best food in the area – always packed and specializing in seafood at reasonable prices.

a freshwater spring and a taverna. A boat excursion is the only way to continue south, to visit the spectacular coast and the waterfall **Krémasto Neró** ('hanging water').

The Sanctuary of the Great Gods

t 255 104 1474; both the site and museum are open Tues–Sun 8.30–3; adm.

The Great Gods of the Thracians were chthonic, Underworld deities, older and more potent than the Olympian upstarts. Their Greek history began in the 8th century BC when Aeolians from Mytilíni came and mingled peaceably with the Thracians, and picked up the cult of the Kabeiri, the Great Gods. Homer knew of them, and by the mid-5th century BC, Samothráki was the religious centre of the North Aegean. But as in Eleusis no one dared to reveal their Mysteries, beyond their secret names: Axieros, Axiokersos, Axiokersa and Kadmilos, whom the Greeks identified with Demeter, Hades, Persephone-Kore and Hermes. St Paul stopped by in AD 49 but failed to convert the locals who kept their sanctuary running until the 4th century, when Theodosius the Great closed all pagan temples.

The Mysteries took place by torchlight and included initiation rites similar to those at Eleusis. Anyone, male or female, free or slave, could join and undergo the two levels of initiation, the *myesis* and the *epopteia*. The *epopteia* began with a confession (unique in the Greek world), baptism, and the winding of a purple sash below the abdomen, and was topped off with the sacrifice of a ram. Initiation was thought to be sovereign against drowning; in ancient times a hall in the sanctuary was full of sailors' ex-votos. Lysander of Sparta and Herodotus were initiates, but the Sanctuary knew its greatest fortune after Philip II fell in love with Olympias of Épirus, mother of Alexander the Great, during an initiation ceremony. As the only pan-Hellenic shrine in Philip's orbit, he was keen to promote it, to demonstrate his 'Greekness' to the world.

The French, of course, bagged the prize, the *Victory of Samothrace*, found in 1863 by Champoiseau, the French consul at Adrianople; the **museum** has a plaster consolation copy sent over from the Louvre, along with good vases and an Archaic-style frieze of temple dancers donated by Philip. A path leads down to the sanctuary, in an idyllic setting under the jagged mountain. The first large building, the rectangular **Anaktoron**, dates from the 6th century BC and was rebuilt twice, lastly by the Romans; first-level initiations were held here, and only the initiated, or *mystai*, were allowed in its inner sanctum or Holy of Holies on the north side. A torch base, now under glass, is a relic of the Kabeiroi's nocturnal rites. Adjacent, by the Sacred Rock, is the **Arsinoëion**, at 66ft in diameter the largest circular structure ever built by the Greeks. It was dedicated in 281 BC by Queen Arsinoë II, wife and sister of Ptolemy Philadelphos, and had one door and no windows; scholars are stumped as to what could have happened in here. The rectangular foundation south of the Arsinoëion belonged to the **Temenos**, where ceremonies may have taken place; adjacent stand the five re-erected Doric columns of the **Hieron** of 300 BC where the upper level of initiation was held for the *mystai*. Only the outline remains of the theatre on the hill; here too is the **Nike Fountain**, where the *Winged Victory* was dedicated by Demetrios Poliorketes in 305 BC after a victory over Ptolemy II at Cyprus. Ptolemy II, not to be outdone, donated the monumental gateway to the sanctuary, the **Propylae Ptolemaion**. Near here is a circular **Tholos** of uncertain use and a Doric building, dedicated by the Hellenistic rulers of Macedonia.

Just up the road, plane trees cover **Palaeópolis**, the city that served the sanctuary (*open daily 8.30–8.30; free*); the island's medieval Genoese bosses, the Gattaluzi, used much of its stone to build their walls on the hill. After Palaeópolis, the road continues east to the delightful little spa of **Thérma** (or **Loutrá**). Like much of this corner of Samothráki, Thérma is immersed in ancient chestnut and plane trees, with places to stay and eat among the rushing streams. Follow the signs to **Gría Vathrá** – a short walk through a canopy of trees to a natural pool and little waterfall that flows even in the summer. From Thérma, a path leads up in four hours to the top of **Mount Fengári** (or Sáos) where you can enjoy the same view as Poseidon, a stunning panorama from the Troad (around Troy) in the east to Athos in the west.

The road from Thérma continues east to the medieval tower in the little delta of the **Foniás**, a river filled with eels and crabs that flows year round; there's a 30-minute path up its boulder-strewn ravine to a waterfall, where nymphs wouldn't look at all out of place. After this oasis, the road braves the increasingly arid coast and ends at the shadeless black pebble beach at **Kýpos**, closed off by merciless cliffs of lava.

The Cyclades

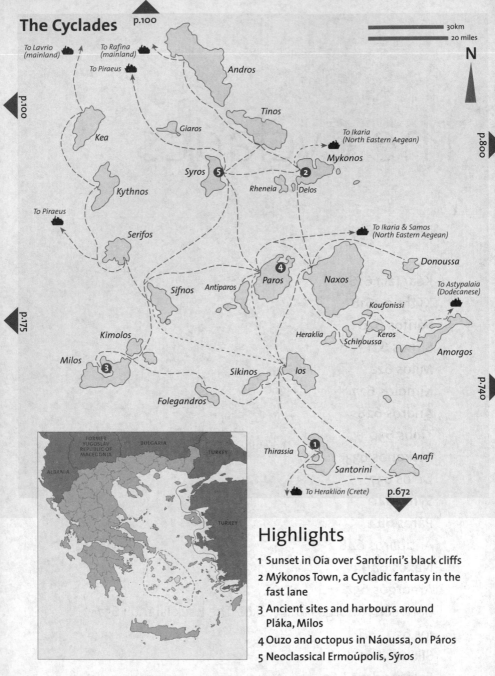

The Cyclades

N

p.100

30km
20 miles

To Lavrio (mainland)
To Rafina (mainland)
To Piraeus
To Piraeus

Andros
Tinos
Giaros
Kea
Syros **5**
Mykonos **2**
To Ikaria (North Eastern Aegean)
Rheneia
Delos
Kythnos
Serifos
To Piraeus
Donoussa
To Ikaria & Samos (North Eastern Aegean)
Sifnos
Antiparos
Paros **4**
Naxos
Koufonissi
To Astypalaia (Dodecanese)
Kimolos
Heraklia
Keros
Schinoussa
Amorgos
Milos **3**
Sikinos
Ios
Folegandros
Thirassia
Santorini **1**
Anafi
To Heraklion (Crete)
p.672

p.100
p.800
p.175
p.740

FORMER YUGOSLAV REPUBLIC OF MACEDONIA
BULGARIA
TURKEY
ALBANIA
TURKEY

Highlights

1 Sunset in Oía over Santoríni's black cliffs
2 Mýkonos Town, a Cycladic fantasy in the fast lane
3 Ancient sites and harbours around Pláka, Mílos
4 Ouzo and octopus in Náoussa, on Páros
5 Neoclassical Ermoúpolis, Sýros

Say 'Greek islands' and most people picture the Cyclades: barren rocks soaking in the blue Aegean, with white sugar-cube villages, bathed in luminous light. Close enough for the next one to be always visible on the horizon, the 24 Cyclades (the name means 'circling', with sacred Délos in the centre) come in as many flavours as a box of chocolates. Mýkonos is as jet-setty as can be, with Páros in second place; spectacular Santoríni gets the most cruise ships and honeymooners; on party-mad Íos you'll feel old at 25; Náxos offers splendid walks to match its beaches; Tínos is a mecca for Greek pilgrims and dovecote-fanciers. Pocket-sized Sérifos, Sífnos and Sýros are lesser known and all the better for that. The islands closest to Athens – Kéa, Kýthnos and Ándros – are favourites of yachtsmen and Greeks. A few Cyclades come under the heading of 'almost away from it all': Folégandros, Mílos and Amorgós, or the tiny Back Islands of Koufoníssi, Schinoússa and Heráklia. From July to September all are naturally air-conditioned by the *meltémi* wind, which can keep ships in port. Or you can fly: Páros, Mýkonos, Mílos, Santoríni, Náxos and Sýros have airports.

History

Inhabited since 6000 BC, the Cyclades were the first off the mark in Greece in the early Bronze Age (3000 BC), when they developed a culture with a strikingly modern sense of design, famous for its elegant white marble idols. In myth, Minos of Crete conquered the islands in order to rid himself of his overly-just brother Rhadamanthys, whom he sent to administer the new territories, a story that corresponds nicely to the Minoan influence that marks the Middle Cycladic style. The Late Cycladic period coincides with the rise of the Mycenaeans. In the subsequent Dark Age, some islands fell under the Dorians and others the Ionians; by the end of the 8th century BC, many, especially Náxos and Páros, were in the forefront of the Archaic cultural awakening.

With the rise of Persia, many Ionian Greeks in Asia Minor fled to Attica, leaving the islands vulnerable; in the subsequent wars, some sided expeditiously with the Persians. To prevent future breakaways, Athens obliged the islands in 478 BC to join a maritime league based at the holy Cycladic island of Delos. But what began as a league of allies gradually turned into vassals paying tribute to Athens, whose fleet was the only one capable of confronting the constant Persian menace. Cycladic resentment often flared into revolt and the Athenians had to work ever harder to extort their contribution of money and ships.

During the Peloponnesian War, many jumped at the chance to support Sparta. But when Athens recovered from the war in 378 BC, it was only to form a second Delian League. Most of the islands turned to Philip II of Macedon as a saviour. The Romans finally brought peace to the Cyclades; their empire's fall spelt centuries of hardship. Constantinople lacked the navy to protect them, leaving them to fend for themselves.

When Constantinople fell to the Crusaders in 1204, the Venetians claimed the Aegean as their share. Marco Sanudo, nephew of Doge Enrico Dandolo, styled himself Duke of Náxos and gave his loyal thugs the smaller Cyclades as fiefs. The Sanudos gave way to the Crispi dynasty in 1383, but, threatened by pirates and the growing Ottoman empire, Venice herself stepped in to police the Cyclades at the end of the 15th century. There was little even Venice could do against the fierce 16th-century admiral Khair-ed-din-Barbarossa, who decimated the islands; from then on they would pay tribute to the Ottomans. Venetian priests had converted many on the Cyclades to Catholicism, and under the Ottomans both Orthodox and Catholic monasteries thrived. When the Greek War of Independence broke out, the Cyclades offered naval support and a safe harbour for refugees; the islands with large Catholic populations were placed under French protection and remained neutral. Nevertheless, the Cyclades were soon incorporated into the new Greek state, and Ermoúpolis on Sýros became the country's leading port; today it remains the largest town and administrative centre of the Cyclades.

Because of the archipelago's size, we start with the western Cyclades, i.e. those closest to Athens, and then take in the eastern Cyclades, from north to south.

Kéa/Tzía (ΚΕΑ/ΤΖΙΑ)

Kéa, with lush valleys, terraces of vines, orchards and dairy cattle, isn't your typical Cycladic island of pristine white Cubism on the rocks. Only four hours from Athens, it is an island of summer villas – and guaranteed to have no room on weekends, when jeeps, dogs, boats and windsurfers pile off the ferries and gin palaces fill the port to bursting; for a short visit, try mid-week.

Kéa was settled by 3000 BC, and in *c.* 1650 BC the Minoans founded a colony at Ag. Iríni, the ruins of which reveal a chronicle of trade between Crete and the older Cycladic culture, continuing well into Mycenaean times. Classical Kéa was divided into four towns: Ioúlis, Karthaea, Poiessa and Korissía, and they produced the great poet Simonides (557–467 BC) who wrote the epigram on Thermopylae. Kéa was also famous for its retirement scheme, the *geroktonia* that required citizens to take a glass of conium (like hemlock) when they reached 70. The island made the headlines again on 21 November 1916, when the *Britannic*, sister ship to the *Titanic*, sank offshore after a still unexplained explosion. It went down in only 55 minutes, three hours faster than the *Titanic* (although with only a few casualties). Jacques Cousteau found the wreck in 1975, and there is talk of making it into world's first underwater museum.

Korissía and Ag. Iríni

The port **Korissía** has a few pretty neoclassical buildings and a lovely church, but otherwise it's an ordinary little place with an art gallery, tavernas and a folklore museum (*t 228 802 1435*). The bay sweeps round to a so-so beach; a footpath over the headland leads north to small, sandy **Gialiskári Beach**, bristling with gated villas, guard dogs and a taverna in the pines. A kilometre north on Ag. Nikólaou Bay, **Vourkári**, an old fishing village, has morphed into a smart resort, with yachties loafing on their sundecks. Around the bay, on the peninsula of **Ag. Iríni**, are the remains of the **Minoan–Mycenaean settlement** (local guidebook available); it has a narrow temple, first constructed in the Bronze Age, a late Minoan megaron, late Bronze Age houses, fortifications and a spring chamber outside the walls. From here the coastal road continues to the delightful beach resort at **Otziás**.

Ioúlis (Chóra), the Happy Lion and Around

High above Korissía, hidden from passing pirates, Kéa's trendy capital **Ioúlis** has stunning views down the terraced hills. Surrounded by the largest collection of **windmills** in the Cyclades (26), the houses in a maze of alleys and archways have

Getting There and Around

By sea: at least four daily **ferry** and **Flying Cat** (75mins) connections with Lávrio (*see* p.159); three to four times a week with Kýthnos and once a week to Sýros. Daily **hydrofoils** in summer with Kýthnos and Piraeus (Zéa). **Port authority: t** 228 802 1344.

By road: bus three to four times daily from Ioúlis to Vourkári. **Taxis: t** 228 802 2444.

Tourist Information

Tourist police: Korissía, **t** 228 802 1100, two blocks in from the Karthea Hotel.

Where to Stay and Eat

Most accommodation is in family-style apartments or simple rooms. The town hall (*dimarchio*) near the port has a list. Kéa is still very Greek; tavernas serve up good Greek fare.

Korissía ✉ 84002

Korissia, t 228 802 1484, **f** 228 802 1355 (*E; moderate*). In a quiet backwater with a terrace, bar and large rooms/studios. *Open May–Oct*.
Karthea, off the harbour, **t** 228 802 1222, **f** 228 802 1417 (*C; inexpensive*). A bit gloomy, but clean and quiet.
United Europe Furnished Flats, t 228 802 1362, **f** 228 802 1122 (*expensive–moderate*). A smart self-catering option close to the beach. Others worth trying are: **To Korali, t** 228 802 1268 (*moderate*), and **To Oneiro, t** 228 802 1118 (*moderate; open year round*).
I Apolavsi ('The Enjoyment'), **t** 228 802 1068 (*inexpensive*). Comfortable, basic studios and a huge sun terrace overlooking the harbour.

Apotheki. In a whitewashed ruin, popular, with a large choice of dishes.
Ouzerie Lagoudera. In a neoclassical house at the harbour; tasty prawn *saganáki*.

Vourkári/Otziás ✉ 84002

At **Vourkári**, apartments to let (*all expensive–moderate*) include: **Nikitas, t** 228 802 2303/1193, on the waterfront; **Lefkes, t** 228 802 1443; and **Petrakos, t** 228 802 1197.
Aristos (€15). Yachties moor next to their tables. Try the delicious *kakavia* (Greek *bouillabaisse*) if it's on the menu.
Nikos, next to the art gallery, **t** 228 802 1486. A cheaper choice.
I Strofi (€15). Otziás' favourite fish taverna, with a romantic touch.

Ioúlis ✉ 84002

Ioulis, t 228 802 2177 (*C; moderate*). One of the few hotels here, full of character.
Piatsa Restaurant. In a lovely setting through the main archway.
Ioulis, on the town hall square. For a grilled lunch with sensational views.
O Kalofagás ('The Good Eater'), in the square. Popular and aptly named.

Písses/Koúndouros ✉ 84002

Galini, t 228 803 1316 (*moderate*). Furnished apartments in Písses. If they are full, try the others run by the Polítis family, **t** 228 803 1343/1318.
Kea Camping, t 228 803 1332. Kea's only campsite. A pleasant site with rooms.
Simitis and **Akroyiali**. Two good fish tavernas; the latter has rooms, **t** 228 803 1301.
Nikolas Demenegas, Koúndouros, **t** 228 803 1416 (*moderate*). Tidy studios in a garden.

red-tiled roofs, flower-filled balconies and covered galleries. At the top, the **Kástro** quarter occupies the acropolis; it has some ancient bits, a few Venetian mansions and Byzantine churches. The highlight of the **Archaeological Museum** (*t 228 802 2079; open Tues–Sun 8.30–3; adm free*) are the finds from Ag. Iríni. Tall Bronze Age terracotta female figures in the Minoan goddess style, painted bright yellow, white and red, hail from the 14th-century BC temple and are the oldest yet found in the Aegean. A 10-minute walk east of Ioúlis stands the benignly smiling 6th century BC **Lion of Kéa**, 10ft high and 19ft long. Some say Zeus sent a lion to chase off murderous nymphs and the Kéans carved him in stone, to make sure they stayed away.

The region north of Ioúlis, the **Paraméria**, still has its oak woods and simple, traditional country houses. Above Paraméria the lush valley of Spathí ends at sandy **Spathí Bay**. Another road east from Ioúlis branches for three fine beaches: **Sykamiá**, **Psíli Ammos** and **Orkós**. The road south of Ioúlis leads 5km through rolling country to the ruined monastery of **Ag. Marína**, built around a three-storey Hellenistic tower. From here the road goes to the west-coast resort of **Písses**; its sandy beach is one of the island's finest. The next bay along, **Koúndouros**, is just as lovely. On the southeast shore, high on the headland at Póles Bay, stood **Karthaea**, once Kéa's most important city, where Simonides had his poetry school, but little remains of its walls and temple of Apollo. The Hellenistic road from **Káto Meriá** to **Elliniká** is lovely to walk.

Kýthnos (ΚΥΘΝΟΣ)

Like Kéa, Kýthnos attracts more Greeks than foreigners, many of whom come to soak in the spa at Loutrá. Once known for its iron mines (which closed in 1940), Kýthnos is now proud to be the first Greek island (1982) to get all of its electricity from renewable sources – wind in the winter and sun in the summer, inspiring similar projects on Mýkonos, Kárpathos, Samothráki and Crete. It has quiet sandy beaches, and a rugged interior great for walks. Perhaps because of their frugal lives, Kythniots celebrate with gusto (15 August and 8 September are the big *panegýria*, at Kanála). Best of all, the people are welcoming; it's an island where the old men still offer to take you fishing.

Life on Kýthnos may be austere, but it has been going on a long time: a Mesolithic settlement (7500–6000 BC) by Loutrá currently holds the title of oldest in the Cyclades. Much later the Minoans arrived, followed by the Driopes (hence the town of Dryopída), a semi-mythical tribe whose king Kýthnos gave the island his name. In the 15th–17th centuries Kýthnos was owned by the Cozzadini, who, rather than take sides, paid taxes both to the Venetians and Turks. To this day the family lives happily in Bologna...is there a lesson there?

Beaches, Chóra and Loutrá

Mérichas, Kýthnos' port, is a typical Greek fishing harbour, a laid-back, cheerful place, kept tidy by the village elders who also tend the ducks that live on the beach. Up the steps from the harbour, a short walk off the Chóra road, is nicer **Martinákia Beach** with an excellent taverna. Just to the north are the unexcavated Hellenistic ruins of **Vyrókastro**, set on the headland above the lovely beaches at **Episkópi** and **Apókrousi**. The prettiest sandy beach, **Kolona**, is just beyond; caiques make the trip.

The 7.5km bus trip north from Mérichas to the capital **Chóra** (or Messária), winds through terraced hills, deep wrinkles filled with oleanders, wider ones with fruit trees and vines, and the occasional dovecote. Chóra is a charming workaday village, where every square inch of pavement is painted with white mermaids, fish, flowers and patterns. It has several pretty churches including **Ag. Sávvas**, founded in 1613 by the Cozzadini and still wearing their coat-of-arms. Just outside Chóra is the power plant, a solar park and modern windmills.

Getting There and Around

By sea: daily **ferry** connections with Piraeus, Sérifos, Sífnos and Mílos, two to three times a week with Lávrio, Kéa, Kímolos, Folégandros, Síkinos, Íos and Santoríni. All ships put in at Mérichas on the west coast, but if the winds are strong they'll come in to Loutrá in the northeast. **Hydrofoil**: daily to Kéa and Piraeus. Port authority: t 228 103 2290.

By road:the island's two **buses** run regularly to Chóra and Loutrá and to Drýopida and Panagía Kanála. **Milos Express Travel**, t 228 103 2104, f 228 103 2291, has **car and bike rentals**. **Taxis**: Kýthnos, t 228 103 1272; Drýopida, t 228 103 1290.

Tourist Information

Tourist police: Chóra, t 228 103 1201.
GATS Travel, t/f 228 103 2055, in Mérichas, arranges accommodation, and the **Cava Kythnos** doubles as a bank branch.

Where to Stay and Eat

Mérichas ✉ 84006

O Finikas, behind the supermarket, t 228 103 2323 (*expensive*). Upmarket rooms done out in Cycladic style, in a garden setting, are the most comfortable.
Kythnos, t 228 103 2092 (*moderate–inexpensive*). Friendly but basic, with smart blue and white striped canopies, slap on the waterfront over a excellent *zacharoplasteío*.
Paradissos, t 228 103 2206 (*moderate–inexpensive*). Comfortable rooms with vine-shaded terraces and stunning views over the bay.
Martinakia, on the beach of the same name, t 228 103 2414. With a friendly parrot in the garden, rooms to let (*moderate*) and serving good *kalamária* and grills.
Yialos (or Sailors), back in Mérichas, t 228 103 2102. Tables on the beach and specialities such as *kalogíros*, a casserole of meat, aubergines, tomatoes and feta.
Ostria, close to where the ferry docks (€12, around €20–25 for a lobster dinner). A new grill restaurant, serving everything from *tzatziki* to lobster.
To Kantouni, t 228 103 2220. Tables at the water's edge where they specialize in grills and *sfougáta*, light rissoles made from the local cheese, and barrelled retsina.

Chóra/Drýopida ✉ 84006

Chóra has no rooms but a couple of tavernas, **To Steki** and **To Kentro**.
Taverna Pelegra (€12), in Dryopída, behind the butcher's shop (basic, but at least the meat's fresh); look out for local sausages drying on the balcony next door.

Loutrá ✉ 84006

Porto Klaras apartments, t 228 103 1276, f 228 103 1355 (Λ; *expensive–moderate*). Beautifully appointed family suites or doubles. All have sea-view terraces.
Meltemi, t 228 103 1271, f 228 103 1302 (*C; moderate*). Rather more modest flats.
Taverna Despina. Good fresh fish and fish soup, and meat from Kýthnos.
Taverna Katerina. At Schinári Beach, with stunning views.

Kanála ✉ 84006

Oneiro, t 228 103 2515, and **Nikos Bouritis**, t 228 103 2350. Both have pleasant, inexpensive rooms. The tavernas here specialize in fish.
Yiannis Kallilas, at Ag. Dimítrios, t 228 103 2208. Rooms and restaurant by the sea.

Buses continue to **Loutrá**, a straggling windswept resort and the most important spa in the Cyclades; the iron impregnated springs in the **hydrotherapy centre** (*t 228 103 1277; open July and Aug 8–noon*) are good for gout, rheumatism, eczema and gynaecological problems. Ancient marble baths inside the Xenia Hotel send steaming water bubbling down a gully. There's a sandy beach and over the headland two more bays, pebbly **Ag. Iríni** and windy **Schinári**. The Mesolithic settlement was on the promontory just to the north. A hard hour's walk north from Loutrá leads to the evocative if derelict medieval citadel **Kástro Katakéfalos**.

Dryopída and Kanála

The other bus out of Mérichas heads to **Dryopída**, Kýthnos' old capital, located near the **Katafíki Cave** where people hid when pirates came. There are two districts, **Péra Rouga** by the river valley and **Galatás**, the upper village, a labyrinth of crazy-paved lanes and red-tiled houses. Dryopída was once an arty place; in the 17th century the icon-painting Skordílis family lived here, and left the iconostasis in **Ag. Mínas**, among other works. Ceramics were big too, although now only the Milás pottery is still in business. It takes an hour to walk to Chóra along the old cobbled way, or to go down to the beaches at **Ag. Stéfanos**, with an islet linked by a causeway, or **Léfkes**, where there are rent rooms. The bus terminates at pine-shaded **Kanála**, a Greek summer resort. The church of **Panagía Kanála**, the island's most important, has a venerated icon, attributed to St Luke. There are wonderful views over to Sýros and Sérifos and the water is so shallow that you can almost walk across. A rough track leads to **Flamboúria Beach** on the west coast with rooms to let.

Sérifos (ΣΕΡΙΦΟΣ)

Sérifos, 'the barren one', can intimidate at first with its stark rocks, so rich in iron and copper that in antiquity the little island had the wherewithal to mint its own coins. A violent miners' strike in 1916, followed by a decline in profits, led to the abandon-ment of the mines, and since the 1960s the population has decreased to around 1,500 people year-round. As for the rest, Sérifos is pure Cycladic; foreign yachties love it, but beware of water shortages in August.

The appealing port **Livádi** is the island's green spot, with a long pebbly-sandy beach lined with tamarisks and rent rooms. Other beaches are nearby: crowded **Livadákia**, and, a 30-minute walk south over the headland, **Karávi**, popular with nudists. The bus or ancient stair link Livádi to **Chóra**, the capital, 6km up, spread like white icing over Sérifos' forbidding slopes. It's a fascinating jumble of houses and churches, many built of stone salvaged from the Byzantine-Venetian castle; 12ft geraniums grow in between. There's a pretty neoclassical square, with a **town hall** built in the moneyed days of 1908. Old windmills still turn, and in the spring you may find a rare carnation that grows only on Sérifos. From Chóra a 20-minute walk down a path (or road) brings you to to **Psilí Ámmos**, an excellent beach with tavernas on the east coast.

The road continues past Chóra to **Megálo Chorió**, the ancient capital, guarded by a ruined marble Hellenistic tower. **Megálo Livádi** below (beach and tavernas) once had loading docks for the mines. The road continues to **Koutalás**, where a '**Cave of the Cyclops**' has two stalactite chambers and a lake (bring a light). **Malliádiko** and **Gánema Beaches** are nearby. A second road passes **Panagía**, named after the oldest church on Sérifos (10th century). At **Galaní**, the **Taxiárchos Monastery** (*t 228 105 1027*), built in 1500, contains a precious altar and 18th-century frescoes by Skordílis. Nearby **Kalítsos**, with almonds, olives and vines, is the garden of Sérifos, and there's a beach, **Platýs Gialós**, just beyond the monastery. On the other side of Galaní, **Sikamiá Bay** is a good hideaway with a beach, taverna, shade and fresh water.

Getting There and Around

Daily **ferry** connections with Piraeus, Kýthnos, Mílos and Sífnos; four times weekly with Kímolos, three times weekly with Santoríni, Folégandros, Síkinos and Íos; twice weekly with Mýkonos and Páros; once weekly to Sýros and Tínos. **Port authority**: t 228 105 1470. Six daily **buses** join Chóra and Livádi; other villages, once daily in summer.

Where to Stay and Eat

For help, try the **Rent Rooms Association**, in Livádi, t 228 105 1520, or **Krings Travel**, Livádi, t 228 105 1164, f 228 105 1488, *corglli@mail.otenet.gr.*

Livádi ✉ 84005

Asteri, t 228 105 1891, f 228 105 1191, *asteri@otenet.gr (B; expensive).* Balcony with sea view for every room, TVs and a restaurant.

Areti, t 228 105 1479, f 228 105 1547 *(C; moderate).* Handy for the ferries, with a quiet garden and comfortable rooms with terraces overlooking the sea. *Open April–Oct.*

Albatross, t 228 105 1148 *(D; moderate).* Smothered in oleander; further around the bay, but the owner meets the ferry with a minibus. *Open April–Oct.*

Naias, t 228 105 1749, f 228 105 2444, *naias@otenet.gr (C; moderate).* In true Cycladic style; no distance from the beach; balconies, and breakfast. *Open all year.*

Captain George Rooms, near the square, t 228 105 1274 *(inexpensive).* Good value.

Korali Camping, Livadákia Beach, t 228 105 1500. Good facilities and bungalows.

Takis, on Livádi's waterfront under an enormous tamarisk. Popular with locals and tourists alike, offering excellent dishes and friendly service.

Mokka, at the end of the port where the locals, yachties, tourists, and an assortment of cats and dogs mingle happily; a pleasantly zany atmosphere, with good food.

Ouzerie Meltemi. Vast choice of nibbles, including the 'married yellow pea'.

Chóra ✉ 84005

Petros, t 228 105 1302. A local favourite with a traditional, reliable menu.

Stavro. Food by the bus stop with accompanying view. Try their potent red wine, which the owners (and some locals) swear leads to wedding bells.

Sífnos (ΣΙΦΝΟΣ)

Sífnos is the most popular island in the western Cyclades – a place of peaceful serendipity, with gentle green hills, vineyards, olive groves, watermelon patches, charming villages and long sandy beaches, all kept spick and span by its 2,000 inhabitants. It is famous for pottery and its cooks, ever since Sifniot Nikolas Tselemntes wrote the first modern cookery book (to this day any cookbook in Greece is a *tselemntes*). One of the best things to do here is walk: the landscape is strewn with Venetian dovecotes, windmills, 300 chapels and 52 ancient towers (more than the rest of the Cyclades combined) left over from a 5th-century BC signalling system.

History: the Island that Laid Golden Eggs

Sífnos has the oldest gold mines yet discovered in Europe, worked by the Phoenicians who called the island Meropia. The Minoans had a colony at Minoa near Apollónia; they were in turn supplanted by Ionians, who were wealthy enough to build their agora in Parian marble. Delphi got wind of it and demanded an annual tithe, in the form of a solid gold egg, and in 530 BC the Sifniots built a magnificent treasury to house them (*see* p.395). But then they got greedy and sent a gilded egg of

Getting There and Around

By sea: daily **ferry** connections with Piraeus, Kýthnos, Sérifos and Mílos; four times a week with Kímolos, two to three times a week with Íos, Santoríni, Folégandros and Síkinos, once a week with Páros, Tínos, Kárystos (Évia) and Rafína. **Excursion boats** from Kamáres to Váthi and Chersónissos; also round the island tours. **Port authority: t** 228 403 1617.

By road: frequent **buses** between Kamáres, Apollonía, Artemónas and on Platýs Gialós; not as often to Fáros, Káto Petáli, Kástro and Váthi. **Taxis: t** 228 403 1656/1793/1626. For **car or mopeds** try seaside **Krinas**, in Kamáres, **t** 228 403 1488, **f** 228 403 1073. Kiosks sell a good **map** showing all the island's footpaths.

Tourist Information

Kamáres tourist office: t 228 403 1977. With the helpful Sofia; has bus schedules.

Aegean Thesaurus: in the main square in Apollonía, **t** 228 403 3151, **f** 228 403 2190, *thesauros@travelling.gr*. Walking tours.

Where to Stay and Eat

Try Sífnos' *revíthia tou foúrno* (baked chick peas), *revithokeftedes* (chickpea patties), *xyno-myzíthra* (wine-steeped cheese), and *ambelofásoula*, made from green beans.

Kamáres ✉ 84003

Boulis, t 228 403 2122, **f** 228 403 2381 (*C; expensive–moderate*). Beachside, with a lawn!

Kamari Pension, t 228 403 3383, **f** 228 403 1709 (*C; moderate*). A good bet on the waterfront.

Dimitris and Margarita Belli, t 228 403 1276 (*inexpensive*). Good rooms with sea view.

Makis Camping, by the beach, **t** 228 403 2366.

Kapetan Andreas, t 228 403 2356 (€12–18). On the harbour, serving the freshest of fish, caught by the owner. *Open Easter–Oct.*

Da Claudio, t 228 403 1761. Excellent Italian trattoria, with great antipasti. *Open June–Sept, eves only.*

Apollonía ✉ 84003

Petali, above the centre, **t/f** 228 403 3024, *patali@par.forthnet* (*B; expensive*). Small,

peaceful, traditionally styled hotel with beautiful views (*open all year*) and a good restaurant serving fine local dishes (*open eves only, May–Sept*).

Angelo's Rooms, t 228 403 1533. Cheap, with garden views.

Orea Sifnos, by the bus stop, **t** 228 403 3069. Tasty food, good wine, and a garden.

Artemónas ✉ 84003

Windmill Villas, t 228 493 2098, *www.windmill-villas.gr* (*moderate*). Self-catering air-conditioned studios around a huge windmill, which sleeps four – book well in advance to bag it. *Open April–Oct.*

Artemonas, t 228 403 1303, **f** 228 403 2385 (*C; moderate*). A charming little place, with a cool courtyard. *Open April–Sept.*

Liotrivi ('Olive Press'), **t** 228 403 2051/1246. One of the best restaurants on the island; specialities with local capers and chickpeas.

Kástro ✉ 84003

To Astro, t 228 403 1476 (€12). Set in the back-streets. Try lamb in red wine.

Fáros/Chrissopigí ✉ 84003

Blue Horizon, t 228 407 1442, **f** 228 407 1441 (*B; luxury*). Ten new apartments.

Sifneiko Archontiko, t 228 407 1454, **f** 228 407 1454 (*D; moderate–inexpensive*). The old standby, as well as some of the cheapest rooms on the island.

Tsapis, on the beach at Chrissopigí, **t** 228 407 1272. Delicious pies and other dishes that confirm Sífnos' culinary traditions.

Zambelis, Fáros, **t** 228 407 1434. On the water, with a very tasty lamb casserole; the owner was Christina Onassis' personal chef. Lovely in the evenings. *Open April–Sept.*

Platýs Gialós ✉ 84003

Platys Yialos, t 228 407 1324, **f** 228 407 1325 (*B; luxury*). Built in traditional Cycladic style with well-equipped bungalows, all facilities and sports. *Open April–Oct.*

Angeliki, near the bus stop, **t** 228 403 1288 (*moderate*). Nice little rent room place.

Camping Platys Yialos, t 228 407 1286. In an olive grove set back from the beach.

Sofia, t 228 407 1202 (€15). Suckling pig, lobster with spaghetti and good wines.

lead, or at least that was the excuse Polykrates of Sámos made in 525 BC when he took over the mines, which soon sank and gave out, empty (*sífnos* in Greek).

In 1307 the Da Coronia ruled the island for Venice; in 1456 the Cozzadini lords of Kýthnos married into the family and kept Sífnos until the Turks took over 1617. In the late 1600s, the 'School of the Holy Tomb' was founded to keep ancient Greek alive. This cultural mission produced two poets: the 19th-century satirist Cleánthis Triandáfilos and Ioánnis Gypáris (d. 1942), who, along with Caváfy, was the first to espouse demotic Greek in literature.

From Kamáres to Apollonía and Artemónas

The port of Sífnos, **Kamáres**, is set between two cliffs that belie the fertility inland; it has a safe sandy beach, tavernas and pottery shops. Sífnos has exceptionally fine clay, and the islanders have always been expert potters; one researcher has shown that every living Greek potter has a Sifniot in the family tree. In the late 1940s there were some 90 workshops in the island, employing 600 potters, and, after nearly dying out, the craft is undergoing a revival.

The bus makes the climb up to the capital **Apollonía**, a Cycladic idyll wrapped in bougainvillaea. The town is named after a 7th-century BC Temple of Apollo, its stone reused in the 18th century to build the church **Panagía Ouranofóra** in the highest part of town. In the bus stop square the **Museum of Popular Arts and Folklore** offers pottery, embroideries and costumes (*ask for the key's whereabouts*). As Artemis is Apollo's twin sister; so **Artemónas**, a pretty mile walk away, is Apollónia's twin village. Beneath its windmills, cobbled lanes wind past neoclassical houses and churches. The church of **Kochí**, with its cluster of domes, occupies the site of a Temple of Artemis; little 17th-century **Ag. Geórgios tou Aféndi** contains fine icons, and **Panagía ta Gourniá**, near the bridge, has a beautiful interior (*key next door*).

Kástro to Panagía Chrissopigí

On the east coast, 3km from Artemónas by road or the coastal path, **Kástro** was the ancient and medieval capital of Sífnos, where tall narrow houses are backed by Byzantine walls, many with Venetian coats-of-arms. The churches have attractive floors, among them **Panagía Koímmissi** (1593), whose altar is decorated with Dionysian bulls' heads. The Venetian church of Sant' Antonio houses the **Archaeological Museum** (*t 228 403 1022; open Tues–Sun 9–2; out of season, ask the lady opposite*). A path leads down to **Serália**, with remnants of the medieval port and a lovely beach. On the road to Platýs Gialós, the monastery of **Ag. Andréas** sits on a hill, amid ruined double walls of the ancient citadel, and a little further north a path from Katavatí continues up (2 hours) to Sífnos' highest peak (2,234ft), named after its 8th-century monastery **Profítis Ilías** (with a 12th-century iconostasis).

Further south, from the laid-back village of **Fáros**, a footpath leads to the rocky cape with Sífnos' most famous monastery, **Panagía Chrissopigí**, built in 1650. The long beach here, **Apókofto**, has golden sands, while **Fasoloú** is popular with nudists.

Platýs Gialós and Other Beaches

Broad sandy **Platýs Gialós** is the busiest beach on Sífnos. One of the island's oldest working potteries is here, that of Franzesko Lemonis, founded in 1936. A cliff top convent, **Panagía tou Vounoú**, affords gorgeous views over the bay; note the Doric columns in the church. There are boats and buses from Kamáres to the fishing hamlet of **Vathí**, a pretty place with a lovely clean beach, shallow water and rent rooms. **Chersónissos**, on the island's windy northern tip, is also best reached by boat. Here master potter Kóstas Depastás upholds the ceramics tradition, his kiln fired by driftwood. There's a taverna if you feel peckish.

Mílos (ΜΗΛΟΣ)

Like Santoríni, Mílos is a volcanic island. But whereas the former is a glamorous beauty associated with tales of Atlantis, Mílos is a sturdy fellow whose fiery origins lie in working for a living, with its precious veins of obsidian, sulphur, kaolin, barium, alum, bensonite and perlite. Mílos also has fantastical rocks in Fauvist colours, miles of pale golden sands and turquoise inlets like mini-fjords, some bubbling with hot springs; electricity is provided by a geothermal station. Walks through the gently undulating countryside lead down to tiny whitewashed chapels by the sea or hamlets with colourful boat garages below their balconies. With its new airport, more tourists come every year: go soon.

History

Some 10,000 years ago, Neolithic voyagers in papyrus boats mined Mílos' abundant veins of obsidian, that hard black volcanic glass prized for the manufacture of Stone Age tools. The oldest town at Phylakope came under Minoan and later Mycenaean rule. Later inhabitants were Dorian and were famous for raising the toughest cockerels for cockfights. When Mílos declared itself neutral in the Peloponnesian War, Athens sent envoys whose might-makes-right speech (the 'Milian Dialogue' in Thucydides) is still moving and depressingly contemporary. However, it failed to convince Mílos to join Athens; Athens sent in troops and when Mílos surrendered they massacred all the men, enslaved the women and children, and resettled the island with Athenians. In 1206 the Sanudo brothers took Mílos for Venice. In 1680, when a band of islanders emigrated to London, James, Duke of York, granted them land to build a church – the origin of Greek Street in Soho.

Adámas and the Beaches around the Bay

If you come by sea, you'll be greeted by the **Arkoúdes** ('bears'), a rock formation on the left as you turn into the **Bay of Mílos**, the largest natural harbour in the Mediterranean, used by the French in the Crimean War and the Allies in the First World War. The port, bustling **Adámas**, has most of the island's facilities (including a roller-skating rink); it was founded in 1836 by Cretan refugees from Sfakiá who brought their icons, now in the churches of **Ag. Tríada** and **Ag. Charálambos**.

Getting There and Around

By air: at least one flight daily from Athens. Olympic Airways is just past the *plateía* in Adámas, **t** 228 702 2380; for **airport information**, **t** 228 702 2381. A taxi from the airport to Adámas will set you back around €8.

By sea: two or more **ferries** daily to and from Piraeus, with daily connections to Sífnos, Kýthnos and Sérifos; once a week with Folégandros and Santoríni; **taxi boat** five times a day from Pollónia to Kímolos in season. **Port authority**: **t** 228 702 2100.

By road: hourly **buses** from Adámas square to Pláka, via Tripití; nine times a day to Pollónia by way of Filikopi and Pachera; seven times to Paleóchora via Zefýria and Provatás. For a **taxi**, call **t** 228 702 2219. Or **rent** your own wheels: ask at Vichos Tours, **t** 228 702 2286, **f** 228 702 2396, or STOP, hard by the port, **t** 228 702 2440.

Tourist Information

Municipal tourist information: Adámas quay, **t** 228 702 2445.

Where to Stay and Eat

If you get stuck, call the **Rooms Association**, **t** 228 702 3429.

Adámas ✉ 84800

Kapetan Georgadas, **t** 228 702 3215, **f** 228 702 3219 (*C; expensive*). Re-vamped traditional-style apartments with satellite TV, mini-bars, air-conditioning and pool. *Open all year.*
Portiani, on the sea, **t** 228 702 2940, **f** 228 702 2766, *sirmalen@otenet.gr* (*C; moderate*). Comfy, with sumptuous buffet breakfast.
Delfini, **t** 228 702 2001, **f** 228 702 2688 (*D; moderate*). Friendly family-run hotel with a nice breakfast terrace. *Open all year.*
Semiramis, **t** 228 702 2118, **f** 228 702 2117 (*D; moderate*). Excellent with a pretty vine-clad terrace bar, transfer minibus and rent-a-bike service. *Open all year.*
Kanaris, a little inland, **t** 228 702 2184 (*inexpensive*). A good budget choice, and the owner will pick you up at the port.
Trapatseli's (€15). Fish feed beneath the terrace here and show up on the menu: try *spetsofái* fish stew or *soupiés*, cuttlefish *stifádo*, as well as the local *dópio* cheese.
Ta Pitsounakia. Spit-roasts of all kinds of meats and *kokorétsi* .

Pláka/Tripití/Klíma ✉ 84800

Plakiotiki Gonia, in Pláka. A sweet little taverna with local dishes like cheese pies and country bread with tomatoes.
Popi's Windmill, in Tripití, **t** 228 702 2287, **f** 228 702 2396 (*expensive*). Has rooms that sleep 4–5 in two converted mills. *Open June–Sept.*
Ergina, Tripití, **t** 228 702 2532 (€15). Traditional dishes, served with Mílos' cheeses on a terrace over the water. *Open June–Sept.*
Panorama, Klíma, **t** 228 702 1623, **f** 228 702 2112 (*C; moderate*). Has rooms and a dining terrace with great views; good for lunch.

An interesting **Mining Museum** (**t** *228 702 2481; open daily 9.30–1 and 5–8*) has opened south along the waterfront. West of town you can wallow in the warm sulphurous **spa baths**, in a cave divided into three rooms (*open daily 8–1; take a towel; adm*). Beyond is popular **Lagáda Beach**, and further on reed-beds with gurgling mud pools mark the route to the 'volcano', a steaming fissure in the rock. Don't miss the round-island **excursion boats** that take in Mílos' crazy and colourful rock formations.

The big bay is fringed with sandy beaches such as **Papikinoú**, backed by hotels. It's quieter at **Alýkes**, the salt marshes before the Mávra Gremná ('black cliffs'); at several places the sea bubbles from hot springs. Past the airport stretches the spectacular beach at **Chivadólimni**, the island's longest, in front of a saltwater lagoon.

Pláka: Ancient Melos, its Catacombs and the Venus di Milo

Buses head up the 4km for **Pláka**, the sugar-cube island capital, built on the acropolis of Melos, while the ancient city itself is covered by modern **Tripití**. The Milians converted early to Christianity, in the 1st century AD, and built the only **catacombs** in Greece (*t 228 702 1625; open Tues–Sun 8–2*), still preserving some original inscriptions and graffiti. Building catacombs (as in Rome) had more to do with the presence of soft volcanic tufa than notions of persecution and secret rites; interring the dead underground saved valuable land. A path from here leads to a marker by a fig tree, where the **Venus de Milo** was discovered in 1820 by a farmer. A French officer sketched her; when the French consul in Constantinople got word, he was determined to buy her for France. Meanwhile, the farmer sold the statue to the Prince of Moldavia. It was in a caique, ready to be placed aboard a ship for Moldavia when the French sailed into Adámas. After brisk bargaining (some say a scuffle), the French won. She made her Louvre debut on 1 March 1821, but somewhere along the line lost her arms (one hand held an apple) and pedestal inscribed *Aphrodites Nikephoros*, 'Victory-bringing Aphrodite'. The path continues past the handsome ancient walls to the well-preserved **Roman theatre**, where spectators had a lovely view over the sea. From here an old *kalderími* path leads down to the fishing hamlet of **Klíma**, with its brightly painted boat garages, *syrmata*, carved into the tufa, and rickety balconies above.

By the bus stop, the **Archaeological Museum** (*t 228 702 1620; open Tues–Sun 8.30–3; adm*) has a plaster Venus, a consolation prize from Paris, the *Lady of Phylakope*, a decorated Minoan-style goddess, and artefacts going back to the Early Cycladic. Signs in Pláka itself point the way to the **Historical and Folklore Museum** (*t 228 702 1292; open Tues–Sat 10–1 and 6–8, Sun 10–1; adm*). On the edge of a cliff to the west, **Panagía Korfiátissa** was re-assembled from old stones from Zefyría (*see* below). Steps lead up to the Venetian **Kástro** set high on a volcanic plug, where houses form the outer walls. There are stunning views from here, and from the lovely church of **Panagía Thalassítras** (1228), where the lintel bears the arms of the Crispi, who overthrew the Sanudi as dukes of the archipelago; it contains icons by Emmanuel Skordílis.

Near Pláka, **Triovassálos** merges into **Péra Triovassálos**, where churches contain icons from Zefyría. Tracks lead down to beaches, some with wonderfully coloured rocks; **Pláthiena** has dazzling orange and white formations. **Mandrákia**, under Triovassálos, is a stunning little cove studded with *syrmata*. Further north, **Firopótamos** is a pretty fishing hamlet.

The North Coast: Phylakope and Pollónia

The road from Pláka to Pollónia offers tempting stops. The bleached moonscape of **Sarakíniko** has a tiny beach and inlet, and east of the fishing hamlets of **Pachaina** and **Ag. Konstantínos** it's a short walk to **Papafrángas Cave**, actually three sea caves, where the turquoise sea is enclosed by the white cliffs of a mini-fjord. After that is **Phylakope**, one of the great centres of Cycladic civilization. Urban improvements characterized the Middle Cycladic period: a wall was built around the more spacious and elegant houses, some with frescoes of flying fish (in Athens' Archaeological Museum). A Minoan-style palace contained fine ceramics from Knossós, and there was trade with Asia Minor. Then bronze completely replaced obsidian, and Phylakope declined.

The bus ends up at Apollo's old town, **Pollónia** on the east coast, a popular resort with a tree-fringed beach. There's lots of new holiday development on the **Pelekóuda** cape, a favourite with windsurfers. Water taxis leave Pollónia harbour for Kímolos five times a day, weather permitting. **Voúdia Beach** to the south has a unique view of the island's mining activities.

Zefýria and the Rest of Mílos

Zefýria was the capital of Mílos from 800 until 1793, when a plague struck (a curse, they say, brought down by a fornicating priest) and all the survivors moved to Pláka. Today it is quiet with old crumbling houses, surrounded by olive trees. The bus continues to popular sandy **Paleochóra Beach**; quieter **Ag. Kyriakí** has tavernas.

Dry, southwestern Mílos is mountainous. Just south of Chivadólimni, **Provatás** has another sandy beach, new hotels and a spa, **Loutrá Provatá**, recommended by Hippocrates, with some Roman mosaics. **Kípos**' 5th-century **Panagía tou Kipou** is the island's oldest church. West, in the unpopulated Chalákas region, woods of rare snake root and cedars survive in canyons. Southwest is the monastery of **Ag. Ioánnis Theológos Siderianós**, St John 'of iron'. When pirates attacked, the people took refuge in the church and the saint saved them by turning the church door to iron. He's still on guard. In April 1945 a shell from an English warship zapped through the church door and embedded itself in the wall without exploding.

Kímolos (ΚΙΜΩΛΟΣ)

Kímolos was once Mílos' Siamese twin, connected by an isthmus with a Mycenaean town that sank, leaving a kilometre-wide channel. Once known as Echinousa, or sea urchin (proudly depicted on its coins), the island's modern name means chalk (*kimolía*), the origin of 'cimolite', a mineral similar to chalky Fuller's Earth, used in the dyeing of cloth. Kímolos remains one of the world's top producers, and if it hasn't rained lately the island may be coated with fine white dust – the despair of local housewives. With its 720 souls it is a quiet, very Greek place with beaches but few tourists, even in August. Generally barren, there are patches of green with 140 species of rare plants, mostly on the southeast coast, and rare blue lizards.

From the pretty little port **Psáthi**, it's a 2km 15-minute walk up to blizzard-white **Chóra**, a tangle of paved lanes with flowers at every turn. The houses of **Mésa Kástro** or **Palío Choró** form the inside of the fortress which has loophole windows and four gates. The outer village, **Éxo Kástro** or **Kainoúrio Choró**, has a beautiful domed church, **Panagía Evangélistra**, built in 1614. Other pretty ones are **Panagía Odygítria** (1873), **Taxiárchis** (1670) and **Chrisóstomos**. One of the windmills still grinds wheat, the last

Getting There

A **ferry** connects five times a week with Piraeus, Mílos, Kýthnos, Sérifos and Sífnos, less often with Folégandros, Síkinos, Íos and Santoríni; **water taxi** three to five times daily to Pollónia on Milos; in summer **caiques** to beaches. Tickets in Psáthi, **t** 228 705 1214.

Where to Stay and Eat

Most visitors are day-trippers. Up in **Chóra** three tavernas serve standard Greek fare: one, **Boxoris**, also has rooms.

In **Alíki**, tavernas offer simple rooms. Try **Taverna Alíki**, **t** 228 705 1340.

working one in the Cyclades. From Chóra, you can walk up to Marco Sanudo's hilltop castle, its walls holding the island's oldest church, **Christós**, of 1592. Another walk by way of **Alíki Beach** ends at **Ag. Andréas** and the **Ellinikó necropolis** – all that survives of the sunken city, with graves from the Mycenaean period to the early years AD. Another path from Chóra descends to **Goúpa**, a pretty hamlet with a good beach. Beyond Goúpa there's a lovely beach at **Klíma** and 7km north at **Prássa**, where the cimolite is extracted, are radioactive springs good for rheumatism.

Ándros (ΑΝΔΡΟΣ)

Lush and green in the south, scorched and barren in the north, Ándros is the second largest of the Cyclades. Only the narrowest of straits separates it from Tínos, while in the north the blustery Cavo d'Oro Channel divides the island from Évia. The same irksome wind makes Ándros one of the coolest spots in the Aegean in July and August. Shipping magnates descend for the summer and breed horses on their estates in the wooded hills. Water gushes from the marble fountains and mossy springs, and flowers, orchards and forests cover the south. Fields are divided by distinctive dry stone walls, *xerolithiés*, split from the local schist.

Ándros was colonized in 1000 BC by Ionians, but was often a square peg in a round archipelago. It supported Xerxes, but later assisted the Greeks at Plateía. Athens held a grudge, however, and in 448 BC Pericles gave part of the island to Athenian colonists, who taxed the locals so heavily that Ándros sided with Sparta in the Peloponnesian War. It resisted the Romans, too, who banished the entire population and gave Ándros to Attalos I of Pergamon. Things improved in Byzantine times. In the 400s Ándros had a neo-Platonic academy, and in the 11th century it exported gold-embroidered silks, an industry that lasted into the 18th century. Later Venetian rulers were so nasty and incompetent that Barbarossa took the island without a fight in 1530s. In 1943 the Germans bombed the island for two days when the Italians refused to surrender.

Gávrion and the West Coast

Ferries dock at **Gávrion**, where Athenian summer villas blossom around the beaches. A 40-minute walk east leads to Ándros' best preserved antiquity, the **Pyrgós Ag. Pétros**, a mysterious 70ft Hellenistic tower with a corbelled dome. The *xerolithiés* walls here resemble giant caterpillars squirming over the land. **Kybí**, south of Gávrion, has a fine sandy beach and a turn-off for the 14th-century convent of **Zoodóchos Pigí**, where the nuns sell weavings (*open until noon*). Further down the coast, **Batsí**, in a sweeping sandy bay, is the island's biggest resort, oozing contrived charms; for an all-over tan take the track to **Delavóyas Beach**. From Batsí a road ascends to the shady garden village of **Arnás**, on the slopes of Ándros' highest peak, 3,261ft Mount Pétalo. **Palaiópolis**, 9km down the coast on a steep hill, was founded by the Minoans and served as the capital until AD 1000; 1,039 steps lead down to ancient walls and ruined temples. The road to Chóra goes through rolling countryside dotted with dovecotes and the crumbling tower-houses of the Byzantine and Venetian nobility.

Getting There and Around

By sea: several daily **ferry, catamaran** and **hydrofoil** connections with Rafína, Tínos and Mýkonos, and daily via Mýkonos to Náxos, Páros, Íos, Santoríni and Sýros. Infrequently with Amorgós and Chíos. **Port authority**: Gávrion, **t** 228 207 1213.

By road: buses (**t** 228 202 2316) run from Chóra to Batsí, Gávrion, Apíkia, Strapouriés, Steniés and Kórthi; buses for Batsí, Chóra and Kórthi leave from near the dock at Gávrion, linking with the ferries. **Car and bike rentals** are widely available. **Taxis**: in Gávrion, **t** 228 207 1561; in Batsí, **t** 228 204 1081.

Tourist Information

There is an occasional tourist office in a dovecote in Gávrion, **t** 228 207 1785.

Where to Stay and Eat

Bátsi is the tourist centre, but charming Ándros Town is more Greek.

Gávrion ✉ 84501

Ándros Holiday, **t** 228 207 1443, **f** 228 207 1097, *Ándroshol@otenet.gr* (*B; luxury*). The smartest in town, on the beach: half-board, pool, tennis, sauna and gym.

Galaxias, on the waterfront, **t** 228 207 1228 (*D; moderate–inexpensive*). Also has a good taverna, with house specialities (€12).

Camping Ándros, **t** 228 207 1444. In an attractive site along the Batsí road with a mini-market, swimming pool, excellent taverna and a van to meet the ferries.

Karlos. Halfway to the campsite, a bit hidden away, where locals come (try *froutália*, an omelette made with potatoes and sausage).

Batsí ✉ 84503

Aneroussa, **t** 228 204 1044, **f** 228 204 1444 (*expensive–moderate, inc. breakfast*). Tops

the cliff at Apróvato and has its own private sands next to Delavóyos Beach.

Skouna, **t** 228 204 1240 (*C; expensive*). Small but a good seafront bet.

Chryssi Akti, **t** 228 204 1236, **f** 228 204 1628 (*C; moderate*). Reasonable; on the beach.

Stamatis. Good food and rooftop views over the harbour (€12).

Takis (€12–15). The town's hotspot for fish.

Chóra ✉ 84500

Paradise, **t** 228 202 2187, **f** 228 202 2340 (*B; expensive*). Graceful, neoclassical confection, with a large pool, tennis and air-conditioned rooms. *Open April–Oct*.

Aegli, **t** 228 202 2303, **f** 228 202 2159 (*C; moderate*). Traditional and air-conditioned. *Open all year*.

Irene's Villas, by the sea, **t** 228 202 3344, **f** 228 202 4554 (*expensive–moderate*). Charming, set in lush gardens.

Cabo del Mar, at Embório, **t** 228 202 5001. The smartest place to dine on Ándros, in an absolutely stunning setting; contemporary Med cuisine. *Open May–Sept*.

Archipelagos, towards Giálya Beach. Great traditional food and good prices (€10).

Palinorio, at Embório. Popular with locals, serving everything from beans to lobster.

Apíkia ✉ 84500

Pigi Sarisa, **t** 228 202 3799, **f** 228 202 2476, *pighi@athserve.otenet.gr* (*B; moderate*). Swish, at the mineral spring; pool, games, restaurant and minibus. *Open all year*.

Restaurant Tassos, at Ménites. Tables overlooking the stream, and specialities like *froutália* and tomatoes stuffed with chicken.

Kórthi ✉ 84502

Korthion, **t** 228 206 1218, **f** 228 20 61118 (*C; moderate–inexpensive*). Family-run, spotless and right on the sea, with a restaurant.

Villa Korthi, **t** 228 206 1122, **f** 228 206 2022 (*moderate*). A good choice, all blue and white and in spitting distance of the sea.

Ándros Town/Chóra

Ándros Town sits on a narrow tongue of land, lined with the neoclassical mansions of ship-owning families; the locals once owned one of every five Greek merchant ships. One of their legacies is a lofty sense of public spiritedness – note the marble-paved main street. At the town's edge the Venetian castle, Mésa Kástro, was damaged in the German bombardment. Káto Kástro, the maze of streets that form the medieval city, and the mansions of the Ríva district are wedged between sandy but windswept Parapórti and Embório Bays, reached by steps from central Plateía Kaíri. The ship-owning Goulándris family endowed the nearby **Archaeological Museum** (*t 228 202 3664; open Tues–Sun 8.30–3; adm*) housing the outstanding *Hermes Psychopompos*, a 2nd-century BC copy of a Praxiteles original discovered in Palaiópolis, the *Matron of Herculaneum*, finds from Zagora and Palaiópolis and architectural illustrations. The Goulándris also built the island's other gem, the **Museum of Modern Art** (*t 228 202 2650; open Wed–Mon 10–2 and 6–9*), which hosts international exhibitions.

Villages Outside Chóra

Lovely villages surround Chóra: **Steniés**, 6km north, is the island's most beautiful, its flower-scented lanes closed to traffic. A few mulberries remain; in the old days the precious silk cocoons would be brought into the houses in the winter to keep them warm. Above, the famous Sáriza mineral water flows in the hill village of **Apíkia**. Other villages are in the fertile **Messariá valley** to the west. **Messariá** has a fine Byzantine church, **Taxiárchis**, built in 1158. Further west, lush nightingale-haunted **Ménites** has a church called **Panagías tis Kóumoulous**, the 'Virgin of the Plentiful', which is believed to stand on a Temple of Dionysos, famous in ancient times for a five-day festival where a fountain ceaselessly flowed with wine. At Aladinó, you can visit a stalactite cave called Cháos – bring a light. The lush **Bay of Kórthion**, 30km southeast of Chóra, has a beach and modest tourist development. To the north, the ruined Venetian **Castle of the Old Woman** is where a gritty old lady who abhorred the Venetians secretly opened the door to the Turks. Appalled at the subsequent slaughter, she leapt from the castle and landed on a rock known as 'Old Lady's Leap'. The inland villages of **Kapariá** and **Aidónia** have the prettiest dovecotes on the island.

On the west coast, **Zagora** was inhabited until the 8th century BC, when it boasted a population of 4,000. It was well defended; sheer cliffs surround it on three sides, while on the fourth the Zagorans built a mighty wall. Some remains of their small, flat-roofed houses survive.

Tínos (ΤΗΝΟΣ)

If Delos was the sacred island of the ancients, Tínos, the Lourdes of Greece, occupies the same place in the hearts of their descendants. Delos in its day probably had much the same feel as Tínos – a permanent carnival atmosphere, inns and so-so restaurants, shaded stoas (here awnings), and merchants selling holy pictures, *támata* (votives), to throngs of pilgrims. The rest of the island is dotted with 1,007 Venetian dovecotes, little white towers of embroidered stone, inhabited by clouds of white doves. You almost believe the locals when they say there's a hole in the ozone layer giving them a direct line to the Almighty – if chapels are God's phone booths, Tínos has one for every ten inhabitants.

History

Originally infested with vipers (its name comes from the Phoenician *Tunnoth* 'snake'), Tínos was settled by the Ionians in Archaic times. There were once two Tínos Towns; Mithridates of Pontus ended the confusion by destroying both in 88 BC. After 1204 the island's Venetian masters, the Gizzi, built the fortress of Santa Elena at Exómbourgo. The strongest in the Cyclades, it withstood eleven Turkish assaults, but in 1715, long after the rest of Greece had submitted, a massive Turkish fleet arrived, the fortress surrendered, and the Turks blew it up. In 1822, a nun, Pelagía, had a vision of the Virgin directing her to an icon with extraordinary healing powers. It was the second year of the Greek War of Independence, and to many the icon was proof of divine favour. A church, the Evangelístra, was built over the find spot and quickly became the most important pilgrimage site in Greece. In 1940, during the pilgrimage,

Getting There and Around

By sea: several daily **ferry**, **hydrofoil** and/or **catamaran** connections with Piraeus, Rafína, Mýkonos, Sýros and Ándros; five times a week with Amorgós via Náxos and Páros, two to three times with Thessaloníki and Skiáthos. Two landing areas operate, often simultaneously; check you find the right one. **Port authority**: t 228 302 2220.

By road: excellent bus service all over the island from the big square near the Hotel Delfinia by the ferry dock, t 228 302 2440, and plenty of **taxis**: t 228 302 2470. For **car and bike rental**, try Vidalis, 16 Aiavanou St, t 228 302 3400, f 228 302 5995.

Tourist Information

Tourist Council: t 228 302 3780.
Tourist police: 5 Plateía L. Sóchou, t 228 302 2180/2255.
Or try *www.pigeon.gr*.

Where to Stay

Tínos ✉ 84200

To witness the greatest pilgrimage in Greece, book ahead for August 14–15, but don't expect any elbow room. At other times, a chorus of rooms people greets ferries.

Tinion, t 228 302 2261, f 228 302 4754 (*B; expensive*). Neoclassical mansion converted into a hotel, with plenty of old-fashioned atmosphere. *Open May–Oct*.

Aeolos Bay, t 228 302 3339, f 228 302 3086 (*B; expensive*). Smart, friendly hotel with a pool overlooking Ag. Fokás Beach.

Leándros, 4 L. Lamera, t 228 302 3545, f 228 302 4390 (*C; moderate*). A favourite, with friendly owners.

Vincenzo Rooms, t 228 302 2612, f 228 302 3612, *vincenzo@pigeon.gr* (*expensive studios and moderate rooms*). Friendly owners, who know all there is to about Tínos.

Andriotis, t 228 302 4719 (*D; inexpensive*). Rooms surrounding a charming courtyard.

Golden Beach, at Ag. Fókas, t 228 302 2579, f 228 302 3385 (*C; expensive*). Offers well-furnished studios and a bus into town.

Porto Tango, at Ag. Ioánnis Pórto, t 228 302 4411, f 228 302 4416, *www.portotango.gr* (*A; luxury–expensive*). A major complex, with tennis, pool and sauna. *Open April–Nov.*

Camping Tinos, t 228 302 2344 or t 228 302 3548. A good site south of town.

Eating Out

To Koutouki tis Elenis, t 228 302 4857. Lovely place that's been there for donkeys' years, with Tiniot specialities.

Pallada, by the harbour, t 228 302 3516. Good cheap fills in pots and pans.

O Rokkos, in Vólax, t 228 304 1989 (€12). The island's best, serving exquisite local delicacies with their own white wine, in a gorgeous setting. *Open Feb–Nov.*

Platanos, in Steni. A gastronomic gem, whose farmer/owner serves his own meat, produce and cheese, just the way the locals like it.

an Italian submarine sneaked into the harbour and sank the Greek cruise boat *Elli* –
a prelude to Mussolini's invasion of Greece.

Tínos Town: Panagía Evangelístra

As you pull into the port, the yellow church of Panagía Evangelístra and its neon-lit
cross floats above the town. The modern Sacred Way below, Evangelístra Street,
becomes a solid mass of pilgrims on 25 March and especially 15 August, when an
average 17,000 descend on Tínos. The icon itself goes out for an airing in a jewelled
pavilion, carried by Greek sailors and accompanied by a military band and national
dignitaries. The most devout cover the entire distance from the ferry to the church on
all fours, with padded knees and arms, crawling in penance for the health of a loved
one – a raw, moving and often disturbing sight.

Wander up Evangelístra, past the stalls of candles, tin *támata*, holy water bottles
and one of the finest displays of kitsch this side of Italy. A red carpet covers the
church's grand marble stair; join the queue to light a candle and kiss the icon.
Through the smoke the church glimmers like Aladdin's cave, full of precious offerings:
a silver and gold tree, lamps dangling ships, a foot, a truck and a bucket (blind pilgrims
pledge to give the icon an effigy of whatever they first see if their sight is restored).
The icon itself, the *Megalóchari* or Great Grace, is so smothered in gold, diamonds and
pearls that you can barely see the dark slip of the Virgin's face.

In the courtyards, hostels care for pilgrims waiting for healing dreams sent by the
Virgin. The crypt, where Ag. Pelagía discovered the icon, has a spring with curative
properties; parents from all over Greece bring their children in August to be baptized
in the font. Next to the chapel the victims of the *Elli* lie in a mausoleum, beside a fragment of the fatal Fascist torpedo. Art donations fill several **museums** (*t 228 302 2256;
all open 8–3.30; free*): an art gallery, with works from the Ionian school, a reputed
Rubens and a dubious Rembrandt, a Sculpture Museum and a Byzantine Museum.

Around Tínos Town

There's more than pilgrims. Tínos has a **Folklore Museum** on Loutrá Street (*open
9–12 and 4–7; adm free*) and, by a pine grove, an **Archaeological Museum** (*t 228 302
2670; open Tues–Sun 8–3; free*) with a sundial, a sea monster, Archaic vessels and other
finds from the **Sanctuary of Poseidon and Amphitrite**. This site (*t 228 302 2670; open
Tues–Sun 8–2; free*) is 4km west, by the beaches at **Kiónia**. Founded in the 4th century
BC after the sea god sent a flock of storks to devour the island's snakes, it was famous
for its cures; you can poke around the ruins of two temples, treasuries, baths, fountains and inns. Further west, there's a little beach under **Gastriá Cave**. East of town,
the closest beach is shingly **Ag. Fokás**; a few minutes further east at **Vryókastro** are
ancient walls and a Hellenistic tower. Further east are better beaches at **Ag. Sostis**
and sandy **Ag. Ioánnis Pórto**.

Around the Island

Between the mountains and ravines, Tínos is all sloping terraces, lush and green
until May and golden brown in the summer, brightened by the ubiquitous dovecotes.

Having one was originally a privilege of the nobility. When the Venetians, during their last decades on the island, let just anyone build one, everyone did.

North of Tínos Town is the massive 12th-century **Kechrovoúni Convent**, where Pelagía had her visions and was canonized in 1971; her cell contains her embalmed head. The nearby villages **Arnados** and **Dío Choriá** are delightful. Of **Exómbourgo** (2,100ft) and the Venetian fortress of Santa Elena, only ruined houses, churches and a fountain remain, but the view is superb. Head up the valley to the charming villages of **Smardákito** and **Tarambádos**, with the island's best dovecotes. North of Exómbourgo, pretty **Loutrá** has a 17th-century Jesuit monastery (Tinos may be sacred to the Orthodox, but it still has lots of Catholics). At lovely little **Vólax**, basket makers work amid weird granite outcrops. **Mount Tsikniás**, looming above, is the reputed tomb of Calais and Zetes, the sons of the North Wind that keeps Tínos cool, even in August. From **Kómi**, another attractive village, a long valley runs down to the sea at **Kolymbíthres**, a horseshoe bay with sandy beaches.

A paved road follows the ridge along the southwest coast. Tínos is famous for its green marble; some examples are in a **sculpture museum** in **Istérnia** (*open Tues–Sun till 3*). The old grammar school is now a school of fine arts, and a shop near the square exhibits student work. A road leads down to popular **Ormós** or **Ag. Nikíta Beach** (rooms and tavernas). Buses continue to **Pánormos Bay**, with a great taverna (Ag. Thalassa) and rooms. **Marlás**, further north, is in the centre of the old marble quarries. From the wild, barren northwest tip of Tínos watch the red sunsets and be bowled over by the drama – and the wind.

Mýkonos (ΜΥΚΟΝΟΣ)

Dry, barren and windy, but graced with excellent beaches and a beautiful town, cosmopolitan Mýkonos has the most exciting nightlife in Greece. It doesn't bat a mascaraed eyelid as the crowds roll in, having made the transformation long ago from a traditional economy to one dedicated to every whim of the international set. It also has the distinction of being one of the most expensive islands and the first officially to sanction nudism on some of its beaches, as well as being the Mediterranean's leading gay resort and the setting for the film *Shirley Valentine*.

The ancient Ionians built three cities on Mýkonos but, during the war between the Romans and Mithridates of Pontus all three were destroyed. Chóra was rebuilt during the Byzantine period, fortified by the Venetians, but in 1537 it fell without resistance to Barbarossa. Mýkonos then came into its own as a pirate island, settled with pirate families who grew rich fencing plunder to European merchants; even so, it was on the front lines in the War of Independence, its fleet of 22 ships led by Mantó Mavrogenous, who donated her considerable fortune to the cause.

Chóra

The island's picture-perfect capital **Chóra** is gleaming and whitewashed, with brightly painted wooden trim. At night it vibrates. A bust of Mantó Mavrogenous guards the main square and the town's pelican mascot, the successor of the original Pétros, often preens himself in the shadow of the small church here. On the hill overlooking the harbour are several thatched **windmills**; one from the 16th century has been restored (*open June–Sept 4–6*). They are a favourite subject for artists as is **Little Venice**, where tall picturesque houses are built directly on the sea; each now accommodates a cocktail bar for sunset views.

The most famous of Mýkonos' 400 churches, snow-white **Panagía Paraportianí**, is just beyond Little Venice, an asymmetrical masterpiece of four churches melted into one. Opposite, the **Folklore Museum** (*t 228 902 2591; open Mon–Sat 4–8, Sun 5–8*) houses old curiosities, along with a traditional bedroom and kitchen, and an exhibition,'Mýkonos and the Sea'. The **Nautical Museum** (*t 228 902 2700; open summer 10.30–1 and 6.30–9.30; adm*), in the centre, has rooms containing ships' models from ancient times plus paintings, prints and coins. Nearby, **Lena's House** (*t 228 902 2591; open April–end Oct 7–9pm*), is a branch of the Folklore Museum: the 19th-century middle-class home of Léna Sakrivanoú, preserved as she left it, down to her chamber pot. Over Ag. Anna Beach, the **Archaeological Museum** (*t 228 902 2325; open 9–3.30, Sun 10–3, closed Tues; adm*) offers boldly decorated ceramics from the necropolis islet of Rhéneia (*see* Délos, p.637) and a great 7th-century BC funeral *pithos* with relief scenes from the Fall of Troy, showing the death of Hector's son and a delightful warrior-stuffed Trojan horse, fitted with aeroplane windows.

Mýkonos

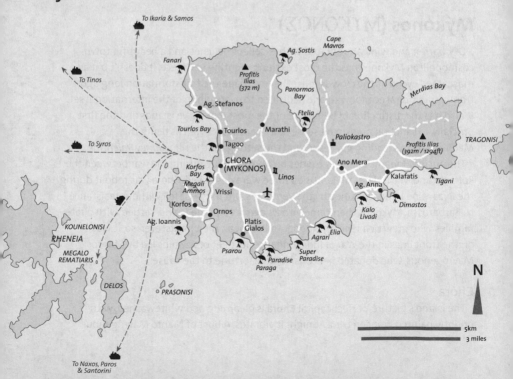

Getting There and Around

By air: several flights daily with Athens, several a week with Thessaloníki, Santoríni, Rhodes and Heráklion. The Olympic office at the end of Ag. Efthimiou street, **t** 228 902 2490. Buses stop by the **airport**: **t** 228 902 2327.

By sea: several **ferry** and **hydrofoil** connections daily with Piraeus, Rafína, Ándros, Tínos, Sýros, Náxos, Páros, Íos and Santoríni; at least three times a week with Heráklion, Amorgós and Sífnos; less frequently with Mílos, the Back Islands, Thessaloníki and Skiáthos; **excursion boats** to Délos daily between 8.30am and 1pm, except Monday; also to Paradise, Super Paradise, Agrari and Eliá from both Chóra and Platýs Gialós. **Port authority**: **t** 228 902 2218.

By road: **buses** run frequently from two bus stations. The one by the archaeological museum serves Ag. Stéfanos, Tourlos, Áno Merá, Eliá, Kalafátis and Kaló Livádi. The one by Olympic Airways is for Ornós, Ag. Ioánnis, Platýs Gialós, Paradise Beach, Psaroú, the airport and Kalamopódi. Information, **t** 228 902 3360. **Taxis**: **t** 228 902 3700 or **t** 228 902 2400. **Car and bike hire** is easy; just don't expect a bargain.

Tourist Information

Tourist police: on the quay, **t** 228 902 2482.

Where to Stay and Eat

Mýkonos is expensive. Most hotels open from Greek Easter till October, and provide airport transfer. On arrival, beware of offers for the isolated, ugly rooms above Chóra; the accommodation desks on the quay may throw up something better.

Chóra (Mýkonos Town) ✉ 84600

Belvedere, **t** 228 902 5122, **f** 228 902 5126, *www.belvederehotel.com* (*A; luxury*). Superb resort hotel just above the centre with great views; traditional architecture and two fine restaurants: a classy sushi bar and Remvi, serving Syrian dishes. *Open all year*.

Semeli, just above town, **t** 228 9027466, **f** 228 907467, *semiliht@otenet.gr* (*A; luxury*).

Elegant Cycladic hotel in a beautiful garden setting, posh rooms. *Open all year*.

Lefteris, **t** 228 902 3128, **f** 228 902 7117, *lefterishot@yahoo.com* (*E; expensive*). With a roof terrace, kitchen facilities and the wonderfully laid-back Kosta.

Rania, **t** 228 902 2315, **f** 228 902 2370, *rania-ap@otenet.gr* (*moderate*). Tasteful, quiet rooms and studios above Taxi square, with very helpful owners.

Philippi, 32 Kalogéra St, **t** 228 902 2294, **f** 228 902 4680, *chriko@otenet.gr* (*D; moderate*). Delightful hotel in the heart of Chóra. Play 'spot the celebrity' in the lovely garden restaurant (**t** 228 902 2295 to book; €30).

Interni, **t** 228 902 6333 (€50). Exquisite fusion cuisine in a beautiful setting – the home from June to September of a trendy Athenian restaurant. *Open eves only*.

Sea Satin, below the windmills, **t** 228 902 4674 (€25). Delicious food, served market-style; and a party atmosphere that carries on to the wee hours. *Open eves only*.

Chez Maria's, Kalogera St, **t** 228 902 7565 (€30–35). Elegant, in a bougainvillaea garden setting. Seafood pasta a speciality, but there's lots more.

Katrine's, **t** 228 902 7391 (€25). Again, centrally placed but not much lighter on the wallet; has many good French specialities; book.

Niko's Taverna, behind the town hall, **t** 228 902 4320. If you need to be reminded that you're in Greece, head here for good dinners in the €12 range.

North of Chóra: Tagoo ✉ 84600

Cavo Tagoo, **t** 228 902 3692, **f** 228 902 4923, *cavotagoo@hol.gr* (*A; luxury*). The award-winning Cubist beauty, 'pour les lucky few', with seawater pool, beautiful view of Mýkonos and the chance to rub shoulders with the stars.

Apanema, **t** 228 902 8590, **f** 228 907 9250, *www.apanemaresort.com* (*A; luxury*). Beautiful new small Cycladic-style hotel, wih a charming pool and friendly service. Good breakfasts and lunches, too. *Open Easter–Oct*.

Spanelis, **t** 228 902 3081 (*D; expensive*). Expensive, but less so. Small, older hotel.

North of Chóra: Toúrlos ✉ 84600

Rhenia, t 228 902 2300, **f** 228 902 3152, *www.rhenia-bungalows.com* (*B; luxury*). Tranquil, sheltered bungalows and pool, overlooking Chóra and Délos.

Olia, t 228 902 3123, **f** 228 902 3824 (*B; expensive*). Pleasing, traditionally styled rooms and pool nearer the sea.

Sunset Hotel, t 228 902 3013, **f** 228 902 3931 (*D; expensive–moderate*). Smaller, with a terrace café where they will cook to your order.

North of Chóra: Ag. Stéfanos ✉ 84600

Kastro, t 228 902 3176, **f** 228 902 6690 (*B; expensive*). Charming little hotel and big rooms with lots of attention to detail, and fabulous views from the pool.

Vangeli, further north, just before Fanári at Choulakia Beach, **t** 228 902 2458, **f** 228 902 5558 (*expensive*). Quiet, small and very Greek, with a good restaurant (€15).

South Coast Beaches: Ag. Ioánnis and Ornós ✉ 84600

Manoula's Beach, at Ag. Ioánnis, **t** 228 902 2900, **f** 228 902 4314 (*C; luxury*). Pretty bungalow complex where they filmed *Shirley Valentine*.

Kivotos, Ornós, **t** 228 902 4094, **f** 228 902 2844, *www.kivotosclubhotel.gr* (*luxury*). One of the 'Small Luxury Hotels of the World' with squash courts, wooden schooner for guests, seawater pool, gourmet restaurant, **La Medusse**.

Yannaki, t 228 902 3393, **f** 228 902 4628 (*C; expensive*). Away from Ornós centre, with a tranquil pool and mod cons.

Platýs Gialós ✉ 84600

Petinos Beach, t 228 902 4310, **f** 228 902 3680, *george@petinos.myk.forthnet.gr* (*A; luxury*). Ritzy pastel paradise with every facility, including pool and watersports.

Argo, t 228 902 3405, **f** 228 902 4936, *argo@otenet.gr* (*E; expensive*). Friendly, clean and possibly a pool by the time you get there.

Mykonos Camping, Parága Beach, **t** 228 902 4578. With good facilities and minibus and boat service from Platýs Gialós.

Further East: Kalafátis and Áno Merá ✉ 84600

Anemoessa, at Kalafátis, **t** 228 907 1420, **f** 228 907 2280, *anemoessa@otenet.gr* (*B; luxury*). Family hotel, with pool and a big buffet breakfast. But you need a car.

Aphrodite Beach, Kalafátis, **t** 228 907 1367, **f** 228 907 1525, *www.aphrodite-mykonos.com* (*A; luxury*). Low-key, old-fashioned resort hotel on the beach where Onassis and Jackie Kennedy stayed. Beautiful grounds, excellent seafood taverna.

Ano Mera, at Áno Merá, **t** 228 907 1113, **f** 228 907 1276, *gats-sa@gats.gr* (*A; luxury–expensive*). Cavernous, offering remarkable value given its Olympic-size pool, disco and restaurant (€15), recommended for its meat dishes.

Dafni, on the square in Anó Merá, **t** 228 907 2222 (around €25). Great new resturant serving the classics from the finest ingredients – including the best chips on the island. *Open daily Feb–Sept, and Fri–Sun only Oct–Nov.*

Entertainment and Nightlife

The international and gay set still bop the night away in venues ranging from the cosy to the crazy. Get started at sunset along the waterfront from Cathedral Square to Paraportiani; try the **Galleraki Bar**, or **Kastro's** in Little Venice, famous for its classical sounds and strawberry daiquiris; if you prefer piña coladas, try **Katerina's** next door. **Bolero**, in the centre, has good music and cocktails.

Piano Bar above Taxi Square offers live music and snazzy cocktails, but get there early for a seat; **Mona Lisa**, also here, plays lots of salsa and other Latin numbers.

High-tech **Astra Bar** is a cool place to be seen, along with **Aígli**, opposite. The **City Club** has a nightly transvestite show, although the sexiest stuff struts its way along the bar at **Icarus**, above Pierro's (*see* below). The perennial favourite, **Mykonos Dancing Bar**, plays Greek music, while **Zorba's** has live *rembétika*. **Pierro's,** just back from the main waterfront, remains the most frenzied; **Cava Paradiso**, on the rocks, hosts superstar DJs.

Around Mýkonos: Inside and Around the Edges

In ancient times Mýkonos was famous for its baldies and, suspiciously, today's old fishermen never want to take off their caps. You may find a few old chaps to chat up inland at **Áno Merá**, the island's other town, where the 16th-century **Panagía Tourlianí Monastery** has Cretan icons, a Florentine altarpiece and a marble steeple. Below, sandy windswept **Panórmos Bay** has ancient ruins and **Fteliá** and **Ag. Sostis**, wild beaches favoured by windsurfers.

North of Chóra, the beaches at **Tagoo**, **Toúrlos** and **Ag. Stéfanos** are always crowded, but **Fanári** to the north is quieter. The nearest beaches south of Chóra are **Megáli Ámmos**, **Kórfos** and **Ornós**, all built up, especially Ornós, with its cute port. The biggest resort is **Platýs Gialós**, to the east, with boat excursions to the other beaches and Délos, while jet setters jet-ski at **Psaroú**, just before Platýs Gialós. **Paradise**, with a campsite, diving school and Cavo Paradiso (a pool-bar-restaurant Hard Rock Café clone), and **Super Paradise** are the once notorious nudist beaches, both much less notorious now. **Eliá**, a once quiet beach accessible by bus, is divided into straight and gay precincts; just inland sprawls **Watermania** (*t 228 907 1685*), the answer to all your aquatic desires (*open April–Oct*). **Ag. Ánna** is a quieter beach, and there's also the fishing hamlet and the family beach at **Kalafátis**.

Délos (ΔΗΛΟΣ)

t 228 902 2259; open Tues–Sun 8.30–3; adm. Major sites are labelled; guide books are on sale. You need two or three hours. Tourist boats from Mýkonos leave between 8.30am and 1pm daily (except on Mon), returning between noon and 3pm, for around €6 return. Agencies offer guided tours (€15), or alternatively hire a private boat at the harbour. Take water, or even a picnic.

Mýkonos could have no greater contrast than its neighbour Délos, the hub of the Cyclades, the holy island of the ancient Greeks and centre of the great Panhellenic alliance of the Athenian golden age. Today it is deserted except for the lonely guardian of the ruins, the boatloads of day-trippers, and little lizards, darting among the poppies and broken marble.

The Birthplace of Apollo

In myth, Delos began as Adelos, 'the invisible', an islet floating just under the waves. When the ever-ready Zeus impregnated the goddess Leto, his angry wife Hera vowed that Leto would not give birth anywhere under the sun. Poor Leto wandered the world but no country would risk Hera's wrath to help her. Finally at Zeus' request Poseidon raised and anchored the floating islet just for her, making it Delos or 'visible'. Yet Delos too hesitated, but Leto promised that her son would make the island the richest sanctuary in Greece. So Leto gave birth to Artemis, goddess of the hunt and virginity, and then nine days later to Apollo, god of reason and light.

By 1000 BC Delos was already an important Ionian cult centre. With the rise of Athens, notably under Pisístratos, Delos knew both its greatest glory and its biggest headaches as the Athenians invented myths to connect them to the islet: their king Erechtheus had led the first delegation to Delos, Theseus stopped off after slaying the Minotaur, and so on. In 543 BC the Athenians tricked (or bribed) Delphi into ordering the island's purification and removing all tombs, a ploy designed to alienate the Delians from their past and diminish the island's importance.

In 478 BC the Athenians organized an Amphictyonic League headquartered at Delos, that modern historians call the Delian League. With the only fleet capable of taking on the Persians, the Athenians promised to defend the Greek city-states, who in return would contribute a yearly sum. It was effective, but no one was fooled in 454 BC when Pericles, to 'protect' the league's treasury, removed it to Athens and then dipped into it to build the Parthenon. The plague that then hit Athens was attributed to the wrath of Apollo, so a second purification of Delos (not Athens, mind) was called for in 426 BC. This time both birth and death were forbidden; the pregnant and dying had to go to nearby Rheneia. The Delians turned to Sparta for aid; Sparta declined, saying that a rock where inhabitants couldn't be born or die wasn't a real home. In 422 BC Athens punished Delos for courting Sparta and exiled the population. In 403 BC, when Sparta defeated Athens, Delos had a 10-year breather before Athens formed the second Delian League. Fifty years later, the Delians demanded Athens' ousting. But the league's leader, Philip II of Macedon, refused, wishing to appease the city that hated him most. Well, Leto did say the 'richest sanctuary', not the happiest.

After the death of Alexander, Delos flourished. By 146 BC it was the centre of all east–west trade, and the Romans declared it a 'free port'. New quays and piers were constructed; the slave markets thrived. In the battle of the Romans against Mithridates of Pontus in 88 BC, Delos was decimated and lost much of its business to Rhodes. In AD 363, Emperor Julian the Apostate tried to jump-start paganism one last time on Delos until the oracles warned: 'Delos shall become Adelos'. A Christian community survived until the 6th century. Then pirates took over and Delos became a handy marble quarry; its once busy markets pastures.

The Excavations

The ruins cover about a thousand years of history. Left of the landing stage is the **Agora of the Competalists**, i.e. of the Roman citizens or freed slaves who worshipped the Lares Competales, patrons of Roman trade guilds. The **Sacred Way** is lined on the left by the foundations of the once tall and splendid **Philip's Stoa** (210 BC), a gift of Philip V of Macedon. The kings of Pergamon built the **Southern Stoa** in the 3rd century BC, and you can make out the remains of the **Delians' Agora**, too. Past the 2nd-century BC marble **Propylaea** (gate) to the left, is the 6th-century BC **House of the Naxians** where only the pedestal remains of a huge *kouros*; another huge dedication, a bronze palm erected by Athens (symbolic of the tree clutched by Leto in giving birth) toppled over and crushed it.

The main event, the **Sanctuary of Apollo**, was once crowded with votives and statues. It had three temples in a row. The first and largest, the **Great Temple of Apollo**, was begun by the Delians in 476 BC. The second was an **Athenian Temple** of Pentelic marble, built during the Second Purification; the third, and smallest, of

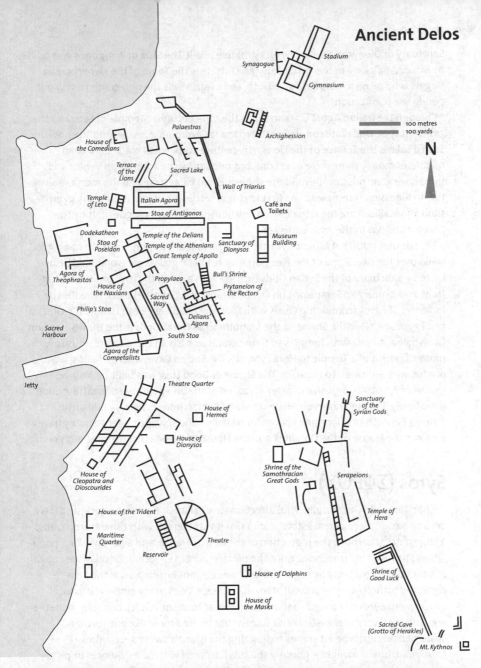

Ancient Delos

Stadium

Synagogue

Gymnasium

Palaestras

Archighession

House of
the Comedians

100 metres
100 yards

N

Terrace
of the
Lions

Sacred Lake

Wall of Triarius

Temple
of Leto

Italian Agora

Stoa of Antigonos

Café and
Toilets

Dodekatheon

Stoa of
Poseidon

Temple of the Delians

Temple of the Athenians

Great Temple of Apollo

Sanctuary of
Dionysos

Museum
Building

Agora of
Theophrastos

House of
the Naxians

Propylaea

Sacred
Way

Bull's Shrine

Prytaneion of
the Rectors

Philip's Stoa

Delians'
Agora

Sacred
Harbour

South Stoa

Agora of the
Competalists

Jetty

Theatre Quarter

House of
Hermes

Sanctuary
of the
Syrian Gods

House of
Dionysos

House of
Cleopatra and
Dioscourides

Shrine of the
Samothracian
Great Gods

Serapeions

House of the Trident

Temple of
Hera

Maritime
Quarter

Theatre

Reservoir

House of Dolphins

Shrine of
Good Luck

House of
the Masks

Sacred Cave
(Grotto of Herakles)

Mt. Kythnos

porous stone, was the 6th-century **Temple of the Delians**, built by the Athenian tyrant
Pisistratos. Demetrios Poliorketes contributed the nearby **Bull's Shrine**, which held a
model trireme in honour of the sacred delegation ship – the one used by Theseus to
return to Athens after slaying the Minotaur. The area also included the **Prytaneion of
the Rectors** and the **Councillors' House**. Towards the museum is the 4th-century BC

Sanctuary of Dionysos, flanked by lucky marble phalli. The **Stoa of Antigonos** was built by Macedonia's king in the 3rd century BC. Outside is the **Tomb of the Hyperborean Virgins**, who came to help Leto give birth, and as such was the only tomb to stay put during the purifications.

Through the **Italian Agora** you can reach the 6th-century BC **Temple of Leto** and the 3rd-century BC **Dodekatheon**, dedicated to the 12 Olympian gods. Beyond the now dry **Sacred Lake** is the **Terrace of the Lions**, 7th-century BC ex-votos made of Naxian marble; originally there were nine lions, but one sits by the Arsenale in Venice and three have gone missing. Beyond the shore are two **Palaestrae** and the foundation of the **Archigession**, a temple to the first mythical settler on Delos. Besides the **gymnasium** and **stadium** are the remains of a few houses and a **synagogue** built by the Phoenician Jews in the 2nd century BC.

The summit (370ft) of Mount Kýthnos has a settlement dating to 3000 BC and good views over the site. Some of the free port's more exotic gods were worshiped below: there's a **Sanctuary of the Syrian Gods** (100 BC) with a small theatre, and the first of three 2nd-century BC **Serapeions** on Delos; Serapis was a synthetic deity created by Ptolemy I of Egypt (combining Osiris with Dionysos) to please both Hellenistic Greeks and Egyptians. Near the **Shrine to the Samothracian Great Gods** is the third Serapeion (with half a statue), with temples to both Serapis and Isis. In the area are houses with mosaic floors, and a **Temple to Hera** (500 BC). The **Sacred Cave**, where Apollo gave oracles, was dedicated to Heracles. The **Shrine of Good Luck** was built by Arsinoë Queen of Egypt. An exclusive quarter surrounded the 2nd-century BC **theatre**; beside it is a lovely 8-arched **reservoir**. Hellenistic and Roman houses here all had private cisterns beneath the floor, and spaces for oil lamps and sewage systems; many have mosaics; the **House of the Dolphins** and the **House of the Masks** are especially good.

Sýros (ΣΨΡΟΣ)

Inhabitants of Sýros (locally, Sýra) affectionately call their home 'Our rock', and it *is* a dry and barren piece of real estate. But in 1821 it was blessed with three trump cards: a large natural harbour, the protection of the king of France, and a hardworking population. The result is Ermoúpolis, once the premier port in Greece, and today the capital of the Cyclades. No Cycladic sugar cubism here: elegant Ermoúpolis is the best-preserved 19th-century neoclassical town in Greece. With many employed in local government Sýros can afford to snap its fingers at tourism, but it's booming nonetheless. Still, it's a very Greek island and tourists are treated more like guests than customers, except when it comes to flogging the island's sweet specialities, *loukoúmia*, Turkish delight – gummy squares flavoured with roses, quinces or pistachios smothered in icing sugar – or *halvadópittes*, which resemble nougat.

History

Poseidon was the island patron and in connection with his cult one of the first observatories in Europe, a heliotrope (a kind of sundial), was constructed in the 6th century BC by the local philosopher, Ferekides. Pythagoras' teacher, Ferekides imparted a mix of astrology, philosophy and beliefs in the immortality of the soul; he was also the first Greek to write in prose. In Roman times the population emigrated to present-day Ermoúpolis, at that time known as 'the Happy' with its splendid harbour and two prominent hills. After the collapse of the *pax romana*, Sýros was abandoned until the 13th century, when Venetians founded Áno Sýros on one of the hills.

Because it was Catholic the island enjoyed the protection of the French, and remained neutral at the outbreak of the War of Independence in 1821. War refugees from Chíos, Psará and Smyrna brought their Orthodox faith with them and founded settlements on the other hill, Vrondádo, and down by the harbour. This town boomed as the 'warehouse' of the new state for cotton from Egypt and spices from the East, and as the central coaling station for the eastern Mediterranean. When it was time to name the new town, Ermoúpolis – 'Hermes city' (the god of commerce) – seemed the natural choice. For 50 years it ran much of the Greek economy; fortunes were spent on mansions, schools, public buildings and the first theatre in modern Greece; cemeteries abound with extravagant monuments. By the 1890s, however, oil replaced coal and Piraeus replaced Ermoúpolis as Greece's main port. Sýros declined, but still supported itself with shipyards and industries, prospering just enough to keep its grand old buildings occupied, but not enough to tear them down to build new concrete blocks.

Ermoúpolis

Greece was reborn in Ermoúpolis.
                          Elefthérios Venizélos

Ermoúpolis (pop. 12,000), is a sweeping crescent meringue of a city rising in twin peaks, one for each religion; older Catholic **Áno Sýros** to your left (or north), and Orthodox **Vrondádo**, on the right. Down below, stately neoclassical buildings, re-painted in their original colours, softly illuminated by old street lamps, form a rare urban idyll. Yet there's no doubt that the city works for a living; prominent on the harbour are the Neórion shipyards.

Central **Plateía Miaoúlis** is the most elegant in Greece, with worn lustrous marble paving, cafés and a statue of revolutionary hero Admiral Miaoúlis. In *Aegean Greece*, Robert Liddell wrote that he could think of no square 'except St Mark's that more gives the effect of a huge ballroom, open by accident to the sky.' The grand neoclassical **town hall** was designed in 1876 by Ziller. Up the steps to its left, the **Archaeology Museum** (*t 228 108 8487; open Tues–Sun 8.30–3*) contains proto-Cycladic to Roman-era finds. To the right, behind the square, the **Apóllon Theatre**, a copy of La Scala in Milan, was the first opera house in Greece. Up the street, the **Velissarópoulos Mansion** is one of the few you can get into to see the painted ceilings and murals characteristic of old Ermoúpolis. In the lanes above the square, the **Metamórphosis** is the Orthodox cathedral, with a pretty *choklakía* courtyard and surprisingly Baroque interior. Chíos Street, descending towards the port, contains the town's bustling **market**. By the port, just up from the bus terminal, the church of the **Annunciation**, built by refugees from

Getting There and Around

By air: three daily flights from Athens. The Olympic office is port side at 52 Andistasios, **t** 228 108 2634. **Airport: t** 228 108 7025. Taxis into town: around €5.

By sea: several **ferry** connections daily with Piraeus, Tínos, Mýkonos, Páros and Náxos; at least twice a week to Amorgós and the Back Islands, Kýthnos, Kéa, Folégandros, Síkinos, Santoríni, Crete and Astypálaia; at least once a week to the Dodecanese. Summer **hydrofoils** to Rafína and Délos.

Port authority: t 228 108 8888.

By road: good **bus** service, **t** 228 108 2575, departing from by the port. Regular buses circle the island, via Azólimnos (1½ hrs), then pass through all the beach villages except Kíni, which has a separate service. **Taxi** rank: **t** 228 108 6222.

Tourist Information

Teamwork, in the port, **t** 228 108 3400, **f** 228 108 3508, *teamwork@otenet.gr*. Organizes accommodation and guided tours of Ermoúpolis, as well as car and bike rentals.

Where to Stay and Eat

The **Rooms and Apartments Association**, **t** 228 108 2252, has a booth near the port.

Ermoúpolis ✉ 84100

Archontikó Vourli, 5 Mavorkordatou, **t** 228 108 1682, **f** 228 108 8440 (*B; luxury–expensive*). Traditionally furnished Vapória mansion of 1888, plus an exquisite breakfast.

Diogenis, Plateía Papágou, just to the left of the ferry dock, **t** 228 108 6301, **f** 228 108 3334 (*B; expensive*). Swish and new, with 43 neoclassical-style rooms.

Hermes, Plateía Kanári, **t** 228 108 3011, **f** 228 108 7412 (*C; expensive*). Smart rooms with bath and balconies right over the sea.

Omiros, 43 Omirou, **t** 228 108 4910, **f** 228 108 6266 (*A; expensive*). A gorgeous 150-year-old neoclassical mansion, the family home of sculptor Vitális. *Open Mar–Oct.*

Paradise, 3 Omirou, **t** 228 108 3204, **f** 228 108 1754 (*moderate*). Well-appointed rooms with a flower-filled courtyard and roof terrace with big views. Off-season discounts.

Ariadne, 9 Filini, **t** 228 108 0245 (*moderate*). Just off the waterfront by the bus depot; convenient if you arrive at an ungodly hour.

Avra Rooms, 7 Afrodíti, **t/f** 228 108 2853 (*moderate*). Near to the port, friendly

Psará, contains a rare icon of the *Assumption* painted and signed by Doménikos Theotokópoulos (*aka* El Greco) after he left for Venice.

Stretching off to the northeast, the elegant **Vapória** quarter is chock-a-block with old shipowners' mansions with marble façades, where marble steps descend to the beach. In the centre of Vapória, in front of blue- and golden-domed **Ag. Nikólaos**, a lion-topped memorial by Vitális is the world's first **Monument to the Unknown Soldier**.

Crowning **Vrondádo Hill** (take the main street up from behind Plateía Miaoúlis), the Byzantine church **Anástasis** has a few old icons and superb views stretching to Tínos and Mýkonos. Excellent tavernas are spread over its steps. More remote – 870 cobbled steps (or a hop on the bus or taxi to start from the top) – is its older twin, **Áno Sýros**, a whitewashed pedestrian-only enclave, mostly Catholic since the Crusades; the **Cathedral of St George**, or Ai-Giórgi, tops the hill. The large, handsome **Capuchin Convent of St Jean** was founded there in 1635 by France's Louis XIII as a poorhouse and contains archives dating from the 1400s; the Jesuits, just above at 16th-century **Panagía Karmilou**, have a cloister from 1744. The famous *rembétika* composer Márkos Vamvakáris was born in Áno Sýros; his bust graces his square. On your way down the hill (the main 'streets' have a white marble strip in the centre), don't miss the **Orthodox cemetery of Ag. Geórgios**, with its elaborate marble mausoleums.

management, good rooms with air-conditioning, TV and hairdryers.

Lillis, in Áno Sýro, **t** 228 108 8087. Wonderful views, excellent food and *rembétika* at weekends. *Open eves only.*

Bailas, 55 Lelas Karagianni, **t** 228 108 5580. Delicious food baked in clay pots. *Open eves only, Oct–May Fri and Sat only.*

Bouba's, opposite the ferry port. A fine old island *ouzerie*, serving exquisite barbecued octopus and local sharp *kopanistí* cheese on *paximádia* (rusks).

Ta Yiannena Psistaria, on the quay, **t** 228 108 2994. For the best roasts and barbecues, with *kokorétsi*, chicken and vegetable dishes.

Kíni ✉ 84100

Sunset, t 228 107 1211 (*C; moderate*). Right on the sea with fine views. *Open all year.*

Harbour Inn, t 228 107 1377, **f** 228 107 1378, *tboukas@otenet.gr* (*moderate–inexpensive*). Six rooms close to the water.

Delfini's. Good place to enjoy delicious stuffed aubergines at the twilight hour.

Galissás ✉ 84100

Benois, **t/f** 228 104 2833, **f** 228 104 2944 (*C; moderate*). Newish and open all year.

Dendrinos, near Akti Delfiniou, **t/f** 228 104 2469 (*moderate–inexpensive*). Friendly, family-run place; rooms have fridges and a *máti* (electric ring for making coffee).

Two Hearts Camping, t 228 104 2052/2321. With bungalows. It meets the ferries.

Posidonía and Around ✉ 84100

Eleana, t 228 104 2601, **f** 228 104 2644, (*C; moderate*). On the beach. *Open all year.*

Chroussa, up in the little village of the same name. Some of the best food on Sýros.

Acapulco, on Fínikas marina, **t** 228 104 3008. For fish.

Entertainment and Nightlife

There's lots on Sýros, from culture at the **Apollon Theatre**, movies at the **outdoor cinema** near the market and bars ranging from sophisticated to rowdy, clustered on the waterfront. The evening *vólta* in Plateía Miaoúlis is still important; once the square was specially paved so that the unmarried knew on which side to stroll to show they were available. Trendy Ermoúpolis flocks to the **Rodo Club**, 2km out of town.

For *rembétika* music head to **Lillis** and **Xanthomalis** in Áno Sýros. **Argo Café** in Galissás has live Greek music.

A 45min walk from Ermoúpolis leads to the pretty seaside church of **Ag. Dimítrios**; all ships coming into port hoot as they pass and a bell is rung in reply. In **Díli**, just above, are the remains of a **Temple of Isis** built in 200 BC. Across the harbour at **Lazarétta** are bits of a 5th-century BC Temple of Poseidon; it may have been the Poseidonia mentioned in the *Odyssey*.

Around Sýros

'Our Rock' isn't altogether barren; olives, pistachios and citrus grow, and the bees make an excellent thyme honey. To the north, at lagoon-like **Grámmata Bay** (by boat only), sailors from Classical times engraved epigrams, still legible on the rocks. The Bronze Age necropolis of **Chalandriani** (2600–2300 BC) yielded many important Early Cycladic finds; the Bronze Age citadel of **Kástri**, an hour's walk north, has ruins of walls, six towers, and houses. The **cave** where philosopher Ferekides whiled away the summer is just south of Chalandriani.

Buses ply the seaside resorts: **Kíni**, a small west coast village (two sandy beaches) is popular for sunsets. North over the headland is **Delfíni Beach** for that all-over tan. In the middle of the island, **Episkópio** boasts **Profítis Ilías**, the oldest Byzantine church on Sýros. Foreign tourists concentrate in **Galissás**, with a sheltered crescent of sand fringed by tamarisks; the rest is all mini-markets and heavy metal, backpackers and bikers. Nearby **Arméos** is for nudists. Further south, **Fínikas**, settled by the Phoenicians and mentioned in Homer, is another popular resort with a gritty roadside beach.

Ermoúpolian grandees built their ornate summer houses at **Dellagrácia** or **Posidonía**, a genteel resort with a serene film-set atmosphere. Further south, quieter **Agathopés** has a sandy beach and an islet opposite. **Mégas Gialós** is a pretty family resort, with shaded sands. **Vári** to the east is now a major resort, but still has its fishing fleet. **Azólimnos** is particularly popular with the Syriani for its *ouzeries* and cafés. Inland, **Chroússa** is a piney village with shipowners' villas, while nearby **Faneroméni** has panoramic views of the island.

Páros (ΠΑΡΟΣ)

Despite the hordes who descend on fashionable Páros each summer, it never seems to lose its charms; its Cycladic houses, narrow lanes, little bridges and flowered balconies somehow absorb the invasion. Famed for its golden beaches and excellent windsurfing, it is also one of the more fertile Cyclades, with vineyards, wheat and barley fields, citrus and olive groves. Páros also means marble, or more specifically the finest, most translucent marble in the world, which led to its prosperity in Early Cycladic times. The Ionians arrived in the 8th century BC and Páros boomed again, and the islanders colonized gold-rich Thássos. Famous Parians include the 7th-century BC poet Archilochos (the first to write in iambic meter) and the Hellenistic sculptor Skopas. Páros supported the Persians in 490 BC, and when Miltiades, the victor at Marathon, came to punish them he failed in his siege and developed the gangrene that killed him. After the Romans, life was unsettled, and the island often deserted; in the 1670s it was the base of Hugues Chevaliers, the inspiration for Byron's *Corsair*.

Parikiá

Parikiá the port has quintupled in size in the last couple of decades, so the locals have put up signs to the 'Traditional Settlement', its core. Once found, it shows itself as a Cycladic beauty, if an unusually flat one, traversed by a long, winding main street. The walls of the **Venetian Kástro**, built from the white marble Temples of Apollo and Demeter, form an attractive collage of columns and pediments. Three windmills close off the waterfront on the south where the *ouzeries* are a popular evening rendezvous. Most of Parikiá sprawls with hotels, bars and restaurants in the direction of **Livádia** and its tamarisk-lined beach. In the course of building a new pier, a Doric temple with foundations the size of the Parthenon has been unearthed.

Set back between Livádia and the old town is Páros' greatest monument, the cathedral **Ekatontapyliani** or 'Hundred Doors', restored to its original appearance in 1966 (*open 8–1 and 4–9, robes provided for the scantily clad*). Founded by St Helen in the 4th century, what stands today is the 6th-century church built by Ignatius, an apprentice of the master builder of Ag. Sophia. When the master came to view his work, he was consumed by jealousy and pushed Ignatius off the roof – but not before Ignatius had

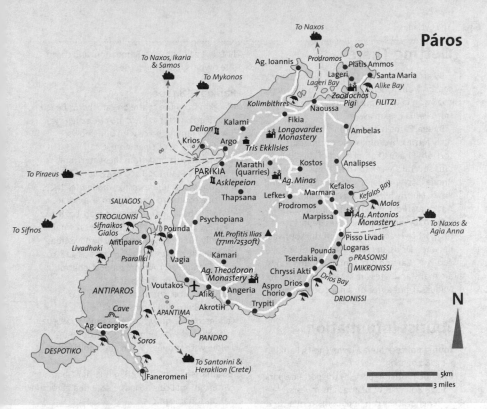

Páros

seized his foot and dragged him down as well; two bizarre stone figures under the columns of the north gate represent the architects. Another tradition says only 99 entrances have been found (the count must include mouse holes!) but, once the 100th is discovered, Constantinople will be Greek again. The **Baptistry** to the right of the church has a 4th-century sunken cruciform font – the oldest one in Orthodoxy.

In front of the church is the **Byzantine Museum** (*t 228 402 1243; open 9–1 and 5–9; adm*); behind the church, a row of sarcophagi marks the **Archaeological Museum** (*t 228 402 1231; open Tues–Sun 8.30–2.30; adm*). One exhibit is a section of the renowned 'Parian Chronicles' – an art-orientated history of Greece from Kerkops (*c.* 1500 BC) to Diognetos (264 BC) carved in marble tablets; to read the rest you'll have to go to the Ashmolean in Oxford.

Around Parikiá

Northeast of Parikiá, a marble foundation and altar mark the **Temple of Delian Apollo**, which was lined up geomantically with Temples to Apollo on Delos and Náxos to form a perfect equilateral triangle. Equally strange, the triangle's altitudes extend to some key places: Athos, Mycenae and Rhodes Town, site of the Colossus – the biggest of all the statues of Apollo.

Just south of Parikiá, by a spring, are the ruins of a small Classical-era **Asklepeion**. The road south continues 6km to **Psychopianá** ('Valley of the Butterflies'), where swarms of tiger moths set up housekeeping in July and August and fly up in clouds as

Getting There

By air: two to seven Olympic flights daily in season from Athens, **t** 228 402 1900; **airport**: **t** 228 409 1256. Frequent bus service to and from Parikiá, 14km away.

By sea: Páros is an Aegean crossroads, with daily **ferries**, **hydrofoils** and **catamarans** to/from Piraeus, Rafína, most of the Cyclades, plus several a week to Thessaloníki, Sámos, Rhodes, Astypálaia, Kos, Kálymnos, Crete and Ikaría. Hourly ferries from Poúnda go to Antíparos. **Port authority**: **t** 228 402 1240.

By road: very frequent **buses** depart from the port to everywhere, except the south coast between Dríos and Alíki; info in Parikiá, **t** 228 402 1395. **Car and bike rentals** abound. **Taxis** are many and rates are reasonable (€6–8 to Náoussa), but agree on a price beforehand.

Tourist Information

Tourist police: Plateía Mavroyénous, Parikiá, **t** 228 402 1673.

Cycladic Tourist Agency: by the portside park, **t** 228 402 1738, **f** 228 402 2146, *mpizas@ otenet.gr*. They can find rooms, rent a car or bike, and arrange horse-riding.

Information office: by the bus station in Náoussa, **t** 228 405 2158, **f** 228 405 1190. For up-to-date details of events, pick up a copy of *The Foreigner*.

Where to Stay and Eat

Páros is packed in July and August. Try the **Rooms Association**, **t/f** 228 402 4528; for hotels, **t** 228 402 4555. Some room and camp-site owners meet the ferries.

Parikiá ✉ 84400

Iria, 3km from the centre on Parasporos Beach, **t** 228 402 4154, **f** 228 402 1167 (*A; expensive*). A good family choice with bungalows, tennis, and pool. *Open April–Oct.*

Argonauta, just back from the waterfront, **t** 228 402 1440, **f** 228 402 3442, *hotel@ argonauta.gr* (*C; expensive–moderate*). Nice, with a courtyard littered with amphorae.

Vayia, set back on the Náoussa road, **t** 228 402 1068, **f** 228 402 3431 (*C; moderate*). A small family-run hotel, surrounded by olive trees.

Dina, in the old town, **t** 228 402 1325, **f** 228 402 3525 (*moderate*). A more modest, charming place with simple rooms.

Eleni, **t** 228 402 2714, **f** 228 402 4170 (*moderate*). Balconied rooms near the beach.

Kondes, on the quay, **t** 228 402 1096, **f** 228 402 2390 (*moderate–inexpensive*). A done-up oldie with fridges, TV and air-conditioning in each room.

To Tamarisko, **t** 228 402 4689 (€12–15). Good international cuisine in the secluded garden at reasonable prices.

Argonauta, in the big square by the National Bank, **t** 228 402 3303. Well known for its fresh fresh food and grills.

Porfyra, by the ancient cemetery, **t** 228 402 3410 (€15–20). In a courtyard under vines, serving a wide array of seafood including shellfish and pasta dishes.

Náoussa and Around ✉ 84401

Astir of Páros, Kolymbíthres Beach, **t** 228 405 1976, **f** 228 405 1985, *www.ila-chaeau.*

you walk by (*t 228 409 1211; open June–Sept 9–8; adm*). At **Poúnda** there is a beach and the small ferry to Antíparos. There's another quieter beach at **Alíki** – and the airport.

Náoussa

On the north coast, the fishing village turned jet-set hang-out **Náoussa** surrounds the half-submerged ruins of a Venetian castle, where caiques bob below and octopi dry on the lines of a dozen *ouzeries*. On the night of 23 August, boats lit by torches re-enact the islanders' battle against the pirate Barbarossa, storming the harbour; all ends in merriment, music and dance. Náoussa's church **Ag. Nikólaos Mostrátos** has an excellent collection of icons. There are more in the **Byzantine Museum** (*t 228 405 3261*), while traditional life is covered in the small **Folk Art Museum** (*t 228 405 3453*).

com/astir/ (A; luxury). The island's most luxurious hotel, with a few golf holes. *Open mid-April–Oct.*

Antrides, t 228 405 1711, **f** 228 405 2079 (B; luxury). Posh neo-monastic, comfortably constructed around a pool. *Open April–Oct.*

Petres, t 228 405 2467, **f** 228 405 2759, www.greekhotel.com/cyclades/paros/naoussa/petres (C; expensive). Comfortable air-conditioned rooms, 2km out of town, with views and a pool.

Stella, t/f 228 405 1317, hotelstella34@hotmail.com (D; moderate). Plain, clean rooms in the old town round a shady courtyard.

Senia Apartments, t 228 405 1971 (moderate). New and airy, with large balconies.

Náoussa is one of the most picturesque places to eat in Greece with *ouzeries* chock-a-block by the water; a place to rub shoulders with celebrities.

Papadakis, t 228 405 1047 (€15–22; book). A wonderful fish restaurant.

Barbarossa, t 228 405 1391 (€12–20). Serving tasty fresh fish. Try the mussel soup.

Christos, t 228 405 1901 (€20–30). Lovely courtyard dining, with Greek and international dishes. People come here to be seen.

Diamantis, just up the hill. Good food at good prices, with draught wine.

Písso Livádi and East Coast Beaches
✉ 84400

Aloni, t 228 404 3237, **f** 228 404 2438 (C; expensive–moderate). A nicely done complex with cool blue rooms and some bird's-eye views.

Anna Agourou, t 228 404 1320, **f** 228 404 3327 (moderate). Air-conditioned rooms and apartments with good watery views.

Albatross, just south in Logarás, **t** 228 404 1157, **f** 228 404 1940, albapar@otenet.gr (C; expensive). Family-oriented bungalow complex with pool.

Free Sun, Logarás, **t** 228 404 2808, **f** 228 404 2809 (moderate). A more modest choice.

Afendakis Apartments, in Márpissa, **t/f** 228 404 1141, info@hotelafendaki.gr (C; expensive). Beautifully appointed accommodation.

Haroula's, in the old town. As the name promises, dining is a joy here.

Paros Philoxenia, Tserdakiá Beach, **t** 228 404 1778, **f** 228 404 1978 (B; luxury). Hotel-bungalow complex with surf club, sea sports, and pool.

ΘΕΑ family taverna, nearby in Messáda, makes tasty dishes from home-grown fare.

Poseidon, in Chryssí Aktí, **t** 228 404 2650, **f** 228 404 2649, www.poseidon-paros.gr (luxury). Luxurious apartment complex in spacious grounds; great location. *Open May–Sept.*

Entertainment and Nightlife

Páros has something for everyone. In Parikiá, try **Black Barts** and the **Salon d'Or** for cocktails on the strip; **Pirate's** for jazz, and a complex of four disco bars of the **Paros Rock** complex. The music is altogether gentler at **Pebbles** and **Evinos,** on the waterfront. In Náoussa, **Varrelathiko** is one of the trendiest clubs in Greece. The **Golden Garden** at Chryssí Aktí is a popular, laid-back bar with a range of international sounds; in Písso Livádi **Remezzo** is a favoured watering hole.

There are beaches within walking distance of Náoussa, or you can make sea excursions to others, notably **Kolimbíthres**, with bizarre, wind-sculpted rocks. Lágeri Beach is nudist, a mix of gay and straight. **Santa Maria** is even further around the coast, with good windsurfing; the fishing village of **Ambelás** has sandy coves, an ancient tower and three hotels. The wetlands west of Náoussa are a winter flamingo haven.

Into the Land of Marble

The quarries at **Maráthi** produce the famed Parian *lychnites* or 'candlelit marble' that admits light 3.5cm into the stone (Carrara's finest is 2.5cm). Such stone was used in the Temple of Solomon, the *Venus de Milo*, the *Hermes* of Praxiteles, the *Victory of Samothrace* and Napoleon's tomb; blocks and galleries, some with ancient inscriptions, lie off the road. Nearby is the island's attractive medieval capital **Léfkes**, with churches from the 15th century, including one, Ag. Triáda, made of marble. East of Léfkes, **Pródromos** is an old farming village and **Mármara** has some streets paved with marble. Above pretty white **Márpissa** and its windmills moulder a Venetian fortress and the 16th-century frescoed **monastery of Ag. Antónios**, larded with ancient marble. Ancient Páros city stood nearby.

Down on the east coast is the port of **Písso Livádi** (excursion boats to Náxos, Mýkonos and Santoríni). It is the centre of the island's beach colonies: **Mólos**, just north, **Poúnda** just south. The winds blow fiercely in July and August, and the next beach, **Tserdakia** (or **Néa Chryssí Aktí**), hosts the Professional Windsurfers' World Cup every August. Just to the south **Chryssí Aktí**, 'Golden Beach', has half a mile of sand. Further south, **Driós** is a pretty green place with a duck-pond, tavernas, sandy coves, and the remains of ancient shipyards.

Antíparos (ΑΝΤΙΠΑΡΟΣ)

Just a mile to the west, mountainous little Antíparos, *'opposite Páros'*, was known as Oliaros when it was first a base of Phoenician merchants of Sidon. A deep cave full of stalactites was discovered in antiquity, and ever since it has been a must-stop place for every traveller in the region. Antíparos is also the octopus capital of Greece; perhaps the tasty eight-legged, sucker-bedecked mollusc is an unsung aphrodisiac, considering the little island's current reputation. Even the local year-round population is rising, and that, in the Cyclades, is rare.

Lacking defences, Antíparos was uninhabited after the fall of Rome until the Venetians built a small castle, and **Kástro** is the alternative name of the main settlement. The Kampiara, a wide street, links the port to a charming square, lined with *ouzeries* and bars. Kástro has a good beach, **Psaralíki**, just south. In the late afternoon wander over to **Sifnaíkos Gialós**, or Sunset Beach. The best beach, **Ag. Geórgios**, just south of the cave, is a little resort.

The **cave** (*open daily 10.45–3.45; adm*) remains the star attraction. Some 400 steps descend 210ft into the fantastic, spooky chamber where past visitors have smoked and carved their names, including Byron and King Otto of Greece (1840).

Getting There and Around

Every two hours or so by **caique** from Parikiá and hourly **car ferry** from Poúnda. **Buses** link the port with the cave. **Port authority** (Páros): t 228 406 1202.

Where to Stay and Eat

Antíparos ✉ 84007
Antíparos has a desk at Parikiá port, so you can book accommodation before you go.

Artemis, t 228 406 1460, f 228 406 1472 (*C; expensive–moderate*). 500 yards from the port; all rooms have fridges and balconies.

Chryssi Akti, t 228 406 1220 (*C; moderate*). Small, elegant hotel on the beach.

Antíparos, t 228 406 1358, f 228 406 1340, *antiparos1@otenet.gr* (*E; moderate*). Simple, all rooms with shower; restaurant and bar.

Antíparos Camping, t 228 406 1410, f 228 406 1221. Famously laid-back campsite, clothes optional; freelancers are tolerated away from town.

Garden and **Anargyros** have good food.

One stalagmite attests in Latin to a Christmas mass celebrated in the cavern by the French ambassador Count Novandel in 1673, attended by 500 (paid) locals. Many inscriptions were lost in 1774, when Russian officers chopped off stalactites as souvenirs, and in the last war, when the Italians and Germans used it for target practice. The entrance church, **Ag. Ioánnis**, dates from 1774.

Náxos (ΝΑΞΟΣ)

Fertile Náxos is the largest of the Cyclades, and the highest, with Mount Zas at 3,294ft. Its 17,000 year-round residents grow much of their own food; sacred to Dionysos, the wine is excellent, as is the local Kítron, a fragrant liqueur made from citrons. The entire west coast is lined with silvery sands. Byron loved its rugged mountains and lush valleys, sprinkled with the ruins of the ancient Greeks, the gilded Byzantines and his beloved Venetians. There are plenty of tourists, but they leave the hinterland to wanderers and poets. Good times to come are 14 July, when the island fêtes its current patron Nikódimos, and the first week of August, when it remembers its ancient patron in the Dionysia festival.

Getting There and Around

By air: two–three flights a day from Athens with Olympic and charters from London and Manchester. **Airport**: t 228 502 3292. **Zas Travel** at the port, t 228 502 3330, f 228 502 3419, *zas-travel@nax.forthnet.gr*, handles Olympic Airways.

By sea: in high season, several **ferries** and **hydrofoils** connect per day with Piraeus; daily with Rafína, Páros, Íos, Santoríni, Mýkonos and Sýros; smaller craft almost daily with Amorgós via Heráklia, Schinoússa, Koufoníssi and Donoússa; less frequent connections with Sámos, Kos and Rhodes. **Port authority**: t 228 502 2300.

By road: **bus** services from Náxos Town dock, t 228 502 2291, every half hour to Ag. Prokópios and Ag. Ánna; several a day to Filóti, Chalkí, Apíranthos, Apollónas, Kóronos, Pirgáki and Kastráki; two to three times to Komiáki and Mélanes. **Taxi** rank by the bus station, t 228 502 2444. Taxis are not metered, so agree on a price first.

Tourist Information

Náxos Tourist Information Centre: by the quay, t 228 502 5201, f 228 502 5200, . Organizes accommodation and has luggage-storage and laundry facilities.

Naxos Tours, t 228 502 3043, f 228 502 3951, *naxostours@naxos-island.com*. Nearby, and helpful, too.

Waterfront Zoom Bookstore sells Christian Ucke's useful *Walking Tours in Náxos*.

Where to Stay and Eat

The **Hotel and Rooms Association** kiosk on the quay is good; another kiosk has **camping** information. Ferries are met by campsite and room owners, milling about in minibuses. Question closely just where their rooms are and if they will bring you back.

Náxos Town ✉ 84300

Château Zevgoli, t 228 502 6123, f 228 502 5200, *chateau-zevgoli@forthnet.gr* (*C; expensive*). Lots of steps for this plush mansion, small and exclusive with roof garden.

Nikos Verikokos, on the Kástro hill, t 228 502 2025 (*rooms, moderate; studios, expensive*). A less expensive choice by the Pantanássa church, offering views.

Anixis, by the Kástro, t 228 502 2932, f 228 502 2112, *hotelanixis@nax.forthnet.gr* (*D; moderate*). Moderate, with views from verandas.

Panorama, Amphitris St, t/f 228 502 4404 (*C; inexpensive*). One of the small hotels in Boúrgos, just outside the Kástro's walls. Pleasant, with a marvellous sea view.

Sofi, three-minutes from the docks, t 228 502 3077, f 228 502 5582 (*moderate*). Attractive, with a very loyal clientele.

Oniro, Plateía Bradóuna, t 228 502 3846 (€15). Candlelit tables in a courtyard, and a roof garden; try the *arni bouti yemistó*, lamb stuffed with garlic and bacon.

Delfini, on the Kástro hill under the wall (€15). Café/bar with a lovely garden setting, serving great generous drinks, snacks, Indian and Thai curry dishes.

Stou Lefteri, t 228 506 1333. Behind the pastry shop, with lovely views over the countryside.

Náxos was a major centre of the Cycladic civilization. Around 3000 BC, as now, the main settlements were near Chóra and at Grótta, where the sea-eroded remains can still be seen in the clear water. One of the first islands to work in marble, it produced the lions of Delos, the Sphinx at Delphi and the largest *kouros* statues ever found. But big was beautiful here; in 523 BC the tyrant Lugdamis declared he would make Náxos' Temple of Apollo the highest building ever; only the massive lintel survives as proof.

In 1207 the Venetian Marco Sanudo captured the island and declared himself Duke of Náxos. When Venice refused to grant him the title, he hitched his wagon to the Roman emperor and took the title Duke of the 'Archipelago' (a corruption of *Aigaíon Pélagos*; under Sanudo's successors, the word gained its current meaning). After 1564 the dukes remained in Náxos, although paying tribute to the sultan.

Excellent food, great atmosphere. *Open April–Oct.*

Meltemi, five minutes from the docks towards Ag. Geórgios, **t** 228 502 2654 (€12–15). Excellent waterfront taverna that has served delicious Greek meals for 25 years.

Néa Chóra and Ag. Geórgios ✉ 84300

Nissaki Beach Hotel, t 228 502 5710, **f** 228 502 3876, *nissaki@naxos.island.com* (*C; expensive*). Rooms circling the pool, with restaurant-bar.

Irene Pension, t 228 502 3169, **f** 228 502 5200, *irenepension@hotmail.com* (*inexpensive*). Quiet, good value and air-conditioned.

Panos Studios, 20m from the beach on a quiet street, **t** 228 502 6078, **f** 228 502 6502, *studiospanos@in.gr* (*moderate*). Run by the Koufópoulos family, whose warm welcome includes a free ouzo, coffee and advice.

Camping Náxos, t 228 502 3500, **f** 228 502 3502. By the beach and has a pool

Kavouri. A favourite old (over 40 years) taverna on Ag. Geórgios Beach.

Beaches South of Chóra: Ag. Prokópios ✉ 84300

Kavouras Village, t 228 502 5580, **f** 228 502 5800 (*B; luxury*). Flower-bedecked studios and villas, with a pool.

Ag. Ánna ✉ 84300

Iria Beach Apartments, t 228 504 4178, **f** 228 504 2602 (*C; luxury–expensive*). Right by the beach, with facilities including car hire.

Ag. Anna, t 228 504 2576, **f** 228 504 2704 (*C; inexpensive*). Also right by the sea, with verandas and fruits of the orchard.

Paradise Taverna. A terrace shaded by a vast pine tree and an infectious atmosphere.

Gorgonas, on the beach, **t** 228 504 1007 (€15–20). For fish, including lobster.

Pláka and Mikrí Vígla ✉ 84300

Villa Medusa, at Pláka, **t** 228 507 5555, **f** 228 507 5500 (*A; expensive*). A favourite of sophisticated windsurfers; rooms have antiques, mini bars and satellite TV.

Aronis Taverna, on the Ag. Ánna–Pláka Beach road, **t** 228 504 2019, **f** 228 504 2021 (*expensive–moderate*). Clean studios by the sea and a hippy eatery; one of many here.

Mikri Vigla, at Mikrí Vígla, **t** 228 507 5241, **f** 228 507 5240, *www.euripiotis.gr* (*B; expensive*). Newish seaside mini-resort in Cycladic style, with a pool and surfing centre.

Apollónas and Órmos Ábram ✉ 84301

Flora's Apartments, t 228 506 7070 (*moderate*). Pleasant, built around a garden.

Efthimios, at Órmos Ábram, **t** 228 506 3244 (*moderate–inexpensive*). A getaway/taverna.

Entertainment and Nightlife

Náxos has a buzzing nightlife with masses of bars; smartish **Veggera,** near the OTE, is popular. In Chóra, **Lakridi Jazz Bar,** Old Market Street, is the mellowest in the evening. Alternatively, you can dance the night away at the **Ocean Club** on the sea, or at **Cream,** or the thumping **Super Island,** in Grótta. In Ag. Ánna, **Enosis, t** 228 502 4644, is a popular club in an old warehouse playing Greek music.

Náxos Town

Náxos Town, the capital, is a bustling place sprawling under the old town's conical hill. By the port, its huge Π-shaped landmark, the **Portára** of the unfinished **Temple of Apollo** (522 BC), stands enigmatically like a door to another dimension. The other waterfront landmark, the 11th-century church of **Panagía Pantanássa,** is famous for its early icon of the Virgin. Old Náxos, just above, is a fine Cycladic town; its narrow twisting streets and tunnels were just the thing to confuse invaders. It had three distinct neighbourhoods: Greek **Boúrgos,** Jewish **Evraiki,** and, up above, **Kástro,** where the Venetian nobility lived. In Boúrgos, the Orthodox cathedral, **Zoodóchos Pigí,** was created in the 18th century out of a temple and older churches. Archaeologists would gladly knock it down; as it is they've had to be content with the ruins of the

Mycenaean town under the adjacent square (*open Tues–Sun 8–2*). The cathedral looks down over **Grótta**, the cave-pocked coast; one hollow is the 'Bath of Ariadne', a reminder of the Cretan princess jilted here by Theseus, and found by Dionysos.

The Evraiki was just above Boúrgos, but traces of its former inhabitants have been obliterated. At the top, the **Kástro** preserves one of its seven towers, guarding one of three entrances into its jumble of stunning houses, flowers and dark alleys. Some 19 Venetian houses still bear their coats-of-arms – something you'll never see in Venice proper, where such displays were frowned upon; current residents claim Venetian descent, and many of the tombstones in the 13th-century **Catholic cathedral** boast grand titles. The cathedral, clad in pale grey marble, was founded by Marco Sanudo, whose ruined palace is directly across the square.

The Kástro's school of commerce, run by friars, was attended for two years by Níkos Kazantzákis. Now the **Archaeological Museum** (*t 228 502 2725; open Tues–Sun 8–2.30; adm*), it houses artefacts from the 5th millennium BC to 5th century AD, including a superb collection of Cycladic art, Mycenaean pottery, and a Roman mosaic of Europa. The nearby **Venetian Museum** (Domus Della-Rocca-Barozzi) preserves a traditional Kástro house (*t 228 502 2387; open Tues–Sun 10–3 and 6–10; adm*) and offers guided tours in English. Just below the museums, the **Antico Veneziano** antique shop is in an 800-year-old mansion, using 2,000-year-old Ionian columns original to the house.

South of Náxos Town

South of the waterfront, a new neighbourhood, Néa Chóra, has sprung up around popular **Ag. Geórgios Beach**, with shallow waters and long curl of sand, with a more homey atmosphere than the big beaches further south. The road then skirts the **Livádi** plain, where Náxos grows its spuds; here, near the airport, a **Temple of Dionysos** was discovered in 1986. Further south are **Ag. Prokópios** (nice, coarse, non-sticky sand), then popular **Ag. Ánna**, sheltered from the *meltémi*, and then **Pláka**, considered by many the best in Náxos. From Ag. Ánna, boats and dirt roads continue south to more beaches; the asphalt road diverts inland, by way of **Ag. Arsénios**. Vast white sandy beaches begin at **Parthéna**, excellent for surfing and swimming, followed by **Mikrí Vígla**, where the sea is brilliantly clear; **Sahára** is well equipped for sea sports, and merges into **Kastráki**, with white sands. Above the road stands **Pírgos Oskéllou**, a ruined Mycenaean fortress, built over a Cycladic acropolis. For something remote, try the strip of sand beyond Kastráki on either side of **Cape Kouroúpia**.

Inland Villages

The interior of Náxos is full of surprises. **Galanádo**, southeast of Náxos Town, has the Venetian **Belonia Tower** and church of **St John**, with a Catholic chapel on the left and an Orthodox one on the right. The arrangement was also employed at the island's first cathedral, the 8th-century **Ag. Mámas**, a short walk from the road to **Sangrí**. Sangrí gets its name from 'Sainte Croix', as the French called its 16th-century tower monastery Tímiou Stavroú. A pretty mile's walk south of Áno Sangrí are the ruins of a 6th-century BC **Temple of Demeter**. A more strenuous walk southeast will take you up to **T'Apaliróu**, the Byzantine castle that defied Marco Sanudo for two months.

From Sangrí the road rises up to the Tragéa plateau, planted with fruit trees and lilacs. Olive groves engulf the villages, including **Chálki**, where both the Byzantines and Venetians built tower houses. Up a steep, difficult path, the Venetian **Apáno Kástro**, sitting on Cyclopean foundations, was Marco Sanudo's summer hideaway. Geometric and Mycenaean tombs have been discovered just to the southeast; there's even a menhir. Chálki has fine frescoed churches: 12th-century **Panagía Protóthronis** and 9th-century **Ag. Diasorítis**, and in a shady glade the striking 5th-century **Panagía Drossianí**, crowned with corbelled domes of field stones (*open most mornings; donation*). Chálki is also in the heart of Kítron territory; visit the **Vallindras Náxos Citron distillery** (*t 228 502 2227; open July and Aug, Mon–Fri am and weekends*). West of Chálki is lovely **Áno Potámia**, another well-watered town, with a taverna (Paradise Garden).

The main road continues on to attractive **Filóti**, on the slopes of Mount Zas, the largest village in the Tragéa, which produces the island's best cheese. Monuments include the Venetian towerhouse of the De Lasti family, the churches **Koímisis tis Theotókou**, with a fine carved marble iconostasis, and **Panagía Filótissa**, with a marble steeple. A path leads up the slopes of **Mount Zas**, with great views and a cave sacred to Zeus near the summit (bring a light). A three-hour, mostly paved route from Filóti follows the mountain south to the excellently preserved Hellenistic **Tower of Chimárou**, built by Ptolemy of Egypt of white marble blocks.

From Filóti the road skirts Mount Zas to **Apíranthos**, with Venetian towers. Many residents today are descended from Cretans who came in Turkish times to work in Greece's only emery mines. It's the most beautiful village on Náxos – Byron wished he could die here – with narrow winding lanes paved with marble. The churches, to SS. Geórgios, Sofía and Ilías, are built on ancient Temples to Ares, Athena and Helios respectively. Visit the small **Cycladic Museum**, devoted to Neolithic finds (*open 9–3; adm*), and a **Geological and Folklore Museum** (*same hours*) in the school. The emery, used in ancient times to polish Cycladic statues, is now brought down from the mountains by a rope funicular to the port of **Moutsoúna**. This has a fine beach, and a dodgy dirt road south to the remote beach of **Psilí Ámmos**.

Naxian marble is almost as fine as Parian, and is still quarried to the west at **Kinídaros**. A beautiful walk begins here; the path descends past a chapel of the woodland goddess-saint Ag. Artemis, and follows the lush Xerotakari river (the only one in the Cyclades to flow in August) down to Egarés. Expect little waterfalls and turtles. Archaic Náxos took pride in producing the biggest statues in Greece, although they weren't always a success. The ancient quarries are west at **Mélanes**; signposted off the road lies a 7th-century BC 20ft-high *kouros*, abandoned because of a broken leg; a second one, 300m south, is in poorer shape. At Mélanes you can pick up the road along the north coast, passing the isolated beaches of **Pachiá Ámmos** and idyllic **Órmos Ábram** (taverna and rooms) and a curious giant marble head abandoned on a rock (but when the *meltémi* roars you'll want to give them a miss). **Apollónas** further north is a dreary little town with a (very) public sandy beach and tavernas heavily patronized by tour buses. Ancient marble quarries are carved out of the mountain, and steps lead up to a colossal but flawed 33ft *kouros*, abandoned in the 7th century BC. Above, the road twists up to pretty **Komiakí**, highest of the island's villages.

Amorgós (ΑΜΟΡΓΟΣ)

Easternmost of the Cyclades, delightful Amorgós is also one of the most rugged islands, with a south coast of cliffs plunging into the sea, the setting for a unique monastery. It was virtually two islands, with the main port of Katápola almost a stranger to Aegiáli in the northeast, until a paved road introduced them in 1995 . After years as an island of exile, Amorgós became a destination for the adventurous, then whoosh! – in 1988 Luc Besson filmed his cult movie *The Big Blue* and travellers arrived en masse and ended up camping in the streets. Still, out-of-season Amorgós is a great choice to savour the fast-disappearing Cycladic way of life.

In ancient times a commonwealth of three city-states shared Amorgós, each minting its own coins and worshipping Dionysos and Athena: Kástri (modern Arkesíni) was settled by Naxians, Minoa by Samians, and Aegiáli by Milians. After Alexander the Great, Amorgós was ruled by Ptolemy of Egypt, and it was a centre of worship of the gods Serapis and Isis. The Romans used the island as a place of exile, beginning a long decline. Amorgós prospered in the 17th century, through the export of exquisite embroideries; some are in the Victoria and Albert Museum in London.

Middle Amorgós: Katápola and Chóra

Katápola, the southern port, sits on a deep horseshoe bay looking out towards the islet of Keros; there's a good beach here and two others at **Xylokeratídi**, the fishing port at the northern side of the bay. Katápola is an attractive, workaday place with smallholders selling produce from their trucks and locals lounging in the coffee-

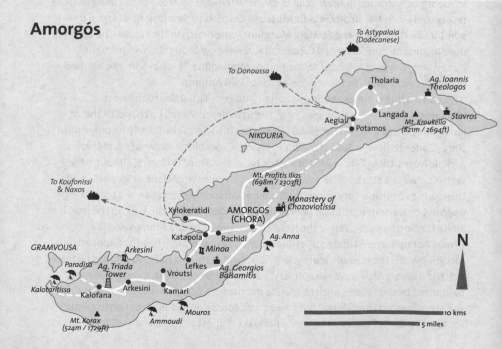

Amorgós

Getting There and Around

By sea: daily **ferry** in summer from Náxos, via Heráklia, Schinoússa, Koufoníssi and Donoússa to Katápola, four to five times a week to Aegiáli. Infrequent summer **hydrofoils** from Sýros, Páros, Íos and Santoríni call at Katápola only. Always check with the **Port authority**: Katápola, **t** 228 507 1259, and Aegiáli, **t** 228 507 3260.

By road: frequent **bus** service daily from Katápola to Chóra (Amorgós Town) and Aegiáli; others via Chóra to the Chozoviótissa Monastery, Ag. Ánna, Paradísi and Kalotaritíssa Beaches. For a **taxi** in Katápola; call **t** 228 507 2205; in Aegiáli, **t** 228 507 3570. There are **cars and motorbikes for rent** in both towns.

Tourist Information

Try Naomi at the **Aegialis Tourist Information Bureau**, **t** 228 507 3394, or Penelope at **Synodinos Travel** in Katápola, **t** 228 507 1201, *synodinos@nax.forthnet.gr*.

Where to Stay and Eat

Katápola ✉ 84008

Eleni, **t** 228 507 1628, **f** 228 507 1543 (*C; moderate*). On the western edge of town, with unimpeded views of the bay and the sunset.

Big Blue, **t** 228 507 1094 (*C; moderate*). In the centre of town. Large rooms, each with its own balcony and a common terrace for guests to gather and share the view.

Voula Beach, **t** 228 507 4052 (*inexpensive*). Set around a shaded garden full of geraniums, near the port police; all rooms have baths.

Villa Catapoliana, **t** 228 507 1064, *Katapol@otenet.gr* (*moderate–inexpensive*). In a courtyard around a small archaeological dig; quiet rooms with fridges and a roof garden.

Minos (€12). At the quieter south end of the waterfront, with a glassed-in side garden for when it's windy. Good home-cooking; try the *pattáto* casserole.

Chóra ✉ 84008

The Yannakos family have quite a monopoly on rooms (**t** 228 507 1367/1277).

Pension Chora, on the edge of the village, **t** 228 507 1110 (*moderate*). Comfortable, with a minibus pick-up service.

Liotrivi, **t** 228 507 1700. In an old olive press with fine views, serving well-prepared baked and stewed dishes. *Open May–Oct*.

Kastanis. Tiny, good, inexpensive and very Greek taverna.

Aegiáli/Langáda/Tholária ✉ 84008

Lakki, **t** 228 507 3253, **f** 228 507 3244 (*B; moderate*). Set back from the beach in a garden. Cycladic-style, immaculate rooms, excellent food from their taverna.

Aegialis, **t** 228 507 3393, **f** 228 507 3395, *www.aegialis.com* (*B; moderate*). An isolated complex across the bay, with enchanting views, pool and taverna, and minibus service.

Mike, **t** 228 507 3208, **f** 228 507 3633, *hotelmik@otenet.gr* (*C; moderate*). The port's first hotel, but has recently had a facelift.

Camping Aegiali, **t** 228 507 3500. Off the Tholária road, with decent facilities.

To Limani, but known to all as **Katerina's** (€12–15). The favourite grazing ground, packed out for its great food, wine from the barrel and mellow sounds.

Korali (€15). Tasty fish and sunset views.

Nikos, in Langáda, **t** 228 507 3310 (*inexpensive*). Clean, comfortable rooms and bougainvillaea on the terrace; it specializes in roast kid and baked aubergines.

Vigla, in Tholária, **t** 228 507 3288, **f** 228 507 3332 (*B; moderate*). Views and restaurant.

houses. From Katápola you can walk up the hill to ancient **Minoa**, where walls, bits of the acropolis, a gymnasium and remains of a Temple to Apollo can still be seen. Beyond Minoa is the little village of **Léfkes**, from where you can visit **Ag. Geórgios Balsamítis**, with good frescoes, built on the site of an ancient 'aquatic' oracle where people came to have their fortunes told by signs on the surface of a sacred spring. There's an old Venetian towerhouse and watermill nearby.

The island capital, **Chóra**, is a typically Cycladic town, perched more than 1,300ft above sea level, with a neat spinal ridge of decapitated windmills – each family had its own. It has a perfect *plateía* and more churches than houses; note the ancient and Byzantine inscriptions and reliefs incorporated over the doors. One, with three vaulted aisles, melts like a meringue into its back wall; another, **Ag. Iríni**, only slightly larger than a phone box, is the smallest church in Greece. There is a tiny **Archaeological Museum**, too (*t 228 507 1831; open Tues–Sun 9–1 and 6–8.30*). Steps lead up a huge rocky thumb to the **Apáno Kástro**, the Venetian fortress built by Geremia Gizzi in 1290 (get the key before you go, either from the town hall or the coffee shop in the square).

The Monastery of Chozoviótissa and the South

*t 228 507 1294; open 8–1 and 5–7; donation. Strict dress code,
although long gowns are available if you fail to meet it.*

To get to the astonishing Monastery of Chozoviótissa, take the *kalderími* path from Chóra, zig-zagging down a natural amphitheatre, or the bus; both leave you a steep 20-minute walk up to the door. Built into sheer 600ft orange cliffs, the monastery is a smooth, stark eight-storey white fort, supported by two enormous buttresses. Within are some 50 rooms, two churches, and a library, but only the small museum and chapel are open to the public. It was founded *c.* 800 by monks from Hozova in the Middle East, fleeing the Iconoclasm with a miraculous icon reputedly painted by St Luke; they were guided to the site by a mysterious nail stuck in the cliff. Rebuilt by Emperor Alexis Comnenus in 1088, the monastery once had 100 monks but now gets by with just three; their assistants provide a warm welcome in the form of brandy and/or water. Below the bus continues down to the pebble beaches at **Ag. Ánna**.

The occasional bus continues south into Káto Meriá, the least visited and most traditional part of Amorgós. The landscape is dotted with curious old churches, sometimes three or four linked together. Tombs, walls, a subterranean aqueduct and houses of ancient **Arkesíni** are near the mountain village of **Vroútsi**. The easiest way to get there is to get off the bus at **Kamári** – there's a taverna – and head north. A well-preserved 4th-century BC Hellenistic tower, the **Pírgos Ag. Triáda**, is near modern Arkesíni. **Kalofana** is remote, but near the delightful beaches of **Paradísi** and **Kalotarítissa** on the west coast.

Aegiáli

Small, charming **Aegiáli**, a picture-perfect Cycladic town, is Amorgós' northern port and main resort, thanks to the island's one genuine sandy beach. From Aegiáli you can take in the scant remains of ancient Aegiáli or take the bus to pretty **Tholária**, named for its vaulted tombs from the Roman period, and **Langáda**, one of the island's most attractive villages, under a rocky thumb similar to Chóra's; a circular walk along the herb-scented hill ridge links them and the port. From Langáda a path leads up to the windmills by way of a frescoed cave church, **Yero Stavros**; another path leads out east in about an hour to frescoed **Ag. Ioánnis Theológos**, an 8th-century monastery, recently restored; one window is a replica of the Ag. Sophia.

Between Amorgós and Náxos: The Back Islands

Between Amorgós and Náxos lie the tiny islands known as the Back Islands because they're in the back of beyond – Schinoússa, Koufoníssi, Donoússa and Heráklia (or Iráklia) are the four inhabited ones. Once a hide-out for pirates, they are now firmly on the holiday map. All have post offices to change money and most have tourist agencies. The islands are quiet in low season, with sandy beaches and wonderful walking country, but be warned – book in August.

Koufoníssi (ΚΟΥΦΟΝΗΣΙ)

Koufoníssi is tiny and flat – you can walk around it in three hours. It has a thriving fishing fleet and exerts such a compelling charm on its visitors that it gets jammed in July and August with Italians and Scandinavians into spear-fishing and perfecting their tans. The beautiful white village, on a low hill above the quay, has its back to the sea, and the tavernas and *ouzeries* on the cobbled main street are lively in summer. Koufoníssi has gorgeous beaches, some tucked under golden rocks eroded into bulging *mille feuille* pastries. **Fínikas**, east of the village, is crowded in high season; **Porí** has a Caribbean air; at wild Cape Xylobatis, you can swim through a 100ft natural tunnel, in an uncanny blue light. There are daily excursions to **Káto Koufoníssi**, the island just opposite, for skinny dipping and lunch at the only taverna, and the occasional excursion to the beaches on **Kéros**. The ruins of a Neolithic settlement at **Daskálio** produced the famous 'Harpist' in the Archaeological Museum in Athens.

Schinoússa (ΣΧΟΙΝΟΥΣΣΑ)

Schinoússa is less attractive scenically than the other small islands, but it's still very Greek and charming. There are only 85 inhabitants in winter, most of them farmers. Ferries dock at tiny **Myrsíni** with a taverna and rooms, but the main settlement is **Chóra**, about a mile up the hill, linked by road or cobbled mule track. From Chóra, a steep track runs down to the grey sand beach at **Tsigoúra**, fringed by tamarisk trees, with a rather expensive taverna and disco. There are other beaches, some bleak and littered by the wind, but **Psilí Ámmos** is worth the 45-minute walk from Chóra via the ghost hamlet of **Messariá**. Schinoússa is blessed with fresh springs and a species of mastic bush grows on its relatively flat terrain.

Donoússa (ΔΟΝΟΥΣΑ)

Remote Donoússa, east of Náxos, is more mountainous than Schinoússa and Koufoníssi, and a good place for lonely walks. The port has rooms to let, tavernas, a summer-only bakery and a shop; the sandy beach **Kédros** is a 15-minute walk. There are fine sandy beaches, at **Livádi** and **Fýkio**, reached in two hours' walk via the hamlets of **Charavgí** and **Mersíni** (or 20 minutes by caique).

Getting There

The islands are served daily in summer by the *Skopelitis*, which rolls its way between Náxos and Amorgós, and the occasional **ferry** from Piraeus. Wherever you are coming from, and whatever your destination, if you get off at one of the Back Islands, you'll be spending the night there.

Port authority (Naxos): **t** 228 502 2300.

Tourist Information

Koufoníssi ✉ 84300

Prassinos agency: by the post office, **t** 228 507 1438. Changes money; sells ferry tickets on the quay, and runs excursions.
Koufonissi Tours: **t/f** 228 507 4091. Helpful.

Schinoússa ✉ 84300

Grispos Tourist Center, a (cum mini-market) agency in Chóra, **t** 228 507 1930, **f** 228 507 1176. At the top of the mule path from Myrsíni. Arranges accommodation, ferry tickets and round-island trips.

Where to Stay and Eat

Koufoníssi ✉ 84300

Small new hotels and studios are sprouting up like crazy, and most offer generous off-season discounts, dropping from expensive in August to inexpensive in June.
Keros Studios, **t** 228 507 1600 (*expensive in season*). With a garden and bar by the sea.
Christina's House, **t** 228 507 1736 (*moderate*). Similar but on a more modest scale.
Villa Ostria, at Ag. Geórgiou, **t/f** 228 507 1671 (*expensive*). Has a pretty veranda over the sea and 10 comfortable rooms, with phones, fridges and music.
Finikas, **t** 228 507 1368 (*C; moderate*). Self-contained double rooms in a cluster of white buildings near Fínikas Beach; the owner meets ferries.
Katerina, **t** 228 507 1455 (*moderate*). Just up from the port, with ebullient landlady.
Camping Charakópou, **t** 228 507 1683. With simple facilities.
Melissa (€10–12). On the main street; tasty Greek favourites served on the terrace.
Giannis Venetsanos, **t** 228 507 4074 (€10–20). Pretty stone house on the beach, featuring lobster dishes and traditional kid from Kéros. *Open June–Sept.*

Schinoússa ✉ 84300

Provaloma, **t** 228 507 1936 (€10–12), just outside Chóra (*moderate*). Fine views, mini bus service, rooms with bath, and a good taverna with a stone oven.
Panorama Taverna. Rooms to let (*inexpensive*), home cooking and views to Tsigoúra.
To Kentro. General store and *kafeneíon* where the locals play backgammon; serves beer, snacks and pungent home-made cheese.
Taverna Myrsini, in Myrsíni, **t** 228 507 1154 (€12–15). Its spartan kitchen conjures up delicious seafood in the evenings and it doubles as a left-luggage store by day.

Heráklia ✉ 84300

At Livádi: **Gavalos Tours**, **t/f** 228 507 1561, may help you find a room.
Melissa, in Ag. Geórgios, **t** 228 507 1539/1561. Taverna with a good budget menu, *kafeneíon* and general store. Has basic, inexpensive rooms upstairs.
Kordalou Taverna, **t** 228 507 1488. Also with inexpensive rooms above.
Zografos, 700m back from the sea in Livádi, **t** 228 507 1946 (*moderate*). Rooms with verandas, baths, fridges and a communal barbecue to grill your own fish.
Livadi, on the beach. Serves good food and plays old *rembétika* songs; also has rooms to let (*inexpensive*). Owner Geórgios organizes boat trips to Alimniás Beach.

Heráklia (ΗΡΑΚΛΕΙΑ)

Heráklia, or Iraklía, the most westerly and largest of the Back Islands, is an hour's ferry from Náxos, but even in mid-August it remains quiet – though come for the Assumption on August 15 and witness three days of eating, drinking and dancing.

There are rooms to let in the attractive port, **Ag. Geórgios**, set in a crook in the hills, with a small tamarisk-lined beach. From here it's a 20-minute walk to the sandy beach at **Livádi**, popular with Greek families and campers. The old Chóra, **Panagía**, is a sleepy and primitive but pretty place about an hour's walk into the hills, but you might hitch a lift with the baker. From Panagía a path leads to sandy **Alimniás Beach**. Another excursion is the three-hour walk southwest from Ag. Geórgios to the stalactite cave of **Ag. Ioánnis**, with two chambers over 240ft long (*bring a flashlight*).

Íos (ΙΟΣ)

Íos is a mecca for throngs of young people who spend their days lounging on the great beaches and their evenings staggering from one watering hole to another. The Irish invasion is so great that the name may as well stand for 'Ireland Over Seas'. Despite the loveliness of the island, its glorious sands and pretty Chóra, you'll feel disenchanted if you don't want to party. In early spring, though, you might find Íos as Lawrence Durrell did, full of 'silences, fractured only by some distant church bell or the braying of a mule'.

Gialós and Íos Town (Chóra)

The Ionians built cities here when the island was famous for its oak forests. Over the centuries the oaks became ships and Íos became a rockpile trimmed with beaches. The port, **Gialós**, or Ormós, is a resort, a quiet one compared to Chóra. Its Turkish nickname was 'Little Malta' because it was a favourite loafing place for young pirates (some things never change). Gialós has a beach, but it tends to be windy; you're better off walking 15 minutes or catching the bus to **Koumbára**, where a long stretch of sand ends at a big rock that's fun for snorkelling.

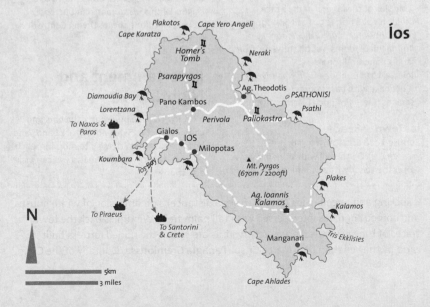

Getting There and Around

By sea: daily **ferry** and summer **hydrofoil** with Piraeus, Santoríni, Páros, Náxos and Mýkonos, six a week with Rafína and Sýros, four with Folégandros and Síkinos, once with Heráklion. **Port authority**: t 228 609 1264.

By road: the **bus** service is excellent, calling at Koumbára, Gialós, Íos Town to Milapótas Beach every 10 minutes day and night; 3-day unlimited travel cards are available. Excursion buses daily to Manganári Bay; less frequently to Ag. Theodótis Beach.

Tourist Information

In Gialós, t 228 609 1028 (opens when ferries arrive for bookings). Also in Íos Town by the town hall, t 228 609 1505, *www.iosgreece.com*.

Where to Stay and Eat

Íos can be reasonable, though the unprepared have paid very dearly; if you can't find a place try the **Rooms Association**, t 228 609 1205. Before Guinness, Íos' speciality was *meyífra*, a hard white cheese, mixed with perfume and fermented in a goatskin.

Gialós (Ormos) ✉ 84001
Petra Apartments, t/f 228 609 1049 (*C; moderate*). A lovely luxurious Cycladic village complex at the far end of the beach.
Poseidon, t 228 609 1091, f 228 609 1969, *poseidht@otenet.gr* (*C; moderate*). Immaculate rooms just off the waterfront and a panoramic pool.
Violetta, t 228 609 1044 (*E; inexpensive*). Cheapest, with basic rooms.
Psarades (€12–15). A good place for fish.

Íos Town ✉ 84001
Sunrise, t 228 609 1074, f 228 609 1664 (*C; expensive*). On the hill with stunning views over the town, with swimming pool and bar.

Homer's Inn, t 228 609 1365, f 228 609 1888 (*C; moderate*). A good bet, with a pool.
Afroditi, t/f 228 609 1546 (*D; moderate–inexpensive*). One of the best rooms places for value.
Pithari, by the church. Excellent food and barrelled wine. Just stroll into the kitchen and point out what you want.
Pinocchio's. Serves great pasta and pizza under lovely bougainvillaea.
Ios Club, on the footpath up from the harbour. Renowned for sunset views over Síkinos, good drinks, classical music and jazz.

Milopótas Beach ✉ 84001
To discourage late-night revellers, four campgrounds have been provided, but rows of sleeping bags by night and naked bodies by day are still the norm.
Ios Palace, t 228 609 1224, f 228 609 1082, *ios@matrix.kapatel.gr* (*B; luxury–expensive*). On the beach, designed and decorated in the old island style; two pools, tennis, billiards, and views. *Open May–Sept*.
Far Out, t 228 609 1446, f 228 609 1701, *farout@otenet.gr* (*C; expensive*). Named because of guests' reactions to the view; comfortable rooms in Cubist style clustered on the hillside, with a pool.
Markos Beach, t 228 609 1571, f 228 609 1671 (*C; expensive–moderate*). Standard rooms with showers, on the beach.
Far Out Camping, t 228 609 1468, f 228 609 1560. With a restaurant, minibus, pool, sports facilities, the **Ios Diving Centre** and bungee jumping.

Entertainment and Nightlife

Íos Town is one huge party, the bars and clubs competing with videos, rock bands and happy hours that stretch into morning; each posts its nightly programme so you can pick and choose.

Rocking and a-reeling **Íos Town** is (from a distance) a dream vision of white houses and domed churches interspersed with tall palm trees. Windmills back the town, traces of the ancient walls are preserved, as are bits of the ruined fortress built in 1400 by the Venetian boss Marco Crispi. **Panagía Gremiotissa**, 'Our Lady of the Cliffs', at the very top houses a miraculous icon that floated to Íos from Crete. Discos, bars, fast food stands and shops selling rude T-shirts fill the rest of the space, although a new **theatre** hopes to instill a bit of culture.

Beaches Around Íos, and Homer Too

Íos has 35 beaches, but few see any reason to go further than superb **Milopótas**, with every conceivable water sport. Don't count on getting much shut-eye near the sands. For something less Babylonian, take a bus, hire a motorbike or catch one of the excursion boats from Gialós for the golden crescents of **Manganári Bay**, where nudism rules and new hotels have been planted. Long sandy/pebbly **Kalamós Beach** is a 30-minute walk north on a track (do-able on a motorbike) beginning at the pretty church of **Ag. Ioánnis Kálamos**.

Ag. Theodótis to the east has a fine beach, under the ruined 15th-century Venetian fortress of **Paliokástro**. The road continues to the coarse golden sands of **Psáthi**, a favourite for windsurfing and loggerhead turtle nests. **Perivóla** in the middle of Íos has the island's fresh-water springs and trees. **Páno Kámbos**, once inhabited by a hundred families but today reduced to three or four, is another pretty place. Nearby, at **Helliniká**, are monoliths of mysterious origin. Tradition has it that the mother of Homer came from Íos, and it was here that the great poet came at the end of his life. His tomb was at **Plakotós** to the north, and although earthquakes have left only the rock on which it was built, the epitaph was copied out by ancient travellers: 'Here the earth covers the sacred head of the dean of heroes, the divine Homer.'

Síkinos (ΣΙΚΙΝΟΣ)

When newspapers and noise get you down, try Síkinos. An 'Ecosystem of European Importance', it hosts wild pigeons, black-headed hawks, sea birds, rare cat vipers and sand snakes; monk seals live in its sea caves. Traditional farming and fishing are still

Getting There and Around

Several **ferry** connections a week with Piraeus and nearby Cyclades; summer tourist boats to Folégandros and Íos. **Port authority**: t 228 605 1222. The island **bus** meets most ferries and runs hourly to Chóra and Kástro.

Where to Stay and Eat

Aloprónia ✉ 84010

Porto Síkinos, t 228 605 1247, f 228 605 1220 (*B; expensive*). Right on the beach, smart and prettily laid out in traditional island design, with a bar, restaurant and tourist office.

Flora, up the hill, t 228 605 1239/1214 (*C; moderate*). Lovely Cycladic-style development of eight self-contained rooms built round a courtyard with wonderful views.

Kamares, t/f 228 605 1281 (*moderate*). Charming traditional rooms.

Panayiotis Kouvdouris, t 228 605 1232. Simple rooms by the sea.

Meltemi. Where the fishermen gather, for a simple lunch, coffee or ouzo.

Chóra ✉ 84010

To Kastro. The main taverna with a roof garden and excellent home-cooking;

Klimateria. Pretty restaurant and *kafeneíon* which does meals, snacks and omelettes.

the mainstay. Síkinos was once called Oenoe, 'wine island', and the local stuff still packs a punch.

Ferries dock at sleepy **Aloprónia** or **Skála**, with a sandy beach, shallow sea, fishing boats and a few tavernas. **Chóra**, the capital, is one of the most authentic villages in the Cyclades and a good hour's walk up if the bus hasn't put in an appearance. The 300 inhabitants are proud of their cathedral, with icons by the 18th-century master Skordílis. In the main square, bees buzz in the trees by the church of the **Pantánassa** and the 18th-century stone **mansions**, some with bright wooden balconies. Up the nearby next hill is **Kástro** with labyrinthine lanes, ruined windmills, tiny rent rooms and *kafeneíons*. There's a **Folk Museum** run by expat John Margétis in memory of his mother, Kaliópe (*open July–Aug pm*).

From Chóra a road leads past ruined **Cyclopean walls** southwest to **Moní Episkópi**. Once a 3rd-century mausoleum, it was converted to the Byzantine church of Koimísis Theotókou in the 7th century. A rough path to the northeast leads (in an hour and a half) to the scant remains of a Classical fortress at **Paliókastro**, near the sandy beach **Málta**. Tracks lead south to the sandy beaches of **Ag. Geórgios** (taverna) and **Ag. Nikólaos** (a caique in summer).

Folégandros (ΦΟΛΕΓΥΝΔΡΟΣ)

With sheer cliffs and a breathtaking Chóra, little Folégandros (with only 300 winter inhabitants) is one of the most alluring of the Cyclades, the base since 1984 for the Cycladic Centre of Art. Much of the landscape looks as if it has been whipped to a froth by a furious god; the locals added the labyrinthine paths across it, designed to confound invaders. Nevertheless, it has been discovered, but in a relaxing, low-key way.

Boats land at tiny **Karavostássi**, with a tree-fringed pebbly beach. Shady **Livádi Beach** is a 15-minute walk away, while **Katérgo Beach**, one of the nicest, is another 45 minutes. Above waits **Chóra**, a stunning sight, perched on the 1,000ft pirate-proof cliffs; the tall houses turn their backs on the sea, fused along the ridge of the cliff; cars have to circle around. Life, especially in the evening, revolves around four interlinking squares. The third has *kafeneía* frequented by locals, and **Ag. Antónis** church with a charming portal. An arcade leads into the fortified **Kástro** quarter, built in the 13th century by Marco Sanudo, a maze of dazzling paved alleys filled with geraniums and bougainvillaea, and white houses sporting distinctive wooden balconies.

From Chóra, a path zig-zags up the hill to the landmark church of the **Panagía**, set on a sheer cliff over the sea (key from the town hall). According to legend, pirates once stole a silver icon of the Virgin and kidnapped an islander, only to capsize and drown, while the local clung to the icon and floated to shore. Every year the icon goes on an island tour, to bless the houses and bring the fishermen luck. Beyond is a large grotto, **Chríssospiliá** ('Golden Cave'), with huge stalactites. A bus, departing from the far side of town, serves **Áno Meriá** to the west, which is a string of hamlets, with an excellent taverna (Kyra Maria), wonderful sunsets and a good **Folk Museum** (*t 228 604 1387;*

Getting There and Around

The **ferry** connects four to five times a week with Piraeus, Íos and Santoríni; less frequently with Mílos, Sífnos, Sérifos, Kýthnos, Páros, Náxos and Síkinos. Caique excursions to beaches and to Sikínos. **Port authority**: t 228 604 1249. The island **buses** link the port Karavostássi to Chóra and meet all the ferries, no matter how late; another bus goes from Chóra to Angáli and Áno Meriá.

Tourist Information

Sottovento: in Chóra, t 228 604 1444, f 228 604 1430.

Maraki Travel: t 228 604 1273. Exchanges money in lieu of a bank and offers Internet services.

Where to Stay and Eat

There's never enough space in the summer (even in the campsite), so do book.

The restaurants are better than average, thanks to a lack of package hotels and day-trippers.

Karovostássi ✉ 84011

Aeolos, t 228 604 1205, f 228 604 1336, book in Athens t 210 922 3819 (*C; moderate*). Immaculate rooms overlooking the beach and a lovely garden.

Camping Livadi, 1km beyond Karavostássi, t 228 604 1204.

Chóra ✉ 84011

Castro, in the Kástro, t 228 604 1414, f 228 604 1230, (*B; expensive*). A gem – a 500-year-old house with pebble mosaic floors. Rooms look down the sheer cliffs to the sea. *Open June–Sept.*

Anemomílos Apartments, t 228 604 1309, f 228 604 1407, *www.greekhotel.com* (*B; expensive*). Newly built in the traditional style, with balconies overhanging the sea. *Open May–Sept.*

Folegándros Apartments, t 228 604 1239, f 228 604 1366, *www.fole-aps.gr* (*C; expensive– moderate*). Built in Cycladic style around a courtyard. *Open May–Sept.*

Odysseus, t 228 604 1276, f 228 604 1366 (*C; moderate*). Pleasant, located on the cliffs.

Fani-Vevis, t 228 604 1237 (*C; moderate*). Old mansion, now renovated.

Pavlo's Rooms, t 228 604 1232 (*inexpensive*). A budget option on the road to Chóra, with basic chalet-style accommodation in converted stables, set in a lovely garden.

Pounta, t 228 604 1063 (€12–15). At the entrance to Chóra, with tables in a charming courtyard; tasty home-style cooking and a choice of vegan dishes.

Nikos 'Turbo Service' (€12). Next to the Kástro. Anything you can imagine, washed down with barrelled wine, presided over by the wise-cracking Nikolas.

Kritikos, t 228 604 1219. On the third square. Delicious chicken and other local meats on the spit; a very Greek hang-out.

I Piatsa. The place for backgammon as well as delicious food.

open daily 5–8) with exhibits of traditional life. You can walk down to remote beaches at **Ampeli**, **Livadáki** and **Ag. Geórgios Bay**. Between Áno Meriá and Chóra a road descends to the main sandy beach, **Angáli**. Next door is quieter, sandy **Ag. Nikólaos Beach** with pines and a taverna, specializing in octopus stewed in wine.

Santoríni/Thíra (ΣΑΝΤΟΡΙΝΗ / ΘΗΡΑ)

Everything seems more intense on Santoríni; forget *Under the Volcano*, here you're teetering on the edge. The mix of sinister precipices and the most brilliant white, trendiest bars and restaurants in the country gives the island a splendid kind of schizophrenia. Nothing beats arriving by sea. As your fragile ship sails into the caldera, the island looms up like a chocolate layer cake with an enormous bite taken out of it, frosted with coconut cream towns that slide over the edge, while the islets opposite look as infernal as the charred gunk in your oven. Santoríni has had its ups and downs, and human endeavours have fared similarly: you can visit no fewer than three former 'capitals': the Minoan centre of Akrotíri, a favourite candidate for Atlantis; the Doric capital Thera at Mésa Vouná; and the medieval Skáros. Even the modern town of Fíra, perched on the rim, was flattened by an earthquake in 1956.

History

Santoríni was once a typically round volcanic island called Strogyle whose original inhabitants were chased away by the Minoans. One of their towns was at Akrotíri, and its rediscovery came about through archaeological detective work that started in Crete. In 1939, while excavating Amnisós, the port of Knossós, Spirýdon Marinátos realized that only a massive natural disaster could have caused the damage he found, which included a 3–20mm layer of volcanic tephra over New Palace sites. Another clue came from Solon, who in 600 BC wrote of his journey to Egypt, where he heard about the lost land of Atlantis, made of red, white and black volcanic rock (like Santoríni) and spoke of a city vanishing in 24 hours. In the *Critias*, Plato described Atlantis as being composed of one round island and one long island, a sweet country of art and flowers connected by one culture and rule (Santoríni and Crete, under Minos?). Lastly, Marinátos studied the eruption of Krakatoa in 1883, which blew its lid with such force that it could be heard 3,000 miles away. Krakatoa formed a caldera of 8.3 sq km, and as the sea rushed in to fill it, it created a *tsunami* or tidal wave over 200m high that destroyed everything in a 150km path. The present bay of Santoríni is 22 sq km – almost *three* times as big. Since French archaeologists had discovered Minoan vases at Akrotíri in the 19th century, Marinátos began to dig there in 1967, seeking to prove his theory: that Minoan civilization owed its sudden decline to the eruption, earthquakes, and tidal waves caused by the explosion of Stogyle in *c.* 1450 BC. Marinátos hoped to unearth a few vases. Instead he found an entire Minoan colony buried in tephra, complete with dazzling frescoes.

The island returned to history in the 9th century BC, when the Dorians settled it, calling it Thera. The Byzantines covered the island with castles, but the Venetians under the Crispi got it anyway. Skáros near Imerovígli was their capital and Irene their patron saint, hence the island's second and more common name, Santoríni.

Fíra (ΦΗΡΑ)

Buses from the port and airport leave visitors in Fíra's Plateía Theotóki to be processed and fattened on fast food before being sacrificed to the volcano god. Cruise ships anchor beneath the towering cliffs and motor launches ferry passengers to the tiny port of **Skála Fíra**; there, donkeys wait to bear them up the winding path to town 885ft above. An Austrian-built **cable car** (*every 15 mins from 6.45am to 8.15pm; €3*) does the donkey-work in two minutes.

Bright white Fíra spills down the volcano's rim on terraces, dotted with blue-domed churches, all enjoying the sublime view. The little lanes are chock-a-block with shops, bars, hotels and restaurants. Fíra blends into quieter **Firostefáni**, just north; here are

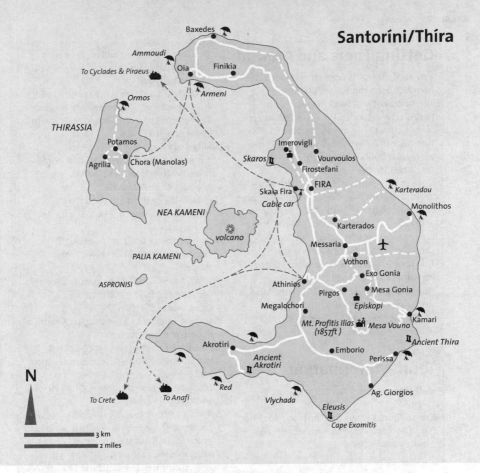

some magnificent old *skaftá*, barrel-roofed cave-houses, Santoríni's speciality, now equipped with all mod cons. The old **Archaeological Museum** (*t 228 602 2217; Tues–Sun 8.30–3; adm*) is on the north side of town with finds going back to the 9th century BC. Opposite the bus station, the new **Museum of Prehistoric Thíra** (*t 228 602 3217; same hours*) has Early Cycladic figurines found in the local pumice quarries and lovely vases, ceramics, jewellery and a few frescoes from Akrotíri, including the great 16ft frieze of a flotilla, a unique record of sailing in the prehistoric Aegean. The **Mégaron Gýzi Museum** (*t 228 602 2244; open daily 10.30–1.30 and 5–8pm, Sun 10.30–4; adm*), located in a beautiful 17th-century mansion, houses exhibits on the island's history – manuscripts, costumes, and photographs of Fíra before the 1956 quake.

Way Down South: Akrotíri, the Minoan Pompeii

Akrotíri, a wine village, was a Venetian stronghold and has beaches on either coast, and a path along the caldera rim. In the 1860s, while digging pumice here for the rebuilding of Port Said, the French found that ancient walls kept getting in the way. In 1967 Spyrídon Marinátos (*see above*) dug as well, and found a strange and wonderful **Minoan city**, buried in c. 1550 BC (*buses from Fíra end up here; t 228 608 1366/2217; open*

Getting There and Around

By air: daily flights from Athens; four a week from Mýkonos; three a week from Thessaloníki; two a week in season from Heráklion and Rhodes. The Olympic Airways office in Fíra: **t** 228 602 2493; **airport**: **t** 228 603 1525. Aegean Airlines: **t** 228 602 8500. There are regular buses from the airport to Fíra, or take a taxi for €6–8.

By sea: daily **ferry** connections with Piraeus, Íos, Páros, Náxos and Mýkonos; frequent (three or four times a week) **hydrofoil** connections with Rafína and other Cyclades; two to three times a week with Heráklion, Kássos, Kárpathos, Chálki; twice a week with Thessaloníki and once a week with Skiáthos. **Port authority**: **t** 228 602 2239.

By road: great **bus** service: in Fíra the bus stop is opposite the museum, down from Plateía Theotokopoúlou. **Taxis**: **t** 228 602 2555 (€8 from Fíra to Oía).

Tourist Information

Markozanes Tours, Fíra, **t** 228 602 3660. Helpful.

Kamari Tours, Kamári, **t** 228 603 1390, **f** 228 603 1497, *kamaritours@san.forthnet.gr*. Have offices everywhere.

Where to Stay and Eat

Fíra ✉ 84700

Fíra is expensive, and, unless otherwise noted, places close from November to March. Out of season, you can wheel and deal with the room owners who mug you as the Athiniós bus pulls into town. Try Santoríni's specialities: fava bean soup and *pseftokeftédes*, made of deep-fried tomatoes, onion and mint.

Tsitouras Collection, Firostefáni, **t** 228 602 3747, **f** 228 602 3918, *tsitoura@otenet.gr* (*A; luxury; €420–600*). Five Venetian houses from 1780; the House of Nureyev (he stayed there) has *the* view. *Open all year.*

Santoríni Palace, Firostefáni, **t** 228 602 2771, **f** 228 602 3705, *www.santoriniplacehotel.gr*

(*A; luxury*). Luxurious and modern, with pool and panoramic views of the sea and town. *Open April–Nov.*

Kallisti Thira, **t** 228 602 2317, **f** 228 602 2962, *kavalht@otenet.gr* (*C; expensive*). Very nice family hotel, on the quiet end of Fíra, with gardens and a pool.

Galini, **t** 228 602 2095, **f** 228 602 3097, *galini-htl@otenet.gr* (*C; expensive*). Nice rooms with caldera views, and transfers to the port. *Open Mar–Nov.*

Tataki, in the centre, **t** 228 602 2389 (*D; moderate*). Cheaper but view-less. *Open all year.*

Argonaftis, **t** 228 602 2055 (*moderate*). Friendly, with breakfast served in the garden.

Stella's, **t** 228 602 3464 (*inexpensive*). Rooms are plain but have a kitchen and views to the other side of the island.

Camping Santoríni, **t** 228 602 2944. Nearby, a superb site with pool.

Selini, **t** 228 602 2249 (€25–35). Excellent restaurant, with imaginative dishes which make delicious use of the island's small tomatoes, cheese and capers. Great views; book. *Open eves only.*

Sphinx, **t** 228 602 3823 (€30). Another romantic caldera setting, serving excellent seafood, much of it with pasta; some meat dishes.

Koukoumavlos, **t** 228 602 3807 (€25–35). Perhaps the most innovative of Fíra's restaurants, full of delicious surprises. Lovely dining rooms, great cellar.

Nikolas, **t** 228 602 4550 (€12–15). A great place for traditional, excellent Greek food. Locals swear by it, proved by frequent queues.

South: Akrotíri/Megalochóri ✉ 84700

Villa Mathios, **t** 228 608 1152, **f** 228 608 1704, *vmathios@otenet.gr* (*expensive in Aug; otherwise good value*). Comfortable, with a pool, air-conditioning and TV.

Pension Karlos, **t** 228 608 1370, **f** 228 608 1095 (*moderate*). En-suite rooms with balconies.

Kapetan Dimitris, Fáros, **t** 228 608 2210. The captain bags the fish and game, the Mrs supplies the fresh vegetables and cheese. *Open Mar–Oct.*

Vedema, in Megalochóri, **t** 228 608 1796, **f** 228 608 1798, *www.vedema.gr* (*A; luxury*). One of the Small Luxury Hotels of the World: a converted winery with marble baths, in-house movies and a private beach 3km away with minibus service. Its restaurant (€40) promises fine dining, and doesn't disappoint.

Períssa ✉ 84700

Sellada Beach, on the sands, **t** 228 608 1859, **f** 228 608 1492 (*expensive*). Handsome traditional rooms and flats with pool.
Ostria, **t/f** 228 608 2607 (*moderate*). Good-value apartments by the sea.
Blue Albacor, **t** 228 608 1654 (*moderate*). Similar to the Ostria, and cheap out of season.

Kamári ✉ 84700

Rose Bay, **t** 228 603 3650, **f** 228 603 3653, *www.greekhotel.com* (*B; expensive*). At one end of the black sands, peaceful Cycladic-style hotel with a pool and BBQ nights.
Andreas, **t** 228 603 1692, **f** 228 603 1314 (*D; moderate*). Modest, but has a lush garden.
Atmosphere, **t** 228 603 1368 (€22). Swedish chefs and waitresses serve up modern dishes, including a few from their homeland.
Kamari. Good, inexpensive family-run taverna, serving *fáva* soup.

Messariá ✉ 84700

Archontiko Argyrou, **t** 228 603 1669, **f** 228 603 3064 (*A; expensive*). Occupying a lovely 1860s mansion with rooms on the ground floor. The first floor has its own museum.

Imerovígli ✉ 87400

Heliotropos, **t** 228 602 3670, **f** 228 602 3672, *www.heliotropos.net/hotel* (*A; luxury*). Intimate, elegant, Cycladic hotel built into the cliff, with a restaurant, views, and large rooms, all with kitchenette. Free Internet.
Astra, **t** 228 602 3641, **f** 228 602 4765, *www.astra.gr*. (*luxury*). Apartments with more sublime views and a pool.
Villa Spiliotica, **t** 228 602 2637, **f** 228 602 3590 (*expensive*). Similar views, lower prices for its apartments and studios; mirrors on the ceilings of its honeymoon suites.
Blue Note. Good bet for dinner with grand views.

Oía ✉ 84702

Perivolas, **t** 228 607 1308, **f** 228 607 1309, *perivolas@san.forthnet.gr* (*A; luxury*). Fourteen lovely traditional houses, with a unique 'infinity' pool on the edge of the cliff.
Fanari Villas, below the windmill, **t** 228 607 1008, **f** 228 607 1235 (*luxury–expensive*). Swish, luxury *skaftá*, with small bar, and steps to Ammoúdi Bay.
Ikies, **t** 228 607 1311, **f** 228 607 1953, *www.ikies.com* (*luxury–expensive*). Rooms, studios and maisonettes on the edge of town, with more privacy than most and a small pool.
Ammoudi Villas, **t** 228 607 1507, **f** 228 607 1509 (*expensive*). Highly recommended, tranquil, offering all mod cons in traditional apartments with verandas.
1800, **t** 228 607 1485 (€25–35). For a romantic dinner by candlelight, in a shipowner's house on the main street, serving lovely imaginative cuisine.
Kastro, **t** 228 607 1045 (€25). If you want aperitifs and dinner overlooking one of the most glorious sunsets in Greece, book. The food is lovely too, with a fusion touch.
Katina, **t** 228 607 1280 (€10–15). Descend to Ammoúdi for the excellent fish and island specialities at this taverna. The President of Greece likes it. Probably likes the prices, too.
Blue Sky Taverna. Reasonable and deservedly popular.

Entertainment and Nightlife

In Fíra, **Bebis** is the bar for a loony young crowd, and **Kira Thira** appeals to lovers of jazz, blues and *sangria*. **Franco's**, playing gentle classical music, is *the* place to laze in deckchairs for sunset, even if the prices are sky-high. The **Mamounia Club** plays Greek hits, or you can rock away at **Tithora Club** in the main square.

Kamári throbs with bars: **Valentino's**, with Greek music, always has a large crowd. Drop in at **Albatross** and dance till dawn.

Tues–Sun 8.30–3; adm). It is still being liberated from its thick sepulchral shell of tephra. Protected by a huge modern roof, a carpet of volcanic dust silences footsteps on paved lanes laid 3,500 years ago, amid houses that stand up to three storeys high, some of rubble masonry, some in fine ashlar, with stone stairways, doors and windows. In general the size of the storage areas and cooking pots suggests a communal life and collective economy. The residents must have had ample warning that the island was about to blow: no jewellery or other valuables were found, and the only skeleton unearthed so far belonged to a pig. As they escaped they must have shed more than a few tears, for life at Akrotíri was sweet judging by the ash imprints of their elaborate wooden furniture, their ceramics and frescoes full of colour and life. In one of the houses is the grave of Marinátos, who died after a fall on the site.

Below, the road continues to **Mávro Rachidi**, where cliffs as black as charcoal offer a stark contrast to the white chapel of Ag. Nikólaos; a path over the headland leads to **Kókkino Paralía** or Red Beach, with sun beds under startling blood-red cliffs.

The Southeast: Embório, Eríssa and Ancient Thira

East of Akrotíri, farming villages encircle Mount Profítis Ilías. Many make Santoríni's excellent white wine; because of the wind the vines are kept low, protected by woven cane; some fields look as if they're growing baskets. In **Megalochóri** you can taste the results at Boutari's winery, restaurant and shop (*t 228 608 1011*). **Embório** still has its Venetian fort; with its lone palm, it looks like something out of the Sahara. Outside the village, the church of **Ag. Nikólaos Marmarinós** was a 3rd-century BC Temple of the Mother of the Gods, and still uses the original ceiling. Another 3km east of Embório, in a pretty setting under the seaside mountain Mésa Vouna, the black beaches of **Eríssa** have attracted a good deal of development; they can be pleasant at either end of the season as the sand warms quickly in the sun. The coastal road south of Eríssa leads to **Cape Exomítis**, guarded by one of the best-preserved Byzantine fortresses of the Cyclades. The road ends by the wild cliffs at **Vlycháda**.

Pírgos, another old village, has interesting barrel-roofed houses, Byzantine walls and a Venetian fort. Vineyards swirl up the flanks of **Mount Profítis Ilías**, Santoríni's highest point (1,857ft). The locals say the **monastery** (1712; *cover your knees and shoulders*) is the only place that will stay above sea level when the rest of Santoríni sinks. At the foot of Profítis Ilías, by Mésa Goniá, the 11th-century **Panagía Episkopí** has fine Byzantine icons and holds the biggest *panegýri* on the island on 15 August. North, another black beach and a million sun beds announce big brash **Kamári**, with 300 hotels. Yet a mile away women in straw hats thresh fava beans in the field.

Kamári was the port of **ancient Thera** (*t 228 602 2217; open Tues–Sun 9–3*), spread over its great terraces on the rocky headland of Mésa Vouna. Although inhabited since the 9th century BC, most of what you see dates from the Ptolemies (300–150 BC), who used Thera as a base for meddling in the Aegean. The north side of the city, with the Ptolemies' **barracks**, **gymnasium** and **governor's palace**, are reached by way of the **Temenos of Artemidoros of Perge**, a sacred area dedicated by an admiral of the Ptolemies, with symbols of the gods in relief. Below, Thera's long main street passes through impressive remains of the vast **agora**, with the base of a Temple of Dionysos and altar of Ptolemy Philometor. The long, well preserved **Royal Stoa** with its Doric columns was last restored in AD 150. Behind it, **houses** have mosaics and toilets; note the one with a phallus dedicated 'to my friends.'. The nearby **theatre** has a dizzying view down to the sea. The road along the headland passes Roman baths past the Column of Artemis and the 6th-century BC **Temple of Apollo Karneios**. Some of the oldest graffiti in Greek (7th century BC) may be seen on the **Terrace of Celebration**, recording admiration and lust for the naked male dancers (the *gymno paidiai*).

The coastal road north leads past the airport to **Monolíthos**, a soft grey sandy beach with a big isolated lump of rock draped with a few ruins, tamarisks and windsurfers. **Messariá** is an important wine and market village.

North of Fíra to Oía

Imerovígli almost merges into Firostefáni and can be a good base if you prefer your caldera quiet. It is by the startling, vertiginous site of **Skáros**, the medieval capital, once defended below by an impregnable castle of 1207, until a volcanic eruption in 1650 destroyed the town. The road north continues to trendy **Oía**, the third port of Santoríni. Its houses, painted in rich, Fauvist colours, are nearly all restored and piled on top of one another over the jumble of broken red and white cliffs. There's a half-ruined Venetian fort where everyone gathers to watch the sunset; if you want the sea, it's 286 steps down to **Arméni Beach**, with a little clutch of houses, or 214 steps down to **Ammoúdi Beach**, with tavernas and a hotel; here you can fill your pockets with pumice souvenirs. The third option is a 3km bus trip to **Baxédes**, with coarse blackish sand and shade. A mansion in Oía houses the **Nautical Museum** (*t 228 607 1156; open Wed–Mon 12.30–4 and 5–8.30; adm*), with ships' models and figureheads.

Islets Around the Caldera

Crusts of land mark the rim of Santoríni's spooky 10km wide and 1,250ft deep caldera. The largest, curving around the northwest, is **Thirassía**, part of Santoríni until the two were blasted apart in 236 BC. The main business on Thirassía, pop. 245, is growing tomatoes and beans on the fertile plateau; the largest village, **Manolás**, has tavernas and rooms to rent by the sea. Excursion boats from Oía also make trips out to the 'burnt isles', **Palía Kaméni** (appeared in AD 157) and **Néa Kaméni** (born in 1720), both still volcanically active.

Anáfi (ΑΝΑΦΗ)

Anáfi, the most southerly of the Cyclades, looks like a tadpole, but with a tail swollen like the Rock of Gibraltar. It's friendly, unpretentious and peaceful. Islanders go about their lives as they always have – but note that if the weather breaks you could get marooned, so allow plenty of time to get back. Some scholars have found in the Anáfiots' songs and festivals traces of the ancient worship of Apollo; the biggest one happens on 8 September, at the monastery.

Getting There and Around

Several **ferry** connections a week with Santorini, Íos, Náxos, Páros and Piraeus, twice with Folégandros and Sýros. Weekly connection in summer with the Dodecanese. **Port authority: t** 228 606 1216.

In season, **caiques** in Ag. Nikólaos go to local beaches.

Buses are few and there are no taxis. For **motorbike rentals**, call **t** 228 606 1292.

Tourist Information

Zeyzed Travel, t 228 606 1253, **f** 228 606 1352. Can help with accommodation.

Where to Stay and Eat

Anáfi ✉ 84009

Room-owners travel down from Chóra by bus or car to meet ferries.

Villa Apollon, above Klisídi Beach, **t** 228 606 1348, **f** 228 606 1287 (*moderate; open May–Oct, out of season* **t** 210 993 6150). The classiest; a garden, and fridges.

Ta Plagia, up by Chóra, **t** 228 606 1308, out of season **t** 210 412 7113 (*inexpensive; open May–Sept*). Similar, with a restaurant.

Anatoli, in Chóra, **t** 228 606 1279 (*moderate–inexpensive*). Rooms with verandas.

Tavernas are simple. In the Chóra, try **Alexandra** or **Kyriakos**.

The one village, quiet **Chóra** (pop. 260), is an amphitheatre of white domed houses and windmills, a short but steep walk up from the landing, **Ag. Nikólaos**. Guglielmo Crispi's half-ruined **Kástro** is to the north of the village. There are attractive **beaches** along the coast around Ag. Nikólaos, from **Klisídi** east of the port to a range of bays signposted from the Chóra road.

The favourite path runs east of Chóra to **Kastélli** (about 2 hours), site of the ancient town and the chapel **Panagía tou Doráki**, decorated with a pair of Roman sarcophagi. Another hour's walk from Kastélli, past the ruined hamlet of **Katalimátsa**, will bring you to the summit of the tadpole-tail, **Mount Kálamos**. Along the way, huge square blocks mark the Temple of Apollo Aiglitos, dedicated, they say, by Jason. On top of Kálamos, the 16th-century **Monastery of Panagía Kalamiótissa** (1,476ft over the sea) enjoys tremendous views, especially sunrises (bring supplies and a sleeping bag). Nearby you can poke around in an old dragon's lair, the stalagmite **Drakontóspilo**.

Crete

18

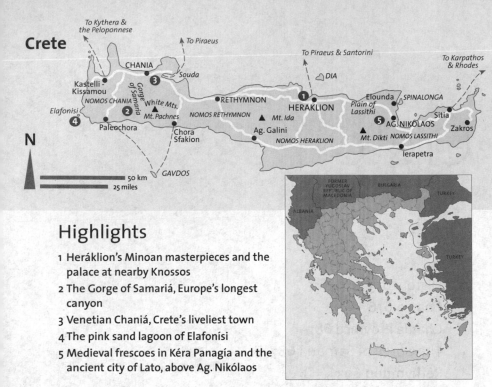

Crete

Highlights

1 Heráklion's Minoan masterpieces and the palace at nearby Knossos
2 The Gorge of Samariá, Europe's longest canyon
3 Venetian Chaniá, Crete's liveliest town
4 The pink sand lagoon of Elafonísi
5 Medieval frescoes in Kéra Panagía and the ancient city of Lato, above Ag. Nikólaos

Crete is Greece's largest island (roughly 260 by 50km), and in many ways its oldest; the birthplace of Zeus, Crete gave Greece its first myths, and nurtured the delightful Minoans, the first civilization on European soil. Its hot climate and lovely beaches make it a major holiday destination from early spring until October.

Crete's popularity is a tribute to its charms. Four mountain ranges lend it a dramatic grandeur out of all proportion to its size; the White Mountains hold the Gorge of Samariá, the longest canyon in Europe. Some 1,500 kinds of wild flowers brighten the landscape; vines, olive and citrus groves cover the coastal plains and hillside terraces; cereals, potatoes, pears, apples, walnuts and chestnuts come from the mountain plains; and greenhouses provide vegetables and fruit for the rest of Greece. Cretan art and architecture afford an equally rich feast: the fabled Minoan sites and art in Heráklion's superb museum; Byzantine churches glowing with frescoes and icons by the Cretan School; the Venetian and Turkish quarters of Chaniá and Réthymnon.

Although it may come as a surprise to holidaymakers who never budge from their resort hotels, Crete has the sharpest sense of identity of any Greek island, manifest in its own culture, dialect, music and dances, and in the works of its most famous sons, El Greco, Elefthérios Venizélos, Níkos Kazantzákis and Míkis Theodorákis. Old men in the villages still don breeches, high boots and black-fringed headbands. On feast days, people sing *matinádes* (improvised couplets) or *rizítika* ('songs from the roots') full of Cretan patriotism. And such patriotism is far from dead. Many young Cretans are taking an active role in preserving their traditions, even moving back up to their ancestral villages, where EU subsidies assure them a living from grandfather's olives.

How Crete is Divided

Lofty mountain ranges neatly divide the island into four sections. These have become modern Crete's political divisions and are used for reference in this book. West of the White Mountains is the *nomós* (province) of Chaniá; between the White Mountains and Psilorítis (Mount Ida) is the province of Réthymnon; between Psilorítis and the Lassíthi Mountains lies the province of Heráklion; and east of the Lassíthi Mountains is the province of Lassíthi, of which Ag. Nikólaos is the capital. This chapter describes Crete in a west-to-east order.

History

The first Cretans arrived from Asia Minor in *c.* 8000 BC. They worshipped fertility goddesses in caves, especially on mountains, and over the millennia they (probably aided by new arrivals from the Middle East) created Europe's first literate civilization, which Arthur Evans, who excavated Knossos, labelled **Minoan**. New dating techniques make the Minoans older than Evans thought; their **Pre-Palatial period** (coinciding with the Early Helladic) goes back to 2600–1900 BC, when they built the first tholos tombs and peak sanctuaries. By 2100 BC they were producing exquisite work in gold, semi-precious stones and sealstones, some bearing writing in ideograms.

The **Old Palace period** (1900–1700 BC) saw a hitherto unheard-of concentration of wealth in Crete. Power, too, was concentrated in the palaces of Knossos, Mália, Phaistos and Zákros, kitted out with the earliest plumbing and decorated with frescoes. Bulls played a major role in religion: the palaces were decorated with U-shaped 'horns of consecration' and several works of art, most notably the famous fresco in the Heráklion museum, showing Minoans grabbing bulls by the horns and vaulting over them. Another archetypal figure was the goddess, as mistress of wild animals and earth; as mistress of the underworld (holding a snake); and as mistress of the sky (with doves). Towns and palaces were unfortified, and traded extensively with Cyprus, Egypt and the Aegean islands. Writing was in ideograms, as on the Phaistos disc (*see* p.707). Paved roads linked settlements, plains were irrigated and art reached new heights. Then in 1700 BC an earthquake devastated everything.

Getting to Crete

By Air

Heráklion, and to a lesser extent Chaniá, are linked by UK **charters**. Major carriers Olympic and Aegean have frequent daily flights from Athens to Heráklion and Chaniá, several times a week from Thessaloníki. Both airlines also operate flights several times a week from Heráklion to Rhodes and Santoríni. Olympic has three flights a week from Athens to Sitía.

By Sea

Large comfortable **ferries** – among the finest in Greece – link Heráklion, Chaniá and Réthymnon to Piraeus daily, and sail fairly frequently to Ag. Nikólaos and Sitía. The 10–12-hour journey through the night isn't bad at all, especially with a cabin. There are daily ships in the summer from Santoríni, and frequently from the other Cycladic islands: others, sometimes calling at Ag. Nikólaos and Sitía, sail to Kárpathos, Kássos, and Rhodes; five times a week there are ferries from Thessaloníki and less frequently from Skýros and Skiáthos. Another twice weekly or so line links western Kastélli-Kíssamou with Kýthera, as well as with Gýthio and Kalamáta in the Peloponnese.

Crete in Myth: a Lot of Bull

As Cronos, the ruler of the world, had been warned that he would be usurped by his own child, he swallowed every baby his wife Rhea, daughter of the Earth, presented to him. After this had happened five times, Rhea determined on a different fate for her sixth child, Zeus. When he was born she smuggled him to Crete and gave Cronos a swaddled stone to swallow instead. She hid the baby in the Diktean Cave and set young Cretan warriors called Kouretes to guard him; they were ordered to shout and dance and beat their shields to drown out the baby's cries. And, as prophesied, Zeus grew up and dethroned his father by castrating him with a sickle.

When a Phoenician princess, Europa, caught Zeus' fancy, the god disguised himself as a beautiful bull and carried her off to Crete, where she bore him three sons: Minos, Rhadamanthys and Sarpedon, then gave her name to an entire continent. When Minos became the king of Crete at Knossos, he was asked to prove that his claim to the throne had divine sanction. Minos remembered the form his father had taken and asked Poseidon to send him a bull from the sea to sacrifice. Only the bull was so magnificent that Minos didn't kill it, but sent it to service his herds.

The kingdom of Minos prospered, exacting tribute from across the Mediterranean. But Poseidon, weary of waiting for the promised sacrifice, caused Minos' wife Pasiphaë to fall in love with the bull. Pasiphaë confided her problem to the inventor Daedalus, who constructed a hollow wooden cow covered with hide for her to enter. Their union resulted in the Minotaur, born with the head of a bull and the body of a man. Minos hid him in another invention of Daedalus, the Labyrinth, a maze of corridors under his palace, and fed it his enemies. Among these were seven maidens and seven youths from Athens, sent to Crete as tribute every nine years.

Two tributes had been paid when Theseus, the son of King Aegeus of Athens, demanded to be sent as one of the victims, and he was so handsome that Minos' daughter Ariadne fell in love with him. She asked Daedalus to help her save his life, and the inventor gave her a ball of thread. Unwinding the thread as he went, Theseus made his way into the labyrinth, slew the Minotaur with his bare hands and thanks to the thread escaped, taking Ariadne and the other Athenians with him.

Minos angrily threw Daedalus and his son Icarus into the Labyrinth. Although they found their way out, escape from Crete was impossible, as Minos controlled the seas. But Daedalus fashioned wings of feathers and wax for himself and Icarus, and off they flew. All went well until an exhilarated Icarus flew too close to the sun. His wings melted, and he plunged and drowned off the island that took his name.

In the **New Palace period** (1700–1450 BC) the Minoans rebuilt their palaces better than ever, as a warren of rooms lit by light wells, overlooking central and western courts. Wooden beams and columns were combined with stone to make them resistant to tremors. Workshops and store-rooms clustered nearby, their contents recorded on clay tablets in Linear A. Apart from the palaces, there were fancy villas, centralized farms, towns and ports. Minoan trade centres were established across the Aegean. They had weapons, although land defences were still non-existent.

The Heráklion museum is jammed full of the exuberant art of the period. The Minoans delighted in fluid, natural forms, and portrayed themselves with wasp waists and long black curls, the men clad in codpieces and loincloths, the women in breast-flaunting bodices, flounced skirts and exotic hats. Their culture spread to the mainland, now occupied by Greek speakers (the future Mycenaeans); the Minoans communicated with them in what seems to have been the lingua franca of the day, in Linear B – proto-ancient Greek.

But c. 1450 BC (or earlier) Santoríni blew its top (*see* p.664) and left Crete in ruins again; on the north coast a 20cm layer of ash was found – *under* structures belonging to the Late Minoan or **Post-Palace period** (1450–1100 BC). The old theory that the Mycenaeans took advantage of the disarray to invade Crete has lost favour before the idea of a long period of co-existence. Of the great palaces, Knossos alone was rebuilt, only to burn down once and for all in c. 1380 BC; in other places, such as Ag. Triáda, typical Mycenaean megarons were built. Linear B became the dominant script and the graceful motifs of the New Palace period became ever more stylized.

In the Aftermath: Dorians, Romans, Byzantines and Saracens

By 1100 BC, as Minoan-Mycenaean civilization ground to a halt, Dorians armed with the latest iron weapons invaded Greece, and then Crete (the **proto-Geometric period**, 1100–900 BC). The last Minoans, the Eteocretans or 'true Cretans', took to the hills; in Praisós they left inscriptions in the Greek alphabet, still waiting to be translated.

By the **Geometric period** (900–650 BC) Crete was divided into a hundred city-states, according to ancient sources. The Minoan goddess in her various aspects joined the Greek pantheon – Atana became Athena, Britomartis became Artemis, her son and consort Welchanos became Zeus. The first bronze statuettes attributed to 'Daedalos' appear, with wide eyes, thick hair and parted legs. The style reached its peak in the **Archaic period** (650–550 BC), but afterwards the Cretans seemed to go into hibernation and all but slept through the **Classical Age**. By the 2nd century BC the island's coasts were little more than pirates' bases, until Quintus Metellus Creticus subdued Crete for Rome (69–67 BC). With the Romans, the centre of power shifted south to Gortyn, the new capital of the Roman province of Crete and Cyrene (Libya). With peace, the population of Crete soared. Christianity arrived when St Paul appointed his Greek disciple, Titus, to found the first church at Gortyn in AD 58.

In 823, **Saracens** from North Africa conquered Crete. One lasting feature of their stay was the building of a castle at Heráklion, called Kandak ('deep moat'), or Candia, a name that became synonymous with Crete (and eventually with the honey and nuts it exported, hence 'candy'). In 961 the future emperor Nikephóros Phokás regained the island for Byzantium. Greek soldiers colonized the land; Emperor Aléxis Comnenus later sent his own son and other young aristocrats, establishing a ruling class.

Venetian and Ottoman Crete

With the conquest of Constantinople in 1204, Crete was awarded to Boniface of Montferrat. He sold it to the Venetians, who, after a brief tussle with Genoa, held it until 1669. At first faced with violent uprisings, often led by the Byzantine nobles, the

Orthodox and Catholics (some 10,000) somehow learned to live together in harmony, especially after the fall of Constantinople in 1453. As a refuge for Byzantine scholars and painters, Crete became a key point of contact with the Italian Renaissance, producing, most famously, Doméniko Theotokópoulos (El Greco). Cretan-Venetian schools and academies, architecture, theatre, literature, song and romantic epic poetry blossomed, culminating in the epic poem *Erotókritos* by Vicénzo Kornáros.

After several attempts, the Ottomans finally caught the island by surprise. In 1645, Sultan Ibrahim sent a fleet against the Knights on Malta. The Venetian commander at Kýthera sent word to allow the fleet safe passage; as the ships began to sail past, they turned their guns on the city. Chaniá and the rest of Crete soon fell – except for Heráklion, which held out until 1669, after a 21-year siege.

The most fertile lands were given to Turkish colonists, and many Cretans became crypto-Christians, publicly converting to Islam to avoid the punishing taxes that turned them into serfs. Those who could emigrated to the Venetian-held Ionian islands; those who couldn't revolted more than 400 times.

In 1898, Greece declared war on Turkey, and the Turks made the mistake of killing the British consul and 14 British soldiers in Heráklion. As British, French, Russian and Italian troops subdued the island, Prince George was appointed High Commissioner of an independent Crete. His imposition of a foreign administration led in 1905 to a revolt led by Elefthérios Venizélos. In 1909 Venizélos was appointed Prime Minister of Greece, and he secured Crete's union with Greece after the Balkan Wars in 1913.

The Battle of Crete

But Crete was to suffer one last invasion. As the Germans overran Greece, the government took refuge on Crete (23 April 1943), with 30,000 British and ANZAC troops. Crete's own battalions were trapped near Albania. But then again, no-one suspected what Goering had in store; after a week of bombing, Nazi paratroopers launched the world's first successful invasion by air on Crete on 20 May 1941. The Allies, along with hundreds of men, women and children, put up such resistance that the Germans had to expend their finest forces over the next 10 days – at the cost of 170 aircraft, 4,000 trained paratroopers, and their 7th airborne division. The later Cretan Resistance, aided by British agents, was legendary, especially the abduction of General Kreipe by Patrick Leigh Fermor and Billy Moss, who spirited Kreipe to Egypt.

Chaniá (XANIA)

Chaniá, Crete's second city (pop. 73,000), is the most seductive of the island's four capitals, with its Venetian, Turkish and neoclassical streets. Unfortunately, many buildings were lost in the Battle of Crete; fortunately, perhaps, the ruins stood neglected for so long that they've now been incorporated into unique garden settings for bars and restaurants. The inner and outer Venetian harbours become magnets in the evening, where dawdling over a drink can easily become addictive.

Buildings in the Kastélli quarter go back to 2200 BC, and archaeologists are sure that the Minoan palace and town, KY-DO-NI-JA, referred to on a Linear B tablet, lie under

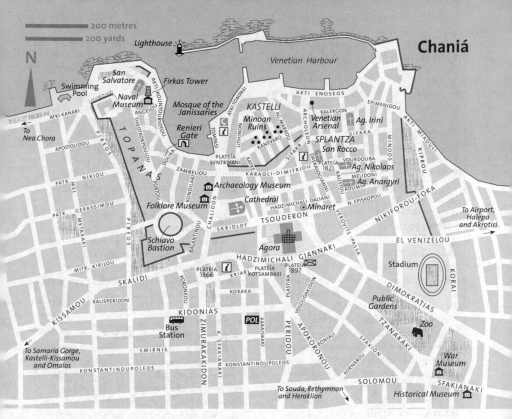

the modern town. In Greek, *kydóni* means quince, a fruit loved by the Minoans: the word (like 'hyacinth', 'labyrinth', and 'sandal') may well have come from their language.

Quince Town survived the rest of Cretan history to get a mention in Homer, to know glory days in the Hellenistic and Roman periods, then to decline so far that it was called 'Rubbish City'. Revived under the Venetians, it was so splendid that it became Crete's capital from 1850–1971, and it prospered as the fief of Elefthérios Venizélos.

Into Old Chaniá

The vortex of daily life in Chaniá is its covered market, the **Agora** (1911). Just west are **Skrídlof** Street, jam-packed with shops selling traditional leather goods, and Chalídon Street, Chaniá's jewellery-shop-lined funnel to the sea. At 21 Chalídon, the Gothic church of San Francesco contains Chaniá's excellent **Archaeological Museum** (*t 282 109 0334; open Tues–Sun 8.30–3; adm*). Its prize is a seal (*c. 1450 BC*) showing a Minoan mortal or god, standing over the sea as it breaks against the gates of a city. Other exhibits include a 3rd-century AD mosaic floor, the gold necklaces of Sossima, who perished in childbirth around the 3rd century BC, and Linear A and Linear B tablets.

Across the street, the sad-looking building with baby bubble domes is a Turkish bath, next to a square holding the **Trimartyr Cathedral**. In the 1850s a soap factory belonging to Mustafa Nily Pasha stood here; as a rare gesture of reconciliation he gave it to the Christians, plus the money to build a church. From here Chalídon Street flows into the crescent of the **outer port**, lined with handsome Venetian buildings.

Getting There and Around

By air: Chaniá's **airport** is on the Akrotíri peninsula, **t** 282 106 3264; a taxi to the centre is about €15. The Olympic Airways office is at 88 Stratigoú Tzanakáki, **t** 282 105 7700; buses from here coincide with Olympic flights. Aegean/Cronus is at the airport, reservations **t** 280 120 000, and in town at 12 El. Venizélou, **t** 282 105 1100.

By sea: **ferry** tickets from Soúda to Piraeus are available from ANEK (departs daily at 8pm) on El. Venizélou, in the market square, **t** 282 102 7500, and from Minoan (three times a week, at 7.45pm), also in the market square, **t** 282 104 5911. The nightly Piraeus–Chaniá ferry pulls in around 6am and is met by early-bird local buses. Every Tues am, Poseidon Lines call at Soúda on route to Cyprus and Israel. **Port authority: t** 282 104 3052.

By road: the **bus station** is at Kidonías, just west of central Plateía 1866. Buses travel at least once a day to all the larger villages of the province and there are hourly departures for Heráklion and Réthymnon, at least hourly along the Stalos/Ag. Marina/Platanías/Gerani route and almost as often to Kolimbári. For information call **t** 282 109 3052.

Tourist Information

Tourist police: 23 Iraklion St, **t** 282 105 3333.

Where to Stay

Chaniá ✉ 73100

Luxury
Villa Andromeda, 150 El. Venizélou, **t** 282 102 8300, **f** 282 102 8303, *villandro@otenet.gr* (*B*). Out east in the Halepa quarter, the former German consulate, divided into 8 suites; a lush garden, Turkish bath and pool.
Casa Delfino, 9 Theofánous, **t** 282 108 7400, **f** 282 109 6500, *casadel@cha.forthnet.gr*, *www.casadelfino.com* (*B*). Classy conversion of a 17th-century town house, with jacuzzis.

Expensive
The Contessa, 15 Theofánous, **t** 282 109 8566, **f** 282 109 8565 (*A*). Has the intimate air of an old-fashioned guesthouse, furnished in traditional style; book well in advance.
Doma, 124 El. Venizélou, **t** 282 105 1772, **f** 282 104 1578 (*B*). Comfortable rooms in a neo-classical mansion, decked out in antiques and Cretan rusticana. *Open Mar–Oct*.
Bozzali Studios, Gavaládon (a quiet lane off Sífaka), **t** 282 105 0824 (*A*). 15 elegant rooms in a lovingly restored house. *Open Mar–Nov*.
El Greco, 49 Theotokopoúlou, **t** 282 109 0432, **f** 282 109 1829, *hotel@elgreco.gr* (*B*). A pretty place draped in creeper, on Chaniá's prettiest street; book well in advance.

Moderate
Palazzo, 54 Theotokopoulou, **t** 282 109 3227, **f** 282 109 3229 (*A*). For those seeking divine inspiration, this is the place, with each room named after a god.
Pension Theresa, 8 Angélou, **t/f** 282 109 2798 (*B*). Charming rooms and studios oozing with character, and a tempting roof terrace in another restored Venetian house.

Inexpensive
Konaki, 43 Kondiláki, **t** 282 108 6379. Eight rooms in a quirky house – the two ground-floor ones are en suite and open on to the banana garden.
Kydonia, 20 Chalídon, **t** 282 107 4650. Well-designed doubles, triples and quads in a quiet courtyard next to the archaeological museum.
Meltémi, 2 Angélou, **t/f** 282 109 2802. Above the mellow *Meltémi* café, with big rooms, some of which have views. *Open all year*.
Stella, 10 Angélou, **t** 282 1073 756. Airy, traditional rooms with fridges and air-conditioning, perched above the eponymous boutique.

The neighbourhood west of the port, **Topanás**, has landmark status, although the interiors are now bars and restaurants. The **Fírkas Tower** at the far end saw the raising of the Greek flag over Crete in November 1913 in the presence of King Constantine and Prime Minister Venizélos and contains the **Naval Museum** (*t 282 109 1875; open*

Youth Hostel, 33 Drakonianoú, **t** 282 105 3565. Decent and quiet, on the edge of the city (take the Ag. Ioánnes bus, leaving every 15mins from in front of the market; no card necessary).

Camping Chaniá, Ag. Apóstoli, 5km west of town, **t** 282 103 1138, **f** 282 103 3371 (city bus from Platéia 1866). By the beach, with a pool and a bar, both of which can be noisy.

Eating Out

To Pigadi tou Tourkou, 1 Kalliníkou Sarpáki, **t** 282 105 4547 (€18–22). In the old Turkish quarter , with delightful, cooked-to-order specialities from Egypt, Lebanon and Tunisia.

Dino's, 3 Aktí Enóseos and Sarpidóna, **t** 282 104 1865 (€20–25). A long-time favourite overlooking the inner harbour, specializing in fish, but also has a selection of meat dishes.

Aeriko, Aktí Miaoúli, **t** 282 105 9307 (€18–20). A good choice and considerably cheaper than the above, with some seafood on the menu and chicken on a spit.

Tholos, 36 Ag. Déka, **t** 282 104 6725 (€18–20). Excellent Greek specialities in the ruins of a Venetian mansion.

Monastiri, **t** 282 105 5527 (€20), behind the Mosque of the Janissaries. Serves fresh fish, traditional Cretan dishes and barrelled wine and frequented by ex-prime ministers.

Mirovolos, 19 Zambelíou, **t** 282 109 1960 (€18–22). In the lovely courtyard of a Venetian building from 1290, featuring ample well-prepared dishes and Cretan dancing to live music.

Tamam, 49 Zambelioú, **t** 282 109 6080. Located in an old Turkish hammam and offers a variety of vegetarian dishes including courgette rissoles and *dákos* with olives and spices.

Akrogiali, 19 Akti Papanikoli, **t** 282 107 3110 (€12–15). Grab a taxi for excellent seafood at low prices.

Nikterida, 7km east at Korakiés on the Akrotíri peninsula, **t** 282 106 4215 (around €12 per person). One of Crete's best tavernas: Chaniots have headed up here since 1938. Lively music and dancing on Saturday nights; book well in advance. *Closed Sun*.

Bars and Nightlife

Chaniá is delightful after dark, just for strolling. The inner harbour, especially around Sarpidóna with its bars, is also inner fashionwise:

Neorion, Sarpidóna. Very trendy, popular with the young Chaniots.

Trilogy, 16a Radamánthous, by the northeast bastion. Chaniá post-modern design.

Synagogi, Atmospheric bar housed in the old Jewish baths.

Ideon Andron, 26 Chálidon. Classical or jazz records in a pretty inner courtyard.

Tsikoudadiko, 31 Zambelioú. For a more distinctly Cretan experience; *rakí* and excellent *mezédes*.

Fortetza, by the lighthouse. A music bar with its own shuttle boat to ferry punters about .

Music and Clubs

Kriti, 22 Kallergón. A hole-in-the-wall local institution; from 8.30pm there's Cretan music for the price of a *rakí* and *mezé*.

The Face, nearby at 12 Kallergón. The newest and reputedly the best club in town.

Fedra, 7 Isóderon, **t** 282 104 0789. Offers blues and jazz.

Volcano, 6 Soúrmeli by the outer harbour. Air-conditioned club in an old Venetian building with a 26ft-high ceiling; music alternates between Greek pop and commercial techno.

Street, 51 Aktí Koundourioti, **t** 282 107 4960. Another very popular music bar, one of the oldest in Chaniá, with a DJ after midnight. The same people own the nearby Bora Bora.

Ekentro Club, 16 Soúrmeli. Plays everything from hip-hop to trance.

NRG, Schiavo Bastion, www.otenet.gr/nrgclub. The only big club in town; bass-pounding techno beats and celebrity DJs.

Tues–Sun 10–4; adm). Crete, naturally, is the focus; there are photos, models of Venetian galleys and fortifications, and mock-ups of key Greek naval victories through the ages. The first floor has evocative photographs from the Battle of Crete.

Behind the tower, the church of **San Salvatore** belonged to the Franciscans and, like most in Chaniá, was converted into a mosque. Near here begins **Theotokopoúlou Street**, Chaniá's prettiest, lined with Venetian houses; the **Byzantine Museum** at No. 78 (*open Tues–Sat 8.30–3; adm*) has Cretan icons, pottery, coins and mosaics. Further south stood the Jewish ghetto, with a dilapidated synagogue on Kondiláki Street; in 1944 the Germans herded its last 400 residents onto a ship that would never be seen again. At the top of Kondiláki, along Portoú Lane, are Chaniá's **walls**. In 1538, after Barbarossa devastated Réthymnon, the Venetians had fortifications wizard Michele Sammicheli surround Chaniá with walls and an enormous moat, 147ft wide and 28ft deep; yet in 1645, the Turks captured the city in two months.

The **east end** of the outer port has Chaniá's landmarks: a graceful Venetian **lighthouse** and the **Mosque of the Janissaries** (1645), crowned with ostrich- and chicken-egg domes. Here the Christian-born slave troops of the Ottoman empire worshipped, although it did little to improve their character; not only did they terrorize the Greeks, but in 1690 they murdered the Pasha of Chaniá and fed his body to the dogs. In 1812, the Sublime Porte had had enough and sent Hadji Osman Pasha, 'the Throttler', to Crete to hang the lot of them, an act that so impressed the Greeks that rumours flew around that 'the Throttler' must be a crypto-Christian.

Behind the mosque, the **Kastélli** quarter embraces the inner harbour. **Excavations** along Kaneváro Street revealed a complex of Minoan buildings, most with two storeys, flagstoned floors and grand entrances; the discovery of Linear A and B tablets suggest the proximity of a palace. Kastélli took the brunt of the Luftwaffe bombs, but on the top of Ag. Markoú are the ruins of the Venetian cathedral, and below rise seven of the original 17 vaults of the **Venetian Arsenal** (1600).

Just east of Kastélli is **Splántza**, or the Turkish quarter. Interesting churches are concentrated here, such as the underground **Ag. Iríni** from the 15th century, in Roúgia Square. South in Vourdouba Street, near a huge plane tree, the 14th-century church of **Ag. Nikólaos** was converted into an imperial mosque to shelter a magical healing sword (still there). Note the *tugra*, or Sultan's stylized thumbprint, on the entrance and the minaret–campanile. The little **Mosque of Ahmet Aga** still stands in Hadzimichali Daliáni Street, while to the east 16th-century **Ag. Anargyri**, in Koumi Street, was the only functioning Orthodox church in Chaniá during the Venetian and most of the Turkish period. Venetian walls survive along Minos Street, on what remains of the Koum Kapissi bastion. Just outside them, the now fashionable **Koum Kapi quarter** was first settled by Bedouins, during a brief period (1831–40) when Egypt's Mehmet Ali was the Sultan's surrogate in Crete.

Chaniá's Newer Quarters and Beaches

From the covered market, Tzanakáki Street leads southeast to the shady **Public Gardens**, with a small zoo and outdoor cinema, often showing films in English. On the corner of Tzanakáki and Sfakianáki, the **War Museum** (*open Tues–Sat 9–1*) chronicles the islanders' remarkable battle history, with photos and weapons. In Plateía Venizélos to the east stands the house of Venizélos, the government palace built for Prince George (now the court-house), and a Russian Orthodox church donated by the mother of a former governor. Further east, by the sea, is the fancy **Halepa** quarter, dotted with neoclassical mansions and ex-consulates from Crete's years of autonomy.

The town beach, **Néa Chorá**, is a 15-minute walk west of the Fírkas tower. Although sandy and safe for children, it's not very attractive. The beaches improve to the west; city buses from Plateía 1866 go as far as lovely sandy **Oasis Beach** and **Kalamáki**.

Chaniá Province

Chaniá Province is the land of the White Mountains, which hit the sky at 8,041ft and are sliced down the middle by the magnificent Gorge of Samariá, the classic day-walk that emerges by the Libyan Sea. The best sands are on the far west coast, from Falassarná to the lagoon of Elafonísi, a tropical beauty only a 15-minute drive from chestnut forests. In between the mountains and sea you'll find orange groves, olives, vineyards and cypresses, Byzantine churches and landscapes more Tuscan than Greek.

South of Chaniá: Venizélos and Citrus Villages

South of Chaniá, the rugged 18km **Thérisson Gorge** saw the Revolution of Therisso in 1905, led by Venizélos in response to the reactionary policies of Prince George.

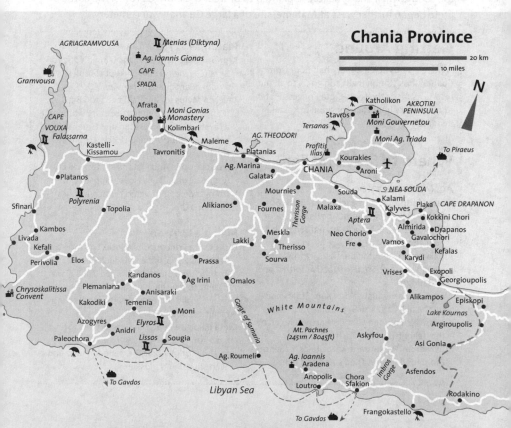

Venizélos was born nearby, in sleepy **Mourniés**, and served as Greek prime minister most of the time between 1910 and 1932. Before he was born, his mother dreamed that he would liberate Crete and named him Elefthérios ('Freedom').

The best oranges in Crete grow in the lush Keríti valley south of Chaniá. Near **Alikianós**, just off the main Chaniá–Omalós road, a memorial honours the Cretans who kept on fighting here, unaware that the Allies were in retreat; their ignorance enabled the majority of British and ANZAC troops to be evacuated from the Libyan coast. The wedding massacre of Kantanoléo's Cretans (*see* opposite) took place at Alikianós' ruined Venetian tower; next to the tower, the little church of **Ag. Geórgios** (1243) has exceptional frescoes, painted in 1430 by Pávlos Provatás.

Chaniá to Cape Spáda

Not a single hotel existed along this coast when a rain of white parachutes fell on 20 May 1941. Few signs of the battle remain, although 2km west of Chaniá stands the monument of the diving eagle, known locally as the **Kakó Poulí**, or 'Bad Bird', the German memorial to the 2nd Parachute Regiment. Just beyond, the beach strip of **Káto Stálos** merges with that of **Ag. Marína**, looking out over **Ag. Theódori** islet with a gaping cave. Just west, **Plataniás** has two faces: an old village above and a resort by the sandy beach and cane forest, planted to protect the orange groves. The Battle of Crete began further west at **Máleme**; site of a large German war cemetery.

Getting Around

There's a **bus** at least every half hour from Chaniá's bus station (**t** 282 109 3052) to all the resorts as far as the Louis Creta Princess Hotel; roughly every hour they continue to Kastélli-Kíssamou.

Where to Stay and Eat

Ag. Marína ✉ 73100
Santa Marina, on the beach, **t** 282 106 8460, **f** 282 106 8571, *info@santamarina-hotels.gr* (*B; expensive*). Set in a lovely garden with a pool and gym.
Alexia Beach, near the beach, **t** 282 106 8110 (*C; inexpensive*). Small, attractive, with a pool and fridges.
Alector's Rooms, just east in Káto Stalós and up the hill, **t** 282 106 8755 (*moderate–inexpensive*). A garden villa, immaculately run by the delightful Helen Zachariou.
Stavrodromi Restaurant, Káto Stalós, **t** 282 106 8104. For delicious fried squid and fish.

Plataniás ✉ 73014
Kronos Apartments, **t** 282 106 8630, **f** 282 106 8574 (*C; expensive*). Well-kept complex, with a pool near the sea. *Open April–Oct.*
Taverna Mylos (or Keratas), **t** 282 106 8578 (€20–25). Converted 15th-century water mill; a lovely place with Cretan and Greek spit-roasted meats where desserts are always on the house.
Haroupia, up in Áno Plataniás, **t** 282 106 8603 (€15). Not only enjoys lovely sunset views from its creeper covered terrace, but has delicious Cretan food.

Máleme ✉ 73100
Louis Creta Princess Club Hotel, **t** 282 106 2702, **f** 282 106 2406, *maleme-beach@cha. forthnet.gr* (*A; luxury*). Shaped like a giant trident to give each of its 414 rooms a sea view. Family-orientated, plus windsurfing facilities. *Open April–Oct.*
Creta Paradise Beach, in Geráni, **t** 282 106 1315, **f** 282 106 1134, *cretpar@sail.vacation. forthnet.gr* (*A; luxury*). Opened in 1992 and even slicker and glossier.

At the foot of rugged Cape Spáda, just before the road to Kastélli splits into old and new, **Kolimbári** has a beach of smooth pebbles and, a short walk north, the most important monastery in western Crete. **Moní Gonías** (*open Sun–Fri 8–12.30 and 4–8, Sat 4–8*) was founded in 1618 by hermits, who clubbed together and built a walled monastery over a sandy cove (*gonías*). The monks were often besieged by the Turks; a cannon ball fired in 1866 is embedded in the seaward wall. The church contains a fine gilt iconostasis and a *Last Judgement* painted on wood. From here, the road veers dizzyingly up the coast of Cape Spáda to **Afráta**; you can follow the unpaved track north with a jeep to **Diktyna**, where an unexcavated shrine to Artemis dates back to the Minoans and remained in business until the end of the Roman empire.

Kastélli-Kíssamou and the West Coast

West of Cape Spáda, the coastal plain and knobbly hills are swathed with olives and vineyards: the difference between its lush greenery and the arid hills of Crete's far east couldn't be more striking. The wild western coast offers not only some of Crete's loveliest beaches, but also a chance to find a lonesome strand of your very own, while the slopes above are covered with dense chestnut forests.

Kastélli-Kíssamou (ΚΑΣΤΕΛΛΙ ΚΙΣΣΑΜΟΥ)

A working wine town, Kastélli-Kíssamou is set in a deep, rectangular gulf, lined by a long beach. Its name recalls its predecessor Kissamos, the port of ancient Polyrenia. Excavations behind the health centre unearthed a lovely mosaic floor from the 2nd century AD; an **archaeological museum** is being arranged in the Venetian commandery. In 1550 the Venetians dismantled Kissamos' temple and theatre to build a castle – hence Kastélli. It has a melodramatic history: when the Cretan Kaptános Kantanoléo captured it, the Venetians pretended to recognize Kantanoléo's authority and offered a highborn Venetian girl as his son's bride. At the wedding the Cretans were given drugged wine, and the Venetians slit their throats and took Kastélli back.

Eight kilometres south of Kastélli, **Polyrénia** on a natural balcony is as old-fashioned as a Cretan village can get, but is even older than it looks. Founded in the 8th century BC by Dorians from the Peloponnese, Polyrénia survived the Romans with the attitude that if you can't beat 'em, join them: a Roman tower of older bits and bobs stands at the village entrance, and up on the acropolis stands the massive base of a 4th-century temple and altar of dressed stone, now supporting a church.

Way Out West

Crete's west coast is starkly outlined by mountains plunging into the sea. They give way to a plain of plastic tomato tunnels and beautiful sandy beaches at **Falassarná**, 15km from Kastélli. North of the beach at Koutrí stood **ancient Falassarná**, Polyrénia's bitter rival. You can measure how much western Crete has risen – Falassarná's port, with its defence towers, is now 200m from the sea. Further up, there's a bathhouse and a **stone throne** from Hellenistic times; it may have been dedicated to Poseidon.

Getting Around

Kastélli's **port** (2km from the centre) has regular ANEN **ferries** with: Kalamáta, Gýthio, Monemvassía and Neápolis in the the Peloponnese, plus two weekly sailings to Piraeus and three to Kýthera and Antikýthera, **t** 282 102 4148, **f** 282 102 8200, *www.anen.gr*; tickets from Xyroukákis in Kastélli, **t** 282 202 2655, or Omalós Tours, Plateía 1866, Chaniá, **t** 282 109 7119.

Buses from Kastélli: three a week (*Mon, Wed, Fri*) to Polyrénia, three a day to Falassarná, five to Chóra Sfakíon, six to Paleochóra, three to Omalós and one morning bus to Chrysoskalítissa and Elafonísi. Note, too, that there is a daily direct bus to Elafonísi from Chaniá at 7.30am.

Where to Stay and Eat

Kastélli ✉ 73400
Galini Beach, at the far end of the beach, **t** 282 202 3288, *info@galinibeach.com, www.galini beach.com* (*inexpensive*). Quiet rooms and organic breakfasts from their own farm.
Coco Beach Camping, just before Kastélli on the main road from Chaniá, **t** 282 402 2940, *katntagk@otenet.gr*. Plenty of facilities, including those for the disabled.
Plaka, **t** 282 202 3322. Set back in a garden by the beach, a favourite for lunch and has live Cretan and Greek music twice a week.

Stimadóris, at the west end of town, **t** 282 202 2057. Fresh fish caught by the owners and a tasty pickled red seaweed salad. *Open eves and lunch in summer.*

Falassarná ✉ 73400
New buildings with flats or rooms have sprouted up higgledy piggledy like toadstools: **SunSet Rooms and Studios**, **t** 282 204 1204. Right on the beach, with a good taverna.
Romantica, **t** summer: 282 204 1089 winter: **t** 282 109 4710 (*moderate*). Small apartments for 4–5, verandas with sea views.
Aqua Marine, **t** 282 204 1414, *aquamarine@ kissamos.net* (*moderate–inexpensive*). New and spotless, all rooms en suite.
Plakures, **t** 282 204 1581. Good for a splurge, serving Greek and Cretan specialities.
Kalabriani, 5km west of Kissamos, **t** 282 202 3204. Set on a beautiful terrace overlooking the sea, serving excellent food; also rooms.

Élos ✉ 73400
Mília, in Vlátos Kissámou, **t/f** 282 205 1569 (*moderate*). Experience the rural Crete of centuries past. Stone dwellings in a chestnut forest hamlet; rooms furnished with antiques, heated by wood stoves and lit by candles. Also delicious organic food, mostly produced on site. *Open all year.*
Kastanofolia, **t** 282 206 1258. 10 bright and spacious rooms to rent.
Filoxenia, **t** 282 206 1322. A favourite with the locals for *mezédes*.

From Kastélli you can hire a caique to sail around wild **Cape Voúxa** (with a gorgeous beach) to the harbour of **Gramvoúsa**, an islet topped by a Venetian fortress. Like Néa Soúda and Spinalonga to the east, it held out against the Turks until the 18th century, when the Venetians gave up hope of reconquering Crete. The Renaissance church is intact and the huge reservoirs, unused for 250 years, are full to the brim.

Down to Elafonísi and the Chestnut Villages

South of Falassarná, the partially paved but easy coastal road takes in spectacular scenery over the sea. There are a couple of beach chances, at **Sfinári** and **Kámbos**, where a 3km track leads down through a ravine to the wild sandy beach of **Livádia**. Towards the Libyan Sea, a sheer rock supports the **convent of Chrysoskalítissa**, 'Our Lady of the Golden Stair' (*open 7am–8pm*). Only persons without sin can see which of the 90 steps is made of gold; a rather more prosaic version says that the Patriarch ordered the convent to sell off the golden step in the 15th century to pay off his debts. Another 5km southwest, you can wade to the islet of **Elafonísi** and its beaches through a shallow, almost tropical lagoon that comes in a spectrum of turquoise, blue and violet, rimmed by pink sand. Children love it. Although a little less virgin every year, it has so far managed to hold off the advances of the big resort hotels.

Rather than backtrack along the coast, consider returning north by way of Crete's chestnut country, where the lush mountains are reminiscent of Corsica. One village, **Kefáli**, has magnificent sea views and fine frescoes in its church, **Metamórphosis tou Sotírou** (1320), located down a track: note the English graffiti from 1553. **Élos**, the largest village, is set amid plane and chestnut trees, and has rooms to stay.

The Southwest: Paleochóra and the Sélino

The White Mountains only let a few roads breach their rocky fastness. Those to the southwest run into the Eparchy of Sélino, where Paleochóra is the star attraction, along with a score of decorated medieval churches, especially around Kándanos. Most are locked, but asking in the nearest *kafeneíon* may produce an 'Open Sesame'.

From Tavronítis to Kándanos to Paleochóra

Of the three roads that wriggle down to the Sélino, the main one from Tavronítis gets the most takers. En route lies lush **Kándanos** with the highest rainfall in Crete.

Getting Around

Paleochóra is served by five **buses** a day from Chaniá. **Small boats** leave Paleochóra for Gávdos three times a week; on Fri and Sun a larger boat sails from Paleochóra to Soúgia, Ag. Roúmeli and Gávdos. Other boats leave Paleochóra for Chóra Sfakíon, Loutró, Soúgia, Pachiá Ámmos Beach and Elafónisos. **Port authority**: t 282 304 1214.

Two **buses** run daily between Chaniá and Soúgia; Soúgia is also linked daily by **boat** to Ag. Roúmeli when the Gorge of Samariá is open.

Tourist Information

Paleochóra: El. Venizélos, t 282 304 1507; *open 10–1 and 6–9, closed Tues.*

Where to Stay and Eat

Paleochóra ✉ 73001

Elman, on the sandy beach, t/f 282 304 1412 (*B; expensive*). Big, modern, with apartments. *Open all year.*

Efthisis Sfinarolákis, t 282 304 1594 or 282 304 1596 (*expensive*). Classy studios and apartments.

Aris, t 282 304 1502, f 282 304 1546, *Arishotel@ cha.forthnet.gr* (*B; moderate*). A good bet, 800m from the sandy beach.

Ostria, in the middle of the sandy beach, t 282 304 1055. Inexpensive rooms and a taverna with Greek dancing on Thursday nights.

Paleochóra Campsite, by the pebble beach, t 282 304 1120. Simple with shade. Good cheap breakfasts next door. but the club opposite can make evenings noisy.

Pizzeria Niki, in the centre. Good, fresh and cheap pizzas, with some seating outside.

The Third Eye, by the sandy beach, t 282 304 1055 (€12). For spicy Asian and Mexican specialities. They also serve fish.

Soúgia ✉ 73009

Santa Irene, t 282 305 1181, f 282 305 1182 (*moderate*). A small and friendly complex of apartments and rooms, with a breakfast bar.

Lissos, t 282 305 1244. Pleasant, inexpensive rooms, all with fridges and air-conditioning.

Liviko, on the waterfront. Popular and serves excellent Greek favourites; try the delicious stuffed courgette flowers. Live music nightly.

Although inhabited since Roman times, nothing here is over 50 years old; in the Battle of Crete the people defended themselves with such ferocity that the Germans retreated, only to return with reinforcements the next day, shooting everyone and burning the town to the ground.

Five Byzantine churches lie within the next three or four kilometres on the road to **Anisaráki**; **Taxiárchos Michaíl**, near Koufalotó, was frescoed in 1327 by the excellent Ioánnis Pagoménos. Anisaráki itself has three 14th-century frescoed churches, as well as **Ag. Anna** from the 1460s; the dedication is intact, and among the pictures is a fine one of St Anne nursing baby Mary and St George on horseback. Just south of Kándanos, in **Plemanianá**, **Ag. Geórgios** has frescoes of the *Last Judgement* from 1410.

Further south is the town the Venetians called Castello Selino, the Bride of the Libyan Sea. The Greeks call it simply Old Town, or Paleochóra, a pleasant place straddling two beaches – one stony, the other sandy, with superb windsurfing. On the tip of the peninsula, the Venetians built the Castello Selino in 1279 to police the ornery locals; now only empty walls defend the poppies that fill it every April. There are quieter beaches to the west; the nearby greenhouses keep them off the postcards.

Unspoiled mountain villages wait nearby. Pretty **Ánidri** is home to Ag. Geórgios, frescoed by Pagoménos in 1323. In the same direction, towards Soúgia, **Azogyrés** offers green surroundings and gurgling streams, a fascinating one-room **historical museum** (*ask for Mr Prokopi, the keyholder*) and one of Crete's rare **evergreen plane trees**, growing next to the 19th-century cliff-side chapel of the Ag. Páteres: it has a charming iconostasis, carved by a local Douanier Rousseau (Mr Prokopi has the key).

Europe at its Southernmost: Gávdos

If you suffer from *mal de civilisation*, catch one of the small ferries from Paleochóra or Chóra Sfakíon that sail to the islet of **Gávdos**, at 35°10' the southernmost point in Europe. The current population is around 55. Beware that it can get hot, and that the unpredictable sea can easily make your stay longer than you intended. Out of season ferries are so irregular that you'll have to stick around Chóra Sfakíon and wait for one to appear. Renting a moped to take with you isn't a bad idea, as none are available on Gávdos. There are beaches, especially sandy **Sarakiníkos** with a few rooms and tavernas (a 40min walk north of the port). A pierced rock, **Tripití** or 'Three Holes', marks the southern end of Europe.

Along the Road from Chaniá to Soúgia

It's an hour's caique ride from Paleochóra to Soúgia, but if you're coming from Chaniá the road branching at Alikianós is quicker. It ascends the west edge of the Omalós plateau to **Ag. Iríni**, a village immersed in trees at the top of a beautiful, walkable 8km gorge, to Soúgia (the Chaniá tourist office has a map). South of Ag. Iríni, the walls of ancient **Elyros**, one of the most pugnacious Dorian settlements on Crete, lie scattered, unexcavated; the church of the Panagía sits on top of a temple, re-using its mosaic floor. Four km west, **Teménia** has a photogenic old church, the Sotír, and the double Cyclopean walls of another ancient city, **Irtakína**. Further along, **Moní** has a church, Ag. Nikólaos, frescoed by the indefatigable Ioánnis Pagómeno.

Soúgia is a higgledy-piggledy wannabe resort endowed with a long pebble beach. The port of Elyros, its ancient name was Syia or 'pig town' for the porkers it raised, when the region was covered with oak forests; to this day the nude beach is known rather unflatteringly as the 'Bay of Pigs'. There are ruins from Syia's Roman past, and a 6th-century mosaic floor, re-used in the church. Another church, **Ag. Antónios** (1382), has frescoes, and a nearby cave, **Spyliara**, is another Cyclops candidate.

From Soúgia you can sail or make a pretty 1½hr walk to **Lissós**. In ancient times renowned for its medicinal springs, its Asklepeion (3rd century BC) was so successful that it could afford to mint gold coins. The sanctuary has a fine mosaic floor and a pit for sacred snakes. The population of Lissós is exactly one: the caretaker, who watches over the theatre, baths and two basilicas with mosaic floors, rebuilt in the 1200s.

The Gorge of Samariá (ΦΑΡΑΓΓΙ ΣΑΜΑΡΙΑΣ)

The single most spectacular stretch of Crete is squeezed into the 18km Gorge of Samariá, the longest in Europe and home to rare fauna and flora, especially rare chasm-loving plants (*chasmopphytes*), *kri-kri* goats (but you'd be lucky to see one), Griffon vultures, Lammergeiers, buzzards and eagles. It takes most people between 5

Getting Around

Buses leave Chaniá for Omalós at 6.15, 7.30 and 8.30am and at 4.30pm; from Kastélli-Kíssamou at 5, 6 and 7 in the morning and Réthymnon at 6.15 and 7 in the morning. **Tour buses** leave almost as early (you can, however, get a slight jump on the crowds by staying in Omalós). Once through the gorge, **boats** from Ag. Roúmeli will take you to Chóra Sfakíon, Soúgia and Paleochóra, where buses retun to the north coast (5.30, 6 and 7pm for Réthymnon). Consider paying the bit extra for a tour bus, to make sure you have a seat on the return journey.

Practicalities

The gorge is open from 6am to 4pm when weather permits, usually around the beginning of May to 31 Oct, during which time the water is low enough to ensure safe fording of the streams. Staff of the National Forest Service patrol the area. Although last admission to the gorge is at 3pm, almost everyone starts much earlier, to avoid the midday heat and to make the excursion a single day's round-trip outing. It is **absolutely essential** to wear good walking shoes and socks; a hat and

a bite to eat are only slightly less vital, and binoculars are a bonus. Dressing appropriately is difficult: it's chilly at Omalós and sizzling at Ag. Roúmeli. Remove rings in case your hands swell. Streams along the gorge provide drinking water at regular intervals, unless dry; take water in case. Mules and a helicopter landing pad are on hand for emergency exits; tickets are date-stamped and must be turned in at the lower gate, to make sure no one is lost. A less strenuous (and less rewarding) alternative is walking an hour up from Ag. Roúmeli to the Sideróportes. **Information**, t 282 106 7179.

Where to Stay and Eat

Omalós ✉ 73005
Neos Omalós, t 282 106 7590, f 282 106 7190 (*C; inexpensive*). Recently built, central heating, bar and restaurant. *Open all year.*
To Exari, t 282 106 7180, f 282 106 7124 (*C; inexpensive*). A bit larger and almost as nice.

Ag. Roúmeli ✉ 73011
Ag. Roúmeli, t 282 509 1241 (*C; inexpensive*). Rooms and a restaurant. *Open Mar–Oct.*
Tara, t 282 509 1231. Similar.

and 8 hours to walk from Omalós south to Ag. Roúmeli on the Libyan Sea, and twice as long if they're very fit, or crazy, and walk up. Not a few return from Samariá having only seen their own feet and the back of the person in front. Staying in Ag. Roúmeli may be the answer, by allowing you more time to enjoy the gorge.

Just getting there is part of the fun. On the early buses, dawn usually breaks just as you reach the most vertiginous section of the road as it climbs 3,937ft before descending to the Omalós Plateau, no shorty itself at 3,543ft. Snows from the fairy circle of White Mountains often flood it, but its one village, **Omalós**, manages to stay dry. The Samariá **Tourist Pavilion**, a few kilometres south, hangs over the edge of the chasm, overlooking the limestone face of 6,834ft Mount Gýnglios. Just after dawn, the first people of the day begin to trickle down the **Xylóskalo**, a stone path with a wooden railing. The name Samariá derives from Ossa Maria, a chapel (1379) and village halfway down the gorge, now used as the guardians' station and picnic ground. Towards the end rise the **Sideróportes** ('iron gates'), where the sheer walls rise almost 1,000ft on either side of a passage only 9ft wide. Beyond is old **Ag. Roúmeli**, abandoned after a torrent swept through in 1954. Recently, some of the empty houses are now stalls selling Greece's priciest cold drinks. When tourists began to appear in the 1960s, a **new Ag. Roúmeli** obligingly rose out of the cement mixer like a phoenix (toadstool is more apt), another blistering 2km away, on the coast. This new Ag. Rouméli is built over ancient Tarra, where Apollo hid from the wrath of Zeus right after slaying Python at Delphi. Here he fell so in love with a nymph that he forgot to make the sun rise and got into an even bigger jam. A sanctuary of Tarranean Apollo marked the spot, now under a church built by the Venetians.

East of Chaniá: Akrotíri (ΑΚΡΩΤΗΡΙ)

Akrotíri, the busiest of Chaniá's three headlands, shelters the island's safest port, Soúda. Its strategic position has assured it plenty of history and, now that Crete is safe from imminent invasion, the access road (Eleftheríou Venizélou) from Chaniá's Halepa quarter is often chocked with locals heading out to Akrotíri's beaches, clubs and villas. Outside these suburban tentacles, Akrotíri is a moody place, dusty and junky with military zones towards the airport, lonely and wild around its monasteries.

First stop should be **Profítis Ilías** church (4.5km from Chaniá), Crete's **memorial to Elefthérios Venizélos** (1864–1936) and his son Sophoklís (1896–1964), who both asked to be buried here to look over Chaniá for eternity. But they had patriotic reasons as well: in 1897, Profítis Ilías was a Revolutionary Military Camp, located just within the Great Powers' 6km exclusion zone around Chaniá. To rout out the Greeks, the British, French, Italian and Russian navies bombarded it. The admirals were so impressed by the Cretans, who held up the Greek flag with their bare hands after it was shot off its pole, that they stopped and applauded. Afterwards a Russian bomb destroyed the monastery, but Elijah (Ilías) got his revenge when the Russian ship was blown up the next day. When the news reached Europe that the Powers had bombed brave Christians, it caused such a stir that it led the Allies to offer Crete its autonomy.

Where to Stay and Eat

Akrotíri's first seaside playgrounds are **Kalathás** and **Tersanás**, rimmed with villas. **Stavrós**, further north, has a lovely circular bay with shallow water; it was used for the beach scenes in the film of *Zorba the Greek*. East of Stavrós, immaculate olive groves and a tree-lined avenue announce **Moní Ag. Triáda**, or Tzagaróliou (*open officially 6–2 and 5–7; adm*). The cruciform church has an austere, colonnaded Venetian façade, and in the narthex an inscription in Greek and Latin tells how Ag. Triáda was refounded in 1634 by Jeremiah Zangarola, a Venetian who became an Orthodox monk. Tangerine trees scent the courtyard and a museum contains a 17th-century *Last Judgement*.

A second monastery, fortified **Moní Gouvernétou** (*open 7–2 and 4–8; adm*), stands on a remote plateau, 5km above Ag. Triáda along a narrow road that just squeezes through the rocky terrain. Gouvernétou played a major role in reconciling Cretans and Venetians at the end of the 16th century; the grotesque heads on the portal, blasted by the sun and wind, are Venetian fancies far from home. Below Gouvernétou are two older, fascinating places. An easy path leads in 10 minutes to the ruins of a hermitage by the cave named **Arkoudiótissa** ('Bear') after a bear-shaped stalagmite, worshipped since pre-Minoan times in the cult of the Mistress of the Wild Animals. The stone bear leans over a cistern, filled by dripping stalactites. A corner in the cave has a small 16th-century chapel dedicated to Panagía Arkoudiótissa, 'Our Lady of the Bear'.

From here the path continues down steeply 20 minutes or so, past a rock shaped like a boat (a pirate ship petrified by the Virgin) to the **Cave of St John the Hermit**. This John sailed from Egypt to Crete, founded a score of monasteries and retired here, becoming so stooped from his poor diet of roots that a hunter shot him, mistaking him for an animal (7 October 1042 – the anniversary still brings crowds of pilgrims). In this wild ravine, he gouged a monastery into the precipice, straddled by a stone bridge. Anchorites lived here until 17th-century pirates made it unsafe. A path descends to a delightful swimming nook, where you postpone the walk back up.

Soúda and Cape Drápanon, Vrises, Georgioúpolis, Lake Kournás and Around

Greater Chaniá trickles scrubbily along the road to **Soúda**, its port, tucked in the magnificent bay, bedecked with naval bases. Signs point the way to the immaculate seaside **Commonwealth War Cemetery**, where 1,497 British and ANZAC troops lie,

Where to Stay and Eat

Kalýves/Almirída ✉ 73003

Kalives Beach, in Kalýves, t 282 503 1285, f 282 503 1134 (*B; expensive*). The pick of the hotels.

Koumos Taverna, in the hills just above Kalyves, t 282 503 2257. A fascinating oddity built by an imaginative stonemason over 13 years, with lots of eccentricities.

Almyrida, on the sea, t 282 503 2128, f 282 503 2139, *Almyrida_beach@internet.gr* (*B, expensive–moderate*). With an indoor pool.

Dimitra, t 282 503 1956, f 282 503 1995 (*A; expensive*). Another stylish hotel, with pool, bar and tennis.

The Enchanted Owl, t 282 503 2494. The English owners serve dishes (Mexican, Indian or Italian) not offered by their Greek neighbours, and roast dinners every Sunday.

Vámos

Vámos S.A. Pensions, t/f 282 502 3100 (*expensive*). A cooperative run by locals, who have converted old stone olive presses and stables into traditional-style accommodation with a kitchen and living room. *Open all year.* In addition, they organize walks to caves and monasteries nearby and offer lessons in Greek dancing, cooking, language, ceramic making and icon painting. They also run the taverna **I Sterna tou Bloumosofi** (around €20–25), serving Cretan specialities baked in the wood oven, plus wine from its own barrels in the cellar.

Georgioúpolis ✉ 73007

Come prepared: it's not unusual to see hotels in Georgioúpolis advertising mosquito nets.

Mare Monte, t 282 506 1390, f 282 506 1274 (*A; luxury*). One of the coast's most luxurious hotels.

Pilot Beach, t 282 506 1002, f 282 506 1397, *resv@pilot-beach.gr* (*A; expensive*). A stylish complex with a pool, good for families but spread out in different buildings.

Mina', at Kourvrá, t 282 506 1257 (*C; moderate*). A pleasant, medium-sized hotel.

Georgis, as you enter the resort from the main road. The best charcoal-grilled meats.

Arolithos, up from the beach. A wide choice of pasta, and Greek or international dishes.

---

killed in the Battle of Crete. Two kilometres west of Soúda, a road forks south for the 16th-century **Moní Chryssopigí** (*open 3.30–6*); the church and museum house exceptional icons, and a superb cross decorated with gold filigree and precious stones.

The Venetians fortified the bay's islet, **Néa Soúda**, so well that they only surrendered to the Turks in 1715 by way of a treaty, in spite of frequent attacks and a pyramid of 5,000 Christian heads piled around the walls. The Turks had an excellent, if rather frustrating, view of it from their fortress of **Idzeddin**, east of Soúda on Cape Kalámi. Now Chaniá's prison, Idzeddin was built of stone from **Aptera**, high on the plateau, above **Megála Choráfia**. Mentioned in Linear B tablets (A-pa-ta-wa), Aptera (*open Tues–Sun 8.30–3*) was one of the chief cities of Crete until shattered by an earthquake in AD 700. Cyclopean walls, often compared to Tiryns (*see* p.260), wind 4km over the slopes, and in the weeds are a theatre, the base of a Temple of Demeter and the skeleton of a Roman basilica; the Monastery of St John sits atop two vaulted Roman cisterns the size of cathedrals. Aptera's name ('featherless') came from a singing contest held between the Muses and the Sirens. The Sirens were sore losers, and tore out their feathers and plunged into the sea, turning into the islets in Soúda Bay.

East of Aptera, the highway dives inland, missing lovely Cape Drápanon, where rolling hills are draped with vines, olive groves and cypresses . A pair of resort towns dot the north coast: **Kalýves**, with a long beach under the Apokoróna fortress, built by the Genoese when they tried to pinch Crete from Venice, and **Almirída**, smaller, with a curved sandy beach, tiny harbour, and good windsurfing. From here, it's 4km to

Gavalochóri, well worth a stop for its **Folklore Museum** (*t 282 502 3222; open Mon–Sat 9–7, Sun 10–1.30 and 5–8; adm*), where exhibits inspired local women to revive the local silk industry, in hibernation since the departure of the Turks. East of Almirída, the road swings in from the rocky coast to picturesque **Pláka** and straggly **Kókkini Chório**, the latter used for most of the village scenes in the film *Zorba the Greek*.

Inland, the cape's sleepy villages reek of past grandeur, with old villas, towers and gates. **Douliáná**, **Xerostérni** and **Kefalás** are three of the best. The largest village, **Vámos**, seems urban in comparison, its main street dark from the shade of trees, a godsend on a hot day. In **Karýdi**, 4km south of Vámos, the **Metóchi Ag. Georgióu** (*open 7–3 and 4–7, Wed 3–7, Sun 4–7*) is both a working monastery and an impressive Venetian complex of buildings, including a huge olive press, with charming domes. If you're heading towards Georgioúpolis from here, put off lunch until you reach **Exópoli**, where the tavernas enjoy a breathtaking view down to the sea.

Just south of the highway from Vámos, **Vrises** is the pleasant crossroads between Chaniá, Réthymnon and Chóra Sfakíon, with lofty plane trees and café terraces lining the torrential Almirós river. The road follows the Almirós down to the genteel resort of **Georgioúpolis**, a minute's walk from the coastal highway, tucked in the crook of Cape Drápanon and shaded by eucalyptus trees. Named in honour of Prince George, the High Commissioner of autonomous Crete, it has a long, sandy (if sometimes rough and windy) beach, part of the intermittent strand that extends to Réthymnon.

Inland, the old Chaniá–Réthymnon road heads into the barren hills. They form a striking amphitheatre around Crete's only lake, **Kournás**, deep and eerie and full of eels. South (turn at Episkopí), the hill town of **Argiroúpoli** overlooks the sea. This was Dorian Lappa, destroyed by the Romans in 67 BC. In the later war between Octavian and Mark Antony, Lappa supported Octavian, and was rewarded with money to rebuild when he became Augustus. Ruins of the baths and aqueduct survive; a canopy protects a geometric mosaic in the upper part of town.

Just down the Asi Gonía road you'll find the **Mýli** or 'Watermills', where Réthymnon's water supply spills through the little troglodytic chapel of Ag. Dínami and down a stepped waterfall in a grove of plane trees, with tavernas serving trout (try **Paleo Mýli** or **Athívoles**). From here the road rises through a narrow gorge to a famous nest of Cretan dare-devilry, **Asi Gonía**, an old village and a slightly introspective one now that there isn't an enemy for its brave *pallikári* to fight.

South to Sfakiá and Chóra Sfakíon

Sfakiá, once isolated under the White Mountains, was the cradle of Crete's most daring and most moustachioed desperados, who clobbered each other in blood feuds but became the bravest freedom-fighters in times of need. Now connected to civilization by a dramatically beautiful road, the Sfakiots have sheathed their daggers, and prey no more than any other Cretans on invading foreigners. Although most tourists see Chóra Sfakíon only as the bus stop after the boat ride after the Gorge of Samariá,

Getting Around

Chóra Sfakíon is linked by four **buses** a day to Chaniá, Omalós, Georgioúpolis and Réthymnon and two a day to Plakiás. Two or three buses a day go from Chaniá to Anópolis, Frangokástello and Skalotí. In season, four **boats** a day sail between Chóra Sfakíon and Ag. Roúmel for the Gorge of Samariá, and three/four times a day to Soúgia and Paleochóra. Morning **excursion boats** link Chóra Sfakíon to Sweetwater Beach. **Port authority: t** 282 509 1292.

Where to Stay and Eat

Chóra Sfakíon ✉ 73011

Livikon, on the quay next to the Samaria hotel, **t** 282 509 1211 (*C; moderate*). New, stylish and comfortable, with a harbour-side taverna. There are also plenty of rooms.

Limani, by the port, offers a fish fry or mixed grill and salad for €12–15. The nearby bakery has Sfakiá's famous *myzithrópittes* (*myzithra* cheese pies).

Delphini Restaurant, on the beach. First-class service and a great view.

Porto Loutró 1 & 2, in Loutró, **t** 282 509 1433 or 282 509 1444, **f** 282 509 1091 (*B; expensive*), Two hotels, same English–Greek owners. New, very comfortable, with water sports facilities. *Open April–Oct*.

Blue House, Loutró, **t** 282 509 1127, **f** 282 509 1035 (*moderate–inexpensive*). Pleasant rooms and restaurant.

Cave, at Komitades, 10km east of Sfakía. Retreat from the summer heat in this cool cave taverna.

you may want to linger on this sun-bleached coast, dotted with beaches, gorges and places to explore; it's also a congenial spot for being incredibly lazy.

South from Vrises to Chóra Sfakíon (ΧΩΡΑ ΣΦΑΚΙΩΝ)

From Vrises (*see* above) the road ascends the Krapí valley (prettier than it sounds) to the edge of the **Langos tou Katre**, a 2km ravine known as the Thermopylae of Sfakiá. This was a favourite spot for a Cretan ambush, one that spelt doom to 400 Turkish soldiers (*see* below), and then again in 1866 to an army of Turks fleeing south after the explosion of Arkádi. It opens onto the striking plateau of **Askýfou**, where the ruined fortress of Koulés cast a long shadow over the fields. Further south, the Libyan Sea sparkles into view as the road noodles through the steep **Ímbros Gorge** and over the last mountain crusts to Chóra Sfakíon.

A one-time viper's nest of vendettas and revolutionaries, Chóra Sfakíon is now given over to the needs of tourists. With few resources of their own, the Sfakiots took everyone else's: smuggling, sheep-rustling and piracy brought home the bacon for centuries. The Venetians constructed Frangokástello in 1317 to try to control them, then, after the revolt of 1570, they added the castle at Chóra. In the Battle of Crete, the locals helped the rearguard ANZAC soldiers to flee to North Africa; a monument by the sea commemorates the evacuation, while a memorial just above town honours the locals executed by the Germans for their role. The World War, however, was only an intermission in a private war between two Sfakiot families known as the 'vendetta of the century', which took some 90 lives before it ended in 1960.

Around Chóra Sfakíon

Buses leave at 11am and 6pm for **Anópolis**, a rustic village on a plateau, where a statue honours Daskaloyánnis, who organized the first revolt against the Turks in

1770. It went all wrong; promised aid from Russia never arrived, and in March 1771 Daskaloyánnis gave himself up, hoping to spare Sfakiá from reprisals; the pasha ordered him to be flayed alive. From Anópolis, it's 4km west to the bridge that spans the dizzying gorge, making the once arduous journey to **Arádena** a snap. Ironically, the bridge arrived too late for Arádena, now a near-ghost town after a bloody feud. Arádena has a famous Byzantine church, the **Astratigos**, dedicated to St Michael, sporting a dome that looks like a tiled toupée. If a Sfakiot was suspected of sheep-rustling, he would be brought here to be questioned before the stern-eyed saint.

Loutró, linked to the rest of the world only by several boats a day from Chóra Sfakión, may be that quiet get-away-from-it-all spot you've been looking for. Loutró bay is sheltered and transparent; it doesn't have much of a beach, although there are a number of nearby coves. Besides the regular boat trips to Mármara Beach, others go to Glykó Neró, or **Sweetwater Beach**, under sheer cliffs. True to its name, springs provide fresh water, and there's a taverna for more substantial needs.

The Ghosts of Frangokástello (ΦΡΑΓΚΟΚΑΣΤΕΛΛΟ)

The Venetians built it, but as medieval Greeks called all Westerners Franks, the 14th-century fortress of Ag. Nikítas is known as Frangokástello. Set on a long sandy beach 14km east of Chóra Sfakíon, it was the scene of a famous event in 1828, during the Greek War of Independence, when an Epiróte insurgent, Hatzimichális Daliánis, took Frangokástello with 650 Cretans. Soon 8,000 Turks arrived to flush them out, and all the Greeks were slain. But bands of Cretans who had remained outside captured the passes and wreaked a terrible revenge on the Turks when they marched north.

The Massacre of Frangokástello has given rise to one of the most authenticated of all Greek ghost stories. On 17 May, the anniversary of the massacre (or sometime during the last ten days of May), phantoms of the Cretan dead, the *Drosoulités* or 'dew shades', rise up at dawn from the cemetery of Ag. Charalámbos, mounted and fully armed, and proceed silently towards the now empty shell of the fortress, before disappearing into the sea. Thousands have seen them, but many more thousands haven't; the morning must be perfectly clear. Meteorologists pooh-pooh the ghosts – mere heat mirages from the Libyan desert, they say.

Réthymnon (ΡΕΘΥΜΝΟ)

Réthymnon, Crete's third city (pop. 26,000), is the only one that 'weds the wave-washed sand', but for centuries the price it paid for its sand was the lack of a proper port; the Venetians dug a cute round one, but it kept silting up. Like Chaniá, it has a Venetian and Turkish centre; but, unlike Chaniá, Réthymnon escaped the attentions of the Luftwaffe. The fortress peering over its shoulder and its minarets lend an exotic touch. Scholars who fled Constantinople came to Réthymnon and made it the 'brain of Crete'; today it's the home of the University of Crete's arts faculty.

Getting There and Around

ANEK ferries sail to Piraeus daily (250 Arkadíou, t 283 102 9874, f 283 105 5519, www.anek.gr). Port authority: t 283 102 2276. In season, sailings to Santoríni twice a week.

The bus station is on the west end of town, between Igoum Gaviil and the Periferiaki, t 283 102 2212; besides serving the province, those labelled 'El Greco/Skaleta' depart every 20min or so for the 10km stretch of hotels east of town. Olympic Airways buses link Réthymnon to Chaniá airport twice a day, from Olympic's office at 5 Koumoundoúrou, t 283 102 2257, f 283 102 7352.

Tourist Information

EOT: along the town beach at E. Venizélou, t 283 102 9148; open Mon–Fri 8–2.30. Tourist police: next door, t 283 102 8156.

Festivals

Réthymnon is the festival capital of Crete, throwing the best carnival on the island. In July it hosts the two-week Cretan wine festival, t 283 102 2522, and in late August–September an increasingly popular Renaissance festival, t283 105 0800, with lots of music and performances.

Sports and Activities

Hellas Bike Travel, 67 Venizeloú, t 283 105 2764, www.hellasbike.com. If you'd love to cycle down Mount Ida or the White Mountains, but not up.
Anopolis Water City, south of the airport, t 281 078 1316. A water park with slides.

The Happy Walker, 56 Tombázi St, t 283 105 2920. Organized treks in western Crete.

From the Venetian harbour, t 51 643 or 71 140, the corny Pirate Ship makes daily excursions to Maráthi, a little fishing village in Eastern Akrotíri; its sister ship, the Popeye, sails to Balí.

Where to Stay

Réthymnon ✉ 74100

Luxury
Creta Beach, 4km east of Réthymnon, t 283 105 5181, f 283 105 4085, www.grecotel.gr. Lavish hotel and bungalow complex with an indoor pool and two outdoor ones, lit tennis courts and lots of sports, especially for children, who even have their own campground. Open Mar–Nov.
Rithymna Beach Hotel and Bungalows, in Ádele (7km east), t 283 107 1002, f 283 107 1668, www.grecotel.gr (A). Also owned by Grecotel and nearly as plush. On a lovely beach with similar facilities, it fills up early in the spring and stays that way, so book early. Open Mar–Oct.

Expensive
Mythos Suites, in town at 12 Plateía Karaóli, t 283 105 3917, f 283 105 1036, mythoscr@ otenet.gr (B). 10 suites furnished in a traditional style, sleeping 2–5 in a 16th-century manor house; all are air-conditioned and there's a pool in the sunny central patio.
Palazzo Rimondi, 21 Xanthoúdidou, t 283 105 1289, f 283 105 1013, Rimondi@otenet.gr (A). Suites in a renovated mansion, built around a courtyard with small pool. Open April–Oct.
Palazzo Vecchio, Plateía Iroon Politechniou, t 283 103 5352, f 283 102 5479,

The Old Town

Although Réthymnon has been inhabited since Minoan times (the name, Rithymna, is pre-Greek), its oldest monuments are Venetian, beginning with the Guóra Gate, just below the Square of the Four Martyrs. Built in 1566 by the Venetian governor, the gate is the sole survivor of the walls erected after the sackings by Uluch Ali in 1562 and 1571. Outside the gate, the 17th-century Valide Sultana mosque was dedicated to the Sultan's mother; after 1923, the attached cemetery was converted into the Municipal Garden, where the cool, melancholy paths seem haunted by discreet slippered ghosts

palazzovecchio@europe.gr. Charmingly restored Venetian building, in a quiet corner by the Fortezza, with a small pool. *Open April–Oct.*

Moderate

Leo, Váfe 2, t 283 102 6197. Charming bed and breakfast inn, in traditional Cretan style.

Brascos, at Ch. Daskaláki and Th. Moátsou, t 283 102 3721, f 283 102 3725, *brascos@aias.gr* (B). Slick and clean. *Open all year.*

Ideon, Plateía Plastíra, t 283 102 8667, f 283 102 8670, *ideon@otenet.gr* (B). Enjoys a fine spot overlooking the dock and has a small pool; advisable to reserve.

Garden House, 83 N. Fokás (near the Fortezza), t 283 102 8586. Small but delightful rooms in a Venetian residence, with a fountain; book well in advance.

Inexpensive

Zorbas Beach, at the east end of the town beach, t 283 102 9868, f 283 102 8540 (C). Good for peace and quiet and the price.

Zania, Pávlou Vlasátou (a block from the sea), t 283 102 8169. A handful of pleasant rooms in a traditional house.

Ralia Rooms, at Salamnós and Athan. Niákou, t/f 283 105 0163. More atmospheric than most rooms places, with lots of wood.

Sea Front, 161 Arkadiou, t 283 105 1062. Run by friendly Ellotia Tours next door; nice pine-clad rooms; the one at the top benefits from a terrace.

Youth Hostel, 41 Tombázi, t 283 102 2848, *www.rethymno.com (reception hrs 8–12pm and 5–9pm)*, Exceptionally nice and convenient. No card required; breakfast and cooking facilities available.

Elizabeth Camping, a few kilometres east of Réthymnon at Misíria, t/f 283 102 8694, *www.sunshine-campings.gr.*

Eating Out

With its tiny fish restaurants, the **Venetian harbour** is the obvious place to dine in the evening, but expect to pay at least €25–30 for the privilege. Scan the menus – some places offer lobster lunches for two for €35–55.

Veneto, 4 Epiméndou, t 283 105 6634 (€30–35). The city's most beautiful restaurant, in the cellar of a 13th-century Venetian building, serving Greek and Cretan specialities.

Avli, 22 Xanthoúdidou, t 283 102 4356. Set up on different levels in a garden, this is one of the prettiest places to eat but can get busy with groups; book in advance.

Natalka, 24 Fotáki, t 283 105 8629. A small but excellent Russian restaurant serving up delicious Greco-Russian cuisine; try the *borscht* or dumplings.

Sunset, on the west side of the Fortezza (about €12 for fish, €6 for pizza). Has good solid Greek food and an extensive wine list and a splendid view of you know what.

Caribbean, by Rimondi fountain in the old town, t 283 105 4345. With Greek, Italian, Spanish and Latin American dishes, served up to live jazz and piano music.

Samaria, t 283 102 4681. An exception to the mediocre restaurants by the beach; good *giovétsi* and lamb *kléftiko*.

O Kompos, 3km southwest of Réthymnon in Atsipópolou, t 283 102 9725. An old favourite for its delicious, inexpensive Cretan food served out in a shady garden.

Kosmikos Kentro Kontaros, on the Chaniá road, t 283 105 1366. Excellent grilled food, good barrelled wine and live Cretan music; a favourite wedding party venue.

Taverna Protohelidoni, 5km west in Petrés, t 283 106 1577. A popular fish restaurant serving up the day's catch overlooking one of the prettiest beaches on the north coast.

– except during the wine festival, when it overflows with Dionysian imbibers. From the Guóra Gate, Ethnikís Antistáseos leads past **San Francesco** (now part of the University of Crete) where Pétros Filágros, the only Cretan pope, began his career (*see* p.729); he paid for its elaborate Corinthian portal. Further down is the Venetian lion-headed **Rimondi Fountain** (1629) at the junction of several streets, now packed with bars. It marked the heart of town, and all the finest buildings were close by. The **Nerandzes Mosque**, with a graceful rocket of a minaret on Manoúli Vernárdou, retains a monumental portal from its days as the Venetian church of Santa Maria. On its conversion into a mosque in 1657, it was capped with three domes; today the city uses it as a concert hall. The handsome Venetian **Loggia** (1550s), nearby on Arkadíou, was a club where the nobility and landowners would meet and gamble; it now does duty as an exhibition hall. Just northeast, the bijou **Venetian harbour** is lined with seafood restaurants, patrolled by black and white swans.

The Fortezza and Archaeological Museum

In ancient times, when Cretans were bitten by rabid dogs they would resort to the Temple of Artemis Roccaéa on Réthymnon's acropolis, and take a cure of dog's liver or seahorse innards. All traces of this were obliterated in the late 16th century, when the Venetians decided that Réthymnon had been sacked once too often and forced the locals to build the **Fortezza** (*open daily 9–4; adm*). It is one of the largest Venetian castles in Crete, with room for the entire population; yet in 1645, after a bitter two-month siege, it was forced to surrender to the Turks. The church, converted into a mosque, is intact, and is used for concerts in the Renaissance festival.

Near the entrance, the **Archaeological Museum**, in the former Turkish prison (*t 283 105 4668; open Tues–Sun 8.30–3; adm*), is beautifully arranged. The most dazzling pieces hail from the Late Minoan cemetery at Arméni: a boar-tooth helmet, bronze double axes, delicate vases, fragile remains of a loop-decorated basket from 1200 BC, and *larnaxes* (sarcophagi), including one painted with a wild goat and bull chase. A coin collection covers most of the ancient cities of Crete. On Vernadoú St, the **Historical and Folk Art Museum** (*t 283 102 9572; open Mon–Sat 9.30–2; adm*) offers a fine collection of costumes, photos, and pottery from ancient times to 40 years ago. Nearby, on Chimáras, the **Municipal Centre of Contemporary Art** (*t 283 102 1847; open Tues–Sun 10–2 and 5–8*) features exhibitions of Greek art from the last 200 years.

Réthymnon Province

Crete's smallest province, Réthymnon is also the most mountainous, wedged between the island's highest peaks, the White Mountains and 8,044ft Mount Ida, or Psilorítis. On the south coast, the main draws are Ag. Galíni, a picturesque seaside resort, and Moní Préveli in a lush and beautiful setting. The fortress-monastery Arkádi is a popular day trip from Réthymnon, or you can venture into the lovely Amári valley to find Crete at its most traditional. A string of old mountain villages en route to Heráklion also provide a day's exploration, with ancient sites and caves.

Moní Arkádi

Four buses a day (three at weekends) go up the flanks of Psilorítis to **Moní Arkádi** (*t 283 108 3076; open daily 8am–8pm; adm*), a sacred shrine for Cretans. Founded in the 11th century, the monastery was mostly rebuilt in the 17th century, although the sun-ripened Mannerist church dates from 1587. It had money then: Arkádi was a repository for ancient Greek manuscripts spirited out of Constantinople. It resembles a small fort, and in 1866 Cretan freedom fighters chose it for a base. The Turks

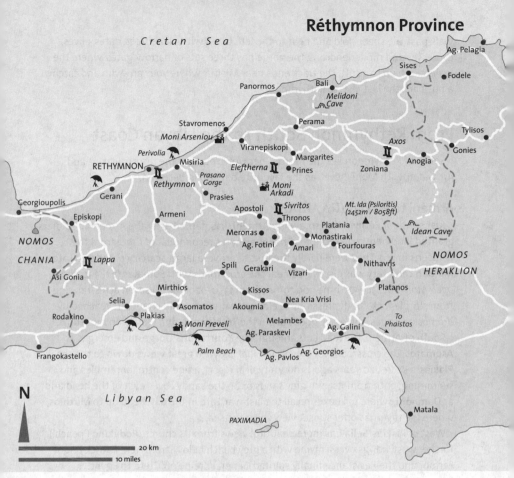

Cretan Sea

Ag. Pelagia

Sises

Fodele

Panormos

Bali

Melidoni Cave

Stavromenos

Perama

Axos

Tylisos

Moni Arseniou

Gonies

Perivolia

Viranepiskopi

Anogia

RETHYMNON

Misiria

Eleftherna

Margarites

Zoniana

Prines

Prasano Gorge

Rethymnon

Moni Arkadi

Gerani

Prasies

Apostoli

Sivritos

Mt. Ida (Psiloritis) (2452m / 8058ft)

Georgioupolis

Thronos

Platania

Episkopi

Armeni

Idean Cave

Meronas

Monastiraki

NOMOS

Ag. Fotini

Amari

Fourfouras

CHANIA

Lappa

Nithavris

NOMOS

Asi Gonia

Spili

Gerakari

Vizari

HERAKLION

Platanos

Mirthios

Kissos

Selia

Asomatos

Akoumia

Nea Kria Vrisi

Rodakino

Plakias

Melambes

To Phaistos

Moni Preveli

Ag. Paraskevi

Ag. Galini

Frangokastello

Palm Beach

Ag. Pavlos

Ag. Georgios

N

Libyan Sea

Matala

PAXIMADIA

20 km

10 miles

demanded that the abbot hand over the rebels; he refused. An army marched on Arkádi nad the population took refuge in the monastery's walls. On 7 November, the Turks attacked, and after two days they breached the walls. Rather than surrender, Abbot Gabriel set fire to the powder magazines, blowing up 829 Turks and Greeks. The news caused a furore in Europe, and many, led by Swinburne and Victor Hugo, took up the cause of Greek independence. The Gunpowder Room, where the blast left a gaping hole in the roof, may be visited, and there's a **Historical Museum** (*adm*), containing the holey, holy banner, portraits of the heroes of 1866 and the vestments of Abbot Gabriel. A windmill was made into an ossuary, displaying a stack of skulls blasted with holes.

The Prasanó Gorge

Just east of Réthymnon, the pretty **Prasanó Gorge** was formed by the Plataniás river, which courteously dries up between mid-June and mid-October so you can walk down the gorge (allow 4 to 5 hours, wear sturdy shoes and bring water). Take the early Amári bus as far as the first bend in the road after Prasiés, where the track begins;

walk past the sheep-fold and bear to the left. Lined with plane trees, dates, olives, cypresses and rhododendrons, the gorge has three sets of narrow 'gates' where the walls climb up to 480ft. The track ends near Misiriá, where you can swim and catch a bus back the last 5km to Réthymnon.

From Réthymnon South to the Libyan Coast

South of Réthymnon lies the narrow 'neck' of Crete and the resorts Plakiás and Ag. Galíni, with Moní Préveli as the favourite day trip in between.

Arméni to Plakiás (ΠΛΑΚΙΑΣ)

Just south of Réthymnon, sprawling **Arméni** was named after the Armenian soldiers granted land here by Nikephóros Phokás after his reconquest of Crete from the Saracens in 961. They were hardly the first to arrive: a large, scarcely plundered **Late Minoan cemetery** was discovered near the crossroads with Somatás (*t 283 102 9975; open Mon–Fri 8.30–3*). Some 200 tombs from 1350–1200 BC fill seven acres, ranging from simple rock-cut depressions to elaborate underground chambers reached by *dromos* passages; the grave goods are in the Réthymnon and Heráklion museums.

South of Arméni, the road cuts through the **Kourtaliótis Gorge** and emerges at **Asómatos**, the crossroads for Préveli and Plakiás, with great views down to the sea. **Plakiás**, a secret 20 years ago, is now a typical resort, a fine centre for rambles and swimming, both from its own grey sands or on the sandy coves east of the headland at **Damnóni**, where pill boxes recall the last war. Late in the day, head up to **Mírthios**, where the tavernas offer sunset views over the sea.

West of Plakiás, **Selía** has more beautiful views from its church. **Rodákino** ('peach'), further west, hangs over a ravine with a grey beach below; from here Patrick Leigh Fermor and the Resistance finally spirited General Kreipe off Crete to Egypt.

Moní Préveli

Moní Préveli is the beauty spot on the central Libyan coast. Its road passes palm groves along the Megálo Pótamos river and the abandoned lower half of the monastery, known as **Káto Préveli**. In the early 19th century, after Daskaloyánnis' aborted revolt in Sfakía (*see* p.693), its abbot Melchisedek Tsouderos began to collect arms for a new revolt. The Turks got wind of it, and in 1821, shortly before the War of Independence, they came to destroy the monastery. Abbot Melchisedek welcomed the Turks with open arms and plied them with drink until they fell asleep, so the monks were able to flee before the Turks woke and pillaged the monastery.

The 'Back' monastery, **Píso Préveli**, is another 3km on, high on the coast (*t 283 203 1246; open 8–1 and 3–7; adm*). The original Byzantine church was demolished by the monks in the 1830s, after the Turks kept refusing them permission to make repairs. They did, however, preserve the furnishings: the gilt iconostasis and a miraculous piece of the True Cross. Note the famous Byzantine palindrome NIΨONANOMH-MATA MHMONANOΨIN ('Cleanse your sins, not only your face') on the fountain.

Getting Around

Plakiás has seven **buses** a day to Réthymnon, plus two a day west along the south coast as far as Chóra Sfakíon, by way of Frangokástello, and two buses a day to Prévéli. Ag. Galíni has five buses from Réthymnon, as well as connections to Heráklion, Phaistos and Mátala by way of Míres. Boats make the daily excursion to Prevéli. Note that Plakiás has no banks or cash dispensers.

Where to Stay and Eat

Plakiás ✉ 74060

Damnoni Bay, t 283 203 1373, **f** 283 203 1002 (*C; expensive*). Studios, a pool, water sports and a seafood restaurant, and the advantage of having a view that doesn't include the Damnoni Bay resort.

Alianthos Beach, t 283 203 1196, **f** 283 203 1197 (*C; moderate*). Neo-Minoan family hotel, with a pool.

Lamon, t 283 203 1425, **f** 283 203 1424 (*B; moderate*). Blue and white, at the bottom of the price range.

Pension Sokrates, t 283 203 1489. Inexpensive rooms near Damnóni Beach.

Youth hostel in Plakiás, **t** 283 203 2118, *www. yhplakias.com*. Set back in an olive grove.

Apollonia Camping, t 283 203 1318, **f** 283 203 1607. Pool, laundry and mini-market. *Open April–Oct.*

Ariadni, Oniroú, **t** 283 203 1640 (€20). A small place that does Cretan specialities such as *monastiráko* (pork with mushrooms, peas and prunes) and *erofilí* (lamb with artichokes and potatoes).

Taverna ChiluJior hy the little port, **t** 283 203 1472,. Does a roaring tráde with the locals.

Sophia B, on the waterfront (€15). A choíce of 32 starters, pasta, meat or fish courses, irrigated with a long Cretan wine list.

Kri Kri, on the waterfront. Good charcoal-grilled food.

Galini, t 283 203 2103. In the palms by Soúda Beach; traditional food and occasional live music.

Spíli ✉ 74200

Green Hotel, t 283 202 2225 (*C; moderate*). A delightful refuge when the coasts are sizzling; book early in the summer.

Costas Inn, near the fountains. Serves tasty Cretan mountain food; rooms for rent.

Ag. Galíni ✉ 74056

Don't arrive in Ag. Galíni without a reservation. Places generally not block-booked are:

Galíni Mare, t/f 283 209 1358 (*C; moderate*). Good views and facilities.

Aktaeon, Kountouriótou, **t** 283 209 1208 (*E; inexpensive*). Private baths and good views over the town; good value.

Argiro's Studios and Rooms, t 283 209 1470 (*D; inexpensive*).

Madame Hortense, up on the second floor. Looming over the waterfront. Lined with photographs of old Ag. Galíni, serves well-prepared French and Greek dishes with a glamorous touch (€20).

Ariston. Good *stifádo*, moussaka and an excellent aubergine salad (€12 for a full meal).

Onar. One of Ag. Galíni's favourites, with excellent Cretan food cooked by mama.

La Strada, in the centre. Has a real pizza oven, and serves it up to jazz music.

Throughout Crete's revolts in the 19th century, Píso Préveli took in refugees until boats could ferry them to Greece. In 1941, the monks performed a similar good deed, sheltering hundreds of Allied troops until they could be picked up by submarine; in gratitude the British gave Préveli two silver candlesticks and a marble plaque, now lovingly cared for by the last monk. It's a dangerous scramble down to **Palm Beach** just below, with lovely sands lined with groves of date palms at the mouth of the Kourtaliótis Gorge. Although the invaders it faces these days, mostly on boat excursions from Plakiás or Ag. Galíni, are more peaceful, there are far too many of them. Up the gorge, the stream forms delightful pools, just the right size for one or two people to lie in on a summer's day, but by the end of summer it usually stinks.

Spíli and Ag. Galíni

Past the Plakiás turn-off, the road to Ag. Galíni continues to **Spíli**, a charming village immersed in greenery; the centrepiece is a long fountain, where water splashes from 17 Venetian lion-heads. At Akoúmia a road (rough towards the end) leads down in 10km for pristine **Ag. Paraskeví**, while further east at Néa Kría Vrísi you can turn for lovely **Ag. Pávlos**, sheltered and sandy, with rooms and a yoga holiday centre.

Ag. Galíni, is easily the most photogenic village on Crete's south coast, with its jumble of houses spilling down the hill. Although the beach is puny, boat excursions sail to others, at Moní Préveli, Mátala, **Ag. Geórgios** (shingly with three tavernas) and Ag. Pávlos (50mins), as well as to the pebble-beached islets called **Paximáthia** for their resemblance to the crunchy, twice-baked rusks that Cretans love.

Amári: The Western Slopes of Mount Ida

Wedged under Mount Ida, the ancient province of Amári consists of two charming valleys that time forgot, filled with cherry orchards, olive groves and frescoed churches. The main road leads south into the valleys by way of Prasiés and **Apóstoli**, with grand views and a frescoed church, Ag. Nikólaos, from the 1300s; **Ag. Fotiní** just beyond marks the crossroads of the east and west valleys. Nearly all the **west valley** villages were torched by the Germans during the war, although they have been rebuilt pretty much as they were. In **Méronas** the church of the **Panagía** has a Venetian Gothic doorway, with the arms of the Kallergis, one of the most prominent Cretan families. Inside (*the key's across the road*) are early 14th-century frescoes, painted in the then new, more naturalistic artistic trends from Constantinople. **Gerakári**, famous for cherries, is the starting point for a stunning drive over the Kédros Mountains to Spíli (*see* above). If you have to choose one route, the **east valley** is lovelier, a proper Cretan Brigadoon. **Thrónos** is the heir of ancient Sybrito, a city destroyed by the Saracens in 824. The setting, especially the acropolis, is superb, and in the centre of Thrónos the mosaic carpet of a basilica overflows from under the little church of the **Panagía,** which has exceptional frescoes (late 13th and early 15th centuries). Just south, medieval **Moní Asómati** has a pretty Venetian church.

Back on the main route, the University of Crete is excavating a Minoan Proto-Palatial villa, a 5min walk from **Monastiráki**. After Chaniá and Réthymnon, this is the most important site yet discovered in western Crete (and still off limits to visitors). **Amári**, the old capital, is a lovely village, surrounded by enchanting views. **Ag. Ánna**, isolated outside the village, has the oldest dated frescoes in Crete (1225).

Réthymnon to Heráklion: the Coastal Route

Between Réthymnon and Heráklion you can choose between the highway, with a few resorts squeezed below on the coast; or the old roads over the northern slopes of Mount Ida. Just before the mountains block the sea, the highway arrives at **Pánormos**, a pretty place with a small beach at the mouth of the Milópotamos river, guarded by a Genoese fort of 1206. Pánormos made its fortune in the last century exporting carob beans – once essential in the manufacture of film. Further east, **Balí**, in part thanks to the cachet of its name, has been transformed from a fishing village overlooking a trio of lovely sandy coves to a jam-packed resort. On the hill over the town, the 17th-century **Monastery of Balí** has a lovely Renaissance façade and fountain.

Eight kilometres in from Balí, the **Melidóni Cave** (bring non-slip shoes) has a small mouth that belies the size: the ceiling, ragged with stalactites, rises 990ft overhead. The Minoans worshipped in its gloom, and to the right of the entrance is a 3rd-century BC inscription to Hermes. In 1824, when the Turks were doing their best to cut short Crete's participation in the Greek War of Independence, 324 women and children and 30 revolutionaries took refuge in the cave. When the Greeks refused to surrender; the Turks built a fire at the entrance and asphyxiated them. With its crumbling altar and broken ossuary, the cave still seems haunted.

The **Old Road** between Pérama and Heráklion is pure rural Crete, where charcoal-burning is alive and well. Sleepy **Fódele**, in orange groves between the Old and New Roads, has a pretty Byzantine church of the Panagía (1383) and was, according to tradition, the birthplace in 1541 of Doménikos Theotokópoulos (El Greco). The '**House of El Greco**' (*open Tues–Sun, 9–5*) contains displays about the master. Although El Greco never returned after he sailed off in 1567 to make his career in Venice, Rome and Spain, he always signed his paintings in Greek, often followed by KRES, or CRETAN. East of Fódele, the highway continues to the junction for the upmarket resort of **Ag. Pelagía**, strewn like chunks of coconut over the headland and protected sandy beach that marks the outer gate of the Bay of Heráklion.

Where to Stay and Eat

Pánormos ✉ **74057**
Villa Kynthia, t 283 405 1148, winter f 281 022 2970 (*B; expensive*). Intimate luxury in a carob bean merchant's mansion of 1898; lovely rooms furnished with antiques and a pool. *Open Mar–Oct.*
Panorma Beach, t 283 405 1321, f 283 405 1403 (*C; moderate*). A typical beach hotel.
Lucy's, t 283 405 1212. Inexpensive rooms.
To Steki. One of the best places to eat.

Balí ✉ **74057**
Because of packagers, most of these places are only available in the off-season.
Bali Village, t 283 409 4210, f 283 409 4252, *Balibeach@her.forthnet.gr* (*B; expensive*). One of the first hotels here and still one of the nicest.
Sophia, t 283 409 4202 (*moderate–inexpensive*). Good value apartments, with pool and family-run taverna.

Ag. Pelagía ✉ **71500**
Capsis Beach and Sofitel Palace, t 281 081 1212, f 281 081 1076, *root@capsis-crete@her.forthnet.gr* (*A; luxury*). Large complex on the peninsula, with three beaches, several pools, a waterfall, riding, and a watersports school.
Peninsula, t 281 081 1313, f 281 081 1291, *Peninsula@her.forthnet.gr* (*A; luxury*). Perched on the rocks, overlooking the beach, with a 'do-it-yourself hairdressing salon'.
Alexander House, t 281 081 1303, f 281 081 1381, *Alexhh@iraklio.hellasnet.gr* (*A; expensive–moderate*). Comfortable rooms with satellite TV, mini bars and balconies, and a good Chinese restaurant.
Panorama, t 281 081 1002, f 281 081 1273 (*B; moderate*). Friendly, large hotel with a pool, water sports and tennis.
Muragio, t 281 081 1070, on the waterfront. Delicious fish.
Valentino, t 281 081 1106. Has similar, and pizzas made in a real Italian *forno*.

Réthymnon to Heráklion: the Inland Route

A choice of roads skirts the northern flanks of Ida, and to see everything requires some backtracking. At Stavroménos, on the coast, you can pick up the road for **Viranepiskopí**, with a 10th-century basilica near a Sanctuary of Artemis and a 16th-century Venetian church. Higher up, 7km south, colourful **Margarítes** is home to a thriving pottery industry (they even make huge *pithoi*) and two frescoed churches, 14th-century **Ag. Demétrius** and 12th-century **Ag. Ioánnis**, with a stone iconostasis.

Another 4km south, **Eléftherna** is just below the ancient city of the same name, founded by the Dorians in the 8th century BC. The setting, above two tributaries of the Milopótamos, is spectacular; mighty walls and a formidable tower, rebuilt in Hellenistic times, kept out most foes. According to historian Dio Cassius, the Romans under Metellus Creticus were only able to capture Eléftherna after the tower was soaked in vinegar(!). Nearby is a section of the aqueduct, which fed two Roman cisterns capable of holding 10,000 cubic metres of water. At the bottom of the glade there's an ancient bridge, with corbelled arches.

Even more precipitous, **Axós** (30km east) was founded *c.* 1100 BC by Minoans fleeing the Dorians. It was the only Cretan city still to have a king of its own into the 7th century BC, and it continued to thrive into the Byzantine period, when it counted 46 churches; 11 survive. Antonia Koutantou (*t 283 406 1311*), who runs a shop, has the key to the churches. Ancient Axos was huge. The acropolis is scattered on terraces above its 8th-century BC walls. On the road east of Axós, a splendid panorama of hill towns opens up. Just below the first one, **Zonianá**, the **Sendóni Cave** (*open 8 to sunset, closed hols; adm*) contains remarkable stalactites, cave draperies and petrified waves.

Anógia and the Idean Cave

The next village east is **Anógia**, where the inhabitants of Axós moved in the Middle Ages. A stalwart Resistance centre, it was burned by both the Turks and the Germans, the latter in reprisal for hiding the kidnapped General Kreipe, when all the men in the village were rounded up and shot. Today rebuilt in an upper, modern town and lower, traditional-looking town, Anógia lives off its weavings; brace yourself for a mugging by little old ladies (including a few surviving widows of the martyrs).

Just east of Anógia begins the 26km road to the **Ideon Cave**, 5,052ft, on the beautiful Nida plateau. Back in Archaic times, this cave took over the Diktean Cave's thunder, so to speak, as the 'birthplace of Zeus'. Ancient to the ancients, the Idaean rites were presided over by Dactyls, or 'finger men'. Pythagoras was initiated by them into the Mysteries of Zagreus (Zeus fused with the mystic role of Dionysos), which may have been behind his mystical theories on numbers and vegetarianism; votive offerings found in the cave date from 3000 BC to the 5th century AD. A ski centre is nearby, and there's a track from the cave to the summit of **Psilorítis**, Crete's highest peak (8,057ft), about 7 hours' round trip if you're an experienced hiker. There are shelters: at Prinos (3,609ft; *t 281 022 7609*) and Toumbotos Prinos (4,921ft; *t 283 102 3666*).

From Anógia, the road continues east to **Goniés**, a village at the entrance to the Malevízi, which produced Malmsey, a favourite wine in medieval Venice and England.

Near here, at **Sklavokámbos**, a Minoan villa went up in flames so intense that its limestone walls were baked as if in a kiln; its ruins are right next to the road.

The Minoan Villas of Týlisos

Much more remains to be seen further east at **Týlisos**, where three large Minoan villas (*t 281 022 6092; open daily 8.30–3; adm*) are set in a landscape swathed in olives and vineyards. Built in the prosperous New Palace period and destroyed *c*. 1450 BC, the villas stood two or three storeys high and had extensive storage space; palatial elements such as light wells, lustral basins, colonnaded courts and cult shrines are produced here in miniature. The Minoan love of twisting corridors is further complicated here by the fact that the Dorians built a town re-using many of the walls. Rectangular Villa B, nearest the entrance, is the oldest and least intact; Villas A and C are built of finely dressed stone: door jambs, stairs, pillars and the drainage system survive. The presence of elaborate villas in Týlisos and Sklavokámbos suggests that the Minoan nobility had country retreats, but the fact that they stand on the Knossos–Idean Cave road may be the true key to their purpose.

Heráklion (ΗΡΑΚΛΕΙΟ)

Bustling Heráklion (pop. 127,000) is Crete's capital and Greece's fourth city – the kind of place that most people go on holiday to escape. But Heráklion boasts two unmissable attractions: a museum containing the world's greatest collection of Minoan art, and the grand palace of Knossos in its suburbs.

Heráklion began modestly as Minoan Katsamba, the smaller of Knossos' two ports, and took on its current name in the Classical period. In the 800s the Saracens saw the potential of the site and built their chief town here, naming it Kandak ('the moats') after the trench they dug around its walls. By the time it was reconquered by Nikephóros Phokás, Kandak was the leading slave market in the Mediterranean. The Venetians made Kandak into Candia, or Candy, and kept it as the capital of Crete; the mighty walls they built around it so impressed the Cretans that they called it Megálo Kástro, the 'Big Castle'. The Turks kept it as their seat of government until 1850, when they transferred this to Chaniá. When Crete became autonomous, the Classical name, Heráklion, was revived and it took back its capital role in 1971.

Venetian Heráklion

When Crete won its autonomy in 1898, Arthur Evans, already a hero for his news reports in Britain on Turkish atrocities, persuaded the Cretans to safeguard their Venetian heritage, and it's a good thing he did because otherwise Heráklion would be a mess. The **Venetian Harbour**, 200m west of the modern ferry docks, still offers the best introduction to the city, guarded by the 16th-century fortress **Rocco al Mare** (or Koules) still wearing its Lion of St Mark (*t 281 028 9935; open Tues–Sat 8.30–3, Sun 10–3; adm*). The **Arsenali**, or shipyards, recall Venetian seamanship and superior facilities at sea that supplied Heráklion during the great 21-year siege.

Heráklion

Rocco al Mare

Venetian Harbour

MAKARIOU

Historical Museum

KALOKAIRINOU

K. PALEOLOGOU

THEOTOKOPOULOU

SKORDILON

CHANDAKOS

1878

SFAKION

MIRIONOU

KAZANTZAKI

MINOTAVROU

KORONEOU

VIRONOS

25 AVGOUSTOU

Catholic Church

P. ANTONIOU

EPIMENIDOU

E

B

D

Parko El Greco

Morosini Fountain

Ag. Titos

AGIOU TITOU

Loggia

MIRABELOU

MALIKOUTI

Battle of Crete and Resistance Museum

BOFOR

MICHELIDAKI

PSAROMILIGON

CHANDAKOS

ANDROGEO

HATZIDAKI

DOUKOS

G

Ag. Markos

DAEDOLOU

IDOMENEOS

XANTHOUDIDOU

Archaeology Museum

IKAROU

KALOKERINOU

ZAMPELIOU

GRAMVOUSAS

ARGIRAKI

IDIS

DIKEOSINIS

AGIOU MINA

PLATEIA EKATERINIS

Ag. Ekaterina

1896

Market

POL

GIANARI

PLATEIA ELEFTHERIAS

MONIS KARDIOTISIS

KATEHAKI

1821

KARTEROU

EVANS

M

ZOGRAFOU

OTHONOS

TRIS KAMARES

Ag. Minas Cathedral

PLATEIA FEREOU

MARKOPOULOU

THESSALONIKIS

PLATEIA ARKADIOU

AVEROF

DIMOKRATIAS

TOBAZI

GIANITSOU

VIKELA

M. MOUSOUROU

PLATEIA KORNAROU

TRIFISTOU

PEDIADOS

SPINALOGAS

Bembo Fountain

VIANION

EVANS

K. GIABOUDI

P. NIKOUSIOU

NIKOLAOU PLASTIRA

KENOURIA PORTA

KOMENO BENTENI

Tomb of Nikos Kazantzakis

PLATEIA KIPROU

F

To the Natural History Museum

MARTINENGO

To **A** and **C**

MIRELOU

Ag. Titos

To A and C

N

To the Natural History Museum

Bus departures

A Airport–Amnissos, No 1
B Knossos, No 2
C Gortyna–Phaistos
D Malía–Ag. Nikolaos–Ierapetra–Sitia
E Rethymnon–Chania
F Kastelli–Viannos
G Archanes

200 metres
200 yards

Getting There and Around

By air: Heráklion's airport, 4km east of the city in Amnísos, t 281 024 5644, is linked to the city by bus no.1, beginning at Pórta Chaníon and passing through the centre; a taxi costs €8. Olympic bus connects to all Olympic flights from Plateía Eleftherías. For Olympic information, call t 281 022 3400 or t 281 022 9191. Aegean/Cronus at the airport, t 281 022 2217; in town at 11 Dimokratías, t 281 034 4324.

By sea: travel agents line Odós 25 Avgoustou, at the Venetian harbour. Ferries sail daily to Piraeus on Minoan Lines, t 281 022 9602, f 281 033 0855, *www.minoan.gr*, and ANEK, t 281 022 3067, f 281 034 6379. **Port authority**: t 281 024 4956.

By road: Heráklion has several **bus** stations. Buses for Knossos and destinations **east** of Heráklion (including Ierápetra and the Lassíthi Plateau) depart from the station just east of the Venetian port, t 281 024 5017. The station for points **west** – Réthymnon and Chaniá – is across the street, t 281 022 1765. From just outside the Pórta Chaníon on the west end, buses head **southwest** to Ag. Galíni, Gortyn, Phaistos, Mátala, Týlisos, Anógia and Milapótamos, t 281 025 5965. From outside the Evans Gate (Plateía Kíprou) buses go to Áno Viános, Mýrtos and Thrapsanó. Buses for Archánes depart from central Plateía Venizélou. Buses for the nearest beaches depart from the Astoria hotel in Plateía Eleftherías; for Ammoudári to the west (no. 6); for Amnisós to the east take bus no.7, just opposite.

There are no end of **car rental** agencies along 25 Avgoustou and Doukos Bofor; rates are reasonable, but be prepared to haggle. Try Auto Europe, t 281 033 0627.

Tourist Information

Tourist police: 10 Dikeosínis St, t 281 028 3190.
Hospitals: Panelisteimiako, t 281 039 2111; Venizélou, t 281 036 8001.
Immediate Help Centre: t 281 022 222.
Left luggage: in the east and southwest bus stations and at the airport.
Post office: Plateía Daskaloyiánnis, t 281 028 2276.

Where to Stay

Heráklion ✉ 71500

Luxury
Atlantis Hotel, 2 Igías (near the Archaeological Museum), t 281 022 9103, f 281 022 6265, *www.grandhotel.gr* (A). Luxurious air-conditioned rooms, pool, and roof garden.
Astoria Capsis Hotel, Platía Eleftherías, t 281 034 3080, f 281 022 9078, *www.astoria-capsis.gr* (A). Similarly priced and just as smart, with rooftop pool and bar.
Candia Maris, Ammoudára, t 281 031 4632, f 281 025 0669, *www.maris.gr* (L). Plush rooms and bungalows at a price (€310 a head); there is even a thalassotherapy centre.
Grecotel Agapi Beach, Ammoudára, t 281 031 1084, f 281 025 8731, *www.grecotel.gr* (A). Offers all the fancy beach accessories you could desire.

Expensive
The Galaxy, 67 Demokratías (just outside the walls to the southeast), t 281 023 8812, f 281 021 1211, *galaxy@galaxy_hotels.com* (A). Contemporary serenity; ask for a room overlooking the pool.
Lato Hotel, 15 Epimenídou, t 281 022 8103, f 281 024 0350, *info@lato.gr* (A). Well kitted-out, modern rooms with lovely sea views from the balconies.
Atrion, 9 Chronaki St., t 281 229 225, f 281 223 292 (B). Relatively new, moderate-sized and air-conditioned, with a garden, patio and underground garage.
Minoa Palace, Amnisós, t 281 038 0404, f 281 038 0422, *minoapalace@akashotels.com* (A). Big fancy beachside complex with a floodlit tennis court, and a score of activities. *Open April–Oct.*

Moderate
Most of these are located near the port and bus stations. Among the best are:
Ilaira, 1 Ariádnis, t 281 022 7103 (C). Traditionally decorated rooms with balcony, and a cafeteria roof terrace.
Daedalos, 15 Daedálou Street, t 281 024 4812, f 281 022 4391 (C). Plain and modern, but convenient for the archaeological museum, on a pedestrian-only street.

Kris, 2 Doúkos Bófor, t 281 022 3211 (C). Friendly, with cheerful blue-and-red colour scheme and well-positioned rooms with fridge/sink.

Inexpensive

Rea, 1 Kalimeráki, t 281 022 3638, f 281 024 2189 (D). One of the nicest, near the sea and quiet.

Atlas, 6 Kandanoléontos, t 281 028 8989 (E). A touch of streamlined Art Deco on a noisy pedestrian-only street near the centre; so-so rooms. Open April–Oct.

Lena, 10 Lahaná, t 281 022 3280, f 281 024 2826 (E). Clean, simple rooms on a quiet street west of 25 Avgoustou.

Hellas, 11 Kandanoléontos, t 281 022 5121. Pleasant, friendly and has a courtyard.

Idaeon Andron, behind the Venetian Loggia, on 1 Perdikári, t 281 028 1795. Pleasant small rooms and a tiny courtyard.

Youth hostel at 5 Víronos, t 281 028 6281. Well run and convenient.

Rent Rooms Hellas, 24 Chandáka, t 281 028 0858. In the old youth hostel building.

Camping Heráklion, 5km west on Ammoudára Beach, t 281 025 0986. Large, with all facilities.

Eating Out

Trendies in Heráklion have created a car-free haven for themselves in the narrow streets between **Daedálou** and **Ag. Títou**. Prices are a bit over the odds, but the food is better, too. The ten or so tavernas jammed between Odós 1866 (the market street) and **Evans Street** are a favourite place to dine, at moderate prices. The picturesque places around the Morosini Fountain are strictly for tourists.

Loukoulous, 5 Korái, t 281 022 4435 (€25–30). An elegant Italian restaurant in a beautifully restored mansion.

Giovanni, 12 Korái, t 281 034 6338 (€20–25). A choice of fixed-price menus for two: fish, Italian, Greek and vegetarian dishes; extensive wine list.

Karavolas, 108 Sófokli Venizélou, t 281 025 5449 (€12). The cult place for a cheap fish lunch.

Merastri, 17 Chrysóstomou, t 281 022 1910 (€18). Great new restaurant serving some of the

best Cretan food on the island. Open eves only except Sun, June–Sept.

Ionia, 3 Evans, t 281 028 3213 The oldest taverna in town, serving some unusual mountain dishes, such as goat with chestnuts and liver with rosemary.

Kyriakos, Leof. Demokratías, t 281 022 4649. A Heráklion institution, for its well prepared 'urban' cusine. Closed Sun eve.

Taverna Anissara, at Goúves. Delicious Greek specialities in a tranquil garden setting.

Petroussas, out west in Ammoudára, on the main drag. Serves excellent Greek food,

Toumbrouk, in Karterós, east of Amnisós. An excellent fish taverna.

Chryssomenos, Ag. Iríni, just after Knossos. A good place for lunch after doing the site.

Entertainment and Nightlife

When the Herakliótes want to spend a night on the town, they usually leave it; the clubs and discos west of the city are especially popular. Popular bars are concentrated around Plateía Venizélou, El Greco Park and Chándakos.

Kastro, Doúkos Bofor. Famous for Cretan music and dancing.

Taverna I Palia Argli at the end of Theríssou, t 281 025 2600. Often has live rembétika music.

Café Amália, 37 Idomeneos, t 281 022 6146. Rembétika on Tues, Thurs and Fri.

Café Veneto, on Epimenídou. Elegant nightspot with a roof terrace overlooking the port.

Apan in Odós Ag. Titos. Trendy music bar.

Portside Club, on the seafront. Cross-shaped bar, very popular with Greeks.

Limeniko Café, on seafront at west end of Makariou St. Mercifully isolated from the traffic, plays popular as well as traditional Greek music.

Loft Club, next door. Opens its doors to the masses at midnight.

Envy or **Privilege**, both on Ikarou, in town. For those who are still full of beans late at night.

Ariadne and **Castello**, out on the road to Knossos, host big Cretan music and dance evenings.

The main street up from the Venetian Harbour, **25 Avgoustou,** lined with shipping agents and banks, also has the church of **Ag. Títos.** It owes its cubic form to the Turks, who made it a mosque and rebuilt it after several earthquakes. The chapel to the left of the narthex houses the island's most precious relic, the head of St Titus, a disciple of St Paul and the apostle of Crete. When forced to give up Crete, the Venetians took Titus' skull and only returned it when Pope Paul IV obliged them to, in 1966.

It takes a bit of imagination to reconstruct, but the Venetians designed what is now **Plateía Venizélou,** at the top of 25 Avgoustou, as a miniature Piazza San Marco. Heráklion's Town Hall occupies the **Venetian Loggia** (1628), built as a meeting place for the nobility and completely reconstructed after taking a direct hit in the Battle of Crete. **San Marco** (Ag. Márkos), the first Venetian church on Crete (1239), was twice rebuilt after earthquakes, stripped of its campanile and converted into a mosque; it's now used as an exhibition centre. Water dribbles from the lions' mouths of the **Morosini Fountain,** erected in 1626 by governor Francesco Morosini, who brought water in from Mount Júktas. Although the fountain is minus its figure of Neptune, the remaining creatures make up some of the finest Venetian work on Crete.

South of Plateía Venizélou, the city's **outdoor market** runs along Odós 1866, a testimony to the big islands's extraordinary fecundity. Several stalls sell Cretan wedding bread – golden wreaths decorated with scrolls and rosettes. Similar forays into the Baroque await at the south end of the market in Plateía Kornárou, in the **Bembo Fountain** (1588), assembled by the Venetians from ancient fragments; the Turks added the charming kiosk-fountain, or **Koúbes,** now a café, and the Cretans added the statues of Erotókritos and Arethoúsa, hero and heroine of their national epic poem.

The Archaeological Museum

t 281 022 6092; open 8–7, Mon noon–7; adm exp. If you get overwhelmed (or hungry) you can go out and return with your date-stamped ticket.

A few blocks east of Plateía Venizélou, on the north side of hemicyclical **Plateía Eleftherías,** this ungainly coffer of a building holds the masterpieces of the Minoans. Thanks to a law passed in the early days of Crete's autonomy, every important antiquity found on the island belongs to the museum. The result is dazzling, delightful and entirely too much to digest in one visit.

The collection is chronological. In **Room I,** containing Neolithic (from 5000 BC) and Pre-Palatial periods (2600–2000 BC), the craftsmanship that would characterize the Minoans is already apparent in the delicate gold pendants, the polished stone ritual vessels, the bold, irregularly fired red and black Vasilikí pottery and carved sealstones. Early Cycladic idols and Egyptian seals found at Mesara point to a precocious trade network. **Rooms II** and **III** are devoted to the Old Palace period (2000–1700 BC), when the Minoans made their first Kamares-ware vases, marrying form and decoration with motifs from the natural world and virtuoso 'eggshell-ware' cups. One case displays the Knossos Town Mosaic: faïence plaques of Minoan houses. The clay **Phaistos Disc** (*c.* 1700 BC) is the world's first example of moveable type: 45 different symbols, believed to be phonetic ideograms, are stamped on both sides in a spiral.

Items from the Minoans' Golden Age, the New Palace period (1700–1450 BC), are divided geographically in **Rooms IV–IX**. Potters turned to even freer, more naturalistic designs. Stone carving became ever more rarefied as the Minoans used porphyrys and semi-precious stones, cutting and polishing them to bring out their swirling grains. **Room IV** contains masterpieces, such as a bull's head rhyton carved in black steatite, the leopard axe from Mália, and bare-breasted snake goddess statuettes; the draughtsboard in ivory, rock crystal and blue glass paste; and the exquisite ivory bull leaper, the first known statue of a freely moving human figure. **Room V** contains finds from Knossos that just pre-date its destruction in 1450 BC, including a model of a Minoan palace. Artefacts from cemeteries fill **Room VI**, where figurines offer hints about funerary practices, banquets and dances; an ivory *pyxis* shows a band of men hunting a bull. Goldwork reached its height in this period; see the Isopata ring, showing four ladies ecstatically dancing. The Mycenaeans are made to answer for the weapons – the boar-tusk helmets and 'gold-nailed swords' as described by Homer.

Items found in central Crete are displayed in **Room VII**. The show-stoppers here are the gold jewellery, particularly the pendant of two bees depositing a drop of honey in a comb from Mália, and the three steatite vessels from Ag. Triáda, decorated in low reliefs: the Harvesters' Vase shows men with winnowing rods; on the 'Cup of the Chieftain', a young warrior reports to a long-haired chieftain; and a rhyton has four zones of athletic scenes: boxing, wrestling and bull sports. The contents of **Room VIII** come from Zákros, the only palace that escaped the ancient plunderers. The stone vases are superb, most notably a rock crystal amphora (it was in over 300 pieces when found) and a rhyton showing a Minoan peak sanctuary. **Room IX** has items from ordinary Minoan houses. The seal engravers achieved an astounding technique; suspicions that they had to use lenses to execute such tiny detail were confirmed when one made of rock crystal was found in Knossos.

After the Golden Age, the Post-Palace period artefacts in **Room X** (1450–1100 BC) show an artistic coarsening and heavier Mycenaean influences. Figures lose their *joie de vivre*; the goddesses are stiff, their flouncy skirts reduced to smooth bells. One goddess wears an opium poppy hat; Minoan use of opium and alcohol may possibly explain a lack of the aggression typical of other 'cradles of civilization'.

The Dorians heralded the decline apparent in **Room XI** (1100–900 BC); the quality of the work is poor all round, whether made by pockets of unconquered Minoans or by the invaders. The pieces in **Room XII** show an improvement in the Mature Geometric and Orientalizing periods (900–650 BC), as familiar gods make an appearance: Zeus holding an eagle and thunderbolts on a pot lid, Hermes with sheep and goats on a bronze plaque. Orientalizing pottery shows the Eastern influences that dominated Greece in the 8th–7th centuries; one vase shows a pair of lovers, presumed to be Theseus and Ariadne. **Room XIII** contains Minoan *larnaxes*, or terracotta sarcophagi. Minoans were laid out in a foetal position, so they are quite small.

The Frescoes and Ag. Triáda Sarcophagus

The Minoans also excelled at frescoes, displayed upstairs in **Rooms XIV–XVI**. Almost as fascinating as the paintings themselves is the work that went into their reconstruction by the Swiss father-and-son team hired by Evans. Cretan artists followed Egyptian conventions in colour: women are white, men are red, monkeys are blue, a revelation that led to the re-restoration of *The Saffron Gatherers*, one of the oldest frescoes, originally restored as a boy and now reconstructed as a monkey picking crocuses. From the palace of Knossos, the nearly completely intact *Cup-Bearer* is from the huge *Procession* fresco, which is estimated to have had 350 figures. Here, too, are *The Dolphins*, *The Prince of the Lilies*, *The Shields*, and also the charming *Partridges* found in the 'Caravanserai' at Knossos. The 'miniature frescoes' in the other two rooms include the *Parisienne*, as she was dubbed by her discoverers in 1903, with her eye-paint, lipstick and 'sacral knot' jauntily tied at the back. Take a good look at the most famous fresco, *The Bull Leapers*, with a border that doubled as a calendar.

Occupying pride of place, the Ag. Triáda Sarcophagus is the only one in stone ever found on Crete, but what really sets it apart is its elaborately painted layer of plaster. The subject is a Minoan ritual: a bull is sacrificed while a woman makes an offering on an altar next to a sacred tree with a bird, the epiphany of the goddess. On the other long side, two women bear buckets, perhaps of bull's blood, accompanied by a man in female dress, playing a lyre. On the right, three men are bearing animals and a model boat, which they offer to either a dead man, wrapped up like a mummy, or an idol (*xoanan*). Near the sarcophagus is a wooden model of Knossos, and the entrance to the Giamalakis collection (**Room XVII**), containing unique items from all periods.

Downstairs, products of ancient Crete's last breath of artistic inspiration in the bold, powerfully moulded 'Daedalic style' (700–650 BC) are contained in **Rooms XVIII** and **XIX**. There is a striking frieze of warriors and lavish bronze shields and cymbals from the Idaean Cave. The bronze figures of Apollo, Artemis and Leto from Dreros are key works: the goddesses are reduced to anthropomorphic pillars, rather like a salt-and-pepper set. Yet the real anticlimax is reserved for **Room XX**, the Classical Greek and Graeco-Roman periods (5th century BC–4th century AD), when Crete was a backwater.

Other Museums in Heráklion

The **Battle of Crete and Resistance Museum** (*t 281 034 6554; open Mon–Fri 8–3*) is just behind the archaeological museum, on the corner of Doukós Bófor and Hatzidáki Streets, with a collection of weapons, photos and uniforms.

Across town, on Lisimáhou Kalokairinoú, the fascinating **Historical Museum of Crete** (*t 281 022 8708; open Mon–Fri 9–5, Sat 9–2, closed Sun and hols; adm exp*) picks up where the archaeological museum leaves off, with artefacts from Early Christian times. The basement contains delightful 18th-century Turkish frescoes of imaginary towns, bits salvaged from Venetian churches. On the ground floor are 14th-century murals from Kardoulianó Pediádos, and, in a room all to itself, the *Imaginary View of Mount Sinai and the Monastery of St Catherine* (*c.* 1576) by Doménikos Theotokópoulos (El Greco), his only painting in Crete. The first floor has pictures of Cretan *kapetános*, each more mustachioed than the last, and the library of Níkos Kazantzákis. Other rooms contain traditional arts, in particular intricate red embroideries and weavings, one of the most noteworthy artistic achievements by Ottoman Cretans.

Outside the walls, southwest of town, the **Natural History Musem of Crete** (*157 Knossos, t 281 032 4711; open daily 9–7; adm*), run by the University of Crete, takes a serious look at the flora and fauna of the island, with a botanical garden.

The Cathedral and Byzantine Museum

West of Plateía Venizélou, the overblown cathedral dedicated to Heráklion's patron **Ag. Miná** (1895) dwarfs its convivial predecessor, old Ag. Miná; the latter has a beautiful iconostasis and an icon of Ag. Minas on his white horse, long the protector of Heráklion (martyrologies say Minas was a 3rd-century Egyptian soldier, but one can't help wondering if his name and cult might have had something to do with the memory of Minos in this ancient port of Knossos).

Around the back, the sun-bleached **Ag. Ekaterína** (1555) was an important monastic school linked to St Catherine in the Sinai. One subject taught here was icon-painting (El Greco studied here) and today the church, appropriately, holds a **Museum of Byzantine Icons** (*t 281 028 8825; open Mon–Sat 9.30–2.30, also Tues, Thurs and Fri 4.30–6.30; adm*). The museum is proudest of its six icons by Mikális Damaskinós, a contemporary of El Greco who went to Venice but returned to Crete; in his *Last Supper*, Damaskinós placed a Byzantine Jesus in a setting from an Italian engraving – a bizarre effect heightened by the fact that Christ seems to be holding a hamburger.

The Venetian Walls and the Tomb of Kazantzákis

Michele Sammicheli, the greatest military architect of the 16th century, designed Candia's walls so well that it took the Turks from 1648 to 1667 to breach them. From the beginning the Venetians tried to rally Europe to the cause of defending Candia as the last Christian outpost in the East, but only received occasional, ineffectual aid from the French. Stalemate characterized the first 18 years of the siege; the sultan found it so frustrating that he banned the mention of Candia in his presence. In 1667 both sides, keen to end the stalemate, sent in their most brilliant generals, the Venetian Francesco Morosini (uncle of the Morosini who blew the top off the Parthenon) and the Turk Köprülü, whose arrival with 40,000 troops finally nudged the Europeans to action, but all too little, too late. Morosini negotiated the city's surrender with Köprülü, and with 20 days of safe conduct sailed away with most of the inhabitants (many ended up on the Ionian Islands) and the city's archives – an outcome that had cost the lives of 30,000 Christians and 137,000 Turks.

Brilliantly restored, Sammicheli's massive walls are nearly as vexing to get on top of today as they were for the besieging Turks – 2½ miles long, in places 44ft thick, punctuated with 12 fort-like bastions. Tunnels have been punched through the old gates, although the **Pórta Chaniá** (Chaniá Gate) at the end of Kalokairinoú preserves much of its original appearance. From Plastirá Street, a side street leads up to the Martinengo Bastion and the simple **tomb of Níkos Kazantzákis**, who died in 1957 and chose his own epitaph: 'I believe in nothing, I hope for nothing, I am free.' In the distance you can see the profile of Zeus in Mount Júktas (*see* p.715).

Heráklion Province

This province, cradled between Psilorítis and the Diktean Mountain, was the core of Minoan Crete, home to Knossos, Mália, Phaistos, Archánes and Ag. Triáda, and countless smaller sites. Besides the finest Cretan art and culture, the province also contains much of the dark side of what the last 40 years have wrought – the resorts along the north coast, thrown up in the first flush of mass tourism in the 1960s, about which you often hear people say that what the Venetians, Turks and Germans couldn't conquer, money has undone without a fight.

Beaches Around Heráklion

Heráklion is surrounded by sand, and you have a choice of backdrops for your beach idyll: a power plant, cement works and hotels just west at **Ammoudára** and, to the east, suburbs and airport behind the unexceptional city beach **Karterós** (7km) and **Amnisós**, the first of the string of resorts east of Heráklion, which overlooks the islet of Día, once sacred to Zeus and now a sanctuary for Crete's endangered ibexes, or *krikri*, who somehow have learned to cope with all the charter flights.

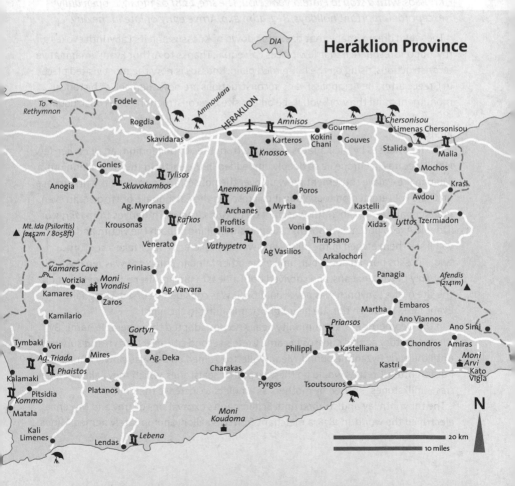

Heráklion Province

Amnisós, in fact, has been a busy place since Neolithic times. Minoan Amnisós had two harbours, on either side of a hard-scrabble hill, now topped by the ruins of a Venetian village. The east end has the fenced-off villa of 1600 BC that yielded the *Fresco of the Lilies* in the museum; on the northwest side is an Archaic Sanctuary of Zeus Thenatas. In the 1930s, while excavating the Minoan 'Harbour Master's Office', Spyridon Marinátos discovered a layer of pumice, the evidence he needed to support his theory that Minoan Crete had been devastated by ash from Santoríni (*see* p.664).

One kilometre from Amnisós is the **Cave of Eileithyia**, goddess of childbirth (to visit, inquire at the Heráklion Archaeological Museum). Few divinities had her staying power; the cave attracted women from the Neolithic era to the 5th century AD. Stalagmites resembling a mother and her children were the main focus; pregnant women would rub against a third one, resembling a pregnant belly with a navel.

Knossos (ΚΝΩΣΟΣ)

Every 10mins a city bus (no.2) departs from Heráklion's main bus station for Knossos, with a stop in Plateía Venizélou. The site, t 281 023 1940, is open daily except for important holidays, 8–7; adm exp. Arrive early or late in the day.

The weird dream image that has come down of Knossos and its Labyrinth evokes a mythopœic resonance that few places can equal. Thanks to Arthur Evans' imaginative reconstructions, rising on the hill-girded plain, Knossos is now the most visited place in Greece after the Acropolis. Evans' reconstructions are now themselves historical monuments, and the work you'll see on the site is reconstructions of reconstructions.

History

The first houses by the Kairatos river date from the 7th millennium BC, or earlier; few Neolithic sites in Europe lie so deeply embedded in the earth. In the 3rd millennium, a Minoan Pre-Palace settlement grew up over the houses, and *c.* 1950 BC the first palace on Crete was erected on top. When it collapsed in the earthquake of 1700 BC, an even grander palace, the Labyrinth, was built on its ruins. 'Labyrinth' derives from *labrys*, or 'Double Axe', a potent symbol that suggests the killing of both the victim and slayer; you'll see them etched in the pillars and walls. In 1450 BC (give or take a century or two) Knossos burned down but, unlike the other Minoan palaces, it was repaired, probably by Mycenaeans, and survived until at least 1380 BC. After a final destruction, the site of the Labyrinth was never built on; it was considered cursed. The guards Evans hired to watch the site heard ghosts moaning in the night.

In the Geometric era, a community near Knossos adopted the venerable name. By the 3rd century BC this Knossos became Crete's second city after Gortyn and survived until the early Byzantine period. Meanwhile, the ruined palace was slowly buried, but not forgotten. Cretans would go there to gather sealstones, which they called *galópetres* – 'milkstones' – prized by mothers as amulets to increase their milk.

The Labyrinth lay undisturbed until Schliemann's excavations of Troy and Mycenae electrified the world. In 1878, a merchant from Heráklion, appropriately named Mínos

Kalokairinós, dug the first trenches into the palace of his namesake, at once finding walls, enormous *pithoi* and the first Linear B tablet. Schliemann heard the news and in 1887 he negotiated the purchase of the site. However, the Turkish owners were impossible and Schliemann gave up in despair; in 1890 he died.

The field thus cleared, Evans, then curator of the Ashmolean Museum in Oxford, arrived in Crete in 1894. Doggedly, he spent the next five years buying Knossos, while supplying reports of Turkish atrocities to the press. The purchase coincided with Cretan independence, and in March 1900 Evans got permission to dig. Within three weeks the throne room had been excavated, along with Linear A tablets, belonging to a civilization older than the Mycenaeans, which Evans labelled 'Minoan' for ever after.

The Site

In 1908, Evans used his considerable inheritance to 'reconstitute' part of Minos' palace. Scholars dispute the accuracy of his reconstructions, the labels Evans assigned to the rooms, and his interpretation of the Minoans as peaceful sophisticates. Yet his reconstructions do succeed in his goal of making Knossos come alive, evoking the grandeur of a 1,500-room Minoan palace of *c.*1700 BC that none of the unreconstructed sites can match; a visit here makes Phaistos or Mália easier to understand.

Unlike their contemporaries in the Near East, the Minoans oriented their palaces to the west, not the east, and the entrance is by way of the **West Court**. The three pits were grain silos, once protected by domes. A porch on the right from the West Court leads to the **Corridor of the Procession**, named after the fresco found here, and to the **Propylon**, or south entrance, with reproductions of its frescoes. A stair from the Propylon leads to an upper floor, which Evans called the '**Piano Nobile**'. Of all his reconstructions, this is considered the most fanciful. The **Tripartite Shrine**, with its three columns, is a typical feature of Minoan palaces, and may have been used to worship the Goddess in her aspects of mistress of heaven, earth and the underworld.

A narrow staircase descends to the **Central Court**, measuring 190 by 95ft. Originally this was closed in by buildings, which may have provided seats to view the bull leaping, although like so much in Knossos, this is problematic: how did they lead bulls through the Labyrinth? How could they squeeze in all the action? Or was this Homer's 'dancing floor of Ariadne'? The sacral horns here were a universal Minoan symbol. From the Central Court, enter the lower levels of the West Wing, site of the tiny **Throne Room** where Evans uncovered a scallop-edged throne where it stood 3,800 years ago; judges of the Court of International Justice in The Hague sit on reproductions. On either side are gypsum benches and frescoes of Mycenaean griffons. The **Lustral Basin**, like others throughout Knossos, may have held water used in rituals, or reflected light from light wells. Evans found evidence here of what appeared to be a last-ditch effort to placate the gods as disaster swept through Knossos.

The stair south of the antechamber of the Throne Room ascends to an upper floor, used in part for storage, as in the **Room of the Tall *Pithos*** and the **Temple Repositories**. The pillars thicken near the top, unique to Minoan architecture and similar to the trunk of the 'horizontal' cypress native to the Gorge of Samariá. Returning to the

Knossos

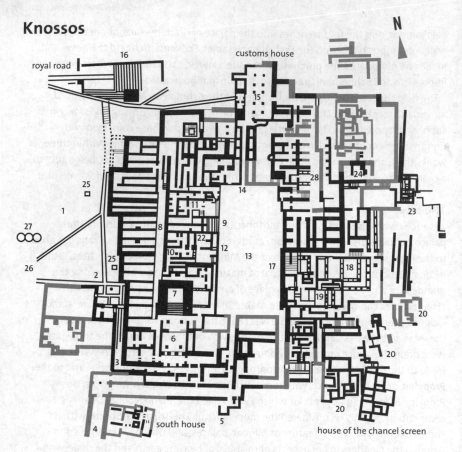

royal road

customs house

N

south house

house of the chancel screen

1	West Court	11	Throne Room	21	north lustral basin
2	west porch	12	Tripartite Shrine	22	temple repositories
3	Corridor of the Procession	13	Central Court	23	east bastion
4	stepped porch	14	north entrance passage	24	store rooms of giant pithoi
5	south entrance	15	North Pillar Hall	25	altar
6	south Propylon	16	theatre	26	bust of Arthur Evans
7	Grand Stair	17	Grand Staircase	27	storage silos
8	store room corridor	18	Hall of the Double Axes	28	Corridor of the
9	stair	19	Queen's Megaron		Draughtboard
10	pillar crypts	20	southeast house		

Central Court, note the high relief fresco copy of the '**Prince of the Lilies**' to the south, at the end of the Corridor of the Procession.

Evans, who took monarchies for granted, had no doubt that the more elaborate **East Wing** of the palace contained the 'Royal Apartments'. Here the **Grand Staircase** and **Central Light Well** are an architectural *tour de force*; almost five flights of broad gypsum steps are preserved. However, descending to the two lower floors (which were found intact) it is hard to imagine that anyone of any class would choose to live with little light and air. The rooms did have something that modern royals couldn't live without: plumbing, visible under the floor in the **Queen's Megaron** and its bathroom, complete with a flush toilet. The King's Megaron, also known as the **Hall of the Double Axes** owing to the many carvings on the walls, opens on to the **Hall of the Royal Guard**, decorated with a copy of the fresco of cowhide figure-of-eight shields.

North of the royal apartments, the **Corridor of the Draughtboard** is where the game-board in the Heráklion Museum was found; here you can see the clay pipes from the Mount Júktas aqueduct. Here too are the impressive **Magazines of Giant Pithoi**. As you leave through the north, there's a relief copy of the bull fresco, and near this the **Customs House**, supported by eight pillars, which may have been used for processing imports and exports. Below is the oldest paved road in Europe, the **Royal Road**, ending abruptly at the modern road; originally it continued to the Little Palace and beyond. It begins at the so-called **Theatre** (it looks like a large stair), where 500 people could sit to view religious processions or dances, as pictured in the frescoes.

Around Knossos

Other Minoan buildings have been excavated outside the palace. Nearest are the reconstructed three-storey **South House**, complete with a bathroom and latrine, the **Southeast House**, and the **House of the Chancel Screen**, both perhaps residences of VIPs – the latter has a dais for a throne or altar. Other sites require special permission to visit, such as the **Royal Villa**, with its throne and beautifully preserved Pillar Crypt. The **Little Palace**, just across the modern road, had three pillar crypts and was used after the Minoans as a shrine; the magnificent bull's head rhyton was found here.

To the south, a sign on the road points the way to the **Caravanserai**, as Evans named it, believing travellers would pause here to wash the dust from their feet in the stone trough; it has a copy of the lovely partridge fresco. Further south are four pillars from the aqueduct, and south of that the **Royal Temple Tomb**, where the natural rock ceiling was painted blue and a stair leads to a temple on top. The **House of the Sacrificed Children**, found in 1980, was named after a large cache of children's bones bearing the marks of knives. The Minoans, having been found guilty of human sacrifice at Archánes (*see* p.716), now had cannibalism to answer for. But it may be that that the children had already died and their bones were being stripped of any flesh before re-burial – a custom that survived in parts of Greece into the 19th century.

South of Knossos: Archánes

One of the ancient proofs of Epimenides' paradox 'All Cretans are liars' was the fact that immortal Zeus was born on Crete, but buried here as well; the profile of his bearded face is easily discerned in Mount Júktas as you head south of Knossos. The road follows a Minoan highway, and has seen some modern history as well: at the Archánes crossroads, Cretan Resistance fighters and the British officers Patrick Leigh Fermor and Captain W. Stanley Moss kidnapped General Kreipe on 26 April 1944.

Handsome **Archánes** has often been called on to supply the thirsty north with wine and water; the Minoan aqueduct to Knossos began here, as did the Venetian one to Heráklion. In the centre, the church of the **Panagía** has an exceptional collection of

16th–19th-century icons (*open mornings*). The **Cretan Historical and Folklore Museum**, signposted 3km from Archánes (*t 281 075 1853; open Wed–Mon 9.30–2*), has tools, costumes and memorabilia from the Battle of Crete, as well as personal belongings of General Kreipe and displays relating to his abduction. Just south of town, the lovely church of the **Asómatos** is decorated with excellent frescoes dated 1315.

Evans surmised the existence of a 'summer palace' in Archánes, and in 1964 Ioánnis and Éfi Sakellarákis found it, and more. The **palace**, unfortunately, is smack in the centre of town (the largest visible section lies between Mákri Sokáki and Ierolóchiton Streets). Dating from *c.* 1700–1450 BC, it was multi-storey and luxurious; only in Knossos and Phaistos were similarly coloured marbles, gypsum and other materials used. It had elaborate frescoes, a drainage system and a cistern built over a spring. A 'theatrical area' and an archive of Linear A tablets were also found.

In Minoan times, a paved road from the palace led to the **Necropolis of Phourní** (*open daily 8–2, but ring ahead, t 281 075 1907*), set atop a ridge 1.5km to the southwest (a very steep walk up; by car you can take the rural road up from Káto Archánes). A major prehistoric cemetery, in use for 1,250 years (2500–1250 BC), it had three tholos tombs. Tholos A was used as a hiding place in the Second World War, but tucked in a side chamber behind a false wall lay a priestess or royal lady from the 14th century BC, buried in a gold-trimmed garment, with gold and ivory jewellery, a footstool decorated with ivory and the remains of a sacrificed horse and bull, carved into bits. The bottom layer of the collective burials in Tholos C goes back to 2500 BC and yielded marble Cycladic figurines and jewellery in the same style as the Treasure of Priam that Schliemann found at Troy. The Mycenaean grave enclosure with seven shaft tombs and three stelae is unique on Crete. Its libation pit was so saturated with offerings that the Sakellarákis team were overwhelmed by 'the unbearable stench'.

Five kilometres southwest of Archánes, above the town dump, on the promontory of **Anemospiliá** (*open daily 8am–8pm*), the Sakellarákises discovered an isolated **tripartite shrine**. Often depicted in Minoan art, this was the first and, so far, the only one ever found. The middle room contained a pair of clay feet from a *xoanon*, an idol made from wood and other perishable materials, worshipped in Greece since Neolithic times; Pausanius wrote that the Greeks believed they were first made by Daedalos on Crete. The eastern room was apparently used for bloodless sacrifices. The western room, however, produced one of the most startling finds in nearly a century of Minoan archaeology: it contained bodies of people caught as an earthquake struck *c.* 1700 BC. The skeleton of a 17-year-old boy was found bound on an altar, next to a dagger; examination by the University of Manchester showed that he had probably had his throat cut. The other skeletons belonged to a man wearing an iron ring and a woman, of fine breeding. By a fourth skeleton, a Kamáres-ware vase was found; it may have been full of blood, perhaps an offering to appease the Earth-shaking god.

The Anemospiliá findings came as a shock. Evans' Minoans seemed too sophisticated for such barbarities, despite hints of human sacrifice in myth. But perhaps such extreme acts were resorted to only in extraordinary situations, where the sacrifice of one is made in the hope of saving many. Even then, the practice may have been so disagreeable that it was hidden behind the doors of the shrine.

Two kilometres south of Archánes, vines surround the villa complex of **Vathýpetro** (*open mornings only; check at the Iouktas café*), set on a spur facing Mount Júktas. In plan it resembles a baby Knossos, with a small west court and larger central court, a tripartite shrine, and a three-columned portico with a courtyard, closed off by a fancy, recessed structure of a type found nowhere else, supported by symmetrical square plinths. Built *c*. 1580 BC, the villa was shattered by an earthquake soon after, and was rebuilt, perhaps as a craft centre; loom weights and potters' wheels were found, along with the oldest wine press in Greece. To this day, local vintners repeat a ritual that may well be as old as Vathýpetro: every 6 August the first fruits of the harvest are offered to the deity on **Mount Júktas**. A good road just before Vathýpetro leads up to the church where it all happens, the Christian replacement for the Minoan peak sanctuary of **Psilí Korfí** just to the north. A young Poseidon was one of the gods worshipped here; the mountain was an important navigational landmark.

The broad road south of Vathýpetro continues to **Ag. Vasílios** and **Moní Spiliótissa**, a convent with a frescoed church built into a cave, hidden in a lush grove of plane trees. A short walk away is the simple church of **Ag. Ioánnis**, with frescoes dated 1291. You could return to Heráklion from here by way of Crete's pretty wine region, Pezá, and the village of **Myrtiá**, set over a majestic landscape (if you come from Heráklion, turn-off just before the road to Archánes). Myrtiá has the **Kazantzákis Museum** (*t 281 0741 689; open daily 9–1 and Mon, Wed, Sat and Sun 4–8, closed Thurs; adm*): photos, documents and memorabilia evoke the life and travels of Crete's greatest novelist, the author of *Zorba the Greek*. He died in 1957 after he was nominated one last time for the Nobel Prize (the Church lobbied against him, and he lost by one vote to Camus).

Southwest of Heráklion

The road from Heráklion to Gortyn, Phaistos and Mátala passes through dense vineyards. On the way, at **Veneráto** you can make a 2km detour to the convent of **Palianí**. Besides early Christian capitals and 13th-century frescoes, Palianí has the Holy Myrtle; the nuns claim there's an icon of the Virgin in the heart of the tree. To the south, the large, straggling village of **Ag. Varvára** stands amid cherry orchards at approximately the geographical centre of the big island; a chapel sits atop a large rock known as the *'omphalos'*, or navel, of Crete. The weather here can be dramatic: at Mégali Vríssi, to the east, Crete's first aeolian park harnesses the cross-island winds.

A lovely road west of Ag. Varvára skirts the groves and orchards on the southern flanks of Psilorítis. Nearly all the villages here began as Minoan farming communities, among them **Zarós**, a local beauty spot and source of bottled mineral water; the

Where to Stay and Eat

Zarós ✉ 70002
Idi Hotel, t 289 403 1302, f 289 403 1511 (*C; moderate*). Lovely mountain hotel, with a verdant garden surrounding pools.

Taverna Votomos, t 289 403 1071 (€15). With lovely views of the valley. Fresh salmon and trout, served with delicious rice, hold pride of place on the menu.

Romans built an aqueduct from here to Gortyn so they wouldn't have to drink anything else. The **Gorge of Zarós** is a good place for a picnic: the walk begins at the monastery of **Ag. Nikólaos**. Another monastery to the west, **Moní Vrondísi**, was burned by the Turks in 1821, but it still has a pretty gate, a charming 15th-century Venetian fountain and a massive plane tree, blasted hollow by lightning and now housing a café. The church's 14th-century frescoes are only a shadow of the treasures it once had – having had a premonition of its sacking, the abbot sent its finest works, by Michael Damáskinos, to Ag. Kateríni in Heráklion, where they remain. **Moní Valsamonérou**, 5km west, is reached by path from **Vorízia**, another village rebuilt after being obliterated in Nazi reprisals (the guardian lives here, although he's usually at the church on weekday mornings). Once important, Valsamonérou is now reduced to an enchanting assymetrical church dedicated to Ag. Fanoúrios, in charge of heaven's lost and found; the exceptional 14th-century frescoes are by Konstantínos Ríkos.

The road continues to **Kamáres**, the base for the 3–4-hour walk up Mount Ida to the **Kamáres Cave** (5,003ft), an important Minoan cave sanctuary. Its gaping mouth, 66ft high and 130ft wide, is visible from Phaistos; Minoan pilgrims brought their offerings in the colourful pottery first discovered here – hence 'Kamáres ware' (*see* p.707).

The Mesará Plain and Gortyn (ΓΟΡΤΥΣ)

Gortyn is open daily 8–7; adm; t 289 203 1144. If you're arriving by bus, get off at the Gortyn entrance and make your way back towards the village of Ag. Déka.

Tucked under the southern flanks of Mount Ida, the long, densely populated Mesará Plain is the breadbasket of Crete. After the Dorian invasion, its biggest town **Gortyn** (or Gortys) gradually supplanted Knossos as the ruling city of Crete. Hannibal's brief sojourn here in 189 BC after his defeat by Rome may have given the inhabitants some insight to the future, because they helped the Romans capture Crete. In reward, Rome

> ## Human Rights, Dorian-style
>
> The first block of engraved limestone, discovered in a mill stream in 1857, was purchased by the Louvre. At the time no-one had ever seen such an ancient inscription in Greek, and the translation, using the writing on ancient coins as a guide, took years. No one suspected that there was more until one summer's day in 1884, when the Italian archaeologist Halbherr noticed a submerged building – the Odeion – while cooling his feet in the same mill stream. The rest of the code, over 600 lines on 12 blocks, was found soon after in a field, minus a few minor bits.
>
> The code, written in *boustrophedon*, 'as the ox ploughs' – from left to right, then right to left – is in the Doric dialect of *c.* 500 BC. Thanks to it the civil laws of Archaic Crete are better known in their specific detail than Roman law. The code was made for public display, and significantly, in spite of a different set of rules for citizens, serfs (the Minoans) and slaves, the Gortyn Code allows women important property rights; slaves had recourse against cruel masters, and there was a presumption of innocence until guilt is proven long before this became the core of Anglo-American law.

made Gortyn the capital not only of Crete but also of their province of Cyrenaica, which included much of North Africa. In AD 828 the Saracens wiped it off the map.

In its prime, Gortyn counted 300,000 souls. Its ruins are scattered through a mile of olive groves. The apse is all that survives of the 6th-century **Basilica of Ag. Títos**, once one of the most important in Greece but now a roosting place for local birds. Titus, originally buried here, was one of Paul's favourite disciples and first bishop of Gortyn. Nearby, built into the walls of the elegant **Roman Odeion** (reconstructed by Trajan in AD 100), is Gortyn's prize, the **Law Code of Gortyn**, now covered by a shelter.

Just up and behind the Law Code is the famous Cretan evergreen **Plane Tree** of Gortyn, by the Lethaios river. The story goes that it has kept its leaves for modesty's sake ever since Zeus in bull disguise brought the Phoenician princess Europa into its shade, resulting in the birth of Minos, Rhadamanthys and Sarpedon.

The rest of Gortyn is outside the enclosed area. If it's not too hot, consider climbing the **Acropolis** with the remains of an 8th-century BC temple and altar, Roman walls and a well-preserved defensive building, perhaps built at the expense of the **Theatre**, chewed away in the hillside below. A few minutes' walk down to **Mitrópolis** reveals an Early Byzantine church with a mosaic floor, cut in two by the modern road. Signs point to the ruins in the olive groves: a **Temple of Isis and Serapis**, the Egyptian gods popular in the late empire, and the elaborate **Temple of Pythian Apollo**, the most important in Gortyn and often rebuilt since Archaic times; the inscription is another segment of Gortyn's Law Code, written in an even older dialect. The imposing 2nd-century AD **Praetorium**, seat of the Roman governor, continued in use as a monastery until Venetian times. Part of the complex includes the **Nymphaeum**, where the waters from the Zarós aqueduct flowed into the city. Further south are the ruins of the gate, amphitheatre, stadium and cemetery, while the main path leads to the village **Ag. Déka**, named after 10 martyrs of c. AD 250. The block on which they were beheaded is kept in the church, and their tombs are the subject of much devotion.

Mires, 9km to the west, is a lively agricultural town that has taken over Gortyn's role as the centre of the Mesará. If you're relying on buses, count on spending time here, waiting for changes for Phaistos, Mátala, Ag. Galíni, the Amári Valley or Réthymnon.

Phaistos (ΦΑΙΣΤΟΣ)

t 289 204 2315; open daily 8–7; adm exp. Arrive early or late to avoid the crowds. A pavilion on the site has a café, food, and rooms, t 289 204 2360.

Superbly overlooking the Mesará plain and Psilorítis, Phaistos was the fief of Minos' brother Rhadamanthys. The first palace was constructed in c. 2000 BC, and destroyed in an earthquake in 1700 BC; the second palace was built over the first and destroyed in turn in c. 1450 BC. Like Knossos but on a smaller scale, it was built of alabaster and gypsum and, although its workshops produced exquisite art, no frescoes were found. Below the palace, 50,000 people lived and worked. Phaistos remained an independent little city-state, until Gortyn crushed it once and for all in the 3rd century BC.

Purists dismayed by Evans' reconstructions at Knossos will breathe a sigh of relief at Phaistos, where only your imagination will reconstruct the three-storey palace from the low, complicated walls and foundations; because the second palace was built over the first means that you need an especially good imagination (or opt for a guided tour). Visits begin in the northwest, in the **Upper Court** with its raised **Processional Way**. This continues down steps into the **West Court**, originally part of the Old Palace – the only section the architects of the New Palace re-used. Otherwise the lines of the building were completely reorientated; the lower façade of the Old Palace survives just before the Grand Stairway. The West Court has the eight tiers known as the **Theatre**, and two formerly-domed granaries or silos.

The **Grand Stairway** was carved partly from the living rock; note how the steps are slightly convex, to allow rainwater to run off. At the top, the **Great Propylon**, the main entrance to the West Wing, stands just before a light well with three columns. Another stair descends to the **Antechamber of the Store Rooms**, which yielded a huge cache of sealstones, while beyond are the **Store Rooms**; one, covered with a roof, still contains its giant *pithoi*, along with a stone stool for standing on to scoop out the contents, and a built-in vessel in the floor to collect wine or oil run-offs. An important corridor separated the storage areas from the main **Shrine**, lined with stone benches.

From the Antechamber of the Store Rooms opens the **Central Court**, its long sides originally sheltered by porticoes; buildings on all sides would have hidden the tremendous views it enjoys today. A stepped block in the northwest corner may have been the platform used by bull dancers for 'diving leaps'. To the southwest is a series of rooms fenced off and mingled with bits of the Old Palace and the foundations of a Classical temple. Landslides have swept away much of the **East Wing**, but the small chamber just to the north, with a bathroom and lustral basin with steps, earned it the name of 'Prince's Apartment'. A horseshoe-shaped **forge**, built in the Old Palace era, is at the end of the corridor to the north, the earliest one yet discovered in Greece.

North of the Central Court, a grand entrance with niches in the walls and another corridor leads to yet more **'royal apartments'**, paved with alabaster and gypsum and now fenced off to prevent wear; you can barely make out the **Queen's Megaron** and its alabaster benches. An open peristyle court tops the **King's Megaron**, with a royal view to the Kamáres Sanctuary (that dark patch between the twin summits). The Phaistos Disc was found nearby, in the mud-brick 'archives' of the Old Palace.

The 'Summer Villa' of Ag. Triáda (ΑΓ. ΤΡΙΑΔΑ)

Just 3km west of Phaistos, a road runs to the car park just above the smaller Minoan palace of Ag. Triáda (*t 289 209 1360; open daily 8.30–3; adm*), named after a diminutive Venetian church on the site. No-one knows why such a lavish little estate was built so close to Phaistos. Guesses are that a wealthy Minoan simply fell in love with the splendid setting, or it may have been a summer palace; Phaistos can turn into a frying pan in the summer and Ag. Triáda usually has a sea breeze. In Minoan times, the sea came further in and the ramp under the villa may have led down to a port. It's certainly an old site; Neolithic dwellings were discovered under the 'palace', which was built around 1600 BC. It burned in the island-wide destruction of 1450 BC. The Minoans rebuilt it and the Mycenaeans added a megaron and a village, dominated by a building that looks like a stoa – a row of shops under a porch – 1,000 years before they were invented. The site has yielded some of the Minoans' finest art, including frescoes, the Harvesters' Vase and the sarcophagus of Ag. Triáda.

The intimate scale and surroundings – and lack of tour groups – make Ag. Tríada the most charming of the major Minoan sites. The villa had two wings. The north–south wing, overlooking the sea, was the most elaborate, with flagstone floors and gypsum and alabaster walls and benches. One room had frescoes (such as the stalking cat), another had built-in closets. *Pithoi* still stand intact in the store rooms. At the entrance, **Ag. Geórgios Galatás** (1302) has good frescoes (the guardian has the key).

Around the Southwest Coast

This corner of Crete offers more than the exquisite fossils of long-lost civilizations. Just to the north of Phaistos, the old village of **Vóri** hopes to waylay you with its superb **Museum of Cretan Ethnology** (*t 289 209 1394; open 10–6; adm*), the best place on the island to learn about traditional life in Crete with excellent detailed descriptions in English. Charmless **Tymbáki**, 3km west, combines tomatoes under plastic with dogged tourism, thanks to its long ugly beach, **Kókkinos Pírgos**, the 'red tower', a name that predates its career as the Ketchup Coast.

Elsewhere, this is a wild shore. One road south of Phaistos leads to **Mátala**, the once notorious beach enclosed by sandstone cliffs, riddled with cave tombs from the 1st and 2nd centuries AD. In the early 1960s Americans bumming around on a dollar a day found that the caves made a perfect place to crash in the winter, and before long they were joined by an international hippy colony, banished in the killjoy 1990s. If you stay overnight, something of their spirit lingers in Mátala's laid-back atmosphere, otherwise grannies hawking rugs may be your strongest memory. If the town beach is a massive body jam, a path and a scramble will take you in about 20 minutes to **Kókkinos Ámmos**, 'red sand', with caves (inhabited, this time); excursion boats sail south to other small beaches at Ag. Farago and Vathí. Avoid walking on the beaches on summer nights, when loggerhead turtles make their nests.

Mátala has been a midwife of tourism for **Pitsídia**, and more recently for **Kalamáki**, an embryonic resort just down by the long beach north of Mátala. At the south end of this beach (easiest reached by a track from Pitsídia) is **Kómmo**, with remains of the

Where to Stay and Eat

Mátala ✉ 70200

Valley Village, t 289 204 5776 (*B; moderate*). With a pool, Greek dancing shows and barbecue nights.

Zafira, t 289 204 5112 (*D; moderate*). Handy for town and beach, but completely booked in season.

Nikos, t 289 204 5375 (*E; inexpensive*). With a garden, a pleasant choice on a whole lane of rent rooms.

Mátala Camping, t 289 204 5720. Just behind the beach, offering shade and low prices.

Syrtaki (€12). On the seaside, serving Greek favourites at reasonable prices.

Zeus Beach Taverna (€10–12). Right on the beach, dishes made by mama, and you can feed your extra bread to the ducks.

Giorgio's Bar, at the end. Cocktails to go with Mátala's famous sunsets.

Kivotos, up in Sivas, **t** 289 204 2744 (€12–15). Oven dishes and live music daily in the summer.

largest Minoan port discovered on the south coast. Although not officially open for visits, you can see a massive building of dressed stone, believed to have been a warehouse, dry docks with five slips, houses (one with a wine press) and a paved road with worn ruts that led to Phaistos. Near the beach stood an important sanctuary, sacred long after the Minoans: the Dorians built a temple here in the 10th century BC, as did the Phoenicians and the Classical and Hellenistic-era Greeks.

Phaistos' rival Gortyn had several ports to the east, including **Kalí Liménes**, the 'Fair Havens', down a steep winding drive. This is where the ship carrying St Paul put in on its way to be wrecked off Malta; it now hosts oil tankers. Ruins of another of Gortyn's harbours, **Levín** (or Lebena) lie near the ramshackle fishing village of **Léndas**. The hot springs east of the village (now pumped elsewhere) led to the construction in the 4th century BC of an Asklepeion; there are mosaics, bits of a temple, and a pool where patients once wallowed in the waters. Nearly all the wallowing these days happens 3km west at **Yerókambos**, a magnificent long beach; a few tavernas rent rooms.

Southeast of Heráklion: Villages of Mount Díkti

The western foothills of Mount Díkti are linked by a good road south of Chersónisos. **Káto** and **Páno Karouzaná** are 'traditional villages' offering Greek nights; but south just before Kastélli, follow signs for 'Paradise Tavern' to lovely **Ag. Pandeleímonos**, built in AD 450 over a temple to Asklepios (the taverna owners will summon the caretaker). Once said to have had 101 doors, it was rebuilt on a more modest scale in c. 1100 after being ravaged by the Saracens. The nave is supported by columns from ancient Lyttos, including one made of nothing but Corinthian capitals.

Kastélli is the largest village here. A short detour west to **Sklaverochóri** has its reward in the 15th-century church **Eisódia tis Theotókou**, decorated with excellent frescoes: a fairytale scene with St George and the princess, allegories of the river gods in the Baptism and a benign Catholic intruder – St Francis. Four kilometres east of Kastélli, ancient **Lyttos** (modern Xidás) was a fierce rival of Knossos after the Dorian invasion and remained sufficiently wealthy to mint its own coins until 220 BC when Knossos, allied with Gortyn, demolished it. Lyttos is just beginning to be investigated; it has Hellenistic walls, a theatre and a frescoed church built over an early basilica.

Potters in **Thrapsanó** (8km west) have made *pithoi* for centuries; their technique for making the great jars, on wheels set in the ground, is the same as in Minoan times. A cave in **Arkalochóri**, just south, yielded Minoan gold axes, one engraved with Linear A, the other with symbols similar to those on the Phaistos Disc – which put paid to notions that the disc was a forgery.

Áno Viánnos and the Southeast Coast

Beyond Mártha (where you can pick up the road to Gortyn, *see* above), **Áno Viánnos** hangs on the southwest flanks of Mount Díkti. Inhabited since early Minoan times, it founded a colony on the Rhône – the main route to the tin mines of Britain – which still bears its Cretan name: Vienne. It was a citadel of resistance against the Turks and Germans; the latter executed 820 people in the area. On the acropolis of Áno Viánnos are the ruins of a Venetian castle and Turkish tower; in the Pláka area are little Ag. Pelagía (1360) and 14th-century Ag. Geórgios, both with frescoes. The latter is near a plane tree, believed to be the oldest in Greece after the granddaddy on Kos.

Two kilometres west, near Káto Viánnos, a good road descends to **Keratókambos**, an attractive fishing village by the beach used by the Saracens to invade Crete in 823. To make sure it wouldn't happen again the Venetians built a fort by the sea and another just east known as **Kastrí**. All the locals come here to swim. A rough-and-tumble road links Keratókambos to **Árvi,** although the road from Amirás east of Áno Viánnos is much easier; at the Amirás crossroads stands a monument to the 600 Cretans killed by the Germans on 14 September 1943. Set in the cliffs, Árvi is enclosed in its own toasty little world, at the head of a valley of banana plantations. It has a pebble beach, and a monastery built on several tiers that originally supported a Temple of Zeus. Other beaches are tucked away along a track to the east.

Lastly, if you continue east, you'll find a sign pointing north for tiny **Áno Sími**, from where a narrow track leads a few kilometres up to three terraces and an altar of a temple dedicated to Aphrodite and Hermes that remained open for business between 1600 BC and AD 300. Beyond, the main road descends through porphyry-coloured badlands where nothing grows, towards the oasis of Mýrtos (*see* p.738).

Heráklion's East Coast: Chersónisos and Mália

East of Heráklion and Amnisós (*see* p.711), Europa, once raped on Crete by Zeus, gets her revenge on Crete. Even more depressing than the god-awfulness of the architecture of this coast are the rusting rods curling out of the roofs, promising more layers of the same, and the skeletons of future monstrosities, usually crumbling away in a patch of litter and weeds – some wannabe Cesare Ritz's grubby field of dreams.

Yet there are a couple of reasons to brake. At Vathianó Kambó, the Minoan villa **Nírou Cháni** or House of the High Priest (**t** *289 707 6110; open Tues–Sun 8.30–3*) has two paved courts with stone benches, perhaps used in ceremonies; 40 tripods and double axes were found here. In **Goúves**, signs point the way to Skotinó, and the enormous **Cave of Skotinó**; the path begins by a white chapel. The cave has a 180ft-high ballroom lit by sun pouring through the cave mouth, with a stalagmite mass in the centre. A huge amount of Minoan cult activity took place in the chambers at the back, around natural altars and formations such as the 'head of Zeus'.

Further east, **Chersónisos**, or Liménas Chersonísou, is a popular synthetic tourist ghetto from end to end, complete with a Cretan museum village, the **Lychnostatis Museum** (**t** *289 702 3660, with a multilingual guided tour; open 9.30–2, closed Sat; adm exp*). An $8 million 18-hole golf course and 'Golf Academy' are due for completion in March 2003. Once the port of ancient Lyttos, little remains of its ancient glories: a reconstructed Roman fountain by the beach, a Roman aqueduct (at Xerokámares) and, on the west side, a 5th-century basilica, seat of one of Crete's first bishops.

Where to Stay and Eat

Chersónisos (Liménas Chersonísou) ✉ 70014

Don't expect to find any cheap rooms here, or even a hotel in season without booking.

Creta Maris, t 289 702 2115, f 289 702 2130, *www.maris.gr (L; luxury)*. Aegean-style and the most luxurious, with lots of sports, six bars, free kindergarten, and well-equipped rooms. *Open Mar–Nov.*

Knossos Royal Village, t 289 702 3375, f 289 702 3150, *www.aldemarhotels.gr (L; luxury)*. Glossy, with outer and indoor pools, water slide, floodlit tennis courts. *Open Mar–Nov.*

Cretan Village, t 289 702 3750, f 289 702 2300, *www.aldemarhotels.gr (A; luxury)*. Traditional village-style two-storey houses.

Silva Maris Bungalows, in quieter Stalís, t 289 702 2850, f 289 702 1404, *www.maris.gr (A; luxury)*. Built like a Cretan village with an attractive pool, water sports and frequent buses to Heráklion.

Katrin, in Stalís, t 289 703 2137, f 289 703 2136, *katrin@hrs.forthnet.gr (B; moderate)*. The pick of this category, with three pools, but book well in advance.

Youth Hostel, El. Venizélou, t 289 702 3521 *(inexpensive)*. Well-run.

Artemis, t 289 703 2131. By the beach in Stalís; serves Greek and Cretan specialities.

Ta Petrina, Ano Chersónisos, in upper Chérsonisos, t 289 702 1976 (€15). Pleasant courtyard setting, with tasty meat and home-grown vegetarian dishes.

Mália ✉ 70007

Ikaros Village, t 289 703 1267, f 289 703 1341, *Ikaros@hrs.forthnet.gr (A; expensive)*. Large complex, designed as a Cretan village; with pool, tennis and sea sports. *Open April–Oct.*

Grecotel Mália Park, towards the Minoan palace, t 289 703 1461, f 289 703 1460 (A; luxury). Plush, air-conditioned bungalows, watersports and a mountain-bike centre.

Ibiscus, just along the main road, t 289 703 1313, f 289 703 2042 *(inexpensive)*. Has a pool.

Youth Hostel, just east of town, t 289 703 1555. Very nice, but fills up fast.

Mália (ΜΑΛΙΑ)

East of Chersónisos, in a wide sandy bay, Mália is now the noisiest, most party-driven holiday sprawl on Crete. There is an older, wiser village of Mália inland, and, oldest of all, the **Minoan Palace of Mália** (*t 289 703 1597; open daily 8.30–3; adm*), near a quiet stretch of beach 3km further east (any bus to Ag. Nikólaos will drop you nearby). The legendary fief of Minos' brother Sarpedon, Mália controlled the fertile coastal plain under the Lassíthi mountains. Its history follows the same pattern as Knossos: inhabited from the Neolithic era, the first palace was built in 1900 BC. When it was devastated by an earthquake 200 years later, another palace was built over the first, then ruined in the catastrophe of *c.* 1450 BC. Compared to Knossos and Phaistos, Mália is 'provincial', built from local stone rather than alabaster, marble and gypsum. On the other hand, the lack of later constructions makes it easy to understand.

The entrance is the **West Court**, crossed by the usual raised flagstones of the Processional Way. Eight grain 'silos', originally covered with beehive domes, are at the south end. The **Central Court**, re-used from the Old Palace, had galleries at the north and east ends; in the middle are the supports of a hollow altar, or sacrificial pit. A Grand Stairway led up into the important **West Wing**, which may have had a ritual role: the raised **Loggia**, where ceremonies may have been performed, is near a myste-rious round stone stuck in the ground. The **Treasury**, behind it, yielded a sword with a rock crystal pommel and a stone axe shaped like a panther. The **Pillar Crypt** has double axes, stars and tridents carved in its square pillars. The four broad steps here may have been a theatre, while in the southwest corner is the unique limestone *kernos*, a round altar with a hollow in the centre and 34 smaller hollows around the edge. Its similarity to the *kernos* used in classical times is striking, and it may have been the Minoans who originated the rite of *panspermia*, or offering of the first fruits.

A portico of square stone pillars and round wooden columns ran along the east side of the Central Court. Mália had no lack of store rooms, and the narrow ones that take up most of the East Wing are equipped with drainage channels from the first palace. North of the centre, the **Pillar Hall** was the largest room in the palace; the chamber above it, reached by the surviving stair, may have been for banquets. Behind it is another pillar room and the **oblique room**, its orientation suggesting some kind of astronomical or lunar observation. A suite of so-called **royal apartments**, with a stepped, sunken lustral basin, are in the northwest corner. Linear A tablets were found in the **Archive Room**, with the base of a single pillar. A paved road leads north to the so-called **Hypostyle Crypt**; no one has the foggiest idea what went on here.

If Mália seems poor next to Knossos and Phaistos, the Minoan estates found in the outskirts were sumptuous, especially the one to the northeast, where the only fresco at Mália was found. In the cemetery by the sea, the **Chrysolakkos tomb** may have been the family vault of Mália's rulers; although the 'gold pit' was looted for centuries, it yielded the Mália twin bee pendant, now in the Heráklion museum.

Lassíthi (ΛΑΣΙΘΙ) Province

The name of Crete's easternmost province comes from the Greek pronunciation of the Venetian La Sitía, one of its chief towns. Lassíthi doesn't have the altitudes that characterize the rest of Crete, but it manages to be the most varied province on the island, framed at its western end by a plateau hanging in the clouds and irrigated by white-sailed windmills, while its east coast ends at Vaï with a palm-lined tropical beach. Ag. Nikólaos, set in the magnificent Gulf of Mirabélo, has the island's poshest hotels in its environs. But traditional Crete, as always, awaits only a few miles inland.

Lassíthi was densely populated in Minoan times: the unplundered palace of Zákros is the most spectacular find, and town sites such as Gourniá, Paleokástro, Vasilikí, Fournoú Korifí and Móchlos have provided clues about everyday Minoan life. Sitía is one of Crete's most delightful towns, and if Ierápetra, on the plastic-coated southeast coast, is perhaps the least pleasant, it has plenty of beaches and a tropical islet.

The Plateau of Lassíthi and the Birthplace of Zeus

The spectacular Plateau of Lassíthi is one of the high points of Crete, both in altitude and atmosphere; although accommodation is a bit paltry, you may want to spend a night there after the tour groups have gone. For it is unique: a green carpet hemmed in by the Díktean Mountains, snowcapped into April and irrigated by windmills designed by Venetian engineers in 1564; the hundreds that still turn make a splendid sight. The uncanny cave where Zeus was born is the main attraction, while Karphí, a Minoan last refuge, is weird, harder to get to, and unvisited.

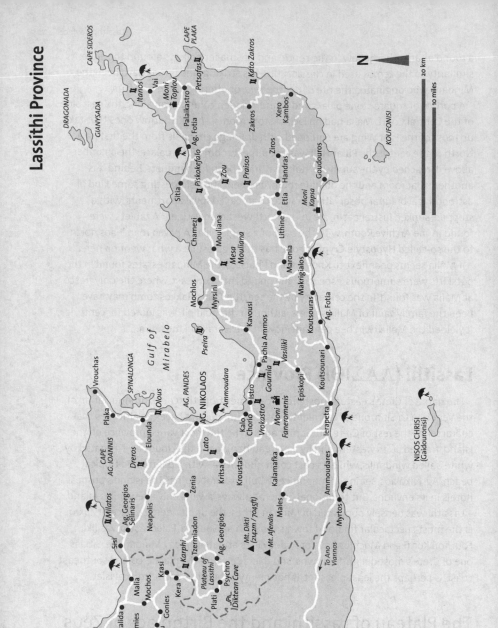

Lassíthi Province

The Lassíthi Plateau: Approaches from the West

With your own transport you have a choice of scenic routes. The main one from Chersónisos passes the old village of **Potamiés**, where the lovely church at abandoned Moní Gouverniótissa has excellent 14th-century frescoes, including a Pantocrator who stares holes into sinners (key at the *kafeneíon*). Frescoes from the same period decorate Ag. Antónios at **Avdoú**, a pretty village dotted with Byzantine churches.

The road from Stalída east of Chersónisos is far more abrupt. After 8.5km of bird's eye views over the sea, **Mochós** is a pleasant antidote to the coastal cacophony. There are a few places to stay, mostly occupied by Swedes, who know Mochós through their assassinated prime minister Olaf Palme; his Villa Palme is now a local shrine. South of Mochós, **Krási** is famous for its spring and plane tree, some 2,000 years old, that once had a café with three tables inside its trunk. Near Krási, in **Kerá**, the **Convent of Kardiótissa** was founded in the 1100s and contains an icon that was twice carried off by the Turks to Constantinople but made its way home on its own (the third time the Turks chained it to a column, but it flew back to Crete with column and chain attached). The column is in the courtyard and the chain hangs on the iconostasis. It has beautiful 14th-century frescoes, with a portrait of the lady donor.

The Villages of the Plateau

Beyond the stone windmills, the road descends into the strange, dream-like bowl of the Lassíthi plateau. An emerald chequerboard, the plateau was farmed by the Minoans and later by the Dorians of Lyttos, but in 1293 it was such a nest of resistance that the Venetians demolished the villages and persecuted anyone who came near. Only in 1543 were Greek refugees from the Peloponnese permitted to resettle the plateau. To re-establish the orchards, the Venetians built 10,000 white-sailed irrigation windmills. In the 1970s they were a remarkable sight, but, sadly, since then most have become derelict in favour of the more reliable petrol pump.

Getting There and Around

One or two daily **buses** from Heráklion, Mália and Ag. Nikólaos wind their way up to the plateau, taking in most of the villages and ending up at the Diktean Cave.

Where to Stay and Eat

Avdoú ✉ 75005
Villa Avdou, t 289 705 1606, f 289 705 1374, www.avdou.com (expensive). Stay in a well appointed studio or villa on an organic farm, offering courses in organic farming, Cretan cookery, and more.

Tzermiádon/Ag. Geórgios ✉ 72052
Kourites, in Tzermiádon, t 284 402 2194 (B; inexpensive). The smartest place to stay on the plateau.
Lassithi, t 284 402 2194 (E; inexpensive). Owned by the same family, and has a restaurant. Open all year.
Rhea, in Ag. Geórgios, t 284 403 1209 (E; nexpensive).

Psychró ✉ 72052
Hotel Zeus, t/f 284 403 1284 (D; inexpensive).
Dikteon Andron, t 284 403 1504 (E; inexpensive).

Sísi ✉ 72400
Minos Imperial, 5km east, t 281 024 2082, f 281 024 3757, www.minosimperial.gr (L; luxury). Opened in June 2001, a hotel and bungalow complex for couples or families, with several pools, tennis, children's activities, water sports, big buffets for breakfast and dinner.
Kalimera Kriti, t 284 107 1134, f 284 107 1598, Kalimera@compulink.gr. (A; luxury). Set in 27 hectares of gardens, with two private beaches, outdoor and indoor pools and tennis courts.
Zygos Apts, t 284 107 1279 (C; moderate). Reasonable, smaller choice with kitchenettes.
Angela Hotel, t 284 107 1176, f 284 107 1121 (C; moderate). With pool and bar.
Elite Restaurant, run by George Sevadalis. Has an excellent reputation.

Eighteen hill villages surround the plateau, leaving the best land on the plateau itself for farming. The largest, **Tzermiádon**, is near a sacred Minoan cave, **Trápeza**, used from 5000 BC (bring a light, or take a local guide). The loftiest Minoan peak sanctuary (3,800ft) is an hour's walk up a strenuous path (a dirt road goes part way, marked 'Tinios Stavros'): this is **Karphí**, the 'nail', an accurate description of its weird mountain. Excavated by John Pendlebury between 1937 and 1939 – his last project before he was killed, fighting alongside the locals, in the Battle of Crete – Karphí was the refuge of some 3,000 Minoans or Eteocretans ('True Cretans'), during the Dorian invasion in 1100 BC. For a century they tried to keep their civilization alive, before the harsh winters apparently got to them. Pendlebury found 150 small houses, a temple, a chieftain's house with a porch and hearthroom, a tower and barracks and a shrine that contained five of the very last Minoan clay idols of the goddess (*c.* 1050 BC, now in Heráklion), distorted, like Alice in Wonderland when she was mistaken for a serpent.

Clockwise from Tzermiádon, **Ag. Konstantínos** has the most souvenir shops on the plateau, while just above it the 13th-century **Moní Kristalénias** enjoys a lovely panorama. In **Ag. Geórgios**, an old farmhouse contains a **Folk Museum** (*open June–Aug 10–4*), complete with everything a Cretan family needed to get by, including a wine-press that doubled as a bed; it also has a collection of photos of Kazantzákis.

Psychró, to the southwest, is the base for visiting the **Díktean Cave**, the birthplace of Zeus (*t 284 403 1316; open 10–5; adm*). From the car park it's a 1km ascent up a rocky path; donkeys are available, and local guides at the entrance hire lanterns in case you haven't brought your own, although it's wise to set a price from the start. Rubber-soled shoes are essential; the descent is slippery.

If you get there before or after the groups, the cave is a haunting, other-worldly place worthy of myth. Only rediscovered in the 1880s, it contained cult items from Middle Minoan up to Archaic times; its role as the birthplace and hiding place of Zeus from his cannibal father Cronos was confirmed by the discovery in Paleókastro of an inscription of the *Hymn of the Kouretes* (the youths who banged their shields to drown the baby's cries). Down in the cave's damp, shadowy bowels the guides point out formations that, if you squint, resemble the baby god, his cradle, his mantle and the place where the nanny goat Amaltheia nursed him; to help conceal the birth, Rhea, his mother, spurted her own breast milk into the heavens, creating the Milky Way. Tradition has it that Minos came up here to receive the Law of Zeus every nine years, and that Epimenides the Sage lived here as a hermit, having strange visions.

Between Mália and Ag. Nikólaos

After Mália, the New Road cuts inland, avoiding the rugged Cape Ag. Ioánnis. This is good news for the last two resorts, Sísi and Milátos, which are free of the grind of traffic that bedevils the coast to the west. **Sísi** is like a chunk of southern California with its modern pastel architecture, sandy beaches and cute port – a turquoise creek under the cliffs, lined with palms and a cascade of tavernas and bars.

Paralía Milátou is just the opposite: low-key, a bit dumpy, with a pebble beach. In 1823, during the War of Independence, the large stalactite **Cave of Milátos** (on the edge of a wild ravine, 6km drive from the beach then a 10-minute walk from the parking area) served as a refuge for two weeks for 3,600 people. The Turks besieged them, and after two battles the Greeks surrendered, only to be massacred or enslaved. Under the bulbous rock at the entrance, the cave has a low, smoke-blackened ceiling supported by stalactites; a chapel contains a reliquary full of bones.

Immersed in almond groves, **Neápolis** is the largest town on the Heráklion–Ag. Nikólaos road. In its former incarnation as Karés, it was the birthplace of Pétros Fílagros in 1340, professor of Greek at the University of Paris, elected Pope Alexander V in 1409 during the Great Schism. Karés predeceased him, however, in 1347, when the Venetians destroyed it after a revolt. The rebuilt 'new town', Neápolis, has a leafy square and a **museum** (*open Tues–Sun 10–1 and 6–9; adm*), housing crafts and finds from ancient **Dreros**. Dreros is north (cross under the New Road and follow signs for Kouroúnes; from the tiny parking area, a path leads up to a saddle between two peaks). There's an Archaic agora and, under a shelter, a 7th-century BC Geometric Temple to Apollo Delphinios that yielded the oldest hammered bronze statues in Greece (in Heráklion) and Eteocretan inscriptions – Minoan words in Greek letters.

Ag. Nikólaos (ΑΓ. ΝΙΚΟΛΑΟΣ)

When Ag. Nikólaos was chosen as capital of Lassíthi in 1905, only 95 people lived in its amphitheatre, overlooking a round lake and the Gulf of Mirabélo. It didn't even have a proper port until 1965, and what has happened since is not exactly hard to guess: the resident population of Agnik, as the Brits call it, has multiplied by 100. In the 1980s it was the first place on Crete to cross over the courtesy threshold; in response, the mayor mounted a campaign to civilize the place, and it worked – the rowdies and louts now home in on Mália, leaving Agnik older, wiser and noticeably nicer.

Originally the port of ancient Lato, the town overlooks the islet of **Ag. Pándes**, with a population of *kri-kri* goats. The other vortex is circular **Lake Voulisméni**, the 'bottomless'. It was often stagnant until 1867, when the local pasha connected it to the sea. Behind the tourist office, there's a small but choice **Folk Art Museum** (*t 284 102 5093; open Sun–Fri 10–4; adm*), with icons, embroideries, instruments and stamps from independent Crete. Aktí S. Koundoúrou follows the waterfront to a beach at the end and the little church that gave the town its name, **Ag. Nikólaos**, with rare 9th-century geometric frescoes from the Iconoclastic period (key at the Minos Palace hotel).

The **Archaeological Museum** (*t 284 102 4943; open Tues–Sun 8.30–3; adm*), up the hill at 68 K. Paleológou, has artefacts from eastern Crete: a Neolithic phallus-shaped idol from Zákros, an Early Minoan pinhead 'Goddess of Myrtos', lovely gold jewellery from Móchlos, a vase from Mália in the form of a triton shell, engraved with two demons making a libation, a Daedalic bust from the 7th century BC that looks like Christopher Columbus and a lamp from Olous with 70 nozzles. In the last room, a 1st-century AD skull has a gold burial wreath embedded in the bone of its brow.

Getting Around

Olympic Airways is at 20 Plastíra, **t** 284 102 8929. LANE, 5 K. Sfakianákis St, **t** 284 102 5249, **f** 284 102 7052, operates two **ferries** a week to Piraeus and Sitía, and one to Kárpathos, Kássos, Mílos. **Port authority: t** 284 102 2312. **Bus station (t** 284 102 2234), Sof. Venizélou.

Tourist Information

Tourist office: 20 Aktí S. Koundoúrou, **t** 284 102 2357; *open daily in season.*
Tourist police and **lost property:** 47 Erithoú Stavroú, **t** 284 102 6900.

Where to Stay

Ag. Nikólaos ✉ 72100

St Nicholas Bay, spread over a narrow peninsula 2km from Ag. Nikólaos, **t** 284 102 5041, **f** 284 102 4556, *www.stnicolas.gr* (*L; luxury*). A 130-bungalow complex which has a private sandy beach, three pools, and every comfort, including an art gallery. *Open Mar–Nov.*

Minos Beach, on the secluded promontory of Ammoúdi, **t** 284 102 2345, **f** 284 102 2548, *www.mamhotel.gr* (*L; luxury*). Although built back practically in the Minoan era by Agnik standards (1962), it is still one of the best; some bungalows are directly on the sea. The complex includes an imaginative French restaurant and three bars, and a patch of private beach.

Coral Hotel, on the waterfront along Aktí Koundoúrou, **t** 284 102 8363, **f** 284 102 8754, *ermis1@ath.forthnet.gr* (*B; expensive*). A smart town option, with pool and terrace.

Hermes, Aktí Koundoúrou, **t** 284 102 8253, **f** 284 1028754 (*expensive*). Central, large, modern rooms with views.

Ormos, near the sea, **t** 284 102 4094, **f** 284 102 5394, *www.ormos-crystal.gr* (*B; expensive*). Family-orientated, with air-conditioning, pool, playground; rates plummet off-season.

Panorama on Aktí Koundoúrou, **t** 284 102 8890, **f** 284 102 7268 (*C; moderate*). Good view over the harbour.

Miramare Apts. Sleep up to five over Kitroplateía Beach, through Knossos Travel, **t** 284 102 2146, **f** 284 102 8114 (*moderate*).

Adonis, just off the centre of Aktí S. Koundoúrou, **t** 284 105 1525 (*C; moderate*)). A pleasant guesthouse.

Doxa, 7 Idomeneos, **t** 284 102 4214, **f** 284 102 4614 (*C; inexpensive*). A good year-round bet.

Green House, 15 Modátsou, **t** 284 102 2025 (*E; inexpensive*). A cheapie, with little rooms leading out to a small courtyard, overflowing with greenery, and patrolled by a small army of cats.

Perla, **t** 284 102 3379 (*E; inexpensive*). Pleasant, clean guesthouse in the centre.

Rea, on the corner of Marathónos and Milátou, **t** 284 109 0330, (*B; inexpensive*). A good value hotel with character and sea views.

Eating Out

Pelagos, on Str. Kóraka just inland from Aktí Koundoúrou, **t** 284 102 5737 (€20). Trendy seafood and a long list of tasty *mezédes*.

Pefko. A favourite with Greeks who want to dine on the lake; reasonable taverna food.

Itanos, next to the cathedral on Str. Kíprou, **t** 284 102 5340. Wide selection of old-fashioned ready dishes (the lamb and spinach in egg-lemon sauce is excellent).

Aovas, halfway up to the archaeological museum, on K. Paleológou. Small, inexpensive and good, serving Cretan dishes in a green shady courtyard.

Trata, on M. Sfakianáki near Kitroplateía Beach. Tuck into dishes such as fish soup, Trata chicken *kleftíko* and casserole dishes.

Ofou to lo, **t** 284 102 4819, at the far end of Kitroplateía. Unusual Greek/Cretan dishes.

Dolphini, down at Ammoúdi Beach (€9). Good food served by jovial twin waiters.

Synantysi, along the Old Road to Heráklion, **t** 284 102 5384. Popular with locals for its excellent array of *mezédes*, including mussels, mushrooms, scampi and squid.

The Embassy, Kondiláki Street, **t** 284 108 3153. A wide variety of reasonable vegetarian and fish dishes, plus Sunday lunch. *Open till 2am.*

New Kow Loon, 1 Pasifais St, **t** 284 102 3891. The only Chinese restaurant in town, but a bit pricey.

La Strada, 5 Plastira, **t** 284 102 8451. Italian trattoria that prides itself on its wide-ranging menu; try the spaghetti with cuttlefish in its ink along with a variety of herby breads.

Tourists are surprised to discover that Agnik was asleep when God was handing out beaches: there's shingly **Kitroplateía** and pocket-sized **Ammoudara** at the end of Aktí S. Koundoúrou, while near the bus station, sandy **Ámmos** is clean, but not very atmospheric. To the south is the crowded **municipal beach** (*fee for beach club facilities*); from here, a path leads past **Gargardóros Beach** and beyond that to **Almyrós**, the best.

Eloúnda, Olous and Spinalónga

Tantalizing views across the Gulf of Mirabélo unfold along the 12km from Ag. Nikólaos north to Eloúnda; below, the rocky coastline is interspersed with tiny coves, draped with some of Greece's most glamorous hotels. **Eloúnda** attracts a high percentage of Brits, many of whom never drift too far from the bars in the square or the nine-hole golf course at the Porto Elounda Hotel. On the south edge of Eloúnda, a bridge crosses the channel dug by the French in 1897; along this, under the windmills, lies **Olous**, the port of ancient Dreros and goal of the 'sunken city' excursions from Ag. Nikólaos. The mosaic floor of an Early Byzantine basilica is near the Canal Bar.

The tiny island of **Spinalónga** (*t 281 024 6211; adm*) is a half-hour caique trip from Eloúnda, or an hour by excursion boat from Ag. Nikólaos. Venetian engineers detached it from the promontory in 1579, and their fortress there held out against the Turks, like the islet forts of Nea Soúda and Gramvoúsa, until 1715. When the Turks left in 1904, Spinalónga became a leper colony – the last in Europe – until 1957. Today the poignant little streets, houses and lepers' church are forlorn. **Pláka**, opposite the islet, was the supply centre for the lepers and now has a tiny laid-back colony of its own, dedicated to relaxation by the pebble beach.

Where to Stay and Eat

Eloúnda ✉ 72053

Eloúnda Beach, t 284 104 1412, f 284 104 1373, *www.eloundabeach.gr* (*L; luxury*). One of the top holiday hotels in the world: fab rooms, cinema, diving expeditions, fitness centre, heated pool and other luxuries, including champagne breakfast, the best restaurant on Crete (Dionyssos), Jaguar limousine service, and a helicopter, sailboat, or private island also available. *Open April–Oct.*

Elounda Mare, t 284 104 1102, f 284 104 1307, *mare@eloundahotels.com* (*L; luxury*). A member of the prestigious Relais & Chateaux complex with 50 hotel rooms and 40 bungalows – and 40 private swimming pools on the seafront.

Candia Park Village, between Ag. Nikólaos and Eloúnda, t 284 102 6811, f 284 102 2367, *info-candia@mamhotel.gr* (*A; expensive*). Recently built and perfect for families, with a wide range of sports and a small aqua park; all rooms are air-conditioned with kitchenettes.

Akti Olous, near the causeway, t 284 104 1270, f 284 10 41 425 (*C; expensive*). Popular place, with a pool and roof garden.

Korfos Beach, t 284 104 1591, f 284 104 1034 (*C; inexpensive*). Near the strand, with water-sports on offer.

Vritomartis, t 284 104 1325 (€22). On an islet in Eloúnda's port, for well-prepared fish and lobster.

Kalidon, t 284 104 1451 (€15–20). Romantically located out on a small pontoon, with a good selection of vegetarian dishes and *mezédes*.

Poulis, t 284 104 4151. Reasonably priced fish and friendly ducks.

Café Ellas. Live Greek music on Friday nights.

O Mylos. A good taverna at Pinés; it's a scenic drive, and the windmills still work.

Spinalonga Village, in Pláka, t 284 104 1285 (*A; expensive*). Bungalows with personalities and views, ideal for families.

Above Ag. Nikólaos

From Ag. Nikólaos, it's a short hop up to Kritsá and, 1km before the village, the church of **Kéra Panagía** (*t 284 105 1525; open Mon–Sat 9–3, Sun 9–2; adm*). It looks like no other church on the island: the three naves, coated with centuries of whitewash, trailing triangular buttresses and crowned by a simple bell tower and drum. Within, the entire surface is alive with Crete's finest frescoes, illustrating the evolution of Byzantine art. The central aisle, dedicated to the Virgin, dates from the 12th to mid-13th centuries: on the northwest pillar look for *St Francis*, who was introduced by the Venetians and was a favourite of the Cretans. The two side aisles are later, painted in the more naturalistic style of the early 14th century. The south aisle is devoted to St Anne and has scenes based on the apocrypha. The north aisle belongs to Christ Pantocrator; a *Last Judgement* covers most of the nearby vaults. Among the saints here, don't miss the donors with their daughter, rare portraits of medieval Cretans.

In 1956, Jules Dassin chose the lovely white village of **Kritsá** for his film *He Who Must Die* starring Melina Mercouri, and ever since its role has been as something of a film set – a traditional Cretan village swamped by Agnik tourists, who are in turn swamped by villagers selling them tablecloths. It's three km up to Dorian **Lato** (*t 284 102 5115; open Tues–Sun 8.30–3*), curling down the saddle between the hills. Founded in the 7th century BC, Lato gave birth to Nearchus, Alexander the Great's admiral, before it was abandoned in favour of its port, Lato Kamara (Ag. Nikólaos). Lato displays some unusual Minoan influences on Dorian design: the double gateway, the street of 80 steps lined with small houses and workshops, and the architecture of its agora, with its column-less sanctuary and cistern. The wide steps that continue up to a peristyle court and *Prytaneion* date from the 7th century BC and may have been inspired by Minoan 'theatres'. Monumental towers stood on either side of a narrower stair leading up to the altar. On the second hill stands a beautiful, column-less temple, an isolated altar and a primitive theatre.

East of Ag. Nikólaos: The Gulf of Mirabélo

The coastline that lends Ag. Nikólaos its panache owes its name to the Genoese fortress of Mirabélo, 'Beautiful View', demolished by the Turks. Frequent buses run the 12km out to the sandy beach of **Kaló Chório**; the road east continues past the up-and-coming resort of **Ístro** to the turn-off for the 12th-century **Moní Faneroménis**, possessing a stupendous view over the gulf. The monastery is built like a fortress into the cliff, sheltering a frescoed cave church. East of Ístro, the road passes directly below the striking hillside site of **Gourniá** (*t 284 209 4604; open 8.30–3, closed Mon & hols; adm*), excavated between 1901 and 1904 by American Harriet Boyd, the first woman to lead a major dig. Gourniá reached its peak at c. 1550 BC, and was never rebuilt after a fire in c. 1225 BC. Paved lanes meander past workshops and houses. At the highest point, a small 'palace' with store rooms surrounds a court; there's a mini theatrical area and Shrine of the Snake Goddess, with a shelf for long, tube-like snake vases.

From Gourniá, it's a short drive to **Pachiá Ámmos**, with an often rubbish-strewn beach, at the beginning of the road bisecting the 12km isthmus of Crete, separating the Aegean and Libyan Seas. As Gourniá wasn't a palace, archaeologists suspect one must be near, especially as the Minoans were here early on; by 2600 BC, they had a settlement at **Vasilikí**, 5km south of Pachiá Ámmos. Excavations here have been taken up again in search of clues to the Minoans' origin, as Vasiliki is one of the few sites from the period that was abandoned (2000 BC) and never rebuilt.

Pachiá Ámmos is also the crossroads for Sitía, some 47km east down a corniche road that slithers high above the Gulf of Mirabélo. **Plátanos** has a wonderful belvedere over the gulf and a pair of tavernas. Beyond, signs point the way down to **Móchlos**, a fishing village with a pebbly beach, set between barren cliffs and a small islet barely a stone's throw from the shore. The Minoans here specialized in pots with lid handles shaped like reclining dogs; some were in the seven intact chamber tombs cut into the cliffs. One building is called 'the House of the Theran Refugees' for its similarities to the houses of Akrotíri (*see* p.664); pot shards from Akrotiri littered the floor *on top of* a 20cm layer of volcanic ash. Life obviously went on after the Big Bang.

Yet another Minoan settlement existed from 3000 BC on **Pseíra**, 2km offshore, where the inhabitants used the pumice that floated ashore from Santoríni to build up the floor of their shrine. Pseíra's House of the Pillar Partitions, with a bathroom with a sunken tub, plughole and drains, is the most elegant in eastern Crete.

Sitía (ΣΗΤΕΙΑ)

Sitía is a pleasant town, with an economy based on sultanas and wine. Its Byzantine, Genoese and Venetian walls fell to earthquakes and the bombardments of Barbarossa, leaving only a restored Venetian fortress as a souvenir. The pranks of its pet pelicans and general schmoozing along the waterfront make it a paradise for lazy visitors. But *la dolce vita* is nothing new here; under the fortress you can see the ruins of a Roman fish tank, where denizens of the deep were kept alive for the table. The **Archaeological Museum**, set among garages at the top of Ítanos Street (*t 284 302 3917; open Tues–Sun 8.30–3; adm*), has Minoan larnaxes, a wine press and Linear A tablets from Zákros, and offerings from the 7th century in the Daedalic style. Some of the newest finds are some from Pétras, just south of Sitía, where a large structure from the New Palace period is being explored.

South of Sitía: the Last True Cretans and a Venetian Villa

Along the main road south, 2km past whitewashed **Maronía**, the road forks for Néa Praisós, just below ancient **Praisós**, the last stronghold of the Eteocretans – the 'true Cretans' – who took refuge here during the Dorian invasion and survived into the 3rd century BC, running their shrine of Diktean Zeus at Palaíkastro and keeping old cults alive on their three acropoli. When Praisós began to compete with Dorian Ierapytna (Ierápetra) in 146 BC, it was decimated. Ironically, this last Minoan town was one of the very first to be discovered, in 1884 by the Italian Federico Halbherr who was

Getting There and Around

Sitía's **airport**, 1km out of town, is linked to Athens three times a week; a taxi costs around €5. The Olympic Airways office is by the marina, **t** 284 302 2270. For **airport information**, **t** 284 302 4666. **Ferries** run four times a week to Kárpathos and Kássos, Ag. Nikólaos and Piraeus. **Port authority**: **t** 284 302 2310.

The **bus station** is at the south end of the waterfront, **t** 284 302 2272, and has connections five times a day to Ag. Nikólaos and Ierápetra, four to Vaï and three to Káto Zákro.

Tourist Information

Municipal tourist office: **t** 284 302 8300, on the marina; *open Mon–Fri 9.30–2.30 and 5.30–9.*
Tourist police: **t** 284 302 4200.

Where to Stay and Eat

Sitía ✉ 72300
Apollon, 28 Kapetan Sifi, **t** 284 302 2733 (*C; moderate*). Air-conditioning and breakfast.

Marianna, 67 Misonos, **t** 284 302 2088 (*C; moderate*). Charming rooms and does a buffet breakfast.
Stars, 37 M. Kolyváki, **t** 284 302 2917 (*D; inexpensive*). Fairly quiet, and convenient for ferries.
Archontiko, 16 Kondiláki, **t** 284 302 8172 (*D; inexpensive*). A quiet little hotel on the western edge of town, by the whitewashed steps.
Youth Hostel, 4 Theríssou St, **t** 284 302 2693. Just east of town and again very pleasant and friendly, with kitchen facilities and a garden.
Balcony, just up Kazantzaki from the water, **t** 284 302 5084 (€25). A great menu which changes every season and includes some delicious Asian dishes, pasta with seafood and roast meats.
Mixos, two streets in from the port (€12). Serves lamb baked or on the spit with barrelled wine.
Neromilos, 4km east of Sitía in Ag. Fotia. A favourite, located in a water mill, with good views.

mystified by the inscriptions in Greek letters, now generally held to be in the native Minoan language of Linear A. The scenery is lovely, the ruins pretty sparse.

The slightly more substantial remains of another vanished civilization may be seen further south in **Etiá**. In the Middle Ages Etiá was the fief of the Di Mezzo family, who in the 15th century built themselves a fortified villa, the most beautiful on Crete, with vaulted ceilings and intricate decorations. Now partially restored, the entrance, ground floor and fountain house offer a hint of the villa's grandeur.

East of Sitía: the Monastery of Toploú

Officially Panagía Akroteriani, Toploú ('cannoned' in Turkish) more aptly evokes this fortress of the faith, 3.5km from the Sitía–Palaíkastro road. It started off with a chapel dating from Nikephóros Phokás' liberation of Crete (961); the monastery itself (*open 9–1 and 2–6*) dates from the 15th century. The gate in its mighty walls is under a hole named *foniás* ('killer'), for pouring boiling oil on attackers. The building stone came from ancient Itanos: note the inscription on the façade, from the 2nd century BC.

Toploú has a history of revolution and resistance. At the beginning of the War of Independence in 1821, the Turks hanged 12 monks over the gate as a warning, although it only made the Cretans mad as hell and by the end of the war Toploú was theirs again. During the Second World War, the abbot was shot by the Germans for operating a radio transmitter. Artefacts from Toploú's battles are on display in the museum (*adm*); the finest icon is a masterpieces of Cretan art: the *Great is the Lord* by Ioánnis Kornáros (1770) has 61 lively, intricate scenes illustrating an Orthodox prayer.

Palaíkastro, Vaï and Itanos

All roads on the east coast converge at **Palaíkastro**, a popular place to stop, with a fine beach below. En route to Chiona Beach, at **Roussolakos**, was a Late Minoan settlement similar to Gourniá. Later, the inhabitants moved up to **Kastrí**, where in the ruins of the famous 4th-century BC Temple to Diktean Zeus – the same one controlled by Praisós – the very ancient *Hymn of the Kouretes* was found engraved on a stone.

Palaíkastro is the last bus stop before **Vaï**. Its silver sands are lined with Europe's only wild palms, a species unique to Crete. A banana plantation completes the Caribbean ambience, but the only way to avoid sharing this tropical paradise with thousands is to get there at the crack of dawn, come out of season or star in the next Bounty ad. Beaches around Vaï act as overflow tanks and free campsites. Three with a few palms of their own are north of Vaï, 1.5km up Cape Sideros near ancient **Itanos**. The Ptolemies used it as a naval station, but pirates forced its abandonment in the 8th century; best preserved are a basilica and Hellenistic wall of finely cut stone.

The Minoan Palace of Zákros

t 284 309 3323; open daily 8–7 in season, otherwise 8–2.30; adm.

From Palaíkastro, the road south cuts through olives and sleepy hamlets to **Zákros**. Here a rich Minoan villa of the New Palace era, with wall paintings, wine presses and cellars, was found near the head of the 'Valley of Death', named not for tourists with broken necks but after the Minoan tombs from 2600 BC cut into the cliffs. In reasonable shoes it's a not terribly difficult 8km walk down to **Káto Zákros**. The road is plied by two or three buses a day from Sitía.

Where to Stay and Eat

Palaíkastro ✉ **72300**

Marina Village, 1 km out of town and 500m from the sea, t 284 306 1284, f 284 306 1285, *Relakis@sit.forthnet.gr* (*C; expensive*). A little resort complex with its own snack bar, pool and tennis.

Hellas, near the square, t 284 306 1240, f 284 306 1340, *Hellas_h@otenet.gr* (*C; inexpensive*). Good value; restaurant. *Open all year.*

Thalia, t 284 306 1217, f 284 306 1558 (*D; inexpensive*). On a side street, smothered in bougainvillaea.

Zákros ✉ **72300**

George, Káto Zákros, t 284 309 3201 (*inexpensive*). Clean, tastefully furnished rooms and a terrace.

Athena, on the sea at the end of the beach road, t 284 309 3458 (*inexpensive*).

Nikos Platanákis, near the archaeological site, t 284 302 6887. The owner, a gourmet cook, hangs all his fruit and veg in the trees and cuts them off when he needs them (€15).

Maria's. Another good choice, serving fresh fish under the tamarisks.

Zákros

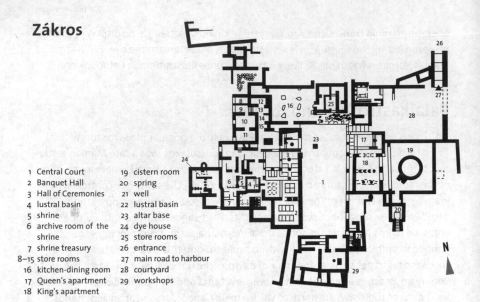

1. Central Court
2. Banquet Hall
3. Hall of Ceremonies
4. lustral basin
5. shrine
6. archive room of the shrine
7. shrine treasury
8–15. store rooms
16. kitchen-dining room
17. Queen's apartment
18. King's apartment
19. cistern room
20. spring
21. well
22. lustral basin
23. altar base
24. dye house
25. store rooms
26. entrance
27. main road to harbour
28. courtyard
29. workshops

N

The fourth major Minoan palace, the **Palace of Zákros**, was discovered in 1961 by Níkos Pláton. The surrounding town was probably the chief port for Egypt for the 'Keftiu' (as the Egyptians called them, and as the Minoans may have called themselves); the importance of trade for Zákros is highlighted by the fact that the valley could never have supplied such a large settlement with enough to eat. Pláton found large quantities of unworked ivory; sculpting it may have been a local speciality.

The palace, built in c. 1700 BC, collapsed and burned down in the catastrophe of 1450 BC, and was never rebuilt or plundered; the discovery of cult items suggests that disaster overwhelmed the residents. The slow subsidence of the east coast of Crete has left the once important harbour under the sea. The original harbour road enters the northeast court; the covered area is a foundry predating the palace. A corridor leads into the long **Central Court**, which preserves the base of an altar. As usual, there are sanctuaries and ritual chambers in the West Wing, entered by way of a monolithic portal near the altar. **Store Rooms** of *pithoi* are to the northwest, while the large **Hall of Ceremonies** extends to the west, with a light well and two windows. The many wine vessels found in the room to the south led the archaeologists to dub it the **Banquet Hall**. Behind this are a **Shrine** and **Lustral Basin**, probably used for purification, and the **Shrine Treasury**, where Pláton found the rock-crystal vase now in the Heráklion Museum. Boxes of Linear A tablets came out of the shrine's **Archive**, but the wet dissolved most into a clay mass. **Workshops** closed in the southern end of the Central Court. In the southeast corner, a **well** with worn steps was used for sacrificial offerings; here Pláton found a bowl of perfectly preserved Minoan olives, which apparently tasted pretty good. The East Wing of the palace is tentatively identified as the **Royal Apartments**. Behind the apartments, the **Cistern Room,** with a balustrade and steps leading down to the paved floor, is even more of an enigma: guesses are that it was a swimming pool, a fish pond or a basin to float an Egyptian-style sacred ship. Nearby, steps lead down to a '**well-fashioned spring**', as Pláton called it after Homer's description, which may have been a shrine connected to the spring that fed the cistern. At the north end is a large **kitchen** – the only one ever found in a palace.

As a protected archaeological zone, the little fishing hamlet of **Káto Zákro** is idyllic. The pebbly beach is fine for a swim, but if it is remote soft white sands you have a yen for, make your way 10km south down the tortuous coastal road to **Xerókambo**.

Ierápetra (ΙΕΡΑΠΕΤΡΑ) and Around

By rights, **Ierápetra**, as the southernmost town in Europe – a mere 370km from Africa – and main market centre for Crete's banana, pineapple and winter veg crops, should be a fascinating place instead of a dull dodoburg with a grey beach. Under Dorian tutelage the city bullied its way into ruling much of eastern Crete by Hellenistic times, and it was strong and contrary enough to hold out against the Romans after they had conquered all the rest of Crete. Piqued, the Romans flattened it; then, to show there were no hard feelings, rebuilt it. The Byzantines made it a bishopric, but it was sacked by the Saracens and toppled by an earthquake in 1508.

Dominating the seafront, the Venetian **Kastélli** stands on the mole of the ancient harbour, once Roman Crete's chief port for Africa, now bobbing with pleasure craft. Near here, the domed church of **Aféndi Christós** was first built in the 1300s and has a fine wooden iconostasis. Behind, in a warren of narrow streets, is a house where Napoleon supposedly spent the night of 26 June 1798, before sailing to Egypt. The

Getting There

The **bus station** is on Lasthénou, t 284 202 8237: there are frequent connections to Sitía (by way of Makrigialós), Gourniá and Ag. Nikólaos, Mýrtos, Koustounári, and Ferma.

Where to Stay and Eat

Ierápetra ✉ 72200

Petra Mare, close to town on the edge of the beach, t 284 202 3341, f 284 202 3350 (*A; expensive*). Modern, with a water park and indoor pool.

Astron, 56 M. Kothrí, on the so-so town beach, t 284 202 5114, htastron@otenet.gr, (*B; expensive–moderate*). Pleasant and pristine; all rooms are air-conditioned, with sea view balconies.

Iris, 36 Kothrí, t 284 202 3136 (*D; moderate*). By the water. Typical for price and comfort.

Cretan Villa, by the bus station at Lakérda, t 284 202 8522 (*D; inexpensive*). Rooms in a 19th-century house.

Napoleon, on the waterfront (around €18 for fish). A great favourite with authentic Greek and Cretan food. Fresh fish (the owner has his own caique) and varieties of snails are specialities.

Siciliana, near the beach, t 284 202 4185 (€12). A real pizza oven that produces a good honest pie.

Lambrakis, 1km east, t 284 202 3393. Good meat and fish grills, and delicious Cretan cheese pies.

Mýrtos ✉ 72200

Mýrtos, t 284 205 1227, f 284 205 1215 (*C; moderate*). Has a good restaurant. *Open all year.*

Esperides, t 284 205 1207, f 284 205 1298 (*C; moderate*). New and large hotel, 200m from the sea.

Mertiza, t 284 205 1208 (*moderate–inexpensive*). Furnished apartments.

most beautiful things in Ierápetra are a Minoan *larnax* painted with scenes of animals and a hunt, and a charming Roman Demeter, both in the **Archaeological Museum**, Plateía Dimarchéiou (*t 284 102 4943; supposedly open Tues–Sat 9–3; adm*).

The best thing to do in Ierápetra is leave – take a boat to the golden sands of **Nisos Chrisí**, an uninhabited islet with one of Crete's last natural cedar forests. The sea deposits shells by the million on Chrisí's shores; a taverna wards off starvation. Boats also go to **Koufonísi**, a remote island to the east, where the seashells were mostly of the murex variety, used to dye cloth royal purple. This made it a prize, and Ierápetra and Itanos fought over it endlessly; a theatre and settlement have been excavated.

Developments are sprouting up **east of Ierápetra**. Old houses at **Koutsounári** have been restored to let, near the dull resort at **Férma**; **Ag. Fotiá** is far more attractive, with a good beach. The best beach, at **Makrigialós**, has fine sand and shallow waters.

Along the Costa Plastica to Mýrtos

Spain has its Costas, so it seems only fair that Crete should flaunt the assets of its southeastern coast: sand and plastic, the latter to force endless tomatoes to redden before their time. West of Ierápetra, the Costa Plastica is almost metaphysically dull. In the hills, however, are pretty villages such as **Kalamáfka**; the hill just above it is said to be the only spot where you can see both the Libyan and Cretan Seas. Things were no doubt prettier back when the early Minoans lived at Néa Mýrtos, at a site known as **Fournoú Korifí**. A proto-town of close to 100 rooms, it was occupied in two periods between 2600 and 2100 BC, when it was destroyed by fire. Finds here proved vital in reconstructing the Pre-Palatial period. A few imported goods such as metal, obsidian from Mílos and stone vases from Mochlós suggest that such valuables were exchanged as dowries or gifts. Cereals, grape pips, olive stones and the bones of cattle, goats and sheep confirm that the essentials of the Cretan diet were already in place; the oldest potter's wheel in Greece was found here, from 2500 BC, with discs turned by the potter's hands, predating the later, spindle-turned wheels. Further west, **Mýrtos** is the one place along this coast where you may want to linger: although burned by the Germans it was rebuilt as it was, with a good deal of charm thrown in.

The Dodecanese

19

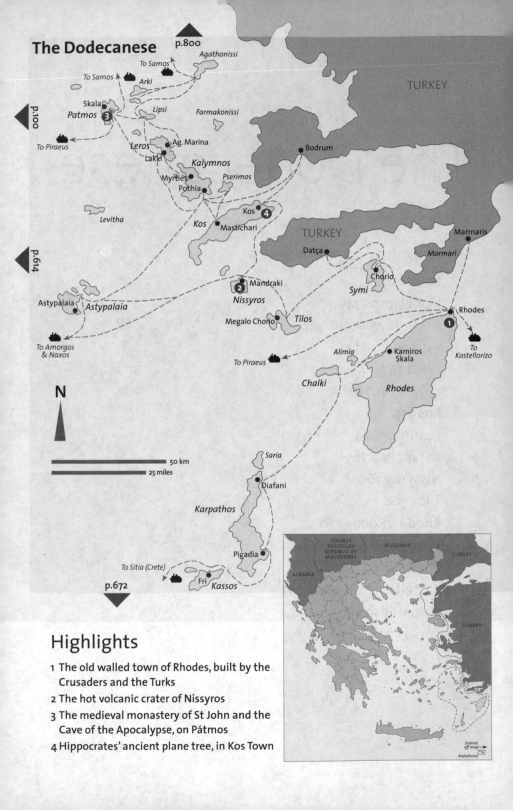

The Dodecanese

p.800
p.100
p.614
p.672

Agathonissi
To Samos
To Samos
Arki
Skala
Patmos **3**
Lipsi
Farmakonissi
To Piraeus
Leros
Ag. Marina
Lakki
Kalymnos
Myrties
Pserimos
Pothia
Levitha
Kos **4**
Kos
Mastichari
Astypalaia
Astypalaia
To Amorgos
& Naxos
Mandraki **2**
Nissyros
Megalo Chorio
Tilos
To Piraeus
Alimia
Chalki
TURKEY
Bodrum
TURKEY
Datça
Marmaris
Marmari
Chorio
Symi
Rhodes **1**
Kamiros
Skala
To
Kastellorizo
Rhodes
Saria
Diafani
Karpathos
Pigadia
To Sitia (Crete)
Fri
Kassos

N

50 km
25 miles

Highlights

1 The old walled town of Rhodes, built by the Crusaders and the Turks
2 The hot volcanic crater of Níssyros
3 The medieval monastery of St John and the Cave of the Apocalypse, on Pátmos
4 Hippocrates' ancient plane tree, in Kos Town

FORMER
YUGOSLAV
REPUBLIC OF
MACEDONIA
BULGARIA
TURKEY
ALBANIA
TURKEY
(Islands off map)
Kastellorizo

The Dodecanese, the 'twelve islands' (although there are 16 inhabited ones), were only added to Greece in 1948. Their distance from the mainland and their long separation from the mainstream of Greek history have dealt them a unique deck to play with – Catholic Crusaders, Ottoman Turks and Fascist Italians, all of whom contributed to their distinct history and architecture. Add a sunny climate, long sandy beaches and a striking individualism, and the holiday possibilities on the Dodecanese are infinite, from the feverish five-star cosmopolitan resorts of Rhodes and Kos to the low-key, very Greek pleasures of Lipsí, Chálki, Kárpathos or Níssyros. Striking Sými and Pátmos attract upmarket crowds; while Astypálaia, Léros, Kálymnos and Tílos remain well-kept secrets. Kastellórizo has an end-of-the-world atmosphere that draws more people every year; Kássos has a similar air but attracts nobody. Connections are excellent between the islands, making it easy to get around and even to pop over to Turkey for a day or two.

History

The first known inhabitants of the Dodecanese were the Carians (from nearby Asia Minor), who were either subjects or allies of the seafaring Minoans, and then of the Mycenaeans. The Dorians, next on the scene, founded powerful city-states on Rhodes and Kos, and formed a powerful Dorian Hexapolis (see p.771) with trade connections all over the Mediterranean. After the Persian defeat in 479 BC, the Dodecanese joined the maritime league at Délos, although their great distance from Athens gave them more autonomy than most members. The Dodecanese burst into full bloom in the Hellenistic and Roman eras, when Kos was world famous for its Hippocratic school of medicine and Rhodes erected its famous Colossus (164 BC). Rhodes then made an alliance with Rome, enabling her to acquire her own mini-empire of Greek islands; her schools of art, science and philosophy outshone Athens. Two centuries later Rome exiled St John to Pátmos, where he penned the *Book of Revelations*.

In 1095, the Dodecanese got their first taste of a more aggressive brand of Christianity, when Crusaders made them a port of call en route to the Holy Land. When the Knights of St John, who ran a hospital for pilgrims, were left homeless after the fall of Jerusalem in 1291, they purchased the Dodecanese from a Genoese pirate. They built a new hospital on Rhodes and castles on all the islands, while raiding the coast and preying on Muslim shipping. In 1522, Suleiman the Magnificent had had enough and attacked Rhodes with an enormous army, and after a bitter siege the Knights were forced to surrender and move on to Malta.

The Turks favoured the Dodecanese more than any other island group, and were sad to go in 1912 when Italy took 'temporary possession', made 'permanent' after 1923 by the second Treaty of Lausanne. Mussolini poured money into his new colonies, sponsoring massive public works, reforestation, archaeological excavations and historical reconstructions. Whereas Turkish rule had often been capricious, the Fascists were far worse in the eyes of the Greeks for outlawing their religion and language. With Italy's surrender in 1943, Churchill sent in British troops to prevent German occupation, but failed. A treaty signed in March 1948 finally united the Dodecanese with Greece, its last territorial gain.

Pátmos (ΠΑΤΜΟΣ)

Of all the Greek islands, beautiful volcanic Pátmos is the most sacred to Christians, because it hosted Jesus' beloved apostle John. After the Crucifixion he lived in Ephesus as Jesus' appointed guardian of Mary. During Domitian's persecutions he was sent to Rome, and then exiled to Pátmos in AD 95, where he lived in a cave and received the vision he described in the *Apocalypse*, or *Book of Revelations*. He may have only spent a year on Pátmos, but in that time John provided not only an accurate prophecy of the fall of the Roman empire, but enough material to keep fire-eating preachers in business ever since. Jump ahead nearly a thousand years, when things were going badly for Alexis Comnenus – 'born to the purple', but so battered by fate he had nothing but the blues. A hermit named Christódoulos nevertheless predicted his ascent to the throne, and Alexis promised him a wish should it come true. Of course it did, and in 1088 Christódoulos asked for Pátmos. Alexis provided the island, the building funds for a monastery, and a charter providing tax exemptions and the right to engage in sea trade. It became more influential than any Greek monastery outside of Athos. The Venetians and Turks respected its charter, and as an autonomous monastic state Pátmos flourished; its school of theology and liberal arts, founded in 1713, was one of the few to function in the open. Monastic control lessened as the islanders took over the sea trade, and in 1720 the monks and laymen divided the land.

Today the port gets busy with cruise passengers being hauled up to the monastery, and there are plenty of very secular shops to make sure they don't leave empty-handed. Yet Pátmos still has something of its otherworldly feel, especially out of season, perhaps because a local law bans 'promiscuity and looseness'; so don't come to the island of the Apocalypse expecting to wake the dead at its clubs.

Skála

All boats drop anchor at **Skála**, the island's main resort, and a smart and upmarket one it is, too. Visitors are greeted by a statue of Protergatis Xanthos Emmanuel, who led an uprising in 1821. Skála didn't even exist until that year, so fearsome were the pirates. Near the beach, a red buoy is a reminder of another troublemaker, the magician Yenoupas, who at the urging of priests of Apollo challenged St John to a duel of miracles. Yenoupas' miracle was to dive into the sea and bring back effigies of the dead; John's was to ask God to turn the magician to stone, which ended the contest. Even petrified, Yenoupas is a menace to shipping and stinks of sulphur. Behind Skála, one of the world's largest desalination plants has been replaced by a reservoir. You can also hike up to the site of the ancient city, **Kastélli**, for stunning views, a few Hellenistic walls and the chapel of **Ag. Konstantínos**; the sunsets are lovely.

The Monastery of St John the Theologian

t 224 703 1398. Opening times may vary; at the time of writing May–Nov daily 8–2 and Tues, Thurs, Sun also 4–6. Try to get there first thing in the morning before the crowds. Shorts prohibited; women must wear skirts. Expect a grumpy welcome; apparently no one told the monks when they

Getting There and Around

By sea: ferries connect daily with Piraeus, Kálymnos, Léros, Kos and Rhodes; frequently with Sámos, Ikaría, Agathónissi and Arki, and weekly with Níssyros, Náxos, Páros, Sýros Chálki, Kárpathos, Kássos; **hydrofoil:** regular in summer to Léros (Ag. Marína), Kálymnos, Kos, Lipsí, Ikaría and Sámos' three ports; **excursion boats** to Arki, Maráthi, Sámos (Pythagório) and Lipsí. **Port authority: t** 224 703 1231.

By road: buses depart from the ferry dock in Skála for Chóra, Gríkou and Kámbos. **Taxis, t** 224 703 1225, from the central square.

Tourist Information

Municipal office: in Skála, **t** 224 703 1666.
Astoria Travel, in Skála, **t** 224 703 1205, **f** 224 703 2975. *www.astoria.gr.*

Where to Stay and Eat

Skála ✉ 85500

Room owners meet the ferries, although many places are out in the boondocks.
Skala, t 224 703 1343, **f** 224 703 1747, *skalahtl@12net.gr (B; expensive–moderate).* Set in attractive gardens with a pool and restaurant, just two minutes from the ferry.
Romeos, t 224 703 1962, **f** 224 703 1070, *romeosh@12net.gr (B; expensive–moderate).* Traditional style rooms 500m from the port, with a pretty pool; all have sunset views.
Hellinis, t 224 703 1275, **f** 224 703 1846, *skalahtl@12net.gr (C; moderate).* Nice en suite rooms on the waterfront with views of the monastery. *Open April–Oct.*
Blue Bay, t 224 703 1165, **f** 224 703 2303, *bluebayhotel@yahoo.com (C; moderate).* All the mod cons in a quiet waterside spot on the road to Gríkou. *Open April–Oct.*
Australis, t 224 703 1576 *(inexpensive).* Friendly and prettily decorated.
Benetos, on the waterfront at Sapsila, **t** 224 703 3089 (€16–22). The island's finest: chef Benetos flies over from Miami to create lovely dishes from the sea and his own garden. Must book. *Open June–Sept.*
Grigoris, by the ferry. Tasty, cheap and cheerful with excellent charcoal-grilled fish.

Aspri, at Aspri Beach, **t** 224 703 2240 (€16–22). Fish taverna with a wonderful view of the castle; delicious lobster with pasta. *Open June–Sept, eves only.*

Chóra ✉ 85500

Archontika Irini, t 224 703 2826 *(expensive).* An old stone mansion, with traditional furniture, fireplaces and wood-burning stove, sleeping 6 to 10. *Open all year.*
Olympia, Plateía Ag. Leviás, **t** 224 703 1543 (€12–15). Good food, and plenty to look at.
Aloni. Traditional bouzouki and dancing.

Méloi Beach (Giordami) ✉ 85500

Porto Scoutari, t 224 703 3123, **f** 224 703 3175, *www.12net.gr/scoutari/ (B; expensive).* Overlooking the bay, with a pool; romantic and quiet apartments, with big beds, TVs and minibus into town. *Open Mar–Oct.*
Rooms and Taverna Méloi, known to all as Stefanos, **t** 224 703 1888. Almost on the beach; basic facilities, but good food.
Campsite, t 224 703 1821. With bamboo-shaded pitches, mini-market and cafeteria.

Kámbos ✉ 85500

Patmos Paradise, 200m from Kámbos, **t** 224 703 2624, **f** 224 703 2740 *(B; luxury–expensive).* Beautiful sea views and all the frills: restaurant, pool, squash, tennis, sauna and fitness centre. *Open mid-April–mid-Oct.*

Gríkou ✉ 85500

Petra Hotel and Apartments, t 224 703 1035 *(C; luxury–expensive).* Just back from the beach with huge terraces; air-conditioned rooms with minibars and phones.
Panorama Apartments, t 224 703 1209, **f** 224 703 2120, *panorama-patmos@excite.com.* Old favourite by the sea. Minibus service.
Joanna Hotel and Apartments, t 224 703 1031, **f** 224 703 2031, book in Athens **t** 210 981 2246 *(moderate).* Newly renovated, nice complex.
Athena, t 224 703 1859, **f** 224 703 2859 *(moderate).* Family-run place on the hillside, with lovely views from its balconies.
Stamatis, t 224 703 1302. For old favourites such as moussaka and stuffed tomatoes.
Flisvos, up on the hill. Small and family-run, with well-cooked Greek staples and a few rooms *(inexpensive).*

dedicated their lives to God that it meant being museum guards and trouser-police. Adm for the Treasury.

Above Skála, whitewashed Chóra clings to the castle walls of the monastery. Buses and taxis make the ascent in a few minutes, but it isn't too strenuous to walk up the old cobbled path if you aren't in a hurry. Once within the mighty walls, the monastery's intimate scale and intricate little corridors are delightful – but can easily become unbearably stuffy when tour groups march through. A charming court of 1698 incorporates the exo-narthex of the church; just inside this is the chapel-tomb of its founder, the Blessed Christódoulos. Designed as a Greek cross set in a square, the church still retains its original marble floor; its icon of St John was a gift from Emperor Alexis. Frescoes cover every surface, although only those in the 12th-century **Chapel of the Theotókos** are as old as the church; others are in the Refectory, off the inner courtyard. The **Treasury Museum** displays the monastic charter – a chrysobul, signed and sealed; an inscription from the Temple of Artemis, stating that Orestes sought refuge here from the Furies; exquisite gifts – gold and silver crosses, croziers and stoles; superb icons, including one from the 11th century left by Christódoulos; and ship pendants made of diamonds and emeralds donated by Catherine the Great. The library contains hundreds of rare codices and manuscripts, including the 6th-century *Codex Porphyrius*, St Mark's Gospel written on purple vellum, but may only be visited with permission from the abbot. Lastly, if it's open, climb up to the roof terrace for a commanding view over the Aegean.

Chóra and down to the Monastery of the Apocalypse

Chóra is a lovely, almost Cycladic village, with a maze of alleys and white mansions built by merchants and captains, often hiding startlingly lavish interiors. You could spend a day finding its 40 or so churches wedged in between: especially good are the **Convent of Zoodóchos Pigí** (1607) with fine frescoes (*open mornings and late afternoons*), the **Convent of the Evangelismós** (*follow the signposts west of town; open mornings*) and 11th-century **Ag. Dimítrios**, but it's likely to be locked. Nor is hunting out the caretaker easy, as Chóra is one of those old, silent places where the streets are often deserted once the daytrippers have gone.

This changes dramatically on Greek Maundy Thursday, when Chóra is packed with visitors and TV crews for the *Niptíras* ceremony, when the abbot re-enacts Christ's washing of his disciples' feet – a rite once performed by the Byzantine emperors. It's a short walk down to the **Monastery of the Apocalypse** (*open Mon, Tues, Thurs and Sun, 8–2 and 4–6; other days 8–2*), built by the cave where John lived and dreamed and dictated to his follower, Próchoros; you can see the rock where the saint rested his head and hand (though he must have been something of a contortionist), and the roof, split in three sections by the voice of God, symbolizing the Holy Trinity. If you're walking up from Skála, follow the ΑΠΟΚΑΛΥΨΟΣ signs.

Beaches and Villages around Pátmos

The closest beach to Skála, **Méloi**, is 2km north, pleasant and tree-shaded but often crowded; for something more peaceful if less shady, look for the sign to **Agriolivádi**, a quiet cove with a pair of tavernas. Pátmos is fine walking country, especially around this dramatic shore, with **Áno Kámbos** the centre of the trail network. This is the only other real village on the island, although there are beaches in every direction. **Kámbos** to the east is sandy, with watersports; **Léfkes** to the west is often windswept; to the north **Lámbi**, also reached by excursion boat, has lovely multi-coloured pebbles and a good fish taverna.

Roads from Skála and Chóra go to Pátmos' principal resort, **Gríkou**, overlooking a beautiful bay. On its south end, the **Kalikátsou rock** has carved rooms and stairs in unlikely places and may have been an 11th-century hermitage. Inland, at **Sykamiá**, there's an old Roman bath said to have been used by St John to baptize his converts. The south road peters out at Diakofti, where Pátmos is only a few hundred yards across. There's a beach here, but a half-hour's tramp (or caique from Skála) will take you to lovelier **Psilí Ámmos**, with fine white sand. West of here, a seaside grotto on **Cape Yenoúpas** was the home of the evil magician, and even today it's hot and smelly.

Lipsí/Lípsos (ΛΕΙΨOI)

Lipsí is the star of an archipelago of islets between Léros and Pátmos, and it's not surprising that Odysseus put off his homecoming for seven years to linger here with Calypso. It does have a certain unworldly magic: for centuries it was owned by the monastery on Pátmos, and the blue domes of the churches bubble over a horizon of soft, green hills. The lovely beaches are a magnet for excursions from Pátmos and Léros, yet by evening the island regains its tranquillity.

Getting There

By sea: ferries connect three times a week with Piraeus, Sámos, Pátmos, Léros and Kálymnos, twice with Kos, Agathoníssi and Arkí, once with Níssyros, Tílos, Sými, Rhodes and Ikaría; **excursion boats** to Léros, Pátmos, Arkí, Maráthi and Makrónissi caves; **hydrofoils** from Pythagório (Sámos), Kos, Kálymnos, Léros and Pátmos.

Port authority: t 224 704 1240.

By road: buses depart almost hourly in season as far as Platís Gialós and Katsadiá Beaches.

Tourist Information

At the town hall, **t** 224 704 1209.
Laid Back Holidays, t 224 704 1141, **f** 224 704 1343, *www.otenet.gr/lbh*. A mine of local information.

Where to Stay and Eat

Lipsí ✉ 85001

Aphrodite, t 224 704 1000, **f** 224 704 1002 (*moderate*). Rooms with kitchens and balconies on the beach, 100m from the port.

Rena's Rooms, t 224 704 1242. Immaculate and owned by John and Rena, who lived in America and run the *Rena II*.

Studios Dream, by Lendoú Beach, **t** 224 704 1271. With kitchenettes and balconies.

Studios Kalymnos, on the far side of the village, a 2min walk from the centre, **t** 224 704 1102/1141. Peaceful, set in a garden and lovely views over the countryside.

Kalypso. Dine under the vines in dishevelled style, chez the famous Mr Mungo.

O Theologos. Specializes in fish and lobster, and prices won't break the bank.

Kali Kardia, further along towards the ferry dock. Popular, with a lovely terrace.

Maria, a few doors along. Excellent restaurant and less frenetic at lunchtime.

Lipsí village greets arrivals with a tidal splash of Fauvist colour, all kept pin bright, as if the locals were competing in a tidy island contest. You can imagine their surprise in July 2002 when the police turned up and arrested the white haired, avuncular 'Michelis Economou, maths professor', alias Alexandros Yiotopoulos, a student radical in Paris in the 1960s who then became the alleged leader of the November 17 terrorist organization. Apparently he had spent the last 16 summers on Lipsí with his French wife – in his now famous red (naturally) house.

Day trippers head straight for the sands, while the Greeks usually stop first to visit **Ag. Ioánnis** and its miraculous icon. The story goes that the Virgin granted a woman's prayer. Being poor, she had nothing to offer in return but a lily, which she humbly placed near the icon. In time the lily withered, but on the day of the Virgin's acceptance into heaven, 24 August, it burst into bloom and has flowered on that day ever since. The ancient stalk can clearly be seen under the glass. Opposite, in the *dimarchíon* (town hall), the small **Nikoforeion Ecclesiastical Museum** (*open Mon–Fri 9.30–1.30 and 4–8, Sat and Sun 10–2*) has a collection of motley stuff and a letter written by Admiral Miaoúlis on the night of his famous sea battle. There is also a **carpet factory** to visit, one of a score set up to employ young women in rural areas.

Lipsí is a miniature world you can walk across in two hours, past walled fields and blue and white chapels. The town beach at **Lendoú** is shaded by trees, but you'll find more peaceful sands by walking over the dusty headland to **Kámbos** or beyond to **Kimissí**. Buses run to the island's best-known beach, the white cove of **Platís Gialós** (3km) which has a pretty church, or take you south to **Katsadiá**, with its succession of sandy coves; both have tavernas.

Arkí (ΑΡΚΟΙ) and Maráthi (ΜΑΡΑΘΙ)

Arkí, a hilly little island with 40 inhabitants, sees occasional caiques from Pátmos and Lipsí and one or two ferries a week. Facilities are minimal – water is shipped in, but a little solar plant now provides electricity. There are quiet coves and a **Blue Lagoon**, good for snorkelling in the vivid waters. **Taverna Asteria** has rooms and the only phone, t 224 703 2371.

Even smaller **Maráthi** has a natural harbour popular with fishermen and yachts, but no ferry; once or twice a week excursion boats from Pátmos and Lipsí link it to the world. Maráthi has a long sandy beach and two tavernas: Greek-Australian **Pantelis Marathi**, t 224 703 2609, with comfortable, en suite rooms (*inexpensive*), and **Mihalis Kavouras**, t 224 703 1580 (*inexpensive*), which is more basic, but has its own charm, owing to a Golgotha of goat skulls used for decoration in the trees.

Agathónissi (ΑΓΑΘΟΝΗΣΙ)

Northeast of Pátmos, steep little Agathónissi (pop. 130) tucked up next to Turkey may be the ticket if you've been seeking a very Greek island with just a tad of civilization. Literally 'thorn island', Agathónissi does have its share, but water is scarce. The

Getting There

A **ferry** links Agathónissi with Sámos (Pithagório), Pátmos, Lipsí, Léros, Kálymnos and Kos twice a week; **hydrofoil**: once a week to Kos, Kálymnos, Léros (Ag Marína), Pátmos and Sámos (Pythagório).
Port authority: t 224 702 3770.

Where to Stay and Eat

Agathónissi ✉ 85001

Maria Kamitsi, Ag. Giórgios, **t** 224 702 3690. A nice pension set in a flower-filled garden set back from the waterfront.

George's, Ag. Giórgios, t 224 702 4385. Rooms (*inexpensive*) and excellent food.

Ioannis Taverna. Ioannis grills his own fish.

Katsoulieris Pension, in Megálo Chorió, **t** 224 702 4385.

port of **Ag. Giórgios** has a pebbly, grotty beach, but there's a better one at **Spília**, in a sheltered cove to the west. Most people live in pleasant **Megálo Chorió** and about 10 live in tiny **Mikró Chorió**, linked by a cement road. Boat excursions in high season visit remote beaches. There are the remains of a medieval granary at **Thóli**, and an excellent place to swim. You can walk (in sturdy shoes) in about 90 minutes to pebbly **Choklakiá**, or to the deserted fishing village of **Kathóliko**, with great views of Sámos and Turkey. There's a small beach, so you can take the plunge on arrival.

Léros (ΛΕΡΟΣ)

With a coastline as serrated as a jigsaw puzzle piece, tree-fringed beaches and unspoiled villages, Léros is a beautiful island that has long been the butt of jokes in Greece. Because of its mental hospitals its name evokes the same reaction as 'Bedlam' in Britain; to make matters worse, Léros sounds like *léra*, 'filth' or 'rogue'. Since the famous 1989 Channel 4 exposé on the grim conditions in the hospitals, the situation has improved dramatically; a care-in-the-community scheme was set up and you may see patients in the villages. But they are not at all intrusive, and Léros is anything but downbeat. The people are friendly, and exceptionally musical; the folk songs of the local Hajiadákis dynasty have influenced Greece's leading composers. It's not at all rare to hear the hammer dulcimer (*sandoúri*), or the bagpipes (*tsamboúna*). Léros has a special atmosphere you either love or hate; and the bad press actually helps to preserve its charm.

History

Léros was sacred to Artemis, and Robert Graves notes that its inhabitants' refusal to adopt the patriarchal religion of Olympus gave them a bad press even in ancient times. A contemporary epigram went: 'The Lerians are all bad, not merely some Lerians, but every one of them – all except Prokles, and of course he is a Lerian too'. Property has always been passed down through the female line (a nod to Artemis?), to the extent that most of Léros is owned by women.

In Roman times, local pirates captured a young lawyer named Julius Caesar on his way back to Rome from Bithynia, where he had had a dissolute affair with the governor; released after a month when his ransom was paid, Caesar got his revenge

Getting There and Around

By air: daily from Athens with Olympic, **t** 224 702 2844/4144. **Airport: t** 224 702 2777.

By sea: ferry connections six times a week with Piraeus, Patmos, Kálymnos, Kos and Rhodes, less often with Níssyros, Tílos, Sými, Lípsi, Arkí, Kastellórizo, Sámos, Náxos, Páros and Sýros. **Caique** daily in high season from Xirókambos to Myrtiés, Kálymnos. **Port authority:** Lakkí, **t** 224 702 2234.

By road: taxi ranks: Lakkí, **t** 224 702 2550; Ag. Marína, **t** 224 702 3340; Plátanos, **t** 224 702 3070 (prices are more or less fixed and reasonable). **Buses** run five times daily in season between Plefoúti, Parthéni, Alínda, Plátanos, Lakkí and Xirócampos.

Tourist Information

Tourist office: Ag. Marína quay; *open 8.30–12 and 3–4.30, Wed 2.30–3.30.*

Where to Stay and Eat

Bring bug-goo: lush Léros is invaded by airborne Lilliputian vampires at night.

Lakkí/Xirókambos ✉ 85400

Katikíes, t 224 702 3624, **f** 224 702 4645 (*A; expensive*). Lovely studios and apartments

in traditional style, set away from the road and sleeping up to six.

Miramare, t 224 702 2053, **f** 224 702 2469 (*D; inexpensive*). Gilds the lily with its gold cornice, but is both central and comfortable.

Katerina, t 224 702 2460, **f** 224 702 3038 (*E; inexpensive*). Nearby, all in cool marble.

Petrinos, t 224 702 4807 (€15). A touch of class, specializing in refined meat dishes. The owner-chef Giorgos trained in Belgium; Lerians flock here all year.

Efstathia, in Xirókambos, **t** 224 702 4099, **f** 224 702 5660 (*C; moderate*). Roomy studios with pool.

Vromólithos ✉ 85400

Tony's Beach, t 224 702 4742, **f** 224 702 4743 (*C; inexpensive*). Often has rooms in Vromólithos, although the rest tend to be block-booked.

Frangos, slap on the beach. Legendary for traditional food.

Pantéli ✉ 85400

Rosa, t 224 702 2798 (*inexpensive*). Nice pension overlooking the harbour.

Cavos, t 224 702 3247 (*inexpensive*). Marginally preferable alternative: rooms and studios.

Psaropoula, on the beach, **t** 224 702 5200 (€15–20). As the name suggests, it's bites from the briny on the menu; try the seafood with rice.

by crucifying every brigand around Léros. In 1316 the island was sold to the Knights of St John and governed as part of the monastic state of Pátmos. In the last century, Léros paid a high price for its excellent anchorages. After 1912 the Italians built their main air and naval ordnance bases at Lépida and based their Eastern Mediterranean fleet in Lakkí Bay; when Churchill sent the British to occupy the island after the Italian surrender in 1943, Hitler sent in an overwhelming force of paratroopers to take it back (12–16 November). Under the *junta*, Communist dissidents were imprisoned in a notorious camp in Parthéni; during the Cyprus dispute the Greek government dismantled its military installations to show that it had no warlike intentions against Turkey.

Lakkí and South Léros

Arriving at **Lakkí** by ferry, usually at night, is an experience, with its extraordinary Fascist buildings reflected in the calm gulf. If Fellini had been Greek, it would have been one of his favourite sets. The wide streets of Mussolini's dream town are usually empty and forlorn – the grandiose cinema, school and old Hotel Roma (later the Leros Palace) all abandoned by the Greeks for the more convivial Plátanos. Many commute

Drossia. Less touristy than some, with fish almost leaping from the family nets.

Plátanos/Ag. Marína/Krithóni
✉ 85400

Eleftheria, Plátanos, t 224 702 3550 (*C; moderate*). Quiet family apartments and doubles.

Kapaniri, Ag. Marína. The place to sample a selection of *mezédes* with your ouzo.

Neromylos, just outside Ag. Marína. New and popular for its traditional food.

Krithoni Paradise, Krithóni, t 224 702 5120, f 224 702 4680 (*B; expensive*). Swish complex with a pool, gardens and piano bar. Relaxing and recommended.

Nefeli Apartments, t 224 702 4001, f 224 702 2375 (*C; moderate*). Another stylish upmarket establishment designed by a woman architect.

Esperides, next to the Paradise, t 224 702 2537. A tasty taverna.

Álinda ✉ 85400

Archonitkó Angelou, t 224 702 2749, f 224 702 4403, *ArchontikoAngelou@hotmail.com* (*C; moderate*). Built in 1895, lovingly restored by the friendly owners and set in a cool, flowery garden. Good home-made breakfast.

Boulafendis Bungalows, t 224 702 3515, f 224 702 4533 (*C; moderate*). Pleasant, spacious studio development around a traditional mansion and pool-bar area.

Ara, t 224 702 4140, f 224 702 4194 (*C; moderate*). Set up high with lofty views of both 'seas'; studios and apartments, restaurant, pool and Internet access.

Papafotis, t 224 702 2247 (*inexpensive*). Friendly owner, with cheaper, clean rooms and studios; the ones facing the mountains are fanned by the *meltémi*.

Alinda, t 224 702 3266 (€10–14). The best taverna for traditional fare, served on the veranda or in the courtyard.

Finikas, t 224 702 2695. An old seaside favourite.

Entertainment and Nightlife

In summer, look for performances in traditional costume by **Artemis**, a society dedicated to the revival of the island dances. There is a **bouzouki club** on the road up to Plefoútis; otherwise Pantéli has a disco and the cool **Savanna** bar at the end of the harbour. In Ag. Marína, **Faros** plays great world music. In Alínda, succumb to a sundae at **Palatino**, with good music and live Greek variety on weekends, or at **Cosmopolitan** with live music and international DJs in season. For a bit of a dance, locals and tourists head for **Puerto Club** in Lakkí.

---

to Lakkí, however, to work in the three mental hospitals built by the Italians. The park around the institutions is open to visitors; one building was intended as the Duce's summer villa. By the waterfront there's a monument to the many who perished in 1943 when a Greek ship, the *Queen Olga*, was bombed by German planes and sank in Lakkí's harbour. A path from the jetty goes to the nearest beach, **Kouloúki**.

South, overlooking **Xirókambos**, is the fort **Paliokástro**, built near an earlier castle from the 3rd century BC. The church inside has mosaics and Xirókambos itself, a simple fishing village, has a pleasant sandy beach to the west. North of Lakkí, it's only 3km to the popular sandy beach of **Vromólithos** ('Dirty Rock'), in a deeply wooded fold. Just around the bay, picture postcard **Pantéli** is a fishing village and nightly rendezvous of seafood-lovers, with tables on the beach.

Plátanos and Ag. Marína

The capital **Plátanos** is near the centre of Léros, a pretty place with a smattering of neoclassical and traditional houses; the views over Pantéli are especially stunning as the lights blink on at night. Its ancient acropolis was taken over by the **Kástro**, a

Byzantine fortress renovated by the Venetians, the Knights and the Greek military, before they upped sticks for another hill. A rough asphalt road rises to the top, or there's 370 steps, lined by houses and fragrant gardens. From the top, the four bays of Léros are spread at your feet. Within the *kástro*'s walls, the church of the **Megalóchari Kyrás Kástrou** (*open 8.30–12.30 and Wed, Sat and Sun 3.30–7.30*) houses a miraculous icon. The story goes that during the Turkish occupation the icon came from Constantinople on a boat with a candle. The inhabitants carried both grandly to the cathedral. The next day, however, the icon had vanished and the Turkish captain of the *kástro* found it, candle still blazing, in his powder store, even though the door had been locked. The icon was taken back to the cathedral, but the following nights decamped to the arsenal again and again, until the Turkish governor was convinced it was a miracle and gave the powder storeroom to the Christians. They made it a church and the icon has been happy ever since.

Ag. Marína, the seaside extension of Plátanos, is easily reached by the main street, but to avoid the motorbike Grand Prix, walk down the lane that runs parallel to the pottery. Ag. Marína has an often windswept harbour, full of fishermen and excursion boats; there are plenty of tavernas and accommodation by the beach at **Krithóni**.

Álinda and the North

Álinda, once the commercial port of Léros, is the island's principal package destination, although still low-key by Kos standards. There's a long sandy beach, with water sports, and plenty of seafront cafés and tavernas. The mosaics of an Early Christian basilica lie in the forecourt of the town hospice, while nearby is the immaculate **British war cemetery** where 183 soldiers lie. In the 1920s many notables of Léros fled to Cairo, and Álinda's folly, the **Bellini Tower**, was built by one of them; it now houses a good **Historical and Folk Museum** (*open daily 10–1 and 6–9; adm*). North of Álinda, a track leads to the secluded beaches at **Panagies** and sandy **Kryfós**, where you can skinny-dip. Or seek out the coves by Léros's answer to Corfu's Mouse Island, **Ag. Isidóros**, a white chapel perched on an islet reached by a causeway.

From Álinda, a eucalyptus-lined road leads north to **Parthéni** ('the Virgins'), former centre of the guinea fowl cult associated with Artemis, but now a very masculine military base. Above, only a few ruins remain of the **Temple of Artemis** (near the church of Ag. Kyrás) but they enjoy a superb setting, where you can sit under a sacred myrtle tree and look at the airport. Further north there's a family beach and taverna at **Plefoúti**, while over the headland at **Kioúra** are pebble coves reached via the chapel gates. You could easily do an island trip by car past **Drymónas** with lovely coves, an oleander gorge and the **Sotos** fish taverna, then over the mountain back to Lakkí.

Kálymnos (ΚΑΛΥΜΝΟΣ)

Sailing into Kálymnos from Kos just as the sun sets and the moon rises in the east is sublime. Even if you miss the magic twilight hour, you may well breathe a sigh of relief when you get to the port Pothiá – for, unlike Kos, this is the real Greece. One street back from the waterfront lies a busy Greek town, where carpenters hammer, tailors stitch, bakers bake and grocers have the old spicy Greek smell of coffee and herbs. The island also strikes a geographical equilibrium: emerald valleys wedged in its rocky face (its highest point, Mount Profítis Ilías, is the driest spot in the Dodecanese) sweep down to Scottish-style lochs.

Even the most casual visitor can't help but notice that this island is preoccupied with sponges: Kálymnos has Greece's last fleet of sponge-divers. Such was its claim to fame until 2001, when word leaked out about the biggest archaeological find in years: a trove of sculpture that 4th-century Christians had buried under a now ruined basilica. So far the site has only been partially excavated, but has already yielded a beautiful 6th-century BC *kouros*, a giant head of Asklepios and a hermaphrodite. The cultural czars in Athens demanded that Kálymnos cough them up, but so far the mayor is doing all he can to put them on display in a museum here, citing the same arguments the government has been using for the return of the Parthenon marbles.

History

Kálymnos was colonized by Mycenaean Argos, who named the capital after their mother city; the Dorians who followed had their city just northeast of Pothiá, at Dímos. An ally of Persia, the queen of Halicarnassus, conquered the island at the

---

To Sponge, or Not to Sponge

In their natural state, sponges are smelly and black; they have to be stamped, squeezed and soaked until their skeletons (the part you use in the tub) are clean. Many are then bleached in vitriol to achieve a yellow colour – but if you're out to buy opt for the natural brown ones, which are much stronger. Look for the densest texture and the smallest holes. The shop should have a bucket of water on hand so you can squeeze your potential purchase.

Diving for these primitive porifers is a dangerous art. In ancient times divers strapped heavy stones to their chests to bear them down to the sea bed, where they speared the sponges with tridents, then, at a signal, were raised to the surface by a lifeline. As modern equipment permitted divers to plunge to new depths, cases of the 'bends' were frequent, and it was common to see Kalymniots crippled or paralysed. These days divers wear oxygen tanks and surface with decompression chambers. But politics limiting access to sponge beds, a deadly sponge virus, overfishing and synthetic substitutes have undermined Kálymnos's traditional livelihood. In the last century, many divers emigrated to Florida to exploit sponge beds off Tarpon Springs.

In the past the sponge fleet left for seven months to work off the coast of North Africa. Today, only a few boats depart for a four-month tour in Aegean and Cretan waters. The week before they set out (traditionally just after Orthodox Easter, but it varies with the weather) is known as the Iprogrós or Sponge Week, devoted to giving the sponge-divers a rousing send-off, with plenty of food, drink, traditional costumes and dances. Their last night, *O Ípnos tis Agápis*, the 'Sleep of Love', ends with the pealing of church bells, calling the divers to their boats. They circle the harbour three times, caps waving, and sail away.

Getting There and Around

An airport at Kanoúni will take small planes ('ask God when, because only he knows'). In the meantime, the quickest way to get there is to fly to Kos and catch a hydrofoil.

By sea: ferries connect daily with Piraeus, Rhodes, Kos, Léros and Pátmos; four to five times weekly with Sámos and Lipsí; frequently with other Dodecanese, twice a week to Bodrum (Turkey), Ikaría and Fourní; once with Mýkonos, Sýros, Náxos, Páros and Kastellorízo. Frequent summer **hydrofoil** and **catamaran** links with Kos, Rhodes, Sými, Tílos, Níssyros, Léros, Lipsí, Pátmos, Ikaría and Sámos. Daily **boats** to Psérimos, Platí and Vathí; daily **caiques** from Myrtiés to Xirókambos, Léros; three ferries a day from Mastichári, Kos; local caiques from Myrtiés to Télendos and Emborió. **Port authority: t** 224 302 4444/9304.

By road: the **bus** station in Pothiá is next to the domed *dimarchíon*. Buses every hour to Myrtiés and Massoúri, five times a day to Vlichádia, 3–4 to Vathí, Árgos, Platís Gialos and Emborió. **Taxis:** the main rank is up Venizélou Street, in Plateía Kýprou; drivers offer tours of the island, **t** 224 302 9555/4222.

Tourist Information

Information booth: on Pothiá's waterfront, **t** 224 302 9310, *www.kalymnos-isl.gr*; *open in summer Mon–Fri 7–2.30*.

Town hall info: t 024 305 9141.

Premier Travel, Myrtiés, **t** 224 304 7830, **f** 224 304 8035.

Where to Stay and Eat

Pothiá ✉ 85200

Themelina, t 224 302 2682 (*moderate*). A lovely 19th-century villa with gardens and pool by the archaeological museum; traditional rooms but your only chance of one is in the off season; it's block-booked May–Oct.

Panorama, in the back streets, **t** 224 302 3138 (*C; moderate*). Lovely décor, and all rooms have balconies with magnificent views.

Greek House, t 224 302 3752 (*inexpensive*). Near the sponge factory, friendly with cosy, wood-panelled rooms.

Patmos, t 224 302 2750 (*inexpensive*). In a relatively quiet side street by the tourist office, with self-catering facilities.

In Pothiá, most restaurants are on 'Octopus Row' at the far end of the quay.

Vouvali's (€16–22). Decorated with nautical bric-à-brac with seawater tanks from where you can choose your own lobster or fish – or try their excellent fish casseroles.

Xefteries, in a back street by the cathedral (€15). In the same family for over 85 years; fresh fish, roast lamb or *stifádo* in a garden.

O Barba-Petros, at the end of the port, **t** 224 302 9678 (€15–22). Popular dining spot with Kalymniots, who come from all over the island for the fish.

Argos, in nearby Árgos. Authentic; try the *moori*, lamb cooked in a clay pot.

Kantoúni/Pánormos/Eliés

Kaldyna Island, t 224 304 7880, **f** 224 304 7190, by Kantoúni (*B; moderate*). Air-conditioned and set back a bit from the sea, with a big

---

beginning of the 5th century BC, but after Persia's defeat Kálymnos joined the maritime league at Delos. Kálymnos next enters history in the 11th century, when Seljuk Turks launched a sudden attack and killed almost everyone. The Knights of St John, when they came, strengthened the fortress of Kástro, but abandoned it to succour Rhodes. During the Italian occupation, attempts to close down the Greek schools resulted in fierce opposition; prominent citizens were either jailed or exiled. The women of Kálymnos, who over the centuries had become fiercely independent with their menfolk away at sea for so long, held protest marches and in a show of defiance painted everything in sight Greek blue and white. In 1996, Kálymniot patriotism nearly landed Greece in the soup with Turkey, over two tiny uninhabited islets to the east; fortunately the warships went home, just in the nick of time.

pool and sea sports. Multi-room bungalows are great for families. *Open May–Oct.*

Domus, Kantoúni Beach, **t** 224 304 7959. Terrace dining with superb view, serving island specialities and a mix of Greek and international fare. *Open May–Oct.*

Elies, 1km from the beach by Panórmos, **t** 224 304 7890, **f** 224 304 7160, *aquanet@klvm. forthnet.gr* (*B; moderate*). With a restaurant and a pool. *Open May–Oct.*

Taverna Marinos, Eliés. Specializes in roast stuffed lamb in the evenings and has an inventive and reasonably priced menu.

Myrtiés

Delfini, **t** 224 304 7514 (*C; moderate*). Central.

Hermes, **t** 224 304 7693, **f** 224 304 8097 (*C ; moderate*). Also a good bet.

Myrties, **t** 224 304 7512 (*D; inexpensive*). In the heart of things and open all year.

Drossia, Melitsacha Beach, **t** 224 304 8745. *Psarotaverna* renowned for swordfish and excellent lobster dishes.

Babis Bar, in the square. Good snacks and breakfast and the perfect place to wait for buses, taxis and the boat to Télendos.

Massoúri

Plaza, **t** 224 304 7134, **f** 224 304 7178 (*B; moderate*). In the more peaceful Arméos area, perched high over the bay with a pool and fine views. *Open May–Oct.*

Studios Tatsis, **t** 224 304 7887 (*C; moderate*). Stylish with great views over Télendos.

Niki's Pension, **t** 224 304 7201 (*moderate*). Between the two resorts. Great views, but is set up steps over rough terrain.

Noufaro, in the north part of town, **t** 224 302 7988 (€15–20). Worth a stroll up here for a hint of sophistication, friendly service and view; Greek and international dishes.

Punibel, near the square, **t** 224 304 8150 (€12–15). For some good Greek dishes, but the emphasis is on pizza.

To Iliovasilema. Owned by the local butcher; dishes here used to walk, not swim.

Mathaios. Does all the Greek favourites well.

Télendos Island

Rita, **t** 224 304 7914 (*inexpensive*). Rooms over the friendly cafeteria that bakes cakes.

Pension Uncle George's, **t** 224 304 7502 (*inexpensive*). Above the excellent restaurant.

Café Festaria, **t** 224 304 7401 (*inexpensive*). Further along; en suite doubles.

Dimitrios Harinos, **t** 224 304 7916 (*inexpensive*). Village rooms in a pretty garden.

Ta Dalinas. Good value taverna with Greek music on Wed and Sat.

Emborió

Harry's Pension/Taverna Paradise, **t** 224 304 7483 (*C; moderate*). Lovely secluded gardens.

Vathí

Galini, in Rína, **t** 224 303 1241 (*C; inexpensive*). Immaculate rooms and home-baked bread, served on a restful terrace overlooking the fjord-like harbour.

Pension Manolis, **t** 224 303 1300 (*inexpensive*). Higher up to the right, with a communal kitchen and nice garden. Manólis is an official guide and a mine of information.

Harbour Taverna. Excellent for seafood.

Pothiá (Kálymnos Town)

Colourful **Pothiá**, Kálymnos' port and the third largest city in the Dodecanese, wraps around hills and stretches along the valley back to the old capital Chorió. Pines close off one end; churches hang on cliffs as dry as biscuits; the landmark is a huge cement cross on a hill, illuminated at night. The police occupy a domed pink Italian villa (the former governor's mansion), rivalled by the silver domes of the 18th-century cathedral **Chrístos Sotíros**. Pothiá's oldest quarter is just behind here, while, by the decaying Italian administration buildings, a stone building houses the **sponge-diving school**. Being born to the career has made the Kalymniots tough hombres. They fish with dynamite and regale you with stories of friends who blew themselves to smithereens; at Easter Pothiá becomes a war zone as rival gangs celebrate the Resurrection with home-made bombs.

Not surprisingly, Pothiá has an excellent hospital as well as one of Greece's few orphanages, where Orthodox priests once came to choose a bride before they were ordained. Nor was culture neglected: the waterfront also has the **Muses Reading Room**, with Corinthian columns and bronze reliefs, which was founded in 1904. The Italians destroyed all the Greek books and turned it into the Café Italia, which in turn was damaged in the war. The club started up again in 1946 and the building was restored to house documents and books, including some in English.

Lovely old mansions and walled orchards rise along Pothiá's back streets. A five-minute walk up from the sea – allow fifteen for getting lost – the **Archaeological Museum** (*t 224 302 3113; open Tues–Sun 10–2*) is housed in a neoclassical mansion belonging to the Vouvális family, the first merchants to export sponges overseas, in 1896; the 'Victorian' furnishings and panoramas of Constantinople tend to stick in the mind more than the prehistoric finds. Don't expect to see the Kálymnos marbles, though – they're still in boxes.

There is a small **beach** near the yacht club, and beyond that a spa at **Thérma**. Around the headland, the beach at **Vlycháda** is one of the island's nicest spots. From Pothiá caiques sail south to **Néra** islet, with a taverna, and to **Képhalas Cave**, a 30-minute walk from the sea (alternatively taxis go as far as the **Monastery of Ag. Kateríni**, where you can pick up a 2km path). The cave has colourful stalactites and was once a sanctuary of Zeus; a huge stalagmite resembles the king of the gods enthroned.

Up to Chorió

Inland, Pothiá's suburb **Mýli** greets visitors with three monumental derelict wind-mills. On a hill here is the ruined Castle of the Knights, **Kástro Chryssochéria** ('Golden-handed'), named after a church built over a temple of the Dioscuri. Mýli blends imperceptibly into the pretty white **Chorió**, the medieval capital, lying under the citadel **Péra Kástro**; on a gloomy day it looks more Transylvanian than Greek. The only intact buildings are nine whitewashed chapels; the views from the top, over the coast, are wonderful. The **Cave of the Nymphs** at the foot of Mount Flaská (near Chorió's hospital) has never been thoroughly explored, but with a torch you can see the holes in the rock where supplicants poured libations. The old cathedral, **Panagía tis Kechaitoméni**, contains columns from a Hellenistic Temple of Apollo; its founda-tions lie just beyond Chorió and the Árgos crossroads: most of its stone went into the 6th-century **Christós tis Ierúsalim**, a church built by the Emperor Arkadios after he found shelter at Kálymnos during a storm; only part of the apse and the mosaic floor survive. The Mycenaean settlement was at **Árgos**, where they left rock-cut tombs.

West Coast Beaches and North Kálymnos

North of Chorió wait Kálymnos' so-so beaches, small fringes of grey sand shaded with tamarisks, although the deep blue coves offer excellent swimming. The resort strip starts at **Kantoúni**, with a sandy beach enclosed by hills, and **Panórmos**, the latter running into **Eliés**, named after its olive groves, all fast becoming package play-grounds. **Linária** is next, with a few bars and tavernas and a path down to a seaweedy bay. Beyond the giant rock, **Platís Giálos** and **Melitzáchas** are a bit more upmarket. The road then plunges down to **Myrtiés**, the heart of the island's tourist strip, where the blood-red sunset over the islet of Télendos opposite is one of the wonders of the Dodecanese. Myrtiés blends into **Massoúri**, a surprisingly brash Golden Mile with neon-sign bars belting out music and local lads racing up and down on motorbikes. Yet the end of Massoúri towards **Arméos** is less frenetic: goatbells tinkle and women crochet in their shops.

From Myrtiés jetty (buses every hour from Pothiá) frequent caiques make the short trip to the craggy **Télendos**, which broke off from Kálymnos in a 6th-century AD earthquake. Its nickname, the Lady of Kálymnos, comes from its profile, best viewed from Kastélli (*see* below). Up a narrow lane from the port you'll find the attractive church of the Panagía, ruined Roman houses and, high above, a Byzantine Monastery. Of several pebble beaches, Chokláka (through the village and down steep steps in the cliff) is the most popular. Most of the islanders are fishermen and, apart from its daytime visitors, Télendos is a good place to get away from it all: it has a handful of seafood tavernas, rooms to rent and a few new holiday villa developments.

North of Massoúri, **Kastélli** was the refuge of survivors of the 11th-century Seljik massacre, and overlooks the sea in a landscape of cave-mouths full of fangs. North of here, limestone cliffs plunge abruptly into the sea and attract rock climbers from around the world. The coastal road is spectacular, overlooking fish farms on its way to the fjord-like inlet at **Arginónta**, the perfect base for treks in the quiet hills. The small beach is pebbly and peaceful, the small taverna is ideal for lunch and there are rooms to rent. The northernmost village on Kálymnos, **Emborió**, is a pretty fishing hamlet with a small beach (bus twice a day from Pothiá, caiques from Myrtiés), within walking distance of some exceptional countryside. The **Kolonóstilo Cave** (or Cyclops Cave) is nearby, with vast curtains of stalactites unfortunately damaged by treasure-hunters with dynamite. The remains of a **Venetian castle** are close by. The tower may have been built on a Neolithic temple; a sacrificial altar was found in the vicinity.

Vathí: the Fjord of Kálymnos

Nothing on the island properly prepares you for the sudden vision of 'the Deep', **Vathí**: a lush volcanic valley containing walled groves of mandarins and lemons and vegetable gardens (the tomatoes are famous) three charming villages, Rína, Plátanos and Metóchi, superbly situated over a magnificent fjord. **Rína** has a charming harbour with a few tavernas and rooms, a working boatyard and a mysterious 'throne' carved in the rock. **Plátanos**, named for its enormous plane tree, has Cyclopean walls. Near the mouth of the fjord, the **Cave of Daskaleío**, accessible only by sea, has yielded a trove of Neolithic-to-Bronze Age items.

Kos (ΚΩΣ)

Dolphin-shaped Kos, with its wealth of antiquities, flowers and orchards, sandy beaches and comfortable climate, is Rhodes' major Dodecanese rival in the tourist trade. The streets are packed with T-shirt and tatty gift shops and swarms of rent-a-

Kos

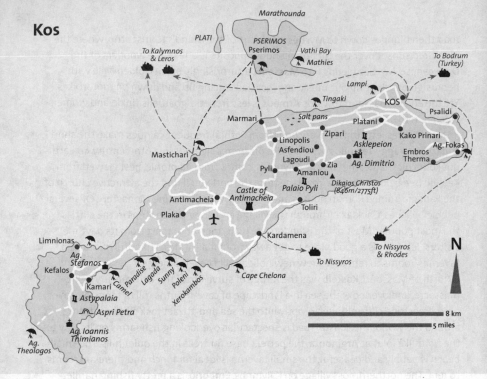

bikes rev up the streets. The big, self-contained resort hotels and countless discos are packed out in season. Even the architecture isn't particularly Greek, although a pair of minarets rising from the mosques add an aura of *cosmopolitana* to the capital. Inland, Kos in summer looks uncannily like a mini California: sweeping golden hills with a few vineyards, groves and orchards, grazing cattle and sheep, and pale cliffs, contrasting with the rashes of building – pseudo-Spanish villas are the rage – crowding the countless sandy coves that ruffle the coasts.

History

Ancient Kos had a number of name changes – Meropis, after its mythical king; Karis, for its shrimp shape; and Nymphaeon, for its nymphs. In the 11th century, the Dorians arrived and made Astypálaia their capital, and in 700 BC they joined the Dorian Hexapolis (*see* p.771). Poised between East and West, the island flourished with the trade of precious goods – and revolutionary ideas. Nearby Halicarnassus was the birthplace of Herodotus, the 'father of history', and in the 5th century BC Kos produced an innovating papa of its own, Hippocrates, the father of medicine, who declared that diseases were not punishments from the gods but had natural causes. His school on Kos, where he taught a wholesome medicine based on waters, special diets, herbal remedies and relaxation, was renowned throughout the ancient world, and he set the standard of medical ethics incorporated in the Hippocratic oath. When he died, the Asklepeion (dedicated to the healing god) was founded, and people from all over the Mediterranean came to be cured in its hospital-sanctuary.

Getting There and Around

By air: countless European charters and four flights a day from Athens. Olympic's office is at 22 Leof. Vass. Pávlou, t 224 202 8331. For one-way tickets home, try Plotin, in town, t 224 202 2871, f 224 202 5154. The airport is 26km from town. Olympic buses from Kos Town depart two hours before each flight and transport arriving Olympic passengers into town or Mastichári. Or there are infrequent public buses (the stop is outside the airport gate – ask for Taverna Panorama) to Kos Town, Mastichári, Kardámena and Kéfalos.
Airport: t 224 205 1229.

By sea: daily ferry connections with Piraeus, Rhodes, Kálymnos and Pátmos, six times a week with Léros, three to four times with Astypálaia, Níssyros, Tílos and Sými, less frequently with Kastellórizo, Chálki, Agathónissi, N.E. Aegean islands and Náxos, Páros and Sýros; daily excursions from Kos Town to Psérimos, Bodrum (Turkey), Níssyros, Platí and Léros. Port authority: t 224 202 6594.

By road: flat Kos Town and the small roads out west are especially suited to bicycles and there is no lack of shops that hire them. The city bus runs every 15 minutes at peak times from the waterfront (7 Akti Koundouriotou, t 224 202 6276) to Ag. Fokás and Lampi; roughly every hour to the Asklepeion; and eight times a day to Messaria (buy tickets in the office). Buses to other points leave from the terminal behind the Olympic Airways office, t 224 202 2292, but arrive early in season or find yourself at the wrong end of a long queue waiting for a taxi.

In theory you can summon a radio cab, t 224 202 3333/7777, but keep an eye on the meter.

In 411 BC, during the Peloponnesian War, the Spartans played a nasty trick; pretending to be friends, they entered the capital Astypálaia and sacked it. In 366 BC the survivors moved to the site of Kos Town, conveniently near the by-now flourishing Asklepeion. The next few centuries were good ones; besides physicians, Kos produced a school of bucolic poetry, led by Theocritus, a native of Sicily (319–250 BC). Apelles, the greatest painter of Alexander's day, was a native of Kos, as was Philetas, inventor of the Alexandrine and teacher of Ptolemy II Philadelphos, king of Egypt; many subsequent Ptolemies were sent over to Kos for their education. The Romans prized Kos for its translucent purple silks, wines and perfumes and St Paul brought Kos religion, in a big way; so far 21 early basilicas have been discovered.

Kos' wealth and strategic position made it a prize for invading Saracens, pirates and Crusaders. The gods themselves, it seems, were jealous, and earthquakes in AD 142, 469 and 554 levelled it. In 1315 the Knights of St John took control, and in 1391 began fortifications using the ancient city as a quarry, incorporating even marble statues from the Asklepeion in their walls. In 1457 and 1477 the Turks besieged Kos without success, but they gained the fortress in 1523 by treaty after the fall of Rhodes; its history then follows the rest of the Dodecanese.

Kos Town

Arrive by sea to view Kos Town at its most enchanting, with its castle and multitude of flowers and palms in the foreground, mountains blue in the background and the Turkish coast filling the horizon. Up close, the town is notable for its collection of Italian colonial Art Deco buildings, all postdating an earthquake in 1933; the same quake also revealed, under the rubble, large swathes of ancient Kos, now surrounded by throbbing holiday fleshpots.

One block up from the harbour, main **Plateía Eleftherías** has been freed of cars, leaving it eerie and empty, like a Pirandello character in search of a play. Here you'll find the 18th-century **Defterdar Mosque** (still used by Kos' 50 Muslim families), and the Art Deco **Archaeological Museum** (*t 224 202 8326; open Tues–Sun, 8.30–3; adm*), laid out like a Roman house, where fittingly the prize is a 4th-century BC statue of Hippocrates with a compassionate expression. There's a 2nd-century AD seated Hermes, with a pet ram and red thumb; a statue of Hygeia, the goddess of health, feeding an egg to a snake; and a fine mosaic of the god Asklepios, stepping from a boat and being welcomed by Hippocrates.

Plateía Eleftherías also has the city's **market** – walk through it to Ag. Paraskeví square, with its cafés and superb bougainvillaea. Buying and selling is old hat here; in Plateía Eleftherías you'll find the entrance into the ancient **Agora**, by way of the **Pórta tou Foroú**, draped with another massive bougainvillaea. This was where the Knights of St John built their town and auberges, just as in Rhodes (*see* p.773). When these

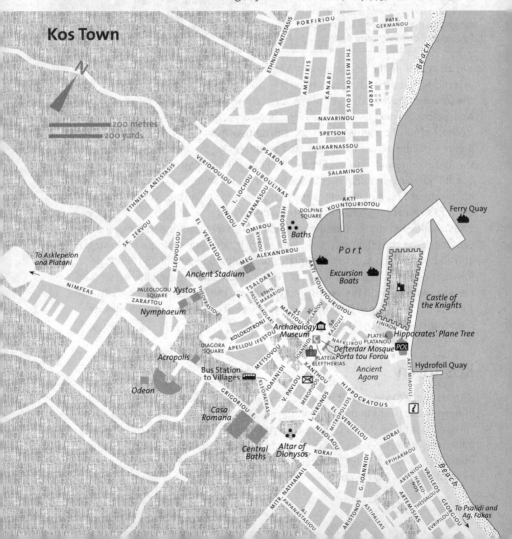

Tourist Information

Municipal tourist office: on Vass. Georgíou,
t 224 202 6585/8724, f 224 202 1111; *open
Mon–Fri 8am–8.30pm, Sat–Sun 8–3.*
Tourist police: t 224 202 6666. They share the
yellow edifice opposite the hydfroils with
the police, t 224 202 2222.
Post office: 14 Venizélou.
British Consulate: in Aeolos Travel, 8 An.
Laoumtzi St, t 224 2026 203.

Sports

Learn to **dive** at the Kos Diving Centre, 5
Koritsas Square, t 224 202 0269/2782; if you
already know how, go out with the Dolphin
Divers, t 224 209 454 8149. The proximity of
Turkey makes for lovely **sailing**: contact
Sunsail, 3 Artemisias, t 224 202 7547, or Kavos
Moorings, 7 Themistokleous, t 224 202 7115,
f 224 202 7116.

Where to Stay

Kos Town ✉ 85300

Be sure to book. If you want a room in the
centre and sleep, buy earplugs. Package
companies hog everything in the moderate
range, so splurge or slum.

Luxury

These are all A class and out in Psalídi.
Kipriotis Village, t 224 202 7640, f 224 202
3590, *www.kipirotis.com.* Spacious and
packed with amenities: an Olympic-sized
pool and a heated indoor one; hammam;
tennis; gym; new golf course and rooms for
the disabled. *Open Mar–Nov.* The same
people own the plush Panorama (same
website) with a thalassotherapy centre.
Hippocrates Palace, t 224 202 4401, f 224 202
4410. The Olympic Health Centre spa, indoor
and outdoor pools, and largest conference
hall in southeastern Europe. *Open April–Oct.*
Oceanis, t 224 202 4641, f 224 202 3728,
www.oceanis-hotel.gr. Another beachside
all-in complex set in a tropical garden, with
four pools and endless activities.
Platanista, t 224 202 7551, f 224 202 5029,
www.platanista.gr. Highly rated Neo-
Venetian palazzo, with tennis, massive pool,
gymnasium, tennis, etc.

Expensive

Ramira Beach, t 224 202 2891, f 224 202 8489
(A). Slightly more affordable and still well
endowed with facilities.

Inexpensive

Afendoulis, 1 Evripílou, t 224 202 5321, f 224 202
5797 *(C).* Friendly and comfortable guest

---

collapsed in the earthquake, they revealed the ancient market and harbour quarter, a
Temple of Aphrodite Pandemos, and a 5th-century Christian basilica.

On the north end of the Agora, Plateía Platánou is almost entirely filled by
Hippocrates' plane tree, its trunk 52ft in diameter, its boughs supported by an intricate scaffolding. At an estimated 700 years old it may be the oldest in Europe, and
Hippocrates just may have taught under its great-grandmother, for he believed, as do
modern Greeks, that of all the trees the shade of the plane is the most salubrious. The
Turks loved the old plane, too, and built a fountain out of a sarcophagus and the
lovely **Mosque of the Loggia** (1786) to keep it company.

The Castle of the Knights

A stone bridge off Plateía Platánou crosses the former moat (now a palm grove) to
the **Castle of the Knights of St John** (*t 224 202 8326; open Tues–Sun 8.30–3; adm*). This,
and the fortress across the strait in Bodrum, Turkey, were the main outer defence of
Rhodes. After an earthquake in 1495, Grand Master Pierre d'Aubusson rebuilt the walls
and added the outer enceinte. Since he used stone from the Agora, the castle is a
curious patchwork quilt of ancient inscriptions and knightly coats-of-arms. Some are

house with a fragrant terrace in a quiet road near the sea, run by Ippokrátis.

Pension Alexis, 9 Irodótou, t 224 202 8798, f 224 202 5797 (*E*). The Mecca for backpackers. Alex is amazingly helpful; his large veranda positively reeks of jasmine.

Manos, 19 Artemisias, t 224 202 8931, f 224 202 3541 (*C*). Rooms with balconies.

Kos Camping, t 224 202 3910, 3km from the port. Well-run site with a wide range of facilities from laundry to bike hire. A minibus meets the ferries.

Eating Out

Hamam, 3 Diagora Square, t 224 202 8323 (€18–22). A sumptuously restored Turkish bath with a garden terrace; the food has an appropriate Byzantine-Anatolian touch; pricey but excellent wine list.

Otto e Mezzo, 21 Apellou, t 224 202 0069 (€15–20). Fresh pasta dishes; intimate indoor dining and summer garden.

Platanos, t 224 202 8991. International and traditional dishes and live music at enticing tables around Hippocrates' beloved tree. Atmospheric but pricey.

Antonis, at Koutarys St, behind Hotel Anna. A real neighbourhood taverna with good food, big portions and low prices.

Taverna Ambavri, a 10min walk south of the Casa Romana. Excellent traditional dishes.

Nick the Fisherman, at Averof and Alikarnassou, t 224 202 3098. Nick's catch comes at good prices, accompanied by the bouzouki when he's in the mood.

Arap, outside town in Platáni. The best of the handful of tavernas here serving Turkish food; excellent aubergine with yoghurt, *borek*, shish kebab and chicken.

Entertainment and Nightlife

Kos is one big party at night. The Agora is alive with the thumping sound of house music from 'Disco Alley' on Navklírou Street, where every establishment is a bar pumping out plenty of bass. Discos go in and out of fashion, but **Kalua** and **Heaven**, both at Lámpi, have a watery backyard and garden and remain popular. **Aesolos** café-bar on the waterfront nearby plays mellow music. For Greek music and *rembetika*, there's **Happy Club**, 1 Navarinou. **Jazz Opera**, 5 Arseniou, is a great place playing jazz, funk, reggae and the blues. Films play at **Orpheus**, with an indoor screen in Plateía Eleftherías and an outdoor screen along Vas. Georgíou St, t 224 202 5713.

in the castle's **antiquarium**, joining stacks of other defunct columns and marbles that nobody seems to know what to do with. The castle's dishevelled weeds and wildflowers and the stillness of the noonday sun attracted director Werner Herzog, who set his first black and white film, *Signs of Life* (1966), within its walls.

Hellenistic and Roman Kos

Strabo wrote 'The city of the Koans is not large, but one lives better here than in others, and it appears beautiful to all who pass it by in their ships'. To see more of it, take Vas. Pávlou St from Plateía Eleftherías to the Seraglio quarter (don't expect any harem girls); here, opposite the Olympic Airways office, stands a ramped Hellenistic **Altar of Dionysos** and, across Grigoríou Street, the ruins of the **Central Baths** (fed by the Vourina spring, praised by Theocritus) and the **Casa Romana** (*t 224 202 3234; open Tues–Sun 8.30–3; adm*), both victims of the earthquake of AD 554 and reconstructed in grim concrete shell by the Italians in 1940. The house, begun in the Hellenistic era, has fine mosaics of panthers and offers an idea of the spacious elegance to which the wealthy could aspire; even on the hottest days it remains cool inside. To the west along Grigoríou St, the **Roman Odeion** has its rows of white marble seats; the statue of Hippocrates was discovered here. More good living is evident in the **Western Excavations** just opposite. Hellenistic walls surround the **acropolis** (now studded with a minaret); on the other side you can pick out the marble-paved *Cardo* and *Decumanus*, the main arteries of the Roman city. Although the Italians took many of the best mosaics off to Rhodes, good ones remain (often under a protective layer of sand), especially the **House of Europa**. Just north of this, lining the *Cardo*, are an elegant 3rd-century BC **nymphaeum**, or fountain house, which supplied water to the **public lavatory** with marble seats. The gymnasium has a **xystos**, a running track covered by a marble colonnade – a luxury that even Kos' luxury hotels can't match. The Romans even had a heated pool, near the **baths**. Part of this was transformed into a church in the 5th century; the lintel has been rebuilt and the baptistry has a well-preserved font. At the north end, an unidentified 3rd-century BC building contains mosaics of battling bulls, bears and boars. The **stadium** is a block north, along Tsaldári St, and has a well-preserved starting gate.

Beaches near Kos Town

The sandy and pebbly town beaches are packed with rows of sunbeds; in places along Vas. Georgíou the smell of gallons of sun lotion is overpowering. The city bus will take you in a few minutes to better, less crowded beaches to the north at **Lampí**; the closest strands to the south are at **Psalídi**, 3km away, and **Ag. Fokás** (8km), both sporting fancy hotel complexes. For something more remote, get your own transport to continue to **Embrós Thermá** (13km), where volcanic black sands and thermal springs make the bathing a few degrees warmer; a new spa may soon replace the old hot pit where the water oozes out.

The Asklepeion and Platáni

4km west of Kos town, reached by city bus; t 224 202 8763; open Tues–Sun 8.30–3; adm.

Along with Epidauros (*see* p.262) this was one of antiquity's most important shrines to Asklepios. It was served by the Asklepiada, a secret order of priests (Hippocrates was one), who found that fresh water and air and beautiful surroundings did much to remedy the ills of body and soul, along with healing herbs, dreams, hallucinogens and the power of suggestion. The cult symbol was the snake, the ancestor of the same one on the modern medical symbol, twining itself around the caduceus. The sanctuary was built after the death of Hippocrates, who left a school of disciples behind him, but most of the buildings date from Hellenistic times, when the earthquake-damaged Asklepeion was last reconstructed. Many of the structures were cannibalized by the Knights, who found it too convenient a quarry.

Set on a hillside, the Asklepeion is built in a series of terraces split by a grand stair. On the lowest level are Roman baths. The next level, once surrounded by a huge portico, has the main entrance and another bath; here was the medical school, and a museum of anatomy and pathology, with descriptions of cures and votive offerings from grateful patients. Near the stair are the remains of a temple dedicated by the

Kos-born physician G. Stertinius Xenophon, Emperor Claudius' personal doctor who, according to Tacitus, murdered his patient in AD 54 by sticking a poisoned feather down his throat (so much for the Hippocratic oath!) before retiring on Kos as a hero, thanks to the many privileges granted the island by Claudius. On this level, too, was the sacred spring of the god Pan, used in the cures. On the next terrace is the altar of Asklepios and Ionic temples dedicated to Apollo and Asklepios; on the top stood a 2nd-century BC Doric Temple of Asklepios, the most sacred of all, enjoying a view that in itself might cure the blues. In August, for the *Hippocratia* festival, teenagers don chitons and garlands to re-enact the old rituals and recite the Hippocratic oath.

Just up the road, the **International Hippocrates Foundation** is dedicated to medical research. In 1996, several Nobel Prize winners attended the first 'International Medical Olympiad' here. The five rings of the Olympic symbol were used to sum up Hippocratic philosophy: 'Life is short. Science is long. Opportunity is elusive. Experiment is dangerous. Judgement is difficult.'

On the way back to Kos Town, down the cool cypress-lined avenue, stop for refreshments in **Platáni**, Kos' Turkish settlement. It's busy and a bit touristy, like everything on Kos, but the Turkish food is excellent. A little out of Platáni, on the road back to the harbour, the **Jewish Cemetery** stands in a pine grove near the Muslim graveyard. The inscriptions on its headstones end abruptly after 1940. Without any parishioners, the pretty synagogue back in Kos town (4 Alexándrou Diákou) has been converted into the civic cultural centre.

Around Kos

The northeast of Kos is flat, with fields of watermelons and tomatoes. Beyond the reach of the city bus, **Tingáki** is a smart little resort overlooking the island of Psérimos. In March and April, the nearby salt pans, **Alíkes**, are a favourite port of call for flamingoes, while the sandy coast and estuary are a loggerhead turtle nesting area. At the far end of the wet lands, **Marmári** offers a generous sandy beach and a chance to explore local byways on horseback at its **Riding Centre** (*t 224 204 1783*). Just inland, two ruined Byzantine basilicas lie on the outskirts of **Zipári**; above, Kos' spinal ridge has a bumpy, curiously two-dimensional profile.

But these are real mountains, not a child's drawing. From Zipári the road climbs to the **Asfendíou**, a cluster of five hamlets with flower-filled gardens. The highest of the five, **Ziá**, is a pretty place with fresh springs, fruit and walnut groves – the bucolic Pryioton described by Theocritus – now converted into a 'traditional village' for coach parties, who come for the sunsets and 'Greek Nights' in the schlocky tavernas; but there are others, too, minus the dancing waiters. Ancient marble quarries dot Kos' highest peak, **Díkaios Christós** (2,775ft), which can be climbed without too much difficulty in about three hours from Ziá. From the Asfendíou a road runs across country to **Lagoúdi** and continues to **Amaníou**, where there's a turn-off to **Palaió Pýli**, the abandoned Byzantine capital on a crag. Within its walls is the church of Panagía Ypapandí, built in the 11th century by the Blessed Christódoulos before he went to Pátmos; it and two others, Ag. Antonio and Ag. Nikólaos, have 14th-century frescoes. Another road, just west of Amaníou, leads to the **Charmyleion**, a tholos tomb hero shrine with twelve mini-vaults, re-used as a church crypt. **Pýli** below is a farming town, although the upper part has a great taverna by a spring-fed fountain (or *pygí*) built in 1592. On 23 April, for the feast of St George, Pýli holds a horse race with an Easter egg as prize, cracked on the brow of the winning horse – a custom going back to antiquity.

Further west, in a wild setting, the **Castle of Antimácheia** was built as a prison for bad knights in the mid-1300s. Within its battlemented, triangular walls are two churches (one with a fresco of St Christopher), cisterns and, over the gateway, the arms of Pierre d'Aubusson. The sprawling village of **Antimácheia**, near the airport, has the island's last working windmill. Opposite is a **traditional house** (*open 8–4.30*); the typical boxed-in beds were often even higher than this so olives and wine could be stored underneath. Even better, head up to **Pláka**, a favourite picnic spot, with wild peacocks and great sunsets.

There are more beaches on either coast: to the south, the sand stretches between **Tolíri** and much hotter **Kardámena**, once a charming fishing village famous for its

Where to Stay and Eat

Tingáki ✉ 85300

Park Lane, 150m from the beach, **t** 224 206 9170 (*B; moderate*). Book through Aeolos Travel in Kos Town, **t** 224 202 6203. Package-dominated family hotel, with pool.
Meni Beach, **t** 224 206 9217, **f** 224 206 9181 (*C; inexpensive*). By the sea with a pool.

Marmári ✉ 85300

Caravia Beach, **t** 224 204 1291, **f** 224 204 1215 (*A; expensive*). Super club hotel set in beautiful grounds a little out of town with a vast range of facilities. *Open May–Oct.*
Tam Tam Beach Taverna, between Marmári and Mastichári, by Troulos Beach. A lovely place for lunch or dinner.

Mastichári ✉ 85301

Mastichari Bay, **t** 224 205 9300, **f** 224 205 9307 (*A; expensive*). Good for families, with nice pool and beach, playground, floodlit tennis, open-air theatre and satellite TV.
Mastichari Beach, **t** 224 205 9252 (*C; inexpensive*). Plain, clean and near the harbour.
Evagelia Argoula, **t** 224 205 9047 (*inexpensive*). Cheap, clean and cheerful studios.
Kalikardia. The oldest taverna in town, and still good.
Taverna Makis, just off the waterside. Long-established and popular.

Kardámena ✉ 85302

Unless you go on a package you may only find rooms on the edges of the season.
Porto Bello Beach, **t** 224 209 1217, **f** 224 209 1168, *portobello@kos.forthnet.gr* (*A; expensive*). Luxurious setting with views of Níssyros, an enormous pool and private beach.
Andreas. Refuses to pander to tourists, serving a good ethnic range of dishes.
Christopoulos Taverna, by the beach, is also recommended.
Kardámena lives it up with happy hours and has something for night owls of all ages, seasoned with good old-fashioned seaside Brit vulgarity.

Kéfalos ✉ 85301

Club Méd Kos, **t** 223 207 1311, **f** 224 207 1561, *www.clubmed.com* (€400–890 per person a week, all meals and sports included). One of the French club's most popular resorts, on two superb beaches. *Open May–Oct.*
Panorama, perched above packageville overlooking Kastrí island, **t/f** 224 207 1524 (*inexpensive*). Quiet studios that live up to the name and a garden; breakfast included.
Paradise Pension, down in town, **t** 224 207 1068 (*inexpensive*). Cheap rooms with fridge, kettle, balcony and a café below.
Esmeralda, in the hill village. Quails and liver as well as more usual Greek fare.

ceramics and golden sand, and now a heaving resort on the Costa Brava scale. On the north coast, **Mastichári** is quieter and has boats for Kálymnos and Psérimos; between the Achilles complex and the sea lie the ruins of a 5th-century **basilica of Ag. Ioánnis** with a partly visible mosaic floor.

More mosaics (under a layer of sand), Ionian columns and remains of baptistries survive of the lovely twin 5th-century basilicas of **Ag. Stéfanos**, near the beach at **Kamári**, towards the dolphin's tail. In the bay you can contemplate the islet of **Kastri**, a natural volcanic bulwark, often surrounded by the butterfly wings of windsurfers. A long fringe of sand runs under the cliffs to the east with a few access roads; the steepest descent is to pretty **Camel Beach**, and the easiest to **Paradise Beach** (or 'Bubble Beach' after the bubbles that rise to the surface). Further along the headland to the left, the beaches **Lagáda** (or Banana; the most beautiful), Sunny, attractive **Poléni** (or Magic) and **Xerókambos** are much quieter.

The road twists up to **Kéfalos**, high up on the headland of the dolphin's tail, where the bus terminates. Another castle looks over Kamári and isn't particularly impressive, although Mandeville in his *Travels* claims it was the lair of a dragon (who was really Hippocrates' daughter, enchanted by Artemis) awaiting a knight brave enough to kiss her to transform her back into a maiden. South, just off the road, there's a Byzantine chapel of the Panagía built out of a temple that belonged to the ancient capital **Astypálaia** (signposted Palatia), the birthplace of Hippocrates. A few bits of the ancient city remain, including a theatre. A paved road descends to **Ag. Theológos** beach, offering secluded swimming (but often waves) and a taverna. The road passes through dramatic scenery, past sheer cliffs and a telecommunications tower, then ends at the charming **Monastery Ag. Ioánnis Thimianós**, 6km from Kéfalos.

Psérimos (ΨΕΡΙΜΟΣ)

Psérimos, wedged between Kos and Kálymnos, has a beautiful sandy beach, which its 70 residents have come to regard as a curse, as day in and day out it becomes invisible under rows of day-trippers resembling well-oiled sardines in a tin. Excursion boats from Kos Town, Mastichári and Kálymnos queue up to dock, the tavernas are thronged and the islanders short-tempered. It becomes even more crowded on 15 August, when hundreds of pilgrims attend the *panegýri* at its monastery Grafiótissa. If you are staying (when the day boats have gone, the people become quite friendly), you'll probably want to hide in the interior by day, or hunt up the smaller pebbly strands on the east coast. Some boats now head instead to the adjacent islet of **Platí**, with another sandy beach, and make a day of it by stopping for lunch in Kálymnos.

Where to Stay and Eat

Psérimos ✉ 85200

If the rooms are full, you can sleep out on the beach, a kilometre from the village. **Katerina Xiloura, t** 224 302 3497. Rooms.

Tripolitis, t 224 302 3196. On the sea, located over Mr Saroukos' taverna.
Pension Niki-Ross. Worth a try (Ross is Australian Greek).
The unnamed taverna with the garden area does excellent fresh *kalamári*.

Astypálaia (ΑΣΤΥΠΑΛΑΙΑ)

Butterfly-shaped Astypálaia, halfway between Kos and Amorgós, offers the perfect transition from the Cyclades, with its austere rocky geography and sugar-cube houses spilling down the hill. Yet it nurtures a very Dodecanesian valley called Livádia in its bosom, which Homer called 'the Table of the Gods', and has equally fertile fishing along its wildly indented coastline. Astypálaia's relative inaccessibility makes it a good place to escape; although it gets busy in August, it remains a friendly, jovial island that moseys along at its own pace.

The capital of the island is divided between **Skála** (or **Pera Gialós**), the port, and **Chóra**, the old town, which curls gracefully down from the Venetian castle to a sandy

Getting There and Around

By air: four flights a week from Athens: book early in season. Olympic Airways: **t** 224 306 1328/1588; **airport: t** 224 306 1665. Buses run between Skála, Chóra and the airport; a taxi costs around €10.

By sea: ferries connect four times a week with Piraeus, less often with Kos, Rhodes, Kálymnos, Náxos, Páros, Amorgós and Níssyros; **hydrofoil** once a week from Rhodes. Port Authority: **t** 224 306 1208.

By road: there are two **buses** a day between Skála, Chóra, Livádia and Maltézana. **Taxis** are also available at reasonable rates. Skála has three **car rental** agencies.

Tourist Information

Tourist office: by the port opens when ferries arrive, and otherwise may be found in a windmill at Chóra, **t** 224 306 1412; *open June–Sept 9.30–1 and 6–9.*
Astypalea Tours: t 224 306 1571, under Vivamare Hotel. Helpful agency.

Where to Stay and Eat

Skála/Chóra ✉ 85900

Kilindra, t 224 306 1966, **f** 224 306 1131, *www.astypalaia.com/kilindra* (*luxury–expensive*). Built into the rock under the castle in Chóra, traditionally furnished apartments with lovely views and home-made breakfasts. *Open all year.*
Kostas Vaikousis, in Chóra, **t/f** 224 306 1430 (*expensive–moderate*). Three houses, with

lots of island charm and character. Ask in the antique shop at the port. *Open April–Oct.*
Titika, t 224 306 1677, **f** 214 306 1430 (*expensive–moderate*). Also in Chóra; a beautifully kept traditional house, offering comforts and privacy for 2–6 people. *Open April–Oct.*
Vivamare, t 224 306 1571, **f** 224 306 1328 (*C; moderate–inexpensive*). Inland from the harbour; comfortable studios with a kitchen.
Maistrali, t 224 306 1691 (*moderate–inexpensive*). Attractive hotel in classic island style; the restaurant (€12–20) serves local dishes, pasta and fish, including lobster.
Camping Astypálaia, t 224 306 1338. Just out of town near the Mármaris; follow the signs (a minibus usually meets ferries).
Monaxia (or **Vicki's**) (€12). Good simple taverna in a small street back from where the ferry docks, with excellent home cooking.
Akroyiali (€12–15). A tourist favourite on the beach at Pera Gialós, with lovely views up to Chóra after dark when the Kástro is bathed in golden light.

Livádi ✉ 85900

Gerani, t 224 306 1484, *gerani72@hotmail.com* (*inexpensive*). Studios; restaurant (€15–20) has tasty home-made dishes and fish, served on its airy tamarisk terrace.
Stefanida, on the beach, **t** 224 306 1510. Fresh lobster, fish and local meat dishes.

Maltezána ✉ 85900

Ovelix, 150m from the sea, **t** 224 306 1260 (*inexpensive*). Studios and rooms. The taverna (€12–18) serves the best fish on the island – including excellent *kakavia* (fish soup). *Open eves only, Greek Easter to Sept.*

beach. Skála has everything you need – an ATM machine, an antique shop selling foreign papers, and a pair of pelicans. Just above the bus stop, the **Archaeological Museum** (*open in season Tues–Sun 10–2 and 6–10; adm*) contains finds from the Kástro as well as from four Mycenaean chamber tombs. The best architecture, however, is up in Chóra, marked by restored windmills along the ridge of the butterfly wing. The lanes are lined with whitewashed houses, many sporting painted wooden balconies. Halfway up, nine little barrel-vaulted chapels are stuck together in a row to hold the bones of Chóra's oldest families.

The citadel, or **Kástro**, was built between 1207 and 1522 by the Quirini of Venice who ruled the island as the Counts of Stampalia. On either side of the narrow entrance, a pair of new buttresses support the high walls; from here you can see what a tight corset squeezes Astypálaia's middle. Among the ruined houses are two white churches: **St George**, on the site of an ancient temple, and the **Panagía Portaïtíssa**, one of the most beautiful in the Dodecanese, topped with a white-tiled dome (*usually open late afternoons in season*). Archaeologists have dug up the rest, finding temple foundations and drains from the 6th century BC. Don't miss the Castro bar just under the walls, with a goat's skull over the door.

West of the windmills, **Livádi** in a wide lush valley has a shingly, sandy beach popular with Greek families. Little roads through farms lead back to the barren mountains to an unexpected little lake with trees and ducks. An unpaved road starting at the windmills goes to **Ag. Ioánnis** on the west coast, a lush spot with orchards, a ruined Byzantine castle and excellent beach. North of Skála, the road passes over the waist of the butterfly, or Steno, and ends up after 9km near the airport at wannabe resort **Maltezána**, once a lair of Maltese pirates. By the olive groves seek out the **Roman baths** with their zodiac mosaics. On the far wing, **Vathí**, on a fjord-like bay, is a favourite if lonely yachting port, a hamlet with a fish taverna and rooms to rent.

Níssyros (ΝΙΣΥΡΟΣ)

In the great war between gods and giants, Poseidon ripped off a chunk of Kos and hurled it on top of the fiery Titan Polyvotis. This became the island of Níssyros, and the miserable Polyvotis, pinned underneath, sighs and fumes, unable to escape. The story is geologically sound: volcanic Níssyros was once part of Kos. When it erupted in 1422 the centre imploded, forming the fertile Lakkí plain. Dormant these days – the last eruption was in 1933 – the volcano still dominates the island. Its rich soil holds tight to water so Níssyros is lush and green, its terraces thick with olives, figs, citrus groves and almonds (someone once called it the Polo mint island – green outside, white inside, with a hole in the middle). The volcano brings summer visitors, but its gypsum and pumice keep the economy going year round.

Mandráki and Around

Mandráki, the capital and port, is as cute as a button, especially the **Langadáki** district where the lanes, cobbled or picked out with pebble mosaics and designed to confound pirates, twist under the balconies of the tall, brightly painted houses. Seawards the lanes aim for **Plateía Ilikioméni** with its bars. On top is the ancient **Kástro** (or **Enetikon**), taken over by the Knights, and, within its walls, the monastery of 15th-century **Panagía Spilianí** (*open daily 10.30–3*). Its beautiful iconostasis holds a venerated icon, loaded with gold and silver. On the stair to the monastery a small **Historical and Popular Museum** is open when the owner's around. Higher up, a rough path leads from Langadáki to the 7th-century BC Doric **Paliokástro**, a spectacular site with Cyclopean walls hewn from volcanic rock, with views out to Gialí and Kos. Below, a path leads to pebbly **Chochláki Beach** under the monastery cliffs. Other good beaches are east: **Miramare** and **Gialiskári** (alias **White Beach**) with black and white crystals, by the spa of **Loutrá** where the hot springs from the volcano ease arthritis.

Further along the coast the pretty fishing village of **Páli** has a succession of dark volcanic sandy beaches, rudimentary catacombs and an incongruous central roundabout. Boats in the harbour are often surrounded by bobbing pumice stones, although in August when the *meltémi* blows fiercely the beaches can be littered with less attractive junk. About an hour's walk or twenty minutes by moped along the road

Getting There and Around

By sea: ferry connections several times a week to Kos, Kálymnos, Tílos, Sými and Rhodes, and once to Astypálaia, Léros, Pátmos, Piraeus, Sými, Sýros, Páros and Náxos; daily **taxi boat** and *Nissiros Express* to Kardaména, Kos; **hydrofoil**: almost daily from Rhodes and Tílos, variable with Kos, Kálymnos and Sými. **Port authority:** t 224 203 1222.

By road: buses, t 224 203 1204, go from the harbour to Páli via White Beach, but buses for Emborió and Nikiá leave early morning and return mid-afternoon only. Níssyros also has two **taxi** firms, Bobby's, t 224 203 1460, and Irene's, t 224 203 1474. A round-island tour costs €20; to the volcano €14.

Tourist Information

Enetikon Travel: t 224 2031 180, f 224 203 1168, on the right as you head up from the harbour. Offers a range of excursions.

Where to Stay and Eat

Níssyros ✉ 85303
    It can be very difficult to find a room in July and August, so book ahead.
Xenon, t 224 203 1011 (*moderate*). By the seaside, inviting and handy for ferries.

Haritos, over the road, t 224 203 1322, f 224 203 1122 (*C; moderate*). Friendly pension with spacious rooms, sea-view balconies and direct-dial phones. *Open all year.*
Miramare Apartments, on the coast road to Páli, t 224 203 1100, f 224 203 1254 (*moderate*). New and luxurious by island standards, beautifully appointed with a terrace.
Porfyris, further into the village opposite the orchard, t/f 224 203 1376 (*C; moderate, inc. breakfast*). The most comfortable and well-priced bet with a sea water pool.
I Drossia, t 224 203 1328 (*inexpensive*). Waves crash on the rocks below your balcony.
White Beach, at Gialiskári, t 224 203 1497/8, f 224 203 1389 (*C; moderate*). Ungainly, but right on the black sands. *Open May–Sept.*
Karava, next to Enetikon Travel. Wide choice of good food, *soumáda* (a local almond drink which tastes like marzipan) and sea views.
Captain's Taverna, further along the front. Excellent home-made dishes including mouthwatering chick pea fritters and wild caper salad made to Granny's recipe.
Taverna Nissyros. In the village centre, one of the most popular eateries with its vine-clad canopy and jolly atmosphere.
Irini, in lively Platéia Elikioméni, the centre of Mandráki nightlife. Good value with friendly service and a menu from *laderá* to roasts.
Angistri, in Páli, on the far edge of the beach. Mama makes a knock-out moussaka.

brings you to the best beaches: the bronze sands of **Lýes** with a cantina and free camping, and **Pachiá Ámmos**, an expanse of reddish sands reached via a scramble over the headland. With mining operations for a backdrop, the islets **Gialí** and **Ag. Antónis** have white crystal sand and are great for snorkelling, with curious rocks.

Into and Around the Volcano

The excursion not to be missed, however, is to the volcano (wear sturdy shoes). Buses leave the port as the tourist boats arrive; if you want more solitude, take the village bus to Nikiá in the morning and walk down. Here the green terraces offer a stunning contrast to the vast crater, an extra-terrestrial landscape of pale greys and yellows, the smell of sulphur so pungent that you can almost see cartoon stink lines snaking up. The tour buses stop near the fuming heart of **Stéfanos**, the largest of five craters – 80ft deep and 1,150ft across. A zigzag path descends to its floor and bubbling fumeroles. You can feel the heat and turmoil of the gases beneath the crust; in some places it's fragile, so if you have children don't let them stray.

Above, two very different villages cling to the rim of the crater. **Emborió** above Páli (linked by a cobbled pathway) only has a handful of inhabitants but they have a free mod con in their basements: natural volcanic saunas. If you want to partake, there's a public sauna in a cave on the outskirts. A ruined Byzantine fort offers memorable views of the crater 1,000ft below. In contrast, **Nikiá** is all dazzling blue and white paintwork, gardens and views over Tílos as well as the crater in all its ghostly enormity. The square has a lovely *choklákia* mosaic and there's a taverna and hostel. The path down to the crater is steep and takes about 40 minutes. On the way, watch out for the **Calanna** rock, said to be a witch turned to stone; a safer place to rest is the **Moní Ag. Ioánnis Theológos**, with trees and picnic benches.

Tílos (ΤΗΛΟΣ)

Tílos is something of a best-kept secret, with good unspoiled beaches, friendly people and wonderful walking country. Although at first glance rugged and barren, it shelters orchards and small farms, watered by fresh springs. It's even a lot cheaper than neighbouring islands. Life goes on with few concessions to tourism, although it's beginning to trickle in. It's a fine place to do nothing; a dreaminess surrounds all activities, and watches seem superfluous.

The port **Livádia** is all vintage 1930s, and has a mile of tree-fringed pebble beach and water clear as gin. Along the beach road you'll find the tiny early basilica of **Ag. Panteleímon** with a mosaic floor, while **Ag. Anna**, further back, has 13th-century frescoes. At the far side of the bay the little sheltered harbour of **Ag. Stéfanos** often hosts a handful of yachts.

Megálo Chorió, 8km up from Livádia, stands on the site of ancient Tílos; near the castle Pelasgian walls date back to 1000 BC. The pretty whitewashed village looks over a fertile plain. The town hall has the key to the church of the **Taxiarchos** (1826), with a double Arabic arch, and a 16ft Hellenistic wall just behind. When Tílos broke away

Getting There and Around

By sea: **ferry** connections four to five times a week with Rhodes, Kos and Kálymnos, less frequently with Sými, Níssyros, Piraeus, Pátmos, Léros, Kastellórizo, Náxos, Páros and Sýros. By **hydrofoil**: regularly in summer with Rhodes, Níssyros, Kos, Kálymnos, Sými and Chálki. **Port authority**: t 224 104 4350.

By road: there's a **bus** service from Livádia to Megálo Chorió, Ag. Antónis and Éristos. Tílos Travel, t 224 105 3259, rents out motorbikes and boats.

Tourist Information

Stefanákis Travel: **t** 224 104 3310/4360, **f** 224 104 4315, by the quay.

Where to Stay and Eat

Livádia ⊠ 85002

Tilos Mare, t 224 104 4100, f 212 104 4005 (*B; expensive*). New, furnished air-conditioned studios, with a pool and restaurant.
Irini, t 224 104 4293, f 224 104 4238 (*C; moderate*). Tastefully tricked out in ethnic style and set back from the beach in lovely gardens.
Eleni, t 224 104 4062, f 224 104 4063 (*C;moderate*). Pleasant and right on the beach.
Marina Beach, a 20min walk around the bay at Ag. Stéfanos, t 224 104 4064 (*moderate*). Excellent A-class rent rooms, if a bit far-flung, but does good food.

Panorama Studios, t/f 224 104 4365 (*moderate*). Smart lodgings, perched on the hillside above the village, with great views from the flower-filled terrace.
Trata. First choice for fish and seafood, but a bit pricier than most.
Irina, on the beach. Good Greek home cooking, a wide choice of dishes and cheap beer. Great for lunch with tables on the sand shaded by trees.
Sophia. Excellent food and friendly service, popular with Brits.

Megálo Chorió ⊠ 85002

Miliou Apartments, in the centre, t 224 102 1002, f 224 104 4204 (*moderate*). Pleasant rooms with a traditional touch in a lush garden with an aviary full of budgies.
Sevasti, t 224 105 3237 (*inexpensive*). Budget rooms next door to the Kali Kardia Taverna.

Éristos ⊠ 85002

Eristos Beach Apartments, t 224 104 4336, f 224 104 4024 (*inexpensive*). Simple, but all apartments have fans and verandas.
Tropicana, t 224 105 3242. Peaceful haven in a tropical garden with chalet-type rooms. Fresh seafood and local vegetable dishes served in a rose-covered arbour.

Ag. Antónis ⊠ 85002

Australia, t 224 105 3296 (*D; inexpensive*). Immaculate and run by Greek-Australian brothers who meet guests from the ferry with their transit van.
Delfini Fish Restaurant. Owned by fishermen; they also do stuffed kid.

from Asia Minor *c.* 10,000 years ago, elephants trapped on the island adapted to the limited food supply by shrinking. They co-existed with Tílos' Stone Age dwellers, but the humans killed them all – the last elephants in Europe – by 4000 BC. A small **museum** contains their pygmy bones and has a video, accompanied by an ancient song by Erinna of Tílos, 'the female Homer', whose poetry was said to rival that of Sappho. The **Kástro** on top was built by the Venetians, who incorporated a Classical gateway and stone from the acropolis.

From here the road drops down to the fertile plain and meanders to the long sandy beach at **Éristos**. Further north is the deserted village of **Mikró Chorió**, abandoned when everyone moved to Livádia (they even took their roofs) – although it comes alive on summer nights when the ruins turn into a club. The church of **Timía Zóni** has charming 18th-century frescoes.

From Megálo Chorió the road runs to windswept **Ag. Antónios**, which has the island's petrol station (*open afternoons only, 3–5*) and an enormous tamarisk. Along the beach, look for Tílos' other fossils – human skeletons 'baked' into the rock, perhaps of sailors caught in the lava when Níssyros erupted in 600 BC. From here a road winds its way to the **Monastery of Ag. Panteleímon**, founded in 1407, set in a lush oasis, 660ft above the west coast. Defended by a stone tower and even taller cypresses, it has fine 15th-century frescoes and a beautiful old marble fountain fringed by pots of basil. The bus driver arranges trips up on Sundays. On 25–27 July, a huge three-day festival or *panegýri* takes place here, not to be missed.

Rhodes/Ródos (ΡΟΔΟΣ)

Rhodes, 'more beautiful than the sun' according to the ancient Greeks, is the largest of the Dodecanese, ringed by sandy beaches, bedecked with flowers, blessed with some 300 days of sun a year and dotted with handsome towns and monuments evoking a long, colourful history. All, in a nutshell, that it takes to sit securely throned as the reigning queen of tourism in Greece. As a year-round resort for cold northerners, it's not quite fair to compare it with other Greek islands: Rhodes is Europe's increasingly glitzy answer to Florida.

History

Rhodes had a close connection with Crete in history as well as myth. The Minoans had colonies at Filérimos, Líndos and Kámiros, until they were supplanted by the

Getting There and Around

By air: Rhodes airport is the third busiest in Greece, t 224 108 3400, receiving nearly a million charter passengers a year. From Athens, there are at least seven daily flights with Olympic and Aegean, plus several a week from Heráklion, Thessaloníki, Mýkonos, Santoríni, Kárpathos, Kastellórizo and Kássos. Olympic is at 9 Iérou Lóchou, Rhodes Town, t 224 102 4571; Aegean, at No.5 25 Martíou, Rhodes Town, t 224 102 5444. **Airport flight information desk**: t 224 108 3214, 024 108 3200 or 224 108 3202. The bus to Parádissi passes near the airport every 30mins or so until 11pm; taxi fares to town are around €8–10.

By sea: **ferry** connections daily with Piraeus, Kos, Kálymnos, Léros and Pátmos, four times a week with Chálki, Níssyros, Sými and Tílos, three with Kárpathos, Kássos and Sitía (Crete), twice with Kastellórizo, Mílos and Ag. Nikólaos (Crete), once with Sámos, Chíos, Mytilíni and Límnos. **Excursion boats** from Mandráki Harbour go to Líndos, Sými and a variety of beaches. Daily **caiques** ply their way from Kámiros Skála on the west coast to Chálki; for Marmaris, Turkey, there are daily **hydrofoils** (currently around €42 return) and ferries. **Port authority**: t 224 102 8695 and 224 102 8888.

By road: East-coast **buses** (t 224 102 4129) are yellow and depart from Plateía Rimini in Rhodes Town; they serve Faliraki (18 times daily), Líndos and Kolymbia (eight to 10 times), Genadi and Psinthos (three to five times). West coast buses (t 224 102 7706) are white and blue, departing from around the corner by the market for Kalithéa Thermi (16 times), Koskínou (10 times), Salakós (five times), and Kámiros, Monólithos and Embónas (once). **Taxis** are plentiful: the central rank is in Plateía Alexandrias, Rhodes Town, t 224 102 7666. Radio taxis: t 224 106 4712, 224 106 6790 or 224 106 4734. Everything from **beach buggies** to **motorbikes** are available for hire; note that **petrol stations** are closed on Sunday, holidays and after 7pm.

Mythic Founders, with Flippers

The first inhabitants of Rhodes were the nine Telchines, enchantresses with dog heads and flippers. They made the sickle that Cronos used to castrate Uranus, carved the first statues of the gods, and founded the cities of Kámiros, Ialysós and Líndos before moving to Crete where they forged Poseidon's trident. Poseidon fell in love with the Telchines' sister Alia, and their daughter Rhodos became mistress of the island, although it couldn't stay afloat. Later, while the Olympians were dividing up the world, Zeus realized to his dismay that he had forgotten to set aside a portion for Helios the sun god. He asked Helios what he wanted, and he replied that he knew of an island just re-emerging from the sea off the coast of Asia Minor which would suit him admirably. Helios married Rhodos and their son re-founded the ancient cities.

Mycenaeans, followed in the 12th century BC by the Dorians. Positioned along the main Mediterranean trade routes, Rhodes soon became a major power, and around 1000 BC its three city-states – Líndos, Ialysós and Kámiros – formed a Dorian Hexapolis, a 'Six City' union with Kos, Cnidos and Halicarnassus. United politically, religiously and economically, the Hexapolis established colonies from Naples to the Costa Brava.

In 408 BC, in order to prevent rivalries, Líndos, Ialysós and Kámiros united to found a central capital, Rhodes, 'the Rose'. Hippodamos of Miletus designed the new town, and the result was considered one of the most beautiful cities in the world. Schools of philosophy, philology and oratory were founded, and the port had facilities far in advance of its time. Rhodes hitched its wagon to the rising star of Alexander the Great in 336 BC, and Alexander in turn favoured Rhodes at the expense of hostile Athens. The island dominated Mediterranean trade; its navy ruled the waves, and founded trade counters all over the known world; its trade and navigation laws were later adopted by the Romans and remain the basis of maritime law today. Perhaps not surprisingly, the Rhodians were also famous braggarts, the Texans of antiquity.

In the struggles between Alexander's successors, Rhodes was allied to Ptolemy of Egypt. When another Macedonian general, Antigonas of Syria, ordered Rhodes to join him against Ptolemy, the Rhodians refused. To change their minds, Antigonas sent his son Demetrios Poliorketes (the Besieger) at the head of an army of 40,000 and the Phoenician fleet. The ensuing siege (305–304 BC) was a famous battle of wits. As often as Dimitrios came up with a new strategy, such as the 10-storey siege tower, the Rhodians (who tripped it up with a hidden ditch) foiled him, until after a year both sides wearily made a truce. So Dimitrios departed, leaving his vast siege machinery behind. This the Rhodians either sold or melted down to construct a great bronze statue of Helios, their patron god. A sculptor from Líndos, Chares, was put in charge of the project, and in 290 BC, after 12 years of work and at a cost of 20,000 pounds of silver, Chares completed the Colossus, or didn't quite: he found he had made a miscalculation and committed suicide just before it was cast. Standing somewhere between 100 and 140ft tall (the Statue of Liberty is 111ft), the Colossus did not straddle the entrance of the harbour, as is popularly believed, but probably stood near the present Castle of the Knights. But of all the Wonders of the Ancient World the Colossus had the shortest lifespan; in 225 BC, an earthquake cracked its knees and brought it

Rhodes

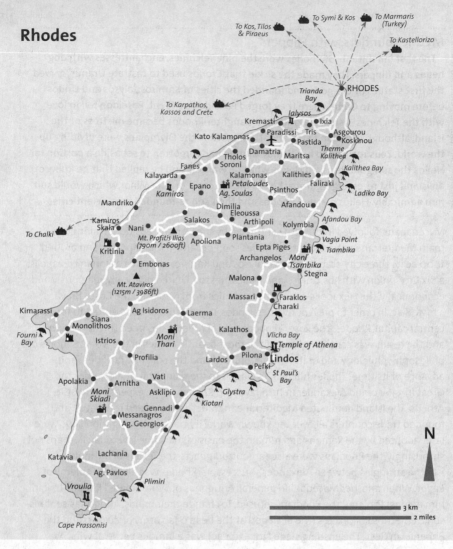

To Kos, Tilos & Piraeus
To Symi & Kos
To Marmaris (Turkey)
To Kastellorizo

RHODES

Trianda Bay

To Karpathos, Kassos and Crete

Ialysos
Kremasti
Paradissi
Tris
Ixia
Asgourou
Koskinou

Kato Kalamonas
Pastida
Therme Kalithea
Damatria
Maritsa
Tholos
Soroni
Fanes
Kalamonas
Kalithies
Kalithea Bay
Kalayarda
Epano
Petaloudes
Psinthos
Faliraki
Kamiros
Ag. Soulas
Ladiko Bay
Mandriko
Dimilia
Afandou
Eleoussa
Kamiros
Skala
Nani
Salakos
Arthipoli
Kolymbia
Afandou Bay
To Chalki
Mt. Profitis Ilias (790m / 2600ft)
Apollona
Plantania
Vagia Point
Kritinia
Epta Piges
Tsambika
Embonas
Archangelos
Moni Tsambika
Mt. Ataviros (1215m / 3986ft)
Malona
Stegna
Massari
Kimarassi
Ag Isidoros
Laerma
Faraklos
Charaki
Siana
Monolithos
Fourni Bay
Istrios
Kalathos
Moni Thari
Vlicha Bay
Profilia
Lardos
Pilona
Temple of Athena
Apolakia
Vati
Pefki
Lindos
St Paul's Bay
Arnitha
Asklipio
Glystra
Moni Skiadi
Kiotari
Gennadi
Messanagros
Ag. Georgios
Katavia
Lachania
Ag. Pavlos
Vroulia
Plimiri
Cape Prassonisi

N

3 km
2 miles

crashing down (Delphi told the Rhodians to leave it there and so it remained until 653 when the Saracens sold it as scrap; according to legend, it took 900 camels to transport the bronze).

In 164 BC, the Rhodians signed a peace treaty with Rome. Alexandria was their only rival in wealth, and tiny Délos, with its duty-free concessions, their only rival in trade. Pompey, Cicero, Cassius, Julius Caesar, Brutus, Cato the Younger and Mark Antony attended the island's school of rhetoric. When Caesar was assassinated, Rhodes as always backed the right horse, in this case Augustus, only this time the wrong horse, Cassius, was in the neighbourhood; he sacked the city, captured its fleet, and sent its treasures to Rome (43–42 BC). Rhodes never recovered its former glory. In AD 57 St Paul converted many of the inhabitants; by the end of the Roman empire the island was a backwater.

Two Hundred Years of Knights

Invaders and adventurers passed through Byzantine Rhodes: Arabs and Saracens, Genoese, Venetians and Crusaders. Of these, the Knights Hospitallers of St John, an order dedicated to protecting pilgrims and running hospitals in the Holy Land, would stay the longest. After the fall of Jerusalem to the Saracens in 1291, they took refuge on Cyprus, then asked the Emperor Andronicus Paleológos to cede them Rhodes in return for their loyalty. After 1204, however, the Byzantines knew better than to trust them, so the knights took the matter into their own hands and purchased the Dodecanese from their current occupants, Genoese pirates, then spent three years subduing the natives.

Once secure, the knights built their hospital and eight inns (*auberges*), one for each 'tongue' in the Order (England, France, Germany, Italy, Castile, Aragon, Auvergne and Provence). Each had a bailiff and the eight bailiffs elected the Grand Master, who lived in a palace. Already wealthy, they were given a tremendous boost in 1312 when Pope Clement V and Philip the Fair of France dissolved the Knights Templars, confiscated their huge fortune and gave the Hospitallers a hefty share. The knights used the money to rebuild the fortifications of Rhodes Town, improving them constantly and with reason – their freebooting ways against Muslim shipping and pilgrims heading to Mecca made them such a menace that the Sultan of Egypt in 1444 and then Mehmet the Conqueror besieged Rhodes without success. Then in 1522 Suleiman the Magnificent moved in with 200,000 troops; the Rhodian defenders (there were 6,000 of them, plus 1,000 Italian mercenaries and 650 knights) bitterly joked that the Colossus was now coming back at them, in the form of cannon balls. After a six-month siege, Suleiman was on the point of sailing away when a traitor informed him that only 180 knights survived. The sultan redoubled his efforts and the knights were forced to surrender. In honour of their courage, Suleiman permitted them to leave in safety, with their Christian retainers and possessions. They made their new headquarters in Malta – at the rent of a falcon a year.

The Ottomans loved Rhodes as a pleasure island, so when it attempted to join the War of Independence in 1821 the Turks reacted with atrocities; their popularity dropped even more in the Great Gunpowder Explosion of 1856, when lightning struck a minaret and exploded a powder magazine, killing 800 people. During the confusion of the Balkan Wars in 1912, the Italians took Rhodes, claiming the island as their inheritance. After 1943 the Germans took over and sent the island's 2,000 Jews to the concentration camps. Rhodes, with the rest of the Dodecanese, joined Greece in 1948.

Rhodes Town

Spread across the northern tip of the island, Rhodes Town (pop. 55,000), the capital of the Dodecanese, celebrated its 2,400th birthday in 1993. It divides neatly into Old and New Towns. Tourism reigns in both, although these days the New Town is filling up with designer boutiques – VAT is 5 per cent lower than on the mainland. The medieval city is so remarkably preserved it looks like a film set, and has often been used as such. It also presents an opulent face to the sea: the massive medieval walls of the Old Town, crowned by the Palace of the Grand Masters, rise out of a subtropical garden; graceful minarets and the arcaded waterfront market add an exotic touch. Monumental pseudo-Venetian public buildings, trying to look serious, decorate the shore to the left, while opposite three 14th-century **windmills** turn lazily behind a forest of masts in the smallest of three harbours, **Mandráki**, used by yachts, small ferries and excursion boats. This is guarded by the fort of **Ag. Nikólaos** (1460s) and a **bronze stag and doe**, marking where the Colossus may have stood. Hydrofoils leave from **Kolona** harbour further on, and larger ferries, boats to Turkey and cruise ships anchor in the **commercial harbour** nearer the Old Town walls.

These **walls** are a masterpiece of fortification, but access is by guided tour only (*t 224 102 5500; Tues and Sat, meet in front of the Palace of the Grand Master at 2.30; adm exp*). Constructed over the Byzantine walls, they stretch 4km and average 38ft thick. Curved to deflect missiles, the landward sides were safeguarded by the 100ft-wide dry moat. Each nation of knights was assigned its own bastion and towers, except the Italians, who as the best sailors were in charge of the fleet. Of the many gates, the most magnificent is the **Gate of Emery d'Amboise** near the Palace of the Grand Masters, built in 1512 (entrance off Papágou Street). Under the Turks, all Greeks had to be outside it by sundown or forfeit their heads.

The Old Town (ΠΑΛΑΙΑ ΠΟΛΗ)

The Old Town was dilapidated when the Italians took charge and began to restore it, but fortunately they lost the war before they could get on with their plan to widen the streets for cars. To keep any such future notions at bay, UNESCO has made the Old Town a World Heritage Site and is providing funds for restoration and infrastructure.

Within the aforementioned Gate d'Amboise lies the inner sanctum, the **Collachium**, where the Knights could retreat if the outer curtain wall were taken. At the highest point, a castle within a castle, stands the **Palace of the Grand Masters** (*t 224 102 5500; open Tues–Fri 8–7, Sat and Sun 8–3, Mon 12.30–7; adm exp*), built in 1346 over a Temple to Helios. It was modelled after the Popes' palace in Avignon – not by accident: 14 of the 19 Grand Masters on Rhodes were French. The Turks used it as a prison, even after the Great Gunpowder Explosion of 1856, when the first floor caved in, and the Italians did the same until Mussolini, fancying himself a new Grand Master, ordered its reconstruction. The Italians filled it with lovely Roman mosaics from Kos, Renaissance furniture, and installed a lift and plumbing, but the war broke out and ended before the Duce could swan around its 158 rooms (don't panic: only a tenth are open to the public). On the ground floor are two exhibitions on the history of Rhodes, detached frescoes, coins and the tombstone of the Grand Master Villier de l'Isle Adam, who defied Suleiman for six months even though outmanned nearly 40 to one.

The main street from the palace into the heart of the Collachium is a favourite of film makers: evocative, cobblestoned **Odós Ippotón** (Knights' Street). It passes under the arcaded **Loggia** that originally linked the Palace to the 14th-century cathedral of St John, where the Grand Masters were buried; after being shattered in the Gunpowder Explosion, a Turkish school was built in the ruins. Ippotón is lined with the Knights' inns, each emblazoned with the arms of the Grand Master in charge when it was built. The **Inn of Provence** is on the left and the two buildings of the **Inn of Spain** on the right, followed by the French chapel and elaborate **Inn of France** (1509), adorned with crocodile gargoyles; there were always more French knights than any other 'tongue'. The **Inn of Italy** (1519) stands at the foot of the street.

Two squares open up at the end of the street; just to the right, on the corner of Plateía Moussíon, stands the much restored **Inn of England** (1483), abandoned in 1534 when the Pope excommunicated Henry VIII. It was hit by an earthquake in 1851, rebuilt by the British, bombed and rebuilt again in 1947. The British Consul of Rhodes (*see* p.778 for the address) has the key. Opposite stands the Flamboyant Gothic hospital of the Knights, built between 1440 and 1481 and restored by the Italians in 1918 to house the **Archaeological Museum** (*t 224 102 5500; open Tues–Sun 8–2.30; adm*). The long vaulted ward where the surgeons (all commoners) cared for patients now shelters the 3rd-century BC *Marine Venus* (a bit sea-eroded) that inspired Lawrence Durrell's book about the island, and the kneeling *Aphrodite of Rhodes* (90 BC), combing out her wet hair; also note the bust of Helios from the 2nd century BC, with holes for his metal sunrays. Ceramics, stelae, Mycenaean jewellery and mosaics round off the collection. In the square, 11th-century **Panagía Kástrou** contains a little **Byzantine Museum** (*open Tues–Sun 8.30–3; adm*), with frescoes and icons.

Through the arch, charming Plateía Argyrokástro has the loveliest inn, the 15th-century **Inn of Auvergne** (now a cultural centre), with a fountain made from a Byzantine baptismal font. Here, too, is the 14th-century **Palace of the Armeria**, constructed by Grand Master Roger de Pins as the Knights' first hospital on Rhodes, and the **Museum of Decorative Arts** (*open Tues–Sun 8.30–3; adm*) with folk arts and handicrafts from all over the Dodecanese. Nearby, in Plateía Sýmis, the **Municipal Art Gallery** (*open Mon–Sat 8–2*), houses 20th-century Greek paintings and engravings. Also in the square are the ruins of a 3rd-century BC **Temple of Aphrodite**, discovered by the Italians in 1922. Fragments of another temple of the same epoch, dedicated to **Dionysos**, are in a corner behind the Ionian and Popular Bank.

The Turkish Town

South of the Collachium of the Knights was the former Turkish bazaar, where bustling **Sokrátous Street** is still thick with shops; don't miss the old-fashioned Turkish *kafeneíon* at No. 17. At the top of Sokrátous Street stands the slender minaret of the lovely, faded red **Mosque of Suleiman** (*now closed*), built in 1523 by Suleiman to celebrate his conquest. The **Muselman Library** (1793; *open Mon–Fri 7.30–2.30 and 6–9, Sat and Sun 8–noon*) opposite contains rare Persian and Arabian manuscripts and illuminated Korans. Behind Suleiman's mosque, the Byzantine clock tower, **To Roloi**, has splendid views over the town if you're lucky enough to find it open. South of Sokrátous Street, the Turkish quarter dissolves into a zigzag of narrow streets, where charming latticework balconies project beside crumbling stone arches. On scruffy Plateía Arionos, off Archeláos Street, the **Mustafa Mosque** keeps company with the atmospheric **Mustafa Hammam** (*open Tues–Fri 11–7, Sat 8–6; bring own soap and towel; adm*), built in 1558 and remodelled in 1765. Heated by a ton of olive logs a day,

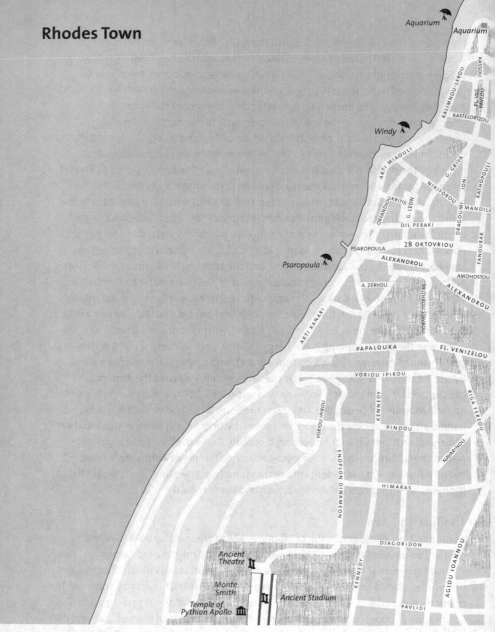

Rhodes Town

Aquarium

Aquarium

Windy

AKTI MIAOULI

KALIMNOU-LEROU

KASSON

PL. VAS. PAVLOU

KASTELORIZOU

G. GRIVA

NIKIFOROU

ION.

KATHOPOULI

ORLANDIOU

KRITIS

G. LEON

DRAGOUMI

MANDILA

FANOURAK

DIL PERAKI

PSAROPOULA

28 OKTOVRIOU

Psaropoula

ALEXANDROU

AMOHOSTOU

A. ZERVOU

ALEXANDROU

FILELLINON

SOLOMOU

AKTI KANARI

PAPALOUKA

EL. VENIZELOU

VORIOU IPIROU

VORIOU IPIROU

KENNEDY

RIGA FEREOU

PINDOU

NAVARINOU

ENOPLON DINAMEON

HIMARAS

DIAGORIDON

AGIOU IOANNOU

Ancient
Theatre

Monte
Smith

KENNEDY

Ancient Stadium

Temple of
Pythian Apollo

PAVLIDI

it has mosaic floors and marble fountains and a lovely ceiling, divided into men's and women's sections. Another mosque, **Ibrahim Pasha** (1531), is off Sofokléous Street; executions once took place in front of it.

On Hippocrátes Square, where Sokrátous turns into Aristotélous Street, is the picturesque Gothic-Renaissance **Kastellania**, built by Grand Master d'Amboise in 1507, perhaps as a tribunal or exchange. It stands at the head of Pithágora, the main street of **Evriakí**, the Jewish quarter. According to the historian Josephus, the community

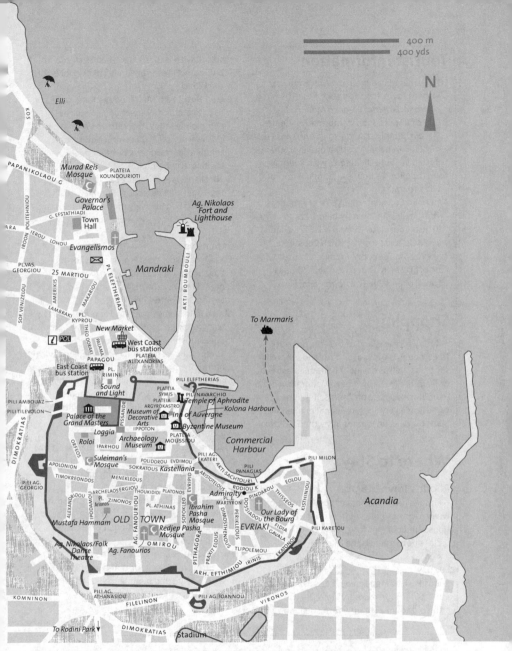

400 m
400 yds

N

Elli

PAPANIKOLAOU G

Murad Reis
Mosque

PLATEIA
KOUNDOURIOTI

Governor's
Palace

G. EFSTATHIADI

Town
Hall

Ag. Nikolaos
Fort and
Lighthouse

Evangelismos

PL.VAS.
GEORGIOU

25 MARTIOU

Mandraki

AKTI BOUMBOULI

New Market

POL

West Coast
bus station

PLATEIA
ALEXANDRIAS

To Marmaris

East Coast
bus station

PAPAGOU

PL.
RIMINI

PILI ELEFTHERIAS

PILI AMBOUAZ

PILI TILEVOLON

Sound
and Light

Palace of the
Grand Masters

Loggia

Roloi

PISSANDR

PLATEIA
SYMIS

PLATEIA
ARGYROKASTRO

Museum of
Decorative
Arts

IPPOTON

Archaeology
Museum

IPARHOU

PILI NAVARCHIO

Temple of Aphrodite

Inn of Auvergne

Byzantine Museum

PLATEIA
MOUSSIOU

Kolona Harbour

Commercial
Harbour

DIMOKRATIAS

Suleiman's
Mosque

APOLONION

TIMOKREONDOS

PILI AG.
GEORGIO

ORFEOS

POLIDOROU EVDIMOU

SOKRATOUS Kastellania

MENEKLEOUS

ARISTOTELOUS

AKTI SACHTOURI

PILI AG.
EKATERI

RODIOU K

PILI
PANAGIAS

PILI MILON

Acandia

ALEXANDRIOU

IPODAMOU

PL.
Arionos

ZINONOS

ARCHELAOS ERGIOU

THOUKIDIDI PLATONOS

PL. ATHINAS

EVRIPID

SOFOKLEO

Admiralty

MARTYRON

PINDAROU THISSEOS

DOSIADOU

PERIKLEOUS

EOLOU

KISTHINIOU

Mustafa Hammam

OLD TOWN

AG. FANOURIOU

Ibrahim
Pasha
Mosque

Redjep Pasha
Mosque

OMIROU

Our Lady of
the Bourg

EVRIAKI

FIDIA

GAVALA

PILI KARETOU

Ag. Nikolaos/Folk
Danse
Theatre

Ag. Fanourios

PITHAGORA

PRAXITELOUS

DIMOSTHENOUS

TLIPOLEMOU

EKATONOS

KOMNINON

PILI AG.
ATHANASIOU

FILELINON

ARH. EFTHIMIOU IRINIS

PILI AG. IOANNOU

VIRONOS

To Rodini Park

DIMOKRATIAS

Stadium

dates from the 1st century AD; later chronicles cite the Jews among Rhodes' defenders against the Turks. To the east **Plateía Evrión Martyrón** (the Square of Hebrew Martyrs) honours those sent to die in the concentration camps. Just south stands the lavishly decorated **synagogue**, still in use.

The so-called **Admiralty** (which was more likely the Catholic bishop's palace) is back on the square, behind a bronze seahorse fountain. From here, Pindárou Street continues to **Our Lady of the Bourg**, built by the Knights in thanksgiving for their

Tourist Information

EOT: corner of Papágou and Makaríou Sts, Rhodes Town, t 224 102 3655, f 224 102 6955, *eot-rodos@otenet.gr*; *open Mon–Fri 8–3*.
City of Rhodes Tourist Information Centre: Plateía Rimini, t 224 103 5945; *open Mon–Sat 9–8, Sun 9–noon*. Mostly a money exchange. Both distribute the free English *Ródos News*.
Tourist police: 24-hour multilingual number, t 224 102 7423.
American Consulate: the Voice of America station at Afándou may help, t 224 105 2555.
British Consulate: Mr and Mrs Dimitriádis, 3 P. Méla, t 224 102 7247. **Irish Consulate**: Mr Skevos Mougros, 111 Amerikís, t 224 102 2461.
Post office: on Mandráki harbour, Rhodes Town; *open Mon–Fri 7.30am–8pm*.

Shopping

It may be the island of the sun, but duty-free Rhodes is packed with fur and umbrella shops, as well as designer boutiques, especially in the New Town near Mandráki. A big market takes place on Zefiros St (by the cemetery) every Sat am. A smaller one takes place on Wed, on Vironas St by the Stadium.

Where to Stay

Rhodes Town ✉ 85100

Rhodes has a plethora of accommodation; *www.helios.gr/hotels/* offers online descriptions and bookings for a selection of luxury to C-class hotels across the island.

Luxury

Rodos Park, 12 Riga Fereou, t 224 102 4612, f 224 102 4613, *www.rodospark.gr* (*L*). In the park by the old town, elegantly furnished rooms and suites, with jacuzzis, pool, health club, and ballroom. One of the Small Luxury Hotels of the World.
Grand Hotel, Aktí Miaoúli, t 224 105 4700, f 224 103 5589, *grand@otenet.gr* (*L*). Recently completely renovated with an emphasis on classical simplicity, a central hotel with tennis and indoor and outdoor pools, casinos, and nightclub.
S. Nicolis, 61 Ippodámou, t 224 103 4561, f 224 103 2034, *nikoliss@hol.gr*. Rooms with canopied bed in lovely medieval houses, and a rooftop terrace; book ahead.

Expensive

Plaza Hotel Best Western, on Ierou Lóchou, t 224 102 2501, f 224 102 2544, *plaza@otenet.gr* (*A*). Refurnished with a pool, babysitting and buffet breakfast.
Marco Polo Mansion, 42 Ag. Fanouríou, t/f 224 102 5562, *marcopolomansion@hotmail.com*. Big atmospheric rooms in a converted Turkish house, tastefully furnished and with hammam; good breakfasts.
Marie, 7 Kos, near Élli Beach, t 224 103 0577, f 224 102 2751 (*C*). Recently renovated, offering a pool, sea sports and satellite TV.

Moderate

Victoria, No.22 25 Martiou, t 224 102 4626, f 224 103 6675 (*C*). Central, family-run, and the owner's son, a UK-trained doctor, has consulting rooms next door.
Popi, Stratigou Zisi and Maliaraki 21, near the Old Town , t 224 102 3479, f 224 103 3453. Studios in the old-fashioned Greek style, each sleeping four.
Paris, 88 Ag. Fanouríou, t 224 102 6356, f 224 102 1095 (*D*). Nice rooms and a courtyard with orange and banana trees, and prices at the bottom of this range.

defeat of the Turks in 1480, but left in ruins by a British bomb in the Second World War. The gate at the end of Pithágora Street, **Píli Ag. Ioánnou**, or Red Door, is another impressive demonstration of the walls' strength.

The New Town

Outside the walls, a row of cafés look enticingly over Mandráki harbour, but are shamefully overpriced. Just behind them, the Italian-built octagonal **New Market** has

Inexpensive

Ambassadeur, 53 Othonos and Amalías, t 224 102 4679, f 224 102 4679 (*C*). One of the best for value in this category.

Andreas, 28D Omírou, t 224 103 4156, f 224 107 4285 (*E*). Recommended, under friendly French-Greek management and with uplifting views of the Old Town.

Attiki, Haritos and Theofiliskou, t 224 102 7767 (*E*). In a medieval building in the heart of the Old Town; a bit dishevelled but children welcome. *Open all year.*

La Luna, t/f 224 102 5856 (*E*). With a bar, in a perfectly quiet courtyard with hammam, next to a tiny church on Ierokléous St, just off Orfeos St. *Open all year.*

Iliana, 1 Gavála, t 224 103 0251 (*E*). In an old Jewish family house, with a small bar and terrace; no charge for childen under 10.

Minos Pension, 5 Omírou, t 224 103 1813. Pristine with a panoramic roof-garden.

Beaches near the City: Ixiá and Triánda

This is one long stretch of hotels, with the prime luxury compounds in Ixiá.

Hilton Rhodes Imperial, t 224 107 5000, f 224 107 6690, (*L; luxury*). Vast and luxurious, with top restaurants, watersports, fitness club, children's club, *syrtáki* dance lessons, squash, language courses, cabaret. *Open Mar–Nov.*

Miramare Wonderland, t 224 109 6251/4, f 224 109 5954, *mamtour@otenet.gr* (*L; luxury*). 'Paradise on earth': swish cottages slap on the beach, all facilities and a train around the complex. *Open April–Oct.*

Rodos Palace, t 224 102 5222, f 224 102 5350, *www.rodos-palace.com* (*L; luxury*). Twin digital state-of-the-art communications systems, catering for the conference trade and meetings of European heads of state. It has all the trimmings, including a domed, heated Olympic-size indoor pool, gym, tennis, and more. *Open Mar–Nov.*

Rodos Bay, t 224 102 3661, f 224 102 1344 (*A; expensive*). Sprawling over a hillside, with a pool and bungalows by the beach; the rooftop restaurant has splendid views.

Galini Hotel Apartments, in Ialysós, t 224 109 4496, f 224 109 1251 (*B; moderate*). Apartments for two to six, pool, children's pool and playground. *Open May–Oct.*

Eating Out

The Rhodians are the Parisians of the Greek islands; they love fashionable food trends.

New Town

Thavma en kero, 16-18 El. Venizélou St, t 224 102 5569 (€25). Famous fusion cuisine in a new location: Swedish chefs, and seriously good Eastern- and Mediterranean-inspired daily specials. *Open Mar–Oct, eves only.*

Palia Istoria, Mitropóleos and Dendrínou Sts, south of the new stadium, t 224 103 2421 (€18–25). Award-winning restaurant famous for lobster linguini. Excellent wine list; book.

Ellinikon, 29 Alexándrou Diákou, t 224 102 8111 (€15–20). Popular, serving a choice of Greek and international dishes.

Christos, out in the suburb of Zéfiros beyond the commercial harbour. One of the best and most authentic tavernas – excellent food, accompanied by a vast range of ouzos.

Dania, 3 Iroon Polytechniou, near the Royal Bank of Scotland, t 224 102 0540. For a taste of Denmark; traditional herring dishes and a *smorgasbord* on Sunday evenings.

Old Town

Alexis, 18 Sokrátous, t 224 102 9347 (€20–30). Old taverna serving some of the most sublime seafood in Greece. *Open Feb–Nov.*

Fotis Melathron, Parodos Sokrátous, t 224 102 4272 (€18–22). Excellent Greek and

been taken over by *souvláki* stands. Further along Mandráki is an austere ensemble of Fascist buildings from the 1920s – post office, theatre and town hall. The Italians also left Rhodes the rather more lighthearted **Governor's Palace**, a pseudo-Doge's Palace decorated with a garish red diaper pattern, and the cathedral **Evangelísmos**, a copy of the one blown up in the gunpowder accident. The Gothic fountain is a copy of Viterbo's Fontana Grande.

international cuisine in an elegant setting, with classy private dining rooms.

Nireas, 22 Plateía Sofokléous, t 224 102 1703. Ace for Greek home cooking; book.

Araliki, 45 Aristofánous. Home cooking and superb *mezédes* in a medieval setting.

Dodekanissos, 45 Plateía Evrión Martyrón, t 224 102 8412. Homely atmosphere, moderately priced seafood and an exceptional shrimp *saganáki*.

Dinoris, 14 Plateía Moussíou, t 224 103 5530. An old but pricey favourite, tucked down a narrow alley by the museum, with a romantic garden patio and lovely fish.

Fotis, 8 Menekleóus St, t 224 102 7359 (€20–30). Courtyard dining, with excellent grilled fish – plus delicacies such as sea urchin salad and steamed mussels.

Cleo's, on Ag. Fanouríou, t 224 102 8415. One of the most elegant places to dine in the heart of the medieval city, serving upmarket Italian and French cuisine. Book.

Meraklis, 32 Aristotélous. Join the workers for a bowl of *patsás* soup – if you dare.

Triánda and Ixiá

Ta Koupia, in Triánda by Ialysós (take a taxi), t 224 109 1824 (€25–35). Lovingly decorated with Greek antiques – excellent *mezédes* and upmarket Greek dishes.

La Rotisserie, in the Rodos Palace, t 224 102 5222 (€30–40). *The* place for French and Greek nouvelle cuisine, with an exquisite wine list; great set-price lunch.

Marco Polo, Hilton Rhodes, t 224 107 5000 (€30). The new sensation for local foodies: exquisite and imaginative Mediterranean-Asian cuisine by a German chef. *Eves only.*

Trata, on Triánda Beach (€16–22). Extremely good fish, and kinder to the pocket.

Sandy Beach Taverna, right on the beach in Ialysós. Favourite lunchtime haunt with a garden terrace; try its *kopanistí*, cheese puréed with cracked olives.

Tzaki, in Ixiá. Known for its *mezédes* and bouzouki music.

Entertainment and Nightlife

The history of Rhodes unfolds at the **Son et Lumière** in the Palace of the Grand Masters (*in English on Mon and Tues at 8.15pm, Wed, Fri and Sat at 9.15pm, Thurs 10.15pm*).

Alternatively, watch **Greek folk dances** by the Nelly Dimogloú Company in the Old Town Theatre, Androníkou (*May–Oct Mon, Wed and Fri 9.20pm–11pm; t 224 102 0157 or t 224 102 9085; lessons available*).

Rhodes Town has 600 **bars** with music offerings from traditional folk to funk, soul, house and rap to vintage Elvis. Traditional Greeks head for the **bouzoúki club** at Élli Beach, while the **Grand Hotel** on Aktí Miaoúli has the **Moons Rock**, featuring top singers, and a **casino**, t 224 102 4458, although it now has to compete with a casino operated by Playboy in the Hotel des Roses, a 1930s landmark.

Orfanídou Street just in from Akti Miaoúli is the street of bars, and **Diákou Street** to the south heaves with Britons and Scandinavians spilling out of them. Rockers should head for the ever popular **Sticky Fingers**, 6 A. Zervou, south of Psarópoula; to live out your fantasies in a tropical themed environment, try the **Blue Lagoon Pool Bar**, No.2 25 Martíou.

In the Old Town, join the smart set in the clocktower, **To Roloi**, up the ramp on Orféos, or follow the cognoscenti to the fabulous **Karpouzi**, in a medieval building off Sokrátous with *rembetíka*, wine and *mezédes*. Bop till you drop at **Le Palais** disco or **Privato**, 2 Iliadon, t 224 103 3267.

The Turks regarded Rhodes as a paradise on earth, and many exiled Muslim notables (including a Shah of Persia) chose to spend the rest of their lives here. Many lie buried in the cemetery north of the theatre, next to the **Mosque of Murad Reis**, named after the admiral who was killed during the siege of Rhodes in 1522 and who is buried in a turban-shaped tomb. The mosque has a lovely minaret reconstructed by the last people you would expect – the Greek government. Stretching along the shore is Rhodes' busiest strand, shingly **Élli Beach**, packed chock-a-block with sunbeds.

At the northernmost tip of the island is the **Aquarium** (*open daily in season 9–9, otherwise 9–4.30; adm*), built by the Italians in 1938. It has tanks of Mediterranean fish and sea turtles, a pair of which are over 100 years old, and a startling collection of victims of amateur taxidermy. On the headland, **Aquarium Beach** has deep water, but its breezes make it more popular for windsurfing than sunsoaking. Further south, **Psaropoúla** is a safe, sandy beach.

Just Outside Rhodes Town

City bus no.5 heads south of the New Town to the acropolis of ancient Rhodes, now known as **Monte Smith** after Admiral Sydney Smith who kept track of Napoleon's Egyptian escapades from here; today, most people come up for the romantic sunset. On the way (North Epírou St) are the ruins of an **Asklepeion**, dedicated to the god of healing, and a **Cave of the Nymphs**. On the top of Monte Smith, the Italians partly reconstructed a 2nd-century BC Doric **Temple of Pythian Apollo**, and a 3rd-century BC **stadium**, which sometimes hosts classical dramas in the summer. A few columns remain of Temples of Zeus and Athena. The reconstructed **ancient theatre** is the only square one on the islands.

City bus no.3 will take you the 2km out to **Rodíni Park** and **Deer Park** (the Delphic oracle told the ancient Rhodians to import deer to solve their snake problem and they have been here ever since). Rodíni Park marks the spot where Aeschines established his celebrated school of rhetoric in 330 BC, where the likes of Julius Caesar and Cicero learned the art of oratory. There's a rock-cut tomb from the 4th century BC, the so-called 'Tomb of Ptolemy', and ruins of an aqueduct. The Knights grew medicinal herbs here, and merry drinkers can join Rodíni's peacocks for the **Rhodes Wine Festival** for three weeks in late July–early August with music, dance and food. Special buses transport revellers from Mandráki harbour.

Western Suburbs: Rhodes Town to Ancient Ialysós and Mt Filérimos

Southwest of Rhodes Town, **Ixiá** and **Triánda** are the Miami Beach of Rhodes: the seafront lined with hotels and luxury complexes, neon-lit bars, fast-food places, and signs for English breakfasts and smorgasbord. The beaches are a favourite of wind-surfers, the sea is a lovely turquoise and there are fine views of Turkey.

Triánda village occupies the site of **ancient Ialysós**, the least important of the three Dorian cities. The Phoenicians were here first, feeling secure because of an oracle that said they would leave only when crows turned white and fish appeared inside the water jars. Iphicles, who besieged the town, heard about it and planted fish in the amphorae and daubed a few birds with plaster. The Phoenicians duly fled (and what-ever the Dorian word for 'suckers' might have been, we can be sure Iphicles said it). Ialysós' garden acropolis-citadel above Triánda, on **Mount Filérimos** (*t 224 109 2202; open Tues–Sun 8–6; adm; wear modest dress to visit the monastery*), has the remains of the great 3rd-century BC **Temple of Athena Polias and Zeus Polieus**, built over a Phoenician temple and partly covered in turn by Byzantine churches. A **Doric fountain** with lionhead spouts has been reconstructed, and up a flight of steps is the monastery of **Our Lady of Filérimos**, converted by the Knights from a 5th-century basilica and heavily restored by the Italians. It wears the coat-of-arms of Grand Master d'Aubusson; the church once had both Catholic and Orthodox altars. Don't miss the tiny underground chapel of **Ag. Geórgios**, with frescoes from the 1300s. The monks will be pleased to sell you a bottle of their own green liqueur called Sette, made from seven herbs.

Down the East Shore

Like the windier west shore, the sandy shore southeast of Rhodes Town is lined with fancy hotels, beginning with the beaches of **Réni Koskinoú**. The inland village of **Koskinoú** is known for its houses with decorative cobblestoned floors and courtyards in pebble mosaics, or *choklákia*, a technique introduced by the 7th-century Byzantines. En route, industry has taken over **Asgouroú**, a Turkish village; the mosque was originally a church of St John.

Further along the coast, the coves of **Kalithéa** are a popular spot for snorkelling. Its waters were recommended by Hippocrates, and its magnificent kitsch Italianate-Moorish spa from the 1920s is being restored. Beyond, holiday La-La Land begins in earnest at **Faliráki Bay North**, with upmarket hotel complexes and a shopping mall, while the original **Faliráki**, with its sweeping golden sands, struggles hard to be the Blackpool of the Aegean. **Ladiko Bay** just south has a small cove known as Anthony Queen (*sic*) Beach after the actor who bought land while filming *The Guns of Navarone*. Next door, the hidden village of **Afándou** is less frenetic and has a rarity in Greece – an 18-hole golf course (*t 224 105 1255*), plus a 7km pebble beach, crystal waters and excellent fish tavernas. Just south, an avenue of eucalyptus leads to **Vágia Point** with great beaches south of the headland. Local farms are irrigated by a nymph-haunted lake fed by the **Eptá Pigés**, the 'Seven Springs', 5km inland, a beauty spot with strutting peacocks, lush vegetation and a wonderful taverna. You can walk to the lake

Where to Stay and Eat

Kalithéa ✉ 85100
Paradise Royal Mare, t 224 106 6060, **f** 224 106 6066 (*L; luxury–expensive*). After a facelift in 1999, this resort in the gardens by the sea is now one of the most stylish on Rhodes. Villas with private pools, pools, waterslides, hammam and more. *Open April–Oct.*

Faliráki ✉ 85100
There are droves of C-class hotels here (any package operator can set you up) plus:
Grecotel Rodos Royal, t 224 108 5412, **f** 224 108 5091, *www.grecotel.gr* (*luxury–expensive*). A truly vast luxury complex near the sea, with four outdoor pools, one indoors, and every

amenity and service to spoil you rotten. *Open April–Oct.*
Faliráki Camping, t 224 108 5516. Rhodes' only campsite, with every comfort.
After dark, Faliráki is one big party.
Champers, t 224 108 5939, is the eighth wonder of the world for young package ravers: karaoke and dancing on giant barrels.

Afándou ✉ 85103
Lippia Golf Resort, t 224 105 2007, **f** 224 105 2367 (*A; expensive–moderate*). An all-inclusive air-conditioned resort hotel, with indoor and outdoor pools and tennis.
Reni Sky, t 224 105 1125, **f** 224 105 2413 (*B; inexpensive*). Good-value, with a pool.
Reni's, t 224 105 1280. The jet-set head here for exceptional seafood dishes.

through ankle-deep water in a tunnel dug by the Italians (claustrophobes have an alternative route, by road).

The long sandy bay at **Tsambíka** is very popular, with its tiny white monastery high on the cliffs above. Rhodes' answer to fertility drugs, the monastery's icon of the Virgin attracts childless women who make the barefoot pilgrimage and pledge to name their babies Tsambíkos or Tsambíka – names popular enough in the local phone book, so it must really work. A rugged coastal path, redolent of Cornwall, offers rewarding walks: from Tsambíka to Faraklós takes around 3 hours. Next stop south on the main road, ceramic-making **Archángelos** has a North African feel, its little white houses spread under a chewed-up castle of the Knights. Its churches, **Archángelos Gabriél** and **Archángelos Micháel**, are two of Rhodes' prettiest; another, **Ag. Theodóroi**, has 14th-century frescoes, but all three are usually shut. Fiercely patriotic, the villagers have even painted the graveyard blue and white. They also have a reputation for their anti-snake goatskin boots. Local cobblers can make you a pair; they fit either foot but don't come cheap.

South, the ruined **Castle of Faraklós** is dramatically set on the promontory below **Malónas**. Even after the rest of the island fell to Suleiman, Faraklós held on, the Knights only surrendering after a long, determined siege. The nearby fishing hamlet of **Charáki** has a pretty shaded esplanade running along a crescent pebble beach, and makes a welcome stop after the coastal walk. There are good fish tavernas, excellent swimming and postcard views of Líndos.

Líndos

With its sugar-cube houses wrapped around the fortified acropolis high over the sea, dramatically beautiful Líndos owes its integrity to the fact that the whole town is classified as an archaeological site; even painting the shutters requires a permit. Líndos was a magnet in the swinging sixties, when, they say, you could hear the clink of cocktail glasses as far away as Rhodes Town. It still has a few showbiz Brits (e.g. Pink Floyd's Dave Gilmour), plus Italians, Germans and Saudi princes and diplomats, who have snapped up the lovely old captains' houses. Incredibly beautiful as Líndos is, there's little left of real village life. In July and August the cobbled streets are heaving with day-trippers and you can literally be carried along by the crowds – around half a million visitors are siphoned through each year. And if you can't take the heat, be warned: Líndos is the frying pan of Rhodes. The nightlife also sizzles.

Líndos was the most important of the three ancient cities of Rhodes; the first temple on its precipitous acropolis was erected by 1510 BC. Four times the size of the present town, the city owed its importance to its twin natural harbours, and to the foresight of its benevolent 6th-century BC tyrant Cleoboulos, one of the Seven Sages of Greece, famous for his beauty, his belief in the intellectual equality of women, and his maxims, one of which, 'Measure is in all the best' (nothing in excess), was engraved at Delphi. The reservoir and rock tunnels dug by his father, King Evander, supplied water to Líndos until only a few years ago.

St Paul brought Christianity to Líndos; the Knights fortified it; and, under the Turks, Lindian merchants handled most of the island's trade. The sea captains built

Getting There and Around

Besides daily **boats** from Rhodes Town, Líndos has its own direct **hydrofoil** to Sými and to Marmaris, Turkey; book through Pefkos Rent-a-Car, **t** 224 403 1387. **Donkey taxis** to the Acropolis cost €5; the possibility of buying a photo of the experience comes with the deal. If you're staying, 3-wheeled vehicles will transport your luggage.

Tourist Information

Plateía Eleftherías, **t** 224 403 1900, **f** 224 403 1282; *open daily 7.30am–10pm.*

Where to Stay

Líndos ✉ 85107

In Líndos, all but a few houses bear the name of a British holiday company: **Direct Greece** is one of the bigger operators (book from the UK; *see* p.96). Local **Pallas Travel**, **t** 224 403 1494, **f** 224 403 1595, can also arrange villas and rooms.

Lindos Sun, **t** 224 403 1453, **f** 224 402 2019 (*C; expensive–moderate*). Offering tennis and pool from April to Oct.

Kyria Teresa's, **t** 224 403 1765 (*moderate*). More modest, pretty garden rooms.

Electra, **t** 224 4031 266 (*moderate–inexpensive*). A winner, with a shady garden.

Katholiki, adjacent, **t** 224 403 1445 (*inexpensive*). Rooms in a traditional house built in 1640 (shared bathroom).

Near Líndos

Lindos Memories, 1.5km from Líndos, **t** 224 403 5000, **f** 224 404 8156 (*A; luxury–expensive*). By a quiet beach, spanking new and very plush, with two pools.

Atrium Palace, Kálathos, **t** 224 403 1601, **f** 224 403 1600, *atrium@otenet.gr* (*L; luxury*). The big noise here, with every conceivable amenity.

Lindos Bay, Vlícha Bay, **t** 224 403 1501, **f** 224 403 1500 (*A; luxury*). On the beach with great views of Líndos, tennis, watersports, pool and wheelchair access.

Steps of Lindos, Vlícha Bay, **t** 224 403 1062, **f** 224 403 1067 (*A; expensive*). Luxury rooms and facilities, and offering a variety of watersports.

Lydian Village, on the beach by Lárdos, **t** 224 404 7361, **f** 224 404 7364 (*B; luxury– expensive*). Club-type complex, exquisitely designed, with houses clustered around courtyards. Furnishings are luxurious but with an ethnic feel.

Eating Out

Mavrikos, just off the square, **t** 224 403 1232 (€18–25). Established in 1933; an imaginative menu with exceptionally good Greek, French and Italian dishes. *Open daily April–Nov, other times weekends only.*

Archontiko, **t** 224 403 1992. Romantic restaurant in a captain's house of 1605, with lovely views of the acropolis and lovely food. Save room for dessert. *Eves only, April–Oct.*

Dionysos Taverna, in the centre. All the usual Greek favourites in a rooftop setting, for a more modest budget.

To Spitaki, in the centre. Greek dishes with a cordon bleu touch in peaceful gardens.

Butcher's Grill, at Péfki, run by family butchers from Lárdos. Excellent fresh meat and traditional village cooking.

Entertainment and Nightlife

Líndos has all types of bars, many in old sea captains' mansions: try the **Captain's House**, with the most elaborate doorway in Líndos, decorated with birds, chains and pomegranate flowers. The 400-year-old **Lindian House**, with painted ceiling and lovely windows, is a grand place, and **Socrates** opposite is in another attractive captain's house. **Jody's Flat**, encompassing a tree, with English papers and board games, is full of character. **Lindos By Night** is an institution, on three floors with lovely roof gardens, laying out superb acropolis views. Three clubs reverberate at night: **Namas** and **Akropolis**, halfway down to the beach, and **Amphitheatre** on the hillside.

mansions around courtyards with elaborate pebbled mosaics (*choklákia*), secluded behind high walls and imposing doorways; the cables carved around them represented the number of ships a captain owned. Many are now holiday homes or bars, which take full advantage of their flat roofs. Some houses have collections of Lindian ware, delightfully painted with stylized Oriental motifs; the Knights once captured a ship full of Persian potters and wouldn't let them go until they had taught their craft to the islanders. The Byzantine church of the **Assumption**, restored by Grand Master d'Aubusson in 1489–90, has frescoes of the Apostles, painted in 1779. One, oddly, has a camel head. The back wall is covered with a scene of the *Last Judgement*, with St Michael weighing souls and a misogynistic St Peter welcoming the Elect to heaven.

The Acropolis of Líndos

High over Líndos, the **Temple of Lindian Athena** (*t 224 403 1258; open in season Mon 12.30–6.40, Tues–Fri 8–6.40, Sat and Sun 8.30–2.40; rest of the year Tues–Sun 8.30–2.40; adm exp*) is one of the most stunning in Greece, accessible by foot or by 'Lindian taxi' – a donkey. The steep route up is a gauntlet of billowing blouses, tablecloths and pushy saleswomen. Líndos' reputation for embroidery dates back to the time of Alexander, and if you look hard you may find some hand-made work, but the vast majority is mass-produced, imported and overpriced.

The Knights contributed the stair to the top that begins near the prow of a trireme carved into the rock. This once served as a podium for a statue of Agissándros, priest of Poseidon; the inscription says that the Lindians gave Agissándros a gold wreath for judging their games. At the top of the stair are two vaulted rooms, and a crumbling 13th-century church of **St John**. Continue straight on for the Doric **Stoa of Lindian Athena**. Lindian Athena was a chaste goddess; to go any further, menstruating or sexually active women had to bathe, heads had to be covered, and men were obliged to have clean bare feet or to wear white shoes not made of horsehair. From the stoa, the 'Stairway to Heaven' leads up to the mighty foundations of the **Propylaea** and, on the edge of the precipice, the **Temple of Athena**. Both were built by Cleoboulos, rebuilt after a fire in 342 BC and reconstructed by the Italians. The temple was celebrated for a primitive wooden statue of Athena, capped with gold, and its golden inscription of Pindar's Seventh Olympian Ode. On the northern slope of the Acropolis, bullocks were sacrificed in honour of Athena in the **Voukópion**, a recess in the rock. The views from the acropolis are stunning, especially of the azure round pool of **St Paul's Bay**, where the apostle landed in AD 58. Below this, the **Grand Harbour** with the decent beach and small, trendy **Pallas Beach** were once home to Líndos' navy, 500 triremes strong. On the far end of this, the cylindrical so-called **Tomb of Cleoboulos** actually pre-dates the king, and in the Middle Ages was converted into the church of Ag. Aililiános.

Around Líndos, and the Southern Tip

Out of eyeshot of Líndos there's no lack of holiday development: at **Péfki**, just south, with a sandy beach fringed by the pine trees, and sprawling **Lárdos**, to the west, with a pretty village as its core and a beach on sweeping **Lárdos Bay**, with sand dunes bordered by reeds and marshes. **Laerma**, 12km inland, is 4km from the 9th-century

Moní Thari – the oldest on Rhodes, now reoccupied by monks from Pátras. The monastery is said to have been founded by a princess held hostage by pirates, who had a dream from the Archangel Michael promising her that she would soon be free. The princess had a gold ring, and in turn she promised St Mike to build as many monasteries as cubits that she flung her ring. She threw it so far she lost it, and ended up building only Thari. The church has some of the finest frescoes on Rhodes, dating back to the 12th century; in places they are four layers thick.

You can still find very peaceful, even deserted beaches south of Lárdos: **Glystra** is a gem, a perfect sheltered cove. **Kiotári** now has isolated upmarket hotels, while its beach stretches for miles in front of the hills. A detour inland leads to the medieval hill village of **Asklipío** huddled beneath yet another castle. Its **Monastery of Metamórfossi** (*open daily 9–6*) dates from 1060, and has 15th-century frescoes of the Old Testament, arranged like comic-strips around the walls. Further south, buses go as far as **Gennádi**, with a beach which looks like a vast pebble mosaic. Inland, **Váti**, with its huge plane tree in the centre, is typical of the new Rhodes; only 35 people hold the fort during the week, while everyone else has a flat in the city and returns at weekends. An arty crowd of German ex-pats have livened up the similar one-horse village of **Lachaniá**. **Plimíri** has a spanking-new marina, a fish farm and a popular fish restaurant . Some wonderful deserted beaches dot the California-like coast.

Kataviá, the southernmost village on Rhodes, has the only petrol station for miles, a good taverna (Martina's) and in July and August windsurfers coming out of its ears, all heading to the sandy isthmus of **Cape Prassonísi**. Near here stand the ruins of a 7th–6th-century BC walled settlement at **Vroulia**, set on a panoramic shelf over the sea. For more grand views over both coasts, take the corniche road from Kataviá to **Messanagrós**, an old-fashioned mountain village. Just west, if you get stuck, you can spend the night at **Moní Skiádi**, a hilltop monastery sheltering an icon which flowed blood when a 15th-century heretic stabbed the Virgin's cheek. The wound and stains are still visible. The unpaved road continues down to the west coast, where there are spectacular views but a wind-battered sea. Sheltered in a valley, **Apolakiá**, famous for its watermelons and weddings, has a few rooms to rent.

Up the West Coast

Monólithos, Embónas and Mount Atáviros

Monólithos, the big village in these parts, is named after a fantastical 700ft spur rising sheer above the sea, capped spectacularly by a **castle** built by Grand Master d'Aubusson and reached by a precarious winding stair. Five kilometres below the castle, down a tortuous road, the shady bay of **Foúrni** has a sandy beach. The sunsets at Monólithos are fabulous; a pair of tavernas have front row seats. There are more good views from nearby **Siána**, an attractive old village on a hillside, famous for its wild honey and *suma*, the local schnapps. You can sample both at roadside cafés, where the oldest houses have roofs made of clay. The church of **Ag. Pantéléimon** has a beautiful interior and basil by the door.

Where to Stay and Eat

Thomas, in Monólithos, t 224 606 1291, f 224 102 8834 (*D; inexpensive*). *Open all year.*

Loukas, Kámiros Skála. Good and jolly place to wait for the Chálki ferry.

Taverna New Kamiros, by the sea on the old Kámiros road. Not much to look at but serves good seafood and meat dishes.

Nymfi, Sálakos, t 224 602 2206 (*B; moderate*). A real oasis with four traditional rooms: the perfect island hideaway. *Open all year.*

Near Arthípoli, indulge in a cool, prolonged lunch at **Psinthos, Pigi Fasouli** under the plane trees or **Artemida**, with charcoal grills and good house wines.

Taverna Oasis, at Eleoússa. Another fine choice, lost in the trees.

Renowned for its wine, olives and tobacco, the mountain village of **Embónas** has tried to preserve its traditional ways – its dances are exceptionally graceful and the *panegýria* in August are among the best on the island. Some older people still wear local costumes, but only those who don't mind being camera fodder for the Greek Nights coach parties. Embónas is home to the winemaking cooperative **CAIR** and the **Emery Winery** (*t 224 604 1208; tastings Mon–Fri 9–3*). The wine that has made them famous, white Villaré, owes its distinctness to indigenous grape *athiri* that refuses to grow outside its own microclimate, at 2,296ft, on the slopes of the island's highest peak, **Mount Atáviros** (3,986ft); its summit is a tough 3hr climb, but offers eagle-eye views of the whole island – you can (they say) see Crete on a clear morning. While up on the roof of Rhodes, head for **Ag. Isidóros**, a quieter version of Embónas.

Legend says Althaemenes (*see* below) founded the village below Embónas, **Kritiniá**, and named it in honour of his native Crete. Just below Kritiniá lies **Kámiros Skála**, a fishing harbour with two good tavernas that served as the port of ancient Kámiros and is now used by local ferries for Chálki. Towering high above, the Knights' **castle** (Kástro Kritiniás) is an impressive ruin, set above lemon groves and pinewoods and affording spectacular views.

Ancient Kamiros

When an oracle predicted that King Katreus of Crete, the grandson of Minos, would be slain by his offspring, his son Althaemenes fled to Rhodes, set up a colony in Kamiros and surrounded it with metal bulls that would bellow if it were invaded. In later life Katreus sailed to Rhodes to visit his son, but arrived at night, and, what with the bellowing of the metal bulls, Althaemenes failed to recognize his father and fellow Cretans and slew them. When he realized his error, he begged the Earth to swallow him, which she did. Kamiros went on to become one of Rhodes' three Dorian cities, until it was destroyed by an earthquake in the 2nd century BC, abandoned and forgotten. Then farmers discovered a few graves, and in 1859 the British Consul and a French archaeologist began excavating. The city they brought to light was the Pompeii of Rhodes (*t 224 104 0037; open Tues–Sun 8.30–5; adm*). An excellent water and drainage system, supplied by a large reservoir, served 400 families; also to be seen are the baths, the agora with its rostrum for public speeches, a large stoa with Doric columns, Roman houses, two temples – one 6th-century BC dedicated to Athena and the other Doric from the 3rd century – and an altar dedicated to Helios. To see the portable finds, however, you'll have to go to the British Museum.

Inland, the village of **Sálakos** is beloved for its shade and fresh water from the Spring of the Nymphs. With its cedar and pine forests, this makes lovely walking country. **Mount Profítis Ilías** (2,592ft) above has two derelict chalet hotels. The chief settlements on its slopes are **Apóllona** with a Museum of Popular Art and **Eleoússa** with a pretty Byzantine church. Nearby **Arthípoli** is a favourite oasis for lunch.

Back on the Northwest Coast

North of Kámiros, the built-up strip in **Theológos** (or **Thólos**) announces the proximity of Rhodes Town and the **airport**. Neighbouring **Kremastí** is famous for its wonder-working icon, **Panagías Kremastí**, occasioning a huge *panegýri* from 15 to 23 August; on the 23rd villagers don traditional costumes and dance a very fast *sousta*.

Inland, a road between Theológos and Paradíssi leads to **Káto Kalamónas** and from there to one last enchanting spot, more so if you manage to get there before or after the coach parties: **Petaloúdes**, the **valley of the butterflies** (*open May–Sept daily 8.30–7; adm*). Sliced by a stream and waterfalls, the narrow gorge is crowned by a roof of fairytale storax trees, whose resin is used to make frankincense. From June to September the scent attracts rare *Callimorpha quadripuntaria* moths, named for the Roman numeral IV on their wings. This is one of their two breeding grounds in the world, but in recent years their numbers have declined because of tourists clapping their hands to see their wings: every flight weakens them, so resist the urge.

You can follow the trail up the valley to the monastery of the **Panagía Kalópetra**, built in 1782 by Alexander Ypsilántis, grandfather of the two brothers who wanted to be kings at the start of the Greek War of Independence. It's a tranquil place, well worth the uphill trek, with wonderful views and picnic tables in the grounds. From here another wooded trail leads to the **Monastery of Ag. Soúlas**, just off the road down to **Soroní**. Here they have a giant festival on 30 July with donkey races immortalized in *Reflections on a Marine Venus*.

Sými (ΣΥΜΗ)

Inevitably there's a fusillade of clicking cameras when the ferries swing into Sými's harbour, the crisp brightness illuminating an amphitheatre of neoclassical mansions on the barren hills. Over the years the island has become the Hýdra of the Dodecanese, with big-name performers drawn to the Sými festival in July–September, fancy restaurants, and a dedicated following among the sailing fraternity. Hundreds arrive on excursion boats from Rhodes, but at night when they've gone and the lights come on, Sými is pure romance. Avoid August when the island is heaving; because it's in a basin and the heat bounces off the rocks, it sizzles like a cat on a hot tin roof. On the other hand, it stays warm into October and is lovely in spring.

History

Sými, they say, was the daughter of King Ialysos on Rhodes; she was abducted and brought here by Glaukos, an eminent sponge-diver and sailor who also built the *Argo* for Jason – and the islanders inherited all his skills. Homer tells how Sými mustered three ships for Troy, led by King Nireus, the most beautiful of all the Greeks after Achilles. In historic times the island was dominated by Rhodes. The Romans fortified the acropolis at Chorió; the Byzantines converted it into a fort, which was renovated by the Knights. From here they could signal to Rhodes, and they favoured swift Symiot skiffs for their raiding activities. When Suleiman the Magnificent came in 1522, the Symiots, the most daring divers in the Aegean, pre-empted attack by offering him the most beautiful sponges he had ever seen. The gratified sultan made the island the official sponge provider to his harem and a free port. Large mansions were constructed; shipbuilders bought forests in Asia Minor; schools thrived. Even after certain privileges were withdrawn after 1821, Sými continued to flourish, until the Italians closed access to Asia Minor and the steamship killed the demand for wooden ships; the population nosedived from 23,000 to 600 by the outbreak of the Second World War. At its end the treaty giving the Dodecanese to Greece was signed on Sými on 8 May 1945, and ratified on 7 March 1948.

Gialós and Chorió

Sými is divided into down, up and over – busy Gialós around the harbour, Chorió, the older settlement high above, Kástro even higher, and Pédi clustered round the bay over the hill. In **Gialós**, arrivals are greeted by the elaborate free-standing clock tower, surrounded by *choklákia* pavements. In honour of the Treaty of the Dodecanese, a copy of the trireme from Líndos was carved into the rock with the inscription: 'Today freedom spoke to me secretly; Cease, Twelve Islands, from being pensive. 8th May, 1945.' Behind the recreation ground next to the bridge, a neoclassical mansion houses the **Nautical Museum** (*open Mon–Sat 10–3; adm*), with models of Sými's sailing ships, sponge-diving equipment and old photos.

At the end of the harbour, behind the clock tower and bronze fishing boy, the road leads around Charani Bay, still a hive of industry where caiques are built or repaired while chickens strut and cats lurk. Bombed in the Second World War, many of the houses have been renovated with elegant plasterwork in blues, greys, yellows and Venetian red. At the end, **Nos Beach** is small and usually packed; for more peace, walk further along the coastal path to **Nimborió**, a tree-shaded harbour with a good taverna, loungers and a pebbly shore.

Gialós dates from the 19th century, while a jumble of older houses with neoclassical elements incorporated into their doorways and windows dominate the **Chorió**. Many have lovely interiors with carved woodwork and Turkish-style *moussándra*, beds on raised platforms. The lower part can be reached by road from Gialós; the alternative is the 375-step **Kalí Stráta**, which starts by Plateía Oekonómou. Worn smooth, the steps can zap even the fittest visitor in summer, even though local grannies trip up and down like mountain goats (bring a light for after dark, though). Near the derelict windmills a Spartan **monument** commemorates a victory over the Athenians off Sými's coast. Further up, there's a 19th-century **pharmacy**, and the churches of **Ag. Panteleímon** and **Ag. Giórgios** with pebble mosaics of evil mermaids. Follow the signs to the **museum** (*t 224 107 1114; open Tues–Sun 10–2; adm*), which houses icons,

Getting There and Around

By sea: the island's ferries, *Symi I* and *Symi II*, leave Mandráki harbour, Rhodes, daily early evening and return to Rhodes in the early morning. There are at least three daily tourist boats from Rhodes, some calling at Panormítis Monastery, and a daily hydrofoil. Excursion boats visit different beaches, and there's a weekly trip to Datcha (Turkey) run by Symi Tours (*see* below).

Port authority: t 224 107 1205.

By road: the island has four taxis and the Sými Bus, t 224 107 2666, departing from the east end of the harbour hourly from 8.30am to 10.30pm to Pédi via Chorió. There are various places rent motorbikes.

Tourist Information

The police share the post office building near the Clock Tower, t 224 107 1111. Pick up a copy of the free *Sými Visitor*. Look out for Mr Noble's *Walking on Sými*, too.

For Sými festival information, contact the municipality, t 224 107 1302.

Symi Tours, t 224 107 1307, f 224 107 2292, www.symi-island.com. Villas and rooms to rent, and organized walking excursions.

Where to Stay and Eat

Sými is very expensive in July and August. Cheaper rooms are often let on condition that you stay three nights or more.

Gialós ✉ 85600

Aliki, t/f 224 107 1665 (*A; luxury–expensive*). A fine sea captain's mansion, lovingly restored with a roof garden and air-conditioning in some rooms. *Open April–Oct.*

Dorian, t 224 107 1181, f 224 107 2292 (*A; luxury–expensive*). Similar; up the steps just behind the Aliki; nine self-catering studios.

Opera House, t 224 107 1856, f 224 107 2035 (*A; expensive*). Family suites with air-conditioning back from the harbour in a garden.

Albatros, t 224 107 1707, f 224 107 2257 (*C; moderate*). Well decorated rooms with air-conditioning.

Les Katerinettes, t 224 107 2698. Rooms in an eccentric traditional house with painted ceilings. Downstairs, try the octopus and *pikilía*, or selection of *mezédes*.

Egli, at the base of the stairway to Chório, t 224 107 1392 (*inexpensive*). Clean, no frills.

Meraklis, in the backstreets beyond the bank. Authentic taverna with excellent Greek cooking and reasonable prices.

Mylopetra, t 224 107 2333 (€25–35). Elegant Mediterranean dishes, home-made bread

coins, pottery and a 19th-century Symiot room. At the top, the **Kástro** sits on the acropolis. Its church, **Megáli Panagía**, replaces one blown up by the Germans when they discovered an arms cache; one of the bells is made from a bomb.

Around Sými

From Chorió it's a half-hour walk downhill to **Pédi** into the most fertile area of the island. Where the road forks, a small beach and excellent taverna await to the left, while the more developed beach and fishermen's cottages are to the right. A path goes over the headland, where you can swim out to **Ag. Marína**, a chapel used as a secret Greek school under the Turks. Water taxis from Pédi buzz to **Ag. Nikólaos**, with a tree-fringed beach and *cantina*.

A new road from Chorió goes to the south tip of Sými and the 18th-century **Monastery of Taxiárchis Michael Panormítis** (*open daily 9–2 and 4–8, but try to avoid 11–12 when tourist boats from Rhodes descend*), set in cypresses and pines. The monastery's colourful bell-tower was built in 1905; its *choklákia* courtyard is strewn with flags. The church has a remarkable **iconostasis** with a stern, larger-than-life

and pasta. Part of the floor is glass, and looks down into a 50 BC tomb.

Ellinikon, just back from the bridge, t 224 107 2455 (€18–22). Unusual *mezédes* and main courses (try sea bass with pesto sauce) and 150 Greek wines.

O Tholos, out on the headland, t 224 107 2033 (€15–20). An impressive menu in a romantic setting, serving great *mezédes* and grills.

Chorió ✉ 85600

Horio, t 224 107 1800, f 224 107 1802 (*B; expensive–moderate, inc. breakfast*). Built in traditional style with smart air-conditioned rooms and stunning views, surrounded by fields.

Metapontis, in upper Chorió, t 224 107 1491 (*B; expensive–moderate*). In a very old Sými house with traditional features like the *moussandra* sleeping gallery.

Taxiarchis, t 224 107 2012, f 224 107 2013 (*C; moderate*). Elegant neoclassical apartments with a small bar, terrace, and breathtaking panorama of Pédi. *Open April–Oct.*

Fiona, lower down the village, t 224 107 2088 (*moderate*). Comfortable and tasteful bed and breakfast; the owner plays the *sandouri* – Zorba's instrument.

Georgio's Taverna. An institution at night, famous for exquisite Sými shrimps and the man himself on the accordion.

Pédi ✉ 85600

Lemonia, t 224 107 1201, f 224 107 2374 (*expensive*). Small, pretty and blue, with views of the bay; rooms with balcony, sitting area, kitchenette, ceiling fans and phone.

Taverna Tolis, on the beach next to the boat yard. The best for food and atmosphere.

Nimborió ✉ 85600

Taverna Metapontis, t 224 107 1820. A pretty spot for lunch (their boat *Panagióta* will take you back to Gialós), with rooms.

Entertainment and Nightlife

Sými buzzes at night. The *ouzerie* **Paco's** is an institution but has a rival in **Elpida**, which does *mezédes* in Mouragio. **Mina's** and former rival **Vapori** have clubbed together, attracting yachties and up-market Brits. The excellent **Τεμβελα Σκαλα** ('Lazy Steps') on the harbour sometimes sees local jam sessions. Chilled night owls head for the **Roof Garden**, for mellow sounds and views. In Chorió, **Jean and Tonic** still reigns supreme for happy hour and nightcaps. You can bop at **The Club** in Gialós, or here bouzouki at the **Alethini Taverna** on the road to Pédi. Further along, **Valanidia** also has bouzouki with top singers in season.

silver-plated icon of St Michael of 1724. In the Orthodox church, Michael is a busy archangel: weigher of souls and patron of sailors and the Greek Air Force, he can also be called upon to help in storms and induce fertility; the many gold and silver ship ex-votos and wax babies attest to his prowess. There are two small **museums** (*adm*), one filled with ex-votos, prayers in bottles that floated to Panormítis, Chinese plates and a stuffed mongoose. The second contains antique furniture and the British radio operated by the abbot and two members of the Resistance, executed by the Germans in 1944. **Seskli**, the islet facing Panormítis, was ancient Teutlousa, where the Athenians took refuge after their defeat by the Spartan navy during the Peloponnesian War. It has a long pebbly beach shaded with tamarisks and barbecue trips from Gialós.

Chálki (ΧΑΛΚΗ)

With neoclassical houses in pastel shades overlooking a gentle horseshoe harbour, barren and rocky Chálki is a miniature Sými, topped by a fairytale Crusader castle on a pointed peak. Only here traditional island life still ambles on – fishing and goat-

Getting There

Three to four **ferry** connections a week with Rhodes; twice with Piraeus (30hrs!), Kárpathos and Kássos, once with Kos, Kálymnos, Mílos, Sitía and Ag. Nikólaos (Crete). Daily boat to and from Kámiros Skála, Rhodes, connecting with the bus to Rhodes Town.
Port authority: t 224 604 5220.

Tourist Information

Regular police: **t** 224 604 5213.
Halki Tours, **t** 224 604 5281. Also worth a try.

Where to Stay and Eat

Chálki ✉ 85110
Most accommodation is now taken up by the holiday companies.
Captain's House, t 224 604 5201 (*moderate*). Turn-of-the-century mansion with three lovely en suite rooms, run with nautical precision by Alex Sakellarídes, ex-Greek Royal Navy, and his English wife Christine; breakfast served on the cool terrace.
Xalki, t 224 604 5390, **f** 224 604 5208 (*C; inexpensive*). Converted olive press to the left of the harbour, offering a sun terrace, snack bar/restaurant, and swimming off the rocks.
Kleanthi, t 224 604 5334 (*B; moderate*). Rooms and studios in a traditional stone house.
Argyrenia, t 224 604 5205 (*inexpensive*). Self-contained chalets set in shady gardens on the way to the beach.
Nick Pondomos, t 224 604 5295 (*inexpensive*). Rooms and taverna overlooking the bay.
Omonia. The place for fresh fish, seafood and grills (€15).
Mavri Thalassa ('Black Sea'). In from the (Aegean) sea, with an assortment of Greek and international cuisine, popular with all (€12–15).
Maria. Maria and her triplet daughters serve Greek oven dishes and good *souvláki*.

herding, supplemented by small-scale tourism. Chálki is famous for its old music traditions, and on occasion you'll hear singers improvise *matinádes*, impromptu songs with 15-syllable verses. Pronounce their island 'Chalky' at your own risk; the name comes from *chalkí*, 'copper', which used to be mined here. It's a quiet place; there are no newspapers, and only a few pick-up trucks and bikes.

The main claim to fame of the port and one town **Emborió** is that its church Ag. Nikólaos has the tallest bell tower in the Dodecanese; it also has a magnificent *choklákia* courtyard. From Emborió a 15-minute walk along 'Boulevard Tarpon Springs' (paid for by sponge fishermen who now ply their trade in Florida and just wide enough for a delivery van) takes you to sandy **Póndamos Beach**, with sunshades and Nick's Taverna by the sea. Determined sightseers should continue walking up another hour for **Chorió**, a ghost-town abandoned in 1950. Here the Knights of St John built their castle; on a clear day you can see Kárpathos and Crete.

A new road makes the once-gruelling 3–5-hour trek to the **Monastery of Ag. Ioánnis Pródromos** less of a slog; you can stay overnight in one of the cells (a family there is in charge). Other beaches can be reached with brothers Michális and Vassílis Pátros on their high-speed launch *Yiánnis Express*. They also sail to the green isle of **Alimniá**, with another castle and a deep harbour where Italian submarines hid during the war. British Special Boat Services commandoes, sent to scupper the submarines in 1943, were captured by Nazis, taken to Rhodes and executed. You can still see the machine-gun strafing as well as paintings of submarines in the ruined houses. The kindly islanders, appalled by the executions, moved to Chálki and vowed never to return, leaving Alimniá to flocks of sheep, barbecuing holidaymakers and the occasional yacht, all in all a beautiful place to laze about, swim and picnic.

Kastellórizo/Mégisti (ΜΕΓΙΣΤΗ)

'Europe begins here,' says the sign welcoming you to Greece's easternmost point, Kastellórizo, six hours – 110km – east of Rhodes, within spitting distance of Turkey. It is the smallest inhabited island of the Dodecanese, 3 by 6km, yet the mother hen of its own small clutch of islets, hence its official name, Mégisti, 'the largest'. Ruined by a long streak of bad luck, its once very lonely 170–200 permanent inhabitants have been officially adopted by Athens. Its success as a film set – for the Italian film *Mediterraneo* – has given the economy a new life; landladies now cry '*Stanza? Stanza?*' as the ferry arrives. Some old houses are being repaired, mostly by Australian 'Kazzies'. However, it remains a quirky backwater in a sea brimming with marine life – including oysters, a rarity on Greek islands.

History

The Dorians built two forts, by the present town and on the mountain at Palaeokástro. This was also the acropolis, where Dionysos was a favourite: 42 rock grape presses were found, linked to conduits that fed the juice into underground reservoirs. The Byzantines repaired its walls, and their work was continued by the Knights of St John, who named the island after their Castello Rosso where they imprisoned misbehaving members of the order. It had various owners – the sultan

Getting There

By air: three flights a week from Rhodes. Olympic Airways, **t** 224 604 9241. **Airport**: **t** 224 604 9238. A bus meets planes.

By sea: twice a week from Rhodes; once a week with Sými, Tílos, Níssyros, Kos, Kálymnos, Léros and Piraeus. Also an overpriced, unofficial boat to Kaş (Kastellórizo is not an official port of entry). **Port authority**: **t** 224 604 9270.

Tourist Police

Regular police: in the harbour by the post office, **t** 224 604 9333.

Where to Stay and Eat

Kastellórizo ✉ 85111

Megisti, **t** 224 604 9272, **f** 224 604 9221 (*C; expensive*). At the end of the harbour, all rooms overlook the sea. *Open Greek Easter–Oct.*

Poseidon, **t** 224 604 9257, **f** 224 604 9257, *www.holidayrentals.gr* (*expensive*). Lovely studios in a restored neoclassical house by the sea. *Open year round.*

Kastellorizo, **t** 224 604 9044, **f** 224 604 9279, *www.kastellorizohotel.gr* (*B; expensive–moderate*). New well-run apartment complex by the sea, with a small pool. *Open Mar–Oct.*

Mavrothalassitis, **t** 224 604 9202 (*inexpensive*). Simple, with en suite facilities.

Akrothalassi, **t** 224 604 9052. A favourite for its delicious and inexpensive daily specials, a cut above traditional taverna fair.

Platania, up the hill on Choráfia Square, **t** 224 604 9206. Unpretentious and picturesque, with tasty island dishes. It featured in the film *Mediterraneo*.

of Egypt in 1440, the king of Naples in1450, the Turks by 1512, the Venetians twice, in 1570 and in 1659. Even so, Kastellórizo was doing fine; it had a population of 15,000 who lived from the sea and holdings along the neighbouring Lycian coast.

Things began to go wrong with the Greek War of Independence. The islanders were the first in the Dodecanese to join the cause, and seized the two fortresses from the Turks. The Powers forced them to give them back in 1833. In 1913 Kastellórizo revolted again only to be squashed by the French, who used the island as a base for their war in Syria – hence drawing bombardments from the Turkish coast. In 1927 an earthquake caused major damage but the Italians, then in charge, refused to do any repairs, as Kastellórizo failed to cooperate with their de-Hellenization programme. By 1941 only 1,500 inhabitants remained. During the war, the isolated Italian garrison was captured by the Germans (the subject of *Mediterraneo*). When the Allies shipped the Greek population to refugee camps in Gaza, British soldiers pillaged the empty houses. To hide their looting, the British (or the British claim, Greek pirates) ignited a fuel dump as they pulled out, leading to a fire that destroyed over 1,500 homes. The ship carrying the refugees home after the war sank. Those who survived discovered that, although they had achieved Greek citizenship, they had lost everything else and there was nothing to do but emigrate, mostly to Australia. The immediately postwar population was reduced to five families, who survived thanks to the Turks in Kaş, who sent over food parcels. British compensation for damages came in the 1980s, but there are still bad feelings over the way it was distributed; none actually went to the people who stuck it out on the island.

Kastellórizo Town

There is only one town on the island, also called Kastellórizo, full of ruined houses and mansions, some displaying traces of the island's old wealth. Tavernas line the waterfront, in high season packed with Italians and yachties. The red **castle** is still in place; the ladder to the top leads to a fine view of the Turkish coast; every day an islander climbs up to raise the flags of Greece and the EU flags at the easternmost extremity of both. A tomb nearby yielded a golden crown, and in the castle keep a small **museum** (*open Tues–Sun, 7.30–2.30*) exhibits photographs of the prosperous town before everything went wrong, a few frescoes, folk costumes and items found in the harbour – including Byzantine tableware. The path along the shore leads up to a **Lycian tomb** cut into the rock, with Doric columns; the whole southwest coast of modern Turkey is dotted with similar, but this is the only one in Greece. The church **Ag. Konstantínos and Heléni** re-uses granite columns from a Temple of Apollo. A steep path rises to the Palaeokástro, the Doric fortress and acropolis. On the gate is an inscription from the 3rd century BC; walls, a tower and cisterns also remain.

There are no beaches, but there are a multitude of islets to swim to, and a million sea urchins to step on. The unmissable excursion by caique is to the **Blue Cave** (**Perásta**), the island's answer to Capri's Grotto Azzuro. The effects are best in the morning when light filters in the low entrance, the reflections turning the walls and stalactites an uncanny blue; wear your swimming gear. The same boats often go out to **Rho**, a hunk of rock with a beach and a flagpole.

Kárpathos (ΚΑΡΠΑΘΟΣ)

Halfway between Crete and Rhodes, Kárpathos offers two islands for the price of one: austere and rugged in the north and soft and fertile in the south, linked by a vertebra of cliffs. The road between the two dates from 1979, ending the isolation of the northern village of Ólympos, a goldmine of traditions lost elsewhere in Greece – even the local dialect is Homeric. From the earliest days, Vróntis Bay hid pirate ships that plundered passing vessels; the island's name may derive from *Arpaktos*, or 'robbery'; the Venetians slurred it into *Scarpanto*, a name you may spot on old maps. One town, Arkássa, was their chief slave market. Today, the natives have one of the highest rates of university education in Europe. Although many live elsewhere, they love Kárpathos so much that they ship their bodies back to be buried.

Pigádia and the South

The friendly capital, **Pigádia**, shelters in the old pirate cove, mountain-ringed Vróntis Bay. Once the ancient city of Possidion, inhabited by the Mycenaeans, it was abandoned in the Byzantine era. The modern town is just that – modern, but it's no accident that the National Bank branch has such an air of prosperity: Kárpathos receives more money from its emigrants than any other island. Beyond the Fascistic port building, it's a short walk to the long beach that rims **Vróntis Bay**, lined with trees and dotted with tavernas. Within an enclosure several columns of a 5th-century basilica, **Ag. Fotiní**, have been re-erected.

South of Pigádia, the land is desolate, the few trees bent over from the wind. The coast softens after 7km at **Ammopí**, a resort where sandy coves are decorated with rock formations. Further south, a ship run aground is an advertisement for Kárpathos' windblasted windsurfing 'paradise', **Afiárti**. Above Ammopí, colourful **Menetés** has a small ethnographic museum (ask at Taverna Manolis) and a church in a dramatic setting. Beyond, the road continues to the west coast and **Arkássa**, with little beaches and hotels at the mouth of a jagged, cave-riddled ravine. A few minutes south on the road are the ruins of its predecessor, **Arkessia**, where a Mycenaean acropolis with Cyclopean walls stands on the rocky headland. The city was inhabited into Byzantine times; the 5th-century church **Ag. Anastásia** has a mosaic floor.

Just north, **Finíki** is a bijou little fishing port with a good restaurant and sandy beach nearby; the sponge divers of Kálymnos call here, and caiques depart for Kássos, if the sea isn't too rough. The road north passes several tempting strands and mini fjords far below in the pines (one spot, **Adia**, has an excellent taverna) en route to **Lefkós**, the nicest beach on the west coast – reached by daily bus from Pigádia. Tucked in the rocks, Lefkós has white sand, pines and a scattering of antiquities. Packagers have arrived, but so far nothing too drastic.

Inland Villages and the East Coast

The beautiful road north of Pigádia rises first to opulent **Apéri**. The capital of Kárpathos up to 1896, it is reputed to be the richest village in Greece; nearly everyone

Getting There and Around

By air: daily flights with Rhodes and Athens, twice a week with Kássos (the shortest scheduled flight in the world: it takes 5 minutes) and twice a week with Sitía (Crete); also charters – even from Slovenia. Olympic office in town, by the square, **t** 224 502 2150. **Airport**: **t** 224 502 2057/8. Taxis to the airport cost around €12.

By sea: three to four **ferry** connections per week with Rhodes and Kássos, often with Chálki, Mílos, Ag. Nikólaos and Sitía (Crete); **boats** in the summer go to Diafáni, leaving Pigádia at 8.30am. At weekends a **caique** goes from Finíki to Kássos.

Port authority: **t** 224 502 2227.

By road: The often appalling state of the roads makes car and motorbike hire dear and the only petrol pumps are in Pigádia. **Buses** from Pigádia go to Ammopí, and Pilés by way of Apéri, Voláda and Óthos, and one or two go on to Finíki and Arkássa and Lefkós.

Tourist Information

Municipal tourist office: **t** 224 502 3841.
Tourist police: Eth. Anastasis in Pigádia, **t** 224 502 2218.

Where to Stay and Eat

If you get stuck, ring the **Association of Hotel Owners**, **t** 224 502 2483.

Pigádia ☑ 85700

Possirama Bay, on the sandy beach of Affoti, **t** 224 502 2916, **f** 224 502 2919 (*A; expensive*). Air-conditioned apartments sleeping 2–4 with large balconies. *Open April–Oct.*

Miramare Bay, in the same area, **t** 224 502 2345, **f** 224 5022 631 (*B; expensive*). Another new operation, with pool, sea views and good breakfast included.

Romantica, **t** 224 502 2461, **f** 224 502 3267 (*C; moderate*). Charming studios in a grove of citrus trees, and a short walk from the beach; it serves delicious breakfasts.

Pavilion, up in town, **t** 224 502 2818, **f** 224 502 3319 (*C; moderate*). A favourite of Americans, with cocktails served in the roof garden.

Blue Bay, by the beach, **t** 224 502 2479, **f** 224 502 2391 (*C; moderate*). Rooms (some with disabled access), a pool, bar and children's playground.

Kárpathos, **t** 224 502 2347 (*D; inexpensive*). An older, cheaper choice, open all year.

Mike's (€10–12). An old favourite for lunch or dinner.

has lived in New Jersey, including the family of Telly Savalas. If you have a chance to peek into a house don't miss it; the Karpathiots lavishly furnish their homes with colourful carpets, mirrors, portraits, antiques and elevated wood beds (*souphas*). Delightful **Voláda** has a ruined castle built by the Cornaros of Venice. From here the road climbs to wine-making **Óthos**, the highest village of Kárpathos, its houses decorated with carved balconies. One has a small **Ethnographic Museum**, run by Ioannis T. Hapsis, who also paints, and sells his pictures by size for €6–60. To the west, **Pilés** is prettier than it sounds and has views over Kássos and makes delicious honey.

Caiques from Pigádia call at the east coast beaches, but you can brave some of them by road. A steep zigzag from Apéri leads down to lovely **Acháta**, with white pebbles. The road north of Apéri takes in the majestic coast, with a serpentine road winding from Katodio to **Kyrá Panagía**, a lovely wide beach, also accessible by a 45-minute walk down through the lush greenery from **Myrtónas**. Another rotten road descends from Myrtónas to **Apélla**, a crescent of fine sand and turquoise water, set in wild boulders ravaged in the Clash of the Titans. The road ends at **Spóa**, at the crossroads to Ólympos; a track from Spóa descends to the overbuilt, overcrowded beach of **Ag. Nikólaos**. Another Wild West road from Spóa circles **Mount Kalílimni** (3,898ft),

Oraia Kárpathos. The best *makarounes* (pasta with fried onions and cheese) in town.
Aeraki (€14–18). Good island specialities – pumpkin fritters, stuffed mushrooms, onion pies, *manouli* cheese and more. **Anemoussa** upstairs serves good Italian food.

Ammopí ✉ 85700

Long Beach, t 224 502 3076, **f** 224 502 2095 (*C; moderate*). With pool and tennis.
Poseidon, south of Ammopí, **t/f** 224 502 2020 (*C; moderate*). In traditional style with a garden terrace; ideal if you're a windsurfer.
Ammopi Beach, t 224 502 2723 (*inexpensive*). Simple, remarkably cheap rooms.

Arkássa ✉ 85700

Arkesia, t 224 506 1290, **f** 224 506 1307 (*B; moderate*). Plush, all mod cons and pool.
Dimitrios, t 224 506 1313 (*B; moderate*). Also comfortable, but with fewer facilities.

Finíki/Lefkós ✉ 85700

Fay's Paradise, t 224 506 1308 (*inexpensive*). Lovely rooms near the harbour.
Pine Tree, north in Adia. Great pasta, chickpea soup and fresh-baked bread.
Small Paradise, in Lefkós, **t** 224 507 1171. Good food and beach-side studios.

Kyrá Panagía ✉ 85700

Book to have a chance at any of these.
Kyra Panagia Studios, t 224 503 1473 (*B; expensive*). Upscale, with a bar.
Sofia's Paradise, t 224 503 1300, **f** 224 503 1099. Good cooking, cheap fish, and figs drowned in raki. Also pleasant rooms with breakfast (*moderate*) and a boat for outings.
Studios Acropolis, t 224 503 1503 (*moderate*). Popular, with lovely views.
Klimateria, up in Voláda. Good taverna fills under a pergola.

Diafáni ✉ 85700

Chryssi Akti, opposite the quay, **t** 224 505 1215 (*E; inexpensive*). Clean and basic.
Delfini, t 224 505 1391 (*inexpensive*). A bit further back, quiet and friendly.

Ólympos ✉ 85700

Olympos, t 224 505 1252 (*inexpensive*). Three traditional en suite rooms; great views.
Aphrodite, t 224 505 1307 (*inexpensive*). Again with lovely views.
Mike's, t 224 505 1304 (*inexpensive*). With a restaurant serving traditional dishes.
Milos. In a windmill; try the pasta stuffed with cheese and spinach.

the highest peak in the Dodecanese, then descends on a corniche to **Messochóri**, set in an amphitheatre, with the pretty 17th-century church of Ag. Ioánnis.

Ólympos and Northern Kárpathos

As the Byzantines lost control of the seas, **Ólympos** became the refuge in the north. Draped over a stark mountain ridge topped by ruined windmills, it is one of the most striking villages in Greece, isolated for so long that linguists in the 19th century found people using pronunciations and expressions that went back to ancient Doric and Phrygian dialects. Houses with carved balconies are stacked one on top of another and doors are opened with wooden locks and keys that Homer himself might have recognized. Many of the men are noted musicians, but because so many have had to go abroad to work, women rule the roost. Property goes to the eldest daughter, the *kanakára*, who can be recognized by the gold coins she wears on chains during feast days along with her traditional costume, among the most beautiful in Greece. Twenty years ago all the women wore a simpler version of it every day. Before the road, visitors had no effect on traditional life, but tens of thousands a year are another story; stay overnight or come in the off-season if you can. The easiest way to get there from Pigádia is by caique to the little port of **Diafáni**, with a connecting minibus.

From Ólympos you can drive most of the way to **Avlóna**, a village that wouldn't look out of place in Tibet but is inhabited only during the harvest. From Avlóna it is a rough walk down to **Vrykoús**, the ancient city remembered today by a stair, rock-cut tombs and walls. Boats from Diafáni sail to **Sariá**, the islet that dots the 'i' of Kárpathos, with ruins of a pirate base.

Kássos (ΚΑΣΣΟΣ)

The southernmost of the Dodecanese, Kássos (pop. 1,500) is a barren rock with steep coasts, ravines and sea grottoes, plus a beach or two wedged in between, practically untouched by tourism. Almost autonomous under the Turks, Kássos was famed for its fleet that fought in the Greek War of Independence until 7 June 1824, when Ibrahim Pasha of Egypt, on his way to crush the Peloponnese (*see* p.178), stopped at Kássos and decimated the island, slaying all the men and taking the women and children as slaves. The few who managed to escape went to the islet of Gramboúsa by Crete, where they turned to piracy, flying the Greek flag until Gramboúsa was returned to Turkish rule. Every year on 7 June a ceremony is held in memory.

Charmingly woebegone **Fri** is the capital, where the main occupation, fishing, is much in evidence. Boats make the excursion out to the **Armathiá**, an islet just north of Kássos, with five beaches. Apart from a few dwarf olives, trees on Kássos never recovered after Ibrahim set the island ablaze, but many lighthouses, testimony to the tricky seas, stick out above the rocks. The bus goes to **Emborió**, the old commercial port, and **Panagía**, where ship captains' houses erode away. **Póli**, on the island's acropolis, has a crumbling Byzantine castle. Kássos' most accessible if mediocre beach is at **Ammoúa**, by the **Hellenokamára**, a lovely stalactite cave.

Getting There and Around

By air: three flights a week to and from Rhodes, one a week to Athens and four twice a week to Kárpathos. Olympic Airways, t 224 504 4330.

By sea: **ferry** connections two to three times a week with Piraeus, three to four times with Rhodes and Kárpathos, twice with Chálki, Mílos and Ag. Nikólaos (Crete); weekend caique from Finíki, Kárpathos. **Port authority**: t 224 504 1288.

By road: three taxis and an irregular bus service in the summer are all you get.

Tourist Information

Kássos Maritime Tourist Agency, t 224 504 1323, *www.kassos-island.gr*.

Where to Stay and Eat

Kássos ☒ 85800

Anagennissis, t 224 504 1323, f 224 504 1036 (*C; moderate–inexpensive*). Comfortable and run by an engaging Kassiot-American. *Open all year.*

Anessis, t 224 504 1201 (*C; moderate–inexpensive*). Similar, but you'll pay a bit less.

Borianoula Apartments, t 224 504 1495, f 224 504 1036. A self-catering option.

Oraia Bouka. Taverna overlooking the port in Fri, and as good as it looks.

Kassos, by the town hall. Newly refurbished, serving good standard dishes.

Milos, t 224 504 1825, facing the sea and **Karayiannakis**, t 224 504 1390, behind the Anagennissis, are also recommended for Greek classics and fish.

The North Aegean Islands

20

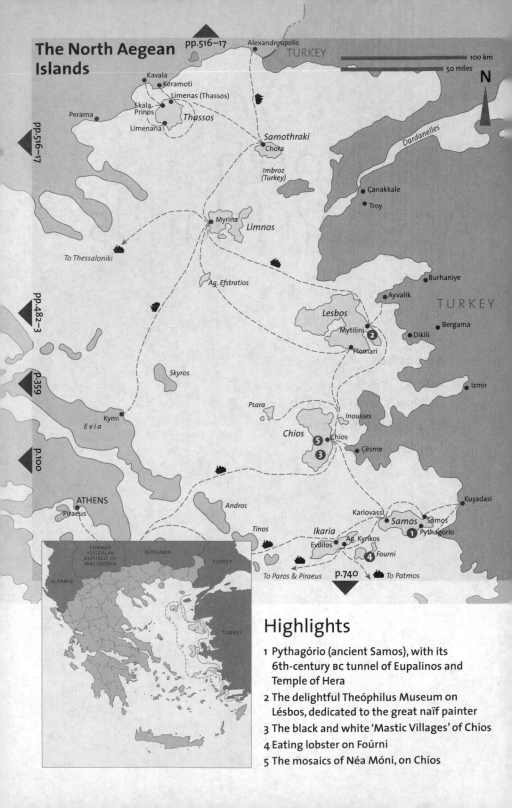

The North Aegean Islands

Highlights

1 Pythagório (ancient Samos), with its 6th-century BC tunnel of Eupalinos and Temple of Hera
2 The delightful Theóphilus Museum on Lésbos, dedicated to the great naïf painter
3 The black and white 'Mastic Villages' of Chíos
4 Eating lobster on Foúrni
5 The mosaics of Néa Móni, on Chíos

The North Aegean islands – Ikaría, Sámos, Chíos, Lésbos and Límnos plus a handful of islets – have such strong personalities that they have only their location near Turkey in common. Their city-states were among the most important in Greece between the 7th and 6th centuries BC, and they seeded their share of Western civilization, led by the likes of Pythagoras, Sappho and probably Homer himself. Although prosperous, fertile and famous for their wine, these islands slipped into obscurity as they fell prey to the greater powers – Persians, Athenians and then the Ottomans – until they were annexed to Greece in 1912. With the exception of Sámos and its package holiday playgrounds, the North Aegean is the last frontier in Greek island tourism; although they have all the ingredients – beaches, scenery, art, charming villages and even airports – their economies are strong enough to do without it. Rarely cat-calendar cute, they defy the stereotypes, and are all the better for it. For Samothráki and Thássos, *see* **Northern Greece**, pp.610–12 and 595–600.

Ikaría (IKAPIA)

A long mountain in the sea, its peaks often lost in billowing cloud, Ikaría swims in one of the wildest corners of the Aegean; if it's calm on one side of the mountain it's blustery on the other, whipping up rainbows of sea mist. Forget the myth: it was the wind that downed Icarus here. Yet what looks forbidding from the sea is often beautiful close up: both the north coast (with a monopoly on sandy beaches) and the south are watered by springs that keep them under oak, pine and plane trees. Best of all, life here is at such a slow pace that the locals joke about living in their own time zone. Development, too, has been slow, and in recent years Ikaría has been held up as a microcosm of environmental and economic sustainability.

Under the Byzantines the island was used to exile court officials; over time the population began to take the airs of those 'born in the purple', and to this day Ikarians retain a reputation for mild eccentricity. On 17 July 1912 (today the occasion for the island's biggest festival) the local doctor and priest led the island's velvet revolution (they put the handful of Turkish administrators on a boat and said farewell) and for five months Ikaría was an independent state with its own flag, stamps and anthem. During the Civil War (1946–9) and junta (1967–74) Ikaría was a dumping ground for left-wing dissidents; at one point there were 15,000, twice the number of Ikarians. Like the Byzantine nobles, their presence influenced the locals; although the Communists rarely win elections on the 'Red Rock', they are strong enough to decide who does.

Ag. Kýrikos and the South Coast
Ag. Kýrikos is the port and commercial heart of Ikaría, a town 'obviously designed by a drunken postman', according to Lawrence Durrell. It has a tiny centre of shops, rooms, banks, travel agents and a bakery unchanged since the 1930s. Outside of this little knot, forget urban density; every Ikarian cultivates his or her own garden in the mountain amphitheatre above. If you arrive by sea, the first thing you'll see are two tall girders holding a nose-diving metal *Icarus* as if in a pair of giant tweezers.

For decades tourism on Ikaría has meant **Thérma**, a seaside spa just east of Ágios, where hot springs – the most radioactive in Europe – bubble up from the earth at 33–55°C and are used to treat chronic rheumatism; one spring called Artemidas is so strong (790 degrees of radiation) that it's closed to the public. From here, the new airport road leads east out to **Fanári**, a slice of old Greece with a row of ramshackle bars overlooking a shingly beach and shallow sea safe for children. A dirt road continues towards the very end of the cape, marked by the best preserved **Hellenistic tower** in Greece; an entire castle stood here, until Admiral Miaoúlis sailed by during the War of Independence and used it for target practice. It protected the ancient **Drakanón**, a town sacred to Dionysos, but only a few 5th-century BC walls survive.

The cliff-ridden coast west of Ag. Kýrikos has more springs; one by the beach at **Thérma Lefkáda** (signposted 'hot water' by the road) bubbles out of the sea so hot that picnickers use it to boil their eggs. The road then passes below the **Evangelístrias** monastery (1775), with a pretty slate-roofed church and precisely one nun. The little theatre by the sea was first used in June 2001 to light the torch for the Ikariad Games, dedicated to non-motorized air sport, which take place every four years around the world. Tucked on the coast beyond a granite spur, **Xilosírti** is spread out among apricot orchards with a beach of large smooth pebbles; to the west a rock by the beach at Livádi marks the spot where Icarus plummeted into the sea. Above Xilosírti the road climbs to **Chrysóstomos** and **Playa**, with a big yellow church. After a rough patch, there's a fork in the road: the dramatic new paved road to the north side of Ikaría passes through wild west scenery on the way to **Kosíkia**, guarded by the ruined 10th-century Byzantine **Nikariás castle**; or, if you have a jeep, you can continue west along the south coast through a tunnel to **Manganítis** (or go by caique from Ágios). The rubble from blasting the tunnel is now a stunning beach dubbed **Seychelles**.

Ikaría's North Coast

Ikaría's northern half attracts far more tourists, with its forests, vineyards, sandy beaches and excellent roads. From Ag. Kýrikos a long, winding road climbs up to the barren mountain pass with its seven windmills, taking in views as far as Náxos before

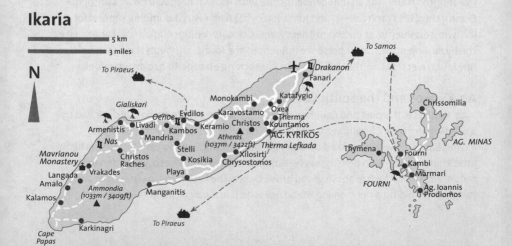

Ikaría

Getting There and Around

By air: the airport is at Fanári, t 227 502 2981, 13km east of Ag. Kýrikos; Olympic has connections four times weekly with Athens, six times in the summer (tickets t 227 502 2214). A bus (€3) links Ag. Kýrikos to flights.

By sea: Ikaría has two ports, and ships serve one or the other. In summer, NEL Superfast Ferries (t 210 411 5015) from Piraeus take only 4½ hours to either Ag. Kýrikos or Évdilos en route to Sámos. Year-round daily ferries cost half as much, but take 12hrs. Summer **hydrofoils** run four times a week to Pátmos, and three times to Sámos. **Port authority**: Ag. Kýrikos, t 227 502 2207; Évdilos, t 227 503 1007.

By road: buses run once or twice a day from Ag. Kýrikos to Évdilos, with summer connections to Armenistís (the trip takes over an hour). **Taxis** are used to making long-haul trips and sharing is common. There are car hire places in both ports.

Tourist Information

Ikariada Travel: t 227 502 3322, in Ag. Kýrikos.
Nas Travel: t 227 503 1947 in Évdilos, and t 227 507 1396 in Armenistís.

Where to Stay and Eat

Ag. Kýrikos ⊠ 83300

Maria Elena, t 227 502 2835, f 227 502 2223 (*B pension; moderate*). Pristine and pleasant just above town, with 16 airy rooms and seven studios, all with balcony.
Kastro, t 227 502 3480/3770, f 227 502 3700 (*C; moderate*). In the centre; tasteful.
Adam's, t 227 502 2418 (*C; moderate*). Similar comfort and prices. *Open all year.*
Isabella's, t 227 502 2839 (*E; inexpensive*). Right in the centre, with a restaurant and pool.
Klimataria. Reliable old restaurant serving delicious moussaká and old-fashioned *ládera* in the heart of Ágios. *Open all year.*
Filoti. Also in the centre, specializing in excellent pizzas and pasta dishes.

Évdilos ⊠ 83302

Atheras-Kerame, t 227 503 1434, f 227 503 1926, winter in Athens t 210 685 8096 (*B; expensive–moderate*). A handsome hotel, partly in a 19th-century building, with a restaurant and bar, pool, gym. Also 20 apartments by the beach. *Open May–Oct.*
Evdoxia, t 227 503 1502, f 227 503 1571 (*C; moderate–inexpensive*). Up the hill

swooping down in a corniche to villages immersed in the trees and **Évdilos**, a picturesque port, with a town beach, **Fytema**, to the west. Just inland lies **Kámbos**, on the site of Oenoe, the ancient capital of Ikaría, famous in Homer for its wine. Exiled Byzantine princelings installed themselves here; the columns and arches of their palace remain, as well as their slate-roofed church, **Ag. Iríni**. The adjacent museum (Vassílis Dionysos has the key; he may well throw in a free guided tour) houses local finds and a 5th-century BC inscription reading 'All Ikarians are liars', modified over the years to 'Jews' or 'Turks' or whoever was out of favour. In the nearby village of **Pygí**, the slate-roofed **Moní Theoktisti** has the finest frescoes on the island.

Further west along the coast, **Gialiskári** has Ikaría's most beautiful sandy beaches: **Messakti**, where a tiny blue-domed church sits on a spit of land, and **Livádi**, over the next headland. The old fishing village of **Armenistís** is now a big resort – big by local standards at any rate. Above it waits the lovely forested region of Rachés, where the main village, wine-growing **Christós Rachés**, is the most Ikarian of Ikaría's villages, and famous for keeping very late hours in its old-fashioned shops and tavernas. This is also one of the best places for walks, with some 24km of trails; a local group has produced a good map, with explanations in English. One excursion is to the 13th-century convent at **Mounté** with wall paintings. An unpaved road to the south leads towards Pezi and a pretty little **lake**.

overlooking the port, all rooms with balcony, mini bar and TV; plus a restaurant.

Dionysos, in Kámbos, **t** 227 503 1300 (*inexpensive*). Out by ancient Oenoe; comfortable rooms owned by the irrepressible and very knowledgeable Vassilis.

To Fytema (tis Popis), **t** 227 503 1928. Lush garden and home-grown ingredients: try *soufikó* (Ikarian ratatouille) and the stuffed courgette flowers. *Open Mar–Nov.*

Armenistís and Gialiskári ✉ 83301

Erofili Beach, near Livádi Beach, **t** 227 507 1058, **f** 227 507 1483, *www.islandikaria.com/erofili.htm* (*A; expensive*). Intimate, beautifully appointed hotel (most rooms have sea views) with indoor seawater pool and jacuzzi; buffet breakfasts. *Open May–Oct.*

Messakti Village, Gialiskári, **t** 227 507 1331, **f** 227 507 1330, in Athens **t** 210 621 9112, **f** 210 621 6684 (*B; expensive–moderate*). Attractive island architecture and slate floors; rooms have kitchenettes and overlook the pool and sandy beach.

Daidalos, **t** 227 507 1390, **f** 227 507 1393, in Athens **t** 210 922 9034, **f** 210 923 5453 (*C; moderate*). Traditionally furnished , with a pool, garden and restaurant.

Dimitris Ioannidopoulos, **t** 227 507 1310 (*inexpensive*). Hillside studios and apartments amongst a veritable forest of flowers.

Atsahas, above Livádi beach, **t** 227 507 1049. A refreshing setting and light Ikarian delicacies such as carrot pies (*karotópita*). They also have rooms. *Open May–Sept.*

Paskalia (aka Vlachos), **t** 227 507 1302. Some of the best food in Armenistís comes from this kitchen; good-value rooms above.

Kelari (Kastanias) at Gialiskári, **t** 227 507 1227. The best of several fish tavernas overlooking the little port, patrolled by well-fed cats.

Christós Rachés ✉ 83301

Raches, **t** 227 504 1269 (*B; moderate*). Peace and quiet and meals in the evening. *Open June–Oct.*

Nas ✉ 83301

Anna, **t** 227 507 1489. The first taverna on the right when coming from Armenistís; delightful owners and excellent traditional Ikarian dishes, wine and seafood.

Astra, **t** 227 507 1255. Views over the beach and seafood (including tender octopus), courgette *beignets* and other dishes, with excellent local wine.

West of Armenistís, **Nas** (from *naos*, or temple) is marked by excellent fish tavernas on a ledge, and a path leads down to a pebble beach in the ancient harbour, where you can swim (costume optional) into a series of caves for some excellent snorkelling. Behind, by the Chalaris river , are the platform and foundations of the 5th-century BC **Temple of Artemis Tavrópolio**. A marvellous statue of the goddess, with eyes that followed the viewer from every angle, was discovered in the 19th century – but the local priest immediately had it thrown in the lime kiln. Beyond Nas, a white road continues southwest to the sweet whitewashed, slate-roofed **Monastery of Mavrianoú**, next to an old threshing floor; the village above, **Vrakádes**, has a pair of cafés. If you're feeling especially adventurous, carry on south to **Karkinágri**, an isolated village with a tiny port (boat three times a week to Ag. Kýrikos), a taverna and a few rooms. This whole area is a good place to find 'pirate houses'– low stone buildings, often under huge boulders, where people hid when they spied the Jolly Roger.

Foúrni (ΦΟΥΡΝΟΥΣ)

If Ikaría is too cosmopolitan, try Foúrni, a rugged, friendly and utterly Greek mini-archipelago midway between Sámos and Ikaría. The larger, hook-shaped island embraces a huge sheltered bay used by pirates to pounce on passing ships; modern

Greeks only dared to settle here in 1775. By then Foúrni had been denuded by charcoal burners from Sámos and Ikaría. But the sea here is 'the lair of fish', especially of red mullet and clawless Mediterranean lobster which, although plentiful, isn't cheap. Many fish by night, using bright lamps that set the sea aglitter.

Half of Foúrni's 1,600 souls live around the port, **Foúrni**, a picturesque web of lanes with a winsome ramshackleness: nearly everyone meets in the lovely plane-shaded square with its old-fashioned *kafeneía*. Just north, up the steps, a path leads to the beaches of **Psilí Ammo** and **Kálamos**. Further, the new road ends up at **Chrissomiliá**; the perfect retreat to write your next novel, with beaches, rooms and two tavernas.

A 15min walk south of the port, **Kámbi**, the 'capital', is a pleasant little place under trees, with a few rooms and a tamarisk-lined beach. From here you can arrange boat trips to **Marmári**, a cove just south, where the ancients quarried marble to build Ephesus, or sail further south to Vlycháda beach. At Foúrni's baby islet **Thýmena**, you'll be stared at if you disembark; bring your own food and sleep under the stars.

Sámos (ΣΑΜΟΣ)

The 'Isle of the Blest', famed for its wine, ships and enormous Temple of Hera, Sámos has always been a very important island. Pines, olives and vines cover its emerald hills, so fertile that Menander wrote in the 4th century BC 'even the hens give milk'. Landscapes range from bucolic to spectacular; the coast is indented with sandy coves and two mountains, Ámbelos (3,740ft) and Kérkis (4,740ft), furnish imposing backdrops. Two famous couples, Zeus and Hera and Antony and Cleopatra, chose Sámos for their dallying, and even today it caters to honeymooners, in hotels instead of gilded barges. Nevertheless, take gold, not gilt; this is an expensive island, and one where you definitely need to book a bed.

History

When Ionians fleeing the Dorian invasion of mainland Greece arrived in Sámos in the 11th century, they found it had two tremendous advantages: its fertility and its position on the only safe all-weather route across the Aegean – a position that made

Getting There and Around

By air: charters from northern Europe, plus five daily flights from Athens on Olympic (t 227 302 7237 in Sámos) and Aegean/ Cronus. Olympic also flies twice weekly to Thessaloníki. The **airport, t** 227 306 1219, is linked by bus four times a day to Sámos (17km) and Pythagório (4km). Consider a taxi.

By sea: Sámos has three ports – Sámos (Vathí), Karlóvassi and Pythagório. In summer, NEL Superfast Ferries (**t** 210 411 5015) cut the journey down to 5½ hours. Slow ferries link Sámos daily with Piraeus, Ikaría and Pátmos, five to six times a week with Kálymnos, Kos,

Léros and Lipsí; also with Chíos, Lésbos, Agathónissi, Mýkonos, Rhodes, Sýros, Páros, Náxos, Límnos, Thessaloníki and Alexandroúpolis. **Port authority**: Sámos (Vathí), **t** 227 302 7890; Karlóvassi, **t** 227 303 0888; Pythagório, **t** 227 306 1225.

By road: from the **bus** station on Ioannou Lekáti St (a 10min walk from the dock at Sámos Town), **t** 227 302 7270, buses run to Pythagório, Ag. Konstantínos, Karlóvassi, Kokkári, Tsamadoú; five to six times a day to Mytilíni and Chóra; four to Heréon and the airport; and once to Marathókampos, Votsalákia and Pírgos. **Taxis**: Sámos, **t** 227 302 8404, Pythagório, **t** 227 306 1450.

it the eternal rival of Miletus in Asia Minor. Early on the islanders invented a swift warship, the *sámaina*, and sailed to Libya and Egypt; in 640 BC, one of them, Kolaios, became the first Greek to pass through the Straits of Gibraltar. In 550 BC, the tyrant of Seamos Polykrates, according to Herodotus the first to understand sea power, ruled the Aegean with his 150 *samainae*, extracting tolls and protection money. Polykrates lavishly patronized the arts and poetry (the great poet Anacreon lived in his court, although he quarrelled with his great contemporary Pythagoras) and funded vast public works, including the great Temple of Hera; the Samians loved luxury so much that they tore down their *palaestra* to build pleasure dens with names like 'Samian Flowers' and the 'Samian Hotbed'. The party ended when Polykrates was lured to the mainland by a Persian satrap, and crucified. In 480 BC the Persian fleet occupied Sámos, until it was defeated by the Greeks in the Battle of Mykále. Sámos then became a democracy and Athenian ally – until Miletus joined the alliance. Sámos reneged, and defeated an Athenian fleet sent by Pericles in 441, before finally capitulating in 391 BC. When the island tried to regain its independence in 365, Athens exiled every last person, replacing them with Athenians until Alexander ordered their return in 321. Later the Ptolemies of Egypt favoured it, and after 129 BC so did Rome.

After the sack of Constantinople, Sámos was ruled by the Venetians and Genoese. When the Turks took it in 1453, the inhabitants left virtually en masse for Chíos. With promises of privileges and a certain amount of autonomy, the Ottomans repopulated the island with Greeks from elsewhere (reflected in many village names). They later joined the revolution and defeated the Turks at a second Battle of Mykále in 1824. Although the Powers excluded Sámos from Greece in 1830, it was granted semi-independence under a Christian governor until union in 1912.

Sámos Town

Sámos Town (or 'Vathí' on ferry schedules) has a magnificent harbour under an amphitheatre of green hills. The older, upper part of town, **Vathí**, with its white and pastel houses under weathered tile roofs, has the monopoly on atmosphere but,

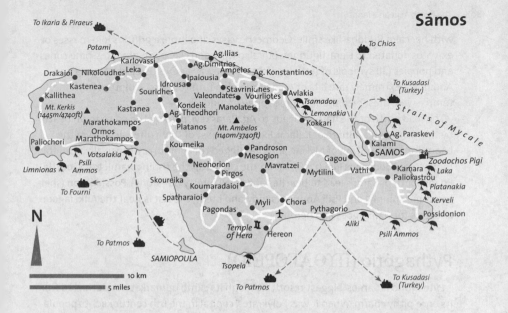

Map labels:

To Ikaria & Piraeus · Potami · Karlovassi · Leka · Nikoloudhes · Drakaioi · Kastenea · Kallithea · Mt. Kerkis (1445m/4740ft) · Kastanea · Idrousa · Souridhes · Marathokampos Ormos · Marathokampos · Paliochori · Votsalakia · Psili Ammos · Limnionas · Skoureika · Spatharaioi · To Fourni · Koumeika · Neohorion · Pirgos · Koumaradaioi · Pagondas · Myli · Temple of Hera · Hereon · SAMIOPOULA · Tsopela · To Patmos · Ag.Ilias · Ag.Dimitrios · Ampelos · Ag. Konstantinos · Ipaiousia · Stavriniides · Valeondates · Vourliotes · Avlakia · Kondeik · Ag. Theodhori · Manolates · Tsamadou · Lemonakia · Platanos · Ag. Theodhori · Mt. Ambelos (1140m/3740ft) · Kokkari · Pandroson · Mesogion · Mavratzei · Chora · Pythagorio · Aliki · Gagou · Mytilini · Vathi · SAMOS · Kalami · Ag. Paraskevi · Zoodochos Pigi · Kamara · Laka · Paliokastrou · Platanakia · Kerveli · Possidonion · Psili Ammos · To Chios · To Kusadasi (Turkey) · Straits of Mycale · To Kusadasi (Turkey) · To Patmos

N · 10 km · 5 miles

down by the sea, life buzzes around palmy **Plateía Pythagório**, guarded by an apt stone lion; Pythagorians believed that the lion was the highest animal a transmigrating soul could lodge in (the highest plant, if you took a botanical route, was laurel). By the municipal gardens, the superb **Archaeological Museum** (*t 227 302 7469; open Tues–Sun 8–2.30; adm*) gives top billing to a set of Archaic statues known as the Geneleos Group (*c. 550 BC*). Made of local marble and dressed in pleats as fine as pinstripes, they are a prelude to the majestic 18ft *kouros* from the Temple of Hera,

Tourist Information

EOT: Martíou St, Sámos Town, **t** 227 302 8530; *open 9–2 Mon–Fri*. The free *Summer Days* suggests good walks.
Tourist police: Sámos Town, **t** 227 302 7333.
British Vice Consulate: 15 Themístokli Sofoúli St, Sámos Town, **t** 227 302 7314.

Where to Stay and Eat

Sámos ✉ 83100

Hotels get block-booked in season; try at the travel offices lining the waterfront if you arrive and everywhere seems full.
Kirki Beach, **t** 227 302 3030 (*B; expensive*). A new, upmarket hotel at Kalámi, with a swimming pool.
Aeolis, 33 Them. Sofoúli, **t** 227 302 8904, **f** 227 302 8063, *aeolis@gemini.diavlos.gr* (*B; moderate*). Stylish, on the water, with petite pool and rooftop bar. *Open all year*.
Galaxy, inland a bit, **t** 227 302 2665, **f** 227 302 7679 (*C; moderate*). Rooms facing a leafy pool. *Open Mar–Oct*.
Samos, by the port, **t** 227 302 8377, **f** 227 302 8482, *hotsamos@otenet.gr* (*C; inexpensive*). Impersonal, but good value and sea views from the roof (with pool and bar).
Avli, **t** 227 302 2939 (*inexpensive*). Delightful; a former convent with a shady courtyard. The simple rooms are deliciously at odds with red moulded bathroom capsules.
Kotópoula, in the centre of town on Mykális and Vlamaris, 5mins up Lekáti Street, **t** 227 302 8415. Excellent vine-covered taverna and favourite of the locals.
Agrabeli, Áno Vathí. Under the vines, sample local specialities, such as fried chickpea balls.

with her calm Buddha-like smile. Geometric vases and bronze griffons join masses of ex-votos donated to Hera: figurines, but also ivory and clay pomegranates, pine cones and poppies (all symbols of fertility), from as far away as Cyprus, Egypt, Etruria and Andalucía. Extremely rare bits of Archaic wooden furniture and sculpture from the temple were preserved thanks to the soggy ground.

The road north of the harbour leads to **Ag. Paraskeví**, passing the so-so town beach, by the fashionable suburb of **Kalámi**. Excursions east of town offer views over the beautiful, narrow Strait of Mykále and the rugged coast of Turkey, especially from the monastery **Zoodóchos Pigí** (1756), set on the cliffs over the fishing hamlet of **Mourtiá**. Roads south of Sámos lead to beaches at **Kervelí** (pretty but stony), **Possidónion** (sheltered and shingly) and **Psilí Ámmos** (sandy, and busy); the last is near the **Áliki** lagoon, a reserve for flamingoes and herons.

Pythagório (ΠΥΘΑΓΟΡΕΙΟ)

Pythagório is Sámos' biggest resort, although its climb upmarket has detracted from its once pithy charm. When it was Polykrates' capital in the 6th century BC, its population was 300,000; by the 20th century it was just another fishing village called Tigáni, 'frying pan', after its circular harbour. In 1955 Tigáni was renamed again to honour is most famous son, synonymous with the theorem that made him famous in every school in the world. It was not just a brilliant theorem, but the very first theorem: Pythagoras was the first to apply the philosophical 'proofs' of earlier philosophers to mathematics. But he was hardly the last one on Sámos to think daring thoughts: in the 5th century BC Melissus wrote of the essential unity of creation; and two centuries

Tourist Information

Tourist information office: on the Pythagório main street, t 227 306 1389, f 227 306 1022; *open 8am–10pm*. Help with accommodation, day trips and excursions.
Tourist police: Pythagório, t 227 306 1333.

Where to Stay and Eat

Pythagório ✉ 83103
Doryssa Bay, Potokáki, t 227 306 1360, f 227 306 1463, *doryssa@gemini.diavlos.forthnet.gr* (*A; luxury*). Luxurious hotel rooms or air-conditioned bungalows; pool, tennis courts, watersports and a mini golf course. *Open April–Oct.*
Glycoriza Beach, t 227 306 1321, f 227 306 1596, *glbeach@gemini.diavlos.gr* (*C; moderate*). Another good out-of-town choice by the sea with pool.

Hera II, t 227 306 1879, f 227 306 1196 (*C; moderate*). Cool, pink establishment; elegant with panoramic town and sea views.
Areli Studios, t 227 306 1245, f 227 306 2320 (*inexpensive*). Some of the most pristine studios in the Aegean, with an olive grove and flowers between you and the road.
Alexandra Rooms, t 227 306 1429 (*D; inexpensive*). Simple, shaded and charming.
Stratos, t 227 306 1157, f 227 306 1881, *vasiliades@aol.com* (*C; inexpensive*). Non-smoking; rooms of varying prices under the aegis of an affable Greek American.
Maritsa, t 227 306 1957, just in from the harbour. Excellent octopus, slow service.
Platania, under plane trees in the main square. Huge portions and good *saganáki*.
Psarades, east of Heréon at Ag. Nikoláos, t 227 303 2489. Excellent fresh fish along with dreamy sunsets over the sea.
Consider taking a taxi up to Chóra for its tavernas, **Andonis** or **Sintrofia**.

Pythagoras: Geometry, Beans and the Music of the Spheres

As fundamental as Pythagoras is to a great deal of later Greek thinking, he never wrote anything down, so we only know him through the writings of his friends or enemies. Born on Sámos around 580 BC, he visited Egypt and Babylonia, before or after a quarrel with Polykrates sent him packing to Croton in southern Italy. There, he and his followers formed a brotherhood 'of the best' and ruled the city for 20 years. It was a secret society, like Freemasonry, and spread throughout the Greek world; members recognized each other by a symbol – the pentangle. Pythagoras taught that after death the soul transmigrated into new humans or plants and animals. By purifying the soul one might improve it, and perhaps escape the need for reincarnation. There were prohibitions on eating meat and, surprisingly, fava beans – although it has recently been shown that he wasn't talking beans at all; the Greeks used letters for numbers, and what reads 'lay off fava beans' is really another theorem, on angles.

Pythagoras was the first to apply *kosmos*, meaning arrangement and ornamentation (hence our 'cosmetics') to the universe. This order was based on the connections of its parts called *harmonia*, and *harmonia* was based on numbers. He discovered that music could be expressed mathematically by ratios and the tuning of the seven-string lyre, and he extended that *harmonia* to 'the music of the spheres', the motions of the seven planets (the five visible ones, and the moon and sun) – and to the Golden Mean, the base of the proportions of Classical architecture and sculpture. The key idea was that the study of the order of the Cosmos and its harmony would help to eliminate the disorder in our souls. No one agreed more than Johannes Kepler, who formulated the Third Law of Planetary Motion (1619): 'The square of the period of revolution is proportional to the cube of the mean distance from the sun.' Kepler noted that the varying speeds of the planets' revolutions corresponded with the ratios in Renaissance polyphonies; in 1980, NASA scientists packed aboard *Voyager* for its journey out of our solar system a computer-generated recording of Pythagoras' and Kepler's music of the spheres.

later the brilliant Aristarchus, attempting to account for the retrograde motion of Mars, concluded that the Earth was a mere planet among planets and that they all circled the sun. This proved to be too radical for many people at the time, as it would be when Copernicus declared the same thing in the 16th century.

The 1,180ft **harbour mole** built by Eupalinos of Mégara, Polykrates' engineering genius, was considered a marvel in its day. It now supports a new harbour wall, where yachts bask instead of sharp-bowed *samainae*. Behind that, at the beginning of a long sand and pebble beach, Lykúrgos Logothétis, a hero of the 1821 revolution, built the **castle**, mostly at the expense of the Temple of Hera. There's a small **Archaeological Museum** in the town hall (*t 227 306 1400; open Tues–Sun 8.45–2*), housing local Archaic-era finds. West of town, little remains of the **Roman Baths** (*t 227 306 1400; open Tues–Sun 8.30–2.45*), but in summer the nearby ancient **theatre** has concerts. A road from here leads up to a **cave** where the sybil Phyto prophesied one true god, a justification for later Christian interest in pagan antiquity; it now shelters the church of **Panagía Spilianí**. The left branch of the road from the theatre leads in 500m to the extraordinary **Eupalinion Tunnel** (*open Tues–Sun 8.45– 2.40; adm*) which brought water to the town. Under Eupalinos two crews of slaves started digging through almost a kilometre of solid rock and met only a few inches off total Channel Tunnel perfection. The tunnel's pipes worked fine until the 6th century AD, after which the tunnel was forgotten until it was rediscovered in the 1890s. Lamps and tools were found in the parallel maintenance tunnel, just where workmen had left them. Visitors are allowed in the first 700m, to where the tunnel has collapsed. You can follow the traces of the city's **long walls** up the slope from here; they once measured 7km.

The Temple of Hera

An 8km **Sacred Way** (now 90 per cent under the airport), entirely paved in marble by an unknown Roman emperor, led from Pythagório, past 2,000 statues, tombs and monuments to the **Temple of Hera** (*t 227 3069 5277; open Tues–Sun 8.30–2.45; adm*). Worship here goes back to 2500 BC, and at some point the deity assumed the name of Hera, a powerful fertility goddess who renewed her virginity (and thus nature) yearly in the Imbrassos river. Her cult 'statue' was a crudely painted plank that fell from heaven, too sacred to be touched, so the priests tied it with twigs of osier to carry it. Twice a year great celebrations took place: the Heraia, in honour of her marriage to Zeus (Sámos hosted their 300-year-long wedding night), and the Tonea, recalling the attempt by pirates to snatch the sacred plank, only to be thwarted by the goddess, who nailed their ship to the waves. Her earliest temples were of mud, wood and bricks, until 560 BC, when a huge Ionic temple in stone was built. There may have been some problem with the marshy ground because soon after Polykrates replaced it with a colossus, the third largest ever built by the Greeks (354 by 165ft). Raiding Herulians in the 4th century AD damaged it; earthquakes and builders looking for ready-cut stone finished it off. Out of the original 155 columns, only one, resembling a stack of breath mints, was spared as a landmark for ships. Around it lie foundations of small temples or treasuries, stoas, statue bases, and the apse of a Christian basilica, along with the base of the monumental 140ft **altar**. The remains of animal sacrifices here yielded no thigh bones, confirming Homer's descriptions of the treatment given to that cut of meat.

Héreon and Southeast Sámos

The nearby seaside village of **Héreon** has hotels on a shingle beach that can get crowded, although caiques run south to the quieter beach of **Tsopela**. Inland villages offer respite as well, especially lively **Chóra**, the island capital from 1560 to 1855. To the north, the road passes through a steep valley to the sprawling village of **Mytilíni**, where fossils dating back 15 million years are gathered in Greece's only **Palaeontological Museum** in the Dimarchíon (*open Mon–Sat 9–2 and some after-noons; call ahead, t 227 305 2055*). The prize exhibit, among the skulls of prehistoric hippopotami and rhinoceroses, is a 13-million-year-old horse brain. Lemon groves surround **Mýli**, the source of the Imbrassos river, where a Mycenaean tomb was found near the school. From well-watered **Pagóndas**, the road circles through fine untamed scenery en route to **Spatharáioi** (7.5km) and **Pírgos** (another 6km), with a lush ravine whose clear waters and cool air should attract nymphs but instead get tour buses at its lovely taverna. From Pírgos you can circle around back towards Pythagório without retracing your steps by way of **Koumaradáioi**, where a track leads up to the **Moní Megális Panagías**, founded in 1586. North of here, **Mavratzeí** is one of Sámos' pottery villages, specializing in goofy 'Pythagorean Cups'; the main road heads back to Chóra.

Along the North Coast and Western Sámos

Celebrated in antiquity but neglected in the Middle Ages, Samian wine began its comeback under the Greek settlers brought over by the Ottomans in the late 1500s. By the 18th century its muscat was imported in large quantities to Sweden and even to France; in 1982, its prized light, amber Grand Cru Vin Doux Naturel was given a French *appellation* (the only Greek wine so honoured). Wines are aged in oak barrels in handsome stone warehouses called *tavérnes* in and around **Malagári**, on the bay west of Sámos Town; since 1933, it has been the seat of the island cooperative. Ten km west of Vathí, the erstwhile fishing village of **Kokkári**, beautifully set on two narrow headlands, is package-holiday heaven, with its own beach and others at **Lemonákia**, a 20-minute walk away, and **Tsamadoú** (partly nudist), a beautiful pebble crescent 2km west, then a steep descent. Further west, **Avlákia** is a delightfully low-key place to stay and a good base for exploring the ravishing hinterland (although scarred by a forest fire in 2000), where cypresses and pines rise up like towers along the lovely slopes of **Mount Ámbelos** or 'Mount Vineyard' (3,783ft). The north-facing villages here are Sámos' top wine-growers, where vines are planted on terraces up to 2,624ft and, like all quality dessert wines, have an extremely low yield. From the handsome wine village of **Vourliótes**, it's a delightful, leafy 3km walk up to Sámos' oldest monastery, **Panagía Vrontiáni**, founded in 1560. Just west, a road leads up to **Manolátes**, a beauty spot overlooking a valley beloved by nightingales. Or you can head down to anticlimactic **Ag. Konstantínos**, quieter and rawer than the other beach resorts.

Karlóvassi and Western Sámos

Wallflower **Karlóvassi**, Sámos' second city, was once a tanning centre; empty warehouses along the port offer a baleful hello. It's divided, in descending order of interest, into old, middle and new (Paléo, Meséo and Néo). Visitors prefer the picturesque old quarter, also called Limáni, although Néo Karlóvassi has the bus stop, banks, post office and the timeless **Paradise** *ouzerie*. A city bus goes to the fine sweep of beach and fish tavernas at **Potámi**, 2km west, where a stream joins the sea; naturalists flock here for its butterflies, dragonflies and rare orchids.

Less visited western Sámos is rich in the scenery and beach departments. A track from Potámi leads back to the 10th-century **Panagía tou Potamoú**, Sámos' oldest church, and, if you carry on, to a magical river canyon with chilly rock pools and tiny

Tourist Information

Tourist police: Kokkári, t 227 309 2333; Karló-vassi, t 227 303 3333.

Where to Stay and Eat

Kokkári ✉ 83100

Most of the accommodation here, and there is plenty, is packaged in season.

Kalidon Palace, t 227 309 2800, f 227 309 2573, *www.kalidonpalace.gr (A; expensive)*. Beautiful setting and views over Kokkári Bay, and a short walk to the beaches. *Open 15 April–Oct.*

Arion, 500m above Kokkári, t 227 309 2020, f 227 309 2006, *arion@gemini.diavlos.gr (A; expensive)*. Traditional style, with shady lawns; pool, sauna and shuttle bus to Kokkári. *Open May–Oct.*

Olympia Village, t 227 309 2420, f 227 309 2457, *www.olympiavillage.gr (expensive)*. Bungalows in a flowery complex. *Open May–Oct.*

Paradisos, t 227 309 2162 *(moderate)*. Moderately priced studios near the Arion.

Kima, on the water's edge (€12). Tasty, freshly prepared Greek dishes.

Avlákia/Vourliótes/Manolátes ✉ 83100

Avlákia, in Avlákia, t 227 309 4230 *(C; inexpensive)*. Very pleasant old-fashioned hotel right on the beach, with **Oscar,** its restaurant, on the strand.

Markos, Vourliótes, t 227 309 3291 *(inexpensive)*. A peaceful and quiet place away from the sea.

Pigi Pnaka, Vourliótes, t 227 309 3380. Taverna next to a spring in a charming setting; try the chicken. *Open May–Oct.*

Angela's Studio, Manolátes, t 227 309 4478 *(inexpensive)*. Another peaceful spot; Angela has a shady, grassy garden from which to contemplate the hills.

Filia, Manolátes, t 227 309 4678. One of the best on Sámos, with especially tasty vegetarian dishes, packed full of flavour. Open lunch only. *Open May–Oct.*

Giorgides, Manolátes, t 227 309 4239. Delightful taverna spilling out on both sides of the street.

Loukas, at the top of Manolátes with views of hills and sea; home-made olive oil, cheese, wine and *suma* (a local schnapps), plus stuffed courgette flowers in season.

Karlóvassi ✉ 83200

There are cheap rooms in Limáni, on the pedestrian lane behind the port road.

Samaina Inn, in Limáni, t 227 303 0401, f 227 303 4471 *(A; expensive)*. An international chain-style hotel with smart, cool rooms, large pool area and crèche. *Open May–Oct.*

Samaina Bay, t 227 303 0812 *(B; expensive)*. Same owners, less flashy but still with pool.

Aspasia, towards Potámi beach, t 227 303 2363, f 227 303 4777 *(B; moderate)*. Smart, with air-conditioning, a pool, roof garden and shuttle bus. *Open April–Oct.*

Merope, in Néo Karlóvassi, t 227 303 2650, f 227 303 2652 *(B; inexpensive)*. Old-world service; amazingly good value, with period rooms and collectors' TVs, as well as pool.

Kyma. Well-prepared *mezédes* by the seaside.

Ormos Márathokámpos ✉ 83102

Anthemousa Studios, t 227 303 7073 *(inexpensive)*. Up by the church in olive groves above the port, with views; the owner also has seafront studios and offers boat trips.

Kleopatra Studios, t 227 303 7486 *(inexpensive)*. Plain but decent; upstairs maisonettes have balconies and the kind owner has more flats right by the sea along the road.

Kerkis Bay, t 227 303 7202, f 227 303 7372 *(B; inexpensive)*. Plain, but a good restaurant.

There are also some 15 rooms to rent up in pretty **Plátanos.**

Limnionas ✉ 83102

Limnionas Bay, t 227 303 7057 *(moderate)*. Low-lying, whitewashed hotel with pool.

Limnionas Studios, t 227 303 1294 *(inexpensive)*. Beautifully secluded, with views.

Limnionas Taverna, on the beach. Small place with fish and traditional fare.

Sophia's Taverna. Just past the turning down to Limnionas on the main road.

waterfalls – but don't expect to have it to yourself in high season. There are superb sandy beaches at **Mikró Seitáni** (1km beyond Potámi) and **Megálo Seitáni** (4km) at the foot of a striking ravine (wear hiking shoes and pack your own provisions). The same path, one of the most stunning on Sámos, continues 8km along the towering west shore as far as **Drakáioi**, a farming village and time-capsule glimpse of traditional Greece served by a rough road from Marathókampos (rare buses). South of Drakáioi the road continues round, past **Kallithéa**, with rooms and food.

A rare bus runs from Karlóvassi to **Plátanos**, the island's second wine-growing area, then down to the sea via **Koumeïka** to a sand-pebble beach with shade known as **Ormós Koumíkou** or **Bállos**. A more westerly road south of Karlóvassi curls around the soaring mass of **Mount Kérkis**, a dormant volcano often crowned with a halo of mist like a remembrance of eruptions past; on hot days aim for **Kastanéa**, with chestnut groves and brooks. To the south, **Márathokámpos** is an attractive village of tiny lanes with some restored houses for guests. Below is the pleasantly low-key resort **Órmos Márathokámpos**, from where caiques sail several times a week to Samiopoúla, a tiny islet with a fine stretch of sand. West is the long white sandy beach of package resort **Votsalákia**, lined with tack and flashing lights. You can follow the path to the **Convent of the Evangelístria**, and beyond to the summit of Mount Kérkis (about six hours there and back, if you're fit). Or head west to the shallow seas at **Psilí Ámmos** and the sandy coves beyond, accessible by foot or boat. If you have a car, drive on to the delightful cove of **Limnionas**, with excellent swimming and relaxation guaranteed.

Chíos (ΧΙΟΣ)

Chíos, beloved of Poseidon, was named after the snow (*chioni*) that fell when the god was born. A wealthy island, celebrated for its cheerful good nature, shipowners and gum mastic that grows nowhere else in the world, Chíos runs the gamut from lush plains, pine forests and unspoiled beaches to scrublands and startlingly barren mountains that bring to mind the 'craggy Chíos' of Homer, a poet whom Chíots claim

Getting There and Around

By air: Olympic has four flights a day from Athens, two a week to/from Lésbos and Thessaloníki. Olympic at the airport: t 227 102 4515, in Chíos Town at 50 Leof. Aegeou, t 227 104 4727. The 4km journey between Chíos Town and runway can be made by taxi (under €12) or the blue Kondári–Kaifas bus (10 a day).

By sea: daily **ferry** connections with Piraeus, Lésbos and Inoússes; daily in summer to Çegme (Turkey), less frequently out of season; also with Límnos, Psará, Thessaloníki, Kavála, Ikaría, Kos, Rhodes, Mýkonos and Sýros; in summer **excursions** to Psará and Inoússes

(contact Miniotis Lines, 21 Neorion St, t 227 102 4671). Travel agents also offer organized tours to Turkey.

Port authority: Chíos Town, t 227 104 4433.

By road: urban blue **buses** (t 227 102 2079) make five to six trips daily to the Kámbos area, Karfás beach and Vrontádos. Green buses depart near Plateía Vounáki (t 227 102 4257) six to eight times daily to Pirgí, Mestá, Kalamotí, Katavakris and Nenita; four times to Kómi, Emborió, Kardámila, Lagáda and Ag. Fotiá. **Taxis**: t 227 104 1111. **Car rental**: the Travel Shop, 56 Leof. Aegeou, t 227 104 1031, f 227 104 1443, *travelshop@otenet.gr*. For **bikes** try Mr Psaras at 9 Omirou, t/f 227 102 5113.

Chíos

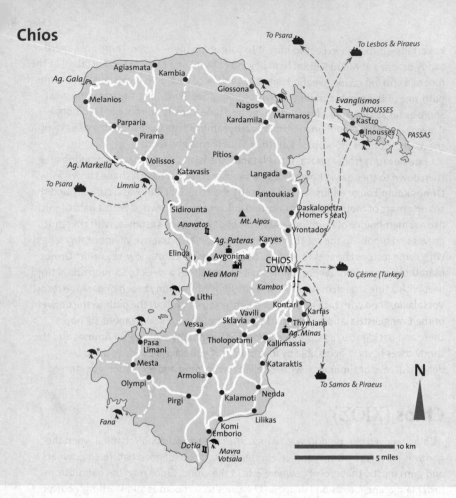

To Psara

To Lesbos & Piraeus

Ag. Gala
Agiasmata
Kambia
Giossona
Melanios
Nagos
Parparia
Pirama
Kardamila
Marmaros
Evanglismos
INOUSSES
Kastro
Inousses
PASSAS
Pitios
Ag. Markella
Volissos
Katavasis
Langada
To Psara
Limnia
Pantoukias
Sidirounta
Daskalopetra
(Homer's seat)
Anavatos
Mt. Aipos
Vrontados
Ag. Pateras
Karyes
Elinda
Avgonima
CHIOS
TOWN
Nea Moni
To Çesme (Turkey)
Kambos
Lithi
Kontari
Karfas
Vavili
Vessa
Sklavia
Thymiana
Ag. Minas
Tholopotami
Kallimassia
Pasa
Limani
Mesta
Kataraktis
Armolia
Olympi
Nenda
Pirgi
Kalamoti
Lilikas
Fana
Komi
Emborio
Dotia
Mavra
Votsala
To Samos & Piraeus

N

10 km
5 miles

as their own. The local architecture is just as beautiful and unique, from exquisite
Byzantine Néa Moní and Genoese country villas to the black and white *sgraffitoed*
Mastichoria. Tourism is not at all on the front burner here; the islanders want visitors
to share their deep love for Chíos rather than just take their money.

History

Settled by Pelasgians (*c.* 3000 BC), Mycenaeans and Ionians in turn, Chíos emerged
in Archaic times as a thriving, independent kingdom, renowned for mastic, wine,
sculpture (soldering was invented here) and its system of government, which Solon
adapted for his Athenian reforms. On the downside, Chíots were the first Greeks to
trade in slaves. The island managed to remain fairly independent in antiquity,
although it was ravaged by Athens when it pulled out of the Delian confederacy in
412 BC. In the 4th century AD Chíos defied Constantine the Great, and lost; as his booty
he carried off its famous statues, including the four bronze horses that ended up on
the front of St Mark's in Venice (according to the locals, but *see* Delphi, p.396). In 1261

the Emperor Michael Paleológos gave Chíos to the Giustiniani of Genoa. In 1344, the Giustiniani chartered a trading company of merchants and shipowners called the Maona, who governed until 1566 when Chíos was lost to the Turks.

The Sultans loved Chíos, especially its sweet mastic, and they granted it more privileges than any other island. It became renowned for its doctors and chess players; and in less fortunate Greece, the Chiots' cheerfulness was equated with foolishness. The laughter stopped in 1822 when a band of 2,000 ill-armed Samians disembarked on Chíos, proclaimed independence and forced the unwilling locals to join the struggle. The furious Sultan then ordered his admiral Kara Ali to make an example of Chíos: some 30,000 Greeks were slaughtered and 45,000 taken into slavery. The Sultan's harem's sweet tooth dictated that only the mastic villages survived. News of the massacre shook Europe; Delacroix painted his stirring canvas (now in the Louvre) and Victor Hugo sent off reams of rhetoric. On 6 June of the same year, the Greek Admiral Kanáris got revenge by blowing Kara Ali and 2,000 men up with his flagship. In 1840 Chíos attained a certain amount of autonomy under a Christian governor, but in 1881 it suffered another tragedy in an earthquake that killed nearly 4,000.

Chíos Town (Chóra)

Chíos Town rose from the earthquake rubble of 1881, slick, glossy, full of fast-food places and pool halls run by Greek Americans. Not what you expect on a Greek island, but after the first surprise the town – Genoa's sister city, for old time's sake – is a very likeable place. The surviving old town is enclosed in the walls of the **Byzantine fortress**. After 1599 only Turks and Jews could live inside; the Greeks had to be outside the gate or **Porta Maggiore** by sundown. In a closet-sized **prison** by the gate the bishop and 75 leading Chiots were held hostage before being hanged by the Turks in 1822. By a ruined mosque, the cemetery has the **tomb of Kara Ali**, author of the massacre of Chíos, surprisingly unvandalized. The **Kastro Justinian Museum**, nearby in Plateía Frouríou (*t 227 102 2819; open Tues–Sun 9–3; adm*), contains frescoes, carvings and early Christian mosaics.

Main **Plateía Vournakíou** (or **Plastíra**) has cafés under the plane trees, the new **Homerium** cultural centre and a mosque marked with a *Tugra*, the swirling 'thumbprint of the Sultan' that denotes royal possession and a mark of the special favour Chíos once enjoyed. Inside, the **Byzantine Museum** (*t 227 102 6866; open Tues–Sun 10–1, Sun 10–3; adm*) has art, tombstones and medieval odds and ends. South of Plateía Vournakíou, the **Folklore Museum** (*same hours*) is the collection of London scholar Philip Argéntis, scion of an old Genoese-Chiot family who got tired (with reason) of looking at his family's portraits; other displays feature Chiot costumes and crafts. The **Archaeological Museum**, 5 Michálon Street (*t 227 104 4139; open 8.45–3, Sun 9.30–2.30, closed Tues; adm*), contains a miscellany of finds, some bearing ancient Chíos' symbol, the sphinx, plus a letter from Alexander the Great. The **Maritime Museum**, 20 Stefanou Tsouri (*open Mon–Sat 10–1*), is a shipping fanatic's fantasy, housed in the Patéras family pile.

Tourist Information

Tourist office: 11 Kanári St, t 227 104 4389, f 227 104 4343; *open Mon–Fri 7–2.30 and 7–10, Sat 10–1 and Sun 7–10am*.
Tourist police: t 227 104 4427, quayside.

Where to Stay and Eat

Chíos Town ✉ 82100

Hotels in town are all open year round.
Chíos Chandris, E. Chandri, t 227 104 4401, f 227 102 5768, *www.chandris.gr (B; expensive)*. A large harbour-front pile. Many rooms overlook the port.
Kyma, E. Chandrí, t 227 104 4500, f 227 104 4600, *kyma@chi.forthnet.gr (C; moderate)*. The core of the hotel is an Italianate villa; a luscious buffet breakfast is included.
Diana, 92 Venizélou, t 227 104 4180, f 227 102 6748 (*C; moderate*). Modern, utilitarian, and friendly. Back rooms are quieter; great bathrooms too.
Chíos Rooms, 1 Kokáli, t 227 102 6743 (*moderate–inexpensive*). Series of rooms in a renovated neoclassical shipowner's house.
Filoxenia, Roidou, t 227 102 2813 (*D; inexpensive*). Clean and simple place to flop.
Hotzas, 3 G. Kondíli St, a 15-minute walk from the quay, t 227 104 2787. Ask directions to Chíos' oldest taverna; excellent food and good barrelled retsina. *Eves only*.
Theodosiou, 33 Neoreiou, at the north end of the port. The best of the waterfront

restaurants, relying on good food rather than designer décor for its loyal clientèle.
Two Brothers, in from the waterfront at 38 Livanoú St, t 227 102 1313 (€10–12). Ordinary-looking, but the surprise is the charming back garden and good, cheap food.
Karatza, on Karfás Street, t 227 103 1221 (*inexpensive*). Has a terrace where you can look over to Turkey while feasting on grilled or ready-prepared food for around €12–15.

Kámbos

Villa La Favorita, t/f 227 103 2265 (*A; expensive–moderate*). Genoese villa with 13 beautiful air-conditioned rooms; minibars and a courtyard waterwheel. *Open May–Oct*.
Perleas, Vitiadou St, t 227 103 2217, f 227 103 2364 (*A; expensive*). Friendly family guest-house in restored mansion with five rooms in a fruit grove, serene and civilized.
Perivoli, 11 Argénti, t 227 103 1513/1973, f 227 103 2042 (*A; moderate*). Quiet traditional pension with a good, popular restaurant (€14–20). *Open all year*.

Karfás

Golden Sand, on the beach, t 227 103 2080, f 227 103 1700, *goldsand@compulink.gr (A; expensive)*. A large pool in a seaside complex.
Benovias, t 227 103 1457 (*moderate*). Uphill, with eight apartments.
Markos' Place, t 227 103 1990, *www.marcosplace.gr (inexpensive)*. For an altogether atmospheric and restful stay in an ex-monastery just south; book. *Open May–Oct*.

Kámbos: Genoese Gentility

The Genoese favoured the well-watered plain south of town that they called the Campo, or **Kámbos**. Here, along with the local Chiot aristocracy, they built villas and plantations of citrus fruit, mastic bushes and mulberries for silk, an important source of income until the 19th century. Best explored by pedal bike, Kámbos remains an enchanting and evocative mesh of narrow lanes, walled gardens, and gates bearing coats-of-arms or the telltale stripes of the Genoese nobility. Many have their own slowly turning waterwheels, while outside the walls flowering meadows, wooden bridges and ancient trees create a rare sense of elegaic serenity, especially at day's end. **Sklaviá**, named after the Genoese's Greek slaves, is especially lush. Towards the modern village of **Vavíli**, the octagonal domed church **Panagía Krína** (1287) contains fine frescoes by the Cretan school.

The nearest beach to Chíos Town and Kámbos is at **Karfás**, reached by frequent blue buses, and so far the only major concession to mass tourism on Chíos. The sand is 'as soft as flour', but for a lower-key beach continue south to **Kómi** (*see* below), beyond **Moni Ag. Minás** (*closed afternoons until 6*). During the massacre in 1822, 3,000 women and children took refuge there; a small, hopeless battle took place before all were slain. Their bones are now in an ossuary; their blood still stains the church floor.

The Mastikochória: Mastic Villages of the South

Continue southwest of Kámbos and you're in mastic land. These bushy little trees (*Pistacia lentiscus*, related to the pistachio) refuse to be transplanted, even to northern Chíos; they'll grow, but not a drop of mastic will they yield. The bark is 'needled' three times between July and September, allowing the sweet, glistening sap to ooze from the wounds like diamonds. Considered a panacea in antiquity, mastic puts the chew in gum and the jelly in the beans that kept the bored inmates chomping in Turkish harems; Roman women used toothpicks made of the wood to sweeten their breath. In the more mundane West it was used in varnish; the Syrians still buy it as an ingredient in perfume. On Chíos they use it to flavour a sweet sticky liqueur, spoon sweets, chewing gum and MasticDent toothpaste, the perfect Chíos souvenir.

The twenty villages where mastic is grown, the Mastikochória, were carefully spared by the Turks in 1822. The Genoese designed them as tight-knit defensive labyrinths around a central keep, the houses sharing a common outer wall with few entrances. The most prosperous are decorated with *xistá*, the *sgrafitto* decoration learned from the Genoese; walls are first covered with mortar containing black sand from Emborió, then coated with white plaster, which is scraped off into geometric, floral or animal-based designs. The first of the Mastikochória is **Armoliá**, defended by the Byzantine

Where to Stay and Eat

Kómi ✉ 82102
Bella Mare, above the restaurant on the beach, t 227 107 1226 (*moderate*). Friendly and family-run; en suite rooms and a free supply of sun loungers. *Open May–Oct.*
Mika's, t 227 107 1335 (*inexpensive*). An alternative just south of town. *Open May–Oct.*
Nostalgia, t 227 107 0070. 'Free umbrellas'. Fresh fish and lobster on the strand.

Pirgí ✉ 82102
Rita Valas Rooms, near the main square, t 227 107 2479/2112 (*moderate–inexpensive*). Quiet, clean rooms and shared kitchen facilities.
Lila Rooms, on the main road, t 227 107 2291, f 227 107 2107 (*moderate–inexpensive*). Run by the dynamic Lila; en suite rooms with a garden.
'Balcony'. Café/restaurant in a house decorated with *xistá*.

Emborió ✉ 82102
Vassiliki, t 227 107 1422 (*inexpensive*). Apartments set back from the harbour.
Themis Studios, t 227 107 1810 (*inexpensive*). Just above the portlet.
Volcano, t 227 107 1136. Delicious food on a shady terrace.

Mestá ✉ 82102
The following (*all moderate–inexpensive*) all have rooms within the fortress: **Lambriní**, t 227 10 7 6226; **Popi**, t 227 107 6262; and **Déspina Almiroúdi**, t 227 107 6388.
Pefkákia. Epitome of the family taverna, set among pines.

Líthi ✉ 82102
Medusa Rooms, t 227 107 3289, f 227 102 3634 (*inexpensive*). Traditionally furnished.
Kira Despina Murina, on the beach, t 227 107 3373 (*inexpensive*). Handful of rooms and great fish, fish soup and big breakfasts.

Kástro tis Oréas (1440), a castle named for its beautiful châtelaine who, like a black widow spider, seduced men, then executed them. **Kalamotí** has tall stone houses on narrow cobbled streets and two attractive Byzantine churches, Ag. Paraskeví and the 12th-century **Panagía Sikelia**. The closest beach to both towns is **Kómi**, a darkish stretch of sand with tavernas and rooms.

In the largest mastic village, **Pirgí**, nearly every house is beautifully decorated with *xistá*; the main square is particularly lavish. Of the equally pretty churches, the 12th-century **Ag. Apóstoli**, a miniature version of Néa Moní, has frescoes from 1655 (*open most mornings*). **Emborió**, 5km from Pirgí, was the old mastic port and is near ruins dating back to 3000 BC, possibly of Levkonion, a rival of Troy; the wealth of amphorae found in the sea here hints at the extent of the Chian wine trade. East of the port, under the Profítis Ilías chapel are bits of a 7th–4th century BC **temple of Athena Polias** and the acropolis. Two beaches five minutes from Emborió are called **Mávra Vótsala** (black pebbles); one is spoiled by power lines, but the one around the headland is better. Back from the shore are the ruins of an early **Christian basilica** with a marble cross-shaped font and a few mosaics.

The last two mastic villages have impressive defences: **Olýmpi**, built around a 68ft tower, and **Mestá**, the ultimate fortress village, with no ground-floor windows facing out and only one entrance into its maze of lanes and flower-filled yards. Two churches are worth a look: the medieval **Ag. Paraskeví** and the 18th-century **Mikrós Taxiárchis**, with a beautiful iconostasis. The southwest coast is dotted with exquisite wild beaches; **Fana**, to the south, derives its name from the long gone Great Temple of Phaneo Apollo, which had an oracle consulted by Alexander. The road north from Mestá to Chíos Town passes Mestá's port of **Pasá-Limáni** and picturesque medieval **Véssa**, on the valley floor. From here, a road leads north to **Lithí** (4.5km), a charming village with a so-so sandy beach below, tavernas and a few rooms. Further up the west coast you can swim at **Elínda** and circle back to Chíos Town by way of Néa Moní.

Inland from Chíos Town: Néa Moní (NEA MONH)

Beautiful **Néa Moní** high in the pines (*t 227 107 9370; open 8–1 and 4–8; women should wear knee-length skirts*) is easiest reached by car (buses only go as far as **Karyés**, 7km away). It was 'new' in 1042, when Emperor Constantine VIII Monomachos replaced an older monastery after the monks found a miraculous icon that prophesied that Constantine would return from exile and gain the throne. In gratitude, the emperor sent architects and artists from Constantinople, who built a subtle, complex church, in which pilasters, niches and pendentives support a great dome atop an octagonal drum. Its richly coloured mosaics shimmer in the penumbra: the *Washing of the Feet*, *The Saints of Chíos*, *Judas' Kiss* and *The Life of Christ* are stylistically similar to those at Dáfni in Athens and among the most beautiful examples of Byzantine art. A chapel has the bones of some of the 5,000 victims (among them 600 monks) of Kara Ali's massacre; all had sought sanctuary in the monastery.

From here, a rough road leads to the monastery **Ag. Patéras**, honouring the three monks who founded Néa Moní. Further up, **Avgónima** has three tavernas to stop at before you zigzag up the granite mountain to the 'Mystrá of Chíos', a striking Byzantine village and castle of **Anávatos**. In 1822 most of the villagers threw themselves off the 1000ft cliff rather than wait to be slaughtered by the Turks. Now only a handful of residents live in this haunted spot.

North of Chíos Town

Northern Chíos is another world, mountainous and barren, its forests decimated by shipbuilders and fires. At **Vrontádos**, 4.5km north of Chíos Town, locals proudly show the **Daskalópetra** (the Teacher's Stone), a rough rock throne on a terrace over the sea where they say Homer sang and taught his poetry to disciples. Killjoy archaeologists say it was really part of an altar dedicated to the Great Goddess. Nonetheless, the International Society of Homeric Studies is based here, and there's a small **Folklore Museum** (*open daily 5–7pm*). Further north is **Langáda**, an attractive fishing village, popular in summer, with an array of bars and tavernas. Jagged rocks surround **Kardámila**, the largest northern village and cradle of the shipowners, which is divided into picturesque upper town and pleasant seaside **Mármaros**. Further north, pretty **Nagós Beach** is set in a green amphitheatre, its name a corruption of a long gone *naos* (temple) dedicated to Poseidon. At nearby **Gióssona**, named after Jason of the Argonauts, there's a pebble beach with turquoise water and a taverna.

Where to Stay and Eat

Vrontádos ✉ 82100

Kyveli Apartments at Daskalópetra, t 227 109 4300, f 227 109 4303, *goldsand@compulink.gr* (*A; expensive*). Large, bland apartments with pool. *Open April–Oct.*

Ag. Markella, in Vrontádos proper, t 227 109 3763, f 227 109 3765, *ag.Markel@otenet.gr* (*B; moderate*). Quirky place with dinky pool.

Velonas, t 227 109 3656, f 227 109 3656 (*inexpensive*). One of many rooms for rent, with clean petite studios just up from the sea.

To Limanaki, t 227 109 3647. Serves delicious fresh fish.

Pantoukios, a short drive north in Pantoukias, t 227 107 4262. For lobster.

Langáda ✉ 82300

Stellios, t 227 207 4813. For excellent octopus, on the waterfront.

O Passos, next door. Popular all round for the best food.

Kardámila ✉ 82300

Kardamyla, t 227 202 3353, f 227 202 3354, *kyma@chi.forthnet.gr* (*B; expensive*). A good base for exploring the unspoiled north, on its own shady beach with watersports, a restaurant, and a friendly owner. *Open April–Oct.*

Volissós ✉ 82300

Stella Tsakiri, t 227 402 1421, f 227 402 1521, *volissos@otenet.gr* (*expensive–moderate*). English-speaking establishment with stylish, well-equipped renovated houses for rent in the village.

Latini Apartments, on the road to Límnos and the beach, t 227 402 1461, f 227 402 1871 (*expensive–moderate*). Apartments closest to the beach, with a lovely garden and terrace.

Taverna Anemi, near the *plateía*. Shady, and an adjacent bar with great music.

Akroyálli, in Límnos. Taverna that serves fresh fish dishes.

Mountainous **Pitiós**, Homer's 'birthplace' has his 'house' and olive grove. The landscape towards Chíos Town is lunar in its emptiness. Further west, past the striking 13th-century **Moní Moúdon**, stands the castle of **Volissós**, founded by Justinian's general Belisarius and the place where Byzantine nobles were exiled; what you see is a Genoese makeover, much of it now in ruins. Volissós also claims Homer, and in ancient times it was the chief town of his (probably spiritual) descendants, the Homeridai. Sandy **Skála Volissoú** or **Limniá** is one of the island's finest beaches and has caiques several times weekly to Psará. There are good beaches nearby: pebbly, nudist **Chóri** just south, and **Límnos**, en route to the **monastery of Ag. Markélla**, the islanders' favoured pilgrimage destination.

A deserted road north of Volissós leads to little **Piramá**, with a medieval tower and the church of Ag. Ioánnis with old icons. On the northwest shore, the village of **Ag. Gála** ('Holy Milk') is named after a frescoed 15th-century Byzantine church in a cave (ask for the key), which drips whitish deposits, said to be the milk of the Virgin; the chapel has a superb iconostasis. For more terrestrial secretions, make your way along the rough coastal road east to **Agiásmata** where Chiots come in the summer to soak in the magic baths.

Inoússes (ΟΙΝΟΥΣΣΕΣ) and Psará (ΨΑΡΑ)

A ferry leaves Chíos daily for nearby **Inoússes**, the 'wine islands'. Only the largest (30 square km) is inhabited, and it's the richest island in Greece: the Inoussans comprise some 60 of the 180 Greek shipowning families. Most began as goatherds or wine makers in Kardámila, Chíos, who after the Second World War cannily parlayed a handful of wartime Liberty ships into a fleet of 500 ships and tankers. Although fancy yachts congregate in Inoússes' sheltered harbour each summer, the town itself is unpretentious and immaculately shipshape. The shipowners have set up a **Maritime Museum** by the quay that opens when it feels like it. There are small, undeveloped beaches in walking distance.

One road crosses to the western cliffs, where in the 1960s Katíngo Patéras, a member of a prominent shipowning dynasty, built the multi-million-dollar **Convent of the Evangelismós** (*adm only to women with long sleeves, headscarves and long skirts*) after her 20-year-old daughter Iríni died of Hodgkinson's Disease, having prayed to take the illness and die instead of her afflicted father. When her body was duly exhumed after three years, she was mummified. Her failure to decompose convinced her mother, now the abbess, that she was a saint (a fact recently confirmed by the Orthodox church) and, like Sleeping Beauty, she is kept in a glass case on display with the remains of her father, who died a few years later.

Psará, one of Greece's martyred islands, is much further away than Inoússes: a 4-hour journey from Chíos Town, or two hours from Limniá (*see* p.820). In the 18th century, independent-minded Chiots moved here and developed a commercial fleet, rivalled only by those of Hýdra and Spétses. When the War of Independence broke out, Psará enthusiastically contributed its ships and one of the war's heroes, Admiral Kanáris, and was such a nuisance that on 20 June 1824 the Sultan sent 25,000 troops to wipe it off the map. Only 3,000 of its 30,000 men, women and children managed to escape. Today 500 people fish and keep bees. Feet are your main transport to the island's beaches: the best is **Límnos**, a sandy strand 20 minutes' walk away.

Lésbos/Mytilíni (ΛΕΣΒΟΣ/ΜΥΤΙΛΗΝΗ)

Sappho's island of Lésbos (or Mytilíni), the third largest island after Crete and Évia, hangs off the coast of Turkey like a gingko leaf. Its vineyards produce Greece's best ouzo, its undulating hills support an astonishing 13 million olive trees, while the higher peaks are swathed in chestnuts and pines; in Sigri you'll find Europe's biggest petrified forest. Fifteen villages have been declared traditional settlements, and the islanders are easygoing, lyrical and fond of horses and drink, ready to break into song or dance whenever the mood (*kéfi*) takes them. Music and poetry run deep in Lésbos' soul, and contribute to its well-known bewitching quality. In myth, the head of Orpheus (*see* p.582) floated here from Thrace and was placed in a cave where it prophesied so well that people bypassed Delphi, until a miffed Apollo ordered the head to shut up. Besides Sappho, other great musicians and poets hailed from here: the quasi-mythological Arion, inventor of the dithyramb (and who in a sticky spot with pirates was rescued by dolphins after he enchanted them with his song); Terpander, 'the father of Greek music'; aristocratic Alcaeus; Longus (the 3rd-century BC author of *Daphnis and Chloe*); and Nobel Laureate Odysséas Elýtis. Known as the Red Island for its left-wing politics, Lésbos has now become something of a mecca for gay women, attracted by its beauty and the power of its ancient name.

History

Like many islands off the Asia Minor coast, Lésbos has been tugged between east and west. An ally of Troy, it was raided by Odysseus and Achilles in the *Iliad*. In the 10th century BC Aeolians from Thessaly colonized the island, and it became an artistic centre, especially under Pittakos (598–79 BC), one of the Seven Sages of Greece. In 527 Lésbos came under the rule of Persia, then after its defeat joined the Delian League. The destructive rivalry between the island's two city states, Mytilíni and Míthymna, came to a head in 428 BC, when Mytilíni took the Spartan side in the Peloponnesian War. Míthymna, seeing a chance to destroy its rival, went at once to Athens, and

Lésbos/Mytilíni

To Chios

To Limnos

MYTILINI

Ag. Marina
Kratigos
Ag. Ermougenis
Varia
Loutra
Moria
Skala Loutron
Ag.
Pamfilla
Thermi
Misstegna
Neas Kydonies
Aspropotamos
Gulf of Geras
Loutra Geras
Perama
Pappados
Paliokipos
Palios
Limani
Tsonia
Ag. Stefanos
Pigi
Messagros
Skopelos
Plomari
Skala Sikaminias
Sikaminia
Klio
Pelopi
Kapi
Mantamados
Ag. Paraskevi
Keramia
Achladeri
Aglassos
Ag. Isidoros
Tarti
Mt. Lepetimnos (968m)
Temple of Mesi
Mt. Olympos (964m / 3162ft)
Ampeliko
Megalochori
Molyvos (Mithymna)
Eftalou
Stypsi
Kalloni
Vassilika
Paralia Drotas
Melinta
Avlaki
Petra
Skoutaros
Skala Kalloni
Polichnitos
Ano Stavros
Anaxos
Ag. Ignatios Limonos
Gulf of Kalloni
Skala Polichnitou
Vatera
Naxos
Skalochori
Parakila
Vrissa
Cavathas
Antissa
Vatoussa
Agra
Nyfida
Lapsarna
Antissa
Chidira
Mesotopos
Tavari
Apothikes
Cape Ag. Fokas
Ipsilou
Petrified Forest
Eressos
Sigri
Skala Eressou
Faneromeni
NISIOPI

N

10 km
5 miles

Getting There and Around

By air: numerous European charters; three (or more) daily flights from Athens on Olympic and Aegean/Cronus; daily from Thessaloníki, three times weekly from Límnos and twice from Chíos. Olympic: 44 Kavétsou, t 225 102 8660; Aegean/Cronus: at the airport, t 225 106 1120. The airport, t 225 106 1490, is 8km from Mytilíni town; a taxi is around €8.

By sea: daily **ferries** with Piraeus and Chíos; almost daily with Sámos, at least once a week with Thessaloníki, Alexandroúpolis, Rafína, Ag. Efstrátios, Ikaría, Psará, Rhodes, Kos and Pátmos. In summer, there is a daily boat to Ayvalik, Turkey (three-day tours to ancient Pergamon are on offer, too).

Port authority: t 225 102 4115.

By road: **buses** to distant villages, t 225 102 8873, depart at the south end of the harbour, by the public gardens (three to four daily to the tourist spots on the west of the island in season; five daily to Plomári, two to Skála Eressoú). Frequent buses to the suburbs and closer villages, t 225 104 8725, depart from the centre of the harbour.

Taxis: Mytilíni, t 225 102 3500/t 225 102 5900. **Car hire**: Holiday Car Rental, 21b Archipelagous St, t 225 104 3311, f 225 102 9581.

Tourist Information

EOT: 6 James Aristarchou St, t 225 104 2511 or 225 104 2513; *open weekdays 8–2.30 and 6–8.30*. At the airport: t 225 106 1279.
Tourist police: t/f 225 102 2776, near the dock; *open 8–3*.
Hoteliers' Union: t 225 104 1787, f 225 104 0008, *www.filoxenia.net*. For booking accommodation.

Lésbos also has an excellent website: *www.greeknet.com*.

Where to Stay

The **Tourism and Travel Agency**, at 5 Konstantinoupoleos St, t 225 102 1329, f 225 104 1268, arranges village rooms. **Sappho Rented Rooms Association**, t 225 104 3375, offers rooms in town. Book ahead.

Mytilíni Town ✉ 81100

Pyrgos of Mytilene, 49 Venizélou, t 225 102 5069, f 225 104 7319. *www.pyrgoshotel.gr (A; expensive)*. The smartest mansion-hotel, with 12 luxurious rooms done in the Second Empire style; parking available.
Villa 1900, 24 Vostáni, t 225 102 3448, f 225 102 8034 *(A; moderate–inexpensive)*. An atmospheric neoclassical mansion, a 10-minute walk south of the harbour. *Open April–Oct*.
Heliotrope, 2.5km out at Vigla Beach, t 225 104 5857, f 225 104 4272, *www.heliotrope.gr (B; moderate–expensive)*. A complex with sea water pool, children's pool, restaurant, bars, and satellite TV. *Open all year*.
Sappho, Prokimea St, on the waterfront, t 225 102 8415 *(C; moderate)*. Lovely views from a modern block. *Open all year*.
Salina's Garden Rooms, 7 Fokiás, t 225 104 2073 *(inexpensive)*. Good; a lovely garden.

Around Mytilíni Town

Loriet, Variá, near the beach, t 225 104 3111, f 225 104 1629, *loriet@hotmail.com (A; luxury)*. Ten suites in a charming stone mansion; pool. *Open all year*.
Akrotiri, t 225 102 6452 *(inexpensive)*. Cheaper rooms on offer in Variá.
Votsala, north in Thermi, t 225 107 1231, f 225 107 1179, *votsala@otenet.gr (B; expensive–moderate)*. A garden-seaside spot; friendly, shuttle service to town. *Open April–Oct*.

Eating Out

The island is famous for sardines, giant prawns, *kakávia* (fish soup), *astakós magiátikos* (lobster with vegetables), and *skoumbri foúrnou* (baked mackerel).
Navagio, on the waterfront at 23 Archipelagous, t 225 104 2609 *(€18–24)*. Restaurant with balcony and ambience: try shrimp, smoked trout, lamb kléftiko, or pasta.
Kalderimi, 2 Thassou, at the central market, t 225 104 6577 *(€12)*. In an old town alley; a mecca for local *ouzerie* connoisseurs, great *mezédes* and atmosphere.
To Fanari, t 225 104 6417. A fish taverna on the south end of the harbour, with a wide selection of wines and knowledgeable owner.
Apolafsi, near the above, t 225 102 7178. *Mezédes*, grilled meat and fresh fish.

Athens duly sent troops to massacre the Mytilinians. For once, however, they reconsidered and sent a second ship countermanding the massacre.

In the 4th century BC Lésbos changed hands frequently. Its best ruler was the eunuch and mercenary Hermeias of Arteneus, who governed according to the precepts of Plato's *Republic*. He invited Aristotle to found an academy in Assos (just opposite Lésbos, in Asia Minor); Aristotle then married Hermeias' niece Pythias and moved to Mytilíni, where he set up another academy with his friend Theophrastus, a native of Lésbos. The local flora and fauna inspired his pioneering work in biology before he left in 342 BC to tutor Alexander (*see* p.552).

Like Chíos, Lésbos in 1354 was given by the Emperor John Paleológos to the Genoese captain Francesco Gattilusio. In 1462 Mehmet the Conqueror captured it, despite the heroic resistance by Mólyvos' Lady Oretta d'Oria, who donned her husband's armour and won one skirmish, and the island remained Turkish until 1912.

Mytilíni

In the island capital, **Mytilíni**, magnificent mansions, impressive public buildings and beautiful gardens collide with dusty, higgledy-piggledy, cacophonous lanes. Nor, apart from a few ticket agencies and hotels, is it the slightest bit bothered with tourism. It has two harbours, one to the south still in use, and an abandoned one to the north. In ancient times a canal called the 'Euripos of the Mytilineans' flowed between the two, a fact dramatically proved when a marble bridge and a trireme were found buried under a street in the middle of town.

On a waterfront traffic island a prettily restored house holds the **Museum of Traditional Arts and Crafts** (*open by request, t 225 102 8501; adm*), with lace, weapons, ceramics, tools and costumes. The lofty dome that dominates the skyline belongs to **Ag. Therápon** (1850) first built over a Temple of Apollo in the 5th century. In front is the interesting **Byzantine Museum** (*t 225 102 8916; phone to check hours; adm*) stocked with icons from the 13th to 18th centuries, including one by Theóphilos (*see below*). The delightful green and shady **municipal gardens** are nearby, along with the **municipal theatre**. The quarters south (Sourada and Kióski) are dotted with grand beautifully restored Victorian or Bavarian neoclassical mansions (*archontika*) built by olive and ouzo barons; some are now hotels.

At 8 Novembriou St, the **Archaeological Museum** (*t 225 102 8032; open Tues–Sun 8.30–3; adm*) is housed in another aristocratic mansion, and prides itself on reliefs found in a Roman house depicting scenes from the comedies of Menander, Greek mosaics found at Chórafa, Roman mosaics from Ag. Therápon and prehistoric finds from Thérma. Rescue finds, including some excellent mosaics, fill a new **annexe** up the same street (*same hours*).

The ancient acropolis is now crowned by a sprawling **Byzantine-Genoese castle** or **Kástro** (*t 225 102 7970; open 8–2.30; adm*), founded in the 6th century by Justinian who is said to have blinded every prisoner he sent here. In 1373 the Genoese repaired it, placing columns from the Archaic Temple of Apollo willy-nilly in the stones. Inside are a Roman cistern, a Turkish *medrese* (Koranic school), prisons and a monk's cell. Excavations have revealed an Archaic **Thesmophorion**, where women held their annual fertility bash, sacrificing piglets in pits to Demeter and then digging them up days later to mix the rotten flesh with seed corn on the altar. More appetizing are the concerts held here in summer, where on one memorable occasion heart-throb singer George Dalaras had his trousers ripped off by ardent female fans. Below is a pay beach at **Tsamákia**, and a large statue of *Freedom* which greets arrivals by sea.

North of the *kástro*, in the Old North Port or **Páno Skála** area, is the forlorn **Yení mosque**, with a truncated minaret, surrounded by carpenters and metalworkers in grimy shops, a bustling market and antiques shops. By the pines at the end of Theátrou Eschílou St is the 15,000-seat Hellenistic **theatre**, one of the largest of its kind. Just south are the remains of a Roman aqueduct, and near the cemetery of **Ag. Kyriakí** are some of the walls of ancient Mytilíni.

South of Mytilíni Town

Buses go hourly to **Variá**, birthplace of the divine Theóphilos Hadzimicháíl (1873–1934). Dwarfed, a lisper and left-handed (considered a curse back then), he left Variá and lived destitute, wandering the Pélion peninsula for 30 years (*see* p.491), earning ouzo and dinner in exchange for Greece's most passionate modern paintings – on shop walls, tins or rags. Since 1964 an old school has housed the charming **Theóphilos Museum** (*t 225 104 1644; open Tues–Sun 9–2.30 and 6–8; adm*), displaying some of his best work. He wrote descriptions around each scene so there's no mistaking the subject, whether from mythology, the lives of the saints, the Greek War of Independence, or a local festival. The museum has 19th-century photos of Greeks posing in the same splendid costumes that Theóphilos loved to paint; he himself enjoyed dressing up as Alexander the Great.

A stone's throw away, the modern **Tériade Museum and Library** (*t 225 102 3372; open Tues–Sun 9–2 and 5–8; adm*) was founded in 1979 by Stratís Eleftheriádes, better known by his French name Tériade. Born in Mytilíni in 1897, he went to study law in Paris at age 18, stayed, and in 1937 launched a publishing house, *VERVE*, printing art books and a respected quarterly review that lasted until 1971. Inspired by medieval illuminated manuscripts, Tériade produced a series of 'Grands Livres' with lithographs by Picasso, Miró, Léger, Chagall, Roualt, Giacometti, Henri Laurens and Juan Gris, hand-printed on handmade paper in limited editions. Many are on display here, along with minor paintings by the same names (although a burglary has put a dent in the collection). On the ground floor there are more paintings by Theóphilos, whom Tériade 'discovered' in 1930 when the artist was dying, unknown and penniless.

South of Variá are lovely beaches bracketing **Ag. Ermougénis** (a good taverna on the hill too). From Skála Loutrón, a **ferry** crosses the Gulf of Géras for Pérama; try the warm waters at **Loutrá Géras**, the gentlest of Lésbos' five spas (*sex segregated; open daily 8–8; adm*).

North of Mytilíni

The East Coast Route

North of Mytilíni, the road first passes **Mória**, with arches of a Roman aqueduct intact, and then **Thérmi**, with the 12th-century church of **Panagía Troulloutí** and hot iron-rich springs; five levels of civilization were excavated here, dating to 3000 BC. A Turkish tower stands near the baths, and there are rooms and a beach nearby.

After the strands at Néa Kydonies and Néa Aspropótamos, this road goes to **Mantamádos**, a large village of grey stone houses famous for yoghurt and a black icon of St Michael that is said to smell of wildflowers, housed in the 18th-century church **Taxiárchis Michael**. The faithful press a coin to the icon; if it sticks, their prayer will be granted. Echoing an older religion, Mantamádos ritually sacrifices a bull on the third Sunday after Easter. Further north, **Kápi**, on 3,176ft Mount Lepétimnos, is the start of a new hiking trail through ravishing, luxuriant ravines. Further north lies the village of **Sikaminiá** and, at the end of the road, **Skála Sikaminiás**, the quintessential island

Getting Around

Excursion boats join Mólyvos to Skála Sikaminiás and beaches; from Sígri, caiques visit Nisiópi islet. A **bus** runs between Eftaloú and Náxos, stopping at Mólyvos, Pétra and the beaches in between. Timetable at the Mólyvos tourist office or at Petra Tours. Mólyvos **taxis**: opposite the bus station, **t** 225 107 1480; in Pétra, **t** 225 104 2022.

Tourist Information

On the main street in Mólyvos, **t** 225 307 1347/1069, **f** 225 307 2277, *mithimna@ aigaio.gr*; open weekdays 7.30–4. They can even find you a room.
Molyvos Watersports, **t** 225 107 1861, has parasailing, waterskiing and windsurfing. Try **donkey trekking** with dinner with Michaelis, **t** 225 307 1309.

Where to Stay and Eat

Skála Kalloní ✉ 81107

Pasiphae, **t** 225 302 3212, **f** 225 302 3154 (*B; expensive*). Comfortable hotel with a saltwater pool, one of several family-orientated complexes on the gulf. *Open April–Oct.*
Arivisi, **t** 225 302 2456, **f** 225 302 3530 (*expensive–moderate*). Apartments. *Open May–Oct.*

Mólyvos/Eftaloú ✉ 81108

Accommodation is plentiful, in converted stone houses on the beach (often block-booked), on the port, and in the old town, car-free so you have to schlep your bags.
Panselinos, **t** 225 307 1905, **f** 225 307 1904 (*B; luxury*). By the sea in Eftaloú, with the works, including wheelchair access. *Open May–Oct.*
Sun Rise, 2km from Mólyvos, **t** 225 307 1713/1779, **f** 225 307 1791, *sunrise@otenet.gr* (*B; expensive*). A complex with pool, tennis, and shuttlebus bus service to the sea. *Open May–Oct.*
Delfinia, just outside Mólyvos, **t** 225 307 1373, **f** 225 307 1524, *delfinia@otenet.gr* (*B; expensive*). With a pool, tennis, beach sports and lazy terrace. *Open all year.*
Olive Press, **t** 225 307 1646, **f** 225 307 1647 (*B; expensive*). A lovely conversion of an olive press, with tennis court, charming café and dining terrace. *Open May–Oct.*
Sea Horse, **t** 225 307 1630, **f** 225 307 1374 (*C; expensive–moderate*). Harbour accommodation; the airy front-facing rooms have views of the day's catch. *Open April–Oct.*
Mólyvos I, by the beach, **t** 225 307 1496, **f** 225 307 1640 (*B; moderate*). Cool terracotta-floored, traditional rooms with a terrace overlooking the beach. *Open April–Oct.*
Mólyvos II, in Eftaloú, **t** 225 307 1534, **f** 225 307 1694 (*B; moderate*). A children's playground, sports, pool, and bus service from Mólyvos I in town. *Open April–Oct.*

fishing village. Although you can swim here, the nearest good beach – a strand of rose-tinted sand – is at **Tsónia** to the southeast, but you have to go by way of Klió to get there on wheels. There's a footpath through the olives from Skála.

The Inland Route

The buses from Mytilíni to Mólyvos (2hrs) take the shorter, inland road. It passes **Keramiá**, a village beloved for its cool springs and centuries-old trees. Further along, it skirts the wide Gulf of Kallorí, whose cultivated plain is dotted with Lombardy poplars. A signposted road leads to the foundations and column drums of the Ionic **Temple of Mesi**, built in the 4th or 3rd century BC and dedicated to Aphrodite. **Kalloní** replaces the ancient city of Arisbe, whose acropolis now wears a medieval *kástro*. **Skála Kalloní** is a quiet family resort, its sandy beach ideal for children. Humans as well as wading birds and storks come for its fresh sardines and anchovies.

West of Kalloní, the 16th-century monastery **Ag. Ignatios Limónos** was a secret Greek school under the Turks. The frescoes in the central church are for men only,

Adonis, t 225 307 1866, **f** 225 307 1636 (*C; moderate*). Nice, amid trees. *Open all year.*

Evangelía Tekés, at the port near the Sea Horse, **t** 225 307 1158, **f** 225 307 1233 (*moderate–inexpensive*). Air-conditioned rooms in a restored stone house.

Posidon, near the beach, **t** 225 307 1981, **f** 225 307 1570 (*C; inexpensive*). Quiet, good value and some rooms have picture-postcard castle views. *Open May–Oct.*

To Xtapodi. The harbour in Molyvos. By far the most atmospheric, but touristy, fish restaurant, and not overpriced, although it appears on most of the island's postcards.

Faros, at the end of the harbour. Very good as well, serving tasty seafood specialities.

T'Alonia Taverna, outside Mólyvos near the Eftaloú road. Excellent, cheap and very popular with the locals; besides traditional Greek dishes it also cooks up breakfast.

Vafios and **Ilias**, both in Vafiós (the village just above Mólyvos). Traditional meat tavernas with wide menus, good local pies and wine from the barrel.

Eftaloú Taverna, t 225 307 1049. One of the best places to eat on Lésbos; home of delicious stuffed courgette flowers and more, served in a garden; neither expensive nor touristy.

Pétra ✉ 81109

Clara, at Avlaki (1.5km from Pétra, with a shuttle bus), **t** 225 304 1532, **f** 225 304 1535, www.klarahotel.gr (*B; luxury–expensive*). Hotel and bungalows around a pool, plus views.

Theofilos, t 225 304 1080, **f** 225 304 1493 (*C; expensive*). Large, with a pool. *Open April–Oct.*

Studios Niki, on the beach, **t** 225 304 1601 (*inexpensive*). Plain, clean and quiet accommodation set in a garden of flowers and birds.

Women's Agrotourist Cooperative, t 225 304 1238, **f** 225 304 1309, womes@otenet.gr. A hundred nice guest rooms in private houses, starting at €20 for a double. Their taverna has scrumptious food. *Open all year.*

Niko's (€15). Recommended for seafood.

Entertainment and Nightlife

Besides an open-air cinema, a summer theatre festival and music and dancing in the castle, there's the **Gatelousi** nightclub between Mólyvos and Pétra, resembling a cruise liner with its deck projecting from the rock face. It has a restaurant and a shuttle service that runs from 10pm to 5am. **Conga** is an open-air club by the waves, while **Bazaar**, near the harbour, has an atmospheric little terrace.

In Pétra, the **Machine Dancing Bar**, in an ex-olive factory, oozes atmosphere.

but both sexes can visit the 40 other chapels, St Ignatius' own room, and the petrified wood, folk art and ecclesiastical artefacts in the excellent little museum. From Kallóni a road leads east up to the village of **Ag. Paraskeví**, where, in an ancient rite (as at Mandamátos), a bull is bedecked with flowers and ribbons, paraded through the village, sacrificed, and eaten in the three-day feast in late May of Ag. Charálambos that, here, includes horse races. Apart from having an unusually old-time feel, the village is best known for olive oil. Presses dot the surrounding country. Further north, the green Ligona ravine below **Stýpsi**, on the slopes of Mount Lepétimnos, boasts 20 ruined water mills and is a favourite venue for 'Greek Nights'.

Míthymna/Mólyvos and the North Coast Resorts

Míthymna or Mólyvos (its Venetian name), at the north tip of Lésbos, was Mytilíni's ancient rival and is today Lésbos' prettiest and most popular town. During the Trojan War, Achilles besieged Míthymna unsuccessfully, until the daughter of the king fell in love with him and opened the city gate, a kindness Achilles rewarded by having her slain for betraying her father. Now dark-grey stone houses with red-tiled roofs, brightly coloured shutters and gardens full of flowers cascade down to the lovely harbour and beach. In the centre, known as the **Agorá**, steep cobbled lanes canopied with vines and wisteria are lined with boutiques; taverna terraces are perched high on stilts with wonderful views of Turkey. A small **Archaeological Museum** (*t 225 307 1059; open Tues–Sun 8.30–3*) sits en route to the striking **Genoese Castle** (*same hours*). In 1373, Francesco Gattilusi repaired this Byzantine fortress, but it still fell to Mehmet the Conqueror in 1462. The fine, long pebble beach lined with tamarisks gradually becomes shingly sand at the end, the nudists' spot. East of Mólyvos, its sidekick **Eftaloú** has a tree-fringed beach and a bathhouse with hot thermal springs.

Pétra and Ánaxos

South of Mólyvos, pretty **Pétra** has winding lanes, wooden balconies, a fine sweep of beach and a sheer rocky spike, carved with 114 steps and crowned by the church of **Panagía Glykofiloússa**, 'Virgin of the Sweet Kiss' (1747). Her icon belonged to a sea captain, but it insisted on staying atop this pinnacle, sneaking away every night even after the frustrated captain nailed it to his mast. So the church was started. A boy

A Minor Revolution

Since antiquity the upper-class women of Lésbos have enjoyed more independence than most Greek women, but their rural sisters, burdened by the dowry tradition, were virtual slaves to the land and their homes. In 1983 the women of Pétra, desperate for change, founded the first women's agricultural cooperative in Greece to provide B&B accommodation in traditional houses, and incidentally to slow the march of the concrete mixer. The idea spread: a national Women's Agricultural Cooperative Council was set up in 1985; on Lésbos alone there are now cooperatives in Asomatos, Agiássos and Polichnítos. The Council seeks to preserve old customs, handicrafts and local cuisine (they sell sweets, liqueurs, olives, salted vineleaves, pasta, and embroideries), encouraging women to play an active part in public life.

bringing *raki* for the workers slipped and fell over the precipice, but the Virgin caught him in a puff of air and took him to safety, without a drop of the raki spilled, either. Pilgrims tackle the climb on 15 August, when they're rewarded with the traditional *keskesi*, made of meat, grain, onions and spices.

Other beaches lie within striking distance of Pétra: **Avláki**, 1km west, small and sandy with two tavernas, and **Ánaxos**, 3km away, fine sand for nearly a kilometre with fabulous views of Mólyvos, although an ugly resort. From **Náxos** a lovely path skirts the dark volcanic shore to the west, leading to **Mikrí Tsichránta** and then **Megáli Tsichránta**, hamlets on a charming bay. This is oak country, with big oak warehouses; in the path's next village, **Kaló Limáni**, the warehouses have been turned into homes.

Western Lésbos and the Petrified Forest

Lésbos' volcanic northwest quarter, barren at first glance, is brimming with wild herbs and birdlife: rose-coloured starlings, bee eaters, hoopoes and golden orioles. The modern village of **Ántissa** has inherited the name of the Bronze Age city, up on the north coast: to get there, follow the road as far as **Gavathás** and then walk east on a 1km path skirting the coast. Terpander, the 'father of Greek music', was born in Ántissa *c.* 710 BC, and is credited with the invention of choric poetry and the *kithera* (a seven-string lyre, which gave its name to the guitar). The Romans destroyed the town for supporting the Macedonians; its meagre remains lie below **Ivriókastro**, a Genoese fort facing the sea. Wonderful quiet beaches with views over to Mólyvos are the main reason for the trek, and if you're lucky you'll hear nightingales. West of Ántissa, the monastery **Ag. Ioánnis Theológos Ipsiloú** is stunningly set on the promontory of an extinct volcano. Founded in the 9th century and rebuilt in the 12th, it shares its pinnacle with military buildings and has a museum of religious items.

Tourist Information

Eressos: t 225 305 3557; *open Mon–Fri 10–noon and 7–9, Sat 10–noon.*

Where to Stay and Eat

Sígri ✉ 81105
Vision, 1km outside Sígri, t 225 305 4226, f 225 305 4450 (*C; moderate*). Well-designed hotel; all rooms have sea view and benefit from the pool, but there's no beach.
Remezzo. Among the spread of tavernas in Sígri; classy, with the largest lobster tank.
The Golden Key. Unbeatable *yigántes* and other home-baked dishes.
To Kendro. Great *kafeneíon* for *souvlaki, tavli* and watching the world go by.

Skála Eressoú ✉ 81105
Sappho Travel, t 225 305 2140, f 225 305 2000, *sappho@otenet.gr*, organize accommodation; also try their website, *www.lesvos.co.uk*.
Aeolian Village, sprawled between Eressoú and Skála Eressoú, t 225 305 3585, f 225 305 3795 (*A; luxury*). Large pools and a supervised children's club. *Open April–Oct.*
Sappho the Eressian, in Skála Eressoú, t 225 305 3495, f 225 305 3233 (*C; moderate*). An orange, lesbian-only haven. *Open April–Oct.*
Galini, t 225 305 3138, f 225 305 3137, *www.aegeas.gr* (*C; moderate*). Good-value air-con rooms set back from the beach amongst trees and flowers. *Open April–Oct.*
Eressos, t 225 305 3560 (*inexpensive*). Clean rooms with a subterranean reception area.
Soulatso, on the waterfront. For fresh fish and great barbecued octopus.

Sappho: the Tenth Muse

Sappho was born in Eressós in the 7th century BC; later, her city proudly minted coins bearing her portrait. She was an aristocrat, married to Kerklyas of Ándros, and ran a marriage school for young ladies, to whom she dedicated many of her poems. Like her fellow islander and contemporary Alcaeus, she wrote personal and choral lyrics with complex rhythms intended to be sung at select private parties. One of her songs dedicated to a young girl is the first known description of passion: 'Equal to the gods seems that man who sits opposite you, close to you, listening to your sweet words and lovely laugh, which has passionately excited the heart in my breast. For whenever I look at you, even for a moment, no voice comes to me, but my tongue is frozen, and at once a delicate fire flickers under my skin. ..' Her influence was so powerful that Plato called her the 'Tenth Muse'. Yet fragments of her poems only just survived; considered morally offensive in 1073, all known copies were burned.

Continuing west to the end of Lésbos (a 2hr drive from Mytilíni), **Sígri** is a delight (if an often windy one): a bustling fishing village and resortlet, complete with 18th-century Turkish castle and a gently shelving, sheltered sandy beach. Within an hour's walk either side of Sígri there are plenty of other coves and beaches, including **Fanerómeni**, which has contrastingly deep water. Sígri is best known, however, for its 20 million-year-old **petrified forest**, unique in Europe and at 37,000 acres even larger than the one in Arizona. These pines, beeches and sequoias were fossilized after being buried in volcanic ash; as it erodes, the trunks have slowly become visible, although most are still buried. The offshore islets of **Nisiópi** (a sandy beach to which caiques venture) and Sarakína also boast remnants. Some excellent specimens are near Sígri along a fenced-in, 2.3km trail; some trunks are standing, others fallen, so you can see their wonderful colours. They are also the subject of a new **Natural History Museum** (*t 225 305 4434; open daily 8–8; adm*). For more on Sígri, its intriguing water cistern, forests and walks, pick up a copy of Roy Lawrence's *Where the Road Ends: Sígri*.

The forest extends to the attractive village of **Eressós**, overlooking a lush emerald plain. Its shady square has cafés, tavernas, and lots of old timers. Bits of ancient Eressós stand 4km east of **Skála Eressoú**, down an avenue of whitewashed trees. Skála itself has a long, steeply shelving sand beach, lined with tamarisks and serviced by a lively if modern seaside village, a favourite of Greek families and gay women. In the attractive square is a bust of Theophrastus of Eressós (372–287 BC), Aristotle's friend, botanist and author. The inland road from Sígri to Eressós is an epic, primeval drive scented by sea daffodils, with scarred rock faces and ancient contoured stone walls, and an amazing sense of space and purity.

Southern Lésbos

Southern Lésbos, between the inland seas of Kallóni and Géras, is dominated by 3,172ft **Mount Olympos**, one of 19 Mediterranean mountains with that name. In its shadow, reached by a delightfully bucolic road, is lovely **Agiássos**, a coach tour stop but still worth while (park at the foot of the village; it's easier). It has a medieval castle and creeper-shaded market streets; carry on up to the bakery for excellent baklava and cheese pies. Founded in the 1100s, the church of the **Panagía** houses an icon, said to have been made by St Luke from mastic and wax. The present church (1812) has one of the most beautiful 19th-century interiors of any Greek church, all grey and gilt, lit by hundreds of suspended lamps and chandeliers. There's a small **Byzantine Museum** (*open 8–8; adm*) to the right of the church. A lovely path leads from Agiássos to Plomári on the coast, passing by way of the ruins of **Palaiókastro**, of uncertain date, and the pleasant village and fountains of **Megalochóri**.

Chestnut and pine groves cover much of the region, and the road west to humdrum **Polichnítos** is especially attractive. The village has a new **Municipal Folklore and Historical Museum** (*t 225 204 2992*), not to mention the thermal spa, **Gera Yera**, oozing out the hottest waters in Europe (91°C), good for arthritis and gynaecological disorders (*t 225 204 1229; open 7–11am and 4–7pm in season; adm*). Near the harbour of **Skála Polichnítou**, there's a beach with noticeably warmer water than off the exposed coastal strips. **Nyfída** is another good beach near the mouth of Kallonís Bay.

South of Polichnítos, **Vríssa** was the home town of Briseis, the princess who caused the rift between Achilles and Agamemnon at Troy. Only a wall remains of the Trojan town destroyed in 1180 BC, and a Genoese tower stands to the west; the modern town can only claim a *kafeneíon*. Ruins of a 1st-century BC Doric temple of Dionysos Vrysageni, 'Born of the Springs', stand on Cape Ag. Fókas, marking the start of **Vaterá** beach, 9km of sand, dotted with seasports facilities, pensions, tavernas and sea daffodils. Walk up the path marked with yellow circles, beginning at the Voúrkos river, to **Áno Stavrós** and **Ampelikó**, a charming village in a ravine under Mount Olympos, with Roman ruins, a castle, pretty church and cafés. In 1998 an extraordinary cache of fossils was discovered here, one tortoise shell the size of a VW Beetle. Finds are displayed at Vríssa (*t 225 206 1711*). Back along the coast to the east, **Plomári**, Lésbos'

Where to Stay and Eat

Polichnítos/Skála Polichnítou ✉ 81300

Gera Yera spa, t 225 204 1229 (*inexpensive*). Tranquil rooms.

Polikentro Taverna, at the entrance to the village. The best place for food.

A handful of tavernas line the harbour and strand serving some of the freshest fish on the island; the *mezédes* are delicious and customers seem to linger forever.

Tzitzifies. A good bet, with the blue and red tablecloths.

Taverna Tsitsanos and **Iotis**, down at Nyfída. Both are excellent.

Vaterá ✉ 81300

Vatera Beach, t 225 206 1212, f 225 206 1164, *hovatera@otenet.gr* (*C; expensive*). Run in relaxed fashion by the inimitable Barbara and George in a tranquil floral setting; the beach-side restaurant has vegetarian options to boot. *Open May–mid-Oct.*

Aphrodite, t 225 206 1288, f 225 206 1128, *www.aphroditehotel.gr* (*C; moderate*). Well-equipped hotel/studios by the beach, with sports, children's activities and more.

Mylos. Soporific café-bar decked out in reggae colours on the beach.

Plomári ✉ 81200

Almost everything is block-booked by Vikings; the **Rented Rooms Union**, t 225 203 1666, should be able to help if you can't find shelter.

Okeanis, t 225 203 2469, f 225 203 2455 (*C; moderate*). 100m from the sea.

Lida I or **II**, t/f 225 203 2507 (*B; inexpensive*). Traditional housing.

second city, has attractive wooden galleried houses. The centre is as funky as Mytilíni Town and reeks of Greece's favourite aperitif – Kéfi, Veto, Tikelli and Barbayiánni ouzos are distilled here, and thoroughly enjoyed by tourists in situ under the palms. Plomári has a beach, but **Ag. Isídoros** just to the east has an even better one. The inland roads are attractive and woodsy; from the main road, an unpaved one descends to the very pretty sandy cove at **Tárti**, with a good taverna. At Pérama, you can catch a ferry across the gulf to Skála Loutrá, by Mytilíni Town.

Límnos (ΛΗΜΝΟΣ)

Límnos doesn't fit many Greek island stereotypes. Almost flat, it's dotted with vineyards, fields of grain, quirky scarecrows and beehives, and it is one of the few islands to support a herd of deer. A magnificent natural harbour near the mouth of the Dardanelles has ensured its military importance over the years. It was sacred to the smithy god Hephaistos, worshipped on Mount Móschylus, which in ancient times emitted a fiery jet of asphaltic gas. Today, Límnos still has astringent hot springs and the sulphuric 'Limnian earth', found near Repanídi, used from ancient times until the Turkish occupation for healing wounds and stomach aches.

Límnos' Malodorous Myths

Deformed Hephaistos so offended his mother Hera that she hurled him from Mount Olympos. He splashed down near Límnos, where the sea goddess Thetis adopted him. Years later, when Hera noticed Thetis wearing a magnificent brooch made by Hephaistos, she reinstated him on Olympos, marrying him off to the lovely Aphrodite, a joke neither partner enjoyed. Hephaistos then took his mother's part in a quarrel with Zeus and Zeus hurled him onto Límnos itself, which crippled him forever. The myth probably reflects a practice in the early days of metallurgy, when smiths were so valued that they were hobbled with chains to keep them from wandering off.

The Limnians loved Hephaistos more than his parents and when Aphrodite betrayed him with the war-god Ares, the Límnian women angrily tossed her cult statue into the sea. Aphrodite promptly made their breath and underarms stink (was it because they worked with woad, a putrid-smelling blue dye?). When their men turned up their noses and turned to Thracian concubines, the ladies doctored their wine, slit their throats, and carried on as independent Amazons. Then Jason and his crew dropped by; the women decided a shipload of sailors was just what they needed. So the kindest courtesy (and perhaps head colds) won over the Argonauts. Jason's son Euneus became king of Límnos during the Trojan War.

Another stinky story features Philoctetes, Heracles' son and inheritor of his bow. When he and the Troy-bound Achaeans landed on Límnos, nasty Hera sent a snake to bite him on the ankle. He was abandoned in a cave because his fellows could not stomach the stench of his wound, until an oracle declared Philoctetes' bow necessary to victory. Odysseus tried to get it from him by trickery (see Sophocles' *Philoctetes*) but in the end Philoctetes himself took the bow to Troy and slew Paris with it.

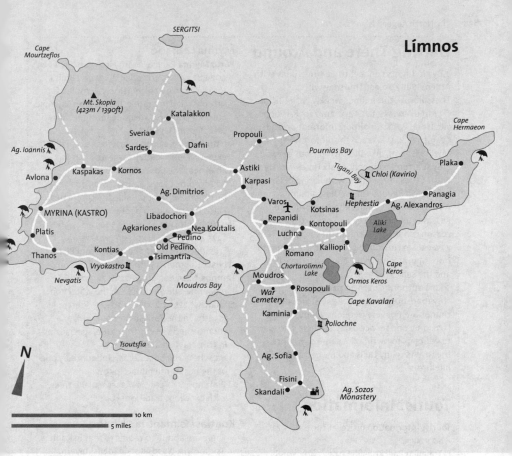

History

Herodotus wrote that the Limnians were Tyrrhenian – related to the Etruscans of Italy. This claim has been given substance by burial customs and pre-6th-century BC inscriptions found on Límnos that show similarities to Etruscan. Whoever they were, they were around a long time. At Polióchne, oval huts date back to 4000 BC – the most advanced Neolithic civilization yet discovered in the Aegean. These precocious Limnians may have even colonized Troy.

During the Persian Wars, the Limnians captured some Athenian women. When their children belittled their native half-siblings, the Limnians slaughtered them and their mothers, giving rise to the expression 'Limnian deeds', for atrocious acts. The gods punished them by making their wives and animals barren. The Limnians consulted Delphi, where the oracle said the only cure for it was to surrender their independence to Athens if the Athenians ever sailed to Límnos in a single day. It seemed a fair hedge, until Athens conquered territory near Mount Athos and did arrive from there in a day to claim their prize.

The Venetians took Límnos in the 13th century, but it was soon regained by the Byzantines. In 1475 Mehmet the Conqueror sent troops to Límnos, but they were

Getting There and Around

By air: flights connect three times daily with Athens, daily except Thursday with Thessaloníki, three times weekly with Lésbos. Olympic Airways, **t** 225 402 2114/2078, is opposite Hotel Paris; for **airport information**, call **t** 225 403 1204. To reach the airport from Mýrina (22km), take the Olympic bus or taxi.

By sea: **ferry** connections six times weekly with Lésbos, three times with Rafína, less often with Piraeus, Chíos, Thessaloníki, Alexandroúpolis, Psará, Rhodes, Sámos and Kos; four ferries a week and day excursions in season run to Ag. Efstrátios. In summer, there's a weekly **excursion** to Mount Áthos. **Caiques** from Mýrina's north harbour go to beaches and the sea caves at Skála.

Port authority: t 225 402 2225.

By road: buses (**t** 225 402 2464) around Límnos are not very frequent. Many villages have only one service a day, so there's no way to get back to Mýrina the same day, hence the town's many taxis and moped and car hire firms.

Tourist Information

Tourist information office: at the port, **t** 225 402 2935.

El Travel, 11 Ralli Kopsídi St, **t** 225 402 4988, **f** 225 402 2697, *eltravel@lim.forthnet.gr*.

Where to Stay and Eat

Accommodation on Límnos is limited and upmarket; book in July and August.

Mýrina ✉ 81400

Porto Myrina Palace, nearby in Avlon bay, **t** 225 402 4805, **f** 225 402 4858 (*L; luxury*) Built in 1995 around a 4th-century BC Temple of Artemis; clad in marble, it boasts an Olympic outdoor pool and an indoor one, and all mod cons. *Open May–Oct.*

Kastro Beach, **t** 225 402 2772, **f** 225 402 2784 (*B; expensive–moderate*). Large and comfortable, near the post office.

Villa Afrodite, **t** 225 402 4795, **f** 225 402 5031 (*A; expensive*). Just outside the centre near Platís Beach, with a pool and gardens.

Ifestos, 17 Eth. Antistasseos, **t** 225 402 4960, **f** 225 402 3623 (*C; expensive–moderate*). Friendly, well-designed, 100m from Platís beach; all rooms with fridge and balcony.

Lemnos, **t** 225 402 2153, **f** 225 402 3329 (*C; moderate–inexpensive*). On the waterfront.

O Glaros, **t** 225 402 2220 (€20–25). Pretty taverna in the Turkish harbour, with a veranda and view of the castle, specializing in fish, crayfish and lobster.

Avra, where the boat docks. Undoubtedly one of the best dinner deals in town.

O Platanos. By a pair of massive plane trees, with excellent traditional fare.

Kontiás/Tsimántria ✉ 81400

There are about 20 rooms to rent in Kontiás; in Tsimántria, **Nasos Kotsinadelis' Taverna** is famous for its chicken grilled over coals.

Moúdros ✉ 81401

To Kyma, **t** 225 407 1333, **f** 225 407 1484 (*B; expensive*). Traditional hotel and a tranquil place to stay, with a reasonable restaurant and bar. *Open all year.*

---

repelled by the heroine Maroúla, who seized her dying father's weapons and uttered a blood-curdling battle cry. In 1478 Mehmet came in person and took the island. During the First World War, Moúdros Bay was the naval base of the Allies at Gallipoli.

Mýrina

Small Mýrina, the island's appealing port and capital, is Límnos' only real town, its landmark a romantic castle built over the rocky promontory in the midst of the sandy shore. A long shopping street noodles up from the commercial harbour in the south. Although a new boutique or shop opens every year, on the whole Mýrina still very much belongs to the Límnians and offers the distinct sights and smells – cologne, freshly ground coffee and pungent herbs – of old Greece. There isn't much to see, but the walk up to the **Kástro** offers a fine view over much of the low rolling island and across the sea to Athos. The castle foundations date to classical times, when it bore a Temple of Artemis; the walls were built in 1186 by Andronicus Comnenus I, then rebuilt by the Venetians in the 15th century, and the Turks a century later.

The *kástro* divides the waterfront into two: a 'Turkish' beach on the south side near the commercial port and, to the north, the main long, sandy Romaíkos or 'Greek beach', with tavernas and much of Mýrina's nightlife. The north port is closed by Cape Petassós and the pretty beach of **Aktí Mýrina**, with an exclusive bungalow hotel on the spot where Límnian women hurled their dead husbands into the sea. Off Romaíkos Beach, the **Archaeological Museum** (*t 225 402 2990; open Tues–Sun 9–3; adm*) has a superb collection. Upstairs are prehistoric relics from Polióchne, divided into four different periods by colour, beginning with the 'Black' period, from 4000 BC. Downstairs are more recent discoveries.

Around Límnos

There are beaches north and south of Mýrina, where discreet free camping is usually tolerated. North of Mýrina the beaches are pebbly but safe, especially **Riha Néra**, with watersports, **Avlónas**, with a bungalow development, and **Ag. Ioánnis**, with tavernas. The more popular beaches are past the army base to the south on the beautiful buxom bays below **Platís** and **Thános** (a lovely golden stretch of sand). Or aim for **Nevgatis**, a kilometre of fine sand kissed by a crystal, shallow sea. **Kontiás** is the island's liveliest and prettiest village, home of Kontiás ouzo. In the summer it fills up with returned immigrants from South Africa and Australia. Just south is an old Mycenaean tower called the **Vryókastro**; **Evgáti** is a decent sandy beach.

East of Kontiás, **Néa Koutális** has a **Nautical Tradition Museum** (*t 225 409 2383 for hours*) and the best beach with pine trees and restaurants, on the vast natural harbour of **Moúdros Bay**. In April 1915 the Anglo-French fleet launched its ill-fated attack on the Dardanelles from here, a campaign planned partly on Límnos by Winston Churchill, then First Lord of the Admiralty. East of gloomy **Moúdros**, the island's second largest town, is the immaculately kept **British Commonwealth war cemetery**; the 800 graves belong to wounded personnel brought back to Moúdros, only to die there in hospital. Límnos' airport (civil and military) is at the north end of the bay, where the island is only a few kilometres wide.

Older Limnians preferred the island's easterly wings. Northeast, on Pournías Bay, **Kótsinas** was the walled medieval capital. A statue of the heroine Maroúla stands here and a spring with good water flows down a long stairway by the church, **Zoodóchos Pigí**. A couple of pleasant bars overlook the fishing port, while from the top of the village there are views east to the **Aliki** and **Chortarolimni lagoons**, a winter resort for flamingoes, bee-eaters, falcons, swans, herons and the ruddy shelduck. **Ormos Kéros** has a sandy stretch of beach, the most popular on the island with swimmers and (experienced) windsurfers. It has dunes all the way to **Kontopoúli** built on ancient Mýrina's rival, **Hephestía**, named after the god who crash-landed here. Parts of the theatre, houses, the acropolis and tombs, mostly unexcavated, remain.

Across little Tigáni Bay from Hephestía, **Chloï** (*open 9.30–3.30*) is better known these days as **Kavírio** after the sanctuary of the Underworld deities, the Cabiri, who later moved to Samothráki (*see* p.611). Archaic foundations stand around a 6th–7th-century BC temple of initiation in a graceful setting, with a beach below. Under the sanctuary a trail leads to the so-called **Cave of Philoktétis**. Beyond is the pleasant village of **Pláka** at the tip of Cape Hermaeon. About 30m out are the submerged ruins of ancient **Chryse**, visible on calm days from a boat. Pláka has good beaches, but there are no real tourist facilities.

Polióchne, one of the most important archaeological sites in the Aegean (*open 9.30–5.30*), is signposted from **Kamínia**, on Límnos' southeast wing. Of its seven different layers of civilization, the oldest Neolithic town predates the Egyptian dynasties and the earliest level of Troy; walls and houses remain of the second town of 2000 BC which can claim the oldest known baths in the Aegean; the third city dates back to the Copper Age, while the top Bronze Age settlement was the Límnos of Homer, from 1500 to 100 BC. There's little to see, but the explanations in English help bring the site to life. Between Polióchne and the abandoned cliff-top monastery of **Ag. Sózos** stretches a sandy expanse called the 'Sahara of Límnos'.

Ag. Efstrátios (ΑΓ. ΕΥΣΤΡΑΤΙΟΣ)

The remote, partly dry, partly green, little volcanic triangle of **Ag. Efstrátios** (locally known as **t'Aïstratí**) lies 21 nautical miles southwest of Límnos. It is linked by ferry four times a week, but as the port is too shallow for big boats, be prepared to transfer into caiques. Rich in minerals (including petroleum), the islet has been inhabited from Mycenaean times. From 1936–62 Ag. Efstrátios played Alcatraz to scores of Greek Communists, but after an earthquake wreaked havoc in 1968, the island's 250 inhabitants all moved next to a wide, sandy beach in a dreary village of concrete huts thrown up after the disaster. The sea – transparent and rich in fish – brings in most of their income. Besides the pleasant village beach, there are several others perfect for Robinson Crusoes, but you will need to hike for at least an hour or hire a caique. For real isolation try the long, sandy beach at Ag. Efstrátios' baby islet, **Vélia**. If you want to stay, the **Xenonas Aï-Strati** (*t 225 409 3329; inexpensive*), is a good bet and occupies one of the very few houses to survive the quake; there are also rooms, tolerated free camping, a small shop or two and a couple of tavernas with limited menus.

Language

Greek holds a special place as the oldest spoken language in Europe, going back at least 4,000 years. From the ancient language, Modern Greek, or Romaíka, developed into two forms: the purist or *katharévousa*, literally translated as 'clean language', and the popular, or Demotic *demotikí*, the language of the people. However, while the purist is consciously Classical, the popular is as close to its ancient origins as say, Chaucerian English is to modern English.

These days few purist words are spoken but you will see the old *katharévousa* on shop signs and official forms. Even though the bakery is called the *foúrnos* the sign over the door will read ΑΡΤΟΠΟΛΕΙΟΝ, bread-seller, while the general store will be the ΠΑΝΤΟΠΟΛΕΙΟΝ, seller of all. You'll still see the pure form on wine labels as well. At the end of the 18th century, in the wakening swell of national pride, writers felt the common language wasn't good enough; archaic forms were brought back and foreign ones replaced. Upon independence, this somewhat stilted, artificial construction called *katharévousa* became the official language of books, documents and even newspapers.

The more vigorous and natural Demotic soon began to creep back; in 1901 Athens was shaken by riots and the government fell when the New Testament appeared in *demotikí*; in 1903 several students were killed in a fight with the police during a *demotikí* performance of Aeschylus. When the fury subsided, it looked as if the Demotic would win out by popular demand until the Papadópoulos government (1967–74) made it part of its puritan 'moral cleansing' of Greece to revive the purist *katharévousa*. It was the only language allowed in secondary schools and everything from textbooks to matchbook covers had to be written in the pure form.

The great language debate was eventually settled in 1978 when Demotic was made the official tongue.

Greeks travel so far and wide that even in the most remote places there's usually someone who speaks English, more likely than not with an American, Australian or even South African drawl. On the other hand, learning a bit of Greek can make your travels much more enjoyable.

Usually spoken with great velocity, Greek isn't a particularly easy language to pick up by ear. However, even if you have no great desire to learn Greek, it is very helpful to know at least the alphabet – so that you can find your way around – and a few basic words and phrases.

Greekspeak

Sign language is an essential part of Greek life and it helps to know what it all means. Greekspeak for 'no' is usually a click of the tongue, accompanied by raised eyebrows and a tilt of the head backwards. It could be all three or a permutation. 'Yes' is usually indicated by a forward nod, head tilted to the side. If someone doesn't hear you or understand you properly they will often shake their heads from side to side quizzically and say '*Oríste?*' Hands whirl like windmills in conversations and beware the emphatic open hand brought sharply down in anger.

A circular movement of the right hand usually implies something very good or in great quantities. Greek people also use exclamations which sound quite odd but actually mean a lot, like *po, po, po!* an expression of disapproval and derision; *brávo* comes in handy for praise while *ópa!* is useful for *whoópa!* look out! or watch it!; *sigá sigá* means slowly, slowly; *éla!*, come or get on with you; *kíta!* look.

The Greek Alphabet

Pronunciation		English Equivalent
Α	α	*álfa*	short 'a' as in 'father'
Β	β	*víta*	v
Γ	γ	*gámma*	guttural g or y sound
Δ	δ	*délta*	always a hard th as in 'though'
Ε	ε	*épsilon*	short 'e' as in 'bet'
Ζ	ζ	*zíta*	z
Η	η	*íta*	long 'e' as in 'bee'
Θ	θ	*thíta*	soft th as in 'thin'
Ι	ι	*yóta*	long 'e' as in 'bee'; sometimes like 'y' in 'yet'
Κ	κ	*káppa*	k
Λ	λ	*lámtha*	l
Μ	μ	*mi*	m
Ν	ν	*ni*	n
Ξ	ξ	*ksi*	'x' as in 'ox'
Ο	ο	*ómicron*	'o' as in 'cot'
Π	π	*pi*	p
Ρ	ρ	*ro*	r

Pronunciation		English Equivalent
Σ	σ,ς	*sigma*	s
Τ	τ	*taf*	t
Υ	υ	*ípsilon*	long 'e' as in 'bee'
Φ	φ	*fi*	f
Χ	χ	*chi*	ch as in 'loch'
Ψ	ψ	*psi*	ps as in 'stops'
Ω	ω	*oméga*	'o' as in 'cot'

Diphthongs and Consonant Combinations

ΑΙ	αι	short 'e' as in 'bet'
ΕΙ	ει, ΟΙ οι	'i' as in 'machine'
ΟΥ	ου	oo as in 'too'
ΑΥ	αυ	av or af
ΕΥ	ευ	ev or ef
ΗΥ	ηυ	iv or if
ΓΓ	γγ	ng as in 'angry'
ΓΚ	γκ	hard 'g'; ng within word
ΝΤ	ντ	'd'; nd within word
ΜΠ	μπ	'b'; mp within word

Useful Phrases

Yes	*né/málista* (formal)	Ναί/Μάλιστα
No	*óchi*	Οχι
I don't know	*then kséro*	Δέν ξέρω
I don't understand... (Greek)	*then katalavéno... (ellinsiká)*	Δέν καταλαβαίνω... (Ελληνικά)
Does someone speak English?	*milái kanis angliká?*	Μιλάει κανείς αγγλικά;
Go away	*fíyete*	Φύγετε
Help!	*voíthia!*	Βοήθεια!
My friend	*o fílos moo (m)*	Ο φίλος μου
	ee fíli moo (f)	Η φίλη μου
Please	*parakaló*	Παρακαλώ
Thank you (very much)	*evcharistó (pára polí)*	Ευχαριστώ (πάρα πολύ)
You're welcome	*parakaló*	Παρακαλώ
It doesn't matter	*thén pirázi*	Δενπειράζει
OK, alright	*endaxi*	Εντάξει
Of course	*vevéos*	Βεβαίως
Excuse me, (as in 'sorry')	*signómi*	Συγγνώμη
Pardon? Or, from waiters, what do you want?	*oríste?*	Ορίστε;
Be careful!	*proséchete!*	Προσέχετε!
What is your name?	*pos sas léne? (pl & formal)*	Πώς σάς λένε;
	pos se léne? (singular)	Πώς σέ λένε;
How are you?	*ti kánete? (formal/pl)*	Τί κάνεται;
	ti kanis? (singular)	Τί κάνεις;
Hello	*yásas, hérete (formal/pl)*	Γειάσας, Χέρεται
	yásou (singular)	Γειάσου
Goodbye	*yásas, (formal/pl), andío*	Γειάσας, Αντίο
	yásou	Γειάσου

Good morning	kaliméra	Καλημέρα
Good evening/good night	kalispéra/kaliníchta	Καλησπέρα/Καληνύχτα
What is that?	ti íne aftó?	Τι είναι αυτό;
What?	ti?	Τί;
Who?	piós? (m), piá? (f)	Ποιός; Ποιά;
Where?	poo?	Πού
When?	póte?	Πότε;
Why?	yiatí?	Γιατί;
How?	pos?	Πώς;
I am/You are/He, she, it is	íme/íse/íne	Είμαι/Είσαι/Είναι
We are/You are/They are	ímaste/ísaste/íne	Είμαστε/Είσαστε/Είναι
I am lost	échasa to thrómo	Έχασα το δρόμο
I am hungry/I am thirsty	pinó/thipsó	Πεινώ/Διψώ
I am tired/ill	íme kourasménos/árostos	Είμαι κουρασμένος/άρρωστος
I am poor	íme ftochós	Είμαι φτωχός
I love you	s'agapó	Σ'αγαπώ
Good/bad/so-so	kaló/kakó/étsi ki étsi	καλό/κακό/έτσι κι έτσι
Fast/big/small	grígora/megálo/mikró	γρήγορα/μεγάλο/μικρό
Hot/cold	zestó/crío	ζεστό/κρύο
Nothing	típota	Τίποτα

Shops, Services, Sightseeing

I would like...	tha íthela...	Θα ήθελα...
Where is...?	poo íne...?	Πού είναι...;
How much is it?	póso káni?	Πόσο κάνει;
bakery	foúrnos/artopoleion	φούρνος/Αρτοπωλείον
bank	trápeza	τράπεζα
beach	paralía	παραλία
church	eklisía	εκκλησία
cinema	kinimatográfos	κινηματογράφος
hospital	nosokomío	νοσοκομείο
hotel	xenodochío	ξενοδοχείο
hot water	zestó neró	ζεστό νερό
kiosk	períptero	περίπτερο
money	leftá	λεφτά
museum	moosío	μουσείο
newspaper (foreign)	efimerítha (xéni)	εφημερίδα (ξένη)
pharmacy	farmakío	φαρμακείο
police station	astinomía	αστυνομία
policeman	astifílakas	αστυνομικός
post office	tachithromío	ταχυδρομείο
plug, electrical	príza	πρίζα
plug, bath	tápa	τάπα
restaurant	estiatório	εστιατόριο
sea	thálassa	θάλασσα
shower	doush	ντους
student	fititís	μαθητής, φοιτητής
telephone office	Oté	ΟΤΕ
theatre	théatro	θέατρο
toilet	tooaléta	τουαλέτα

Time

What time is it?	ti óra íne?	Τί ώρα είναι
month/week/day	mína/evthomáda/méra	μήνα/εβδομάδα/μέρα
morning/afternoon/evening	proí/apóyevma/vráthi	πρωί/απόγευμα/βράδυ
yesterday/today/tomorrow	chthés/símera/ávrio	χθές/σήμερα/αύριο
now/later	tóra/metá	τώρα/μετά
it is early/late	íne norís/argá	είναι νωρίς/αργά

Travel Directions

I want to go to ...	thélo na páo ston (m), sti n (f)...	Θέλω να πάω στον, στην...
How can I get to...?	pós boró na páo ston (m), stin (f)...?	Πως μπορώ να πάω στον, στην...?
Where is...?	poo íne ...?	Πού είναι...?
How far is it?	póso makriá íne?	Πόσο μακριά είναι
When will the... come?	póte tha érthi to (n), ee (f), o (m)...?	Πότε θα έρθει το, η, ο...?
When will the... leave?	póte tha fíyí to (n), ee (f), o (m)...?	Πότε θα φύγει το, η, ο...?
From where do I catch...?	apó poo pérno...?	Από πού πέρνω...?
How long does the trip take?	póso keró pérni to taxíthi?	Πόσο καιρό παίρνει το ταξίδι?
Please show me	parakaló thíkste moo	Παρακαλώ δείξτε μου
the (nearest) town	to horió (to pió kondinó)	Το χωριό (το πιό κοντινό)
here/there/near/far	ethó/eki/kondá/makriá	εδώ/εκεί/κοντά/μακριά
left/right	aristerá/thexiá	αριστερά/δεξιά
north/south/east/west	vória/nótia/anatoliká/thitiká	βόρεια/νότια/ανατολικά/δ

Driving

Where can I rent ...?	poo boró na nikiáso ...?	Πού μποπώ νά? νοικιάσω ...?
a car	éna aftokínito	ένα αυτοκινητο
a motorbike	éna michanáki	ένα μηχανάκι
a bicycle	éna pothílato	ένα ποδήλατο
Where can I buy petrol?	poo boró n'agorásso venzíni?	Πού μπορώ ν'αγοράσω βενζίνη?
Where is a garage?	poo íne éna garáz?	Που είναι ένα γκαράζ?
a mechanic	énas mihanikós	ένας μηχανικός
a map	énas chártis	ένας χάρτης
Where is the road to...?	poo íne o thrómos yiá...?	Που είναι ο δρόμος για...?
Where does this road lead?	poo pái aftós o thrómos?	Που πάει αυτός ο δρόμος?
Is the road good?	íne kalós o thrómos?	Είναι καλός ο δρόμος?
EXIT	éxothos (th as in 'the')	ΕΞΟΔΟΣ
ENTRANCE	ísothos (th as in 'the'	ΕΙΣΟΔΟΣ
DANGER	kinthinos (th as in 'the')	ΚΙΝΔΥΝΟΣ
SLOW	argá	ΑΡΓΑ
NO PARKING	apagorévete ee státhmevsis	ΑΠΑΓΟΡΕΥΕΤΑΙ Η ΣΤΑΘΜΕΥΣΙΣ
KEEP OUT	apagorévete ee ísothos	ΑΠΑΓΟΡΕΥΕΤΑΙ Η ΕΙΣΟΔΟΣ

Numbers

one	*énas (m), mía (f), éna (n)*	ένας, μία, ένα
two	*thío*	δύο
three	*tris (m, f), tría (n)*	τρείς, τρία
four	*téseris (m, f), téssera (n)*	τέσσερεις, τέσσερα
five	*pénde*	πέντε
six	*éxi*	έξι
seven/eight/nine/ten	*eptá/októ/ennéa/théka*	επτά/οκτώ/εννέα/δέκα
eleven/twelve/thirteen	*éntheka/thótheka/thekatría*	έντεκα/δώδεκα/δεκατρία
twenty	*íkosi*	είκοσι
twenty-one	*íkosi éna (m, n) mía (f)*	είκοσι ένα, μία
thirty/forty/fifty/sixty	*triánda/saránda/penínda /exínda*	τριάντασαράντα/πενήντα/ εξήντα
seventy/eighty/ninety	*evthomínda/ogthónda/ enenínda*	ευδομήντα/ογδόντα/ ενενήντα
one hundred	*ekató*	εκατό
one thousand	*chília*	χίλια

Months/Days

January	*Ianooários*	Ιανουάριος
February	*Fevrooários*	Φεβρουάριος
March	*Mártios*	Μάρτιος
April	*Aprílios*	Απρίλιος
May	*Máios*	Μάιος
June	*Ioónios*	Ιούνιος
July	*Ioólios*	Ιούλιος
August	*Avgoostos*	Αύγουστος
September	*Septémvrios*	Σεπτέμβριος
October	*Októvrios*	Οκτώβριος
November	*Noémvrios*	Νοέμβριος
December	*Thekémvrios*	Δεκέμβριος
Sunday	*Kiriakí*	Κυριακή
Monday	*Theftéra*	Δευτέρα
Tuesday	*Tríti*	Τρίτη
Wednesday	*Tetárti*	Τετάρτη
Thursday	*Pémpti*	Πέμπτη
Friday	*Paraskeví*	Παρασκευή
Saturday	*Sávato*	Σάββατο

Transport

the airport/aeroplane	*to arothrómio/aropláno*	το αεροδρόμιο/αεροπλάνο
the bus station	*ee stási too leoforíou*	η στάση του λεωφορείου
the railway station/the train	*o stathmós too trénou/to tréno*	ο σταθμός του τρένου/το τρένο
the port/port authority	*to limáni/limenarchío*	το λιμάνι/λιμεναρχείο
the ship	*to plío, to karávi*	το πλοίο, το καράβι
the steamship	*to vapóri*	το βαπόρι
the car	*to aftokínito*	το αυτοκίνητο
a ticket	*éna isitírio*	ένα εισιτήριο

Glossary

acropolis fortified height, usually the site of city's chief temples

acroteria figures on pedestals on the top and corners of a pediment

agíos, agía, agíi saint/saints, abbreviated Ag.

agora market and main civic area

áno/apáno upper

archaía ancient ruins

ávaton holy of holies, where only the priests could enter

bouleuterion council chamber

caique small wooden boat

cavea the concave seating area of an ancient theatre

cella innermost room of a temple

Cyclopean used to describe walls of stones so huge that only a Cyclops could carry them

choklakía black and white pebble mosaic

chóra 'place'; often what islanders call their 'capital' town

chorió village

chthonic pertaining to the Underworld

dimarchíon town hall

entablature all parts of an architectural order above the columns

entasis convex curving of a column that gives the illusion of the column being straight

EOT Greek National Tourist Office

eparchía eparchy, an Orthodox diocese, now used to refer to an area outside a big city

exonarthex outer porch of a church

heroön a shrine to a hero or demigod, often built over a tomb

hoplite foot soldier with a large circular shield, often interlocked with other hoplites to form a unit called a phalanx

iconostasis in an Orthodox church, the decorated screen between the nave and altar

kalderími stone-paved pathways

kástro castle or fort

katholikón monastery chapel

káto lower

kore Archaic statue of a maiden

kouros Archaic statue of a naked youth

krater large bowl for mixing wine and water

larnax Minoan clay sarcophagus, resembling a bathtub

limáni port

limenarchíon port authority

loutrá hot spring, spa

megaron Mycenaean palace 'unit'

metopes sculpted panel on a frieze

moní monastery or convent

náos temple

narthex entrance porch of a church

néa new

nisí/nisiá island/islands

nomós province

odeion concert hall, originally roofed

ósios blessed

OTE Greek National phone company

paleo old

palaestra area of a gymnasium set aside for wrestling

panagía the 'all holy': the Virgin Mary

panegýri saint's feast day

Pantocrator the Almighty: a figure of the risen Christ in Byzantine churches

paralía beach or waterfront

pithos large storage jar

peripteral building surrounded by a colonnade supporting the roof

plateía square

polis city-state

pronaos temple porch

propylon entrance gate; a **propylaea** has more than one door

pýrgos tower

rhyton drinking horn

skála port

spílio cave or grotto

stathmós station, for buses, trains or petrol

stoa a portico not attached to a large building; in an agora, often lined with shops

stylobate base of a colonnade

temenos sacred precinct

tholos circular building; often a Mycenaean beehive tomb

Further Reading

In addition to the following, don't ignore the many works by Greek publishers in English, available in Greek bookshops, notably the series of modern Greek fiction translated into English by Kedros Press and the regional architectural guides by Melissa.

Angelomatis-Tsougarakis, Helen, *The Eve of the Greek Revival: British travellers' perceptions of early 19th-century Greece* (Routledge, 1990). Attitudes on the verge of the War of Independence.

Andrewes, Antony, *Greek Society* (Penguin, 1967). Good introduction to ancient Greek society, divided into bite-sized topics.

Andrews, Kevin, *Castles of the Morea*. *The* castle book, complete with drawings; try your local library. Also his *Flight of Ikaros*, (Penguin, 1984) written about travelling in the Peloponnese writing about castles during the Greek Civil War.

Burkert, Walter, *Greek Religion* (Basil Blackwell, Oxford, and Harvard University Press, 1987) – ancient religion, that is, by one of the great authorities in the field.

Byron, Robert, *The Station* (Phoenix, 2000). Reprint of the lively 1928 classic on Athos.

Castleden, Rodney, *Minoans: Life in Bronze Age Crete* (Routledge, 1990).

Chadwick, John, *The Decipherment of Linear B* (Cambridge University Press, 1991). A detective story: how Michael Ventris broke the code that was Mycenaean Linear B.

Cheetam, Nicolas, *Medieval Greece* (Yale University Press, 1981, out of print). Good coverage on the time after the Romans to Greece's strange Frankish interlude.

Clogg, Richard, *A Short History of Modern Greece* (Cambridge University Press, 1992). Best, readable account of a messy subject.

Dalby, Andrew, *Siren Feasts: A History of Food and Gastronomy in Greece* (Routledge, 1996). Very detailed account of ancient Greek diet and feasts.

De Bernières, Louis, *Captain Corelli's Mandolin* (Martin Secker & Warburg, London 1994). Gorgeous humane novel set in Kefalonía during the Second World War.

Dodds, E. R., *The Greeks and the Irrational* (University of California Press). Puts Homer's Olympian religion 'on the couch' and examines the impulses underlying its apparently rational structure.

Davidson, James, *Courtesans and Fishcakes* (Fontana, 1998). Erudite and amusing study of ancient Greek sexual gymnastics and lust for seafood.

Drews, Robert, *The Coming of the Greeks* (Princeton, 1988). Careful tracing of Indo-European migrations to Greece.

Durrell, Gerald, *My Family and Other Animals* (Viking/Penguin). Charming account of expat life on Corfu in the 1930s.

Durrell, Lawrence, *The Greek Islands, Prospero's Cell* and *The White House* (both on Corfu); *Reflections on a Marine Venus* (on Rhodes) (Faber & Faber and Viking/Penguin). Evocative works by an old prose maestro.

Fermor, Patrick Leigh, *The Mani* and *Roumeli: Travels in Northern Greece* (both Penguin). Beautiful books that wear their wisdom and excellent scholarship lightly.

Finley, M. I., *The World of Odysseus* (Penguin/Viking). Mycenaean history and myth.

Grant, Michael, *The Classical Greeks* and *The Rise of the Greeks* (both Phoenix). Very readable accounts of the Greeks in their heyday, and how they got there.

Graves, Robert, *The Greek Myths* (Penguin, 1955, but often reprinted). The classic, down to the often off-the-wall footnotes.

Greenhalgh, Peter and Eliopolis, Edward, *Deep Into Mani* (Faber and Faber, 1985). A tour de force, terrific on the *myrologia*.

Hammond, N. G. L., *Alexander the Great* (Bristol Press, 1980). General biography by one of the finest Alexander scholars, with a detailed section on ancient Macedonia.

Harrison, Jane Ellen, *Themis: A Study of the Social Origins of Greek Religion* and *Prolegomena to the Study of Greek Religion.* Widely available reprints of the wonderful pioneering classics on Greek religion.

Higgins, Reynold, *Minoan and Mycenaean Art* (Thames and Hudson, 1981). Compact and well illustrated overview.

Kazantzakis, Nikos, *Zorba the Greek, Report to Greco, Christ Recrucified, Freedom or Death* (Faber & Faber/Simon & Schuster). The soul of Crete in fiction.

Keeley, Edmund and Philip Sherrard, translators, *A Greek Quintet* (Denis Harvey and Co., Évia, 1981). Fine translations of Cavafy, Sikelianos, Seferis, Elytis and Gatsos.

Kremezi, Aglaia, *The Foods of the Greek Islands* (Houghton Mifflin, 2000). Kremezi set herself the task of discovering recipes on the verge of extinction, while prowling the kitchens of elderly housewives.

Lane Fox, Robin, *Alexander the Great* (Penguin, 1986). Sweeping, sympathetic and fluent epic account of the 'last Homeric hero.'

Leontis, Artemis, ed. *Greece: A Traveler's Literary Companion* (Whereabouts Press, 1997). Insightful selection of Greek short stories: a great introduction into the obsessions of modern Greece.

McKirahan Jr., Richard D., *Philosophy Before Socrates* (Hackett Indianapolis, 1994). Know your pre-Socratics and discover there really isn't anything new under the sun.

Manessis, Nico, *The Illustrated Greek Wine Book.* Annually updated guide in English to Greek wines, lavish and packed with photos.

Mazower, Mark, *Inside Hitler's Greece* (Yale University Press, 1995). Vivid account of life during the Occuption. His *The Balkans* (Phoenix, 2002) offers a concise background to the Macedonian issue.

Meier, Christian, *Athens: A Portrait of the City in Its Golden Age* (Pimlico, 2000). Wide-ranging and knowledgeable overview of a unique period and people.

Miller, Henry, *The Colossus of Maroussi* (New Directions). A passionately enthusiastic love letter to Greece, written on the eve of the Second World War.

Osborne, Robin, *Greece in the Making 1200–479 BC* (Routledge, 1996). Excellent, meaty account of the Archaic period.

Pausanias, *Guide to Greece* (two volumes), trans. by Peter Levi (Penguin). The ultimate source, plus Levi's detailed footnotes show just how often Pausanias was spot on.

Pettifer, James, *The Greeks: The Land and People Since the War* (Penguin, London and New York, 200). Good general account.

Renfrew, Colin, *The Cycladic Spirit* (Thames & Hudson). A study of Cycladic art.

Rice, David Talbot, *Art of the Byzantine Era* (Thames & Hudson). A classic.

Runciman, Steven, *The Great Church in Captivity* (Cambridge University Press, 1968). Not for the faint-hearted, but he is one of the few who can explain the Greek church to Westerners; in this case, he examines its tricky role under the Turkish oOccupation.

Sagan, Eli, *The Honey and the Hemlock* (Princeton University, 1991). Study of democracy using the Athenian model. The really scary part is how little we have changed.

Slater, Philip E., *The Glory of Hera* (Princeton University Press, 1968). A witty and gripping Freudian analysis of Greek mothers, their inferior status and how it affects their boys .

Spivey, Nigel, *Greek Art* (Phaidon, 1997). Intriguing account of the evolution of Greek art and its political undercurrents.

Storace, Patricia, *Dinner with Persephone*, (Pantheon, New York 1996/Granta, London 1997). New York poet tackles the contradictions of modern Greece

Vrettos, Theodore, *The Elgin Affair* (Secker and Warburg, 1997). Lively, unbiased account of Elgin's removal of the Parthenon marbles.

Walbank, F. W., *The Hellenistic World* (Fontana/Harvard University Press). The lively period from Alexander to the Romans.

Ware, Timothy Callistos, *The Orthodox Church* (Penguin). All you've ever wanted to know about the national religion of Greece, told clearly and concisely by a believer.

Woodhouse, C. M., *Modern Greece: A Short History* (Faber & Faber, 1992).

Zaidmann, Louise and **Pantel, Pauline**, *Religion in the Ancient Greek City* (Cambridge University Press, 1992). Covers the brass tacks of practical ancient Greek religion.

Index

Main page references are in **bold**. Page references to maps are in *italics*.

Acknowledgements

Dana Facaros extends big thanks to the hundreds of kind locals along the way who made this book a pleasure to research; to Mike and Brian for the hospitality, dog-kisses and ouzo; to Lily and Jerry for checking out Crete; to Linda for persevering in the face of the worst bureaucracy Greece can throw up; to Dominique and Linda for their editing prowess; to Kate the famous cat-sitter, and to my dear Paco who somehow survived my prattling about Greece for over a year.

Linda Theodorou would like to thank Nikos, who put up with long mountain treks and endless queries about stresses and never lost his cool, not even when the Passat did. Ann and Russ Burdon turned fact-finding forays into delightful excursions, and Dana, as ever, provided motivation, good advice, and a hard act to follow. And then there are my wonderful fellow citizens, the Greeks themselves, who were everywhere helpful, always hospitable, and so tactful that no one ever made me feel uncomfortable about my heavily accented Greek.

Greece touring atlas

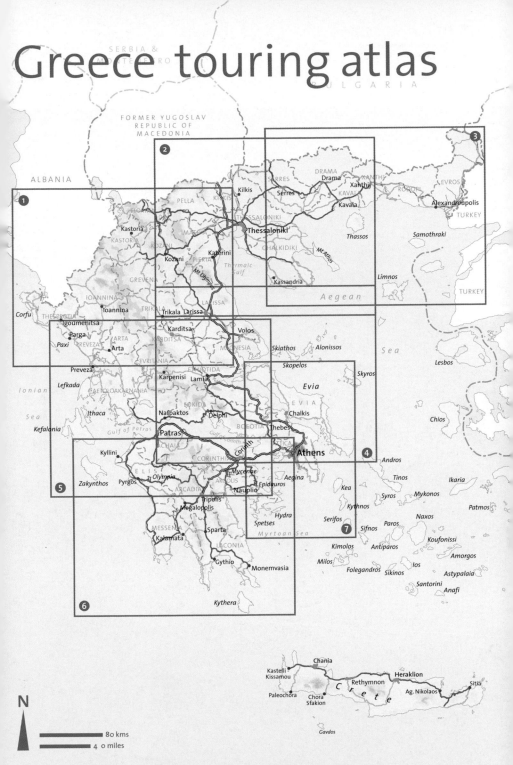

N

80 kms

4 o miles

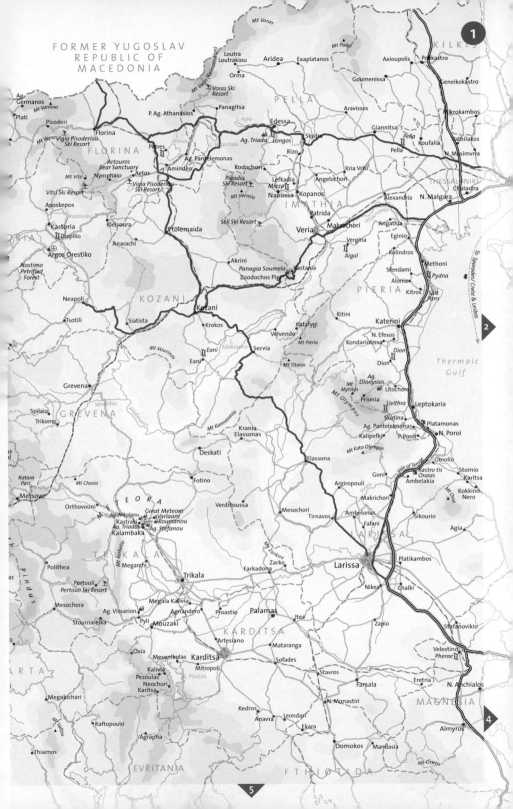

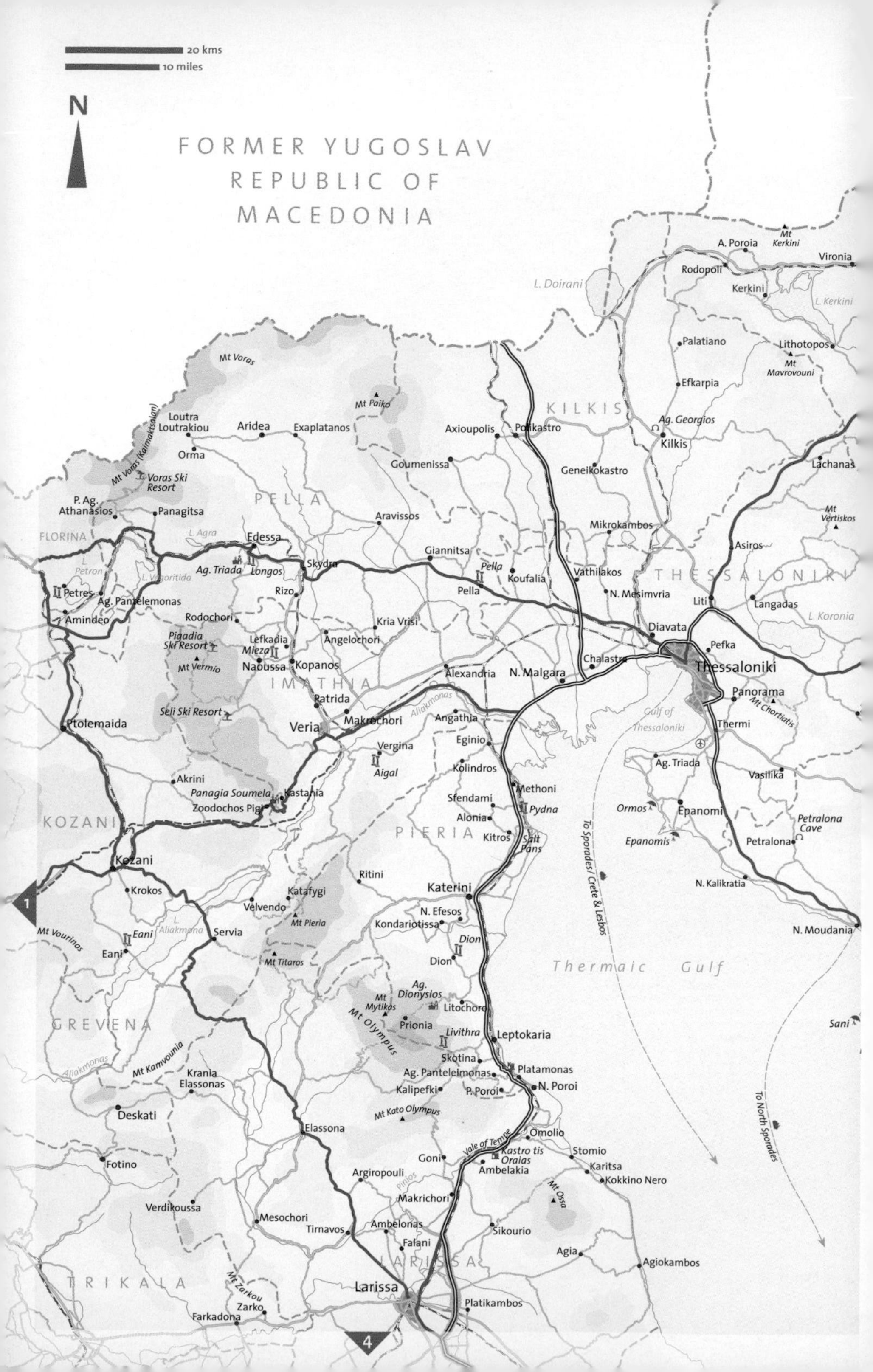

20 kms
10 miles
N
FORMER YUGOSLAV REPUBLIC OF MACEDONIA
A. Poroia
Mt Kerkini
Vironia
Rodopoli
Kerkini
L. Kerkini
L. Doirani
Palatiano
Lithotopos
Mt Mavrovouni
Efkarpia
Mt Voras
Mt Paiko
KILKIS
Ag. Georgios
Kilkis
Loutra Loutrakiou
Aridea
Exaplatanos
Axioupolis
Polikastro
Orma
Goumenissa
Geneikokastro
Lachanas
Mt Voras (Kaimaktsalan)
Voras Ski Resort
P. Ag. Athanasios
Panagitsa
PELLA
Aravissos
Mikrokambos
Mt Vertiskos
FLORINA
L. Agra
Edessa
Giannitsa
Asiros
L. Petron
L. Vegoritida
Ag. Triada
Longos
Skydra
Pella
Koufalia
Vathilakos
THESSALONIKI
Petres
Ag. Pantelemonas
Rizo
Pella
N. Mesimvria
Liti
Langadas
Amindeo
Rodochori
Kria Vrisi
L. Koronia
Diavata
Pigadia Ski Resort
Lefkadia
Mieza
Angelochori
Pefka
Mt Vermio
Naoussa
Kopanos
Chalastra
Thessaloniki
Alexandria
N. Malgara
IMATHIA
Aliakmonas
Panorama
Patrida
Mt Chortiatis
Seli Ski Resort
Gulf of Thessaloniki
Ptolemaida
Veria
Makrochori
Angathia
Thermi
Vergina
Eginio
Aigal
Kolindros
Ag. Triada
Vasilika
Akrini
Panagia Soumela
Kastania
Methoni
Zoodochos Pigi
Sfendami
Pydna
Ormos
Epanomi
Petralona Cave
KOZANI
Alonia
To Sporades/ Crete & Lesbos
PIERIA
Kitros
Salt Pans
Epanomis
Petralona
Kozani
Ritini
Katerini
N. Kalikratia
Krokos
Katafygi
Velvendo
N. Efesos
Mt Pieria
Kondariotissa
Mt Vourinos
L. Aliakmona
Servia
Dion
N. Moudania
Eani
Eani
Dion
Mt Titaros
Thermaic Gulf
Ag. Dionysios
Mt Mytikas
Litochoro
Mt Olympus
Prionia
Sani
GREVENA
Livithra
Leptokaria
Aliakmonas
Mt Kamvounia
Skotina
Krania Elassonas
Platamonas
Ag. Panteleimonas
Kalipefki
P. Poroi
N. Poroi
Deskati
Mt Kato Olympus
To North Sporades
Elassona
Omolio
Vale of Tempe
Stomio
Kastro tis Oraias
Fotino
Goni
Ambelakia
Karitsa
Argiropouli
Kokkino Nero
Pinios
Mt Ossa
Makrichori
Verdikoussa
Mesochori
Ambelonas
Tirnavos
Sikourio
Falani
Agia
LARISSA
Agiokambos
TRIKALA
Mt Zarkou
Larissa
Platikambos
Zarko
Farkadona
1
4

2

BULGARIA

Zagrantenia Forest

Karandere Forest · Elatia

Western Rodopi

Thermata

Potami · Skaloti

Promachonas · Mt Orvilos · K. Nevrokopi

Louta Sidirokastrou · Mt Vrondous Lailia Forest · Volakas · Mt Falakro · Nestos · Pachni

Sidirokastro · Vrondou Ski Resort · K. Vrondou · DRAMA · Paranesti · Ioniko · Sminthi

Mt Menikio · Kokinogia · Mt Lekani

Chrysopigi · Eleonas · Maara · Prosotsani · Drama · Nikiforos · Lekani · Stavroupolis · XANTHI

SERRES · Timiou Prodromou · Dokato · Livera · Xanthi

Serres · Alistrati · Ag. Athanasios · Paradeisos · Toxotes · Domidia

Monoklisia · N. Zichni · Alistrati Cave · Philippi · Krioneri · Krini · Timbario

Ag. Eleni · Stathmos Angistis · Krinides · Zygos · KAVALA · Xerias · Exochi

Strymonas · Angistis · Ikosifoinissis · Karvali · Chrisoupolis · Eflalo · Avdira

Nigrita · Proti · Mt Pangaion · Nikisiani · Ag. Silas · Skala

Achinos · Rodolivos · Eleftheroupolis · Kavala · N. Erasmio · Kotza Orman Forest

Ivira · Kipia · Panagia · P. Tsifliki

Mesoropi · Avli · N. Iraklitsa · Keramoti

Sochos · Amphipolis · Ofryniou · Mt Simvolon · N. Peramos · Limenas (Thassos) · To Is. Samothraki

Nea Kerdilia · Skala Prinos · Panagia

Askos · Mt Kerdilio · Touzla · Skala Kallirachis · Prinos · Skala Potamias

Mt Volvis · Asprovalta · Loutra Elevtheron · Kallirachis · Maries · Potamia · Is. Thassos

L. Volvi · Stavros · Mt. Ipsarion

Apollonia · Rendina · Limenaria

Zangliveri · Olympiada · Stageira · Potos · Moni Archangelou

Paleochori · Ierissos Gulf

Mt Cholomondas · Arnea

CHALKIDIKI · Gomati · Ierissos

Polygyros · N. Roda · Esfigmenou

Chelandariou

Amouliani · Ouranoupoli · Vatopediou

Olynthos · Metangitsi · Pirgadikia · Is. Amouliani · Zographou · Koutloumousiou

Konstamonitou · Karies · Stavronikita

Metamorfosi · Ormos Panagias · Docheiariou · Xenofondos · Skiti Ag. Panteleimonos

N. Potidea · Nikiti · Is. Diasporos · Gulf · Xiropotamou · Daphni · Filotheou

Kalogria · Karydi · Simonopetra · Ag. Dionysiou · Great Lavra

N. Fokea · Spathies · Vourvourou · M. Ag. Paviou · Mt Athos

Sani · Elia · Parthenonas · Kavourotrypes · Platanitsi

Afytos · N. Marmaras · Sarti

Kallithea · Kassandra Gulf

Kipsa · Kassandra · Is. Kelifos · Porto Carras · Skala Sikias

Kassandra Peninsula · Toroni · Kalamitsi

N. Skioni · Loutra · Porto Koufo

C. Paliouri

To Limnos

3

20 kms
10 miles

N

B U L G A R I A

Karandere Forest · Zagrantenia Forest
Elatia
Western Rodopi
Thermata

Potami · Skaloti

Promachonas · Mt Orvilos
K. Nevrokopi

Louta Sidirokastrou
Mt Vrondous Lailia Forest
Volakas
Mt Falakro
Nestos
Pachni

Sidirokastro
Vrondou Ski Resort
K. Vrondou
D R A M A
Paranesti
Ioniko
Sminthi

Mt Menikio
Chrysopigi
Kokinogia
Mt Lekani
Stavroupolis
X A N T H I

S E R R E S
Eleonas
Timiou Prodromou
Maara · Prosotsani
Drama
Nikiforos
Lekani
Livera · Xanthi

Serres
Alistrati
Dokato
Toxotes · Domidia
Paradeisos · Krini · Timbario

Monoklisia
N. Zichni
Alistrati Cave
Ag. Athanasios
Philippi · Krioneri
Xerias
Exochi

Ag. Eleni
Stathmos Angistis
Krinides
Zygos
K A V A L A
Avdira

Strymonas
Proti
Ikosifoinissis
Karvali
Chrisoupolis
Eflalo
Skala

Nigrita · Achinos
Angitis
Mt Pangaion
Nikisiani
Ag. Silas
Kavala
N. Erasmio
Kotza Orman Forest

Ivira
Rodolivos
Eleftheroupolis
Kipia
Avli
Panagia · P. Tsifliki
Kavala Gulf
Keramoti

Sochos
Mesoropi
N. Iraklitsa
N. Peramos
Limenas (Thassos)

THESSALONIKI
Askos
Mt Kerdilio
Nea Kerdilia
Amphipolis
Ofryniou
Mt Simvolon
Skala Prinos
Panagia

Mt Volvis
L. Volvi
Touzla
Skala Kallirachis
Prinos · Skala Potamias
Maries · Potamia
Is. Thassos

Apollonia
Rendina
Asprovalta
Stavros
Orfanos Gulf
Loutra Elevtheron
Kallirachis
Mt. Ipsarion

Olympiada · Stageira
Limenaria
Potos

Moni Archangelou

Paleochori
Arnea
Ierissos Gulf

Mt Cholomondas
CHALKIDIKI
Polygyros
Gomati
Ierissos
N. Roda

Esfigmenou
Chelandariou

Olynthos
Metangitsi
Pirgadikia
Is. Amouliani
Amouliani
Ouranoupoli
Zographou
Vatopediou
Koutloumousiou

Metamorfosi
Ormos Panagias
Is. Diasporos
Agiou Orou Gulf
Konstamonitou
Docheiariou
Xenofondos
Karies · Stavronikita
Skiti Ag. Panteleimonos

N. Potidea
Nikiti
Karydi
Xiropotamou
Daphni
Filotheou

N. Fokea
Kalogria Spathies
Elia
Vourvourou
Simonopetra
Ag. Dionysiou
M. Ag. Paviou
Mt Athos
Great Lavra

Sani · Afytos
Kallithea
Parthenonas
Kavourotrypes
Platanitsi

Kipsa · Kassandra
Kassandra Gulf
N. Marmaras
Is. Kelifos
Sarti

Porto Carras
Skala Sikias

Toroni
Kalamitsi

N. Skioni
Porto Koufo

Loutra
C. Paliouri

Kassandra Peninsula
Sithonia Peninsula

2

4

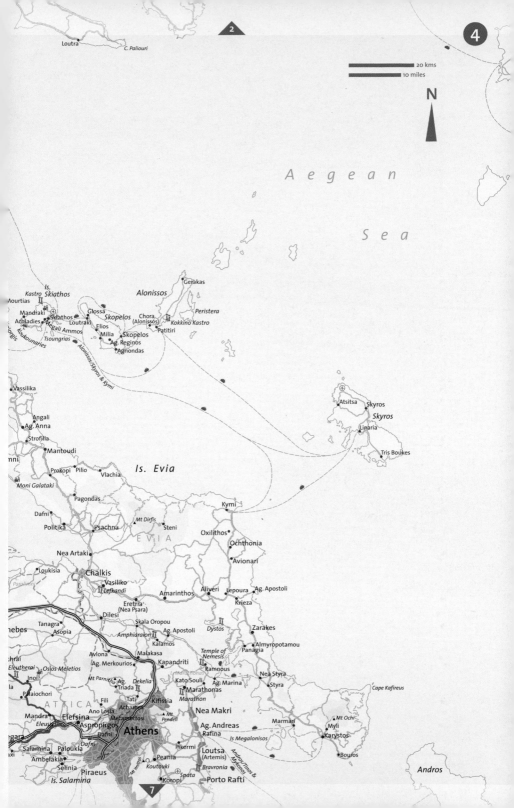

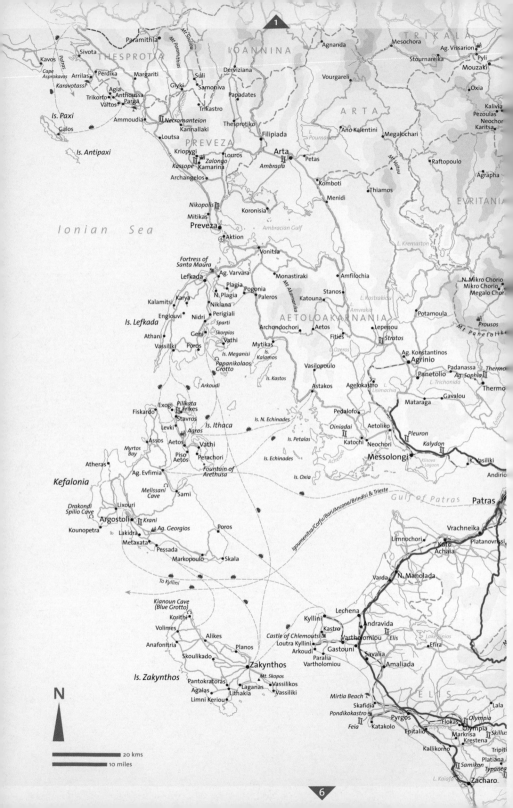

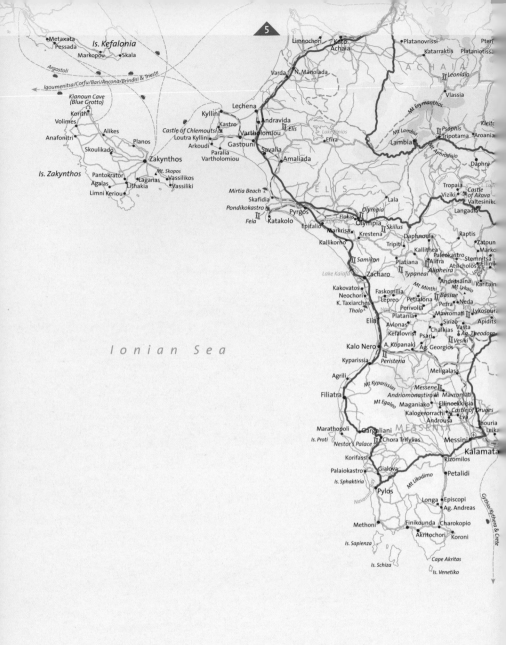

Is. Kefalonia
Metaxata
Pessada
Markopou Skala

Argostoli

Igoumenitsa/Corfu/Bari/Ancona/Brindisi & Trieste

Kianoun Cave
(Blue Grotto)
Korithi
Volimes
Anafonitri   Alikes
Skoulikado   Planos
                  Zakynthos
Is. Zakynthos Pantokrator   Mt. Skopos
               Agalas Lithakia Laganas Vassilikos
               Limni Keriou   Vassiliki

Kyllini
Kastro
Castle of Chlemoutsi
Loutra Kyllini
Arkoudi
Paralia
Vartholomiou

Lechena
Andravida
Vartholomiou Elis
Efira
Gastouni
Savalia
Amaliada

Limnochori Kato
            Achaia
Varda N. Manolada

Mt Erymanthos

Lala

Mirtia Beach
Skafidia
Pondikokastro
Feia Katakolo

Flokas
Olympia
Olympia Skillus
Epitalio
Markrisa
Kallikorho
Krestena
Tripiti

Platanovrissi Pteri
Katarraktis Plataniotissa
ACHAIA
Leonidio
Vlassia
Mt Lambia Psophis   Kleito
Lambia   Tripotama Aroania
Aphrodisio
Daphni
Tropaia
Viziki Castle
        of Akova
        Valtesiniko
Langadia

Daphnoula
Raptis
Zatoun
Marko
Kallithea Paleokastro
           Stemnitsa
Platiana Alifira Atsicholos Ellini
Typaneai Alipheira
Andritsaina Karitain
Mt Minthi Mt Lykaio
Faskomilia Bassae
Lepreo Petialona Petra Neda
Perivolia   Lykosoura
Platania   Apidits
Avlonas Sirizo
Kefalovrisi Psari Vasta Ag. Theodora
Chalkias   Vesiki
A. Kopanaki Ag. Georgios

Samikon
Lake Kaiafa
Zacharo
Kakovatos
Neochori
K. Taxiarches
Tholo
Elia
Kalo Nero

Kyparissia Peristeria
Agrili
Meligalas
Filiatra Mt Kyparissias
          Andriomonastiro Messene
Mt Egaleo Maganiako Ellinoekklisia
           Kalogerorrachi Castle of Druges
           Ahdrousa Eva
Marathopoli Gargaliani   MESSENIA Thouria
Is. Proti Chora Trifylias   Leika
Nestor's Palace   Messini
Korifassi   Kalamata
Palaiokastro Gialova Rizomilos
Is. Sphaktiria   Petalidi
              Mt Likodimo
              Pylos
Navarino Bay Longa Episcopi
                     Ag. Andreas
Methoni Finikounda Charokopio
         Akritochori Koroni
Is. Sapienza

Cape Akritas
Is. Schiza
         Is. Veniko

Ionian Sea

N

20 kms
10 miles

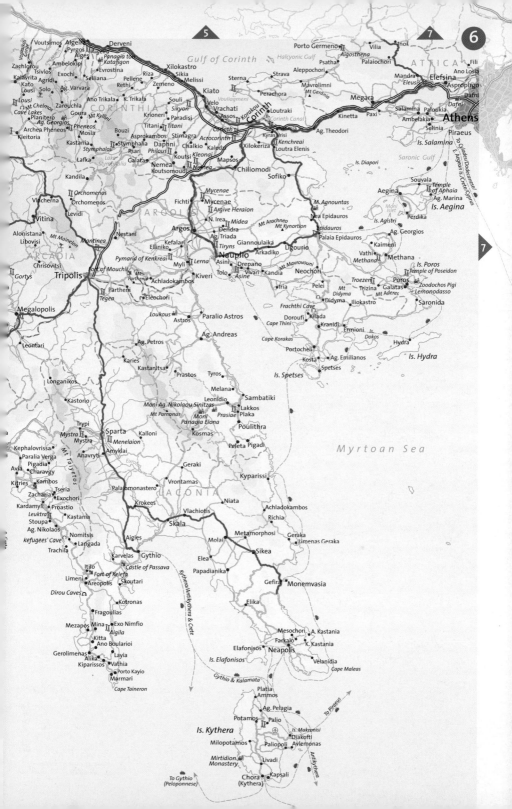

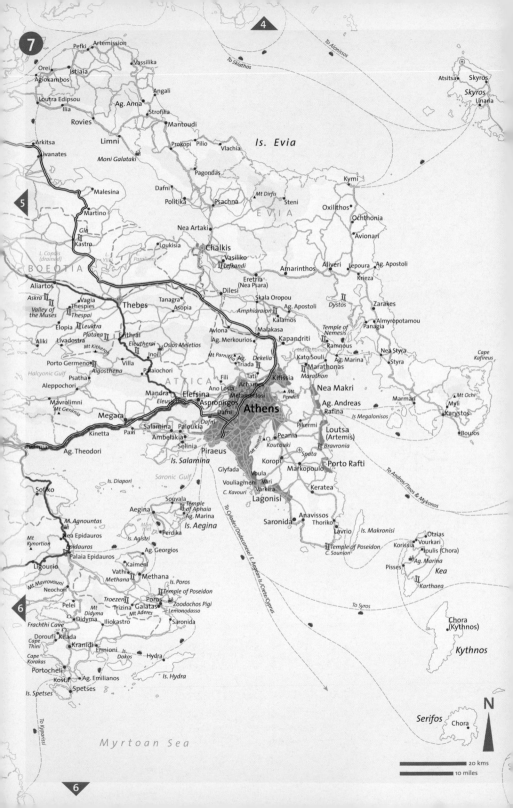

One call...

Car Rental Services
- Over 4,000 locations worldwide
- Travel into Eastern Europe
- Long-term leasing

Prestige and Sports Cars
- Large selection of vehicles
- Available throughout Europe

Chauffeur Services
- Hourly, half day and full day services
- Airport transfers

European Air & Hotel Packages
- Over two thousand 2, 3, and 4-star hotels
- Airfares from major US cities available

Online Reservations
- Browse and request all of our services from our website
- Affiliate program with commissions